What's New in This Edition

The first edition of *Microsoft Office 97 Unleashed* enjoyed a successful run and was the object of many rave reviews from readers and reviewers. To ensure that this book contains only the most timely and accurate information, I put together this special Professional Reference Edition, which boasts a wide array of changes and additions. Here's a summary of what to expect:

Better organization: I revamped the book's outline to make things easier to find, and I grouped topics in a more logical manner. For example, all the information relating to Office's common features has been grouped in Part II.

Expanded Internet material: This edition includes an extra Internet chapter that shows you how to set up an Office-based Web site using Personal Web Server and Microsoft FrontPage.

Improved networking coverage: Networking is a crucial yet confusing topic. To help you get over this often formidable hurdle, I've expanded the networking coverage to include information on setting up a network connection, using network resources, and sharing your data.

Deeper coverage of Office integration: To help you get more out of Office, the integration material has been consolidated into a single section (Part IX), and I've expanded the material.

More VBA chapters: VBA is a big part of unleashing Office, so I've added a few chapters and many more tips and techniques throughout. You'll find more information on how to use the new Visual Basic Editor; separate chapters on the object models of Word, Excel, PowerPoint, and Access; how to control menus and toolbars programmatically; how to program the Outlook Inbox; and how to trap errors and debug programs.

More appendixes: This edition has six new appendixes.

Paul McFedries'
Microsoft® Office 97
Professional Reference Edition

Paul McFedries

SAMS
PUBLISHING

201 West 103rd Street
Indianapolis, IN 46290

UNLEASHED

Copyright © 1997 by Sams Publishing

PROFESSIONAL REFERENCE EDITION

International Standard Book Number: 0-672-31144-5

Library of Congress Catalog Card Number: 97-67507

2000 99 98 97   4 3 2

Interpretation of the printing code: the rightmost double-digit number is the year of the book's printing; the rightmost single-digit, the number of the book's printing. For example, a printing code of 97-1 shows that the first printing of the book occurred in 1997.

Composed in AGaramond and MCPdigital by Macmillan Computer Publishing

Printed in the United States of America

President, Sams Publishing	*Richard K. Swadley*
Publishing Manager	*Dean Miller*
Managing Editor	*Brice P. Gosnell*
Indexing Manager	*Johnna L. VanHoose*
Director of Marketing	*Kelli S. Spencer*
Product Marketing Manager	*Wendy Gilbride*
Associate Product Marketing Manager	*Jennifer Pock*
Marketing Coordinator	*Linda Beckwith*

Acquisitions Editor
Kim Spilker

Development Editor
Brian-Kent Proffitt

Software Development Specialist
Patricia J. Brooks

Production Editor
Gayle L. Johnson

Copy Editor
Kris Simmons

Indexer
Kelly Talbot

Technical Reviewers
John Charlesworth
Susan Teague

Editorial Coordinators
Mandie Rowell
Katie Wise

Technical Edit Coordinator
Lynette Quinn

Editorial Assistants
Carol Ackerman
Andi Richter
Rhonda Tinch-Mize

Cover Designer
Jason Grisham

Book Designer
Gary Adair

Copy Writer
David Reichwein

Production Team Supervisor
Brad Chinn

Production
Paula Lowell
Tim Osborn
Carl Pierce
Ian A. Smith

Contents

Part IV Unleashing Excel

15 Working with Ranges 371

16 Manipulating Formulas and Functions 389

Part IX   Unleashing Office Integration

48   Office Integration and OLE   1079

Acknowledgments

Writing books is endlessly fascinating for me, because what begins as just a few thoughts ends up as a physical, tangible thing that gets sent out (hopefully) to the far-flung corners of the world. Of course, the trip from thought to thing is a long one, and lots of people get their fingers in a book's pie before it's ready to ship. This book was no exception, so I'd like to thank not only the long list of people you'll find near the front of this book, but also the following hard-working souls:

Dean Miller: Dean is a Publishing Manager, so it's his job to coordinate the publishing program and make sure that all bases and markets are covered. I'd like to thank Dean for including me as a coauthor in the original incarnation of this book, and then for having the confidence to turn the entire project over to me for this Professional Reference Edition.

Kim Spilker: Kim is the Acquisitions Editor, who pulled the whole project together and made sure I had all the resources I needed to get the job done. Kim also had the thankless task of making sure I toed the line and met my deadlines. (This is important, because I often agree with Douglas Adams: "I like deadlines; I especially like the sound they make as they go whooshing by.")

Brian-Kent Proffitt: Brian's job as Development Editor was to work with me in setting up the book's outline and overall structure, to ensure that all relevant topics were covered, and to make sure that these topics were discussed in some sort of sensible order. Brian's keen intellect and excellent book instincts made him a pleasure to work with.

Patty Brooks: I like to think my books are worth the price of admission all by themselves, but these days you have to give people a few extra goodies. The CD-ROM material that comes with this book is chock-full of such goodies, and it was Patty's job as Software Development Specialist to pull everything together. That's no easy task, because it involves negotiating with software developers, keeping track of updates, planning the structure of the CD, coordinating with authors and editors, and getting everything to production on time. Thanks, Patty, for all your hard work.

Gayle Johnson: Whenever I do a project for Sams, I always ask that Gayle be the Production Editor. That's because she is one of the most professional and conscientious editors I've ever worked with, and the books that she shepherds through the production process are always of the highest quality.

Kris Simmons: Gayle can't do *everything*, so Kris eased her workload a little by checking punctuation, spelling, and grammar in many of the chapters. Her efforts are appreciated.

Susan Teague and John Charlesworth: A computer book usually stands or falls on the quality of its information. Sams ensures that its books contain accurate and useful information by hiring experts—called Technical Editors—to "field test" the content and make sure that things work as advertised. Susan and John put this book through its paces, so you can be assured that you're getting the straight goods.

I extend big-time thanks to all these people for their competence and hard work. I hope you enjoy the book!

About the Author

Paul McFedries is a computer consultant, programmer, and freelance writer. He has worked with computers in one form or another since 1975, he has a degree in mathematics, and he can swap out a hard drive in seconds flat, yet he still, inexplicably, has a life. He is the author or coauthor of more than two dozen computer books that have sold over one million copies worldwide. His books include the Sams Publishing titles *Paul McFedries' Windows 95 Unleashed* and *Visual Basic for Applications Unleashed.* Other hats worn by McFedries on occasion include video editor, animator, bread maker, Webmaster, brewmaster, cruciverbalist, and neologist. He has no cats, and his favorite hobbies are shooting pool, taking naps, riding his motorcycle, and talking about himself in the third person.

Tell Us What You Think

As a reader, you are the most important critic of and commentator on our books. We value your opinion and want to know what we're doing right, what we could do better, what areas you'd like to see us publish in, and any other words of wisdom you're willing to pass our way. You can help us make strong books that meet your needs and give you the computer guidance you require.

If you have access to the World Wide Web, check out our site at `http://www.mcp.com`.

NOTE

If you have a technical question about this book, call the technical support line at (317) 581-3833 or send e-mail to `support@mcp.com`.

As the team leader of the group that created this book, I welcome your comments. You can fax, e-mail, or write me directly to let me know what you did or didn't like about this book, as well as what we can do to make our books stronger. Here's the information:

Fax: (317) 581-4669

E-mail: `opsys_mgr@sams.mcp.com`

Mail: Dean Miller
           Comments Department
           Sams Publishing
           201 West 103rd Street
           Indianapolis, IN 46290

Introduction

Knowledge is of two kinds. We know a subject ourselves, or we know where we can find information upon it.

—*Samuel Johnson*

The sheer size and scope of the Microsoft Office suite is enough to give even the best thesaurus a run for its money. Choose just about any "large" or "complex" adjective—massive, sprawling, gargantuan, disk space-usurping, labyrinthine, brain-bending—and it's bound to seem just right to describe the Office gestalt.

With so many features, utilities, and technologies in the Office package, you need some sort of guide that not only tells you what these knickknacks are, but also shows you how to get the most out of them so that you can get the most out of your Office investment. And that's precisely where this book comes in. I've scoured Office from head to toe, rung its bells and blown its whistles, and generally just pushed the entire package to its limits to see what would happen. The result is the book you're holding—a book that offers the following coverage to help you unleash your Office productivity:

- How to use the components and commands that are new to Office 97
- Advanced material on each of the Big Four Office applications: Word, Excel, Access, and PowerPoint
- In-depth coverage of the other Office programs, including Outlook, the graphing and drawing tools, and more
- Dedicated coverage of all the Internet and Web page publishing features of Office 97
- How to integrate the Office applications using Binder, OLE, and other techniques
- How to use Office in a networked environment
- Extensive coverage of Visual Basic for Applications so that you can program the Office applications both individually and collectively

Through many real-world examples, I've translated my own hard-won experiences in developing custom Office solutions to give you a leg up on creating solutions that will help you leverage the full power of the Office suite.

What You Should Know Before Reading This Book

My goal in writing *Microsoft Office 97 Unleashed* was to give you extensive coverage of the Office programs and technologies, as well as numerous examples for putting the suite to good use. Note, however, that this book isn't an Office tutorial per se. So although I cover the entire Office suite, many relatively low-level topics are presented quickly so that we can get to meatier topics. Therefore, although you don't need to have Office experience in order to read this book, knowledge of some of the basics would be helpful.

I've tried to keep the chapters focused on the topic at hand and unburdened with long-winded theoretical discussions. For the most part, each chapter gets right down to brass tacks without much fuss and bother. To keep the chapters uncluttered, I've made a few assumptions about what you know and don't know:

- I assume that you have knowledge of rudimentary computer concepts such as files and folders.
- I assume that you're familiar with Windows and that you know how to launch applications and use accessories such as Control Panel.
- I assume that you're comfortable with the basic Windows 95 interface. This book doesn't tell you how to work with tools such as pull-down menus and dialog boxes.
- I assume that you can operate the peripherals attached to your computer, such as the keyboard, mouse, printer, and modem.
- I assume that you've installed Office 97 and are ready to dive in at a moment's notice.
- I assume that you have a brain and are willing to use it.

How This Book Is Organized

To help you find the information you need, this book is divided into a dozen parts that group related tasks. The next few sections offer a summary of each part.

Part I: Introducing Microsoft Office 97

The two chapters in Part I give you a "big picture" view of the Office suite. Chapter 1 introduces the entire Office package, giving you brief summaries of what's in each Office version (Standard, Professional, Small Business, and Developer). Chapter 2 focuses on Office 97 and tells you what new features you can expect in this significant upgrade.

Part II: Unleashing Office 97's Common Features

Part II looks at a number of features that are implemented throughout the Office suite. After a quick summary of some routine tasks in Chapter 3, subsequent chapters discuss printing, the OfficeArt tools, Microsoft Graph, the Office Assistant, the Office Shortcut Bar, and more. Part II closes with a look a how to customize the office menu's and toolbars.

Part III: Unleashing Word 97

Word 97 is Microsoft's flagship word processing application, and it's one of the most powerful applications available on any platform. The price of all this power is complexity, and it's the goal of the chapters in Part III to help you manage that complexity. To that end, the first couple of chapters give you lots of information on working with documents, including advanced topics such as columns, tables, footnotes, frames, lists, indexes, and outlines.

Subsequent chapters cover the various Wizards available in Word, techniques for turning Word documents into forms, mail merge, document layout considerations, and customization.

Part IV: Unleashing Excel

Number crunchers get their turn in Part IV. Here you'll find no less than nine chapters that cover just about every aspect of Excel. The first two take some basic Excel concepts—ranges, formulas, and functions—and show you how to extend them to create advanced worksheets.

The next few chapters cover crucial Excel topics such as charts, lists, pivot tables, and querying external databases with Microsoft Query. You also learn how to wield Excel's powerful data analysis tools and how to customize Excel's options.

Part V: Unleashing Access

If you need to work with data, but Word's tables and Excel's lists aren't powerful enough for you, you'll probably want to graduate to using an Access database. The chapters in Part V will get you up to speed. Coverage includes extensive background on database design; how to plan, build, and populate tables; how to extract data with sophisticated queries; and how to design and work with forms and tables.

Subsequent chapters cover Access macros, techniques for working with multiple tables, and a summary of the various Access program options.

Part VI: Unleashing PowerPoint

Once you've finished writing documents in Word, performing calculations in Excel, and assembling data in Access, you'll often want to bring everything together as part of a PowerPoint presentation. Part VI shows you how it's done, from designing an effective presentation to creating the slides to running the show. You'll also learn some valuable techniques for incorporating multimedia into your presentations, as well as how to customize the program.

Part VII: Unleashing Outlook

Outlook is the powerful new desktop information manager that replaces both the Exchange e-mail client and the Schedule+ organizer. The seven chapters in Part VII serve to get you up and running with this fascinating new tool. The first chapter shows you how to get Outlook set up for the way you work. From there, you learn how to use all of Outlook's e-mail and fax features, and how to work with the other Outlook folders: Calendar, Contacts, Tasks, Journal, and Notes.

Part VIII: Unleashing the Office Internet Tools

Microsoft completely retooled Office 97 so that the Internet would be an ubiquitous part of the landscape. You can now embed hyperlinks in just about any Office document, convert Office documents into Web pages, work with ActiveX controls, and much more. All of these topics are grist for the mill in Part VIII. You'll begin with a Web page primer that gives you the basics of Web documents and HTML. From there, you'll learn how to work with hyperlinks, navigate the Web with Internet Explorer, and convert Office documents into HTML. Other chapters show you how to create Web pages within Word, how to set up Web forms, and how to use Personal Web Server and FrontPage to manage an Office Web site.

Part IX: Unleashing Office Integration

Part IX takes you through the crucial topic of integrating Office applications and sharing data. I give you some background on OLE technology and provide basic techniques for linking and embedding objects. From there, you learn how to use the Binder application and how to use the specific integration tools found in each Office application.

Part X: Unleashing the Networked Office

The days of the lone computer operating in splendid isolation are rapidly coming to a close. In business settings, it's now more likely that your machine will be attached to a network and that you'll need to collaborate with other Office users on that network. Although this book explains network-related concepts throughout, the two chapters in Part X focus on specific areas such as mailing and routing documents from within the Office programs and sharing data with other users.

Part XI: Office Application Development with VBA

With Office 97, the Visual Basic for Applications (VBA) programming language is now available in all the major applications: Word, Excel, Access, and PowerPoint. Part XI consists of seven chapters that show you how to take advantage of VBA's power and ease of use to build Office-based applications. You'll begin with some basic programming concepts, and then you'll progress to the objects available in the four major applications, controlling your code, and creating custom user interfaces.

Part XII: Appendixes

To round out your Office education, Part XII presents a few appendixes that contain extra goodies. You'll find information on the contents of the Office ValuPack, a summary of what you get in both the Small Business Edition and the Developer Edition, lists of all the VBA statements and functions, and the ANSI character set.

Bonus Chapters on the CD

You'll also find seven bonus chapters on the CD that comes with this book. The first chapter shows you how to set up Office for a networked environment, share resources, and more. The next five chapters will be of interest to VBA developers. They show you how to control Web page objects using VBScript (a subset of VBA), program the Outlook Inbox, debug your VBA procedures, program databases, and integrate Office applications programmatically. The last bonus chapter shows you how to set up an Internet connection.

This Book's Special Features

Microsoft Office 97 Unleashed is designed to give you the information you need without making you wade through ponderous explanations and interminable technical background. To make your life easier, this book includes various features and conventions that help you get the most out of the book and Office 97 itself.

Steps: Throughout this book, each Office task is summarized in a step-by-step procedure.

Sidebars: Note, Tip, and Caution sidebars draw your attention to important (or merely interesting) information.

Toolbar buttons: Whenever a toolbar button is mentioned, a picture of that button appears in the margin.

Things you type: Whenever I suggest that you type something, what you type appears in a monospace font.

Placeholders: Placeholders are words that stand for what you will actually type. Placeholders in regular text appear in *italic*. Placeholders in code appear in *italic monospace*.

Arguments: In lines of code, required arguments appear in ***bold italic monospace***. Optional arguments appear in *italic monospace*.

Commands: I use the following style for application menu commands: File | Open. This means that you pull down the File menu and select the Open command.

The code continuation character (➥): When a line of VBA code is too long to fit on one line of this book, it is broken at a convenient place, and the code continuation character appears at the beginning of the next line.

 The CD icon: This icon tells you that the file, workbook, or spreadsheet being discussed is available on the CD that comes with this book.

IN THIS PART

Introducing Microsoft Office 97

PART

I

Office 97: The Big Picture

IN THIS CHAPTER

CHAPTER 1

His eye, like his mind, sought an extended view.

—*Dumas Malone*

In the 16-plus years that personal computers have been a part of the technological landscape, business productivity software (the programs that help you create memos, spreadsheets, and other documents that are a fundamental part of the workaday world) has evolved considerably. This evolution occurred not only in response to the increasing sophistication of the underlying hardware, but also in response to user needs and demands. With the benefits of 20/20 hindsight, we can look back at this history and recognize a five-stage phylogeny of productivity applications:

Stage 1—Rugged individualism: The brave and hardy souls who were early adopters of PC technology not only had to deal with the esoterica of the DOS command line, but also suffered from a lack of productivity applications. As a result, mediocre products such as WordPerfect, Lotus 1-2-3, and dBASE were runaway bestsellers and commanded the lion's share of their respective markets.

Stage 2—Swiss army knives: As computers became more popular and, in particular, began to invade the home, two problems arose with the productivity programs associated with Stage 1: These large applications were overkill for many people, and it was a hassle to have to close down one program in order to work with another. The solution was the *integrated package,* a sort of Swiss army knife application that combined productivity tools such as a word processor, spreadsheet, and database into a single, low-cost package.

Stage 3—More bang for the buck: Integrated packages enjoyed a successful run, but their popularity waned after a while. Why? Well, for one thing, the computer quickly became a mainstream business tool, and the scaled-down modules in the integrated packages were no match for their stand-alone counterparts. For example, a secretary could compose basic letters in Microsoft Works' word processing module, but she really needed Microsoft Word to do her job properly. For another, the easy access afforded by the all-in-one nature of the integrated package was obviated by Windows' multitasking capabilities. As a result, powerful stand-alone Windows productivity applications such as Word and Excel dominated the software sales charts. (Also, the death knell was sounded for DOS applications and for companies who were late getting their Windows versions to market.)

Stage 4—Suite deals: With stand-alone productivity applications once again on top of the computing world, pressure began to mount to reduce the onerous costs of these software behemoths. Instead of paying $500 for each of three applications, users wondered why developers couldn't bundle them and offer the whole package at a reduced price. Not only was this just good old-fashioned capitalism, but the software companies reasoned that it would be an excellent way of building a user base for lesser categories such as presentation graphics and databases. Thus did the phrase "productivity suite" enter the computing lexicon.

Stage 5—Integration redux: With suites firmly ensconced as the product of choice in the business software market, the trend over the past few years has been to supply higher levels of integration among the suite's individual components. This integration usually involves one or more of the following:

- Making the application interfaces as similar as possible.
- Implementing shared tools—such as spell-checkers—across the applications.
- Enabling data sharing via technologies such as object linking and embedding.

This brings us to the present. A survey of the current productivity suite landscape shows an almost prairie-like expanse, which is the result of two things: a huge installed base of some 40 million users, and the total domination of Microsoft Office, thanks to its whopping 80 percent market share.

As you'll see in this chapter and, indeed, throughout the rest of this book, Microsoft's near-monopoly in the suite market is well-deserved, because the individual Office components are uniformly excellent and, perhaps more importantly, because of Microsoft's aggressive and successful implementation of the Stage 5 integration.

A Brief Tour of the Office 97 Package

Microsoft Office is a truly massive software package. A complete installation of the Professional Edition will litter your hard drive with dozens of components and usurp a little under 200 MB of disk real estate. Sounds like a colossal case of *bloatware,* right? Well, not necessarily. Although it's true that the Big Four—Word, Excel, PowerPoint, and Access—are getting fatter with each Office iteration (for example, the executable file for Excel 97 weighs in at a positively obese 5.3 MB), Microsoft has engineered Office 97 to share a lot of code among the applications. This reduces code duplication and lets you customize your Office installation as never before. So although Office may never be described as svelte, it's at least somewhat efficient with its resources.

In the end, your evaluation of Office 97 must come down to a "return on investment" equation. In other words, what are you getting in return when you invest your hard-earned cash? (I call it the "bauble per buck" ratio.) Office certainly isn't cheap, but it comes with a spectacular list of features. If enough of these bells and whistles are essential for helping you work more productively, investing in Office is a no-brainer. To help you make that decision, this section takes a quick look at the feature sets and system requirements for each flavor of Office: Standard, Professional, Small Business, and Developer.

Office 97 Standard Edition

At the time I wrote this, Office 97 Standard Edition was priced at $499 for new users. Upgraders must fork over $249.

NOTE: SOME PRICE POINTS

There are three things to remember about these and all other prices quoted in this chapter:

- These are list prices; street prices will almost certainly be lower.
- Most upgrade packages include some sort of mail-in rebate coupon.
- Deals can always be struck on volume purchases.

Here's what you get for your money:

Word 97: A best-of-breed word processor with a truly impressive feature set, including on-the-fly spelling and grammar checking, a built-in thesaurus, tables, indexing, edit tracking, columns, multiple-page views, tables of contents, envelopes and labels, numerous formatting features, and many Wizards for automating tasks. Part III, "Unleashing Word," takes you through many of these features.

Excel 97: A world-class spreadsheet program that comes with in-cell editing, charting, data maps, flat-file database capabilities, grouping and outlining, pivot tables, spell checking, edit tracking, Goal Seek, scenarios, Solver, and many Wizards. Most of these features are covered in Part IV, "Unleashing Excel."

PowerPoint 97: The *de facto* standard in presentation graphics software, PowerPoint makes it easy to create professional-looking presentations and slide shows thanks to its helpful Wizards and predefined color schemes, layouts, designs, and animations. See Part VI, "Unleashing PowerPoint."

Outlook: This is Microsoft's new "desktop information manager." It integrates e-mail, a scheduling tool, a contacts database, a to-do list, a journal for tracking activities, and more. When used in conjunction with an Exchange Server network, Outlook supports custom messaging applications, shared folders, message filtering, and other advanced groupware features. Part VII, "Unleashing Outlook," runs through all the Outlook modules.

Binder: This is an OLE container application that lets you combine multiple Office documents from multiple Office applications into a single file (see Figure 1.1). I'll show you how to work with Binder in Chapter 49, "Packaging Office Documents with Binder."

Clipart: Office Standard comes with a huge collection of clip art images, as well as a Clip Gallery application that makes it easy to preview and select images. See Chapter 7, "More Office Tools," for more information.

FIGURE 1.1.

A binder file containing Word, Excel, and PowerPoint documents.

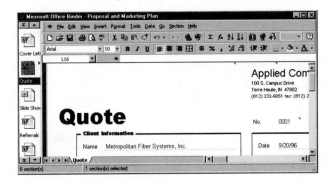

Equation Editor: This applet lets you insert mathematical formulas and equations into your Office documents. See Chapter 7.

Graph: This is a charting tool that lets you graph any type of numeric data in any Office application. See Chapter 6, "Working with Microsoft Graph."

Internet Explorer: This is Microsoft's World Wide Web browser. I'll show you how to use it in Chapter 44, "The Office 97 Internet Tools."

Office Shortcut Bar: This is a toolbar that gives you one-click access to many of the most common Office features and applications (see Figure 1.2). I'll show you how it works in Chapter 7.

FIGURE 1.2.

The Office Short-cut Bar.

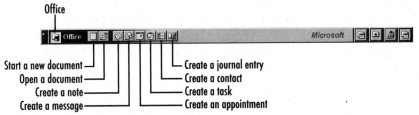

Organization Chart: This is another charting tool, but this one specializes in creating organizational charts. See Chapter 7.

Photo Editor: This is an image manipulation tool that lets you crop, resize, and rotate images, as well as apply numerous effects. You can also use Photo Editor to scan materials into Office documents. See Chapter 7.

Query: You use this tool to access and query external data sources from within Excel (although it can also be used as a stand-alone application). See Chapter 21, "Using Microsoft Query."

Visual Basic for Applications (VBA): This is Microsoft's common macro language and Office development environment. You can use it to automate routine tasks as well as create full-blown Office applications. I cover VBA in detail in Part XI, "Unleashing Office Application Development with VBA."

WordArt: This is an applet that creates impressive text effects that you can insert into any Office document (see Figure 1.3). See Chapter 7 for details.

FIGURE 1.3.

WordArt lets you insert interesting text effects into your Office documents.

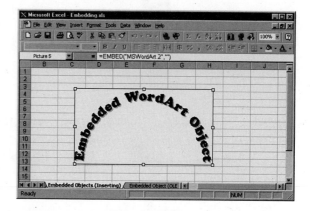

Office 97 Professional Edition

The Professional Edition of Office 97 will set you back $599 if you're a new user, and $349 if you're upgrading. There's also a version of the Professional Edition that comes with Microsoft's new IntelliMouse. This upgrade costs $379. The Professional Edition includes all of the components I listed for the Standard Edition, as well as the following:

Access 97: This is a state-of-the-art relational database system that lets you create sophisticated tables, relationships, queries, forms, and reports. Access also comes with a number of database tools, including table and performance analyzers, security, and replication. I discuss Access in detail in Part V, "Unleashing Access."

Microsoft Bookshelf Basics: This is a scaled-down version of Microsoft Bookshelf 1996-1997. It comes with the *American Heritage Dictionary,* the original *Roget's Thesaurus,* and the *Columbia Dictionary of Quotations.* It also includes "preview" versions of the *Concise Columbia Encyclopedia,* shown in Figure 1.4, the *Concise Encarta World Atlas,* the *People's Chronology* (a timeline of historical events), the *World Almanac and Book of Facts,* and the *Internet Directory.*

FIGURE 1.4.

Bookshelf Basics includes a preview version of the Concise Columbia Encyclopedia.

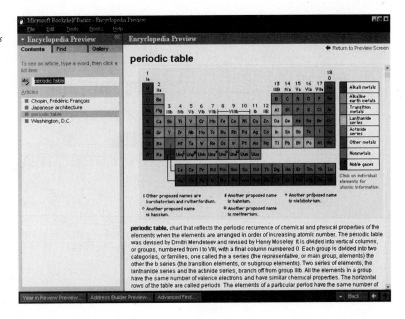

IntelliMouse: This is the latest in a long line of Microsoft mouse products. The big news in this new version is a small rubber wheel that lies between the two mouse buttons. You can use this wheel to scroll up and down in documents, zoom in and out of spreadsheets, and much more. I'll talk more about the IntelliMouse in Chapter 7.

Office 97 Small Business Edition

The Small Business Edition of Office 97 is designed to meet the needs of small-business owners and the self-employed. New users can buy this edition for $499, while upgraders will pay $249. The Small Business Edition includes the Standard Edition components, plus the following tools:

Publisher 97: This is a powerful page layout program you can use to create newsletters, flyers, business cards, letterheads, postcards, greeting cards, and Web sites.

Small Business Financial Manager: This is a set of add-ins to Excel that gives you extra tools for importing data from various accounting packages, creating customizable financial reports, and performing what-if analysis (see Figure 1.5).

FIGURE 1.5.

*The Small Business
Financial Manager.*

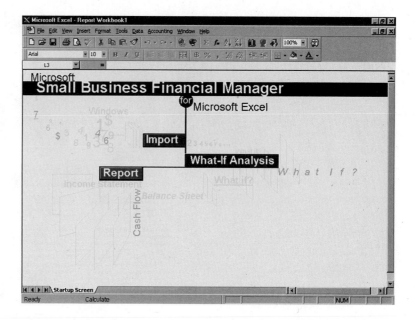

Automap Streets Plus: This is a collection of highly detailed street maps for U.S. cities. You can use these maps to find specific addresses, add maps to your Publisher documents, and even find the best route from here to there. It also includes addresses for tens of thousands of restaurants and over 12,000 hotels.

Doing Business on the Internet: This is an electronic book that tells you how to get your business on the Internet, how to set up your Web site, and how to attract customers to your site.

Business templates: The Small Business Edition comes with dozens of templates for memos, letters, faxes, reports, forms, financial models, and more.

I talk about the Small Business Edition in depth in Appendix B, "Office 97 Small Business Edition."

Office 97 Developer Edition

The Office 97 Developer Edition is suited for developers who create Office-based applications and solutions. For new users, this edition costs $799. Upgraders pay $499. The Developer Edition comes with all the Professional Edition components, plus the following extras:

Royalty-free Access runtime engine: This engine lets you distribute Access applications and run them on machines that don't have Access installed.

Setup Wizard: This Wizard is an Access application that leads you through the steps necessary to create a custom setup program that will install your Office application, as shown in Figure 1.6. This setup program will not only install the appropriate files, but it will also create shortcuts and update the appropriate Registry settings.

1

FIGURE 1.6.

*The Setup Wizard
makes it easy to create
installation disks for
your application.*

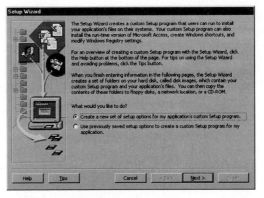

Replication Manager: This tool provides a graphical interface that makes it easier to replicate and synchronize databases across remote sites.

Visual SourceSafe integration: With the Developer edition, you can integrate your application with a source-code control system—such as Visual SourceSafe—that allows developer teams to work together. It supports team coordination, version tracking, and reusable code.

ActiveX controls: You get a number of ready-to-use ActiveX controls that you can drop directly into your custom forms. The available objects include CommonDialog control, Internet Transfer control, ProgressBar control, StatusBar control, Toolbar control, and Winsock control.

Help Workshop: Provides a front end for building custom Windows Help files.

Win32 API Viewer: This utility provides an interface to the Win32 Application Programming Interface. You get easy access to the constants, data types, and `Declare` statements used with all the Win32 functions.

Developer documentation: This includes two printed manuals—*Microsoft Office 97 Visual Basic Programmer's Guide* and *Building Applications with Microsoft Access 97*—that provide information, tips, and techniques for creating Office applications.

For detailed coverage of the Developer Edition, see Appendix C, "Office 97 Developer Edition."

Office 97 System Requirements

As I mentioned earlier, Office 97 isn't shy about using up your system's resources. Taking full advantage of its features requires a fast processor, lots of memory, and acres of hard disk space. How much is enough? Table 1.1 presents a rundown of the minimal and reasonable system requirements you'll need in order to install and work with the various editions of Office 97.

Table 1.1. System requirements for Office 97.

System Component	What You Need
Windows version	**Minimum:** Windows 95 or Windows NT Workstation 3.51 with Service Pack 5. **Reasonable:** To get the most out of the Office 97 interface, you should install it on a system running Windows 95 or Windows NT Workstation 4.0 with Service Pack 2 or later.
Processor	**Minimum:** 33 MHz 486. **Reasonable:** 133 MHz or better Pentium or 166 MHz or better Pentium Pro. The more muscular your processor, the easier time it will have lifting those heavy Office files.
Memory	**Minimum:** Windows 95: 8 MB, or 12 MB if you'll be running Access. Windows NT: 16 MB. **Reasonable:** To run multiple Office applications, you'll need at least 16 MB. For snappy performance, consider upgrading to 24 MB or even 32 MB.
Hard disk free space	**Minimum:** If you run the Typical install, here's the amount of disk space you'll need for each edition of Office 97: Standard: 102 MB Professional: 121 MB Small Business: 196 MB Developer: 140 MB **Reasonable:** If you run a Custom installation, here are the minimum and maximum values for hard disk-space used by each edition:
Video	**Minimum:** VGA, 14-inch monitor. **Reasonable:** Super VGA, 17-inch monitor. If you plan on running multiple applications, you'll want to maximize screen space. To do this, you should have a video card and monitor capable of displaying 256 colors at 1,024×768 resolution. If you plan on using Office 97's multimedia features (such as video), a video card that can handle true color (16 million colors) is a must.

Edition	Minimum	Maximum
Standard	67 MB	167 MB
Professional	73 MB	191 MB
Small Business	67 MB	246 MB
Developer	92 MB	210 MB

System Component	What You Need
Peripherals	**Minimum:** Microsoft-compatible mouse; CD-ROM drive. **Reasonable:** The new IntelliMouse has some nice features. For the Office 97 Web-based features, you'll need Internet access, via either your corporate network or a modem. To take advantage of Office 97's built-in sound support, you'll need a sound card, speakers, and a microphone. If you plan on using Office 97's workgroup features, your system must have a network interface card installed. Also note that some of Outlook's advanced groupware features require Microsoft Exchange Server on your network.

Who's Using Microsoft Office: A User Survey

Microsoft claims that it invested over 25,000 hours of research in Office 97. This research includes user surveys, "instrumented versions" of Office (special versions of the software that track specific user actions, such as keystrokes, mouse clicks, and dialog box choices), analysis of technical support calls, usability studies, user suggestions, and more. You'll see the results of this prodigious labor when I take you on a tour of the new Office 97 features in the next chapter. For now, this section will examine Microsoft's published research findings, which show, among other things, who uses Office and how.

NOTE: VIEWING THE SURVEY RESULTS

The results of Microsoft's Office survey are available online at the following Web address:

```
http://www.microsoft.com/msoffice/office97/documents/o97revgd/userre/
➥userre.htm
```

Question #1: Gender of the respondents.

In a breakdown by gender, Microsoft found that 59 percent of Office users were male, and 41 percent were female. This question applied to general Office users. It would have been more interesting to break this down further by application to see if there are major gender differences between the users of, say, Word and Access, but this was not done (or Microsoft isn't telling us).

Question #2: Age of the respondents.

Table 1.2 shows the breakdown of Office users by age group. (Note that the results add up to only 99 percent. Either this was a rounding error, or the missing one percent were under 21.)

Table 1.2. Office users by age group.

Age Group	Percent
21 to 34	33 percent
35 to 44	36 percent
45 to 54	22 percent
55 and over	1 percent
No answer	7 percent

Question #3: How long have you been using Microsoft Office?

Microsoft next asked the respondents to state how long they had been using Office. Table 1.3 shows the results. Interestingly, over half the respondents had more than a year's worth of Office use under their belts, and therefore could be considered experienced users. This is, I think, a reflection of the immediate popularity of Office 4.0, which was released in 1993.

Table 1.3. Office users by experience.

Office Experience	Percent
3 to 6 months	19 percent
6 to 12 months	27 percent
More than 12 months	54 percent

Question #4: On a scale of 1 to 4, how frequently do you use each Microsoft Office product?

This question is slightly problematic for us, because Microsoft's published documentation doesn't say what the numbers 1 through 4 mean. For example, does a rating of 1 mean that the respondent *never* used the application, or that he used it only rarely? I've taken the liberty of interpreting these figures as follows: 1 means rarely, 2 means occasionally, 3 means regularly, and 4 means frequently.

Given this interpretation, Table 1.4 shows the results: 97 percent of the respondents use Word regularly or frequently, compared with 90 percent for Excel, 50 percent for PowerPoint, and only 40 percent for Access.

Table 1.4. Office applications by frequency of use.

Frequency	Word	Excel	PowerPoint	Access
Rarely (1)	2 percent	2 percent	30 percent	50 percent
Occasionally (2)	1 percent	8 percent	20 percent	10 percent
Regularly (3)	22 percent	40 percent	40 percent	25 percent
Frequently (4)	75 percent	50 percent	10 percent	15 percent

Question #5: From what medium do you run Microsoft Office?

Microsoft wanted to know what percentage of users run Office from their hard drive, from their CD-ROM drive, and from a network server. Table 1.5 shows the numbers.

Table 1.5. Media used to run Office.

Medium	Percent
Hard drive	50 percent
Network server	42 percent
CD-ROM drive	8 percent

Question #6: Which Excel features are used at least once?

Earlier I mentioned that Microsoft used instrumented versions of Office software to track user actions such as mouse clicks and keypresses. In this survey, Microsoft installed an instrumented version of Excel and tracked which features users accessed. They then ranked these features by the number of users who accessed them at least once during the day. As you can see from Table 1.6, this ranking is dominated by basic file-maintenance features such as opening, closing, and saving documents, and copying, cutting, and pasting data.

Table 1.6. Excel features ranked by usage (the number of respondents who used the feature at least once).

Rank	Command	Rank	Command
1	File Open	14	Undo
2	Paste	15	Cell Alignment
3	Save	16	Font Properties
4	Copy	17	Select Cells
5	Print	18	Font
6	Close Document	19	File New
7	Cut	20	Activate Object
8	Format Cells	21	AutoFill
9	Delete	22	Run
10	Save As	23	Insert
11	Print Preview	24	Close Window
12	Page Setup	25	Cancel Copy
13	Clear		

Question #7: Which Excel features are used most often?

The second part of the instrumented version study tracked the frequency with which each feature was used. Although basic chores again ranked near the top, as shown in Table 1.7, note the number of Excel-specific features that made the list, including Run Macro, AutoFill, Activate Object, and Select Cells.

Table 1.7. Excel features ranked by frequency of use.

Rank	Command	Rank	Command	Rank	Command
1	Paste	9	Activate Object	17	Font Properties
2	Copy	10	Print	18	Print Preview
3	Run Macro	11	Cut	19	Font
4	File Open	12	Select Cells	20	Calculate Now
5	Save	13	Insert	21	Repeat
6	AutoFill	14	Close Document	22	Cell Borders
7	Delete	15	Cell Alignment	23	Undo
8	Clear	16	Page Setup	24	Close Window

Online Resources for Office 97

Although this book is crammed with all kinds of useful information and techniques, the daunting bulk of Office 97 makes it impossible to cover absolutely everything. Besides, the Office world is in a constant state of flux, so keeping up with what's new is a full-time job. To help you keep your head above water, this section presents a list of some online sites that offer practical information, the latest news, and first-rate shareware and other files.

The World Wide Web

Many Office-related Web pages offer files, how-tos, tips, news, troubleshooting, white papers, freebies, and much more. Table 1.8 lists a few of the pages I think you'll find useful.

Table 1.8. Office-related Web sites.

URL	*Description*
`http://www.microsoft.com/office/`	Microsoft Office home page (see Figure 1.7)
`http://www.microsoft.com/word/`	Microsoft Word home page
`http://www.microsoft.com/excel/`	Microsoft Excel home page
`http://www.microsoft.com/powerpoint/`	Microsoft PowerPoint home page
`http://www.microsoft.com/access/`	Microsoft Access home page
`http://www.microsoft.com/outlook/`	Outlook home page
`http://www.microsoft.com/office/sbe/`	Microsoft Office Small Business Edition home page
`http://www.microsoft.com/officedev/`	Microsoft Office Developer Forum home page
`http://www.microsoft.com/vba/`	Visual Basic for Applications home page
`http://www.microsoft.com/officefreestuff/`	Office Free Stuff
`http://www.microsoft.com/kb/`	Microsoft Knowledge Base (see Figure 1.8)

FIGURE 1.7.

The World Wide Web home page for Microsoft Office.

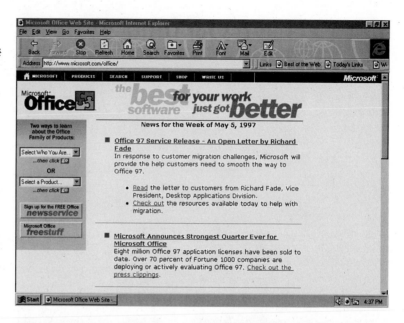

FIGURE 1.8.

This Web page lets you search the Microsoft Knowledge Base for information on an Office product.

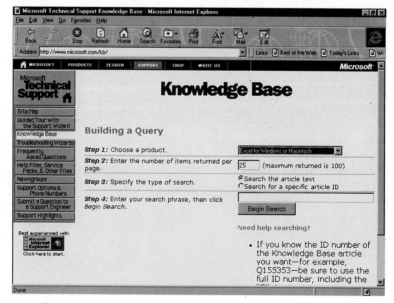

Usenet Newsgroups

If you need help with a specific Office question, fumbling around various Web sites looking for the answer might not be the best way to go. In some cases, posting a question to the appropriate Usenet newsgroup is often a better approach. Table 1.9 summarizes the Microsoft newsgroups that focus on Office.

Table 1.9. Usenet's Office-related newsgroups.

Newsgroup	Description
microsoft.public.office.binders	Discussions related to the Binder.
microsoft.public.office.misc	Miscellaneous Office topics that don't fit anywhere else.
microsoft.public.office.setup	Covers issues related to Office installation.
microsoft.public.office.shortcutbar	How to use and customize the Shortcut Bar.
microsoft.public.officedev	Covers Office application development.

Summary

This chapter presented a "big-picture" view of the Microsoft Office application suite. After a brief history of suites, I took you through the features that are found in all four flavors of Microsoft Office: Standard, Professional, Small Business, and Developer. You then learned about the system requirements for running Office. Next I summarized the results of a Microsoft user survey that showed a few interesting facts about how people use the Office applications. I closed with a look at some online resources for Office.

Here's a list of related chapters:

■ I'll tell you about Office 97's new bells and whistles in Chapter 2, "What's New in Office 97."

■ For a more in-depth look at the Small Business Edition, see Appendix B, "Office 97 Small Business Edition."

■ I cover the features specific to the Developer Edition in Appendix C, "Office 97 Developer Edition."

What's New in Office 97

IN THIS CHAPTER

CHAPTER 2

After climbing a great hill, one only finds that there are many more hills to climb. I have taken a moment here to rest, to steal a view of the glorious vista that surrounds me, to look back on the distance I have come.

—Nelson Mandela

On August 24, 1995, Microsoft shipped an updated version of Office. The problem, however, was that the glare from the hype of the Windows 95 launch on that same day prevented anyone from seeing the new Office upgrade, and its own launch turned out to be a non-event. Even when people did finally turn their attention away from Windows 95 to focus on Office 95, they were underwhelmed, to say the least. Aside from a few extra goodies thrown into the mix, Office 95 was really just a 32-bit upgrade that brought the suite's applications in line with the Windows 95 world. Yawn.

I think it's safe to say that this fate does *not* await the latest version of Office, called Office 97. The Microsoft programmers spent the year-and-a-half after Office 95 was released fine-tuning every aspect of the suite, cramming lots of great new programs into the box, and implementing some slick technology that is sure to keep Office 97 at the forefront of the applications suite pack. The fact that Office 97 sold a stunning 8 million licenses in its first quarter—an all-time Office record—along with the fact that at the time of this writing it had penetrated 70 percent of Fortune 1000 companies, is proof that folks realize this is no mere incremental upgrade.

To help you get a handle on the new features and technologies found in the Office 97 package, this chapter takes you on a tour of most of them. I'll discuss the new interface enhancements, review the new Internet technologies, examine the new features found in Word, Excel, PowerPoint, and Access, and much more.

New Interface Features

As I mentioned in the last chapter, Microsoft invested some 25,000 hours of research into Office 97. Much of this research was geared toward improving and optimizing the user interface of the entire Office suite. Here's a summary of the interface enhancements you'll find in Office 97:

> **Consistent menus and toolbars:** The point of a well-designed application suite is not just to let you create professional-caliber documents, but also to let you create them quickly and efficiently. One way to do this is to give each application in the suite more or less the same look and feel. That way, the transition between programs is smooth, and you spend less time learning each program and less time trying to find what you need. To that end, the menus and toolbars of each Office 97 application were tweaked to the point where they all share the same basic structure. As you can see in Figure 2.1, for example, the toolbars of the Big Four applications look remarkably similar, and they all share the same seven or eight menus (File, Edit, View, and so on).

FIGURE 2.1.

Each Office application uses the same basic menu and toolbar structure.

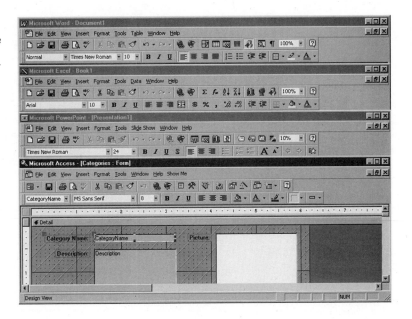

Shared Objects: Another way that Office 97 implements a consistent interface is through the use of Shared Objects. These are a set of cross-application tools that, according to Microsoft, allow the Office programs to share more than 50 percent of their code. There are a number of Shared Objects in the Office 97 suite, but the biggest are the following:

- Command Bars (shared menu and toolbar code)
- FindFast (a document indexing and search engine)
- Hyperlinks (document-based hyperlinks and Web browser-like navigation)
- OfficeArt (drawing objects and tools)
- Office Assistant (an "intelligent" front end for the Office Help system)
- Visual Basic for Applications (a macro programming and application development environment)

Command Bars: This is an object model that combines all the Office 97 menus and toolbars under a single roof. So, as mentioned earlier, not only does this result in a more consistent layout, but it also gives you a common mechanism for customizing toolbars and menus. As you'll see in Chapter 8, "Customizing the Office Menus and Toolbars," this new mechanism is both easier to use and more powerful.

Menu bar graphics: The Office applications display the Standard and Formatting toolbars by default, but they contain many other toolbars designed for specific tasks. In addition, you can add icons to any toolbar for quick access to the commands you use most often. However, this is handy only if you know that a particular command has a toolbar button available. To help out, if a particular command has a toolbar icon available, the Office 97 menus display the icon to the left of the command, as shown in Figure 2.2.

FIGURE 2.2.

An icon appears to the left of commands that have toolbar equivalents.

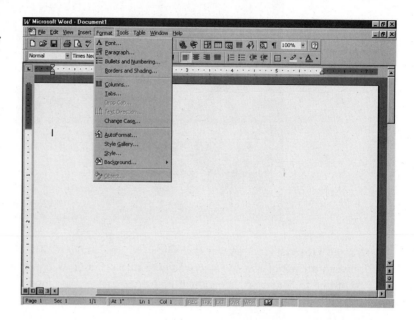

Tear-off menus: The Command Bars model blurs the distinction between menu bars and toolbars. For example, some toolbar buttons display menus when clicked. Similarly, some cascade menus do double duty as toolbars. The latter are called *tear-off menus,* and you recognize them by looking for a gray bar at the top of a cascade menu, as shown in Figure 2.3. If you drag this gray bar, Office "tears off" the menu to create a floating toolbar.

Scrollable menus: If you work on a notebook computer or on a desktop that uses a low screen resolution (640×480), you might often find that there isn't enough screen real estate to fully display long menus. To handle these situations, the Office 97 menus can now scroll up or down, as shown in Figure 2.4. You simply click the menu's up and down arrows to scroll to the other menu items.

Better dialog boxes: Many of the Office dialog boxes were given a complete overhaul to make them easier to navigate and more efficient. The Microsoft designers made extensive use of tabs to group related functions yet still maintain a clean, uncrowded look. For example, Figure 2.5 shows Word 97's new Find and Replace dialog box, which combines three features: Find, Replace, and Go To. Note, too, that the default dialog box has an extremely simple layout that won't intimidate novice users, and power users can click the More button to access the sophisticated features, as shown in Figure 2.6.

FIGURE 2.3.

In Office 97, you can "tear off" cascade menus to turn them into floating toolbars.

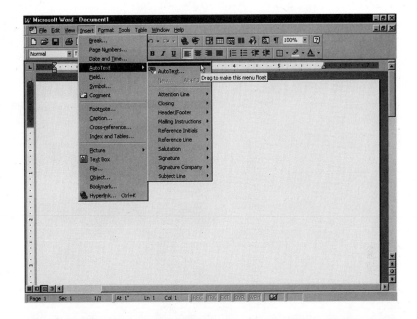

FIGURE 2.4.

The Office 97 menus can now scroll up or down.

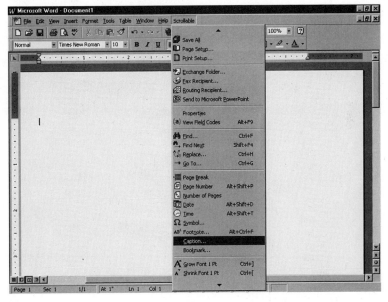

IntelliSense: Microsoft has spent untold millions of dollars researching ways to make applications more responsive to the needs of users. Although this research is ongoing, much of what has been learned has found its way into Office 97 under the IntelliSense banner. In Excel, for example, you can now refer to cells based on row and column labels (such as "January Sales"). In Outlook, you can use natural-language dates—such as "next Thursday" or "the last day of the month"— and these are translated into actual dates. In Word, spelling *and* grammar are checked on-the-fly. In all Office 97 applications, help is offered under specific circumstances. In Figure 2.7, for example, Word recognizes that I'm beginning a letter and offers to help.

FIGURE 2.5.

Word 97's new Find and Replace dialog box houses three separate functions.

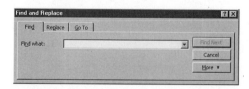

FIGURE 2.6.

Clicking the More button expands the dialog box to reveal advanced features.

FIGURE 2.7.

Office 97 "watches" what you're doing and offers help if you need it.

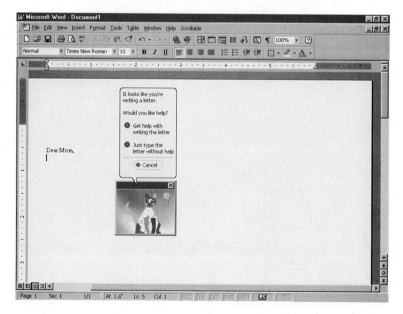

ToolTips everywhere: When toolbars first appeared a few years ago, they were praised for the one-click access they provided for common commands. However, they were also panned, because it was difficult to remember what each icon stood for. The solution was to use ToolTips—small banners that presented a short description when you hovered the mouse pointer over an icon. But toolbar buttons weren't the only obscure and potentially confusing interface elements. So in Office 97, Microsoft has associated ToolTips (they're actually called ScreenTips) with just about every element on the screen (see Figure 2.8).

FIGURE 2.8.

There are ScreenTips associated with just about every interface element.

2

WHAT'S NEW IN OFFICE 97

New Internet Features

Although Office 97 is crammed with new interface enhancements and, as you'll see later in this chapter, a myriad of new features and programs, if there's one area that will define the essence of the Office 97 upgrade, it's the Internet. Ever since Microsoft's belated realization (in late 1995) that the Internet was a phenomenon unlike any other in the history of the PC, its programmers have been working feverishly to build a full and robust roster of Internet products and establish Microsoft as a (if not *the*) dominant force in cyberspace.

Office, as Microsoft's flagship applications suite and the undisputed market leader in productivity programs, is a major component of this strategy. Microsoft's overarching design goal for Office 97 was to imbue the entire suite with the spirit of the Internet and to accomplish the nontrivial task of taking Office's acknowledged prowess in creating high-quality local documents and transferring this ability to publishing high-quality Web-based (and intranet-based) documents. Here's a summary of just a few of the enhancements added to Office 97 in an attempt to achieve this goal:

Internet Explorer: Office 97 ships with Internet Explorer, Microsoft's full-featured Web browser. This gives you a mechanism by which to surf local, Web-based, and intranet-based HTML files.

Internet Explorer "knows" Office documents: Thanks to ActiveX, you can now view Office 97 documents in their native format using Internet Explorer. So besides viewing HTML-based Web pages in Explorer, you can now also use Explorer to browse Excel 97 workbooks, Word for Windows 97 documents, and PowerPoint 97 presentations. Figure 2.9 shows Internet Explorer displaying an Excel workbook. Note, in particular, that all of the Excel interface is present, which means you can work with the document directly from Internet Explorer.

FIGURE 2.9.

Internet Explorer can now display native Office documents.

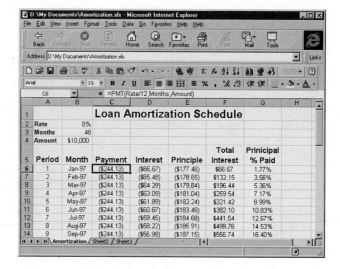

Hyperlinks: The Web's hyperlink mechanism has been extended to Office documents. You can now embed links in any Office document—links that will take you not only to Internet sites, but also to other documents on your computer, intranet, or local area network. Access 97 now has a Hyperlink field type that lets you create fields that contain clickable links.

The Save as HTML command: All the major Office applications come with a Save as HTML command that lets you convert existing Office documents into HTML format.

Web toolbar: The Big Four Office applications also come equipped with a Web toolbar that you can use to either load Web sites (via Internet Explorer) or browse Office documents. Figure 2.10 shows the Web toolbar in Excel. Note, in particular, the browser-specific features: the Back and Forward buttons, the Address box, the Go menu, and so on.

Word's Web tools: Word 97 is now a full-fledged HTML editor. You can use it to craft sophisticated Web pages either in WYSIWYG mode or by tweaking HTML tags manually. If you're looking for a quick start, Word 97's new Web Page Wizard, shown in Figure 2.11, comes with a number of templates and options that make it easy to create simple, easily customizable pages.

FIGURE 2.10.

You can use the new Web toolbar to browse Office documents or launch Web sites.

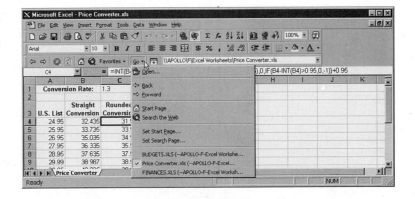

FIGURE 2.11.

The Web Page Wizard makes it easy to get simple HTML documents up and running.

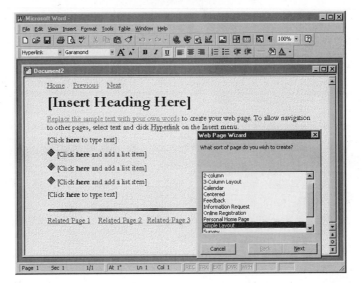

Excel's HTML extensions: Excel 97 brings a few HTML extensions to the table (literally!). For example, the FORMULA attribute lets you insert Excel formulas into HTML tables. When you view the page in Excel, these formulas work just like they would in an Excel worksheet cell, as shown in Figure 2.12. Similarly, the AUTOFILTER attribute lets you filter HTML tables in-place, and the CROSSTAB attribute lets you create pivot tables based on HTML tables.

Working with FTP sites: In the major Office 97 applications, the Open and Save As dialog boxes have been modified to work directly with FTP sites, as shown in Figure 2.13. This lets you view documents stored on an FTP server, as well as save your documents to an FTP storage site.

FIGURE 2.12.

You can add formulas to HTML tables that you view in Excel.

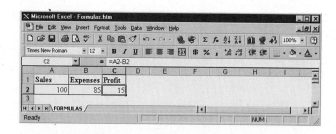

FIGURE 2.13.

Office 97 applications can now work with FTP sites directly.

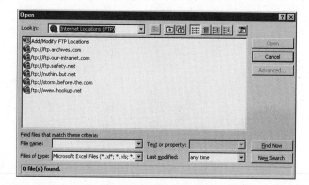

NOTE: OFFICE 97 INTERNET INFO

I cover all of these Internet features and quite a few more in Part VIII, "Unleashing the Office Internet Tools."

What's New in Word 97

With over 35 million users and counting, Microsoft Word is by far the world's best-selling Windows word processor. For those of us who use Word on a daily basis, it's gratifying to know that Microsoft isn't content to rest on its laurels. Instead, it built dozens of new features and enhancements into Word 97 in an effort to make what was often an unwieldy application into a more efficient one. Here's a list of just a few of the major new features you'll find in Word 97:

> **Improved AutoFormat:** Word 97's AutoFormat feature has been beefed up to include automatic bulleted and numbered lists, Internet and e-mail addresses, network paths, and conversion of emphasis markers to real formatting (such as converting *bold* to **bold**). AutoFormat also preserves formatting in lists. For example, if you use bold at the beginning of the first item in a bulleted list, AutoFormat will automatically apply bold to the beginning of each subsequent bullet.

Improved AutoCorrect: AutoCorrect—the on-the-fly spell checker introduced in Word 95—is one of the nicest features in Word. In Word 97, this features comes with a few improvements: correction of accidental cAPS lOCK sequences, multiple-word replacements, common grammatical mistakes, and right-click access to corrected spellings.

AutoComplete: With this new feature, Word 97 suggests text based on your typing. For example, if you type Sept, Word 97 displays September in a ScreenTip banner, as shown in Figure 2.14. If you then press Enter, AutoComplete fills in the rest of the word. AutoComplete recognizes days of the week, months, and all the defined AutoText entries.

2

WHAT'S NEW IN OFFICE 97

FIGURE 2.14.

AutoCorrect recognizes the start of some common words and offers to finish them for you.

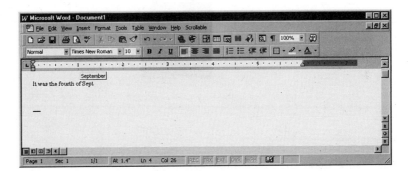

Improved spell checking: Word's spell checker has been updated to reduce wrongly flagged misspellings. For example, the dictionary now includes Fortune 1000 company names, ethnic names, many recently coined words (such as *downsizing*), computer terminology, and the names of countries and large U.S. towns.

On-the-fly grammar checking: Word 95's on-the-fly spell checking was such a big hit that Microsoft decided to add on-the-fly grammar checking to Word's arsenal. Grammatical errors are flagged with a wavy green line, and you need only right-click to access corrections, as shown in Figure 2.15. Also, Microsoft's advanced linguistic group developed its own natural-language grammar engine that theoretically improves accuracy (although my own informal testing doesn't bear this out).

FIGURE 2.15.

Word questions you about improper grammar.

Wizards, wizards, and more wizards: Word 97's waiting room is crowded with numerous wizards waiting in the wings to help you accomplish a number of Word tasks. These tasks include writing a letter or memo, composing a fax, creating newsletters and résumés, and more. Also, as you can see from Figure 2.16, the wizards boast a new, more efficient design.

FIGURE 2.16.

The new look of the Word 97 Fax Wizard.

Improved table creation tools: The Table feature has been completely revamped in Word 97. Instead of specifying a grid based on a number of rows and columns, you now "draw" the table's borders and cells using the mouse. This is a completely intuitive way to construct tables, and the updated Tables and Borders toolbar makes it a snap to adjust table boundaries and format cell borders and backgrounds.

Style previews: The Style drop-down list in the Formatting toolbar now shows you a preview of what each style looks like, as shown in Figure 2.17.

FIGURE 2.17.

The Style list now shows previews of each style.

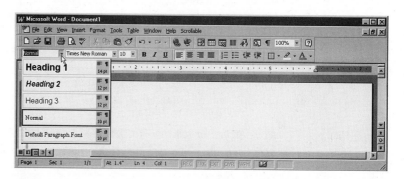

More document collaboration features: If you share documents among several people, Word 97 has many new features that make this process easier. You can add in-place comments to the document, highlight text, track changes by user, use versioning to maintain the working history of a document, and more.

More text effects: Besides text highlighting, other new text effects in Word 97 include borders applied to individual words or phrases, character scaling, double strike-through, new font formatting effects such as outline and shadow, and animated text.

Built-in macro virus detection: Word 97 now automatically detects and eradicates macro viruses such as the Concept virus.

Document Map: Navigating long documents has always been problematic. To help, Word 97 includes a new Document Map feature, which splits the window into two sections, as shown in Figure 2.18. The left side shows an outline of the headings in the document, and the right side shows the document text. To navigate the document, you need only click the headings in the left pane.

FIGURE 2.18.

The Document Map feature shows an outline of your document's headings.

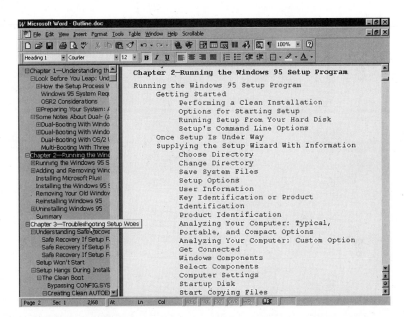

NOTE: WORD INFORMATION

Head for Part III, "Unleashing Word," to learn more about using Word 97.

What's New in Excel 97

Microsoft Excel has been the best (and most popular) spreadsheet application on the market for some time, and Excel 97 will only serve to strengthen that position. That's because the new version is loaded with user interface enhancements and new analysis features. Here's a summary:

Larger capacity: You can now enter up to 32,767 characters in a single cell (compared to just 255 in previous versions), a worksheet can now contain up to 65,536 rows (increased from 16,384), and a data series in a 2-D chart can now include up to 32,000 points (up from 4,000 points).

Natural-language formulas: To make worksheets easier to read, Excel 97 now supports natural-language formulas based on the sheet's row and column headers. For example, if you have a column labeled January and a row labeled Sales, you can refer to the intersecting cell as January Sales.

AutoCorrect comes to formulas: Many worksheet formula errors are common ones that occur repeatedly. These include missing or double parentheses, repeated operators, and transposed cell references. Excel 97 now includes an AutoCorrect feature that recognizes these common errors and offers to fix them for you automatically, as shown in Figure 2.19.

FIGURE 2.19.

Excel 97's AutoCorrect feature can fix many common formula errors.

Range Finder: This new feature gives you a visual summary of the cells involved in a calculation. When you double-click a cell containing a formula, Range Finder adds colored frames around the cells and ranges used in the calculation. You can also use the mouse to alter the size and shape of any of these ranges.

Conditional Formatting: With previous versions of Excel, you could apply, for example, a particular color to a cell based on the value of that cell. However, this required defining complicated custom formats for each cell. Excel 97 saves you that drudgery by introducing the new Conditional Formatting feature. This feature lets you apply a particular format to any cell that meets one or more criteria, as shown in Figure 2.20.

FIGURE 2.20.

Conditional Formatting takes the drudgery out of formatting cells based on their value.

Multiple Undo: Excel 97 now lets you undo up to the last 16 actions.

Custom Cells: Text inserted into worksheet cells is now more flexible. You can rotate text, indent text, merge cells, and have text sized automatically so that it fits inside a cell.

Improved charting: Charting is one of the most commonly used features in Excel, and it has been enhanced considerably in Excel 97. Improvements include a streamlined and more powerful Chart Wizard, an enhanced Chart toolbar, Chart Tips (ToolTip-like banners that provide information such as the exact value of a data marker), and new chart types (such as Bubble, Pyramid, Conical, and Cylindrical). Also, the OfficeArt component is now integrated with the charting module so that you can add background pictures, textures, and gradient fills (see Figure 2.21).

FIGURE 2.21.

The addition of OfficeArt to Excel's charting module lets you create fancier graphs.

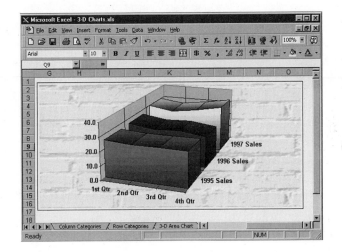

PivotTable improvements: Excel 97 PivotTables come with quite a few useful enhancements. These include the preservation of formatting during a pivot (a long overdue feature), the ability to include calculated fields and items, server-based page fields (queries that use server data to update page fields dynamically), customizable page field layouts, and more options for sorting PivotTable data.

Built-in data validation: In the past, validating data entry required either macro or VBA programming. Excel 97 now comes with data validation features built right into the program. These features let you ensure that data entry values fall with a specified range and are of the correct type (such as a number, as shown in Figure 2.22). You can also define custom input and error messages.

Cell Notes are now Comments: The old Cell Notes feature has been replaced by the Comments feature, which tells who entered the comment and allows other users to respond to the comment.

Workgroup features: For collaborative efforts, Microsoft built many new features into Excel 97, including the following: workbook sharing, the ability to track changes (as well as to accept or reject those changes), workbook merging, timed updates, and personal view settings.

FIGURE 2.22.

Data validation is built into Excel 97.

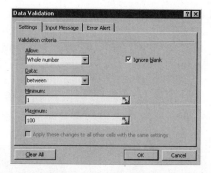

NOTE: EXCEL CHAPTERS

I cover Excel's features in Part IV, "Unleashing Excel."

What's New in PowerPoint 97

If you spend any amount of time at any type of conference or meeting just about anywhere on the planet, you'll almost certainly end up sitting through a PowerPoint presentation or two. PowerPoint seems to be one of those applications that has gone beyond best-sellerdom and is now firmly ensconced in ubiquity. This exalted status hasn't gone to Microsoft's head, however, because it was only too happy to toss a fistful of improvements into the PowerPoint package:

> **Enhanced AutoContent Wizard:** The AutoContent Wizard in PowerPoint 97 has been beefed up considerably. It has a much larger selection of presentation types, and the overall design of the Wizard has been streamlined, as shown in Figure 2.23.

FIGURE 2.23.

PowerPoint 97 comes with an improved AutoContent Wizard.

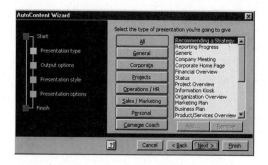

> **More presentation templates:** PowerPoint 97 has many presentation templates to choose from, including 30 new designs, 10 templates with preset animations, and lots of coordinated color schemes.

Expand Slide: One of the most common problems users face when putting together presentations is ending up with too much information on a single slide. Rather than making you fiddle with the font size or delete important data, PowerPoint 97 has a new Expand Slide feature. Expand Slide divides a single slide into multiple slides where the main headers become slide titles and all other bullets are moved up one level.

Summary Slide: A typical presentation incorporates some kind of summary slide at the end of the show. The normal process of creating such a slide is to copy titles or main headings from the presentation's other slides. To help automate this process, PowerPoint comes with a Summary Slide feature that creates the summary based on your selections.

Slide Comments: This feature lets users collaborating on a presentation add notes or suggestions to one or more slides.

Slide Finder: Many PowerPoint users reuse slides from other presentations (their own or those created by others and stored on a server). The problem, however, is finding a slide needle in a haystack of presentations. The new Slide Finder, shown in Figure 2.24, is designed to solve that. You can open and display a quick view of a presentation and then add it to your list of "favorites." From there, you can view your favorites and select individual slides for use in your current presentation.

FIGURE 2.24.

The Slide Finder makes it easier to reuse slides from existing presentations.

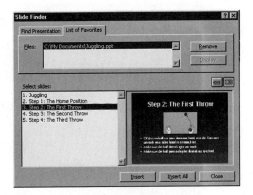

More multimedia: The days of the static title-and-a-few-bullet-points slides, while not exactly over, are at least numbered. Many PowerPoint users are keeping their audience's eyes from glazing over by incorporating multimedia elements into their presentations. PowerPoint 97 provides a number of tools that help you create professional-quality multimedia elements: Custom Animation, shown in Figure 2.25, makes it a breeze to add sophisticated animation and transition effects to any slide object. Voice Narration lets you record narration that plays during the show, and Custom Soundtracks lets you assign background music or sound effects that play during the show.

2

WHAT'S NEW IN OFFICE 97

FIGURE 2.25.

The Custom Animation feature comes with dozens of preset animation and sound effects.

Multiple levels of Undo: PowerPoint can now reverse up to the last 150 actions.

PowerPoint Central: This is a set of resources that gives PowerPoint users access to tutorials, new templates, multimedia clips, and more. As you can see from Figure 2.26, PowerPoint Central is a slide show that uses a browser-like interface. You can either run through the show normally or click the links to jump to specific sections. You can even download updated versions of PowerPoint Central from Microsoft so that you always have access to the latest information.

FIGURE 2.26.

PowerPoint Central offers quick access to the latest tutorials, files, and more.

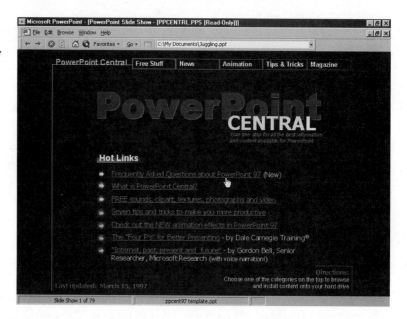

NOTE: POWERPOINT COVERAGE

You'll find this book's PowerPoint material in Part VI, "Unleashing PowerPoint."

What's New in Access 97

Although Access 97 still has plenty to recommend it, it doesn't come with the long list of new and enhanced features found in the other Office applications. The Access improvements are concentrated in three areas: performance, ease of use, and data sharing. Here's a summary:

Improved performance: Access has gone from being one of the slowest desktop relational database systems to one of the fastest. With each new iteration, the Access programmers seem to squeeze a bit more performance out of the Access database engine. Access 97 is no exception, because it's noticeably faster than its predecessors. (Microsoft claims speed increases of up to 50 percent.)

Updated Database Wizards: Access now ships with 22 different Database Wizards that cover everything from simple address books to sophisticated inventory control systems (see Figure 2.27).

FIGURE 2.27.

Access 97 has nearly two dozen Database Wizards for easy database setup.

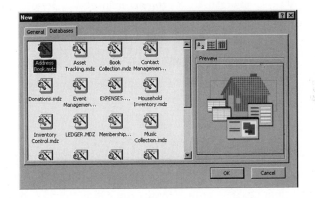

Design tables in datasheet view: With Access 97, you can now make design changes to a table while in datasheet view. For example, you can insert, delete, and rename fields.

Filter by Form: All Access 97 forms have a Filter by Form mode that lets users filter a table using familiar form controls (see Figure 2.28).

Filter by Selection: With this filter, users can select a value in a field and then filter the entire table to show only records that use that value.

Replication enhancements: You can now replicate databases over the Internet and replicate partial tables.

FIGURE 2.28.

All Access 97 forms have a Filter by Form mode.

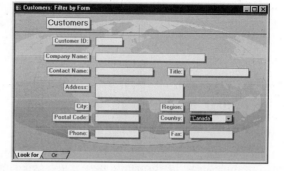

NOTE: ACCESS CHAPTERS

For information on using Access, see Part V, "Unleashing Access."

Outlook: A DIM View

In the never-ending quest to straighten out our lives, we've seen no shortage of software solutions, from personal organizers to contact managers to personal information managers. Now, with Outlook, we have yet another category of organizing software: the *desktop information manager.* As its name (but not its unfortunate "DIM" acronym) implies, this new category operates on a more general level than its predecessors. So, yes, you can use Outlook to store names and phone numbers, and you can use it to set up appointments and remind you of birthdays. But Outlook also offers the following:

- E-mail features integrated throughout
- One-click access to a contact's Web site
- The ability to view and work with disk files and folders
- Full support for the groupware features found in Microsoft Exchange Server
- The ability to track your activities (including the files you work with and the phone calls you make)

The seven chapters in Part VII, "Unleashing Outlook," show you how to unleash all these features. For now, though, here's a quick look at each of the major features of Outlook:

Inbox: This is Outlook's e-mail client (see Figure 2.29). Like Exchange, the Outlook client supports multiple e-mail systems, including Internet Mail, Microsoft Mail, Exchange Server, and the Microsoft Network. However, Outlook goes well beyond Exchange (the Windows 95 version, that is) by offering many advanced features, such as multiple views, message filtering and grouping, rules, and automatic signatures.

FIGURE 2.29.

The Outlook Inbox.

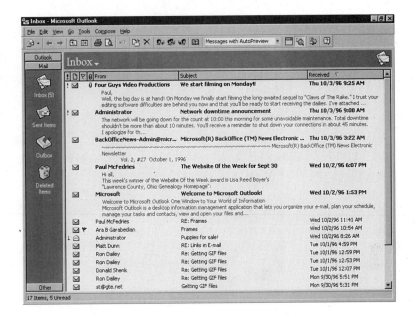

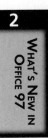

Calendar: This is Outlook's scheduling tool (see Figure 2.30). It lets you define both one-time-only and recurring appointments and events. The interface is extremely flexible in that not only does it support the standard daily, weekly, and monthly views, but you can also view any number of days. Also, the new AutoDate feature lets you enter natural-language dates (such as next Tuesday) and have them translated into the correct dates. As with Schedule+, you can also have Outlook remind you of upcoming appointments. The Meeting Planner is a handy tool that takes much of the confusion and guesswork out of organizing a large meeting.

Contacts: This folder is a very powerful contacts database (see Figure 2.31). There are over 100 fields that you can track, including e-mail addresses and Web sites. You can phone contacts using your modem, send e-mail messages, plan meetings, and even surf to Web sites, all within this folder.

Tasks: This is your Outlook "to-do" list. Not only can you set up personal tasks, but you can also send "task requests" via e-mail to other people. If they accept these requests, each person's Tasks folder is updated automatically. For ongoing tasks, the other person can send you "status reports" to keep you apprised of his or her progress. (Again, Outlook updates the task's status automatically.)

Journal: This is one of Outlook's most interesting features. The Journal is a record of various tasks you've performed, such as sending an e-mail message, making a phone call, or submitting a meeting request. A timeline shows you when you performed each activity. You can also set up Journal to show you when you worked with Office documents and for how long.

FIGURE 2.30.

Outlook's Calendar module.

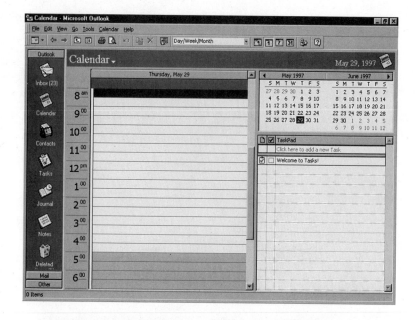

FIGURE 2.31.

Outlook's Contacts module.

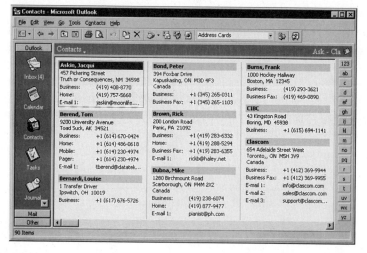

Notes: This is Outlook's answer to sticky notes. A Note is a small window in which you enter some text, such as a scrap of conversation, a quotation, or an idea. These Notes are independent of the Outlook window, so you can keep them in view all the time.

Exchange Server support: The groupware tools in Exchange Server are fully supported in Outlook. This means that you can set up public folders for global contact lists and shared schedules. And you can create newsgroup-like folders in which messages are posted to the folder, not to individuals.

NOTE: OUTLOOK

I discuss all of Outlook's features in detail in Part VII.

New VBA Features

VBA 5.0 is no mere incremental upgrade. Since the previous version was released with Office 95, Microsoft has spent its time revamping the interface and cramming the VBA tool chest with countless new programming gadgets and gewgaws. (In case you're wondering, the "5.0" designation doesn't mean all that much. It just synchronizes the version numbers of VBA and the latest incarnation of Visual Basic.) I'll show you how to take advantage of many of these new features in Part XI, "Unleashing Office Application Development with VBA," but let's begin with a sneak preview so you'll know what to expect:

VBA is now Office-wide: VBA is now the common macro language for the entire Microsoft Office suite. This means that you can leverage your existing knowledge of VBA syntax, statements, and functions and put it to immediate use with the objects exposed by Word and PowerPoint. But that's not all. Thanks to the wonders of OLE Automation, other Office tools expose their objects to VBA. This means, for example, that you can compose and send e-mail messages programmatically by manipulating the appropriate objects in Outlook.

A new integrated development environment: Word, Excel, and PowerPoint now share a new integrated development environment (IDE). This is a separate VBA window that gives you a "big-picture" view of the current VBA project. As you can see in Figure 2.32, this view includes a Project Editor that lists the application objects (documents) in the current file and a Properties window that lists the available properties for the current object. You can use this IDE to add new modules and forms to the project, write code, and debug your procedures.

Internet/intranet support: The Internet and intranet features built into Office 97 are fully supported in VBA. This means that your procedures can create and work with hyperlinks, incorporate Internet Explorer's browser objects, send e-mail, and more. Also, you can use VBScript—a subset of the VBA language—to validate Web page form input and establish lines of communication between Web page objects.

Support for ActiveX controls: VBA can work with any of the ActiveX controls (formerly known as OLE controls) that are installed on your system. This lets you set up dynamic forms and dialog boxes with richer content.

Improved code editor: The editor you use to write VBA code has been beefed up with some welcome new features. In addition to existing features such as on-the-fly syntax checking and color-coded keywords, the new editor also includes the *IntelliSense* feature, which provides syntax help on-demand. In Figure 2.33, for example, you can see that the editor displays a pop-up menu that shows you a list of the properties and methods you can use to complete a line of code. The editor also displays the appropriate arguments when you enter a function or statement.

FIGURE 2.32.

You now work with VBA in a separate IDE.

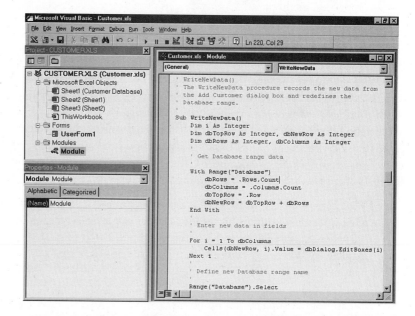

FIGURE 2.33.

The new IntelliSense feature provides syntax help on-demand.

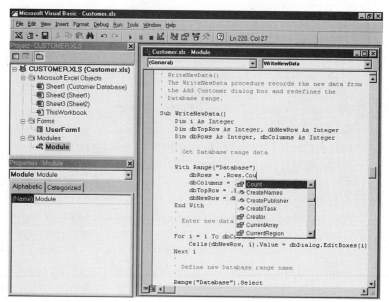

A common forms-building tool: For interactive applications, Word, Excel, and PowerPoint share a common forms-building tool that you can use to create feedback forms and dialog boxes. The objects you use to build these forms have a number of properties, methods, and events, so you can control any aspect of a form programmatically.

The new and improved Object Browser: Objects are at the heart of VBA, and the vast majority of your VBA procedures will manipulate one or more objects in some way. However, Office exposes well over 500 objects and untold thousands of properties, methods, and events. To help you keep everything straight, the Object Browser, shown in Figure 2.34, has been greatly improved. It now groups each object's properties, methods, and events (with separate icons for each type), lets you search for objects and members, provides hypertext links to related objects, and lets you view the associated Help topic for the current item.

FIGURE 2.34.

The new Object Browser.

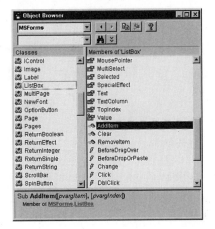

Improvements to Data Access Objects: The Data Access Objects (DAO) model has been enhanced to improve performance, support database replication, and provide better support in multiuser environments. In addition, you can use a new client/server connection mode called ODBCDirect to establish a direct connection to an ODBC database without loading the Jet database engine.

Command bars: Working with menu bars, toolbars, and shortcut menus has been streamlined in VBA 5.0. A new *command bars* object model encapsulates each of these objects into a single structure with common properties and methods.

Class modules: VBA now lets you use *class modules* to set up your own objects. Procedures and functions defined within a class module become the methods and properties of the user-defined object.

Improved security: To prevent users from accessing (and possibly modifying) your code, you can now set up VBA projects with password protection. Because VBA modules and forms are separate from the document objects (for example, Excel no longer has module sheets), securing your project in no way restricts the user from working with the underlying document.

Conditional compilation: Your VBA procedures can now use *conditional compilation* to control which statements get compiled. For example, if you use the Windows API, you'll need to differentiate between 16-bit calls and 32-bit calls. Similarly, you might want to include debugging "flags" in your code and use conditional compilation to turn certain debugging features on when you're testing and off when you distribute the application.

NOTE: VBA PROGRAMMING TUTORIAL

This book comes with an extensive tutorial on VBA programming. You'll find it in Part XI.

Other New and Improved Features

To complete our look at the Office 97 enhancements, here's a list of a few other goodies that are either new or improved:

Office Assistant: The Office Assistant acts as a sort of general-purpose Help system front end, albeit a very sophisticated one. Among other things, the Office Assistant can provide on-the-fly advice while you work (this is tied in with the IntelliSense feature I discusses earlier; see Figure 2.7), and it lets you ask natural-language questions (such as How do I compose a fax?; see Figure 2.35). Not only that, but the Office Assistant is both customizable and programmable via VBA.

FIGURE 2.35.

The Office Assistant accepts non-geek questions.

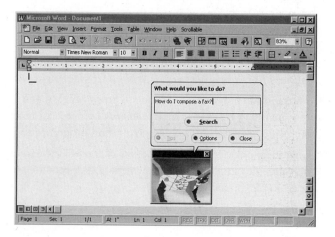

OfficeArt: The Office drawing tools have been completely revamped into their present OfficeArt configuration. You get many new features, including a more efficient Drawing toolbar, AutoShapes (prebuilt shapes such as boxes, stars, arrows, and flowchart symbols), extensive fill effects (including gradients and textures), Bezier curves, 3-D effects, shadows, and much more.

Clip Gallery: This is a new one-stop shop for all your clip art and multimedia file needs. As you can see from Figure 2.36, the Clip Gallery displays not only standard clip-art files, but also picture files (BMP, GIF, JPEG, and so on), sound files, and video files.

FIGURE 2.36.

The Clip Gallery makes it easy to add clip art, images, sounds, and videos to a document.

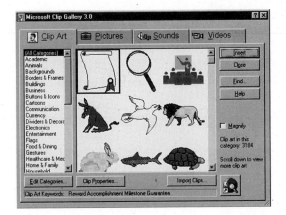

Enhanced Office Binder: The Binder has a few new features, including the ability to specify common headers, footers, and margins, and the ability to print each Binder document in a single print job.

The IntelliMouse: Microsoft's new IntelliMouse includes a small wheel between the two buttons. Within any Office document, you can use this wheel to scroll up and down or zoom in and out.

Summary

This chapter closed our introduction to Office 97 by running through what's new and improved. I began by showing you the new interface and Internet features, and then I went through the enhancements to Word, Excel, PowerPoint, Access, Outlook, and VBA. Here's a list of chapters where you'll find related information:

- I show you how to wield the OfficeArt tools and the Clip Gallery in Chapter 5, "Using the OfficeArt Tools."

- For information on the Office Assistant and the IntelliMouse features, see Chapter 7, "More Office Tools."

■ Head for Part III, "Unleashing Word," to learn more about using Word 97.

■ I cover Excel's features in Part IV, "Unleashing Excel."

■ For information on using Access, see Part V, "Unleashing Access."

■ This book's PowerPoint material is in Part VI, "Unleashing PowerPoint."

■ I discuss Outlook's features in Part VII, "Unleashing Outlook."

■ I cover all the Office 97 Internet features in Part VIII, "Unleashing the Office Internet Tools."

■ I show you how to use Binder in Chapter 49, "Packaging Office Documents with Binder."

■ You'll find VBA information in Part XI, "Unleashing Office Application Development with VBA."

IN THIS PART

II

PART

Unleashing Office 97's Common Features

Day-to-Day Office Basics

IN THIS CHAPTER

CHAPTER 3

Where the telescope ends, the microscope begins. Which of the two has the grander view?

—*Victor Hugo*

Now that you and Microsoft Office have been properly introduced, it's time for the two of you to get acquainted. To that end, the chapters here in Part II will take you through all the features that are common throughout the Office suite. You'll learn about printing techniques; how to use Microsoft Graph, OfficeArt, the Office Assistant, and other tools; and how to customize the Office menus and toolbars.

For starters, though, this chapter gives you the goods on a few workday Office chores, including opening, saving, and starting a new document; working with document windows and properties; formatting and finding text; and spell-checking your work.

Creating a New Document

When you launch an Office application, the program will either load a new document automatically (in the case of Word and Excel) or prompt you to either create a new document or open an existing one (in the case of PowerPoint and Access).

NOTE: THE GENERIC DOCUMENT

Throughout this chapter (and, indeed, throughout this book), I'll be using the word *document* in its most generic sense. In other words, a document will be any file that you create using Word, Excel, PowerPoint, or Access. So, yes, a document can be a memo or letter created in Word, but it can also be an Excel workbook, a PowerPoint presentation, or an Access database.

Creating a New, Default Document

Once you've started an application, however, you can create a new document at any time. To begin, first select File | New. The application will then display the New dialog box, the format of which depends on the program. Figure 3.1 shows Word's New dialog box.

FIGURE 3.1.

Word's New dialog box.

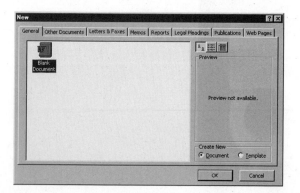

You have two choices at this point:

■ If you want to create a new document based on the application's default template (such as Normal.dot in Word), make sure the "Blank" icon is highlighted (the name of this icon varies among the applications), and then click OK.

> **TIP: FASTER DEFAULT TEMPLATE DOCUMENTS**
>
> There are two quicker ways to create a new document based on the application's default template: Either click the New button on the toolbar, or press Ctrl-N.

■ To use another template as the basis for the new document, open one of the other tabs in the New dialog box, highlight the template you want to use, and click OK. Depending on the template, either you'll get a fresh document or a Wizard will load to lead you through the steps necessary to set up the new document.

Creating a New Document Outside of the Application

Although you'll normally create new documents within an Office application, it's possible to create them outside of any Office program. Office itself gives you two methods:

■ Select Start | New Office Document.
■ Click the New Office Document button on the Office Shortcut Bar (see Chapter 7, "More Office Tools").

Either way, Office loads the New Office Document dialog box, from which you can create a default document or a template-based document for any Office application.

You can also use Windows Explorer to create a new document. It's not surprising that you can create new folders in Explorer—after all, this is a common task in any file management system—but it's certainly unusual that you can create new files. However, this is in keeping with Windows 95's "think documents, not applications" approach. Explorer "understands" certain file types, so it's easy for it to create new, empty files.

To create a new Office document in Explorer, first highlight the folder in which you want the new document stored. Now, either select File | New or right-click inside the file list and choose New. (The latter technique also works on the Windows desktop.) The cascade menu that appears contains a number of commands, as shown in Figure 3.2, but you'll see a few that are Office-specific. For example, you can choose Microsoft Word Document to create a new, empty Word file.

FIGURE 3.2.

You can create new Office documents from within Explorer.

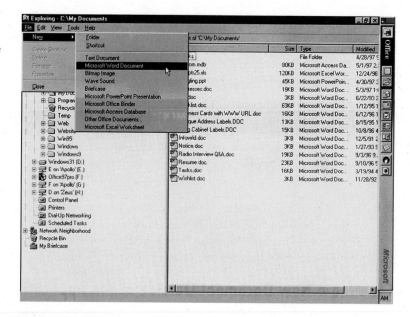

Opening a Document

Instead of using a new, blank document, you'll often have to open an existing document to make changes or view the document's data. There are three techniques you can use to start this process:

- Select File | Open.
- Press Ctrl-O.

- Click the Open toolbar button.

Whichever method you choose, the Open dialog box appears, as shown in Figure 3.3.

FIGURE 3.3.

Use the Open dialog box to open an existing document.

The Open Dialog Box

With the Open dialog box displayed, you use the Look in lists to find the document you need. Use the top drop-down list to choose the appropriate drive and folder, and use the lower list to highlight the document. When that's done, click OK to open the file.

To help you locate the file you need, the Open dialog box lets you specify simple search criteria using the following controls:

File name: If you know the name of the file, enter it in this text box. That way, the dialog box won't display any files that don't match this name.

Files of type: Use this drop-down list to choose the type of file you want to open.

Text or property: If you know the document you need contains a specific word or phrase, or a specific value in a document property, enter the word, phrase, or value in this text box. If you enter a phrase, be sure to enclose it in quotation marks (for example, `"shopping list"`).

Last modified: Use this drop-down list to select a date range in which to search (such as `today` or `last month`).

Find Now: Click this button to have the application search for files that meet your criteria.

New Search: Click this button to clear your search criteria and return to the default Open dialog box values.

The Open dialog box also includes several buttons that control navigation and the file display. Table 3.1 provides a summary.

Table 3.1. Open dialog box buttons.

Button	Name	Description
	Up One Level	Click this button to display the parent of the current folder. For example, if the current folder is C:\My Documents\ Memos, clicking this button will display C:\My Documents. You can also move up one folder level by pressing the Backspace key.
	Search the Web	This button launches Internet Explorer and displays the Find it Fast page that lets you search the World Wide Web for a document (see Chapter 44, "The Office 97 Internet Tools").

continues

Table 3.1. continued

Button	Name	Description
	Look in Favorites	Click this button to display the Favorites folder. Once you've displayed Favorites, click this button again to return to the original folder.
	Add to Favorites	Click this button to add either the current folder or the currently selected file to the Favorites folder.
	List	Click this button to display the document list with filenames only.
	Details	Click this button to display the document list with filenames, file size, file type, and the date and time each file was last modified.
	Properties	Click this button to display a separate pane that shows the document properties of the highlighted file (see Figure 3.4).
	Preview	Click this button to display a separate pane that shows a preview of the highlighted document.
	Commands and Settings	Click this button to access various commands and defaults (see "Using the Open Dialog Box Commands and Settings").

FIGURE 3.4.

The Open dialog box showing document properties.

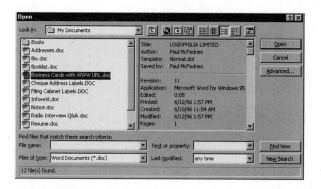

Opening Multiple Documents

If you regularly work with multiple documents, you don't need to run a separate Open command for each file. Instead, the Open dialog box lets you choose multiple files at once. Here are the three methods you can use to select multiple documents:

- To select nonconsecutive documents, hold down the Ctrl key and click each document.

- To select consecutive documents, click the first document, hold down the Shift key, and click the last document.

- You can also select a group of documents by "boxing" them with the mouse. Move the mouse pointer to the right of the first document's name (make sure that it's not over the document's name or icon), and then drag the mouse pointer down and to the left. As you're dragging, you'll see a dotted-line box; every document that falls at least partially within that box gets highlighted. When all the documents you need are highlighted, release the mouse button.

File Maintenance from the Open Dialog Box

You'll probably use Windows Explorer as the base of operations for basic file maintenance such as copying, renaming, and deleting files. However, you can perform many of these chores right in the Open dialog box. Here's a summary of the various techniques you can use:

Renaming a file: Either highlight the file and press F2, or right-click the file and choose Rename. Use the text box that appears to edit the filename, and then press Enter.

Copying a file: Either highlight the file and press Ctrl-C, or right-click the file and choose Copy. Now move to the folder in which you want the copy to appear, and then either press Ctrl-V or right-click inside the folder and choose Paste.

Moving a file: Either highlight the file and press Ctrl-X or right-click the file and choose Cut. Now move to the folder in which you want to move the file, and then either press Ctrl-V or right-click inside the folder and choose Paste.

Deleting a file: Either highlight the file and press Delete or right-click the file and choose Delete.

Printing a file: Right-click the file and choose Print.

Using the Open Dialog Box Commands and Settings

The new Open dialog boxes have so many features that they're really mini-applications in themselves. They even come with a few built-in commands you can run and options you can set. To view these features, click the Commands and Settings button to display the menu shown in Figure 3.5. Here's a summary of what's available on this menu:

Open Read-Only: Opens the highlighted document in read-only mode (which means you won't be able to save any changes to the file).

Open as Copy: Makes a copy of the highlighted document, appends `Copy of` to the filename, and then opens this new file.

Print: Prints the highlighted file.

Properties: Displays the file properties of the highlighted document.

Sorting: Displays the Sort By dialog box, shown in Figure 3.6. Use the drop-down list to choose the sorting field, and then select either Ascending or Descending and click OK.

TIP: SORTING IN DETAILS VIEW

If you display the Open dialog box in Details view, you can sort the files by clicking the headers that appear at the top of each column. Keep clicking the header to toggle between an ascending and descending sort.

Search Subfolders: For the simple search criteria that I outlined earlier, the Open dialog box looks only in the current folder. If you also want it to check the subfolders, choose this command.

Group files by folder: If you have the Search Subfolders command enabled, the found files are grouped by folder. To see an ungrouped list of the found files, deactivate this command.

Map Network Drive: You can use this command to map a network drive to a local drive letter on your computer.

Add/Modify FTP Locations: This command lets you work with Internet FTP sites in the Open dialog box. See Chapter 44 for details.

Saved Searches: You'll see in the next section that the Open dialog box lets you save search criteria for later use. If you have any saved searches, this command displays them in a cascade menu. To run any search again, select it from this menu.

FIGURE 3.5.

The Commands and Settings menu of the Open dialog box.

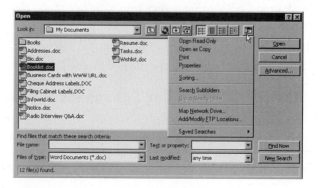

FIGURE 3.6.

Use this dialog box to specify the sort order for the files shown in the Open dialog box.

Advanced Document Searching

The simple criteria available in the Open dialog box combined with the search-related commands discussed in the preceding section should satisfy most of your document-searching needs. However, you'll need a more powerful tool if your searching requires any of the following:

- The ability to specify wildcard characters for filenames or text
- The ability to specify multiple criteria
- The ability to search specific document properties
- The ability to save search criteria for future use

For all of these conditions and more, you'll need to turn to the Advanced Find dialog box, shown in Figure 3.7. To display this dialog box, click the Advanced button in the Open dialog box. The next few sections show you how to work with the various Advanced Find controls.

FIGURE 3.7.

Use the Advanced Find dialog box for more sophisticated searches.

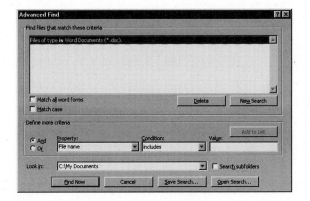

Step 1: Specifying a Location

By default, the Advanced Find dialog box searches in whatever folder was currently displayed in the Open dialog box. The name and path of this folder appear in the Look in text box. If you want to select a different folder, use the drop-down list to find the one you need.

Also note that Advanced Find has a Search subfolders check box. If you activate this option, Advanced Find will search not only the current folder, but also all of its subfolders.

3

DAY-TO-DAY
OFFICE BASICS

Step 2: Defining Criteria

The next step is to specify one or more criteria to use as the parameters of your search. Creating a single criterion involves working with the following controls in the Define more criteria group:

Property: Use this drop-down list to select the property you want to search.

Condition: Use this drop-down list to choose the criterion operator (the available operators depend on the property you chose).

Value: Use this text box to enter the value that you want Advanced Find to match. Note that you can use wildcards and other operators:

- For text values, use a question mark (?) to substitute for a single character, and use an asterisk (*) to substitute for any string of characters. For example, pa?t matches *past, part,* and *pant,* while pa*t matches *parent, pageant,* and *parliament.*

- For numeric values, if you select the any number between condition, use and to specify a range of numbers (such as 1 and 10).

- For date values, if you select the any time between condition, use and to specify a range of dates (such as August 1, 1997 and August 31, 1997).

When your criterion is ready, click Add to List to add it to the list of criteria at the top of the dialog box.

If you want to define another criterion, you first need to decide if it should be an "And" criterion or an "Or" criterion:

And: In this case, Advanced Find matches a document only if it satisfies both criteria.

Or: In this case, Advanced Find matches a document only if it satisfies one or both of the criteria.

> **NOTE: WORKING WITH CRITERIA**
>
> If you change your mind and decide you don't want a particular criterion in the search definition, highlight the criterion and click Delete.
>
> If you'd prefer to start the whole thing over again, click the New Search button.

Step 3: Finishing Up

Advanced Find gives you two more options that apply to all of the criteria:

Match all word forms: Activate this check box to have Advanced Find match all the variations for your criteria text (except filenames). For example, if your criterion includes the word move, Advanced Find will match documents that contain not only move, but also *moved, moving, mover, moves,* and so on.

Match case: Activate this check box to make your search case-sensitive. For example, if reed is part of your criteria, a case-sensitive search will match documents containing *reed,* but not those containing *Reed.*

If you want to save these search criteria to use again at a later time, click Save Search, enter a name for the search in the Save Search dialog box that appears, and click OK.

NOTE: RUNNING A SAVED SEARCH

There are two methods you can use to run a saved search:

- In the Open dialog box, click the Commands and Settings button, click Searches, and then click the saved search you want to run.

- In the Advanced Find dialog box, click Open Search, highlight the search you want to use in the Open Search dialog box that appears, and then click Open. When you're back in the Advanced Find dialog box, click Find Now.

With all of that out of the way, you're now ready to run the search, which you can do by clicking the Find Now button.

Saving a Document

When you open a document, the application copies it into your computer's random access memory (RAM). This makes things much faster (memory chips operate blindingly fast compared to hard disks) but inherently more dangerous because the contents of memory are purged whenever you turn off your computer. This means that a program crash or power failure could wipe out all your work in the blink of an eye.

The Save Command

To be safe, you should regularly save a copy of your work to the relatively safe confines of your hard disk. Happily, saving a file in any Office application is only a couple of mouse clicks or keystrokes away:

- Select File | Save.
- Press Ctrl-S.

- Click the Save toolbar button.

If you've saved the document before, the application will write your changes to the hard disk file and then return you to the document. If you're saving a new file, however, you'll see the Save As dialog box, discussed in the next section.

The Save As Command

One of the fundamental axioms of computer productivity is "Don't reinvent the wheel." If you have, say, a nicely formatted spreadsheet that works properly, and you need something similar, don't start from scratch. Instead, you can use the Save As command to save a copy of the existing document under a different name.

To do this, select File | Save As to display the Save As dialog box, shown in Figure 3.8. It is much like the Open dialog box you saw earlier. Use the Save in list to choose a location for the file, use the File name text box to name the document, and click Save.

FIGURE 3.8.

The Save As dialog box appears either when you're saving a new document or when you select File | Save As.

TIP: CREATING FOLDERS ON-THE-FLY

One of the handiest features of the new Save As dialog box is that you can use it to create a folder without having to switch to Windows Explorer. Simply click the New Folder button, enter a name for the folder, and press Enter.

Creating a Template

You saw earlier how you can create new documents based on existing templates. A template is a document that contains a basic layout (formatting, styles, default text, macros, and so on) that you can use as a skeleton for similar documents. A template ensures that the documents you use frequently all have a consistent look and feel. For example, if you need to consolidate budget numbers from various departments, your task will be much easier if all the Excel work-books have the same layout. To that end, you can issue each department a budget template containing the layout you want everyone to use.

Creating a template is similar to creating any other document. The following procedure outlines the required steps:

1. Set up the document with the settings you want to preserve in the template. You can either use an existing document or create a new one.

2. Select File | Save As to display the Save As dialog box.

3. Enter a name for the template in the File name text box (you don't need to add an extension—see step 4).

4. In the Save as type drop-down list, select the Template option. In Word, for example, you'd select Document Template (*.dot). The application displays the Templates folder (this is a subfolder within your main Microsoft Office folder).

5. Use the Save in list to select the appropriate folder for the template. For example, the templates that ship with Excel are stored in the Spreadsheet Solutions folder.

6. Click Save.

Once that's done, you can follow the instructions provided earlier to create a new document based on your template.

Working with Document Windows

As a user of the Windows environment, you know what an advantage it is to have multiple applications running in their own windows. Most Windows applications take this concept a step further by letting you open multiple documents in their own windows. However, the Office applications (except Access) go one better by letting you open multiple windows for the *same* document.

When you open a second window on a document, you're not opening a new file; you're viewing the same file twice. You can navigate independently in each window, so you can display different parts of a document at the same time. The application even lets you change the document display for every window.

Opening a New Document Window

To open another window for the current document in Word, Excel, or PowerPoint, select Window | New Window. When the application opens the new window, it changes the names that appear in the document title bar. The application appends :1 to the title of the original window and :2 to the title of the second window. Figure 3.9 shows an example using the 1996 Sales workbook. Notice that the original window now has the title 1996 Sales:1, and the new window has the title 1996 Sales:2.

The number of windows you can open for a document is limited by your computer's memory. (With Windows 95's improved memory handling, however, you shouldn't have any trouble opening as many windows as you need.) Any window you open can be moved and sized to suit your taste. Because each window is a view of the same document, any editing or formatting changes you make in one window are automatically reflected in all the other windows.

FIGURE 3.9.

*Two windows con-
taining the same
document.*

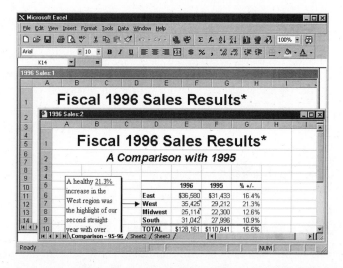

> **NOTE: USE MULTIPLE WINDOWS FOR EXCEL DATA ENTRY**
>
> You can use multiple windows to make Excel data entry easier. Open one window for the
> data-entry area, and then use other windows to display, say, a list of data codes (for
> example, part numbers or general ledger accounts).

Navigating Document Windows

After you've opened two or more windows, you'll need to switch between them. Use any of the
following techniques to navigate among document windows:

- Click any visible part of a window to activate it.
- From the Window menu, select one of the windows listed at the bottom of the menu.
  The application displays a check mark beside the currently active window.
- Press Ctrl-F6 to move to the next window. Press Ctrl-Shift-F6 to move to the preceding window.

Arranging Document Windows

One of the problems with having several windows open at once is that they tend to get in each
other's way. In most cases, it's preferable to give each window its own portion of the work area.
Even though you can move and size windows yourself, you might prefer to have the application
handle this task for you. You can do this by selecting Window | Arrange All in Word or
PowerPoint or Window | Arrange in Excel.

For the latter, you'll see the Arrange Windows dialog box, shown in Figure 3.10. The Arrange section contains the following options:

Tiled: Divides the work area into rectangles of approximately equal size (called *tiles*) and assigns each open window to a tile.

Horizontal: Divides the work area into horizontal strips of equal size and assigns each open window to a strip.

Vertical: Divides the work area into vertical strips of equal size and assigns each open window to a strip.

Cascade: Arranges the windows so that they overlap each other and so that you can see each window's title bar.

FIGURE 3.10.
Use Excel's Arrange Windows dialog box to arrange your open windows.

If you have other documents open at the same time and you want to arrange only the current document windows, activate the Windows of active workbook check box in the Arrange Windows dialog box. This tells Excel to apply the selected Arrange option to the current document windows only. When you're done, click OK to arrange the windows.

Formatting Characters

The Office applications have dozens of ways to spruce up drab, lifeless documents. Many of these formatting techniques are specific to each application, but the one area that is common to the entire Office suite (aside from OfficeArt, which I cover in Chapter 5, "Using the OfficeArt Tools") is character formatting.

This section shows you how to work with the extensive font capabilities found throughout Office. You'll learn about the various font attributes and how to apply them to your documents. Throughout this section, the emphasis is on selecting fonts that improve the impact and effectiveness of your documents.

Learning About Fonts

Back in the days when DOS dinosaurs dominated the PC landscape, people rarely had to pay much attention to the characters that made up correspondence and memos. Outside of a measly few effects (such as making words bold), there wasn't a whole lot you could do with individual letters and symbols, so they became mere foot soldiers in any given war of words.

The advent of the graphical interface changed all that, however. With Windows, it suddenly became a snap to alter the size and shape of letters and numbers and therefore impart an entirely different atmosphere to writings. The engine behind this newfound typographical prowess was, of course, the *font.*

I always like to describe fonts as the "architecture" of characters. When you examine a building, certain features and patterns help you identify the building's architectural style. A flying buttress, for example, is usually a telltale sign of a Gothic structure. Fonts too are distinguished by a unique set of characteristics. Specifically, four items define the architecture of any character: the typeface, the type size, the type style, and the character spacing.

Font Architecture I: Typeface

A *typeface* is a distinctive design that's common to any related set of letters, numbers, and symbols. This design gives each character a particular shape and thickness (or *weight,* as it's called in type circles) that's unique to the typeface and difficult to classify. However, three main categories serve to distinguish all typefaces: serif, sans serif, and decorative.

A *serif* typeface contains fine cross strokes (called *feet*) at the extremities of each character. These subtle appendages give the typeface a traditional, classy look that's most often used for long stretches of text. Windows 95 comes with Times New Roman, and Office adds Bookman Old Style and Garamond.

A *sans serif* typeface doesn't contain these cross strokes. As a result, sans serif typefaces usually have a cleaner, more modern look that works best for headings and titles. Arial is an example of a sans serif font that comes with Windows 95, and Office adds Arial Narrow, Haettenschweiler, and Tahoma.

Decorative typefaces are usually special designs that are supposed to convey a particular effect. So, for example, if your document needs a fancy, handwritten effect, something like Brush Script would be perfect. (Unfortunately, the Brush Script typeface doesn't come with Windows 95 or Office. However, lots of companies sell font collections that include all kinds of strange and useful fonts.)

Figure 3.11 shows examples of a few typefaces. As you can see, they can produce dramatically different effects.

Here are some general rules for selecting document typefaces:

- Use sans serif typefaces for numbers, headings, and titles. Sans serif characters tend to be wider and cleaner-looking than their serif counterparts, which is helpful when you're displaying numbers or brief but large text entries. (A sans serif typeface—Arial—is the default typeface used by Excel.)
- Use serif typefaces for lengthy sections of text. The elegant serif design makes smaller characters easy to read. (The serif typeface Times New Roman is the default typeface used in Word.)

- When choosing a typeface for a report, take your audience into consideration. If you're presenting a report to a business group, you should use more conservative typefaces, such as Bookman Old Style or Times New Roman. In more relaxed settings, you can try AvantGarde or even (in small doses) a calligraphic font such as Brush Script.

- Try to limit yourself to two typefaces (at most) in a single document. Using more makes your reports look jumbled and confusing. It's much more effective to vary type size and style within a single typeface than to use many different typefaces.

FIGURE 3.11.

Some sample typefaces in Word.

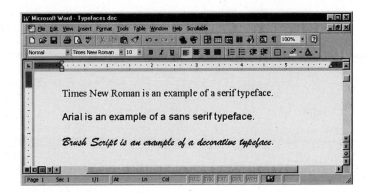

Font Architecture II: Type Size

The *type size* measures how tall a font is. The standard unit of measurement is the *point;* there are 72 points in an inch. So, for example, the letters in a 24-point font would be twice as tall as those in a 12-point font. Technically, type size is measured from the highest point of a tall letter, such as f, to the lowest point of an underhanging letter, such as g. Figure 3.12 shows a few examples of type sizes. (In case you're wondering, this book is laid out in a 10.5-point AGaramond font.)

FIGURE 3.12.

Some sample type sizes.

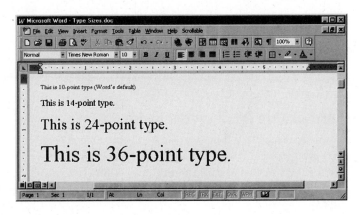

Use different type sizes in your documents to differentiate titles and headings from data:

- Use 24- or even 36-point type for document titles, but remember that your title must fit on a single page. If your report has a subtitle, use a type size that's slightly smaller than the one used in the main title. For example, if your title is in 24-point type, make the subtitle 18-point type.

- In Excel, column and row labels look good in 12- or 14-point type, but, again, watch the size. If your labels are too large, you'll have to widen your columns accordingly.

- For most reports, the standard 10-point type is fine for your data, although you'll probably have to switch to a larger type (such as 12-point or even 14-point) if you plan to present your work on a slide or overhead.

Font Architecture III: Type Style

The *type style* of a font refers to extra attributes added to the typeface, such as **bold** and *italic*. Other type styles (often called type *effects*) include <u>underlining</u> and ~~strikeout~~ (sometimes called *strikethrough*). These styles are normally used to highlight or add emphasis to sections of your documents.

Figure 3.13 shows an Excel worksheet that implements several type styles. As you can see, fonts are a powerful way to improve your document design.

FIGURE 3.13.

Using fonts effectively can greatly improve the appearance of your documents.

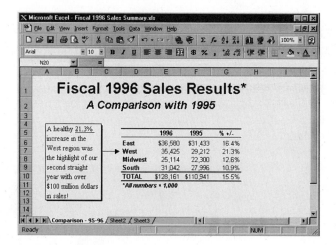

Font Architecture IV: Character Spacing

The *character spacing* of a font can take two forms: *monospaced* or *proportional.* Monospaced fonts reserve the same amount of space for each character. For example, look at the Courier New font shown in Figure 3.14. Notice how skinny letters such as i and l take up as much space as wider letters such as m and w. Although this is admirably egalitarian, these fonts tend to look like they were produced with a typewriter (in other words, they're *ugly*).

FIGURE 3.14.
Monospaced versus proportional character spacing.

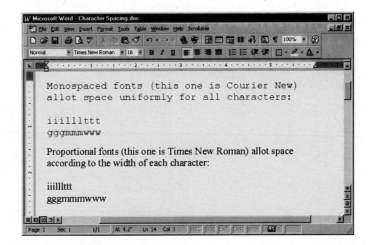

In contrast, in a proportional font, such as the Times New Roman font shown in Figure 3.14, the space allotted to each letter varies according to the width of the letter. This gives the text a more natural feel.

Using Fonts

In the Office applications, you're free to use as many fonts as you like, although, in practice, a presentation-quality report should use only a few fonts. (To be clear, a font is a specific combination of typeface, type size, and type style. This means that 10-point Arial is a different font than 24-point Arial Bold.)

To select a font in any Office program, first perform one of the following tasks:

- If you want to apply the formatting to new text, position the cursor where the new text will begin.

- If you want to format existing text, select the characters you want to work with. In Excel, you can select a cell, a range, or a group of characters inside a cell.

NOTE: SELECTING INDIVIDUAL CELL CHARACTERS

To select characters inside a cell, press F2 or double-click the cell to activate in-cell editing. Then use the mouse or keyboard to highlight the characters you want to format. Note that you can format individual cell characters only if the cell contains text. The characters in formulas and numbers all use the same formatting.

Selecting Fonts Via the Font Tab

Select Format | Font (in Excel, select Format | Cells) and then select the Font tab in the dialog box that appears. The layout of this tab will vary among the applications, but Word's, shown in Figure 3.15, is more or less representative of the species.

FIGURE 3.15.

Use the Font tab to set your font options.

Here's a summary of the common controls you'll see in your Office font formatting travels:

Font: Use this list to select the typeface (in Office, the terms *font* and *typeface* are used interchangeably).

Font style: Use this list to choose a style of text.

Size: Use this list to select a point size.

Color: Use this list to select a color for the text.

Effects: Use these check boxes to toggle various text effects on and off. The number of options available varies from program to program.

When you're done, click OK to put the new font settings into effect.

Selecting Fonts Via the Formatting Toolbar

Besides using the Font tab, you can set many of the font attributes using the Formatting toolbar, which contains the following font tools:

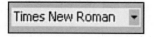   Use the Font drop-down list box to select a typeface.

    Use the Font Size drop-down list box to select a font size.

B   Click the Bold tool to apply the bold font style.

I   Click the Italic tool to apply the italic font style.

U   Click the Underline tool to apply the underline font style.

A ▾   Drop down the Font Color tool to apply a color.

Selecting Fonts Via Shortcut Keys

If you don't have a mouse, or if you prefer to use the keyboard, you can use the various keyboard shortcuts that Office provides to select font attributes. Table 3.2 lists these shortcut key combinations.

Table 3.2. Shortcut keys for selecting font attributes.

Shortcut Key	Result
Ctrl-B	Toggles the bold style on and off
Ctrl-I	Toggles the italic style on and off
Ctrl-U	Toggles the underline effect on and off

Finding and Replacing Text

If you've ever found yourself lamenting some long-lost text adrift in some huge mega-document, the folks who designed Office can sympathize (probably because it has happened to *them* once or twice). In fact, they were even kind enough to build a special Find feature into the Office applications to help you search for missing records. Find can look for all or part of a word or phrase in a document, and it has various options for matching case and using wildcard characters.

The Office applications also come with a Replace feature that lets you easily replace one or more instances of one piece of text with another. The next two sections discuss both features in depth.

Finding Text

If you need to find text in a relatively small document, it's usually easiest just to scroll through the file using the mouse or keyboard. But if you're dealing with a large document, don't waste your time rummaging through the whole file. The Find feature lets you quickly and easily search the entire document for a key word or phrase.

When you're ready to begin, either select Edit | Find or press Ctrl-F to display the Find dialog box. Again, the layout of this dialog box varies among the Office applications.

The Word Find and Replace Dialog Box

Figure 3.16 shows Word's default Find and Replace dialog box. Click the More button to get the expanded dialog box shown in Figure 3.17.

FIGURE 3.16.

Use the Find and Replace dialog box to track down text in a document.

FIGURE 3.17.

Click the More button to expand the Find and Replace dialog box.

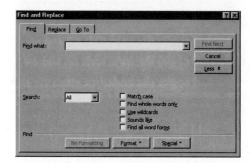

Here's a summary of the various controls in the expanded dialog box:

Find what: Use this text box to enter the word or phrase you want to find.

Search: If you suspect that the text you want to find is below the current cursor position, select Down. If you think the text is above the current cursor position, select Up. If you're not sure, select All to search the entire document.

Match case: Activate this check box to make your search case-sensitive.

Find whole words only: When this check box is deactivated, Word will look for text that *contains* the search text. If you only want to find words that match the search text exactly, activate this check box.

Use wildcards: Activate this check box if you want to use Word's pattern-matching feature, which supports the following wildcard characters:

Character	What It Matches
?	Any single character. For example, pa?t finds *part* and *past*.
*	Zero or more characters. For example, pa*t finds *parent* and *parakeet*.
[character-list]	Any single character in *character-list*, which can be either a series of characters (such as [aeiou]) or a range (such as [a-m]). For example, pa[cn]t finds *pact* and *pant*.
[!character-list]	Any single character not in *character-list*. For example, pa[!r]t doesn't find *part*.
{n}	Exactly *n* occurrences of the previous character. For example, pat{2}er finds *patter* but not *pater*.
{n,}	At least *n* occurrences of the previous character. For example, pat{1,}er finds *patter* and *pater*.
{n,m}	From *n* to *m* occurrences of the previous character. For example, 50{1,3} finds *50, 500,* and *5000*.
@	One or more occurrences of the previous character. For example, pas@*t finds *past* and *passe-partout*.
<	The beginning of a word. For example, <pat finds *patent* and *pattern,* but not *spat* or *dispatch*.
>	The end of a word. For example, >pat finds *spat* but not *patter* or *dispatch*.

TIP: SEARCHING FOR WILDCARD CHARACTERS

To search for one of the wildcard characters, precede the character with a backslash (\). For example, use \< to search for the less-than sign.

Sounds like: Activate this check box to perform a "soundex" search that matches words that sound like the search text. For example, if you enter past as your search text, Word will match both *past* and *passed*.

Find all word forms: Activate this check box to find not only the search word, but all its related forms. For example, if your search text is find, Word will match not only *find,* but also *found, finding, finds,* and so on.

Format: Use this button to search for text formatting. When you click this button, Word displays a list of formatting categories. Clicking a category displays a dialog box that you use to select the formatting you want to search for.

Special: Use this button to select a special character to search for. These characters include paragraph marks, tabs, page breaks, and more.

Find Next: Click this button to start the search. If the text that Word finds (assuming the search is successful) isn't the instance you want, click Find Next again to find the next instance of your search text. (In this case, "next" depends on whether you're searching up or down.)

If Word can't find the search text, it lets you know when it has reached the bottom of the document (if you're searching down) or the top of the document (if you're searching up) and asks if you want to continue the search. Click Yes to search the rest of the document. If Word still can't find the search text, it displays a message to let you know.

The Excel Find Dialog Box

Excel's Find dialog box, shown in Figure 3.18, gives you a few extra options that are specific to searching worksheets:

Search: Use this drop-down list to choose the direction in which Excel should search. If you select By Rows, Excel searches across each row and moves down through the sheet. If you select By Columns, Excel searches down each column and across the sheet (left to right).

Look in: Use this list to specify what part of each cell Excel should examine: formulas, values, or comments.

Find entire cells only: If you activate this check box, Excel's search will be successful only if it can exactly match the search text with the entire cell (not just part of the cell).

FIGURE 3.18.

Excel's version of the Find dialog box.

The PowerPoint Find Dialog Box

The PowerPoint Find dialog box is shown in Figure 3.19. As you can see, there are no special options, so searching is straightforward. Note, however, that PowerPoint's Find feature applies to the entire presentation, not just to the current slide.

FIGURE 3.19.

PowerPoint's Find dialog box.

The Access Find Dialog Box

The Access Find feature lets you search for a word or phrase in any field to find what you need. For example, suppose you have a table of invoices and you need to find invoice number 1234567. No problem. You'd simply tell Access to look in the Invoice Number field (or whatever it's called) for the value *1234567*. Similarly, if you want to find a customer named "Fly By Night Travel," you'd search in the Customer Name field for *fly by* or *night travel*. (As you've seen, your searches have to match only part of the name, and you don't have to worry about uppercase and lowercase.)

Before starting an Access search, you should move into the field you want to use for the search. This is optional, because Access can find data anywhere in the table. However, you'll find that this makes the search much faster. When you're ready to begin, either select Edit | Find, press Ctrl-F, or click the Find button on the toolbar. The Find dialog box appears, as shown in Figure 3.20.

FIGURE 3.20.

Use the Access Find dialog box to hunt for a record in a table.

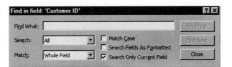

Here's a summary of the unique controls in this dialog box:

Match: The three options in this drop-down list tell Access where in the field you want to search. Any Part of Field looks for the search text anywhere in the field. Whole Field tells Access that the search text must exactly match the entire field (not just part of the field). Start of Field looks for the search text at the beginning of the field.

Search Fields As Formatted: Activate this check box if you want to search for data based on its display format and not its underlying value.

Search Only Current Field: Activate this check box to tell Access to conduct its search only in the field you selected. If you want Access to search the entire table, deactivate this check box.

When you start the search, Access moves to the record if it finds a match. If this is the record you want, click Close. Otherwise, you can continue searching by clicking the Find Next button.

3

DAY-TO-DAY
OFFICE BASICS

Finding and Replacing Text

One of the Office features you'll probably come to rely on the most is *find and replace.* This means that the application seeks out a particular bit of data and then replaces it with something else. This might not seem like a big deal for a replacement or two, but if you need to change a couple of dozen instances of *St.* to *Street,* it can be a real time-saver.

Happily, replacing data is very similar to finding it. You begin by either selecting Edit | Replace or by pressing Ctrl-H to display the Replace tab. Again, the layout of this tab varies among the applications. Figure 3.21 shows the Word version. Enter the data you want to search for in the Find what text box, and enter the data you want to replace it with in the Replace with text box. The other options are similar to those in the Find tab. When you're ready to go, click one of the following buttons:

Find Next: Finds the next matching record without performing the replacement.

Replace: Replaces the currently highlighted data and then moves to the next match.

Replace All: Replaces every instance of the search text with the replacement value.

FIGURE 3.21.

Use the Find and Replace dialog box to search for and replace data in a document.

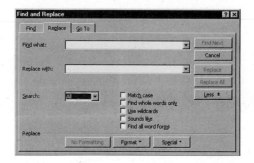

Spell-Checking Text

One of the easiest ways to lose face in the working world is to hand in a report or display a slide that contains spelling mistakes. No matter how professionally organized and formatted your document appears, a simple spelling error will stick out like a sore thumb. But mistakes do happen, especially if your document is a large one. To help you catch these errors, the Office applications include a spell-checking utility.

Using the Spell Checker

Before launching the spell checker, first decide what you want to check. If you want to check just a word or a section of text, highlight the text. If you want to check the entire document, move the cursor to the top of the file.

To invoke the spell checker, use any of these methods:

- Select Tools | Spelling.
- Press F7.

- Click the Spelling toolbar button.

When you invoke the Spelling command, the application compares each word in your selected text or document with those in its standard dictionary. If it doesn't find a word, it displays the Spelling dialog box, shown in Figure 3.22.

FIGURE 3.22.

The Spelling dialog box appears if a misspelled word is found.

The Spelling dialog box contains the following elements:

Not in Dictionary: This information box shows the word that the application couldn't find.

Change to: This text box contains the word that the application has determined is closest to the unknown word. If you turn off the Always suggest option, the application displays the unknown word. In either case, you can enter your own correction in this box.

Suggestions: This list box contains all the words that the application has determined are close to the unknown word. No suggestions appear if you turn off the Always suggest option.

Ignore: Click this button to skip this instance of the word.

Ignore All: Click this button to skip all instances of the word.

Change: Click this button to change the unknown word to the word displayed in the Change to box.

Change All: Click this button to change all instances of the unknown word to the word displayed in the Change to box.

Add: Click this button to add the unknown word to the dictionary shown in the Add words to box.

Suggest: Click this button to have the application suggest corrections. This button is active only if you turn off the Always suggest option.

AutoCorrect: Click this button to add the unknown word and the correction shown in the Change to box to your list of AutoCorrect entries. (I'll discuss AutoCorrect in Chapter 11, "Word Assistance.")

Add words to: This box displays the current custom dictionary (see the next section).

The other controls in the Spelling dialog box vary with the application. The Excel Spelling dialog box, which you just saw in Figure 3.22, has the following options:

Ignore UPPERCASE: Select this option to have the application skip uppercase versions of words that are found in the dictionary in lowercase.

Always suggest: Activate this check box to have the application display suggestions for every unknown word.

Cell Value: This information box displays the full contents of the cell containing the unknown word.

In other versions of this dialog box, you'll see an Options button that gives you some extra settings. For example, Figure 3.23 shows you the dialog box that Word displays. (See Chapter 14, "Customizing Word," for details on the options available in this dialog box.)

FIGURE 3.23.

When you're checking spelling in Word, clicking the Options button displays this dialog box.

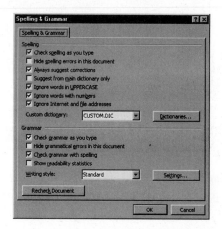

Using Custom Dictionaries

The dictionary that Office uses to check spelling is extensive and has been beefed up considerably in Office 97. For example, Office used to flag your name, the names of countries and companies, and many technical terms. In Office 97, however, the dictionary now includes Fortune 1000 company names, ethnic names, many recently coined words (such as *downsizing*), computer terminology, and the names of countries and large U.S. towns.

That still leaves out a large chunk of the English language, however. To account for this, you can use custom dictionaries to hold words you use frequently that Office doesn't recognize. You have two ways to proceed:

Add words to the default custom dictionary: The default custom dictionary is called CUSTOM.DIC. If you click Add in a Spelling dialog box, the application inserts the unknown word into this dictionary.

Create a new custom dictionary: To do this, display the Spelling dialog box and use the Add words to text box to enter the name of the new dictionary.

You can create as many different dictionaries as you need. For example, you could have a dictionary for technical terms used in your industry, another for employee or customer names, and another for common abbreviations. Keep in mind that you can use only one custom dictionary at a time.

NOTE: CUSTOM DICTIONARY MAINTENANCE

Word has a Custom Dictionaries dialog box that lets you create, edit, and delete custom dictionaries. I'll show you how to use this feature in Chapter 14.

NOTE: LOOKING FOR AUTOCORRECT INFORMATION?

If you're looking for instructions on using AutoCorrect—the on-the-fly spell checker that's common to all the Office applications—head for Chapter 11. That chapter shows you how to wield not only AutoCorrect, but also Word's handy AutoText feature.

3

DAY-TO-DAY OFFICE BASICS

Summary

This chapter began your look at the common Office features by examining a few techniques for workaday tasks. These included creating, opening, and saving documents; creating templates; juggling multiple document windows; formatting text; finding and replacing text; and running the spell checker.

Here's a list of chapters where you'll find related information:

- Another common day-to-day chore—printing—is covered in Chapter 4, "Printing Options and Techniques."
- OfficeArt is the subject of Chapter 5, "Using the OfficeArt Tools."
- See Chapter 11, "Word Assistance," to learn how to work with the AutoCorrect feature.

Printing Options and Techniques

CHAPTER 4

IN THIS CHAPTER

Some said, John, print it; others said, Not so:
Some said, It might do good; others said no.

—*John Bunyan*

Remember when all this high-falutin' computer technology was supposed to result in the pro-verbial "paperless office" of tomorrow? Clearly, tomorrow never came. If anything, we're awash in more paper than ever since computers took over. It's just like all the other pipe dreams from those "here's-what-the-future-will-bring" flicks from the '50s. By the time the '90s roll around, they assured us, we'll all have endless leisure hours to spend rocketing around in flying cars. As someone once said, we always overestimate change in the long term and underestimate it in the short term.

I suspect one of the reasons for this plenitude of paper is that we all have a real need for hard copy. For one thing, it just feels good to create something tangible, something we can literally get our hands on. For another, I don't think we trust our computers fully. Electronic files, with their unfortunate tendency to get wiped out by the merest power surge or an accidental press of a Delete key, seem so fragile. Printouts, on the other hand, seem heartier and, well, *safer*.

I say if we're going to be printing fools, we might as well be wise printing fools. Happily, as this chapter will show you, such wisdom is fairly easy to come by thanks to Windows 95's easy and consistent approach to printing. You'll begin with some printing basics, and then you'll gradu-ate to some intermediate and advanced techniques that help you unleash your Office docu-ment printing.

Installing a Printer with the Add Printer Wizard

Windows 95 is the control freak of the computer world. It has to know absolutely *everything* about your machine and whatever peripherals—especially printers—are along for the ride. This isn't a bad thing, though, because it actually makes your life easier. How? For example, in the anarchic world of DOS, every program has its own particular printing agenda. Although there's nothing wrong with such digital individualism, the downside is that you have to perform the rigmarole of setting up your printer for every DOS program.

Windows 95 is different because it performs the printing drudgery itself. As a result, you only have to tell Windows what kind of printer you have and then you're in business. Windows applications handle print jobs by simply passing the buck to the printing subsystem, so there's no need to perform separate printer setups for all your programs.

As with any device, you need to install a driver to get Windows 95 to print properly. If you didn't do this during the Windows 95 installation, or if you have a new printer to set up, you can use the Printers folder to do it from the desktop. Here are the steps you need to follow:

1. Select Start | Settings | Printers to open the Printers folder. (You can also open the Printers folder by double-clicking the Printers icon in Control Panel.)
2. Open the Add Printer icon to start the Add Printer Wizard.

3. Click Next.

4. If your computer is on a network, the wizard asks if you want to set up a local printer or a network printer. Choose the appropriate option and click Next.

5. If you chose the Network printer option, the wizard prompts you to enter a network path. Enter the appropriate UNC path, or use the Browse button to choose the printer from a dialog box. The wizard also wants to know if you print from DOS programs. Select Yes or No as appropriate and click Next.

6. The next wizard dialog box, shown in Figure 4.1, lists the manufacturers and printers that Windows 95 supports. Use these lists to track down your printer and highlight it. If your printer isn't in the list, you have two choices:

   ■ Check your printer manual to see if the printer works like (*emulates*) another printer. If it does, see if you can find the emulated printer in the list.

   ■ If your printer comes with a disk, click Have Disk and follow the on-screen prompts.

FIGURE 4.1.

Use this wizard dialog box to highlight your printer.

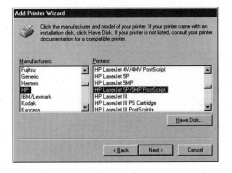

7. Click Next.

8. In the next wizard dialog box, shown in Figure 4.2, use the Available ports list to select your printer port and then click Next.

FIGURE 4.2.

Use this wizard dialog box to select the port your printer is attached to.

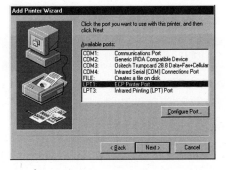

4

PRINTING
OPTIONS AND
TECHNIQUES

9. The next Add Printer Wizard dialog box that appears is shown in Figure 4.3. Use the Printer name text box to enter a descriptive name for the printer. If you've installed other printers, the wizard asks if you want this printer to be the default for all your Windows applications. If so, activate the Yes option. Click Next to continue.

FIGURE 4.3.

Use this dialog box to name your printer and optionally set it as the default printer.

10. Finally, the wizard asks if you want to print a test page. This is a good idea, so select Yes and then click Finish.

11. Follow the on-screen prompts to insert your Windows 95 source disks.

12. After the wizard installs the drivers, it sends the test page to the printer, and a dialog box asks if the page printed properly. If it did, click Yes. If it didn't, select No. In this case, Windows 95 runs the Print Troubleshooter, which will ask you a series of questions in an attempt to track down the problem.

When all is said and done, you are dropped off at the Printers folder. Your new printer has its own icon, as shown in Figure 4.4.

FIGURE 4.4.

For each printer you install, an icon appears in the Printers folder.

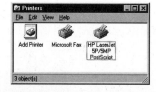

NOTE: PLUG AND PLAY PRINTERS

If you have a printer that is Plug and Play–compliant, installation is easy. Just connect the printer to your computer, turn the printer on, and restart your computer. When Windows 95 starts, it detects the printer, queries it for its device ID, and prompts you for your Windows 95 source disks.

Office Printing Basics

One of Windows 95's principal missions in life is to give all the applications you use a reasonably consistent look and feel. This means that the vast majority of Windows applications use, say, the same dialog box controls, the same method of selecting text, the same command for saving a file, and so on.

Printing is a good example of this consistency. In all the Office applications, you can initiate a print job by using any of the following techniques:

- Select File | Print.
- Press Ctrl-P.
- In the Open dialog box, right-click a document and then choose Print from the shortcut menu.

- Click the Print button on the Standard toolbar.

Note that the latter two techniques send the current document to the printer immediately. The first two methods display the Print dialog box, which looks something like the one shown in Figure 4.5 (this is the one from Excel). The options in this dialog box vary among the Office applications, but the following controls are common:

FIGURE 4.5.

Select File | Print in any Office application to display the Print dialog box. The one shown here is from Excel.

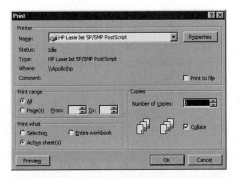

4

PRINTING
OPTIONS AND
TECHNIQUES

Name: This drop-down list tells you the name of the currently selected printer. When you first open the Print dialog box, the Name list displays the default Windows 95 printer. If you prefer to use a different printer (assuming you installed more than one), select it from the list. The other fields in the Printer group give you information about the printer, such as its status and port.

Properties: This button displays a dialog box with a few options that are specific to the current printer. These options let you choose from various printer settings (such as selecting a paper tray).

Print to file: If you activate this check box, the document is saved to a printer (PRN) file instead of going to the printer. When you click OK, the Print to File dialog box appears so that you can enter the filename and select a location. See "Getting a 'Soft' Copy: Printing to a File" later in this chapter for more information on printing to a file.

Print range: All the applications let you print some or all of a document. In Excel, for example, you can print some or all of the sheets in the current workbook. Similarly, in Word you can print the entire document, a range of pages, or the current selection.

Number of copies: You use this spinner to enter the number of copies you want. You can also use the Collate check box to choose whether you want multiple copies *collated.* For example, suppose you want two copies of a three-page document. If you activate the Collate option, you get one copy of all three pages, followed by the second copy. If you don't collate, you get two copies of Page 1, two copies of Page 2, and then two copies of Page 3.

Using Drag and Drop to Print Files

Windows 95's drag-and-drop capabilities can be extremely useful. To my mind, one of the best uses of drag-and-drop is printing a file without opening the source application and loading the document.

All you have to do is drag the document from Explorer or My Computer and drop it on a printer icon in the Printers folder. Alternatively, you can create a shortcut for a printer (by dragging its icon from the Printers folder to the desktop) and then drop your documents on this shortcut.

With either method, the source application loads just long enough to send the document to the printer, and then it shuts down automatically.

Note, too, that in Explorer or My Computer you can print a file by highlighting it and selecting File | Print or by right-clicking the file and selecting Print from the context menu.

TIP: USE THE SEND TO MENU TO PRINT DOCUMENTS EASILY

The drag-and-drop method is interesting, but it means either keeping the Printers folder open all the time or rearranging your windows to get to the desktop shortcut.

A better way is to create a shortcut for your printer in the Windows' Send To subfolder. That way, you can print any document by right-clicking it in Explorer, choosing Send To from the shortcut menu, and clicking the printer.

To create a Send To shortcut, drag your printer from the Printers folder and drop it inside the Send To folder. When Windows asks if you want to create a shortcut, click Yes.

Getting a "Soft" Copy: Printing to a File

What do you do if you don't have a printer? What if you only have a dot matrix printer and you want to print your résumé on a laser printer? If you know someone who has the printer you need, Windows 95 lets you print your document to a file. You can then transport the file to the other computer and print it from there. The other computer doesn't even need the source application.

You saw earlier that you can print to a file by activating the Print to file check box in the Print dialog box. If you prefer a more permanent solution, you can tell Windows 95 to print to a port named FILE instead of, say, LPT1. To do this, use either of the following methods:

- ■ If you haven't installed the printer (that is, the type of printer you'll eventually use to print the file), run the Add Printer Wizard as described earlier. When the wizard asks you to specify a port, select FILE.

- ■ For an installed printer, open the Printers folder and display the properties sheet for the printer you want to use (by highlighting the printer icon and selecting File | Properties or by right-clicking the icon and selecting Properties). Select the Details tab, and then use the Print to the following port list to select the FILE port. Click OK to put the new setting into effect.

When that's done, use any of the methods outlined earlier to print a document. When you do, you see the Print To File dialog box, shown in Figure 4.6. Enter the filename, choose a location, and click OK.

FIGURE 4.6.

Use the Print To File dialog box to enter the name of the file you want to print to.

4

PRINTING OPTIONS AND TECHNIQUES

Once the document has been "printed" to the file, what happens next? Now you copy the file to a floppy disk, head to where the printer is located, and copy the file to the other computer. To print the file, start a DOS session and enter the following generic command:

```
COPY /B filename port
```

The /B switch tells DOS to print a binary file, `filename` is the name of your file, and `port` is the port the printer is attached to. For example, if your file is named PRINT.PRN, and the printer is attached to LPT1, you enter the following:

```
COPY /B print.prn lpt1
```

I assume that the file is in the current folder. If it isn't, you need to include the drive and folder with the filename.

Printing Multiple Files

Although you usually print a single file at a time, you might find that you occasionally need to print multiple files at once. For example, you might need to print a series of reports or workbooks to include in a project or to ship to a customer. Although you can open all the files and print them individually, the Office applications give you an easier method:

1. Select File | Open.

2. Select all the documents you want to print. (See the last chapter for some techniques on selecting multiple files.)

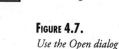

3. Click the Commands and Settings button and then click Print, as shown in Figure 4.7.

FIGURE 4.7.

Use the Open dialog box to print multiple files at once.

Printing from Word

Okay, so much for the common printing experience. If all you need to do is print the occasional Office document, you now know everything you need to know to get the job done without fuss.

However, the Office applications have no shortage of extra printing features that might come in handy. The rest of this chapter looks at a few of the application-specific printing techniques. I begin by looking at the extra printing options and features that you can use to get hard copies of your Word document.

Word's Printing Basics

I begin by looking at the basics of printing Word documents. For starters, if you don't want to print the entire document, use one of the following techniques to choose how much of the document you want to print:

- If you want to print only a single page, place the cursor anywhere inside the page.
- If you want to print a range of text, use the mouse or keyboard to select the text.

Next, select File | Print to display the Print dialog box, shown in Figure 4.8. As you can see, Word's version of the Print dialog box contains all the common controls discussed earlier. Here's a summary of the unique options you can work with:

FIGURE 4.8.

Word's Print dialog box.

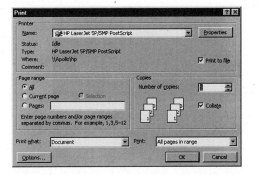

Page range: As described earlier, you use these options to tell Word how much of the document you want to print. Choose All to print the entire file; choose Current page to print only the page that contains the cursor; choose Select to print only the high-lighted text; and choose Pages to print specific page numbers. For the latter, you can enter individual page numbers separated by commas, or page ranges of the form x-y, where x and y are page numbers (x must be less than y).

Print what: Use this drop-down list to choose what part of the document you want printed. Besides the document itself, you can also choose to print the document properties, comments, styles, AutoText entries, or key assignments.

Print: If you're printing a range of pages, use this drop-down list to choose which of those pages to print: All pages in range, Odd pages, or Even pages. (The latter two are useful when you want to print on both sides of a sheet of paper.)

When you're done, click OK to start the print job.

Word's Printing Options

Notice that the Print dialog box has an Options button. Clicking this button displays the Print tab, shown in Figure 4.9. (You can also display this tab from the Options dialog box by selecting Tools | Options.) Here's a rundown of the options in this tab:

Draft output: Activate this check box to print the document with only bare-bones formatting. This lets Windows render the document faster, which should reduce printing time. (The downside, of course, is a loss of document quality. This option is useful for quick-and-dirty printouts.)

Update fields: When this check box is activated, Word updates all field codes before printing the document.

Update links: When this check box is activated, Word updates all DDE and OLE links before printing the document.

Allow A4/Letter paper resizing: When this option is turned on, Word automatically adjusts the printout to match the system's country settings. This is required because Letter size is standard in some countries whereas A4 size is standard in others.

Background printing: This check box, which is activated by default, toggles Word's background printing feature on and off. When it's on, Word uses an extra bit of system memory to spool the print job in the background, which lets you return to work faster.

Print PostScript over text: This option is used with Word for Macintosh files that contain a watermark or other PostScript text that lies "underneath" the regular document text. If you activate the check box, Word prints the PostScript text on top of the existing text.

Reverse print order: If your printer ejects pages facing up, activate this check box. That way, Word prints the pages in reverse order, which means your printout is ordered correctly.

Document properties: Activate this check box to print the document's properties on a separate page after the main document prints.

Field codes: Activate this check box to print the document's field codes instead of the field values.

Comments: Activate this check box to print the document's comments on a separate page after the main document prints.

Hidden text: If you have any text formatted as hidden, activate this check box to include the hidden text in the printout.

Drawing objects: Activate this check box to print the document's graphic objects. If you deactivate this check box, Word displays a blank box in place of each image.

Print data only for forms: When activated, this option tells Word to print only the data in a form, not the form itself. Note that this option applies only to the current document.

Default tray: Use this list to specify which printer tray to use.

FIGURE 4.9.

Use the Print tab to set Word's default printing options.

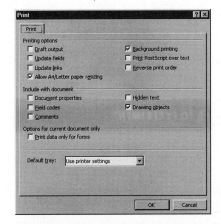

NOTE: WORD'S PAGE SETUP OPTIONS

You can customize the look of your printed page a great deal by taking advantage of the various page setup options provided by Word. For example, you can customize the margin sizes, change the paper size and the paper orientation (landscape or portrait), and much more. See Chapter 9, "Document Concepts," for details. Note, too, that Chapter 9 is the place to go to learn how to define headers and footers in your Word documents.

TIP: USE OUTLINES TO CONTROL WHICH TEXT IS PRINTED

As you'll learn in Chapter 10, "Document Patterns and Presentations," you can use Word's Outline view to break your document into multiple levels (provided you use Word's predefined heading styles). One of the nicest benefits of using outlines is that Word only prints the displayed text. If you want to prevent some text from printing, you need only use the outline to collapse the appropriate section.

Printing Envelopes

While waiting in a bookstore checkout line a few years ago, I happened to notice a woman standing in the paperback bestsellers section. She had a book in each hand and was clearly trying to figure out which one to buy. She stared intently at the covers, read the blurbs on the

4
PRINTING OPTIONS AND TECHNIQUES

back, checked out the price, but she just couldn't decide. Finally, she put the two books spine-to-spine and chose the thicker one!

I recall this story to remind you that most people look at the whole package when they evaluate something. If you're going to mail your documents, applying fancy formatting techniques is only the start. Your package might not even get opened if it arrives in a sloppily addressed envelope (or if it does get opened, your careful prose will almost certainly be read with a jaundiced eye).

This section helps you avoid such a fate by showing you how easy it is to create great-looking envelopes and labels in Word.

NOTE: YOU NEED TO EXPERIMENT

"In theory, theory and practice are the same thing; in practice, they're not." I'm not sure who said that, but he or she must have been a computer user. Why? Well, because in theory, printing envelopes is a breeze; in practice, you usually need to try a few experiments to make sure things come out right.

Defining Your Return Address

Assuming you want your return address to appear on the envelope, you can save yourself a step by defining this address in advance. You do that by selecting Tools | Options, activating the User Information tab, and entering your address in the Mailing address text box, as shown in Figure 4.10. Word uses this address as the default return address for all your envelopes. (As you'll see later, you can easily change the return address when you print your envelopes.)

FIGURE 4.10.

Enter your return mailing address in the User Information tab.

Entering the Delivery Address

The only other task you need to perform is adding the mailing address to the document, as shown in Figure 4.11. (If you want, you can bypass this step; Word also lets you enter the mailing address when you define the envelope, as you'll see in a second.) This is no big deal: You can insert the address just about anywhere that makes sense. Remember, however, that what you type is exactly what appears on the front of the envelope. Make sure the address is complete (including the ZIP or postal code) and contains no spelling mistakes.

FIGURE 4.11.

You can save a step down the road by including the delivery address in your document.

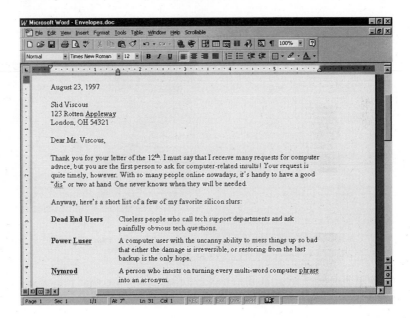

If the delivery address is the only address that appears in the document, no further action is required because Word can find the address automatically. If you have other addresses in the document, however, you need to highlight the entire address before defining the envelope.

Basic Envelope Printing

When you're ready to print the envelope, select Tools | Envelopes and Labels. Word displays the Envelopes and Labels dialog box, shown in Figure 4.12. Enter or adjust the Delivery address and Return address, as necessary. If you don't want the return address to appear on the envelope, activate the Omit check box.

If you want to adjust the size of the envelope, click Options to display the Envelope Options dialog box, shown in Figure 4.13. Use the Envelope size list to choose the appropriate envelope, and then click OK. (I discuss the other options in this dialog box in the next section.)

FIGURE 4.12.

Use the Envelopes and Labels dialog box to print your envelope.

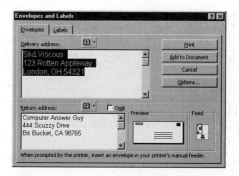

FIGURE 4.13.

You use the Envelope Options dialog box to change the envelope size (among other things).

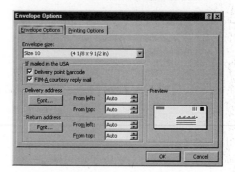

At this point, you can either print the envelope right away or insert it into the current document for later use. Here are the options you have:

■ If you want to print the envelope, first make sure your printer is up and running with the appropriate envelopes loaded (depending on your printer). When you're ready to go, click the Print button.

■ If you want to print the envelope along with the document later on, you can insert the envelope into the document by clicking the Add to Document button. Word adds a new page to the top of the document (by inserting a hard page break) and displays the return and mailing addresses. You can then select File | Print to send both the envelope and the document to the printer.

TIP: ADD IMAGES TO THE ENVELOPE

The Add to Document command is also useful if you want to include an image on your envelope. Once you add the envelope, position the cursor inside the envelope page, insert the image you want, and position it accordingly. (See Chapter 5, "Using the OfficeArt Tools.")

Working with Envelope Options

As usual, Word gives you all kinds of bells and whistles to make sure you get exactly the kinds of envelopes you need. The next few sections take you through the various setup options that are available for envelopes.

Adding Barcodes to Envelopes

The U.S. Postal Service (USPS) uses delivery point barcodes (also known as POSTNET barcodes) to computerize mail sorting and speed up mail delivery. If you do bulk mailings, you can save on postal rates by presorting the envelopes and including the official USPS delivery point barcode as part of the mailing address.

Word also lets you insert a Facing Identification Mark (FIM). This is a barcode that appears on the front of the envelope near the stamp or postmark. It's used on courtesy reply envelopes to define the front of the envelope during mechanical presorting operations.

To add these barcodes to your envelope, click the Options button in the Envelopes and Labels dialog box. In the Envelope Options dialog box that appears, shown in Figure 4.13, activate either or both of the Delivery point barcode and FIM-A courtesy reply mail check boxes, and then click OK. Figure 4.14 shows a sample envelope with both barcode types inserted.

FIGURE 4.14.

A sample envelope showing both types of barcodes.

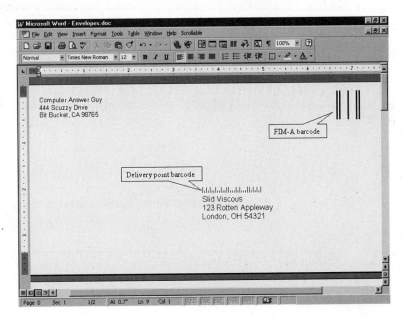

4

PRINTING
OPTIONS AND
TECHNIQUES

Creating a FIM-C Barcode

What do you do if you need a FIM-C barcode? (FIM-C barcodes are used for business reply envelopes.) Word doesn't provide any direct way to do this, but it's not hard. Here are the steps to follow:

1. Set up the envelope with the delivery point barcode and the FIM-A barcode, as described in the last section.

2. Click Add to Document to insert the envelope. (If you've already inserted the envelope, click the Change Document button instead.)

3. Display the envelope, right-click the FIM-A barcode, and click Toggle Field Codes. This displays the BARCODE field definition that Word uses to insert barcodes in an envelope.

4. Edit the field code to change the A to a C, as shown in Figure 4.15.

FIGURE 4.15.

To get a FIM-C barcode, change the BARCODE field from A to C as shown here.

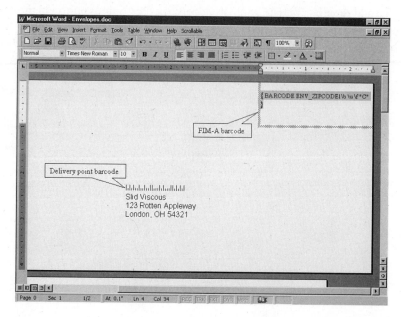

5. To view the FIM-C barcode, right-click the BARCODE field and click Toggle Field Codes.

Changing the Address Font and Position

One of the most common problems with envelopes is that the addresses often don't print where they're supposed to. For example, the mailing address might be too far down or the return address might get truncated on the left. If you don't like where Word is printing the return and mailing addresses on the envelope, you can adjust the address positions. Here's how:

1. Display the Envelopes and Labels dialog box, as described earlier in this chapter.

2. Click the Options button to display the Envelope Options dialog box (see Figure 4.13).

3. Both the Delivery address group and the Return address group have three controls that affect the delivery address and return address:

> **Font:** Click this button to display the Envelope Address dialog box, which is a variation of Word's standard Font tab.

> **From left:** Use this spinner to enter a value in inches from the left edge of the envelope.

> **From right:** Use this spinner to enter a value in inches from the top edge of the envelope.

4. Click OK to return to the Envelopes and Labels dialog box.

5. Print or insert the envelope.

Envelope Printing Options

To close this discussion of the various options Word provides for envelopes, this section examines the Printing Options tab of the Envelope Options dialog box, shown in Figure 4.16. (Recall that you display this dialog box by clicking Options in the Envelopes and Labels dialog box.)

FIGURE 4.16.

Use the Printing Options tab to specify how you feed your envelopes to your printer.

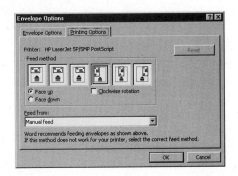

The options in this dialog box vary depending on the printer you're using, but the one shown in Figure 4.16 is typical. These options let you adjust how you feed your envelopes to your printer:

> **Feed method:** Use these controls to specify how you physically feed the envelope into your printer.

> **Feed from:** Use this list to determine how the envelopes are fed. Manual feed is the default, but you can also select a specific printer tray to enable automatic envelope feeding.

Attaching an Image to the Return Address

Earlier I mentioned that you can insert images on your envelopes by adding the envelope to the document and then using the OfficeArt tools to insert and position a graphic. However, Word also lets you associate with your return address an image that is displayed and printed automatically. Here are the steps to follow:

1. Define your return address as described earlier.

2. Click Add to Document to insert the envelope. (If you've already inserted the envelope, click the Change Document button instead.)

3. Display the envelope and position the cursor where you want the image to appear.

4. Insert the image you want to use. (See Chapter 5.)

5. Click the image to select it.

6. Select Insert | AutoText | New to display displays the Create AutoText dialog box, as shown in Figure 4.17.

FIGURE 4.17.

Use the Create AutoText dialog box to define the EnvelopeExtra1 AutoText that Word uses to print an image with your return address.

7. In the Please name your AutoText entry text box, type `EnvelopeExtra1` and then click OK.

Word now inserts the image defined by EnvelopeExtra1 automatically each time it prints an envelope.

Printing Labels

Instead of printing an address directly on an envelope, you can instead place the address on a label and then stick the label on the envelope. This is handy if you're using envelopes that are too big to fit in your printer or if you're using padded envelopes that could cause a printer to choke. Of course, there are many other uses for labels: name tags, floppy disks, file folders, and so on. The next couple of sections show you how to define labels and enter text into them.

Basic Label Printing

As with envelopes, your first task is to add the mailing address to the document. (You can bypass this step because Word lets you enter the mailing address when you define the label.)

Remember that if you have multiple addresses in the document, you must highlight the entire address before printing the label. Now follow these steps:

1. Select Tools | Envelopes and Labels to display the Envelopes and Labels dialog box.
2. Select the Labels tab, shown in Figure 4.18.

FIGURE 4.18.

Use the Labels tab to set up your label for printing.

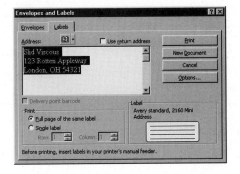

3. Enter or adjust the address as necessary.
4. If you want to use your return address, activate the Use return address check box.
5. The Print group gives you the following options:

   Full page of the same label: Select this option to have Word fill the page with multiple labels.

   Single label: Select this option to print only one label. Use the Row and Column spinners to specify where you want the label printed.

6. To change label type, click Options and then use the Label Options dialog box, shown in Figure 4.19, to choose the appropriate label. Note that you can also use this dialog box to select the printer type and label tray. Click OK when you're done.

FIGURE 4.19.

Use the Label Options dialog box to specify the type of label you want to print.

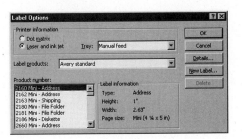

4
PRINTING
OPTIONS AND
TECHNIQUES

Now you can either print the labels right away or write them to a new document for later use:

- If you want to print the labels, click the Print button.
- If you want to print the labels later, click the New Document button. Word creates a new document for the labels.

Merging an Address List to Mailing Labels

The previous section assumes you want to print either a single label or multiple copies of the same label. What if you want to print multiple labels that use different addresses? For this scenario, you need to use Word's Mail Merge feature, which is described in detail in Chapter 13, "Word as a Publisher." For now, however, here are the steps to follow to use Mail Merge to create multiple labels:

1. Select Tools | Mail Merge to display the Mail Merge Helper dialog box.

2. Click Create and then click Mailing Labels in the menu that appears.

3. When Word asks where you want the labels created, click New Main Document. Word then creates a new document that holds the labels and returns you to the Mail Merge Helper.

4. Click Get Data and then choose one of the following commands:

   Create Data Source: Use this command to create a new data source. (See Chapter 13 for details.)

   Open Data Source: Use this command to use an existing list of addresses in a Word document, Excel workbook, Access database, or other data source.

   Use Address Book: Use this command to get the addresses from an Exchange or Outlook address book.

5. Word prompts you to set up the main merge document. Click Set Up Main Document to display the Label Options dialog box (see Figure 4.19).

6. Choose your options and then click OK. Word displays the Create Labels dialog box, shown in Figure 4.20.

FIGURE 4.20.

Use the Create Labels dialog box to add merge fields and barcode data to the label.

7. For each field you want to appear in the label, position the cursor where you want the field to appear and then use the following buttons to add the merge field to the label:

   Insert Merge Field: Click this button to display a list of the possible merge fields. Clicking one of these items inserts a code for the field into the label.

   Insert Postal Bar Code: Click this button to create a barcode for the label.

8. Add text to the label, if necessary.

9. When you're done, click OK to return to the Mail Merge Helper.

10. Click Merge. Word displays the Merge dialog box, shown in Figure 4.21.

FIGURE 4.21.

Use the Merge dialog box to set up the merge operation.

11. To print the label now, use the Merge To list to select Printer. If you prefer to print the labels later, select New document.

12. Select other merge options as necessary.

13. Click Merge. Word creates the labels.

TIP: PRINTING SELECTED LABELS

To print labels for selected recipients only, load or create a mail database from a mail merge and then select Query Options. From this menu, you can specify criteria for selecting the data records.

Creating a Custom Mailing Label

If none of the listed labels match your label's dimensions, you can customize an existing label type to the size you need. To do this, follow these steps:

1. Select Tools | Envelopes and Labels and click the Labels tab.

2. Click the Options button to display the Label Options dialog box.

3. In the Printer information group, select the type of printer you'll use: Dot matrix or Laser and ink jet.

4. Use the Product number list to select a label type that has dimensions that are similar to the label size you need.

5. Click New Label. Word displays a New Custom dialog box similar to the one shown in Figure 4.22.

6. Use the Label name text box to enter a name for your new label.

7. Use the spinners to adjust the dimensions of the label.

8. Click OK to return to the Label Options dialog box.

9. Make sure your custom label is highlighted in the Product number list and then click OK to return to the Labels tab.

4

PRINTING OPTIONS AND TECHNIQUES

FIGURE 4.22.

Use the New Custom dialog box to adjust the dimensions of the label.

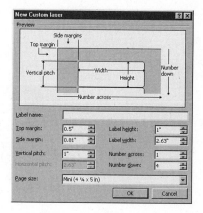

Printing from Excel

Once you set up a workbook the way you want, it's time to print it out for all to see. This section takes you through Excel's printing basics. You'll learn how to select page setup options, define a print area, preview the print job, and more.

Excel's Printing Basics

I start by examining the basic Excel printing technique. If you don't want to print the entire workbook, use one of the following techniques to choose how much of the document you want to print:

- If you want to print only a single sheet, activate that sheet.
- If you want to print two or more worksheets, set up a group that includes just those worksheets.
- If you want to print a cell range, highlight the range.
- If you want to print multiple ranges, you must establish a print area. See "Defining a Print Area" later in this section.

Select File | Print to display the Print dialog box, shown in Figure 4.23. Excel's version of the Print dialog box is fairly standard and includes only the following unique controls:

Print range: Use these controls to set the number of pages or the current selection to print. Select All to print everything, or Page(s) to print a range of pages (which you specify with the From and To spinners).

Print what: These option buttons determine how much of the workbook you want to print. Choose Selection to print only the selected range; choose Active sheet(s) to print the current sheet group; choose Entire workbook to print everything.

When you're done, click OK to start the print job.

FIGURE 4.23.

Excel's Print dialog box.

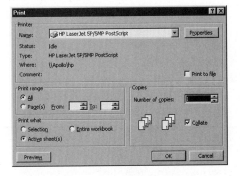

Setting Up Your Pages

Before printing, you need to decide how you want your worksheet pages to look. This includes decisions such as the paper orientation (landscape or portrait), the size of your margins, and the header and footer you want to use. To set these options and more, select File | Page Setup. You see the Page Setup dialog box, as shown in Figure 4.24. The next few sections discuss most of the options in this dialog box. When you finish choosing your options, you have three choices:

- Click Print to display the Print dialog box.
- Click Print Preview to see how your printout will look before you print it.
- Click OK to return to the document and put the new settings into effect.

FIGURE 4.24.

Use the Page tab to choose a paper size and page orientation.

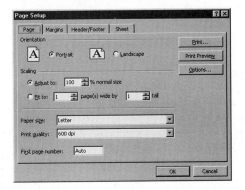

4

PRINTING OPTIONS AND TECHNIQUES

Changing the Page Orientation

The *page orientation* determines how Excel lays out the worksheet data on the page. The Page tab in the Page Setup dialog box gives you two options:

Portrait: Prints along the short side of the page (this is the normal page orientation). Assuming Excel's default margin sizes of 0.75" on the left and right and 1" on the top and bottom, and using letter-size paper (8.5" × 11"), this orientation gives you a print area that is 7 inches wide and 9 inches high on each page.

Landscape: Prints along the long side of the page. With the default margins on letter-size paper, this orientation gives you a page print area 9.5 inches wide and 6.5 inches high.

Scaling Your Worksheet

If you have a PostScript printer or any other printer that accepts scalable fonts, you can scale your worksheets to fit on a page. The idea is that you specify a percentage reduction and Excel shrinks the printed worksheet proportionally while maintaining all layout and formatting options. (You can also enlarge your worksheets.)

To try this feature, make sure the Adjust to option is activated in the Page tab and then use the spinner beside it to choose the percentage you need. To reduce the printout, enter a value between 10 and 100. To enlarge the printout, enter a value between 100 and 400.

If you find you must use a lot of trial and error to get the proper reduction setting, you can save some time by letting Excel do the work for you. In the Page tab, activate the Fit to option and then use the two spinners to enter the number of pages wide and tall you want the printout to be.

Other Options in the Page Tab

Here's a quick summary of the other controls that are available in the Page tab:

Paper size: Use this drop-down list to select a different paper size for your printout. The options in this include standard letter size (8 1/2" × 11") and legal size (8 1/2" × 14"). You also see other sizes depending on the currently selected printer. Make sure that the size you select matches the paper loaded in the printer.

Print quality: Use this list to choose the default print quality for your pages.

First page number: Use this text box to specify the page number Excel should use for the first page of the printout. This is handy if the document you're printing is part of a larger report.

Setting Page Margins

The *page margins* are the blank areas that surround the printed text on a page. By default, Excel decrees the left and right margins to be 0.75 inches and the top and bottom margins to be 1 inch, but you can override that, if you want. Why would you want to do such a thing? Here are a few good reasons:

- If someone else is going to be making notes on the page, it helps to include bigger margins (to give him or her more room for writing).

- Smaller margins all around mean that you get more text on a page. On a long worksheet, this could save you a few pages when you print it out.

- If you have a worksheet that won't quite fit on a page, you can decrease the appropriate margins just enough to fit the extra lines onto a single page.

NOTE: MORE WAYS TO PRODUCE FEWER PAGES

See "Fitting More Data on a Page" later in this chapter for some other ways to squeeze more data on a page.

CAUTION: DON'T MAKE YOUR MARGINS TOO SMALL

Some laser printers don't allow you to set your margins smaller than 0.25" because of physical limitations.

To adjust the margins, activate the Margins tab in the Page Setup dialog box, shown in Figure 4.25. You can then enter your new margin values using the Top, Bottom, Left, and Right spinners.

FIGURE 4.25.

The Margins tab in the Page Setup dialog box.

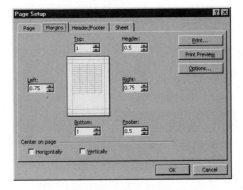

You can also use the Header and Footer spinners to adjust how far the page headers and footers appear from the edge of the page. Use Header to set the distance from the top of the page to the top of the header. Use Footer to set the distance from the bottom of the page to the bottom of the footer.

Finally, the Center on page options tell Excel to center the printout between the margins. Activate the Horizontally check box to center between the left and right margins, and activate the Vertically check box to center between the top and bottom margins.

Adding a Header or Footer

You can add headers or footers that display information at the top (in the case of a header) or bottom (for a footer) of every printed page. This is useful for keeping track of things such as page numbers and the current date and time. The next two sections show you how to work with both Excel's predefined and custom headers and footers.

Adding a Predefined Header or Footer

Excel has a number of predefined headers and footers that can display page numbers, workbook and worksheet names, file revision dates, authors, and more.

To use one of these headers or footers, first activate the Header/Footer tab in the Page Setup dialog box, shown in Figure 4.26. Then use the Header drop-down list to select a predefined header. Your selection appears in the header box above the list.

FIGURE 4.26.

The Header/Footer tab in the Page Setup dialog box.

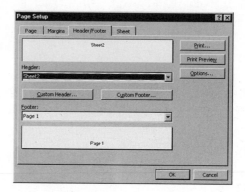

For a footer, use the Footer drop-down list to select a predefined footer. In this case, your choice appears in the footer box below the list.

Creating a Custom Header or Footer

If none of the predefined headers or footers fits the bill, you can create your own custom version. You can enter seven different items in a customized header or footer: text such as a workbook title or other explanatory comments, the current page number and total page count, the date and time, and the workbook and worksheet tab names. You can specify a font for any of these items, and you can place them on the left or right side of the page (or in the center). Here are the steps to follow.

1. To create a custom header, click the Custom Header button to display the Header dialog box, shown in Figure 4.27. To create as custom footer, click the Custom Footer button to display the Footer dialog box.

FIGURE 4.27.

Use the Header dialog box to create a custom header. The Footer dialog box works just like the Header dialog.

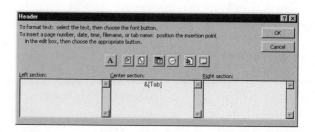

2. Click inside either the Left section, Center section, or Right section text box.

3. Enter text or click one of the buttons to insert a code into the header. Here's a summary of what each button provides:

Button	Code Inserted	Description
	&[Page]	Displays the page number.
	&[Pages]	Displays the total page count.
	&[Date]	Displays the date the workbook is printed.
	&[Time]	Displays the time the workbook is printed.
	&[File]	Displays the workbook filename.
	&[Tab]	Displays the worksheet tab name.

4. (Optional) Select any text you want to format and click the Font button.

5. Repeat steps 2 through 4 to enter any other text or codes.

6. Click OK to return to the Page Setup dialog box. Excel displays the header or footer in the appropriate box.

Defining a Print Area

Once you lay out your pages the way you want, you need to decide how much of the worksheet you want to print. By default, Excel prints the entire document, but you can print only a part of the sheet by specifying a *print area*. A print area is a special range that defines which cells you want to print.

To set it up, first activate the Sheet tab in the Page Setup dialog box, shown in Figure 4.28. In the Print Area text box, use one of the following techniques:

■ Type the range you want to print.

■ Click the Collapse Dialog button (the one on the right side of the text box), and use the mouse or keyboard to select the range on the worksheet. When you're done, click the Collapse Dialog button again to restore the Sheet tab.

FIGURE 4.28.

Use the Sheet tab to define a print area (among other things).

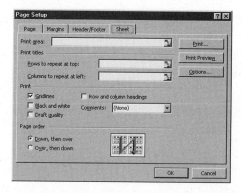

Note that you can enter as many ranges as you need. When you're done, Excel displays a dotted line around the range to mark the print area and names the range Print_Area.

TIP: A FASTER WAY TO DEFINE A PRINT AREA

Rather than use the Page Setup dialog box to define the print area, you can do it right from the worksheet. Just select the range you want to use and then select File | Print Area | Set Print Area.

NOTE: REMOVING A PRINT AREA

If you no longer need a print area, you can remove it with any of the following methods:

- Define a different print area.
- Select File | Print Area | Clear Print Area.
- Select Insert | Name | Define and delete the Print_Area name.
- Select File | Page Setup, activate the Sheet tab, and delete the reference from the Print area text box.

Defining Titles to Print on Every Page

If your printout extends for more than a single page, your row and column titles usually print only on the first page. This can make the subsequent pages confusing and difficult to read. To get around this problem, you can tell Excel to print the appropriate row and column headings on every page. If you select one or more rows, they print at the top of each page; if you select one or more columns, they print on the left of each page.

To define the titles you want to print on every page, head once again for the Sheet tab in the Page Setup dialog box. The Print titles section gives you two text boxes:

Rows to repeat at top: Use this text box to type in the range for the column headings you want to appear at the top of each page. You can also click the Collapse Dialog button and use the mouse or keyboard to select the range on the worksheet.

Columns to repeat at left: Use this text box to type in the range for the row headings you want to appear at the left of each page. Again, you can also click the Collapse Dialog button and use the mouse or keyboard to select the range on the worksheet.

When you put these new settings into effect, Excel displays a dotted line around the range to mark the print title and names the range Print_Title.

NOTE: REMOVING PRINT TITLE

To turn off print titles, try either of the following techniques:

■ Select Insert | Name | Define and delete the Print_Title name.

■ Select File | Page Setup and then delete the references from the Rows to repeat at top and Columns to repeat at left text boxes.

Adjusting the Appearance of Each Page

The Sheet tab in the Page Setup dialog box also gives you several options that affect the look of your printed pages:

Gridlines: Excel usually prints the worksheet gridlines (unless you've turned off the gridlines by selecting Tools | Options). If you prefer not to see the gridlines, deactivate the Gridlines check box.

Black and white: If you added any color formatting to your cells or charts, most printers print these colors as patterns. If this isn't the look you want, activate this check box to tell Excel to print these colors as shades of gray or, for text, as plain black and white.

Draft quality: For faster (but lower quality) printing, activate this check box. Excel speeds up printing by suppressing some graphics and gridlines in the printout.

Row and column headings: If you're printing the worksheet as documentation, you probably want to print the row and columns headings as well. (This is especially true if you display the document's formulas before printing.) You can do this by activating this check box.

Comments: If your workbook contains comments, you can print them along with the workbook by using this drop-down list to select either At end of sheet or As displayed on sheet.

Page order: When you're printing a range that's larger than a single page, Excel works its way down through the range when printing the pages. It then jumps back to the top of the range, moves over to the next group of columns, and then works down again. If you prefer to print across the range first and then down through the rows, activate the Over, then down option button.

Adjusting Page Breaks

Excel breaks up large worksheets into pages, where the size of each page is a function of the paper size, the default font, and the margin settings in the Page Setup dialog box. Using these parameters, Excel sets automatic page breaks to delineate the print area for each page. Although you can't adjust automatic page breaks, you can override them using manual page breaks. This lets you control which data is printed on each page.

TIP: VIEWING AUTOMATIC PAGE BREAKS

To see Excel's automatic page breaks before printing, select Tools | Options, display the View tab, and activate the Page breaks check box.

Before setting a manual page break, you need to position the cell pointer correctly, as shown in Figure 4.29. Here's the basic technique:

- For a horizontal break, position the active cell in column A and remember that Excel inserts the page break at the top of the active cell. If you want a horizontal page break between, say, Rows 9 and 10, make A10 the active cell.

- For a vertical break, position the active cell in Row 1 and remember that Excel inserts the page break at the left edge of the active cell. If you want a horizontal page break between, say, Columns E and F, make F1 the active cell.

- To insert both a horizontal and a vertical page break, position the active cell in the cell below and to the right of the break position you want.

To insert a manual page break, position the cell pointer appropriately for the break you want, and select Insert | Page Break. Excel inserts the page break at the cell you selected.

To remove manual page breaks, move to any cell immediately below a horizontal page break or immediately to the right of a vertical page break, and then select Insert | Remove Page Break.

FIGURE 4.29.

The correct cell positions for inserting manual page breaks.

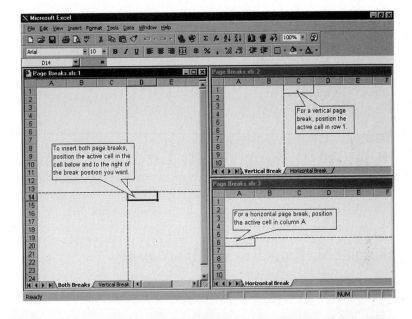

TIP: VIEWING PAGE BREAKS

You can see page breaks easier if you turn off the worksheet gridlines. Select Tools | Options, activate the View tab, and deactivate the Gridlines check box.

Also, automatic and manual page breaks appear as dashed lines on your worksheet. You can tell them apart by noting that automatic page breaks use smaller dashes with more space between each dash.

Fitting More Data on a Page

When you print a worksheet, you often end up with a couple of rows or columns that can't fit on a page. They are printed by themselves on a separate page, which is usually inconvenient and unattractive. Earlier I showed you how to scale worksheets to fit a page. This section examines several other techniques you can use to fit more information on a page.

Adjusting the Normal Font

A worksheet's default column width and row height are functions of the *font* defined in the Normal style. In general, the smaller the type size of the Normal font, the more rows and columns will fit on a single printed page.

For example, 10-point Arial prints 52 standard-height rows on a single page (assuming you're using 8 1/2" × 11" paper). However, if you reduce the Normal type size to 8 points, a single page will print 63 standard-height rows.

Similarly, using a narrower font increases the number of columns printed per page. For example, 10-point Arial prints 9 standard-width columns per page, but this increases to 13 standard-width columns if you use 10-point Arial Narrow.

Setting Smaller Margins

Because margins determine the amount of space surrounding your printed data, reducing margin size (as described earlier in this chapter) means more room on each page for printing. For example, reducing all four margins (right, left, top, and bottom) to 0.25" increases the number of columns printed from 9 to 13 and the number of rows from 52 to 61 (assuming that 10-point Arial is the Normal font).

Changing the Paper Size and Orientation

If you have trouble fitting all your rows on a page, try printing on longer paper. Changing the paper size from 8 1/2" × 11" to 8 1/2" × 14" increases the number of rows per page from 51 to 68 (based on 10-point Arial). Recall from earlier in this chapter that you use the Paper size drop-down list in the Page Setup dialog box to select a different paper size.

If you have trouble getting all your columns to fit on a page, change the page orientation from Portrait to Landscape in the Page tab of the Page Setup dialog box, as described earlier. Excel prints the worksheet sideways and increases the number of columns per page from 9 to 15. Just remember that this orientation reduces the number of rows printed per page.

Adjusting Rows and Columns

Make sure your rows are no taller (and your columns no wider) than they need to be. Select the entire print area and then select both the Format, Row, AutoFit and Format, Column, AutoFit commands. Also, hiding any unnecessary rows and columns lets you fit more important information on each page.

Printing from Access

When working in Access, you can print out datasheets, forms, and reports. Although Access doesn't have the wealth of printing options found in Word and Excel, it does have a few basic settings. I run through these settings and give you the basic Access printing procedure in this section.

Access Printing Basics

Begin by checking out the basic Access printing technique. If you're printing a table or the results of a select query, you have a choice of printing all the records or only selected ones. For the latter, use the datasheet to select the records you want to print before initiating the print job. (See Chapter 25, "Working with Tables," to learn how to select records in a datasheet.)

Now select File | Print to display the Print dialog box, shown in Figure 4.30. The Access version of the Print dialog box is similar to the other Office Print dialog box and includes only the following unique controls:

Print Range: Use these controls to set the number of pages you want to print. Select All to print everything or Pages to print a range of pages (which you specify with the From and To spinners). If you're printing a datasheet, use the Selected Record(s) option to print only the highlighted records.

Setup: Clicking this button displays the Page Setup dialog box, discussed in the next section.

FIGURE 4.30.

The Access Print dialog box.

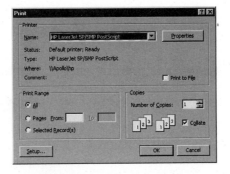

When you're done, click OK to run the print job.

TIP: CREATE PRINT BUTTONS FOR QUICK PRINTING

If you're building Access applications, you can make life a bit easier for your users if you set up command buttons on each form that let the user print records, forms, or reports just by clicking the button.

To set this up, first display your form or report in Design view. Make sure the Control Wizards button is activated in the Access toolbox, and then draw a new command button. (This is all explained in more detail in Chapter 27, "Creating and Using Simple Forms.") When the Command Button Wizard appears, pick one of the following choices:

■ To let the user print the current record from a form, highlight Record Operations and then highlight Print Record.

■ To let the user print the current form, highlight Form Operations and then highlight Print Current Form.

continues

continued

- To let the user print a different form, highlight Form Operations and then highlight Print a Form.

- To let the user print a report, highlight Report Operations and then highlight Print Report.

Setting Up Your Pages

Before printing, you might need to adjust how the printed pages will look. Access lets you modify options such as the margin sizes, the paper orientation (landscape or portrait), the size of your margins, and layout of the columns.

To set these options and more, select File | Page Setup or click Setup in the Print dialog box. You see a Page Setup dialog box, the layout of which depends on the object you're working with. Figure 4.31 shows the dialog box associated with forms and reports. When you finish choosing your options, click OK to return to the database and put the new settings into effect.

FIGURE 4.31.

Use the Page Setup dialog box to set various page options for your printouts.

Setting Page Margins

The *page margins* are the blank areas that surround the printed text on a page. By default, Access uses a 1 inch margin all around. To change this, use the text boxes in the Margins tab to set the new margin sizes in inches. Depending on the current database object, you also see one of the following check boxes:

Print Data Only: If you activate this check box, Access prints only the data contained in a form or report. Labels, borders, gridlines, and images are not printed.

Print Headings: If you activate this check box, Access includes a datasheet's column headings in the printout.

Setting Page Options for Forms and Reports

If the current database object is a form or report, the Page Setup dialog box also includes a
Page tab, as shown in Figure 4.32. Here's a summary of the options in this tab:

Portrait: Prints along the short side of the page (this is the normal page orientation).
Assuming Excel's default margin sizes of 0.75" on the left and right and 1" on the top
and bottom, and using letter-size paper (8.5" × 11"), this orientation gives you a print
area that is 7 inches wide and 9 inches high on each page.

Landscape: Prints along the long side of the page. With the default margins on letter-
size paper, this orientation gives you a page print area 9.5 inches wide and 6.5 inches
high.

Size: Use this drop-down list to select a different paper size for your printout. The
options in this include standard letter size (8 1/2" × 11") and legal size (8 1/2" × 14").
You also see other sizes depending on the currently selected printer. Make sure that
the size you select matches the paper loaded in the printer.

Source: Use this list to choose a printer tray for the print job.

Printer for *Object*: Use this group to set the printer to use for the current database
Object. Either select Default Printer to use the Windows 95 default printer or select
Use Specific Printer and click Printer to choose the printer to use.

FIGURE 4.32.

*Use the Page tab to set
a few options for forms
and reports.*

Customizing the Printout Columns

By default, Access prints form and report data in a single column down the page. If your layout
isn't too wide or if you're using landscape orientation, you can tell Access to print using two or
more columns, which reduces the number of pages in the printout.

You use the Column tab, shown in Figure 4.33, to adjust the printout columns:

Number of Columns: Use this text box to specify the number of columns you want
to use.

Row Spacing: Use this text box to specify the distance, in inches, that Access should use to separate each record.

Column Spacing: Use this text box to specify the distance, in inches, that Access should use to separate the columns. This control is only activated if you enter 2 or more in the Number of Columns text box.

Column Size: By default, Access makes the columns the same width and height as the Details area in the form or report. If you want to specify custom dimensions, deactivate the Same as Detail check box and then use the Width and Height controls to specify the new dimensions.

Column Layout: If you specified 2 or more in the Number of Columns text box, the controls in the Column Layout group are activated. You use these options to determine how Access uses the columns to print the data. Select Down, then Across to print the data down each column and then across the page; select Across, then Down to print the data across the page and then down the columns.

FIGURE 4.33.

Use the Columns tab to customize the printout columns.

Printing from PowerPoint

PowerPoint is designed to create great-looking on-screen presentations, but printing a hard copy is still necessary. For example, you might want to distribute handouts so the audience can follow along, or you might have a few notes that you need to keep handy. This section runs through all of PowerPoint's printing techniques.

PowerPoint Printing Basics

I start by running through the basic PowerPoint printing steps. If you don't want to print the entire presentation, use one of the following techniques to choose how much of the document you want to print:

■ If you want to print only a single slide, activate that slide.

■ If you want to print two or more slides, use the Slide Sorter to select those slides.

■ To print a selection of slides in a particular order, select Slide Show | Custom Shows to create a custom slide show.

Next, select File | Print to display the Print dialog box. PowerPoint's Print dialog box, shown in Figure 4.34, includes all of the standard controls and a few that are unique to PowerPoint presentations:

Print range: Use these controls to set the number of slides to print. Choose All to print every slide; choose Current slide to print only the active slide; choose Selection to print only the slides selected in the Slide Sorter; use the Custom Show list to choose a custom show to print; or use Slides to print a range of slide numbers.

Print what: Use this drop-down list to choose what parts of the presentation—slides, handouts, notes, and so on—you want to print.

Black and white: Activate this check box to print in black and white (where colors are printed as shades of gray).

Pure black and white: Activate this check box to print using pure black and white (color fills are printed as white, pictures are printed as shades of gray).

Scale to fit paper: If you activate this check box, PowerPoint scales slides that are larger or smaller than the page so that they fit the page.

Frame slides: Activate this check box to have PowerPoint display a border around each printed slide.

FIGURE 4.34.

PowerPoint's Print dialog box.

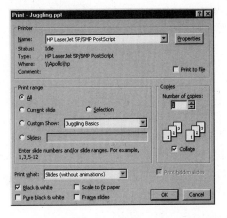

4

PRINTING OPTIONS AND TECHNIQUES

When you're done, click OK to start the print job.

> **NOTE: POWERPOINT'S PRINT OPTIONS**
>
> PowerPoint has quite a few options that define its default print settings. I run through each of these options in Chapter 35, "Customizing PowerPoint."

Modifying the Page Setup for Slides

Before printing, you might want to make some adjustments to the page setup values that PowerPoint uses when printing slides. These values cover the page orientation, slide sizes, and the slide numbers.

To work with these settings, select File | Page Setup to display the Page Setup dialog box, shown in Figure 4.35. Here's a summary of the controls available:

Slides sized for: Use this list to select how you want PowerPoint to size the slides. For printouts, you select either Letter Paper or A4 Paper. Alternatively, use the Width and Height spinners to set custom dimensions for the printed slides.

Number slides from: Use this spinner to set the starting slide number.

Orientation: These options determine how PowerPoint lays out each slide on the page. Portrait prints along the short side of the page, and Landscape prints along the long side of the page.

FIGURE 4.35.

Use the Page Setup dialog box to customize the layout of your printed slides.

When you're done, click OK to put the new settings into effect.

Creating an Outline for Printing

While in Outline view, outlines can be printed as they appear on-screen. Here are some printing variations:

- ■ To print only the slide titles from the outlines, click the Collapse All button.
- ■ To print all levels of text in your outline, click the Expand All button.
- ■ To print outlines without formatting, deactivate the Show Formatting button.

- To increase or decrease the type size of outlines, use the toolbar's Zoom box. You can either type a percentage in the box or pull down the list and choose one of the preset percentages.

- To show headers and footers on printed outlines, select View | Header and Footer. Use the Header and Footer dialog box to choose the items—such as the date and time and the slide number—you want to display in the header and footer.

- To choose options for slides, notes, and handouts, select View | Master and then choose either Slide Master, Handout Master, or Notes Master. PowerPoint then displays the appropriate master.

Printing from Outlook

Outlook, as I mentioned briefly in Chapter 2, "What's New in Office 97," brings some exciting new features to the field of personal information management. I discuss Outlook in depth in Part VII, "Unleashing Outlook," but for now I run through the program's printing options.

Outlook's Printing Basics

As usual, I begin by taking you through the basic printing procedure. Before choosing the Print command, decide what you want to print. If you're in the Calendar folder, for example, select the days or months to include in the printout (assuming, of course, that you don't want to print everything).

Once that's done, select File | Print to display the Outlook Print dialog box. The controls you see in this dialog box depend on the type of Outlook data you're trying to print. Figure 4.36 shows the dialog box that appears when you print from the Calendar folder. In all cases, though, you see a Print style group that lets you choose a page layout for your printout. I discuss this in more detail later. For now, you can see the layout provided by each style by highlighting the style and then clicking the Preview button.

FIGURE 4.36.

The Outlook Print dialog box for the Calendar folder.

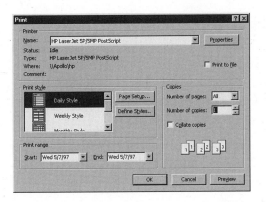

Here's a summary of the unique controls that each folder brings to the Print dialog box:

Inbox: This folder adds a Print options group that gives you two check boxes:

Start each item on a new page: If you activate this check box, Outlook starts a new page for each printed message.

Print attached files with item(s): If you activate this check box, Outlook also prints any files that are attached to a message.

Calendar: This folder adds a Print range group that lets you specify a range of dates to print. Use the Start and End controls to enter the date range.

Contacts: This folder adds a Print range group that lets you choose how many Contacts to print. Choose All items to print the entire folder, or choose Only selected items to print just the contacts you selected before running the Print command.

Tasks: This folder adds a Print range group that lets you choose how many Tasks to print. Choose All rows to print the entire folder, or choose Only selected rows to print just the selected tasks.

Journal: This folder adds a Print options group that gives you the same two check boxes that I described for the Inbox folder.

Notes: This folder also adds a Print options group that displays the same check boxes used with the Inbox folder.

When you're done, click OK to proceed with the print job.

Working with Print Styles

As you saw in the last section, Outlook defines various print styles for each folder. These print styles are a collection of page layout settings that cover options such as the fonts used in the printout, the paper size and orientation, the margins, and the text displayed in headers and footers. This section shows you how to edit Outlook's existing print styles as well as how to create your own.

Modifying an Existing Print Style

To make changes to an existing print style, you need to display the Page Setup dialog box for that style. To do that, activate the folder that contains the print style you want to work with, and then use any of the following techniques:

- Select File | Page Setup and then select the style name in the cascade menu that appears.
- Select File | Page Setup | Define Print Styles, highlight the style in the Define Print Styles dialog box, and click Edit.
- Select File | Print, highlight the style in the Print style list, and click Page Setup.

The controls in the Page Setup dialog box that appears vary from style to style, as you might imagine. Figure 4.37 shows the Page Setup dialog box for the Daily Style (which is one of the Calendar styles).

FIGURE 4.37.

The Page Setup dialog box for the Calendar folder's Daily Style.

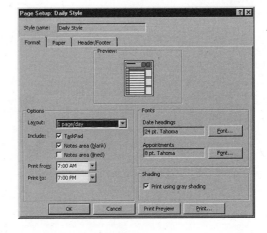

The Format Tab

The controls in the Format tab determine the overall look of the printed pages:

Preview: This box shows you what the print style looks like.

Options: This group provides a few options that are specific to the style.

Fonts: These controls let you set the font used in the printout headings and text. Click the Font buttons to select the font options you want to use.

Shading: When this check box is activated, Outlook prints headings, dates, and other elements using gray-scale shading.

The Paper Tab

The Paper tab, shown in Figure 4.38, controls the paper and page size, the orientation, the margins, and more:

Paper: Use this list to specify the type of paper you use for the printout. You can also use the Width and Height text boxes to set custom page dimensions.

Paper source: Use this drop-down list to select the printer paper tray to use during the print job.

Page: Use this list to specify the page size you want to use. Note that "page" here isn't necessarily the same as a sheet of paper. For example, the Letter Half item prints two "pages" on a single sheet of paper.

Margins: Use these text boxes to specify the page margins you want to use.

Orientation: These options determine how Outlook lays out the data on the page. Portrait prints along the short side of the page, and Landscape prints along the long side of the page.

FIGURE 4.38.

The Paper tab governs various aspects of the printed pages.

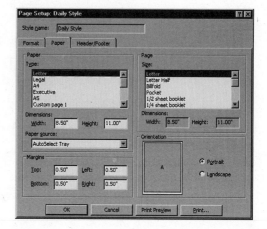

The Header/Footer Tab

Finally, you can use the Header/Footer tab, shown in Figure 4.39, to specify text and codes to print in the top or bottom of each page. Here are the steps to follow:

1. The three boxes associated with both the header and footer represent the left, center, and right of the object. Click inside the section you want to work with.

2. Enter text or select one of the buttons to insert a code into the header. Here's a summary of what each button provides:

Button	*Code Inserted*	*Description*
	[Page #]	Displays the page number.
	[Total Pages]	Displays the total page count.
	[Date Printed]	Displays the date the item is printed.
	[Time Printed]	Displays the time the item is printed.
	[User Name]	Displays your user name.

4. If you want Outlook to reverse the right and left sections on odd and even pages, activate the Reverse on even pages check box.

5. Repeat steps 1 through 4 to enter any other text or codes.

FIGURE 4.39.

Use the Header/Footer tab to construct a header and footer for your printout.

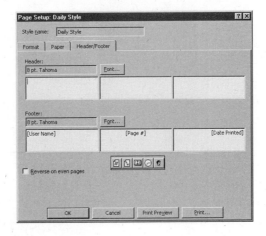

Previewing Your Printouts

When you're working in an application, you often can't see certain elements that will appear on the printed page. In Excel, for example, you can't see page elements such as margins, headers, and footers in the normal screen display. Because these kinds of features play such a large part in determining the look of your printouts, the Office applications offer a Print Preview feature. This feature, by showing you a scaled down, full-page version of your pages, lets you get the "big picture." You can see the effect of each of the page layout and print options you selected. You also have easy access to the Page Setup dialog box, where you can make changes and then immediately see the effect on the printout. Print Preview also lets you adjust your margins visually with the mouse, and you can print right from the preview screen.

To try Print Preview, use either of the following techniques:

■ Select File | Print Preview.

■ Click the Print Preview toolbar button.

You see a screen similar to the one shown in Figure 4.40.

FIGURE 4.40.
Word's Print Preview screen.

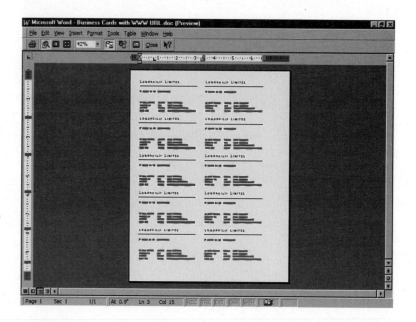

The displayed page is "live" in the sense that you can add, move, or delete text, apply formatting, and perform most other regular document chores (depending on the application). However, the Print Preview window has its own toolbar that provides you with a few preview-related features. Table 4.1 summarizes the role of each button.

Table 4.1. Print Preview's toolbar buttons.

Button	Name	Description
	Print	Prints the document.
	Magnifier	Toggles the mouse pointer between the selection arrow and a magnifying glass. The latter lets you switch the Zoom percentage between 42 percent and 100 percent by clicking the document.
	One Page	Sets the preview window to show only a single page.
	Multiple Pages	Lets you preview two or more pages. When you click this button, a drop-down list appears to give you various display choices.

Button	Name	Description
44%	Zoom	Use this list to select the Zoom magnification used in the preview window.
	View Ruler	In Word, this button toggles the Ruler on and off.
	Shrink to Fit	Clicking this button reduces the number of pages in the document by one. Use this feature to avoid printing only a small amount of data on the last page of the document.
	Full Screen	When you click this button, the application removes most of the Print Preview interface so all that remains is the preview screen and the toolbar. Click Close Full Screen to return to the normal preview screen.
Close	Close	Click this button to shut down Print Preview.

Tips for Saving Paper

As you've seen in this chapter, Windows 95 and Office make printing so easy that you have yet another reason to print too many documents. To keep your paper costs down and save a tree or two, here are some tips that will help you cut down on the amount of paper you use:

- Print a document only when you have to. Too many people print intermediate drafts or whenever they make the slightest change. With Windows' WYSIWYG (What You See Is What You Get) display, you shouldn't need a hard copy until the document is finished.

- Take advantage of the Print Preview feature described in the last section. A sneak peek at the document will save you many a reprint.

- Proofread your documents carefully before printing them. You usually need to reprint because of spelling and grammatical errors that you didn't catch until you read the printout. You can avoid this by giving a document the once-over before printing it. By all means, use the Office spell checker and Word's grammar checker.

- Try to maximize the print area on each page. You can do this by reducing the margins and by using smaller type sizes.

■ Print only what you need. Most applications let you print a selection of text, a single page, or a range of pages. There's no point in printing the entire document if you need only a small chunk of it.

■ If you print a document and then discover a small mistake (such as a spelling gaffe) on one page, just reprint the offending page.

■ Distribute your documents electronically if you can. Rather than send a printout to someone, you can send the file over a network, as an e-mail attachment, or even via floppy disk.

■ Reuse printouts you no longer need. If you're printing an unimportant document that only you will see, turn some used pages around and print on the other side.

Summary

This chapter took you on a tour of Office printing facilities. I began by showing you how to install a printer in Windows 95. You then learned some printing basics that apply to all the Office applications. From there, I discussed the print specifics for Word, Excel, Access, PowerPoint, and Outlook. I closed with a look at the Print Preview feature and a few tips on saving paper. You'll find related information in the following chapters:

■ Chapter 9, "Document Concepts," tells you about Word features such as margins, page setup, and headers and footers.

■ See Chapter 13, "Word as a Publisher," for instructions on using Word's merge feature.

■ Check out Chapter 28, "Designing and Customizing Reports," for some valuable information on setting up an Access report.

■ Chapter 35, "Customizing PowerPoint," runs through PowerPoint's printing options.

■ To learn more about setting up and working with Outlook, see Part VII, "Unleashing Outlook."

Using the OfficeArt Tools

CHAPTER 5

Art! Who comprehends her? With whom can one consult concerning this great goddess?

—*Ludwig von Beethoven*

There are many ways to spruce up a boring document, including formatting the text, adjusting paragraph settings, using bulleted and numbered lists, and so on. However, if you really want to grab the attention of the reader or audience, you can't beat a well-made or well-chosen image. The problem is that most of us are decidedly not professional artists (or even competent amateurs, for that matter), so high-end artwork is out of reach.

Or is it? Office 97 ships with a core component called OfficeArt that's integrated into each Office application. OfficeArt is a powerful set of drawing tools that you can wield to create and enhance graphic objects in your documents. You can add lines, circles, or polygons, add sophisticated effects, import graphics from external sources, and more. With OfficeArt, even those of us who have only a fleeting relationship with our right brain can still produce pleasing images that will pass muster with all but the most discriminating viewer.

This chapter shows you how to use OfficeArt to add graphic objects to your documents, either by drawing them yourself using the Drawing toolbar or by importing graphics from external sources. You also learn a number of useful techniques for editing and enhancing your images.

A Tour of the Drawing Toolbar

Your OfficeArt starting point is the Drawing toolbar, which contains no fewer than 18 tools that let you create and enhance your own images. With these tools, you can draw lines, rectangles, ovals, arcs, and polygons, insert text boxes, AutoShapes, and WordArt images, and set colors, line styles, shadows, and other effects.

To display the Drawing toolbar, use any of the following techniques:

- Select View | Toolbars | Drawing.
- Right-click any toolbar and then choose Drawing from the menu that appears.

- Click the Drawing button on the Standard toolbar.

Table 5.1 summarizes the Drawing toolbar buttons.

Table 5.1. The Drawing toolbar buttons.

Button	Name	Description
Draw ▾	Draw menu	Provides access to a number of drawing-related commands.
▧	Select Objects	When activated, lets you select graphic objects.

Button	Name	Description
	Free Rotate	Lets you rotate an image.
AutoShapes ▾	AutoShapes menu	Provides a menu of predefined shapes.
	Line	You use this tool to draw a straight line.
	Arrow	You use this tool to draw an arrow.
	Rectangle	You use this tool to draw a rectangle or square.
	Oval	You use this tool to draw an ellipse or circle.
	Text Box	You use this tool to insert a text box.
	Insert WordArt	You use this tool to insert a WordArt image.
	Fill Color	Sets the background color for the selected object.
	Line Color	Sets the border color for the selected object.
	Font Color	Sets the font color for the selected object.
	Line Style	Provides a choice of line styles for the selected object.
	Dash Style	Provides a choice of dash styles for the selected object.

continues

Table 5.1. continued

Button	Name	Description
	Arrow Style	Provides a choice of arrow styles for the selected object.
	Shadow	Provides a choice of shadow settings for the selected object.
	3-D	Provides a choice of 3-D settings for the selected object.

Drawing Basic Shapes

OfficeArt comes with dozens of built-in shapes—called AutoShapes—that you can use to quickly and easily create drawings from scratch. In most cases, you just select a shape and then drag on the document to create the object. This section gives you the specific techniques to use for all of OfficeArt's shapes.

Drawing Straight Lines and Arrows

A straight line is probably the most basic shape, and it's useful as a separator, as part of a more complex image such as a company logo, and in many other situations. Arrows are handy for pointing out important document information. Follow these steps to create a straight line or arrow:

1. Click the tool you want to use. If you want to create multiple shapes, double-click the tool. For straight lines and arrows, you have three choices:

   ■ Click the Line tool for a straight line.

   ■ Click the Arrow tool for a one-headed arrow.

   ■ Click AutoShapes | Lines and then click the Double Arrow tool for a two-headed arrow.

2. In each case, the mouse pointer changes to a crosshair. Move the pointer into the document and position the crosshair where you want to begin the line.

3. Press and hold down the left mouse button.

4. Drag the mouse pointer to where you want the line to end.

5. Release the mouse button. OfficeArt inserts the line or arrow.

6. If you're drawing multiple lines, repeat steps 2 through 5.

7. To finish drawing multiple lines, click an empty part of the worksheet or press the Esc key.

Figure 5.1 demonstrates some ways to use lines in an Excel worksheet.

FIGURE 5.1.

Some line objects in a worksheet.

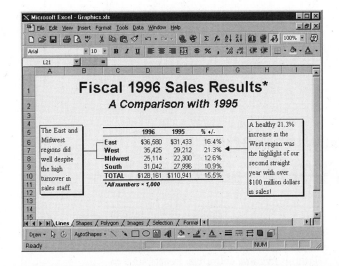

TIP: KEYS FOR SPECIAL LINES

Here are some keys to use along with the mouse:

■ To restrict straight lines and arrows to 15-degree increments, hold down the Shift key while you draw.

■ To create a line that extends in two directions from your starting point, hold down Ctrl while you draw.

■ To align your shapes with Excel's worksheet gridlines, hold down the Alt key while drawing.

NOTE: CANCELING A SHAPE

With any OfficeArt drawing tool, if you're in mid-draw and you don't like what you see, press Esc to wipe out the current shape and start again.

Drawing Freehand Lines

As you've seen, OfficeArt makes it easy to draw lines and arrows—too easy, some might say. For a real challenge, try using the Scribble tool to draw freehand lines that follow the mouse pointer. Here's what you do:

1. Click AutoShapes | Lines and then click the Scribble button.

2. Move the mouse pointer into the document and position it where you want the line to start. The pointer changes to a crosshair.

3. Hold down the left mouse button and drag the mouse. As you drag, the mouse pointer changes to a pencil icon, and a line follows your every move.

4. When you're done, release the mouse button.

Drawing Rectangles, Ovals, and Other Enclosed Shapes

OfficeArt comes with two basic enclosed shapes: a rectangle and an oval. However, the AutoShapes menu also provides a large number of predefined shapes:

Basic Shapes: These tools let you draw simple shapes such as diamonds and other regular polygons, cylinders, hearts, and moons.

Block Arrows: These tools provide you with arrows in block (enclosed polygon) format.

Flowchart: Use these tools to draw flowchart symbols.

Stars and Banners: This is a collection of starbursts and banner images.

Callouts: Use these shapes to add callouts to your documents. A callout is an object containing text that points to another object in the document.

TIP: DISPLAYING THE AUTOSHAPES TOOLBAR

If you plan to use the AutoShapes frequently, you might find the AutoShapes toolbar a more convenient access point. To display this toolbar, select Insert | Picture | AutoShapes.

Follow the steps outlined here to create a shape:

1. Click the tool you want to use. If you want to create multiple shapes, you have to tear off the menu and then double-click the tool. (See the next section to learn more about tear-off menus.) You have three choices:

■ Click the Rectangle tool for a rectangle or square.

■ Click the Oval tool for an oval or circle.

■ Click AutoShapes and then select a tool from the menus provided.

2. Move the mouse pointer into the document and position it where you want to begin drawing the shape.

3. Press and hold down the left mouse button.

4. Drag the mouse pointer until the shape has the size and form you want.

5. Release the mouse button. OfficeArt draws the shape.

6. If you create a callout, OfficeArt displays a cursor so you can enter the text. See "Working with Text" later in this chapter.

7. If you're drawing multiple shapes, repeat steps 2 through 5.

8. To finish drawing multiple shapes, click an empty part of the worksheet or press the Esc key.

TIP: KEYS FOR SPECIAL SHAPES

Here are some keys to use along with the mouse:

■ To make your rectangles square or your ellipses circular, hold down the Shift key while drawing.

■ To make your starting point the center of the shape, hold down Ctrl while drawing.

■ To align your shapes with Excel's worksheet gridlines, hold down the Alt key while drawing.

NOTE: CHANGING A SHAPE

If you create a shape and then decide that a different shape is preferable, you don't have to delete the original shape and start over. Instead, click the shape and then select Draw | Change AutoShape in the Drawing toolbar. Use the cascade menu that appears to select a new AutoShape.

You can use shapes to create your own custom worksheet formatting. For example, instead of using Excel's cell borders, create your own with the Rectangle button, as shown in Figure 5.2. This figure also shows some examples of shapes used in a worksheet.

FIGURE 5.2.

Some sample shapes on a worksheet.

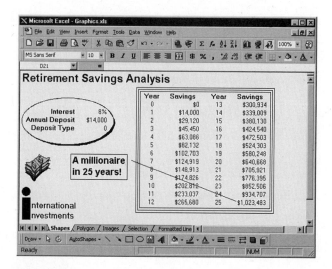

Working with Tear-Off Menus

Before I discuss more of the OfficeArt drawing tools, take a slight detour to check out the new tear-off menus in Office 97. A tear-off menu is a collection of items that usually appears as a cascade menu that branches from a pull-down menu or a toolbar. However, you can drag these menus from their normal position so that they become a separate toolbar that remains on screen. This is handy if you need to use multiple tools from the same menu, and as you saw in the last section, it's a must if you want to draw multiple shapes with a single tool.

For example, each of the cascade menus that you see on the Drawing toolbar's AutoShapes menu is a tear-off menu. To turn one of these into a floating toolbar, follow these steps:

1. Click AutoShapes and then choose a command to display one of the cascade menus.

2. Move the mouse pointer into the cascade menu and place it over the gray bar that appears at the top of the menu. The bar changes to dark blue.

3. Drag the mouse. The menu detaches itself and OfficeArt displays a gray outline that represents the floating toolbar.

4. When the outline is in the position you want, release the mouse button to display the toolbar.

Figure 5.3 shows the Basic Shapes tools as both a cascade menu and a floating toolbar.

Drawing Bezier Curves

For more complex or custom shapes, you often need to draw curves. The OfficeArt tools are very flexible in that they let you draw precise Bezier curves with any number of vertices. Here are the steps to follow to create a curve:

FIGURE 5.3.

If a cascade menu has a bar at the top, it means you can drag the menu to display it as a floating toolbar.

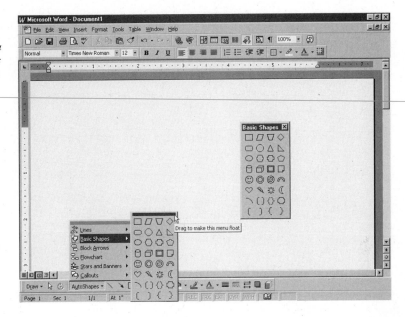

1. Click AutoShapes | Lines and then click the Curve tool.

2. Move the mouse pointer into the document, position the crosshair where you want to begin the curve, and click.

3. Move the mouse pointer to draw the initial line. This is the line that you will curve.

4. When the line is the length you want, click to set it.

5. Move the mouse pointer to curve the line.

6. When the curve is the way you want it, click to set it.

7. Repeat steps 5 and 6 to add more curves to the line.

8. Double-click to finish drawing the curve.

9. If you're drawing multiple curves, repeat steps 2 through 8.

10. To finish drawing multiple curves, press the Esc key.

Drawing Freeform Polygons

OfficeArt also lets you draw complex, freeform polygons with any number of sides. Here are the steps to follow to create a freeform polygon:

1. Click AutoShapes | Lines and then click the Freeform tool.

5

USING THE OFFICEART TOOLS

2. Move the pointer into the document and position the crosshair where you want to begin the polygon.

3. You can begin with a freehand line by pressing and holding down the left mouse button. To draw a straight line instead, click the left mouse button.

4. Move the mouse pointer to draw the initial segment.

5. To finish freehand drawing, release the mouse button. To finish drawing a straight line, click the left mouse button.

6. Repeat steps 3 through 5 to add other freehand or straight lines.

7. To finish drawing the polygon, either double-click or enclose the polygon by joining the last segment to the starting point.

8. If you're drawing multiple polygons, repeat steps 2 through 7.

9. To finish drawing multiple polygons, press the Esc key.

Working with Text

OfficeArt is mostly about drawing and inserting pictures, but that doesn't mean your left brain can't have any fun. In fact, OfficeArt gives you three different ways to create shapes that include text:

Callouts: As I mentioned earlier, callouts are shapes that include some sort of descriptive text as well as a pointer that associates the callout with another document object. When you finish drawing a callout, OfficeArt automatically places a cursor inside the callout so you can add your text.

AutoShapes: You can add text to most of the other AutoShapes as well. To add text to an AutoShapes, right-click the shape and then choose Add Text from the shortcut menu. This puts a cursor inside the shape so you can type your text.

Text boxes: These are rectangular boxes that are designed to hold text. To draw a text box, first either click the Text Box button on the Drawing toolbar or else select Insert | Text Box. You then follow the same method I outlined earlier for drawing a rectangle. When you finish drawing a text box, OfficeArt automatically places a cursor inside the callout so you can add your text.

Creating Linked Text Objects

Most of the text objects you draw are islands unto themselves with no connection to each other. However, sometimes you might need to break up a large text object into two or smaller objects. Similarly, you might need to space a single narrative across multiple text objects throughout your document.

Given these and similar situations, it would be nice if you could treat the text in all the related text objects as a whole. This means that if you, say, insert some text in one text object, the text in the other text objects is pushed down accordingly (in the same way that text inserted into a Word document pushes down the rest of the document text).

With Office 97, you can do this quite easily by creating linked text objects. Here are the steps to follow:

1. Create any of the text objects discussed in the last section.
2. Create an empty text object. (You can set up a link only to an empty text object.)
3. Click the first text object to select it. You see the Text Box toolbar.
4. Click the Create Text Box Link button.
5. Click the second text object. OfficeArt creates a link between the two text objects.
6. Repeat as necessary to create more links. For example, create a third text object, click the second text object, click Create Text Box Link, and click the third text object.

Here are a few techniques for working with linked text objects:

■ You can type all your text in the first of the linked text objects. If your typing extends beyond the boundaries of this object, OfficeArt wraps the text into the next linked object.

■ Any text inserted or deleted in any of the linked objects causes the text to adjust accordingly.

■ To move forward through the linked objects, click Next Text Box in the Text Box toolbar.

■ To move backward through the linked objects, click Previous Text Box in the Text Box toolbar.

■ To break a link between two text objects, click the object that is first in the link and then click Break Forward Link in the Text Box toolbar.

Inserting Pictures

Although the drawing tools that come with OfficeArt are handy for creating simple graphics effects, a more ambitious image requires a dedicated graphics program, such as Windows Paint or CorelDRAW!. With these programs, you can create professional-quality graphics and then import them into your document. If the application supports object linking and embedding (OLE), you can maintain a link between the object and the original program.

You can use two methods to import a graphic object into a document:

■ You can use the Clipboard to copy and paste the object from the original application to the OfficeArt worksheet. This method is useful if you need to use only part of a graphic image. I show you how to use the Clipboard and OLE in Chapter 48, "Office Integration and OLE."

■ Select Insert | Picture to insert an image from one of the following sources:

Clip Art: This command launches the Clip Gallery application. See "Inserting an Image from the Clip Gallery" later in this chapter.

From File: This command lets you insert an image from an existing file. See "Inserting an Image from a File."

WordArt: This command starts the WordArt text effects component. I show you how to use this program later in "Inserting a WordArt Image."

From Scanner: Use this command to capture an image from a digital scanner. See "Inserting an Image from a Scanner."

Chart: This command loads Microsoft Graph so you can create a chart. See Chapter 6, "Working with Microsoft Graph."

Inserting an Image from the Clip Gallery

If you don't have the time or the skill to create your own images, consider using a clip art library. Clip art is professional-quality artwork that is commercially available in libraries of several hundred or more images. Because you have Microsoft Office, you don't need to purchase clip art because you get thousands of images free as part of the Office package. You'll find the clip art files in two places:

■ In the Clipart subfolder of your main Microsoft Office folder. This folder contains only a small number of files.

■ On the Office CD-ROM in the Clipart folder. This is the main source for clip art files.

Rather than work with clip art files directly, Office provides the Clip Gallery application. Here are the steps required to insert an image via the Clip Gallery:

1. Select where in your document you want the image to appear.

2. Insert your Office CD-ROM.

3. Select Insert | Picture | Clip Art. Figure 5.4 shows the window that appears.

4. Select one of the tabs—Clip Art, Pictures, Sounds, or Videos.

5. Use the Categories list on the left side of the window to choose a clip category. The objects in the selected category appear in the clip window.

6. Click the object you want to insert.

7. While an object is highlighted, you can use the following techniques:

■ To get a closer look at a clip art image or picture, activate the Magnify check box.

- To find out the object's size and other properties, click the Clip Properties button.

- To hear a sound or play a video, click the Play button.

FIGURE 5.4.

The Clip Gallery provides a convenient method for finding the Office clip art, picture, sound, and video files.

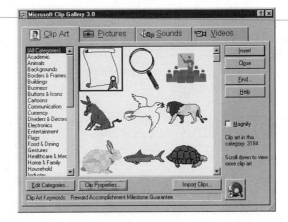

8. Click Insert to insert the image into your document.

NOTE: IMPORTING CLIP ART

If you have other images on your computer, you can add them to the Clip Gallery for easy access. To do this, click the Import Clips button, select one or more files, and then click Open.

If you have access to the World Wide Web, Microsoft also maintains a Web site called Clip Gallery Live that maintains a large collection of images for users of Microsoft Office. To view this site, use either of the following techniques:

- Click the Internet Explorer icon in the Clip Gallery window and then click OK in the dialog box that appears.

- Enter the address `http://www.microsoft.com/clipgallerylive/` into your Web browser.

When the page appears, click the Accept button to accept the license agreement and move to the Clip Gallery Live site. As you can see in Figure 5.5, the left side of the screen has four buttons that correspond to the Clip Art, Pictures, Sounds, and Videos tabs in the Clip Gallery window. Click one of these buttons, select a category, and click Go to display the files. If you see one you like, click the link below the image to save it to your computer.

5

USING THE OFFICEART TOOLS

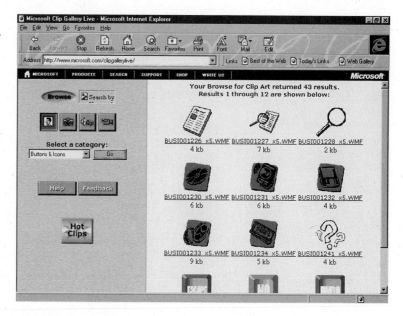

Inserting an Image from a File

Rather than go through the Clip Gallery, you might prefer to insert an existing graphics file directly into your document. Here are the steps to follow:

1. Select where in your document you want the image to appear.

2. Choose Insert | Picture | From File. OfficeArt displays the Insert Picture dialog box.

3. Highlight the graphics file you want to use. A preview of the picture appears, as shown in Figure 5.6.

FIGURE 5.6.

*Use the Insert Picture
dialog box to insert a
graphics file into your
document.*

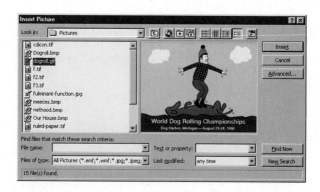

4. Click Insert. OfficeArt inserts the file into the document.

Inserting an Image from a Scanner

If you have a digital scanner, you can use it to acquire an image, touch up that image in Microsoft Photo Editor, and insert the image into your document. Here are the steps to follow:

1. Select where in your document you want the image to appear.
2. Select Insert | Picture | From Scanner. OfficeArt launches Microsoft Photo Editor, which in turn loads the TWAIN Source Manager software that you use to acquire scanned images.
3. Use the scanner to scan a final image. The image is loaded into Photo Editor, as shown in Figure 5.7.

FIGURE 5.7.

Once you've acquired the scanned image, it's loaded into Photo Editor for retouching and other effects.

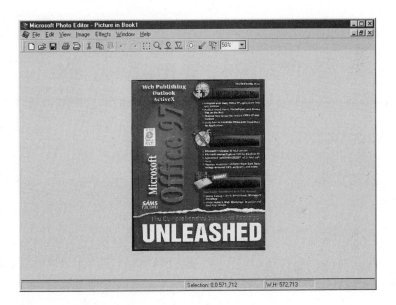

4. Use the Photo Editor commands to enhance the image as needed.
5. When you're done, select File | Exit and Return to *Document*, where *Document* is the name of your document.

Inserting a WordArt Image

You saw in Chapter 3, "Day-to-Day Office Basics," that the Office applications boast quite a few font-related options for improving the look of your document text. Good-looking and well-used fonts are a must for any quality document, but if you want real eye-catching text effects, you need to turn to WordArt. This OLE server application can apply various special effects to text, most of which would otherwise require a high-end graphics application.

Here are the steps you need to follow to insert a WordArt object into a document:

1. Select the location in your document where you want the WordArt image to appear.

2. Start WordArt using either of the following techniques:

   ▪ Select Insert | Picture | WordArt.

   ▪ Click the Insert WordArt button on the Drawing toolbar.

3. In the WordArt Gallery window that appears, shown in Figure 5.8, click the style you want and then click OK.

Figure 5.8.

Use the WordArt Gallery to choose the style you want.

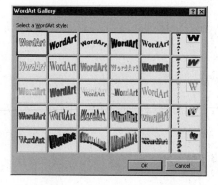

4. Next you see the Edit WordArt Text dialog box, as shown in Figure 5.9. Use the Text area to enter the text you want to use. You can also select a font, size, and bold and italic effects. When you're done, click OK to insert the image.

Figure 5.9.

Use the Edit WordArt Text dialog box to enter your text and set up the font you want.

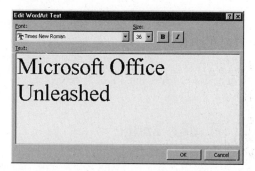

Figure 5.10 shows an example of an inserted WordArt image. Notice that the WordArt toolbar also appears. Table 5.2 summarizes the WordArt toolbar buttons.

FIGURE 5.10.
*An inserted WordArt
image.*

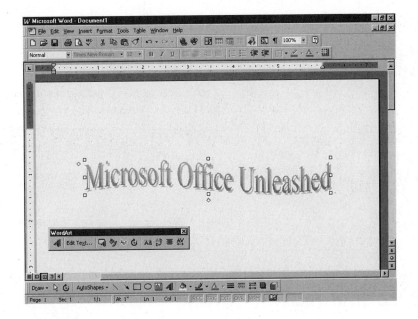

Table 5.2. The WordArt toolbar buttons.

Button	Name	Description
	Insert WordArt	Inserts another WordArt image.
Edit Text...	Edit Text	Displays the Edit WordArt Text dialog box.
	WordArt Gallery	Displays the WordArt Gallery window.
	Format WordArt	Displays the Format WordArt dialog box. (I discuss the various object formatting options later in this chapter.)
Abc	WordArt Shape	Displays a menu of shapes that WordArt can apply to the text.
	Free Rotate	Lets you rotate an image.

continues

Table 5.2. continued

Button	Name	Description
Aa	WordArt Same Letter Heights	When this button is activated, WordArt displays each letter using the same height.
A b b↵	WordArt Vertical Text	Toggles the text between vertical and horizontal orientation.
≡	WordArt Alignment	Displays a menu of text-alignment options.
AV ↔	WordArt Character Spacing	Displays a menu of character-spacing options.

Formatting and Editing Graphic Objects

The OfficeArt tools aren't difficult to use, but chances are that the objects you create or insert won't look just the way you want. You might need to adjust the size or position of an object, change the color of the border or background, add a drop shadow, or rotate the image. OfficeArt lets you do all these editing and formatting chores; I'll use the rest of this chapter to explain the appropriate techniques.

Selecting Graphic Objects

Before you can work with a graphic object, you must select it. The following procedure lists the steps to follow to select a graphic object:

1. Activate the Select Objects button on the Drawing toolbar.

2. Position the mouse pointer over the border of the graphic. You know the mouse is positioned properly if you see a four-headed arrow at the tip of the pointer.
3. Click the object.

Every graphic object has an invisible rectangular *frame.* For a line or rectangle, the frame is the same as the object itself. For all other objects, the frame is a rectangle that completely encloses the shape or image.

When you select an object, OfficeArt displays several "handles" around the object's frame, as shown in Figure 5.11:

■ Every object displays a number of *selection handles*—the small white rectangles in Figure 5.11. You use these handles to change the size of the image (as discussed later).

■ AutoShapes also display one or more *adjustment handles*—the yellow diamonds in Figure 5.11. You use these handles to adjust the appearance of the shape. With a WordArt object, for example, you can use an adjustment handle to make the text lean more to the left or right.

FIGURE 5.11.

Selected objects display handles around the object's frame.

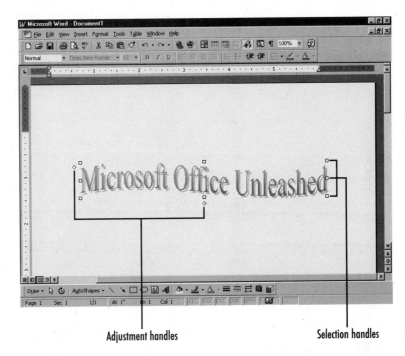

Adjustment handles   Selection handles

Selecting Multiple Graphic Objects

If you use graphics often, you can easily end up with a dozen or more objects in a worksheet. If you want to rearrange or reformat a worksheet, it becomes time-consuming to move or format each object individually. To get around this problem, OfficeArt lets you select all the objects you want and work with them simultaneously.

OfficeArt offers a couple of methods for selecting multiple objects. If you want to work with only a few objects, or if the objects you need are scattered widely throughout the document, hold down the Shift key and click each object individually.

If the objects you want are grouped in the document, you can use the mouse to "lasso" all the objects in one shot. The following procedure takes you through the necessary steps:

1. Activate the Select Objects button on the Drawing toolbar.

2. Position the mouse pointer at the top-left corner of the area you want to select.

3. Press and hold down the left mouse button.

4. Drag the pointer to the bottom-right corner of the area you want to select. As you drag the pointer, OfficeArt indicates the selected area with a dashed border, as shown in Figure 5.12.

Figure 5.12.

Make sure that the selection area completely encloses each object you want to select.

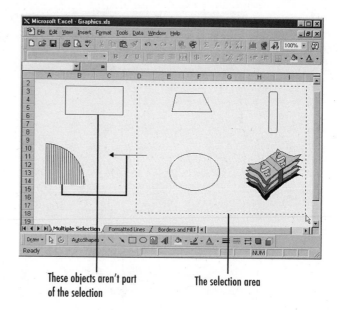

These objects aren't part of the selection

The selection area

5. Release the mouse button. OfficeArt places selection handles around each object in the selection area.

NOTE: LASSO THE ENTIRE OBJECT

The selection area must completely enclose an object to include it in the selection.

TIP: ADDING TO THE SELECTION

If you miss any objects, make sure the Select Objects button is still active and then, while holding down the Shift key, repeat steps 2 through 5 for the other objects you want to include.

After you've made a multiple selection, you can format, size, move, copy, or delete all the objects at once. Note, however, that you must format lines and shapes separately because they use different formatting options. To exclude an object from the selection, hold down the Shift key and click the object's border. To exclude several objects from the selection, hold down Shift and use the lassoing technique to deselect the objects.

TIP: SELECTING ALL WORKSHEET OBJECTS

To select all the graphic objects in an Excel worksheet, select Edit | Go To and then click the Special button in the Go To dialog box. In the Go To Special dialog box that appears, activate the Objects option and select OK. To deselect all objects, click any empty part of the worksheet or press the Esc key.

Formatting Shapes

All of the OfficeArt shapes come with a number of formatting options that let you set colors, line styles, and more. You find these options in the Format AutoShape dialog box, which you can display using any of the following techniques:

- Select the object and then select Format | AutoShape.
- Right-click the object and then choose Format AutoShape from the shortcut menu.
- Double-click the object.

Formatting Lines

I begin the formatting portion of the show with a look at the various options available for lines and borders. You find these options in the Colors and Lines tab of the Format AutoShape dialog box, shown in Figure 5.13. (Note that this dialog box has a slightly different layout among the various Office applications. The dialog box shown in Figure 5.13 is from Word.)

FIGURE 5.13.

Use the Colors and Lines tab to set various formatting options for lines and shape borders.

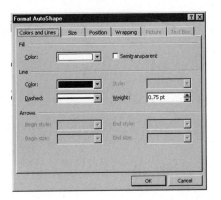

In the Line section, you have the following options:

Color: Use this drop-down list to set the color of the line or border.

Style: Use this drop-down list to choose a style for the line or border.

Dashed: Use this drop-down list to change the line or border to a dashed or dotted format.

Weight: Use this spinner to set the thickness of the line or border.

If you're working with an arrow, use the following controls in the Arrows section:

Begin style: Use this drop-down list to set the look of the arrow's starting point.

Begin size: If you select an arrow or other "non-line" item from the Begin style list, use this list to set the arrowhead size and shape.

End style: Use this drop-down list to set the look of the arrow's ending point.

End size: If you select an arrow or other "non-line" item from the End style list, use this list to set the arrowhead size and shape.

OfficeArt also provides several buttons in the Drawing toolbar that give you easier access to many line formatting options, as shown in Table 5.3.

Table 5.3. Line formatting buttons in the Drawing toolbar.

Button	Name	Description
	Line Color	Click this button to set the line or border to the currently displayed color. Click the downward-pointing triangle to display the color palette. (See "Working with Colors.") Click Patterned Lines to display the Patterned Lines dialog box, shown in Figure 5.14.
	Line Style	Click this button to see a selection of line styles.
	Dash Style	Click this button to see a selection of dash styles.
	Arrow Style	Click this button to see a selection of arrow styles.

FIGURE 5.14.

Use this dialog box to set a pattern for the line. (You need a thick line to see the pattern.)

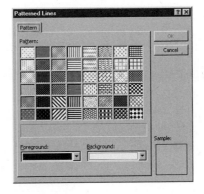

Working with Colors

All of the formatting options let you turn a plain, unformatted document into an attractive, professional-quality report. The final touch often involves adding just the right amount of color to your presentation. With colors, you can emphasize important results, shape the layout of your page, and add subtle psychological effects.

OfficeArt makes it easy to apply colors quickly to borders and fills (the interior of a shape), but it also comes with some excellent tools for creating sophisticated color effects.

Applying a Color from the Palette

In the preceding section I showed you how to set line colors. To apply a quick fill color, use one of the following methods:

- In the Format AutoShape dialog box, drop-down the Fill section's Color list to display the palette, and then click the color you want. Note that this section also has a Semi-transparent check box. If you activate this option, you can see text or other data that sits "behind" the shape, as shown in Figure 5.15.

FIGURE 5.15.

An example of a semi-transparent shape.

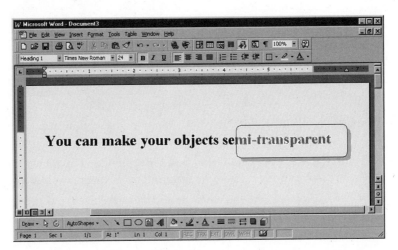

■ Click the Fill Color button to set the fill to the currently displayed color. To choose a different color, click the downward-pointing triangle to display the color palette and then click a color square.

Applying a Non-Palette Color

If the colors available in the default palette don't suit your needs, OfficeArt has plenty more to choose from. When you display the palette, click More Fill Colors (or More Line Colors if you're setting the color of a line) to display the Colors dialog box, shown in Figure 5.16. Click the color you want and then click OK to apply it.

Figure 5.16.

Use the Standard tab to click on the new color you want to use.

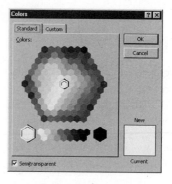

For more control over the new color, use the Custom tab shown in Figure 5.17. In this tab, you can use any of the following three methods to select a color:

Figure 5.17.

Use the Custom tab for greater control over the new color.

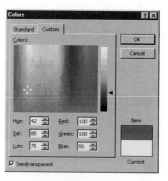

■ Click inside the Colors box. Note, too, that the vertical strip to the left of this box controls the luminosity (brightness) of the color.

■ Enter values in the Red, Green, and Blue spinners. This method utilizes the fact that you can create any color in the spectrum by mixing the colors red, green, and blue.

■ The Custom tab lets you enter specific numbers between 0 and 255 for each of these colors. A lower number means the color is less intense, and a higher number means the color is more intense. To give you some idea of how this works, Table 5.4 lists the first eight colors of the default palette and their respective red, green, and blue numbers.

Table 5.4. The red, green, and blue numbers for eight default palette colors.

Color	Red	Green	Blue
Black	0	0	0
White	255	255	255
Red	255	0	0
Green	0	255	0
Blue	0	0	255
Yellow	255	255	0
Magenta	255	0	255
Cyan	0	255	255

NOTE: GRAY-SCALE COLORS

Whenever the red, green, and blue values are equal, you get a gray-scale color. Lower numbers produce darker grays, and higher numbers produce lighter grays.

■ Enter values in the Hue, Sat, and Lum spinners. With this method, you're setting three different attributes—hue, saturation, and luminance:

> **Hue:** This number (which is more or less equivalent to the term *color*) measures the position on the color spectrum. Lower numbers indicate a position near the red end, and higher numbers move through the yellow, green, blue, and violet parts of the spectrum. As you increase the hue, the color pointer moves from left to right.

> **Saturation:** This number is a measure of the purity of a given hue. A saturation setting of 240 means that the hue is a pure color. Lower numbers indicate that more gray is mixed with the hue until, at 0, the color becomes part of the gray-scale. As you increase the saturation, the color pointer moves toward the top of the color box.

> **Luminance:** This number is a measure of the brightness of a color. Lower numbers are darker, and higher numbers are brighter. The luminance bar to the right of the color box shows the luminance scale for the selected color. As you increase the luminance, the slider moves toward the top of the bar.

When you're done, click OK to apply the custom color.

Working with Fill Effects

Besides applying solid colors to a fill, OfficeArt also lets you apply a variety of fill effects, including gradients, textures, patterns, and pictures. To view these effects, click Fill Effects in the color palette to display the Fill Effects dialog box, shown in Figure 5.18.

FIGURE 5.18.

The Fill Effects dialog box lets you apply sophisticated color effects to your fills.

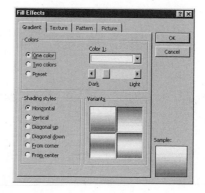

Applying a Gradient

A gradient is a shading effect in which one color gradually morphs into a second color. You use the controls in the Gradient tab to set up this attractive effect.

The Colors group gives you three choices:

One color: Activate this option to use just one color in the gradient. Use the Color 1 list to choose the base color from the palette. Use the slider to set the morph shade to Dark or Light.

Two colors: Activate this option to use two colors in the gradient. In this case, you use the Color 1 and Color 2 palettes to choose the gradient colors.

Preset: Activating this option displays the Preset colors drop-down list from which you can choose among several predefined gradients.

The Gradient tab also has two other controls to further customize the gradient effect:

Shading styles: These options determine the direction of the gradient.

Variants: These boxes give you some variations on the selected shading style.

Applying a Texture

Rather than work with colors, you might prefer to apply one of the built-in OfficeArt textures. Some of these textures are realistic representations of various material, including newsprint, marble, and granite, whereas others are simply interesting abstract patterns.

To apply a texture, activate the Texture tab in the Fill Effects dialog box, shown in Figure 5.19, click a texture box, and then click OK.

FIGURE 5.19.

Use the Texture tab to apply various material effects to the fill.

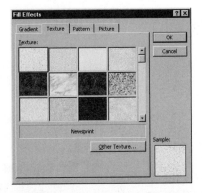

NOTE: MORE TEXTURES

You can add images to the Texture tab by clicking the Other Texture button and then choosing the image you want from the Select Texture dialog box. Note that you'll find a few interesting textures in the \Clipart\Backgrounds subfolder of your main Microsoft Office folder.

Applying a Pattern

Another variation on the fill effects theme is the fill pattern. A pattern is a two-color effect in which one color serves as the background and the other color applies a foreground design. To assign a pattern, follow these steps:

1. Activate the Pattern tab in the Fill Effects dialog box, shown in Figure 5.20.

FIGURE 5.20.

Use the Pattern tab to construct fill patterns.

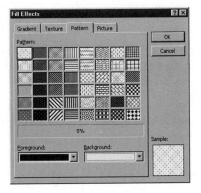

2. Use the Pattern boxes to choose the type of pattern you want to use.
3. Use the Foreground palette to choose the foreground color.
4. Use the Background palette to choose the background color.
5. Click OK to apply the effect.

Applying a Picture

The final fill effect involves setting the background of the shape to a picture file. Here are the steps to follow:

1. Activate the Picture tab in the Fill Effects dialog box.
2. Click Select Picture to display the Select Picture dialog box.
3. Highlight the image file you want to use and then click OK. OfficeArt displays the picture in the Picture tab, as shown in Figure 5.21.

FIGURE 5.21.

Use the Picture tab to apply an image file as a fill effect.

4. Click OK to apply the effect.

Using Color Effectively

You now know how to apply fill colors, but that's only half the battle. Colors that are poorly matched or improperly applied can make a document look worse, not better. This section examines a few basics of using colors effectively in your document.

With so many colors available, the temptation is to go overboard and use a dozen different hues on each page. However, using too many colors can confuse your audience and even cause eye fatigue. Stick to three or four colors at most. If you must use more, use different shades of three or four hues.

Before finalizing your color scheme, you need to make sure that the colors you selected work well together. For example, blue and black are often difficult to distinguish and green/red combinations clash. Other color combinations to avoid are red/blue, green/blue, and brown/black. On the other hand, color combinations such as red/yellow, gray/red, and blue/yellow go well together, as do contrasting shades of the same color, such as black and gray.

> **NOTE: AVOID RED/GREEN COMBINATIONS**
>
> Another good reason to avoid using green and red in your worksheets is that approximately 8 percent of the male population suffers from red-green color blindness.

When selecting colors, think about the psychological impact your scheme will have on your audience. Studies have shown that "cool" colors such as blue and gray evoke a sense of dependability and trust. Use these colors for business meetings. For presentations that require a little more excitement, "warm" colors such as red, yellow, and orange can evoke a festive, fun atmosphere. For a safe, comfortable ambience, try using brown and yellow. For an environmental touch, use green and brown.

If you're putting together several related documents for a report or presentation, settle on a color scheme and then use it consistently throughout your presentation. Charts, clip art, and slides should all use the same colors.

Adding Shadow Effects

Previous Office versions let you add only a simple drop shadow to your images. If you wanted a more sophisticated look, you had to create a separate shadow object (that is, a filled rectangle or polygon) by hand and adjust the z-order to put the shadow object "behind" the main object.

With Office 97, however, that drudgery is a thing of the past. OfficeArt offers no fewer than 20 different pre-fab shadows that you can apply to any object, and it even comes with a separate set of shadow-related tools that let you set precise shadow positions, change the shadow color, and more.

Here are the steps to follow to add a shadow to an object:

1. Select the object or objects you want to work with.
2. Click the Shadow button on the Drawing toolbar. OfficeArt displays a selection of shadow styles, as shown in Figure 5.22.
3. Click the shadow style you want to use.

The palette of shadow styles also includes a Shadow Settings command. Clicking this item displays the Shadow Settings toolbar, which gives you the half dozen tools outlined in Table 5.5.

FIGURE 5.22.
Click the Shadow button to see a selection of shadow styles.

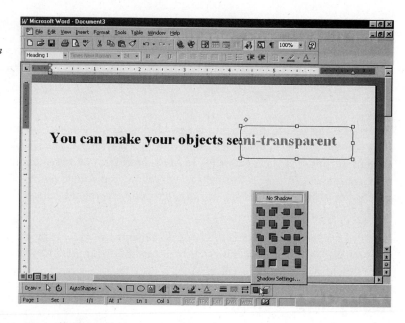

Table 5.5. The Shadow Settings toolbar buttons.

Button	Name	Description
	Shadow On/Off	Toggles the shadow on and off.
	Nudge Shadow Up	Click this button to move the shadow up 1 point.
	Nudge Shadow Down	Click this button to move the shadow down 1 point.
	Nudge Shadow Left	Click this button to move the shadow left 1 point.
	Nudge Shadow Right	Click this button to move the shadow right 1 point.
	Shadow Color	Click this button to display a color palette from which you can select the shadow color. You can also click the Semi-transparent Shadow command to apply the semi-transparent effect to the shadow.

TIP: A BIGGER SHADOW NUDGE

If you hold down the Shift key while clicking any of the Nudge buttons, OfficeArt moves the shadow 6 points in the specified direction.

Adding 3-D Effects

As with shadows, earlier Office versions had no tools for creating 3-D effects. If you wanted to make an image appear three-dimensional, you had to attach properly angled polygons to the image border, which was laborious at best and unprofessional-looking at worst.

However, OfficeArt rides to the rescue once again by providing you with 20 built-in 3-D styles and numerous tools for creating custom 3-D effects.

Here are the steps to follow to add a built-in 3-D effect to an object:

1. Select the object or objects you want to work with.
2. Click the 3-D button on the Drawing toolbar. OfficeArt displays a selection of 3-D styles, as shown in Figure 5.23.

FIGURE 5.23.

Click the 3-D button to see a selection of 3-D effects.

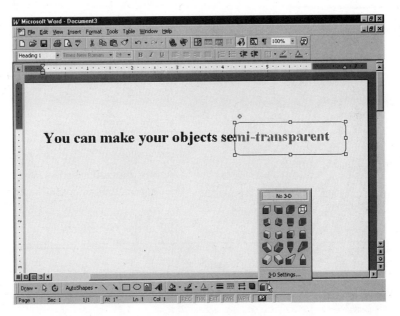

3. Click the 3-D style you want to use.

Notice, too, that the 3-D palette also includes a 3-D Settings command, which you can use to display the 3-D Settings toolbar. Table 5.6 offers a summary of each button on this toolbar.

Table 5.6. The 3-D Settings toolbar buttons.

Button	Name	Description
	3-D On/Off	Toggles the 3-D effect on and off.
	Tilt Up	Rotates the 3-D effect 6 degrees up relative to the horizontal axis.
	Tilt Down	Rotates the 3-D effect 6 degrees down relative to the horizontal axis.
	Tilt Left	Rotates the 3-D effect 6 degrees left relative to the vertical axis.
	Tilt Right	Rotates the 3-D effect 6 degrees right relative to the vertical axis.
	Depth	Displays a selection of depths, measured in points, for the 3-D effect.
	Direction	Displays a selection of directions for the 3-D effect to extrude from the image.
	Lighting	Displays a palette that lets you choose the direction from which the light source falls on the image. Also offers a selection of light intensities.
	Surface	Displays four surface types for the 3-D effect: Wire Frame, Matte, Plastic, and Metal.
	3-D Color	Displays a color palette from which you can select the color of the 3-D effect.

TIP: A BIGGER 3-D TILT

If you hold down the Shift key while clicking any of the Tilt buttons, OfficeArt rotates the 3-D effect by 45 degrees in the specified direction.

Wrapping Text Around an Object in Word

When you create or insert an image in a Word document, the image obscures any existing text. To make your document looks its best, you probably want to set things up so the regular document text flows smoothly around the object. This is known as *wrapping* the text around the object.

Fortunately, OfficeArt gives you a number of options for wrapping text in your Word documents. To view these options, display the Format AutoShape dialog box for the object you want to work with and then click the Wrapping tab, shown in Figure 5.24. This dialog box is divided into three groups:

> **Wrapping style:** These boxes determine how the text wraps around the object. You can wrap the text around the object's frame (the Square option), around the object's contours (Tight), around the object's border only (Through), or at the top and bottom edge of the object (Top & bottom). To revert to the default unwrapped style, select None.

> **Wrap to:** These boxes set where the text wraps in relation to the object. You can have the text wrap around the Left side of the object, the Right side, or Both sides. For irregular objects, select Largest side to wrap the text along the side with the largest dimension.

> **Distance from text:** Use these spinners to set a white space buffer between the object and the wrapped text.

FIGURE 5.24.

Use the Wrapping tab to ensure that the text in your Word documents wraps around a graphic object.

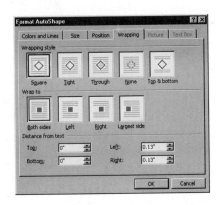

Formatting Text Boxes

OfficeArt uses the term "text box" to refer to any shape that includes text, including AutoShapes, callouts, and, of course, text boxes. There aren't many formatting options associated with text boxes, but you can work with what few there are by displaying the Format AutoShape dialog box for a text object and then clicking the Text Box tab, shown in Figure 5.25. Here are the controls available:

Internal margin: These spinners control the amount of white space (margin size) OfficeArt places around the text.

Format Callout: If the object is a callout AutoShapes with a "leader" (a line that points to something), click this button to display the Format Callout dialog box, shown in Figure 5.26. You use the controls in this dialog box to set the type of callout and a few other options.

Convert to Frame: In Word, click this button to convert the text object to a frame.

Figure 5.25.

Use the Text Box tab to set various options related to text objects.

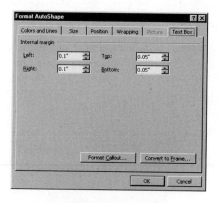

Figure 5.26.

Use the Format Callout dialog box to customize your callout shapes.

Formatting Pictures

To complete the discussion of the OfficeArt formatting options, this section examines the various settings available for formatting pictures. With these settings, you can adjust the picture's brightness and contrast, crop the picture, convert the picture to a watermark, and more.

You work with these settings via the Picture tab in the Format Picture dialog box (see Figure 5.27), which you can display by using either of the following techniques:

- Select the picture and then select Format | Picture.
- Right-click the picture and then choose Format Picture from the shortcut menu.

FIGURE 5.27.

*Use the Picture tab to
format a picture in your
document.*

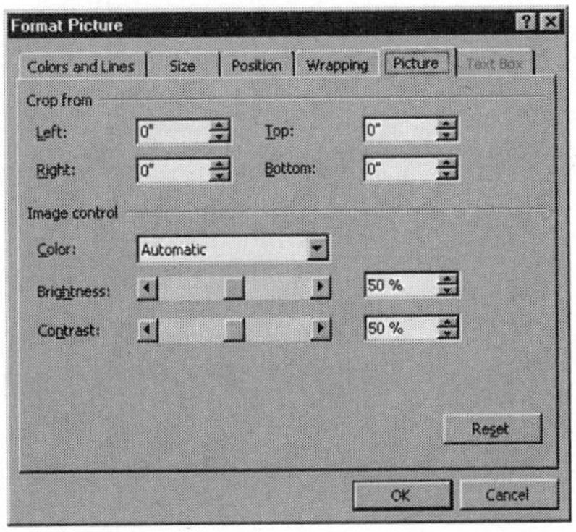

Here's a rundown of the controls in this tab:

> **Crop from:** Use these spinners to crop the image from the Left, Right, Top, or
> Bottom.
>
> **Color:** Use this drop-down list to set the color scale of the object Grayscale, Black &
> White, or Watermark.
>
> **Brightness:** Use this slider to set the brightness of the colors in the image. You can
> also use the spinner to specify a brightness percentage.
>
> **Contrast:** Use this slider to set the contrast (also known as the *saturation* or the
> *intensity*) between the light and dark areas of the image. You can also use the spinner
> to specify a contrast percentage.
>
> **Reset:** Click this button to reset the image attributes to their original values.

NOTE: COMPLETING THE WATERMARK

A watermark is a faint image that sits "under" the regular document text. However, setting
a picture's color to Watermark isn't enough to convert the image to a true watermark. To
do that, you must do two more things:

1. In the Wrapping tab, select None.
2. In the Drawing toolbar, select Draw | Order | Send Behind Text.

OfficeArt also includes a set of tools for working with picture attributes directly. You'll find
these tools on the Picture toolbar, and Table 5.7 gives you a brief description of each button.

5

**USING THE
OFFICEART TOOLS**

Table 5.7. The Picture toolbar buttons.

Button	Name	Description
	Insert Picture	Displays the Insert Picture dialog box so you can insert another picture.
	Image Control	Displays a list of the color scales.
	More Contrast	Increases the color intensity.
	Less Contrast	Decreases the color intensity.
	More Brightness	Adds more light to the picture.
	Less Brightness	Darkens the picture.
	Crop	Crops the picture. Click this button and then drag a selection handle to crop the picture.
	Line Style	Provides a choice of line styles for the picture's frame.
	Text Wrapping	Displays a list of wrapping options (described earlier).
	Format Picture	Displays the Format Picture dialog box and activates the Picture tab.
	Set Transparent Color	Specifies a color as transparent, which lets you see anything behind that color. Click this tool and then click the color you want to make transparent.
	Reset Picture	Resets the image attributes to their original values.

Sizing Graphic Objects

You can resize any graphic object to change its shape or dimensions. The following procedure outlines the steps to follow:

1. Select the object you want to size. OfficeArt displays selection handles around the object's frame.

2. Position the mouse pointer over the handle you want to move. The pointer changes to a two-headed arrow. To change the size horizontally or vertically, use the appropriate handle on the middle of a side. To change the size in both directions at once, use the appropriate corner handle.

3. Drag the handle to the position you want. As you drag the mouse, the pointer changes to a crosshair and OfficeArt shows a dashed outline that represents the new frame dimensions.

4. Release the mouse button. OfficeArt redraws the object and adjusts the frame size.

TIP: KEYS FOR SIZING

To keep the same proportions when sizing an object, hold down the Shift key and drag a corner handle. To size an object in relation to its midpoint, hold down Ctrl while sizing. To size an object along the gridlines in an Excel worksheet, hold down the Alt key while sizing.

For more precise sizing, display the Format AutoShape (or Format Picture) dialog box and then activate the Size tab, shown in Figure 5.28. Here's a summary of the controls:

Size and rotate: If you want to adjust the object's dimensions directly, use the Height and Width spinners in this group. If you also want the object rotated, use the Rotation spinner to set the number of degrees of rotation.

Scale: If you want to change the size by a percentage of the object's dimensions, use the Height and Width spinners in this group.

Lock aspect ratio: Activate this check box if you want to scale the object and keep the same relative dimensions between the height and width.

Relative to original picture size: If you're working with a picture object, activate this check box to scale the picture relative to its original dimensions (that is, the size of the picture when you first inserted it into the document).

Reset: Click this button to reset the image to its original size.

Editing Freehand Lines, Curves, and Polygons

To change the size or shape of a freehand line, curve, or polygon, you can use the procedures outlined in the preceding section to adjust the object's frame. However, you can also "edit" any of these objects by moving, adding, or deleting the so-called *edit points* of the object. The edit points are the vertices of the object, the points where you clicked while drawing the original shape or changed direction while drawing a freehand line.

FIGURE 5.28.

Use the Size tab for precision sizing.

To edit a freehand line, curve, or polygon, first use either of the following techniques:

■ Select the shape, and in the Drawing toolbar, select Draw | Edit Points.

■ Right-click the shape and then choose Edit Points from the shortcut menu.

OfficeArt displays the edit points as small black rectangles at each vertex of the selected object. (Several edit points appear along each freehand line, and one edit point appears at the beginning and end of every straight line.) You can then move, add, or delete edit points to get the shape you want. Here are the methods to use:

■ To move an edit point, first position the mouse pointer over the edit point. The pointer changes to a four-headed arrow, as shown in Figure 5.29. Drag the edit point to the position you want, and release the mouse button. OfficeArt redraws the object to reflect the new edit point position.

FIGURE 5.29.

The mouse pointer for moving an edit point.

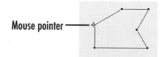

■ To add an edit point, position the mouse pointer where you want the new point to appear (the pointer changes to a crosshair with a black square in the middle, as shown in Figure 5.30), hold down the Ctrl key, and click. OfficeArt adds the edit point.

FIGURE 5.30.

The mouse pointer for adding an edit point.

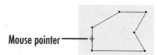

■ To delete an edit point, position the mouse pointer over the edit point (the pointer changes to an X, as shown in Figure 5.31), hold down the Ctrl key, and click. OfficeArt deletes the edit point and redraws the polygon.

FIGURE 5.31.

The mouse pointer for deleting an edit point.

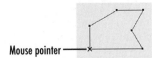

Mouse pointer ———×

Setting Up the Grid

OfficeArt has a grid that you can use for precision moving and sizing of graphic objects. When the grid is turned on, OfficeArt moves or sizes objects by snapping the mouse pointer to the grid points.

You can activate and customize the grid by selecting Draw | Grid on the Drawing toolbar. The Snap to Grid dialog box that appears, shown in Figure 5.32, gives you the following options:

Snap to Grid: Activate this check box to turn on the grid.

Horizontal spacing: Use this spinner to set the horizontal distance between each grid point.

Vertical spacing: Use this spinner to set the vertical distance between each grid point.

Horizontal origin: Use this spinner to specify the left starting point for the grid.

Vertical origin: Use this spinner to specify the top starting point for the grid.

Snap to shapes: Activate this check box to align objects using the gridlines that pass through the horizontal and vertical edges of AutoShapes.

FIGURE 5.32.

Use the Snap to Grid dialog box to activate and customize the OfficeArt grid.

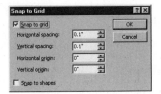

Moving Graphic Objects

You can move any graphic object to a different part of the document. OfficeArt gives you four different methods:

■ You can use the mouse to drag the object.

■ You can "nudge" the object to move it in small increments.

5

USING THE
OFFICEART TOOLS

- You can rotate or flip the object.
- You can align the object with other objects in the document.

Moving an Object by Dragging

You can drag an object to move it by following these steps:

1. Select the object you want to move.

2. Position the mouse pointer on any edge of the object. The pointer changes to a four-headed arrow.

3. Drag the object to the position you want. As you drag the object, a dashed outline shows you the new frame position.

4. Release the mouse button. OfficeArt redraws the object in the new position.

TIP: KEYS FOR MOVING

To move an object only horizontally or vertically, hold down the Shift key while dragging. To move an object along Excel's worksheet gridlines, hold down the Alt key while dragging.

Nudging an Object

OfficeArt also has a "nudge" feature that lets you move an object in small increments. To use this feature, select the object and then select Draw | Nudge in the Drawing toolbar. The cascade menu that appears gives you four commands: Up, Down, Left, and Right. These commands move the object in the specified direction as follows:

- If the Grid feature is turned on (see "Setting Up the Grid" earlier in this chapter), the object is moved one grid point.
- If the Grid feature is turned off, the object is moved one pixel.

Rotating or Flipping an Object

To get the look you want, you might need to either rotate an object around its axis or flip the object. You can do this in OfficeArt by selecting Draw | Rotate or Flip in the Drawing toolbar. The cascade menu that appears gives you the following commands:

Free Rotate: If you select this command, OfficeArt adds rotation handles to the four corners of the object's frame. To rotate the object, move the mouse pointer over a rotation handle and then drag the handle. Note that you can also activate this feature by clicking the Free Rotate button on the Drawing toolbar.

> **TIP: FREE ROTATING ABOUT A CORNER**
>
> When the Free Rotate feature is activated, if you hold down Ctrl while dragging the mouse, OfficeArt rotates the object around the opposite handle. For example, if you drag the upper-left rotation handle, the object rotates around the lower-right handle.

Rotate Left: Select this command to rotate the object to the left by 90 degrees.

Rotate Right: Select this command to rotate the object to the right by 90 degrees.

Flip Horizontal: Select this command to flip the object 180 degrees around its horizontal axis.

Flip Vertical: Select this command to flip the object 180 degrees around its vertical axis.

Aligning Graphic Objects

Objects often look best when they are aligned in apple-pie order. The simplest way to do this is to use the various Align commands offered by OfficeArt. These commands let you align objects according to the left edges, top edges, and more.

To try this feature, first select all the objects you want to align. Select Draw | Align or Distribute on the Drawing toolbar. In the cascade menu that appears, choose one of the following commands:

Align Left: Adjusts the horizontal position of all the selected objects so that they line up on their left edges.

Align Center: Adjusts the horizontal position of all the selected objects so that the center of each object is aligned.

Align Right: Adjusts the horizontal position of all the selected objects so that they line up on their right edges.

Align Top: Adjusts the vertical position of all the selected objects so that they line up on their top edges.

Align Middle: Adjusts the vertical position of all the selected objects so that the middle of each control is aligned.

Align Bottom: Adjusts the vertical position of all the selected objects so that they line up on their bottom edges.

Distribute Horizontally: Moves the selected objects so they're aligned horizontally with equal horizontal spacing between each object.

Distribute Vertically: Moves the selected objects so they're aligned vertically with equal vertical spacing between each object.

Relative to Page: Activate this command to make all these alignment commands operate in relation to the document edges.

Copying Graphic Objects

If you want multiple copies of the same object, you don't have to draw each one. Instead, follow these steps to make as many copies of the object as you need:

1. Select the object you want to copy.
2. Hold down the Ctrl key and position the mouse pointer on any edge of the object. The pointer changes to an arrow with a plus sign.
3. Drag the pointer to the position you want. As you drag the mouse, a dashed outline shows you the position of the copied object.
4. Release the mouse button. OfficeArt copies the object to the new position.

Deleting Graphic Objects

To delete a graphic object, select it and then either select Edit | Clear or press Delete.

Grouping Graphic Objects

OfficeArt lets you create object *groups*. A group is a collection of objects you can format, size, and move—similar to the way you format, size, and move a single object. To select an entire group, you just need to click one object in the group.

To group two or more objects, select them and then choose Draw | Group in the Drawing toolbar. OfficeArt creates an invisible, rectangular frame around the objects.

OfficeArt treats a group as a single graphic object with its own frame. In Figure 5.33, for example, a circle, a rectangle, and a text box are grouped. Any sizing, moving, or copying operations act on each member of the group.

FIGURE 5.33.

OfficeArt treats grouped graphics as a single object.

To ungroup objects, select the group and then choose Draw | Ungroup. OfficeArt removes the group but leaves the individual objects selected.

Controlling Object Placement in Excel

When you're working with Excel, most of your graphic objects are probably positioned in relation to their specific worksheet cells. For example, you might have a text box with an arrow to explain the contents of a cell, or you might have a rectangle around a worksheet table. In either case, when you move or size the worksheet cells, you want the graphic to move or size along with the cells.

Follow these steps to attach an object to its underlying cells:

1. Select the object.
2. Choose Format | Object to display the Format Object dialog box.
3. Select the Properties tab.
4. Activate the placement option you want:

    Move and size with cells: Attaches the object to the cells underneath the object. When you move or size the cells, the object is moved or sized accordingly. This is the default option for drawn objects.

    Move but don't size with cells: Attaches the object only to the cell underneath its top-left corner. When you move this cell, the object moves with it but doesn't change size. This is the default option for embedded charts and pictures.

    Don't move or size with cells: The object isn't attached to the cell underneath it.
5. Click OK.

NOTE: THE PRINT OBJECT OPTION

The Properties tab has a fourth option: Print object. Deactivate this option when you don't want the selected object to print with the worksheet.

To illustrate object placement, Figure 5.34 shows three copies of a graphic image. Each copy has a different placement option, as described by the label above the object. Figure 5.35 shows the same graphics after one row is inserted and another has its height increased.

Ordering Overlapped Graphic Objects

When you insert objects, you usually want to avoid overlapping them. However, sometimes you might want objects to overlap. For example, if you add two or more pictures, you might be able to produce interesting effects by superimposing one picture over another.

FIGURE 5.34.

Three objects with different placement options.

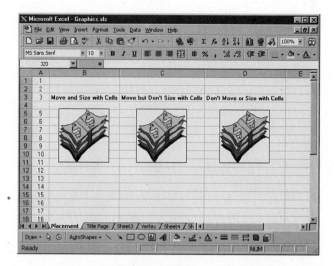

FIGURE 5.35.

The placement options determine how an object is affected by cell movement or sizing.

Row inserted here —

Row height increased —

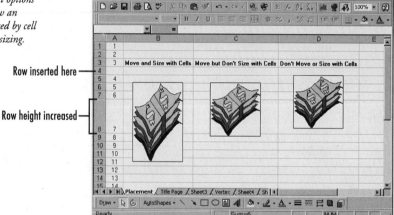

When you have two objects that overlap, the most recently created object covers part of the other object. The newer object is "in front" of the older one. The overlap order of these objects is called the z-order. (Think of the z-axis in a graph.) To change the z-order, select one of the overlapping objects and then choose Draw | Order. The cascade menu that appears gives you the following choices:

Bring to Front: Moves the object to the top of the z-order, which places it in front of every other object.

Send to Back: Moves the object to the bottom of the z-order, which places it behind every other object.

Bring Forward: Moves the object one position toward the front of the z-order.

Send Backward: Moves the object one position toward the back of the z-order.

Bring in Front of Text: In Word, this command displays the object on top of the document text.

Send Behind Text: In Word, this command displays the object behind the document text.

Summary

This chapter showed you how to work with graphic objects in OfficeArt. I showed you how to add the various object types (lines, rectangles, and so on), and I showed you various methods for formatting and manipulating objects. Here's a list of some related chapters to check out:

- Graphic objects can turn a plain worksheet into a thing of beauty, but you shouldn't ignore the other Office formatting options. I told you about many of them in Chapter 3, "Day-to-Day Office Basics."

- For the full scoop on working with Microsoft Graph objects, see Chapter 6, "Working with Microsoft Graph."

Working with Microsoft Graph

IN THIS CHAPTER

CHAPTER 6

A picture shows me at a glance what it takes dozens of pages of a book to expound.

—*Ivan Turgenev*

In the Office universe, the number cruncher of choice is, of course, Excel. And when you want to convert those dry-as-dust numbers into an attractive visual display, Excel's charting module is the easiest way to go. Even if you need to display the chart in a document created in another Office application, you could still use Excel to create the chart and then use OLE to link or embed the chart into your document or slide. (See Chapter 48, "Office Integration and OLE," to learn the basics of linking and embedding data.)

But what if you have just a few numbers residing in, say, a table in a Word document, and you want to graph them? Or what if you want to add a quick chart to a PowerPoint slide? For these simpler scenarios, the lengthy process of loading Excel, building a chart, and transferring the data seems like overkill. A better approach would be to use the Microsoft Graph application. Graph is like a miniature version of Excel in which you enter a few numbers and headings using a simple datasheet; those values are automatically converted into a chart. You can then format the chart to your liking with Microsoft Graph's limited (but still useful) formatting options. Microsoft Graph is an OLE server application, so the resulting chart is embedded into your document and can easily be modified. This chapter shows you how to use Microsoft Graph to create, format, and embed charts in your Office documents.

Getting Started

Without further ado, let's get Microsoft Graph up and running. How you begin depends on the application you're using:

- In Word, if you want to chart an existing table, first select the table. Otherwise, position the cursor where you want the chart to appear. Then select Insert | Picture | Chart.

- In PowerPoint, either double-click a slide's chart object, or select Insert | Chart.

- For all applications (that is, all applications that can act as OLE containers), select Insert | Object, highlight Microsoft Graph 97 Chart in the Object type list, and click OK.

Microsoft Graph performs three actions at this point, as shown in Figure 6.1:

- It embeds a new chart object.

- It displays a datasheet that contains the numbers used to construct the chart. (If you highlighted a Word table in advance, the datasheet contains the table values.)

- It adjusts the menus and the Standard toolbar to give you access to the charting features.

FIGURE 6.1.

When you launch Microsoft Graph, it embeds a chart, displays the datasheet, and modifies the application's interface.

Datasheet

Embedded chart object

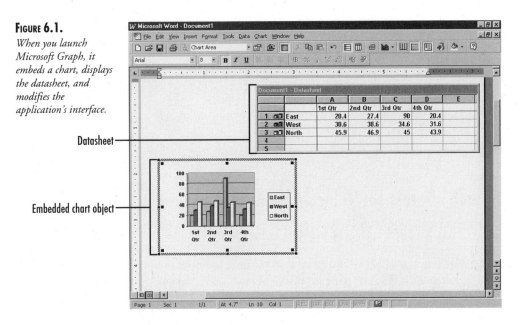

Entering Chart Data

You use Microsoft Graph's datasheet to enter the data that appears in the chart. If you've used Excel in the past, you'll recognize that the datasheet uses the same row-and-column layout that you see in an Excel worksheet. The Excel techniques you're used to for navigating and selecting cells, entering and formatting data, adjusting column widths, and so on are basically the same in Microsoft Graph.

Understanding the Datasheet

In case you're new to the worksheet concept, let's examine the sample data provided by Microsoft Graph to understand the layout of the datasheet and see how it's used to create the chart. The sample data is from a fictional company that has three divisions: East, West, and North. The datasheet shows numbers (which could be sales figures, budget targets, or whatever) for each division by quarter (1st Qtr, 2nd Qtr, and so on). Using this data as an example, here's a summary of the datasheet components:

■ The rows are labeled 1, 2, 3, and so on, and each one represents a *data series,* which can be defined as a collection of related values. The data series in row 1, for example, is a collection of values related to the East division.

■ The columns are labeled A, B, C, and so on, and each one represents a *data category,* which subdivides the data into groups. The data category in column A, for example, groups the data by first quarter.

- The intersection of each row and column is called a *cell*; it's these cells that hold the datasheet values. Each cell has its own address that identifies it uniquely. This address is created by combining the letter and number of the column and row that define the cell. In the sample data, the cell at the intersection of column A and row 1 has the address A1 and the value 20.4.

- The first column of the datasheet is used for the *data series names,* which are the names you assign to each data series.

- The first row of the datasheet is used for the *data category labels,* which are the names you assign to each category.

How the Datasheet Values Appear in the Chart

Before you begin modifying data and entering new values, let's take a moment to see how the datasheet values correspond to the chart elements:

- In the sample data, the chart's vertical columns are divided into four groups of three columns each. Each of these groups represents a data category (that is, a datasheet column; see Figure 6.2).

FIGURE 6.2.

Microsoft Graph groups data category values in the chart.

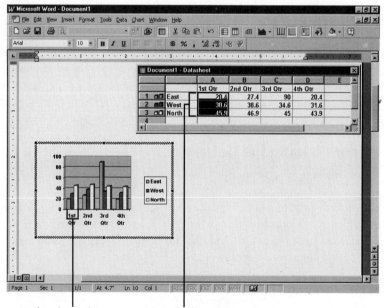

These data markers...   ...represent this data category

- The data category labels (the headings at the top of each column in the datasheet) are displayed along the horizontal axis of the chart to help you identify each category. This axis is known as the *category axis* (it's also called the *x-axis*).

- In the chart categories, each column represents a cell value from the datasheet. These columns are called *data markers.*

- The data markers are plotted against the vertical axis, which is known as the *value axis.* (In a 2-D chart, this is also called the *y-axis;* in a 3-D chart, it's called the *z-axis.*)

- Each data series (a row in the datasheet) is displayed in the chart using columns of a particular color (see Figure 6.3). When you insert a chart into Word, for example, the sample data for the North division is plotted using yellow columns. The box to the right of the chart is called a *legend;* it tells you which colors correspond to which data series.

FIGURE 6.3.

Microsoft Graph uses a unique color to plot each data series. The legend tells you which color corresponds to which series.

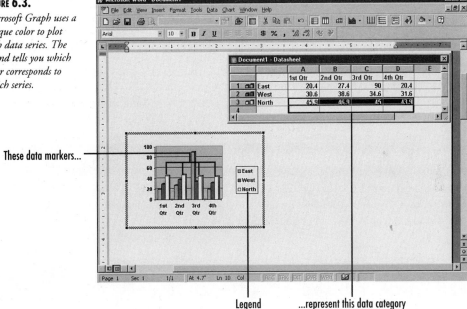

These data markers...

Legend   ...represent this data category

Datasheet Navigation Keys

Data entry is much faster if you can navigate the datasheet quickly. Table 6.1 lists the most commonly used navigation keys.

Table 6.1. Datasheet navigation keys.

Key(s)	Which Way They Move
Arrow keys	Left, right, up, or down one cell
Home	To the beginning of the current row
End	To the end of the current row
Page Up	Up one screen
Page Down	Down one screen
Ctrl-Home	To the first data cell (B2)
Ctrl-End	To the bottom-right corner of the datasheet
Ctrl-arrow keys	In the direction of the arrow to the next nonblank cell if the current cell is blank, or to the last nonblank cell if the current cell is nonblank

Entering Data

Entering data in a datasheet cell is straightforward. All you do is move the active cell to the cell you want to use and then start typing. A cursor appears inside the cell to show you where the next character or number you type will appear. When you're done, either press Enter or click another cell to confirm the new data.

TIP: USE ARROW KEYS TO CONFIRM ENTRIES

When entering numbers or text, you can also confirm your entry by pressing any of the arrow keys. The active cell will then move in the direction of the arrow. This is handy if you have, say, a lengthy column of data to type in.

NOTE: IMPORTING A WORKSHEET

If the data you need already exists in an Excel worksheet or some other file, you can import the data into the Microsoft Graph datasheet.

To begin, either select Edit | Import File or click the Import File button on the toolbar. Use the Import File dialog box to select the file, and then click Open. If you selected an Excel workbook, the Import Data Options dialog box will appear so that you can choose the worksheet or range you want to import.

Entering Numbers

Numbers are what datasheets are all about, since they form the guts of the chart. For the most part, you can enter numeric values without any special techniques. However, here are a few tips that might make your numeric data entry chores easier:

- You can enter percentages by following the number with a percent sign (%). Note that although Microsoft Graph shows the percentage, it stores the number internally as a decimal. For example, if you enter 15%, you'll see 15% in the cell, but the number is stored internally as 0.15.

- You can use scientific notation when entering numbers. For example, to enter the number 3,879,000,000, you could enter 3.879E+09. Similarly, you could enter 0.003879 as 3.879E–03.

- For negative numbers, either precede the value with a minus sign (–) or surround the number with parentheses. If you make an entry such as (125), Microsoft Graph assumes you mean –125.

- You can enter commas to separate thousands, but you must make sure that each comma appears in the appropriate place. Microsoft Graph will interpret an entry such as 12,34 as text.

- If you want to enter a fraction, you need to type an integer, a space, and then the fraction (5 1/8, for example). This is true even if you're entering only the fractional part. In this case, you need to type a zero, a space, and then the fraction, or Microsoft Graph will interpret the entry as a date. For example, 0 1/8 is the fraction one-eighth, but 1/8 is January 8.

NOTE: FORMATTING NUMBERS

Although you can specify a numeric format by the way you enter a number, you can also convert a number to any of Microsoft Graph's dozen formats. To do so, select the range you want to work with and then select Format | Number. Use the Format Number dialog box that appears to select the numeric format you want, and then click OK.

Also note that Microsoft Graph's Formatting toolbar boasts a few buttons that give you quick access to some common numeric formats.

Entering Dates and Times

If you need to enter a date or time, use any of the formats outlined in Table 6.2.

Table 6.2. Microsoft Graph date and time formats.

Format	Example
m/d/yy	8/23/97
d-mmm-yy	23-Aug-97
d-mmm	23-Aug (Graph assumes the current year)
mmm-yy	Aug-97 (Graph assumes the first day of the month)
h:mm:ss AM/PM	10:35:10 PM
h:mm AM/PM	10:35 PM
h:mm:ss	22:35:10
h:mm	22:35
m/d/y h:mm	8/23/94 22:35

TIP: DATE AND TIME SHORTCUTS

Here are a couple of shortcuts that will let you enter dates and times quickly. To enter the current date in a cell, press Ctrl-; (semicolon). To enter the current time, press Ctrl-: (colon).

Editing Cell Contents

If you make a mistake when entering data, or you have to update the contents of a cell, you need to edit the cell to get the correct value. One option you have is to highlight the cell and begin typing the new data. This will erase the previous contents with whatever you type. Often, however, you need to change only a single character or value, so retyping the entire cell would be wasteful. Microsoft Graph lets you modify the contents of a cell without erasing it. To edit a cell, follow these steps:

1. Select the cell you want to edit.
2. Double-click the cell or press F2. A cursor appears inside the cell.
3. Edit the contents of the cell.
4. Confirm your changes by clicking another cell or by pressing Enter. To cancel the edit without saving your changes, press Esc.

Selecting Multiple Cells

Instead of working with just a single cell, you might prefer to work with two or more cells at once. A selection that includes multiple cells is called a *range*.

Most ranges are rectangular groups of adjacent cells, but you can select ranges with noncontiguous cells. Ranges speed up your work by allowing you to perform operations on many cells at once instead of one at a time. For example, suppose you want to delete the contents of an entire row. If you worked on individual cells, you might have to perform the deletion procedure dozens of times. However, by creating a range that covers the entire row, you could do this with a single deletion.

Here's a review of the methods you can use to select multiple cells:

- To select a rectangular range or contiguous cells, drag the mouse over the cells.
- To select a noncontiguous range, hold down the Shift key and click each cell.
- To select an entire row, click the row heading. For example, to select row 1, click the button labeled 1 on the left side of the datasheet. To select multiple rows, drag the mouse across the row headings.

TIP: SHORTCUT FOR SELECTING A ROW

Press Shift-Spacebar to select the current row.

- To select an entire column, click the column heading. For example, to select row A, click the button labeled A at the top of the datasheet. To select multiple columns, drag the mouse across the column headings.

TIP: SHORTCUT FOR SELECTING A COLUMN

Press Ctrl-Spacebar to select the current column.

- To select the entire datasheet, either press Ctrl-A or click the button in the upper-left corner of the datasheet.

Clearing a Range

If you no longer need the contents of a cell or range, you can clear it using any of the following techniques:

- Edit the cell to delete the current value.
- Select the cell or range and press the Delete key.
- Select the cell or range and choose Edit | Clear | All.
- To delete only the cell contents and leave the cell formatting intact, select the cell or range and choose Edit | Clear | Contents.
- To delete only the cell formatting and leave the contents intact, select the cell or range and choose Edit | Clear | Formats.

Inserting and Deleting a Range

When you first work with a datasheet, you use up rows and columns sequentially as you add data and formulas. Invariably, however, you'll need to go back and add some values or labels that you forgot or that you need for another part of the datasheet. When this happens, you need to insert ranges into your datasheet to make room for your new information. Conversely, you often have to remove old or unnecessary data from a datasheet, and that requires you to delete ranges. The next couple of sections describe methods of inserting and deleting ranges in Microsoft Graph.

Inserting an Entire Row or Column

The easiest way to insert a range into a datasheet is to insert an entire row or column. First, you need to select where you want to insert the new row or column:

- If you're inserting a row, select the column above which you want the new row to appear.
- If you're inserting a column, select the column to the left of which you want the new column to appear.

If you want to insert multiple rows or columns, select the appropriate number of rows or columns. For example, if you select two rows, Microsoft Graph will insert two new rows.

You can now use any of the following techniques to insert the new row or column:

- Select Insert | Cells.
- Press Ctrl-+ (plus sign).
- Right-click the selection and choose Insert from the shortcut menu.

If you're inserting a row, Microsoft Graph shifts the selected row down. If you're inserting a column, Microsoft Graph shifts the selected column to the right.

Inserting a Cell or Range

In some datasheets, you might need to insert only a single cell or a range of cells so as not to disturb the arrangement of surrounding data. Here's the procedure to follow:

1. Select the range where you want the new range to appear.
2. Use any of the insertion techniques outlined in the preceding section. Microsoft Graph displays the Insert dialog box, shown in Figure 6.4.

FIGURE 6.4.

Use the Insert dialog box to tell Microsoft Graph which direction you want the existing cells shifted.

Working with Microsoft Graph

CHAPTER 6

183

6

WORKING WITH
MICROSOFT
GRAPH

3. Select either Shift cells right or Shift cells down.

4. Click OK to insert the range.

Deleting a Range

Deleting a range is similar to inserting one. In this case, however, you'll want to exercise a little more caution, since a hasty deletion can have disastrous effects on your datasheet. (Of course, you can select Edit | Undo if you make any mistakes.)

First, select the range, row, or column you want to delete, and then use any of the following methods:

- ■ Select Edit | Delete.
- ■ Press Ctrl–– (minus sign).
- ■ Right-click the selection and choose Delete from the shortcut menu.

Hiding the Datasheet

Once you've entered and edited your data, you might prefer to hide the datasheet so that it doesn't get in your way. Use either of the following techniques to toggle the datasheet on and off:

- ■ Select View | Datasheet.

- ■ Click the View Datasheet toolbar button.

Selecting a Chart Type

By default, Microsoft Graph uses a column chart to display your data. However, you might decide that the standard chart type doesn't display your data the way you want. Or you might want to experiment with different chart types to find the one that best suits your data. Fortunately, the chart type isn't set in stone; it can be changed at any time. Depending on the chart, you can use either of the following methods to select a different chart type:

- ■ Use the Chart Type dialog box.
- ■ Use the Chart Type tool's palette of types.

Selecting a Chart Type from the Chart Type Dialog Box

Follow these steps to use the Chart Type dialog box to select a chart type:

1. Click the chart to activate it.

2. Select Chart | Chart Type, or right-click the chart background and choose Chart Type from the shortcut menu. Microsoft Graph displays the Chart Type dialog box, shown in Figure 6.5.

FIGURE 6.5.

Use the Chart Type dialog box to assign a different chart type.

3. Use the Chart type list to select a new chart type.

4. Chart subtypes are variations on the main chart type that display your data in slightly different ways. To select a chart subtype, click one of the boxes in the Chart sub-type group. (Note that the Custom Types tab boasts a few other types of charts.)

5. Click OK.

Using the Chart Type Tool to Select a Chart Type

This section shows you how to select a chart type using the Chart Type tool. Here are the steps to follow:

1. Click the chart to activate it.

2. Click the Chart Type tool's downward-pointing arrow. Microsoft Graph displays a palette of chart types, as shown in Figure 6.6.

3. Click the chart type you want. Microsoft Graph redraws the chart.

TIP: TEAR OFF THE CHART TYPE PALETTE

If you want to experiment with various chart types, you can "tear off" the Chart Type tool's palette. Drop the palette down and place the mouse pointer inside the bar at the top of the palette (the bar will turn blue). Now drag the mouse pointer until the palette separates. When you release the mouse button, the Chart Type toolbar appears as a floating palette.

Figure 6.6.

Drop down the Chart Type toolbar list to see a palette of chart types.

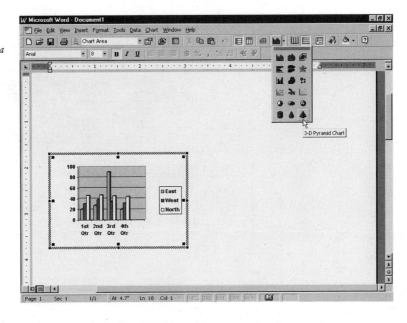

Switching Data Series and Categories

By default, Microsoft Graph plots rows as the data series and columns as the data categories. However, you can reverse this order to use columns as the data series and rows as the data categories by using either of the following methods:

- Select Data | Series in Columns.

- Click the By Columns toolbar button.

Figure 6.7 shows the sample data plotted with the columns as the data series.

To return to the default layout (rows as data series), use one of these techniques:

- Select Data | Series in Rows.

- Click the By Rows toolbar button.

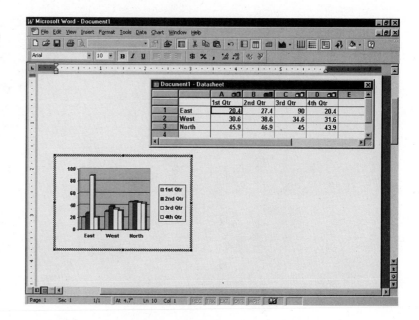

FIGURE 6.7.
The Microsoft Graph sample data plotted using the columns as the data series.

Including the Data with the Chart

Although you'll usually only want to display the chart by itself in your documents, Microsoft Graph lets you include the data as well. You do this by attaching a data table to the chart, as follows:

■ Select Chart | Chart Options to display the Chart Options dialog box, go to the Data Table tab, and activate the Show data table check box.

■ Click the Data Table toolbar button.

Figure 6.8 shows the sample data with a data table attached.

FIGURE 6.8.

To show the data along with your chart, attach a data table.

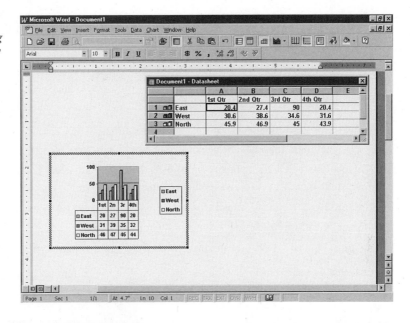

Selecting Chart Elements

A Microsoft Graph chart is composed of elements such as axes, data markers, gridlines, and text, each with its own formatting options. Before you can format an element, however, you need to select it. Microsoft Graph offers two techniques:

- Use the Chart Objects list on the toolbar. Just drop down the list and click the element you want to work with.

- Use the mouse to click the element you want to work with. Table 6.3 lists the mouse techniques for selecting various chart items.

Table 6.3. Mouse techniques for selecting chart elements.

Action	Result
Click an empty part of the plot area.	The plot area is selected.
Click an axis or an axis label.	The axis is selected.
Click a gridline.	The gridline is selected.
Click any marker in the series.	The data series is selected.
Click a data marker once and then click it a second time.	The data marker is selected.
Click an object.	The object is selected.

Converting a Series to a Different Chart Type

If you want to create a combination chart not found among Microsoft Graph's built-in chart types, or if you have chart formatting you want to preserve, you can easily apply an overlay effect to an existing chart. Microsoft Graph lets you convert individual data series into chart types; just follow these steps:

1. Click the chart to activate it.
2. Click any data marker in the series you want to convert.
3. Select Chart | Chart Type (or right-click the series and select Chart Type from the shortcut menu) to display the Chart Type dialog box.
4. In the Options group, make sure that the Apply to selection check box is activated.
5. Select the chart type and subtype you want to use for the series.
6. Click OK. Microsoft Graph converts the series to the chart type you selected.

Figure 6.9 shows the sample data where each series uses a different chart type.

FIGURE 6.9.

The sample data showing a different chart type for each series.

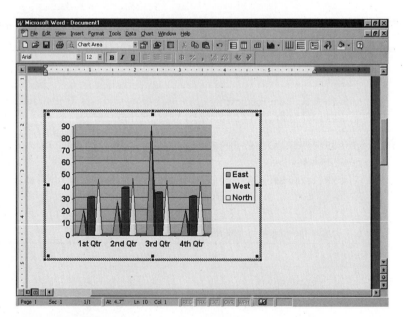

Formatting Chart Axes

Microsoft Graph provides various options for controlling the appearance of your chart axes. You can hide axes; set the typeface, size, and style of axis labels; format the axis lines and tick marks; and adjust the axis scale. You can find most of the axis formatting options in the Format Axis dialog box, shown in Figure 6.10. To display this dialog box, select the axis you want to format and then choose Format | Selected Axis.

FIGURE 6.10.
Use the Format Axis dialog box to enhance the look of your chart axes.

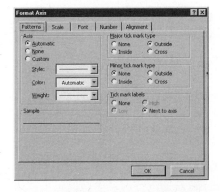

TIP: ACCESSING THE FORMAT DIALOG BOX

For any chart object, Microsoft Graph gives you a number of methods to access the appropriate Format dialog boxes quickly:

■ Double-click the object

■ Select the object and press Ctrl-1

■ Right-click the object and select Format *Object* from the shortcut menu

■ Select the object and click the Chart toolbar's Format *Object* button

Formatting Axis Patterns

The Patterns tab in the Format Axis dialog box lets you set various options for the axis line and tick marks. Here's a summary of the control groups:

■ Axis: These options format the axis line. Select None to remove the line, or select Custom to adjust the style, color, and weight. The Sample box shows you how the line will look.

■ Major tick mark type: These options control the position of the major tick marks. The options in the Minor tick mark type group perform the same functions for the minor tick marks.

■ Tick mark labels: These options control the position of the tick mark labels.

NOTE: MAJOR VERSUS MINOR TICK MARKS

The major tick marks carry the axis labels. The minor tick marks appear between the labels. See the next section to learn how to control the units of both the major and the minor tick marks.

Formatting an Axis Scale

You can format the scale of your chart axes to set things such as the range of numbers on an axis and where the category and value axes intersect.

To format the scale, select the Scale tab of the Format Axis dialog box. If you're formatting the value axis, you see the layout shown in Figure 6.11. These options format several scale characteristics, such as the range of values (Minimum and Maximum), the tick mark units (Major unit and Minor unit), and where the chart floor crosses the value axis. For the last of these characteristics, you have two choices:

- Activate the check box labeled Floor (XY plane) and enter a value in the text box labeled Crosses at.

- Activate the check box labeled Floor (XY plane) crosses at minimum value. This places the x-axis at the bottom of the chart.

FIGURE 6.11.

The Scale tab for the value axis.

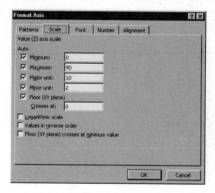

For the category axis, the Scale tab appears as shown in Figure 6.12. These options mostly control the frequency of categories:

Number of categories between tick-mark labels: This text box controls the major tick mark unit. For example, an entry of 5 puts a tick mark label every five categories.

Number of categories between tick marks: This text box controls the total number of tick marks. For example, an entry of 1 provides a tick mark for each category.

Categories in reverse order: Activating this check box displays the categories along the x-axis in reverse order.

Formatting Axis Labels

You can change the font, numeric format, and alignment of the labels that appear along the axis. To change the label font, select the Font tab in the Format Axis dialog box, and then select the font options you want.

FIGURE 6.12.
The Scale tab for the category (X) axis.

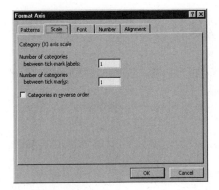

To change the numeric format of axis labels (assuming, of course, that the labels are numbers, dates, or times), you have two choices:

- Format the data series that generated the labels. Microsoft Graph uses this formatting automatically when it sets up the axis labels.

- Select the Number tab in the Format Axis dialog box, and then select a numeric format from the options provided.

To format the alignment of the axis labels, select the Alignment tab in the Format Axis dialog box, and then select the option you want from the Orientation group.

TIP: USE THE FORMATTING TOOLBAR

You can also use the tools on the Formatting toolbar (such as Bold and Currency Style) to format the labels of a selected axis.

Formatting Chart Data Markers

A *data marker* is a symbol that Microsoft Graph uses to plot each value (data point). Examples of data markers are small circles or squares for line charts, rectangles for column and bar charts, and pie slices for pie charts. Depending on the type of marker you're dealing with, you can format the marker's color, pattern, style, or border.

To begin, select the data marker or markers you want to work with.

- If you want to format the entire series, click any data marker in the series, and then select Format | Selected Data Series. Microsoft Graph displays the Format Data Series dialog box.

- If you want to format a single data marker, click the marker once to select the entire series, and then click the marker a second time. (Note, however, that you don't double-click the marker. If you do, you just get the Format Data Series dialog box. Click the marker once, wait a couple of seconds, and then click it again.) Then choose Format | Selected Data Point to display the Format Data Point dialog box.

Whichever method you choose, select the Patterns tab to display the formatting options for the series markers. Figure 6.13 shows the Patterns tab for a data series that uses the area, bar, column, pie, or doughnut chart type.

FIGURE 6.13.

The Patterns tab for area, bar, column, pie, and doughnut chart data series.

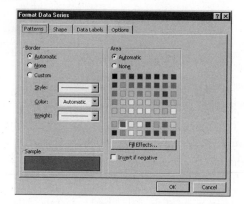

Use the Border group to either turn off the border (None) or define the style, color, and weight of the marker border. Use the Area section to assign marker colors and patterns.

You get a different set of options when you format line, XY, or radar chart markers, as shown in Figure 6.14. Use the Line section to format the style, color, and weight of the data series line. The Smoothed line option (available only for line and XY charts) smoothes out some of a line's rough edges. Use the Marker section to format the marker style as well as the foreground and background colors.

FIGURE 6.14.

The Patterns tab for line, XY, and radar charts.

Formatting the Plot Area and Background

You can format borders, patterns, and colors of both the chart plot area and the background. To format either of these areas, follow this procedure:

1. Select the plot area or chart background.
2. Select either Format | Selected Plot Area or Format | Selected Chart Area to display the appropriate Format dialog box.
3. In the Patterns tab, select the options you want in the Border and Area groups.
4. If you're in the Format Chart Area dialog box, you can also select the Font tab to format the chart font.
5. Click OK.

Options That Affect the Entire Chart

Microsoft Graph has quite a few options that affect the chart as a whole, including settings related to chart titles, axes, gridlines, and the legend. The rest of this chapter discusses these options.

Adding Chart Titles

It often improves the readability of your chart if you include titles for the chart itself and for the axes. To do this, follow these steps:

1. Select Chart | Chart Options to display the Chart Options dialog box, shown in Figure 6.15.

FIGURE 6.15.

Use the Titles tab to add titles to your chart.

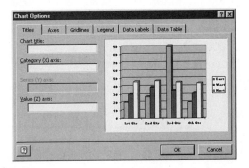

2. Select the Titles tab.

3. Depending on the type of chart you're dealing with, the Titles tab provides you with some or all of the following options:

Chart Title	Adds a title centered above the chart
Value (Y) Axis	Adds a title beside the value axis
Value (Z) Axis	Adds a title beside the value axis of a 3-D chart
Category (X) Axis	Adds a title below the category axis
Series (Y) Axis	Adds a title beside the series axis of a 3-D chart
Second Value (Y) Axis	Adds a title to a second value axis

4. Click OK.

Displaying and Formatting Chart Gridlines

Adding horizontal or vertical gridlines can make your charts easier to read. For each axis, you can display a major gridline, a minor gridline, or both. The positioning of these gridlines is determined by the numbers you enter for the axis scales. For a value axis, major gridlines are governed by the Major Unit option, and minor gridlines are governed by the Minor Unit option. (The Major and Minor Unit options are properties of the value axis scale. To learn how to adjust these values, see the section "Formatting an Axis Scale.") For a category axis, major gridlines are governed by the number of categories between tick labels, and minor gridlines are governed by the number of categories between tick marks.

Displaying Gridlines

To display gridlines, use any of the following techniques:

■ Click this toolbar button to toggle the chart's vertical gridlines on and off.

■ Click this toolbar button to toggle the chart's horizontal gridlines on and off.

■ Select Chart | Chart Options and then select the Gridlines tab in the Chart Options dialog box, shown in Figure 6.16. Activate the check boxes for the gridlines you want to display, and then click OK.

Formatting Gridlines

Once your gridlines are in place, you can format their style, color, and weight by following these steps:

1. Select a gridline.
2. Select Format | Selected Gridlines to display the Format Gridline dialog box.
3. Use the Patterns tab to select the gridline options you want (Style, Color, and Weight).
4. Click OK.

FIGURE 6.16.
Use the Gridlines tab to activate chart gridlines.

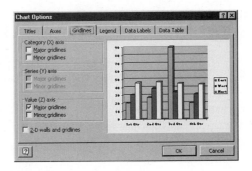

Adding and Formatting a Chart Legend

If your chart includes multiple data series, you should add a legend to explain the series markers. This makes your chart more readable and makes it easier for others to distinguish each series.

To add a legend, you have two choices:

■ Select Chart | Chart Options, activate the Legend tab in the Chart Options dialog box, and activate the Show legend check box.

■ Use the Chart toolbar's Legend tool to toggle the legend on and off.

You can format your legends with the same options you used to format chart text. Select the legend, and then choose Format | Selected Legend to display the Format Legend dialog box. You can then use the Patterns and Font tabs to format the legend. You can also use the options in the Placement tab to change the position of the legend.

Changing the 3-D View

When you use 3-D charts, sometimes certain data points in the back of a chart get obscured behind taller data markers in the chart's foreground. This can mar the look of an otherwise attractive chart. Fortunately, Microsoft Graph lets you change a number of aspects of the 3-D view to try to get a better perspective on your data.

Microsoft Graph's 3-D View dialog box, shown in Figure 6.17, handles these adjustments. To display this dialog box (which is available only when you're working with 3-D chart types), select Chart | 3-D View.

FIGURE 6.17.
Use the 3-D View dialog box to change the view for a 3-D chart.

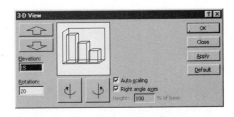

Within this dialog box, you can set five options: Elevation, Rotation, Auto scaling, Right angle axes, and Height.

Elevation: This value, which is measured in degrees, controls the height from which you look at the chart. For most 3-D charts, you can enter an elevation value between −90 and 90. A 0-degree elevation puts you on the floor of the plot area, 90 degrees means that you're looking at the chart from directly overhead, and −90 degrees means that you're looking at the chart from directly underneath. For 3-D bar charts, the allowable range of elevation is between 0 and 44 degrees. For pie charts, the range is from 10 to 80 degrees.

Rotation: This value, also measured in degrees, controls the rotation of the chart around the vertical (Z) axis. For most 3-D charts, you can enter a value between 0 and 360 degrees. A 0-degree rotation puts you directly in front of the chart, 90 degrees brings you to the side of the chart, and 180 degrees shows you the back of the chart with the series in reverse order. For 3-D bar charts, the acceptable range of rotation is between 0 and 44 degrees. For pie charts, the rotation represents the angle of the first slice. 0 degrees puts the left edge of the slice at 12 o'clock, 90 degrees puts it at 3 o'clock, and so on.

Auto scaling: Activating this option tells Microsoft Graph to scale the chart automatically so that it always fills the entire chart window. This check box is available only when the Right angle axes check box is selected.

Right angle axes: This option controls the orientation of the chart axes. When you activate this check box, Microsoft Graph draws the axes at right angles to each other.

TIP: STRAIGHTEN CHART LINES

If your chart lines appear overly jagged, activate the Right angle axes option. The chart lines that define the walls and markers then run horizontally and vertically and should appear straight.

Height *x* % of base: This text box controls the height of the vertical (Z) axis. The height is measured as a percentage of the category (X) axis. This option is unavailable when you select Auto scaling.

Summary

This chapter got you up to speed with Microsoft Graph's charting capabilities. I began by showing you a number of techniques for entering and editing values in the data sheet. From there, you looked at all kinds of formatting options for each of the chart elements. Here are a few other chapters to read for related information:

■ To learn about working with graphic objects, see Chapter 5, "Using the OfficeArt Tools."

■ If you need an organization chart, use the Organization Chart application as described in Chapter 7, "More Office Tools."

■ The techniques you use with Microsoft Graph are almost identical to those used in Excel's charting module. See Chapter 18, "Working with Charts," for details.

■ I cover OLE theory and techniques in Chapter 48, "Office Integration and OLE."

More Office Tools

IN THIS CHAPTER

CHAPTER 7

Give us the tools, and we will finish the job.

—*Winston Churchill*

Unleashing the Office suite consists mostly of mastering the common interface elements and features (see Chapters 3 and 4), learning the ins and outs of the major applications (see Parts III through VII), and understanding how best to integrate your data (see Part IX). However, there's also a fourth component that's necessary for unleashing Office: learning how to wield the large number of ancillary tools that ship with the Office package.

You've already made some headway in that direction. Chapter 5 showed you how to use the OfficeArt drawing tools, the Clip Gallery, and WordArt, and Chapter 6 showed you how to work with Microsoft Graph. This chapter continues the process by taking you through another half dozen Office tools: the Office Assistant, the Office help system, the Office Shortcut Bar, the new IntelliMouse, Organization Chart, and Equation Editor.

Intelligent Help: The Office Assistant

Over the years, Microsoft has attempted to build "intelligence" into its help systems. A couple of Office versions ago, for example, we saw the introduction of the Tip Wizard. This was a toolbar that monitored mouse and keyboard activity and displayed tips that provided more efficient methods for accomplishing your tasks.

Then came the debut of the ill-fated Microsoft Bob, which served as a shell replacement for Windows. Although Bob failed, it had many new and interesting characters, including animations, that took you through various tasks.

In Office 97, Microsoft tried to bridge the gap between the Spartan suggestions offered by the Tip Wizard and the in-your-face omnipresence of Bob's helpers. The result is the Office Assistant, which acts as a general purpose help system front end. Like the Tip Wizard, the Office Assistant monitors your activity and offers on-the-fly advice while you work, but the Assistant goes one better by also letting you ask natural-language questions. Unlike Bob, the Office Assistant doesn't take over your screen but resides quietly in its own window until called upon. It even moves and resizes itself if it detects that it's getting in your way.

The next few sections show you how to get the most out of the Office Assistant.

Invoking the Office Assistant

The Office Assistant is activated by default and should appear on your screen automatically whenever you launch an Office application. If you don't see the Office Assistant, use any of the following methods to display it:

- Pull down the Help menu and select *Application* Help, where *Application* is the name of the Office program you're using (such as Microsoft Word).
- Press F1.

■ Click the Office Assistant button on the Standard toolbar.

As you can see in Figure 7.1, the Office Assistant appears inside a small window.

FIGURE 7.1.

The Office Assistant appears in a small window whenever you run an Office application.

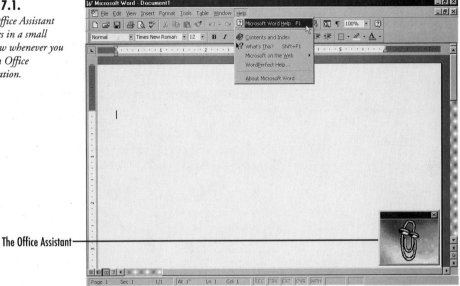

The Office Assistant

NOTE: HIDING THE ASSISTANT

Once you finish with the Office Assistant, you might prefer to hide it until the next time you need it. To do that, right-click the Office Assistant window and choose Hide Assistant from the shortcut menu that appears.

NOTE: ANIMATING THE ASSISTANT

As you work, the Office Assistant randomly displays various animations. If you've got some time to kill, you can run some of these animations by hand. Just right-click the Office Assistant window and choose Animate! from the shortcut menu.

Choosing Your Assistant

The Office Assistant is a cartoon character that comes with a repertoire of animations and sound effects. The default is a paper clip character, but you can choose from several other characters.

If you plan to leave the Office Assistant on-screen full-time, pick a character that won't drive you insane after five minutes. Follow these steps to select a different Office Assistant:

1. Right-click the Office Assistant window and select Choose Assistant from the shortcut menu. The Office Assistant dialog box appears.

2. Make sure the Gallery tab is displayed.

3. Click the Next and Back buttons to run through the available characters. For each character, Office displays a sample animation and sound effect, as well as a description of the character, as shown in Figure 7.2.

FIGURE 7.2.

Use the Gallery tab to choose your Assistant.

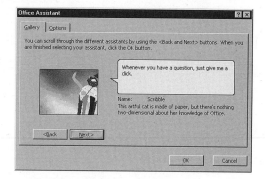

4. When you've found an Assistant you can live with, click OK.

5. If the Office Assistant asks you to insert your original Office CD-ROM, follow the instructions on the screen.

NOTE: CHANGES AFFECT ALL OFFICE PROGRAMS

The Office Assistant is shared by all the Office applications. Any changes you make to the Office Assistant in one application also affect the Office Assistant in the other Office programs.

TIP: DOWNLOAD MORE ASSISTANTS

If none of the default Assistants strike your fancy, you can find a few more online at the following Web page:

http://www.microsoft.com/officefreestuff/office/assistants.htm

Double-click the downloaded .EXE file and the new Assistant is installed automatically. (In other words, the Assistant's .ACT (Actor) file is decompressed into the \Office\Actors subfolder of your main Microsoft Office folder.)

Using the Assistant to Search for Help

Later in this chapter, I show you how to use the regular Office help system to find topics and perform keyword searches. These are powerful techniques, but the interface is often cryptic and the required syntax is often arcane.

In an effort to put a better face on the help system, the Office Assistant lets you ask natural-language questions, such as How do I create an envelope? or Tell me how to build a table. To enter a query, first use any of the following methods:

- Click the title bar in the Office Assistant window.
- Pull down the Help menu and select *Application* Help, where *Application* is the name of the Office program you're using (such as Microsoft Word).
- Press F1.
- Click the Office Assistant button on the Standard toolbar.

In each case, the Office Assistant displays a dialog box similar to the one shown in Figure 7.3.

FIGURE 7.3.

The Office Assistant lets you ask natural-language questions.

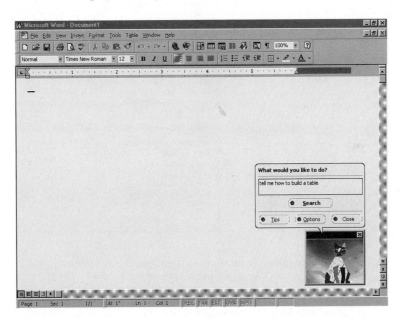

Use the text box to enter your question, and then click Search. The Office Assistant scours the help system for topics related to your query and then displays a list of those topics, as shown in Figure 7.4. Click a topic to launch the help system and display the topic text, as shown in Figure 7.5.

FIGURE 7.4.

The Office Assistant parses your question and then displays a list of related topics.

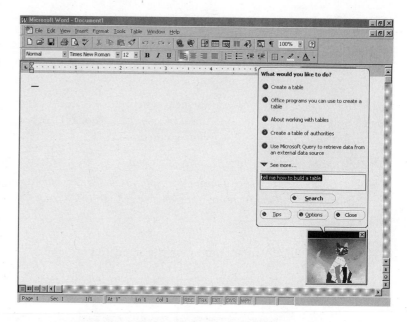

FIGURE 7.5.

Clicking a topic launches the help system and displays the topic text.

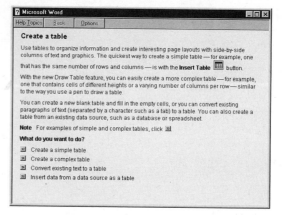

Note, too, that the Office Assistant is context-sensitive. This means that if you invoke the Office Assistant while performing some action, the dialog box that appears contains topics related to that action. For example, if you invoke the Office Assistant while the cursor is inside a table cell in Word, the dialog box that appears includes a couple of table-related topics, as shown in Figure 7.6.

FIGURE 7.6.

The Office Assistant provides context-sensitive help.

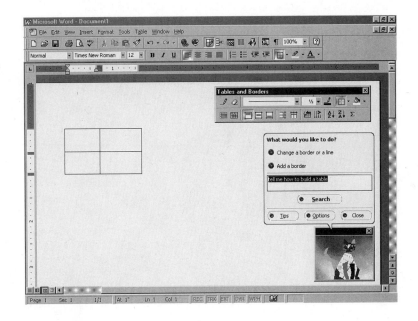

Office Assistant and IntelliSense

I mentioned earlier that the Office Assistant monitors your work and tries to offer help accordingly. This is part of Microsoft's IntelliSense technology, which is designed to make software intelligently proactive.

One of the ways the Office Assistant accomplishes this is to look for certain entries or actions that are indicative of a larger purpose. For example, if you type Dear Mr. Smith, and press Enter, that certainly looks like you're starting a letter. Similarly, if you type 1. Part I and press Enter, it is reasonable to assume that you're starting a numbered list. The Office Assistant recognizes these and other indicators and acts accordingly.

One of the things the Office Assistant does is convert your typing into what it thinks is the appropriate format. In Figure 7.7, for example, you can see that the Office Assistant converted the typing into a numbered list. If that's okay with you, click Cancel to continue. Otherwise, you can click No, change it back to how it was to remove the automatic formatting.

For more complex tasks, the Office Assistant offers to provide you with help related to what you're doing. In Figure 7.8, for example, you see that the Office Assistant recognizes the beginning of a letter and offers to provide help on writing the letter. Again, you can continue on your own or you can choose to accept the Office Assistant's help. In the letter-writing example, accepting the offer of help means the Office Assistant launches the Letter Wizard, as shown in Figure 7.9.

FIGURE 7.7.

The Office Assistant often converts your typing into what it thinks is the appropriate format.

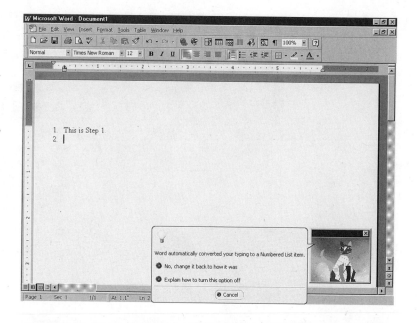

FIGURE 7.8.

For trickier tasks, the Office Assistant asks if you want help.

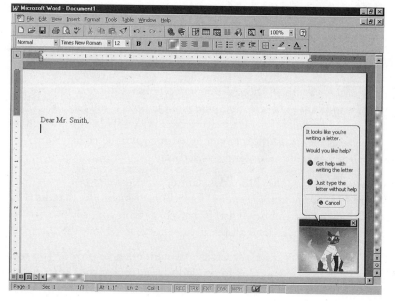

Figure 7.9.

If you accept the Office Assistant's help, it often launches a wizard to take you through the task.

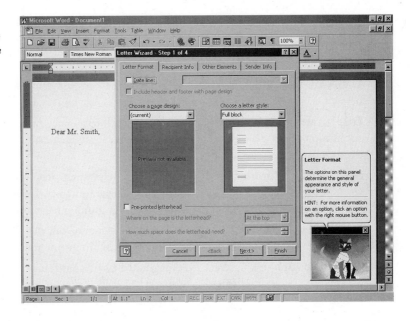

Office Assistant Options

You saw earlier how you can choose from the gallery of available Office Assistant characters. The Office Assistant also comes with quite a few other options so you can customize it to suit the way you work. To see these options, use any of the following methods:

- Click the title bar in the Office Assistant window and then click Options.
- Right-click the Office Assistant window and choose Options from the shortcut menu.

In both cases, you see the Options tab in the Office Assistant dialog box, shown in Figure 7.10.

Figure 7.10.

Use the Options tab to customize the Office Assistant.

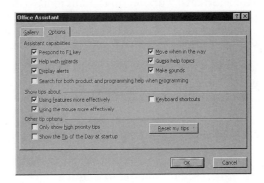

7

More Office Tools

Here's a rundown of the check boxes available in the Assistant capabilities group:

Respond to F1 key: If you deactivate this check box, pressing F1 bypasses the Office Assistant and takes you directly to the help system.

Help with wizards: This option determines whether the Office Assistant provides help when you run an Office wizard.

Display alerts: When this check box is activated, the Office Assistant displays all the application's alert dialog boxes. If you deactivate this check box, the application displays its normal alert dialogs.

Search for both product and programming help when programming: When you work in the Visual Basic Editor, activate this check box to make the Office Assistant search both the regular help topics and the programming help topics.

Move when in the way: When this check box is turned on, the Office Assistant window moves and resizes itself to avoid obscuring the work area.

Guess help topics: This check box toggles the Office Assistant's context-sensitive help on and off. If you deactivate this option, the Office Assistant no longer suggests help topics.

Make sounds: This check box toggles the Office Assistant character's sound effects on and off.

The Show tips about group contains three check boxes that govern the Office Assistant's on-the-fly help:

Using features more effectively: If you deactivate this check box, the Office Assistant won't monitor your activity and so won't offer help for tasks such as writing a letter.

Using the mouse more effectively: If you deactivate this check box, the Office Assistant won't show tips that are related to using the mouse.

Keyboard shortcuts: Turn on this option to have the Office Assistant suggest keyboard equivalents for the actions you perform.

Finally, the Other tip options group contains the following controls:

Only show high priority tips: If you find the Office Assistant is a bit too chatty for your liking, activate this check box. This tells the Office Assistant to display only the most important tips.

Show the Tip of the Day at startup: If you turn on this option, the Office Assistant displays a tip when you launch each Office application, as shown in Figure 7.11. Note that you might need to restart the application to put this setting into effect.

Reset my tips: Click this button to start the Tip of the Day from the beginning.

FIGURE 7.11.

If you activate the Tip of the Day feature, you see a short tip each time you start an Office application.

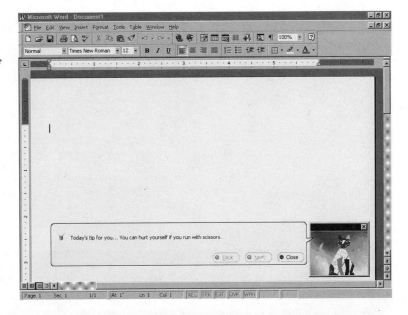

TIP: VIEWING TIPS

If you activate the Tip of the Day feature, you can view the tips at any time by using either of these techniques:

■ Click the Office Assistant window title bar and then click Tips.

■ Right-click the Office Assistant window and choose Tips from the shortcut menu.

Bypassing the Assistant: The Office Help System

If you find the Office Assistant a bit too cute or obtrusive, or if you need more in-depth information, you need to get past the Office Assistant and into the help system proper. The good news is that latest Office help system is a decided improvement over the one used in pre-Windows 95 versions. The topics are easier to navigate, the topic search is more complete, and you can even search for specific keywords. The next few sections introduce you to these welcome improvements.

Invoking the Help System

To bypass the Office Assistant and get to the help system, select Help | Contents and Index. You see the Help Topics window, the contents of which depend on the application. Figure 7.12 shows the Help Topics window for Microsoft Word.

FIGURE 7.12.

The Help Topics window appears when you select Help | Contents and Index.

> **NOTE: WHAT'S THIS? HELP**
>
> Some dialog boxes have a question mark (?) button in the upper-right corner. If you click this button and then click a dialog box control, a pop-up box appears that tells you a bit about the control. This is called, appropriately enough, *What's This?* help.

Navigating Help Topics

The help system windows give you a list of items, and the icons to the left of these items tell you what you're dealing with:

- If the item has a question mark icon, it's a help topic.
- If the item has a book icon, it's a help category (called a *book* in help system parlance) that contains either help topics or more books.

To get to the topic you want, open the appropriate book either by double-clicking it or by highlighting it and clicking the Open button. If the book displays more books, keep opening them until you get to the subject area you need. When you find your topic (see Figure 7.13), display it either by double-clicking it or by highlighting it and clicking the Display button.

After you choose a topic, help opens a new window and displays the topic text. In Word, for example, opening the What's new in Word 97 topic displays the help window shown in Figure 7.14. Besides reading the displayed text to get the information you need, you can also perform any of the following actions:

- If you see a word in green text with a dashed underline, you can click that word to display a pop-up box containing the word's definition. When you've read the definition, press Esc to close the pop-up box.

FIGURE 7.13.

Open the help system "books" to display the topics.

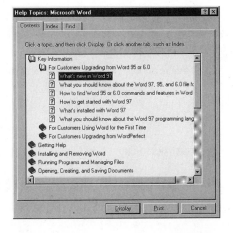

FIGURE 7.14.

A typical help topic window.

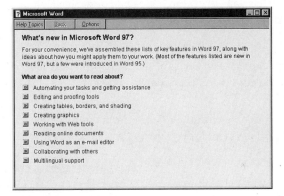

■ Click Related Topics (if available) at the bottom of the window to see a new help window with information related to the current topic. This is an example of a help system *hyperlink,* a button or piece of text that takes you to another topic (also known as *jumps*).

■ Click the Back button to see the previous help topic.

■ Click the Help Topics button to return to the topics window.

■ Click the Options button to set various help system options. The Annotate command lets you add your own notes to a topic; the Copy command copies the entire topic to the Clipboard; the Print Topic command prints the topic; the Font command lets you change the topic's font size (Small, Normal, or Large); the Keep Help on Top command determines whether the topic window remains on top of other windows; and the Use System Colors command tells Office to use the system's currently defined background and text colors for the topic window.

7

MORE OFFICE
TOOLS

TIP: MORE TOPIC TIPS

Another way to access the various help topic options is to right-click anywhere inside the topic and select a command from the context menu that appears.

The Copy command copies the entire topic, but what if you want to copy just part of the topic? Easy: Use the mouse to highlight the text you want to copy and then press Ctrl-C.

■ Click the Close (×) button to close help.

Searching for Help Topics in the Index Tab

As handy as the help system is, it can become a bit of a maze when you start jumping from topic to topic. To make it easier to find what you want, the help system includes an Index feature that lets you either search for a help topic in an alphabetical list of topics or simply type a keyword. Here's how it works:

1. In a Help Topics window, select the Index tab.
2. Type the first few letters of the topic you want. For example, if you type env in the Word help system, the Index list highlights the envelopes topic, as shown in Figure 7.15.
3. Either double-click the topic you want, or highlight it and click the Display button. The help system displays the topic.

FIGURE 7.15.

In the Index tab, enter the first few letters of the topic you want to find.

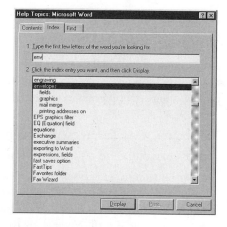

Searching for Help Topics in the Find Tab

The Index tab is well constructed, so it should suffice for finding most topics. What if your keyword doesn't correspond to an appropriate topic? What if you want to find a topic that satisfies multiple keywords (a *keyphrase*)? What if you want to see a list of *all* the help topics that contain a keyword or a keyphrase?

For these situations, Office has an excellent help system search engine. This engine works by building a database of words from the help topics and cross-referencing each word with the particular topic (or topics) from which it came. If you enter a word, help checks the database and displays every help topic that contains the word. If you enter multiple words, help finds either all the topics that contain each word or all the topics that contain at least one of the words (your choice).

To try this, select the Find tab in the Help Topics dialog box. The first time you select this tab, the Find Setup Wizard appears, as shown in Figure 7.16. This dialog box gives you three options:

FIGURE 7.16.

Use the Find Setup Wizard dialog box to choose the Find option you want to use.

Minimize database size (recommended): This option leaves out certain parts of the help system (such as the text from definition pop-ups) and reduces some of Find's capabilities. (I explain what happens later, in the section called "Find Options.") Still, Find remains a powerful search tool, so this option suits most people.

Maximize search capabilities: This option indexes every help system word and includes every possible Find option. If you have sophisticated search needs and a lot of free hard disk space, select this option.

Customize search capabilities: Select this option to tailor Find to suit your needs. This option provides Find capabilities somewhere in between the first two options.

When you've made your selection, click Next. If you chose either Minimize database size or Maximize search capabilities, click Finish in the next Find Setup Wizard dialog box that appears. If you chose Customize search capabilities, the Find Setup Wizard takes you through a series of dialog boxes. (The options in these dialog boxes might make more sense after you've read the next couple of sections.)

NOTE: CHANGING THE DATABASE OPTION

If you want to redo the database of help words, you can click the Rebuild button when you get to the Find tab, shown in Figure 7.17. This action displays the Find Setup Wizard again so that you can select a different option.

FIGURE 7.17.

Use the Find tab to search for specific words in the help system.

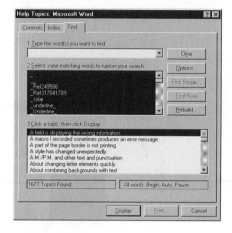

Searching with Find

After Find has built its database of help words (which might take a minute or two, depending on the option you selected and the speed of your computer), you see the Find tab, shown in Figure 7.17. Here's how to search for a topic using this dialog box:

1. In the Type the word(s) you want to find text box, enter the word or words you want to locate. If you want, you can enter just the first few letters of the word. As you type, Find displays a list of words that match.

2. To fine-tune the search, use the Select some matching words to narrow your search list to highlight the word or words you want to find.

3. Use the Click a topic, then click Display list to highlight the topic you want to see.

4. Click the Display button to open the topic.

Find Options

Find boasts various options you can take advantage of for more sophisticated searching. To see these options, click the Find tab's Options button. You see the Find Options dialog box, shown in Figure 7.18.

Figure 7.18.

Use the Find Options dialog box to specify how you want Find to interpret the words you enter.

The Search for topics containing group has three options:

All the words you typed in any order selects topics that contain every word you enter, regardless of the order in which you enter them. For example, if you enter `default font`, Find selects only the topics that contain both the words "default" *and* "font."

At least one of the words you typed selects topics that contain one or more of the words you enter. For example, if you enter `default font`, Find selects only the topics that contain either the word "default" *or* "font" (or both).

The words you typed in exact order selects topics that contain every word you enter, in the same order in which you enter them. For example, if you enter `default font`, Find selects only the topics that contain the phrase "default font."' Note that this option isn't available if you chose the Minimize database size option.

The Show words that drop-down list contains the following items:

begin with the characters you type selects topics that contain words that start with the characters you enter. For example, if you type `inter`, Find selects topics with words that begin with "inter," such as *Internet, internal,* and *international.*

contain selects topics for which the characters you enter are included anywhere in a word. For example, if you type `inter`, Find selects topics with words that contain "inter," such as *Internet, Painter,* and *printers.*

end with selects topics that contain words that finish with the characters you enter. For example, if you type `inter`, Find selects topics with words that end with "inter," such as *pointer* and *printer.*

match selects topics that contain words that exactly match what you enter. For example, if you type `form`, Find selects topics that contain the word "form" but not *forms* or *formatting.*

have the same root selects topics that have the same linguistic root as the word you enter. For example, if you enter `type`, Find selects topics that contain the words *type, types, typing, typed, typist,* and so on. Note that this option isn't available if you chose the Minimize database size option.

The Begin searching group contains options that specify when you want Find to begin searching the database:

>   **After you click the Find Now button:** If you activate this option, Find doesn't search the database until you click Find Now.

>   **Immediately after each keystroke:** If you activate this option, Find begins searching the database as soon as you enter a character and revises its search criteria with each new keystroke. To avoid getting bogged down, you should make sure that the Wait for a pause before searching check box is activated. This tells Find to wait until you stop typing before starting the search.

Find Options also has a Files button that you can use to specify which help files are included in the database. When you click Files, a list of the help files appears. Highlight the files you want to use and click OK.

When you've selected all your options, click OK to return to the Find tab.

Quick Clicks: The Office Shortcut Bar

The Office Shortcut Bar is a special toolbar that gives you one-click access to some common Office tasks and features. It also comes with quite a few customization options that let you set up the Shortcut Bar to suit your style. This section examines the Shortcut Bar and takes you through all its features and options.

Displaying the Shortcut Bar

By default, the Shortcut Bar loads automatically each time you start Windows. If the Shortcut Bar doesn't appear automatically, you can launch it by running the shortcut named Microsoft Office Shortcut Bar in your main Microsoft Office folder. (Office will ask if you want the Shortcut Bar loaded automatically at startup. Click Yes if you do or No if you don't.)

As you can see in Figure 7.19, the Shortcut Bar usually takes up residence down the right side of your screen. If you prefer a different location, drag the title bar to a different edge of the screen until it snaps into place and then release the mouse button. (You can, if you want, drag the Shortcut Bar to the middle of the screen and leave it as a floating toolbar.)

As I mentioned earlier, the Shortcut Bar is a special toolbar. (Technically, the Shortcut Bar is a window that uses a toolbar as its only interface element.) As such, the Shortcut Bar contains a collection of buttons that you click to set various actions in motion. For example, clicking the New Message button launches Outlook and opens a new e-mail message window. (As with all Office toolbars, hover the mouse pointer over a button to see a brief description of what the button does.)

FIGURE 7.19.
The Office Shortcut Bar usually appears on the right edge of your screen.

Toolbar icon

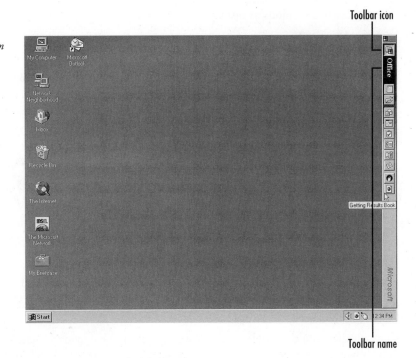

Toolbar name

Working with Shortcut Bar Toolbars

The Shortcut Bar is actually a collection of toolbars. The default toolbar is called Office and it contains buttons related to Office features and programs. However, there are also other toolbars for things like your desktop icons and your Programs folder. This section shows you how to display other toolbars and how to create custom toolbars.

Switching Toolbars

The Shortcut Bar comes with the following toolbars:

Office: Office-related tasks and applications.

QuickShelf: A collection of icons related to Bookshelf Basics.

Desktop: Displays all the icons that are defined on your Windows desktop.

Favorites: Displays the icons in your Favorites folder.

Programs: Displays the icons in your Programs folder.

Accessories: Displays the icons in your Accessories folder.

For each toolbar, Shortcut Bar displays an icon and the toolbar name. (See Figure 7.19.)

You can use two methods to display another toolbar:

- Right-click the toolbar name (or any empty area of the Shortcut Bar) and select the toolbar you want to display.

- Right-click the toolbar name (or any empty area of the Shortcut Bar) and select Customize from the shortcut menu. In the Customize dialog box, display the Toolbars tab, shown in Figure 7.20, activate the check box beside each toolbar you want to see, and then click OK.

FIGURE 7.20.

Use the Toolbars tab to activate the toolbars you want to display.

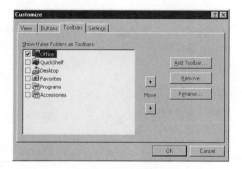

Once you have multiple toolbars displayed, click the toolbar icons to switch between each one. As you switch, the Shortcut Bar changes the toolbar name to reflect the current toolbar, and it also uses a different background color for each toolbar, as shown in Figure 7.21.

FIGURE 7.21.

Click the toolbar icons to switch between the displayed toolbars.

Each icon represents a different toolbar

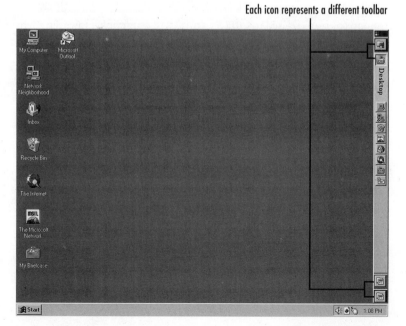

Creating Custom Toolbars

The default Shortcut Bar toolbars are fine, but they might not contain the files or folders you really need. That's not a problem, however, because it's easy to either create your own or customize the existing toolbars. This section shows you how it's done.

Creating a New Toolbar

If you want to start with a new toolbar, here's how to go about it:

1. In the Shortcut Bar, right-click the toolbar name (or any empty area of the Shortcut Bar) and select Customize from the shortcut menu.
2. In the Customize dialog box, display the Toolbars tab.
3. Click Add Toolbar to display the Add Toolbar dialog box, shown in Figure 7.22.

FIGURE 7.22.

Use the Add Toolbar dialog box to define your new toolbar.

4. This dialog box gives you two choices:

   Create a new, blank Toolbar called: Activate this option to create an empty toolbar. Use the text box provided to enter a name for the toolbar.

   Make Toolbar for this Folder: Activate this option to create a new toolbar where each button represents a file residing in a specific folder. Use the text box provided to enter the folder path or else click Browse and select the folder using the dialog box that appears.

5. Click OK to return to the Customize dialog box.

Adding Buttons to a Toolbar

If you created a new toolbar, or if you want to customize the buttons on an existing toolbar, first display the Buttons tab in the Customize dialog box, shown in Figure 7.23. Use the Toolbar list to choose the toolbar you want to work with, and then use any of the following techniques:

■ To add a file to the toolbar (technically, you're adding a shortcut to a file), click Add File, select the File from the dialog box that appears, and click Add.

FIGURE 7.23.

Use the Buttons tab to customize the buttons that appear on a toolbar.

TIP: POSITIONING THE NEW BUTTON

Before running the Add File command, select the toolbar button above which you want the new button to appear.

- To add a folder to the toolbar, click Add File, select the File in the dialog box that appears, and click Add.
- Use the check boxes beside each button to toggle the button on and off in the toolbar.
- To move a button, highlight it and click the up arrow or the down arrow.
- To rename a button, highlight it, click Rename, enter the new name in the Rename dialog box, and click OK.
- To insert a space into the toolbar, select the button above which you want the space to appear, and click Add Space.
- To delete a button, highlight it and click Delete.

Customizing the Shortcut Bar

The Shortcut Bar comes equipped with quite a few options that let you customize the look of the toolbars and buttons, as well as set a few useful options. To display these settings, right-click the toolbar name (or any empty area of the Shortcut Bar), click Customize to display the Customize dialog box, and activate the View tab, shown in Figure 7.24.

FIGURE 7.24.

Use the View tab to change the toolbar colors and customize other Shortcut Bar options.

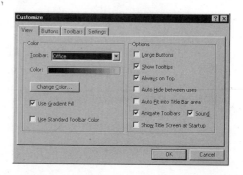

The controls in the Color group determine the background color used with each toolbar. Here's a summary of these controls:

Toolbar: Use this list to choose the toolbar you want to work with.

Color: This box shows the background color used with the selected toolbar.

Change Color: Click this button to select a different background color.

Use Gradient Fill: When this check box is activated, the Shortcut Bar displays the background color as a gradient. Deactivate this check box to display a solid color.

Use Standard Toolbar Color: If you activate this check box, Shortcut Bar uses the default toolbar color (usually gray).

The Options groups contains eight check boxes that controls various aspects of the Shortcut Bar:

Large Buttons: Activate this check box to increase the size of the Shortcut Bar buttons.

Show Tooltips: This option toggles the tooltips on and off.

Always on Top: When this option is turned on, the Shortcut Bar remains in view at all times.

Auto Hide between uses: If you activate this check box, the Shortcut Bar slides off the screen when you move the mouse away from the Shortcut Bar. If you then move the mouse to the edge of the screen (that is, the edge of the screen where the Shortcut Bar is hidden), the Shortcut Bar reappears.

TIP: QUICKER AUTO HIDE

Another, quicker, method for toggling the Auto Hide feature on and off is to right-click the toolbar name (or any empty area of the Shortcut Bar) and then select Auto Hide from the shortcut menu.

Auto Fit into Title Bar area: If you turn on this option, you can drag the Shortcut Bar into the title bar of an application and the Shortcut Bar resizes itself so that it fits into the title bar.

Animate Toolbars: When this check box is activated, the Shortcut Bar shows each toolbar sliding into position as you switch between toolbars.

Sound: When this check box is on, the Shortcut Bar plays a brief sound as you switch between toolbars.

Show Title Screen at Startup: Activate this option to have the Shortcut Bar display its splash screen each time it loads.

7

MORE OFFICE TOOLS

Microsoft Discovers the Wheel: The IntelliMouse

Some versions of Microsoft Office Professional ship with the new IntelliMouse, the latest in a long line of Microsoft mouse products. (The IntelliMouse is also available as a separate product.) The showstopping feature in this new mouse is a small rubber wheel that lies between the two mouse buttons. You can use this wheel to scroll up and down in documents, zoom in and out of spreadsheets, and much more. This section shows you how to use and customize the IntelliMouse.

> **NOTE: INSTALL INTELLIPOINT**
>
> To take advantage of the IntelliMouse features, you must install the IntelliPoint software that comes with the mouse.

Some Basic IntelliMouse Moves

As I write this, the only applications that take advantage of the IntelliMouse features are the Office programs and Internet Explorer. However, it's certain that other applications will build IntelliMouse functionality into their software. Here's a quick summary of the actions that should be universal in any IntelliMouse-enabled program:

To scroll up or down in a document: Rotate the wheel forward to move up through a document a few lines at a time; rotate the wheel backward to move down through a document a few lines at a time.

To zoom in and out of a document: To increase the Zoom percentage, hold down Ctrl and rotate the wheel forward; to decrease the Zoom percentage, hold down Ctrl and rotate the wheel backward.

To expand or collapse outline headings: To expand an outline heading, hold down Shift and rotate the wheel forward; to collapse an outline heading, hold down Shift and rotate the wheel backward.

Word and Excel also support a feature called *panning* that lets you scroll through a document or worksheet and control the speed. To enable panning, click the wheel button:

- Word displays an *origin mark* in the vertical scroll bar, as shown in Figure 7.25. Drag the pointer above the origin mark to scroll up; drag the pointer below the origin mark to scroll down.

- Excel displays an origin mark at the spot you click. (Excel's origin mark is a dot surrounded by four arrows.) To scroll, move the mouse in relation to the origin mark.

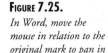

FIGURE 7.25.

In Word, move the mouse in relation to the original mark to pan in that direction.

Origin mark

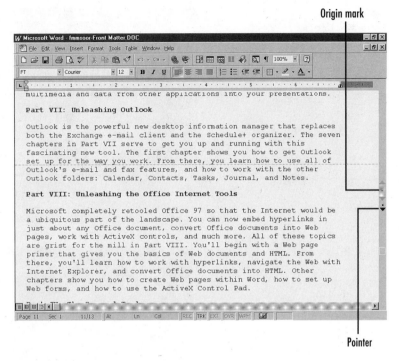

Pointer

In both cases, the greater the distance the pointer is from the origin mark, the faster you scroll. To turn off panning, click the wheel again.

IntelliMouse Options

When you install the IntelliMouse, the setup program adds a new Wheel tab, shown in Figure 7.26, to the Mouse properties sheet. (To display this tab, select Start | Settings | Control Panel, launch the Mouse icon from the Control Panel window, and select the Wheel tab.)

In the Wheel group, use the Turn on the wheel check box to toggle the IntelliMouse wheel on and off. Clicking the Settings button displays the Settings for Wheel dialog box, shown in Figure 7.27. Here's a summary of the available settings:

Direction: If you activate the check box in this group, IntelliPoint reverses the usual wheel directions. (For example, rotating the wheel forward scrolls down through a document.)

Scroll *x* lines at a time: Activate this option to scroll the specified number of lines when you rotate the wheel.

Scroll one "screen" at a time: Activate this option to scroll one screenful at a time when you rotate the wheel.

FIGURE 7.26.

Use the new Wheel tab to customize some IntelliMouse settings.

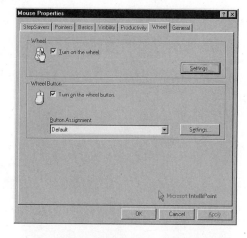

FIGURE 7.27.

Use the Settings for Wheel dialog box to set some wheel-related options.

Here's a summary of the options in the Wheel Button group:

Turn on the wheel button: Use this check box to toggle the IntelliMouse wheel button on and off.

Button Assignment: Use this list to specify what happens when you click the wheel button. Select Default to use whatever default action is defined in the application; if the application has no default action for the wheel button, choose one of the other items.

Settings: Click this button to display the Settings for Wheel Button dialog box, shown in Figure 7.28. Use the slider to set how fast the mouse pointer moves while you hold down the wheel button, and then click OK.

FIGURE 7.28.

Use the Settings for Wheel Button dialog box to set the button of the pointer when the wheel button is pressed.

The Lay of the Company Land: Organization Chart

An organization chart is a visual representation of a corporation's employee hierarchy. Although it is certainly possible to use the OfficeArt tools discussed in Chapter 5, "Using the OfficeArt Tools," to create an organization chart, Office provides an easier way: the Organization Chart application. This is an OLE server application that you use to insert an Organization Chart graphic into any Office document. This section shows you how to use Organization Chart.

Starting Organization Chart

As I mentioned earlier, Organization Chart is an OLE server application. That means you can't use it as a stand-alone program. Instead, you launch Organization Chart from an Office application (or any application that can act as an OLE container, for that matter) and use it to embed an Organization Chart object within the document. (If you're not sure about any of these OLE concepts, turn to Chapter 48, "Office Integration and OLE," to learn everything you need to know.) This object is a graphic image that shows the organization chart you create.

To get started, position the cursor where you want the Organization Chart object to appear. Select Insert | Object to display the Object dialog box, highlight MS Organization Chart 2.0 in the Object type list, and click OK. You see the Organization Chart window, shown in Figure 7.29.

FIGURE 7.29.

The Organization Chart window.

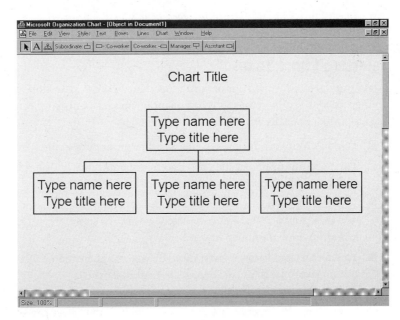

7

MORE OFFICE TOOLS

TIP: INSERTING A CHART IN POWERPOINT

A quicker way to launch Organization Chart in PowerPoint is to select Insert | Picture | Organization Chart.

Creating a Chart: The Basic Steps

Here's a rundown of the steps you have to plow through to create a basic chart:

1. To add a title for the chart, click Chart Title and edit the text accordingly.

2. Each box in the chart represents one employee in the hierarchy. To change the default text in each box, double-click the box and edit the text. Use the first line for the employee's name and the second line for the employee's title. You can also enter one or two comments.

3. To add an employee, click the appropriate button (Subordinate, Co-worker, and so on), and then click an existing box. Make sure you honor the correct relationship in the hierarchy. If you're adding a subordinate, for example, click the box that represents his manager.

4. Use the commands on the Styles, Text, Boxes, Lines, and Chart menus to format the chart as needed. (See "Formatting the Chart.")

5. Repeat steps 2 through 5 until the chart is complete.

6. Select File | Exit and Return to *Document,* where *Document* is the name of the document in which you're embedding the Organization Chart object.

Selecting Chart Boxes

I show you how to format your organization chart in the next section. This often involves selecting either one or more boxes or one or more lines (the ones connecting the boxes), so you need to know about the available techniques:

- To select a single box, click it. (This technique applies to lines as well.)

- To select multiple boxes that are scattered around the chart, hold down Shift and click each box. (This technique applies to lines as well.)

- To select multiple boxes that are grouped together, drag the mouse to create a selection area. Any box that lies completely within the selection area is highlighted. (This technique applies to lines as well.)

- To select related items, choose Edit | Select, and then choose a command from the cascade menu (such as All Managers or All Assistants).

- To select boxes according to their level within the hierarchy, choose Edit | Select Levels, enter the levels you want to work with in the Select Levels dialog box, shown in Figure 7.30, and then click OK.

FIGURE 7.30.

Use the Select Levels box to choose the chart levels you want to work with.

■ To select every box, either choose Edit | Select | All or press Ctrl-A.

Formatting the Chart

Organization Chart comes with quite a few options for formatting a chart. These options include text formatting, line and box formatting, and a few different styles for the chart layout. Most of these are straightforward, so I just provide a summary here.

The Styles menu displays a collection of layout styles that you can use to structure groups of boxes, as well as set up the Assistant and Co-Manager positions.

The text formatting options are all found on the Text menu. Here are the available commands:

Font: Displays the Font dialog box, from which you can select a typeface, type size, and more.

Color: Displays the Color dialog box, from which you can select a color for the text.

Left, Right, and Center: Use these commands to align the text.

Organization Chart's box formatting can be found on the Boxes menu:

Color: Displays the Color dialog box, from which you can set the background color of a box.

Shadow: Displays a menu of shadow styles.

Border Style: Displays a menu of styles for the box border.

Border Color: Displays the Color dialog box, from which you can set the background color of a box.

Border Line Style: Displays a menu of styles for the line that defines the box border.

If you want to format the lines that connect the boxes, use the commands on the Lines menu:

Thickness: Displays a menu of line widths.

Style: Displays a menu of line styles.

Color: Displays the Color dialog box, from which you can set the color of a line.

To set the background color of the chart, select Chart | Background Color and then choose a color from the Color dialog box that appears.

Math for the Masses: Equation Editor

The Equation Editor is another OLE server application, and it lets you insert mathematical formulas and equations into your Office documents. As with Organization Chart, Equation Editor embeds a graphic object that represents your equation. Here are the steps to follow to use this application:

1. Position the cursor where you want the Equation Editor object to appear.

2. Select Insert | Object to display the Object dialog box, highlight Microsoft Equation 3.0 in the Object type list, and then click OK.

3. Equation Editor may display a Tip dialog box. If so, either read the tip or cancel. In any case, a new Equation Editor object is inserted and Equation Editor opens the object in-place, as shown in Figure 7.31.

FIGURE 7.31.

Equation Editor embeds a new object in-place.

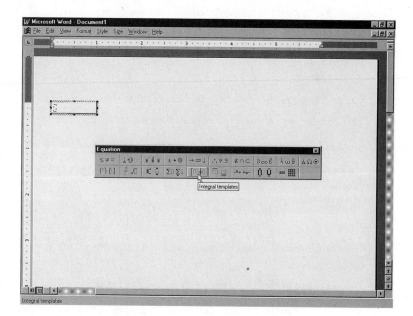

4. To enter text, just type inside the Equation Editor object. Note the following:

   - If you want to type in a different style (such as Greek letters), pull down the Style menu and select the style you want.

   - To change the type size (to get, say, a superscript), use the commands on the Size menu.

5. To enter mathematical symbols, first click the appropriate button on the Equation toolbar. Each button presents you with a palette of symbols or templates (predefined items into which you enter text). Click a symbol or template to add it to the equation.

TIP: VIEW SYMBOL DEFINITIONS

If you're not sure what a particular symbol or template is used for, click the button to display the appropriate palette, move the mouse pointer over the item, and read the descriptive text in the status bar.

6. Repeat steps 4 and 5 until the equation is complete.
7. Click outside the Equation Editor object.

Summary

This chapter examined a few more of the tools that ship with the Office package. You first learned how to work with and customize the Office Assistant and how to get the most out of the regular Office help system. From there, I showed you how to wield the Office Shortcut Bar and the new IntelliMouse. I closed with a look at two OLE servers: Organization Chart and Equation Editor.

Here's a list of chapters where you'll find related information:

- For a complete list of all the Office tools and applications, see Chapter 1, "Office 97: The Big Picture."
- To learn how to use the OfficeArt drawing tools, the Clip Gallery, and WordArt, see Chapter 5, "Using the OfficeArt Tools."
- See Chapter 6, "Working with Microsoft Graph," for information on the Office Graph tool.
- I show you how to work with the Office Internet features in Part VIII, "Unleashing the Office Internet Tools."
- To learn more about using OLE with Office, see Chapter 48, "Office Integration and OLE."
- For information on Binder, head for Chapter 49, "Packaging Office Documents with Binder."
- I discuss some of the extra tools that come with the Small Business Edition in Appendix B, "Office 97 Small Business Edition."
- See Appendix C, "Office 97 Developer Edition," to learn more about the Developer Edition tools.

Customizing the Office Menus and Toolbars

Each man must have his "I"; it is more necessary to him than bread; and if he does not find scope for it within the existing institutions he will be likely to make trouble.

—*Charles Horton Cooley*

The Microsoft programmers designed Office so that the commands and features most commonly used by most people are within easy reach. This means that the setup of the menu system and toolbars reflects what the ordinary user might want. However, no one qualifies as an ordinary user—we all work with Office in our own way. What one person uses every day, another needs only once a year; one user's obscure technical feature is another's bread and butter.

To address these differences, Office provides what might be the most customizable interface on the market today. Office lets you create custom menus either by deleting some of an application's built-in commands or by adding new commands and attaching macros to them. You can also easily configure the toolbars simply by dragging buttons on or off them. You can even create your own button faces with the Button Editor. This chapter explores all of these customization features.

Displaying, Moving, and Sizing Toolbars

I'll lead off with a look at the simplest interface customization techniques, which involve displaying and hiding toolbars, as well as moving and sizing them. First, though, you need to know the difference between docked and floating toolbars.

The Office programs designate the top and bottom of the application window, as well as the left and right sides of the window, as "docking" areas. So a *docked toolbar* is one that is attached to one of these areas. Docked toolbars have the following characteristics:

- The buttons are arranged either in a single, horizontal row (in the case of a toolbar docked at the top or bottom of the window; see Figure 8.1) or in a single, vertical column (in the case of a toolbar docked at the left or right edge of the window).

- The toolbar becomes part of the application window interface, which leaves less room for document windows.

- A *move handle* appears on either the left side of the toolbar (if it's docked at the top or bottom; see Figure 8.1) or the top of the toolbar (if it's docked on the left or right).

On the other hand, a *floating toolbar* is one that resides outside of these docking areas. Floating toolbars have the following characteristics:

- The toolbar forms a small window, and the buttons are arranged according to the shape of the window.

- The toolbar "floats" on top of the application (and can even be moved outside of the application window), so it leaves more room for document windows.

- The toolbar window includes a title bar, a close button, and a border (see Figure 8.1).

FIGURE 8.1.

You can display your toolbars either docked or floating.

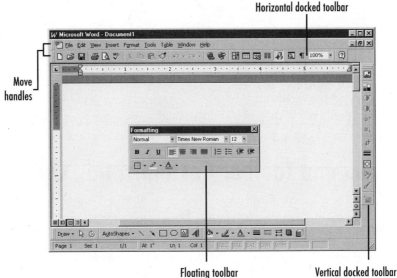

Horizontal docked toolbar

Move handles

Floating toolbar

Vertical docked toolbar

Here's a summary of the various methods you can use to display, move, and size toolbars:

■ To display a toolbar, first either select View | Toolbars or right-click a visible toolbar. From the menu that appears, choose the toolbar you want to display.

■ If the toolbar you want doesn't appear in the list, select Tools | Customize (in Access you have to select View | Toolbars | Customize). In the Toolbars tab, shown in Figure 8.2, activate the check box beside the toolbar you want, and click Close.

FIGURE 8.2.

The Toolbars tab lists all the application's available toolbars.

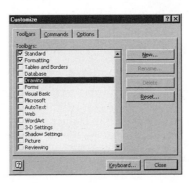

■ To hide a docked toolbar, either select View | Toolbars or right-click a visible toolbar, and then deactivate the toolbar command in the menu that appears.

8

CUSTOMIZING THE
OFFICE MENUS
AND TOOLBARS

- To hide a floating toolbar, either use the procedure just discussed or click the toolbar's Close button.
- To move a docked toolbar, drag its move handle. To turn it into a floating toolbar, drag the toolbar outside of the docking area.
- To move a floating toolbar, drag its title bar. To dock a floating toolbar, drag it to a docking area. When you see the toolbar outline snap into place either horizontally or vertically (depending on the docking area you're using), release the mouse button.
- To size a floating toolbar, drag the toolbar window borders.

Menu and Toolbar Customization Options

Let's now look at a few menu and toolbar customization options that are common to the Office applications. To view these options, first display the Customize dialog box using any of the following methods:

- Select Tools | Customize (this command isn't available in Access).
- Select View | Toolbars | Customize.
- Right-click the menu bar or any toolbar, and then choose Customize from the shortcut menu.

When the Customize dialog box appears, activate the Options tab, shown in Figure 8.3. Here's a rundown of the controls in this tab:

Large icons: Many people have trouble seeing the toolbar icons, either because they're running their screen at a high resolution or because their eyesight isn't what it used to be. If this is the case for you, activate this check box to increase the size of the toolbar icons and make them easier to see.

Show ScreenTips on toolbars: When this check box is activated, Office displays the name of a toolbar button when you hover the mouse pointer over the button for a second or two.

Show shortcut keys in ScreenTips: If you activate this check box, Office checks to see if a toolbar button has a shortcut key equivalent. If it does, Office displays the key combination in the ScreenTip banner.

Menu animations: When you choose a menu from the menu bar, the associated menu normally appears instantly. You can use this drop-down list to make menus appear with an animated flourish. Your choices are Unfold, Slide, and Random.

8

CUSTOMIZING THE
OFFICE MENUS
AND TOOLBARS

FIGURE 8.3.

The Options tab has a few settings for customizing menus and toolbars.

Creating Custom Menus

Office comes with a powerful set of tools called Command Bars that let you modify the Office application menus or create your own from scratch. Here's a list of some of the things you can do with the Command Bars feature:

- Move, rename, or delete existing menu commands.
- Add commands to or delete commands from an existing menu or shortcut menu.
- Create your own custom menus and attach them to any menu bar.
- Delete menus from any menu bar.
- Create your own menu bars.

The next few sections show you how to do all this and more.

> **NOTE: CUSTOM MENU BARS**
>
> To create a custom menu bar, you use the same technique that you use to create a custom toolbar. See "Creating a New Toolbar" later in this chapter.

First, a Game Plan

Before you dive into the menu customization techniques outlined in the next few sections, you need to take a step back and plan what you want to do. For starters, bear in mind that these techniques require that you sit down in front of the computer and work with it directly, so they apply only to the following situations:

- You're the administrator of a small system, or you're a corporate developer and your application is designed for a limited number of employees. (After all, you wouldn't want to tweak the menu systems of a thousand machines!)

- You're a consultant putting together a system for a client.
- You want easier access to some application commands or to the macros and procedures you've developed for your own use.

In each case, I'm assuming you can sit down in front of the computer, load the underlying application, and make the appropriate menu customizations.

On the other hand, there will be plenty of situations in which you can't access the user's computer directly—for example, if you distribute your application electronically or via some other means where you have no direct contact with the user. Similarly, you might be building an application for use on hundreds or thousands of computers, and it's impractical to customize each system by hand. For these and similar cases, you need to use Visual Basic for Applications to customize your menus. I'll tell you how to do this in Chapter 59, "Creating a Custom User Interface."

The next thing you must consider is the layout of your custom menus. You can use three levels of customization:

Menu commands: This level involves adjusting existing commands or tacking new commands onto one or more of the application's built-in menus. Use this level when you have just a few changes to make.

Cascade menus: This level involves adding one or more cascade menus to the application's built-in menu system. Use this level if you have several related procedures that you want to group together.

Menus: This level involves creating an entirely new menu that appears in the application's menu bar. Use this level to create personalized menus or when you have many different procedures and you don't want to cram them all into the application's built-in menus.

Customizing an Existing Menu

If all you need to do is customize one of the application's existing menus, follow the steps outlined earlier to display the Customize dialog box, and then use the following techniques:

- To move a menu item to a different location, drag it within the menu.
- To rename a menu item, click the item, click Modify Selection in the Commands tab, and then use the Name text box to edit the item name.
- To delete a menu item, drag it off the menu.

NOTE: RESETTING THE MENU

If you no longer want to keep your changes, you can revert a built-in menu to its default configuration by right-clicking the menu name and then choosing Reset from the shortcut menu.

Creating a New Menu

If you'll be adding many new commands to the application's menu system, you might not want to bog down the existing menus with too many items. To keep things clean, you can create a custom menu just for your procedures. Here are the steps to follow:

1. Display the Customize dialog box as described earlier.
2. Activate the Commands tab, shown in Figure 8.4.

FIGURE 8.4.

Use the Commands tab in the Customize dialog box to create new menus in the application.

3. In the Categories list, highlight New Menu.
4. In the Commands list, drag the New Menu item up to the menu bar. You'll see a vertical bar that marks the spot where the new menu will appear. When the bar is positioned where you want your menu, drop the New Menu item.
5. Either click Modify Selection or right-click the new menu, and then use the Name box on the shortcut menu to name your new menu, as shown in Figure 8.5. Place an ampersand (&) before whichever letter you want to use as an accelerator key. (Make sure the key you choose doesn't conflict with an accelerator key used by any other menu.)
6. Press Enter.

TIP: QUICKLY REARRANGE MENU BAR ITEMS

If you want to change the order of the menu bar items, you can do so without displaying the Customize dialog box. Just hold down the Alt key and drag the menu bar item left or right. You can also delete a menu bar item by holding down Alt and dragging the item off the menu bar.

8

CUSTOMIZING THE
OFFICE MENUS
AND TOOLBARS

FIGURE 8.5.

Use the Modify Selection menu to rename the new menu bar item.

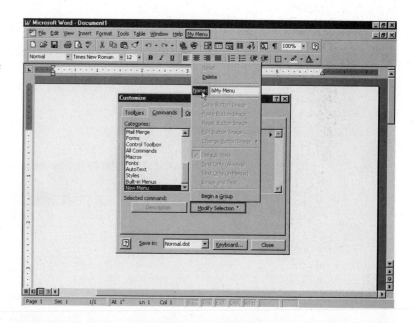

NOTE: DISPLAYING THE MODIFY SELECTION MENU

We'll be using the Modify Selection menu throughout this chapter. Rather than constantly repeating the instructions for displaying this menu, I'll just say, "Display the Modify Selection menu." This means that you use either of the following techniques:

- Highlight the item you want to work with, and then click the Modify Selection button in the Commands tab of the Customize dialog box.
- Right-click the item.

Creating a New Cascade Menu

To work with cascade menus, you have two choices:

- Add the cascade menu to the new menu you created in the preceding section.
- Add the cascade menu to one of the application's built-in menus.

Either way, you follow the steps outlined in the preceding section. However, instead of dragging the New Menu item to the menu bar, drag it to an existing menu. When the menu pulls down, drag the mouse pointer down into the menu to the position where you want the cascade menu to appear. (A black horizontal bar shows you where the menu will be positioned.) When you drop the item, a new cascade menu is created.

To rename the cascade menu item, display the Modify Selection menu and then use the Name text box to enter the new name (including an accelerator key).

Adding Menu Commands

You're now ready to create custom menu commands. Remember that you can create these commands in any of the following locations:

- On a custom menu that you've created
- On a custom cascade menu that you've created
- On one of the application's built-in menus

Here are the steps you need to work through:

1. Follow the steps outlined earlier to display the Commands tab in the Customize dialog box.
2. In the Categories list, highlight the category that contains the command you want.
3. In the Commands list, drag the command you want to a custom menu, a custom cascade menu, or a built-in menu.
4. When the menu opens, drag the item down into the menu and then drop the item at the position where you want the command to appear.

Creating Custom Commands for Macros

In Part XI, "Unleashing Office Application Development with VBA," I'll show you a number of methods for running your VBA macros. However, all these methods assume that you know which task each macro performs. If you're constructing procedures for others to wield, they might not be as familiar with what each macro name represents. Not only that, but you might not want novice users scrolling through a long list of procedures in the Macro dialog box or, even worse, having to access the Visual Basic Editor.

To help you avoid these problems, you can make your macros more accessible by assigning them to custom menu commands, as explained in the next two sections.

Custom Macro Commands in Word, PowerPoint, and Access

Here are the steps you need to follow to add a custom command for a macro in Word, PowerPoint, and Access:

1. Follow the steps outlined earlier to display the Commands tab in the Customize dialog box.
2. In the Categories list, highlight the Macros item. (In Access, select the All Macros item.)
3. In the Commands list, drag the macro you want to work with to a custom menu, a custom cascade menu, or a built-in menu.
4. When the menu opens, drag the item down into the menu and then drop the item at the position where you want the command to appear.

5. Display the Modify Selection menu, and then use the Name box on the shortcut menu to edit the macro name, if necessary. Place an ampersand (&) before whichever letter you want to use as an accelerator key.

6. Press Enter.

NOTE: CREATING COMMAND GROUPS

You've probably noticed that the Office applications group related menu commands by using separator bars. You can do the same for your custom menus. With the Customize dialog box displayed, pull down the menu and click the first command in the group you want to create. Now click Modify Selection and then click Begin a Group. The application adds a separator bar above the selected command.

Custom Macro Commands in Excel

Excel uses a slightly different method for creating custom macro commands:

1. Follow the steps outlined earlier to display the Commands tab in the Customize dialog box.

2. In the Categories list, highlight the Macros item.

3. In the Commands list, drag the Custom Menu item to a custom menu, a custom cascade menu, or a built-in menu.

4. When the menu opens, drag the item down into the menu, and then drop the item at the position where you want the command to appear.

5. Display the Modify Selection menu, and then use the Name box on the shortcut menu to name your new menu. As before, place an ampersand (&) in front of whichever letter you want to use as an accelerator key. (To ensure that the Modify Selection menu remains on-screen, don't press Enter when you're done.)

6. In the Modify Selection menu, click Assign Macro. The Assign Macro dialog box appears, as shown in Figure 8.6.

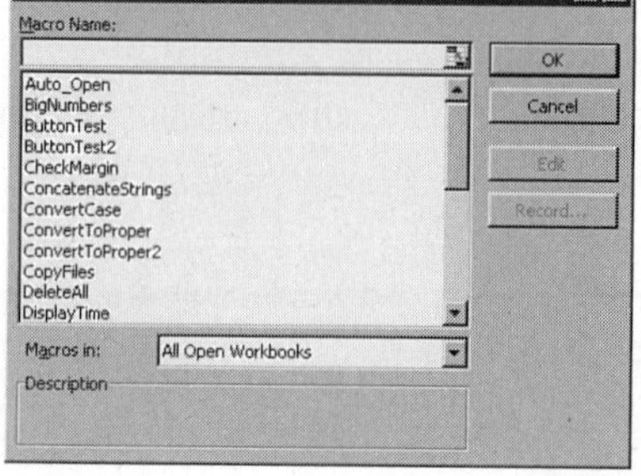

FIGURE 8.6.

Use this dialog box to choose the macro you want to assign to the new menu item.

7. Use the Macro Name list to highlight the macro you want to assign to the new menu command, and then click OK.

Deleting Menus and Menu Commands

If you no longer need a custom menu, cascade menu, or command, you can use a couple of methods to delete these items. First, display the Customize dialog box, and then try either of these techniques:

■ Use the mouse to drag the item off the menu or menu bar and drop it outside the application's menu system.

■ Right-click the item and then choose Delete from the shortcut menu.

Creating Custom Toolbars

Menu commands are fine, but there's nothing like a toolbar's one-click access for making your macros easy to run. This section shows you how to create custom toolbars, populate them with buttons, and assign macros to these buttons.

Customizing an Existing Toolbar

If you want to make changes to one of the application's existing toolbars, display the toolbar, follow the steps outlined earlier to load the Customize dialog box, and then use the following techniques:

■ To move a button to a different location, drag it within the toolbar.

■ To change the size of a toolbar drop-down list, click it and drag either the left or right edge.

■ To change how a toolbar button is displayed, right-click the button and then choose one of the following commands from the shortcut menu:

Default Style: Uses the application's default style (only the button's image is shown).

Text Only (Always): The button displays text (that is, the button name) whether it's displayed on a toolbar or on a menu.

Text Only (in Menus): The button displays text only when it's displayed on a menu.

Image and Text: The button displays both its image and its name.

■ To delete a button, drag it off the toolbar.

Creating a New Toolbar

Theoretically, you *could* add new buttons to the application's built-in toolbars, but you run the risk of overcrowding them and possibly confusing your users. Instead, you can create a toolbar from scratch and add existing commands and custom buttons to it. Here are the steps to follow to create a new toolbar:

1. Follow the steps outlined earlier to display the Customize dialog box.
2. Activate the Toolbars tab.
3. Click the New button. The New Toolbar dialog box appears, as shown in Figure 8.7.

FIGURE 8.7.

Use this dialog box to name your new toolbar.

4. Use the Toolbar name text box to enter the name you want to use for the toolbar.
5. In Word only, use the Make toolbar available to list to assign the new toolbar to a template.
6. Click OK. The application displays a new, empty toolbar.

NOTE: CREATING A NEW MENU BAR

In Office 97, there is no difference between a menu bar and a toolbar. (In fact, you can drag the menu bar from its top docking position and turn it into a floating toolbar.) Therefore, you can use the preceding steps to create custom menu bars as well.

NOTE: CUSTOM TOOLBAR MAINTENANCE

Once you've created a custom toolbar, activate the Toolbars tab in the Customize dialog box, and then use the following techniques to work with it:

- ■ To rename the toolbar, highlight it in the Toolbars list, click Rename, and then enter the new name in the dialog box that appears.
- ■ To delete the toolbar, highlight it in the Toolbars list and click Delete. When the application asks you to confirm the deletion, click OK.

Adding a Toolbar Cascade Menu or Toolbar Button

Once you have your new toolbar, you can start adding cascade menus and buttons to it. This is exactly the same as adding cascade menus and commands to a drop-down menu, so just follow the procedures described earlier. In this case, of course, you drag the menus, built-in commands, or macros and drop them on the toolbar of your choice.

Working with Button Images

If you add a button for a macro to a toolbar, you can leave the button as text, but you might prefer to assign a custom image. You have three ways to do this:

■ Copy an image from another button.

■ Use one of the application's predefined images.

■ Use the Button Editor to edit an existing image or create an image from scratch.

Copying a Button Image

If another toolbar button has an image you want to use, follow these steps to copy the image and assign it to your custom button:

1. Follow the steps outlined earlier to display the Commands tab in the Customize dialog box.

2. Display the toolbar that contains the button image you want if it's not already displayed.

3. Display the Modify Selection menu for the button that contains the image you want.

4. Click Copy Button Image.

5. Display the Modify Selection menu for the button whose image you want to change.

6. Click Paste Button Image.

Assigning a Predefined Button Image

The Office applications come with more than 40 predefined button images that you can assign to your custom toolbar buttons. Follow these steps:

1. Follow the steps outlined earlier to display the Commands tab in the Customize dialog box.

2. Display the Modify Selection menu for the button whose image you want to change.

3. Click Change Button Image.

4. In the cascade menu that appears, click the image you want.

Using the Button Editor

The Office Button Editor lets you modify an existing button image or create your own. The following procedure shows you how it's done:

1. Follow the steps outlined earlier to display the Commands tab in the Customize dialog box.

2. Display the Modify Selection menu for the button whose image you want to edit.

TIP: STARTING WITH ANOTHER BUTTON IMAGE

If another toolbar button has an image that's close to the one you want, use the steps outlined earlier to copy that image to your button. You can then edit this image as necessary using the Button Editor.

---

3. Click Edit Button Image. The application displays the Button Editor dialog box, shown in Figure 8.8.

FIGURE 8.8.

The Button Editor lets you design your own toolbar buttons.

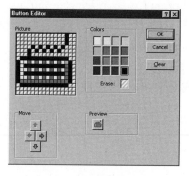

4. If you want to create the button from scratch, click the Clear button.

5. Select a color by clicking one of the boxes in the Colors group.

6. Add the color to the image by clicking one or more boxes in the Picture area. To clear a box, click it again. The Preview area shows you what the button looks like at regular size.

7. If necessary, use the buttons in the Move group to adjust the position of the image.

8. Repeat steps 5 through 7 to draw the complete image.

9. Click OK to assign the new image to the button.

Attaching a Toolbar to an Excel Workbook

If you're working in Excel and you need a custom toolbar only for a specific workbook, you can attach the toolbar to the workbook. This is also useful for developers who want to distribute custom toolbars with their projects. Here are the steps to follow:

1. Activate the workbook to which you want to attach the custom toolbar.

2. Display the Toolbars tab in the Customize dialog box.

3. Highlight your custom toolbar and then click Attach. Excel displays the Attach Toolbars dialog box, shown in Figure 8.9.

FIGURE 8.9.

Use the Attach Toolbars dialog box to attach a toolbar to a workbook.

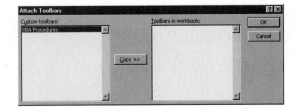

4. Highlight the custom toolbar and click Copy >>.

5. Click OK.

After you've attached a toolbar, it's automatically copied into the Excel workspace whenever you open the workbook.

TIP: REMOVING A TOOLBAR FROM A WORKBOOK

If you accidentally copy a toolbar, it's easy enough to remove it from the workbook. Begin by highlighting the toolbar in the Toolbars in workbook list. The Copy >> button changes to a Delete button. Click this button to remove the toolbar, and then click OK.

Attaching a Toolbar to a Word Document

When you create a new toolbar in Word, the dialog box you use to name the toolbar also contains a Make toolbar available to list (see Figure 8.7). You use this list to choose the document or template in which to store the toolbar. If you select Normal.dot, Word makes the toolbar available to all documents, but if you choose a specific file, the toolbar will be visible only when you work with that file.

If you've attached a custom toolbar to a specific document, you can copy it to any other open document or template, but the procedure is slightly different than the one just described for Excel:

1. Open both the document that contains the custom toolbar and the document to which you want to copy the toolbar.

2. Select Tools | Template and Add-Ins to display the Template and Add-Ins dialog box.

3. Click Organizer. Word displays the Organizer dialog box.

4. Activate the Toolbars tab, shown in Figure 8.10.

FIGURE 8.10.

Use the Organizer's Toolbars tab to copy a custom toolbar to another document.

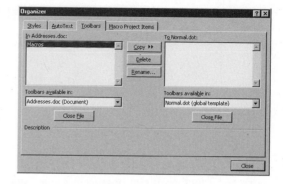

5. Use one of the Toolbars available in lists to select the document containing the custom toolbar.

6. Use the other Toolbars available in list to select the document to which you want to copy the toolbar.

7. Highlight the custom toolbar and then click Copy >>.

8. Click Close.

TIP: DELETING A TOOLBAR FROM A DOCUMENT

To remove a toolbar from a document, follow steps 1 through 5 and then click Delete.

NOTE: OTHER ORGANIZER DUTIES

You can also use the Organizer to copy styles, AutoText entries, and VBA project items (modules, class modules, and forms) from one document to another. Just follow the steps in this section and choose the appropriate tab in the Organizer dialog box (Styles, AutoText, or Macro Project Items).

Summary

This chapter showed you how to set up custom menus and toolbars in the Office applications. I began by showing you some basic techniques for displaying, moving, and sizing toolbars. From there, you learned about a few options related to toolbars and menus. I then showed you how to use the built-in Office tools to create new menus, cascade menus, and menu commands, as well as how to assign macros to custom commands. Next you learned how to customize toolbars and toolbar buttons. I closed by showing you how to attach a toolbar to an Excel workbook.

Here's a list of chapters where you'll find related information:

- You'll learn about some of Word's other customization options in Chapter 14, "Customizing Word."
- Excel's customization features are covered in Chapter 23, "Customizing Excel."
- To customize Access, turn to Chapter 31, "Customizing Access."
- I tell you about PowerPoint's customization features in Chapter 35, "Customizing PowerPoint."
- To learn how to control menus and toolbars programmatically, see Chapter 59, "Creating a Custom User Interface."

PART

III

Unleashing Word

Document Concepts

CHAPTER 9

IN THIS CHAPTER

> *Here is pen and here is a pencil,*
> *Here's a typewriter, here's a stencil,*
> *Here is a list of today's appointments,*
> *And all the flies in all the ointments,*
> *The daily woes that a man endures—*
> *Take them, George, they're yours!*

—*Ogden Nash*

In many ways, Word is the centerpiece of the Microsoft Office suite—partly because it's the oldest of the applications, and partly because almost anyone who uses a computer must have a word processor. In this, the first chapter of this book devoted to Word, you'll be reintroduced to the concept of a document's being more than text. You'll also be given a tour of the new interface, and you'll find information on creating and formatting a document.

This chapter, as well as the others covering Word, uses plenty of illustrations and shows several ways of doing tasks wherever possible. This will help you adapt Word to fit the way you work.

Document Definition

One of the central ideas in Office 97 is designing business solutions with a *document-centric* viewpoint. The document isn't just a collection of text created by a word processor; it's a collection of objects designed to present a central theme. Word fits into this concept as one of the tools for unifying the various elements of a document.

Through various techniques, you can use Word to have information from the other applications tied into a page (or pages) and manage the presentation of that data to the screen or the printer.

Although this chapter mainly shows you how to create text-based documents, later chapters will show you how to add data from the other Office applications, as well as graphics from other sources, to build more complex documents.

Opening Word

There are a number of ways to start Word, depending on what you want to do and your personal preferences. Here are the three most common ways:

- Select Start a new document from the Office shortcut bar and then select a Word template or wizard.
- Double-click a file found in Explorer that is associated with Word (for example, a file that has a .DOC extension).
- Choose Word from the Start menu (select Start | Programs | Microsoft Word).

NOTE: DISPLAYING FILE EXTENSIONS

By default, Windows 95 and Windows NT 4.0 do not display file extensions in either Explorer or the file-related dialog boxes (such as Open and Save As). This can be a pain when you're renaming files (as well as other things), so it pays to turn file extensions on. To do this, select View | Options in Explorer, deactivate the Hide MS-DOS file extensions for file types that are registered check box, and click OK.

If you've used Word before, you'll notice several similarities to previous versions, as well as a number of differences. Although the menu remains very similar, the default toolbars have changed quite a bit. There are quite a few buttons on the default toolbars. Many of them were available in previous Word versions but weren't set up by default.

Looking at the menu, you'll notice that each menu selection has a letter underlined (usually the first letter, but sometimes the second). This letter is known as the *hot key*. By holding down the Alt key and then pressing the key for the underlined letter, you can activate the menu the same as if you used the mouse to pull down the menu. If you run the mouse over the menu options, the options become buttons to indicate that the mouse has chosen that option.

The options on each menu also have underlined letters. By simply pressing that letter's key after you activate the menu, you select the option (again, the same as if you had used the mouse to click it). Some of these menu choices show other keystrokes that can be used to get to the same function directly (such as Ctrl-C to copy or Ctrl-V to paste). These are referred to as *shortcut keys*. They let you keep your fingers on the keyboard while performing common functions.

Often, a menu choice produces a dialog box that contains several items that you can enter. Use the Tab or the left arrow key to move from item to item. You also can hold down the Shift key and press the Tab key to move back to an item (the right arrow key works as well). This keyboard navigation technique works the same way through most of Windows, so learning these keystrokes can shave some time off common chores.

The Helpful Office Assistant

Perhaps the biggest screen difference in Office 97's Word over previous versions is the *Office Assistant*, shown in Figure 9.1. It appears in its own window when you start Word, offering you advice. If you want to remove the Office Assistant and keep it from showing up again, click its close button. It will remain hidden until you click the toolbar's Office Assistant button.

In most cases, you won't use the menu bar's Help option. The Office Assistant generally offers all the help you'll need. When you need help, click the Office Assistant's window and type your question. (The Office Assistant replaces the Answer Wizard from the previous version of Word.) When you type your question, the Office Assistant displays a list of several help topics that might answer your question. Select the topic that most closely matches your request. The Office Assistant displays the familiar Help window.

FIGURE 9.1.

Office Assistant is always ready to give you advice.

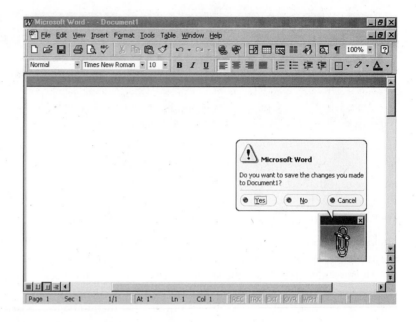

As you type, the Office Assistant moves out of the way if it will cover up something you enter. You can close the Office Assistant to gain more screen real estate and then click the toolbar's Office Assistant button to redisplay the Office Assistant.

If you see a yellow light bulb appear in the Office Assistant's window, click the light bulb to see what Office Assistant is thinking. Usually, it has noticed something you just did and can offer you a better way of doing it.

TIP: WORKING WITH THE OFFICE ASSISTANT

The Office Assistant appears in all the Office 97 programs. You can change its appearance. Click the Office Assistant window and select Options. Click the Gallery tab to select a new Office Assistant character.

Toolbar Highlights

Toolbars often appear beneath the menu bar. Word contains many toolbars, but rarely will you want to display more than two or three at a time. To display or hide a toolbar, first either select View | Toolbars or right-click any displayed toolbar and then activate or deactivate the appropriate toolbar command. To determine what a toolbar button does, rest the mouse over the button for a moment. Word's *ToolTip* box pops up, describing the button.

The top toolbar, called the Standard toolbar, contains many familiar Windows tools. You'll notice a few new ones, such as the Insert Hyperlink and Web Toolbar buttons. These two buttons offer access to the Internet in case you want to use Word to create Web pages.

On the second toolbar, called the Formatting toolbar, most of the items are the same as in previous versions of Word, but a new Font Color button has been added. This is for coloring selected text. With the proliferation of color printers and colorful Web pages, font colors are more important than ever. Clicking the button that has the A lets you color selected text. Clicking the down arrow to the right of this gives you a choice of colors to use; the A's color changes according to your choice. Figure 9.2 shows some text in various colors, as well as the drop-down list of available colors. Although you can't see the actual colors in this figure, the text is purple, green, blue, and pink.

FIGURE 9.2.

Sections of colored text and a menu of text color choices.

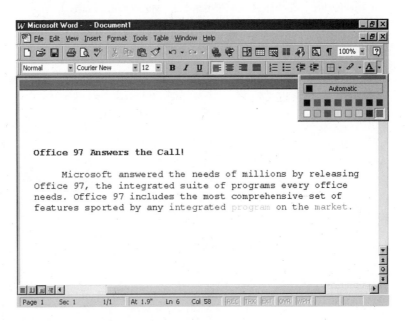

Depending on your program's current setup, you might see Word's horizontal ruler below the menu and the toolbars. The ruler shows you the current left and right margins and any indents or special tab stops defined for the current section of text. If you don't see the ruler, you can display it by selecting View | Ruler.

TIP: DISPLAY THE RULER TEMPORARILY

You can temporarily display the ruler by resting the mouse cursor directly under the formatting toolbar. The toolbar will appear for as long as you leave the mouse there.

9

DOCUMENT
CONCEPTS

Changing Fonts

One of the first things you're likely to change in a document is the font. Although Times New Roman is okay, it might not look that good on your printer, and it certainly isn't recommended for documents that will be viewed electronically, such as on the Internet. The easiest way to change the font is to go to the Formatting toolbar. The middle list (the second from the left) is called the Font box. It contains the currently selected font. Clicking the arrow drops down a list of fonts available on your system.

The problem with using this method to change the font is that you have to already know what the font will look like. If you don't mind a few additional mouse clicks, you can get a preview of the new font. To do so, select Format | Font to display the Font dialog box, shown in Figure 9.3. From here you change the font and also specify other effects. You can also set style and size (which can also be done from the Formatting toolbar). Notice that there is also a tab for Character Spacing, which lets you define how the spacing should be set with that font.

FIGURE 9.3.

The Font dialog box.

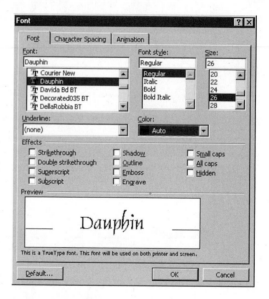

For any of this to work on existing text, you must first select the text you want to change, and then select the options you want to use.

This is a good time to point out a difference between the way Word uses the term *font* and the way most publishers and designers use the term. Normally, a Times New Roman or Arial would be called a *typeface,* and a *font* would be Times New Roman, 12-point, bold italic.

One other area of confusion when it comes to fonts is the term *points.* This term refers to the size of a font. It comes from the printing industry, which measures size in points rather than inches. There are 72 points in an inch, so a 12-point font has six lines of text in a 1-inch section of a printed page. Therefore, larger point sizes result in taller fonts.

One other consideration to make when working with fonts is whether you will be distributing the electronic version of the document. If all you'll be doing is printing the document and sending it around, you should feel free to use any font on your system. If you think you'll be sharing the file, however, you should try to choose a default Windows font. Otherwise, your recipients might not have the font you used. If they don't, your document will end up looking strange, because Word will use a substitute font to replace your font.

Working with Margins and Page Setup

Another common change to a document is to adjust the margins. The easiest way to do this for a paragraph (and for the rest of the document from that point on unless you change it back) is to go to the ruler and drag the margin markers to the new point on the ruler. You can drag the left margin marker, the right margin marker, or both to adjust the margins. Figure 9.4 gives a rather extreme example of how to adjust the right margin. The white area of the ruler shows you the entire document's left and right margin boundaries, and the left and right margin markers adjust to illustrate each paragraph's margins as you select certain paragraphs.

FIGURE 9.4.

An example of changing the margin with the ruler.

Text after margin change —

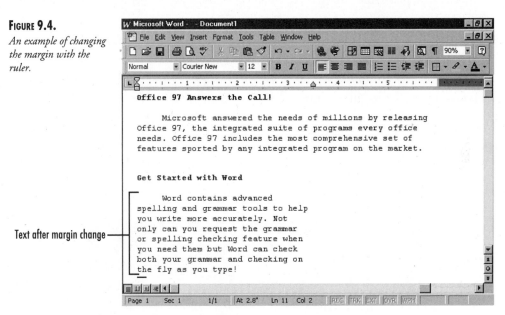

Another way to change margins for a document (or for a particular section) is to select File | Page Setup. Figure 9.5 shows the Page Setup dialog box that appears. The Margins tab is selected.

You can set the top and bottom margins, the left and right margins, and a gutter (the extra margin space allowed for binding a document). All these measurements are based on the distance from the edge of the paper, as defined in the Paper Size tab.

FIGURE 9.5.

The Margins tab of the Page Setup dialog box.

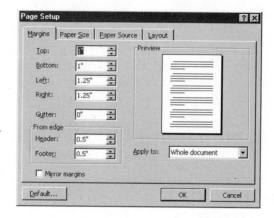

Below these options are the Header and Footer boxes. Remember that these measurements are based from the edge of the page; your top and bottom margins aren't taken into consideration. In other words, make sure you aren't defining your header and footer to print on top of your regular text.

Below the preview page, which shows how your changes affect a page of text, is the Apply To list box, where you can specify whether these changes should apply to the entire document or just to the remaining part of the document from the current point in the text.

This dialog box also has three buttons: OK, Cancel, and Default. OK confirms the changes, Cancel causes Word to ignore your changes, and Default returns the settings to Word's default settings in case you make unintended changes and want to revert to the settings that were in effect before you displayed the dialog box.

Above the buttons is the Mirror margins check box. Figure 9.6 shows how the Page Setup screen changes with this option to allow you to format facing pages.

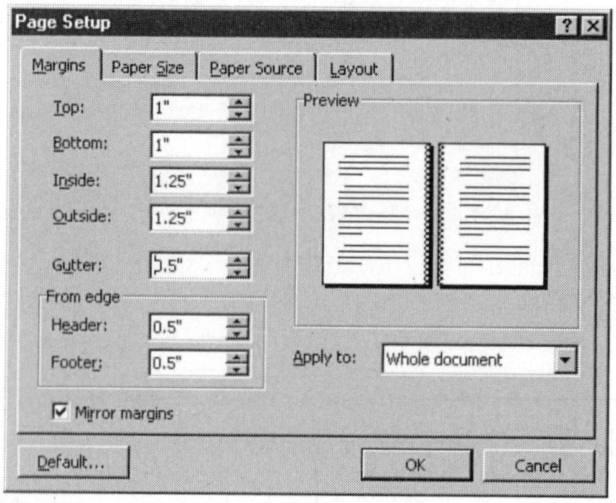

FIGURE 9.6.

The Page Setup dialog box after you select Mirror margins.

Notice the facing page margins: You can adjust the inside (next to the binder) and outside left and right margins. The markings on the inside of the pages represent the *gutter*. When you use a gutter value, reports that you will bound or present with a cover can be formatted appropriately.

The Paper Size tab lets you define the size of paper used when printing. Because the margin settings are relative to the paper size, you need to be accurate in describing the paper size measurements. Several default sizes are already defined. One consideration here is to remember that this is the size of paper that you will be printing to. In other words, suppose that you were creating a fax. You would want to make sure that the paper size matched the options available for the receiving fax.

The next tab is Paper Source, which you'll use mainly if you have a printer with multiple trays. Even in that case, you'll generally set this option once and leave it. This tab also lets you specify a separate tray for the first page. Usually this is for using stationery for the first page and bond paper for the rest.

The Layout tab gives you additional options for applying the setup. When you click the Layout tab, you can set options for sections and vertical alignment, as shown in Figure 9.7. This option is most often used to allow special header and footer setups. You can have different headers and footers for odd and even pages (such as in a book where the section title is on one side and the chapter title is on the other), or you can set up a different header and footer for the first page of the document.

FIGURE 9.7.

The Layout tab of the Page Setup dialog box.

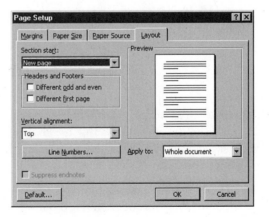

9

DOCUMENT CONCEPTS

The Layout tab's Line Numbers button works great if you have a document in which the line being referenced is important (as with certain legal documents, for example) or if you need to track absolute position in a file. You could also use it for programming, although that would be a rather difficult way to achieve the effect. One other use for this option is if you wanted to create a numbered list of items, particularly a long list.

Headers and Footers

Headers and footers are used to present information such as the date and page number at the top (header) or bottom (footer) of each page. Word even gives you the flexibility to not put everything on every page.

Interestingly, the command for working with headers and footers is on the View menu. Selecting View | Header and Footer brings up the screen shown in Figure 9.8, which is the document in page layout view with the Header and Footer toolbar.

FIGURE 9.8.

The Header and Footer toolbar in Word.

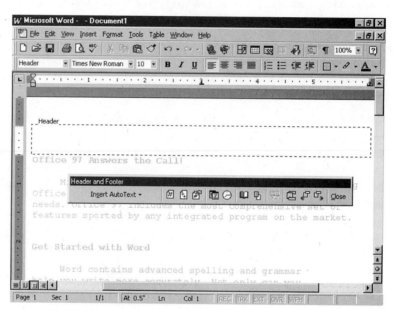

The text for the page you're working with turns gray to indicate that it can't be edited while you're working with a header or footer. Within the Header box that is displayed, you can type in text that you want to display, add graphics, or include fields that automatically add the date or page number. The same is true of the Footer box.

On the Header and Footer toolbar, you'll find a button for switching between the Header and Footer boxes. The Show Previous and Show Next buttons let you move between headers and footers if you have multiple headers or footers for different sections of your document.

The Page Number button has a page with a pound sign (#) on it. This button adds a field reflecting the current page number and places it at the point in the header or footer where the cursor is. Likewise, the Date and Time buttons insert the current date and time in a header or footer.

TIP: ALWAYS PRINT THE DATE AND TIME

Get in the habit of printing the date and time in headers or footers for reports. Later, you'll be able to tell when you printed the report.

The Show/Hide Document Text button can make it a little easier to tell what's part of the header or footer and what isn't.

Click the Close button to return to the view you used before adjusting the header and footer. The Close button makes the text in the main document editable and hides the header and footer.

NOTE: THE INSERT AUTOTEXT BUTTON

The Insert AutoText button displays a drop-down list box that you can use to insert several common editing elements into your header or footer, such as the filename or the name of the person who created the file.

Borders and Shading

A pair of features that can help you emphasize a section of your document are Borders and Shading. These effects can help set off a paragraph or picture.

As with so many features in Word, there are two different ways to bring up Borders and Shading. The first is to click the Tables and Borders toolbar button (the button with a picture of a box with lines and a pencil). This action displays the floating Tables and Borders toolbar, shown in Figure 9.9. As with the Fonts dialog box, using this toolbar is most useful when you already know how to use it and how it will change the appearance of your text.

FIGURE 9.9.

The Tables and Borders toolbar enabled in Word.

Even though this is called the Tables and Borders toolbar, the list box at the right end of the toolbar lets you set shading color preferences. If you haven't used these effects much, you'll probably prefer to start with the menu-based version of these commands by selecting Format | Borders and Shading. This brings up the Borders and Shading dialog box, shown in Figure 9.10, with the Borders tab selected.

You see an example of your screen so that you can get a feel for how your various choices will actually look once they're applied. To see how your changes will affect your document, select one of the dialog box's options and change it to see the result in the preview area. You can also select the thickness of the line used to create the border, as well as line and color options. Use the Page Border tab to add a border to the page. The Shading tab, shown in Figure 9.11, gives you a number of options and a preview of what the end result will look like.

FIGURE 9.10.

The Borders tab of the Borders and Shading dialog box.

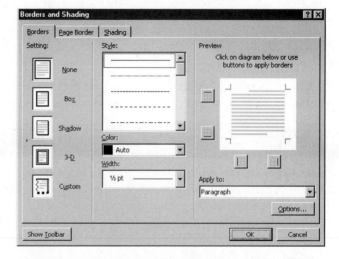

FIGURE 9.11.

The Shading tab of the Borders and Shading dialog box.

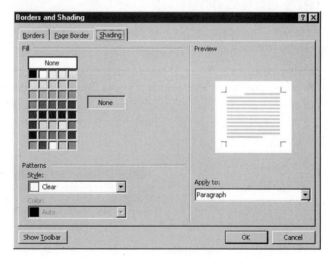

As you can tell by looking at these tabs, there are a number of different options for combining borders and shading to bring out the area you want to show off. One combination is shown in Figure 9.12. The selected paragraph has a 1½-point border with a Shadow preset and a custom shading of 25 percent. Compared to the rest of the text on the page, this paragraph really stands out, and it's still pretty easy to read. In addition, this paragraph should still be legible when printed. You shouldn't make boxes much darker than this unless you change the text color to a color like white. You can do this by clicking the Highlight and Font Color toolbar. Your results when changing these options can be pretty wild, so make sure you have enough time set aside to come up with an attractive result.

FIGURE 9.12.

The end result of using borders and shading on a section of text.

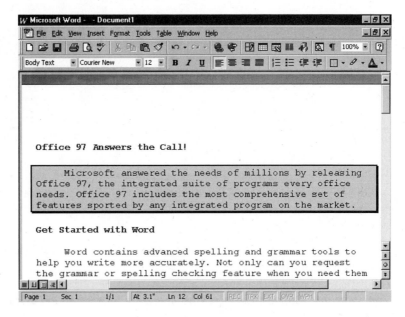

As with any effect, the trick to making it work well in your documents is to use it sparingly. Using this effect to emphasize pictures or sections of text more than once on a page is likely to make these items not stand out much at all.

Columns

Most newspapers, newsletters, and magazines use more than one column of text on a page. Or perhaps you have a large document and you want to break the text into columns to make it easier to read. You can use Word to create columns in a couple of ways.

One way is to use the Newsletter Wizard. Even if you don't want to create a newsletter, you can set up your document with it and then delete the first page that has the logo.

If you want a little more control over the formatting of columns, or if you need some additional effects, select Format | Columns. You'll see the dialog box shown in Figure 9.13, where you can set up a number of different column options.

You'll see five windows along the top. The first three let you choose a simple column setup with one, two, or three even columns. The next two windows let you specify an uneven setup, either to the left or to the right. If you select one of these two options, you can change the number of columns with the Number of columns field.

FIGURE 9.13.

*The Columns dialog
box.*

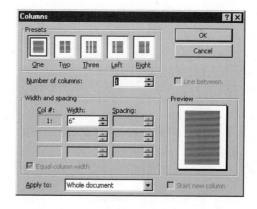

FIGURE 9.13.

*The Columns dialog
box.*

Further down the page is the Width and spacing section, where you can set up each of the columns if you need that level of control (for example, if you want a small central column and two larger columns on each side). Generally, you'll just leave the Equal column width check box selected.

You can choose to apply these changes to either the whole document or from this point on. The Line between check box draws a line between the columns. At the bottom is the Start new column check box, which is used to move text after the current cursor point to the next column (note that you must also select the This point forward option in the Apply to list).

Tables

One of the most common ways of handling data is to make a list. But when a list starts including three or four details for each item, it can quickly get unwieldy. At that point, creating a table to handle your information makes more sense.

The easiest way to add a table is to select Table | Insert Table. You see the Insert Table dialog box, shown in Figure 9.14, where you can define a simple table or use AutoFormat to make your table a little more complex.

FIGURE 9.14.

*The Insert Table
dialog box.*

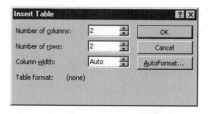

Unless your table is really simple, you'll probably want to select the Draw Table tool on the Tables and Borders toolbar to create a table. The Draw Table tool works just as if you drew a table with a pencil. When you click the Draw Table tool, the mouse pointer changes to a pencil.

Draw your table's rows and columns. Word helps you so that your columns and rows are even and align with each other. Figure 9.15 shows a fairly complex table being drawn with Draw Table.

FIGURE 9.15.

The Draw Table tool makes complex tables a snap.

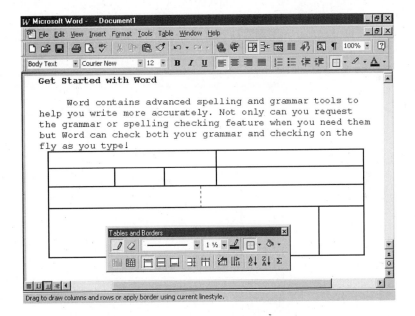

Once you've drawn your table, use AutoFormat to apply one of the standard table styles. Click anywhere within the table you've drawn, and then click the AutoFormat button on the AutoFormat Tables and Borders toolbar. You will see a Table AutoFormat dialog box similar to the one shown in Figure 9.16, with a long list of options for formatting your table. When you consider the various options, try to keep in mind how the table will look on-screen as well as how it will look when you print it. This AutoFormat screen is basically the same as the one that is loaded if you don't use the Table Wizard.

FIGURE 9.16.

The AutoFormat screen for Word tables.

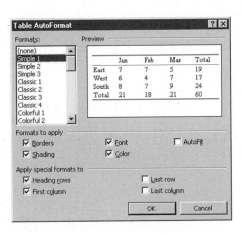

9

DOCUMENT CONCEPTS

Figure 9.17 shows the end result of all the work you might go through to generate a nice table that has subdivisions for Quarter and Month and five rows (one for each division). To enter data into the table, click the cell you want to put a value in and then use the Tab key to move to the next cell. When you've filled a row, press the Tab key again to go to the next row.

FIGURE 9.17.

The final product: a quarterly/monthly table.

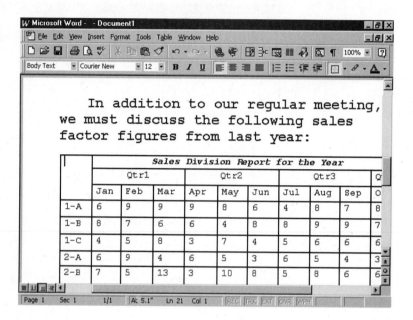

If you don't like how your table looks, simply click somewhere inside the table and select Table | Table AutoFormat and try one of the other selections. If you already have some text that you think will make a good table (for example, a list of items that are separated with tabs), you can select Table | Convert Text To Table to make a table out of the existing text. You get a certain amount of control over how the columns and rows are determined. Notice how AutoFormat cleaned up the preceding table (see Figure 9.18).

You can use the Borders and Shading options discussed earlier to make your tables easier to read. Select the part of the table you want to change, and then select Format | Borders and Shading to add emphasis to your table.

One other way to add a quick table is to click the Insert Table button on the Standard toolbar (it has a little table icon right next to a similar icon with the Excel logo). This brings up an empty group of boxes. Selecting the number of rows and columns you need (Figure 9.19 has 11 rows and 6 columns) designs the subsequent table that Word places in your document when you release the mouse button. Once you place the rows and columns, the rest of the table's formatting is up to you or AutoFormat.

Figure 9.18.

AutoFormat makes a table look good.

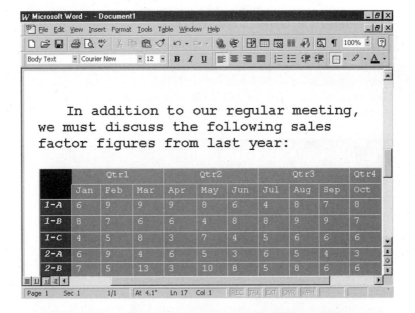

Figure 9.19.

The Insert Table button and a partially selected chart.

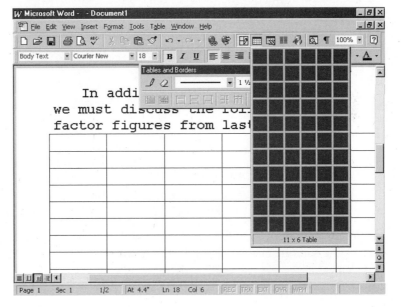

Footnotes and Endnotes

If you're familiar with scientific texts, or if you had to write a thesis when you were in school, you're familiar with using footnotes and endnotes. The idea is that you mark a location in the document with an indicator, and then later in the document you explain what the mark meant. Footnotes are printed at the end of the page, whereas endnotes are printed at the end of the document.

CAUTION: FOOTNOTES VERSUS FOOTERS

Don't confuse the terms *footnote* and *footer*. A footer appears at the bottom of each page, whereas a footnote appears at the bottom of a single page.

Adding footnotes and endnotes is relatively easy. Begin by moving to the point in your document where you want to indicate the footnote or endnote. Then select Insert | Footnote for either type of note. The Footnote and Endnote dialog box, shown in Figure 9.20, appears. Here you can select a footnote or endnote, as well as what type of indicator you want to use in the text. Note that you can also use a custom symbol if you prefer.

FIGURE 9.20.

The Footnote and Endnote dialog box.

Once you've made your decision, you'll see a marker placed in your text. The footnote appears at the bottom of the page, where you can type in the information, as shown in Figure 9.21.

The information you enter here is tied to the marker in your text. When your document is printed, the notes are numbered (if you chose that option) and printed at the end of the page or document.

FIGURE 9.21.

The footnote entry screen.

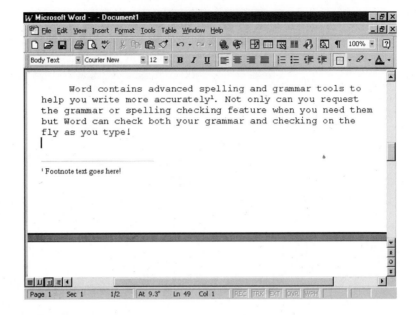

FIGURE 9.21.

The footnote entry screen.

Comments and Revisions

If you're working on documents with other people, you'll want some way for them to make comments or changes without losing your original work. Using comments and revisions are the two methods for doing this.

Comments can be thought of as electronic Post-it notes. They are kept as separate notes that you can view. To include a comment, click the place in the text where you want to make the comment. Then select Insert | Comment. Word displays a yellow comment marker in the text, and an editing area for the comment appears, as shown in Figure 9.22. This figure also shows you how to indicate who made the comment; the comment tag contains the author's initials from the File | Properties page. You can view comments by either double-clicking the comment marker or by selecting View | Comments.

One other thing you might notice on the comment screen is the little cassette tape icon. You can click this icon to record a voice comment if you have a microphone.

FIGURE 9.22.

The comment entry screen with a tag marking the initials of the person who made the comment.

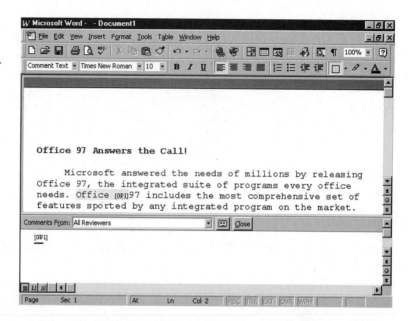

FIGURE 9.22.

The comment entry screen with a tag marking the initials of the person who made the comment.

NOTE: COMMENTS ARE NEW TO WORD 97

Comments replace annotations, found in previous versions of Word.

Once you add a comment (or multiple comments) to text, Word marks the text at the comment's location with a dim yellow highlight to indicate that a comment exists. Right-click the highlight to read, edit, or remove the comment. The comment window will then once again open at the bottom of Word's document window.

Revisions are designed to allow users to make somewhat more forceful suggestions. By turning them on, another person can actually make changes to the document. Then the original author or a third party can choose to accept the changes or return to the original version.

To turn on revisions, select Tools | Track Changes | Highlight Changes. You see the Highlight Changes dialog box, shown in Figure 9.23.

FIGURE 9.23.

The revisions setup.

From here, you can choose several options to affect how revisions are shown. The revisions that you request will appear in a different color through the Word document that the editor works on. In addition to controlling the highlighting, the Track Changes submenu also lets you select Compare Versions, which lets you compare an open document with another file. The Accept or Reject Changes option lets you incorporate revisions or remove revisions and retain the original text.

Summary

In this chapter, you learned the basics of working with Word and Word documents. You should now feel more comfortable with creating documents, making simple formatting changes, and adding special touches such as borders, shading, and tables.

Here are some chapters with related information:

- See Chapter 3, "Day-to-Day Office Basics," to learn about a few basic editing, formatting, and document chores.
- I covered Office printing in Chapter 4, "Printing Options and Techniques."
- To learn how to use OfficeArt to add images and drawings to your Word documents, see Chapter 5, "Using the OfficeArt Tools."
- I showed you how to customize Word's toolbars and menus in Chapter 8, "Customizing the Office Menus and Toolbars."
- In Chapter 10, "Document Patterns and Presentations," you'll learn about the templates (and some of the associated wizards) you can use to create various types of documents in Word, as well as how to use different views to see your document in different ways.
- See Chapter 11, "Word Assistance," to learn more about bookmarks, AutoText, and AutoCorrect.
- I'll show you how to construct forms in Word in Chapter 12, "Building Word Forms."
- Chapter 13, "Word as a Publisher," is home to topics such as managing document layout, tips for business and personal publications, and Mail Merge.
- I cover Word's Options dialog box as well as its keyboard customization techniques in Chapter 14, "Customizing Word."

Document Patterns and Presentations

CHAPTER 10

> *Man is eminently a storyteller. His search for a purpose, a cause, an ideal, a mission and the like is largely a search for a plot and a pattern in the development of his life story.*
>
> — *Eric Hoffer*

Having looked at the basics of creating a word processing document in Chapter 9, "Document Concepts," we'll now look at some of the tools available in Word for creating more complex documents. This includes using templates (as well as the associated wizards for some of them), using the various views in Word to see different things in a document, and other useful tips.

Templates and Wizards

Templates and wizards help you format your documents. Rather than having to face a blank screen and make all the formatting decisions for a document, you can start a new document based on a template or follow the steps of a wizard to start a document with some of your own information or characteristics already filled in.

A template is a special kind of Word document that has various styles, formats, and preferences set; generally, templates have a .DOT extension. When you create a new document based on a template, the new document has all the styles and formats of the template; you don't have to reestablish them on your own. Unless you specify otherwise, new documents use the template NORMAL.DOT, where you can set the styles, formats, and preferences you want for your standard work.

A wizard takes things several steps beyond a template. A wizard walks you through the creation of a particular type of document, stopping to let you enter information or make choices about the document's style or layout. When you've finished with all the steps of a wizard, Word creates the document based on the wizard's template and the information and choices you entered.

So where do you find templates and wizards? You can either select Start a New Document from the shortcut bar, select File | New, or press Ctrl-N. The New dialog box, shown in Figure 10.1, opens with a series of tabs to choose from. These tabs contain templates and wizards, arranged by the type of document. Select a tab and then double-click a template or wizard icon, and you're on your way. Click a template icon for a preview of the formatting of the selected document.

NOTE: NEW DOCUMENT SHORTCUTS USE NORMAL.DOT

Pressing the New button on the Standard toolbar or pressing Ctrl-N opens a new document based on the NORMAL.DOT template. You don't get a chance to select a different template.

FIGURE 10.1.
*The New dia-
log box.*

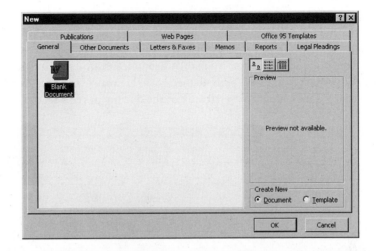

TIP: TEMPLATE "FLAVORS"

Many of Word's document templates come in three "flavors": contemporary, elegant, and professional. By consistently choosing one of these styles, you can maintain that look throughout your work.

Let's compare documents created using a template and those created using a wizard. We'll start a résumé using both of these methods.

A Template-Based Document

To begin a template-based résumé, select File | New. From the New dialog box, select the Other Documents tab. We'll select Elegant Resume.dot as the template for our résumé. Double-click the elegant résumé template to create the new document.

NOTE: IF YOU DON'T SEE EXTENSIONS

If you've left Windows 95's default "extension hiding" on, you won't see the .dot extensions for templates. To see the extensions, launch Windows Explorer, select View | Options, activate the Show all files option, and click OK.

10

That's it. You've started a résumé based on Word's elegant résumé template (see Figure 10.2). As you can see, you're still in for a bit of work. Unless you're Rich Andrews from Southridge, SC, and have that set of work experience, you'll need to do a lot of work to change the résumé. However, all the formatting is there: When you substitute your name for Rich's, your name will be in that typeface, properly aligned with the work experience. Substitute your work experience for Rich's, and the overall look of the document remains the same.

FIGURE 10.2.

A résumé document based on a template.

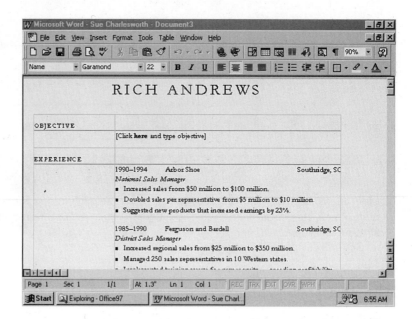

Word does give you a little more help with templates by providing places to personalize, as well as a variety of tips and cues. In the résumé, for instance, under Objective, Word has placed the instruction [Click **here** and type objective]. When you click that area, Word selects the area, and your typing overwrites the instruction.

A Wizard-Based Document

Now we'll look at creating a résumé with a wizard. Select File | New, select the Other Documents tab, and double-click Resume Wizard.wiz. The Résumé Wizard, shown in Figure 10.3, opens. To progress through the wizard, follow the instructions and click the Next > button to move on to the next part.

NOTE: WIZARD EXTENSIONS

Again, if you've left Windows 95's default "extension hiding" on, you won't see .wiz extensions either.

FIGURE 10.3.

The Résumé Wizard.

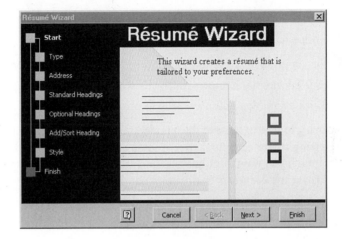

As you move through the wizard, you make a number of choices and fill in some information about yourself:

You determine what type of résumé you want to create.

You supply your name, address, and phone number.

You select what standard headings you want on your résumé.

You add other headings you want.

You change the order of the headings.

You choose from the professional, contemporary, or elegant styles.

When you're done, click the Finish button. Word then creates the résumé shell you specified.

You've still got work to do on your résumé, but you're further along than you were using only the template. In particular, now you have your own personal information and headings that are specific to your experience.

When Should You Use Templates Versus Wizards?

So when would you use a template as compared to a wizard? You should consider using a wizard when

- you have little idea of how to put a particular type of document together
- you want a quick start with a document
- your information fits easily into Word's document format

On the other hand, you should consider using a template when

- you simply want a framework to work in while formatting your document
- your information requires much customization
- your information doesn't readily fit into Word's document format

After having looked at some of the templates available in Word, you might decide you want to create a template for a memo, letter, or some other commonly used document. This is particularly helpful if you want your business documents to have a consistent look. Using a template ensures that each document maintains a consistent style.

A template can contain anything that a document can. Therefore, if you want to use a graphic as a letterhead, you can store it with the template. Any macros you create can also be stored.

The two most common ways to create a template involve building off an existing document. The first way is to load an existing template, make your changes, and save it under a different name. The second way is to set up a document the way you want it to look. After selecting File | Save As, change the Save As type to Document Template. By convention, the file extension should be .DOT to indicate that this is a template. If you want the template to be available from the File | New option or from the shortcut bar, you need to make sure that it is saved in the \Program Files\Microsoft Office\Templates directory in the appropriate folder (such as Letters & Faxes if it's a letter template).

You can create your own wizards if you want to (but this requires some heavy-duty macro writing). As with templates, your best bet is to find a wizard that is close to what you want, edit it to do what you need it to do, and then save it under a new name. The .WIZ extension is traditionally used to indicate a wizard. If you pull up a wizard, you'll notice that many of them are essentially blank documents with a number of macros, two of which (AutoNew and StartWizard) identify a normal wizard. AutoNew is defined to always be the starting macro when you create a new document from a template. You can learn more about macros in Chapter 11, "Word Assistance."

Views

As you might have noticed with both templates and wizards, your document is opened in Page Layout view. This is one of the four standard views you can work in with your Word documents. To switch between the views, you can either click one of the four buttons at the bottom-left of your document (just above the status bar, which shows the page number), or you can use the View menu to choose the appropriate view, as shown in Figure 10.4.

FIGURE 10.4.

The View menu.

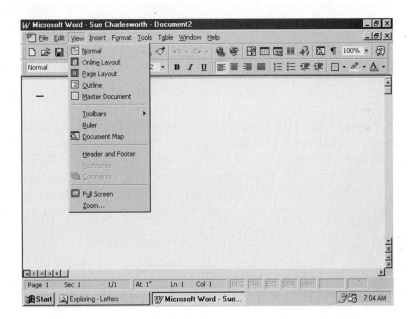

Which view is best depends on what you're doing. Normal view is designed for general-purpose typing, editing, formatting, and moving text around. It gives you a basic feel for the text and elements in your document without trying to provide exact WYSIWYG (What You See Is What You Get) capabilities.

Online Layout view caters to Office 97's ties to the Internet. When you select Online Layout view, Word wraps text to fit the window rather than the printed page. Text is larger, any document background you have selected appears more clearly than in Normal view, and Word opens the Document Map (discussed in just a moment).

Page Layout view tries to achieve WYSIWYG (although it isn't as accurate as Print Preview) by showing how elements such as graphics will be positioned on the printed page.

To easily scroll through a long document, move text around, or see a document's structure, you'll want to use Outline view.

10

DOCUMENT PATTERNS AND PRESENTATIONS

In addition to these standard views, there are three other views you might want to use. If you want to divide a long document into separate files (for example, dividing a book into several chapters), you should use Master Document view.

The Document Map view opens a window to the left of your screen. This window contains an outline of the headings in your document. Clicking one of the headings causes you to "jump" to that location in your document.

> **TIP: DOCUMENT MAP MIGHT BE BETTER**
>
> For scrolling through a long document or checking out a document's structure, try using the Document Map rather than Outline view. If you need to rearrange text or see the text that accompanies headings, use Outline view.

Last, but not least, if you want to see your document on-screen without rulers, toolbars, or other screen elements, choose Full Screen view. You can edit your document in this view. In addition, you have access to all keyboard shortcuts. If you move the pointer to the top of the screen, the normal Word menu appears. Select View and one of the views to restore the toolbars and other screen elements. Alternatively, click the Close Full Screen tool on the small, floating Full Screen toolbar to restore the screen.

Styles

If you've ever worked for a large company, you probably received a new-employee packet on your first day. It probably contained an employee manual, some information on benefits, security information for logging onto the LAN, and other frequently asked questions. Now, imagine that every time someone started working at this large company, someone had to go to several buildings to get the various packets.

The idea behind a style in Word is that if you use a particular format often, you shouldn't have to go through the hassle of defining it every time. Like the new-employee packet, it stores all the various parts that make up the logical whole as one definition.

Like most features in Word, a style can be defined in several ways. One of these ways is to select Format | Style, which brings up the dialog box shown in Figure 10.5. It lets you work with current styles or define new ones.

Clicking the New button takes you to the dialog box shown in Figure 10.6, where you can set the various options that go into a style definition. Notice all the different settings you have access to within a style. Also, note that a new style can be based on an old one.

FIGURE 10.5.

The Style dialog box.

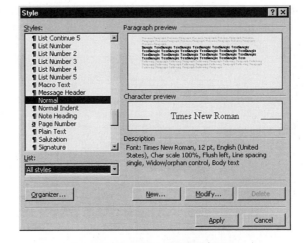

FIGURE 10.6.

The New Style dialog box.

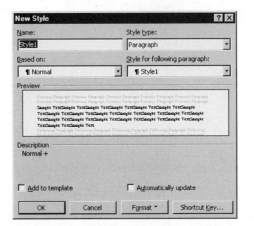

TIP: ADD THE NEW STYLE TO THE TEMPLATE

If you want to add a new style to your template, be sure to enable Add to template. Otherwise, the style will apply only to the current document.

An easier way to define a style is to take a section of text that is already defined the way you want for your style. Select the section of text and then click inside the Style box (located on the far left of the Formatting toolbar, to the left of the Font list). Type the name you want to use for this new style and press Enter. If that name is already being used, you'll get a warning. Otherwise, your new style will become available in the current document and will be saved in NORMAL.DOT (the default template).

10

DOCUMENT
PATTERNS AND
PRESENTATIONS

If you want to see what styles are already available, select Format | Style Gallery. You see a screen like the one shown in Figure 10.7. It lets you preview the various styles available.

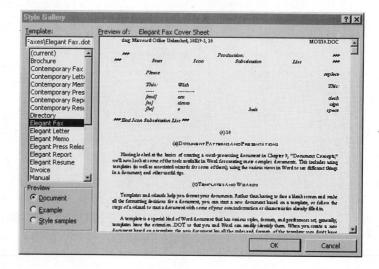

In this example, the Document option has been selected to show how it affects the current document. The Example and Style samples options use defined text to show off the various options for each style.

Text Boxes

Text boxes are new to Word 97, although they are strikingly similar to the frames of earlier versions of Word. Once you've created a text box, you can place text in the box and then move the box around your document, format the flow of the document around the box, and change the box's border and interior colors. The text stays safe inside the box while you move the box or change the rest of the document to fit around it.

To create a text box, select Insert | Text Box. The cursor changes to cross hairs. Click and drag to create a box of the desired size. Without further formatting, the new text box sits on top of the existing text, obscuring what's beneath it (see Figure 10.8). To put text into the box, type it directly into the box, paste a selection in, or insert a file.

NOTE: CONVERTING EXISTING TEXT TO A TEXT BOX

If you create a text box while you have some text selected, Word cuts the selection, creates the text box, and pastes the text in the box. Word places the text box at the left margin and wraps the document around the box.

Figure 10.8.

A new text box.

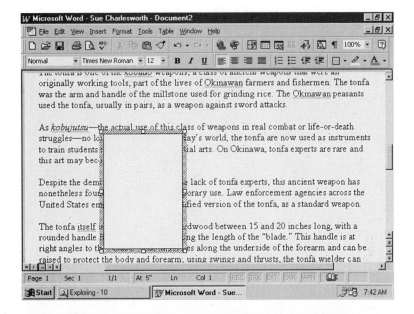

NOTE: VIEW CHANGES WHEN INSERTING TEXT BOXES

When you insert a text box, Word automatically switches to Page Layout view.

CAUTION: TEXT BOXES DON'T APPEAR IN NORMAL VIEW

If you change from Page Layout view to Normal view, your text boxes seem to disappear. Don't panic: Word hasn't eaten them; they just don't show up in Normal view. Switch back to Page Layout view, and your text boxes are right where you left them.

By default, Word places simple line borders around a text box. You have two ways to access text box formatting:

1. Hold the cursor on the border. When the cursor changes to a four-headed arrow, right-click and choose Format Text Box.

2. Click in the box and select Format | Text Box.

Use the various tabs of the Format Text Box dialog box, shown in Figure 10.9, to color and format the box's border and background, change the box's size, wrap document text around the box (see Figure 10.10), and position the box relative to page elements.

10

DOCUMENT PATTERNS AND PRESENTATIONS

FIGURE 10.9.

The Wrapping tab of the Format Text Box dialog box.

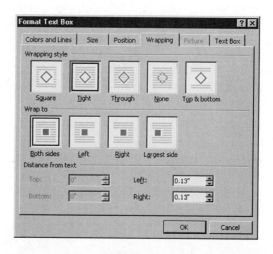

FIGURE 10.10.

A text box with the document wrapped around.

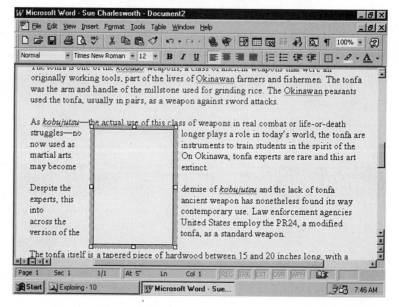

Another significant use of text boxes is to "flow" text from place to place in your document by linking text boxes. To flow text, create a text box and place your text in it. Create a second, empty text box. Click the first box. Open the Text Box toolbar (if it's not already open) by selecting View | Toolbars | Text Box. When the Text Box toolbar appears, click the Create Text Box Link icon. The cursor changes into a full, upright pitcher (see Figure 10.11), indicating that you're ready to "pour" (or flow) text into another text box.

NOTE: THE TEXT BOX TOOLBAR

The Text Box toolbar opens automatically when you insert a text box and stays open as long as a text box is active. However, if you click outside a text box, the toolbar goes away.

FIGURE 10.11.

Ready to flow text for linked text boxes.

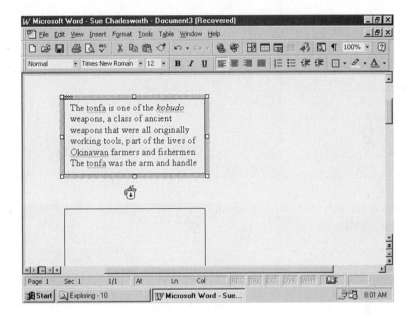

Move the cursor into the second box. It changes into a pitcher that pours letters into the box, as shown in Figure 10.12. Click in the second text box. Whatever text didn't fit within the border of the first text box appears in the second, as shown in Figure 10.13. Your two text boxes are now linked. If you want another text box linked, simply create a third text box and link it to the second. You can create and link further boxes as desired.

If you want to unlink text boxes, thus putting your text in fewer boxes, click in what will be the last box in the chain, and then click the Break Forward Link tool on the Text Box toolbar.

You might be wondering why you should care about linked text boxes. If you've ever created a newsletter or some other kind of document where you wanted to put part of some text in one place and continue it in another, linked text boxes can come in handy. Using these chains of text, you can spread text across locations on multiple pages, and the text will adjust itself to fit the boxes.

10

DOCUMENT
PATTERNS AND
PRESENTATIONS

FIGURE 10.12.

"Pouring" text into the linked text box.

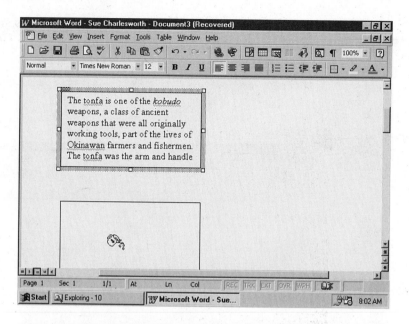

FIGURE 10.13.

The linked text boxes.

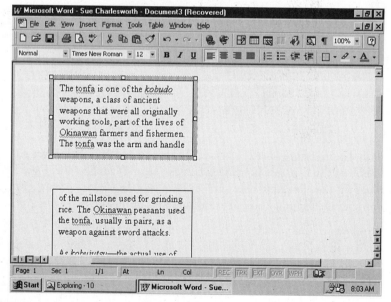

Print Preview

Particularly when you have a number of frames or other specially formatted objects in a document, it's important to select File | Print Preview or click the Print Preview button on the Standard toolbar to see exactly what the end result will be.

A file viewed using the Print Preview option will look something like Figure 10.14. Notice that the image of the page is scaled to fit into the space given. If you want to know how much the image was scaled, look at the toolbar above the image to see the scale list box (31% in this case).

FIGURE 10.14.

The Print Preview of a document.

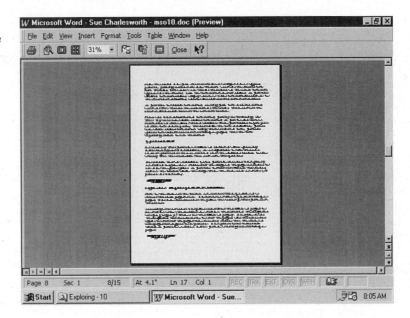

Next to the scale on the toolbar is a button with a picture of a screen that has four pages on it. This button is used to preview multiple pages, which you select from the panel that comes up when you click the button (see Figure 10.15).

Selecting a matrix from this panel determines the number of pages to be shown at once. The results are shown at the bottom of the requester as $n \times n$ Pages, where n is the number of pages. Figure 10.15 shows a 2×3 page preview. The Multiple Page selector is still active to show you the correlation between the two. Notice that the scale of each page has dropped to 15 percent. This option tends to be most useful if you have a similar format that you're checking across multiple pages.

TIP: USE PRINT PREVIEW TO CHECK PAGE ELEMENTS

Use Print Preview and Multiple Pages to check your page breaks and heading placement. You'll be able to easily see if you have only a line or two at the top or bottom of a page.

FIGURE 10.15.

Previewing multiple pages.

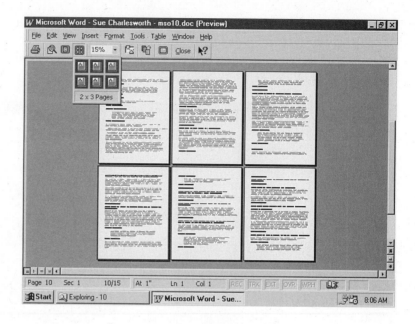

Another button on the toolbar you'll want to use is the one with a small computer screen on it (to the left of the Close button). This is the Full Screen button, and it gives you more screen space to display your image. When you click this button, the ratio jumps to 40 percent, which makes it a little easier to see how your text is affected by different options (in fact, the text is now almost large enough to read).

Just to the left of this button is the Shrink to Fit button. It alters your document to fit into a certain number of full pages, without leaving a partial page at the end. Therefore, instead of having eight full pages and just a couple of paragraphs on the ninth page, your document is changed to make everything fit on eight pages. The trick that Word uses is to scale your font by partial points (for example, it might change a 12-point font to an 11.5-point font). Depending on the document, this feature might work well, or it might really mess things up.

Even though your document looks a little different in Print Preview, it can still be edited in this mode. Of course, you'll have a hard time seeing what you're changing. Therefore, unless you're moving a graphic, you'll probably want to click the Close button to exit Print Preview and then edit from Normal view.

NOTE: ZOOMING IN ON THE PAGE

You can make the text size usable by clicking the magnifier button, choosing the region of text you want to view, and then clicking the magnifier button again. The text zooms to 100% and is quite readable. However, because you're in Print Preview, you don't have the same editing capabilities as you do in Normal view.

Lists

Another useful tool for setting up a document is to create a list using bullets or numbers. Particularly if you're running through a procedure or trying to emphasize the points you're making in a memo, creating a list will mark each point and make it stand out.

The quick way to create a bulleted list is to click the Bullet List button (the one with three squares in front of three lines) on the Formatting toolbar. Every time you press the Enter key, another bullet point is added. Turn bulleted lists off by clicking the Bullet List button again.

Similarly, creating a quick numbered list is a matter of clicking the Number List button (the one with the numbers 1, 2, and 3 in front of three lines). Every time you press the Enter key, another numbered point is added. As with bullets, you turn off the numbered list option by clicking the Number List button again.

As is the case with most things in Word, you can create bulleted and numbered lists using menu options. In this case, select Format | Bullets and Numbering. This brings up the screen shown in Figure 10.16, with the Bulleted tab enabled.

FIGURE 10.16.

The Bulleted tab of the Bullets and Numbering screen.

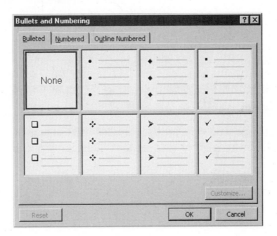

Looking at this screen, you notice that there are a number of different types of bullet symbols to choose from. If these symbols aren't what you want, select one of the bullets and then click the Customize button to bring up the dialog box shown in Figure 10.17. Choose one of the bullet characters (which, for some reason, aren't the same as the ones on the Bulleted tab) and then click the Bullet button to display the characters in the Symbol font (see Figure 10.18). Choose one of the characters to be your bullet, or drop down the Font box to change the display to another font. Click OK to close the Symbol dialog box. Word adds the bullet character you chose to the Bullet character line-up. Click OK to add that bullet to your text.

FIGURE 10.17.

The Customize Bulleted List dialog box.

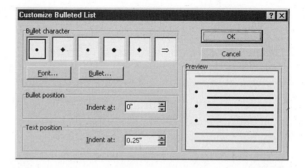

FIGURE 10.18.

Choosing different bullet fonts.

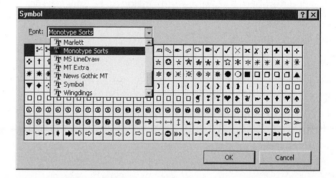

TIP: USE SYMBOLS AS BULLETS

Although you can use letters as bullets, the special symbol or dingbat fonts make the best—and the most fun—bullets. Look for Monotype Sorts, Wingdings, Zapf Dingbats, or similar fonts.

Besides customizing the bullet itself, you can customize the spacing of the bulleted list. In the Customize Bulleted List dialog box, you can specify how far from the margin Word should indent your bullets. You can also specify how far to indent the list text.

TIP: INDENT BULLETS

Use a combination of the bullet indent and a larger text indent to easily create a bulleted list that's indented from the left margin. (See Figure 10.19.)

FIGURE 10.19.

An indented bulleted list.

The Numbered tab, shown in Figure 10.20, is similar to the Bulleted tab. Note that the "numbers" include Roman numerals and alphabetic characters.

FIGURE 10.20.

The Numbered tab of the Bullets and Numbering dialog box.

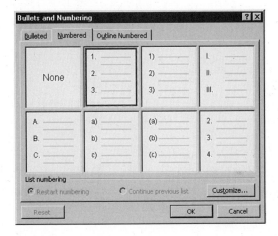

Because the numbered lists use letters and numbers, the modification is different as well. Figure 10.21 shows how numbered lists can be modified. You'll notice that you can define text that occurs before and after the number or letter for each point. So instead of having a list numbered with 1, 2, and 3, you could have a list with Point 1 and Point 2 or Step 1 and Step 2.

One other option on the Bullets and Numbering dialog box is the Outline Numbered tab, shown in Figure 10.22. It lets you create different outlined, numbered, and indented lists. In addition to the varied lists provided, you can customize a list.

10

DOCUMENT PATTERNS AND PRESENTATIONS

FIGURE 10.21.

The Customize Numbered List dialog box and the Font requester, used to change the font for characters or numbers.

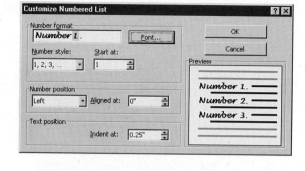

FIGURE 10.22.

The Outline Numbered tab of the Bullets and Numbering dialog box.

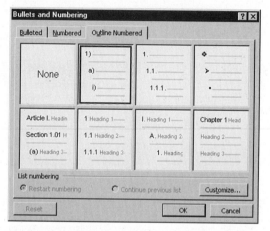

> **NOTE**
>
> Here's a nifty thing about Outline Numbered lists: Word has tied some of its predefined formats to heading styles, so using one of these Outline Numbered lists will automatically cause the various heading levels to be applied. Of course, you can turn off the linking or change the styles that the list links to.

Not only can you use these options to create lists from scratch, but you can also select a section of text to be converted to a list. Simply select the text and then choose one of the options from the toolbar or the Bullets and Numbering dialog box.

Figure 10.23 shows samples of the three kinds of lists. Notice the customizations for the bulleted list (the book symbols as bullets) and the numbered list ("Agenda item" appears before the number).

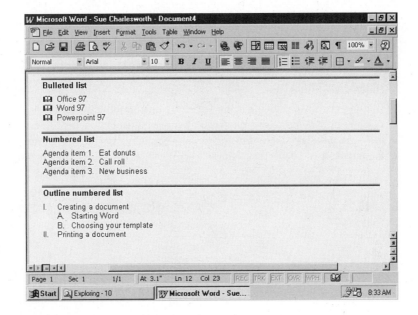

FIGURE 10.23.

Different sample lists.

Tables of Contents

Another type of specialized list is the table of contents for a report or publication. Word makes it easy to create one for your document by doing a scan for the styles you've specified for the headings. Word uses these styles to determine how things in your document relate to each other. You can use the default heading styles (Heading 1 through Heading 9), or you can specify your own heading styles.

To do this, in your document apply the desired heading styles to the headings in your table of contents. Then select the point in the document where you want to insert the table of contents. Select Insert | Index And Tables, and then choose the Table of Contents tab, shown in Figure 10.24.

FIGURE 10.24.

The Table of Contents tab.

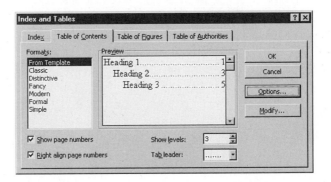

10

DOCUMENT PATTERNS AND PRESENTATIONS

Choose one of the available designs in the Formats list. You can see what it will look like in the Preview window.

> **NOTE**
>
> Clicking the Options button in the Table of Contents tab lets you define your table of contents from styles other than Word's headings (see Figure 10.25). Scroll up and down the Available styles list and assign table of contents (TOC) levels. When Word creates the table of contents, it will pick up your specified TOC levels rather than heading styles.

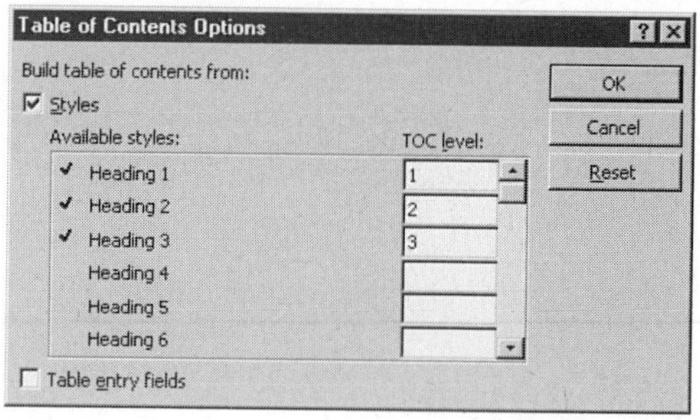

FIGURE 10.25.

Defining table of contents levels.

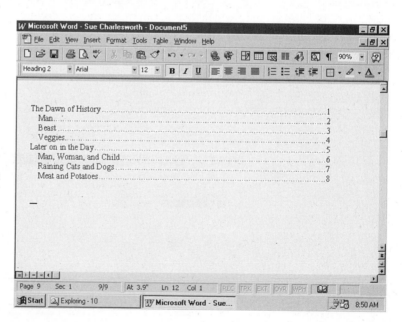

Figure 10.26 shows a simple table of contents.

FIGURE 10.26.

A simple table of contents.

Indexes

Related to the table of contents (and available from the same menu option) is the index. To create an index, you mark the words or phrases you want to include in the index. Using hidden text, Word marks this text as an index entry. When you instruct Word to construct your index, it finds all the index entries and their page numbers and creates a new index section in your document. Now for the specific how-tos.

Select Insert | Index and Tables. The Index and Tables dialog box, shown in Figure 10.27, appears. Select the Index tab and click the Mark Entry button. Word displays the Mark Index Entry dialog box, shown in Figure 10.28. In your document, select the word or phrase you want added to the index, and then click the Mark button. When you've marked all your index entries, click Cancel.

FIGURE 10.27.

The Index and Tables dialog box.

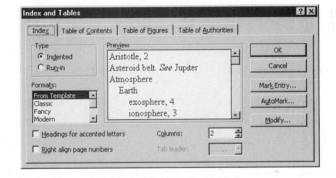

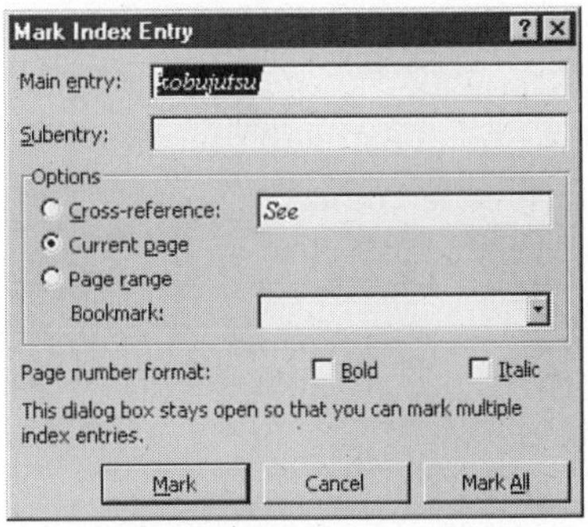

FIGURE 10.28.

The Mark Index Entry dialog box.

TIP: SELECT TEXT TO ENABLE THE MARK BUTTON

Unless you've selected some text before you access the Mark Index Entry dialog box, the Mark button will be inactive. If you select your index text after accessing the Mark Index Entry box, click the Mark button anyway. Word will mark your entry.

10

DOCUMENT
PATTERNS AND
PRESENTATIONS

Now Word can create the index. Position the insertion point where you want your index. Select Insert | Index and Tables, select the Index tab, and click OK. Word adds two continuous section breaks to your document and places the index between them, as shown in Figure 10.29.

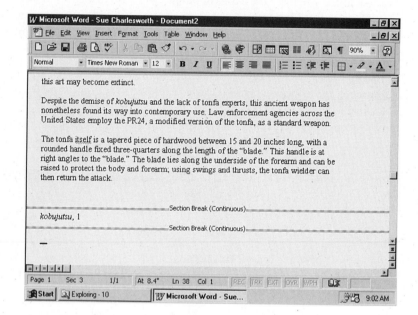

Outlines

Creating an outline using Outline view and setting various levels in your document can be considered an intermediary step between a multilevel list and a master document. You can create an outline of this form by using Outline view to bring up the Outline toolbar. Then you use the icons on the toolbar to set the level of the various items in your outline. Figure 10.30 shows a new document created using Outline view with the initial topic entered.

After adding the next line, select it and then set it to the appropriate style (in this case, Heading 2). You can also use the button that has an arrow pointing to the right to demote the item so that it's not the same level as the chapter title. When you add the next line, you can again assign it to a level (such as Heading 3) or demote it. In this particular case, because there will be no lower levels, the button with a picture of a double-headed arrow pointing right is used to make the item Body Text, which in this case means that it's at the bottom level.

Figure 10.31 shows all the levels expanded to reveal all the current contents of this outline.

By double-clicking the plus sign to the left of the topics that have them, you can collapse your outline. Therefore, if you have a number of items, you can keep them all collapsed except for the one you're currently using or examining.

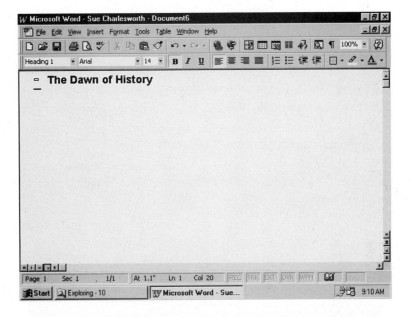

FIGURE 10.30.

Starting to build an outline.

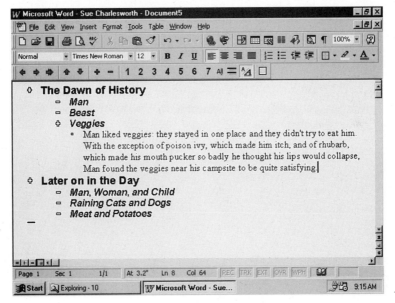

FIGURE 10.31.

An example of an outline in Outline view.

Summary

In this chapter you learned about a number of different techniques for changing how you look at and organize the information in your document. By using different views, you can look at

10

**DOCUMENT
PATTERNS AND
PRESENTATIONS**

an item in different ways, making the item easier to work with and making it easier to figure out how the item will print.

Here are a few related chapters to check out:

- To get more information on templates, see Chapter 3, "Day-to-Day Office Basics."
- For more on printing, see Chapter 4, "Printing Options and Techniques."
- I cover text boxes and other graphic objects in depth in Chapter 5, "Using the OfficeArt Tools."
- With the techniques covered in this chapter, you're ready to move on to Chapter 11, "Word Assistance," which covers additional techniques for working with your document.

Word Assistance

IN THIS CHAPTER

CHAPTER 11

There is never finality in the display terminal's screen, but an irresponsible whimsicality, as words, sentences, and paragraphs are negated at the touch of a key. The significance of the past, as expressed in the manuscript by a deleted word or an inserted correction, is annulled in idle gusts of electronic massacre.

—Alexander Cockburn

This chapter explores some tools that can help make working with Word a little easier.

Bookmarks

Have you ever wanted to mark a place in a document so you could find it easily? If you've ever marked places in your document with an odd string of characters such as @@@@@ and searched for that string (and had to remember to delete the string before finishing your document), or if you've simply used Page Up and Page Down to move from place to place in your document, bookmarks are for you.

Bookmarks, as the name implies, let you place markers in your document, making it easy to return to specific spots in your work. You can mark either a single spot or a block of text. To place a bookmark in your document, move the insertion point to the place where you'd like the bookmark, or select the text you want marked. Select Insert | Bookmark. In the Bookmark dialog box that appears (see Figure 11.1), give your bookmark a name and click Add.

FIGURE 11.1.

Adding a bookmark.

NOTE: WHAT I MEAN BY "TEXT"

When you see references to *text* in this chapter, this doesn't refer to text only. In these instances, consider *text* to mean any aspect of your document, including graphics and tables, or even a mix of document elements.

The Bookmark dialog box also lists all the bookmarks in your document and lets you change the order of the list, as shown in Figure 11.2. Word defaults to listing your bookmarks alphabetically. To see your bookmarks in the order in which they appear in your document, select Location as the Sort by condition.

To return to the spot or text marked by a bookmark, select Insert | Bookmark, select the bookmark name from the list, and click Go To.

FIGURE 11.2.

Sorting bookmarks by location.

TIP: USE BOOKMARKS TO SELECT TEXT FOR COPYING

When you go to a block of text, Word highlights the entire block. This technique can be handy if you know you'll want to repeatedly copy the same block of text and you're not sure it will be in the Clipboard for pasting. Highlight the text, create a bookmark, go to the marked section when you need it, and copy it.

Bookmarks are invisible in the printed document, but you might want to see their locations in your document. Select Tools | Options and select the View tab, shown in Figure 11.3. In the Show box, click Bookmarks. When Show Bookmarks is enabled, bookmarks of a single point appear as a heavy I-bar in your document (see Figure 11.4), and bookmarks of a block of text are marked by heavy square brackets. To disable the showing of bookmarks, select Tools | Options | View and disable the Bookmarks option.

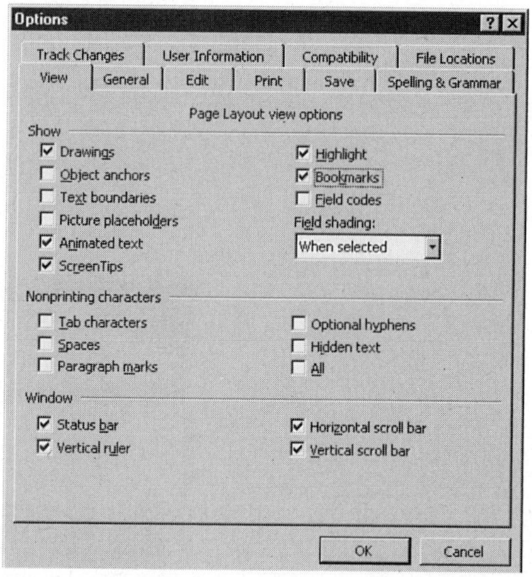

Figure 11.3.

Showing bookmarks.

Figure 11.4.

Bookmarks marked in text.

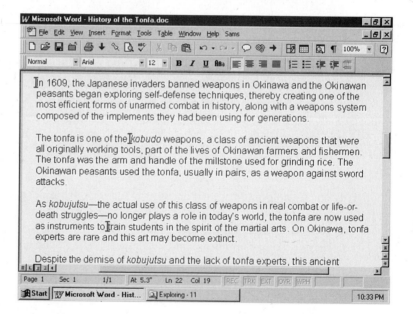

AutoText

Have you ever needed to add the same block of text to different documents? Are you tired of typing in the exact same stuff repeatedly (making the same mistakes each time)? If you've ever had to dig out an old copy of a document to verify some wording, or type something in for the umpteenth time, AutoText is for you.

Creating AutoText Entries

AutoText provides a way to store blocks of text or graphics, often called *boilerplate* material, and insert the stored blocks elsewhere in the same document or in other documents. To create an AutoText entry, highlight the block and select Insert | AutoText | New. In the Create AutoText dialog box, shown in Figure 11.5, give your AutoText a name (Word suggests a name by using the first bit of your text) and click OK.

FIGURE 11.5.
Creating AutoText.

True to form, Word gives you another way to create AutoText. Select Insert | AutoText | AutoText. The AutoCorrect dialog box, shown in Figure 11.6, appears, showing the AutoText tab. This more complete view of AutoText gives you a preview of your AutoText, as well as a list of all your AutoText entries. Again, Word names your entry based on the first bit of the text. Word places this suggestion in the Enter AutoText entries here field. Rename the AutoText if you'd like, and then click Add.

FIGURE 11.6.
The AutoText tab of the AutoCorrect dialog box.

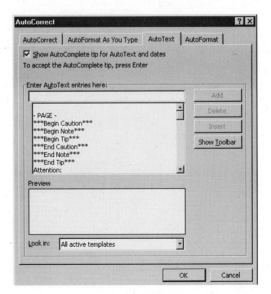

> **TIP: PRESERVE FORMATTING IN AUTOTEXT ENTRIES**
>
> If your AutoText entry has special formatting that you want to preserve, be sure to include the paragraph mark at the end of the text in your AutoText entry.

To change the contents of an AutoText entry, insert the entry into your document, make your changes, select the text, and re-add it as an AutoText entry. Select the entry's original name to save the changes.

Accessing AutoText Entries

Word 97 doesn't just let you add your own AutoText: It provides a whole bunch of AutoText entries commonly used in business and personal documents (for example, there's a letter salutation that says "Dear Mom and Dad"). To see a list of Word's AutoText categories, select Insert | AutoText, as shown in Figure 11.7. The menu items with arrows have further AutoText selections. AutoText entries that you have created also show up among these menu items.

FIGURE 11.7.

AutoText entries.

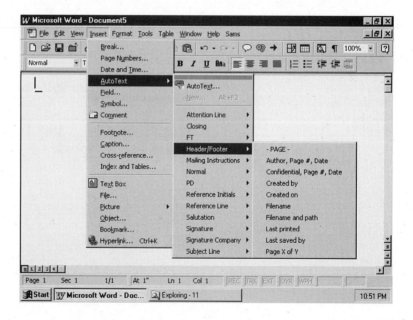

For further convenience, you can display the AutoText toolbar. Do any of the following:

- Select View | Toolbars | AutoText.
- Right-click any toolbar and then activate the AutoText command in the menu that appears.
- Click the Show Toolbar button in the AutoText tab of the AutoCorrect dialog box.

The AutoText toolbar, shown in Figure 11.8, provides easy access to the AutoText tab of the AutoCorrect dialog box and to a drop-down list of AutoText entries. It also helps you create new AutoText entries.

NOTE: VIEWING ENTRIES FOR ALL STYLES

In the list of AutoText entries that you see by selecting Insert | AutoText or by viewing the AutoText toolbar, Word displays only those entries that apply to the current style. To see the complete list, hold down Shift as you select Insert | AutoText, or Shift-click the toolbar. If the current style contains no AutoText entries specific to it, the full list displays.

FIGURE 11.8.
The AutoText toolbar.

The AutoText toolbar ——

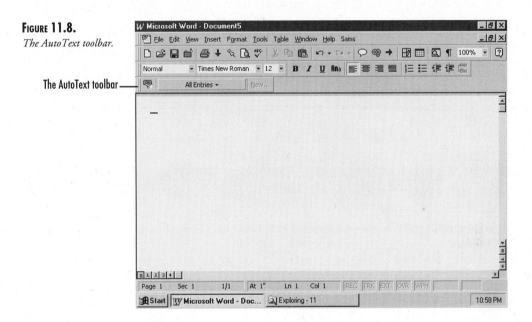

To place an AutoText entry—one of yours or one of Word's—into your document, follow one of these methods:

- Select Insert | AutoText, choose one of the categories from the list, and select one of the entries.

- Select Tools | AutoCorrect, then click the AutoText tab. Scroll through the list of AutoText entries, select an entry, and click OK. You can also get to this dialog box by clicking the AutoText tool on the AutoText toolbar.

- Click the Entries List tool on the AutoText toolbar, select one of the categories, and choose an entry.

Once you've selected a specific AutoText entry, Word adds it to your document at the insertion point.

We're not done yet. You still have two more ways to add AutoText to your document:

■ Use Word's AutoComplete feature. Once you (or Word) have added an AutoText entry, type the name of the AutoText entry in your document. When you've typed enough letters for Word to uniquely identify the AutoText name, a box with the complete entry appears above the insertion point. Press Enter to have Word Auto-Complete the entry.

■ Use F3 to substitute the AutoText entry for the AutoText name. As you type the name of the AutoText entry, Word displays a box with the complete entry. At this point, press F3 to substitute the AutoText entry for its name. If Word doesn't recognize the name and therefore doesn't display the pop-up box, you'll need to type in the complete AutoText name before pressing F3.

TIP: WATCH THE PREVIEW BOX

If you're not sure which AutoText entry you want, look in the Preview box of the AutoText tab (select Tools | AutoCorrect) to see a portion of the entry. Most of the Word-provided entries are self-explanatory, but if you've added some cryptically named entries, this method could help.

TIP: USE AUTOTEXT TO COPY TEXT

The "Bookmarks" section discussed how to use a bookmark to make it easy to repeatedly copy and paste a block of text. AutoText does the same thing: When you insert a block of AutoText, you don't lose your place in your document.

AutoText Examples

Let's look at some AutoText examples. A simple one is your company's address. If you type it in once and save it as AutoText, you'll never have to type it in again. What happens if you want the address to appear at the left margin sometimes and centered at the top of the page other times? Save the differently formatted addresses as separate AutoText entries, making sure to include the paragraph mark at the end of the text, and insert the appropriate address where needed.

As another example, say you put out your company's electronic newsletter. Rather than construct the heading each time you issue the newsletter, or copy and paste it from the last issue, or build a template for the newsletter, simply store the heading as an AutoText entry and insert it each time you create the newsletter. The AutoText in Figure 11.9 includes both text and a graphic.

Here's one final example: Each month you publish a summary of the company's sales by the type of product and region of the country. You build the table framework, including the format of particular cells, right-justify the numeric entries, and save it as an AutoText entry (see Figure 11.10). Each month you can insert the AutoText into your document and fill in the appropriate numbers.

FIGURE 11.9.

AutoText with a graphic.

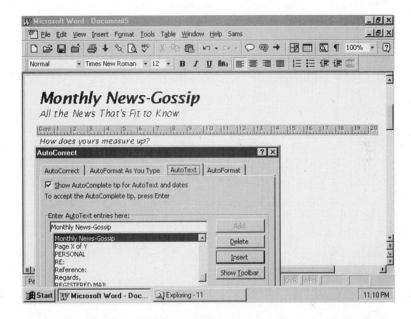

FIGURE 11.10.

An AutoText table.

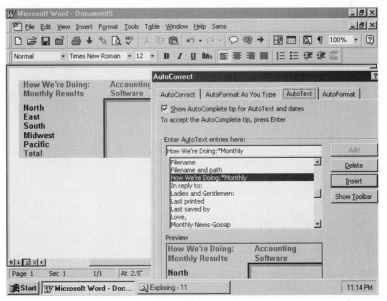

AutoCorrect

Are there words your fingers just won't type correctly? Do you leave the Shift key down just a little too long and type words beginning with two capital letters? Have you ever left that blasted Caps Lock on and had to go back and retype something, or play with changing the case to get everything the way it should be? If so, AutoCorrect is for you.

Select Tools | AutoCorrect to display the AutoCorrect dialog box, shown in Figure 11.11. The AutoCorrect tab lets you choose from a series of common typing corrections (including recovering from Caps Lock) and shortcuts. In addition to these corrections, you can also specify if you want AutoCorrect to replace text as you type.

FIGURE 11.11.

The AutoCorrect dialog box.

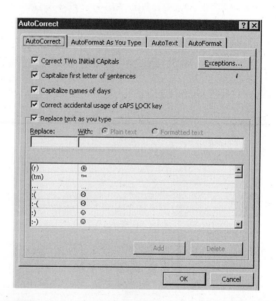

NOTE: AUTOCORRECT FIXES CAPS LOCK ERRORS

In a thoroughly intelligent move, AutoCorrect not only fixes Caps Lock text, but also turns Caps Lock off. Don't worry; Word won't fix words or phrases you want to be in all caps. It only fixes those cases where you start a sentence with a lowercase letter and continue with uppercase letters.

In addition to correcting common typing errors such as typing teh instead of the, AutoCorrect also corrects spelling errors such as *thier* and *recieve*. If your personal bugaboos aren't included in the list Word provides, you can add them. Enter your incorrect way of doing things in the Replace field and the correct way in the With field, as shown in Figure 11.12. Click Add if you want to keep the AutoCorrect dialog box open for further entries or OK if you want to close AutoCorrect and continue with your document. Then, the next time you type one of the Replace entries, AutoCorrect replaces it with the With entry.

FIGURE 11.12.

Adding an Auto-Correct entry.

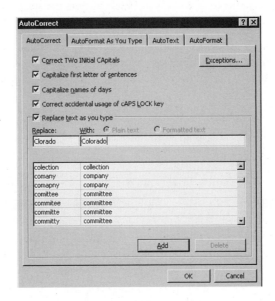

If you don't want to type the entry into the With field, select the text in your document and open AutoCorrect. The text appears in the With field, leaving you to enter the incorrect spelling in the Replace field.

NOTE: MOVE BEYOND THE ENTRY TO REPLACE IT

AutoCorrect doesn't replace text until you continue beyond the Replace entry. Once you type a space or a punctuation mark, AutoCorrect goes to work.

Don't be fooled by AutoCorrect's name: It goes far beyond a simple correction mechanism. Did you notice that the With field in the AutoCorrect dialog box is significantly longer than the Replace field? That's so that you can replace abbreviations with spelled-out text. Instead of typing out a company name each time you reference it (and Amalgamated Architectural Additions does get tiring, doesn't it?), you could create an AutoCorrect entry that would replace `aaa` with `Amalgamated Architectural Additions`. Then, instead of typing you-know-what, you could just type `aaa`.

You can include symbols or graphics in an AutoCorrect entry. To do so, select the symbol or graphic and any other text you want to accompany it. In the AutoCorrect dialog box, Word places your selection in the With field. Add your shortcut text in the Replace field, and you're done.

AutoCorrect also includes some nifty formatting changes. Instead of the clunky-looking fraction 1/2, AutoCorrect substitutes the typographically pleasing ½. 1st becomes 1st and 3rd becomes 3rd. The em dash is much simplified: If you type two hyphens, Word automatically substitutes an em dash when you begin to type the next word. Simple arrows (-->) become arrow symbols. Keyboard "smileys" (:)) become true smiley faces.

If you want AutoCorrect to stop correcting any of the checked items in the AutoCorrect dialog box, simply uncheck that feature. If you want to stop correcting one of your shortcuts or replacements (or one of Word's), go into the AutoCorrect dialog box, select the item in the Replace list, and click Delete.

The "AutoText" section discussed storing a newsletter heading as an AutoText entry. You can also store the heading as an AutoCorrect entry, replacing something like mng with the heading, as shown in Figure 11.13. As with text-only entries, select the text and the graphic to store the new, AutoCorrect entry.

FIGURE 11.13.

AutoCorrect with a graphic.

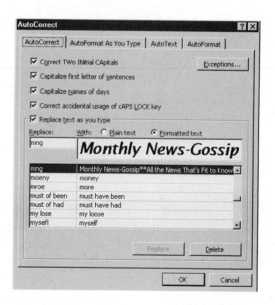

How about replacing your initials with your full name? That could be handy if you type a lot of letters. You also could create an AutoCorrect entry for your address—or anyone else's.

In creating this chapter (and others in this book), I employed a number of AutoCorrect abbreviations. For instance, instead of typing AutoText and AutoCorrect, I used att and ac as their respective AutoCorrect entries. For PowerPoint (I hate typing capital letters in the middle of words), I substituted ppt.

NOTE: AVOIDING THE REPLACEMENT

To intentionally use AutoCorrect the wrong way or to type the code letters without replacement takes some doing. You have a number of options. You have to carefully type the code letters in your document, without putting a space or punctuation after them. You could delete some already-entered text and replace it with your AutoCorrect code. Another option is to press Alt-Backspace until your original text reappears.

I have my favorite mistypings, too. For some reason, I have a terrible time with words that end in "ation"—they come out as "aiton" instead. When I use an "ation" word a lot—and consistently mistype it—I create an AutoCorrect entry for it.

NOTE: AUTOCORRECT DOESN'T DO PARTS OF WORDS

AutoCorrect only deals with whole words. For example, you couldn't tell it to substitute ation for aiton. Similarly, AutoCorrect doesn't handle suffixes: applicaiton and applicaitons require separate AutoCorrect entries, as shown in Figure 11.14.

FIGURE 11.14.
AutoCorrect for suffixes.

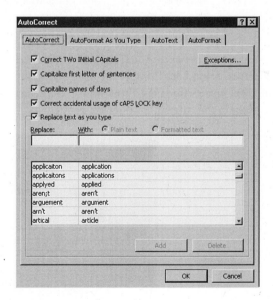

AutoText and AutoCorrect: Which One Should You Use?

Although AutoText doesn't correct misspellings or "expand" abbreviations like AutoCorrect, both tools insert text and graphics into your documents. To add addresses, memo headings, or your name, which should you use—AutoText or AutoCorrect?

Personal preference and working habits determine much of the choice. If you can remember a list of replacement codes and you want Word to insert your repeating blocks of text as you go along, use AutoCorrect. If you don't want to be bothered with remembering lots of codes, or if someone shares your computer and can't be expected to know which AutoCorrect items have been added, use AutoText. It's probably easier to scroll through the list of AutoText entries and identify the text they replace than to scroll through the list of AutoCorrect replacements. Do you prefer to keep your hands on the keyboard as much as possible? Creating AutoCorrect entries with short codes makes inserting repeated text easy and automatic.

CAUTION: AUTOTEXT AND AUTOCORRECT CONFLICTS

What happens if you assign the same name or code to both an AutoText and an Auto-Correct entry? AutoText "wins."

One other difference between AutoText and AutoCorrect is that you can print a list of your AutoText entries. Select File | Print. In the Print dialog box that appears, shown in Figure 11.15, select AutoText entries from the Print what pull-down list. The name and content of each AutoText entry in the current template get printed.

FIGURE 11.15.

Printing AutoText entries.

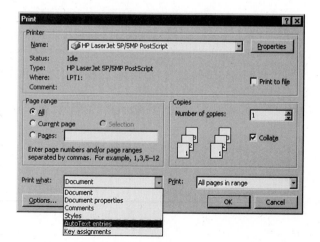

AutoSave

How many times have you heard that you should save your work regularly? How many times have you become so engrossed in your work that you forgot to save it—only to have the power fail after you'd done extraordinary and irreproducible work for two hours? You should activate AutoSave now, before you have another power failure.

To activate AutoSave, select Tools | Options and choose the Save tab, shown in Figure 11.16. Select Save AutoRecover info every and enter a value in minutes. Word will now automatically save your open documents at the increment you specified. You can also activate AutoSave by selecting File | Save As and clicking the Options button. The same Options dialog box appears.

FIGURE 11.16.

Setting AutoSave in the Options dialog box.

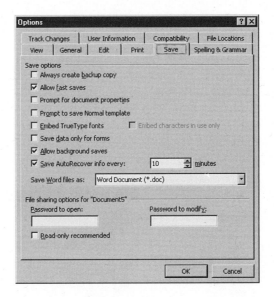

If a power failure or some other problem occurs after you've enabled AutoSave, Word works to recover your documents. After the failure, when you restart Word, it opens all the documents that were active at the time of the failure. Using Save As, save all your documents. You'll lose any work done since the last automatic save, but depending on the AutoSave interval you specified, that could be much better than losing an entire morning's efforts.

TIP: SELECT THE BEST AUTOSAVE INTERVAL

Waiting for Word to AutoSave a document, particularly a long one, can be annoying. Balance your AutoSave interval against the nuisance factor and your memory and other factors. If you can remember (or otherwise have documented) what you've been working

continues

continued

on, and you're not under a time crunch, you might want to set AutoSave for a longer interval. On the other hand, if you can't afford the time or you can't rely on memory to reconstruct your documents, set the interval to a shorter period. If you've set the AutoSave interval to 10 minutes, that's the most you can lose.

Widows and Orphans

Widows and orphans are those annoying single lines or words left by themselves at the top or bottom of a page or paragraph. A *widow* is a single line or word at the top of a page or column, and an *orphan* is the single line or word at the bottom. A widow can particularly distract readers by appearing to be a subhead instead of a line of straggling text. Orphans slow readers down.

Now that you know what widows and orphans are, and that you don't want them in your text, how do you prevent them? Actually, in Word, it's more a case of how to allow them if you really want them in your text. Select Format | Paragraph, and then select the Line and Page Breaks tab, shown in Figure 11.17. In the pagination box, Widow/Orphan control is checked by default; Word automatically prevents single lines at the top or bottom of your text. If you want to allow single lines at either the top or bottom of your text, disable the Widow/Orphan control box to turn widow and orphan prevention off.

FIGURE 11.17.

Widow and orphan control.

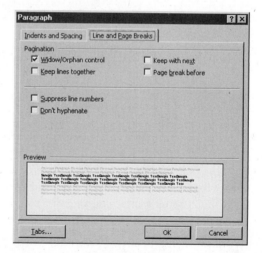

Figure 11.18 shows a section of text with a widow—a single line just below the new page marker. Figure 11.19 shows the same section of text, but with widow/orphan control turned on. Note that Word has repaginated the document so that an additional line joins the former widow. Figure 11.20, similarly, has an orphan—a single line just above the new page marker. Figure 11.21 demonstrates the effect of widow/orphan control on that section of text.

FIGURE 11.18.

A widow.

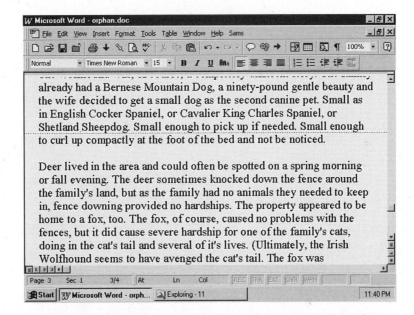

FIGURE 11.19.

The widow controlled.

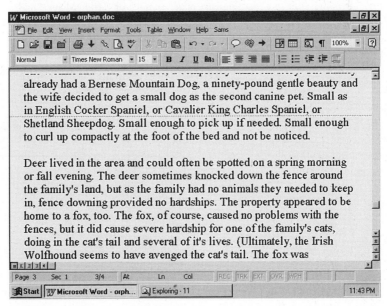

FIGURE 11.20.

An orphan.

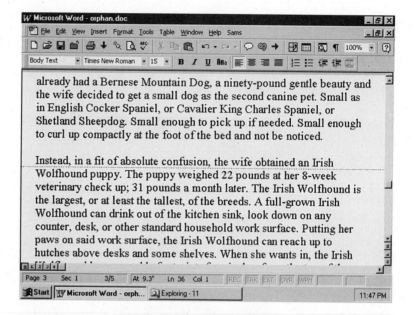

FIGURE 11.20.

An orphan.

FIGURE 11.21.

The orphan controlled.

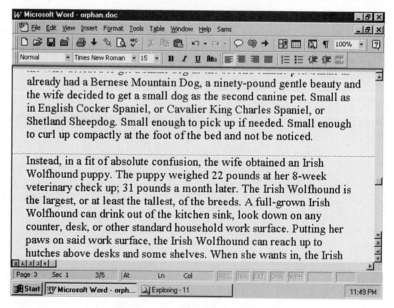

FIGURE 11.21.

The orphan controlled.

Summary

This chapter examined a few tools that can make working with Word a little easier, less tedious, or safer. It first looked at bookmarks, which let you mark places in your document and jump to those marks. Then it explored AutoText, which lets you store boilerplate information for reuse in any document. With AutoCorrect, you can automatically correct common typing and spelling errors. In addition, AutoCorrect lets you create shortcut entries or codes for long phrases or chunks of text and graphics. AutoSave automatically saves your work at intervals you specify. Finally, this chapter looked at widow and orphan control, which controls whether you have single lines at the top or bottom of a page or column.

Here are a couple of related chapters:

- I showed you how to spell check any document in Chapter 3, "Day-to-Day Office Basics."
- I'll tell you about some options related to AutoCorrect in Chapter 14, "Customizing Word."

Building Word Forms

CHAPTER 12

IN THIS CHAPTER

> *We never stop investigating. We are never satisfied that we know enough to get by. Every question we answer leads on to another question. This has become the greatest survival trick of our species.*
>
> —*Desmond Morris*

In this chapter you'll learn how to create a special type of document called a *form*. A form, as the name suggests, is a document that contains a number of fields into which the user enters data, such as his name and address. Once your form is complete, you can either print it and have the user enter the data on paper or send the user the file and have him fill in the blanks on-screen.

A template provides the foundation of an electronic or online form, storing the skeleton of blanks and accompanying text that make up the form. On the template, you add the different types of fields necessary to gather the required information. Then, when you create a new document based on the template, you save the document, and the template remains intact, ready for the form's next use. Protecting the form's template prevents accidental or intentional over-writing of the form.

NOTE: CONSIDER DOCUMENTS FOR PAPER FORMS

If your form will only be used as a paper document, you might want to create it as a document rather than as a template.

Creating a Form

Although you can start your form right at the keyboard and screen, jumping right into entering fields and labels, editing, changing, and rearranging, your job might go smoother if you sketch out your form first—determine what information you want to collect, lay out your fields, and then place your labels and accompanying text.

Word provides the following three types of form fields:

- Text fields
- Check boxes
- Drop-down lists

Each form field type helps you collect different types of information:

- Text field: Free-form alphanumeric information
- Check box: Yes/no, on/off information
- Drop-down list: Selections from predetermined lists of entries

Because you're basing your forms on templates, you'll need to create a template first. On the template, start placing your form fields and text.

To place a form field in your template, first open the Forms toolbar, shown in Figure 12.1, by choosing View | Toolbars | Forms. The Forms toolbar includes buttons that let you perform the following tasks:

■ Create a text field

■ Create a check box

■ Create a drop-down list

■ Open the Options dialog box for form fields

■ Draw tables

■ Insert tables

■ Add frames

■ Shade the form fields

■ Lock (protect) the form

FIGURE 12.1.
The Forms toolbar.

Click one of the three field buttons—text field, check box, or drop-down list—to insert that field type at the insertion point. The inserted field appears as a shaded box. Each field type has options available to further refine and define the field and the information you can place in it. The following sections discuss the options for the different kinds of form fields.

Text Form Field Options

You open the Text Form Field options dialog box, shown in Figure 12.2, by double-clicking a text field, by right-clicking the field and selecting Properties, or by selecting the field and clicking the Form Field Options button on the Forms toolbar. In the Text Form Field Options dialog box, you can specify additional details about the text field. Each text form field has a type, as in the following:

■ Regular text (the default)

■ Number

■ Date

■ Current date

■ Current time

■ Calculation

FIGURE 12.2.

The Text Form Field Options dialog box.

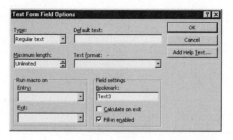

For all text types except current date and current time, you can set a default value, maximum length, and format pattern. (For calculations, Word replaces the default value with an expression.) To change the type, maximum length, or format, click the arrows by the fields and select the new value. For maximum length, click the up and down arrows to increase or decrease the size of the field.

Default values and field lengths of less than five spaces appear in the forms template; Word applies other limitations or formats when you fill out the form.

Check Box Form Field Options

You open the Check Box Form Field options dialog box, shown in Figure 12.3, by double-clicking a check box, by right-clicking the field and selecting Properties, or by selecting the field and clicking the Form Field Options button on the Forms toolbar. In the Check Box Form Field Options dialog box, you can specify additional details about the check box field. For check boxes, you can set the box size and default value.

FIGURE 12.3.

The Check Box Form Field Options dialog box.

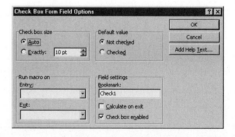

TIP: SET DEFAULT VALUES CAREFULLY

Help eliminate mistakes and relieve your form users of some extra work and aggravation. Set the default check box value to the standard, more common, or more-likely-to-occur value.

Drop-Down Form Field Options

You open the Drop-Down Form Field Options dialog box, shown in Figure 12.4, by double-clicking a drop-down form field, by right-clicking the field and selecting Properties, or by selecting the field and clicking the Form Field Options button on the Forms toolbar. In the Drop-Down Form Field Options dialog box, you can specify additional details about the drop-down field. Drop-down fields let you, the form creator, define a list of valid values for the field, from which the user makes a selection. Enter values in the Drop-down item field, and then click Add. Rearrange the order of items by selecting an item and then clicking the up or down Move arrows. To remove an item from the list, select the item, click Remove, and then delete the text from the Drop-down item field. To edit an item, select it and click Remove. The item text appears in the Drop-down item field. Make your changes and click Add.

FIGURE 12.4.

The Drop-Down Form Field Options dialog box.

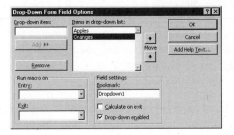

Adding Help Text to a Form

Every type of form field has a button to add help text. In the Form Field Help Text dialog box, shown in Figure 12.5, the Status Bar and Help Key (F1) tabs have the same layout. You may select one of your AutoText entries or enter other text in the Type your own box to be the help text for that field. Status Bar entries appear in Word's status bar when that field is active while you're filling out a form; Help Key entries appear in a Help dialog box when you press F1 while that field is active. You may have both Status Bar and Help Key help for a field.

FIGURE 12.5.

The Form Field Help Text dialog box.

Running Macros from Form Fields

Regardless of the field type, you may specify macros to run when entering or exiting a field. Click the arrow next to the field to see a list of macros available in the template. Word runs the Entry macro when the insertion point enters the field; it runs the Exit macro when the insertion point leaves the field.

> **NOTE: COPY MACROS TO THE TEMPLATE**
>
> Be sure to copy any macros you want to run with a form to the form template.

Preparing the Form for Use

After you finish designing and constructing your form, you want to protect it. To protect a form, click the Protect Form button (the lock) on the Forms toolbar. Alternatively, select Tools | Protect Document and click Forms. Whenever a form is protected, the lock icon on the Forms toolbar is depressed.

Protecting the form prevents someone from overwriting the parts you want to remain static while allowing someone to enter information in the various fields. Protecting the form also sets it up for online use. When you're filling in a protected form, pressing Tab moves the insertion point to the next field.

Using an Online Form

To use an online form, create a new document and choose the template with the form. The document opens with the insertion point positioned in the first field of the form. Enter your information and then press the Tab key to move to the next field. If you try to enter more characters than allowed, Word simply ignores the excess characters. Entering an alphabetic character in a numeric field displays an error message.

Forms Examples

You'll hear references to the "paperless society," or, more in line with the subject of this chapter, the "paperless workplace." Unfortunately, it sometimes seems as if computers and word processors have only made it easier to produce reams of documents and forms. Creating and using online forms can help reduce the amount of paper generated in the workplace.

The following examples help show you how to create forms in Word. While each of the forms could certainly be printed, copied, and filled in by hand, you should give serious thought to incorporating them—or whatever forms suit your needs—into an online system.

Online forms create new storage challenges, such as what to name the completed form, how to manage the hard disk storage of forms, and a host of other issues that have already been solved for paper documents. Don't let this stop you from developing an online forms system. After all, it's probably just as easy to lose a paper form as it is to misplace a file on your hard drive. However, you can use the Windows Find utility to help you locate files; no such help exists for paper copies.

The Job Applicants Form

The first form you will develop is an online job applicant information form. For this example, assume that clerks in a Human Resource office receive job applications and enter an applicant's information into the form. You're concerned with the applicant's name and address, the position for which he or she is applying, whether a cover letter was received, and whether the applicant included salary information.

Figure 12.6 shows the form template. The Name and Address fields have maximum lengths of 45 characters, and the City field has a maximum length of 35 characters. The State field has a maximum length of 2 and defaults to CO. (Why make your form-fillers enter the applicant's state if you know where most of the applicants come from? If you want to use a similar form in an area where you might have applicants from several states, make the field a drop-down list including the likely states, and set the default state to be your state.) The Zip field has five characters.

FIGURE 12.6.

The Job Applicants template with the Position options displayed.

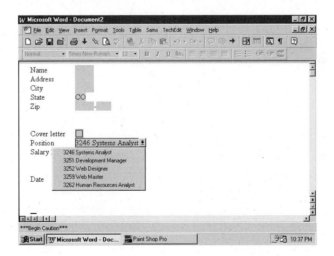

The Cover letter check box is unchecked. You want the clerk to consciously record the existence of a cover letter. The Position field is a drop-down list box. The list contains the advertised positions, as well as an "unspecified" category. Salary history, like Cover letter, requires a conscious effort to check.

Notice that the starting positions of the fields are aligned. This alignment makes the form easier to read and fill in.

For an online form, storing each file by applicant name makes sense; this is how similar paper forms are filed. Windows 95's long filename capabilities let you use the applicant's full name as the filename.

Product Registration Form

Your next form is for phone registrations of software products. When a new call comes in, the user creates a new file with the Phone Product Registration template, shown in Figure 12.7. Word fills in the current date and time. The Call line fields are implemented here as a series of check boxes. This arrangement doesn't force the user to select only one box, and a simple check box seems more appropriate for this function than a drop-down list.

FIGURE 12.7.

The Phone Product Registration template.

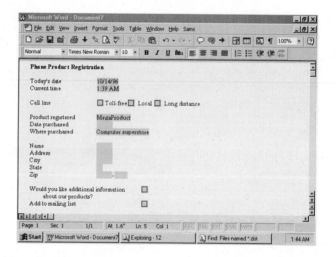

Product registered is a drop-down list box. The box lists products in the order of their popularity, which is another example of making your form easy to fill in. The customer information is similar to that on the job application form, but no default state is supplied (these phone lines take calls from all over the country). The Add to mailing list check box defaults to checked. Unless the customer specifies otherwise, he's added to the mailing list.

Developing a system to store online product registrations might take a bit more work. Consider saving registrations using the customer name as the filename; use different subdirectories to store registrations of different products.

Summary

In this chapter you learned about forms, concentrating on online forms as a means of collecting information. Here are a few chapters where you'll find similar information:

- I cover HTML forms in Chapter 46, "Web Forms and Databases."
- I show you how to build forms for use with VBA procedures in Chapter 59, "Creating a Custom User Interface."

CHAPTER 13

Word as a Publisher

IN THIS CHAPTER

Some said, John, print it; others said, Not so:
Some said, It might do good; others said, no.

—*John Bunyan*

In this chapter you'll look at Word as a publisher, examining its capability to produce documents that are outside the scope of those you create with a typewriter.

Publishing used to mean creating documents that went beyond the capabilities of the typewritten page, using mock-ups and paste-ups, specifying typefaces, submitting the pasted-together document to a printer, reviewing proofs, and hoping that the finished article turned out to be what you intended. With the advent of powerful word processing packages, such as Word, that run on PCs, the nature of publishing has changed.

With Word, you have at your fingertips document formatting capabilities that used to be reserved only for print shops using typesetters and other sophisticated equipment. Although some functions are still best—or only—done by the printer, you can now perform many publishing functions on your own computer, using Word. Some of the "publishing" capabilities available to you through Word include the following:

- Character formatting
- Different fonts and typefaces
- Borders
- Dingbats
- Text boxes and objects
- Linked text boxes and text flow
- Section and column breaks and formatting

All in all, this is a far cry from the typewriter, where your only character "formatting" was all-caps or underlining, and you had one typeface.

Now that you have publishing functions at your fingertips—literally—what types of documents or publications can you create with them? Let's explore.

Business Publications

Businesses need many types of documents, starting with those that establish business identity, such as letterhead and business cards, invoices, statements, estimates, and so on. They also need promotional materials, such as brochures, fliers, coupons, and advertisements. Finally, they need internal and external materials, such as reports to shareholders, catalogs, order forms, press releases, memos, newsletters, and fax sheets, not to mention letters, reports, and product documentation.

These publications influence how outsiders—and insiders—perceive the business. Poorly done, business communications can lose customers; well done, business communications can make the sale. Look at two quick examples. Figure 13.1 shows part of a sample flier for a freelance business writer. The writing is fair and it contains no typos, but does it inspire you to hire the writer? Compare it to Figure 13.2. Same writer, same message, but which one would you be more likely to respond to?

FIGURE 13.1.

A bland flier.

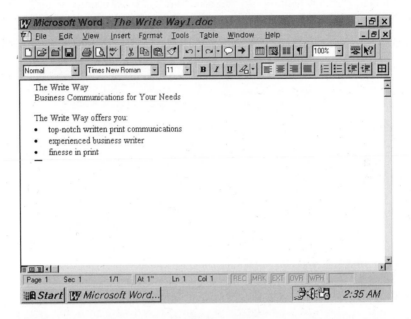

FIGURE 13.2.

A flier with pizzazz.

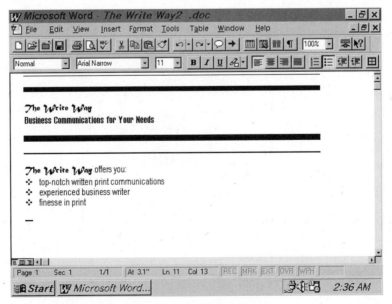

Suppose that you've written a report for your boss—an important report that highlights critical gaps in the company's customer service efforts. Your report is one of five your boss will receive this week just before her quarterly meeting with the board. She'll choose one of the reports to present to the board. Given a choice between the report in Figure 13.3 and the one in Figure 13.4, which one do you think will catch her eye?

FIGURE 13.3.

A bland report.

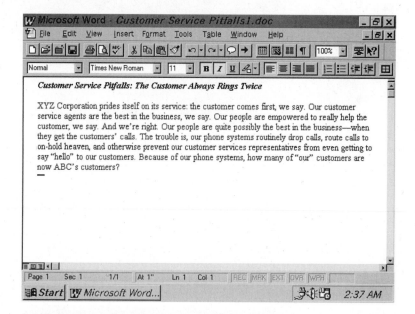

FIGURE 13.4.

An attention-grabbing report.

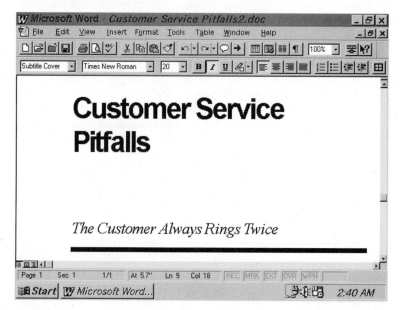

With all the possibilities Word offers for desktop publishing, where do you start when producing your own documents? Look no further than Word's wizards and templates. When you create a new Word document, you can choose from the following wizards:

- Fax
- Letter
- Memo
- Newsletter
- Envelopes
- Mailing list
- Résumé
- Web page
- Legal pleading

That's not counting the templates and wizards included from Office 95: awards, agendas, brochures, directories, invoices, press releases, manuals, and more.

Personal Publications

What works for improving a business's image applies to your personal image, too. Publications you put out can be every bit as important to you as the year-end summary is to the corporation across town. Are you a student, or do you know one? How many essays, papers, or themes does a student generate? Speaking from experience, this former graduate student produced major papers, minor papers, analyses, take-home essay exams, and management models. Cover sheets, charts, graphics, and, of course, a lot of text all figured into the required output. After facing stacks of papers, which paper do you think a professor would see more positively: Student A's, shown in Figure 13.5, or Student B's, shown in Figure 13.6?

Consider another personal publication—one critical in these days of downsizing, layoffs, and buyouts—the résumé. Some sources say you have 30 seconds to make a good impression with your résumé. Which résumé would you rather have make an impression about you—the one shown in Figure 13.7, or the one shown in Figure 13.8?

FIGURE 13.5.

A bland cover sheet.

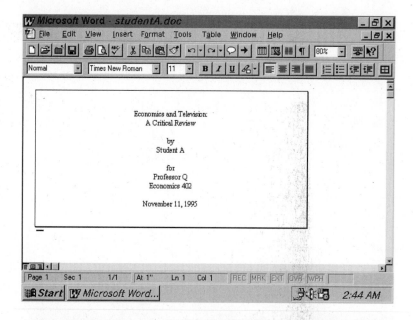

FIGURE 13.6.

*An interesting cover
sheet.*

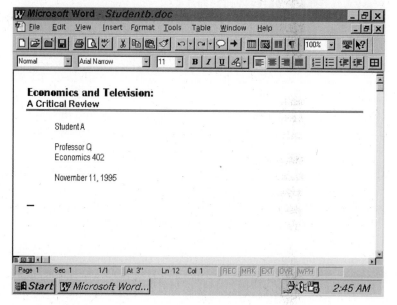

FIGURE 13.7.
A bland résumé.

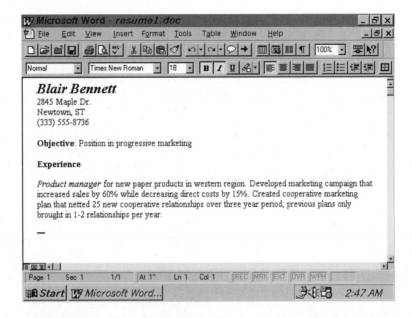

FIGURE 13.8.
A bold résumé.

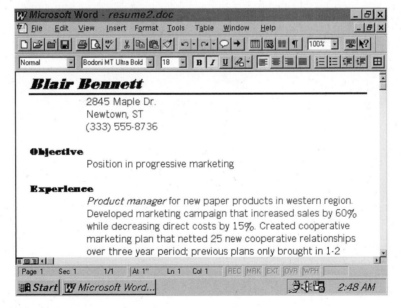

Layout

Knowing what types of documents you can publish is but the first step. As these examples have demonstrated, how you lay out and format a document plays a critical role in its success.

When laying out a publication, keep the following key points in mind:

- White space: White space is the blank areas of a document. It includes side, top, and bottom margins, and the spaces between lines and sections. White space is more than good; it's critical to a publication's success. Cramming as much text as possible on a page doesn't result in more information available to your reader; it results in a non-reader.

- Consistency: Structure your document consistently. When you use consistent formatting for major points, secondary points, sidebar material, introductions, and so on, your reader will know how to key in on those points and more easily find and read the material.

- Contrast: No, this doesn't contradict the preceding point. Both consistency and contrast contribute to a publication's success. Contrast provides interest and helps clarify your publication's structure. Even if your document is consistent in its structure, if all the elements look the same, your reader won't be able to determine the structure. Compare Figure 13.9 and Figure 13.10. Which figure lets you identify structure at a glance? Make sure your contrast does contrast, however. Small differences between document elements don't provide enough contrast to guide the reader.

Figure 13.11 demonstrates ineffective contrast. The document doesn't provide adequate contrast between elements. Compare it to Figure 13.12, where, once again, you can readily identify document elements.

FIGURE 13.9.

A poorly-identified structure.

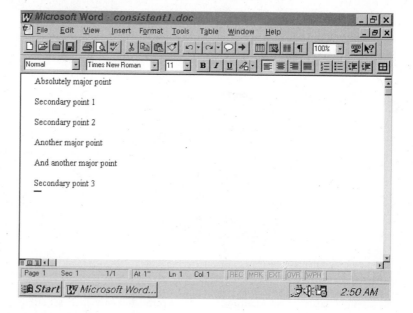

FIGURE 13.10.

A well-defined structure.

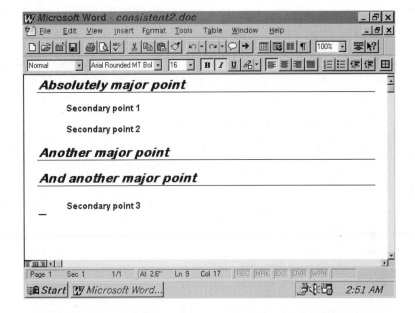

FIGURE 13.11.

Low contrast.

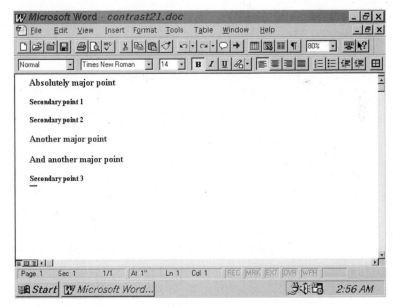

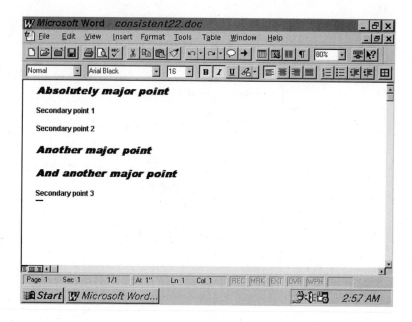

The following list discusses a few things to avoid:

- All caps: Capital letters might have been the only form of contrast and emphasis available on the typewriter, but other forms of emphasis are available now. When we read, we depend on word shape—the pattern of ups and downs created by the ascenders and descenders of letters—to help us distinguish words. Words in all caps have the same shape; thus, we have to work harder to understand what's written.

- Centered text: Our eyes and brain are more comfortable when each line begins at the same place, which makes left-justified text easy reading. In contrast, when lines are centered, each line begins at a different place, making us work harder to read the text.

- Underlined text: Underlining interferes with letters' descenders, thus confusing word shapes and making it more difficult to distinguish between letters and words. Underlining dates back to typewriters and their limited repertoire of emphasis. Find a different way to highlight words or phrases.

- Blocks of script: Long sections of script or italic type do not make for easy reading.

Now that you've been introduced to some page layout and design guidelines, you can explore how to use Word for good page design.

White Space

Set generous margins to ensure adequate white space in your documents. Consider using an extra-wide left margin as a design element, as shown in Figure 13.13. This sample has the left margin set at 3 inches, with the major headings set with an indentation of –2.0 inches. Margins such as these can be especially useful for manuals and other types of teaching documents, giving the reader plenty of room to make notes.

FIGURE 13.13.

Margins as white space.

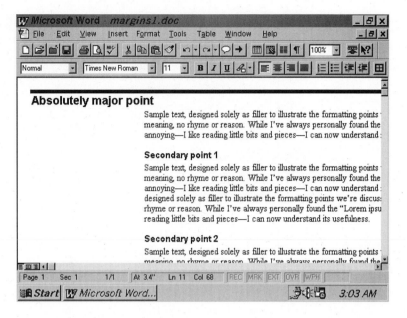

You can also introduce white space when setting the space before and after attributes of paragraphs. Extra space between headings and the text they accompany helps set the headings apart. Be careful to keep the headings "attached" to their text, however, and not to the text above. In Figure 13.14, does the heading belong to the paragraph above it or below it? Figure 13.15 makes the relationship clear.

FIGURE 13.14.

An unclear heading relationship.

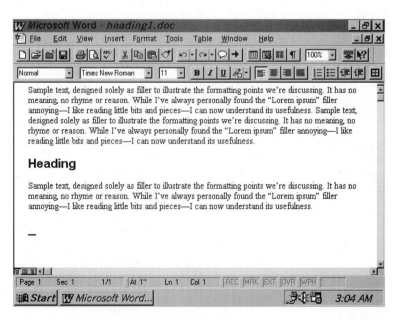

FIGURE 13.15.

*A clear heading
relationship.*

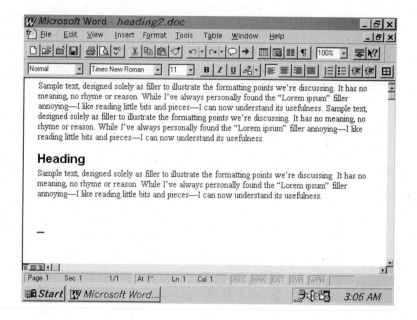

A raging debate among desktop publishers is going on even as you read this: Should you justify your right margins, or should you leave them ragged? The answer is "It depends." Many people perceive a justified right margin as formal and, therefore, more desirable for formal documents. Others insist that the drawbacks of right justification outweigh the perhaps more casual approach of a ragged right margin. White space comes into play here, both as a positive and a negative.

When you set text with a justified right margin, Word forces extra spaces between words to make the right margin even. These extra spaces can cause "rivers" of unwanted white space to run through your text. When you use justified right margins in columns, Word has fewer words to work with and might insert whole blocks of spaces in order to even out the margin. Readers find these blocks extremely distracting. Ragged right margins don't force extra spaces into text and therefore don't cause white rivers and blank areas. Extra white space at the right margin also helps open up your text.

White space in ragged right margins has a drawback, however. Depending on how you set Word's hyphenation, you can end up with extremely ragged right edges. Select Tools | Language | Hyphenation to help control the ragged right margin (see Figure 13.16). Click Automatically hyphenate document to have Word hyphenate automatically. The value in the Hyphenation zone field determines the trade-off between raggedness and the number of hyphens. A smaller hyphenation zone reduces the raggedness of the right margin by hyphenating more words. A larger hyphenation zone decreases the number of hyphenated words but increases the right margin's raggedness. Unfortunately, if you hyphenate to reduce raggedness, you run the risk of having hyphens ending too many lines—another visual distraction. In the Hyphenation dialog box, you can set the number of consecutive hyphenated lines that Word will allow in your document.

Figure 13.16.

The Hyphenation dialog box.

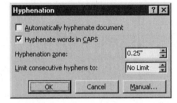

Figure 13.17 shows a paragraph set with a wide hyphenation zone. Notice how ragged the right margin is. Figure 13.18 is the same text with a narrow hyphenation zone; the right margin is much smoother.

Figure 13.17.

A ragged right margin.

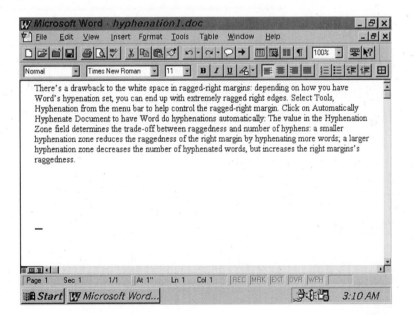

FIGURE 13.18.

A smoother right margin.

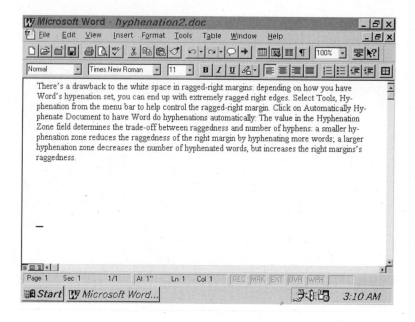

Consistency

Styles are a powerful consistency tool for your documents. Each time you begin a major topic, introduce it with the same style. Similarly, introduce different levels of topics with their own styles. Then, your reader has clues and cues about your document and its content.

Fonts and typefaces can also provide consistency. If you have different types of information to present in your publication, you can establish different fonts for each type of information. For example, many books that teach programming languages use a different typeface to show program code than the typeface used for regular text. As another example, you can effectively identify callouts—those little pieces of text that you place in margins, next to figures, or between paragraphs—by setting them in a different font or surrounding them with distinctive borders.

Contrast

Contrast refers to ways of distinguishing different document elements. You can establish contrast in a variety of ways. Different typefaces often distinguish between a publication's headings and its text. As I stated earlier, make sure you have enough contrast in your contrast. Setting headings in a slightly larger font size doesn't make the differences jump out at your reader. Using two similar serif typefaces doesn't cut it, either.

NOTE: FONT INFO

To learn more about serif and sans serif typefaces and other font particulars, see Chapter 3, "Day-to-Day Office Basics."

You can create effective contrast by using a sans serif typeface for headings and a serif typeface for body text, as was done in this book. Using the same typeface for both headings and text is effective when the headings are significantly larger. Use related type families, too. A bold, condensed version of the body font can introduce headings effectively.

Mail Merge

Remember how form letters used to look? The "form" part had obvious spaces where your name was inserted, or it placed your "personalized" information in stand-alone blocks where differences in information length weren't quite so glaring.

Form letters—then and now—serve exceedingly useful purposes, however. If you're a business owner, a club officer, or an information gatherer, form letters let you produce volumes of documents that are tailored to specific groups of people and that are personalized for individuals within those groups. Using Word, you can create form letters that are highly specific, both to your reader and to you.

Word avoids the use of the unsavory term "form letter" and calls its form-letter-creation process Mail Merge. Mail Merge involves merging data, such as names and addresses, to create various kinds of mailings. We'll explore the how-tos in the next sections.

The Mail Merge Helper

Merging involves the following three documents:

- The data source holds the information about people that you add to your mailing. A table typically forms the data source.
- The main document provides the "form" into which Word adds personalized information.
- Form letters are individual letters or documents that reflect the merging of the data with the form.

Word provides wizards to help you create and format documents. Wizards generally move you through a linear process: You follow steps until you complete a task. Mail Merge is a little different. The process of creating individualized letters doesn't follow a neat linear path. You move

13

back and forth between your main document and the data source until you have both set up to your liking. To guide you through this process, Word provides the Mail Merge Helper.

To display the Mail Merge Helper dialog box, shown in Figure 13.19, select Tools | Mail Merge. You'll follow the helper's steps; however, merging requires a certain amount of "bouncing around" between the main document (number 1) and the data source (number 2). The text in the top box guides you through the merging and offers tips on what to do next.

FIGURE 13.19.

*The Mail Merge Helper
dialog box.*

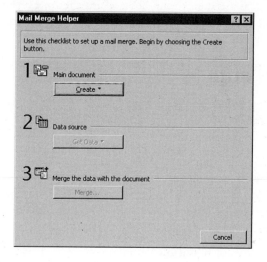

You will begin with the main document. Click Create, and then select what you want to create. Mail Merge lets you create

- ■ Form letters
- ■ Mailing labels
- ■ Envelopes
- ■ Catalogs

Once you've selected the kind of merge document you want to create, Word displays a dialog box where you choose which document—the active one or a new one—will be used as the "form" of your mailing. If you don't want the active document used as the main document, select New Main Document.

You now have a main document that you can edit. Unless you have a large amount of text for your form letter, however, you can do little with your main document at this point. Instead, create your data source so that you know which fields to place in your main document. Click Get Data in step 2 of the Mail Merge Helper and select Create Data Source. Word displays the Create Data Source dialog box, shown in Figure 13.20.

FIGURE 13.20.

The Create Data Source dialog box.

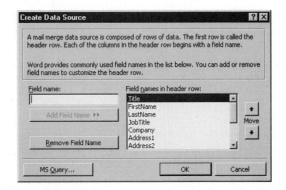

Working with the Data Source

In the Create Data Source dialog box, you specify the titles of the data fields for your mail merge. These titles form the header row of the data source table. Word provides a list of commonly used data fields to get you started. To remove fields you won't use, select the field name and click Remove Field Name. Add new fields by entering their names in the Field name text box and clicking Add Field Name. Change the order of fields by selecting a field name and clicking the Move up arrow or Move down arrow.

NOTE: WATCH THE ORDER OF THE FORM FIELDS

As you specify the fields you want in your form letter, the order of the fields in the data source isn't critical. However, there might be a nuisance factor in having an often-used field at the bottom of the list.

After you specify your data fields, Word recognizes that the data source table is empty and gives you the choice of creating your data records or returning to your main document. What you do at this point is largely a matter of choice. Select Edit Main Document to place field placeholders in your main document. Select Edit Data Source to add data records to your data source table. I want to discuss adding data records first, so click Edit Data Source.

In the Data Form dialog box that appears, shown in Figure 13.21, you create your individual records. Word presents a list of blank data fields in which you enter the value for each field. After you enter all your records, click OK. Click Add New to add the current record and leave the data form open to enter the next record. Click Delete to delete a record. To move from record to record, click the left and right arrow keys next to the Record box. The current record number appears inside the Record box. To find a record with a particular value, click Find, enter the value (or partial value) in the Find What box, and then specify or select the field to search in the In Field. Click Find First and Find Next to move through your records.

13

WORD AS A
PUBLISHER

FIGURE **13.21.**

The Data Form dialog box.

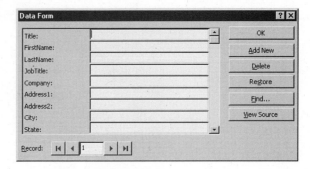

Use the Restore button to undo changes you've made to a record. If you haven't added the record, Restore erases the data you entered and returns the data fields to blanks.

The View Source button closes the Mail Merge Helper and opens the table forming the data source. Word creates the table with your data field names as column headers; the rows contain the information from your records.

Working with the Main Document

After you close your data source, Word returns to your main document. Now that you have names for your data fields, you can add them to your main document.

Click the Insert Merge Field button on the Mail Merge main document toolbar and select the field you want from the list. Word inserts a field placeholder in your main document. Field placeholders appear as the field name surrounded by chevrons (« and »), as shown in Figure 13.22. When you merge your main document with your data source, Word substitutes the value in the individual fields for the field placeholders.

Continue to add text and field placeholders to your main document. If you want to check how a merged record will look, click the View Merged Data button (to the right of the Insert Word Field button) on the Mail Merge main document toolbar. View Merged Data toggles between the main document with its placeholders and a "real" merged document.

To see how your merged documents will look and list any errors encountered during the merge, click the Check for Errors button on the Mail Merge main document toolbar. The Checking and Reporting Errors dialog box, shown in Figure 13.23, offers you a number of options for simulating or running a merge. Once you're happy with the results, click one of the merge radio buttons and then click OK to run your merge.

FIGURE 13.22.
Field placeholders.

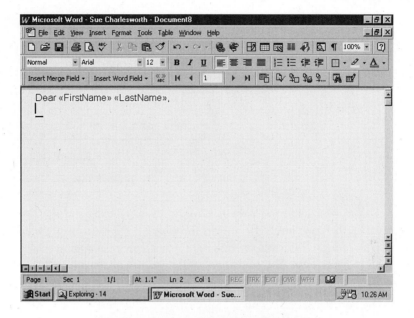

FIGURE 13.23.
The Checking and Reporting Errors dialog box.

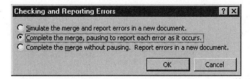

Merging the Data Source and the Main Document

When you click the Merge to New Document button, Word merges the records in the data source with the main document, substituting the value of a field in the field placeholder. Word places the merge results in a single document, with each individual form letter in a separate section. You can then treat this new document as you would any other.

Clicking the Mail Merge button displays the Merge dialog box. In this dialog box, you can select a range of records to merge. Click the Query Options button to open the Query Options dialog box, shown in Figure 13.24. The Filter Records tab lets you select specific records to merge by using field names and comparison values. Using filters, you can choose records in your data source that meet specific criteria. The following are some examples of filters:

- Specific ZIP codes, to target a mailing
- A salary range, to offer special benefit packages
- Children's ages, to tailor a book purchase offer

FIGURE 13.24.

The Query Options dialog box.

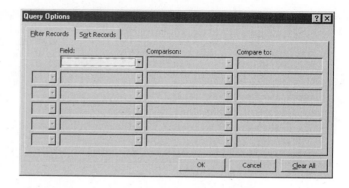

To set up your filter, select the field you want to filter by and the comparison you want to make. In the Compare To field, enter the value by which you want to filter your data field. For instance, for the ZIP code example, you would enter ZipCode (or whatever you've called that field) in Field. Then you would enter Equal to in the Comparison field and a ZIP code in the Compare to field.

In the Sort Records tab, you can specify up to three sort levels. Sorting doesn't affect which records will be used for the merge; it only arranges the newly created records in the order you specify. For example, if you had a database composed entirely of men named John Smith, John Brown, and John Doe, you might want to sort your mail merge by last name, then by middle initial. With this sort, all the John Browns would be listed first. Within the Brown list, the names would be arranged by middle initial. Your list would then move on to the John Does, arranged by middle initial, and then would finish up with the sorted John Smiths.

A Mail Merge Example

Now, let's look at a simple example of a mail merge. Your form letter will go out to individuals in a company who have checked documents out of the company library but haven't returned them. Figure 13.25 shows the data form for your form letter. It consists of the individual's name, company data, the name of the document, the date the document was checked out, and the date the document was checked in.

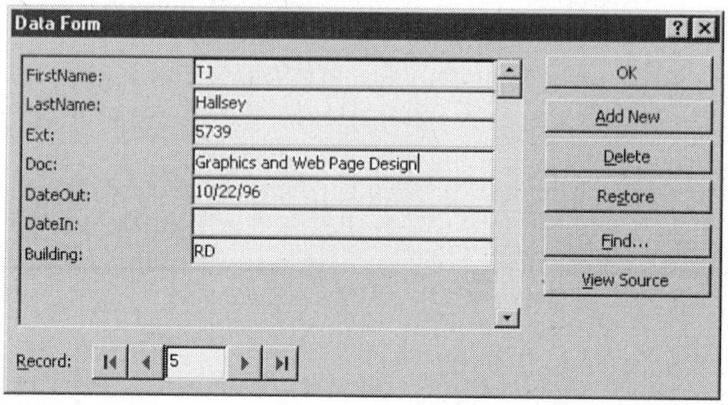

FIGURE 13.25.

The Library data form.

The main document, shown in Figure 13.26, is a simple reminder. You use the individual's name, document name, and check-out date, along with the person's building code, to complete the simple reminder form.

Figure 13.27 shows the merged file.

FIGURE 13.26.

The Library main document.

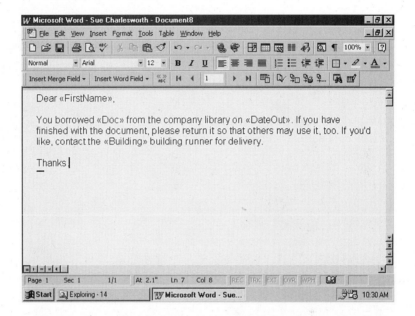

FIGURE 13.27.

The Library merged file.

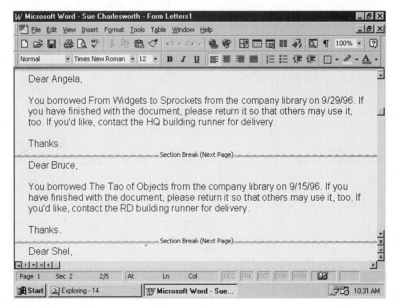

Summary

In this chapter you explored using Word as a desktop publishing tool and learned some of the elements of good document design. You then read about Mail Merge, which lets you create form letters by combining a main document with a data source.

Here are some related chapters:

- For a few formatting basics, see Chapter 3, "Day-to-Day Office Basics."
- For tips and techniques on integrating Word with the other Office applications, see Chapter 50, "Working with the Office Integration Tools."

Customizing Word

IN THIS CHAPTER

CHAPTER

14

That so few now dare to be eccentric, marks the chief danger of the time.

—John Stuart Mill

When you install Word right out of the box, it comes in a basic, one-size-fits-all outfit. This off-the-rack approach is fine for some people, but most people prefer a little more individuality in their Word wear. They want their version of Word to reflect their impeccable tastes, their inimitable personality, and their charming quirks.

Thankfully, Word is only too happy to oblige such rugged individualism. It comes with a large number of settings and options that let you customize the program to your heart's content. This chapter looks at many of these features.

Displaying the Options Dialog Box

The word *fritterware* is often applied to option-laden software that makes you fritter away your time playing with the program's numerous bells and whistles. Word, with its impressive number of customization options, might just be the fritterware champ of the Office suite.

To see what I mean, display the Options dialog box by selecting Tools | Options. As you can see in Figure 14.1, Word's Options dialog box is weighed down with no fewer than 10 tabs, which in turn are home to dozens of settings. The rest of this chapter runs through each tab and briefly describes the available settings.

FIGURE 14.1.

You can use the Options dialog box to change dozens of Word's default settings.

NOTE: NAVIGATING TABBED DIALOG BOXES

Here's a summary of the navigation techniques you use for a multilevel tabbed dialog box:

- Using the mouse, click on a tab to select it.
- Using the keyboard, press Ctrl-Tab to move right and Ctrl-Shift-Tab to move left.

- If the tab name is selected, you can press the right arrow to move right, the left arrow to move left, the up arrow to move up, and the down arrow to move down.

When you finish choosing your options, click OK to return to the worksheet.

Changing the View

The options in the View tab control the default display settings for Word pages, text, and windows.

The check boxes displayed in the Show group vary depending on the current Word view. Here's a summary of all the check boxes you see:

Drawings: This check box, which is available only in Page Layout and Online Layout views, toggles the display of graphic objects on and off. If you have a document with a lot of graphics, activating this option can make it easier to scroll through the file.

Object anchors: If you've anchored a graphic object to a paragraph, activate this check box to display an anchor icon beside the image. Note that you must also activate the All check box in the Nonprinting characters group. This option is available only in the Page Layout and Online Layout views.

Text boundaries: If you activate this option, available only in Page Layout and Online Layout views, Word displays a dotted line around the page margins, columns, and objects.

Draft font: Available only in Normal and Outline views, this check box minimizes the display of document formatting by rendering text formatting as bold and underline and displaying boxes instead of images.

Picture placeholders: Activate this option to show a gray box where a graphic usually appears. If you have a document with a lot of graphics, activating this option can make it easier to scroll through the file.

Animated text: This check box toggles the display of animated text on and off.

ScreenTips: This check box toggles the display of ScreenTips text on and off.

Highlight: This check box toggles the display of text highlighting on and off.

Bookmarks: If you activate this option, Word displays (but doesn't print) bookmarks in your documents. Each bookmark is surrounded by square brackets ([ ]).

Field codes: If you activate this check box, Word displays the codes for each document field instead of the field's result. You can also use the Field shading list to specify when Word displays the field shading (Never, Always, or When selected).

TIP: TOGGLING FIELD CODES

If you just want to take a quick look at a field code, highlight the field and press F9 to toggle the display between the field's code and its result.

The Nonprinting characters group in the View tab sets the display options for various "characters" that appear on-screen but aren't printed:

Tab characters: Activate this option to tell Word to display a right-pointing arrow in place of all tab characters.

Spaces: If you activate this check box, Word displays a small dot in place of each space character.

Paragraph marks: Activate this setting to display the paragraph symbol (¶) at the end of each paragraph.

Optional hyphens: If you activate this option, Word displays the optional hyphen symbol (¬). These hyphens indicate where you want a real hyphen to appear if a word must be broken at the end of a line.

NOTE: HYPHENATING A DOCUMENT

Assuming that you have Word's Hyphenation tool installed, you can have Word automatically hyphenate your document. This means that Word will even out the right-hand margin by breaking up long words when they won't fit on the end of a line. (See Chapter 13, "Word as a Publisher," for details.) In some cases, however, you might want to decide where the hyphens are placed yourself rather than relying on Word. To do this, insert an optional hyphen at the spot where you want a word broken during hyphenation. To insert an optional hyphen, press Ctrl-- (Ctrl-hyphen).

Hidden text: Hidden text is often used to avoid displaying sensitive information, such as payroll figures or passwords. Activating this setting tells Word to display text that has been formatted as hidden. Such text is shown with a dotted underline (although the underline doesn't print).

All: Activate this check box to display all the preceding characters.

The check boxes in the Window group control the display of each Word window: (The available controls depend on the current view.)

Status bar: Deactivate this check box to hide the status bar and give yourself some extra screen real estate.

Vertical ruler: If you deactivate this check box, which is available only in Page Layout and Online Layout views, Word doesn't display the vertical ruler down the left side of the screen.

Horizontal scroll bar: Use this check box to toggle the horizontal scroll bar on and off.

Vertical scroll bar: Use this check box to toggle the vertical scroll bar on and off.

Style area width: Available in Normal and Outline views, this spinner controls the size of the style area, which displays the style used in each paragraph.

Wrap to window: If you activate this check box, Word wraps the document text to the right edge of the document window instead of the right edge of the page. This option is available in Normal, Online Layout, and Outline views.

TIP: MAXIMIZING THE WORK AREA

If you want to maximize the work area, the easiest way to do so is to select View | Full Screen. This command removes everything from the screen, including the menu bar, toolbars, scroll bars, and status bar. To return to the normal view, either click the Close Full Screen toolbar button or press Escape.

Word's General Options

The controls in the General tab, shown in Figure 14.2, offer a wide variety of customization choices:

Background repagination: This check box is activated by default, which means that Word continually repaginates your documents while you work. Note that this option is disabled (and activated) in the Page Layout and Online Layout views, which means that you can't turn off background repagination when working in these modes.

Help for WordPerfect users: When this check box is activated, Word monitors the keyboard for WordPerfect for DOS keyboard shortcuts so it can display the Word equivalent. For example, if you press Shift-F7—the WordPerfect Print command shortcut—Word displays the Help for WordPerfect Users dialog box, shown in Figure 14.3.

TIP: ANOTHER ROUTE TO WORDPERFECT HELP

You can also display the Help for WordPerfect Users dialog box by selecting Help | WordPerfect Help.

Navigation keys for WordPerfect users: Activating this check box turns off the usual Word document navigation keys in favor of the WordPerfect for DOS navigation keys. For example, pressing Home, Home, up arrow returns you to the start of the document (instead of Ctrl-Home).

Blue background, white text: If you turn on this option, Word converts its document windows to mimic WordPerfect's white text on a blue background look.

Provide feedback with sound: When this check box is activated, Word plays sounds associated with various program events, such as opening and closing files.

Provide feedback with animation: When this check box is activated, Word displays animations in the status bar during lengthy operations such as saving, printing, spell checking, background repagination, and more.

Confirm conversion at Open: When this check box is deactivated (the default), Word automatically converts documents you open to its native format. If you activate this option, Word asks you to confirm the conversion.

Update automatic links at Open: When you open a document that contains automatic links to a server document in another application, Word displays a dialog box asking whether you want to update the links. Deactivate this check box to prevent this dialog box from appearing.

Mail as attachment: If you have an e-mail system on your computer and you select File | Send To | Mail Recipient, activating this check box tells Word to send the file as an attachment to the message. If you clear this option, Word inserts the document text into the message.

Recently used file list: Activate this check box to display at the bottom of the File menu a list of the files you used most recently. Use the accompanying spinner to change the number of files displayed.

Macro virus protection: When this check box is activated, Word warns you if a document you're about to open contains macros and checks those macros for viruses.

Measurement units: This drop-down list determines the units used on Word's ruler.

FIGURE 14.2.

The General tab contains a mixed bag of settings.

FIGURE 14.3.

*When WordPerfect
Help is activated, Word
displays this dialog
box in response to
WordPerfect keyboard
shortcuts.*

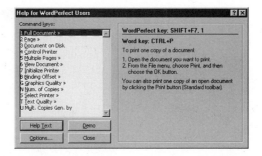

Changing Editing Options

The options in the Edit tab, shown in Figure 14.4, control various text editing settings:

Typing replaces selection: When this check box is activated, Word replaces any highlighted text with whatever character you type.

Drag-and-drop text editing: This option affects what Word does when you drag the mouse over selected text. When this check box is activated, drag-and-drop is turned on so that dragging selected text moves the text along with the mouse pointer. (To copy the text instead, hold down the Shift key while dragging.) Deactivating this option turns off drag-and-drop text editing, so dragging the mouse over selected text only changes the selection.

When selecting, automatically select entire word: This option affects how you select text by dragging the mouse. When this check box is activated, Word selects the entire word once you've highlighted only the first part of it.

Use the INS key for paste: Activate this check box to use the Insert key to paste cut or copied text (this is equivalent to Ctrl-V).

Overtype mode: Activating this check box places Word permanently in overtype mode, which means that your typing replaces existing text. (You can still return to the default insert mode at any time by pressing the Insert key.)

Use smart cut and paste: When this check box is turned on, Word monitors the spacing around words that you cut, paste, and delete. For example, if you paste a word beside another one, Word inserts a space between the words. Similarly, if you delete the last word of a sentence, Word ensures that no space remains before the period.

Tabs and backspace set left indent: When this option is turned on, pressing Tab at the beginning of a line increases the left indent setting. Similarly, pressing Backspace at the beginning of a line decreases the left indent.

Allow accented uppercase French: If you work with French text, activate this check box to enable accent marks in uppercase letters.

Picture editor: This list sets the default graphics software that Word launches when you double-click a picture object.

FIGURE 14.4.

Text editing options can be found in the Edit tab.

NOTE: THE PRINT OPTIONS

If you want descriptions of the options in the Print tab, head to Chapter 4, "Printing Options and Techniques."

Changing the General Workspace Options

The controls in the Save tab, shown in Figure 14.5, affect how Word saves your documents:

Always create backup copy: If you activate this check box, Word backs up the previous version of the document before saving the current version. (The "previous version" means the version of the document that doesn't include any of the changes made since the last save.) This backup copy uses the .BAK extension, and it's saved in the same folder as the document.

Allow fast saves: When this check box is activated, selecting the Save command doesn't save the entire file. Instead, Word just appends any changes you've made to the end of the file. This is much quicker than saving the entire file, but it can also increase the file size considerably. To keep your Word document file sizes down, deactivate this check box.

Prompt for document properties: Activate this check box to have Word display the Properties dialog box whenever you save a new document.

Prompt to save Normal template: When this check box is deactivated, Word saves a modified Normal template automatically the next time you save a document. If you'd rather have Word ask you whether you want the Normal template saved, activate this check box.

Embed TrueType fonts: If this option is turned on, Word embeds information about TrueType fonts right in the document. This is useful if you send the document to someone who might not have the appropriate TrueType fonts.

Embed characters in use only: Activate this option to have Word embed only the TrueType fonts that you actually use in the document. Note that Word enables this check box only if you activate the Embed TrueType fonts setting.

Save data only for forms: If you're using your document as an online form, activating this check box tells Word to save the document as a text file that includes only the form data (in tab-delimited format). This makes it easy to read the form information into a database.

Allow background saves: When this check box is activated, Word saves your documents in the background while you work.

Save AutoRecover info every *x* minutes: With this option activated, Word periodically saves information about the document that lets it recover the file in the event of a system crash. Use the spinner to determine that interval Word uses to save the AutoRecover data.

Save Word file as: This drop-down list determines the default format used when you save a Word file.

FIGURE 14.5.

The Save tab controls govern various settings related to saving documents.

The Save tab also includes several controls that apply only to the current document:

Password to open: If you want others to enter a password to open this document, enter the password (up to 15 case-sensitive characters) in this text box. Note that the opened file is read-only.

Password to modify: If you want others to enter a password in order to make changes to a file, use this text box to enter the password (up to 15 case-sensitive characters).

14

CUSTOMIZING WORD

Read-only recommended: If you activate this check box, Word displays the dialog box shown in Figure 14.6 if anyone attempts to open the file.

FIGURE 14.6.

If a document is set up as read-only recommended, Word displays this dialog box each time the file is opened.

Spell and Grammar Checking Settings

Word comes with a number of options that let you customize both its spell checking and its grammar checking. Here are the options for the spelling check that you find in the Spelling & Grammar tab, shown in Figure 14.7:

Check spelling as you type: This check box toggles Word's on-the-fly spell check on and off.

Hide spelling errors in this document: This check box toggles the misspelled word indicator (the wavy red underline) on and off.

Always suggest corrections: If you deactivate this check box, the spell checker doesn't suggest possible replacements for misspelled words.

Suggest from main dictionary only: If you activate this check box, Word only suggests replacement words from its main dictionary. Words added to custom dictionaries are ignored.

Ignore words in UPPERCASE: When this check box is activated, the spell checker ignores all words typed entirely in uppercase letters.

Ignore words with numbers: When this check box is activated, the spell checker ignores all words that contain numeric values.

Ignore Internet and file addresses: When this check box is activated, the spell checker ignores all words that contain Internet addresses (such as `http://www.mcp.com/`) or file paths (such as `\\Server\user\`).

Custom dictionary: This list displays the names of the active custom dictionaries.

FIGURE 14.7.

*Use the Spelling &
Grammar tab settings
to customize Word's
spelling and grammar
checkers.*

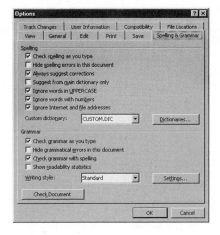

Each time you click Add during a spell check, Word adds the current word to the displayed
custom dictionary. In the Spelling & Grammar tab, you can use the Dictionaries button to
create new custom dictionaries. Here are the steps to follow:

1. Click Dictionaries to display the Custom Dictionaries dialog box, shown in
   Figure 14.8.

FIGURE 14.8.

*Use this dialog box to
create a new custom
dictionary.*

2. Click New. Word displays the Create Custom Dictionary dialog box.
3. Select a location for the new dictionary, enter a name, and click Save.
4. Click OK.

14

CUSTOMIZING WORD

TIP: VIEW CUSTOM DICTIONARY ENTRIES

Custom dictionaries use the .DIC extension, but they're really just simple text files that display each of the added entries on a separate line. To view these entries, display the Custom Dictionaries dialog box, highlight the custom dictionary you want to work with, and click Edit. Word then loads the .DIC file. Feel free to add, edit, or delete any of the entries while the file is open.

Here's a rundown of the grammar-related options in the Spelling & Grammar tab:

Check grammar as you type: Use this check box to toggle the on-the-fly grammar check on and off.

Hide grammatical errors in this document: Use this check box to toggle the grammar error indicator (the wavy green underline) on and off.

Check grammar with spelling: If you activate this check box, Word also checks the document's grammar when you invoke a spelling check.

Show readability statistics: Activating this check box tells Word to calculate various statistics concerning the document's "readability." These statistics are displayed automatically when Word has finished checking the grammar. Figure 14.9 shows an example.

FIGURE 14.9.

The grammar checker's readability statistics.

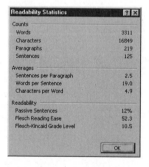

Writing style: Use this list to choose the default writing style the grammar checker should apply during its checks.

Settings: Click this button to display the Grammar Settings dialog box shown in Figure 14.10. You can use this dialog box to customize the options the grammar checker uses for each writing style.

Recheck Document: Click this button to run the grammar check.

FIGURE 14.10.
Use the Grammar Settings dialog box to customize the grammar checker options.

Customizing Edit Tracking Options

Word's edit tracking feature lets you monitor who made changes to a document and when. Changes are indicated by different fonts for different types of edit. You use the Track Changes tab, shown in Figure 14.11, to customize these font settings. For each of the four edit categories—Inserted text, Deleted text, Changed formatting, and Changed lines—use the Mark drop-down list to choose a font effect or other marking scheme, and use the Color drop-down list to specify the color of the edits. In each case, the Preview boxes show you what the edited text will look like.

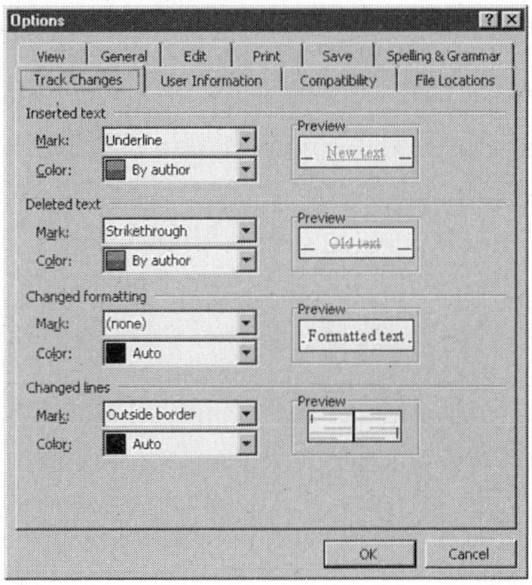

FIGURE 14.11.
The Track Changes tab controls various settings related to the font used for document edits.

14

Entering User Information

Word keeps track of various bits of personal data that it uses within a number of features. You can enter this data in the User Information tab, shown in Figure 14.12:

> **Name:** Enter your user name in this text box. Word uses this name to identify your document edits if you're tracking changes. It also places this data in the Properties dialog box (select File | Properties) and uses it when you create letters and envelopes and insert comments.

> **Initials:** Your initials are used with comments and in some letter and memo templates.

> **Mailing address:** Enter your address here. Word uses this address to automatically fill in your return address in envelopes and letters.

FIGURE 14.12.

Enter your name, initials, and mailing address in the User Information tab.

Word's Compatibility Options

To help ensure compatibility between Word and other word processing programs (or even earlier versions of Word), use the Compatibility tab, shown in Figure 14.13. Here's a summary of the available options:

> **Font Substitution:** If a document contains a font that isn't available on your system, click this button to display the Font Substitution dialog box, shown in Figure 14.14, and see which font Windows is using as a substitute. Use the Substituted font list to change the font. If you want to convert the missing font to the substituted font, click Convert Permanently.

Recommended options for: Use this list to choose the word processing program for which you want to set compatibility options.

Options: Use these check boxes to specify the compatibility options you want activated for the selected word processor.

FIGURE 14.13.

The Compatibility tab options help you maintain compatibility between Word and other word processing programs.

FIGURE 14.14.

The Font Substitution dialog box shows you which fonts Windows is using to display document fonts that are missing from your system.

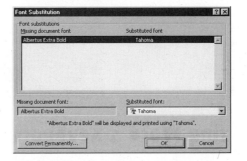

Specifying Where Word Stores Its Files

During installation, Word sets up several default folders to use for storing documents and template, clip art images, and more. Use the File Locations tab, shown in Figure 14.15, to change any of the following default folders. You do this by highlighting the current file type, clicking Modify, and using the dialog box that appears to choose a new folder. Here's a summary of the displayed file types:

Documents: This is the default folder that appears when you display the Save As and Open dialog boxes.

Clipart pictures: This is the default folder that appears when you insert a picture.

14

CUSTOMIZING
WORD

User templates: This is the default folder that appears when you save a template.

Workgroup templates: This is the default folder that's used to store templates that you want to share with network users.

User options: This is the default folder in which Word stores the selected options for each user.

AutoRecover files: This is the default folder that Word uses to store the AutoRecover data for each document.

Tools: This is the default folder for the shared Office tools.

Startup: This is the default folder that Word examines at startup. Any templates or add-ins placed in this folder are opened automatically when you start Word.

Figure 14.15.

Use the File Locations tab to specify new default folders.

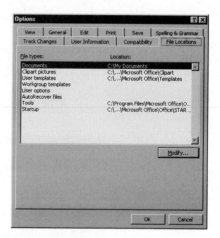

Customizing Word's Keyboard

I showed you various techniques for customizing Word's menus and toolbars in Chapter 8, "Customizing the Office Menus and Toolbars." Unlike the other Office applications, however, Word also lets you customize the third user-interaction element—the keyboard. Specifically, you can assign keyboard shortcuts to any of Word's commands (or change the existing keyboard shortcuts). Here are the steps to follow:

1. Select Tools | Customize.
2. Click the Keyboard button to display the Customize Keyboard dialog box.
3. Use the Save changes in list to choose the document or template in which the new key combination is stored.
4. Use the Categories list to choose the category that contains the command you want to work with.
5. Use the Commands list to highlight the command.

6. Move the cursor into the Press new shortcut key text box. If the command already has a shortcut key assigned, it appears in the Current keys list.

7. Press the key combination you want to use. Word displays the keypress in the text box and tells you whether the key combination is already assigned, as shown in Figure 14.16.

FIGURE 14.16.

Using the Customize Keyboard dialog box, you can assign key combinations to any Word command.

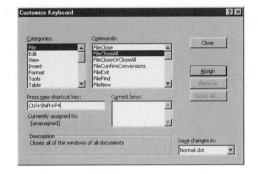

8. If this is the key combination you want to use, click Assign. Otherwise, repeat step 7 until you find a key combination you want.

9. Repeat steps 4 through 8 to assign other key combinations.

10. When you're done, click Close.

Loading Add-Ins

Add-ins are products that provide additional functionality and therefore offer even more ways to customize Word. Add-ins might come from Microsoft or other software vendors, or they might be programs you've written. Because add-ins aren't part of Word—or one of Office's objects—you must install them on your system and then load them into Word before using them.

To load an add-in into Word, select Tools | Templates and Add-Ins. The Templates and Add-ins dialog box appears. In the Global Templates and Add-ins area, select the product you want to load into Word, and then click OK. If you store the add-in product in the Word Startup folder, Word automatically loads the product.

Summary

This chapter gave you the 50-cent tour of Word's extensive customization options. I took you through the Options dialog box, and I also showed you how to customize the Word keyboard and load add-ins.

14

CUSTOMIZING WORD

Here are a few other chapters to read for related information:

- Word's Print tab options are covered in Chapter 4, "Printing Options and Techniques."
- You can also customize Word's menus and toolbars. See Chapter 8, "Customizing the Office Menus and Toolbars."
- To learn how to control Word via VBA, see Chapter 56, "Programming Word."

IV

PART

Unleashing Excel

Working with Ranges

IN THIS CHAPTER

CHAPTER 15

> *In the midst of this chopping sea of civilized life, such are the clouds and storms and*
> *quicksands and thousand-and-one items to be allowed for, that a man has to live, if he*
> *would not founder and go to the bottom and not make his port at all, by dead reckoning,*
> *and he must be a great calculator indeed who succeeds.*

> —*Henry David Thoreau*

Ranges are powerful tools that can unlock the hidden power of Excel, so the more you know about ranges, the more you'll get out of your Excel investment. This chapter reviews some range basics and then takes you beyond the range routine and shows you some techniques for taking full advantage of Excel's range capabilities.

A Review of Excel's Range Selection Techniques

As you work with Excel, you'll come across three situations in which you'll select a cell range:

- When a dialog box field requires range input
- While entering a function argument
- Before selecting a command that uses range input

In a dialog box field or function argument, the most straightforward way to select a range is to enter the range coordinates by hand. Just type the address of the upper-left cell (called the *anchor cell*), followed by a colon and then the address of the lower-right cell. To use this method, you either must be able to see the range you want to select or you must know in advance the range coordinates you want. Because often this is not the case, most people don't type the range coordinates directly; instead, they select ranges using either the mouse or the keyboard.

Selecting a Range with the Mouse

Although you can use either the mouse or the keyboard to select a range, you'll find that the mouse makes the job much easier. The following sections take you through several methods you can use to select a range with the mouse.

Selecting a Contiguous Range with the Mouse

A rectangular, contiguous grouping of cells is the most common type of range. To use the mouse to select such a range, follow these steps:

1. Point the mouse at the upper-left cell of the range (the anchor) and then press and hold down the left mouse button.

2. With the left mouse button still pressed, drag the mouse pointer to the lower-right cell of the range. The cell selector remains around the anchor cell, and Excel highlights the other cells in the range in reverse video. The formula bar's Name box shows the number of rows and columns you've selected.

3. Release the mouse button. The cells remain selected to show the range you've defined, and the Name box shows the address of the anchor cell.

TIP: ADJUSTING THE SELECTED RANGE

Do you have to start over if you select the wrong lower-right corner and your range ends up either too big or too small? Not at all. Just hold down the Shift key and click the correct lower-right cell. The range adjusts automatically.

Selecting a Row or Column with the Mouse

Using the worksheet row and column headings, you can quickly select a range that consists of an entire row or column. For a row, click the row's heading; for a column, click the column's heading. If you need to select adjacent rows or columns, just drag the mouse pointer across the appropriate headings.

What if you want to select every row and every column (in other words, the entire worksheet)? Easy: Just click the Select All button near the upper-left corner of the sheet.

Selecting a Range in Extend Mode with the Mouse

An alternative method uses the mouse with the F8 key to select a rectangular, contiguous range. You can do this by following these steps:

1. Click the upper-left cell of the range.
2. Press F8. Excel enters extend mode (you'll see EXT in the status bar).
3. Click the lower-right cell of the range. Excel selects the entire range.
4. Press F8 again to turn off extend mode.

TIP: VIEWING THE ACTIVE CELL

After selecting a large range, you'll often no longer see the active cell because you've scrolled it off the screen. If you need to see the active cell before continuing, you can either use the scroll bars to bring it into view or press Ctrl-Backspace.

Working with 3D Ranges

A *3D range* is a range selected on multiple sheets. This is a powerful concept because it means that you can select a range on two or more sheets and then enter data, apply formatting, or give a command, and the operation will affect all the ranges at once.

To create a 3D range, you first need to group the worksheets you want to work with. To select multiple sheets, you can use any of the following techniques:

■ To select adjacent sheets, click the tab of the first sheet, hold down the Shift key, and click the tab of the last sheet.

■ To select noncontiguous sheets, hold down the Ctrl key and click the tab of each sheet you want to include in the group.

■ To select all the sheets in a workbook, right-click any sheet tab and choose Select All Sheets from the context menu.

When you've selected your sheets, each tab is highlighted and [Group] appears in the workbook title bar. To ungroup the sheets, click a tab that isn't in the group. Alternatively, you can right-click one of the group's tabs and select Ungroup Sheets from the shortcut menu.

With the sheets now grouped, you create your 3D range simply by activating one of the grouped sheets and then selecting a range using any of the techniques we just ran through. Excel selects the same cells in all the other sheets in the group. (You can prove it for yourself by activating the other sheets in the group.)

You can also type in a 3D range by hand when entering a formula, for example. Here's the general format for a 3D reference:

`FirstSheet:LastSheet!ULCorner:LRCorner`

Here, `FirstSheet` is the name of the first sheet in the 3D range, `LastSheet` is the name of the last sheet, and `ULCorner` and `LRCorner` define the cell ranges you want to work with on each sheet. For example, to specify the range A1:E10 on worksheets Sheet1, Sheet2, and Sheet3, use the following reference:

`Sheet1:Sheet3!A1:E10`

You'll normally use 3D references in worksheet functions that accept them. These functions include AVERAGE(), COUNT(), COUNTA(), MAX(), MIN(), PRODUCT(), STDEV(), STDEVP(), SUM(), VAR(), and VARP().

Using Range Names

Although ranges let you work efficiently with large groups of cells, they have some disadvantages:

■ You can't work with more than one range at a time. Each time you want to use a range, you have to redefine its coordinates.

■ Range notation isn't intuitive. To know what a formula such as =SUM(E6:E10) is adding, you have to look at the range itself.

■ A slight mistake in defining a range can lead to disastrous results, especially when you're erasing a range.

You can overcome these problems by using range names. You can assign names of up to 255 characters to any single cell or range on your spreadsheet. To include the range in a formula or range command, you use the name instead of selecting the range or typing in its coordinates. You can create as many range names as you like, and you can even assign multiple names to the same range.

Range names also make your formulas intuitive and easy to read. For example, by assigning the name AugustSales to a range such as E6:E10, the purpose of a formula such as =SUM(AugustSales) becomes immediately clear. Range names also increase the accuracy of your range operations because you don't have to specify range coordinates.

Besides overcoming the problems mentioned earlier, range names also bring several advantages to the table:

- Names are easier to remember than range coordinates.
- Names don't change when you move a range to another part of the worksheet.
- Named ranges adjust automatically whenever you insert or delete rows or columns within the range.
- Names make it easier to navigate a worksheet. You can use the Go To command to jump to a named range quickly.
- You can use worksheet labels to create range names quickly.

Defining a Range Name

Besides having a maximum length of 255 characters, range names must also follow these guidelines:

- The name must begin with either a letter or the underscore character (_). For the rest of the name, you can use any combination of characters, numbers, or symbols (except spaces). With multiple-word names, separate the words by using an underscore or by mixing case (for example, cost_of_goods or CostOfGoods). Excel doesn't distinguish between uppercase and lowercase letters in range names.
- Don't use cell addresses or any of the operator symbols (such as +, -, *, /, <, >, and &), because these could cause confusion if you use the name in a formula.
- To make typing easier, try to keep your names as short as possible while still retaining their meaning. TotalProfit96 is faster to type than Total_Profit_For_Fiscal_Year_96, and it's certainly clearer than the more cryptic TotPft96.

Defining Range Names by Hand

With these guidelines in mind, follow these steps to define a range name:

1. Select the range you want to name.
2. Select Insert | Name | Define. The Define Name dialog box appears, as shown in Figure 15.1.

FIGURE 15.1.

Use the Define Name dialog box to define a name for the selected range.

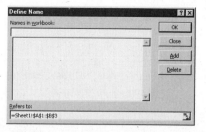

TIP: KEYBOARD SHORTCUT

If you're in a hurry, you can press Ctrl-F3 to open the Define Name dialog box quickly.

3. Enter the range name in the Names in workbook text box.

4. If for some reason the range displayed in the Refers to box is incorrect, you can use one of two methods to change it:

   ■ Type the correct range address (be sure to begin the address with an equals sign).

   ■ Move the cursor into the Refers to box, delete the existing address, and then use the mouse or keyboard to select a new range on the worksheet. As you select the range, Excel displays a smaller version of the Define Name dialog box (showing just the Refers to text box) and updates the range coordinates automatically.

CAUTION: PUT EXCEL IN EDIT MODE BEFORE MOVING AROUND

If you need to move around inside the Refers to box using the arrow keys (for example, to edit the existing range address), first press F2 to put Excel into edit mode. If you don't, Excel remains in point mode, and the program assumes that you're trying to select a cell on the worksheet.

5. Click the Add button. Excel adds the name to the Names in workbook list.

6. Repeat steps 3 through 5 for any other ranges you want to name.

7. When you're done, click the Close button to return to the worksheet.

Defining Range Names Using Worksheet Text

When you select Insert | Name | Define, Excel sometimes suggests a name for the selected range. Specifically, Excel uses an adjacent text entry to make an educated guess about what you'll want to use as a name.

Instead of waiting for Excel to guess, you can tell the program explicitly to use adjacent text as a range name. The following procedure shows you the appropriate steps:

1. Select the range of cells you want to name, including the appropriate text cells that you want to use as the range names.

2. Select Insert | Name | Create. Excel displays the Create Names dialog box.

TIP: KEYBOARD SHORTCUT

The shortcut key for the Create Names dialog box is Ctrl-Shift-F3.

3. Excel guesses where the text for the range name is located and activates the appropriate check box. (For example, if there is text in the leftmost column of the selected range, Excel activates the Left column check box). If this isn't the one you want, deactivate the check box and then activate the appropriate one.

4. Click OK.

Bear in mind that if the text you want to use as a range name contains any illegal characters (such as a space), Excel replaces them with an underscore character (_).

NOTE: REFERRING TO RANGE NAMES

Range names are available to all the sheets in a workbook. This means, for example, that a formula in Sheet1 can refer to a named range in Sheet3 simply by using the name directly. If you need to use the same name in different sheets, you can create *sheet-level* names. These kinds of names are preceded by the name of the worksheet and an exclamation point. For example, Sheet1!Sales refers to a range named Sales in Sheet1, and Sheet2!Sales refers to a range named Sales in Sheet2.

If the named range exists in a different workbook, you must precede the name with the name of the file in single quotation marks. For example, if the Mortgage Amortization workbook contained a range named Rate, you would use the following entry to refer to this range in a different workbook:

```
'Mortgage Amortization'!Rate
```

Working with the Name Box

The Name box in Excel's formula bar gives you some extra features that make it easier to work with range names:

■ After you've defined a name, it appears in the Name box whenever you select the range.

■ The Name box doubles as a drop-down list. To select a named range quickly, drop the list down and select the name you want. Excel moves to the range and selects the cells.

■ You can also use the Name box as an easy way to define a range name. Just select the range and click inside the Name box to display the insertion point. Enter the name you want to use and then press Enter. Excel defines the new name automatically.

Changing a Range Name

If you need to change the name of one or more ranges, you can use one of two methods:

■ If you've changed some row or column labels, just redefine the range names based on the new text (as described earlier) and delete the old names (see the next section).

■ Select Insert | Name | Define. Highlight the name you want to change in the Names in workbook list, make your changes in the text box, and click the Add button.

CAUTION: THE OLD RANGE NAME REMAINS INTACT

Note that these methods don't actually change the name of the range. Instead, they just define a new name for the range while leaving the old name intact. This also means that any formulas that refer to the original range name won't get changed.

Deleting a Range Name

If you no longer need a range name, you should delete the name from the worksheet to avoid cluttering the name list. Just follow these steps:

1. Select Insert | Name | Define to display the Define Name dialog box.
2. In the Names in workbook list, select the name you want to delete.
3. Click the Delete button. Excel deletes the name from the list.
4. Repeat steps 2 and 3 for any other names you want to delete.
5. When you're done, click OK.

Filling a Range

If you need to fill a range with a particular value or formula, Excel gives you two methods:

■ Select the range you want to fill, type the value or formula, and press Ctrl-Enter. Excel fills the entire range with whatever you entered in the formula bar.

■ Enter the initial value or formula, select the range you want to fill (including the initial cell), and select Edit | Fill. Then, select the appropriate command from the cascade menu that appears. For example, if you're filling a range down from the initial cell, select the Down command. If multiple sheets are selected, use Edit | Fill | Across Worksheets to fill the range in each worksheet.

> **TIP: KEYBOARD SHORTCUTS**
>
> Press Ctrl-R to select Edit | Fill | Right and Ctrl-D to select Edit | Fill | Down.

Using the Fill Handle

The *fill handle* is the small black square in the bottom-right corner of the active cell or range. You can use the fill handle to fill a range with a value or formula. Just enter your initial values or formulas, select them, and then drag the fill handle over the destination range. (I'm assuming that the data you're copying won't create a series.) When you release the mouse button, Excel fills the range.

Note that if the initial cell contains a formula with relative references, Excel adjusts the references accordingly. For example, suppose that the initial cell contains the formula =A1. If you fill down, the next cell will contain the formula =A2, the next will contain =A3, and so on.

Creating a Series

Although you can use the fill handle to create a series, you can use Excel's Series command to gain a little more control over the whole process. Follow these steps:

1. Select the first cell you want to use for the series and enter the starting value. If you want to create a series out of a particular pattern (such as 2, 4, 6, ...), fill in enough cells to define the pattern.
2. Select the entire range you want to fill.
3. Select Edit | Fill | Series. Excel displays the Series dialog box, shown in Figure 15.2.

FIGURE 15.2.

Use the Series dialog box to define the series you want to create.

4. In the Series in group, select Rows to create the series in rows starting from the active cell or Columns to create the series in columns.
5. Use the Type group to enter the type of series you want. You have the following options:

>   Linear: This option finds the next series value by adding the step value (see step 7) to the preceding value in the series.
>
>   Growth: This option finds the next series value by multiplying the preceding value by the step value.

Date: This option creates a series of dates based on the option you select in the Date Unit group (Day, Weekday, Month, or Year).

AutoFill: This option works much like the fill handle does. You can use it to extend a numeric pattern or a text series (for example, Qtr1, Qtr2, Qtr3).

6. If you want to extend a series trend, activate the Trend check box. This option is available only if you have selected a Linear or Growth series type.

7. If you have selected a Linear, Growth, or Date series type, enter a number in the Step value box. This number is what Excel uses to increment each value in the series.

8. To place a limit on the series, enter the appropriate number in the Stop value box.

9. Click OK. Excel fills in the series and returns you to the worksheet.

Copying a Range

The quickest way to become productive with Excel is to avoid reinventing your worksheet. If you have a formula that works, or a piece of formatting that you've put a lot of effort into, don't start from scratch to create something similar. Instead, make a copy and then adjust it as necessary.

Copying a Range with the Copy Command

If you prefer the pull-down menu approach, you can copy a range using the Copy command.

CAUTION: DON'T OVERWRITE EXISTING CELLS

Before copying a range, look at the destination area and make sure that you won't be overwriting any nonblank cells. Remember that you can use the Undo command if you accidentally destroy some data. If you want to insert the range among some existing cells, see the next section.

Follow these steps to copy a range using the Copy command:

1. Select the range you want to copy.

2. Select Edit | Copy. Excel copies the contents of the range to the Clipboard and displays a moving border around the range.

3. Select the upper-left cell of the destination range.

4. Select Edit | Paste. Excel pastes the range from the Clipboard to your destination.

TIP: COPY SHORTCUTS

Instead of selecting Edit | Copy, you can press Ctrl-C, right-click the source range and select the Copy command from the Range shortcut menu, or click the Copy button on the Standard toolbar.

Instead of selecting Edit | Paste, you can press Ctrl-V, right-click the destination cell and select the Paste command from the Range shortcut menu, or click the Paste button on the Standard toolbar.

Inserting a Copy of a Range

If you don't want a pasted range to overwrite existing cells, you can tell Excel to *insert* the range. In this case, Excel moves the existing cells out of harm's way before pasting the range from the Clipboard. (As you'll see, you have control over where Excel moves the existing cells.) Follow these steps to insert a copy of a range:

1. Select the range you want to copy.

2. Use any of the methods described earlier to copy the range to the Clipboard.

3. Select the upper-left cell of the destination range.

4. Select Insert | Copied Cells. Excel displays the Insert Paste dialog box, shown in Figure 15.3, so that you can choose where to move the existing cells that would otherwise be overwritten.

FIGURE 15.3.

Use the Insert Paste dialog box to tell Excel in which direction to move the existing cells.

TIP: INSERTION SHORTCUT

You also can insert a copied range by right-clicking the destination cell and selecting Insert Copied Cells from the shortcut menu.

5. Select Shift cells right to move the cells to the right or Shift cells down to move them down.

6. Click OK. Excel shifts the existing cells and then pastes the range from the Clipboard.

15

WORKING WITH RANGES

Moving a Range

Moving a range is very similar to copying a range, except that the source range gets deleted when all is said and done.

Using the Menu Commands to Move a Range

To move a range using the menu commands, you need to cut the range to the Clipboard and then paste it. The following procedure details the steps involved:

1. Select the range you want to move.
2. Select Edit | Cut. Excel cuts the contents of the range to the Clipboard and displays a moving border around the range.
3. Select the upper-left cell of the destination range.
4. Select Edit | Paste. Excel pastes the range from the Clipboard to your destination.

TIP: CUT SHORTCUTS

Instead of selecting Edit | Cut, you can press Ctrl-X, right-click the source range, and select the Cut command from the Range shortcut menu, or click the Cut button on the Standard toolbar.

Inserting and Deleting a Range

When you begin a worksheet, you generally use rows and columns sequentially as you add data, labels, and formulas. More often than not, however, you'll need to go back and add some values or text that you forgot or that you need for another part of the worksheet. When this happens, you need to insert ranges into your spreadsheet to make room for your new information. Conversely, you often have to remove old or unnecessary data from a spreadsheet, which requires you to delete ranges. The next few sections describe various and sundry methods for inserting and deleting ranges in Excel.

Inserting an Entire Row or Column

The easiest way to insert a range into a worksheet is to insert an entire row or column. The following steps show you how it's done:

1. Select the row or column before which you want to insert the new row or column. If you want to insert multiple rows or columns, select the appropriate number of rows or columns, as shown in Figure 15.4.

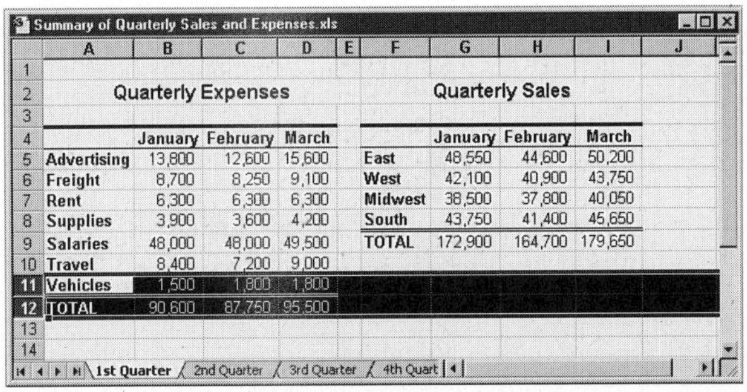

Figure 15.4.

Two rows have been selected at the point where two new rows are to be inserted.

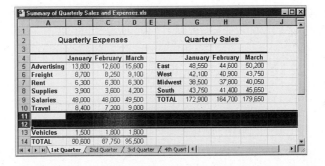

Press Ctrl-Spacebar to select an entire column or Shift-Spacebar to select an entire row.

2. If you're inserting rows, select Insert | Rows. Excel shifts the selected rows down, as shown in Figure 15.5. If you're inserting columns, select Insert | Columns instead. In this case, Excel shifts the selected columns to the right.

Figure 15.5.

When you insert rows, Excel shifts the existing cells down.

To insert a row or column quickly, as soon as you've selected a row or column, press and hold down the Ctrl key and then press the + key. You can also right-click the range and then select Insert from the shortcut menu.

Inserting a Cell or Range

In some worksheets you might need to insert only a single cell or a range of cells so as not to disturb the arrangement of surrounding data. For example, suppose that you want to add a Repair line between Rent and Supplies in the Quarterly Expenses table shown in Figure 15.6.

15

WORKING WITH
RANGES

FIGURE 15.6.

When you insert cells in the Quarterly Expenses table, you don't want to disturb the Quarterly Sales table.

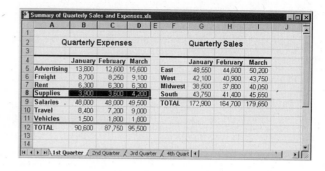

You don't want to add an entire row because it would create a gap in the Quarterly Sales table. Instead, you can insert a range that covers just the area you need. Follow these steps:

1. Select the range where you want the new range to appear. In the Quarterly Expenses example, you would select the range A8:D8.

2. Select Insert | Cells. Excel displays the Insert dialog box, shown in Figure 15.7.

FIGURE 15.7.

Use the Insert dialog box to tell Excel which way to shift the existing cells.

3. Select either Shift cells right or Shift cells down.

4. Click OK. Excel inserts the range.

Deleting an Entire Row or Column

Deleting a row or column is similar to inserting. In this case, however, you need to exercise a little more caution because a hasty deletion can have disastrous effects on your worksheet. (However, keep in mind that you can always select Edit | Undo if you make any mistakes.)

The following procedure shows you how to delete a row or column:

1. Select the row or column you want to delete.

2. Select Edit | Delete. Excel deletes the row or column and shifts the remaining data appropriately.

Deleting a Cell or Range

If you need to delete only one cell or a range to avoid trashing any surrounding data, follow these steps:

1. Select the cell or range you want to delete.
2. Select Edit | Delete. Excel displays the Delete dialog box.
3. Select either Shift cells left or Shift cells up.
4. Click OK. Excel deletes the range.

Clearing a Range

As you've seen, deleting a range actually removes the cells from the worksheet. What if you want the cells to remain, but you want their contents or formats cleared? For that, you can use Excel's Clear command:

1. Select the range you want to clear.
2. Select Edit | Clear. Excel displays a submenu of Clear commands.
3. Select either All, Formats, Contents, Comments, or Hyperlinks.

> **TIP: DELETION SHORTCUTS**
>
> To quickly delete the contents of the selected range, press Delete. You can also right-click the range and select Clear Contents from the Range shortcut menu.

Using Excel's Reference Operators

As you probably know, Excel has various operators (+, *, and &, for example) that you use for building formulas. I'd like to close our look at ranges by talking about some of Excel's *reference operators*. You use these operators when working with cell references, as discussed in the next two sections.

Using the Range Operator

The *range* operator is just the familiar colon (:), which you've been using all along. All you do is insert a colon between two references, and Excel creates a range (for example, A1:C5). Nothing too surprising here.

Until now, though, you've probably been creating your ranges by using the reference on the left side of the colon to define the upper-left corner of the range and the reference on the right side of the colon to define the lower-right corner. There are other ways to create ranges with the range operator, however. Table 15.1 points out a few of them.

Table 15.1. Sample ranges created with the range operator.

Range	What It Refers To
A:A	Column A (that is, the entire column)
A:C	Columns A through C
1:1	Row 1
1:5	Rows 1 through 5

You can also use a range name on either side of the colon. In this case, the named range becomes a *corner* for the larger range. For example, Figure 15.8 shows a worksheet with the named range Rent that refers to B7:D7. Table 15.2 shows some sample ranges you can create with Rent as one corner.

FIGURE 15.8.

The named range Rent used in Table 15.2.

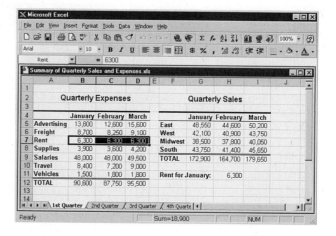

Table 15.2. Sample ranges created with a range name.

Range	What It Refers To
Rent:D12	B7:D12
Rent:A1	A1:D7
Rent:G2	B2:G7
Rent:A13	A7:D13

Using this technique, Excel "fills in" a rectangular range that includes the named range in one "corner" and the specified cell in another corner. For example, consider the range Rent:D12. Excel begins with the Rent range (B7:D7) and extends the range down so that it includes cell D12. The result is the rectangular range B7:D12.

Using the Intersection Operator

If you have ranges that overlap, you can use the *intersection* operator (a space) to refer to the overlapping cells. For example, Figure 15.9 shows two ranges: C4:E9 and D8:G11. To refer to the overlapping cells (D8:E9), you would use the following notation: C4:E9 D8:G11.

FIGURE 15.9.

The intersection operator returns the intersecting cells of two ranges.

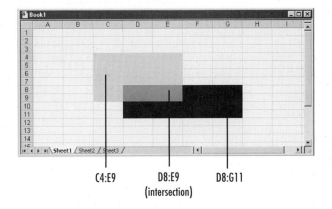

C4:E9   D8:E9   D8:G11
        (intersection)

If you've named the ranges on your worksheet, the intersection operator can make things much easier to read, because you can refer to individual cells by using the names of the cell's row and column. For example, in Figure 15.10, the range B5:B12 is named January and the range B7:D7 is named Rent. This means that you can refer to cell B7 as January Rent (see cell H11).

FIGURE 15.10.

After you name ranges, you can combine row and column headings to create intersecting names for individual cells.

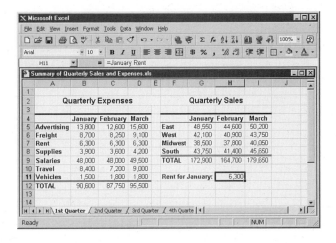

CAUTION: MAKE SURE RANGES OVERLAP

If you try to define an intersection name and Excel displays #NULL! in the cell, this means that the two ranges don't have any overlapping cells.

Summary

This chapter showed you how to get the most out of your worksheet ranges. It showed you a number of ways to select a range. It also told you about range names, the fill handle, creating a series, copying and moving a range, and how to use Excel's reference operators. For related range information, see the following chapters:

- Functions often use range arguments, and you'll be learning about functions in Chapter 16, "Manipulating Formulas and Functions."

- I'll explore some advanced range topics—such as consolidating data—in Chapter 17, "Advanced Worksheet Topics."

- To learn how to control ranges programmatically, see Chapter 57, "Excel VBA Techniques."

Manipulating Formulas and Functions

CHAPTER 16

> *Mathematics may be compared to a mill of exquisite workmanship, which grinds your stuff to any degree of fineness; but, nevertheless, what you get out depends on what you put in; and as the grandest mill in the world will not extract wheat flour from peascods, so pages of formulae will not get a definite result out of loose data.*
>
> —*Thomas Henry Huxley*

A worksheet is merely a lifeless collection of numbers and text until you define some kind of relationship among the various entries. You do this by creating *formulas* that perform calculations and produce results. This chapter takes you through some formula basics, shows you a number of techniques for building powerful formulas, and talks about troubleshooting and auditing formulas.

This chapter also introduces you to Excel's built-in worksheet functions. You'll learn what the functions are, what they can do, and how to use them.

Understanding Formula Basics

Most worksheets are created to provide answers to specific questions: What is the company's profit? Are expenses over or under budget, and by how much? What is the future value of an investment? How big will my bonus be this year? You can answer these questions, and an infinite variety of others, by using Excel formulas.

All Excel formulas have the same general structure: an equals sign (=) followed by one or more *operands*—which can be a value, a cell reference, a range, a range name, or a function name—separated by one or more *operators*—the symbols that combine the operands, such as the plus sign (+) and the greater-than sign (>).

Excel divides formulas into four groups: arithmetic, comparison, text, and reference. Each group has its own set of operators, and you use each group in different ways. In the next few sections I'll show you how to use each type of formula.

Using Arithmetic Formulas

Arithmetic formulas are by far the most common type of formula. They combine numbers, cell addresses, and function results with mathematical operators to perform calculations. Table 16.1 summarizes the mathematical operators used in arithmetic formulas.

Table 16.1. The arithmetic operators.

Operator	Name	Example	Result
+	Addition	=10+5	15
-	Subtraction	=10-5	5
-	Negation	=-10	–10
*	Multiplication	=10*5	50

Manipulating Formulas and Functions

CHAPTER 16

391

16

MANIPULATING
FORMULAS AND
FUNCTIONS

Operator	Name	Example	Result
/	Division	=10/5	2
%	Percentage	=10%	0.1
^	Exponentiation	=10^5	100000

Most of these operators are straightforward, but the exponentiation operator might require further explanation. The formula =x^y means that the value x is raised to the power y. For example, the formula =3^2 produces the result 9 (that is, 3*3=9). Similarly, the formula =2^4 produces 16 (that is, 2*2*2*2=16).

Using Comparison Formulas

A *comparison formula* is a statement that compares two or more numbers, text strings, cell contents, or function results. If the statement is true, the result of the formula is given the logical value TRUE (which is equivalent to any nonzero value). If the statement is false, the formula returns the logical value FALSE (which is equivalent to 0). Table 16.2 summarizes the operators you can use in logical formulas. (Note that you don't have to use only numbers with your comparison formulas; Excel can also compare letters.)

Table 16.2. Comparison formula operators.

Operator	Name	Example	Result
=	Equal to	=10=5	FALSE
>	Greater than	=10>5	TRUE
<	Less than	=10<5	FALSE
>=	Greater than or equal to	="a">="b"	FALSE
<=	Less than or equal to	="a"<="b"	TRUE
<>	Not equal to	="a"<>"b"	TRUE

There are many uses for comparison formulas. For example, you can determine whether to pay a salesperson a bonus by using a comparison formula to compare his actual sales with a predetermined quota. If the sales are greater than the quota, the rep is awarded the bonus. You can also monitor credit collection. For example, if the amount a customer owes is more than 150 days past due, you might send the invoice to a collection agency.

Using Text Formulas

So far, I've discussed formulas that calculate or make comparisons and return values. A *text formula* is a formula that returns text. Text formulas use the ampersand (&) operator to work with text cells, text strings enclosed in quotation marks, and text function results.

One way to use text formulas is to concatenate text strings. For example, if you enter the formula ="soft"&"ware" into a cell, Excel displays software. Note that the quotation marks and ampersand are not shown in the result. You also can use & to combine cells that contain text. For example, if A1 contains the text Ben and A2 contains Jerry, entering the formula =A1 & " and " & A2 returns Ben and Jerry.

Using Reference Formulas

The reference operators combine two cell references or ranges to create a single joint reference. I discuss reference formulas in Chapter 15, "Working with Ranges," but Table 16.3 gives you a quick summary.

Table 16.3. Reference formula operators.

Operator	Name	Description
: (colon)	Range	Produces a range from two cell references (for example, A1:C5).
(space)	Intersection	Produces a range that is the intersection of two ranges (for example, A1:C5 B2:E8).
, (comma)	Union	Produces a range that is the union of two ranges (for example, A1:C5,B2:E8).

Understanding Operator Precedence

You'll often use simple formulas that contain just two values and a single operator. In practice, however, most formulas you use will have a number of values and operators. In these more complex expressions, the order in which the calculations are performed becomes crucial. For example, consider the formula =3+5^2. If you calculate from left to right, the answer you get is 64 (3+5 equals 8, and 8^2 equals 64). However, if you perform the exponentiation first and then the addition, the result is 28 (5^2 equals 25, and 3+25 equals 28). As this example shows, a single formula can produce multiple answers, depending on the order in which you perform the calculations.

To control this problem, Excel evaluates a formula according to a predefined *order of precedence.* This order of precedence allows Excel to calculate a formula unambiguously by determining which part of the formula it calculates first, which part it calculates second, and so on.

The Order of Precedence

Excel's order of precedence is determined by the various formula operators I outlined earlier. Table 16.4 summarizes the complete order of precedence used by Excel.

Manipulating Formulas and Functions

CHAPTER 16

393

16

MANIPULATING
FORMULAS AND
FUNCTIONS

Table 16.4. Excel's order of precedence.

Operator	Operation	Order of Precedence
:	Range	First
(space)	Intersection	Second
,	Union	Third
-	Negation	Fourth
%	Percentage	Fifth
^	Exponentiation	Sixth
* and /	Multiplication and division	Seventh
+ and -	Addition and subtraction	Eighth
&	Concatenation	Ninth
= < > <= >= <>	Comparison	Tenth

From this table, you can see that Excel performs exponentiation before addition. Therefore, the correct answer for the formula =3+5^2, given earlier, is 28. Notice, as well, that some operators in Table 16.4 have the same order of precedence (for example, multiplication and division). This means that it doesn't matter in which order these operators are evaluated. For example, consider the formula =5*10/2. If you perform the multiplication first, the answer you get is 25 (5*10 equals 50, and 50/2 equals 25). If you perform the division first, you also get an answer of 25 (10/2 equals 5, and 5*5 equals 25). By convention, Excel evaluates operators that have the same order of precedence from left to right.

Controlling the Order of Precedence

Sometimes you will want to override the order of precedence. For example, suppose that you want to create a formula that calculates the pre-tax cost of an item. If you bought something for $10.65, including 7 percent sales tax, and you want to find the cost of the item less the tax, you would use the formula =10.65/1.07, which gives you the correct answer of $9.95. In general, this is the formula:

$$\text{Pre-tax cost} = \frac{\text{Total Cost}}{1 + \text{Tax Rate}}$$

Figure 16.1 shows how you might implement such a formula. Cell B5 displays the Total Cost variable, and cell B6 displays the Tax Rate variable. Given these parameters, your first instinct might be to use the formula =B5/1+B6 to calculate the original cost. This formula is shown in cell E9, and the result is given in cell D9. As you can see, this answer is incorrect. What happened? Well, according to the rules of precedence, Excel performs division before addition, so the value in B5 first is divided by 1 and then is added to the value in B6. To get the correct answer, you must override the order of precedence so that the addition 1+B6 is performed first. You do this by surrounding that part of the formula with parentheses, as shown in cell E10. When you do this, you get the correct answer (see cell D10).

FIGURE 16.1.

Use parentheses to control the order of precedence in your formulas.

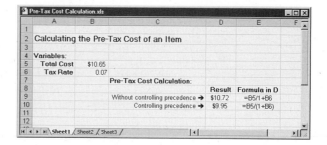

In general, you can use parentheses to control the order that Excel uses to calculate formulas. Terms inside parentheses are always calculated first; terms outside parentheses are calculated sequentially (according to the order of precedence). To gain even more control over your formulas, you can place parentheses inside one another; this is called *nesting* parentheses. Excel always evaluates the innermost set of parentheses first. Here are a few sample formulas:

Formula	First Step	Second Step	Third Step	Result
3^(15/5)*2-5	3^3*2-5	27*2-5	54-5	49
3^((15/5)*2-5)	3^(3*2-5)	3^(6-5)	3^1	3
3^(15/(5*2-5))	3^(15/(10-5))	3^(15/5)	3^3	27

Notice that the order of precedence rules also hold within parentheses. For example, in the expression (5*2-5), the term 5*2 is calculated before 5 is subtracted.

Using parentheses to determine the order of calculations lets you gain full control over Excel formulas. This way, you can make sure that the answer given by a formula is the one you want.

CAUTION: MAKE SURE YOU CLOSE YOUR PARENTHESES

One of the most common mistakes when using parentheses in formulas is to forget to close a parenthetic term with a right parenthesis. If you do this, Excel generates an error message. To make sure that you've closed each parenthetic term, count all the left and right parentheses. If the totals don't match, you know you've left out a parenthesis.

Copying and Moving Formulas

I showed you various techniques for copying and moving ranges. The procedures for copying and moving ranges that contain formulas are identical, but the results are not always straightforward. For an example, check out Figure 16.2, which shows a list of expense data for a company. The formula in cell C11 totals the January expenses. The idea behind this worksheet is to calculate a new expense budget number for 1997 as a percentage increase of the actual 1996 total. Cell C3 displays the INCREASE variable (in this case, the increase being used is 9 percent). The formula that calculates the 1997 BUDGET number (cell C13 for the month of January) multiplies the 1996 TOTAL by the INCREASE (that is, =C11*C3).

FIGURE 16.2.

A budget expenses worksheet.

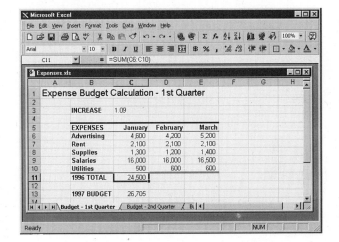

The next step is to calculate the 1996 TOTAL expenses and the 1997 BUDGET figure for February. You could just type each new formula, but you learned in the preceding chapter that you can copy a cell much more quickly. Figure 16.3 shows the results when you copy the contents of cell C11 into cell D11. As you can see, Excel adjusts the range in the formula's SUM() function so that only the February expenses are totaled. How did Excel know to do this? To answer this question, you need to know about Excel's relative reference format.

FIGURE 16.3.

When you copy the January 1996 TOTAL formula to February, Excel automatically adjusts the range reference.

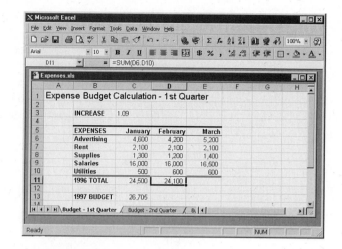

Understanding Relative Reference Format

When you use a cell reference in a formula, Excel looks at the cell address relative to the location of the formula. For example, suppose that you have the formula =A1*2 in cell A2. To Excel, this formula says, "Multiply the contents of the cell one row above this one by 2." This is called the *relative reference format*, and it's the default format for Excel. This means that if you copy this formula to cell A5, the relative reference is still "Multiply the contents of the cell one row above this one by 2," but the formula changes to =A4*2, because A4 is one row above A5.

Figure 16.3 shows why this format is useful. You had to copy only the formula in cell C11 to cell D11, and, thanks to relative referencing, everything comes out perfectly. To get the expense total for March, you would just have to paste the same formula into cell E11. You'll find that this way of handling copy operations will save you incredible amounts of time when you're building your worksheet models.

However, you need to exercise some care when copying or moving formulas. Let's see what happens if we return to the budget expense worksheet and try copying the 1997 BUDGET formula in cell C13 to cell D13. Figure 16.4 shows that the result is 0! What happened? The formula bar shows the problem: the new formula is =D11*D3. Cell D11 is the February 1996 TOTAL, and that's fine, but instead of referring to the INCREASE cell (C3), the formula refers to a blank cell (D3). Excel treats blank cells as 0, so the answer is 0. The problem is the relative reference format. When the formula was copied, Excel assumed that the new formula should refer to cell D3. To see how you can correct this problem, you need to learn about another format: the *absolute reference format*.

Figure 16.4.
Copying the January 1997 BUDGET formula to February creates a problem.

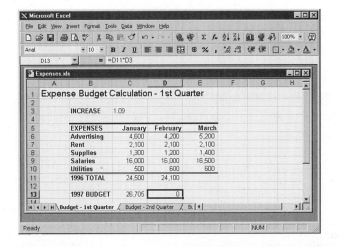

NOTE: MOVING A FORMULA DOESN'T CAUSE THE PROBLEM

The relative reference format problem doesn't occur when you move a formula. When you move a formula, Excel assumes that you want to keep the same cell references.

Understanding Absolute Reference Format

When you refer to a cell in a formula using the absolute reference format, Excel uses the physical address of the cell. You tell the program that you want to use an absolute reference by placing dollar signs ($) before the row and column of the cell address. To return to the example in the preceding section, Excel interprets the formula =$A$1*2 as "Multiply the contents of cell A1 by 2." No matter where you copy or move this formula, the cell reference doesn't change. The cell address is said to be *anchored*.

To fix the budget expense worksheet, you need to anchor the INCREASE variable. To do this, change the January 1997 BUDGET formula in cell C13 to read =C11*$C$3. After you've made this change, try copying the formula again to the February 1997 BUDGET column. You should get the proper value this time.

CAUTION: WATCH FORMULAS WITH RANGE NAMES

Most range names refer to absolute cell references. This means that when you copy a formula that uses a range name, the copied formula will use the same range name as the original, which might produce errors in your worksheet.

You also should know that you can enter a cell reference using a mixed reference format. In this format, you anchor either the cell's row (by placing the dollar sign in front of the row address only—for example, B$6) or its column (by placing the dollar sign in front of the column address only—for example, $B6).

> **TIP: KEYBOARD SHORTCUT**
>
> You can quickly change the reference format of a cell address by using the F4 key. When editing a formula, place the cursor to the left of the cell address and keep pressing F4. Excel cycles through the various formats.

Copying a Formula Without Adjusting Relative References

If you need to copy a formula but don't want the formula's relative references to change, you can use three methods:

- If you want to copy a formula from the cell above, select the lower cell and press Ctrl-' (apostrophe).

- Activate the formula bar and use the mouse or keyboard to highlight the entire formula. Next, copy the formula to the Clipboard (by selecting Edit | Copy or by pressing Ctrl-C), and then press the Esc key to deactivate the formula bar. Finally, select the cell in which you want the copy to appear, and paste the formula there.

- Activate the formula bar and type an apostrophe (') at the beginning of the formula (to the left of the equals sign) to convert it to text. Press Enter to confirm the edit, copy the cell, and then paste it in the desired location. Now, delete the apostrophe from both the source and the destination cells to convert the text back to a formula.

Working with Arrays

An *array* is a group of cells or values that Excel treats as a unit. You create arrays either by using a function that returns an array result (such as DOCUMENTS()—see the section "Functions That Use or Return Arrays") or by entering an *array formula,* which is a single formula that either uses an array as an argument or enters its results in multiple cells.

Using Array Formulas

Here's a simple example that illustrates how array formulas work. In the Expenses workbook shown in Figure 16.5, the 1997 BUDGET totals are calculated using a separate formula for each month:

January 1997 BUDGET	=C11*$C$3
February 1997 BUDGET	=D11*$C$3
March 1997 BUDGET	=E11*$C$3

FIGURE 16.5.

This worksheet uses three separate formulas to calculate the 1997 BUDGET figures.

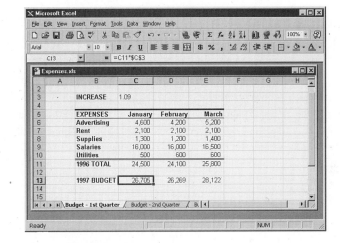

You can replace all three formulas with a single array formula by following these steps:

1. Select the range that you want to use for the array formula. In the 1997 BUDGET example, you select C13:E13.

2. Type the formula, and then in the places where you would normally enter a cell reference, type a range reference that includes the cells you want to use. *Don't*, I repeat, *don't* press Enter when you're done. In this example, you would type
   `=C11:E11*$C$3`.

3. To enter the formula as an array, press Ctrl-Shift-Enter.

The 1997 BUDGET cells (C13, D13, and E13) now all contain the same formula:

`{=C11:E11*$C$3}`

Notice that the formula is surrounded by braces ({ }). This identifies the formula as an array formula. (When you enter array formulas, you never need to enter these braces yourself—Excel adds them automatically.)

NOTE: WORKING WITH ARRAYS

Because Excel treats arrays as a unit, you can't move or delete part of an array. If you need to work with an array, you must select the whole thing. If you want to reduce the size of an array, select it, activate the formula bar, and then press Ctrl-Enter to change the entry to a normal formula. You can then select the smaller range and re-enter the array formula.

Understanding Array Formulas

To understand how Excel processes an array, you need to keep in mind that Excel always sets up a correspondence between the array cells and the cells of whatever range you entered into the array formula. In the 1996 BUDGET example, the array consists of cells C13, D13, and E13, and the range used in the formula consists of cells C11, D11, and E11. Excel sets up a correspondence between array cell C13 and input cell C11, D13 and D11, and E13 and E11. To calculate the value of cell C13 (the January 1996 BUDGET), for example, Excel just grabs the input value from cell C11 and substitutes that in the formula. Figure 16.6 shows a diagram of this process.

FIGURE 16.6.

When processing an array formula, Excel sets up a correspondence between the array cells and the range used in the formula.

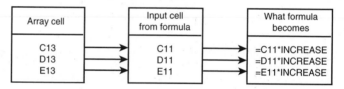

Array formula: ={C11:E11*INCREASE}

Array cell	Input cell from formula	What formula becomes
C13	C11	=C11*INCREASE
D13	D11	=D11*INCREASE
E13	E11	=E11*INCREASE

Array formulas can be confusing, but if you keep these correspondences in mind, you should have no trouble figuring out what's going on.

Array Formulas That Operate on Multiple Ranges

 In the preceding example, the array formula operated on a single range, but array formulas also can operate on multiple ranges. For example, consider the Invoice Template worksheet shown in Figure 16.7. The totals in the Extension column (cells F12 through F16) are generated by a series of formulas that multiply the item's price by the quantity ordered. For example, the formula in cell F12 is this:

```
=B12*E12
```

You can replace all these formulas by making the following entry as an array formula into the range F12:F16:

```
=B12:B16*E12:E16
```

Again, you've created the array formula by replacing each cell reference with the corresponding ranges (and by pressing Ctrl-Shift-Enter).

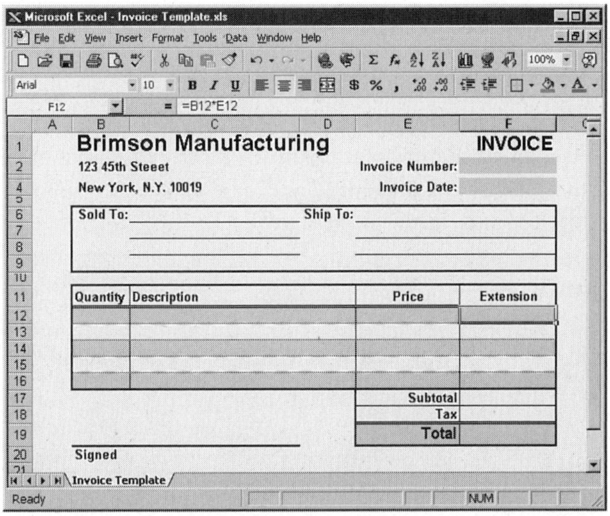

FIGURE 16.7.

This worksheet uses several formulas to calculate the extended totals for each line.

NOTE: YOU CAN ENTER AN ARRAY IN A SINGLE CELL

You don't have to enter array formulas in multiple cells. For example, if you don't need the Extended totals in the Invoice Template worksheet, you can still calculate the Subtotal by making the following entry as an array formula in cell F17:

=SUM(B12:B16*E12:E16)

Using Array Constants

In the array formulas you've seen so far, the array arguments have been cell ranges. You also can use constant values as array arguments. This procedure lets you input values into a formula without having them clutter your worksheet.

To enter an array constant in a formula, enter the values right in the formula and observe the following guidelines:

■ Enclose the values in braces ({ }).

■ If you want Excel to treat the values as a row, separate each value with a semicolon.

■ If you want Excel to treat the values as a column, separate each value with a comma.

For example, the following array constant is the equivalent of entering the individual values in a column on your worksheet:

{1;2;3;4}

Similarly, the following array constant is equivalent to entering the values in a worksheet range of three columns and two rows:

`{1,2,3;4,5,6}`

 As a practical example, Figure 16.8 shows two different array formulas. The one on the left (used in the range E4:E7) calculates various loan payments given the different interest rates in the range C5:C8. The array formula on the right (used in the range F4:F7) does the same thing, but the interest rate values are entered as an array constant directly in the formula.

FIGURE 16.8.

Using array constants in your array formulas means you don't have to clutter your worksheet with the input values.

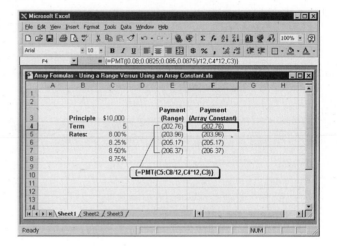

Functions That Use or Return Arrays

Many of Excel's worksheet functions either require an array argument or return an array result (or both). Table 16.5 lists several of these functions and explains how each one uses arrays.

Table 16.5. Some Excel functions that use arrays.

What the Function Uses	Array Argument?	Returns Array Result?
COLUMN()	No	Yes, if the argument is a range
COLUMNS()	Yes	No
CONSOLIDATE()	Yes	No
DOCUMENTS()	No	Yes, if multiple documents are open
FILES()	No	Yes
GROWTH()	Yes	Yes

Manipulating Formulas and Functions

CHAPTER 16

403

16

MANIPULATING
FORMULAS AND
FUNCTIONS

What the Function Uses	Array Argument?	Returns Array Result?
HLOOKUP()	Yes	No
INDEX()	Yes	Yes
LINEST()	No	Yes
LOGEST()	No	Yes
LOOKUP()	Yes	No
MATCH()	Yes	No
MDETERM()	Yes	No
MINVERSE()	No	Yes
MMULT()	No	Yes
NAMES()	No	Yes
ROW()	No	Yes, if the argument is a range
ROWS()	Yes	No
SUMPRODUCT()	Yes	No
TRANSPOSE()	Yes	Yes
TREND()	Yes	Yes
VLOOKUP()	Yes	No
WINDOWS()	No	Yes
WORKGROUP()	Yes	No

When you use functions that return arrays, be sure to select a range large enough to hold the resultant array, and then enter the function as an array formula.

Working with Range Names in Formulas

You probably use range names often in your formulas. After all, a cell that contains the formula =Sales-Expenses is much more comprehensible than one that contains the more cryptic formula =F12-F2. The next few sections show you a few techniques that will make it easier for you to use range names in formulas.

Pasting a Name into a Formula

One way to enter a range name in a formula is to type the name in the formula bar. But what if you can't remember the name? Or what if the name is long and you've got a deadline looming? For these kinds of situations, Excel has a feature that lets you select the name you want from a list and paste it right into the formula. The following procedure gives you the details:

1. In the formula bar, place the insertion point where you want the name to appear.
2. Select Insert | Name | Paste. Excel displays the Paste Name dialog box, shown in Figure 16.9.

Figure 16.9.

Use the Paste Name dialog box to paste a range name into a formula.

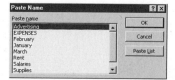

TIP: KEYBOARD SHORTCUT

A quick way to display the Paste Name dialog box is to press F3.

---

3. Use the Paste name list to highlight the range name you want to use.
4. Click OK. Excel pastes the name in the formula bar.

TIP: USE THE NAME BOX

You can bypass the Paste Name dialog box by using the Name box in the formula bar. When you're ready to paste a name, drop down the Name list and select the name you want.

Applying Names to Formulas

If you've been using ranges in your formulas, and you name those ranges later, Excel doesn't automatically apply the new names to the formulas. Instead of substituting the appropriate names by hand, you can get Excel to do the dirty work for you. Follow these steps to apply the new range names to your existing formulas:

1. Select the range in which you want to apply the names, or select a single cell if you want to apply the names to the entire worksheet.
2. Select Insert | Name | Apply. Excel displays the Apply Names dialog box, shown in Figure 16.10.

Figure 16.10.

Use the Apply Names dialog box to select the names you want to apply to your formula ranges.

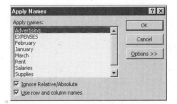

3. Select the names you want applied from the Apply names list.

4. Activate the Ignore Relative/Absolute check box to ignore relative and absolute references when applying names.

5. The Use row and column names check box tells Excel whether to use the worksheet's row and column names when applying names. If you activate this check box, you also can click the Options button to see more choices.

6. Click OK to apply the names.

Naming Formulas

You can apply a naming concept for frequently used formulas, and the formula doesn't physically have to appear in a cell. This not only saves memory, but it often makes your worksheets easier to read as well. Follow these steps to name a formula:

1. Select Insert | Name | Define. Excel displays the Define Name dialog box.

2. Enter the name you want to use for the formula in the Names in workbook edit box.

3. In the Refers to box, enter the formula exactly as you would in the formula bar.

CAUTION: PUT EXCEL IN EDIT MODE

Press F2 to put Excel into edit mode before you move around inside the Refers to box with the arrow keys. If you don't press F2 first, Excel assumes that you're trying to select a cell on the worksheet.

---

4. Click OK.

Now you can enter the formula name in your worksheet cells (rather than the formula itself). For example, the following is the formula for the volume of a sphere (r is the radius of the sphere):

$4\pi r^3 / 3$

So assuming that you have a cell named Radius somewhere in the workbook, you could create a formula named, say, SphereVolume and make the following entry in the Refers to box of the Define Name dialog box:

```
=(4*PI()*Radius^3)/3
```

Working with Links in Formulas

If you have data in one workbook that you want to use in another, you can set up a link between them. This allows your formulas to use references to cells or ranges in the other workbook. When the other data changes, Excel automatically updates the link.

For example, Figure 16.11 shows two linked workbooks. The Budget Summary sheet in the 1995 Budget - Summary workbook includes data from the Details worksheet in the 1995 Budget workbook. Specifically, the formula shown for cell B2 in 1995 Budget - Summary contains an external reference to cell R7 in the Details worksheet of 1995 Budget. If the value in R7 changes, Excel immediately updates the 1995 Budget - Summary workbook.

FIGURE 16.11.

Two linked workbooks.

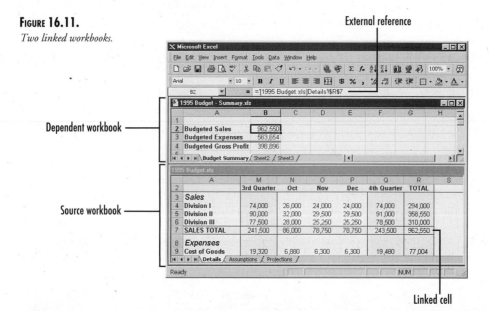

NOTE: LINK TERMINOLOGY

The workbook that contains the external reference is called the *dependent* workbook (or the *client* workbook). The workbook that contains the original data is called the *source* workbook (or the *server* workbook).

Understanding External References

There's no big mystery behind Excel links. You set up links by including an external reference to a cell or range in another workbook (or in another worksheet from the same workbook). In my case, all I did was enter an equals sign in cell B2 of the Budget Summary worksheet, and then I clicked cell R7 in the Details worksheet.

Manipulating Formulas and Functions

CHAPTER 16

407

16

MANIPULATING
FORMULAS AND
FUNCTIONS

The only thing you need to be comfortable with is the structure of an external reference. Here's the general syntax:

```
'path[workbookname]sheetname'!reference
```

path	The drive and directory in which the workbook is located. You need to include the path only when the workbook is closed.
workbookname	The name of the workbook, including an extension. Always enclose the workbook name in square brackets (`[ ]`). You can omit *workbookname* if you're referencing a cell or range in another sheet from the same workbook.
sheetname	The name of the worksheet's tab. You can omit *sheetname* if *reference* is a defined name in the same workbook.
reference	A cell or range reference, or a defined name.

For example, suppose the 1995 Budget workbook is stored in the C:\My Documents\ Worksheets\ folder. If you were to close this workbook, Excel would automatically change the external reference shown in Figure 16.11 to the following:

```
='C:\My Documents\Worksheets\[1995 Budget.xls]Details'!$R$7
```

NOTE: USING QUOTATION MARKS

You need to put single quotation marks around the path, workbook name, and sheet name only if the workbook is closed or if the path, workbook, or sheet name contains spaces. If in doubt, include the single quotation marks anyway; Excel will happily ignore them if they're not required.

Updating Links

The purpose of a link is to avoid duplicating formulas and data in multiple worksheets. If one workbook contains the information you need, you can use a link to reference the data without re-creating it in another workbook.

To be useful, however, the data in the dependent workbook should always reflect what actually is in the source workbook. You can make sure of this by updating the link as follows:

- If both the source and dependent workbooks are open, Excel automatically updates the link whenever the data in the source file changes.

- If the source workbook is open when you open the dependent workbook, Excel automatically updates the links again.

- If the source workbook is closed when you open the dependent workbook, Excel displays a dialog box asking if you want to update the links. Click Yes to update or No to cancel.

- If you didn't update a link when you opened the dependent document, you can update it any time by selecting Edit | Links. In the Links dialog box that appears, highlight the link and then click the Update Now button.

Editing Links

If the name of the source document changes, you'll need to edit the link to keep the data up to date. You can edit the external reference directly, or you can change the source by following these steps:

1. With the dependent workbook active, select Edit | Links to display the Links dialog box.
2. Highlight the link you want to change.
3. Click the Change Source button. Excel displays the Change Links dialog box.
4. Select the new source document and then click OK to return to the Links dialog box.
5. Click Close to return to the workbook.

Auditing Formulas

Some formula errors are the result of referencing other cells that contain errors or inappropriate values. To find out, you can use Excel's auditing features to trace cell precedents, dependents, and errors.

How Auditing Works

If a formula refers to a number of cells, and some of those cells also refer to other cells, tracking down the source of a problem can become a nightmare. To help out, Excel's auditing features can create *tracers*—arrows that literally point out the cells involved in a formula. You can use tracers to find three kinds of cells:

Precedents	Cells that are directly or indirectly referenced in a formula. For example, suppose that cell B4 contains the formula =B2—B2 is a direct precedent of B4. Now suppose that cell B2 contains the formula =A2/2: This makes A2 a direct precedent of B2, but it's also an *indirect* precedent of cell B4.
Dependents	Cells that are directly or indirectly referenced by a formula. In the preceding example, cell B2 is a direct dependent of A2, and B4 is an indirect dependent of A2.

Errors	Cells that contain an error value and are directly or indirectly referenced in a formula (and therefore cause the same error to appear in the formula).

 Figure 16.12 shows a worksheet with three examples of tracer arrows:

■ Cell B4 contains the formula =B2, and B2 contains =A2/2. The arrows (they're blue on-screen) point out the precedents (direct and indirect) of B4.

■ Cell D4 contains the formula =D2, and D2 contains =D1/0. The latter produces the #DIV/0! error. Therefore, the same error appears in cell D4. The arrow (it's red on-screen) points out the source of the error.

■ Cell G4 contains the formula =Sheet2!A1. Excel displays the dotted-line arrow with the worksheet icon whenever the precedent or dependent exists on a different worksheet.

FIGURE 16.12.
The three types of tracer arrows.

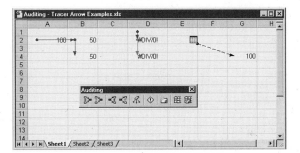

Tracing Cell Precedents

To trace cell precedents, follow these steps:

1. Select the cell containing the formula whose precedents you want to trace.

2. Select Tools | Auditing | Trace Precedents. Excel adds a tracer arrow to each direct precedent.

   You also can click this tool on the Auditing toolbar to trace precedents.

3. Keep repeating step 2 to see more levels of precedents.

TIP: TRACING SHORTCUT

You also can trace precedents by double-clicking the cell, provided that you turn off in-cell editing. You do this by selecting Tools | Options and then deactivating the Edit directly in cell check box in the Edit tab. Now when you double-click a cell, Excel selects the cell's precedents.

Tracing Cell Dependents

Here are the steps to follow to trace cell dependents:

1. Select the cell whose dependents you want to trace.

2. Select Tools | Auditing | Trace Dependents. Excel adds a tracer arrow to each direct dependent.

You can also trace dependents by clicking this tool on the Auditing toolbar.

3. Keep repeating step 2 to see more levels of dependents.

Tracing Cell Errors

To trace cell errors, follow these steps:

1. Select the cell containing the error you want to trace.

2. Select Tools | Auditing | Trace Error. Excel adds a tracer arrow to each cell that produced the error.

You also can click this tool on the Auditing toolbar to trace errors.

Removing Tracer Arrows

To remove the tracer arrows, you have three choices:

■ Select Tools | Auditing | Remove All Arrows to remove all the tracer arrows.

■ Click the Remove All Arrows tool on the Auditing toolbar to remove all tracer arrows.

■ Use the following buttons on the Auditing toolbar to remove precedent and dependent arrows one level at a time:

Click the Remove Precedent Arrows tool on the Auditing toolbar to remove precedent arrows one level at a time.

Click the Remove Dependent Arrows tool on the Auditing toolbar to remove dependent arrows one level at a time.

About Excel's Functions

Functions are formulas that have been predefined by Excel. They're designed to take you beyond the basic arithmetic and text formulas you've seen so far. They do this in three ways:

- Functions make simple but cumbersome formulas easier to use. For example, suppose that you wanted to add a list of 100 numbers in a column starting at cell A1 and finishing at cell A100. Even if you wanted to, you wouldn't be able to enter 100 separate additions in a cell, because you would run out of room (recall that cells are limited to 255 characters). Luckily, there's an alternative: the SUM() function. With this function, you would simply enter =SUM(A1:A100).

- Functions let you include complex mathematical expressions in your worksheets that otherwise would be impossible to construct using simple arithmetic operators. For example, determining a mortgage payment given the principal, interest, and term is a complicated matter at best, but Excel's PMT() function does it without breaking a sweat.

- Functions let you include data in your applications that you couldn't access otherwise. For example, the INFO() function can tell you how much memory is available on your system, what operating system you're using, what version number it is, and more.

As you can see, functions are a powerful addition to your worksheet-building arsenal. With the proper use of these tools, there is no practical limit to the kinds of models you can create.

The Structure of a Function

Every function has the same basic form:

```
FUNCTION(argument1, argument2, ...)
```

It begins with the function name (SUM or PMT, for example), which is followed by a list of arguments separated by commas and enclosed in parentheses. The arguments are the function's inputs—the data it uses to perform its calculations.

For example, the FV() function determines the future value of a regular investment based on three required arguments and two optional ones:

```
FV(rate,nper,pmt,pv,type)
```

rate	The fixed rate of interest over the term of the investment.
nper	The number of deposits over the term of the investment.
pmt	The amount you'll deposit each time.
pv	The present value of the investment.
type	Shows when the deposits are due (0 for the beginning of the period; 1 for the end of the period).

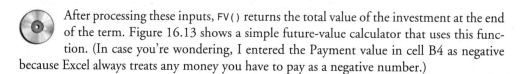

NOTE: FUNCTION SYNTAX

Throughout this part of the book, when I introduce a new function, I show the argument syntax and then describe each argument (as I just did with the FV() function). In the syntax line, I show the function's required arguments in ***bold italic monospace*** type and the optional arguments in *regular italic monospace* type.

After processing these inputs, FV() returns the total value of the investment at the end of the term. Figure 16.13 shows a simple future-value calculator that uses this function. (In case you're wondering, I entered the Payment value in cell B4 as negative because Excel always treats any money you have to pay as a negative number.)

FIGURE 16.13.

The FV() *function in action.*

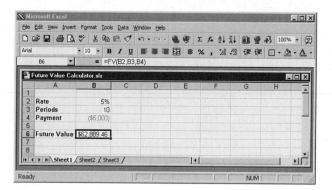

Entering Functions

You enter functions as you do any other data, but you must follow these rules:

- You can enter the function name in either uppercase or lowercase letters. Excel always converts function names to uppercase.

- Always enclose function arguments in parentheses.

- Always separate multiple arguments with commas. (You might want to add a space after each comma to make the functions more readable.)

- You can use a function as an argument for another function. This is called *nesting* functions. For example, the function AVERAGE(SUM(A1:A10), SUM(B1:B15)) sums two columns of numbers and returns the average of the two sums.

Using the Function Wizard

Although normally you'll type in your functions by hand, there might be times when you can't remember the spelling of a function or the arguments it takes. To help out, Excel provides a tool called the Function Wizard. It lets you select the function you want from a list and prompts you to enter the appropriate arguments. The following procedure shows you how the Function Wizard works:

1. To start a formula with a function, either select Insert | Function or click the Function Wizard tool on the Standard toolbar. Excel activates the formula bar, enters an equals sign, and then displays the Paste Function dialog box, shown in Figure 16.14.

FIGURE 16.14.

Use the Paste Function dialog box to select a function.

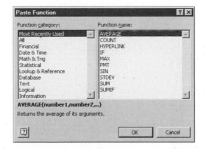

TIP: KEYBOARD SHORTCUT

To skip step 1 of the Function Wizard, enter the name of the function in the cell and then either click the Function Wizard button or press Ctrl-A.

---

2. In the Function category list, select the type of function you need. If you're not sure, select All.

3. Select the function you want to use from the Function name list.

4. Click OK. Excel displays a dialog box that shows the various arguments available for the function.

5. For each required argument and each optional argument you want to use, enter a value or cell reference in the appropriate text box. As shown in Figure 16.15, Excel shows the current argument values and the current function value.

6. When you're done, click OK. Excel pastes the function and its arguments into the cell.

Figure 16.15.

Use the second Function Wizard dialog box to enter values for the function's arguments.

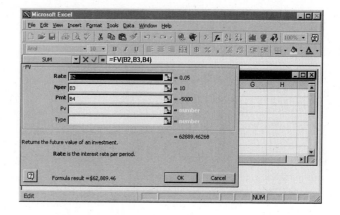

Summary

This chapter showed you how to build better formulas in Excel. For related information on formulas, see the following chapters:

- You'll find you use ranges extensively in your formulas. To make sure that your range skills are at their peak, see Chapter 15, "Working with Ranges."

- Many Excel functions take range arguments. To learn more about ranges and range names, see Chapter 15.

- For more about Excel's database functions, see Chapter 19, "Working with Lists and Databases."

CHAPTER 17

Advanced Worksheet Topics

IN THIS CHAPTER

I know that two and two make four—& should be glad to prove it too if I could—though I must say if by any sort of process I could convert 2 & 2 into five it would give me much greater pleasure.

—*Lord Byron*

Although many of Excel's advanced features are designed with specific groups of users in mind (scientists, engineers, and so on), others are intended to make everyone's life easier. These tools reward a bit of effort in the short term with improved productivity in the long term. Such is the case with the features that are the subject of this chapter: worksheet views, outlines, templates, consolidating data, protecting data, and adding dialog controls to worksheets. All these features have two things in common: They can make your day-to-day work more efficient, and they can help you get more out of your Excel investment.

Displaying Multiple Worksheet Panes

Another way to simultaneously view different parts of a large worksheet is to use Excel's Split feature. You can use Split to divide a worksheet into two or four *panes* in which each pane displays a different area of the sheet. The panes scroll simultaneously horizontally and vertically. You can also freeze the panes to keep a worksheet area in view at all times.

Splitting a Worksheet into Panes

Depending on the type of split you want, you can use one of the following two methods to split your worksheets:

- Use Window I Split to split the worksheet into four panes at the selected cell. (Later, you can adjust the split to two panes if you like.)
- Use the horizontal or vertical split boxes to split the worksheet into two panes at a position you specify (horizontally or vertically).

Using the Split Command

 When you use the Split command, Excel splits the worksheet into four panes at the currently selected cell. How do you know which cell to select? Look at Figure 17.1, which shows the Amortization worksheet with cell C6 selected.

The results of splitting the worksheet by selecting Window I Split are shown in Figure 17.2. Notice that Excel places the *horizontal split bar* on the top edge of the selected cell's row and the *vertical split bar* on the left edge of the selected cell's column. This feature is convenient because now the loan variables are in the upper-left pane, the periods and months are in the lower-left pane, the title and column headings are in the upper-right pane, and the loan data is in the lower-right pane. The panes are synchronized so that as you move down through the loan data, the period and month values also move down.

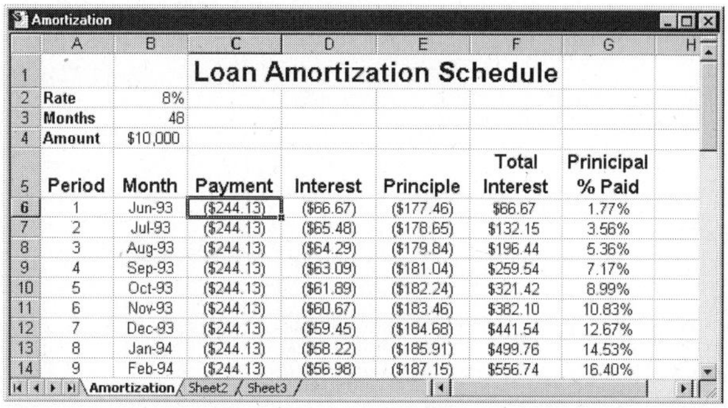

FIGURE 17.1.

The Amortization worksheet before being split.

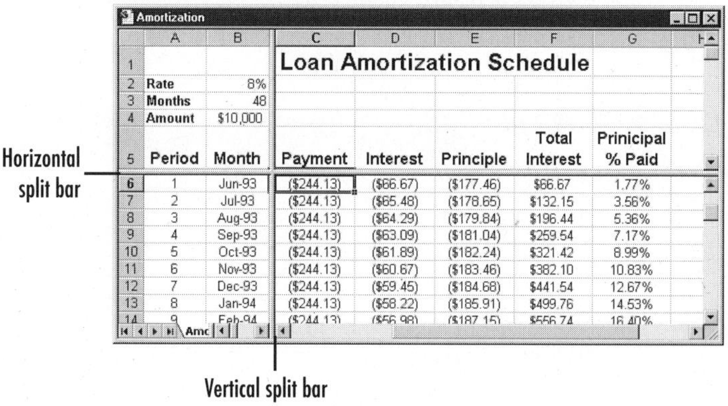

FIGURE 17.2.

The Amortization worksheet after it is split.

Horizontal split bar

Vertical split bar

If the split isn't where you want it, you can always use the mouse to drag the vertical or horizontal split bar. To move both bars at the same time, drag the intersection point.

Using the Window Split Boxes

Using the mouse, you can use the horizontal and vertical split boxes to create a two-pane split. The horizontal split box is the small button located between the vertical scrollbar's up arrow and the window's Close button (see Figure 17.3). The vertical split box is the small button to the right of the horizontal scrollbar's right arrow (again, see Figure 17.3).

Follow these steps to split a worksheet using the split boxes:

1. Position the mouse pointer on the split box you want. The pointer changes to a two-headed arrow.

2. Press and hold the left mouse button. Excel displays a light gray bar to indicate the current split position.

3. Drag the pointer to the desired split location.

4. Release the mouse button. Excel splits the worksheet at the selected location. The split box moves to the split location.

FIGURE 17.3.

You can use the split boxes to split a worksheet.

Horizontal split box

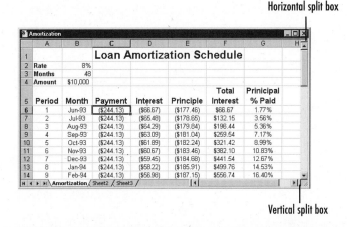

Vertical split box

TIP: REMOVING THE SPLIT

To remove the split, drag the split box back to its original location, or select Window | Remove Split.

Freezing Worksheet Titles

One of the problems with viewing multiple panes is that the work area can get confusing when some of the panes contain the same cells. For example, Figure 17.4 shows the Amortization worksheet split into four panes, in which each pane contains a different cell in its upper-left corner. Clearly, such a display is meaningless. To prevent this situation from happening, you can *freeze* your panes so that areas displaying worksheet titles or column headings remain in place.

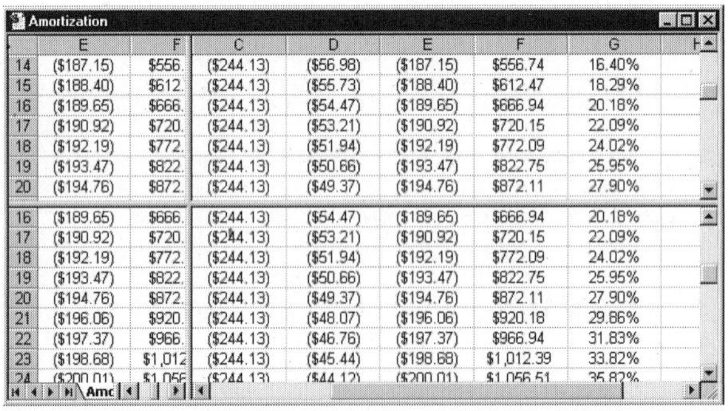

FIGURE 17.4.

Split worksheets often can become confusing.

To try this, first split the worksheet and then arrange each pane so that it shows the desired information (title, heading, and so on). Now select Window | Freeze Panes. Excel replaces the thick gray split bars with thin black freeze bars.

Figure 17.5 shows the Amortization worksheet with frozen panes. In this case, the panes were frozen from the split position shown in Figure 17.2. For this example, the frozen panes provide the following advantages:

- No matter where you move up or down in the worksheet, the column headings and loan variables remain visible.

- As you move up or down in the worksheet, the values in the bottom panes remain synchronized.

- No matter where you move left or right in the worksheet, the period and month values remain visible.

- As you move left or right in the worksheet, the values in the two right panes remain synchronized.

FIGURE 17.5.

The Amortization worksheet with frozen panes.

	A	B	C	D	E	F	G	H
1			**Loan Amortization Schedule**					
2	Rate	8%						
3	Months	48						
4	Amount	$10,000				Total	Prinipcal	
5	Period	Month	Payment	Interest	Principle	Interest	% Paid	
6	1	Jun-93	($244.13)	($66.67)	($177.46)	$66.67	1.77%	
7	2	Jul-93	($244.13)	($65.48)	($178.65)	$132.15	3.56%	
8	3	Aug-93	($244.13)	($64.29)	($179.84)	$196.44	5.36%	
9	4	Sep-93	($244.13)	($63.09)	($181.04)	$259.54	7.17%	
10	5	Oct-93	($244.13)	($61.89)	($182.24)	$321.42	8.99%	
11	6	Nov-93	($244.13)	($60.67)	($183.46)	$382.10	10.83%	
12	7	Dec-93	($244.13)	($59.45)	($184.68)	$441.54	12.67%	
13	8	Jan-94	($244.13)	($58.22)	($185.91)	$499.76	14.53%	
14	9	Feb-94	($244.13)	($56.98)	($187.15)	$556.74	16.40%	

Amortization / Sheet2 / Sheet3

TIP: UNFREEZING PANES

To unfreeze panes without removing the splits, select Window | Unfreeze Panes. To unfreeze panes *and* remove the splits, select Window | Remove Split.

Using Outlines

Outlines? In a spreadsheet? Yes, those same creatures that caused you so much grief in high school English class also are available in Excel. In a worksheet outline, though, you can *collapse* sections of the sheet to display only summary cells (such as quarterly or regional totals, for example), or you can *expand* hidden sections to show the underlying details.

 The worksheet shown in Figure 17.6 displays monthly budget figures for various sales and expense items. The columns include quarterly subtotals and, although you can't see it in the figure, a grand total. The rows include subtotals for sales, expenses, and gross profit.

FIGURE 17.6.

The Budget worksheet showing detail and summary data.

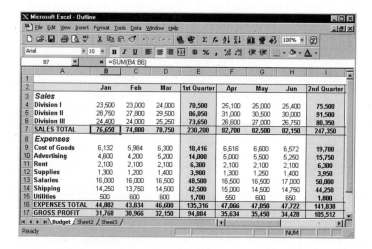

Suppose that you don't want to see so much detail. For example, you might need to see only the quarterly totals for each row, or you might want to hide the salary figures for a presentation you're making. An outline is the easiest way to do this. Figure 17.7 shows the same worksheet with an outline added (I'll explain shortly what the various symbols mean). Using this outline, you can hide whatever details you don't need to see. Figure 17.8 shows the worksheet with data hidden for the individual months and salaries. You can go even further. The view in Figure 17.9 shows only the sales and expenses totals and the grand totals.

One of the big advantages of outlines is that as soon as you've hidden some data, you can work with the visible cells as though they were a single range. This means that you can format those cells quickly, print them, create charts, and so on.

FIGURE 17.7.

The Budget worksheet with outlining added.

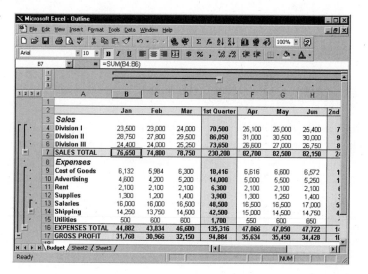

FIGURE 17.8.
Outlining lets you hide detail data you don't need to see.

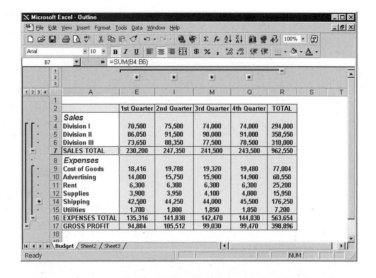

FIGURE 17.9.
Outlines usually have several levels that let you hide even subtotals.

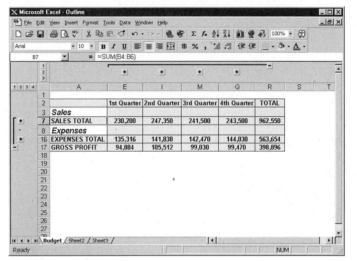

Creating an Outline Automatically

The easiest way to create an outline is to have Excel do it for you. (You can create an outline manually too, as you'll see later.) Before you create an outline, you need to make sure that your worksheet is a candidate for outlining. There are two main criteria:

■ The worksheet must contain formulas that reference cells or ranges directly adjacent to the formula cell. Worksheets with SUM() functions that subtotal cells above or to the left (such as the Budget worksheet presented earlier) are particularly good candidates for outlining.

■ There must be a consistent pattern to the direction of the formula references. For example, you can outline a worksheet containing formulas that always reference cells above or to the left. However, you can't outline a worksheet with, for example, SUM() functions that reference ranges above *and* below a formula cell.

After you determine that your worksheet is outline material, select the range of cells you want to outline. If you want to outline the entire worksheet, select only a single cell. Then choose Data | Group and Outline | Auto Outline. Excel creates the outline and displays the outline tools, as shown in Figure 17.10.

FIGURE 17.10.

When you create an outline, Excel adds outline tools to the worksheet.

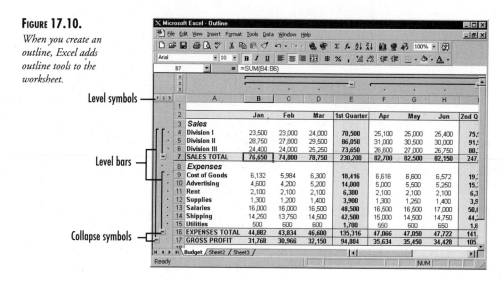

Understanding the Outline Tools

When Excel creates an outline, it divides your worksheet into a hierarchy of *levels*. These levels range from the worksheet detail (the lowest level) to the grand totals (the highest level). Excel outlines can handle up to eight levels of data.

In the Budget worksheet, for example, Excel created three levels for both the column and the row data:

■ In the columns, the monthly figures are the details, so they're the lowest level (level 3). The quarterly totals are the first summary data, so they're the next level (level 2). Finally, the grand totals are the highest level (level 1).

■ In the rows, the individual sales and expense items are the details (level 3). The sales and expenses subtotals are the next level (level 2). The Gross Profit row is the highest level (level 1).

> **NOTE: OUTLINE LEVEL MNEMONIC**
>
> Somewhat confusingly, Excel has set things up so that lower outline levels have higher level numbers. The way I remember it is that the higher the number, the more detail the level contains.

To help you work with your outlines, Excel adds the following tools to your worksheet:

- Level bars: These bars indicate the data included in the current level. Click a bar to hide the rows or columns marked by a bar.

- Collapse symbol: Click this symbol to hide (or *collapse*) the rows or columns marked by the attached level bar.

- Expand symbol: When you collapse a level, the collapse symbol changes to an expand symbol (+). Click this symbol to display (or *expand*) the hidden rows or columns.

- Level symbols: These symbols tell you which level each level bar is on. Click a level symbol to display all the detail data for that level.

> **TIP: KEYBOARD SHORTCUT**
>
> To toggle the outline symbols on and off, press Ctrl-8.

Creating an Outline Manually

If you examine Figure 17.7, you'll see that the Budget worksheet's rows have *four* outline levels, whereas the rows in Figure 17.10 have only three. Where did the extra level come from? I added it manually because I needed some way of collapsing the Salaries row. Because this row isn't a subtotal or some other formula, Excel ignores it (rightfully so) when creating an automatic outline.

If you would like more control over the outlining process, you easily can do it yourself. The idea is that you selectively *group* or *ungroup* rows or columns. When you group a range, you assign it to a lower outline level (that is, you give it a higher level number). When you ungroup a range, you assign it to a higher outline level.

Grouping Rows and Columns

The following procedure shows you how to group rows and columns:

1. If your detail data is in rows, select the rows you want to group. You can select at least one cell in each row, or you can select entire rows (see Figure 17.11), thus saving a step later. If your detail data is in columns, select the columns you want to group.

Figure 17.11.

The Sales detail rows selected for grouping.

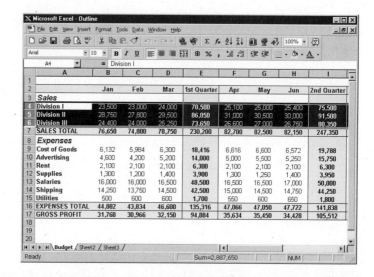

TIP: SELECTING AN ENTIRE ROW

To select an entire row, click the row heading or press Shift-Spacebar. To select an entire column, click the column heading or press Ctrl-Spacebar.

---

2. To group the selection, use any of the following techniques:

   Select Data | Group and Outline | Group.

   Press Alt-Shift-right arrow.

   Click the Group button on the PivotTable toolbar.

   If you selected something other than entire rows or columns, Excel displays the Group dialog box, shown in Figure 17.12. Proceed to step 3 to deal with this dialog box.

   If you selected entire rows or columns, Excel groups the selection and adds the outline symbols to the sheet, as shown in Figure 17.13. In this case, you can skip to step 4.

3. In the Group dialog box, select either Rows or Columns, and then click OK to create the group.

4. Repeat steps 1 through 3 either to group other rows or columns or to move existing groups to a lower outline level.

FIGURE 17.12.

*If you didn't select
entire rows or columns,
Excel displays the
Group dialog box.*

FIGURE 17.13.

*When you group a
selection, Excel adds
the appropriate outline
symbols to the
worksheet.*

	A	B	C	D	E	F	G	H	I
1									
2		Jan	Feb	Mar	1st Quarter	Apr	May	Jun	2nd Qua
3	*Sales*								
4	Division I	23,500	23,000	24,000	70,500	25,100	25,000	25,400	75,50
5	Division II	28,750	27,800	29,500	86,050	31,000	30,500	30,000	91,50
6	Division III	24,400	24,000	25,250	73,650	26,600	27,000	26,750	80,35
7	SALES TOTAL	76,650	74,800	78,750	230,200	82,700	82,500	82,150	247,35
8	*Expenses*								
9	Cost of Goods	6,132	5,984	6,300	18,416	6,616	6,600	6,572	19,78
10	Advertising	4,800	4,200	5,200	14,000	5,000	5,500	5,250	15,75
11	Rent	2,100	2,100	2,100	6,300	2,100	2,100	2,100	6,30
12	Supplies	1,300	1,200	1,400	3,900	1,300	1,250	1,400	3,95
13	Salaries	16,000	16,000	16,500	48,500	16,500	16,500	17,000	50,00
14	Shipping	14,250	13,750	14,500	42,500	15,000	14,500	14,750	44,25
15	Utilities	500	600	600	1,700	550	600	650	1,80
16	EXPENSES TOTAL	44,882	43,834	46,600	135,316	47,066	47,050	47,722	141,83
17	GROSS PROFIT	31,768	30,966	32,150	94,884	35,634	35,450	34,428	105,51
18									
19									
20									

Ungrouping Rows and Columns

If you make a mistake when grouping a selection or you need to make adjustments to your
outline levels, here's how to ungroup rows and columns:

1. If you're working with rows, select the rows you want to ungroup. Again, you can save
   a step if you select the entire row. If you're working with columns, select the columns
   you want to ungroup.

2. To ungroup the selection, use any one of the following techniques:

   Select Data | Group and Outline | Ungroup.

   Press Alt-Shift-left arrow.

   Click the Ungroup button on the PivotTable toolbar.

   If you selected entire rows or columns, Excel ungroups the selection and removes the
   outline symbols. In this case, you can skip to step 4.

   If you selected something other than entire rows or columns, Excel displays the
   Ungroup dialog box. Proceed to step 3 to deal with this dialog box.

3. In the Ungroup dialog box, select either Rows or Columns, and then click OK to ungroup the selection.

4. Repeat steps 1 through 3 either to ungroup other rows or columns or to move existing groups to a higher outline level.

Hiding and Showing Detail Data

The whole purpose of an outline is to let you move easily between views of greater or lesser detail. The next two sections tell you how to hide and show detail data in an outline.

Hiding Detail Data

To hide details in an outline, you have three methods from which to choose:

■ Click the collapse symbol at the bottom (for rows) or right (for columns) of the level bar that encompasses the detail data.

■ Select a cell in a row or column marked with a collapse symbol, and then select Data | Group and Outline | Hide Detail.

 ■ Select a cell in a row or column marked with a collapse symbol and then click the Hide Detail tool on the PivotTable toolbar.

Showing Detail Data

To show collapsed detail, you have four methods from which to choose:

■ Click the appropriate expand symbol.

■ To see the detail for an entire level, click the level marker.

■ Select a cell in a row or column marked with an expand symbol, and then select Data | Group and Outline | Show Detail.

 ■ Select a cell in a row or column marked with an expand symbol, and then click the Show Detail tool on the PivotTable toolbar.

Selecting Outline Data

When you collapse an outline level, the data is only temporarily hidden from view. If you select the outline, your selection includes the collapsed cells. If you want to copy, print, or chart only the visible cells, you need to follow these steps:

1. Hide the outline data you don't need.

2. Select the outline cells you want to work with.

3. Select Edit | Go To to display the Go To dialog box.

4. Click the Special button. Excel displays the Go To Special dialog box.

5. Activate the Visible cells only option button.

6. Click OK. Excel modifies your selection to include only those cells in the selection that are part of the expanded outline.

> **TIP: KEYBOARD SHORTCUT**
>
> You also can select visible cells by pressing Alt-; (semicolon).

Removing an Outline

You can remove selected rows or columns from an outline, or you can remove the entire outline. Follow these steps:

1. If you want to remove only part of an outline, select the appropriate rows or columns. If you want to remove the entire outline, select a single cell.

2. Select Data | Group and Outline | Clear Outline. Excel adjusts or removes the outline.

Working with Templates

A *template* is a document that contains a basic layout (sheets, labels, formulas, formatting, styles, names, and so on) that you can use as a skeleton for similar documents. A template ensures that the worksheets, charts, or macro sheets you use frequently all have a consistent look and feel. For example, if you need to consolidate budget numbers from various departments, your task will be much easier if all the worksheets have the same layout. To that end, you can issue each department a budget template containing the worksheet layout you want everyone to use.

Creating a Template

Creating a template is similar to creating any other workbook. The following procedure outlines the required steps:

1. Set up the workbook with the settings you want to preserve in the template. You can either use an existing document or create a new one from scratch.

2. Select File | Save As to display the Save As dialog box.

3. Enter a name for the template in the File name text box (you don't need to add an extension—see step 4).

4. In the Save as type drop-down list, select the Template (*.xlt) option. Excel displays the Templates folder.

5. Use the Save in list to select the folder for the template. The templates that ship with Excel are stored in the Spreadsheet Solutions folder.

6. Click Save.

Creating a New Document Based on a Template

After you've created a template, you can use either of the following methods to create a new document based on the template:

■ If you saved the template in your Excel startup directory, select File | New to display the New dialog box, shown in Figure 17.14. In the General tab, highlight the template and click OK. (The Workbook template, by the way, creates a default Excel workbook.)

FIGURE 17.14.

When you save a template in the startup directory, its name appears in the New dialog box.

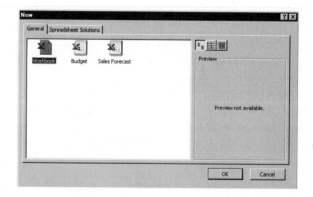

■ To use one of Excel's built-in templates, select File | New, select the Spreadsheet Solutions tab in the New dialog box, highlight the template, and click OK.

In both cases, Excel opens a copy of the file, gives the window the same name as the template, and adds a number. The number indicates how many times you've used this template to create a new document in the current Excel session. For example, if the template is called Budget, the first new document you create is called Budget1, the second is Budget2, and so on.

Making Changes to a Template

When you want to make changes to a template, select File | Open, highlight the template, and select Open. After the template is open, you can make changes as you would to any other workbook. When you finish, save the file. You don't need to specify the template type this time because Excel automatically saves the file as a template.

Consolidating Multisheet Data

Many businesses create worksheets for a specific task and then distribute them to various departments. The most common example is budgeting. For instance, Accounting will create a generic "budget" template that each department or division in the company must fill out and return. Similarly, you often see worksheets distributed for inventory requirements, sales forecasting, survey data, experimental results, and so on.

Creating these worksheets, distributing them, and filling them in are all straightforward operations. The tricky part, however, comes when the sheets are returned to the originating department and all the new data must be combined into a summary report showing company-wide totals. This is called *consolidating* the data, and it's often no picnic, especially for large worksheets. However, as you'll soon see, Excel has some powerful features that can take the drudgery out of consolidation.

Excel can consolidate your data using one of the following methods:

> Consolidating by position: With this method, Excel consolidates the data from several worksheets using the same range coordinates on each sheet. You would use this method if the worksheets you're consolidating have an identical layout.

> Consolidating by category: This method tells Excel to consolidate the data by looking for identical row and column labels in each sheet. So, for example, if one worksheet lists monthly Gizmo sales in row 1 and another lists monthly Gizmo sales in row 5, you can still consolidate as long as both sheets have a "Gizmo" label at the beginning of these rows.

In both cases, you specify one or more *source ranges* (the ranges that contain the data you want to consolidate) and a *destination range* (the range where the consolidated data will appear). The next couple of sections take you through the details of both consolidation methods.

Consolidating by Position

If the sheets you're working with have the same layout, consolidating by position is the easiest way to go. For example, check out the three workbooks shown in Figure 17.15—Division I Budget, Division II Budget, and Division III Budget. As you can see, each sheet uses the same row and column labels, so they're perfect candidates for consolidation by position.

Begin by creating a new worksheet that has the same layout as the sheets you're consolidating. Figure 17.16 shows a new consolidation workbook that I'll use to consolidate the three budget sheets.

FIGURE 17.15.

When your worksheets are laid out identically, use consolidation by position.

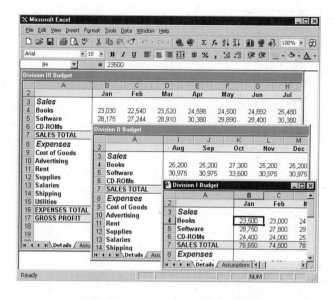

FIGURE 17.16.

When consolidating by position, create a separate consolidation worksheet that uses the same layout as the sheets you're consolidating.

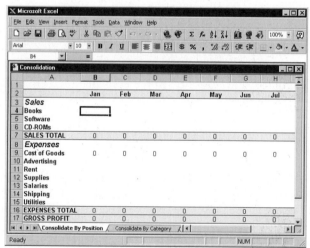

As an example, let's see how you'd go about consolidating the sales data in the three budget worksheets shown in Figure 17.15. We're dealing with three source ranges:

'[Division I Budget]Details'!B4:M6

'[Division II Budget]Details'!B4:M6

'[Division III Budget]Details'!B4:M6

With the consolidation sheet active, follow these steps to consolidate by position:

1. Select the upper-left corner of the destination range. In our Consolidation By Position worksheet, we'd select cell B4.

2. Select Data | Consolidate. Excel displays the Consolidate dialog box, shown in Figure 17.17.

FIGURE 17.17.

The Consolidate dialog box with several source ranges added.

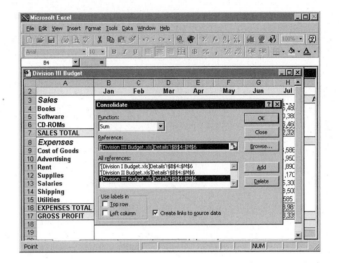

17

ADVANCED WORKSHEET TOPICS

3. Use the Function drop-down list to select the operation to use during the consolidation. You'll use Sum most of the time, but Excel has 10 other operations to choose from, including Count, Average, Max, and Min.

4. In the Reference text box, enter a reference for one of the source ranges. Use one of the following methods:

   ■ Type in the range coordinates by hand. If the source range is in another workbook, be sure to include the workbook name enclosed in square brackets (as shown a moment ago). If the workbook resides in a different drive or folder, include the full path to the workbook as well.

   ■ If the sheet is open, activate it (either by clicking it or by selecting it from the Window menu) and then use the mouse to highlight the range.

   ■ If the workbook isn't open, click the Browse button, highlight the file in the Browse dialog box, and click OK. Excel adds the workbook path to the Reference box. Fill in the sheet name and the range coordinates.

5. Click the Add button to add the range to the All references box.

6. Repeat steps 4 and 5 to add all the source ranges.

7. If you want the consolidated data to change whenever you make changes to the source data, activate the Create links to source data check box.

8. Click OK. Excel gathers the data, consolidates it, and then adds it to the destination range, as shown in Figure 17.18.

FIGURE 17.18.

The consolidated sales budgets.

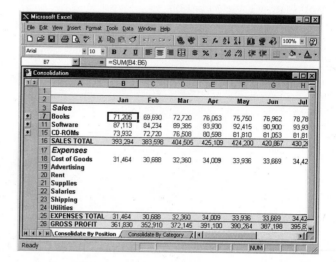

If you chose not to create links to the source data in step 7, Excel just fills the destination range with the consolidation totals. If you did create links, however, Excel does three things:

■ It adds link formulas to the destination range for each cell in the source ranges you selected. (See the section titled "Working with Links in Formulas" in Chapter 16, "Manipulating Formulas and Functions," for details about link formulas.)

■ It consolidates the data by adding SUM() functions (or whatever operation you selected in the Function list) that total the results of the link formulas.

■ It outlines the consolidation worksheet and hides the link formulas, as you can see in Figure 17.18.

If you display the Level 1 data, you'll see the linked formulas. For example, Figure 17.19 shows the detail for the consolidated sales number for Books in January (cell B7). The detail in cells B4, B5, and B6 contain the formulas that link to the corresponding cells in the three budget worksheets (for example, '[Division I Budget.xls]Details'!$B$4).

FIGURE 17.19.

The detail (linked formulas) for the consolidated data.

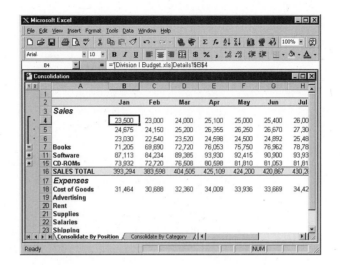

Consolidating by Category

If your worksheets don't use the same layout, you'll need to tell Excel to consolidate the data *by category*. In this case, Excel examines each of your source ranges and consolidates data that uses the same row and/or column labels. For example, take a look at the Sales rows in the three worksheets shown in Figure 17.20. As you can see, Division C sells books, software, videos, and CD-ROMs, Division B sells books and CD-ROMs, and Division A sells software, books, and videos. Here's how you'd go about consolidating these numbers (note that I'm skipping over some of the details I outlined in the preceding section):

1. Create or select a new worksheet for the consolidation and select the upper-left corner of the destination range. You don't need to enter labels for the consolidated data, because Excel will do it for you automatically. However, if you'd like to see the labels in a particular order, it's okay to enter them yourself. (However, make sure that you spell the labels exactly the same as they're spelled in the source worksheets.)

2. Select Data | Consolidate to display the Consolidate dialog box.

3. Use the Function drop-down list to select the operation to use during the consolidation.

4. In the Reference text box, enter a reference for one of the source ranges. In this case, make sure you include in each range the row and/or column labels for the data.

5. Click the Add button to add the range to the All references box.

6. Repeat steps 4 and 5 to add all the source ranges.

7. If you want the consolidated data to change whenever you make changes to the source data, activate the Create links to source data check box.

8. If you want Excel to use the data labels in the top row of the selected ranges, activate the Top row check box. If you want Excel to use the data labels in the left column of the source ranges, activate the Left column check box.

9. Click OK. Excel gathers the data according to the row and/or column labels, consolidates it, and then adds it to the destination range. Figure 17.21 shows the result of the consolidation. Notice, in particular, that you can use the outline symbols to expand the consolidation totals and see the underlying detail.

FIGURE 17.20.

Each division sells a different mix of products, so we need to consolidate by category.

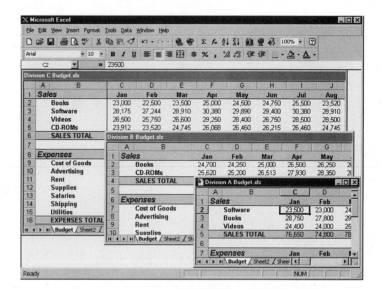

FIGURE 17.21.

The sales numbers consolidated by category.

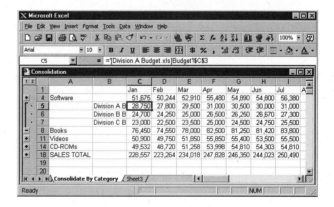

> **NOTE: PIVOT TABLES MIGHT BE A BETTER CHOICE**
>
> Pivot tables are often better for consolidating data by category. See Chapter 20, "Creating and Customizing Pivot Tables," to find out how they work.

Protecting Worksheet Data

When you've labored long and hard to get your worksheet formulas or formatting just right, the last thing you need is to have a cell or range accidentally deleted or copied over. You can prevent this from happening by using Excel's worksheet protection features, which let you prevent changes to anything from a single cell to an entire workbook.

Protecting Individual Cells, Objects, and Scenarios

Protecting cells, objects, and scenarios in Excel is a two-step process:

1. Set up the item's protection formatting. You have three options:

   ■ Cells, objects, and scenarios can be either *locked* or *unlocked.* As soon as protection is turned on (see step 2), a locked item can't be changed, deleted, moved, or copied over.

   ■ Cell formulas and scenarios can be either *hidden* or *visible.* With protection on, a hidden formula doesn't appear in the formula bar when the cell is selected, and a hidden scenario doesn't appear in the Scenario Manager dialog box.

> **NOTE: SCENARIO INFO**
>
> Unfamiliar with scenarios? You'll learn all about them in Chapter 22, "Excel's Data Analysis Tools."

   ■ Text boxes, macro buttons, and some worksheet dialog box controls (see the section "Using Dialog Box Controls on a Worksheet") also can have *locked text,* which prevents the text they contain from being altered.

2. Turn on the worksheet protection.

These steps are outlined in more detail in the following sections.

Setting Up Protection Formatting for Cells

By default, all worksheet cells are formatted as locked and visible. This means that you have three options when setting up your protection formatting:

■ If you want to protect every cell, leave the formatting as it is and turn on the worksheet protection.

■ If you want certain cells unlocked (for data entry, for example), select the appropriate cells and unlock them before turning on worksheet protection. Similarly, if you want certain cells hidden, select the cells and hide them.

■ If you want only selected cells locked, select all the cells and unlock them. Then select the cells you want protected and lock them. To keep only selected formulas visible, hide every formula and then make the appropriate range visible.

Here are the steps to follow to set up protection formatting for worksheet cells:

1. Select the cells for which you want to adjust the protection formatting.

2. Select Format | Cells. In the Format Cells dialog box, activate the Protection tab, shown in Figure 17.22. Excel displays protection options for the range.

FIGURE 17.22.

Use the Protection tab in the Format Cells dialog box to set up the protection formatting for individual work-sheet cells.

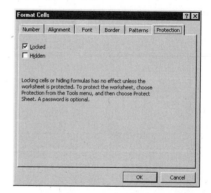

3. To lock the cells' contents, activate the Locked check box. To unlock cells, deactivate this check box.

4. To hide the cells' formulas, activate the Hidden check box. To make the cells' formulas visible, deactivate this check box.

TIP: HIDING CELL CONTENTS

Hiding a formula prevents only the formula from being displayed in the formula bar; the results appear inside the cell itself. If you also want to hide the cell's contents, create an empty custom numeric format (;;;) and assign this format to the cell.

5. Click OK.

Setting Up Protection Formatting for Objects

Excel locks all worksheet objects by default. (It also locks the text in text boxes, macro buttons, and some worksheet dialog box controls. See the section "Using Dialog Box Controls on a Worksheet.") As with cells, you have three options for protecting objects:

- If you want to protect every object, leave the formatting as it is and turn on the worksheet protection.

- If you want certain objects unlocked, select the appropriate objects and unlock them before turning on worksheet protection.

- If you want only selected objects locked, select all the objects and unlock them. Then select the objects you want protected and lock them.

TIP: SELECTING ALL OBJECTS

To select all the objects in a sheet, choose Edit | Go To, click the Special button in the Go To dialog box, and activate the Objects option.

Follow these steps to set up protection formatting for worksheet objects:

1. Select the objects for which you want to adjust the protection formatting.

2. Select Format | Object. In the Format Object dialog box, activate the Protection tab. Excel displays protection options for objects.

3. To lock the objects, activate the Locked check box. To unlock them, deactivate this check box.

4. For text boxes or macro buttons, activate the Lock text check box to protect the text. Deactivate this check box to unlock the text.

5. Click OK.

Setting Up Protection Formatting for Scenarios

Similar to cells, scenarios are normally locked and visible. However, you can't work with scenarios in groups, so you have to set up their protection formatting individually. The following procedure shows you the steps:

1. Select Tools | Scenarios. The Scenario Manager dialog box appears.

2. Highlight the scenario in the Scenarios list and then click the Edit button. Excel displays the Edit Scenario dialog box, shown in Figure 17.23.

17

ADVANCED
WORKSHEET
TOPICS

FIGURE 17.23.

Use the Edit Scenario dialog box to set up protection formatting for a scenario.

3. To lock the scenario, activate the Prevent changes check box. To unlock it, deactivate this check box.

4. To hide the scenario, activate the Hide check box. To unhide the scenario, deactivate it.

5. Click OK. Excel displays the Scenario Values dialog box.

6. Enter new values, if necessary, and click OK.

7. Repeat steps 2 through 6 to set the protection formatting for other scenarios.

8. When you're done, click Close to return to the worksheet.

Protecting a Worksheet

At this point, you've formatted the cells, objects, or scenarios for protection. To activate the protection, follow these steps:

1. Select Tools | Protection | Protect Sheet. Excel displays the Protect Sheet dialog box, shown in Figure 17.24.

FIGURE 17.24.

Use the Protect Sheet dialog box to activate your protection formatting.

2. For added security, you can enter a password in the Password text box. This means that no one can turn off the worksheet's protection without first entering the password. If you decide to enter a password, keep the following guidelines in mind:

   ■ When you enter a password, Excel masks it with asterisks. If you're not sure whether you entered the word correctly, don't worry. Excel will ask you to confirm it.

   ■ Passwords can be up to 255 characters long, and you can use any combination of letters, numbers, spaces, and other symbols.

■ Use a password that's meaningful to you so that it's easy to remember. However, don't use a password that's easy for someone else to guess (such as your name or your spouse's name).

CAUTION: STORE YOUR PASSWORD IN A SAFE PLACE

If you forget your password, there's no way to retrieve it, and you'll never be able to access your worksheet. As a precaution, you might want to write down your password and store it in a safe place.

■ Excel differentiates between uppercase and lowercase letters, so remember the capitalization you use.

3. Select what you want to protect: Contents, Objects, or Scenarios.

4. Click OK.

5. If you entered a password, Excel asks you to confirm it. Reenter the password and click OK.

TIP: NAVIGATING UNLOCKED CELLS

To navigate only the unlocked cells in a protected document, use the Tab key (or Shift-Tab to move backward). Tab avoids the locked cells altogether (which you can still move to by using the arrow keys or the mouse) and always jumps to the next unlocked cell. If you happen to be on the last unlocked cell, Tab wraps around to the first unlocked cell.

To turn off the protection, select Tools | Protection | Unprotect Sheet. If you entered a password, Excel displays the Unprotect Sheet dialog box. Type the password in the Password text box and click OK.

Protecting Windows and Workbook Structures

You can also protect your windows and workbook structures. When you protect a window, Excel does the following:

■ The window's maximize and minimize buttons, control menu box, and borders are hidden. This means that the window can't be moved, sized, or closed.

■ When the window is active, the following commands are disabled on the Window menu: New Window, Split, and Freeze Panes. The Arrange command remains active, but it has no effect on the protected window. The Hide and Unhide commands remain active.

When you protect a workbook's structure, Excel does the following:

- The Edit menu's Delete Sheet and Move or Copy Sheet commands are disabled.
- The Insert menu's Worksheet, Chart, and Macro commands have no effect on the workbook.
- The Scenario Manager can't create a summary report.

Follow these steps to protect windows and workbook structures:

1. Activate the window or workbook you want to protect.
2. Select Tools | Protection | Protect Workbook. Excel displays the Protect Workbook dialog box, shown in Figure 17.25.

FIGURE 17.25.

Use the Protect Workbook dialog box to protect your workbook structure and windows.

3. Enter a password in the Password text box if necessary. Follow the same guidelines outlined in the preceding section.
4. Select what you want to protect: Structure or Windows.
5. Click OK.
6. If you entered a password, Excel asks you to confirm it. Reenter the password and click OK.

Protecting a File

For workbooks with confidential data, merely protecting cells or sheets might not be enough. For a higher level of security, Excel gives you three options (listed in order of increasing security):

- You can have Excel recommend that a workbook be opened as *read-only*. A read-only document can be changed, but you can't save your changes. Or, more accurately, you can save changes, but only to a file with a different name. The original file always remains intact. Note that Excel only recommends that the file be opened as read-only. You can also open the file with full read/write privileges.
- You can assign a password for saving changes. Users who know this password (the *write reservation password*) are assigned write privileges and can save changes to the workbook. All others can only open the file as read-only.

■ You can assign a password for opening a document. This is useful for workbooks with confidential information, such as payroll data. Only users who know the password can open the file.

To set these security options, follow these steps:

1. Activate the workbook and select File | Save As (or press F12).
2. In the Save As dialog box, click the Options button. Excel displays the Save Options dialog box, shown in Figure 17.26.

FIGURE 17.26.

Use the Save Options dialog box to set up various levels of security for a worksheet file.

3. If you want Excel to recommend that the file be opened as read-only, activate the Read-only recommended check box.
4. To prevent unauthorized users from opening the file, enter a password in the Password to open edit box.
5. To restrict the write privileges when opening the worksheet, enter a password in the Password to modify edit box.
6. Click OK.
7. If you entered passwords, Excel asks you to confirm them. Reenter the passwords and click OK. Excel returns you to the Save As dialog box.
8. Click OK. Excel asks whether you want to replace the existing file.
9. Click OK.

Using Dialog Box Controls on a Worksheet

One of the Excel's slickest features is that it lets you place dialog box controls such as spinners, check boxes, and list boxes directly on a worksheet. You can then link the values returned by these controls to a cell to create an elegant method of entering data.

Using the Forms Toolbar

You add the dialog box controls by selecting tools from the Forms toolbar. Table 17.1 summarizes the tools you can use to place controls on a worksheet.

Table 17.1. Excel's Forms toolbar buttons.

Button	Name	Description
	Group box	Creates a box to hold option buttons.
	Check box	Creates a check box. If activated, a check box returns the value TRUE in its linked cell. If it's deactivated, it returns FALSE.
	Option button	Creates an option button. In each group of option buttons, the user can select only one option. The returned value is a number indicating which option button was activated. The value 1 represents the first button added to the group, 2 signifies the second button, and so on.
	List box	Creates a list box from which the user can select an item. The items in the list are defined by the values in a specified worksheet range, and the value returned to the linked cell is the number of the item chosen.
	Drop-down	Creates a drop-down list box. This box is similar to a regular list box; however, the control shows only one item at a time until you click the down arrow to drop the list down.
	Scrollbar	Creates a scrollbar control. Unlike window scrollbars, a scrollbar control can be used to select a number from a range of values. Clicking the arrows or dragging the scroll box changes the value of the control. This value is what gets returned to the linked cell.
	Spinner	Creates a spinner. Similar to a scrollbar, you can use a spinner to select a number between a maximum and minimum value by clicking the arrows. This number is returned to the linked cell.

Adding a Control to a Worksheet

You add controls to a worksheet using the same steps you use to create any graphic object:

1. On the Forms toolbar, click the control you want to create. The mouse pointer changes to a cross hair.
2. Move the pointer onto the worksheet and drag it to create the object.

3. Excel assigns a default caption to group boxes, check boxes, and option buttons. To edit this caption, click the control and edit the text accordingly. When you're done, click outside the control.

Once you've added a control, you can move it and size it as needed.

CAUTION: SELECTING A CONTROL

The controls you add are "live" in the sense that when you click them, you're working the control (activating it and changing its value). To select a control for sizing or moving, you need to hold down the Ctrl key before clicking the control.

Linking a Control to a Cell Value

To use the dialog box controls for inputting data, you need to associate each control with a worksheet cell. The following procedure shows you how it's done:

1. Select the control you want to work with. (Again, remember to hold down the Ctrl key before you click the control.)
2. Select Format | Control to display the Format Control dialog box.

TIP: DISPLAYING THE FORMAT CONTROL DIALOG BOX

There are three quick ways to display the Format Control dialog box: Select the control and press Ctrl-1, right-click the control and select Format Control from the shortcut menu, or click the Properties tool on the Forms toolbar.

3. Activate the Control tab and then use the Cell link box to enter the cell's reference. You can either type in the reference or select it directly on the worksheet.
4. Click OK to return to the worksheet.

TIP: LINKING A CONTROL TO A CELL

Another way to link a control to a cell is to select the control and enter a formula in the formula bar of the form =cell. Here, cell is an absolute reference to the cell you want to use. For example, to link a control to cell A1, you would enter the following formula:

=$A$1

Figure 17.27 shows a worksheet with several controls and their corresponding linked cells. (To make things a little clearer, I added the numbers you see beside the scrollbar and spinner; they don't come with the control.)

Figure 17.27.

A worksheet with several controls and their corresponding linked cells.

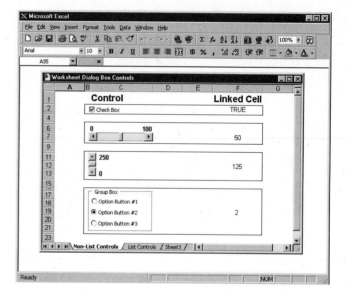

Working with List Boxes

List boxes and drop-down lists are different from other controls because you also have to specify a range that contains the items to appear in the list. The following steps show you how it's done:

1. Enter the list items in a range.

2. Add the list control to the sheet (if you haven't done so already) and then select it.

3. Select Format | Object to display the Format Object dialog box.

4. Activate the Control tab and then use the Input Range box to enter a reference to the range of items. You can either type in the reference or select it directly on the worksheet.

5. Click OK to return to the worksheet.

Figure 17.28 shows a worksheet with a list box and a drop-down list. The list used by both controls is the range A2:A8. Notice that the linked cells display the number of the list selection, not the selection itself. To get the selected list item, you could use the INDEX() function with the following syntax:

INDEX(*list_range*, *list_selection*)

list_range	The range used in the list box or drop-down list.
list_selection	The number of the item selected in the list.

FIGURE 17.28.

A worksheet with a list box and drop-down list control.

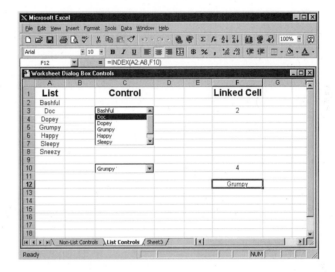

For example, to find out the item selected from the drop-down list box in Figure 17.28, you would use the following formula:

=INDEX(A2:A8,F10)

Summary

This chapter showed you a number of advanced techniques for dealing with Excel worksheets and workbooks. We talked about changing the worksheet view, using outlines, working with templates, consolidating data, protecting worksheets and workbooks, and adding worksheet dialog box controls. If you're still hungry for more info, here are a few other chapters to check out:

■ Data consolidation can add link formulas to the destination range for each cell in the source ranges you selected. See the section "Working with Links in Formulas" in Chapter 16, "Manipulating Formulas and Functions," for details about link formulas.

■ Pivot tables are often better for consolidating data by category. See Chapter 20, "Creating and Customizing Pivot Tables," to find out how they work.

■ Multiple worksheet views are handy for simple "what-if" analyses. See Chapter 22, "Excel's Data Analysis Tools," for more information on what-if analysis.

■ I showed you how to protect your scenarios. If you don't have any scenarios to protect, you can find out how to do so in Chapter 22.

Working with Charts

IN THIS CHAPTER

When producers want to know what the public wants, they graph it as curves. When they want to tell the public what to get, they say it in curves.

—Marshall McLuhan

One of the best ways to analyze your worksheet data—or get your point across to other people—is to display your data visually in a chart. Excel gives you tremendous flexibility when you're creating charts; it lets you place charts in separate documents or directly on the worksheet itself. Not only that, but you have dozens of different chart formats to choose from, and if none of Excel's built-in formats is just right, you can further customize these charts to suit your needs.

After you've created a chart and selected the appropriate type of chart, you can enhance the chart's appearance by formatting any of the various chart elements. This chapter shows you how to format chart axes, data markers, and gridlines.

A Review of Chart Basics

 Before getting down to the nitty-gritty of creating and working with charts, we'll take a look at some chart terminology that you need to become familiar with. Figure 18.1 points out the various parts of a typical chart. Each part is explained in Table 18.1.

Figure 18.1.

The elements of an Excel chart.

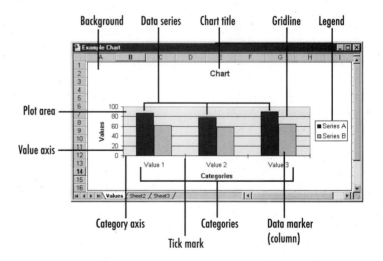

Table 18.1. The elements of an Excel chart.

Element	Description
Background	The area on which the chart is drawn. You can change the color and border of this area.
Category	A grouping of data values on the category axis. Figure 18.1 has three categories: Value 1, Value 2, and Value 3.

Element	Description
Category axis	The axis (usually the x-axis) that contains the category groupings.
Data marker	A symbol that represents a specific data value. The symbol used depends on the chart type. In a column chart, such as the one shown in Figure 18.1, each column is a marker.
Data series	A collection of related data values. Normally, the marker for each value in a series has the same pattern. Figure 18.1 has two series: Series A and Series B. These are identified in the legend.
Data value	A single piece of data. Also called a *data point*.
Gridlines	Optional horizontal and vertical extensions of the axis tick marks. These make data values easier to read.
Legend	A guide that shows the colors, patterns, and symbols used by the markers for each data series.
Plot area	The area bounded by the category and value axes. It contains the data points and gridlines.
Tick mark	A small line that intersects the category axis or the value axis. It marks divisions in the chart's categories or scales.
Title	The title of the chart.
Value axis	The axis (usually the y-axis) that contains the data values.

How Excel Converts Worksheet Data into a Chart

Creating an Excel chart usually is straightforward and often can be done with only a few keystrokes or mouse clicks. However, a bit of background on how Excel converts your worksheet data into a chart will help you avoid some pitfalls.

When Excel creates a chart, it examines both the shape and the contents of the range you've selected. From this data, the program makes various assumptions to determine what should be on the category axis, what should be on the value axis, how to label the categories, and which labels should show within the legend.

The first assumption Excel makes is that *there are more categories than data series*. This makes sense, because most graphs plot a small number of series over many different intervals. For example, a chart showing monthly sales and profit over a year has two data series (the sales and profit numbers) but 12 categories (the monthly intervals). Consequently, Excel assumes that the category axis (the x-axis) of your chart runs along the longest side of the selected worksheet range.

The chart shown in Figure 18.2 is a plot of the range A1:D3 in the Column Categories worksheet. Because in this case the range has more columns than rows, Excel uses each column as a category. Conversely, Figure 18.3 shows the plot of the range A1:C4, which has more rows than columns. In this case, Excel uses each row as a category.

Figure 18.2.

A chart created from a range that has more columns than rows.

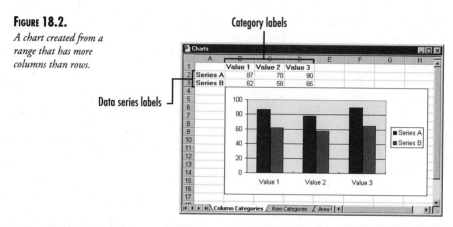

Figure 18.3.

A chart created from a range that has more rows than columns.

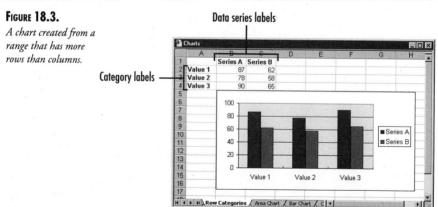

NOTE: SAME NUMBER OF ROWS AND COLUMNS

If a range has the same number of rows and columns, Excel uses the columns as categories.

The second assumption Excel makes involves the location of labels for categories and data series:

■ For a range with more columns than rows (such as in Figure 18.2), Excel uses the contents of the top row (row 1 in Figure 18.2) as the category labels, and the far-left column (column A in Figure 18.2) as the data series labels.

■ For a range with more rows than columns (such as in Figure 18.3), Excel uses the contents of the far-left column (column A in Figure 18.3) as the category labels, and the top row (row 1 in Figure 18.3) as the data series labels.

NOTE: SAME NUMBER OF ROWS AND COLUMNS, PART 2

If a range has the same number of rows and columns, Excel uses the top row for the category labels and the far-left column for the data series labels.

Creating a Chart

When plotting your worksheet data, you have two basic options: You can create an *embedded chart,* which sits on top of your worksheet and can be moved, sized, and formatted, or you can create a separate *chart sheet* by using the automatic or cut-and-paste methods. Whether you choose to embed your charts or store them in separate sheets, the charts are linked with worksheet data. Any changes you make to the data are automatically updated in the chart. The next few sections discuss each of these techniques.

Excel's Chart Wizard tool takes you through the steps necessary for setting up a chart and setting various customization options. The following steps shows you how the Chart Wizard works:

1. Select the cell range you want to plot. (This step is optional because you get a chance to select a range later in the process.)

2. Either click the Chart Wizard tool on the Standard toolbar or select Insert |Chart. Excel displays the first Chart Wizard dialog box, shown in Figure 18.4.

18

WORKING WITH CHARTS

FIGURE 18.4.

Use the first Chart Wizard dialog box to select a chart type.

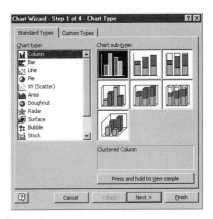

3. Select a chart from the Chart type list, and then select a subtype from the Chart sub-type group. (If you selected your data in advance, you can see a preview of the chart by moving the mouse over the Press and hold down to view sample button, and pressing the mouse button.) Click the Next > button. Excel displays the Source Data dialog box, shown in Figure 18.5.

FIGURE 18.5.

Use this dialog box to select the chart data range.

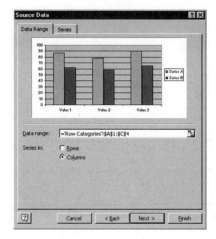

4. If you didn't do so earlier, use the Data range box to enter the range you want to chart. You can either enter the range coordinates by hand or use the mouse to high-light the range directly on the sheet. (For the latter, make sure you click inside the Data range text box first.) Click the Next > button. The third Chart Wizard dialog box, shown in Figure 18.6, appears.

FIGURE 18.6.

Use this Chart Wizard dialog box to format the chart.

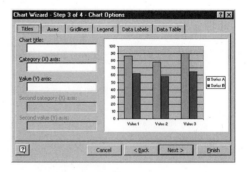

5. This dialog box presents a number of tabs that you can use to format the chart. For example, you can use the Titles tab to define an overall chart title and titles for the category and value axes. I'll discuss the rest of these formatting options later in this chapter. When you're done, click the Next > button to display the final Chart Wizard dialog box, shown in Figure 18.7.

FIGURE 18.7.
Use this Chart Wizard dialog box to specify a location for the new chart.

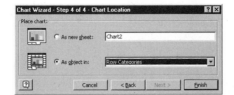

6. To insert the chart as a new chart sheet, activate the As new sheet option and enter a title for the sheet in the text box provided. If you'd prefer to embed the chart on an existing worksheet, activate the As object in option and use the drop-down list to choose the sheet you want to use. When you're done, click Finish. Excel inserts the chart.

NOTE: USING EMBEDDED CHARTS

Because you can print embedded charts along with your worksheet data, embedded charts are useful in presentations in which you need to show plotted data and worksheet information simultaneously.

Activating a Chart

Before you can work with chart types, you need to activate a chart. How you do this depends on the kind of chart you're dealing with:

- For an embedded chart, click inside the chart box. Excel displays selection handles around the chart object's border.
- For a chart sheet, select the sheet tab.

Selecting a Chart Type

After you've created a chart, you might decide that the existing chart type doesn't display your data the way you want. Or you might want to experiment with different chart types to find the one that best suits your data. Fortunately, the chart type isn't set in stone and can be changed at any time. Depending on the chart, you can use either of the following methods to select a different chart type:

- Use the Chart Type dialog box.
- Use the Chart Type tool's palette of types.

18

WORKING WITH CHARTS

Selecting a Chart Type from the Chart Type Dialog Box

Follow these steps to use the Chart Type dialog box to select a chart type:

1. Activate the chart you want to change.

2. Select Format | Chart Type. Excel displays the Chart Type dialog box, shown in Figure 18.8.

FIGURE 18.8.

Use the Chart Type dialog box to assign a different chart type.

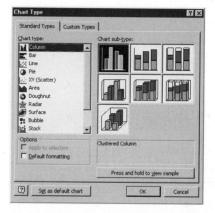

TIP: CHARTING SHORTCUT

You can also display the Chart Type dialog box by right-clicking the chart background and selecting the Chart Type command from the shortcut menu.

---

3. Use the Chart type list to select a new chart type.

4. Chart subtypes are variations on the main chart type that display your data in slightly different ways. To select a chart subtype, click one of the boxes in the Chart sub-type group. (Note that the Custom Types tab boasts a few other types of charts.)

5. Click OK.

Using the Chart Type Tool to Select a Chart Type

The following procedure shows you how to select a chart type using the Chart Type tool:

1. Activate the chart you want to change.

2. Display the Chart toolbar.

3. Drop down the Chart Type tool and select one of the chart types from the palette that appears. Using the selected chart type, Excel redraws the chart.

TIP: TEARING OFF THE CHART TYPE PALETTE

If you want to experiment with various chart types, you can "tear off" the Chart Type tool's palette. Drop the palette down and place the mouse pointer inside the bar at the top of the palette (the bar will turn blue). Now drag the mouse until the palette separates. When you release the button, the Chart Type toolbar appears as a floating palette.

Selecting Chart Elements

An Excel chart is composed of elements such as axes, data markers, gridlines, and text, each with its own formatting options. Before you can format an element, however, you need to select it. Table 18.2 lists the mouse techniques for selecting various chart items.

Table 18.2. Mouse techniques for selecting chart elements.

Action	*Result*
Click the chart background.	The entire chart is selected.
Click an empty part of the plot area.	The plot area is selected.
Click an axis or an axis label.	The axis is selected.
Click a gridline.	The gridline is selected.
Click any marker in the series.	The data series is selected.
Click a data marker once and then click it a second time.	The data marker is selected.
Click an object.	The chart object is selected.

You can also make use of the Chart toolbar's Chart Objects drop-down list. Just drop down the menu and select the chart object you want to work with. Excel selects the object automatically.

Converting a Series to a Different Chart Type

If you want to create a combination chart not found among Excel's built-in chart types, or if you have chart formatting you want to preserve, you can easily apply an overlay effect to an existing chart.

For example, Figure 18.9 shows a chart with three series: sales figures for 1995, sales figures for 1996, and a series that plots the growth from 1995 to 1996. The chart clearly shows that the

Growth series would make more sense as a line chart. Excel lets you convert individual data series into chart types. To do so, follow these steps:

1. Activate the chart you want to work with.

2. Click the series you want to convert.

3. Select Chart | Chart Type (or right-click the series and select Chart Type from the shortcut menu) to display the Chart Type dialog box.

4. In the Options group, make sure that the Apply to selection option is activated.

5. Select the chart type you want to use for the series and click OK. Excel converts the series to the chart type you selected. Figure 18.10 shows the chart in Figure 18.9 with the Growth series converted to a line chart.

FIGURE 18.9.

The Growth series would be better as a line chart.

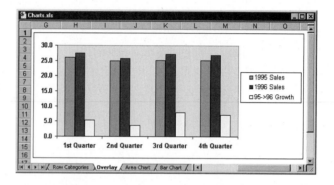

FIGURE 18.10.

The revised chart with the Growth series converted to a line chart.

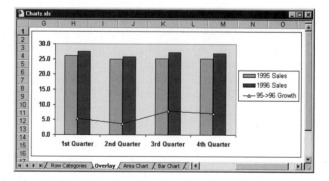

Formatting Chart Axes

Excel provides various options for controlling the appearance of your chart axes. You can hide axes; set the typeface, size, and style of axis labels; format the axis lines and tick marks; and adjust the axis scale. You can find most of the axis formatting options in the Format Axis dialog box, shown in Figure 18.11. To display this dialog box, select the axis you want to format and then choose Format | Selected Axis.

FIGURE 18.11.

Use the Format Axis dialog box to enhance the look of your chart axes.

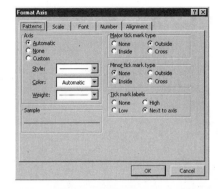

TIP: ACCESSING THE FORMAT DIALOG BOX

For any chart object, Excel gives you a number of methods for accessing the appropriate Format dialog boxes quickly:

■ Double-click the object.

■ Select the object and press Ctrl-1.

■ Right-click the object and select Format *Object* from the shortcut menu.

■ Select the object and click the Chart toolbar's Select *Object* button.

Formatting Axis Patterns

The Patterns tab in the Format Axis dialog box lets you set various options for the axis line and tick marks. Here's a summary of the control groups:

■ Axis: These options format the axis line. Select None to remove the line, or select Custom to adjust the Style, Color, and Weight. The Sample box shows you how the line will look.

■ Tick mark type: These options control the position of the Major and Minor tick marks.

■ Tick mark labels: These options control the position of the tick mark labels.

NOTE: MAJOR VERSUS MINOR TICK MARKS

The major tick marks carry the axis labels. The minor tick marks appear between the labels. See the next section to learn how to control the units of both the major and the minor tick marks.

18

WORKING WITH
CHARTS

Formatting an Axis Scale

You can format the scale of your chart axes to set things such as the range of numbers on an axis and where the category and value axes intersect.

To format the scale, select the Scale tab in the Format Axis dialog box. If you're formatting the value (Y) axis, you see the layout shown in Figure 18.12. These options format several scale characteristics, such as the range of values (Minimum and Maximum), the tick mark units (Major unit and Minor unit), and where the category (X) axis crosses the value axis. For the last of these characteristics, you have three choices:

- Activate the check box labeled Category (X) axis. This places the x-axis at the bottom of the chart (that is, at the minimum value on the y-axis).
- Enter a value in the text box labeled Crosses at.
- Activate the check box labeled Category (X) axis crosses at maximum value. This places the x-axis at the top of the chart.

FIGURE 18.12.

The Scale tab for the value (Y) axis.

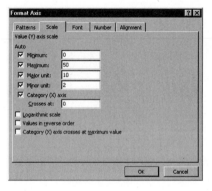

Formatting the value axis scale properly can make a big difference in the impact of your charts. For example, Figure 18.13 shows a chart with a value axis scale ranging from 0 to 50. Figure 18.14 shows the same chart with the value axis scale between 18 and 23. As you can see, the trend of the data is much clearer and more dramatic in Figure 18.14.

FIGURE 18.13.

A stock chart showing an apparently flat trend.

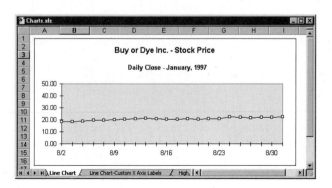

FIGURE 18.14.

*The same stock chart
with an adjusted scale
shows an obvious up
trend.*

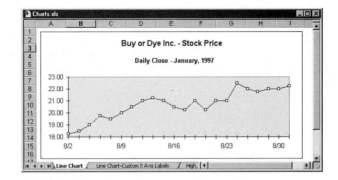

For the category (X) axis, the Scale tab appears as shown in Figure 18.15. These options mostly
control where the value (Y) axis crosses the category (X) axis and the frequency of categories:

- Use the text box labeled Value (Y) axis crosses at category number to control where
  the y-axis crosses the x-axis. For example, an entry of 1 (the default) places the y-axis
  on the left side of the chart. If you prefer to see the y-axis on the right side of the
  chart, activate the check box labeled Value (Y) axis crosses at maximum category.

- The major tick mark unit is controlled by the text box labeled Number of categories
  between tick-mark labels. For example, an entry of 5 puts a tick-mark label every five
  categories.

- The total number of tick marks is controlled by the text box labeled Number of
  categories between tick marks. For example, an entry of 1 provides a tick mark for
  each category.

- When the check box labeled Value (Y) axis crosses between categories is deactivated
  (the default), Excel plots the values on the tick marks. If you activate this check box,
  Excel plots the values between the tick marks.

- Activating the check box labeled Categories in reverse order displays the categories
  along the x-axis in reverse order.

FIGURE 18.15.

*The Scale tab for the
category (X) axis.*

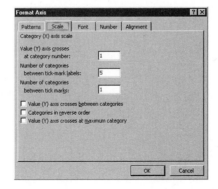

Formatting Axis Labels

You can change the font, numeric format, and alignment of the labels that appear along the axis. To change the label font, select the Font tab in the Format Axis dialog box, and then select the font options you want.

To change the numeric format of axis labels (assuming, of course, that the labels are numbers, dates, or times), you have two choices:

■ Format the worksheet data series that generated the labels. Excel uses this formatting automatically when it sets up the axis labels.

■ Select the Number tab in the Format Axis dialog box, and then select a numeric format from the options provided.

To format the alignment of the axis labels, select the Alignment tab in the Format Axis dialog box, and then select the option you want from the Orientation group.

TIP: USE THE FORMATTING TOOLBAR

You also can use the tools on the Formatting toolbar (such as Bold and Currency Style) to format the labels of a selected axis.

Formatting Chart Data Markers

A *data marker* is a symbol that Excel uses to plot each value (data point). Examples of data markers are small circles or squares for line charts, rectangles for column and bar charts, and pie slices for pie charts. Depending on the type of marker you're dealing with, you can format the marker's color, pattern, style, or border.

To begin, select the data marker or markers you want to work with.

■ If you want to format the entire series, click any data marker in the series, and then select Format | Selected Data Series. Excel displays the Format Data Series dialog box.

■ If you want to format a single data marker, click the marker once to select the entire series, and then click the marker a second time. (Note, however, that you don't double-click the marker. If you do, you just get the Format Data Series dialog box. Click the marker once, wait a couple of seconds, and then click it again.) Then choose Format | Selected Data Point to display the Format Data Point dialog box.

Whichever method you choose, select the Patterns tab to display the formatting options for the series markers. Figure 18.16 shows the Patterns tab for an area, bar, column, pie, or doughnut chart marker. (The corresponding Format Data Point dialog box has only the Patterns and Data Labels tabs.)

FIGURE 18.16.

The Patterns tab for area, bar, column, pie, and doughnut chart data series.

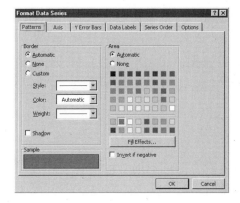

Use the Border group to either turn off the border (None) or define the Style, Color, and Weight of the marker border. Use the Area section to assign marker colors and patterns.

You get a different set of options when you format line, XY, or radar chart markers, as shown in Figure 18.17. Use the Line section to format the Style, Color, and Weight of the data series line. The Smoothed line option (available only for line and XY charts) smoothes out some of a line's rough edges. Use the Marker section to format the marker style as well as the foreground and background colors.

FIGURE 18.17.

The Patterns tab for line, XY, and radar charts.

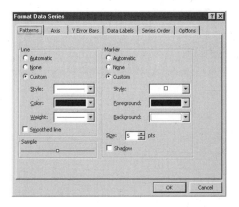

Displaying and Formatting Chart Gridlines

Adding horizontal or vertical gridlines can make your charts easier to read. For each axis, you can display a major gridline, a minor gridline, or both. The positioning of these gridlines is determined by the numbers you enter for the axis scales. For a value axis, major gridlines are governed by the Major Unit option, and minor gridlines are governed by the Minor Unit option. (The Major and Minor Unit options are properties of the value axis scale. To learn how to adjust these values, see the earlier section "Formatting an Axis Scale.") For a category axis, major gridlines are governed by the number of categories between tick-mark labels, and minor gridlines are governed by the number of categories between tick marks.

Displaying Gridlines

The following procedure shows you how to display gridlines:

1. Select Chart | Chart Options and then select the Gridlines tab in the Chart Options dialog box, shown in Figure 18.18.

FIGURE 18.18.

Use the Gridlines tab to activate chart gridlines.

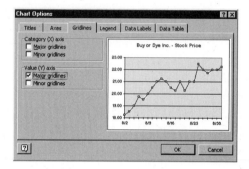

2. Activate the check boxes for the gridlines you want to display.
3. Click OK.

Formatting Gridlines

Once your gridlines are in place, you can format their style, color, and weight by following these steps:

1. Select a gridline.
2. Select Format | Selected Gridlines to display the Format Gridline dialog box.
3. Use the Patterns tab to select the gridline options you want (Style, Color, and Weight).
4. Click OK.

Formatting the Plot Area and Background

You can format borders, patterns, and colors of both the chart plot area and the background. To format either of these areas, follow this procedure:

1. Select the plot area or chart background.
2. Select either Format | Selected Plot Area or Format | Selected Chart Area to display the appropriate Format dialog box.

3. In the Patterns tab, select the options you want in the Border and Area groups.

4. If you're in the Format Chart Area dialog box, you can also select the Font tab to format the chart font.

5. Click OK.

Adding and Formatting a Chart Legend

If your chart includes multiple data series, you should add a legend to explain the series markers. This makes your chart more readable and makes it easier for others to distinguish each series.

To add a legend, you have two choices:

■ Select Chart | Chart Options, activate the Legend tab in the Chart Options dialog box, and then activate the Show legend check box.

■ Use the Chart toolbar's Legend tool to toggle the legend on and off.

You can format your legends with the same options you used to format chart text. Select the legend, and then choose Format | Selected Legend to display the Format Legend dialog box. You can then use the Patterns and Font tabs to format the legend. You also can use the options in the Placement tab to change the position of the legend. (Alternatively, you can drag the legend to a different location.) Figure 18.19 shows a chart with a formatted legend.

FIGURE 18.19.

A chart with a formatted legend.

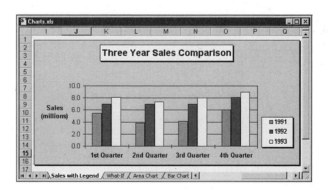

18

WORKING WITH CHARTS

Summary

This chapter got you up to speed with Excel's charting capabilities. After some brief charting theory, this chapter looked at all kinds of formatting options for each of the chart elements. Here are a few other chapters to read for related information:

■ To brush up on your range-selection techniques, see Chapter 15, "Working with Ranges."

■ You can use charts for simple what-if data analysis. Chapter 22, "Excel's Data Analysis Tools," tells you how.

Working with Lists and Databases

CHAPTER 19

Why can't somebody give us a list of things that everybody thinks and nobody says, and another list of things that everybody says and nobody thinks.

—*Oliver Wendell Holmes, Sr.*

These days, there's no shortage of dedicated database programs for the Windows market. There's the Access package that comes with Microsoft Office, of course, and there are also Windows versions of FoxPro, Paradox, and dBASE, to name a few. These high-end programs are full relational database management systems designed to handle complex, interrelated tables, queries, and reports.

Fortunately, when it comes to simple tables of data, you don't have to bother with all the bells and whistles of the big-time database systems. Excel is more than capable of handling flat-file databases (or *lists,* as they're called in Excel) right in a worksheet. You can create simple data-entry forms with a few mouse clicks, and you can sort the data, summarize it, extract records based on criteria, and lots more. This chapter introduces you to Excel lists. You'll learn what lists are, how you can use them, how to create them in your Excel worksheets, and how to work with them.

What Is a List?

A *list* is a collection of related information with an organizational structure that makes it easy to find or extract data from its contents. Examples of lists are a phone book organized by name and a library card catalog organized by book title.

In Excel, the term *list* refers to a worksheet range that has the following properties:

- Field: A single type of information, such as a name, an address, or a phone number. In Excel lists, each column is a field.

- Field value: A single item in a field. In an Excel list, the field values are the individual cells.

- Field name: A unique name you assign to every list field (worksheet column). These names are always found in the first row of the list.

- Record: A collection of associated field values. In Excel lists, each row is a record.

- List range: The worksheet range that includes all the records, fields, and field names of a list.

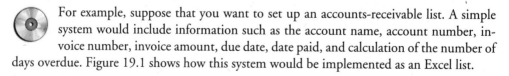 For example, suppose that you want to set up an accounts-receivable list. A simple system would include information such as the account name, account number, invoice number, invoice amount, due date, date paid, and calculation of the number of days overdue. Figure 19.1 shows how this system would be implemented as an Excel list.

NOTE: LIST USES

You can use lists for just about anything you need to keep track of: inventory, accounts payable, books, CDs, and even household possessions.

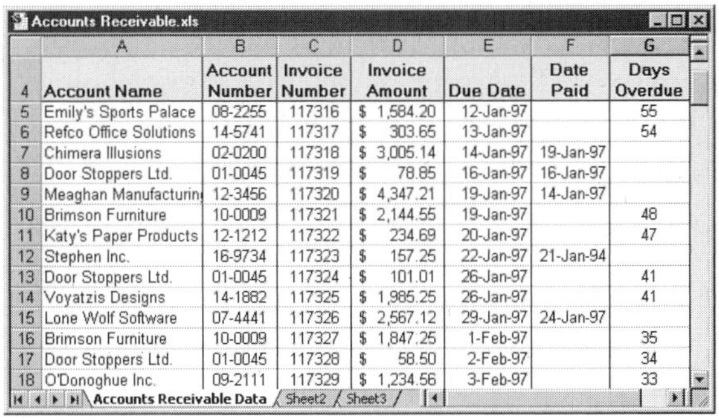

	A	B	C	D	E	F	G
4	Account Name	Account Number	Invoice Number	Invoice Amount	Due Date	Date Paid	Days Overdue
5	Emily's Sports Palace	08-2255	117316	$ 1,584.20	12-Jan-97		55
6	Refco Office Solutions	14-5741	117317	$ 303.65	13-Jan-97		54
7	Chimera Illusions	02-0200	117318	$ 3,005.14	14-Jan-97	19-Jan-97	
8	Door Stoppers Ltd.	01-0045	117319	$ 78.85	16-Jan-97	16-Jan-97	
9	Meaghan Manufacturin	12-3456	117320	$ 4,347.21	19-Jan-97	14-Jan-97	
10	Brimson Furniture	10-0009	117321	$ 2,144.55	19-Jan-97		48
11	Katy's Paper Products	12-1212	117322	$ 234.69	20-Jan-97		47
12	Stephen Inc.	16-9734	117323	$ 157.25	22-Jan-97	21-Jan-94	
13	Door Stoppers Ltd.	01-0045	117324	$ 101.01	26-Jan-97		41
14	Voyatzis Designs	14-1882	117325	$ 1,985.25	26-Jan-97		41
15	Lone Wolf Software	07-4441	117326	$ 2,567.12	29-Jan-97	24-Jan-97	
16	Brimson Furniture	10-0009	117327	$ 1,847.25	1-Feb-97		35
17	Door Stoppers Ltd.	01-0045	117328	$ 58.50	2-Feb-97		34
18	O'Donoghue Inc.	09-2111	117329	$ 1,234.56	3-Feb-97		33

FIGURE 19.1.
An accounts-receivable list.

Planning a List

The most important step in creating a list is determining the information you want it to contain. Although a list can be as large as the entire worksheet, in practice you should minimize the size of the range. This technique saves memory and makes managing the data easier. Therefore, you should strive to set up all your lists with only essential information.

For example, if you're building an accounts-receivable list, you should include only data that relates to the receivables. In such a list, you need two kinds of information: invoice data and customer data. The invoice data includes the invoice number, the amount, the due date, and the date paid. You also include a calculated field that determines the number of days the account is overdue. For the customer, you need at least a name and an account number. You don't need to include an address or a phone number, because this information isn't essential to the receivables data.

This last point brings up the idea of *data redundancy*. In many cases, you'll be setting up a list as part of a larger application. For example, you might have lists not only for accounts receivable, but also for accounts payable, customer information, part numbers, and so on. You don't need to include information such as addresses and phone numbers in the receivables list, because you should have that data in a more general customer information list. To include this data in both places is redundant.

TIP: USE KEY FIELDS FOR CROSS-REFERENCES

Different but related lists need to have a *key field* that is common to each. For example, the accounts-receivable and customer information lists both could contain an account number field. This lets you cross-reference entries in both lists.

After you decide what kind of information to include in your list, you need to determine the level of detail for each field. For example, if you're including address information, do you want separate fields for the street address, city, state, and ZIP code? For a phone number, do you need a separate field for the area code? In most cases, the best approach is to split the data into the smallest elements that make sense. This method gives you maximum flexibility when you sort and extract information.

The next stage in planning your list is to assign names to each field. Here are some guidelines to follow:

- Always use the top row of the list for the column labels.

- Although you can assign names as long as 255 characters, you should try to use short names to prevent your fields from becoming too wide.

TIP: USE WORD WRAP FOR LONG FIELD NAMES

If you need to use a long field name, turn on the Word Wrap alignment option to keep the field width small. Select the cell, choose Format | Cells, select the Alignment tab in the Format Cells dialog box, activate the Wrap Text check box, and click OK.

- Field names must be unique, and they must be text or text formulas. If you need to use numbers, format them as text.

- You should format the column labels to help differentiate them from the list data. You can use bold text, a different font color, a background color, and a border along the bottom of each cell.

The final step in setting up your list is to plan its position in the worksheet. Here are some points to keep in mind:

- Some Excel commands can automatically identify the size and shape of a list. To avoid confusing such commands, try to use only one list per worksheet. If you have several related lists, include them in other tabs in the same workbook.

- If you have any other nonlist data in a worksheet, leave at least one blank row or column between the data and the list. This technique helps Excel identify the list automatically.

■ Excel has a command that lets you filter your list data to show only records that match certain criteria. (See the section "Filtering List Data" for details.) This command works by hiding rows of data. Therefore, if you have nonlist data you need to access, it's important not to place it to the left or right of a list.

Entering List Data

After you've set up your field names, you can start entering your list records. The following sections show you how to enter data directly on the worksheet or by using a data form.

Entering Data Directly on a Worksheet

The most straightforward way to enter information into a list is to directly type data in the worksheet cells. If you've formatted any of the fields (numeric formats, alignment, and so on), be sure to copy the formats to the new records.

Entering and deleting records and fields within a list is analogous to inserting and deleting rows and columns in a regular worksheet model. Table 19.1 summarizes these list commands.

Table 19.1. Some basic list commands.

List Action	*Excel Procedure*
Add a record	Select a row, and then select Insert | Rows.
Add a field	Select a column, and then select Insert | Columns.
Delete a record	Select the entire row, and then select Edit | Delete.
Delete a field	Select the entire column, and then select Edit | Delete.

If you don't want to add or delete an entire row or column (for example, if other worksheet data is in the way), you can insert or delete data within the list range. If you're inserting or deleting a row, select a list record (be sure to include each field in the record). If you're inserting or deleting a column, select a list field (be sure to include each record in the field as well as the field name).

Entering list information can be tedious. Excel offers several shortcut keys to speed up the process; they're summarized in Table 19.2.

Table 19.2. Excel data-entry shortcut keys.

Key	*Action*
Tab	Confirms the entry and moves to the field on the right.
Shift-Tab	Confirms the entry and moves to the field on the left.

continues

19

WORKING WITH
LISTS AND
DATABASES

Table 19.2. continued

Key	Action
Enter	Confirms the entry and moves to the next record.
Shift+Enter	Confirms the entry and moves to the preceding record.
Ctrl-"	Copies the number from the same field in the preceding record.
Ctrl-'	Copies the formula from the same field in the preceding record.
Ctrl-;	Enters the current date.
Ctrl-:	Enters the current time.

TIP: PRESSING ENTER TO MOVE TO ANOTHER RECORD

If pressing Enter or Shift-Enter doesn't move you to another record, select Tools | Options. Then select the Edit tab in the Options dialog box and activate the check box labeled Move selection after Enter. Note, too, that you can use the Direction drop-down list to choose the default direction Excel moves after you press Enter.

Entering Data Using a Data Form

Excel lists are powerful information-management tools, but creating and maintaining them can be tedious and time-consuming. To make data entry easier and more efficient, Excel offers the data form dialog box. You can use this form to add, edit, delete, and find list records quickly.

What Is a Data Form?

A *data form* is a dialog box that simplifies list management in the following ways:

■ The dialog box shows only one record at a time, which makes data entry and editing easier.

■ You can view many more fields in a form than you can see on-screen. In fact, depending on the size of your screen, you can view as many as 18 fields in a single form.

■ When you add or delete records using the data form, Excel automatically adjusts the list range.

■ You get an extra level of safety when you add or delete records. Excel prevents you from overwriting existing worksheet data when you add records, and it seeks confirmation for record deletions.

■ Novice users or data-entry clerks are insulated from the normal list commands. Simple command buttons let users add, delete, and find data.

The good news about data forms is that Excel creates the form automatically based on the layout of your list. To view the form, you select any cell from within the list and then choose Data | Form. (You also can select one of the field name cells or a cell in a row or column immediately adjacent to the list.)

Figure 19.2 shows the data form for the Accounts Receivable list. When constructing the data form, Excel begins with the field names and adds a text box for each editable field. Excel includes fields that are the result of a formula or function (for example, the Days Overdue field in Figure 19.2) for display purposes only; you can't edit these fields. The scrollbar lets you move quickly through the list. The record number indicator in the top-right corner keeps track of both the current list row and the total number of records in the list. This dialog box also includes several command buttons for adding, deleting, and finding records.

FIGURE 19.2.

An Excel data form.

> **NOTE: SORTING DOESN'T AFFECT RECORD NUMBERS**
>
> The record number indicator is unaffected by the list sort order. The first record below the field names is always record 1.

Editing Records

You can use the data form to edit any fields in your list records, with the exception of computed or protected fields. Here are the steps to follow:

1. Display the data form.
2. Select the record you want to edit.
3. Edit the fields you want to change.
4. Repeat steps 2 and 3 for other records you want to edit.
5. Click Close to finish editing the list.

> **CAUTION: CHANGES RECORDED WHEN YOU MOVE TO ANOTHER RECORD**
>
> When you make changes to a record, Excel saves the changes permanently when you scroll to another record. Therefore, before leaving a record, check each field to ensure that it contains the data you want. To restore a record to its original data, select the data form's Restore button before you move to another record.

Adding Records

Adding records with the data form is fast and easy. Here are the steps to follow:

1. Display the data form.
2. Click the New button or press Ctrl-Page Down. Excel creates a blank record and displays New Record as the record number indicator.
3. Fill in the fields for the new record.
4. Repeat steps 2 and 3 for other records you want to add.
5. Click Close to finish adding new records.

When you add records with the data form, Excel adds them to the bottom of the list without inserting a new row. If there is no room to extend the list range, Excel displays a warning message. To add new records, you must either move or delete the other data.

Deleting Records

Follow the steps in this procedure to delete records using the data form:

1. Display the data form.
2. Select the record you want to delete.
3. Click the Delete button. Excel warns you that the record will be deleted permanently.
4. Click OK to confirm the deletion. Excel returns you to the data form.
5. Repeat steps 2 through 4 to delete other records.
6. Click Close to return to the worksheet.

> **NOTE: LIST ADJUSTED AFTER DELETION**
>
> When you delete a record from the data form, Excel clears the data and shifts the records up to fill in the gap.

Finding Records

Although the data form lets you scroll through a list, you might find that for larger lists you need to use the form's search capabilities to quickly locate what you want. You can find specific records in the list by first specifying the *criteria* that the search must match. Excel then compares each record with the criteria and displays the first record that matches. For example, you might want to find all invoices that are over $1,000 or those that are at least one day past due.

> **NOTE: COMPLEX SEARCHES**
>
> You can perform only simple searches with the data form. For more complex search criteria, see "Filtering List Data" later in this chapter.

You construct the search criteria using text, numbers, and comparison operators such as equal to (=) and greater than (>). For example, to find all the invoices that are over $1,000, you would type >1000 in the Invoice Amount field. To find an account named Read Inc., you would type read inc. in the Account Name field. Here are the steps to follow:

1. Display the data form.
2. Click the Criteria button. Excel displays a blank record and replaces the record number indicator with Criteria.
3. Select the field you want to use for the search.
4. Enter the criterion. Figure 19.3 shows the data form with a criterion entered for finding invoices on which the Invoice Amount is greater than 1000.

FIGURE 19.3.

The criteria data form with a sample criterion.

5. Repeat steps 3 and 4 if you want to use multiple criteria (see the following discussion).
6. Use the Find Next and Find Prev buttons to move up or down to the record that matches the criteria.

Sorting a List

One of the advantages of a list is that you can rearrange the records so that they're sorted alphabetically or numerically. This feature lets you view the data in order by customer name, account number, part number, or any other field. You can even sort on multiple fields, which, for example, would let you sort a client list by state and then by name within each state.

For quick sorts, Excel offers a couple of toolbar buttons:

 The Sort Ascending tool.

 The Sort Descending tool.

First, select a cell within the column upon which you want to sort the list. For example, if you want to sort a list of accounts by name, select a cell in the Account Name column. Then simply click either the Sort Ascending or Sort Descending tool.

For more advanced sorts, the sorting procedure is determined by the options in the Sort dialog box, shown in Figure 19.4. It gives you the following choices:

■ Sort by: This drop-down list box contains the list field names. Select a field from this list to determine the overall order for the sort. In Figure 19.4, the Due Date field is selected; therefore, the entire database will be sorted by Due Date.

FIGURE 19.4.

*Use the Sort dialog box
to change the sort order
of your lists.*

■ Then by: This drop-down list also contains the list field names. Select a field from this list to sort records that have the same data in the field specified in Sort by. In Figure 19.4, for example, all the records that have the same due date will be sorted by account name.

■ Then by: Select a field name from this list to sort the records that have the same data in the fields specified by both Sort by and the first Then by field. Figure 19.4 shows that records that have the same due date and the same account name are sorted by the Invoice Amount field.

NOTE: YOU DON'T HAVE TO SORT ON THREE FIELDS

Although Excel lets you sort on as many as three fields, it isn't necessary to enter a field in all three lists. For most sorts, you'll need to choose a field in only the Sort by list.

■ My list has: Excel usually can differentiate between field names (the header row) and data. If Excel finds what it thinks is a header row, it doesn't include it in the sort (and it activates the Header row option). If your list doesn't have a header row (or if you want the top row included in the sort), select the No header row option.

NOTE: HOW EXCEL IDENTIFIES LIST HEADERS

Excel identifies a list's header row by looking for differences in data type (most field names are text entries), capitalization, and formatting. If your list doesn't have a header row, you can still sort by using column headings (Column A, Column B, and so on).

CAUTION: TAKE CARE WHEN SORTING FORMULA CELLS

Be careful when you sort list records that contain formulas. If the formulas use relative addresses that refer to cells outside their own record, the new sort order might change the references and produce erroneous results. If your list formulas must refer to cells outside the list, be sure to use absolute addresses.

For each sort field, you can specify whether the field is sorted in ascending or descending order. Table 19.3 summarizes Excel's ascending sort priorities.

Table 19.3. Excel's ascending sort order.

Type (in Order of Priority)	Order
Numbers	Largest negative to largest positive
Text	Space ! " # $ % & ( ) * + , - . / 0 through 9 (when formatted as text) : ; < = > ? @ A through Z (Excel ignores case) [\ ] ^ _ ' {	} ~
Logical	FALSE before TRUE
Error	All error values are equal
Blank	Always sorted last (ascending or descending)

The following procedure shows you how to sort a list:

1. Select a cell inside the list.

2. Select Data | Sort. Excel displays the Sort dialog box.

3. Enter the sort options you want.

4. Click OK. Excel sorts the range.

Filtering List Data

One of the biggest problems with large lists is that it's often hard to find and extract the data you need. Sorting can help, but in the end you're still working with the entire list. What you need is a way to define the data you want to work with and then have Excel display only those records on-screen. This action is called *filtering* your data. Fortunately, Excel offers several techniques that get the job done.

Using AutoFilter to Filter a List

Excel's AutoFilter feature makes filtering subsets of your data as easy as selecting an option from a drop-down list. In fact, that's literally what happens. If you select Data | Filter | AutoFilter, Excel adds drop-down arrows to the cells containing the list's column labels. Clicking one of these arrows displays a list of all the unique entries in the column. Figure 19.5 shows the drop-down list for the Account Name field in an Accounts Receivable database.

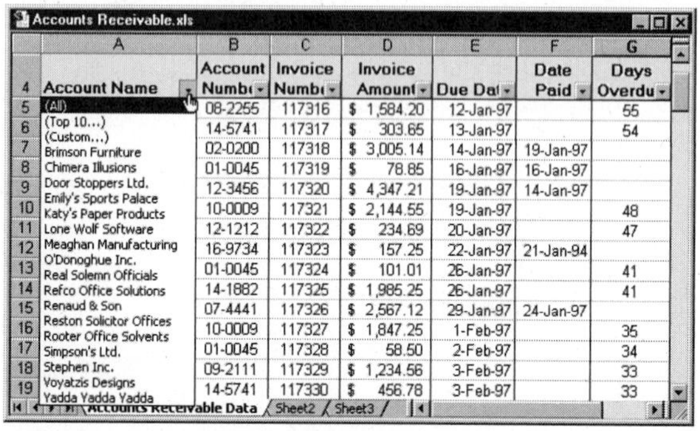

FIGURE 19.5.

For each list field, AutoFilter adds drop-down lists that contain only the unique entries in the column.

> **TIP: USING AUTOFILTER ON A SINGLE FIELD**
>
> If you want to use AutoFilter with only a single field, select that field's entire column before choosing Data | Filter | AutoFilter.

If you select an item from one of these lists, Excel takes the following actions:

■ It displays only those records that include the item in that field. For example, Figure 19.6 shows the resultant records when the item Refco Office Solutions is selected from the list attached to the Account Name column. The other records are hidden and can be retrieved whenever you need them.

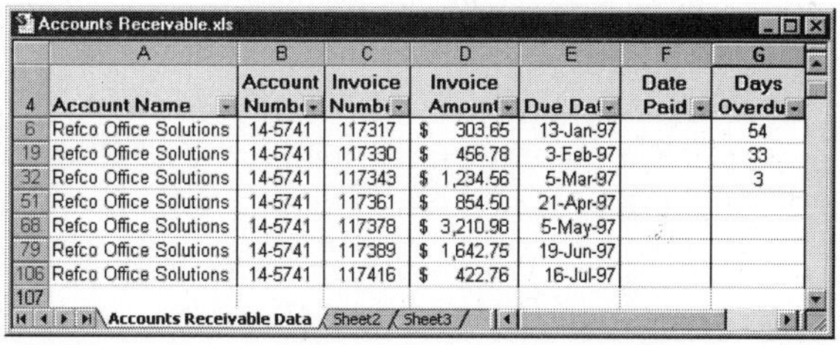

FIGURE 19.6.

Selecting an item from a drop-down list displays only records that include the item in the field.

CAUTION: DATA TO THE LEFT AND RIGHT IS HIDDEN

Because Excel hides the rows that don't meet the criteria, you shouldn't place any important data either to the left or to the right of the list.

■ It changes the color of the column's drop-down arrow. This indicates which column you used to filter the list.

■ It displays the row headings of the filtered records in a different color.

■ It displays a message in the status bar telling you how many records it found that matched the selected item.

To continue filtering the data, you can select an item from one of the other lists. For example, you can select the nonblank cells in the Days Overdue column to see only those Refco Office Solutions invoices that are overdue. (To learn how to select nonblank fields, see the next section.)

AutoFilter Criteria Options

The items you see in each drop-down list are called the *filter criteria*. Besides selecting specific criteria (such as an account name), you also have the following choices in each drop-down list:

■ All: Removes the filter criterion for the column. If you've selected multiple criteria, you can remove all the filter criteria and display the entire list by selecting Data | Filter | Show All.

■ Top 10: Displays the Top 10 AutoFilter dialog box (numeric fields only), shown in Figure 19.7. The left drop-down list has two choices (Top and Bottom), the center spinner lets you choose a number, and the right drop-down list has two choices (Items and Percent). For example, if you choose the default choices (Top, 10, and Items), AutoFilter displays the records that have the 10 highest values in the current field.

19

WORKING WITH
LISTS AND
DATABASES

FIGURE 19.7.

Use the Top 10 AutoFilter dialog box to filter your records based on values in the current field.

- Custom: Allows you to enter more sophisticated criteria. For details, see the next section.

- Blanks: Displays records that have no data in the field. In the Accounts Receivable list, for example, you could use this criterion to find all the unpaid invoices (that is, those with a blank Date Paid field).

- NonBlanks: Displays records that have data in the field. Selecting this criterion in the Days Overdue field of the Accounts Receivable list, for example, finds invoices that are overdue.

Showing Filtered Records

When you need to redisplay records that have been filtered via AutoFilter, use any of the following techniques:

- To display the entire list and remove AutoFilter's drop-down arrows, select Data | Filter | AutoFilter.

- To display the entire list without removing the AutoFilter drop-down arrows, select Data | Filter | Show All.

- To remove the filter on a single field, display that field's AutoFilter drop-down list and select the All option.

Summary

This chapter showed you how to work with lists (or databases, as they used to be called) in Excel. It showed you how to set up a list, how to use forms for data entry, and how to sort and filter a list. For some list-related material, try these chapters:

- If you need to fill in a list field with a series, you can use the Fill handle or Edit | Fill | Series. See Chapter 15, "Working with Ranges," for more information.

- Filtering and list functions are powerful tools for analyzing list data. But for large lists, they might not be enough to help you extract all the information you need. Pivot tables might be the answer, however. They're covered in depth in Chapter 20, "Creating and Customizing Pivot Tables."

- If the data you want to work with is in an external database table (such as an Access or FoxPro file), you can use Microsoft Query to get at it. I explain this in Chapter 21, "Using Microsoft Query."

CHAPTER 20

Creating and Customizing Pivot Tables

IN THIS CHAPTER

> *The real world is not easy to live in. It is rough; it is slippery. Without the most clear-eyed adjustments we fall and get crushed. A man must stay sober: not always, but most of the time.*
>
> —*Clarence Day*

Lists and external databases can contain hundreds or even thousands of records. Analyzing that much data can be a nightmare without the right kinds of tools. To help you, Excel offers a powerful data-analysis tool called a *pivot table*. This tool lets you summarize hundreds of records in a concise tabular format and then manipulate the table's layout to see different views of your data. This chapter introduces you to pivot tables and shows you various ways you can use them with your own data.

How Pivot Tables Work

In the simplest case, pivot tables work by summarizing the data in one field (called a *data field*) and breaking it down according to the data in another field. The unique values in the second field (called the *row field*) become the row headings. For example, Figure 20.1 shows a database of sales by sales representatives. With a pivot table, you can summarize the numbers in the Sales field (the data field) and break them down by Region (the row field). Figure 20.2 shows the resulting pivot table. Notice how Excel uses the four unique items in the Region field (East, Midwest, South, and West) as row headings.

FIGURE 20.1.

A database of sales by sales representatives.

	Region	Quarter	Sales Rep	Sales
1	Region	Quarter	Sales Rep	Sales
2	East	1st	A	192,345
3	West	1st	B	210,880
4	East	1st	C	185,223
5	South	1st	D	165,778
6	Midwest	1st	E	155,557
7	South	1st	F	180,567
8	West	1st	G	200,767
9	Midwest	1st	H	165,663
10	East	2nd	A	173,493
11	West	2nd	B	200,203
12	East	2nd	C	170,213
13	South	2nd	D	155,339
14	Midwest	2nd	E	148,990
15	South	2nd	F	175,660
16	West	2nd	G	190,290

FIGURE 20.2.

A pivot table showing total sales by region.

Sum of Sales	
Region	Total
East	1,463,655
Midwest	1,340,875
South	1,409,544
West	1,477,884
Grand Total	5,691,958

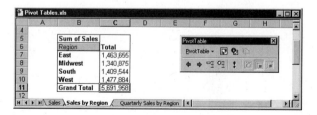

You can further break down your data by specifying a third field (called the *column field*) to use for column headings. Figure 20.3 shows the resulting pivot table with the four unique items in the Quarter field (1st, 2nd, 3rd, and 4th) used to create the columns.

FIGURE 20.3.

A pivot table showing sales by region for each quarter.

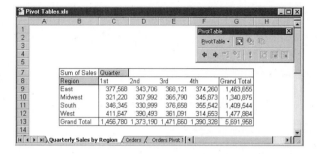

The big news with pivot tables is the *pivoting* feature. If you want to see different views of your data, you can, for example, drag the column field over to the row field area, as was done in Figure 20.4. The result, as you can see, is that the table shows each region as the main row category, with the quarters as regional subcategories.

FIGURE 20.4.

You can drag row or column fields to "pivot" the data and get a different view.

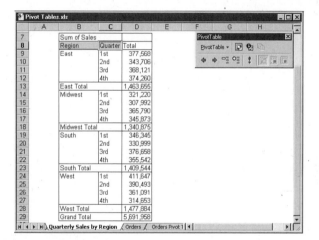

Some Pivot Table Terms

Pivot tables have their own terminology, so here's a quick glossary of terms with which you need to become familiar:

- Source list: The original data. You can use one or more Excel lists, an external database, an existing pivot table, or a crosstab table from Excel 4.0.

- Field: A category of data, such as Region, Quarter, or Sales. Because most pivot tables are derived from lists or databases, a pivot table field is directly analogous to a list or database field.

- Item: An element in a field.

- Row field: A field with a limited set of distinct text, numeric, or date values to use as row headings in the pivot table. In the example you just saw, Region is the row field.

- Column field: A field with a limited set of distinct text, numeric, or date values to use as column headings for the pivot table. In the second pivot table, shown in Figure 20.3, the Quarter field is the column field.

- Page field: A field with a limited set of distinct text, numeric, or date values that you use to filter the pivot-table view. For example, you could use the Sales Rep field to create separate pages for each rep. Selecting a different sales rep filters the table to show data only for that person.

- Pivot table items: The items from the source list used as row, column, and page labels.

- Data field: A field that contains the data you want to summarize in the table.

- Data area: The interior section of the table in which the data summaries appear.

- Layout: The overall arrangement of fields and items in the pivot table.

Building a Pivot Table

Excel provides the PivotTable Wizard to make creating and modifying your pivot tables easy. The PivotTable Wizard uses a four-step approach that lets you build a pivot table from scratch:

1. Specify the type of source list to use for the pivot table.

2. Identify the location of the data.

3. Define the row, column, page, and data fields for the table.

4. Select a location, name, and other options for the table, and then create the table.

Throughout the rest of this chapter, the list shown in Figure 20.5 is used as an example. This is a list of orders placed in response to a three-month marketing campaign. Each record shows the date of the order, the product ordered (there are four types: Printer stand, Glare filter, Mouse pad, and Copy holder), the quantity and net dollars ordered, the promotional offer selected by the customer (1 Free with 10 or Extra Discount), and the advertisement to which the customer is responding (Direct mail, Magazine, or Newspaper).

FIGURE 20.5.

The Orders list that is used as an example throughout this chapter.

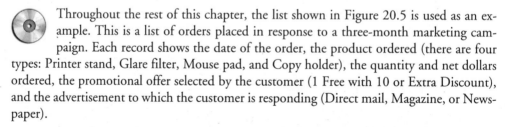

Figure 20.6 shows a simple pivot table for the Orders database. In this example, the quantity shipped is summarized by product and advertisement. The row headings are taken from the Product field, and the column headings are taken from the Advertisement field. The Promotion field is used as the page field to filter the data.

FIGURE 20.6.

A simple pivot table created from the Orders database.

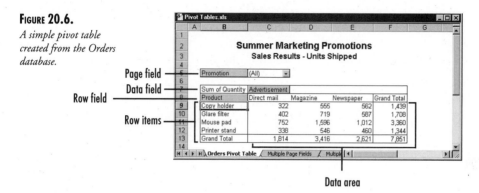

Navigating the PivotTable Wizard

The PivotTable Wizard dialog boxes, like those for other Excel Wizard tools, contain several buttons that let you navigate the PivotTable Wizard quickly. See Table 20.1.

Table 20.1. PivotTable Wizard navigation buttons.

Button	Description
Help	Displays a Help window for the current step.
Cancel	Closes the PivotTable Wizard without creating the table.
< Back	Goes back to the preceding step.
Next >	Goes to the next step.
Finish	Creates the pivot table.

Creating a Pivot Table

The steps you use to create a pivot table vary depending on the source data you're using. You can use four types of data:

- Microsoft Excel list or database: A multicolumn list on a worksheet. This list must have labeled columns.

- External data source: A separate database file in Access, dBASE, FoxPro, SQL Server, or some other format. You retrieve the data from Microsoft Query (as explained in Chapter 21, "Using Microsoft Query").

20

CREATING AND CUSTOMIZING PIVOT TABLES

■ Multiple consolidation ranges: A collection of lists with row and column labels in one or more worksheets. Each range must have a similar layout and identical row and column labels.

■ Another Pivot Table: Another pivot table in the same workbook.

Creating a Pivot Table from an Excel List

The most common source of pivot tables is an Excel list. You can use just about any list to create a pivot table (even, as you'll see, a list in an unopened workbook), but the best candidates for pivot tables exhibit two main characteristics:

■ At least one of the fields contains "groupable" data—that is, the field contains data with a limited number of distinct text, numeric, or date values. In the Sales worksheet shown in Figure 20.1, the Region field is perfect for a pivot table because, despite having dozens of items, it has only four distinct values: East, West, Midwest, and South.

■ Each field in the list must have a heading.

So, given a list that fits these criteria, follow these steps to create a pivot table:

1. Select a cell inside the list you want to use. (This isn't strictly necessary, but doing so saves you a step later.)

2. Select Data | PivotTable Report. Excel displays the PivotTable Wizard - Step 1 of 4 dialog box, shown in Figure 20.7.

   You also can start the PivotTable Wizard by clicking the PivotTable Wizard button on the PivotTable toolbar.

FIGURE 20.7.

The PivotTable Wizard - Step 1 of 4 dialog box, which appears when you start the PivotTable Wizard.

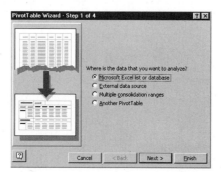

3. Make sure that the Microsoft Excel list or database option is activated, and then click Next >. You see the PivotTable Wizard - Step 2 of 4 dialog box, shown in Figure 20.8.

FIGURE 20.8.

The PivotTable Wizard - Step 2 of 4 dialog box for an Excel list.

4. If you selected a cell in the list, the correct range coordinates should already be displayed in the Range text box. If not, enter the range by either typing the address or selecting the range directly on the worksheet. Click Next > to display the PivotTable Wizard - Step 3 of 4 dialog box, shown in Figure 20.9.

FIGURE 20.9.

The layout used to create the pivot table shown in Figure 20.6.

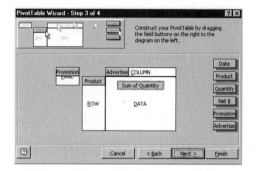

5. Specify the layout of the pivot table by dragging the field labels on the right to the appropriate areas within the dialog box. For example, to add a row field, drag a label and drop it anywhere inside the ROW box. Figure 20.9 shows the layout used to create the pivot table you saw in Figure 20.6. When you're done, click Next > to display the PivotTable Wizard - Step 4 of 4 dialog box, shown in Figure 20.10.

FIGURE 20.10.

Use the PivotTable Wizard - Step 4 of 4 dialog box to specify the table location and display options.

TIP: CUSTOMIZING FIELDS

You can customize each field by double-clicking the label. (You can also customize the fields after you've created the pivot table.)

6. If you want the pivot table displayed in a new sheet, activate the New worksheet option. Otherwise, activate the Existing worksheet option and use the text box provided to enter the address of the cell that you want to use as the upper-left corner of the table. You can type a reference or select it directly on the worksheet (or even on another sheet).

7. To set various pivot table options (such as the name of the table), click Options, fill in the PivotTable Options dialog box, shown in Figure 20.11, and click OK. (Note that you can also access this dialog box after the Wizard is done. To do so, pull down the PivotTable list on the PivotTable toolbar, and then click the Options command.)

FIGURE 20.11.

Use this dialog box to specify various pivot table options.

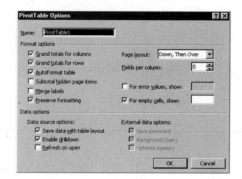

8. Click the Finish button. Excel creates the pivot table in the location you specified and displays the PivotTable toolbar.

Formatting a Pivot Table

For your final pivot-table chore, you need to look at the various ways you can format the table to make it look its best for reports or presentations. The next two sections cover changing the name of a field and changing the numeric format for the data field.

Changing the Data Field's Numeric Format

Numeric formatting applied to the data field using Format | Cells is lost each time you reorganize your pivot tables. To maintain a permanent numeric format in the data field (or to change the existing numeric format), follow these steps:

1. Display the PivotTable Field dialog box for the data field by using either of the following methods:

   ■ Right-click a cell in the data field and choose Field from the shortcut menu.

   ■ Select a cell in the data field and click the PivotTable Field button on the PivotTable toolbar.

2. Click the Number button. Excel displays the Format Cells dialog box.

3. Select the numeric format you want to use.

4. Click OK to return to the PivotTable Field dialog box.

5. Click OK to return to the worksheet.

Changing the Name of a Pivot Table Field

Excel sometimes creates generic names for your pivot table fields. For example, if your pivot table consolidates data from multiple ranges, Excel uses names such as Row, Column, and Page1 for the table fields. Similarly, if you group items based on their labels, Excel creates new fields with names such as Product2 and Promotion3.

To change these generic names, or any row, column, or page field names, you can use either of the following techniques:

- Select the cell containing the field label and use the formula bar to edit the field name.
- Display the PivotTable Field dialog box for the field (use the techniques outlined in the preceding section), edit the field name that appears in the Name text box, and then click OK.

Deleting Fields from a Pivot Table

If you'd like to simplify the pivot table, you can knock things down a dimension by removing a row, column, or page field. (You can also remove a data field if your pivot table has multiple data fields.) Excel gives you three methods for removing a field:

- Drag the field off the pivot table.
- Use the PivotTable Wizard.
- Delete the field from the PivotTable Field dialog box.

Deleting a Field by Dragging

To remove a row, column, or page field from the pivot table, you can use the mouse to drag the field out of the pivot area. (You can't use this method to delete a data field.) The *pivot area* is defined by two ranges:

- The rectangular range that holds the row fields, the column fields, and the data fields.
- The two rows of cells directly above the row fields. (That is, the area where the page field normally appears.)

When you drag a row, column, or page field out of this area, the mouse pointer changes to a field icon with an X through it. When you release the mouse button, Excel deletes the field from the table.

Deleting a Field Using the PivotTable Wizard

You can also use the PivotTable Wizard to remove a row, column, data, or page field from the pivot table. Follow these steps:

1. Select a cell inside the pivot table you want to work with.
2. Select Data | PivotTable Report (or click the PivotTable Wizard button on the PivotTable toolbar) to display the PivotTable Wizard - Step 3 of 4 dialog box.

TIP: PIVOTTABLE WIZARD SHORTCUT

You can also display the PivotTable Wizard - Step 3 of 4 dialog box by right-clicking a pivot table cell and selecting Wizard from the shortcut menu.

3. Use the mouse to drag the field label you want to remove and drop it off the table area.
4. Click the Finish button. Excel removes the new field and redisplays the pivot table.

Deleting a Field Using the PivotTable Field Dialog Box

The third and final method utilizes the PivotTable Field dialog box to delete a row, column, page, or data field. Here are the steps:

1. Select a cell in the pivot table field you want to delete.
2. Display the PivotTable Field dialog box (as described earlier).
3. Click the Delete button. Excel deletes the field and returns you to the worksheet.

Summary

This chapter introduced you to pivot tables and showed you how to create them from Excel lists. You also learned various techniques for customizing your pivot tables. Here are some chapters that contain related information:

- For coverage of creating and working with charts, check out Chapter 18, "Working with Charts."
- To get an explanation of querying external data sources, see Chapter 21, "Using Microsoft Query."
- Pivot tables are just one of Excel's many data-analysis features. To learn more about analysis with Excel, see Chapter 22, "Excel's Data Analysis Tools."

Using Microsoft Query

IN THIS CHAPTER

Information can tell us everything. It has all the answers. But they are answers to questions we have not asked, and which doubtless don't even arise.

—Jean Baudrillard

For the most part, the biggest problem with Excel lists is getting the data onto the worksheet in the first place. If the data doesn't exist in any other form, you have no choice but to enter it yourself. In many cases, however, the data you need already exists in a separate file elsewhere on your computer, or perhaps on a network server.

Excel provides several tools for accessing data files in non-Excel formats. Excel's File | Open command can handle files in xBASE and Lotus 1-2-3 formats, and the TextImport Wizard can convert delimited or fixed-width text files into Excel. These methods, however, often fall short for three reasons:

- If you need only a small piece of a huge file, it's wasteful to import the entire file into Excel. Besides, databases with tens of thousands of records aren't all that uncommon, so a file import might choke on Excel's 16,384-row limit.

- Many databases contain related tables. For example, a database might include a table of customer data and a table of order data related by a common Customer ID field. If you need data from both tables, you're out of luck, because there's no way for Excel to honor the relationships between the two tables.

- The data you need might be in a file format not supported directly by Excel, such as SQL Server or Paradox.

To solve all of these problems, Excel comes with a separate program called Microsoft Query that you can use to access external database files from programs such as dBASE, Access, FoxPro, and SQL Server. This chapter shows you the basics of Microsoft Query and explains how to open external databases, extract the information you need, and return that information to Excel.

About Microsoft Query

Microsoft Query is a small but powerful database application designed to give you easy access to various database formats. You can use Microsoft Query as a stand-alone program or via Excel menus.

A *query* is a request to a database for specific information. It combines criteria conditions with functions to retrieve the data you want to work with. Microsoft Query lets you construct queries easily by using pull-down menu commands and drag-and-drop techniques. Query takes these actions and constructs *SQL* (Structured Query Language) statements that do the dirty work of retrieving and filtering the data.

You can also use Microsoft Query to edit and maintain your database files. You can add and delete records, modify field contents, sort records, join databases, and even create new database files. The beauty of Microsoft Query is that you can do all this with many different database formats and maintain a consistent interface.

Understanding ODBC

The data you can work with in Microsoft Query depends on the *Open Database Connectivity (ODBC) drivers* you installed with Excel. These drivers serve as intermediaries between Query and the external database. They take care of the messy problems of dealing with different database file structures and communication between incompatible systems.

Each ODBC driver is a *DLL* (dynamic link library—a set of subroutines) that tells an ODBC-enabled application (such as Microsoft Query) how to interact (via SQL) with a specific data source. The go-between for the application and the driver is the ODBC Driver Manager, which keeps track of the location of the database, the database filename, and a few other options.

Figure 21.1 shows how Excel, Microsoft Query, the ODBC Driver Manager, the ODBC device driver, and the database fit together.

FIGURE 21.1.
*The relationship
between Excel, Query,
the ODBC components,
and the database.*

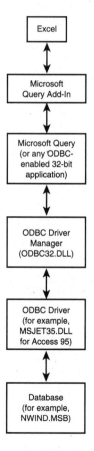

Here are the basic steps you'll follow each time you need to access an external database:

1. Use the Microsoft Query add-in to start Query from Excel.
2. Use the ODBC Driver Manager to specify the database to use.
3. Use Microsoft Query to load tables, filter the data, and format the layout of the data (which is all done via the appropriate ODBC driver).
4. Return the query results to Excel.

Excel provides ODBC drivers for the sources listed in Table 21.1.

Table 21.1. Excel's ODBC device drivers.

Database	*Versions*
Access	1.0, 1.5, 2.0, 7.0, 8.0
dBASE	III, IV, 5.0
Excel (.XLS files)	3.0, 4.0, 5.0, 7.0, 8.0
FoxPro	2.0, 2.5, 2.6
Paradox	3.x, 4.x, 5.x
SQL Server	1.1, 4.2, NT, Sybase 4.2
Text	

Extra drivers for Btrieve (version 5.1), ODBC ODS Gateway, and other databases are available from Microsoft or third-party vendors.

Some Notes About Databases and Tables

Although the terms *database* and *table* are often used interchangeably, they have distinct meanings in Microsoft Query (and, indeed, in relational-database theory as a whole). To wit, a *table* is a collection of data organized into records and fields. It's directly analogous to an Excel *list*, in which a row is the equivalent of a record and a column is the equivalent of a field. A *database* is a collection of tables (and, like Access databases, it can include other objects as well, such as forms and reports).

You'll often find that two or more of a database's tables are "joined" by a *relational key* field. For example, suppose you have a table that contains data for your customers. This data includes the customer ID, the customer name, the customer address, and more. The same database might also have a table of orders placed by these customers. This table probably includes fields for the amount ordered and the date the order was placed, but it also needs to record which customer placed the order. You could enter the customer's name, address, phone number, and so on, but that would be wasteful because all that data already resides in the Customers table. A better approach would be to include the CustomerID field and then relate the two

Using Microsoft Query

CHAPTER 21

493

21

USING
MICROSOFT
QUERY

tables using that field. For example, if an order were placed by a customer with ID 12-3456, you could find out that customer's address simply by looking up 12-3456 in the Customers table. Figure 21.2 shows a graphical representation of this relationship (this figure was taken from a Microsoft Query screen).

The last thing you need to know before beginning is that many tables include a field that contains only unique values. This so-called *primary key field* ensures that no two table records are alike and that there is an unambiguous way to reference each record in the table. For the Customers table, as long as you assign a unique ID number to each customer, you can use the CustomerID field as the primary key. Similarly, you can create an OrderID field in the Orders table, assign unique numbers to the field (such as invoice numbers), and use that as the primary key. As you can see from Figure 21.2, Query displays primary key fields in bold.

FIGURE 21.2.

Two tables related via a common CustomerID field.

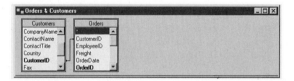

Installing Microsoft Query and ODBC Drivers

As I mentioned earlier, you can run Query either as a stand-alone program or via Excel menu commands. Your concern in this chapter is using Query as an adjunct to Excel, so I won't cover using Query as a separate program. (However, there is enough information here that you could figure out how to use the stand-alone Query on your own.)

NOTE: RUNNING QUERY AS A STANDALONE APPLICATION

To run Microsoft Query as a stand-alone program, use Explorer or My Computer to display the \Program Files\Common Files\Microsoft Shared\MSQuery folder, and double-click the Msqry32.exe file.

If you didn't install Query when you set up Excel, you can load it onto your system by running the Microsoft Office setup program. The following steps show you how to install both Query and the necessary ODBC drivers for the data you are going to work with:

1. Select Start | Settings | Control Panel to open the Control Panel folder, and then double-click the Add/Remove Programs icon.

2. In the Add/Remove Programs Properties dialog box, highlight the Microsoft Office 97 entry in the Install/Uninstall tab and then click Add/Remove. (If Windows asks you to insert your Office CD, insert the disc and click OK.)

3. After Office 97 Setup starts, click Add/Remove.

4. In the Options list, highlight Data Access and ActiveX Controls and then click Change Option.

5. Activate the Microsoft Query check box.

6. Highlight the Database Drivers item and click Change Option. Setup displays a list of the available ODBC drivers, as shown in Figure 21.3.

Figure 21.3.

Use this dialog box to select the ODBC drivers you want to work with.

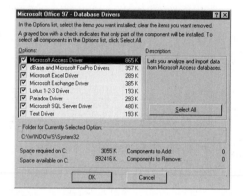

7. Click OK, and then click OK again to return to the main Setup dialog box.

8. Click Continue to install the components.

Unlike previous versions of Excel, you don't need to load an add-in program to use Query from within Excel. Once you've installed Query, Excel modifies the Data menu by adding the Get External Data command. As you'll see in the next section, this command presents a cascade menu from which you start Microsoft Query so that you can work with an external database.

Getting Started

To retrieve data from an external database file, you switch to Microsoft Query and create a query that specifies the information you need. To begin a new query, follow these steps:

1. Select Data | Get External Data | Create New Query. Query loads and then displays the Choose Data Source dialog box, shown in Figure 21.4. If you're starting Query for the first time, this dialog box is blank. Skip to the next section for instructions on setting up a data source.

Using Microsoft Query

CHAPTER 21

495

21

USING
MICROSOFT
QUERY

FIGURE 21.4.

*Use the Choose Data
Source dialog box to
choose the data source
you want to work with.*

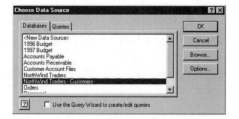

2. Highlight a data source in the Databases tab.

3. If you want to use the Query Wizard to create a data source or edit an existing data source, make sure the Use the Query Wizard to create/edit queries check box is activated. This chapter assumes that you don't use the Wizard, so make sure this check box is deactivated.

4. Click OK to open the source. If the data source contains multiple tables, Query displays the Add Tables dialog box, shown in Figure 21.5.

FIGURE 21.5.

*Use the Add Tables
dialog box to select the
tables you want to
include in your query.*

5. For each table you want to work with, highlight the table in the Table list and click the Add button.

6. When you've finished adding tables, click Close.

Working with Data Sources

A *data source* is a pointer that defines the data you want to work with. This includes the ODBC driver and the location of the file (or files). Data-source locations generally fall into two categories:

- A single database file that includes multiple tables. For example, an Access database file would be a data source.

- A directory (or folder) of database files, each of which contains only a single table. For example, a directory of FoxPro or dBASE (versions III and IV) files would be a data source.

Defining a Data Source

Before you can work with Microsoft Query, you need to define at least one data source. As you saw in step 4 in the last numbered list, you then use this data source to select which tables to include in the query. The following procedure outlines the steps you need to follow in order to define a data source:

1. If you're in the Microsoft Query window, select File | New Query (or click the New Query button on the toolbar) to display the Choose Data Source dialog box.

2. Highlight <New Data Source> and click OK. Query displays the Create New Data Source dialog box.

3. Use the Give your new Data Source a Name text box to name your data source. (This is the name that appears in the Choose Data Source dialog box.)

4. Use the Select a driver for the type of database you want to access drop-down to choose the appropriate ODBC driver.

5. Click the Connect button. Use the dialog box that appears (the layout of which depends on the ODBC driver you selected) to choose the database you want to use:

   ■ If you're defining an Access data source, click the Select button, highlight the database name in the Select Database dialog box that appears, and click OK.

   ■ If you're defining a dBASE, FoxPro, or Paradox data source, use the Version drop-down list to select the version number of the program that created the files, and then choose Select Directory to specify the directory (folder) where the files reside. (Note that you might need to deactivate the Use Current Directory check box first.)

   ■ If you're defining an Excel data source, use the Version drop-down list to select the version number of Excel that created the files, and then choose Select Workbook to specify the workbook file that contains the list or lists.

   ■ If you're defining a text data source, choose Select Directory to specify the directory (folder) where the files can be found. (Again, you might need to deactivate the Use Current Directory check box first.)

   ■ If you're defining a SQL Server data source, use the Server combo box to enter the name of a SQL Server on your network.

6. Click OK. If the Login dialog box appears, enter the Login name and Password that you use to access the data source (if any). Then click OK to return to the Choose New Data Source dialog box.

7. If the data source contains multiple tables, you can use the Select a Default Table for your data source drop-down list to choose a default table. Query will add this table automatically to all queries you create using this data source.

8. To save your login name and password with the data source, activate the Save my UserID and Password in the Data Source definition check box. Figure 21.6 shows a complete Create New Data Source dialog box.

FIGURE 21.6.

Use the Create New Data Source dialog box to define a data source to use with Microsoft Query.

9. Click OK to return to the Choose Data Source dialog box.

10. Make sure your new data source is highlighted, and then click OK. If the data source contains multiple tables, and you didn't define a default table, the Add Tables dialog box appears.

11. For each table you want to work with, highlight the table in the Table list and click the Add button. When you're done, click Close. Query displays a new query file.

A Tour of the Microsoft Query Window

After you've added one or more tables, Microsoft Query creates a new query file and displays it in a window, as shown in Figure 21.7. To get you comfortable with the layout of this window, here's a rundown of the various features (not all of which might be currently visible on your screen):

■ Table pane: The query file's window is divided into three panes. The top pane is the *table pane.* It displays one or more boxes that represent the tables you added to the query from the Add Tables dialog box. Each box displays the name of the table at the top, followed by a list of the database field names. You can toggle the table pane on and off by selecting View | Tables or by clicking the Show/Hide Tables toolbar button.

■ Criteria pane: This is the middle pane, and it's where you define the criteria for your query. Note that the criteria pane isn't displayed when you begin a new query. To toggle the criteria pane on and off, select View | Criteria or click the Show/Hide Criteria button on the toolbar.

■ Data pane: The bottom pane displays the results of the query (called, appropriately
enough, the *result set*). This area is empty initially, so you have to add fields from the
databases included in the query.

■ Navigation buttons: You use these buttons to move from record to record in the
result set.

FIGURE 21.7.

*The Microsoft Query
window.*

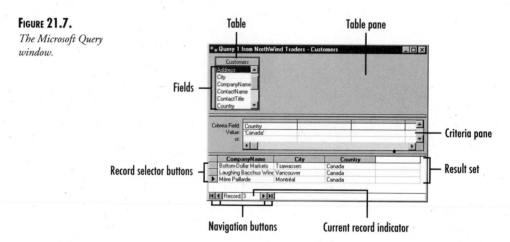

To move from pane to pane, either use the mouse to click the pane you want to work with or
press F6 to cycle through the panes. (You can also press Shift-F6 to cycle backward through
the panes.) To change the size of a pane, use the mouse to drag the bar that separates each pane
from its neighbor.

Adding Fields to the Data Pane

To get the information you want from an external database, you need to add one or more table
fields to the query window's data pane. After you've added fields, you can move them around,
edit them, change their headings, and more. This section shows you various methods of adding fields to the data pane. The next section takes you through the basics of working with table
fields.

Adding a Field with the Mouse

You might find that the mouse offers the most convenient way to add fields to the data pane.
You can try two basic techniques:

■ Double-click a field name. Query adds the fields to the next available column in the
data pane.

21

■ Drag the field from the field list and drop it inside the data pane. Drop the name on an existing field to position the new field to the left of the existing field.

If you want to add multiple fields at once, hold down Ctrl and click each field. (If the fields are contiguous, you can select them by clicking the first field, holding down Shift, and then clicking the last field.) Then drag the selection into the data pane.

If you want to place all the fields inside the data pane, you have two ways to proceed. If you want the fields to appear in the order in which they appear in the table, either double-click the asterisk (*) field or drag the asterisk field and drop it inside the data pane. If you want the fields to appear in alphabetical order, double-click the table name and then drag any of the fields into the data pane.

Filtering Records with Criteria

You can also filter the records in an external database; the process is similar to the one you learned for lists. This section leads you through the basics of filtering records with criteria.

Creating Simple Criteria

As you saw in Chapter 19, "Working with Lists and Databases," Excel's AutoFilter feature lets you set up simple criteria such as showing only records in which the State field is CA or in which the Account Number field is 12-3456. Query lets you create similar filters, and the process is almost as easy, as you'll see in these steps:

1. Move to the column that contains the field you want to use to filter the records.
2. Select the value in the field you want to use as a criterion.
3. Click the Criteria Equals button on the Query toolbar. Query filters the data based on the selected field value.
4. Repeat steps 1 through 3 to filter the records even further.

Entering Simple Criteria in the Criteria Pane

For more sophisticated queries, you can filter your records using the *criteria pane*. You can add field names to this pane and then set up criteria that range from simple field values to complex expressions for compound and computed criteria.

If you use the technique described in the preceding section for entering simple criteria, you'll see that Query displays the criteria pane automatically and adds the field names and values to the criteria pane.

You can also enter simple criteria directly in the criteria pane (this is handy, for instance, if you don't have a mouse and can't use the Criteria Equals tool). The following procedure shows you the necessary steps:

1. Display the criteria pane, if necessary, and move the cursor into the first header of the Criteria Field row.

2. Use the drop-down list to select a field to use for the criterion. (Alternatively, you can drag a field from the table pane and drop it on the criteria pane.)

3. Select the cell below the field name (that is, the cell on the Value row) and enter the field value you want to use for the criterion. Enclose text in single quotation marks (for example, 'Canada'; see Figure 21.7) and dates in number signs (for example, #1995-01-15#). For more information, see the next section.

To run the query, move the cursor to a different cell, select a different pane, or press Enter. This is assuming, of course, that the Automatic Query feature is activated. How do you know if it is? There are two things to look for:

■ The Records | Automatic Query command is activated.

■ The Auto Query toolbar button is pressed.

If Automatic Query is not active, you need to run the query by hand using either of the following techniques:

■ Select Records | Query Now.

■ Click the Query Now button on the toolbar.

Entering Criteria Expressions in Microsoft Query

Entering criteria expressions in Microsoft Query is similar to entering them in Excel. However, you should be aware of the following differences:

■ Enclose text in single quotation marks (for example, 'Canada') rather than double quotation marks. In most cases, Query adds the single quotation marks for you.

■ Enclose dates in number signs (for example, #1994-01-15#). Again, Query usually recognizes a date and adds the number signs for you.

Using Microsoft Query

CHAPTER 21

501

21

USING
MICROSOFT
QUERY

- If you're working with numbers, you can use the normal comparison operators such as equal to (=), not equal to (<>), greater than (>), and less than (<). For example, suppose you have an Invoices table with an Amount field. To filter the table to show only invoices in which the amount is greater than or equal to $1,000, you would add the Amount field to the criteria pane and enter the following criterion: `>=1000`.

- To use wildcard characters, you must include the keyword `Like` and then use an underscore to substitute for a single character or a percent sign to substitute for a group of characters. For example, to find all records in which the NAME field includes the word Office, you would type `Like '%Office%'` in the criteria pane's NAME field.

NOTE: SAVE THE QUERY FOR FUTURE USE

If you think you'll want to use this query again, make sure that you select File | Save to save your work.

Returning the Query Results to Excel

When you have the result set you want, you can import the data into Excel by following these steps:

1. Select File | Return Data to Microsoft Excel or click the Return Data to Excel button. Query switches to Excel and displays the Returning External Data to Excel dialog box, shown in Figure 21.8.

FIGURE 21.8.

Use the Returning External Data to Excel dialog box to set a few options for the external data you're returning.

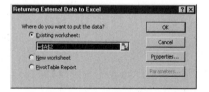

2. You can paste the external data in either a New worksheet, a PivotTable Report, or an Existing worksheet. For the latter, use the text box provided to select the top-left corner of the range you want to use for the data.

3. Click Properties to display the External Data Range Properties dialog box, shown in Figure 21.9.

FIGURE 21.9.

Use this dialog box to set a few options for the data you're returning from Query.

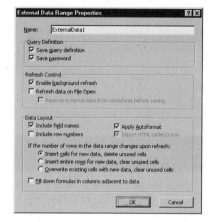

Here's a rundown of the various options in this dialog box:

- Name: Use this text box to enter a name for the external data.

- Query Definition: Activate the Save query definition check box to keep a copy of the query definition in the worksheet. This way, you can refresh the data at any time. Activate the Save password check box to save the data source password with the query definition.

- Refresh Control: These options determine how Excel refreshes the external data. Activate Enable background refresh to have Excel refresh the data without displaying the Query window. Activate Refresh data on File Open to force Excel to refresh the external data each time you open the file.

- Data Layout: These options determine how the external data appears in the worksheet. You can display field names and row numbers, AutoFormat the table, and specify how Excel should handle changes in the number of rows after refreshing the data.

4. Click OK. Excel pastes the result set into the worksheet.

Working with External Data

Once you've pasted external data into a worksheet, Excel gives you a number of methods for working with that data:

■ To update (refresh) the data, highlight a cell within the data range and either select Data | Refresh Data or click the Refresh Data button on the External Data toolbar.

■ If you have multiple external data tables, you can refresh all of them by clicking the Refresh All button on the External Data toolbar.

■ To change the properties of the external data range, highlight a cell within the data range and either select Data | Get External Data | Data Range Properties or click the Data Range Properties button on the External Data toolbar.

■ To edit the query, highlight a cell within the data range and either select Data | Get External Data | Edit Query or click the Edit Query button on the External Data toolbar.

Summary

This chapter introduced you to Microsoft Query, the tool that lets Excel users access external data. It provided an overview of Query and the ODBC drivers that are the nuts and bolts of the whole process. You learned how to start Query, set up a data source, add tables, create a result set using fields and criteria, and then return the results to Excel. If you're looking for related information, here are a few chapters to check out:

■ After you get your external data into Excel, it's treated just like any other Excel list. To learn all about creating, editing, and filtering Excel lists, see Chapter 19, "Working with Lists and Databases."

■ You can create pivot tables directly from external data sources. For more information on pivot tables, check out Chapter 20, "Creating and Customizing Pivot Tables."

CHAPTER 22

Excel's Data Analysis Tools

IN THIS CHAPTER

Information networks straddle the world. Nothing remains concealed. But the sheer volume of information dissolves the information. We are unable to take it all in.

—Günther Grass

Sometimes it's not enough to simply enter data in a worksheet, build a few formulas, and add a little formatting to make things presentable. You're often called on to divine some inner meaning from the jumble of numbers and formula results that litter your workbooks. In other words, you need to analyze your data to see what nuggets of understanding you can unearth.

This chapter looks at a few simple analytic techniques that have many uses. You'll learn how to use Excel's numerous methods for what-if analysis and how to wield Excel's useful Goal Seek tool. This chapter also introduces you to Solver—a sophisticated optimization program that lets you find the solutions to complex problems that would otherwise require high-level mathematical analysis.

What-if analysis, however, is not an exact science. All what-if models make guesses and assumptions based on history, expected events, or whatever voodoo comes to mind. A particular set of guesses and assumptions that you plug into a model is called a *scenario*. Because most what-if worksheets can take a wide range of input values, you usually end up with a large number of scenarios to examine. Instead of going through the tedious chore of inserting all these values into the appropriate cells, Excel has a Scenario Manager feature that can handle the process for you. This chapter completes our look at Excel's data-analysis features by examining this useful tool.

Using What-If Analysis

What-if analysis is perhaps the most basic method of interrogating your worksheet data. In fact, it's probably safe to say that most spreadsheet work involves what-if analysis of one form or another.

 With what-if analysis, you first calculate a formula D, based on the input from variables A, B, and C. You then say, "What if I change variable A? Or B or C? What happens to the result?"

For example, Figure 22.1 shows a worksheet that calculates the future value of an investment based on five variables: the interest rate, period, annual deposit, initial deposit, and deposit type. Cell C9 shows the result of the FV() function. Now the questions begin. What if the interest rate were 7 percent? What if you deposited $8,000 per year? Or $12,000? What if you reduced the initial deposit? Answering these questions is a simple matter of changing the appropriate variables and watching the effect on the result.

NOTE: OPENING ANALYSIS.XLS

The Analysis.xls file contains all the sample worksheets used in this chapter. In particular, it includes the "Iterate" worksheet used later (see the "Using Iteration" section). When you open this workbook, Excel displays a dialog box that complains about the circular reference used in the Iterate sheet. This is perfectly normal. You should click Cancel to open the worksheet as is.

FIGURE 22.1.

The simplest what-if analysis involves changing worksheet variables and watching the result.

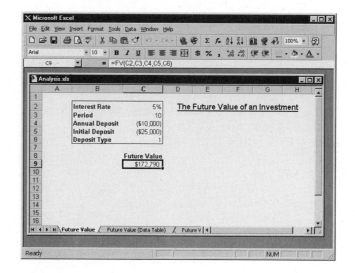

Setting Up a One-Input Data Table

The problem with modifying formula variables is that you see only a single result at a time. If you're interested in studying the effect that a range of values has on the formula, you need to set up a *data table*. In the investment analysis worksheet, for example, suppose that you want to see the future value of the investment with the annual deposit varying between $7,000 and $13,000. You could just enter these values in a row or column and then create the appropriate formulas. Setting up a data table, however, is much easier, as the following procedure shows:

1. Add to the worksheet the values you want to input into the formula. You have two choices for the placement of these values:

    If you want to enter the values in a row, start the row one cell up and one cell to the right of the formula.

    If you want to enter the values in a column, start the column one cell down and one cell to the left of the cell containing the formula. See Figure 22.2.

2. Select the range that includes the input values and the formula. (In Figure 22.2, this would be B9:C16.)

3. Select Data | Table. Excel displays the Table dialog box, shown in Figure 22.3.

4. If you entered the input values in a row, select the Row input cell text box and then enter the cell address of the input cell. If the input values are in a column, enter the input cell's address in the Column input cell text box instead. In the investment analysis example, you enter C4 in the Column input cell, as shown in Figure 22.3.

FIGURE 22.2.

Enter the values you want to input into the formula.

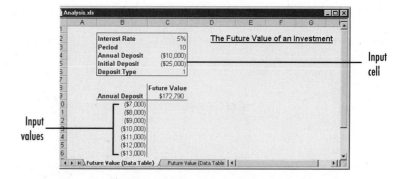

FIGURE 22.3.

In the Table dialog box, enter the input cell where you want Excel to substitute the input values.

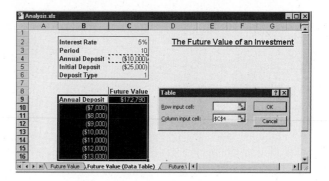

5. Click OK. Excel takes each of the input values, places them in the input cell, and then displays the results in the data table, as shown in Figure 22.4.

FIGURE 22.4.

Excel substitutes each input value into the input cell and displays the results in the data table.

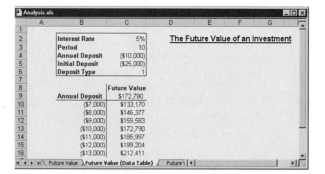

Adding More Formulas to the Input Table

You're not restricted to just a single formula in your data tables. If you want to see the effect of the various input values on different formulas, you can easily add them to the data table. For example, in our future value worksheet, it would be interesting to factor inflation into the calculations so that the user could see how the investment appears in today's dollars. Figure 22.5 shows the revised worksheet with a new Inflation variable (cell C7) and a formula that converts the calculated future value into today's dollars (cell D9).

FIGURE 22.5.

To add a formula to a data table, enter the new formula next to the existing one.

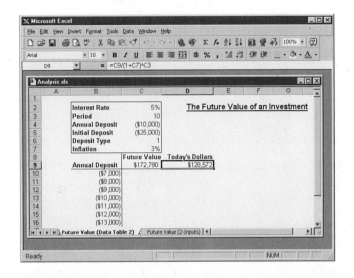

NOTE: CONVERTING A FUTURE VALUE TO TODAY'S DOLLARS

Here is the formula for converting a future value to today's dollars:

`Future Value / (1 + Inflation Rate) ^ Period`

Period is the number of years from now that the future value exists.

To create the new data table, follow the steps outlined earlier. However, make sure that the range you select in step 2 includes the input values and *both* formulas (that is, the range B9:D16 in Figure 22.5). Figure 22.6 shows the results.

FIGURE 22.6.

The results of the data table with multiple formulas.

	A	B	C	D	E	F	G
1							
2		Interest Rate	5%	The Future Value of an Investment			
3		Period	10				
4		Annual Deposit	($10,000)				
5		Initial Deposit	($25,000)				
6		Deposit Type	1				
7		Inflation	3%				
8			Future Value	Today's Dollars			
9		Annual Deposit	$172,790	$128,572			
10		($7,000)	$133,170	$99,091			
11		($8,000)	$146,377	$108,918			
12		($9,000)	$159,583	$118,745			
13		($10,000)	$172,790	$128,572			
14		($11,000)	$185,997	$138,399			
15		($12,000)	$199,204	$148,226			
16		($13,000)	$212,411	$158,053			

NOTE: DATA TABLE WHAT-IF ANALYSIS

After you have a data table set up, you can do regular what-if analysis by adjusting the other worksheet variables. Each time you make a change, Excel recalculates every formula in the table.

Setting Up a Two-Input Table

You can also set up data tables that take two input variables. This option lets you see the effect on an investment's future value when you enter different values for, say, the annual deposit and the interest rate. Here's how you set up a two-input data table:

1. Enter one set of values in a column below the formula and the second set of values in the row beside the formula, as shown in Figure 22.7.

FIGURE 22.7.

Enter the two sets of values you want to input into the formula.

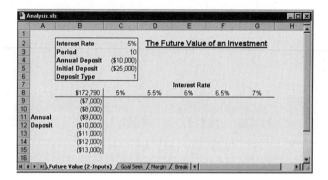

2. Select the range that includes the input values and the formula (B8:G15 in Figure 22.7).
3. Select Data | Table to display the Table dialog box.
4. In the Row input cell text box, enter the cell address of the input cell that corresponds to the row values you entered (C2 in Figure 22.7—the Interest Rate variable). In the Column input cell text box, enter the cell address of the input cell you want to use for the column values (C4 in Figure 22.7—the Annual Deposit variable).
5. Click OK. Excel runs through the various input combinations and then displays the results in the data table, as shown in Figure 22.8.

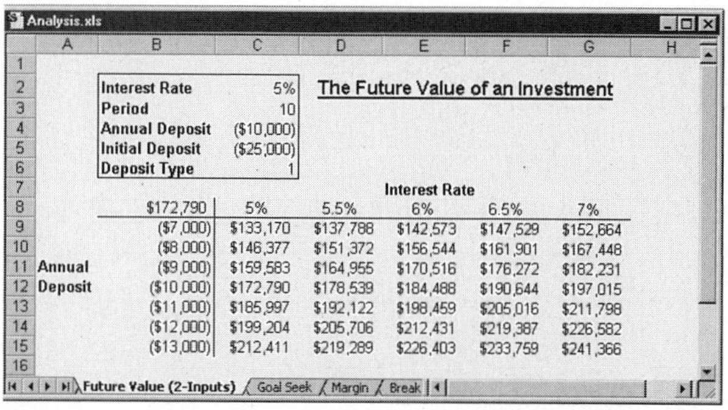

	A	B	C	D	E	F	G	H
1								
2		Interest Rate	5%	The Future Value of an Investment				
3		Period	10					
4		Annual Deposit	($10,000)					
5		Initial Deposit	($25,000)					
6		Deposit Type	1					
7					Interest Rate			
8		$172,790	5%	5.5%	6%	6.5%	7%	
9		($7,000)	$133,170	$137,788	$142,573	$147,529	$152,664	
10		($8,000)	$146,377	$151,372	$156,544	$161,901	$167,448	
11	Annual	($9,000)	$159,583	$164,955	$170,516	$176,272	$182,231	
12	Deposit	($10,000)	$172,790	$178,539	$184,488	$190,644	$197,015	
13		($11,000)	$185,997	$192,122	$198,459	$205,016	$211,798	
14		($12,000)	$199,204	$205,706	$212,431	$219,387	$226,582	
15		($13,000)	$212,411	$219,289	$226,403	$233,759	$241,366	
16								

FIGURE 22.8.
Excel substitutes each input value into the input cell and displays the results in the data table.

> **TIP: CONTROLLING TABLE RECALCULATION**
>
> As I mentioned earlier, if you make changes to any of the variables in a table formula, Excel recalculates the entire table. This isn't a problem in small tables, but large ones can take a very long time to calculate. If you prefer to control the table recalculation, choose Tools | Options, select the Calculation tab, and then activate the Automatic except tables check box. To recalculate a table, press F9 (or Shift-F9 to recalculate the current worksheet only).

Editing a Data Table

When you select Data | Table, Excel enters an *array formula* in the interior of the data table. This formula is a `TABLE()` function with the following syntax:

```
{=TABLE(row_input_ref, column_input_ref)}
```

Here, `row_input_ref` and `column_input_ref` are the cell references you entered in the Table dialog box. The braces (`{ }`) indicate that this is an array, which means you can't change or delete individual elements of the table. (To learn more about arrays, see Chapter 16, "Manipulating Formulas and Functions.") If you want to delete or move the data table, you first must select the entire table.

Working with Goal Seek

Here's a what-if question for you: What if you already know the result you want? For example, you might know that you want to have $50,000 in a college fund 18 years from now, or that you have to achieve a 30 percent gross margin in your next budget. If you need to manipulate only a single variable to achieve these results, you can use Excel's Goal Seek feature. You tell Goal Seek the final value you need and which variable to change, and it finds a solution for you (if one exists).

How Does Goal Seek Work?

When you set up a worksheet to use Goal Seek, you usually have a formula in one cell and the formula's variable—with an initial value—in another. (Your formula can have multiple variables, but Goal Seek lets you manipulate only one variable at a time.) Goal Seek operates by using an *iterative method* to find a solution. In other words, Goal Seek first tries the variable's initial value to see whether that produces the result you want. If it doesn't, Goal Seek tries different values until it converges on a solution. (To learn more about iterative methods, see "Using Iteration" later in this chapter.)

Running Goal Seek

Suppose that you want to set up a college fund for your newborn child. Your goal is to have $50,000 in the fund 18 years from now. Assuming 5 percent interest, how much will you need to deposit into the fund every year? The following procedure shows how to use Goal Seek to calculate the answer:

1. Set up your worksheet to use Goal Seek. Figure 22.9 shows the College worksheet, which I've set up the following way:

    Cell C8 contains the FV() function, which calculates the future value of the college fund. When you're done, this cell's value should be $50,000.

    Cell C6 contains the annual deposit into the fund (with an initial value of $0). This is the value Goal Seek adjusts to find a solution.

    The other cells (C4 and C5) are used in the FV() function; however, for this exercise we'll assume that they're constants.

FIGURE 22.9.

A worksheet set up to use Goal Seek.

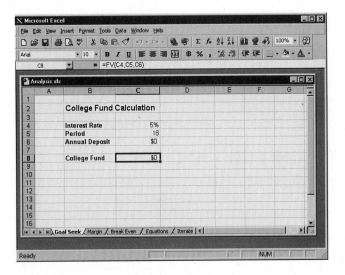

2. Select Tools | Goal Seek. Excel displays the Goal Seek dialog box, shown in Figure 22.10.

FIGURE 22.10.

The completed Goal Seek dialog box.

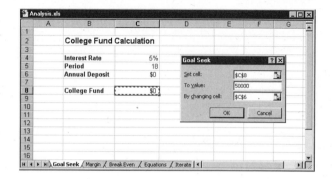

3. In the Set cell text box, enter a reference to the cell that contains your goal. For this example, enter C8.

4. In the To value text box, enter the final value you want for the goal cell. The example's value is 50000.

5. Use the By changing cell text box to enter a reference to the variable cell. In the example, enter C6.

6. Click OK. Excel begins the iteration and displays the Goal Seek Status dialog box, shown in Figure 22.11. When finished, the dialog box tells you whether Goal Seek found a solution. (If a solution was found, the values are entered into the worksheet.)

FIGURE 22.11.

The Goal Seek Status dialog box shows you the solution (if one was found).

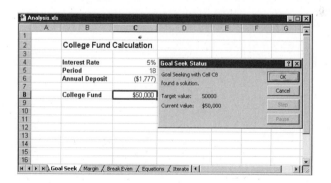

> **NOTE: PAUSING GOAL SEEK**
>
> Most of the time, Goal Seek finds a solution relatively quickly. For longer operations, you can click the Pause button in the Goal Seek Status dialog box to stop Goal Seek. To walk through the process one iteration at a time, click the Step button. To resume Goal Seek, click Continue.

7. If Goal Seek found a solution, you can accept the solution by clicking OK. To ignore the solution, click Cancel.

Goal Seek Examples

Goal Seek is a simple tool, but it can handle many types of problems. This section looks at a few more examples of Goal Seek.

Optimizing Product Margin

Many businesses use product margin as a measure of fiscal health. A strong margin usually means that expenses are under control and that the market is satisfied with your price points. Product margin depends on many factors, of course, but you can use Goal Seek to find the optimum margin based on a single variable.

For example, suppose that you want to introduce a new product line, and you want the product to return a margin of 30 percent during the first year. You make the following assumptions:

- The sales during the year will be 100,000 units.
- The average discount to your customers will be 40 percent.
- The total fixed costs will be $750,000.
- The cost per unit will be $12.63.

Given all this information, you want to know what price point will produce the 30 percent margin.

Figure 22.12 shows a worksheet set up to handle this situation. An initial value of $1.00 is entered into the Price per Unit cell, and Goal Seek is set up in the following way:

- The Set cell reference is C14, the Margin calculation.
- A value of .3 (the Margin goal) is entered in the To value text box.
- A reference to the Price per Unit cell (C4) is entered into the By changing cell text box.

FIGURE 22.12.

A worksheet set up to calculate a price point that will optimize gross margin.

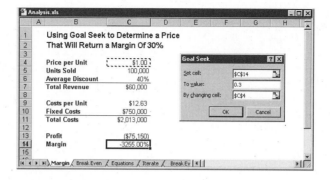

When you run Goal Seek, it produces a solution of $47.87 for the price, as shown in Figure 22.13. This solution can be rounded up to $47.95.

FIGURE 22.13.

The result of Goal Seek's labors.

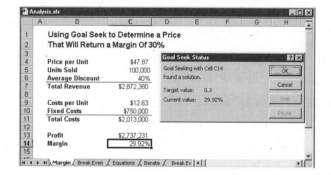

A Note About Goal Seek's Approximations

Notice that the solution in Figure 22.13 is an approximate figure. In other words, the margin value is 29.92%, not the 30% you were looking for. That's pretty close (it's off by only 0.0008), but it's not exact. Why didn't Goal Seek find the exact solution?

The answer lies in one of the options Excel uses to control iterative calculations. Some iterations can take an extremely long time to find an exact solution, so Excel compromises by setting certain limits on iterative processes. To see these limits, select Tools | Options and then select the Calculation tab in the Options dialog box that appears, as shown in Figure 22.14. These two options control iterative processes:

- **Maximum iterations:** The value in this text box controls the maximum number of iterations. In Goal Seek, this value represents the maximum number of values that Excel plugs into the variable cell.

- **Maximum change:** The value in this text box is the threshold Excel uses to determine whether it has converged on a solution. If the difference between the current solution and the desired goal is within this value, Excel stops iterating.

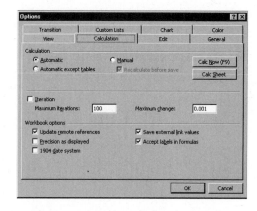

It was the Maximum change value that prevented you from getting an exact solution for the profit margin calculation. On a particular iteration, Goal Seek hit the solution .2992, which put you within 0.0008 of your goal of 0.3. Because 0.0008 is less than the default value of 0.001 in the Maximum change text box, Excel halted the procedure.

To get an exact solution, you must adjust the Maximum change value to 0.0001.

Performing a Break-Even Analysis

In a *break-even analysis,* you determine how many units of a product you must sell so that your total profits are 0 (that is, so that the product revenue equals the product costs). Setting up a profit equation with a goal of 0 and varying the units sold is perfect for Goal Seek.

To try this, we'll extend the example used in the "Optimizing Product Margin" section. In this case, assume a unit price of $47.95 (the solution found to optimize product margin, rounded up to the nearest 95 cents). Figure 22.15 shows the Goal Seek dialog box filled out as detailed here:

- The Set cell reference is set to C13, the Profit calculation.
- A value of 0 (the Profit goal) is entered in the To value text box.
- A reference to the Units Sold cell (C5) is entered into the By changing cell text box.

FIGURE 22.15.

A worksheet set up to calculate a price point that optimizes gross margin.

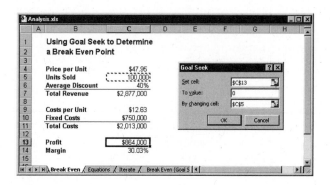

Figure 22.16 shows the solution: 46,468 units must be sold to break even.

FIGURE 22.16.

The break-even solution.

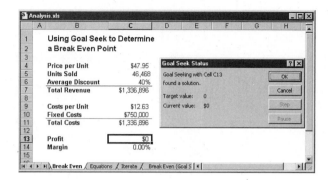

Solving Algebraic Equations

Goal Seek is also useful for solving complex algebraic equations of one variable. For example, suppose that you need to find the value of *x* to solve the following rather nasty equation:

$$\frac{(3x - 8)^2 (x - 1)}{4x^2 - 5} = 1$$

This equation, although too complex for the quadratic formula, can be easily rendered in Excel. The left side of the equation can be represented with the following formula:

```
=(((3*A2 - 8)^2)*(A2-1))/(4*A2^2-5)
```

Cell A2 represents the variable *x*. You can solve this equation in Goal Seek by setting the goal for this equation to 1 (the right side of the equation) and by varying cell A2. Figure 22.17 shows a worksheet and the completed Goal Seek dialog box.

FIGURE 22.17.

Solving an algebraic equation with Goal Seek.

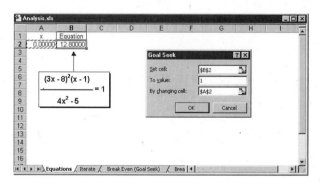

Figure 22.18 shows the result. The value in cell A2 is the solution *x* that satisfies the equation. Notice that the equation result (cell B2) is not quite 1. As I mentioned earlier, if you need higher accuracy, you must change Excel's convergence threshold. In this example, select Tools | Options, and in the Calculation tab, type `0.000001` in the Maximum change text box.

FIGURE 22.18.

Cell A2 holds the solution for the equation in cell A1.

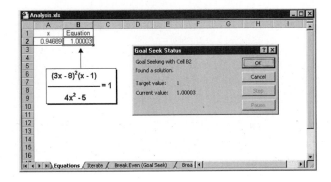

Using Iteration

A common business problem involves calculating a profit-sharing plan contribution as a percentage of a company's net profits. This isn't a simple multiplication problem, because the net profit is determined, in part, by the profit-sharing figure. For example, suppose that a company has a gross margin of $1,000,000 and expenses of $900,000, which leaves a gross profit of $100,000. The company also sets aside 10 percent of net profits for profit sharing. The net profit is calculated with the following formula:

```
Net Profit = Gross Profit - Profit Sharing Contribution
```

This is called a *circular reference formula* because there are terms on the left and right side of the equals sign that depend on each other. Specifically, Profit Sharing Contribution is derived with the following formula:

```
Profit Sharing Contribution = (Net Profit)*0.1
```

One way to solve such a formula is to guess at an answer and see how close you come. For example, because profit sharing should be 10 percent of net profits, a good first guess might be 10 percent of *gross* profits, or $10,000. If you plug this number into the formula, you end up with a net profit of $90,000. This isn't right, however, because 10 percent of $90,000 is $9,000. Therefore, the profit-sharing guess is off by $1,000.

So you can try again. This time, use $9000 as the profit-sharing number. Plugging this new value into the formula gives a net profit of $91,000. This number translates into a profit-sharing contribution of $9,100—which is off by only $100.

If you continue this process, your profit-sharing guesses will get closer to the calculated value (this process is called *convergence*). When the guesses are close enough (for example, within a dollar), you can stop and pat yourself on the back for finding the solution. This process is called *iteration*.

Of course, you didn't spend your (or your company's) hard-earned money on a computer so that you could do this sort of thing by hand. Excel makes iterative calculations a breeze, as you'll see in the following procedure:

1. Set up your worksheet and enter your circular reference formula. Figure 22.19 shows a worksheet for the example just mentioned. If Excel displays a dialog box telling you it can't resolve circular references, click OK.

FIGURE 22.19.

A worksheet with a circular reference formula.

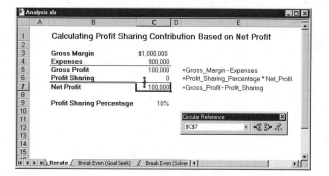

2. Select Tools | Options, and then select the Calculation tab in the Options dialog box.
3. Activate the Iteration check box.
4. Use the Maximum iterations text box to specify the number of iterations you need. In most cases, the default figure of 100 is more than enough.
5. Use the Maximum change text box to tell Excel how accurate you want your results to be. The smaller the number, the longer the iteration takes, and the more accurate the calculation will be. Again, the default value is probably a reasonable compromise.
6. Click OK. Excel begins the iteration and stops when it has found a solution, as shown in Figure 22.20.

TIP: WATCHING THE PROGRESS OF THE ITERATION

If you want to watch the progress of the iteration, activate the Manual check box in the Calculation tab and enter 1 in the Maximum iterations text box. When you return to your worksheet, each time you press F9, Excel performs a single pass of the iteration.

FIGURE 22.20.

The solution to the iterative profit-sharing problem.

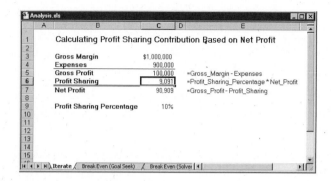

Loading the Analysis Toolpak

Excel's Analysis Toolpak is a large collection of powerful statistical functions and commands that add more than 90 new functions to Excel's already impressive function list. Most of these tools use advanced statistical techniques and will be used by only a limited number of users.

To use the tools and functions in the Analysis Toolpak, you need to load the add-in macro that makes them available to Excel. The following procedure takes you through the steps:

1. Select Tools | Add-Ins. Excel displays the Add-Ins dialog box.
2. Activate the Analysis Toolpak check box in the Add-Ins available list.

NOTE: MAKE SURE YOU INSTALLED THE ANALYSIS TOOLPAK

If you don't see an Analysis Toolpak check box in the Add-Ins available list, you didn't install the Analysis Toolpak when you installed Excel. You need to run the Office Setup program and use it to install the Analysis Toolpak.

3. Click OK.

With the Analysis Toolpak now loaded, you'll see a new Data Analysis command on Excel's Tools menu.

Solving Complex Problems with Solver

Earlier in this chapter you learned how to use Goal Seek to find solutions to formulas by changing a single variable. Unfortunately, most problems in business and science aren't so easy. You'll usually face formulas with at least two and sometimes even dozens of variables. Often a problem will have more than one solution, and your challenge will be to find the *optimal* solution (that is, the one that maximizes profit, minimizes costs, or whatever). For these bigger challenges, you need a more muscular tool. Excel has just the answer: Solver. Solver is a sophisticated optimization program that lets you find solutions to complex problems that would otherwise require high-level mathematical analysis. This section introduces you to Solver (a complete discussion would require a book in itself) and takes you through a few examples.

Some Background on Solver

Solver is a powerful tool that isn't needed by most Excel users. It would be overkill, for example, to use Solver to compute net profit given fixed revenue and cost figures. Many problems, however, require nothing less than the Solver approach. These problems cover many different fields and situations, but they all have the following characteristics:

- They have a single *target cell* that contains a formula you want to maximize, minimize, or set to a specific value. This formula could be a calculation, such as total transportation expenses or net profit.

- The target cell formula contains references to one or more *changing cells* (also called *unknowns* or *decision variables*). Solver adjusts these cells to find the optimal solution for the target cell formula. These changing cells might include items such as units sold, shipping costs, or advertising expenses.

- Optionally, there are one or more *constraint cells* that must satisfy certain criteria. For example, you might require that advertising be less than 10 percent of total expenses, or that the discount to customers be a number between 40 percent and 60 percent.

What types of problems exhibit these kinds of characteristics? A surprisingly broad range, as the following list shows:

- The transportation problem: This problem involves minimizing shipping costs from multiple manufacturing plants to multiple warehouses while meeting demand.

- The allocation problem: This problem requires minimizing employee costs while maintaining appropriate staffing requirements.

- The product mix problem: This problem requires generating the maximum profit with a mix of products while still meeting customer requirements. You solve this problem when you sell multiple products with different cost structures, profit margins, and demand curves.

- The blending problem: This problem involves manipulating the materials used for one or more products to minimize production costs, meet consumer demand, and maintain a minimum level of quality.

- Linear algebra: This problem involves solving sets of linear equations.

Loading Solver

Solver is an add-in to Microsoft Excel, so you'll need to load Solver before you can use it. The following procedure takes you through the steps:

1. Select Tools | Add-Ins. Excel displays the Add-Ins dialog box.
2. Activate the Solver Add-In check box in the Add-Ins available list.
3. Click OK. Excel adds a Solver command to the Tools menu.

Using Solver

So that you can see how Solver works, I'll show you an example. Earlier, you used Goal Seek to compute the break-even point for a new product. (Recall that the break-even point is the number of units that need to be sold to produce a profit of 0.) I'll extend this analysis by computing the break-even for two products: a Finley sprocket and a Langstrom wrench. The goal is to compute the number of units to sell for both products so that the total profit is 0.

The most obvious way to proceed is to use Goal Seek to determine the break-even points for each product separately. Figure 22.21 shows the results.

FIGURE 22.21.

The break-even points for two products (using separate Goal Seek calculations on the Product Profit cells).

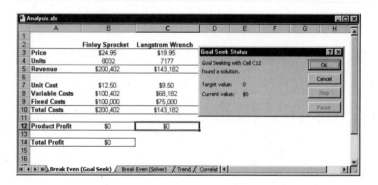

This method works, but the problem is that the two products don't exist in a vacuum. For example, cost savings will be associated with each product because of joint advertising campaigns, combined shipments to customers (larger shipments usually mean better freight rates), and so on. To allow for this, you need to reduce the cost for each product by a factor related to the number of units sold by the other product. In practice, this would be difficult to estimate, but to keep things simple, I'll use the following assumption: The costs for each product are reduced by one dollar for every unit sold of the other product. For instance, if the Langstrom wrench sells 10,000 units, the costs for the Finley sprocket are reduced by $10,000. I'll make this adjustment in the Variable Costs formula. For example, the formula that calculates Variable Costs for the Finley sprocket (cell B8) becomes the following:

```
=B4*B7 - C4
```

Similarly, the formula that calculates Variable Costs for the Langstrom wrench (cell C8) becomes the following:

```
=C4*C7 - B4
```

By making this change, you move out of Goal Seek's territory. The Variable Costs formulas now have two variables: the units sold for the Finley sprocket and the units sold for the Langstrom wrench. I've changed the problem from one of two single-variable formulas, which are easily handled (individually) by Goal Seek, to a single formula with two variables—which is the terrain of Solver.

To see how Solver handles such a problem, follow these steps:

1. Select Tools | Solver. Excel displays the Solver Parameters dialog box, shown in Figure 22.22.

FIGURE 22.22.

Use the Solver Parameters dialog box to set up the problem for Solver.

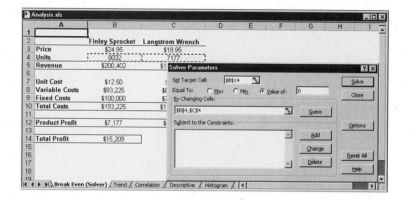

2. In the Set Target Cell text box, enter a reference to the target cell—that is, the cell with the formula you want to optimize. In this example, you would enter B14.

3. In the Equal To section, activate the appropriate option button. Select Max to maximize the target cell, Min to minimize it, or Value Of to solve for a particular value (in which case you also need to enter the value in the text box provided). In this example, you would activate Value Of and enter 0 in the text box.

4. Use the By Changing Cells box to enter the cells you want Solver to change while it looks for a solution. Separate each cell reference with a comma. In this example, you would enter B4,C4.

TIP: WHAT THE GUESS BUTTON DOES

The Guess button enters into the By Changing Cells text box all the nonformula cells referenced by the target cell's formula.

NOTE: CHANGING CELLS MAXIMUM

You can enter a maximum of 200 changing cells.

5. Click Solve. (I discuss constraints in the next section.) Solver works on the problem and then displays the Solver Results dialog box, which tells you whether it found a solution.

6. If Solver found a solution you want to use, activate the Keep Solver Solution option and click OK. If you don't want to accept the new numbers, select Restore Original Values and click OK or just click Cancel.

Figure 22.23 shows the results for this example. As you can see, Solver has produced a Total Profit of 0 by running one product (the Langstrom wrench) at a slight loss and the other at a slight profit. While this is certainly a solution, it's not really the one you want. Ideally, for a true break-even analysis, both products should end up with a Product Profit of 0. The problem is that you didn't tell Solver to solve the problem this way. In other words, you didn't set up any *constraints*.

FIGURE 22.23.

When Solver finishes its calculations, it displays a completion message and enters the solution (if it found one) into the worksheet cells.

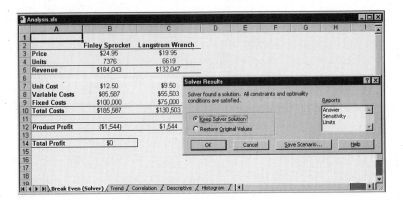

Adding Constraints

The real world puts restrictions and conditions on formulas. A factory might have a maximum capacity of 10,000 units a day. The number of employees in a company might have to be greater than or equal to zero (negative employees would reduce staff costs, but nobody has been able to figure out how to do this yet). Your advertising costs might be restricted to 10 percent of total expenses. All these are examples of what Solver calls *constraints*. Adding constraints tells Solver to find a solution so that these conditions are not violated.

To find the best solution for the break-even analysis, you need to tell Solver to optimize both Product Profit formulas to 0. The following steps show you how this is done.

NOTE: CANCELLING A SOLUTION

If Solver's completion message is still on-screen from the preceding section, click Cancel to return to the worksheet without saving the solution.

1. Select Tools | Solver to display the Solver Parameters dialog box. Solver reinstates the options you entered the last time you used it.

2. To add a constraint, click the Add button. Excel displays the Add Constraint dialog box.

3. In the Cell Reference box, enter the cell you want to constrain. For this example, you would enter cell B12 (the Product Profit formula for the Finley sprocket).

4. The drop-down list in the middle of the dialog box contains several comparison operators for the constraint. The available operators are less than or equal to (<=), equal to (=), greater than or equal to (>=), and integer (int). (Use the integer operator when you need a constraint, such as total employees, to be an integer value instead of a real number.) Select the appropriate operator for your constraint. For this example, select the equal to operator (=).

5. In the Constraint box, enter the value by which you want to restrict the cell. For the example, enter 0. (See Figure 22.24.)

FIGURE 22.24.

Use the Add Constraint dialog box to specify the constraints you want to place on the solution.

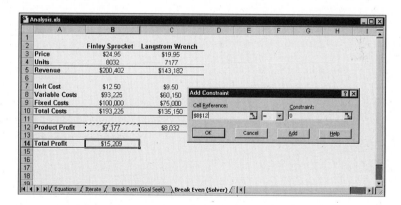

6. If you want to enter more constraints, click the Add button and repeat steps 3 through 5. For the example, you also need to constrain cell C12 (the Product Profit formula for the Langstrom wrench) so that it too equals 0. When you're done, click OK to return to the Solver Parameters dialog box. Excel displays your constraints in the Subject to the Constraints list box.

NOTE: CONSTRAINTS MAXIMUM

You can add a maximum of 100 constraints.

---

7. Click Solve. Solver again tries to find a solution, but this time it uses your constraints as guidelines.

TIP: CHANGING A CONSTRAINT

If you need to make a change to a constraint before you begin solving, highlight the constraint in the Subject to the Constraints list box, click the Change button, and then make your adjustments in the Change Constraint dialog box that appears. If you want to delete a constraint you no longer need, highlight it and click the Delete button.

Figure 22.25 shows the results of the break-even analysis after the constraints are added. As you can see, Solver was able to find a solution in which both Product Margins are 0.

FIGURE 22.25.

The solution to the break-even analysis after constraints are added.

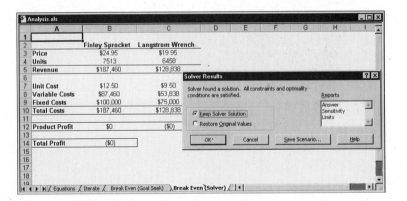

How Scenarios Work

Excel has powerful features that let you build sophisticated models that can answer complex questions. The problem, though, isn't in *answering* questions but in *asking* them. For example, Figure 22.26 shows a worksheet model that analyzes a mortgage. You use this model to decide how much of a down payment to make, how long the term should be, and whether to include an extra principal paydown every month. (A *paydown* is a payment over and above your regular monthly payment that is applied directly to your mortgage principal.) The Results section compares the monthly payment and total paid for the regular mortgage and for the mortgage with a paydown. It also shows the savings and reduced term that result from the paydown.

FIGURE 22.26.

A mortgage-analysis worksheet.

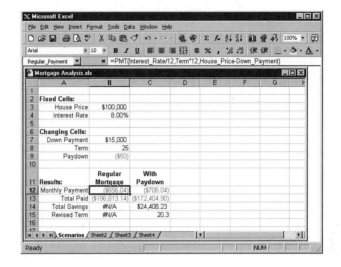

Here are some possible questions to ask this model:

- How much will I save over the term of the mortgage if I use a shorter term and a larger down payment and include a monthly paydown?

- How much more will I end up paying if I extend the term, reduce the down payment, and forego the paydown?

These are examples of *scenarios* that you would plug into the appropriate cells in the model. Excel's Scenario Manager helps by letting you define a scenario separately from the worksheet. You can save specific values for any or all of the model's input cells, give the scenario a name, and then choose the name (and all the input values it contains) from a list.

Setting Up Your Worksheet for Scenarios

Before creating a scenario, you need to decide which cells in your model will be the input cells. These will be the worksheet variables—the cells that, when you change them, change the results of the model. (Not surprisingly, Excel calls these the *changing cells.*) You can have as many as 32 changing cells in a scenario. For best results, follow these guidelines when setting up your worksheet for scenarios:

- The changing cells should be constants. Formulas can be affected by other cells, and that can throw off the entire scenario.

- To make it easier to set up each scenario and to make your worksheet easier to understand, group the changing cells and label them. (Refer to Figure 22.26.)

- For even greater clarity, assign a range name to each changing cell.

Adding a Scenario

To work with scenarios, you use Excel's Scenario Manager tool. This feature lets you add, edit, display, and delete scenarios as well as create summary scenario reports.

Once your worksheet is set up the way you want, you can add a scenario to it by following these steps:

1. Select Tools | Scenarios. Excel displays the Scenario Manager dialog box.
2. Click the Add button. The Add Scenario dialog box, shown in Figure 22.27, appears.

FIGURE 22.27.

*Use the Add Scenario
dialog box to add
scenarios to a
workbook.*

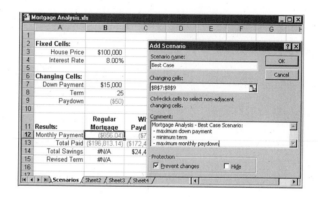

3. In the Scenario name text box, enter a name for the scenario.
4. In the Changing cells box, enter references to your worksheet's changing cells. You can type in the references (be sure to separate noncontiguous cells with commas) or select the cells directly on the worksheet.
5. In the Comment box, enter a description for the scenario. This will appear in the Comment section of the Scenario Manager dialog box.
6. Click OK. Excel displays the Scenario Values dialog box, shown in Figure 22.28.

FIGURE 22.28.

*Use the Scenario Values
dialog box to enter the
values you want to use
for the scenario's
changing cells.*

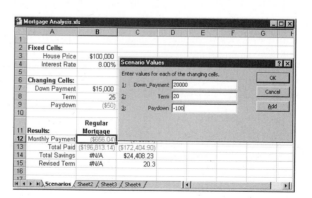

7. Use the text boxes to enter values for the changing cells.

NOTE: NAMED CELLS ARE EASIER TO WORK WITH

You'll notice in Figure 22.28 that Excel displays the range name for each changing cell, which makes it easier to enter your numbers correctly. If your changing cells aren't named, Excel displays the cell addresses instead.

---

8. To add more scenarios, click the Add button to return to the Add Scenario dialog box, and repeat steps 3 through 7. Otherwise, click OK to return to the Scenario Manager dialog box.

9. Click the Close button to return to the worksheet.

Displaying a Scenario

After you define a scenario, you can enter its values into the changing cells by simply selecting the scenario from the Scenario Manager dialog box. The following steps give you the details:

1. Select Tools | Scenarios to display the Scenario Manager, shown in Figure 22.29.

FIGURE 22.29.

When you click Show, Excel enters the values for the highlighted scenario into the changing cells.

2. In the Scenarios list, highlight the scenario you want to display.

3. Click the Show button. Excel enters the scenario values into the changing cells.

4. Repeat steps 2 and 3 to display other scenarios.

5. Click the Close button to return to the worksheet.

Editing a Scenario

If you need to make changes to a scenario—whether changing the scenario's name, selecting different changing cells, or entering new values—follow these steps:

1. Select Tools | Scenarios to display the Scenario Manager.

2. In the Scenarios list, highlight the scenario you want to edit.

3. Click the Edit button. Excel displays the Edit Scenario dialog box (which is identical to the Add Scenario dialog box, shown in Figure 22.27).

4. Make your changes, if necessary, and click OK. The Scenario Values dialog box appears. (Refer to Figure 22.28.)

5. Enter the new values if necessary and then click OK to return to the Scenario Manager dialog box.

6. Repeat steps 2 through 5 to edit other scenarios.

7. Click the Close button to return to the worksheet.

Summary

This chapter covered various Excel techniques for performing data analysis. You learned how to use data tables for what-if analysis and how to use Goal Seek and iteration. This chapter also showed you how to solve complex problems using Excel's powerful Solver tool. Finally, this chapter gave you some background on how scenarios work and how to add, display, and edit them. Here are some related chapters to investigate:

■ To learn more about entering and working with arrays and array formulas, read Chapter 16, "Manipulating Formulas and Functions."

■ For more information on Excel's charting capabilities, check out Chapter 18, "Working with Charts."

■ The Scenario Summary feature can create a pivot table. If you need a refresher course in pivot tables, see Chapter 20, "Creating and Customizing Pivot Tables."

■ The Office 97 Small Business Edition includes an add-in called the Small Business Financial Manager, which gives you extra analysis tools. I'll tell you more about it in Appendix B, "Office 97 Small Business Edition."

Customizing Excel

IN THIS CHAPTER

CHAPTER 23

The mark of our time is its revulsion against imposed patterns.

—Marshall McLuhan

The Microsoft programmers designed Excel so that the commands and features most commonly used by most people are within easy reach. This means that Excel's setup reflects what the ordinary user might want. However, no one qualifies as an ordinary user; we all work with Excel in our own way. What one person uses every day, another needs only once a year; one user's obscure technical feature is another's bread and butter.

To address these differences, Excel provides what might be the most customizable interface on the market today. Excel has dozens of settings you can use to control everything from automatic recalculation to the display of zero values. This chapter runs through each of these customization options and also shows you how to work with Excel add-in utilities.

Displaying the Options Dialog Box

The Options dialog box, shown in Figure 23.1, is the source of many of Excel's customization features. To display it, select Tools | Options. You use the eight tabs to modify Excel's settings and default values.

FIGURE 23.1.

You can use the Options dialog box to change dozens of Excel's default settings.

In case you need a briefing at this point, here's a summary of the navigation techniques for a multilevel tabbed dialog box:

- Using the mouse, click on a tab to select it.
- Using the keyboard, press Ctrl-Tab to move right and Ctrl-Shift-Tab to move left.
- If the tab name is selected, you can press the right arrow to move right, the left arrow to move left, the up arrow to move up, and the down arrow to move down.

When you finish choosing your options, click OK to return to the worksheet.

Changing the View

The View tab options control several display settings for the Excel screen, workbooks, objects, and windows.

The Show group has two check boxes:

Formula bar: Deactivate this check box to hide the formula bar. If you use in-cell editing, turning off the formula bar gives you more room on-screen. The downside is that you lose access to the Name box and the Function Wizard button. You can also hide the formula bar by deactivating View | Formula Bar.

Status bar: Deactivate this check box to hide the status bar and give yourself some extra screen real estate. You can also hide the status bar by deactivating View | Status Bar.

TIP: MAXIMIZING THE WORK AREA

If you want to maximize the work area, the easiest way to do so is by selecting View | Full Screen. This command removes everything from the screen except the menu bar, row and column headers, scroll bars, and sheet tabs. (As you'll soon see, you can use the View tab to turn off these items as well.) To return to the normal view, either click the Full Screen toolbar button or select View | Full Screen again.

The option buttons in the Comments section control the display of cell comments:

None: Activate this option to hide both cell comments and the comment indicators.

Comment indicator only: When this option is activated, Excel displays a small red triangle in the upper-right corner of cells that have comments attached to them. You need to hover the mouse pointer over a cell to view its comment.

Comment & indicator: When this option is activated, Excel displays both the comments themselves and a small red triangle in the upper-right corner of cells that have comments attached to them.

The Objects group in the View tab sets the display options for worksheet objects. If you have a worksheet with a lot of graphics, these options can make it easier to scroll through the sheet:

Show all: Select this option when you want to display the graphic objects normally.

Show placeholders: Select this option to show a gray box where the graphics usually are.

Hide all: Select this option to hide the graphics entirely.

23

CUSTOMIZING
EXCEL

TIP: KEYBOARD SHORTCUT FOR DISPLAYING WORKSHEET OBJECTS

You can also cycle through these options without displaying the Options dialog box. Just press Ctrl-6 repeatedly.

The nine check boxes in the Window Options group control the display of each Excel window:

Page breaks: Activate this check box to display the dashed lines that mark the borders of each printed page.

Formulas: Activate this check box to display cell formulas rather than values.

TIP: KEYBOARD SHORTCUT FOR TOGGLING FORMULAS

You can also toggle between formulas and values by pressing Ctrl-` (backquote).

Gridlines: Use this check box to toggle gridlines on and off. When gridlines are on, you can use the Color drop-down list to select a color for the gridlines.

Row & column headers: Use this check box to toggle the row and column headers on and off.

Outline symbols: If the current worksheet is outlined, use this check box to toggle the outline symbols on and off.

TIP: KEYBOARD SHORTCUT FOR TOGGLING OUTLINE SYMBOLS

You can also press Ctrl-8 to toggle outline symbols on and off.

Zero values: Deactivate this check box to hide cells containing zero.

Horizontal scroll bar: Use this check box to toggle the horizontal scroll bar on and off.

Vertical scroll bar: Use this check box to toggle the vertical scroll bar on and off.

Sheet tabs: Use this check box to toggle the sheet tabs on and off.

Changing the Calculation Options

The Calculation tab, shown in Figure 23.2, contains several settings used to control worksheet calculations.

FIGURE 23.2.

Use the Calculation tab to work with Excel's calculation settings.

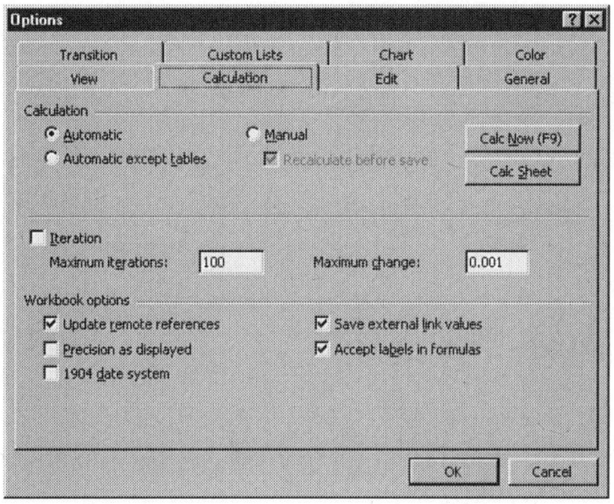

Excel always calculates a formula when you confirm its entry, and Excel normally recalculates existing formulas automatically whenever their data changes. This behavior is fine for small worksheets, but it can slow you down if you have a complex model that takes several seconds or even several *minutes* to recalculate. Use the Calculation group options to set the calculation mode:

Automatic: This is Excel's default calculation mode.

Automatic except tables: If you activate this option, Excel runs in automatic calculation mode, but it ignores all calculations related to data tables.

Manual: If you activate this option, Excel doesn't recalculate automatically, so you must do so by hand (as explained in a moment). You also tell Excel not to recalculate before saving the worksheet. To do so, turn off the Recalculate before Save check box.

With manual calculation turned on, you'll see a `Calculate` message in the status bar whenever your worksheet data changes and your formula results need to be updated. When you want to recalculate, select Tools | Options and choose one of the following from the Calculation tab:

■ Click the Calc Now button to recalculate every open worksheet.

■ Click the Calc Sheet button to recalculate only the active worksheet.

TIP: KEYBOARD SHORTCUT FOR MANUAL RECALCULATION

To recalculate the open worksheets without bothering with the Options dialog box, press F9. If you want to calculate only the active worksheet, press Shift-F9.

23

CUSTOMIZING
EXCEL

If you want to recalculate only part of your worksheet while manual calculation is turned on, you have two options:

■ To recalculate a single formula, select the cell containing the formula, activate the formula bar, and confirm the cell (by pressing Enter or clicking the Enter button).

■ To recalculate a range, select the range, select Edit | Replace, and enter an equals sign (=) in both the Find What and Replace With boxes. (Make sure that the Find entire cells only check box is deactivated.) When you click Replace All, Excel "replaces" the equals sign in each formula with another equals sign. This doesn't change anything, but it forces Excel to recalculate each formula.

Activating the Iteration check box sets up the worksheet for iterative calculations. For example, see the material on circular reference formulas in Chapter 22, "Excel's Data Analysis Tools." You can also use the Maximum iterations and Maximum change text boxes with Goal Seek (which I also covered in Chapter 22).

The Workbook options group contains the following check boxes:

Update remote references: This check box controls whether Excel recalculates formulas that contain references to other applications. If you find that remote references are increasing the time Excel takes to recalculate formulas, deactivate this option. On the other hand, if your links display the #REF! error, you need to activate this check box.

Precision as displayed: When this check box is deactivated (the default), Excel stores values with full (15-digit) precision. When you activate this check box, Excel uses the displayed value in each cell to determine the precision it uses. For example, if a cell contains 1234.567, Excel uses three-digit precision for the cell.

1904 date system: Activate this check box to calculate dates using January 2, 1904, as the starting point (rather than January 1, 1900). Because Excel for the Macintosh uses the 1904 date system, this option lets you work with the same worksheet in both PC and Mac environments.

Save external link values: If this check box is activated (the default) and a workbook contains links to another workbook, Excel saves copies of the linked values from the server workbook in the client workbook. If a large amount of data is involved, the dependent workbook might get bloated beyond a reasonable size. If this happens, deactivate this check box to prevent Excel from storing the source values.

Accept labels in formulas: When this check box is activated, Excel lets you enter label names to refer to cells in your worksheet formulas.

Changing Editing Options

The options in the Edit tab, shown in Figure 23.3, control various cell and range-editing settings:

Edit directly in cell: This check box toggles in-cell editing on and off. If you turn in-cell editing off, Excel's double-click behavior changes. If the cell contains a note, the Cell Note dialog box appears; if the cell contains a formula, the formula's precedents are selected.

Allow cell drag and drop: This check box toggles Excel's drag-and-drop feature. When this check box is activated, you can move or copy a range by dragging it with the mouse pointer.

Alert before overwriting cells: When you use drag-and-drop to move or copy a range, Excel warns you if nonblank cells in the destination range will be overwritten. Deactivate this check box to disable this warning.

Move selection after Enter: If you activate this check box, Excel moves the cell selector after you press Enter (or Shift-Enter). Use the Direction list to specify which direction Excel sends the selector. If you deactivate this check box, Excel stays on the same cell when you press Enter (or Shift-Enter).

Fixed decimal: Activate this check box to cause Excel to automatically insert a decimal place into numbers you enter. Use the Places spinner to specify the location of the decimal. For example, if Places is 2, Excel converts a number entered as 12345 to 123.45.

Cut, copy, and sort objects with cells: Activate this check box to keep graphic objects together with their underlying cells when you cut or copy the cells or when you sort or filter a list.

Ask to update automatic links: When you open a workbook that contains automatic links to a server document in another application (see Chapter 50, "Working with the Office Integration Tools"), Excel displays a dialog box asking whether you want to update the links. Deactivate this check box to prevent this dialog box from appearing.

Provide feedback with animation: When this check box is activated (the default), Excel animates range inserting and deleting. In a deletion, for example, Excel removes the range and then shows the adjacent cells moving to their new position. To turn off this behavior, deactivate this check box.

Enable AutoComplete for cell values: With this check box activated (the default), Excel attempts to complete your cell entries automatically by examining existing cells in the same column. For example, suppose that you enter ACME Coyote Supplies in cell A1. If you then move down to cell A2 and enter A, Excel fills in the rest of the cell with ACME Coyote Supplies.

FIGURE 23.3.

The Edit tab options control Excel's editing settings.

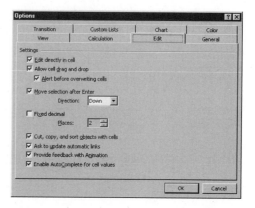

Changing the General Workspace Options

The controls in the General tab, shown in Figure 23.4, affect miscellaneous workspace options:

R1C1 reference style: When this check box is deactivated (the default), Excel uses A1-style cell references. Activate this check box to switch to R1C1-style references.

NOTE: RELATIVE REFERENCES IN R1C1 STYLE

The normal A1 style that you're accustomed to numbers a worksheet's rows from 1 to 16384 and assigns the letters A through IV to the worksheet's 256 columns. In R1C1 style, though, Excel numbers both the rows and the columns. In general, the notation RxCy refers to the cell at row x and column y. Here are some examples:

A1 Style	R1C1 Style
$A$1	R1C1
$D$8	R8C4
$B$4:$E$10	R4C2:R10C5
$B:$B	C2 (that is, column B)
$3:$3	R3 (that is, row 3)

As you can see, these are all absolute references. To use relative references in R1C1 notation, enclose the numbers in square brackets. For example, R[2]C[2] refers to the cell two rows down and two columns to the right of the active cell. Similarly, R[-1]C[-3] refers to the cell one row above the active cell and three columns to the left. Here are a few more examples of relative references:

Relative Reference	Description
R[1]C[-1]	One row down and one column left
R[-5]C[3]	Five rows up and three columns right
R[2]C	Two rows down, same column
RC[-1]	Same row, one column left
R	The current row
C	The current column

Ignore other applications: Activate this check box to cause Excel to ignore Dynamic Data Exchange (DDE) requests from other applications.

Macro virus protection: When this check box is activated, Excel warns you if a workbook you're about to open contains macros and checks those macros for viruses.

Recently used file list: Activate this check box to display at the bottom of the File menu a list of the files you used most recently. Use the accompanying spinner to change the number of files displayed.

Prompt for workbook properties: Activate this check box to have Excel display the Properties dialog box whenever you save a new workbook.

Provide feedback with sound: When this check box is activated, Excel plays sounds associated with various program events, such as opening and closing files.

Zoom on roll with IntelliMouse: Activate this check box to turn on the IntelliMouse Zoom feature. (See Chapter 8, "Customizing the Office Menus and Toolbars.")

Sheets in new workbook: This option specifies the default number of sheets in new workbooks. You can enter a number between 1 and 255.

Standard font: This drop-down list contains the typefaces available on your system. The typeface you select becomes the one Excel uses for all new worksheets and workbooks. You can also set the default type size by selecting a number in the Size list.

Default file location: This option determines the initial folder that appears when you first display the Open or Save As dialog boxes. To make it easy to find your Excel documents, save them all in a single folder and enter the full path in this text box.

Alternate startup file location: Excel uses the \Program Files\Microsoft Office\Office\Xlstart folder as its default startup location. Any files placed in this directory are opened automatically when you start Excel, and any templates in this directory appear in the New dialog box. Use this text box to specify a startup directory in addition to Xlstart.

User name: In this text box, enter the user name you want displayed in the Properties dialog box, scenarios, views, and file sharing.

23

CUSTOMIZING
EXCEL

FIGURE 23.4.

The General tab controls various workspace options.

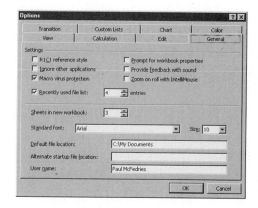

Changing the Lotus 1-2-3 Transition Options

When you import a 1-2-3 file, Excel changes some option settings to make using a 1-2-3 worksheet easier for you. The settings it changes are in the Transition tab of the Options dialog box, shown in Figure 23.5.

FIGURE 23.5.

The Transition tab in the Options dialog box controls settings that make Excel operate more like 1-2-3.

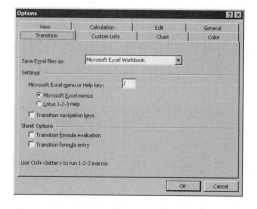

Here's a rundown of the options in the Transition tab:

Save Excel files as: This drop-down list determines the default format used when you save an Excel file.

Microsoft Excel menu or help key: The key entered in this text box activates either the Excel menu bar or the Lotus 1-2-3 help system, depending on which of the two options listed below the text box is activated: Microsoft Excel menu or Lotus 1-2-3 help.

Transition navigation keys: This option changes the functions of some Excel keystrokes. Table 23.1 describes these changes.

Table 23.1. Keys that change when you activate the Transition navigation keys option.

Key Function	Normal Excel Function	Alternative
Home	Moves to the first cell in the row	Moves to cell A1
Tab	Moves right one column	Moves right one page
Shift-Tab	Moves left one column	Moves left one page
Ctrl-right arrow	Moves right to next block	Moves right one screen of data
Ctrl-left arrow	Moves left to next block	Moves left one screen of data
"	N/A	Right-aligns the cell text
^	N/A	Centers the cell text
\	N/A	Fills the cell with the characters that follow

NOTE: LEFT-ALIGN PREFIX ALWAYS WORKS

You can use 1-2-3's left-align prefix (') regardless of whether the Transition navigation keys option is selected.

Transition formula evaluation: Excel also activates this check box. This option causes Excel to handle formula evaluation in the following ways:

- If the lookup value in the HLOOKUP() and VLOOKUP() functions is text, Excel does three things differently: (1) It looks for exact matches rather than the largest value that is less than or equal to the lookup value. (2) The row or column you're using for the search can be in any order. (3) If the third argument (the one that tells Excel how many rows or columns into the table to look for the desired value) is 1, Excel returns the offset of the matched lookup value, not the value itself. For example, if you're using VLOOKUP() and the lookup value is in the fourth row of the lookup column, Excel returns 4 if VLOOKUP()'s third argument is 1.

- Conditional tests return 1 rather than TRUE and 0 rather than FALSE.

- When one of the MOD() function's arguments is negative, MOD() returns different values depending on the setting of this check box. For example, the formula =MOD(-24,10) returns 6 when Transition formula evaluation is off and -4 when it's on.

- Text strings are assigned the value 0.

■ You can't concatenate numeric values. If you try to, Excel returns a #VALUE! error.

■ You can't use string functions on numeric values. If you try, Excel returns a #VALUE! error.

Transition formula entry: Excel activates this check box if there are any macro names on the worksheet. This option causes Excel to handle formula entry in the following ways:

■ If you enter a reference that corresponds to a named range you've defined, Excel automatically converts the reference to the appropriate name after you confirm the entry. Note that this feature works only for contiguous ranges. Because Excel lets you define noncontiguous ranges, this feature might not always work.

■ If a formula contains a range name, activating the formula bar changes the name to its underlying reference.

■ If you delete a range name, formulas containing the name automatically convert to their underlying reference.

■ If you add a dollar sign ($) before a range name, Excel makes the name absolute.

The Custom Lists Tab

You can use the Custom Lists tab to create your own lists for AutoFill series. As you saw in Chapter 15, "Working with Ranges," Excel recognizes certain values (for example, January, Sunday, 1st Quarter) as part of a larger list. When you drag the fill handle from a cell containing one of these values, Excel fills the cells with the appropriate series. However, you're not stuck with the few lists that Excel recognizes out of the box. You're free to define your own AutoFill lists, as described in the following steps:

1. In the Options dialog box, select the Custom Lists tab, shown in Figure 23.6.

FIGURE 23.6.

Use the Custom Lists tab to create your own custom lists.

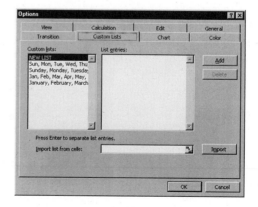

2. In the Custom lists box, select NEW LIST. An insertion point appears in the List entries box.

3. Type an item from your list into the List Entries box and press Enter. Repeat this step for each item. (Make sure that you add the items in the order in which you want them to appear in the series.)

4. Click Add to add the list to the Custom lists box.

TIP: IMPORTING A CUSTOM LIST

If you already have the list in a worksheet range, don't bother entering each item by hand. Instead, use the Import list from cells text box to enter a reference to the range. (You can either type the reference or select the cells directly on the worksheet.) Click the Import button to add the list to the Custom lists box.

NOTE: DELETING A CUSTOM LIST

If you need to delete a custom list, highlight it in the Custom lists box, and then click the Delete button.

Changing the Chart Options

The Chart tab, shown in Figure 23.7, controls several default chart settings. (Note that the Chart tab's options are available only if you've activated a chart, as described in Chapter 18, "Working with Charts.")

FIGURE 23.7.

The Chart tab controls various default chart settings.

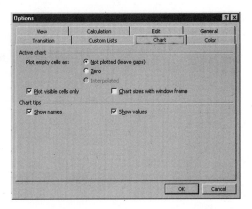

Plot empty cells as: This group specifies how Excel should handle blank cells in a data series. Select Not plotted (leave gaps) to ignore blanks, Zero to plot blanks as zeros, or Interpolated to have Excel draw a straight line between the points on either side of the blank cell.

Plot visible cells only: Excel usually includes in a chart cells that you've hidden yourself or that have been hidden by an outline or filter. Deactivate this check box to exclude hidden cells from the chart data series.

Chart sizes with window frame: If your chart is displayed in a separate chart sheet, activate this check box to cause Excel to change the size of the chart whenever you change the size of the window. You can also size a chart with its window frame by selecting View | Sized with Window. (This command is available only when you activate a chart sheet.)

Show names: When this check box is activated, Excel displays the name of a chart object when you hover the mouse pointer over the object.

Show values: When this check box is activated, Excel displays the value of a data marker when you hover the mouse pointer over the marker.

Working with Custom Color Palettes

When applying colors to your worksheet elements, Excel lets you choose from a palette of 56 colors. The 56 default colors are usually fine for most applications, and you might never need another color. However, if a particular shade might be just right for your presentation, Excel lets you customize the color palette. The Color tab, shown in Figure 23.8, displays the default palette, and you can use this tab to customize the palette.

FIGURE 23.8.

Use the Color tab to customize Excel's color palette.

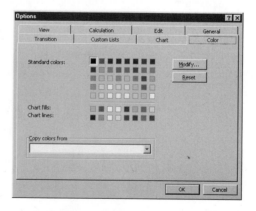

To begin, click the color you want to customize, and then click Modify. In the Colors dialog box that appears, use the Standard tab, shown in Figure 23.9, to click on the color you want, and then click OK.

NOTE: THE CUSTOM TAB

To learn how to work with the Custom tab of the Colors dialog box, see Chapter 5, "Using the OfficeArt Tools."

FIGURE 23.9.

Use the Standard tab to click on the new color you want to use.

Working with Excel's Add-Ins

Excel comes with more bells and whistles than most people know what to do with. Despite Excel's massive feature list, some optional components aren't loaded into Excel automatically. These components, called *add-ins,* toss even more commands, functions, and features into the Excel mix. You've already seen a few of these add-ins (such as the View Manager and the Report Manager), but in this section I'll show you how to install and work with all the add-in files.

Why doesn't Excel just include its entire add-in library as part of the basic program? It's mostly a question of speed and performance. Some of the add-ins are huge, and including them all slows Excel's startup time dramatically. It also puts a much larger burden on your system's memory. By keeping the add-ins as separate programs, you can choose to load only those you need, when you need them. Table 23.2 describes the available Excel add-ins.

Table 23.2. Excel's add-in programs.

Add-In	Description
Analysis ToolPack	Adds dozens of new functions and statistical features to Excel. The Analysis ToolPack is covered in Chapter 22.
Analysis ToolPack - VBA	Gives you access to the Analysis ToolPack from Visual Basic for Applications.

continues

23

CUSTOMIZING
EXCEL

Table 23.2. continued

Add-In	Description
AutoSave	Automatically saves workbooks at regular intervals. Loading this add-in inserts an AutoSave command in the Tools menu; this command displays the AutoSave dialog box, shown in Figure 23.10.
Conditional Sum Wizard	Helps you construct formulas that sum a column of cells based on other values (conditions) in the same list. To run this wizard, select Tools | Wizard | File Conversion.
File Conversion Wizard	Takes you step-by-step through the process of converting one or more files from one format to another. To run this wizard, select Tools | Wizard | Conditional Sum.
Internet Assistant Wizard	Lets you convert Excel data into an HTML file. Select File | Save as HTML to launch this wizard.
Lookup Wizard	Helps you to create formulas that find data in a list. You start the wizard by selecting Tools | Wizard | Lookup.
Microsoft AccessLinks Add-In	Lets you view Excel table data using an Access form or report. Also lets you export Excel data to Access. (This add-in is available only if Access is installed on your computer.)
Microsoft Bookshelf Integration	Places a couple of Bookshelf-related commands on the Excel menus. For example, you can look something up in Bookshelf by selecting Tools | Look Up Reference.
MS Query Add-In...	Lets you access data in external databases. Microsoft Query can handle data sources in various formats, including Access, FoxPro, dBASE, and SQL Server. For full coverage of Query, see Chapter 21, "Using Microsoft Query."
ODBC Add-In	Adds functions for retrieving data from external databases using Microsoft's Open Database Connectivity (ODBC).
Solver Add-In	Generates what-if scenarios based on linear and nonlinear optimization techniques. Head for Chapter 22 to get the details on Solver.

Add-In	Description
Template Utilities	Provides a collection of utilities used by the template worksheets that come with Excel.
Template Wizard with Data Tracking	Creates a template and a database from an existing worksheet. Whenever you enter data into the template, Excel copies it to the database automatically.
Update Add-In Links	Updates links to add-ins created for version 4.0 of Excel. This allows these older add-ins to take advantage of some of Excel's new functionality.
Web Form Wizard	Lets you create an HTML form from an Excel worksheet. Selecting Tools | Wizard | Web Form launches the wizard.

FIGURE 23.10.

The AutoSave add-in saves your workbooks automatically at the time interval you specify.

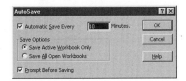

Here are the steps to follow to load one or more add-in programs:

1. Select Tools | Add-Ins. Excel displays the Add-Ins dialog box, shown in Figure 23.11. The Add-Ins Available list shows the add-ins that were installed when you installed Excel. Add-ins with a checkmark beside them are currently loaded.

FIGURE 23.11.

Use the Add-Ins dialog box to select the add-ins you want to load.

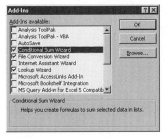

2. To activate an add-in, click it or highlight it and press the spacebar.

3. The displayed add-ins are those found in the \Program Files\Microsoft Office\Office\Library folder. If you've installed an add-in from a third-party developer, click the Browse button, track down the add-in file in the Browse dialog box, and then select OK.

4. When you've activated all the add-ins you need, click OK to return to the worksheet. Excel loads the add-ins.

Summary

This chapter gave you the grand tour of Excel's extensive customization options. I took a thorough look at the Options dialog box, and I also showed you how to work with add-ins.

Here are a few other chapters to read for related information:

■ You can also customize Excel's menus and toolbars. See Chapter 8, "Customizing the Office Menus and Toolbars."

■ For information on Excel's calculation modes, see Chapter 16, "Manipulating Formulas and Functions."

■ To find out more about iteration, circular reference formulas, and Goal Seek, head for Chapter 22, "Excel's Data Analysis Tools."

■ I discuss automatic links in Chapter 50, "Working with the Office Integration Tools."

V

PART

Unleashing Access

CHAPTER 24

An Access Database Primer

IN THIS CHAPTER

> *Information is the oxygen of the modern age. It seeps through the walls topped by barbed wire, it wafts across the electrified borders.*
>
> —*Ronald Reagan*

This chapter introduces you to Microsoft Access 97, the data-organizing component of the Microsoft Office 97 suite. Designed to help you create personal and departmental databases, Access 97 builds on the previous releases of Access in order to provide an easier system to program and use. I'll explain some basic Access concepts—including tables, queries, forms, and reports—run through what's new in Access 97, and show you how to create and open database files in Access.

A Brief Introduction to Access Databases

Access is a *database management system.* This means that Access will not only store your information, but it will also supply you with the means to manage this information (by sorting, searching, extracting, summarizing, and so on). Actually, the official description of Access is that it's a *relational* database management system (RDBMS). The "relational" part means that you can set up relations between various databases. For example, most businesses assign some sort of account number for each of their customers. So a database of customer information would include a field for this account number (as well as the name, address, credit limit, and so on). Similarly, you could also include the account number field in a database of accounts receivable invoices (along with the invoice date, amount, and so on). This lets you relate each invoice to the appropriate customer information. (So, for example, you could easily look up phone numbers and call those deadbeat customers whose invoices are more than 90 days past due!)

However, Access isn't your average RDBMS. It takes a unique approach to the subject that, once you get used to it (which doesn't take long), is certainly convenient and possibly even intuitive. To see why Access is unique, we need to reexamine databases from the Access perspective.

Access Databases: Something a Little Different

In simplest terms, a database is a collection of data with some sort of underlying organization. In most systems, anything related to the data (such as a data entry screen or a report that summarizes the data) is considered a separate piece of the overall pie. Access, though, is different because its databases consist not only of the basic data, but also of related items you use to work with the data.

If you like, you can think of an Access database as a kind of electronic tool shed. In this tool shed you have not only your raw materials (your data) stored in bins and containers of various shapes and sizes, but you also have a number of tools you can use to manipulate these materials, as well as a work area where all this manipulation happens.

Each Access database can contain six different types of objects: tables, queries, forms, reports, macros, and modules. The next few sections introduce you to each type of object.

Tables: Containers for Your Data

In Access databases, you store your information in an object called a *table*. Tables are rectangular arrangements of rows and columns, where each column represents a field (a specific category of information) and each row represents a record (a single entry in the table).

Figure 24.1 shows a table of customer data. Notice how the table includes separate fields (columns) for each logical grouping of the data (company name, contact name, and so on).

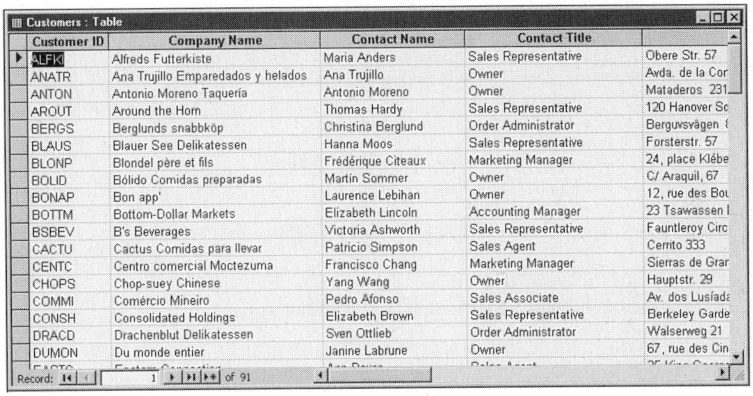

Customers : Table

Customer ID	Company Name	Contact Name	Contact Title	
ALFKI	Alfreds Futterkiste	Maria Anders	Sales Representative	Obere Str. 57
ANATR	Ana Trujillo Emparedados y helados	Ana Trujillo	Owner	Avda. de la Cor
ANTON	Antonio Moreno Taquería	Antonio Moreno	Owner	Mataderos 231
AROUT	Around the Horn	Thomas Hardy	Sales Representative	120 Hanover Sc
BERGS	Berglunds snabbköp	Christina Berglund	Order Administrator	Berguvsvägen 8
BLAUS	Blauer See Delikatessen	Hanna Moos	Sales Representative	Forsterstr. 57
BLONP	Blondel père et fils	Frédérique Citeaux	Marketing Manager	24, place Klébe
BOLID	Bólido Comidas preparadas	Martín Sommer	Owner	C/ Araquil, 67
BONAP	Bon app'	Laurence Lebihan	Owner	12, rue des Bou
BOTTM	Bottom-Dollar Markets	Elizabeth Lincoln	Accounting Manager	23 Tsawassen B
BSBEV	B's Beverages	Victoria Ashworth	Sales Representative	Fauntleroy Circ
CACTU	Cactus Comidas para llevar	Patricio Simpson	Sales Agent	Cerrito 333
CENTC	Centro comercial Moctezuma	Francisco Chang	Marketing Manager	Sierras de Grar
CHOPS	Chop-suey Chinese	Yang Wang	Owner	Hauptstr. 29
COMMI	Comércio Mineiro	Pedro Afonso	Sales Associate	Av. dos Lusíada
CONSH	Consolidated Holdings	Elizabeth Brown	Sales Representative	Berkeley Garde
DRACD	Drachenblut Delikatessen	Sven Ottlieb	Order Administrator	Walserweg 21
DUMON	Du monde entier	Janine Labrune	Owner	67, rue des Cin

Record: 1 of 91

FIGURE 24.1.
In Access databases, tables store the raw data.

See Chapter 25, "Working with Tables," to learn how to create and work with tables.

> **NOTE: THE NORTHWIND SAMPLE DATABASE**
>
> All the examples used in this chapter (and in all of the Access chapters in this book) use the Northwind Traders sample database that ships with Access. You'll find the Northwind.mdb file in your Microsoft Office folder, in the \Office\Samples subfolder.

Queries: Asking Questions of Your Data

By far the most common concern expressed by new database users (and many old-timers, as well) is how to extract the information they need from all that data. If you only need to look up a phone number or an address, Access has powerful search capabilities (which I'll cover later in this chapter).

But what if, for example, you have a database of accounts receivable invoices and your boss wants to know *right away* how many invoices are more than 150 days past due? You could try counting the appropriate records, but if the database is large, you'd probably be out of a job before you finished counting. The better way would be to ask Access to do the counting for you by creating another type of database object: a *query*. Queries are, literally, questions you ask of your data. In this case, you could ask Access to display a list of all invoices more than 150 days past due.

Queries let you extract from one or more tables a subset of the data. For example, in a table of customer names and addresses, what if I wanted to see a list of firms that are located in France? No problem. I'd just set up the following query: "Which records have 'France' in the Country field?" The answer to this question is shown in Figure 24.2.

FIGURE 24.2.

The answer to an Access query that asked "Which records have 'France' in the Country field?".

Company Name	Address	City	Country
Blondel père et fils	24, place Kléber	Strasbourg	France
Bon app'	12, rue des Bouchers	Marseille	France
Du monde entier	67, rue des Cinquante Otages	Nantes	France
Folies gourmandes	184, chaussée de Tournai	Lille	France
France restauration	54, rue Royale	Nantes	France
La corne d'abondance	67, avenue de l'Europe	Versailles	France
La maison d'Asie	1 rue Alsace-Lorraine	Toulouse	France
Paris spécialités	265, boulevard Charonne	Paris	France
Spécialités du monde	25, rue Lauriston	Paris	France
Victuailles en stock	2, rue du Commerce	Lyon	France
Vins et alcools Chevalier	59 rue de l'Abbaye	Reims	France

Record: 1 of 11

I'll show you how to work with queries in Chapter 26, "Querying Data."

Forms: Making Data Entry Easier

Entering data into a table is unglamorous at best and downright mind-numbing at worst. To make this chore easier, you can create Access database objects called *forms*. Forms provide you with a "template" that you fill in whenever you enter a record. The form displays a blank box for each field in the table. Data entry becomes a simple matter of filling in the appropriate boxes. As you can see in the sample form shown in Figure 24.3, each box is labeled so that you always know what type of data you're entering. Best of all, each form is easily customizable, so you can move the fields around to make them look like real-life forms, and you can add fancy effects such as graphics to give your forms pizzazz.

FIGURE 24.3.

You can use Access forms to make data entry easier.

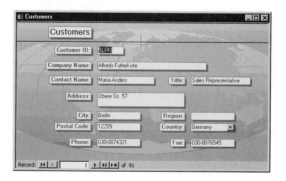

Check out Chapter 27, "Creating and Using Simple Forms," to learn more about using Access forms.

Reports: Making Your Data Look Good

Even though tables are decidedly neater than Post-it Notes and scraps of paper, the information is still "raw" in that it appears in a rather dull and unpolished row-and-column format. To make your data more palatable for others to read, you can create a fourth type of database object: a *report*. Reports let you define how you want your data to appear on the printed page. You can decide which fields to include in the report, where they appear on the page, and which font to use. You can also add your own text and graphics.

Access has a number of wizards to make things even easier. For example, the report shown in Figure 24.4 uses the names and addresses from the Customers table to create mailing labels. You can create a similar report by using the Label Wizard.

FIGURE 24.4.

A sample mailing label report.

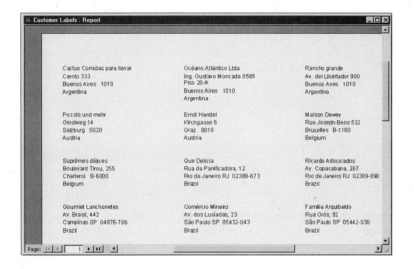

Chapter 28, "Designing and Customizing Reports," tells you everything you need to know about creating and working with reports.

Macros: Automating Repetitive Tasks

Access has a macro feature that you can use to encompass several actions within a single command. Macros operate by running a series of actions that can do anything from beeping the speaker to shutting down the application.

In Figure 24.5, for example, the Add Products macro is associated with a command button on a form. When the user clicks the button, the macro runs and performs a number of actions, including closing the current form (the Close action), opening another form (the OpenForm action; note that the form that gets opened is specified in the Form Name argument), setting an initial value (the SetValue action), and moving the focus to a specific control (the GoToControl action.) See Chapter 30, "Creating Access Macros," for information on Access macros.

FIGURE 24.5.

An example of an Access macro that closes an existing form and opens a new one.

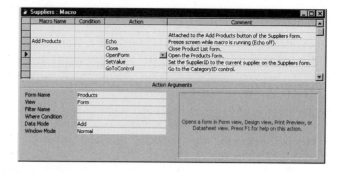

Modules: Programming Access

Macros are handy for automating short, simple tasks, but they aren't suitable for full-scale database applications. For that, you need to move to a higher level, and Access provides one: Visual Basic for Applications (VBA). With VBA, you can program every aspect of Access, from table creation to data entry to queries, forms, and reports. You can even extend VBA by programming your own functions (see Figure 24.6). I'll show you how to program VBA in Part XI, "Unleashing Office Application Development with VBA." I'll focus on Access programming in particular in Chapter E5 on the CD, "VBA Database Programming in Access."

FIGURE 24.6.

An example of a VBA module.

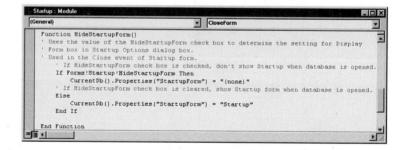

Creating an Access Database

Although the Northwind sample database that ships with Access is great for experimenting and getting to know the program's features, you'll eventually need to create and work with your own databases. This section shows you a couple of methods for cobbling together a database of your own.

Creating a Blank Database

The most direct way to set up a database is to create a blank database container into which you can drop tables, queries, forms, and so on. Access gives you two ways to create a blank database:

■ Each time you start Access, you'll see the dialog box shown in Figure 24.7. To create a blank database, activate the Blank Database option and click OK.

FIGURE 24.7.
You can create a blank database from this Access startup dialog box.

NOTE: ENABLING THE STARTUP DIALOG BOX

If you don't see the dialog box shown in Figure 24.7 when you start Access, select Tools | Options, display the View tab in the Options dialog box, activate the Startup Dialog Box check box, and click OK.

■ If you're already in Access, either select File | New Database, press Ctrl-N, or click the New Database button on the toolbar. In the New dialog box that appears, make sure that the Blank Database icon is highlighted in the General tab, and then click OK.

In either case, Access presents you with the File New Database dialog box. Use the Save in list to select a storage location for the database file, use the File name box to name the file, and click Create. Figure 24.8 shows a blank database container.

FIGURE 24.8.
A blank Access database.

Using the Database Wizard

Instead of a blank database, you may prefer to use the Database Wizard to set up the basic structure of the database. Again, you have two ways to proceed:

■ In the Access startup dialog box (shown in Figure 24.7), activate the Database Wizard option and click OK.

■ If you're already in Access, select File | New Database, press Ctrl-N, or click the New Database button on the toolbar. In the New dialog box that appears (see Figure 24.9), select the Databases tab, highlight the type of database you want to create, and click OK.

FIGURE 24.9.

Access comes with a number of predefined database types that you can use as a starting point.

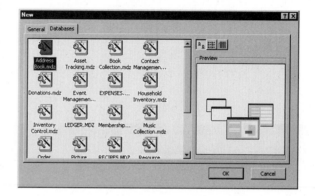

Access then displays the File New Database dialog box. As before, use the Save in list to select a location for the database file, use the File name box to name the file, and click Create.

From here, the Database Wizard loads and takes you through several dialog boxes that let you determine the structure of the tables (such as which fields to include), whether or not you want to include sample data, the style of the input screens (forms) and reports, and a few other odds and ends.

Working in the Database Window

The database window is essentially unchanged in Access 97. You still see the familiar tabs for the six types of Access objects—tables, queries, forms, reports, macros, and modules—and you still display objects by either clicking the appropriate tab or by selecting View | Database Object and selecting an object type from the cascade menu that appears. The next few sections present a quick review of a few techniques that you'll use often when working in a database window.

Changing the Database View

By default, Access just shows you the name of each object in a list format. You can change how Access displays the objects by pulling down the View menu (or by right-clicking an empty part of the database window and selecting View from the context menu) and selecting one of the following commands:

Large Icons: Displays each object as an icon. You can also click the Large Icons toolbar button.

Small Icons: Displays each object as a smaller icon. You can also click the Small Icons toolbar button.

List: This is the default view that shows only a list of the object names. You can also click the List toolbar button.

Details: Displays extra information about each object, including a description, the date and time the object was created and last modified, and the object type (see Figure 24.10). You can also click the Details toolbar button.

FIGURE 24.10.

The database container in Details view.

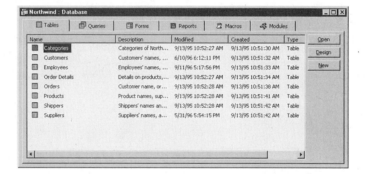

Changing the Object Sort Order

The default sort order for the objects is by name. To choose a different sort order, either select View | Arrange Icons or right-click on an empty part of the database window and select Arrange Icons from the context menu. Now select the sort command you want: By Name, By Type, By Created, or By Modified.

Hiding Objects

If other people have access to the database, you might have certain objects that you don't want them to see. For example, you might have a table that contains sensitive data, or you might have a report that isn't quite finished yet and you don't want anyone else to see it. To offer these objects some (very limited) protection, you can hide them so that they don't appear in the database window.

To do this, first display the object's properties sheet by using any of the following methods:

- Highlight the object and select View | Properties.
- Right-click the object and select Properties from the context menu.

- Highlight the object and click the Properties button on the Database toolbar.

In the properties sheet that appears, shown in Figure 24.11, activate the Hidden check box and click OK. If the object still appears in the database window, select Tools | Options, display the View tab, deactivate the Hidden Objects check box, and click OK.

FIGURE 24.11.

Activating the Hidden check box will prevent the object from appearing in the database container.

To unhide the object, select Tools | Options, display the View tab, activate the Hidden Objects check box, and click OK. Now display the object's properties sheet again and deactivate the Hidden check box.

Creating a Shortcut for an Object

If you have a table or other object that you use frequently, you might find it convenient to create a desktop shortcut for the object. For example, double-clicking a table's shortcut loads Access, opens the appropriate database, and then opens the table.

To create a shortcut, use either of the following techniques:

- Highlight the object and select Edit | Create Shortcut.
- Right-click the object and select Create Shortcut from the context menu.

Either way, you'll see the Create Shortcut dialog box, shown in Figure 24.12. Use the Location text box to select a folder for the shortcut (the default is the Desktop), or click Browse to use a dialog box to select the folder. If this is a network database, make sure that the This Database is on the Network check box is activated and that the Full Network text box shows the full UNC network path for the database file. Click OK to create the shortcut.

FIGURE 24.12.
Use this dialog box to define a shortcut for an object.

With your shortcut in place, double-click it to load the object. Note, too, that the shortcut's context menu (which you can see when you right-click the shortcut) contains various other commands. For example, you could select the Design command to open, say, a form in Design mode. Similarly, you could select Preview to open a report in Preview mode.

Converting an Older Access Database

Access 97 uses a new database structure that is incompatible with earlier versions of Access. This means that any database you create in Access 97 won't work in any previous version of Access. Access 97 can still open older databases, but you won't be able to make any design changes to the database objects. However, you can still enter and edit data in an older database.

If you'll be sharing an existing database with users who work with a previous version of Access, you're better off leaving the database in the older format. If you need to make design changes, you can always do it in the appropriate Access version.

However, if you won't be sharing the database, or if all the users have upgraded to Access 97, you should convert the file to the Access 97 format to take advantage of the new features (such as the ability to add hyperlinks to a table). To get started, use either of the following methods:

■ Select File | Open Database, press Ctrl-O, or click the Open Database toolbar button. Use the Open dialog box to choose the database you want to work with, and then click Open. You should see the Convert/Open Database dialog box, shown in Figure 24.13. Make sure that the Convert Database option is activated, and then click OK. If Access displays another dialog box telling you that you can't make changes to the database objects, click OK.

FIGURE 24.13.
*This dialog box appears
when you attempt to
open an older Access
database.*

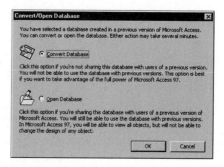

■ Close the current database, if necessary, and select Tools | Database Utilities | Convert Database. In the Database to Convert From dialog box, highlight the database you want to work with and click Convert.

In the Convert Database Info dialog box that appears, use the Save in box to select a location for the converted database, use the File name box to name the new file, and click Save. Access then converts the database (this might take a few minutes, depending on how many objects are in the database) and stores it in the location you specified. Select File | Open to display the new database window.

Securing a Database with a Password

If you're running Access on a stand-alone computer that nobody else uses, you won't have to worry about securing your data from prying eyes. Similarly, security won't be much of an issue if you're on a network but you want your database to be accessible by everyone. However, if you have a database that contains sensitive information (such as payroll data), you'll need to implement some level of security.

The easiest way to restrict access to a database is to assign a password. That way, only those who know the password can open and work with the database. Here are the steps to follow to assign a password to a database file:

1. Select File | Open to display the Open dialog box.

2. Use the Look in box to highlight the database file you want to secure, activate the Exclusive check box, and click Open. (Note that if the database is already open, but it's not open in Exclusive mode, you must close the database and reopen it in Exclusive mode.)

3. Select Tools | Security | Set Database Password to display the Set Database Password dialog box, shown in Figure 24.14.

FIGURE 24.14.
*Use this dialog box to
set a password for the
database.*

4. Enter your password in the Password text box, enter your password again in the Verify text box, and click OK.

5. Close the database to remove the Exclusive lock.

Now, whenever you or anyone else tries to open the database, the Password Required dialog box will appear. Access to the database will be denied if the correct password isn't entered.

If you want to remove the password, open the database again in exclusive mode. Select Tools | Security | Unset Database Password to display the Set Database Password dialog box. Type in the password and click OK.

Replicating a Database

One of Access's handiest features is replication. *Replication* lets you create replicas, or "special copies" of a database, to distribute to users in different locations so that they can work on their copy of the database independent of other users. Replicas allow for data synchronization so that all the replicas can be put together into a single entity, incorporating all the changes that have been introduced in the individual users' copies.

Note, however, that once you convert a regular database into a replicated database, there is no going back—you can't convert it back to a nonreplicable database. Here's a summary of the changes Access makes to a database during replication:

■ Several fields are added to each table. Access uses these fields to keep track of, among other things, changes made to the tables.

■ Several new system tables are added to the database. These tables keep track of errors and conflicts that occur during synchronization.

■ AutoNumber fields (explained in the next chapter) are changed so that they generate random numbers.

■ The original database is converted in a *Design Master,* and a single replica is created. You use the Design Master to make changes to the structure and design of the database objects. When you synchronize the replicas, these changes are propagated through to each replica. You can't use a replica to alter the structure of database objects.

24

**AN ACCESS
DATABASE PRIMER**

The Replication Procedure

Here are the steps to follow to replicate a database:

1. Open the database you want to replicate.

2. Select Tools | Replication | Create Replica. Access informs you that it must close the database in order to create the replica.

3. Click Yes to proceed. Access now asks if you want to create a backup of the database.

4. Since the changes made by the replication process are irrevocable, you should click Yes to create the backup. (The backup has the same name as the original, except that it has a .BAK extension.) When that's done, Access converts the database to the Design Master for the replica and then displays the Location of New Replica dialog box.

5. Use the Save in box to choose a location for the replica (this should be a shared folder), use the File name box to name the replica, and click OK. Access now creates the replica and displays a dialog box when it's done.

6. Click OK. Access displays the Design Master for the replicated database.

If you need to create more replicas, simply select Tools | Replication | Create Replica as often as you wish. Each time you run this command, Access creates a new replica in the location you specify. (The various replicas you create are known as the *replica set.*)

Synchronizing Replicas

To make sure that each replica contains the most current information, you need to *synchronize* the replicas. During synchronization, Access checks the changes made to each replica and then incorporates these changes into each copy of the file.

To perform the synchronization, open one of the replicas or the Design Master and then select Tools | Replication | Synchronize Now. (If Access asks if you want to close any open database objects, click Yes.) In the dialog box that appears (see Figure 24.15), enter a path to the replica that you want to synchronize with (or use the Browse button to choose the file), and click OK.

FIGURE 24.15.

Use this dialog box to select the replica you want to synchronize with the current replica.

When the synchronization is complete, Access will ask if you want to close and then reopen the database. (This is to ensure that all changes are visible.) Click Yes. If any errors occurred during the synchronization, Access will offer to display them. Click Yes if you'd like to examine the conflicts.

NOTE: REPLICATION AND THE BRIEFCASE

The Replication feature can also be used in conjunction with the Briefcase feature found in Windows 95 and Windows NT 4.0.

Analyzing Database Performance

Performance Analyzer is a feature that assists not only the developer, but the end user as well. Performance Analyzer optimizes any or all of the objects in a database. To try it, open the database you want to analyze and then use either of the following methods:

■ Select Tools | Analyze | Performance.

■ Click the Analyze drop-down list in the toolbar and then click Analyze Performance.

Access creates a list of all the objects in the database and then displays the Performance Analyzer dialog box, shown in Figure 24.16. Select the objects you want to analyze (or select the All tab and click Select All to analyze the entire database) and click OK.

FIGURE 24.16.

Use this dialog box to select which database object to analyze.

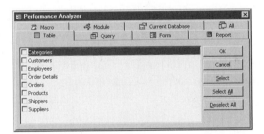

When the analysis is complete, the dialog box shown in Figure 24.17 appears. Three kinds of performance suggestions are displayed in the Analysis Results list. (The various icons beside each item are explained in the Key group. They fall into three categories: Recommendation, Suggestion, and Idea. The Fixed icon appears when you've handled a problem.) When you click one of these items, information about the optimization is presented in the Analysis Notes section. Access can perform Recommendation and Suggestion optimizations for you, but Idea optimizations must be performed manually. Idea optimizations present a list of instructions to follow. Note, however, that Performance Analyzer doesn't provide suggestions for how to improve the system you're running Access on or how to improve Access performance itself.

24

**AN ACCESS
DATABASE PRIMER**

FIGURE 24.17.

*The Performance
Analyzer results
window.*

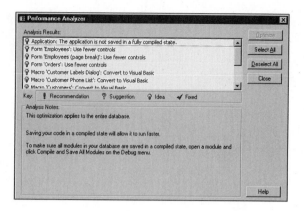

Splitting a Database

The Database Splitter Wizard splits a database into two files: one that contains the tables (or the back-end components) and one that contains the queries, reports, forms, and other Access objects (or the front-end components). This allows an administrator to distribute the front-end files to users while keeping a single source of data on the network. This results in less overhead and traffic on the network, because the only time the network is used is to retrieve or modify data, not whenever a user wants to go to another form or report. This results in a significant performance increase in a multiuser environment.

Before splitting a database, you should make a backup copy. When that's done, open the database and select Tools | Add-ins | Database Splitter. Access displays the Database Splitter dialog box, shown in Figure 24.18. Click the Split Database button. In the Create Back-end Database dialog box that appears, select a location and name for the back-end database and click Split.

FIGURE 24.18.

*Use the Database
Splitter dialog box to
cleave a database into
front-end and back-end
components.*

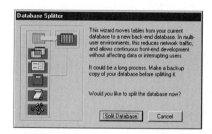

Summary

This chapter introduced you to some of the basic concepts behind Access databases. You also learned how to create new databases and work in the database window. From there, you learned how to convert older Access databases; how to secure a database with a password; and how to replicate, analyze, and split a database.

Here's a list of chapters where you'll find related information:

- I'll show you how to create and work with tables in Chapter 25, "Working with Tables."

- Queries are a great way to make sense of mountains of data. You'll see how they work in Chapter 26, "Querying Data."

- You can make your data-entry chores easier by creating a form. I'll show you how in Chapter 27, "Creating and Using Simple Forms."

- There's nothing like a snazzy report to dress up your data. Check out Chapter 28, "Designing and Customizing Reports," to learn how to create them.

- Macros can reduce wear and tear on your typing fingers by automating repetitive tasks. You'll learn how to create them in Chapter 30, "Creating Access Macros."

- You'll learn about various Access customization options in Chapter 31, "Customizing Access."

- You'll often need to import data from other Office applications, as well as import Office data into Access. Chapter 50, "Working with the Office Integration Tools," shows you how it's done.

- For maximum flexibility and power, you need to use VBA to program Access and create custom applications. I'll give you a primer on Access VBA programming in Chapter E5 on the CD, "VBA Database Programming in Access."

24

AN ACCESS DATABASE PRIMER

Working with Tables

IN THIS CHAPTER

CHAPTER

25

Knowledge in the form of an informational commodity indispensable to productive power is already, and will continue to be, a major—perhaps the major—stake in the worldwide competition for power. It is conceivable that the nation-states will one day fight for control of information, just as they battled in the past for control over territory, and afterwards for control over access to and exploitation of raw materials and cheap labor.

—*Jean François Lyotard*

Once you have an Access database to work with, your starting point is always the humble table, because that's where the data is stored. After all, queries, reports, and modules don't amount to much unless they have some raw data to munch on. This chapter will get you off on the right foot by showing you how to plan and create a table, and then how to enter data, manipulate fields and records, find the information you need, and sort and filter the data.

Designing Your Table

You need to plan your table design before you create it. By asking yourself a few questions in advance, you can save yourself the trouble of redesigning your table later. For simple tables, you need to ask yourself three basic questions:

- Does the table belong in the current database?
- What type of data should I store in each table?
- What fields should I use to store the data?

The next few sections examine these questions in more detail.

Does the Table Belong in the Current Database?

Each database you create should be set up for a specific purpose. It could be home finances, business transactions, personal assets, or whatever. In any case, once you know the purpose of the database, you can then decide if the table you want to create fits in with the database theme.

For example, if the purpose of the database is to record only information related to your personal finances, it wouldn't make sense to include a table of recipes in the same database. Similarly, it would be inappropriate to include a table of office baseball pool winners in a database of accounts payable invoices.

What Type of Data Should I Store in Each Table?

The most important step in creating a table is determining the information you want it to contain. In theory, Access tables can be quite large: up to 255 fields and 1 GB in size. In practice, however, you should minimize the size of your tables. This saves memory and makes managing the data easier. Therefore, you should strive to set up all your tables with only essential information.

For example, suppose you want to store your personal assets in a database. You have to decide whether you want all your assets in a single table, or whether it would be better to create separate tables for each type of asset. If you're only going to be entering basic information—such as the date purchased, a description of each item, and its current value—you can probably get away with a single table. More detailed data will almost certainly require individual tables for each asset. For example, a table of CDs might include information on the record company, the number of tracks, the total running time, and so on. Clearly, such a table wouldn't work for, say, your collection of cubic zirconia jewelry.

When you've decided on the tables you want to use, you then need to think about how much data you want to store in each table. In your CD collection, for example, would you want to include information on the producer, the release date, and the number of people the band thanks in the liner notes? This might all be crucial information for you, but you need to remember that the more data you store, the longer it will take you to enter each record.

What Fields Should I Use to Store the Data?

Now you're almost ready for action. The last thing you need to figure out is the specific fields to include in the database. For the most part, the fields are determined by the data itself. For example, a database of business contacts would certainly include fields for name, address, and phone number. But should you split the name into two fields—one for the first name and one for the last name? If you think you'll need to sort the table by last name, then, yes, you probably should. What about the address? You'll probably need individual fields for the city, state, and ZIP code.

Here are two general rules to follow when deciding how many fields to include in your tables:

- Ask yourself whether you really need the data for a particular field (or if you might need it in the near future). For example, if you think your table of contact names might someday be used to create form letters, a field to record titles (Ms., Mr., Dr., and so on) would come in handy. When in doubt, err on the side of too many fields rather than too few.

- Always split your data into the smallest fields that make sense. Splitting first and last names is common practice, but creating a separate field for, say, the phone number area code would probably be overkill.

NOTE: TABLE DESIGNS AREN'T SET IN STONE

Don't sweat the design process too much. As you'll see, it's easy to make changes down the road (by adding or deleting fields), so you're never stuck with a bad design.

25

WORKING WITH TABLES

Deciding Which Field to Use for a Primary Key

When you create a table, you'll need to decide which field to use as the *primary key*. The primary key is a field that uses a unique number or character sequence to identify each record in the table. Keys are used constantly in the real world. Your Social Security number is a key that identifies you in government records. Most machines and appliances have unique serial numbers. This book (like most books) has a 10-digit ISBN—International Standard Book Number (which you can see on the back cover).

Why are primary keys necessary? Well, for one thing, Access creates an *index* for the primary key field. You can perform searches on indexed data much more quickly than on regular data, so many Access operations perform faster if a primary key is present. Keys also make it easy to find records in a table, because the key entries are unique (things such as last names and addresses can have multiple spellings, which makes them hard to find). Finally, a primary key is a handy way to avoid data-entry errors. Since the entries in a primary key field must be unique, there is no chance for someone to, say, enter the same account number for two different customers.

You can set things up so that Access sets and maintains the primary key for you, or you can do it yourself. Which one do you choose? Here are some guidelines:

- If your data contains a number or character sequence that uniquely defines each record, you can set the key yourself. For example, invoices usually have unique numbers that are perfect for a primary key. Other fields that can serve as primary keys are employee IDs, customer account numbers, and purchase order numbers.

- If your data has no such unique identifier, let Access create a key for you. This means that Access will set up an AutoNumber field that will assign a unique number to each record (the first record will be 1, the second 2, and so on).

Relating Tables

Access is a *relational* database system, which means that you can establish relationships between multiple tables. I talk more about this in Chapter 29, "Juggling Multiple Tables," but a brief introduction here will be useful.

Let's use an example. Suppose you have a database that contains (at least) two tables:

Orders: This table holds data on orders placed by your customers, including the customer name, the date of the order, and so on. It also includes an Order ID field as the primary key.

Order Details: This table holds data on the specific products that comprise each order: the product name, the unit price, the quantity ordered.

Why not lump both tables into a single table? Well, that would mean that, for each product ordered, you'd have to include the name of the customer, the order date, and so on. If the customer purchased 10 different products, this information would be repeated 10 times.

To avoid such waste, the data is kept in separate tables, and the two tables are *related* on a common field called Order ID. Figure 25.1 shows how this works. The first record in the Orders table refers to Order ID 10248. If you look at the Order Details table, you'll see that the first three records also have an Order ID of 10248. Therefore, we know (among other things) that those three products were ordered by Vins et alcools Chevalier.

FIGURE 25.1.

The Orders and Order Details tables are related on the common Order ID field.

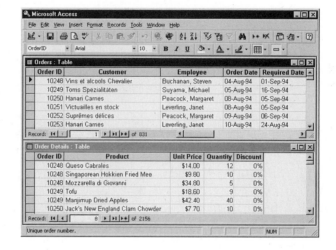

Creating a Table

Now that you've got your tables properly planned, you can get down to brass tacks and start building them. Access gives you four methods to create tables:

- Using the Table Wizard
- Using the Table Design view
- Importing data from an external source
- Linking to an external table

The next few sections show you how to wield the first two of these tools. To learn how to import external data into Access, see Chapter 50, "Working with the Office Integration Tools."

Using the Table Wizard

The Table Wizard—like all the Office Wizards—is a series of dialog boxes. In this case, the dialog boxes take you step-by-step through the process of creating a table. Before you can start

25

WORKING WITH TABLES

the Table Wizard, you need to tell Access that you want to create a new table. (I'm assuming that you already have a database open, as described in Chapter 24, "An Access Database Primer.") You can use any of the following techniques:

- Select Insert | Table.

- In the database window, select the Table tab (if necessary) and click New.

- Pull down the New Object list on the Database toolbar and choose Table.

A dialog box named New Table, shown in Figure 25.2, appears. Highlight Table Wizard and click OK.

Figure 25.2.

Select Table Wizard in this dialog box.

Selecting Fields for Your Table

When the Table Wizard loads, you'll see the dialog box shown in Figure 25.3. The purpose of this first dialog box is to help you decide which fields you want to include in your table. The Sample Tables list gives you a selection of predefined tables that come with Access. There are over two dozen business-related tables and about 20 personal ones. (You switch between the two lists by activating either the Business or Personal option button.)

Figure 25.3.

You use the first Table Wizard dialog box to select fields from one of the sample tables.

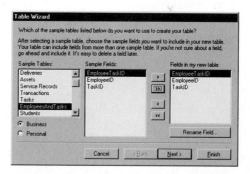

When you highlight a table in the Sample Tables list, Access displays the fields associated with the table in the Sample Fields list. The idea is that you find a sample table that closely matches the table you want to create, and then add fields from the Sample Fields list to the Fields in my new table list. These are the fields that will appear in your table.

NOTE: YOU CAN USE FIELDS FROM OTHER SAMPLE TABLES

Feel free to use fields from more than one sample table. Once you've added fields from one table, go ahead and select another one and begin adding whatever fields you need.

To move fields in and out of your table, use the Table Wizard buttons, described in Table 25.1.

Table 25.1. Table Wizard buttons you can use to add and remove sample fields in your table.

Button	Description
>	Adds the highlighted sample field to your table.
>>	Adds all the sample fields to your table.
<	Removes the highlighted field from your table.
<<	Removes all the fields from your table.

NOTE: YOU CAN ADD MISSING FIELDS BY HAND

If you don't see a field you need among any of the Sample Fields, you have two choices: If you're missing just one or two fields, you can add them yourself later. If you're missing many fields, you might need to create the entire table from scratch. In either case, you'll need to read the section "Working in Design View" later in this chapter to get the appropriate instructions.

When you've added all the fields you need, click Next > to move to the next dialog box, shown in Figure 25.4.

FIGURE 25.4.

The second Table Wizard dialog box.

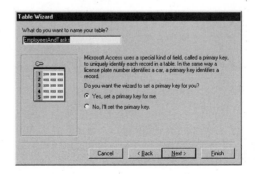

Specifying a Name and a Primary Key Field

The next Table Wizard dialog box serves two purposes. The first is to assign a name to your table. Access suggests a name, but feel free to type your own name in the edit box provided.

NOTE: TABLE NAME RESTRICTIONS

Your table names can have a maximum of 64 characters (including spaces), but they can't include exclamation points (!), periods (.), square brackets ([ ]), or backquotes (`). Also, you can't use the name of an existing table in the same database.

The second purpose of this dialog box is to assign the primary key for the table (as described earlier). If you want Access to create the primary key automatically, activate the Yes, set a primary key for me option. If you'd prefer to set the primary key yourself, activate the No, I'll set the primary key option instead.

When you're ready to continue, click Next >. If you're letting Access set the primary key for you, you can skip the next section.

Setting the Primary Key

If you told Table Wizard that you want to set the primary key yourself, the third dialog box you'll see is shown in Figure 25.5. Use the drop-down list to select the field you want to use for the primary key. Remember that the field you use for the key must contain entries that uniquely identify each record.

FIGURE 25.5.

This Table Wizard dialog box appears if you decided to set the primary key field yourself.

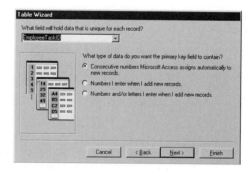

This dialog box also includes several option buttons that tell Access what type of data will appear in the field. You have three choices:

Consecutive numbers Microsoft Access assigns automatically to new records: If you select this option, Access will add numbers to the selected field that increment automatically whenever you add a new record.

Numbers I enter when I add new records: This option tells Access that you'll be entering your own values in the selected key field, and that these values will be numeric entries only.

Numbers and/or letters I enter when I add new records: This option also tells Access that you'll be entering your own key values, but that the entries may be numbers, letters, or combinations of both.

When you're done, click Next > to move to the next step. The dialog box that appears depends on whether you've defined other tables in the database. If you have, you'll see the Table Wizard dialog box shown in Figure 25.6. Otherwise, you can skip to the section titled "Finishing Up the Table."

FIGURE 25.6.

You'll see this Table Wizard dialog box if you have other tables in your database.

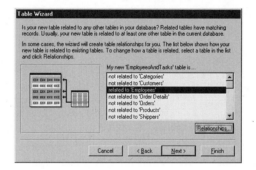

Relating Your Tables

As you learned earlier, you can establish relationships between two or more tables that have at least one field in common. In the dialog box shown in Figure 25.6, Table Wizard first tries to guess at the relationships you want:

- ■ If your new table uses a field that exists in another table, Table Wizard assumes the two are related.

- ■ If your new table has no fields in common with the other tables, Table Wizard assumes there is no relationship.

If these guesses are correct, click Next > to move to the final dialog box. Otherwise, you need to follow these steps to change the relationships:

1. Highlight the relationship you want to change.
2. Click the Relationships button. Table Wizard displays the Relationships dialog box, shown in Figure 25.7.
3. Activate the option button that correctly describes the type of relationship you want to set up.
4. Click OK to put the change into effect.

Figure 25.7.

Use this dialog box to define the relationship between two tables.

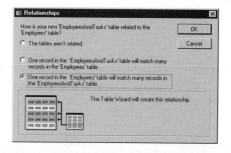

NOTE: MULTIPLE TABLES

See Chapter 29 for more detailed information on the types of relationships you can establish between two or more tables.

Finishing Up the Table

The last Table Wizard dialog box, shown in Figure 25.8, gives you three choices:

Modify the table design: Activate this option button if you want to make changes to the table manually. You'd choose this, for example, if the Table Wizard didn't include one or more fields you needed. The next section tells you how to make changes to your table design.

Enter data directly into the table: Activate this option button if you want to start entering data right away. See "Data Entry Techniques" later in this chapter.

Enter data into the table using a form the wizard creates for me: Activating this option button creates a form you can use to enter data. I'll talk about forms in detail in Chapter 27, "Creating and Using Simple Forms."

To exit the Table Wizard and create the table, click the Finish button.

Figure 25.8.

The last of the Table Wizard dialog boxes.

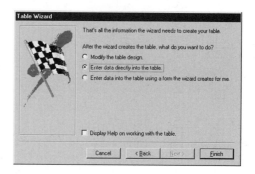

Working in Design View

The Table Wizard makes it easy to create tables, but it's not perfect. For one thing, although it does boast an admirable collection of sample tables, the samples certainly don't cover every possibility. For another, the tables it creates aren't the most efficient structures in the world. For example, if you include a sample phone number field, Table Wizard creates a field capable of holding up to 30 characters!

To get more control over your tables, you need to build them manually using Table Design view. This section shows you how to build your own tables and perform basic maintenance to keep them in top shape.

To get started, use the techniques outlined earlier to begin a new table. When the New Table dialog box appears, highlight Design View and click OK. Access displays the window shown in Figure 25.9.

FIGURE 25.9.

Use Table Design view to construct your table by hand.

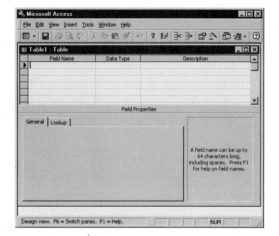

This is called Table Design view, and you use it to set up the fields you want to include in your table. For each field, you need to do four things:

1. Enter a name for the field.
2. Assign the field's data type.
3. Enter a description for the field.
4. Set the field's properties.

The next few sections take you through each of these steps.

25

WORKING WITH
TABLES

TIP: A QUICK WAY TO ADD A FIELD FROM A SAMPLE TABLE

If you like, you can add a field from one of the Access sample tables without having to run through the Table Wizard rigmarole. To try this, click the Build button on the Table Design toolbar. In the Field Builder dialog box that appears, choose a sample table, highlight a sample field, and click OK.

Entering a Name for the Field

You use the Field Name column to enter a name for the field. This is generally straightforward, but there are a few rules you need to follow:

- Names can be up to 64 characters long, so you have lots of room to make them descriptive. One caveat, though: The longer your names, the fewer fields you'll see on-screen when it's time to enter data.

- You can use any combination of letters, numbers, spaces, and other characters, but you can't use periods (.), exclamation points (!), backquotes (`), or square brackets ([ ]).

- Each name must be unique in the table. Access won't let you duplicate field names in the same table.

When you've entered the field name, press Tab to move to the Data Type column (you'll see a drop-down arrow appear in the column).

Assigning a Data Type to the Field

You use the Data Type column to tell Access what kind of data will appear in the field. From the drop-down list (press Alt-down arrow to display it), select one of the following data types:

Text: This is a catch-all type you can use for fields that will contain any combination of letters, numbers, and symbols (such as parentheses and dashes). These fields will usually be short entries (the maximum is 255 characters) such as names, addresses, and phone numbers. For purely numeric fields, however, you should use either the Number or Currency types (discussed in a moment).

Memo: Use this type for longer alphanumeric entries. Memo field entries are usually several sentences or paragraphs long, but they can contain up to 64,000 characters. These types of fields are useful for long, rambling text or random notes. In a table of customer names, for example, you could use a memo field to record customers' favorite colors, the names of their spouses and kids, and so on.

Number: Use this type for fields that will contain numbers only. This is particularly true for fields you'll be using for calculations. (Note, though, that fields containing dollar amounts should use the Currency type, described in a moment.)

Date/Time: This type is for fields that will use only dates and times. Access can handle dates from the year 100 right up to the year 9999. (You can make up your own jokes about missing appointments in the year 10000.)

Currency: Use this field for dollar values.

AutoNumber: This type creates a numeric entry that Access increments automatically whenever you add a record. Because this type of field assigns a unique number to each record, it's ideal for setting up your own primary key.

Yes/No: Use this type for fields that will contain only Yes or No values. For example, in a table of your friends and acquaintances, you could have a field that tells you whether they bought you a birthday present last year.

OLE Object: This type creates a field that can hold data from other programs (such as a graphic image or even an entire spreadsheet).

Hyperlink: This field type is used for links to Internet (or intranet) sites. See Chapter 44, "The Office 97 Internet Tools," for the nitty-gritty on using hyperlinks and other Web-based data in Access.

Lookup Wizard: This type displays a combo box from which the user can select a possible value. Selecting this type loads the Lookup Wizard, which takes you through the process of specifying which values to use. You can either designate a field from another database (Access will display the unique values from the field) or enter the values yourself.

When you've selected the data type, press Tab to move to the Description column.

Entering a Description

Use the Description column to enter a description for the field. You can use up to 255 characters, so there's plenty of room. As you'll see later, the Description field text appears in the status bar when you're entering data for the field.

Setting Field Properties

Your last task for each field is to set up the field's *properties*. These properties control various aspects of the field, such as its size and what format the data takes. The properties for each field are displayed in the bottom half of the design window. To change a property, you click the field you want to work with and then click the property.

Space limitations prevent me from covering every possible property, but here's a quick look at the most common ones:

Field Size: In a Text field, this property controls the number of characters you can enter. You can enter a number between 1 and 255, but the size you enter should only be large enough to accommodate the maximum possible entry. In a phone number field, for example, you'd set the size to 13 or 14. In a Number field, you select the appropriate numeric type, such as Integer or Single.

Format: This property controls the display of dates and numbers. For example, the Long Date format would display a date as Saturday, August 23, 1997, but the Short Date format would display the date as 8/23/97.

25

WORKING WITH TABLES

Default Value: This property sets up a suggested value that appears in the field automatically whenever you add a new record to the table. For example, suppose you have a table of names and addresses and it includes a Country field. If most of the records will be from the same country, you could add it as the default (for example, USA or Canada).

TIP: THE CURRENT DATE AND TIME

In a Date/Time field, you can make today's date the default value by entering =Date() as the Default Value property. For the current time, enter =Time(). To get both the current date and time, enter =Now().

Required: In most tables, you'll have some fields that are optional and some that are required. For required fields, set their Required property to Yes. Access will then warn you if you accidentally leave the field blank.

Indexed: Tables that are indexed on a certain field make it easier to find values in that field. If you think you'll be doing a lot of searching in a field, set its Indexed property to Yes. (See Chapter 3, "Day-to-Day Office Basics," for information on searching an Access Table.)

NOTE: MAKING INDEX ADJUSTMENTS

You can adjust your indexed fields by selecting View | Indexes or by clicking the Indexes button on the Table Design toolbar. In the Indexes dialog box that appears, you can adjust the default sort order for each index, whether only unique field values are indexed, and so on.

Setting the Primary Key

As explained earlier, every table should have a primary key. To set up a primary key, you need to do two things:

1. Create a field that will contain entries that uniquely identify each record. If your data doesn't have such a field (such as invoice numbers or customer account codes), all is not lost. Just set up a new field (you could even name it "Primary Key") and assign it the AutoNumber data type.

2. Place the cursor anywhere in the field row and activate the Edit | Primary Key command (or right-click the row and select Primary Key from the context menu). You can also click the Primary Key button on the Table Design toolbar. Access designates the primary key field by placing a key beside the field name.

Saving the Table

When your table is set up the way you want, you need to save your changes for posterity. To do this, select File | Save, press Ctrl-S, or click the Save button. If you haven't saved the table before, you'll see the Save As dialog box, shown in Figure 25.10. In the Table Name edit box, enter the name you want to use for the table. Table names can be up to 64 characters long, and they can't include exclamation points (!), periods (.), square brackets ([ ]), or backquotes (`). Click OK or press Enter to save the table.

FIGURE 25.10.

Use this dialog box to enter a name for your new table.

Moving a Field

As you'll see later in this chapter, you'll normally enter the data for each record in the same order that you added the fields to the table. If the current field order isn't right for some reason, you need to move the fields to get the correct order. The following steps show you how to move a field:

1. You first need to select the entire field you want to move by using either of the following methods:

   ■ Click the field selection button to the left of the Field Name column (see Figure 25.11).

   ■ Place the cursor anywhere in the field and press Shift-Spacebar.

FIGURE 25.11.

You need to select the entire field before you can move it.

Click here to select the entire field

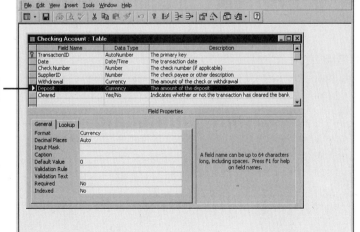

2. Select Edit | Cut to remove the field.

3. Select the field above which you want the moved field to appear. (You can either select the entire field or simply place the cursor in one of the field's columns.) In Figure 25.11, for example, if I wanted the Deposit field to appear above the Withdrawal field, I would select the Withdrawal field.

4. Select Edit | Paste. Access reinstates the field data above the current field.

TIP: USE DRAG-AND-DROP TO MOVE A FIELD

An easier way to move a field is to use drag-and-drop. Select the entire field, drag the field selection button up or down to the position you want, and then release the mouse button to drop the field in the new location.

Adding New Fields

Adding another field to the table is just like adding a field in your original database design. You move to the first empty row and then enter the field name, data type, description, and properties.

However, what if you want to insert the new field somewhere in the middle of the table? You could add the field at the bottom and then move it, but Access gives you a way to save a step. You first select the field above which you want the new field to be inserted. Then either select Insert | Rows or click the Insert Rows toolbar button. Access creates a blank field above the current field.

Deleting Fields

Deleting fields is easy. Simply select the field you want to get rid of and then either select Edit | Delete Rows or click the toolbar's Delete Rows button.

Returning to the Database Window

When you've finished creating your table, you can return to the Database window either by closing the Table Design window or, if you'd prefer to leave the Table Design window open, by clicking the Database Window button on the toolbar. Your new table will appear in the Database window's Table tab.

Modifying the Table

If you need to make changes to your table's design and you've already closed the design window, you can reopen it by highlighting the table name in the Database window's Table tab and then clicking the Design button.

NOTE: ADDING A TABLE DESCRIPTION

If you're using the Details view in the Database window, you'll want to add a description for your new table. To do this, highlight the table and then either select View | Properties or click the Properties button on the toolbar. (You can also right-click the table and choose Properties from the context menu.) In the dialog box that appears, use the Description text box to enter a description for the table, and then click OK.

Data Entry Techniques

When it comes to databases, the *data* is the most important thing. So it's crucial to know a few techniques that not only make data entry easier, but also help ensure that data is entered accurately.

To enter data, you need to open the table's *datasheet*. You do this by highlighting the table name in the Database window's Table tab and then clicking the Open button. Figure 25.12 shows the datasheet window that appears. (In this case, I've opened a table that already contains data so that I can illustrate some of the features of the datasheet window.)

FIGURE 25.12.

You use this window to enter your data.

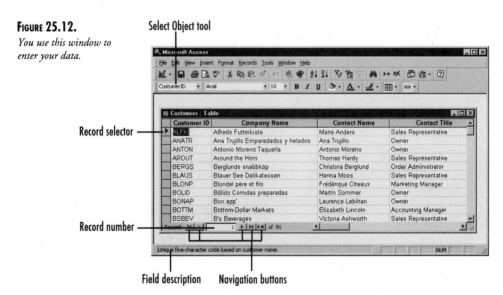

The datasheet window has the following features:

> **Fields:** Each column in the datasheet corresponds to a field you added when you created the table.
>
> **Field Names:** These are the buttons at the top of each column and are the names you assigned to your fields.

Records: Each row in the datasheet corresponds to a record.

Record selector: These buttons run down the left side of the window. You use them to select records. They also show icons that give you more information about the record (as described later in this chapter).

Record number box: This tells you which record is currently selected.

Field description: If you entered a description for your fields, they appear in the status bar as you select each field.

Navigation buttons: These buttons let you navigate the table. See "Navigating Table Records" later in this chapter.

Navigating Fields

To make it easier to enter your data, you should be familiar with the techniques for navigating the datasheet fields. As I've mentioned, with the mouse you can select a field just by clicking it. If you can't see all your fields, you can either use the horizontal scrollbar to bring them into view or drop down the toolbar's Select Object list (see Figure 25.12) and then click the field you want to work with.

Using the keyboard, you can use the keys outlined in Table 25.2.

Table 25.2. Keys to use when navigating fields in the datasheet.

Button	*Description*
Tab or right arrow	Moves to the next field to the right.
Shift-Tab or left arrow	Moves to the previous field to the left.
Home	Moves to the first field.
End	Moves to the last field.
Ctrl-Home	Moves to the first field of the first record.
Ctrl-End	Moves to the last field of the last record.

When you use the keys in Table 25.2 to move into a field that already contains data, Access will highlight the data. If you press any key while the field is highlighted, you'll replace the *entire* entry with that keystroke! If this isn't what you want, immediately press Esc to restore the text. To prevent this from happening, you can remove the highlight by clicking inside the field or by pressing F2.

The keys in Table 25.2 are the Access defaults, but you can change this behavior. To learn how, see the section "Customizing Access Keyboard Behavior" in Chapter 31, "Customizing Access."

Entering Data

Entering data in Access is, for the most part, straightforward. You just select a field and start typing. Here are a few notes to keep in mind when entering table data:

- If you want to replace an entire field value, you can either type in the correct value (Access will automatically replace the highlighted value with your typing) or press Delete to clear the field.

- If you only want to change one or more characters in a field, press F2 or click inside the field to remove the highlight, and then edit the field accordingly.

- If you're editing a field, you can select the entire contents of the cell by pressing F2.

- When you're editing a record, the record selector changes to a pencil icon, as shown in Figure 25.13. This tells you that you've made changes to the record.

FIGURE 25.13.

When you've made changes to a record, the record selector changes to a pencil icon.

- The width of a field's column has nothing to do with how much data you can enter into the field. (This is determined solely by the `Field Size` property, which you learned about earlier in this chapter.) If you approach the edge of the column as you're typing, Access will scroll the first part of the field off to the left.

- If you see a field that contains [AutoNumber], this means that Access will automatically assign numbers to the field, so you can skip it.

- When entering dates, use the format *mm/dd/yy,* where *mm* is the month number (for example, 12 for December), *dd* is the day, and *yy* is the year. For example, 12/25/96 is an acceptable date. The date format you end up with depends on the `Format` property you assigned to the field.

- When entering times, use the format *hh:mm:ss,* where *hh* is the hour, *mm* is the minutes, and *ss* is the seconds. Military types can use the 24-hour clock (for example, 16:30:05), and the rest of us can add *am* or *pm* (for example, 4:30:05 pm). Again, the format that's displayed depends on the field's `Format` property.

TIP: ENTERING THE CURRENT DATE AND TIME

You can add today's date to a field by simply pressing Ctrl-; (semicolon). To add the current time, press Ctrl-: (colon).

- When entering a number in a Currency field, don't bother entering a dollar sign ($); Access will add it for you automatically.

- If you enter a value that Access wasn't expecting (for example, if you type Maybe in a Yes/No field), Access will display an error message.

- You save the current record by moving to a different record. If you'd prefer to save the current record and still remain in edit mode, press Shift-Enter.

Adding More Records

Access always keeps a blank record at the bottom of the table for adding new records (it's the one that has an asterisk in its record selector). The next section tells you how to move around between records, but for now, you can use any of the following methods to select the blank record:

- If you're in the last field of the record directly above the blank record, press Tab.
- Select Edit | Go To | New Record.
- Press Ctrl-+ (plus sign).

- Click the New Record button on the Datasheet toolbar.

Navigating Table Records

Once you've added a couple of records to your table, you need to know how to navigate from one record to another. This becomes even more important once you have dozens or even hundreds of records in the table. Knowing how to navigate all that data can save you lots of time and energy.

If you can see the record you want, click it. (You'll usually click whatever field you want to edit.) If you can't see the record, use the vertical scrollbar on the right side of the datasheet window to bring the record into view.

Mouse users can also use the five datasheet navigation buttons at the bottom of the window. They are explained in Table 25.3.

Table 25.3. The datasheet navigation buttons.

Button	Description
	Moves to the first record.
	Moves to the previous record.
	Moves to the next record.
	Moves to the last record.
	Moves to the new record.

You can also use Record | Go To to navigate the table. When you select this command, a cascade menu appears with the following commands:

First: Takes you to the table's first record.

Last: Takes you to the last record.

Next: Takes you to the next record.

Previous: Takes you to the previous record.

Undoing Field and Record Changes

If you've made changes to a record and, for some reason, you've really made a mess of things, help is just around the corner. Access has a couple of commands that will restore either a single field or an entire record to its original state.

If you've made changes to the current field and you want to restore the field to the value it had before you started editing, select Edit | Undo Typing (or press Esc). Note that this command is available only while you're inside the field. If you move to another field, the command is no longer available.

If you'd prefer to restore the entire record to its original state, first move to a different field to confirm any changes you might have made to the current field. Then select Edit | Undo Current Field/Record (or press Ctrl-Z). Again, you should note that this command is available only as long as you don't move to another record.

You can also undo any changes you made to the last saved record by selecting Edit | Undo Last Saved Record.

Note that, in each of these cases, you can also click the Undo button on the toolbar.

Working with Records

We'll turn our attention now to working with the records in the datasheet. The next few sections tackle the basic record techniques: selecting, copying, and deleting.

Selecting a Record

You first need to select a record before you can work with it. Access, bless its electronic heart, gives you four different methods to choose from:

- Move to any field in the record and select Edit | Select Record.
- Click the record selector to the left of the record you want. You can also use this method to select multiple records: Just drag the mouse pointer over the record selector for each record you want to work with.
- Move to any field in the record and press Shift-Spacebar. To select multiple records, press Shift-Spacebar and then press either Shift-up arrow or Shift-down arrow.
- To select every record, either choose Edit | Select All Records or click the blank button in the upper-left corner of the datasheet (it's just below the window's control menu icon).

With your record (or records) selected, you can proceed with your copying or deleting, as described in the next two sections.

Copying a Record

One of the secrets of computer productivity is the maxim "Don't reinvent the wheel." Specifically, if you have to enter a new record that has almost the same data as an existing record, it's much simpler to make a copy of the existing record and then make your changes to the copy.

To copy a record, select it and choose Edit | Copy. Now select Edit | Paste Append. Access tacks on the record to the end of the table.

Deleting a Record

To keep your tables relatively neat and tidy, you should delete any records you no longer need. To do this, use any of the following techniques:

- Select the record or records you want to toss out, and then select Edit | Delete Record.
- Select the record or records and press Delete.
- Move to any field with the record and press Ctrl-- (minus sign).

- Click the toolbar's Delete Record button.

In all cases, the dialog box shown in Figure 25.14 appears to tell you what you already know: that you've just deleted a record. Click Yes to continue with the deletion.

Formatting the Datasheet

The standard datasheet displayed by Access is serviceable at best. Most people, though, have three major complaints about the default datasheet:

■ Some columns are too small to show all the data in a field.

■ You can't see all the fields in the datasheet window.

■ The characters are a little on the small side, so they're hard to read.

The next few sections show you how to format the datasheet to overcome these problems.

Changing the Datasheet Column Sizes

The default datasheet assigns the same width to every column. Although this so-called *standard width* might be fine for some fields, for others it's either too large or too small. Fortunately, Access lets you adjust the width of individual columns to suit each field.

To change the width, move to the column (it doesn't matter which record) and select Format | Column Width. (You can also display the Column Height dialog box by right-clicking the field name and selecting Column Width from the context menu.) In the Column Width dialog box that appears, shown in Figure 25.15, enter a number in the Column Width text box. (The standard width is 15.6667, but you can enter any number between 0 and 436.) If you want to change a previously modified column back to the standard width, activate the Standard Width check box. If you want the column to be as wide as the widest field value, click the Best Fit button. Otherwise, click OK.

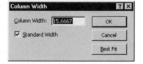

You can also use the mouse to change the width of a column. Move the mouse pointer so that it rests on the right edge of the field name box. The pointer will change to a vertical bar with two arrows protruding from its sides. From here, you have two choices:

■ Drag the mouse to the left to make the column width smaller, or drag it to the right to make the width larger.

■ Double-click to size the column width to accommodate the largest field value.

TIP: ZOOM IN ON YOUR DATA

If you have a field with a large amount of data (a Memo field, for example), it isn't always practical to expand the column width to see all the data. Instead, move to the field and press Shift-F2. Access displays the Zoom dialog box to show you more of your data. If you like, you can also use this dialog box to enter more data or edit the existing data. When you're done, click OK to return to the datasheet.

Changing the Datasheet Row Heights

Another way to see more data in each field is to increase the height of each datasheet row (you can't do this for individual rows). As with column widths, there are two methods you can use:

■ Select Format | Row Height (or right-click any record selector and choose Row Height from the context menu). In the Row Height dialog box that appears, shown in Figure 25.16, enter the new height in the Row Height edit box. The standard height is 12.75 (which you can revert to at any time by activating the Standard Height check box), but you can enter any number between 0 and 1636. Click OK when you're done.

FIGURE 25.16.

Use this dialog box to set the row height for the datasheet.

■ Position the mouse pointer on the bottom edge of any row selector. The pointer will change into a horizontal bar with arrows sticking out the top and bottom. Drag the mouse up to reduce the row height and drag it down to increase the row height.

Changing the Look of the Datasheet

The appearance of the datasheet is governed by two factors: the font used to display the data, and the style of each cell. Here's a quick rundown of the various methods you can use to change the look of your datasheet:

- To change the font, select Format | Font, choose the font you want from the Font dialog box that appears, and click OK. Note that this applies to all the datasheet cells.

- To change the formatting of the individual datasheet cells, select Format | Cells. The Cells Effects dialog box, shown in Figure 25.17, lets you toggle gridlines on and off, change the cell effects, and determine the gridline and background colors.

FIGURE 25.17.

Use this dialog box to format the datasheet cells.

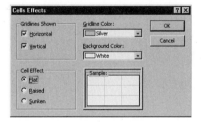

- The Formatting (Datasheet) toolbar boasts a number of tools that put each of these formatting options a mouse click away.

Changing the Table Design

During data entry, you'll often find that you need to make changes to the design of the table. A field might be too large or too small, or you might want to set up a default value for a field. Whatever the case, you can make some design changes right from the datasheet, or you can switch to Design view. Here are the basic techniques:

- To delete a field, select a cell inside the field and then choose Edit | Delete Column.

- To add a new field, first select the entire field to the left of which you want the new field to appear. (You select an entire field either by clicking the field's column name or by selecting a cell inside the field and pressing Ctrl-Spacebar.) Then select Insert | Column.

- To change the name of a field, select a cell within the field and then select Format | Rename column.

- For more advanced changes, you can switch to Design view by selecting View | Design View or by clicking the View toolbar button and choosing Design View.

- When you're ready to return to the datasheet, save your changes and then either select View | Datasheet View or click the View toolbar button and choose Data-sheet View.

Sorting Records

Another way to find records in a table is to *sort* the table. Sorting means that you place the records in alphabetical order based on the data in a field (or numerical order if the field contains numeric or currency data). For example, suppose you have a table of customer names and addresses, and you want to see all the customers who are from California. All you have to do is sort the table by the data in the State field, and all the records with CA in this field will appear together.

Sorting on a Single Field

Since sorting is such a common practice, the Access programmers made it easy to perform quick sorts on a single field. To try this, first select the field you want to sort. Then use one of the following methods:

- Select Records | Sort Ascending to sort on the field in ascending order. Alternatively, select Records | Sort Descending to sort on the field in descending order.

- Right-click the field and choose either Sort Ascending or Sort Descending from the context menu.

- For an ascending sort, click the field and then click the Sort Ascending button on the toolbar.

- For a descending sort, click the field and then click the Sort Descending button on the toolbar.

Sorting on Multiple Fields

Although most of your table sorts will probably be on single fields, there will be times when you have to perform a sort on multiple fields. For example, you might want to sort a table by country and then by postal code within each country. For these more advanced sorts, Access provides the Advanced Filter/Sort tool, which you can load by selecting Records | Filter | Advanced Filter/Sort. Access displays the Filter window, shown in Figure 25.18.

FIGURE 25.18.

Use the Filter window to perform sorts on two or more fields.

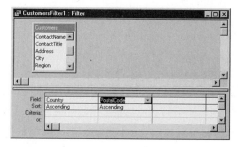

You use the columns in the lower pane to select the fields upon which you want to sort. Each Field cell has a drop-down list that contains the available fields. You choose the field and then use the Sort cell below it to choose either Ascending or Descending. However, be sure that the order in which you select the fields reflects the sort priority you want to use. For example, if you want to sort by country and then by postal code within each country, you'd select the Country field in the first column and then the PostalCode field in the second column.

When you're done, you sort the table either by selecting Records | Apply Filter/Sort or by clicking the Apply Filter toolbar button. To revert the table to its unsorted state, select Records | Remove Filter/Sort.

Filtering Table Data

If you've ever been to a large, noisy gathering, you might have been struck by how easily humans can ignore a cacophony of music and voices around them and concentrate on whatever conversation they're having at the time. Our brains somehow filter out the unimportant noise and let in only what we need to hear.

This idea of screening out the unnecessary is exactly what Access *filters* do. We often want to work with only some of the records in a large table. The other records are just "noise" that we want to somehow tune out. For example, if you have a table of customer invoices, you might want to work with any of the following subsets of the data:

- Only those invoices from a particular customer
- All the invoices that are overdue
- Every invoice with an amount greater than $1,000

A filter can do all this and more. The idea is that you define the *criteria* you want to use (such as having the Amount field greater than or equal to $1,000), and then, when you filter the table, Access will display only those records that meet the criteria. When you filter a table, the resulting subset of records is called a *dynaset*.

For example, consider the Orders table shown in Figure 25.19. This is a table of invoice data for customer purchases. As you can see, the table has over 800 records, so there's plenty of "noise" to filter out.

Figure 25.19.

A table of orders data.

Order ID	Customer	Order Date	Shipped Date	Ship Via	Freight
10248	Vins et alcools Chevalier	04-Aug-94	16-Aug-94	Federal Shipping	$32.38
10249	Toms Spezialitäten	05-Aug-94	10-Aug-94	Speedy Express	$11.61
10250	Hanari Carnes	08-Aug-94	12-Aug-94	United Package	$65.83
10251	Victuailles en stock	08-Aug-94	15-Aug-94	Speedy Express	$41.34
10252	Suprêmes délices	09-Aug-94	11-Aug-94	United Package	$51.30
10253	Hanari Carnes	10-Aug-94	16-Aug-94	United Package	$58.17
10254	Chop-suey Chinese	11-Aug-94	23-Aug-94	United Package	$22.98
10255	Richter Supermarkt	12-Aug-94	15-Aug-94	Federal Shipping	$148.33
10256	Wellington Importadora	15-Aug-94	17-Aug-94	United Package	$13.97
10257	HILARIÓN-Abastos	16-Aug-94	22-Aug-94	Federal Shipping	$81.91
10258	Ernst Handel	17-Aug-94	23-Aug-94	Speedy Express	$140.51
10259	Centro comercial Moctezuma	18-Aug-94	25-Aug-94	Federal Shipping	$3.25
10260	Ottilies Käseladen	19-Aug-94	29-Aug-94	Speedy Express	$55.09
10261	Que Delícia	19-Aug-94	30-Aug-94	United Package	$3.05

Record: 7 of 831

25

WORKING WITH TABLES

Figure 25.20 shows another view of the same table, in which I've set up a filter to show only a subset of records. In this case, my criteria was that the Customer field be equal to "Chop-suey Chinese." This shows me all the invoices for that particular customer.

FIGURE 25.20.

The same table filtered to show only one customer's invoices.

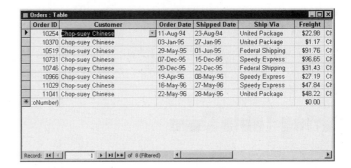

Filtering by Selection

For simple filters, Access has a Filter By Selection feature. You can select a particular value in a field, and Access will filter the table so that it displays only those records that match the selected value. In the example just discussed, I highlighted "Chop-suey Chinese" in the Customer field (see Figure 25.19) and then ran Filter By Selection using one of the following methods:

- ■ Select Records | Filter | Filter By Selection.
- ■ Right-click the value and choose Filter By Selection from the context menu.
- ■ Click the Filter By Selection toolbar button.

NOTE: FILTER EXCLUDING SELECTION

The context menu gives you an alternative to Filter By Selection: Filter Excluding Selection. Choosing this command filters the table to include every record *except* those that contain the selected value.

When you no longer need to work with the filtered list, select Records | Remove Filter/Sort, right-click the table and choose Remove Filter/Sort, or click the Apply Filter toolbar button (to deselect it).

Learning About Filter Criteria

As with sorting, you can create more advanced filters that use multiple fields and calculations. Before I show you how to set up such a filter, let's take a brief look at filter criteria. You use criteria to tell Access what subset of your data you want to see. The basic idea is that you select a field and then enter an *expression* that defines your criteria. In plain English, filters always take the following form:

>Show me all records where *field* is *expression*

Here, *field* is the name of the field you want to use, and *expression* defines the criteria you want to apply to the table records. For example, suppose you select the Customer field and you enter `Chop-suey Chinese` as the criteria expression. Then your filter becomes the following:

>Show me all records where Customer is "Chop-suey Chinese"

Similarly, suppose you want to see only those invoices where the Freight amount is greater than $100. In this case, you'd select the Freight field, and your expression would be >100 (> is the symbol for "greater than"; see Table 25.4). Here's the English equivalent for this filter:

>Show me all records where Freight is greater than 100

In this example, I used the greater than sign (>) as part of the expression. Access has a number of these symbols (called *operators*) that you can use to add tremendous flexibility to your criteria. Table 25.4 lists the most common ones.

Table 25.4. Operators you can use in criteria expressions.

Symbol	Description
=	Equal to
<	Less than
<=	Less than or equal to
>	Greater than
>=	Greater than or equal to
<>	Not equal to

Here are a few sample expressions and the filters they create (I'm using the Orders table for these examples):

Expression	Field	Description
"Bern"	Ship City	Displays records where Ship City is "Bern."
<>"France"	Ship Country	Displays records where Ship Country is not equal to "France."
<="G"	Customer	Displays records where Customer begins with the letters A through G.
10360	Order ID	Displays records where Order ID is 10360.
<100	Freight	Displays records where Freight is less than $100.
>=1000	Freight	Displays records where Freight is greater than or equal to $1,000.
>#1/1/95#	Shipped Date	Displays records where Shipped Date is after 1/1/95.
Null	Ship Region	Displays records where the Ship Region field is empty.

Here are some notes to keep in mind when entering your criteria expressions:

■ If you want your filter to match an exact value, you usually don't have to bother with the equal to symbol (=) in your expression. As the preceding examples show, you can simply enter the value itself.

■ Although the preceding examples show quotation marks around text and number signs (#) around dates, you don't have to bother with these symbols when entering your expressions. Access will kindly add them for you.

NOTE: MORE CRITERIA INFO

This section only scratches the surface of criteria expressions. For a more in-depth treatment, see Chapter 26, "Querying Data."

Creating a Filter

Okay, with those criteria basics in tow, it's time to get down to the business at hand. To start a filter, select Records | Filter | Advanced Filter/Sort. You'll see a filter window, as shown in Figure 25.21.

FIGURE 25.21.

The filter window.

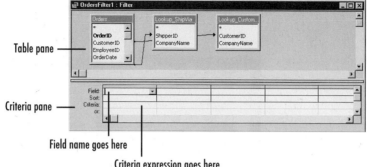

Table pane

Criteria pane

Field name goes here

Criteria expression goes here

As you can see, the filter window is divided into two sections:

Table pane: This is the top half of the window. It contains a box that lists all the fields from your table. You use this box to select which field to use with your criteria.

Criteria pane: This is the bottom half of the window. The field you select appears in the top line (labeled Field), and you enter your criteria in the third line (labeled Criteria).

Adding a Field to the Criteria Grid

Once you have the filter window displayed, your first task is to select the field you want to use for your filter. Use one of these techniques:

- Double-click the field name.
- Drag the field name and drop it in the Field box.
- Use the drop-down list in the Field box to select the field.

Entering Criteria and Applying the Filter

The next step is to enter your criteria. In the criteria grid, select the Criteria line below your field name and type in the criteria. Figure 25.22 shows a filter window set up to display records in the Orders table where the Freight field is greater than or equal to 100.

FIGURE 25.22.

A filter window with criteria.

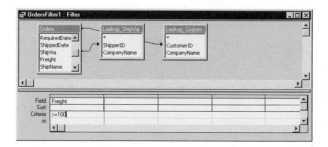

25

When you're done, you filter the table either by selecting Records | Apply Filter/Sort or by clicking the Apply Filter toolbar button. Figure 25.23 shows the result.

FIGURE 25.23.

The filtered table.

Order ID	Customer	Order Date	Shipped Date	Ship Via	Freight
10255	Richter Supermarkt	12-Aug-94	15-Aug-94	Federal Shipping	$148.33
10258	Ernst Handel	17-Aug-94	23-Aug-94	Speedy Express	$140.51
10263	Ernst Handel	23-Aug-94	31-Aug-94	Federal Shipping	$146.06
10267	Frankenversand	29-Aug-94	06-Sep-94	Speedy Express	$208.58
10270	Wartian Herkku	01-Sep-94	02-Sep-94	Speedy Express	$136.54
10277	Morgenstern Gesundkost	09-Sep-94	13-Sep-94	Federal Shipping	$125.77
10286	QUICK-Stop	21-Sep-94	30-Sep-94	Federal Shipping	$229.24
10294	Rattlesnake Canyon Grocery	30-Sep-94	06-Oct-94	United Package	$147.26
10298	Hungry Owl All-Night Grocers	06-Oct-94	12-Oct-94	United Package	$168.22
10303	Godos Cocina Típica	12-Oct-94	19-Oct-94	United Package	$107.83
10305	Old World Delicatessen	14-Oct-94	09-Nov-94	Federal Shipping	$257.62
10316	Rattlesnake Canyon Grocery	28-Oct-94	08-Nov-94	Federal Shipping	$150.15
10324	Save-a-lot Markets	08-Nov-94	10-Nov-94	Speedy Express	$214.27
10329	Split Rail Beer & Ale	15-Nov-94	23-Nov-94	United Package	$191.67

Record: 1 of 187 (Filtered)

Summary

This chapter showed you the ins and outs of working with Access tables. After some theoretical discussion related to table planning and design, you learned how to create a table using both the Table Wizard and Design view. From there, I showed you a few techniques for data entry, working with records, and formatting the datasheet. You also learned how to find data, sort records, and filter a table.

Here's a list of chapters where you'll find related information:

■ Queries are powerful filters that you can save and reuse. To learn how to create them, see Chapter 26, "Querying Data."

■ You can relieve data entry drudgery by creating a form. I'll show you how in Chapter 27, "Creating and Using Simple Forms."

■ See Chapter 29, "Juggling Multiple Tables," for more detailed information on the types of relationships you can establish between two or more tables.

■ I discuss the Access table customization options in Chapter 31, "Customizing Access."

■ To learn how to import external data and link to external tables, check out Chapter 50, "Working with the Office Integration Tools."

Querying Data

CHAPTER 26

When action grows unprofitable, gather information, when information grows unprofitable, sleep.

—*Ursula K. LeGuin*

This chapter gets you up to speed with one of the most powerful concepts in all of Access: queries. Queries are no great mystery, really. Although the name implies they're a sort of question, it's more useful to think of them as *requests*. In the simplest case, a query is a request to see a particular subset of your data. For example, showing only those records in a customer table where the country is "Sweden" and the first name is "Sven" would be a fairly simple query to build. (This type of query is known in the trade as a *select query*.)

In this respect, queries are fancier versions of the filters we looked at in Chapter 25, "Working with Tables." Similar to using filters, you select field names and set up *criteria* that define the records you want to see. However, unlike filters, queries are not simply a different view of the table data. They're a separate database object that actually *extracts* records from a table and places them in a *dynaset*. As you'll see later, a dynaset is much like a datasheet, and many of the operations you can perform on a datasheet can also be performed on a dynaset. (Query results are called dynasets because they're dynamic subsets of a table. Here, "dynamic" means that, if you make any changes to the original table, Access updates the query automatically, or vice versa.)

The other major difference between a query and a filter is that you can save queries and then rerun them anytime you like. Filters, on the other hand, are ephemeral: When you close the table, any filters you've defined vanish into thin air.

Other types of queries are more sophisticated. For example, you can set up queries to summarize the data in a table, to find duplicate records, to delete records, and to move records from one database into another. I'll cover all of these kinds of queries in this chapter.

Creating a Query

As I've said, the end result of a query is a dynaset, which looks and acts very much like a table's datasheet. So you might expect that the process of creating a query would be similar to that of creating a table, and, in fact, it is. Both processes involve three steps:

1. For a table, you begin by creating a new table object. For a query, you create a new query object.

2. A new table is empty, so you have to define its basic structure by adding fields. New queries are also empty and also need fields to define their structure. The difference, as you'll see, is that the query's fields come from an existing table.

3. In a table, you then need to flesh out the structure by entering data into new records. Queries, too, need records to give them substance. In this case, though, you "enter" records into the query by defining the criteria the query uses to extract records from the underlying table.

The next few sections take you through each of these steps.

Creating a New Query Object

To get your query started, activate the Queries tab in the Database window and then click New. A dialog box called New Query appears, as shown in Figure 26.1. Highlight Design View and click OK. (I'll talk about the various Wizards that appear in this list later on in this chapter.) Access then displays the Show Table dialog box, shown in Figure 26.2. Use the list in the Tables tab to highlight the table you want to use, and then click Add. (Note, too, that you could also base your new query on an existing query by using the items in the Queries tab instead.) Add as many tables as you need (I'll talk about multiple-table queries in Chapter 29, "Juggling Multiple Tables") and then click Close.

FIGURE 26.1.

To start your query,
select Design View from
this dialog box.

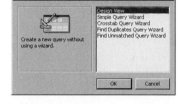

FIGURE 26.2.

Use the Show Table
dialog box to select a
table upon which to
base your query.

TIP: A QUICK WAY TO ADD A TABLE TO A NEW QUERY

You can bypass the Show Table dialog box by opening the table you want to use as the basis for your query, clicking the New Object button on the toolbar, and clicking Query.

Access creates a new query object and displays the query design window, as shown in Figure 26.3. This window is divided into two areas: the *table pane* and the *QBE grid*. The table pane includes boxes for the tables you have added to your query. These boxes contain a *field list,* which is a list of the available fields in each table. As you'll see in the next section, you use this list to add fields to the query.

FIGURE 26.3.

The query design window.

Field list

Table pane

QBE grid

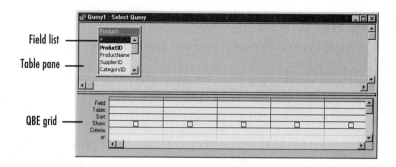

The QBE grid is a collection of text boxes (they're called *cells*) where you define the query. Use the first row (Field) for the query's field names. Use the third row (Sort) for sorting options. Use the fourth row (Show) to determine which fields appear in the query results. Use the rest of the rows (Criteria, and so on) to set up your criteria.

The "QBE" part of QBE grid stands for *query by example,* which is a method that makes it easy to define a query. The idea is that you set up a query by defining an example of what you want each dynaset record to look like. As you'll see in the next few sections, this involves adding the fields you want to a grid and then setting up criteria for one or more of those fields. The alternative to QBE is SQL—Structured Query Language. This is a more complex—but also more powerful—method of querying data, but I won't discuss it in this book. (If you're interested, the Access Help system has a SQL reference. In the Contents tab, look for the book titled *Microsoft Jet SQL Reference.*)

Selecting the Fields to Include in the Query

When you've created a new query object, it's time to add some structure to it. As I've said, you do this by adding fields from the table associated with the query. What fields do you add to the query? To answer that question, you need to ask yourself two other questions:

> What fields do I want to use for the criteria? These are the fields that determine which records you see when you run the query. For example, suppose you have a table of compact discs with an Artist field and you want your query to show only those CDs from a particular group. Then you'd definitely need to include the Artist field in the query.
>
> What fields do I want to see in the dynaset? When you look at the results of the query, you'll usually want to see more than just the fields you used for the criteria. In the compact discs example, you might also want to see the name of the disc, the year it came out, and so on. So you'll need to include in the query each field you want to see.

After you know which fields you want to use in the query, you're ready to go. Access starts with the cursor inside the first cell of the QBE grid, so you can start from there. Simply click the drop-down arrow to display a list of fields from the table, and then click the field you want to use. (If you have more than one table in the query, first use the Table cell to choose the table you want to work with.) Then repeat this procedure in the Field cells of the other columns until you've entered all the fields you need.

You can also select fields from the field list. There are two basic techniques:

- To add a single field, either double-click it in the field list or drag the name from the field list to the appropriate Field cell in the QBE grid.

- To add multiple fields, hold down Ctrl, click each field you want, and then drag any one of the highlighted fields into a Field cell in the QBE grid. Access enters each field in its own cell.

If you add a column by mistake, you should delete it from the QBE grid to avoid cluttering the dynaset. To do this, click inside the column you want to get rid of and then select Edit | Delete Columns.

NOTE: WATCH YOUR FIELD ORDER

When selecting fields, keep in mind that the order in which you select your fields is the order in which they'll appear in the dynaset. If you add fields in the wrong order, you can fix this easily. First, select the QBE grid column you want to move by clicking the bar at the top of the column. With the mouse pointer still inside the bar, drag the column left or right to the new location.

What about the asterisk (*) that appears at the top of the field list? This is a special symbol that means, in effect, "every field in the table." If you want your query to display every field, the easiest way to do it is to drag the asterisk to the QBE grid. That way, the only other columns you have to work with in the QBE grid are those you'll use to define your criteria.

Entering the Query Criteria

The final step in defining your query is to enter the criteria. Type your expressions directly into the Criteria cells in the QBE grid and be sure to press Enter when you're done. You can use the same simple criteria I outlined for filters in Chapter 25. However, I'll be showing you more sophisticated criteria later in this chapter in the section "Understanding Query Criteria."

Excluding a Field from the Query Results

You'll often add fields to the QBE grid for criteria purposes only, and you don't want the field to appear in the dynaset. You can exclude any field from the dynaset by deactivating the appropriate check box in the field's Show cell. For example, Figure 26.4 shows a query where I'm using the UnitsInStock field to look for out-of-stock items (that is, where UnitsInStock equals 0). However, I've already included all the table fields in the dynaset by adding the asterisk to the first column, so I exclude the extra UnitsInStock field by deactivating its Show check box.

FIGURE 26.4.

Deactivate a column's Show check box to prevent it from being displayed in the dynaset.

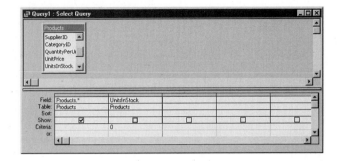

Running the Query

When you have your query set up the way you want, you can run it (that is, display the dynaset) either by selecting Query | Run or by clicking the Run toolbar button. Figure 26.5 displays the results of the query shown in Figure 26.4.

FIGURE 26.5.

The dynaset produced by the query shown in Figure 26.4.

Supplier	Category	Quantity Per Unit	Unit Price	Units In Stock
New Orleans Cajun Delights	Condiments	36 boxes	$21.35	0
Pavlova, Ltd.	Meat/Poultry	20 - 1 kg tins	$39.00	0
Plusspar Lebensmittelgroßmärkte AG	Meat/Poultry	50 bags x 30 sausgs	$123.79	0
Formaggi Fortini s.r.l.	Dairy Products	12 - 100 g pkgs	$12.50	0
G'day, Mate	Meat/Poultry	48 pieces	$32.80	0
				0

Record: 1 of 5

As you can see, the dynaset is really just a datasheet. You navigate and format it the same way (as explained in Chapter 25), and you can even edit the records and add new ones. (Any changes you make are automatically applied to the underlying table.) To return to the query design window, select View | Design View, or click the Design View button on the toolbar.

Understanding Query Criteria

The heart of any query is its criteria. This is a set of expressions that determine exactly the records that appear in the dynaset. In this section, you'll go beyond the simple criteria that you learned about in Chapter 25 and examine more complex examples that will let you unleash the full power of Access queries.

Entering Compound Criteria

For many criteria, a single expression just doesn't cut the mustard. For example, in the query shown in Figure 26.4, I selected all the records in the Products table with no inventory by adding the UnitsInStock field to the QBE grid and entering =0 in this field's Criteria cell.

That works, but what if you want to select only the out-of-stock products that haven't been reordered? For queries like these, you need to set up *compound criteria* where you enter either multiple expressions for the same field or multiple expressions for different fields. The next two sections cover the two basic types of multiple criteria: And criteria and Or criteria.

Entering And Criteria

You use And criteria when you want to select records that satisfy two or more different expressions. So given *expression1* and *expression2*, a record appears in the result only if it satisfies both *expression1* and *expression2* (which is why they're called And criteria).

Let's look at an example. Suppose you want to display all products with no inventory (UnitsInStock=0) *and* that haven't yet been reordered (UnitsOnOrder=0). In this case, you add both the UnitsInStock and UnitsOnOrder fields to the QBE grid, and enter =0 into the Criteria cells for each field, as shown in Figure 26.6.

FIGURE 26.6.

An example of an And *criterion.*

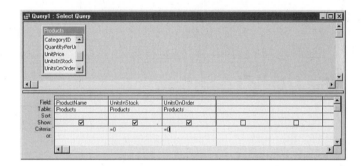

Entering Or Criteria

With Or criteria, you want to display records that satisfy one expression *or* another. If the record satisfies either expression (or both), it appears in the query results; if it satisfies neither expression, it's left out of the results. (Again, you're allowed to use more than two expressions if necessary. No matter how many expressions you use, a record appears in the query results only if it satisfies at least *one* of the expressions.)

Again, an example will help clarify things. Suppose you want to select those products where the inventory is greater than or equal to 100 (UnitsInStock>=100) *or* where the number of units on order is greater than or equal to 100 (UnitsOnOrder>=100). In this case, you add both the UnitsInStock and UnitsOnOrder fields to the QBE grid and enter the criteria expressions *on separate lines* in the QBE grid (that's why the "or" appears under Criteria in the grid). Figure 26.7 shows how you would set up such a query.

FIGURE 26.7.

To use Or *criterion for different fields, enter the expressions on separate lines in the QBE grid.*

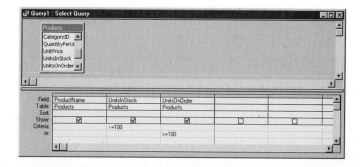

NOTE: OR CRITERIA IN A SINGLE FIELD

If necessary, you can set up Or criteria using a single field. For example, suppose you want to select those products with no inventory (UnitsInStock=0) or those products with over 100 units in stock (UnitsInStock>=100). To set this up, you'd add the UnitsInStock field to the QBE grid, enter =0 in the Criteria cell and enter >=100 in the or cell below it.

Building Criteria Expressions

The queries you've seen so far are simple filters that use literal values to select matching table records. To create more advanced queries, however, you have to go beyond literals and construct full-fledged *expressions* that combine operators, functions, and field names with literal values. Access uses the result of the expression to filter the table.

Most criteria expressions are logical formulas that, when applied to each record in the table, return either TRUE or FALSE. The dynaset contains only those records for which the expression returned TRUE. In fact, you can see that even criteria that use simple literal values are also expressions (albeit not very sophisticated ones). For example, suppose you have a Customer field in the QBE grid and you enter Barney's Beanery as the criterion. This is equivalent to the following logical formula:

```
Customer = "Barney's Beanery"
```

Access constructs the dynaset by applying this formula to each record in the table and selecting only those records for which it returns TRUE (that is, those records where the Customer field contains "Barney's Beanery").

Criteria Identifiers

In Access queries, an *identifier* is a field name from the query's underlying table, surrounded by square brackets. In the Products table, for example, you have a UnitsInStock field and a

ReorderLevel field. If you want to see all the records where the in-stock quantity is less than the reorder level, you'd add the UnitsInStock field to the QBE grid and enter <[ReorderLevel] as the criterion.

Using Operators in Criteria

Access has a few dozen different operators you can include in your expressions. The four types of operators—comparison, logical, arithmetic, and miscellaneous—are covered in the next few sections.

Comparison Operators

You use comparison operators to compare field values to a literal, a function result, or to a value in another field. Table 26.1 lists Access's comparison operators.

Table 26.1. Comparison operators for criteria expressions.

Operator	General Form	Description
=	= Value	Matches records where the field value is equal to Value.
<>	<> Value	Matches records where the field value is not equal to Value.
>	> Value	Matches records where the field value is greater than Value.
>=	>= Value	Matches records where the field value is greater than or equal to Value.
<	< Value	Matches records where the field value is less than Value.
<=	<= Value	Matches records where the field value is less than or equal to Value.

You'll mostly use operators on numeric or date fields, but you can also use them on text fields. For example, the expression < 'D' will match field values that begin with the letters A, B, or C.

Logical Operators

You use the logical operators to combine or modify TRUE/FALSE expressions. Table 26.2 summarizes Access's three logical operators.

Table 26.2. Logical operators for criteria expressions.

Operator	General Form	Description
And	*Expr1* And *Expr2*	Matches records where both *Expr1* and *Expr2* are TRUE.
Or	*Expr1* Or *Expr2*	Matches records where at least one of *Expr1* and *Expr2* are TRUE.
Not	Not *Expr*	Matches records where *Expr* is not TRUE.

The And and Or operators let you create compound criteria using a single expression. For example, suppose you want to match all the records in your Products table where the UnitsInStock field is either 0 or greater than or equal to 100. The following expression will do the job:

```
=0 Or >=100
```

The Not operator looks for records that *don't* match a particular logical expression. In a table of customer data, for example, if you want to find all non-North American customers, you'd add the Country field to the QBE grid and enter the following expression:

```
Not 'USA' And Not 'Canada' And Not 'Mexico'
```

Arithmetic Operators

You use the arithmetic operators shown in Table 26.3 to perform various math operations on a field. For example, suppose you have a sales history table with UnitSales1995 and UnitSales1996 fields. To find all the records where the unit sales in 1996 were at least 10 percent higher than those in 1995, you'd add the UnitSales1996 field to the QBE grid and enter the following expression:

```
>=[UnitSales1995]*1.1
```

Table 26.3. Arithmetic operators for criteria expressions.

Operator	General Form	Description
+	*Value1* + *Value2*	Adds *Value1* and *Value2*.
-	*Value1* - *Value2*	Subtracts *Value2* from *Value1*.
*	*Value1* * *Value2*	Multiplies *Value1* and *Value2*.
/	*Value1* / *Value2*	Divides *Value1* by *Value2*.

The Like Operator

If you need to allow for multiple spellings in a text field, or if you're not sure how to spell a word you want to use, the *wildcard characters* can help. There are two wildcards: The question mark (?) substitutes for a single character, and the asterisk (*) substitutes for a group of characters. You use them in combination with the `Like` operator, as shown in Table 26.4.

Table 26.4. The `Like` operator for criteria expressions.

Example	Matches Records Where the Field Value
`Like "Re?d"`	Matches records where the field value is `Reid`, `Read`, `reed`, and so on.
`Like "M?"`	Matches records where the field value is `MA`, `MD`, `ME`, and so on.
`Like "R*"`	Matches records where the field value begins with `R`.
`Like "*office*"`	Matches records where the field value contains the word `office`.
`Like "12/*/96"`	Matches records where the field value is any date in December, 1996.

The Between...And Operator

If you need to select records where a field value lies between two other values, use the `Between...And` operator. For example, suppose you want to see all the invoices where the invoice number is between (and includes) 123000 and 124000. Here's the expression you'd enter in the invoice number field's Criteria cell:

```
Between 123000 And 124000
```

You can use this operator for numbers, dates, and even text.

The In Operator

The `In` operator is a useful replacement for multiple `Or` criteria. For example, suppose you want to filter a table to show only those records where the Region field equals `NY`, `CA`, `TX`, `IN`, or `ME`. You *could* do this using several `Or` operators, like so:

```
'NY' Or 'CA' Or 'TX' Or 'IN' Or 'ME'
```

However, the following expression is more efficient:

```
In('NY','CA','TX','IN','ME')
```

The Is Null Operator

What do you do if you want to select records where a certain field is empty? For example, an invoice table might have a Date Paid field where, if this field is empty, it means the invoice hasn't been paid yet. For these challenges, Access provides the `Is Null` operator. Entering this operator by itself in a field's Criteria cell will select only those records where the field is empty.

To select records where a particular field is *not* empty, use the `Is Not Null` operator.

NOTE: THE EXPRESSION BUILDER

Instead of entering these complex criteria by hand, Access includes an Expression Builder that provides handy buttons for the various operators. To use the Expression Builder, either right-click the Criteria cell and click Build in the context menu, or click the Build button on the toolbar.

Using Calculations in Queries

Most queries simply display the raw data for the fields included in the QBE grid, probably filtered by some criteria. If you need to analyze the dynaset, however, you'll need to introduce calculations into your query. Access lets you set up two kinds of calculations:

A totals column: A column in the dynaset that uses one of several predefined *aggregate* functions for calculating a value (or values) based on the entries in a particular field. A totals column derives either a single value for the entire dynaset or several values for the grouped records in the dynaset.

A calculated column: A column in the dynaset where the "field" is an expression. The field values are derived using an expression based on one or more fields in the table.

Working with Totals Columns

The easiest way to analyze the data in a table is to use a totals column and one of the predefined *aggregate functions.* There are seven functions in all: Sum, Avg, Max, Min, Count, StDev, and Var. The idea is that you add a single field to the QBE grid and then convert that column into a totals column using one of these functions. Table 26.5 outlines the available functions you can use for your totals columns.

Table 26.5. Aggregate functions available for totals columns.

Total	Field Type	What It Calculates
Sum	Numeric only	The sum of the values in the field.
Avg	Numeric only	The average of the values in the field.
Min	All except Memo	The smallest value in the field.
Max	All except Memo	The largest value in the field.
Count	All	The number of values in the field.
StDev	Numeric only	The standard deviation of the values in the field.
Var	Numeric only	The variance of the values in the field.

Setting Up a Totals Column

The following steps are required to create a totals column:

1. Clear all columns from the QBE grid except the field you want to use for the calculation.

2. Either select View | Totals, or right-click the column and click Totals, or click the Totals button on the toolbar. Access adds a Total row to the QBE grid.

3. Select the field's Total cell and use the drop-down list to select the function you want to use. In Figure 26.8, for example, I've selected the Sum function on the UnitsInStock field.

FIGURE 26.8.

Use the Total cell to choose the aggregate function you want to use for the calculation.

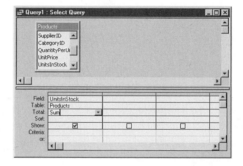

Figure 26.9 shows the result of the Sum calculation on the UnitsInStock field. As you can see, the dynaset consists of a single cell that shows the function result.

FIGURE 26.9.

The dynaset shows only the result of the calculation.

Creating a Totals Column for Groups of Records

In its basic guise, a totals column shows a total for all the records in a table. Suppose, however, that you'd prefer to see that total broken out into subtotals. For example, instead of a simple sum on the UnitsInStock field, how about seeing the sum of the orders grouped by category?

To group your totals, all you have to do is add the appropriate field to the QBE grid to the left of the column you're using for the calculation. For example, Figure 26.10 shows the QBE grid with the CategoryID field from the Products table to the left of the UnitsInStock field. Running this query produces the dynaset shown in Figure 26.11. As you can see, Access groups the entries in the Category column and displays a subtotal for each group.

FIGURE 26.10.

To group your totals, add the field used for the grouping to the left of the field used for the calculation.

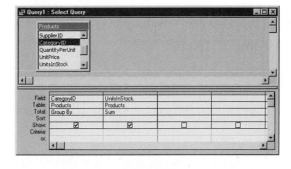

FIGURE 26.11.

Access uses the columns to the left of the totals column to set up its groupings.

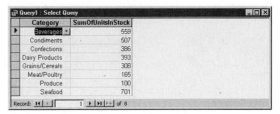

You can extend this technique to derive totals for more specific groups. For example, suppose you want to see subtotals for each supplier within the categories. All you'd have to do is add the SupplierID field to the QBE grid to the left of the UnitsInStock column, but to the right of the CategoryID column, as shown in Figure 26.12. Access creates the groups from left to right, so the records are first grouped by Category and then by Supplier. Figure 26.13 shows the dynaset.

FIGURE 26.12.

You can refine your groupings by adding more columns to the left of the totals column.

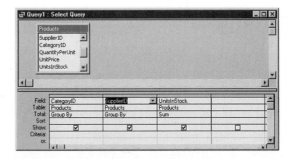

NOTE: COLUMN NAMES AND RELATED TABLES

You might be wondering why Access displays the Category and Supplier columns instead of CategoryID and SupplierID in the dynaset shown in Figure 26.13. That's because the Products table is related to two tables (among others): Categories and Suppliers. Access uses these relationships to display the category and supplier names instead of only the numbers in the CategoryID and SupplierID fields. You'll learn more about how this works in Chapter 29.

FIGURE 26.13.

The dynaset produced by the query in Figure 26.12.

Category	Supplier	SumOfUnitsInStock
Beverages	Exotic Liquids	56
Beverages	Pavlova, Ltd.	15
Beverages	Refrescos Americanas LTDA	20
Beverages	Plusspar Lebensmittelgroßmärkte AG	125
Beverages	Bigfoot Breweries	183
Beverages	Aux joyeux ecclésiastiques	86
Beverages	Leka Trading	17
Beverages	Karkki Oy	57
Condiments	Exotic Liquids	13
Condiments	New Orleans Cajun Delights	133
Condiments	Grandma Kelly's Homestead	126
Condiments	Mayumi's	39
Condiments	Pavlova, Ltd.	24

Record: 1 of 49

Setting Up a Calculated Column

The seven aggregate functions available for totals columns are handy, but they might not be what you need. If you'd like to create columns that use more sophisticated expressions, you'll need to set up a calculated column.

A calculated column is a dynaset column that gets its values from an expression instead of a field. The expression you use can be any combination of operator, identifier, and literal values, and there are even a few built-in functions you can use.

Building a calculated column is simple: Instead of specifying a field name when adding a column to the dynaset, you enter an expression. You type the expression directly into the column header in the QBE grid using the following general form:

```
ColumnName:expression
```

Here, `ColumnName` is the name you want to use for the calculated column and `expression` is the calculation. For example, the Products table contains both a UnitsInStock field and a UnitPrice field. The *inventory value* is simply the quantity in stock multiplied by the price of the product. You could set up a calculated column to show the inventory value by entering the following expression as the header of a new column in the QBE grid, as shown in Figure 26.14:

```
Inventory Value:[UnitsInStock]*[UnitPrice]
```

FIGURE 26.14.

A query set up with a calculated column.

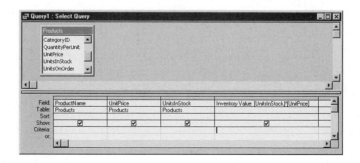

Figure 26.15 shows the result.

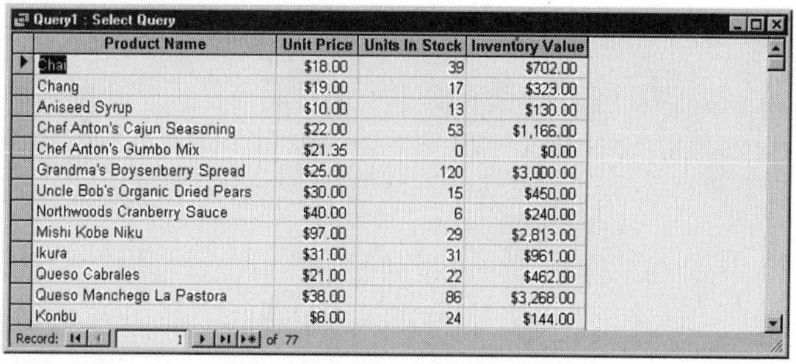

FIGURE 26.15.

A dynaset with a calculated column.

Product Name	Unit Price	Units In Stock	Inventory Value
Chai	$18.00	39	$702.00
Chang	$19.00	17	$323.00
Aniseed Syrup	$10.00	13	$130.00
Chef Anton's Cajun Seasoning	$22.00	53	$1,166.00
Chef Anton's Gumbo Mix	$21.35	0	$0.00
Grandma's Boysenberry Spread	$25.00	120	$3,000.00
Uncle Bob's Organic Dried Pears	$30.00	15	$450.00
Northwoods Cranberry Sauce	$40.00	6	$240.00
Mishi Kobe Niku	$97.00	29	$2,813.00
Ikura	$31.00	31	$961.00
Queso Cabrales	$21.00	22	$462.00
Queso Manchego La Pastora	$38.00	86	$3,268.00
Konbu	$6.00	24	$144.00

Record: |◄| ◄ | 1 | ► |►|| |►*| of 77

NOTE: FILTERING DATA WITH A CALCULATED COLUMN

Keep in mind that you can always use a calculated column for filtering the table. In other words, you can use the calculated column's Criteria cell to enter a criteria expression. For example, if you wanted to see those products where the inventory value is greater than $3,000, you'd enter >=3000 in the Criteria cell of the calculated column.

The preceding two chapters got you up to speed with this query rigmarole by showing you how to work with select queries. However, you'll be happy (or dismayed) to know that Access has more types of queries than you can shake a stick at. Some of these queries are close relatives of the select query, while others are, at best, distant cousins. This chapter covers a few of the more popular members of this extended query family.

Modifying Table Data with Update Queries

In Chapter 25, you learned how to use the Replace command to make global changes to a field. While this command often comes in handy, there are some jobs it simply can't handle. For example, what if you want to replace the contents of a field with a new value, but only for records that meet certain criteria? Or what if your table includes price data and you want to increase all the prices by five percent?

For these tasks, you need a more sophisticated tool: an *update query*. Unlike a select query, which only displays a subset of the table, an update query actually makes changes to the table data. The idea is that you select a field to work with, specify the new field value, set up some criteria (this is optional), and then run the query. Access flashes through the table and changes the field entries to the new value. If you enter criteria, only records that match the criteria are updated. (Queries that make changes to a table are called *action queries*.)

To create an update query, first create a select query that includes the field (or fields) you want to update and the field (or fields) you'll need for the criteria. (Remember, criteria are optional for an update query. If you leave them out, Access will update every record in the table.) When the select query is complete, run it to make sure the criteria are working properly.

To convert the query to an update query, use one of the following methods:

- Select Query | Update Query.
- Right-click an empty part of the table pane or QBE grid and select Query Type | Update Query from the context menu.

- Use the Query Type drop-down list on the toolbar to select Update Query.

Access changes the query window's title bar to Update Query and replaces the QBE grid's Sort and Show rows with an Update To row. Select the Update To cell for the field you want to change and enter the new value. When you run the query, Access displays a dialog box to tell you how many rows (records) will be updated. Click Yes to perform the update.

After you see what update queries can do, you'll wonder how you ever got along without them. For example, one common table chore is changing prices and, in a large table, it's a drudgery most of us can live without. However, if you're increasing prices by a certain percentage, you can automate the whole process with an update query. For example, suppose you want to increase each value in a UnitPrice field by five percent. To handle this in an update query, you'd add the UnitPrice field to the QBE grid and then enter the following expression in the Update To cell:

`[UnitPrice]*1.05`

Enclosing UnitPrice in square brackets ([ ]) tells Access you're dealing with the UnitPrice field. So multiplying this by 1.05 signifies that you want every UnitPrice field entry increased by five percent. You can also, of course, set up criteria to gain even more control over the update. Figure 26.16 shows an update query that raises the UnitPrice field by five percent, but only for those records where the CategoryID field is 1.

FIGURE 26.16.

An update query with criteria.

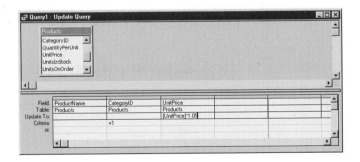

Removing Records from a Table with Delete Queries

If you need to delete one or two records from a table, it's easy enough just to select each record and select Edit | Delete Record (as explained in the Chapter 25). But what if you have a large chunk of records to get rid of? For example, if you sell your prized collection of 8-track tapes, you'll want to delete all the 8-track records from your music database. Similarly, you might want to clean out an Orders table by deleting any old orders that were placed before a certain date. In both examples, you can set up criteria to identify the group of records to delete. You then enter the criteria in a delete query and Access will delete all the matching records.

Before setting up the delete query, you need to create a select query with the following fields:

- The asterisk "field" (the asterisk represents the entire table).
- Any field you need for your deletion criteria.

Enter the criteria and then run the select query to make sure the query is picking out the correct records. If things look okay, you're ready to create the delete query. Return to the query design window, and then use any of the following methods:

- Select Query | Delete Query.
- Right-click an empty part of the table pane or QBE grid and select Query Type | Delete Query from the context menu.

- Use the Query Type drop-down list on the toolbar to select Delete Query.

The title bar changes to Delete Query and Access replaces the Sort and Show lines with a Delete line. The asterisk field will display From in the Delete cell, and each criteria field will display Where in the Delete cell. Figure 26.17 shows a delete query for the Products table that will remove all the records where the Discontinued field contains Yes.

FIGURE 26.17.

A delete query uses the asterisk field and any fields you need for your criteria.

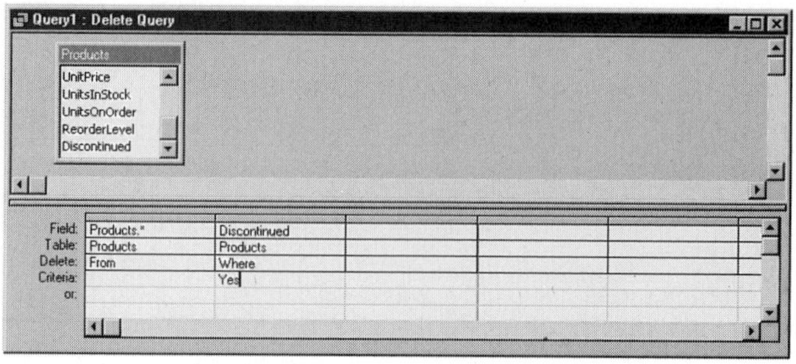

CAUTION: TRY THE SELECT QUERY FIRST

Always make sure you try out the select query before you even think about moving on to the deletion. The records you'll be deleting will be gone for good, and no amount of huffing and puffing will bring them back. Running the select query is an easy way to prevent you from wiping out anything important.

When you run the query, Access analyzes the criteria and then displays a dialog box telling you how many records you'll be deleting. If the number seems reasonable, click Yes to proceed.

Creating New Tables with Make-Table Queries

As I explained earlier, the results of select queries are called *dynasets* because they're dynamic subsets of the table data. When I say "dynamic," I mean that if you edit the query records, the corresponding records in the table also change. Similarly, if you edit the table, Access changes the query records automatically.

This is usually welcome behavior because at least you know you're always working with the most up-to-date information. However, there might be the odd time when this isn't the behavior you want. For example, at the end of the month or the end of the fiscal year, you might want some of your tables to be "frozen" while you tie things up for month- or year-end (this would apply particularly to tables that track invoices).

Instead of letting the new work pile up until the table can be released, Access lets you create a table from an existing one. You could then use the new table for your month-end duties, so the old table doesn't need to be held up. You do this using a *make-table* query.

As usual, you begin by creating a select query that includes the fields you want for the new table as well as any criteria you need. (Be sure to run the select query to make sure the fields and records displayed are the ones you want.) Then use one of the following methods to convert the select query into a make-table query:

- Select Query | Make-Table Query.
- Right-click an empty part of the table pane or QBE grid and select Query Type | Make-Table Query from the context menu.
- Use the Query Type drop-down list on the toolbar to select Make-Table Query.

Access displays the Make Table dialog box, shown in Figure 26.18. Use the Table Name text box to enter the name you want to use for the new table, and then select either Current Database or Another Database (for the latter, enter the filename of the database in the text box provided). When you're ready, click OK.

FIGURE 26.18.

Use the Make Table dialog box to define your new table.

When you run the query, Access displays a dialog box to let you know how many records will be pasted into the new table. Click Yes to create the new table.

Adding Records to a Table with an Append Query

Instead of creating an entirely new table, you might prefer to add records from one table to an existing table. You can accomplish this with an *append query*.

Begin by creating a select query that includes the fields you want for the new table as well as any criteria you need. Run the select query to make sure the fields and records displayed are the ones you want. Now use one of the following techniques to convert the select query into an append query:

- Select Query | Append Query.
- Right-click an empty part of the table pane or QBE grid and select Query Type | Append Query from the context menu.

- Use the Query Type drop-down list on the toolbar to select Append Query.

Access displays the Append dialog box (which is identical to the Make Table dialog box shown in Figure 26.18). Use the Table Name text box to enter the name of the table to which you want the records appended, and then select either Current Database or Another Database (for the latter, enter the filename of the database in the text box provided). When you're ready, click OK. Access adds an Append To row to the QBE grid. For each field in the QBE grid, use the Append To cell to choose the field in the other table to use for the append operation. (If you add the asterisk field, Append To will show the name of the other table. In this case, if you add other fields for criteria purposes, make sure these fields have their Append To cells blank.)

When you run the query Access displays a dialog box to let you know how many records will be added into the new table. Click Yes to append the record.

Query Wizard Queries

With the Query Wizards, you have access to three other types of queries, and you don't have to mess around with the QBE grid. The Query Wizards let you create each query in the usual step-by-step wizard method that you've come to know and love.

You begin by creating a new query object. In the New Query dialog box that appears, select either Crosstab Query Wizard, Find Duplicated Query Wizard, or Find Unmatched Query Wizard, and then click OK. You can then follow the instructions in each Wizard dialog box to create your query. The next three sections describe each of the Query Wizard types.

Crosstab Queries

Crosstab queries take large amounts of complex data and summarize some or all of the information into a handy row-and-column format. For example, consider the Sales Promotion Orders table shown in Figure 26.19. (This table was imported from the Excel workbook named Pivot Tables.xls on this book's CD. I'll show you how to import Excel data into Access in Chapter 50, "Working with the Office Integration Tools.") This table lists orders taken during a sales promotion. The customer could select any one of four products (copy holder, glare filter, mouse pad, printer stand) and two promotions (1 Free with 10, Extra Discount).

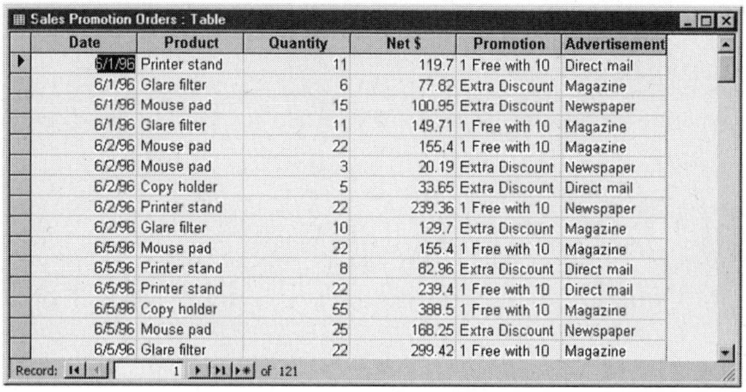

Sales Promotion Orders : Table

Date	Product	Quantity	Net $	Promotion	Advertisement
6/1/96	Printer stand	11	119.7	1 Free with 10	Direct mail
6/1/96	Glare filter	6	77.82	Extra Discount	Magazine
6/1/96	Mouse pad	15	100.95	Extra Discount	Newspaper
6/1/96	Glare filter	11	149.71	1 Free with 10	Magazine
6/2/96	Mouse pad	22	155.4	1 Free with 10	Magazine
6/2/96	Mouse pad	3	20.19	Extra Discount	Newspaper
6/2/96	Copy holder	5	33.65	Extra Discount	Direct mail
6/2/96	Printer stand	22	239.36	1 Free with 10	Newspaper
6/2/96	Glare filter	10	129.7	Extra Discount	Magazine
6/5/96	Mouse pad	22	155.4	1 Free with 10	Magazine
6/5/96	Printer stand	8	82.96	Extra Discount	Direct mail
6/5/96	Printer stand	22	239.4	1 Free with 10	Direct mail
6/5/96	Copy holder	55	388.5	1 Free with 10	Magazine
6/5/96	Mouse pad	25	168.25	Extra Discount	Newspaper
6/5/96	Glare filter	22	299.42	1 Free with 10	Magazine

Record: 1 of 121

FIGURE 26.19.
A table of orders taken during a promotion.

A basic analysis of this table would be to calculate how many of each product were ordered for each promotion. With so many orders, this would be a nightmare to figure out by hand, but a crosstab query like the one shown in Figure 26.20 does the job nicely. In this case, Access took the four unique entries in the Product field and used them as entries in the leftmost column, and it took the two unique entries in the Promotion field and used them as headings for the other columns. It then summed the appropriate Quantity field values and summarized everything in a nice, neat package.

The Crosstab Query Wizard asks you to pick a table and then do the following:

- Select a field whose unique entries will appear in the leftmost column of the query.
- Select a field whose unique entries will appear as the headings for the other columns in the query.
- Select a field to use for the calculations and the type of calculation to use (for example, Sum or Count).
- Assign a name to the query.

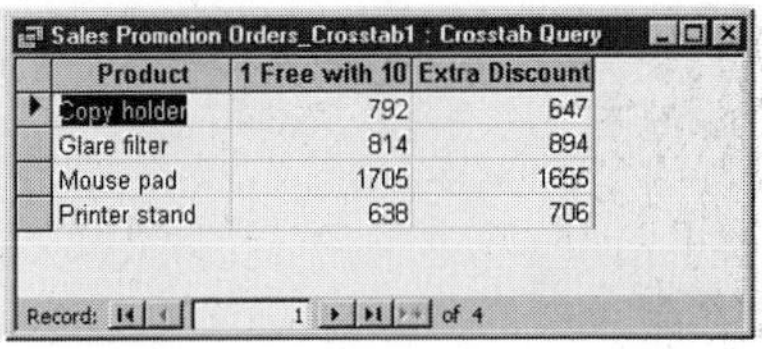
Sales Promotion Orders_Crosstab1 : Crosstab Query

Product	1 Free with 10	Extra Discount
Copy holder	792	647
Glare filter	814	894
Mouse pad	1705	1655
Printer stand	638	706

Record: 1 of 4

FIGURE 26.20.
The table data presented as a crosstab query.

Find Duplicates Queries

If you're concerned about having duplicate records in a table, a Find Duplicates query will scope them out for you. This query displays a list of a table's duplicate entries (if it has any). You can then use this information to return to the table and either edit or delete one or more records to remove the duplication.

After you select the table you want to use, the Find Duplicates Query Wizard then takes you through the following tasks:

- Selecting one or more fields that may contain duplicate information (you can select up to 10 fields).
- Selecting any other fields you want to see in the query.
- Naming the query.

Find Unmatched Queries

The Find Unmatched Query Wizard lets you find records in one table that have no matching entries in another. For example, suppose you have a Products table (with a ProductID field) and an Orders table (also with a ProductID field). This Wizard can examine both tables and, using the common ProductID field as a guide, tell you if any records in the Products table have no matching records in the Orders table. In other words, it gives you a list of the products that haven't been ordered.

When you start this Wizard, it asks you to select the table you want to see in the query results. In the example just mentioned, you'd select the Products table. The next step is to select the table that contains the related records (this would be the Orders table in the example). You then have to do the following:

- Select the fields in each table that contain the matching information (ProductID).
- Select the fields you want to see in the query.
- Enter a name for the query.

Summary

This chapter took you on a tour of Access queries, beginning with the steps involved for creating a query. You then learned all about query criteria, including compound criteria, expressions, and operators. I then showed you how to use calculations in your criteria, including setting up totals columns and calculated criteria. This chapter finished with a look at various query types, including update, delete, make-table, and append queries, as well as a few Query Wizard queries.

Here's a list of chapters where you'll find related information:

■ The query's dynaset is displayed in a datasheet. To learn how to work with Access datasheets, see Chapter 25, "Working with Tables."

■ You can use query results as the basis for a report. I'll show you how to create reports in Chapter 28, "Designing and Customizing Reports."

■ If you have related tables, you might need to work with multiple tables in your queries. To learn how, see Chapter 29, "Juggling Multiple Tables."

■ I discuss various query customization options in Chapter 31, "Customizing Access."

Creating and Using Simple Forms

IN THIS CHAPTER

Form and function are a unity, two sides of one coin. In order to enhance function,
appropriate form must exist or be created.

—Ida P. Rolf

Data entry is the unglamorous side of Access. Sure, entering a record or two isn't so bad, but entering dozens of records quickly becomes a chore you'd do anything to avoid. The datasheet techniques presented in Chapter 25, "Working with Tables," can help, but the datasheet isn't the most attractive way to get information into a table. You can take some of the drudgery out of data entry by using *forms.*

In the real world, we deal with forms of various descriptions all the time—application forms, registration forms, license renewals, deposit slips, traffic tickets (one of my specialties, unfortunately). It's a rare day that goes by without some officious person tossing a form our way and telling us to fill it out in triplicate.

Paper forms, then, are documents with blank boxes that you use to fill in the required information. Each box usually has a label beside it to let you know what kind of information to enter. Access *forms* are basically the same as their paper counterparts. As you can see in Figure 27.1, a form is a window that displays, for each field in the table, a text box, drop-down list, check box, or other control.

FIGURE 27.1.

An example of an
Access form.

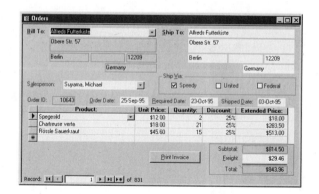

Forms bring a number of advantages to the data entry table:

■ Since the form shows only one record at a time, you can see all the table fields at once (unless your table has a large number of fields). In contrast, you can usually see only four or five columns at a time in a datasheet.

■ Controls such as drop-down lists reduce the possibility of data-entry errors by giving the user a limited set of choices for a field.

■ Access gives you a number of customization options. This lets you create Access forms that look exactly like paper forms, and you can add graphics and other objects to make the forms more interesting.

■ You aren't distracted by other data in the table, so you can give your full attention to the task at hand.

This chapter shows you not only how to create a form, but also how to customize it to your liking.

Creating a Form with AutoForm

By far the easiest way to create a form is to use the AutoForm feature. It lets you create quick-and-dirty data entry forms with just a few clicks of the mouse. AutoForms—which you can use only on existing tables or queries—are fast and ask no questions. Access gives you a number of ways to work with AutoForm (and, as you'll see, the method you use determines the form layout you get):

■ You can create an AutoForm directly from the Tables or Queries tabs.

■ You can run one of the AutoForm Wizards.

■ You can display the form design window and choose an AutoFormat from there.

Running AutoForm Directly on a Table or Query

If all you want is a basic no-muss, no-fuss form, run the AutoForm feature directly from the Tables or Queries tabs. Specifically, highlight the table or query you want to use as the basis for the form, and then use either of the following techniques:

■ Select Insert | AutoForm.

■ Drop down the New Object button on the toolbar and choose AutoForm.

Access analyzes the selected table or query and then creates a simple form like the one shown in Figure 27.2. As you can see, the resulting form uses a columnar layout that shows the name of each field and provides a text box for the data. (Yes/No fields get a check box instead.)

FIGURE 27.2.

A basic form created with AutoForm.

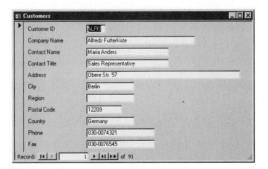

Running an AutoForm Wizard

For more control over the form layout and extra formatting, Access has three AutoForm Wizards that you can use. To try them, use any of the following methods:

- Highlight a table or query (this is optional) and select Insert | Form.
- Highlight a table or query (again, this is optional), drop down the New Object button on the toolbar, and select Form.
- Activate the Forms tab and click New.

Access displays the New Form dialog box, shown in Figure 27.3. Highlight one of the AutoForm Wizards:

AutoForm: Columnar: This wizard creates a form with a columnar layout similar to the one shown in Figure 27.2.

AutoForm: Tabular: This wizard creates a form with a tabular layout that shows the field names at the top and the records in rows.

AutoForm: Datasheet: This wizard creates a form with a datasheet layout.

FIGURE 27.3.

Use this dialog box to choose which of the AutoForm Wizards you want to run.

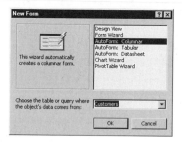

Use the drop-down list to select a table or query to use for the underlying data, and then click OK. Without further ado, the AutoForm Wizard constructs the form. As you can see in Figure 27.4, the forms created by these wizards also include some formatting. (The formatting you see might be different from that shown in Figure 27.4. I'll show you how to change this formatting in the next section.)

FIGURE 27.4.

The AutoForm Wizards create forms that have various formatting frills.

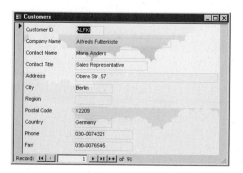

Assigning an AutoFormat in Design View

The AutoForm feature actually has 10 different predefined form layouts (called *AutoFormats*). The AutoForm Wizards always apply the default format. To choose another, you need to enter the form design window:

- If you're starting a new form, highlight Design View in the New Form dialog box, select the table or query, and click OK.

- If your form is already on-screen, either select View | Design View or click the Design View button on the toolbar.

From here, select Format | AutoFormat to display the AutoFormat dialog box, shown in Figure 27.5. The Form AutoFormats control contains a list of the available layouts. Highlight the one you want and click OK. Note that the default layout used by the AutoForm Wizards is always the *last* AutoFormat that you selected in this dialog box.

FIGURE 27.5.

Use this dialog box to select the AutoFormat you want to use.

Note, too, that you can customize these AutoFormats to suit your taste. If you click the Customize button in the AutoFormat dialog box, Access displays another dialog box that lets you perform one of three actions:

- Create a new AutoFormat template based on the formatting used in the current form.

- Change the current AutoFormat template based on the formatting used in the current form.

- Delete the current AutoFormat template.

Creating Simple Forms with the Form Wizard

The AutoForm feature is a fast way to create a form, but it suffers from a lack of interaction. In other words, you have no way of specifying the fields you want to see or the formatting style you want to use. For more control over your forms, you need to use the Form Wizard. The Form Wizard is more like a traditional Office wizard: It displays a series of dialog boxes that take you step-by-step through the entire form-creation process.

27

CREATING AND
USING SIMPLE
FORMS

To access the Form Wizard, start a new form as described earlier. In the New Form dialog box, highlight the Form Wizard item, select a table or query (this is optional), and click OK.

In the first of the Wizard's dialog boxes, shown in Figure 27.6, use the Table/Queries list to choose the underlying data source for the form (if you haven't done so already). Then, for each field you want to include in the form, highlight the field in the Available Fields list and click the > button. (If you want to select all the fields, click the >> button.) When you're done, click Next >.

FIGURE 27.6.

Use this Form Wizard dialog box to select the table or query and the fields you want to use.

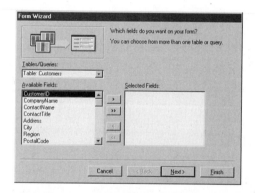

The next Form Wizard dialog box, shown in Figure 27.7, asks you to choose the layout of the fields. You have four choices:

> **Columnar:** The fields are arranged in columns, and only one record is shown at a time.
>
> **Tabular:** The fields are arranged in a table, with the field names at the top and the records in rows.

Datasheet: The fields are arranged in a datasheet layout.

Justified: The fields are arranged across and down the form with the field names above their respective controls.

Choose the layout option you want and click OK.

FIGURE 27.7.

Use this Wizard dialog box to choose the form layout.

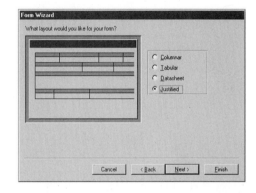

The next Wizard dialog box, shown in Figure 27.8, asks you to select one of the predefined AutoForm templates. Highlight the template you want to use and click OK.

FIGURE 27.8.

Use this dialog box to choose an AutoForm template.

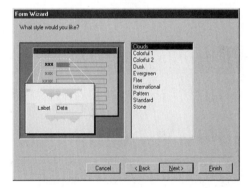

The fourth and last Wizard dialog box, shown in Figure 27.9, lets you modify the name of the form. A suggestion is already in place in the What title do you want for your form? text box; it's based on the name of the underlying table or query. This dialog box also lets you open the form to enter data or to modify the form's design. When you've made your choice, click Finish to complete the form.

FIGURE 27.9.

The last of the Form Wizard's dialog boxes.

This is the end of the Form Wizard. You can create a sophisticated and professional data entry form in a fraction of the time that it would take to create it from scratch. It isn't as fast as an AutoForm Wizard, but it does allow more flexibility in the customization.

Creating a Form in Design View

Although the Form Wizard is a step up from AutoForm in terms of control, the resulting forms still might not satisfy your needs. For example, you might want to build a custom form that mirrors as closely as possible an equivalent paper form. If the Access form resembles the paper form, the person using the form to enter data will feel more comfortable with it and will be less likely to make mistakes.

For maximum form flexibility, you need to use the form design window. How much flexibility do you have in customizing your forms? Well, let's just say that I could probably write an entire book that deals only with Access's customization options. Unfortunately, I have only a chapter, so I'll just cover the basics.

Displaying Design View

Access forms have a *design view* that you can use for your customization chores. How you display this view depends on whether you're dealing with an existing form or a new one.

For an existing form, highlight it in the Forms tab and then click the Design button. If the form is already open, either select View | Design View or click the Design View button on the toolbar.

For a new form, try one of these techniques:

- Highlight a table or query (this is optional) and select Insert | Form.

- Highlight a table or query (again, this is optional), drop down the New Object button on the toolbar, and click Form.

- Activate the Forms tab and click New.

In the New Form dialog box, highlight Design View, select a table or query, and click OK. You'll see a window similar to the one shown in Figure 27.10.

FIGURE 27.10.

The form design view.

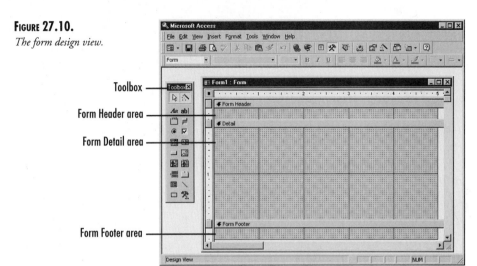

Toolbox

Form Header area

Form Detail area

Form Footer area

A Tour of the Design View Window

Here's a quick overview of the design view screen:

Toolbox: This is a floating toolbar that contains buttons representing the objects you can place inside the form (such as labels and text boxes). If you don't see the toolbox on your screen, either activate View | Toolbox or click the Toolbox button on the toolbar.

Form Header: This is the top part of the form. You can use this area to enter a title for the form. To display this area (and the Form Footer), activate View | Form Header/Footer.

Detail: This area takes up the bulk of the form window. It's where you place the table's fields and their labels.

Form Footer: This is the bottom part of the form. You can use this area for instructions on how to fill out the form, page number data, or whatever.

Adding Controls to a Form

To add a control to a form, click the toolbox button for the desired control. The button will change to its pressed state. Move the mouse pointer onto the form, press and hold down the left mouse button where you want the control located, and then drag the mouse to size the control. You can also simply click the form, and the control will be added using a default size.

If you want to add several controls of the same type to a form, you can "lock down" the toolbox button by double-clicking it. This allows you to add several labels to the form without having to reselect the label tool each time. To release the lock, either click the button again or press the Esc key.

To make a copy of a selected control (or group of selected controls), select Edit | Duplicate. Access will create a duplicate of the selected control(s) directly below the selected control(s).

Types of Controls

An Access form can contain one of three types of controls: bound, unbound, and calculated. This section discusses the differences between these types.

Unbound Controls

An unbound control is used to convey information to the user or to receive from the user input that won't be stored in the database. Here are some examples of using unbound controls:

- A label for a text box is used to describe what the text box represents.
- Text boxes or drop-down list boxes can be used to select different scenarios on a what-if form.
- A line can be placed on a form to separate different sections of the form.
- A company logo can be placed on the form to add graphical effects.

When a control is added using the toolbox and no Control Wizard is activated, the control will automatically be unbound.

Bound Controls

Bound controls are used to display and edit data from the database. The term "bound" refers to the fact that the control is tied to a field of a table, query, or SQL SELECT statement. The most common type of bound control is the text box, but nearly any control can be a bound control (with the exception of lines, rectangles, page breaks, command buttons, image frames, and labels).

A bound control will inherit many of the formatting and text properties defined for the field to which it is bound (for example, Caption, Description, Input Mask, and Default Value). These properties can be changed on the form using the control's property sheet.

NOTE: CONTROL PROPERTY SHEET TECHNIQUES

To display the property sheet for a control, use any of the following techniques:

■ Click the control and then select View | Properties.

■ Right-click the control and select Properties from the context menu.

■ Click the control and then click the Properties button on the toolbar.

To add a bound control to the form, first display the field list using either of the following methods:

■ Activate View | Field List.

■ Click the Field List button on the toolbar.

Figure 27.11 shows the field list for the Customers table.

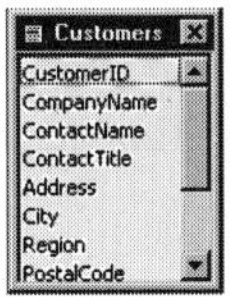

FIGURE 27.11.

The field list for the Customers table.

Follow these steps to add a bound control:

1. Select a single field, a group of fields (by holding down the Ctrl key to select sequential fields or holding down the Shift key to select multiple fields that aren't sequential), or all fields (by double-clicking the title bar of the Field List window).

2. Drag the mouse pointer from the field list to the form. The cursor will change to a small box (or a group of boxes if more than one field is selected). Place the upper-left corner of the box where the upper-left corner of the first bound control should be placed.

3. The control(s) will be placed on the form, and a label will be placed to the left of each control. The text of the label will be the `Caption` property for the field to which the control is bound.

27

CREATING AND
USING SIMPLE
FORMS

You can also change an unbound control to a bound control using the control's Control Source property. Doing so, however, won't cause the control to inherit many of the field's properties (except for ValidationRule, ValidationText, and DefaultValue, which are always enforced for the field).

Calculated Controls

Calculated controls use expressions to derive their data. Expressions are combinations of operators, fields, control names, functions, and constants. Although text boxes are the most common form of calculated controls, any control having the Control Source property can be a calculated control. A calculated control can be used to compute sales tax on an order entry form, for example.

All expressions must begin with an equals sign. An example expression is

=[States]![SalesTaxRate]*[OrderForm]![OrderTotal]

The [States]![SalesTaxRate] part refers to a table of states where one of the fields is SalesTaxRate. The [OrderForm]![OrderTotal] part refers to the control named OrderTotal on the form named OrderForm (probably the current form).

To create a calculated control while in Design view, follow these steps:

1. From the toolbox, select the type of control to be used and position the control on the form (see the section "Adding Controls to a Form").

2. Enter the expression using one of the following methods:

   ■ If the control is a text box, the expression can be entered directly into the control. Click inside the text box portion until the blinking edit cursor is visible. Type the expression into the edit box.

   ■ If the control isn't a text box, or if you don't want to enter the expression directly, double-click the control to open its property sheet. Move to the Control Source property. Here you can enter the expression as text or use the Expression Builder (click the Build button to the right of the ControlSource text box).

TIP: ZOOM IN ON THE CONTROL SOURCE

If you're typing in the Control Source property and need a larger text box, Access provides a Zoom box, which you can activate by pressing Shift-F2.

Of Combo Boxes and List Boxes

Combo boxes and list boxes can make data entry easier and more accurate. Furthermore, if the Control Wizard feature is enabled (that is, the Control Wizard button in the toolbox is pressed), adding one of these controls to a form will cause the Control Wizard to activate, making it easy for you to include these controls in your forms.

The Combo Box and List Box Wizards let you easily bind a combo box or list box to either a list of values or to the field items in another table or query in the database. For example, suppose you're building a form for the Customers table. This table includes a field for the title of the contact person. Rather than having the user type in the titles by hand, you could use a list box or combo box to give him a predefined list of possible titles (Owner, Sales Representative, Marketing Manager, and so on). Let's see how you'd set this up.

First, make sure that the toolbox is visible and that the Control Wizard feature is enabled. Click either the Combo Box button or the List Box button on the toolbox, and then draw the control on the form. When you're done, you'll either see the Combo Box Wizard or the List Box Wizard. (I'll discuss the Combo Box Wizard here, but the two Wizards use the same dialog boxes.)

27

CREATING AND
USING SIMPLE
FORMS

NOTE: COMBO BOX VERSUS LIST BOX

How do you decide between a combo box and a list box? Well, recall that a combo box is a combination of a list box and a text box, so the user can either choose a value from the list or enter a new value in the text box. If you don't want the user to enter values other than those that are part of the list, use a list box. If you want to give the user the flexibility to add new items to the field, use a combo box.

CAUTION: CONTROL WIZARD LIMITATIONS

The Control Wizard won't be activated when you're creating a duplicate. Also, any code associated with a control won't be copied to the new control.

The first Wizard dialog box, shown in Figure 27.12, gives you three options that determine how the combo box relates to the underlying table:

> **I want the combo box to look up the values in a table or query:** Activate this option if you want Access to get the list items from a field in another data source. I'll explain how this option works in Chapter 29.

> **I will type in the values that I want:** Activate this option to specify the values that will appear in the list. This is the option we'll choose for our example.

Find a record on my form based on the value I selected in my combo box:
Activate this option to allow the user to select a record from the underlying table by
entering a value into the combo box.

Click Next > to continue.

FIGURE 27.12.

*This dialog box
determines where the
list box gets its values.*

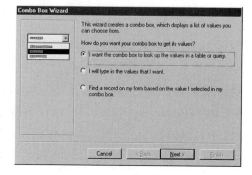

If you chose to derive the combo box values from a table or query, the Wizard will display
three dialog boxes from which you can choose the list values:

1. In the first of these dialog boxes, highlight the table or query you want to use, and
   then click Next >.

2. In the second dialog box, choose the field or fields whose unique values you want to
   use, and then click Next >.

3. Use the next dialog box to adjust the width of the combo box column, as shown in
   Figure 27.13.

FIGURE 27.13.

*Use this Wizard dialog
box to enter the list
items.*

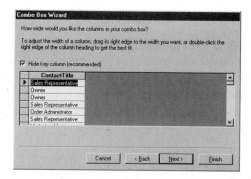

If instead you chose to enter the combo box values by hand, you'll see the Wizard dialog box
shown in Figure 27.14. It presents a small datasheet into which you enter the values you want
to appear in the list. You can also adjust the width of the column. When you're done, click
Next >.

FIGURE 27.14.

Use this Wizard dialog box to enter the list items.

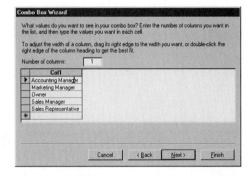

Figure 27.15 shows the next Wizard dialog box. Here, the Wizard wants to know what you'd like Access to do with the value selected in the list box. In this case, activate the Store that value in this field option and then select the appropriate field (ContactTitle in this example) from the drop-down list provided. Click Next > to continue. The final dialog box asks for a name for the field. Enter the name you want to use, and then click Finish.

FIGURE 27.15.

Use this dialog box to choose the field that will store the selected value.

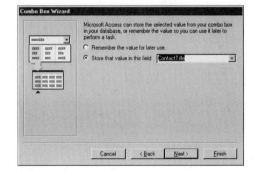

Navigation in a Form

Navigation in a form refers not just to the fields that appear on the form but also to the records within the form. When you're working on a form, you can navigate the form using several different methods. The first is to use the Enter key. The Enter key accepts the data that the user entered into the field and moves the focus to the next field. The Tab key performs the same action, but the user doesn't need to enter any data. If hot keys are associated with buttons on the form, the user can hold down the Alt key and press the corresponding underlined letter.

TIP: ASSIGNING A HOT KEY TO A FIELD

To assign a hot key to a field, edit the field's label and place an ampersand (&) before the appropriate letter. For example, to make the C in Customer the hot key, you'd edit the label to read &Customer.

NOTE: CHANGING THE TAB ORDER

The tab order of the form can affect the way the Tab key and the Enter key move the user around the form. To change the tab order, select View | Tab Order when the form is in Design view.

You can move from record to record by moving to the last field on the current form and pressing Enter. This action will bring you to the first field on the next record. However, this won't work with the Tab key. If you're on the last field on the form and you press the Tab key, the focus is moved back to the first field on the same record. It loops you around all the fields on the same record. You can also use the Page Up and Page Down keys to move to the next sequential record. If you hold down the Ctrl key and press Home or End, you will move to the first and last record in the dataset, respectively.

You can choose to turn on a form's navigation buttons. `Navigation Buttons` is a property that appears on the form's properties sheet, as you can see in Figure 27.16. (To display the form's properties sheet, choose Edit | Select Form (or press Ctrl-R) and then choose View | Properties.)

FIGURE 27.16.

`Navigation Buttons` *is a property of the form.*

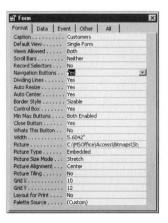

These buttons give you a graphical way of moving around the records. When this feature is turned on, the familiar datasheet navigation buttons appear in the bottom-left corner of the form. (I explained these buttons in Chapter 25.)

Editing Data on a Form

Editing data on a form actually means that you can add, edit, or delete information in individual fields or information on entire records. You can control what the user can do when a form is opened. In Figure 27.17, you see several new properties that give you more flexibility when it comes to allowing users to edit data.

FIGURE 27.17.

A few new properties give the developer more control of editing data.

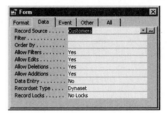

Six properties pertain to the editing of data. They are `Allow Edits`, `Allow Deletions`, `Allow Additions`, `Data Entry`, `Recordset Type`, and `Record Locks`:

- `Allow Edits` is either Yes or No. It lets the user save records when using the form. When turned off (No), it prevents the changing of any of the data displayed by the form.

- `Allow Deletions` is either Yes or No. When this property is set to No, the user can view and edit existing data but can't delete any records. When this is set to Yes, the user can delete records, provided that the referential integrity rules aren't broken.

- `Allow Additions` is either Yes or No. When this is turned on (Yes), the user can add a record to the form. When it is set to No, the user can't add records. The Add Record button in the Navigation Button group is not activated.

- `Data Entry` is set to either Yes or No. This is different from `Allow Additions` in that when this feature is turned on, the form automatically opens to a new, blank record. The user doesn't have the capability to view existing records. Errors will occur if `Allow Additions` is set to No and `Data Entry` is set to Yes. When this feature is set to Yes, the form must have a record source.

- `Recordset Type` can only be set to Dynaset, Dynaset (Inconsistent Updates), or Snapshot. It deals with the multiple tables and their fields being bound to controls on the form. The bound controls can be edited if the `Recordset Type` is set to Dynaset. Snapshot doesn't let the user edit the bound controls. This property is similar to the `AllowUpdating` property in Access 2.0.

■ Record Locks deals with the multiuser application environment. It can only be set to No Locks, All Records, or Edited Record. No Locks means that two or more people can edit the same record. He who saves first wins. All others will get a message stating that the record has been changed. The only option from there is to either dump the changes, overwrite the changes of the person who saved the record first, or copy a version of the changes to the Clipboard and view the saved changes. The Edited Records option allows the user to edit a record while locking out the other users. Depending on the size of the record, Access might also lock down other records stored around the edited record. This prevents other users from editing records that aren't being used by any other user. The All Records option locks all the records in the form and their underlying tables. Only one person at a time is allowed to edit any records on the form.

Using a Form to Open a Form

Although there are a number of ways to open a form, you might not want all of them available to novice users. For example, you might not want users to have access to the Forms tab just in case they accidentally make changes to a form's layout. As an alternative, you can create a separate form that launches other forms.

When forms are opened from other forms, a button usually launches them. A common example of one form being used to launch other forms is a main menu. Main menus may have several different buttons that launch several different forms. The toolbox has a tool called the Command Button. This tool, when coupled with the handy Command Button Wizard, helps developers through the process of setting up a button to launch another form.

TIP: ACTIVATE THE CONTROL WIZARD BUTTON

The Control Wizard button that appears in the upper-right corner of the toolbox must be activated in order for the Command Button Wizard to run. Click the Control Wizard button first and then create the command button.

Click the Command Button tool and then move to the form and drag a small square to the desired size. As soon as the box is drawn, the Command Button Wizard is launched. A button on a form can perform several different actions, as you can see in Figure 27.18. Because this example deals with opening a form, highlight Form Operations in the Categories list, highlight Open Form in the Actions list, and click Next >.

FIGURE 27.18.

Use the first Wizard dialog box to select the action you want to associate with the button.

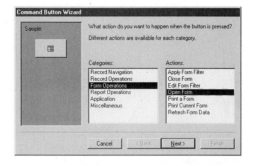

The next dialog box, shown in Figure 27.19, asks for the name of the form that is to be opened when the button is clicked. In this case, the Sales Analysis form will be opened. Click Next > to continue.

FIGURE 27.19.

Use this dialog box to choose the form to open.

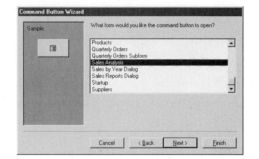

The Command Button Wizard now asks you to choose how the button should appear, as shown in Figure 27.20. You have two choices:

■ Text: Select this option to display a word or phrase on the button. Use the text box provided to enter your text.

■ Picture: Select this option to display a picture on the button. Activate the Show All Pictures check box to see a full list of the available pictures.

FIGURE 27.20.

You can display either text or a picture on the button face.

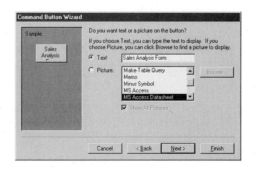

Click Next > to display the final Wizard dialog box. This is where you give the button a name. The suggestion from Access is usually pretty generic, like Command2. It's wise to rename the button to something that reflects what the button does when pressed (for example, Vendors for the button that opens the Vendors form). Click Finish to complete the operation.

Summary

This chapter introduced you to Access forms. You saw how they can take at least a little of the drudgery out of data entry. You learned three ways to create a form: by running AutoForm directly on a table or query, by running an AutoForm Wizard, and by working in Design view. I also showed you how to add controls to a form, work with combo boxes and list boxes, and navigate and edit a form.

Here's a list of chapters where you'll find related information:

■ For basic data entry techniques, see Chapter 25, "Working with Tables."

■ Report design uses many of the same techniques as form design. You can leverage much of your form know-how in Chapter 28, "Designing and Customizing Reports."

■ I'll show you how to use multiple tables in your forms in Chapter 29, "Juggling Multiple Tables."

■ I discuss various form customization options in Chapter 31, "Customizing Access."

Designing and Customizing Reports

IN THIS CHAPTER

CHAPTER 28

Report me and my cause aright.

—*Hamlet (William Shakespeare)*

Printing a report from Access is often the final result of the database effort. No matter how great the user interface, printed output is more easily understood by most people. Even though reports can be rows and columns of Courier text, people have high expectations for the report's appearance. In the days of DOS, people didn't seem to question a report that looked like a teletype printout, but now a report has to be functionally correct as well as cleverly formatted. This chapter focuses on creating the back-end data structures that make up a good report, along with the powerful formatting tools that are included in Access 97.

Access is an excellent tool for data publishing. *Data publishing* is the database equivalent of desktop publishing. Many people use Access just as a publishing tool, publishing data that has been attached to their company mainframe or an existing database. Reports in Access are now created much like laying out newsletters in PageMaker or Quark. Access tools, known as *controls,* are used to create lines, words, and pictures. Knowledge gained from creating the company newsletter can now be used in making the company reports. Microsoft has included functional similarities between desktop publishing applications and Access. For instance, holding down the Shift key while drawing with the Line tool produces a straight line.

Creating a Report Instantly Using the AutoReport Tool

Access has the tools and flexibility that allow beginners to see results quickly and advanced developers to generate complex documents. Microsoft's answer for the I-want-it-now managers is a feature called the *AutoReport,* which is identical to the AutoForm feature for form creation. AutoReport takes a chosen table or query and generates a report with the click of the mouse. Access gives you a number of ways to work with AutoReport (and, as you'll see, the method you use determines the report layout you get):

- You can create an AutoReport directly from the Tables or Queries tab.
- You can run one of the AutoReport Wizards.
- You can display the report design window and choose an AutoFormat from there.

Running AutoReport Directly on a Table or Query

If all you want is a basic no-muss, no-fuss report, run the AutoReport feature directly from the Tables or Queries tab. Specifically, highlight the table or query you want to use as the basis for the report, and then use either of the following techniques:

- Select Insert | AutoReport.

- Drop down the New Object button on the toolbar and click AutoReport.

Access analyzes the selected table or query and then creates a simple report like the one shown in Figure 28.1. As you can see, the resulting report uses a columnar layout that shows the name of each field and the associated data.

FIGURE 28.1.

A basic report created with AutoReport.

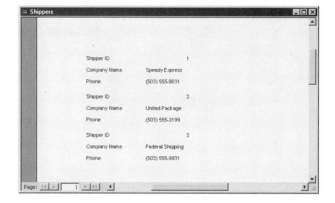

Running an AutoReport Wizard

To give you more control over the report layout and to let you add extra formatting, Access has two AutoReport Wizards. To try them out, use any of the following methods:

- ■ Highlight a table or query (this is optional) and select Insert | Report.
- ■ Highlight a table or query (again, this is optional), drop down the New Object button on the toolbar, and choose Report.
- ■ Activate the Reports tab and click New.

Access displays the New Report dialog box, shown in Figure 28.2. Highlight one of the AutoReport Wizards:

> **AutoReport: Columnar:** This Wizard creates a report with a columnar layout similar to the one shown in Figure 28.1.

> **AutoReport: Tabular:** This Wizard creates a report with a tabular layout that shows the field names at the top and the records in rows.

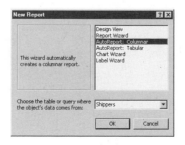

Use the drop-down list to select a table or query to use for the underlying data, and then click OK. The AutoFormat Wizard constructs the report. As you can see in Figure 28.3, the reports created by these Wizards also include some formatting. (I'll show you how to change this formatting in the next section.)

FIGURE 28.3.

The AutoReport Wizards create reports that have various formatting frills.

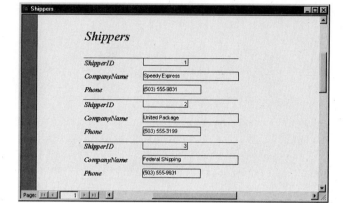

Assigning an AutoFormat in Design View

The AutoReport feature actually has ten different predefined report layouts. The AutoFormat Wizards always apply the default format. To choose another, you need to enter the report design window:

- If you're starting a new report, highlight Design View in the New Report dialog box, select the table or query, and click OK.

- If your report is already on-screen, either select View | Design View or click the Design View button on the toolbar.

From here, select Format | AutoFormat to display the AutoFormat dialog box, shown in Figure 28.4. The Report AutoFormats control contains a list of the available layouts. Highlight the one you want and click OK. Note that the default layout used by the AutoReport Wizards is always the *last* AutoFormat that you selected in this dialog box.

FIGURE 28.4.

Use this dialog box to select the AutoFormat you want to use.

Note, too, that you can customize these AutoFormats to suit your taste. If you click the Customize button in the AutoFormat dialog box, Access displays another dialog box that lets you perform one of three actions:

- Create a new AutoFormat template based on the formatting used in the current report.
- Change the current AutoFormat template based on the formatting used in the current report.
- Delete the current AutoFormat template.

From here, you can display or edit your report. See "Report Creation from the Bottom Up" later in this chapter.

The Architecture of Access Reports

To do complex publishing, the serious developer needs to know the wheres and whys of reporting. As mentioned earlier, the AutoReport feature brings report publishing to beginning users. For elaborate reporting, the developer needs to focus on the source of the data and how the objects and sections in the report interact with each other. This section gives some insight into approaching reports from a molecular level.

How Reports Are Structured

When Access is instructed to run a report, it works with the controls that either the developer or the wizard has inserted into its sections in order to format a page of information. For example, Figure 28.5 displays the Shippers report in Design view, which shows you the various sections (which are often called *bands* or *layers*) generated by the wizard.

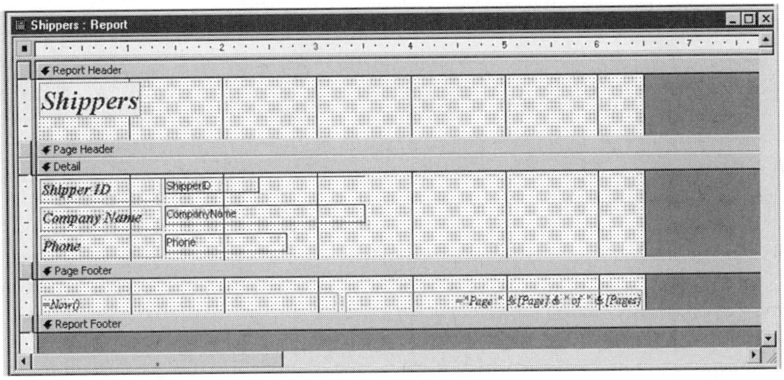

FIGURE 28.5.

The Design view of a columnar Access report.

Notice that the sections begin with the Report Header and end with the Report Footer, and that they then work their way inward. The following diagram represents this sectional construction:

Report Header

Page Header

Detail Section

Page Footer

Report Footer

Compare the report in Design view (see Figure 28.5) to the print preview shown in Figure 28.3. Notice that the controls are printed in their corresponding sections:

- The label called Shippers is in the Report Header; it appears only at the top of the first page of the report.
- Notice that the Page Header is empty, which means that no header will appear on page two.
- The Detail section is where the individual records get printed. The Detail section can also be thought of as where the records get "cycled."
- Notice that there are two controls that have the word *ShipperID* in them. One is a descriptive label, and the other is a bound control that displays data from the underlying table.
- The following section is the Page Footer; notice the text box expressions =Now() and ="Page " & [Page] & " Of " & [Pages]. These expressions display the date/time and page numbering, respectively.
- The final section of all reports is the Report Footer. The Report Footer is zero height, which means that it won't display anything.

NOTE: CONTROLS DEFINED

A *control* is an element placed on forms and reports. Examples include labels, text boxes, OLE picture controls, lines, rectangles, and so on. All controls have properties that can be set in the properties sheets.

Types of Reports

Actually, there is only one type of report: the type with sections that contain controls that are displayed on-screen and ultimately on paper. However, by manipulating a report's section height and width, along with section properties and page setup, you can display a report in many creative ways. After learning the fundamentals of reporting, you will have more control with reporting. Until then, you can use the wizards Microsoft has created, which break the report creation process into five major report categories:

- Columnar report: A report in which one record on each page is displayed vertically.
- Tabular report: A report in which rows of records going across like a spreadsheet are displayed horizontally. Multicolumn reports that snake the text flow in columns is a type of tabular report.
- Grouping report: A report in which data is grouped with totals.
- Label report: A report in which columns of data are spaced out in groups (for example, mailing labels).
- Chart report: A report that has a graph only.

NOTE: CHECK OUT THE NORTHWIND EXAMPLES

An excellent way to learn about reporting is to examine the work of others. The sample Northwind database that ships with Access contains sample reports that are worthy of investigation.

Establishing the Data Source for a Report

An Access report needs a recordset as its underlying source. This recordset can either be a table or a query. If report information comes from more than one table, a query will have to be built first (or the Report Wizard will have to be used). Forms and reports are identical in how they are tied to tables and queries.

TIP: CREATE QUERIES FOR COMPLEX REPORTS

The Report Wizard in this release of Access will create a query if the fields are chosen from two different tables. However, if the report is extremely complex and pulls records from multiple tables, you should create and save a query first.

NOTE: FORMS AND REPORTS ARE MORE OR LESS THE SAME

Treat forms and reports as identical twins when working with them. All the knowledge gained from building forms can be used in building reports. There is substantial similarity in the controls and properties of both. Think of a form as the part of Access that a user views on the monitor, and a report as the part that comes out of the printer.

Report Creation from the Bottom Up

The report wizards are excellent tools for folks new to report building, because they illustrate many important design fundamentals. Even if you're an experienced Access user, the wizards are still handy tools, because they let you get a report off the ground quickly.

Unfortunately, there's only so much each wizard can do. If you want to create intermediate-to-advanced reports, or if you need to extensively customize the default wizard reports, you'll need to go "under the hood" and tweak your reports by hand. The topics covered in this section will show you how to do just that.

Preliminary Foundations

The first step is to question what fields are involved in the report. Do all of the fields for the report reside in a single table, or will a query need to be created to bring these fields into one recordset? If the fields come from more than one table, can the Report Wizard handle the task, or is this situation so complex that it requires query creation? Will this report need subreports?

The second step in the creation of any report is to think about the finished product. In other words, what will the report look like when it is finished? Taking a few minutes to sketch it on paper provides a blueprint from which to work and saves a considerable amount of time in the long run.

NOTE: YOU MIGHT NEED A SUBREPORT

If the report is so complex that it is based on two or more unrelated queries, a subreport might be required.

The third step is optional: Create and test the query that underlies the upcoming report. (I explained queries in Chapter 26, "Querying Data.") Most reports are based on a query, but you can also use an entire table as your data source.

Initiating the Report Generation Process

Here are the steps for generating reports:

1. Click the Report tab in the Database window.
2. Click the New button, located on the right side of the database window.
3. In the New Report dialog box, choose a table or query on which to base the report.

There are now several choices:

- Design View: Use this option to start from scratch with a blank report.
- Report Wizard: Use this option to create a report by answering a series of questions.
- AutoReport: Use these options to create an instant columnar or tabular report (as described earlier).
- Chart Wizard: Use this option to construct a chart using Microsoft Graph.
- Label Wizard: Use this option to build mailing labels.

NOTE: USE A REPORT WIZARD TO GET A GOOD START

I recommend that you use one of the Report Wizards to begin a report. The Wizard saves you time by doing most of the formatting and page setup. Afterwards, go into Design view and customize the report.

Building a Single Table Report Using the Report Wizard

The only way to really learn reporting is to do it. The following is a step-by-step creation of a popular report style—the Grouping report. This report answers this request: "Show me all the contact names of customers of Northwind Traders grouped by title; also display the contact's name, company, country, city, and phone number, sorted by country and then city."

NOTE: WIZARDS AREN'T REQUIRED

Realize that wizards don't have to be used to create reports. Their only purpose is to save developers time in the report creation process. Wizards can be used only with a new report; they can't be invoked again for the same report after the report is finished.

Step 1: Select the Record Source

Click the New button while in the Report tab of the database window. In the New Report dialog box, highlight Report Wizard, select the Customers table, which will be the underlying source of data for this report, and then click OK.

Step 2: Select the Fields

The first Wizard dialog box, shown in Figure 28.6, asks you to select the fields to include in your report. To select fields to be on the report, use the right arrow button (>) to move them from the Available Fields box to the Selected Fields box. For this report select ContactTitle, ContactName, CompanyName, Country, City, and Phone. When you're ready to proceed, click Next >.

FIGURE 28.6.

The first Report Wizard dialog box asks you to select fields for your report.

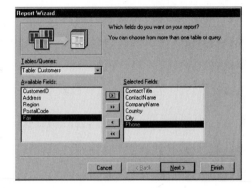

Step 3: Select the Grouping Fields

Now the Wizard asks if you want to add any grouping levels (see Figure 28.7). A *grouping level* is a field upon which the records are grouped. Access determines the unique values in the field, and any records that have the same value in that field are displayed together in the report. In the ContactTitle field, for example, all the contacts who have Owner in this field will be grouped.

FIGURE 28.7.

Use this dialog box to determine how the report records will be grouped.

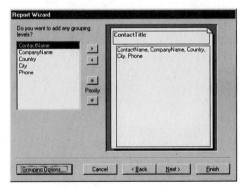

In the list box provided, highlight the field you want to use for the grouping level and then click the right arrow button. For the example, you want to group on the ContactTitle field. (Note, too, that you can also create subgroups within the main group. For example, you could group the unique values in the ContactTitle field by country.) When you're done, click Next >.

Step 4: Determine the Sort Order

By default, the grouping field (ContactTitle, in this case) is sorted alphabetically. The next Wizard dialog box, shown in Figure 28.8, asks you which field or fields determine the sort order *within* the grouping. Use the drop-down lists to select the appropriate fields (the buttons beside the drop-down lists toggle the sort order between ascending and descending). In this example, you'll want to sort by country and then by city. To do this, select Country in the first drop-down list and City in the second drop-down list. Click Next > to proceed.

FIGURE 28.8.

Use this Wizard dialog box to sort the records within the groups.

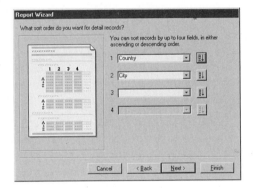

Step 5: Choose the Report Layout

The next Wizard dialog box, shown in Figure 28.9, determines the overall layout of your report. The Layout group has various options for how the group titles will appear and how the records within each group will be laid out. Use the Orientation group to determine whether the records are displayed across the short side of the page (Portrait) or the long side of the page (Landscape). You can also use the check box to force Access to fit all the fields onto the page by adjusting the field widths. Click Next > to move on.

FIGURE 28.9.

Use this dialog box to determine the layout of the report.

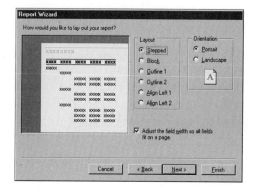

Step 6: Select a Report Style

In the next Wizard dialog box, shown in Figure 28.10, you select the report style you want to use. These styles are the same as the AutoFormat styles you saw earlier. Highlight your choice and click Next >.

FIGURE 28.10.

Use this dialog box to select a report style.

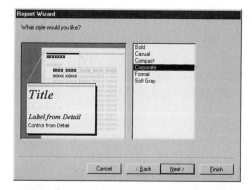

NOTE: FORMS GENERATED BY THE WIZARD CAN BE CHANGED

Remember that *all* the settings that the wizard generates can be modified after the report is finished.

Step 7: Finishing Up

The last wizard dialog box is shown in Figure 28.11. Type in an appropriate title for this report, choose whether you want to see the report in design or preview, and then click the Finish button. Figure 28.12 shows the completed report.

FIGURE 28.11.
The last of the Report Wizard dialog boxes.

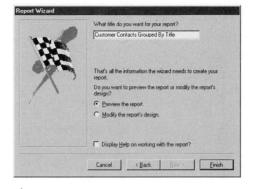

FIGURE 28.12.
The complete report shown in preview mode.

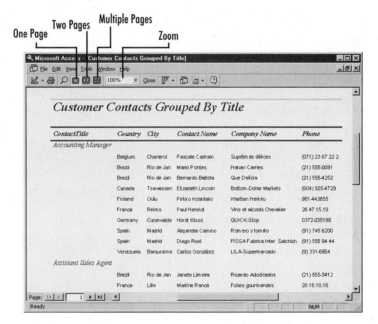

28

DESIGNING AND CUSTOMIZING REPORTS

Print Preview Unleashed

The print preview feature in Access 97 is almost indistinguishable in appearance and features from the print preview in Word. To see a preview of your report, use any of the following techniques:

- ■ In the Database window, activate the Reports tab, highlight the report, and then either click Preview or select File | Print Preview.

- ■ In the report design screen, click the Print Preview button on the toolbar.

After you have the preview window on-screen, here's a list of the various ways you can view your reports:

- Use the mouse as a magnifying glass to zoom in and out on the report by clicking it.
- Use the toolbar's One Page, Two Page, and Multiple Pages tools.
- Use the toolbar's Zoom drop-down list. (Unfortunately, the built-in zoom levels aren't customizable—you can't specify 66%, for example.)
- Use the View | Zoom and View | Pages commands.
- Right-click to bring up the shortcut menu, which also contains the Zoom and Pages options.

How Grouping Works in Reporting

The grouping options you selected during the Report Wizard aren't set in stone. If you want to make changes, display the report in Design view, and then select View | Sorting and Grouping. Access displays the Sorting and Grouping dialog box, shown in Figure 28.13. By examining the previously created report, you can receive some clues as to what the wizard did. Notice that ContactTitle is the first entry in the box, and its Group Header property is set to Yes. This is all that is needed to initiate grouping; it establishes another section in the report. If, say, the Country field's Group Header property is set to Yes, another section appears. From a sorting aspect, Country and City have been chosen, and the Sort Order is ascending.

FIGURE 28.13.

The Sorting and Grouping dialog box defines the report's structure.

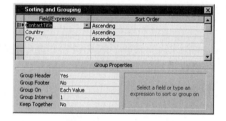

Customizing Reports

Forms and reports are very similar in how they manipulate controls, sections, and properties. An entire book could be written on the tricks and techniques used in form and report design. This section covers the foundations of customization, which should serve as a basis from which you can use your own creativity.

Many developers rush into report creation and assume that the customizing process will be just as intuitive as using the wizards. Unfortunately, they are often left frustrated: They are tricked because 90 percent of the report is built in a few minutes, but the last 10 percent can take several hours. By studying the techniques covered in the following sections, you can drastically cut the time it takes to complete that last 10 percent. For example, you can use the powerful trick of automatically sizing a text box control by double-clicking one of its selection handlebars. The techniques discussed in these sections are best learned through hands-on experimentation.

Manipulating Controls

Selecting, moving, and sizing controls in order to get the desired layout can be a very tedious process. Some powerful features to accelerate the design process are presented in the following secions.

Moving and Sizing Controls

You can move a control and its label together by placing the cursor on the border of a selected control and then dragging. (You can also use Ctrl-*arrow key* to move the control.) You can move a control independently of its label by placing the cursor on the large black square in the left corner of the selected control and then dragging.

NOTE: BYPASSING SNAP TO GRID

Hold down the Ctrl key while moving a control to disable Snap to Grid.

You can size a control by placing the cursor on one of its handlebars and then dragging. (You can also use Shift-*arrow key* to size the control.)

NOTE: AUTOMATIC CONTROL SIZING

To size a control automatically, double-click one of its handlebars.

The Four Methods of Selecting Controls

When more than one control is selected, they can be manipulated, moved, sized, or deleted as a group. Here are the methods of selecting multiple controls:

- Hold down the Shift key while clicking the separate controls.
- Choose View | Select All.
- Click the Reports background and drag a square around the controls to capture them as a group, as shown in Figure 28.14.

FIGURE 28.14.

Dragging a square around a group of controls will select them.

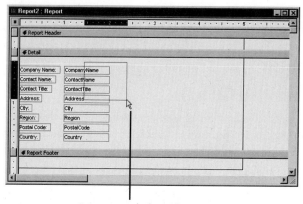

Drag pointer in background

- Click the vertical ruler that lines the left edge of the report. Access will select every object that lies on a horizontal line from the spot you clicked, as shown in Figure 28.15. Similarly, click inside the upper ruler to select items vertically.

FIGURE 28.15.

Shooting the controls by clicking the ruler will select many controls at once.

Click ruler to select horizontally

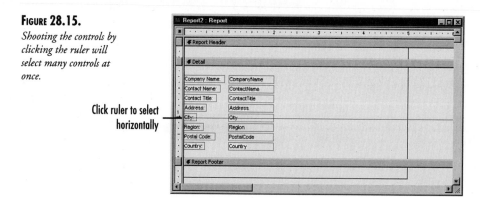

Deleting and Reestablishing Controls

To delete a control, simply select it and press the Delete key.

To reestablish a control, follow these steps:

1. Display the report's field list by choosing View | Field List.
2. Drag the field(s) off the list and onto the report. (Hold down the Ctrl key to select more than one field.)

> **NOTE: THE FIELD LIST**
>
> The field list displays the fields in the underlying table or query. If a field isn't on the field list, it can't be shown on the report.

Creating Controls with the Toolbox

You can display the Toolbox by choosing View | Toolbox or by clicking the Toolbox button on the toolbar. The Toolbox is a construction kit for controls. Reports generally only have label controls, text box controls, and lines for separating the two.

Follow these steps to create any type of control:

1. Display the Toolbox by choosing View | Toolbox.
2. Click a tool (the Line tool, for example).
3. Drag and draw a line. (Hold down the Shift key to draw a straight line.)

Changing Control Properties

Changing control properties is the final step in manipulating a report. Everything in Access has properties. The report has properties, each control has properties, and each report section has properties. By changing a property to Yes or No, you can make changes to the entire struc-ture of the report.

Here are four methods of displaying the properties sheet:

- Select View | Properties.
- Right-click a control and choose Properties.
- Double-click any control or section.

- Click the Properties tool on the toolbar.

The most crucial report property is the Record Source property, shown in Figure 28.16. (Note that first you need to select Edit | Select Report before displaying this dialog box.) If you delete the contents of this property, the report no longer has data to display. If you choose the drop-down list box of the Record Source property, the data source can be redirected to another table or query.

Figure 28.16.

The Record Source *property defines the report's underlying recordset.*

Modifying a Report to Display One Grouping Per Page

Often a page break is needed in an Access report. You can create one by setting the section property called Force New Page. Here are the steps:

1. Open up the Northwind sample database.
2. Double-click the report called Summary of Sales by Year. Notice that each year gets repeated one after the other. The task is to put each year on a separate page.
3. Select View | Report Design.
4. In Design view, click the View menu again and display the properties.
5. Click the background area of the ShippedDate Footer to display its properties.
6. Choose the All tab in the property box.
7. Change the second property down, Force New Page, to After Section. This forces a page break after this section is formatted on the report.
8. Print preview the report to see that each group (that is, each year) is on a separate page.

Aligning and Sizing Multiple Controls

The Format menu changes depending on the report element chosen. If several controls are selected, the Format menu contains the option to align or size them.

TIP: USE THE CONTEXT MENU

Right-clicking a selected control brings up the Align option.

TIP: EASIER CONTROL ALIGNMENT

Here's an aligning secret. Because labels and controls are linked to each other, aligning columns can become very frustrating. Try selecting only the labels, aligning them in the opposite direction, moving one label where the group should align, and then realigning the labels to the desired position.

Redefining the Defaults for Controls

When controls are created from the tools in the Toolbox or dragged off the field list, they assume the default Size and Font properties. As a developer, you have the ability to change these defaults. With the following technique, report-developing time can be radically decreased. Here's how to redefine a text box control's default properties:

1. Set the size, font, and other properties as needed.
2. Select Format | Change Default.

All new text boxes for this report will now assume the new default setting.

Building a Report from Scratch and Modifying Its Controls

Creating a report from scratch is an excellent way to learn what the Report Wizards do and how to harness their power. For the casual user, the following example will be helpful in the occasional report modification; for a developer, it will provide insight into reporting fundamentals. An example of when you would have to rely on building from scratch is when the report needed has to resemble an existing report. The following steps take you through the process:

1. Initialize a blank report: In the database window select the Report tab, click the New button, and click OK. A blank report based on no recordset is generated.

TIP: CHANGING THE DEFAULT TEMPLATE

To change the Normal template for blank reports, select Tools | Options | Forms/Reports. In the Report Template box, type in the name of a report in the database.

2. Set the record source: From the report design window select View | Properties or double-click the square box to the left of the horizontal ruler to display the Report properties. Set the Record Source property to Table Categories.
3. Place the fields: Choose View | Field List to display the field list. Drag each field needed on the form into the Detail section. To drag more than one field at a time, hold down the Ctrl key and click the desired fields.
4. Arrange the fields: Using the customizing techniques discussed earlier in this chapter, move, size, and change the fields inside the Detail section. Don't forget that by selecting individual controls, you can change the Font, Border, Alignment, and Size properties.

TIP: CONTROLLED MOVING AND SIZING

Pressing Ctrl-*arrow* key moves controls in fine increments; Shift-*arrow* key sizes the controls.

5. Display one record per page: Double-click the background of the Details section to show its properties. Set the property Force New Page to After Section.

6. Preview the report and fine-tune it: Click the Print Preview tool to see how the report will be printed.

The Many Ways of Publishing a Report

With the ever-increasing need to distribute information across the Internet and across platforms, Microsoft has given you new ways to take reports out of your computer and share them with others. Publishing a report can take many forms. Printing on paper, which is the classic end result of a report, isn't the only choice anymore.

Publishing on Paper

Although printing the report on paper is an obvious choice, it isn't the only one. By choosing File | Page Setup, you can change the printing parameters for the printed page. Inside the Print Setup box, you will find many consistencies within Office, such as margin settings, printer setup, and paper orientation.

Publishing to E-Mail

Reports can now be embedded into a MAPI-compliant mail package such as Microsoft Exchange. While viewing the report in print preview, select File | Send. Three choices for formatting come up: Formatted Text (RTF), Spreadsheet (XLS), or Text Only (TXT). The next box you see is the Microsoft Exchange E-mail dialog box, complete with the report displayed as a ready-to-ship embedded icon.

Exporting in Another Format

If the report needs to be viewed by someone who doesn't have Access but who has a word processor, spreadsheet, or desktop publisher, export it in a common file format. To do this, choose File | Save As/Export. In the Save As dialog box, select To an External File and click OK. In the bottom of the box you can choose the format to export.

Publishing to Word or Excel Through Office Links

Using the Office Links tool, located in the middle of the toolbar, a report can be published to Word or Excel. Access opens the chosen program and then transports the data to that program.

The Office Links feature of Access can take a report in print preview and turn it into a Word document or an Excel spreadsheet. If you click the Office Links drop-down box and then choose Publish It with MS Word, Access opens Word and transfers the formatted text. The process is the same with Excel.

NOTE: EXPORTING VIA MACROS

The export feature can be performed programmatically through the macro action OutputTo.

TIP: A GOOD REPORT EXAMPLE

To stretch your concept of what a report is capable of, investigate the catalog report in Northwind.

Summary

If you study the techniques and examples in this chapter, you will greatly reduce your report creation time. The tools available in Access 97 allow an incredible amount of creativity in data publishing. With the new freedom in report building, there will also be new frustrations. Because Access can do so much, deciding which tool to use can become confusing. Complex reporting will be easy after you study the literature, read the Help screens, investigate examples, and get lots of practical experience. As with other elements of Microsoft Office, nothing is more beneficial than hands-on experience.

Here's a list of chapters where you'll find related information:

- To learn how to create subreports (reports that include data from two or more related tables), see Chapter 29, "Juggling Multiple Tables."

- I discuss various report customization options in Chapter 31, "Customizing Access."

- For more information on using Access in conjunction with other Office products, see Chapter 50, "Working with the Office Integration Tools."

28

DESIGNING AND CUSTOMIZING REPORTS

Juggling Multiple Tables

CHAPTER

29

The thing that's between us is fascination, and the fascination resides in our being alike.

—*Marguerite Duras*

Most database applications (and *all* well-designed database applications) store their information in multiple tables. Although most of these tables will have nothing to do with each other (for example, tables of customer information and employee payroll data), it's likely that at least some of the tables will contain related information (such as tables of customer information and customer orders).

Working with multiple, related tables presents you with two challenges: You need to design your database so that the related data is accessible, and you need to set up links between the tables so that the related information can be retrieved and worked with quickly and easily. This chapter tackles both challenges and shows you how to exploit the full multiple-table powers of Access.

Relational Database Fundamentals

Why do you need to worry about multiple tables, anyway? Isn't it easier to work with one large table instead of two or three medium-sized ones? To answer these questions and demonstrate the problems that arise when you ignore relational database models, let's look at a simple example: a table of sales leads.

The Pitfalls of a Nonrelational Design

Table 29.1 outlines a structure for a simple table (named Leads) that stores data on sales leads.

Table 29.1. A structure for a simple sales leads table (Leads).

Field	Description
LeadID	The primary key.
FirstName	The contact's first name.
LastName	The contact's last name.
Company	The company that the contact works for.
Address	The company's address.
City	The company's city.
State	The company's state.
Zip	The company's ZIP code.
Phone	The contact's phone number.
Fax	The contact's fax number.
Source	Where the lead came from.
Notes	Notes or comments related to the sales lead.

This structure works fine until you need to add two or more leads from the same company (a not-uncommon occurrence). In this case, you would end up with repeating information in the Company, Address, City, and State fields. (The Zip field would also repeat, as will, in some cases, the Phone, Fax, and Source fields.)

All this repetition makes the table unnecessarily large, which is bad enough, but it also creates two major problems:

- The data entry clerk must enter the repeated information for each lead from the same company.

- If any of the repeated information changes (such as the company's name or address), each corresponding record must be changed.

One way to eliminate the repetition and solve the data entry and maintenance inefficiencies would be to change the table's focus. As it stands, each record in the table identifies a specific contact in a company. But it's the company information that repeats, so it makes some sense to allow only one record per company. You could then include separate fields for each sales lead within the company. The new structure might look something like the one shown in Table 29.2.

Table 29.2. A revised, company-centered structure for the sales leads table.

Field	Description
LeadID	The primary key.
Company	The company's name.
Address	The company's address.
City	The company's city.
State	The company's state.
Zip	The company's ZIP code.
Phone	The company's phone number.
Fax	The company's fax number.
First_1	The first name of contact #1.
Last_1	The last name of contact #1.
Source_1	Where the lead for contact #1 came from.
Notes_1	Notes or comments related to contact #1.
First_2	The first name of contact #2.
Last_2	The last name of contact #2.
Source_2	Where the lead for contact #2 came from.

29

JUGGLING MULTIPLE TABLES

continues

Table 29.2. continued

Field	Description
Notes_2	Notes or comments related to contact #2.
First_3	The first name of contact #3.
Last_3	The last name of contact #3.
Source_3	Where the lead for contact #3 came from.
Notes_3	Notes or comments related to contact #3.

In this setup, the company information appears only once, and the contact-specific data (I'm assuming this involves only the first name, last name, source, and notes) appears in separate field groups (for example, First_1, Last_1, Source_1, and Notes_1). This solves the earlier problems, but at the cost of a new dilemma: The structure as it stands will hold only three sales leads per company. Of course, it is entirely conceivable that a large firm might have more than three contacts—perhaps even dozens. This raises two unpleasant difficulties:

- If you run out of repeating groups of contact fields, new ones must be added. Although this might not be a problem for the database designer, most data-entry clerks generally don't have access to the table design (nor should they).

- Empty fields take up as much disk real estate as full ones, so making room for, say, a dozen contacts from one company means that all the records that have only one or two contacts have huge amounts of wasted space.

How a Relational Design Can Help

To solve the twin problems of repetition between records and repeated field groups within records, you need to turn to the relational database model. This model was developed by Dr. Edgar Codd of IBM in the early 1970s. It was based on a complex relational algebra theory, so the pure form of the rules and requirements for a true relational database setup is quite complicated and decidedly impractical for real-world applications. The next few sections look at a simplified version of the model.

Step 1: Separate the Data

Once you know which fields you need to include in your database application, the first step in setting up a relational database is to divide these fields into separate tables where the "theme" of each table is unique. In technical terms, each table must be composed of only entities (that is, records) from a single *entity class*.

For example, the table of sales leads you saw earlier dealt with data that had two entity classes: the contacts and the companies they worked for. Every one of the problems encountered with that table can be traced to the fact that we were trying to combine two entity classes into a single table. So the first step toward a relational solution is to create separate tables for each class of data. Table 29.3 shows the table structure for the contact data (the Contacts table) and Table 29.4 shows the structure for the company information (the Company table). Note, in particular, that both tables include a primary key field.

Table 29.3. The structure for the Contacts table.

Field	*Description*
ContactID	The primary key.
FirstName	The contact's first name.
LastName	The contact's last name.
Phone	The contact's phone number.
Fax	The contact's fax number.
Source	Where the lead came from.
Notes	Notes or comments related to the sales lead.

Table 29.4. The structure for the Company table.

Field	*Description*
CompanyID	The primary key.
CompanyName	The company's name.
Address	The company's address.
City	The company's city.
State	The company's state.
Zip	The company's ZIP code.
Phone	The company's phone number (main switchboard).

Step 2: Add Foreign Keys to the Tables

At first glance, separating the tables seems self-defeating because, if you've done the job properly, the two tables will have nothing in common. So the second step in our relational design is to define the commonality between the tables.

In our sales leads example, what is the common ground between the Contacts and Company tables? It's that every one of the leads in the Contacts table works for a specific firm in the Company table. So what's needed is some way of relating the appropriate information in Company to each record in Contacts (without, of course, the inefficiency of simply cramming all the data into a single table, as we tried earlier).

The way you do this in relational database design is to establish a field that is common to both tables. You'll then be able to use this common field to set up a link between the two tables. The field you use must satisfy three conditions:

- It must not have the same name as an existing field in the other table.
- It must uniquely identify each record in the other table.
- To save space and reduce data entry errors, it should be the smallest field that satisfies the two preceding conditions.

In the sales leads example, a field needs to be added to the Contacts table that establishes a link to the appropriate record in the Company table. The CompanyName field uniquely identifies each firm, but it's too large to be of use. The Phone field is also a unique identifier and is smaller, but the Contacts table already has a Phone field. The best solution is to use CompanyID, the Company table's primary key field. Table 29.5 shows the revised structure for the Contacts table that includes the CompanyID field.

Table 29.5. The final structure for the Contacts table.

Field	Description
ContactID	The primary key.
CompanyID	The Company table foreign key.
FirstName	The contact's first name.
LastName	The contact's last name.
Phone	The contact's phone number.
Fax	The contact's fax number.
Source	Where the lead came from.
Notes	Notes or comments related to the sales lead.

When a table includes a primary key field from a related database, the field is called a *foreign key*. Foreign keys are the secret to successful relational database design.

Step 3: Establish a Link Between the Related Tables

Once you have your foreign keys inserted into your tables, the final step in designing your relational model is to establish a link between the two tables. This step is covered in detail later in this chapter.

Types of Relational Models

Depending on the data you're working with, you can set up one of several different relational database models. In each of these models, however, you need to differentiate between a *child* table (also called a *dependent* table or a *controlled* table) and a *parent* table (also called a *primary* table or a *controlling* table). The child table is the one that is dependent on the parent table to fill in the definition of its records. The Contacts table, for example, is a child table because it is dependent on the Company table for the company information associated with each person.

The One-To-Many Model

The most common relational model is one in which a single record in the parent table relates to multiple records in the child table. This is called a *one-to-many* relationship. The sales leads example is a one-to-many relation because one record in the Company table can relate to many records in the Contacts table (in other words, you can have multiple sales contacts from the same firm). In these models, the "many" table is the one where you add the foreign key.

Another example of a one-to-many relationship would be an application that tracks accounts-receivable invoices. You would need one table for the invoice data (Invoices) and another for the customer data (Customer). In this case, one customer can place many orders, so Customer is the parent table, Invoices is the child table, and the common field is the Customer table's primary key.

The One-To-One Model

If your data requires that one record in the parent table be related to only one record in the child table, you have a *one-to-one* model. The most common use of one-to-one relations is to create separate entity classes to enhance security. In a hospital, for example, each patient's data is a single entity class, but it makes sense to create separate tables for the patient's basic information (such as his name, address, and so on) and his medical history. This allows you to add extra levels of security to the confidential medical data (such as a password). The two tables could then be related based on a common "PatientID" key field.

Another example of a one-to-one model would be employee data. You would separate the less-sensitive information such as job title and startup date into one table, and restricted information such as salary and commissions into a second table. If each employee has a unique identification number, you would use that number to set up a relation between the two tables.

Note that in a one-to-one model, the concepts of *child* and *parent* tables are interchangeable. Each table relies on the other to form the complete picture of each patient or employee.

The Many-To-Many Model

In some cases, you might have data in which many records in one table can relate to many records in another table. This is called a *many-to-many* relationship. In this case, there is no direct way to establish a common field between the two tables. To see why, let's look at an example from a pared-down accounts-receivable application.

Table 29.6 shows a simplified structure for an Invoices table. It includes a primary key—InvoiceID—as well as a foreign key—CustID—from a separate table of customer information (which I'll ignore in this example).

Table 29.6. The structure for an Invoices table.

Field	Description
InvoiceID	The primary key.
CustID	The foreign key from a table of customer data.

Table 29.7 shows a stripped-down structure for a table of product information. It includes a primary key field—ProductID—and a description field—Product.

Table 29.7. The structure for a Products table.

Field	Description
ProductID	The primary key.
Product	The product description.

The idea here is that a given product can appear in many invoices, and any given invoice may contain many products. This is a many-to-many relation, and it implies that *both* tables are parents (or, to put it another way, neither table is directly dependent on the other). But relational theory says that a child table is needed to establish a common field. In this case, the solution is to set up a third table—called a *relation table*—that is the child of both the original tables. In our example, the relation table would contain the detail data for each invoice. Table 29.8 shows the structure for such a table. As you can see, the table includes foreign keys from both Invoices (InvoiceID) and Products (ProductID), as well as a Quantity field.

Table 29.8. The structure for a table of invoice detail data.

Field	Description
InvoiceID	The foreign key from the Invoices table.
ProductID	The foreign key from the Products table.
Quantity	The quantity ordered.

Enforcing Referential Integrity

Database applications that work with multiple, related tables need to worry about enforcing *referential integrity rules*. These rules ensure that related tables remain in a consistent state relative to each other. In the sales leads application, for example, suppose the Company table includes an entry for "ACME Coyote Supplies" and that the Contacts table contains three leads who work for ACME. What would happen if you deleted the ACME Coyote Supplies record from the Company table? Well, the three records in the Contacts table would no longer be related to any record in the Company table. Child records without corresponding records in the parent table are called, appropriately enough, *orphans*. This situation leaves your tables in an inconsistent state that could have unpredictable consequences.

Preventing orphaned records is what is meant by enforcing referential integrity. You need to watch out for two situations:

- Deleting a parent table record that has related records in a child table.
- Adding a child table record that isn't related to a record in the parent table (either because the common field contains no value or because it contains a value that doesn't correspond to any record in the parent table).

Establishing Table Relationships

Now that you know the theory behind the relational model, you can turn your attention to creating and working with related tables in queries, forms, and reports. The first step, however, is to establish the relation between the two tables, which is what this section is all about.

To get started, either select Tools | Relationships or click the Relationships button on the Database toolbar. You'll see the Relationships window, shown in Figure 29.1. (Note that you'll see this view of the window only if you're working with the Northwind sample database.)

Figure 29.1.

*You use the Relation-
ships window to
establish relations
between tables.*

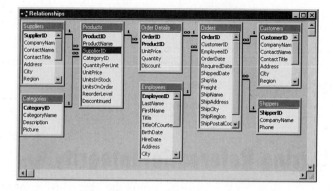

Understanding Join Lines

Because the Northwind sample database is well-designed, all the tables are related to each other
in one way or another. You can tell this by observing the lines that connect each table in the
Relationships window. These lines are called *join lines.* As you can see in Figure 29.1, the join
line connects the two fields that contain the related information. For example, the Suppliers
and Products tables are joined on the common SupplierID field. In this case, SupplierID is the
primary key field for the Suppliers table, and it appears as a foreign key in the Products table.
This lets you relate any product to its corresponding supplier data.

The symbols attached to the join lines tell you the type of relation. In the join between the
Suppliers and Products tables, for example, the Suppliers side of the join line has a 1, and the
Products side of the line has an infinity symbol (∞). This stands for "many," so you would
interpret this join as a one-to-many relation.

Types of Joins

Access lets you set up three kinds of joins: inner joins, outer joins, and self-joins.

> **Inner join:** An *inner join* includes only those records in which the related fields in the
> two tables match each other exactly. This is the most common type of join.

> **Outer join:** An *outer join* includes every record from one of the tables and only those
> records from the other table in which the related fields match each other exactly. In
> our sales leads example, it's possible that there might be companies for which no
> contacts have yet been established. Creating an inner join between the Company and
> Contacts table will show you only those firms that have existing contacts. However,
> setting up an outer join will show *all* the records in the Company table, including
> those where there is no corresponding record in the Contacts table.

NOTE: MORE ON OUTER JOINS

An outer join is also called a *left-outer join*. To see why, consider a one-to-many relation. Here, the left side is the "one" table and the right side is the "many" table. So this type of join includes every record from the "one" (left) side and only those matching records from the "many" (right) side.

You use the term *left-outer join* when you need to differentiate it from a *right-outer join*. In a one-to-many relation, this type of join includes every record from the "many" (right) side and only those matching records from the "one" (left) side.

Self-join: A *self-join* is a join on a second copy of the same table. Self-joins are handy for tables that include different fields with the same type of information. For example, the sample table Employees that comes with Access has an EmployeeID field that lists the identification number of each employee. The same table also includes a ReportsTo field that lists the identification number of the employee's manager. To display the name of each employee's manager, you'd use a second copy of the Employees table and join the EmployeeID and ReportsTo fields.

Adding Tables to the Relationships Window

If you need to establish a new relationship between two tables, your first order of business is to add the tables to the Relationships window. Here are the steps to follow:

1. Select Relationships | Show Table, or click the Show Table button on the toolbar. Access displays the Show Table dialog box, shown in Figure 29.2.

FIGURE 29.2.

Use this dialog box to add tables to the Relationships window.

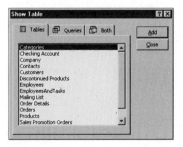

29

JUGGLING
MULTIPLE TABLES

2. Highlight the table you want to add.

3. Click the Add button. Access adds the table to the Relationships window.

4. Repeat steps 2 and 3 to add more tables.

5. Click the Close button to return to the Relationships window.

Joining Tables

To create a join between two tables (or a self-join between two copies of the same table), use the mouse to drag one of the related fields and drop it on the other. Here are the specific steps:

1. Add the tables you want to join.

2. Arrange the table boxes so that you can see the fields you want to use for the join in each box.

3. Drag the related field from one table and drop it on the related field in the other table. Access displays the Relationships dialog box, shown in Figure 29.3.

FIGURE 29.3.

Access displays this dialog box when you drag a related field from one table and drop it on another.

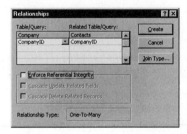

4. If you want Access to enforce referential integrity rules on this relation, activate the Enforce Referential Integrity check box. If you do this, two other check boxes become active:

   Cascade Update Related Fields: If you activate this check box and then make changes to a primary key value in the parent table, Access will update the new key value for all related records in all child tables. For example, if you change a CompanyID value in the Company table, all related records in the Contacts table will have their CompanyID fields updated automatically.

   Cascade Delete Related Fields: If you activate this check box and then delete a record from the parent table, all related records in all child tables will also be deleted. For example, if you delete a record from the Company table, all records in the Contacts table that have the same CompanyID as the deleted record will also be deleted.

5. To set the type of join, click the Join Type button to display the Join Properties dialog box, shown in Figure 29.4. Here, option 1 corresponds to an inner join, option 2 corresponds to a left-outer join, and option 3 corresponds to a right-outer join. Click OK to return to the Relationships dialog box.

6. Click Create. Access sets up the join line between the two fields.

As soon as you have your joins set up, you can add the appropriate fields to the data pane and even filter the data using criteria.

Figure 29.4.

Use this dialog box to establish the type of join.

Editing a Relationship

If you need to make changes to a relationship, Access lets you edit the relation parameters from within the Relationships window. For the relation you want to adjust, either click the join line for the two fields and then select Relationships | Edit Relationship, or right-click the join line and choose Edit Relationship from the context menu. Access displays the Relationships dialog box so that you can make your changes.

Removing a Join

If you no longer need a join, you can remove it either by clicking the join line and selecting Edit | Delete Relationship (or pressing Delete), or by right-clicking the join line and choosing Delete from the context menu.

Multiple-Table Queries

With a properly constructed relational database model, you'll end up with fields that don't make much sense by themselves. For example, the Northwind database has an Order Details table that includes a ProductID field—a foreign key from the Products table. This field contains only numbers and therefore by itself is meaningless to an observer.

The idea behind a multiple-table query is to *join* related tables and by doing so create a dynaset that replaces meaningless data (such as a product ID) with meaningful data (such as a product name).

The good news is that once you've established a relationship between two tables, Access handles everything else behind the scenes. All you have to do is add the appropriate tables to the query. You can either do this at design time (in the Query Wizard or in the Show Table dialog box that appears when you start a new query in Design view), or you can add new tables while in Design view. For the latter, use the same steps that I outlined in the section "Adding Tables to the Relationships Window."

As you can see in Figure 29.5, Access displays join lines between related tables. From here, you simply create the query in the usual way—by adding fields from either table, setting up criteria, and so on. See Chapter 26, "Querying Data," for details.

FIGURE 29.5.

A multiple-table query that shows fields from the Order Details and Products tables.

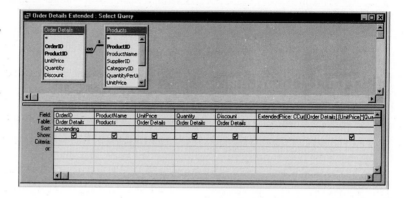

The only thing you have to watch out for is dealing with tables that each have a field with the same name. In Figure 29.5, you can see that both the Order Details table and the Products table have a UnitPrice field. To differentiate between them in, say, a calculated criterion, you need to preface the field name with the table name, like so:

```
[Table Name].[FieldName]
```

For example, consider the formula that calculates the ExtendedPrice field in the Order Details Extended query. The idea behind this formula is to multiply the unit price times the quantity ordered and subtract the discount. Here's the formula:

```
CCur([Order Details].[UnitPrice]*[Quantity]*(1-[Discount])/100)*100
```

To differentiate between the UnitPrice field in the Order Details table and the UnitPrice field in the Products table, the formula uses the term `[Order Details].[UnitPrice]`.

Multiple-Table Forms

Once you set up a multiple-table query, it's straightforward to use this query as the underlying data source in a form. However, there are two other ways that you can use multiple tables with forms: creating subforms, and populating combo boxes and list boxes. The next few sections explain both concepts.

Working with Subforms

One of the handiest uses for related tables is to create a form that displays the related data from both tables simultaneously. For example, the form shown in Figure 29.6 contains data from two sources. The bulk of the form fields displays data from an Orders table query (a few fields from the Customers table are thrown in for good measure), and the datasheet in the middle of the form contains data from the Order Details table. Because the Orders and Order Details tables are related by the OrderID field, the order details shown are just those for the displayed order; when you move to a different order, the order details change accordingly.

FIGURE 29.6.

A form showing data from two related tables.

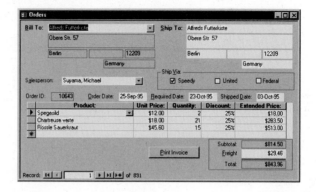

This type of form is actually a combination of two separate forms. The regular form fields (in the example, the ones showing the Orders table data) are part of the *main form,* and the datasheet (the Order Details table data) is called the *subform.* A form/subform combination can be thought of as a main/detail form or a parent/child form.

Subforms are especially effective at showing dependent records from tables or queries participating in one-to-many relationships. In the preceding example, each item in the Orders table can have many related records in the Order Details table. Because of this, most subforms are viewed in datasheet mode, but this isn't a requirement. However, the main form can't be viewed in datasheet mode when a subform is present.

Adding a Subform via the Form Wizard

An easy way to set up a form/subform combination is to use the Form Wizard. Begin a new form using the Form Wizard as described in Chapter 27, "Creating and Using Simple Forms." In the initial Wizard dialog box, first add the fields you want to use for the main form. When that's done, use the Table/Queries list to select the data source you want to use for the subform, and then select the fields that will be used for the subform.

Because you've added fields from multiple sources, the Form Wizard displays the dialog box shown in Figure 29.7. The purpose of this dialog box is to establish which table will be used as the basis for the main form (and, therefore, which table will be used as the basis for the subform). In the How do you want to view your data? list, highlight the item that includes the table you want to use with the main form, and then click Next >.

FIGURE 29.7.

Use this dialog box to establish which tables apply to the main form and the subform.

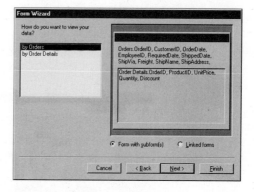

The next Wizard dialog box asks you to select a layout for the subform, as shown in Figure 29.8. Activate either the Tabular or the Datasheet option, and then click Next >.

FIGURE 29.8.

Use this dialog box to choose a layout option for the subform.

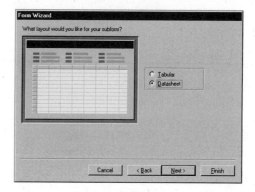

From here, you follow the usual steps for finishing the form. (The only difference is that, in the last dialog box, you need to specify a name for both the main form and the subform.)

Adding a Subform Control

If you've already started your form, you can still add a subform using Design view. In the Toolbox, click on the Subform/Subreport control, and then drag the mouse inside the form to create a box to hold the subform. Access starts the Subform/Subreport Wizard to lead you through the process, as shown in Figure 29.9.

FIGURE 29.9.

The Subform/Subreport Wizard makes it easy to add a subform to an existing form.

You have two ways to proceed:

- If you want to create the subform from a table or query, activate the Table/Query option, click Next >, and then use the next Wizard dialog box to choose the table or query and select the subform fields.

- If you want to use an existing form as the subform, activate the Forms option, use the drop-down list provided to select the form you want to use, and click Next >.

Now you'll see the Wizard dialog box shown in Figure 29.10. You use it to choose the field that links the main form and the subform. As long as the tables are related (which they should be for this to work), Access will establish the correct linking field automatically. (If not, you can always activate the Define my own option and set up the link fields yourself.) Click Next >. Enter a name for the subform and click Finish to complete your work.

FIGURE 29.10.

Use this dialog box to establish the field that links the main form and the subform.

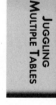

Working with Combo Boxes and List Boxes

Back in Chapter 27, I showed you how to populate a combo box or list box with a series of values that you type in by hand. However, if the available values exist as part of another table, you can get Access to grab these values from the table and use them to populate the list. There are two different situations to consider:

- When the two tables are related
- When the two tables are unrelated

If the two tables are related, Access handles all the dirty work for you. For example, suppose you're building a form for a table that includes an EmployeeID field. It wouldn't be very efficient (or accurate, for that matter) to have the data entry clerk type in the actual identification numbers for each employee. Instead, you would relate your table to the Employees table using EmployeeID as the common field. If you then added the EmployeeID field to your form, Access would do two things automatically:

- It would set up the field as a drop-down list.
- It would populate the list with the name of each employee. That is, it would grab the unique names from the Employees table and use these names in the list.

If the two tables are unrelated, you need to do a bit more legwork. Specifically, you need to specify which table and which field to use for the list items. For example, if you add a combo box to the form, Access loads the Combo Box Wizard. In the first dialog box, activate the I want the combo box to look up the values in a table or query option, and click Next >. From here, subsequent Wizard dialog boxes take you through the process of choosing the table or query and specifying which field contains the values for your list.

Multiple-Table Reports

In Access, the process of creating reports and forms is quite similar: You add fields, insert graphic objects, format text, and so on. This similarity also shows up when you're working with multiple tables. You saw earlier how to create a form/subform combination; the process for creating a report/subreport combination is almost identical. As with forms, you have two ways to proceed:

- If you're using the Report Wizard to create a new report, adding fields from multiple tables will cause the Wizard to detour from its usual routine and ask you about the layout of the report and subreport.

- If you're working in Design view, use the Subform/Subreport tool to draw a box for your subreport. In the Subform/Subreport Wizard that appears, use the steps described earlier to define your subreport.

Summary

This chapter showed you a few techniques for working with multiple tables in Access. You began by learning some important relational database theory, including why a relational design is important, how to implement a proper relational database, and the types of relational models. From there, I showed you how to establish relationships between tables and how to work with multiple-table queries, forms, and reports.

Here's a list of chapters where you'll find related information:

- To learn how to create and work with tables, see Chapter 25, "Working with Tables."
- For information on basic queries, check out Chapter 26, "Querying Data."
- I showed you how to create data entry forms in Chapter 27, "Creating and Using Simple Forms."
- Check out Chapter 28, "Designing and Customizing Reports," to get the nitty-gritty on Access reports.

Creating Access Macros

IN THIS CHAPTER

CHAPTER

30

> *Nature is a self-made machine, more perfectly automated than any automated machine.*
> *To create something in the image of nature is to create a machine, and it was by learning*
> *the inner working of nature that man became a builder of machines.*
>
> *—Eric Hoffer*

In Access you can use macros to automate tasks by building lists of actions that occur in response to events, such as a command button being clicked. You build the list in the order you want these actions to occur. The list can cover all the features available through the menus, as well as some that aren't. By using macros, you can automate the process of importing and exporting data, create buttons that perform complex queries, and other useful functions.

In the rest of this chapter you'll learn about creating simple and complex macros, working with existing macros, associating macros with various events, and troubleshooting your macros.

Writing Access Macros

Unlike writing a VBA program, where you can be as structured or unstructured as you want, writing a macro tends to be a very regimented process. For example, look at Figure 30.1, which shows the initial screen for creating a new macro. You'll notice that each line has an Action and a Comment column. The actions from which you can select are shown in the drop-down list.

FIGURE 30.1.

The opening screen for a new macro.

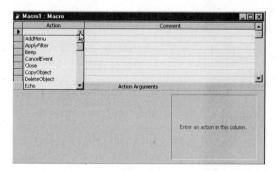

Once you choose a possible action, the arguments for that action appear in the bottom panel, as shown in Figure 30.2. Notice that the default arguments for a TransferDatabase action (which you use to import or export data to a supported database) are already filled in.

Just as there was a list of supported actions for the macro, many of the arguments for an action also have drop-down lists. Figure 30.3 shows that there are quite a few choices for a target database.

Not all of the arguments contain drop-down lists, however, so you still have to be somewhat aware of what you're trying to do. But with all these lists, you can see how easy it is to build sophisticated macros quickly without being too technical.

FIGURE 30.2.

Macro arguments for
`TransferDatabase.`

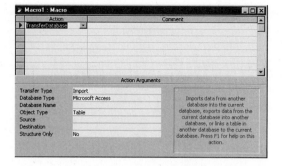

FIGURE 30.3.

*The argument drop-
down list.*

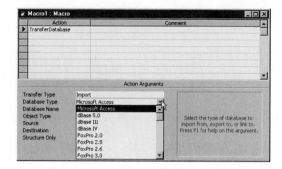

Creating a Simple Macro

To illustrate this a little more clearly, I'll show you how to create a simple macro for importing
a text file. This is one way to bring in data from a larger system.

To get started, use either of the following methods:

- Select the Macro tab from the Database window and click the New button.
- Select Insert | Macro.

- Select Macro from the toolbar's New Object drop-down list.

At this point, your screen should show empty Action and Comment columns (as shown in
Figure 30.1). Now, go into the first Action field and click the button on the right side of the
field in order to access the drop-down list. For this macro, scroll down to the `TransferText`
option and select it. Your screen should now look like the one shown in Figure 30.4, which
shows the `TransferText` action and its default arguments.

Now, click the first argument (`Transfer Type`). This brings up a button you can click for a drop-
down list of the possible values for the argument. The `Specification Name` and `Has Field Names`
arguments also have drop-down lists. The other two arguments (`Table Name` and `File Name`)
have to be typed in. The final version of this macro might look like the example shown in
Figure 30.5.

FIGURE 30.4.

The start of a macro using TransferText.

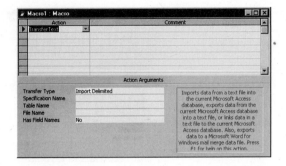

FIGURE 30.5.

The final version of the sample macro.

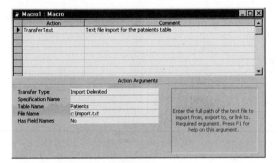

Notice that the comment has also been filled in. This is especially important in longer macros, where you might have several of the same actions for different tables or forms.

Now you can exit the macro. You'll be prompted to save your changes and to name the macro. Because you can use up to 255 characters (including spaces), you should try to use a meaningful name, such as Import for Patients Table.

Part of the trick to writing macros is knowing what actions are available to you. To learn about the actions you can use, check out the online help for Access under the macros topic, or look at your Access user manual. Another way to find out more about the macro actions is to scroll through the drop-down list, select actions that look interesting, and then press the F1 key to bring up more information about that action.

Using the SendKeys Action

SendKeys is one of the more complex actions. By using SendKeys, you can enter information into an open Access dialog box or another active Windows application. An example where this action might be helpful is the import used in the sample macro shown in Figure 30.5. Suppose you are bringing down large amounts of data. You probably don't want to store the data uncompressed because of all the disk space it takes up. Therefore, you would want to keep the data in a zip file and then use a Windows-based unzip program and the SendKeys action to unpack the import file when you need to use it again.

If you're sending literal text data (such as a name), it needs to be enclosed in quotation marks for most arguments (although there are exceptions). To send keystrokes that are used for commands or movements, use the special key arguments listed in Table 30.1.

Table 30.1. Special key arguments.

To Get This Key	Use This Keystroke Argument
Alt	%
Backspace	{BACKSPACE} or {BS} or {BKSP}
Break	{BREAK}
Caps Lock	{CAPSLOOK}
Ctrl	^
Delete	{DELETE} or {DEL}
Down arrow	{DOWN}
End	{END}
Enter	{ENTER} or ~
Esc	{ESC}
Function key	{F*x*} (where *x* is a number from 1 to 16)
Help	{HELP}
Home	{HOME}
Insert	{INSERT} or {INS}
Left arrow	{LEFT}
Num Lock	{NUMLOCK}
Page Down	{PGDN}
Page Up	{PGUP}
Print Screen	{PRTSC}
Right arrow	{RIGHT}
Shift	+
Scroll Lock	{SCROLLLOCK}
Tab	{TAB}
Up arrow	{UP}

continues

30

CREATING ACCESS MACROS

Table 30.1. continued

To Get This Key	Use This Keystroke Argument
Codes for Reserved Characters	
{ or } (braces)	{{} or {}}
[or] (brackets)	{[} or {]}
^ (caret)	{^}
% (percent)	{%}
+ (plus)	{+}
~ (tilde)	{~}

When you press two keys in combination, such as Alt-F, specify this action as

%F

To press Alt-F, followed by P (without Alt), use

%FP

If a key is held down while two or more keys are pressed, enclose the group of following keys in parentheses. The following example is the equivalent of Alt-D-V:

%(DV)

When you want to send the same keystroke many times, add a number specifying how many times to repeat. To move up three times, for example, use this:

{UP 3}

Running Your Macro

There are several ways to run a macro once it's written. The first way is to click the Run toolbar button that appears when your macro is open for editing. You can also select Run | Run. Alternatively, you can "step" through the macro one command at a time by selecting Run | Single Step. However, you'll generally want to use Run—except when you're troubleshooting a macro.

Similarly, you can run a macro by clicking the Macro tab on the database window and then clicking the Run button. If your macro depends on having a particular form already open, you need to open the appropriate form and select Tools | Macro | Macro. Access will display the Run Macro dialog box, shown in Figure 30.6. Select the macro you want to run, and then click OK.

FIGURE 30.6.

The Run Macro dialog box.

You can also have one macro run another macro by using the RunMacro action. In general, though, you'll usually run a macro as a result of a specific event occurring. Here is a list of events that will kick off a macro:

- Clicking a button
- Moving between fields
- Making changes in a record
- Opening or closing tables and forms
- Pressing a shortcut key
- Selecting a custom command from a custom menu

Most macros can be run using any of these methods; however, a particular form or record might need to be active in order for a macro to complete successfully.

Modifying Existing Macros

Once you have a macro, you might decide to make changes to it. Or you might need to modify someone else's macro to perform a specific task for you. To modify an existing macro, activate the Macros tab, highlight the macro you want to edit, and click the Design button. This brings the macro sheet back up.

To modify a macro, you usually have three choices:

- Change the existing actions or comments, or edit the arguments of an existing action.
- Insert a row so that you can add an action between existing actions. Begin by clicking anywhere inside the row above which you want the new action to appear. Then either select Insert | Rows or click the toolbar's Insert Rows button.

- Delete a row that contains an action you no longer need. Select the row you want to remove and then either select Edit | Delete Rows or click the toolbar's Delete Rows button.

Adding Macros to Events

As I mentioned earlier, you'll usually associate a macro with an event. These events can occur throughout the use of an Access database. Depending on what you're trying to do, you might want a macro in a form, in a section of a form, in a report, or in a section of a report. All of these options are covered in this section.

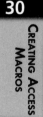

30

CREATING ACCESS MACROS

Adding Macros to Forms

To add a macro to a form, you can either create a control that you associate the macro with or edit the Event properties of the form or field to call the macro. In either case, the form must be opened in Design view to allow changes to be made.

Now display the properties sheet for the control either by clicking the control and selecting View | Properties or by right-clicking the control and choosing Properties from the context menu. (Note, too, that you can also associate macros with form events. In this case, select Edit | Select Form before displaying the properties sheet.)

In the properties sheet, activate the Event tab to see a list of the various events that you can use to trigger the macro. For example, a macro associated with the On Click event will run whenever the user clicks the control. For each event, you have a drop-down list that contains all the available macros, as shown in Figure 30.7.

FIGURE 30.7.

Choosing the macro for the On Click *event.*

If you need to create a macro from scratch, click the button with the three periods to display the Choose Builder dialog box. Highlight the Macro Builder option and then click OK to begin building your macro directly. At the form level, you can also click the Other tab and then associate a macro with the Menu Bar option.

To determine which event to use, think about when you want your actions to occur and then match the macro accordingly. If you're unsure of how a specific event works, click in the field for the event and then press F1 to bring up the online help for the event.

Each section of the form (Header, Detail, and Footer) has its own events. To work with these events, click in the section you want to work with, and then right-click to bring up the floating menu. Select Properties, and then click the Event tab.

Finally, you can use this process to work with events at the field level. To do this, click the field you want to work with and then right-click to bring up the floating menu. Again, select Properties. It's important to remember that these macros are associated only at the level you defined them. In other words, an After Update defined at the field level won't be activated if you update a different field. So, if your macro can be used by more than one field, you'll want it associated with either a section or a form-level event.

Macros can also be associated with controls on the form. The events will vary somewhat, depending on the type of control being worked with. As an example, in Figure 30.7 a command button has been defined, and a macro has been associated with one of its events. You can also associate a macro with a command button when the button is created by specifying it as a Run Macro button in the Command Button Wizard.

Like forms, controls have certain events you tend to use fairly often. You can learn more about these events by pressing the F1 key to access the online help.

Adding Macros to Reports

Reports tend to be another area where macros can be very useful. Just like forms, reports have two levels of events. Figure 30.8 shows the events associated with the report object. You display this dialog box by clicking in an area of the report design window that isn't part of one of the report sections, right-clicking to display the floating menu, and then selecting the Properties option.

FIGURE 30.8.

Events for a report.

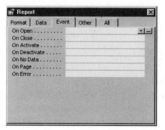

For more details on these events, you can again rely on Access 97's online help to assist you in choosing the proper event for your macro.

Within a report there are also sections, each of which can have the events associated with it set up with a corresponding macro. These events are listed in Table 30.2.

Table 30.2. Report section events.

Event	Description
OnFormat	Runs a macro after Access has accumulated or calculated the data for the section but before it has printed the section.
OnPrint	Runs a macro after the data in a section is laid out but before printing.
OnRetreat	Runs a macro when Access returns to a previous report section during report formatting.

30

CREATING ACCESS MACROS

Troubleshooting Macros

Although it's nice to think that every macro you write will run correctly the first time you code it, the reality is that sometimes it won't. Usually you'll build a simple macro, test it, get it working, and then add more complex statements and so on until you get the final version. One way you'll know that your macro isn't working is when you see the Action Failed dialog box, shown in Figure 30.9. It shows you which macro has failed, what step it was on when it failed, and the arguments that were being used for that step.

FIGURE 30.9.

The Action Failed dialog box.

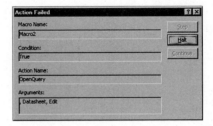

If you get the Action Failed dialog box, you'll want to jot down the macro name and the step as well as any open forms, reports, or queries. Then click the Halt button to close the dialog box. If you don't already have the macro sheet open for the offending macro, you need to open it and see if you can figure out why that step caused the particular failure. Things to look at are whether what you thought should happen matched what appeared to be happening (particularly a problem with reports), whether the logic in the conditions matches what you thought you coded, and whether there was a condition in the data being analyzed that you didn't expect.

After you've looked at these items, if there still is no apparent problem, it's time to try "stepping" through the macro by selecting Run | Single Step. To do this, begin by opening the macro and any forms or reports that would normally be open when it runs. Select Run | Single Step to start the Single Step process. Then run the macro. As the macro goes through each step, you get a dialog box (similar to the one shown in Figure 30.10) that shows the step being executed. The information about that step is displayed in the dialog box.

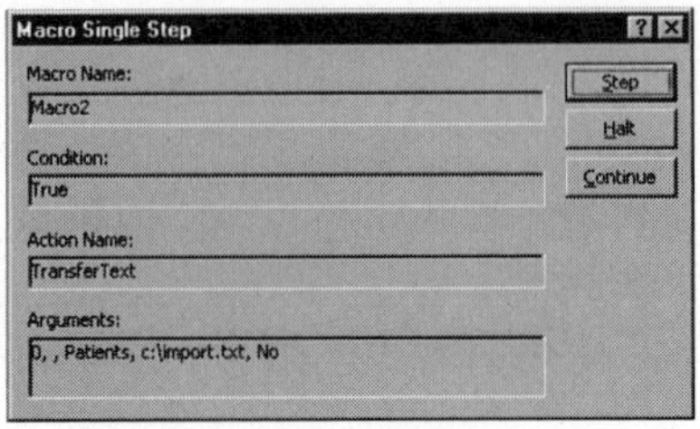

FIGURE 30.10.

The Macro Single Step dialog box.

You have three choices at each step: You can click Step (which is the default) to go to the next action, click Halt to stop execution of the macro, or click Continue to run the macro from that point on without stopping until the end of the macro or until an error is encountered.

Something else you can do to help troubleshoot is use the MsgBox action to display a message at a particular step in the macro. For example, the message can let you know if you've executed an action that you didn't think you would (in which case you should check your Condition statement), or it can give you the value of a variable you're working with.

In longer macros where you might have several similar actions, you probably won't want to single-step through the macro. In this case, you'll want to use the StopMacro action to stop the macro after the point where you think the error is occurring. Then, by moving this action back and forth, you can make sure you're working on the correct action.

Once the macro has been debugged, you'll probably want to finish it by adding a SetWarnings action to the beginning of it with the argument Off. That way, system messages (particularly confirmations for queries) won't appear to the end user. Along the same lines, you might want to add an Echo action to turn off screen updates while your macro is running. This is a good idea, because if you're switching between several forms or reports, your macro will run much faster.

An Example: Opening a Form

In Chapter 27, "Creating and Using Simple Forms," I showed you how to use a command button on a form to open another form. Forms don't have to be opened from a button, however: They can be opened through a macro by using the OpenForm action.

As you can see in Figure 30.11, the OpenForm action has a number of arguments:

- The Form Name argument determines the form to be opened, which comes from the drop-down list. In this case, it's the Customers form.
- The View argument determines how the form is opened. It can be Form, Design, Print Preview, or Datasheet View.
- The Filter Name argument is either a query or a sort order for the records. This is not a required field.
- You can use the Where Condition clause to enter a SQL WHERE clause to select specific records.
- The Data Mode argument is how the form will be opened for the user. It determines whether users will be allowed Add, Edit, or Read Only access to the records in the form.
- Window Mode refers to the size of the window that the form will be displayed in when it's opened. It can be Normal, Hidden, Icon, or Dialog.

FIGURE 30.11.

The Customers form will be opened by this macro action.

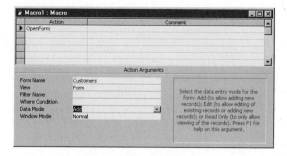

Now that you've filled in all the argument information, close and save the macro. Once the macro has been created, it can be called from a form. Open any form in Design view. Pull up the toolbox and turn off the Control Wizard button. Click the Command Button tool and draw a small box on the form. A blank button will appear on the form. Pull up the properties box for that command button and use the appropriate event to select your macro. In Figure 30.12, for example, the macro is associated with the On Click event.

FIGURE 30.12.

Macro code is attached to an event on a command button that appears on a form.

Summary

In this chapter you've learned about macros—not only what they are, but also the basics of coding, modifying, and troubleshooting them. You should now be more comfortable with deciding when to use them, as well as how to make sure they run when you want them to.

Here's a list of chapters where you'll find related information:

- You can attach actions to a control without having to construct a macro. See Chapter 27, "Creating and Using Simple Forms," for an example.

- You can gain much more control over your database objects by creating Visual Basic for Applications programs. See Chapter E5 on the CD, "VBA Database Programming in Access," for details.

Customizing Access

IN THIS CHAPTER

CHAPTER

31

> *Resistance to the organized mass can be effected only by the man who is as well organized in his individuality as the mass itself.*
>
> *—Carl Jung*

You've seen throughout the chapters here in Part V that Access is unique among the major Office applications: Its interface is different, it doesn't deal with "documents" per se, and so on. This uniqueness also seems to apply to customization. While folks routinely remake Word, Excel, and PowerPoint in their own image, most users seem to prefer working with Access in its default, out-of-the-box garb. That's a shame, because Access comes loaded with all kinds of interesting and useful customization options. This chapter takes you through most of them so you can see for yourself.

Customizing Access Startup

Although Access is primarily used as a database management system, it spends much of its time acting as a database application. In other words, many people never deal with raw Access data; they only see various front-ends to the data, such as forms and reports. Ideally, the user should never suspect that he's running Access. For example, consider the window shown in Figure 31.1. Unless you're very familiar with the Access interface, it's difficult to tell that this application is running inside Access.

FIGURE 31.1.

It's tough to tell, but this application is running inside Access.

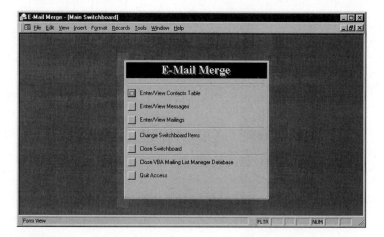

The Startup Dialog Box

How do you accomplish this? Access has a Startup dialog box, shown in Figure 31.2, that lets you change the application title, hide the menu bar and toolbars, and more. To view this dialog box, select Tools | Startup.

Figure 31.2.

Use the Startup dialog box to control the startup options for your Access application.

Here's a rundown of the various controls in this dialog box:

Application Title: This text box determines the text that Access displays in its title bar.

Application Icon: Use this box to enter or select the icon that is displayed both in the upper-left corner of the application window and in the application's taskbar button.

TIP: ICON STASH

You'll find quite a few icon (.ICO) files in the \Office\Forms subfolder of your main Microsoft Office folder.

Menu Bar: If your application contains multiple menu bars, use this drop-down list to choose the menu bar that is displayed with the application.

Allow Full Menus: If you deactivate this check box, Access hides the View, Insert, and Tools menus and any menu commands that would let the user make design changes to the application.

Allow Default Shortcut Menus: Deactivate this check box to disable the Access shortcut (context) menus.

Display Form: This drop-down list determines which form is displayed automatically at startup.

Display Database Window: Deactivate this check box to prevent Access from displaying the application's Database window.

Display Status Bar: Deactivate this check box to hide the status bar.

Shortcut Menu Bar: Use this drop-down list to choose a custom menu bar to be used as the shortcut menu in your application.

Allow Built-in Toolbars: Deactivate this check box to hide the built-in Access toolbars.

Allow Toolbar/Menu Changes: Deactivating this check box hides the Customize command that would otherwise allow the user to make changes to the application's menus and toolbars.

Allow Viewing Code After Error: Click the Advanced>> button to see this option. If you deactivate this check box, Access doesn't let the user view your application's code if a runtime error occurs.

Use Access Special Keys: Click the Advanced>> button to see this option. Deactivating this check box means that Access deactivates the following keys:

Key	Description
F11 or Alt-F1	Displays the Database window.
Ctrl-F11	Toggles between the built-in menu bar and the custom menu bar.
Ctrl-G	Displays the Debug window.
Ctrl-Break	Stops code execution and displays the current code module.

When you're done, click OK and then close and reopen the database to put the changes into effect.

TIP: AVOIDING THE STARTUP OPTIONS

You can bypass all of the startup options discussed in this section by holding down the Shift key while the application loads.

Access Startup Command-Line Options

The Access executable is called Msaccess.exe, and it can be found in the Office subfolder of your main Microsoft Office folder. You can use this executable to launch Access from the command line and specify one or more command-line arguments. Table 31.1 runs through the available arguments.

Table 31.1. Access command-line arguments.

Argument	Description
database	Opens the specified database. If the database isn't in your default Access database folder (see "General Customization Options"), be sure to include the appropriate path information.
/excl	In networked environments, opens the specified database in exclusive mode.
/ro	Opens the specified database for read-only access.
/user *username*	Starts Access using the specified username.

Argument	Description
/pwd `password`	Starts Access using the specified password.
/profile `user profile`	Starts Access using the options in the specified user profile instead of the standard Registry settings created during installation.
/compact `target database`	Compacts the specified database to the target database and then closes Access. If you omit the target database, Access compacts the database to the original database name and folder.
/repair	Repairs the specified database and then closes Access.
/convert `target database`	Converts the specified database (which should be in an earlier Access format) to the target database (which will have the Access 97 database format) and then closes Access.
/x `macro`	Starts Access and runs the specified macro.
/cmd	Specifies that what follows on the command line is the value that will be returned by the Command function. This option must be the last option on the command line.
/nostartup	Starts Access without displaying the initial startup dialog box.
/wrkgrp `file`	Starts Access using the specified workgroup information file.

Customizing the Access View

The rest of this chapter covers the various controls found in the Options dialog box, shown in Figure 31.3. To display this dialog box, select Tools | Options. For starters, here's a review of the options found in the View tab:

Status Bar: This check box toggles the Access status bar on and off.

Startup Dialog Box: Deactivate this check box to prevent Access from displaying at startup its initial dialog box (the one that prompts you to either create a new database or open an existing database).

Hidden Objects: This check box toggles the Database window's hidden objects on and off. (I showed you how to hide database objects in Chapter 24, "An Access Database Primer.")

System Objects: This check box toggles the Access system objects on and off.

Names Column: For Access macros, this check box toggles the Macro Name column on and off (see Chapter 30, "Creating Access Macros").

Conditions Column: For Access macros, this check box toggles the Condition column on and off.

FIGURE 31.3.

The Options dialog box is chock full of Access customization treats.

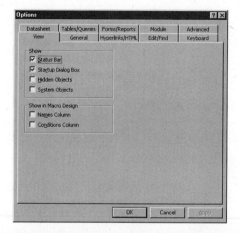

NOTE: MORE VIEW OPTIONS

For more information on changing the Access view—such as sorting the database objects—see the section "Working in the Database Window" in Chapter 24.

General Customization Options

The next stop on our Access customization journey is the General tab in the Options dialog box, shown in Figure 31.4. Here's a summary of the available controls:

Print Margins: These text boxes determine the margins Access uses when printing reports and other data.

Default Database Folder: Use this text box to specify the folder that Access displays by default when you run the Open command or create a new database.

New Database Sort Order: Use this drop-down list to select the default sort order that Access applies to each new database you create.

Provide feedback with sound: Activate this check box to have Access play various sounds to accompany dialog box alerts and tasks such as printing.

FIGURE 31.4.

The General tab.

Setting Datasheet Defaults

In Chapter 25, "Working with Tables," I showed you a few methods for customizing individual datasheets. Rather than requiring you to make the same changes to every new datasheet you create, Access has a number of options that control the default look of your datasheets. You'll find these knickknacks in the Datasheet tab of the Options dialog box, shown in Figure 31.5. Here's a summary:

Default Colors: These drop-down lists control the colors Access uses for the datasheet font, background, and gridlines.

Default Font: Use the controls in this group to specify which font Access uses to display the datasheet text.

Default Gridlines Showing: These check boxes toggle the horizontal and vertical datasheet gridlines on and off.

Default Column Width: Use this text box to specify the standard width that Access should use for all datasheet columns.

Default Cell Effect: These options determine how each cell appears within the datasheet. The default is Flat, but you can also elect to have the cells appear raised above the datasheet background or sunken into the background.

Show Animations: When activated, this check box enables datasheet animations. For example, if you insert a column, Access "slides" the current column to the right.

FIGURE 31.5.

Use the Datasheet tab to set custom defaults for your datasheets.

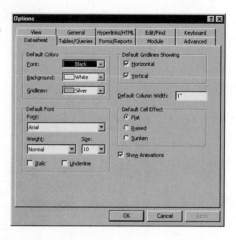

Setting Table and Query Defaults

The next item on our customization agenda involves setting a few defaults for tables and queries. Not surprisingly, these settings can be found in the Tables/Queries tab of the Options dialog box, shown in Figure 31.6. Here's what you get:

Default Field Sizes: Use the Text control to specify the default size for fields that use the Text data type. Use the Number drop-down list to set the default data type for numeric fields.

Default Field Type: Use this list to specify the data type that Access applies to new fields by default.

AutoIndex On Import/Create: The values that appear in this text box determine which fields Access automatically indexes when you import data or create a new table. The idea is that the individual values (which you separate with semicolons) represent either the beginning or ending of field names that you want indexed. For example, one of the default values is ID, which means that any field name beginning or ending with that text (RecordID, for instance) will be indexed automatically.

Show Table Names: This check box toggles the query design grid's Table row on and off. (This only applies to new queries; existing queries aren't affected.) If you use queries that contain multiple tables, you should leave this option activated to make it easier to differentiate the table fields.

Output All Fields: If you activate this check box, Access includes in the query results every field in the underlying table, even if you haven't added all the fields to the query grid. Again, this option applies only to new queries.

Enable AutoJoin: When this check box is activated, Access creates an inner join automatically if two tables in a query have fields with the same name and the same data type. If you'd rather define these relationships by hand, clear this check box.

Run Permissions: These options determine the permissions that are applied when a user runs a select or action query. For example, they might determine whether or not a user can make changes to the data returned by a select query. Select Owner's to use the permissions associated with the owner of the database, or select User's to work with the permissions associated with the user.

FIGURE 31.6.

The controls on the Tables/Queries tab let you set various defaults for Access tables and queries.

Some Form and Report Options

The Forms/Reports tab in the Options dialog box, shown in Figure 31.7, is home to a few settings related to Access forms and reports:

Selection Behavior: As you learned in Chapter 27, "Creating and Using Simple Forms," you can select multiple objects in the form or report design view by dragging the mouse to create a "selection box." If you activate the Partially Enclosed option, the selection box need only cover part of an object to select it. By contrast, if you activate Fully Enclosed, the selection box must completely cover an object before Access will select it.

Form Template: Use this text box to enter the name of the form that you want to use as the template for all new forms (that is, new forms created without the help of the Form Wizard).

Report Template: Similarly, you use this text box to enter the name of a report to use as the template for all new reports (without the help of the Report Wizard).

Always Use Event Procedures: Access gives you three ways to associate code with a form or report object: the Expression Builder, the Macro Builder, and the Code Builder. The latter implements a VBA event procedure. If you always want to use the Code Builder, activate the Always Use Event Procedures check box.

Figure 31.7.

The Forms/Reports tab contains a few settings related to Access form and report objects.

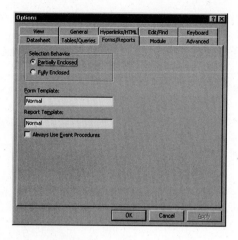

Edit and Find Options

In Chapter 25, I ran through a few techniques for editing table records (see the section "Working with Records") and for finding and replacing data (see the section "Finding Data"). The controls in the Edit/Find tab, shown in Figure 31.8, let you customize the behavior of these operations:

> **Default Find/Replace Behavior:** These options determine the default settings in the Find and Replace dialog boxes. In particular, they determine the settings for the Match drop-down list and the Search Only Current Field check box:

Option	*Match*	*Search Only Current Field*
Fast Search	Whole Field	Activated
General Search	Any Part Of Field	Deactivated
Start of Field Search	Start of Field	Activated

Confirm Record Changes: When activated, this check box tells Access to display a confirmation message when you make changes to a record.

Confirm Document Deletions: When activated, this check box tells Access to display a confirmation message when you attempt to delete any database object.

Confirm Action Queries: When activated, this check box tells Access to display a confirmation message whenever you attempt to run an action query.

Show List of Values In: When you're using Filter by Form, these check boxes determine which fields display a list of values to use as the filter. Activate Local Indexed Fields to display a list of values in all indexed fields, activate Local Nonindexed Fields to display a list of values for each nonindexed field, and activate

ODBC Fields to display a list of values for each field associated with a linked external table. Note that these settings apply only to the currently open database.

Don't display lists where more than this number of records read: The value in this text box determines the maximum number of records Access will read in order to build its Filter By Form value lists. The default value is 1000, which means that Access will stop extracting unique entries for the Filter By Form value lists after 1,000 records. Again, this option applies only to the current database.

FIGURE 31.8.

The Edit/Find tab has a few options related to editing and finding database records.

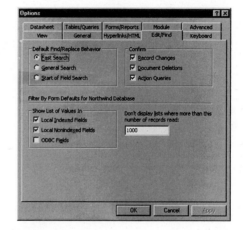

Customizing Access Keyboard Behavior

I showed you a few techniques for navigating datasheets via the keyboard in Chapter 25 (see the section "Navigating Fields"). The Keyboard tab, shown in Figure 31.9, contains a few options that let you customize this navigation:

Move After Enter: These options determine what Access does to the cursor after you press Enter when you've finished editing a field. The default setting is Next Field, which moves you to the field to the right of the current field (or to the first field in the next record if you're on the last field). If you'd prefer that the cursor not move, activate the Don't Move option. Alternatively, you can tell Access to move the cursor down to the same field in the next record by activating the Next Record option.

Arrow Key Behavior: These options determine what Access does when you press either the left or right arrow key while on a field. The default is Next Field, which moves you to the field to the right of the current field (or to the first field in the next record if you're on the last field). If you activate Next Character, Access moves the cursor one character at a time.

Behavior Entering Field: These options determine what Access does when you navigate to a new field. The default is Select Entire Field, which tells Access to select the text in the new field. To avoid this, choose either Go to Start of Field (which places the cursor to the left of the first character in the field) or Go to End of Field (which places the cursor to the right of the last character in the field).

Cursor Stops at First/Last Field: This check box determines what Access does when you attempt to navigate past the first or last field in a record. By default, if you navigate past the last field, Access moves the cursor to the first field in the next record. Similarly, if you navigate past the first field, Access moves the cursor to the last field in the previous record. If you'd prefer that Access just stop at either the first field or the last field, activate this check box.

FIGURE 31.9.

The options in the Keyboard tab let you customize the Access keyboard navigation techniques.

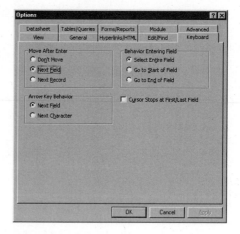

HTML and Hyperlink Options

You'll learn about the new HTML and Hyperlink features that come with Access 97 in Chapter 44, "The Office 97 Internet Tools." For now, here's a rundown of the various options in the Access Hyperlinks/HTML tab that you can work with (see Figure 31.10):

Hyperlink Color: Use this drop-down list to select the color Access uses to display hyperlinks.

Followed Hyperlink Color: Use this drop-down list to select the color Access uses to display hyperlinks that you've clicked.

Underline Hyperlinks: This check box toggles hyperlink underlines on and off.

Show Hyperlink Addresses in Status Bar: When activated, this check box tells Access to display the URL of a hyperlink in the status bar whenever you hover the mouse pointer over the link text. If deactivated, no address is displayed.

HTML Template: This text box determines the default template that Access should use whenever you create an HTML file from Access data.

Data Source Information: Use these text boxes to set up default ODBC data source information for implementing dynamic Web pages associated with Internet Information Server. You need to specify a data source name, a user name (the User to Connect As field), and a password (the Password for User field).

Microsoft Active Server Pages Output: These text boxes determine the settings Access should use when creating Active Server Page (.ASP) files. Use the Server URL text box to specify the default URL of the Web server you'll be using. In the Session Timeout (min) text box, enter a value in minutes after which an inactive Web server session should be timed out.

FIGURE 31.10.

The Hyperlinks/HTML tab contains a few settings concerning the new Web-related features found in Access 97.

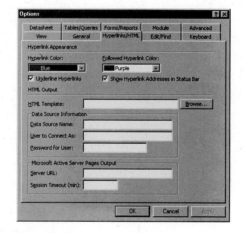

A Few Advanced Options

To complete our look at Access customization options, this section examines the grab bag of power user settings found in the Advanced tab, shown in Figure 31.11:

Default Record Locking: These options determine the record locking that Access employs in networked environments:

- The No Locks option tells Access not to lock the record you're currently editing. If another user makes changes to the record, Access gives you the option of accepting or discarding that person's changes.

- The All Records option tells Access to lock every record in the current table.

- The Edited Record option tells Access to lock only the current record.

Default Open Mode: These options determine the mode Access uses when you open a database in a networked environment. Select Shared to allow other people to open the database at the same time; select Exclusive to prevent others from opening the database.

Ignore DDE Requests: If you activate this check box, Access won't respond to any DDE requests that come in from other applications.

Enable DDE Refresh: When this check box is activated, Access refreshes any open DDE links according to the interval specified in the Refresh Interval text box. DDE links won't be updated if you deactivate this check box.

OLE/DDE Timeout (sec): This value sets the number of seconds Access waits before retrying a failed OLE or DDE connection. The maximum value is 300 seconds.

Number of Update Retries: In a networked environment, this value sets the number of attempts Access will make to save a record that has been locked by a remote user. (The time between each retry is set by the Update Retry Interval value, discussed in a moment.) The maximum value is 10.

ODBC Refresh Interval (sec): In a networked environment, this value sets the interval, in seconds, that Access uses for refreshing external table data retrieved via ODBC. The maximum value is 32,766 seconds.

Refresh Interval (sec): In a networked environment, this value determines how often Access updates the data in a table to reflect changes made by other users. This setting also determines how often Access refreshes DDE links. The maximum value is 32,766 seconds.

Update Retry Interval (msec): In a networked environment, this value sets the amount of time, in milliseconds, that Access waits between each attempt to save a record that has been locked by a remote user. The maximum value is 1000 milliseconds.

Command-Line Arguments: Use this text box to specify one or more Access command-line arguments to use when you load this database. See Table 31.1 for the arguments you can use.

Conditional Compilation Arguments: One or more conditional compilation arguments or constants. (Conditional compilation lets you determine which parts of a VBA module are compiled). If you enter multiple values, separate each one with a colon.

Project Name: Use this text box to specify a name for your application. This name is displayed in the References dialog box and in Object Browser's library list.

Error Trapping: These options determine how Access handles VBA errors:

- Activate Break on All Errors to have Access enter break mode when any error occurs, even if the running procedure contains an `On Error` statement (see Chapter E4 on the CD, "Debugging VBA Procedures").

■ Activate Break in Class Module to have Access enter break mode when an error occurs in a class module, unless the running procedure contains an On Error statement.

■ Activate Break on Unhandled Errors to have Access enter break mode when any error occurs, unless the running procedure contains an On Error statement, or the procedure exists in a class module.

FIGURE 31.11.

The Advanced tab contains miscellaneous options that should appeal to power users.

Summary

This chapter took you on a quick tour of the various Access customization options. I began by showing you how to customize the Access startup, which included the settings in the Startup dialog box and the Access command-line arguments. I then ran through most of the controls in the Options dialog box.

Here's a list of chapters where you'll find related information:

■ To learn how to customize the Access menus and toolbars, see Chapter 8, "Customizing the Office Menus and Toolbars."

■ For information on working with Access databases, see Chapter 24, "An Access Database Primer."

■ I cover tables in Chapter 25, "Working with Tables."

■ Queries are the subject of Chapter 26, "Querying Data."

■ See Chapter 27, "Creating and Using Simple Forms," to learn how to wield the Access form tools.

■ To learn more about using Access in a networked environment, head for Part X, "Unleashing the Networked Office."

VI
PART

IN THIS PART

Unleashing PowerPoint

Designing an Effective Presentation

IN THIS CHAPTER

32

CHAPTER

There are nine and sixty ways of constructing tribal lays,
And every single one of them is right.

—*Rudyard Kipling*

Presentations let you communicate your ideas to groups of people. Using a variety of presentation formats and techniques, you can present textual material, tables, graphs, drawings, and other types of information to your audience to inform, persuade, train, or otherwise influence their thinking. In the Office suite, PowerPoint provides the framework and engine for creating eye-catching presentations.

PowerPoint's presentational building blocks are slides, which are individual "chunks" of information in the form of text, graphics, tables, charts, Internet hyperlinks, media clips, and other Office objects. Slides generally convey information in telegraphic or shorthand style—short phrases or "bursts" of text, pictures, charts, or graphs. Save long sentences and flowing prose for reports—presentations use short, pithy lines to make text easy to grasp.

In this chapter, you'll explore the creation of a PowerPoint presentation with an emphasis on *design* and learn to consciously choose the elements of an *effective* presentation. Here are some of the design topics examined:

- Organizing the presentation's contents using an outline
- Selecting the right template for a presentation
- Determining the layout for individual slides
- Adding animation effects to slides
- Choosing transitions from slide to slide

Outlines: Organizing Content

PowerPoint makes it easy to create sharp-looking presentations. Well-designed templates, predefined slide layouts, and predetermined text placement all help you place your information easily on slides. All the pretty backgrounds and fancy type in the world won't help your presentation make its point if *you* haven't done your work first. In other words, if you haven't put time and thought into the design of the presentation, all the flash in the world won't make it effective. In fact, too much flash can hinder the effectiveness of what you have to say. Often, less is better, so be careful not to add too much clutter to presentations.

In PowerPoint, outlines provide a convenient means of organizing the content of your presentation. The abbreviated style of outlines is ideally suited to presentations, and the hierarchical arrangement of information readily adapts to text slides. In PowerPoint, the top level of an outline's structure becomes the title of a slide and lower levels of the outline form bulleted text hierarchies.

You can create a PowerPoint presentation without developing an outline first. For short presentations where you have a clear picture of the information you want to present and how that information fits together, it might be easier to create slides directly, without going through the outlining stage. But for longer presentations, as with any informative endeavor, an outline helps you organize your content, making it easier for you to create an effective presentation.

Let's now turn our attention to the creation of a presentation, beginning with an outline.

Creating the Outline

When you start PowerPoint, you see the dialog box shown in Figure 32.1. It lets you open an existing presentation or create a new one.

FIGURE 32.1.

The intial Power-Point dialog box.

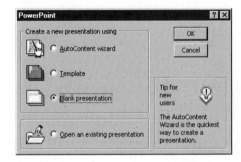

Click the Blank presentation option to start a new presentation, and then press Enter. Select the first AutoLayout preview to create PowerPoint's first blank slide using the slide view. The AutoLayout previews provide several standard presentation formats from which you can choose. The section "Automatic Layouts" explains how to utilize the AutoLayout dialog box.

Perhaps the easiest way to create a new presentation from scratch is to create a presentation outline. In PowerPoint, you can create an outline for your presentation in one of two ways:

- Click the Outline View icon at the bottom of the screen.
- Select View | Outline.

PowerPoint switches to Outline view, automatically opens the Outline toolbar along your screen's left edge, and positions the cursor in the slide for adding text. The first line of a slide in Outline view is the presentation's title. To add lines of outline text, click the demote button to move the text down a level (for the first line of text on the slide) or press Alt-Shift-right arrow. Press Enter to add a new line at the same level as the previous line. Click the promote button to move the text up a level, or press Alt-Shift-left arrow. Continue to add text lines to your slide, changing levels to reflect the hierarchical relationship of your information, as shown in Figure 32.2.

TIP: CREATE SLIDES FROM AN OUTLINE

If you have a text document in an outline format, select Insert | Slides From Outline, and then select the outline document. The outline becomes PowerPoint slides.

FIGURE 32.2.

Use the Outline view to create new presentations.

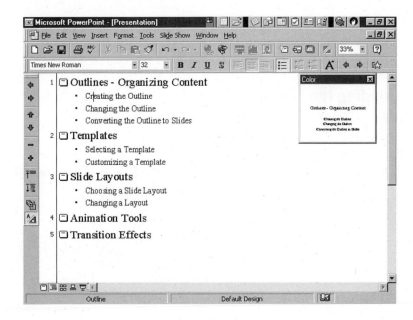

For easier viewing of your slide's titles (which, remember, are the top level of your outline), click the Outline toolbar's Collapse All button. PowerPoint collapses your outline to show only the titles. Click the Expand All button to expand your outline so that all levels display.

If the Common Tasks toolbar (the toolbar looks like a small dialog box) gets in your way, drag it to a different location or close the toolbar's window. If you close the Common Tasks toolbar you can redisplay the toolbar when you need it by selecting View | Common Tasks.

Chapter 50, "Working with the Office Integration Tools," explains how to combine PowerPoint and Word. If you prefer creating your presentation notes in Word initially, PowerPoint lets you easily insert those Word presentation notes into PowerPoint. Word's advanced text-editing tools make composing presentation notes even easier than using PowerPoint's outlining tools.

Changing the Outline

As you develop your outline, PowerPoint makes it easy for you to rearrange the order of information in a level or to shift the position of a slide or group of slides. To change the order of information within a level, move the cursor to the left of the line you want to move. When the cursor changes to a double-headed arrow, click the left mouse button to select the line, and then drag the line to its new position. To change the position of a slide and all its information, move the cursor to the left of a slide title and then click and drag the slide. To move a group of slides, select additional slides by holding down Ctrl (for slides out of sequence) or Shift (for slides in order) and then drag the group.

Converting the Outline to Slides

As you create a presentation's outline, PowerPoint's Color window displays a preview of your current slide. If you want to see the slide full-screen, you can change from an Outline view to PowerPoint's Slide view.

Here are the two ways to change from Outline view to Slide view:

■ Click the Slide View icon.
■ Select View | Slide.

Each major heading from the outline becomes a slide, with the top-level heading becoming the slide's title. Each outline line converts to a bulleted text line, with different levels corresponding to the outline's levels, as shown in Figure 32.3.

FIGURE 32.3.
Making a slide from an outline.

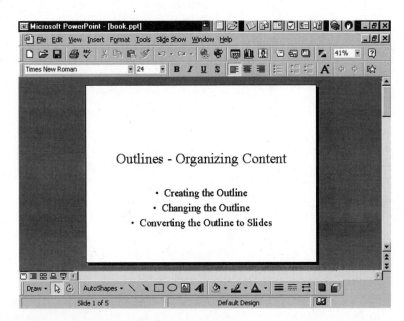

Outlining the MicroMouseMike Presentation

Throughout this chapter—and the rest of the PowerPoint section—we'll be looking at a particular presentation as an example of using PowerPoint. This sample presentation outlines the roll-out plans for a new product—the MicroMouseMike, a combination cordless computer pointing device and hand-held microphone. The presentation is aimed at the employees of Stand Up Routines, the creator of the MicroMouseMike.

Figure 32.4 shows part of the outline for the MicroMouseMike roll-out presentation. The presentation's developers have organized the content into what, when, where, who, why, and how points, followed by a brief business analysis of strengths, weaknesses, opportunities, and threats.

FIGURE 32.4.

Part of the Micro-MouseMike outline.

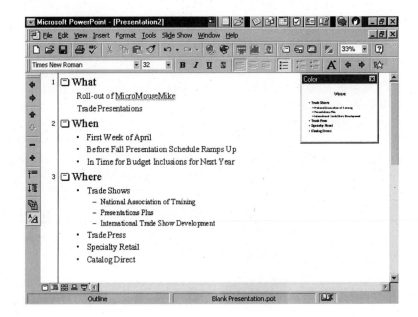

AutoContent

The outline is admittedly a good way to organize your content, but what if you're not sure what your content should be? PowerPoint provides the AutoContent Wizard to give you a starting point for presentations.

CAUTION: AUTOCONTENT VERSUS AUTOLAYOUT

Don't confuse the AutoContent Wizard with PowerPoint's AutoLayout formats. AutoLayout provides several design templates from which you can select when you create new presentations; the AutoContent Wizard walks you through a presentation's design one step at a time.

Use the AutoContent Wizard to help you create the following presentations:

- Recommending a strategy
- Selling a product, service, or idea
- Training

- Reporting progress
- Communicating bad news

You can create many more topics with the AutoContent Wizard. To access it, select the appropriate AutoContent Wizard from the area labeled Create a new presentation using in the opening PowerPoint dialog box, or you can select File | New and then select AutoContent Wizard from the Presentations tab.

AutoContent presentations aren't complete in and of themselves. They provide the layout for a presentation, which includes basic slides within the presentation topic and suggestions for the information to put in each slide. It's up to you to flesh out the presentation.

> **TIP: DELETE THE SUGGESTED TEXT**
>
> Don't forget to delete the suggested text. You don't want development hints to show up as part of your presentation.

Templates

Once you lay out the content of your presentation, it's time to turn your attention to your presentation's appearance. You can, if you choose, design the look of the overall presentation from scratch, designating background colors and patterns, font type and size for each level of information on a slide, bullet shape and color for each level, placement and alignment of the title text, and so on. To be effective, your presentation design should consider the following details:

- The legibility and readability of different fonts at different sizes
- Color theory and psychology
- The presentation medium—color overheads, black-and-white overheads, on-screen slides, Internet HTML Web pages, or 35mm slides
- Placement of headers, footers, and other recurring information

Designing an effective presentation format from scratch takes a lot of work and expertise, encompassing many factors that most of us don't want to deal with. It is for us that PowerPoint includes presentation templates.

PowerPoint's templates address the issues of presentation design and provide professional, predesigned presentation layouts. Fonts and sizes have already been plugged in, with an eye toward legibility and readability. Colors don't clash or send out hostile vibrations. Bullets fit with the feel and color scheme of the rest of the presentation. All you have to do is pick an appropriate template for your purpose, make changes to the template to suit your needs, and then add your information.

Selecting a Template

Next to the content, the overall design of your presentation is probably the most important part of an effective presentation. Starting with a professionally designed template gets you pointed in the right direction. The next issue, however, is *which* template to use.

When you create a new presentation, you select a template. When PowerPoint displays the New Presentation dialog box, shown in Figure 32.5, select the Presentations tab. (You'll see a list of several template designs. If you see the tab labeled Presentation Designs, you'll see additional, and simpler, templates.)

FIGURE 32.5.

A preview of a template.

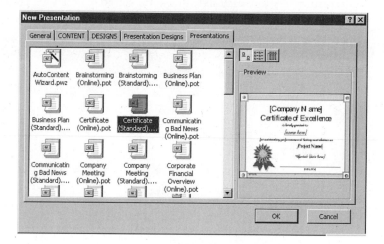

Click over one of the template icons to preview that template in the preview window. You can change the icon display to a list format (and move back once again to the icon display) by clicking the appropriate button above the preview window. Move through the templates to find one you want, and then apply it. That template forms the base of your presentation.

NOTE: THE BLANK PRESENTATION TEMPLATE

You can create a "blank" presentation without a template. Actually, it's a presentation with a template called Blank Presentation.POT. Even then, the template isn't truly blank. The "blank" template provides basic font types and sizes, bullets, and text placement guidelines. Every presentation needs at least that much in its framework.

If you want to change an open presentation's format to a different template, select Format | Apply Design or click the Apply Design button on the toolbar. The Apply Design Template dialog box lists the available templates and previews the template selected. As discussed earlier, preview the different templates and select the one you want to apply to your presentation.

But how do you decide which template to choose? Think about the purpose of your presentation: What information do you want to convey, to whom, and in what kind of setting? What overall tone do you want your presentation to have? A presentation about this quarter's financial results to the Board of Directors will look very different from one delivered at a sales pep rally. When choosing your presentation template, the following points might help:

- Is your presentation formal or informal?
- Is your presentation internal (for your employees or the members of your group) or external (for customers, prospects, students, the Board, or some other set of people)?
- Are you presenting good news or bad?
- Are you going to integrate your presentation to the Internet or to an intranet?
- Are you selling something, or are you summarizing progress on a project?

For example, the Risk template, shown in Figure 32.6, probably wouldn't be suitable for serious, formal presentations, but it might be just right for highlighting this quarter's Las Vegas sales results at an employee meeting. The Who's Who template could be an excellent backdrop for presenting a recruitment meeting training session. Personal Home Page works well for presentations about Web sites. What about that serious, formal presentation for the Board of Directors? Why not use Organization Overview (see Figure 32.7), Project Status, or Reporting Progress?

FIGURE 32.6.

A preview of the Risk template with its dice picture.

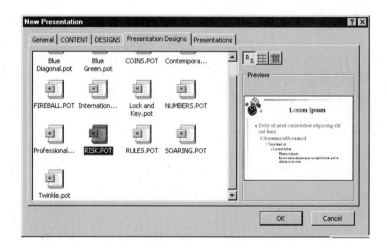

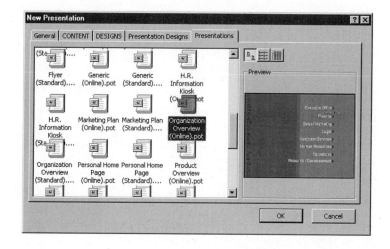

You'll have other considerations when choosing your template, of course, but this discussion offers some starting points.

Customizing a Template

One of PowerPoint's templates might be just right for your presentation. If so, great! Your presentation's design will be one less thing to worry about on your way to an effective presentation. Often, however, a template is just right *except* for the background color or title alignment or font. Or perhaps you need the company's logo to appear each slide. Using the template as a starting point, you can make changes to the overall presentation so that it's just right for your needs.

Every presentation has a Slide Master. The Slide Master is the "control center" for your presentation, setting the base fonts and bullets, including their size and color, and designating where common information appears on slides. Anything you change on the Slide Master, or anything you add, shows up on all slides in your presentation. Put your company's logo (or that of your customer or prospect) on the Slide Master to have it appear on all the slides of your presentation.

To open the Slide Master, do either of the following:

■ Select View | Master | Slide Master.

■ Press Shift and click the Slide View icon.

The Slide Master, shown in Figure 32.8, also displays *placeholders,* which are areas on a slide reserved for particular information. Placeholders on a Slide Master include the following areas:

- Title area
- Object area (where different kinds of Office objects can be placed)
- Date area
- Number area (where slide numbers that are automatically incremented display)
- Footer area (where you can enter the information you want to appear on every slide)

FIGURE 32.8.

The Slide Master.

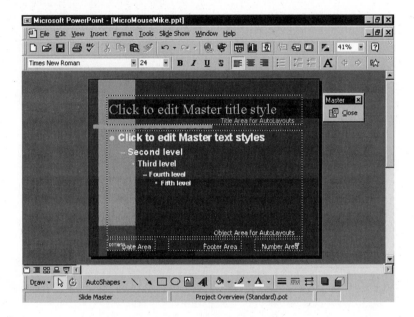

You can change the size and placement of the placeholders.

CAUTION: WATCH FOR OBJECT OVERLAP

When you place objects outside the Slide Master's planned areas, be sure to check all your slides to verify that slide text doesn't conflict with the other objects.

With the Slide Master open, you can also change the background, background colors, and other colors of the presentation. Select Format | Slide Color Scheme (or right-click and select Slide Color Scheme) to change the Slide Master's colors. The dialog box shown in Figure 32.9 appears. The Standard tab offers a number of different predefined color schemes. The Custom tab lets you change the color of individual elements of your presentation. Select Format | Background to change custom background colors, patterns, or textures.

FIGURE 32.9.

The Color Scheme dialog box.

Here are a few more tips for slide design:

- Sans serif typefaces (those without the little "feet" at the letter tips) are more legible than serif typefaces (those with the little "feet"). *Legibility* refers to the ability to easily recognize letters and words. You're aiming for legibility in your slides.

- In general, type that is smaller than 18 points will be too small for your audience to read. If you have a large room, an older audience, or you simply want to ensure that everyone can read your slides, use larger type.

NOTE: DEFAULT TYPE SIZES

PowerPoint type defaults to 32 points for first-level items, 28 points for second-level items, 24 points for third-level items, and 20 points for fourth- and fifth-level items. The type sizes of the first three levels should be adequate for most audiences. If you can spare the room, it wouldn't hurt to bump up each level by four points.

- Use light backgrounds with dark type for overheads, and use dark backgrounds with light type for on-screen slide shows or 35mm slides.
- Make sure you have good contrast between background and type.
- Don't cram too much information on one slide. Limit yourself to main points: Five per slide is close to the maximum. *Retain* your audience; don't *pain* your audience with busy slides.
- Use landscape (horizontal) slides rather than portrait (vertical) slides. Vertical slides require smaller type sizes to fit in information and lend themselves to overcrowded slides. Horizontal slides, with their longer lines, are easier to read and force you to be more compact with your information.

TIP: COLOR SCHEME USAGE

The predefined slide color schemes usually include at least one scheme with a dark background and one with a light background. Use dark backgrounds for on-screen presentations and 35 mm slides; use light backgrounds for overheads.

NOTE: SLIDE MASTER CHANGES

When you make changes to the Slide Master, the changes affect that presentation only—the template itself doesn't change.

TIP: USE A TEMPORARY PRESENTATION

When trying out different templates or backgrounds, create a new, temporary presentation and copy just a few of your slides into it. Check out the proposed changes against these few slides, and you'll see the effects of your changes much faster than if you apply them to your entire presentation. Include slides that represent all your slide types (text, graphic, and chart) to make sure you like all the types with the new colors and styles. When you're happy, go back to your real presentation and make the same changes.

The MicroMouseMike Template

As mentioned earlier, this chapter's sample presentation describes the product roll-out plans for the MicroMouseMike. As you'll recall, the presentation is aimed at the employees of Stand Up Routines, the creator of the MicroMouseMike. The product is ready to hit the shelves, and Stand Up Routines wants to generate enthusiasm and increase product awareness in its employees by promoting the roll-out internally. The presentation will be informative without being "teachy" or "preachy."

After examining all the templates and applying the top template candidates to the MicroMouseMike presentation, Stand Up Routines has decided to use the Project Overview template for the presentation. Project Overview, they feel, gives an unexpected feeling of informality but adds colorful interest to the presentation. They have also decided to change the type face for the body and title of the slides to an interesting sans serif style (Kabel, not provided by Windows) in order to provide good legibility and to continue the feeling of informality and fun. Figure 32.10 shows one of the slides with the Project Overview template.

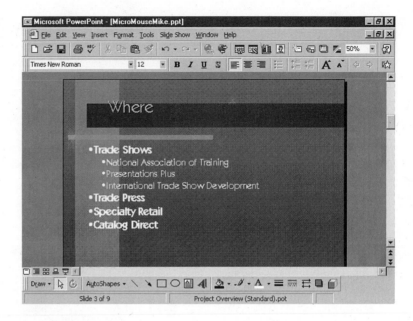

FIGURE 32.10.

A MicroMouseMike slide with the Project Overview template.

Automatic Layouts

Now that the content and overall presentation have been determined, we turn our attention to the layout of the individual slides. When you first create your content outline and change from Outline view to Slide view, all your slides will have a simple bulleted text layout. To change the layout of any slide, select the Slide Layout button from the Common Tasks toolbar window. PowerPoint then displays thumbnails of all the available slide layouts. These slide layouts are called *AutoLayouts* when you create a new blank presentation. Select the layout most suited for the information presented in the slide.

You have slides with bulleted text that you have "created" from your outline, but you probably still have slides you want to add. You might even want to add some pictures, too. Although you can have an effective presentation using text alone, graphics and different visual formats can make your information more interesting. Use one of the following techniques to create new slides:

- Click the Common Tasks toolbar's New Slide option.
- Select Insert | New Slide.
- Click the Insert New Slide button on the toolbar.
- Press Ctrl-M.

PowerPoint opens the Slide Layout dialog box, shown in Figure 32.11, allowing you to choose the layout of your slide.

FIGURE 32.11.

Select from a variety of new slide layouts.

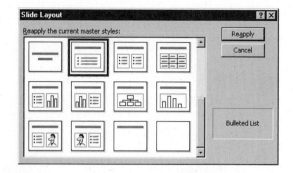

Choosing a Slide Layout

In many cases, the most appropriate layout to use is fairly obvious: Bulleted List for plain text; Table for tabular information; Graph for some form of chart. Other times, however, you'll need to make some design decisions. Do you want a slide of text followed by the chart it describes, or do you want to combine the text and graph on one slide? If so, is the slide more effective with the text on the left or on the right? Because the text area on a two-part slide is obviously going to be smaller, can you effectively make your point in a smaller area with a smaller font size? If you decide to put four objects (clip art, charts, or some other Office object) on the slide, do they complement each other without making the slide look too cluttered or busy?

After creating the layout for a graph or organization chart, double-click in the area indicated on the new slide to open the application and then create the representation of your information. Refer to Chapter 6, "Working with Microsoft Graph," to see how to create graphs and to Chapter 7, "More Office Tools," to see how to create organization charts. Double-clicking in an Object layout opens a list of objects you can place in your slide. In the Table layout, double-clicking sets up the insertion of a Word table.

You can change the layout of a slide at any time by clicking the Common Tasks toolbar's Slide Layout button and selecting a new layout. Common sense tells you that a bulleted list won't translate well into an organization chart. Changing slide layouts is most effective for layouts where you're swapping out the left and right sides or the top and bottom of a slide, or when you've just created the slide and realize that you want a slightly different layout.

Changing the MicroMouseMike Presentation

Looking over their MicroMouseMike roll-out presentation, the folks at Stand Up Routines realize that they need to make a few changes. First of all, the text they entered in parts of the original outline is too long to fit on one slide. Also, they need some visual interest.

To take care of the too-long text, they reconsider the layout of the Who and Threats slides. The Who slide looks too cluttered when they put the To and By sections in two columns on the same slide; therefore, they decide to create a new slide by splitting Who into two slides. For the Threats slide, they change the layout to 2-Column Text and then cut and paste the slide text into two columns, as shown in Figure 32.12. Even though the slide might look a little busy, they decide that they don't want to split the Threats slide into two slides and that the two columns of text are acceptable.

FIGURE 32.12.

The Threats slide with two columns of text.

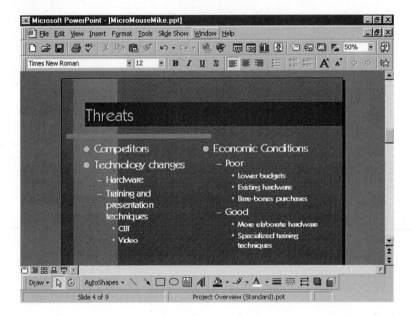

To add visual interest, Stand Up Routines adds clip art to its Where We'll Impact slide. To do this, they select the Text & Clip Art slide layout, double-click in the clip art side, and select the graphic they want for the slide from the Clip Gallery. Figure 32.13 shows the resulting slide.

NOTE: CREATING GRAPHS

This discussion will not cover the creation of the graph. See Chapter 6 for information on graphs.

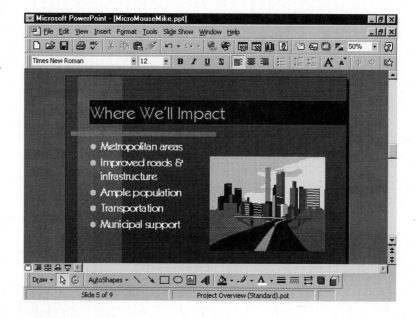

FIGURE 32.13.

The Where We'll Impact slide with a graphic clip art image.

Animation Tools

For on-screen presentations in PowerPoint, you can add animation or action within a slide. *Animation* specifies how text lines, clip art, or other objects appear on a slide.

Before adding animation, activate the Animation Effects toolbar, shown in Figure 32.14, by doing either of the following:

- Click the Animation Effects button on the toolbar.
- Select View | Toolbars and then select Animation Effects.

FIGURE 32.14.

The Animation Effects toolbar.

To add animation for graphics, select an object and then select the desired effect from the Animation Effects toolbar. Repeat this for as many objects on the slide as you want to animate.

When you specify animation for graphics, the animation order increments automatically. If you want your objects to appear in a different order, select the object and then change the number of its order.

To further refine your animation (or to create animation), click the Custom Animation button on the Animation Effects toolbar. In the Custom Animation dialog box, shown in Figure 32.15, you can specify the following items:

- The animation's timing
- Whether or not to animate an object
- The specific effect that is to take place during and after the animation
- What sound, if any, will accompany the effect
- The order of the animation

Figure 32.15.

The Custom Animation dialog box.

NOTE: APPLY EFFECTS INDIVIDUALLY

You must specify the effect for each individual object separately. You can't select a group of objects and then apply an effect to all of them at once. Don't forget this step, or you might find yourself wondering why your sun sets but your moon doesn't rise.

To remove animation for an object such as a graphic image, select the object, click the Custom Animation button on the Animation Effects toolbar, and select the Don't Animate option from the Timing dialog box.

To add animation for text, select the text on the Custom Animation's Timing dialog box and then select the animation effects from the rest of the dialog box's tabs. The text animation you choose affects all text in that text box; therefore, you don't have to (and can't) specify effects by individual lines. You can add animation to either the title or the slide text by clicking the appropriate Animation toolbar button.

TIP: EFFECTS AND PARAGRAPH LEVELS

By default, text effects apply to the first-level paragraphs. Therefore, first-level text will appear using whatever effect you've chosen, followed by any second- or lower-level text. The animation stops before the next first-level paragraph. Use the Custom Animation dialog box to change the levels at which the animation "stops" before requiring your input to continue.

Remove text animation by clicking the Don't Animate option in the Custom Animation Timing dialog box to toggle the effects off. To help verify that you added an appropriate animation, click the Preview button in the Custom Animation dialog box to see the slide's animation.

CAUTION: DON'T OVERDO IT

Animation effects are lots of fun to develop, but a little goes a long way when you're at the receiving end. Use animation effects sparingly to be most effective.

CAUTION: PREVIEW YOUR SLIDE SHOW

Absolutely, positively preview your slide show, complete with animation, before you show it to someone else. It's too easy to choose a text effect that puts up a line of text a letter at a time, blanking out each letter before moving on to the next. This isn't a particularly good way to impress your boss.

Following the same reasoning, assigning random effects to a slide might not work well for your presentation. By definition, you don't know what you'll get with a random effect—there's no way to preview it.

TIP: USE FLYING TEXT IN TITLES

If you want to use flying text, use it in the slide title rather than the body of the slide. This way, you've emphasized the title, which you probably want to do anyway, and haven't detracted from the information in the slide itself.

TIP: LOOK FOR THE ANIMATION ICON

Have you forgotten which slides have animation effects? In the slide sorter view, slides with animation effects have a little animation icon below the slide. In addition, when you select a slide, its animation effect, if any, is displayed in the toolbar.

Animation and MicroMouseMike

Given that right now you're reading a book (a notoriously static medium), seeing examples of animation effects in the MicroMouseMike sample presentation is all but impossible. However, I'll describe the animation effects so that you can get ideas for incorporating them into your presentations.

Since the MicroMouseMike is a wireless, hand-held, combination PC mouse and microphone, why not develop a slide like Figure 32.16? It shows a PC, a mouse, and a microphone (all available from the Office Clip Art Gallery) with plus signs from the Drawing toolbar between them. You can animate the three objects in turn using the flying effect to have them "land" in the appropriate place on the slide.

TIP: CONVERTING IMAGES TO OBJECTS

You can convert a clip art image to a PowerPoint object so that you can use PowerPoint's tools to customize the clip art. Select the clip art and then, from the Draw toolbar, choose Draw | Ungroup.

For a How slide, or a similar one, consider adding the text effect of "moving" through the bulleted points, dimming a line after it's been addressed. To do this, click in the text box, select the Build Slide Text button from the Animation Effects toolbar, and then click the Custom Animation button. Next, click the arrow below After animation and select a shade of gray (or another appropriate color) that is slightly lighter than the background. You can select from the row of color boxes or click Other Colors to see additional color options. In your presentation, as you move through the slide, the previous bullet points are dimmed out.

FIGURE 32.16.

The MicroMouseMike slide.

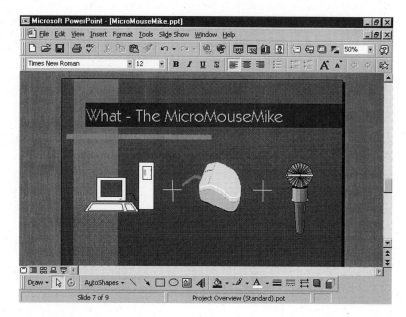

Transition Effects

The last weapon in PowerPoint's visual effects arsenal that we will explore is transition effects. Although animation effects take place within a slide, transition effects occur between slides. Transitions move your presentation gracefully from slide to slide instead of abruptly changing from one slide to another.

To add a transition to a slide, go into Slide Sorter view, as shown in Figure 32.17, and select a slide. You can select multiple slides by holding down Shift while you click over each slide to apply the transition to a group of slides. Click the Slide Transition button on the toolbar or select a transition from the drop-down Transition list. In the Slide Transition dialog box, shown in Figure 32.18, you can specify the following items:

- The effect
- The effect's speed
- How to advance the slide
- A sound

In addition, a preview window shows a demonstration of the effect. When you change an effect, the preview instantly shows the result of your change.

FIGURE 32.17.
The Slide Sorter view.

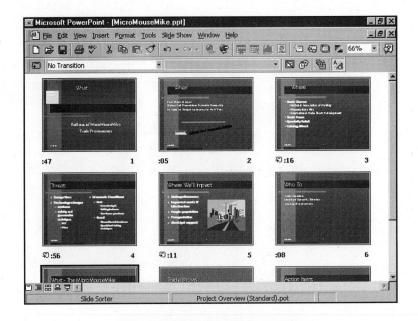

FIGURE 32.18.
The Slide Transition dialog box.

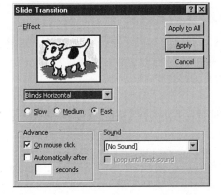

A transition icon appears below the slide. Click the transition icon to preview the transition for that slide. You can also apply a transition while in Slide view by selecting Slide Show | Slide Transition.

CAUTION: WATCH TRANSITION AND ANIMATION COMBINATIONS

Be careful when combining a transition and an animation effect on the same slide. The transition, a pause, and then text flying onto the screen one letter at a time might be too much.

Summary

This chapter explored the design of an effective PowerPoint presentation. It started with using an outline as a means to organize the content of a presentation. Once an outline is created, you can convert the outline to slides. This chapter then explored the way templates add special styles to presentations. PowerPoint's predesigned templates save you from the burden of determining all the pieces of the presentation and their visual components. A template might not address all your needs, but you can customize a presentation through the use of the Slide Master. This chapter then discussed the layout of individual slides and the kinds of information a slide can hold.

Exploring animation and transition effects finished this chapter's look at presentation design. Animation and transitions add further visual interest to an on-screen presentation. Animation occurs within a slide, to either text or graphics, and transitions move the presentation smoothly from one slide to the next.

Throughout this chapter, the MicroMouseMike product roll-out presentation was used as an example to demonstrate design techniques.

Here are a few related chapters to check out:

- OfficeArt is covered in Chapter 5, "Using the OfficeArt Tools."
- To learn how to work with PowerPoint's charting tools, see Chapter 6, "Working with Microsoft Graph."
- I'll cover some techniques for running slide shows in Chapter 33, "Making the Presentation."
- If you want to add sounds and videos to your presentations, see Chapter 34, "Multimedia Presentations."
- Some PowerPoint customization settings are covered in Chapter 35, "Customizing PowerPoint."
- You'll learn how to control PowerPoint via VBA in Chapter 58, "Programming a PowerPoint Presentation."

32

DESIGNING
AN EFFECTIVE
PRESENTATION

Making the Presentation

IN THIS CHAPTER

CHAPTER

33

Speech is power: speech is to persuade, to convert, to compel. It is to bring another out of his bad sense into your good sense.

—*Ralph Waldo Emerson*

Now that you have the content of your presentation settled, along with simple animations and transitions, you can turn your attention to the presentation's mechanics. This chapter explains how to show your presentation and also looks at the issue of notes—how you provide additional information besides what's on your slides, either for yourself (the presenter) or your audience.

Creating and Using Notes

When determining the content of your presentation, you kept the actual amount of information on a slide to a minimum—just the high-level points to provide the framework for the topics you want to present. How, then, do you keep track of the details you want to cover for each slide? What if you want to provide those details to your audience, too? Simple. Use PowerPoint's notes.

Notes let you have paper printouts that contain both your slides and additional information you enter in notes. Consider the following ways you can use notes:

- As your presentation notes.
- As additional detailed handouts for your audience.
- As a copy of your presentation with a blank area for your audience to take their own notes. Have you ever been to a conference where they distribute hard copies of the presentations with three-slides-per-page printouts with lines for notes and wanted to do the same thing? Keep reading and find out how.
- As a student guide. If you use a presentation as your primary teaching medium, you can put additional information on notes pages for your learners.
- As an instructor's guide. Again, if you teach from your presentation, you might have points you wish to make, or other information associated with a particular slide. Add this information as notes, and you have your instructor's guide, perfectly in sync with the information you're giving your learners.

To create notes, select View | Notes Page, or click the Notes Page View button from the icons at the bottom of the screen. The note page displays the current slide with the notes area below the slide, as shown in Figure 33.1. Click in the notes area and type whatever text you want for each slide. Press Page Down and Page Up to navigate through the slide Notes Page views.

TIP: INCREASING THE NOTES SIZE

If the Notes view is too small to read, increase the view's zoom size by selecting View | Zoom. Better yet, roll your IntelliPoint Mouse's zoom roller to adjust the readable view.

FIGURE 33.1.

The Notes Page view displays your presentation's notes.

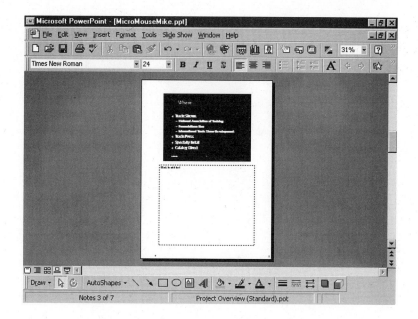

If you're creating handouts for your audience, you might want to consider using the master formatting tools on the Notes Master. Select View | Master | Notes Master, or press Shift while selecting the Note Pages icon to open the Notes Master view. In the Notes Master (Figure 33.2 shows a zoomed Notes Master view), you can specify a header and footer and add the date and page numbers. You can also specify how the text within the note body itself will appear by formatting the font. The information you specify on the Notes Master then prints on every note page.

To print your notes, select File | Print. In the Print dialog box, move to Print what and select Notes Pages from the list. Click Black and White to print the slide in black and white instead of a gray version of your color slide. Notes pages print in portrait layout, with a half-sized representation of your slide on the top portion of the page and your text on the bottom portion.

NOTE: USE BLACK AND WHITE FOR PRINTING

Be sure to check Black and White for printing, even if you're already viewing your slides in black and white. If you don't, your color slides will print in black and gray and look ugly.

Remember that PowerPoint's notes are for the speaker and aren't designed to hand out to your audience. As you present the presentation, you'll see the notes. Use handouts (discussed in a later section) when you want to give your audience presentation handouts.

FIGURE 33.2.

*The Notes Master holds
common note elements.*

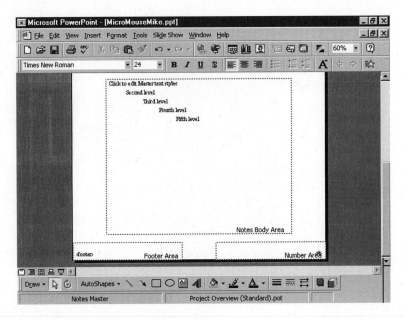

Adding Presentation Comments

PowerPoint comments work like the little yellow sticky notes we often stick all over our screens. When you select View | Comments, PowerPoint displays any comments you might have added to your presentation.

To add a comment, click the Insert Comments toolbar button (or select Insert | Comments). PowerPoint adds a comment note to your presentation, as shown in Figure 33.3. PowerPoint always begins a comment with the author's name, but you can change the name text to something else or erase it. PowerPoint gets the author's name from the Tools | Options | General page's User information section.

As with most Office 97 windows, you can move and resize the comment window. The comments aren't part of your presentation. They won't appear until you display them by selecting View | Comments. Comments are useful for describing the source for presentation numbers and for notes to others who might work on this presentation with you. Once you're done with the comment, delete it by clicking the comment to display its resizing borders and then pressing Delete.

FIGURE 33.3.

Adding a comment to a presentation is as easy as slapping on a yellow sticky note.

The new comment ——

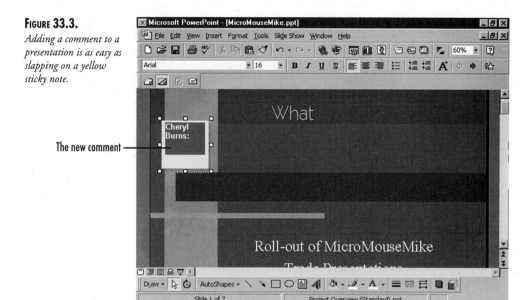

Handout Material

Handouts are simply printouts of your slides—just the slides, no notes. Audience members often appreciate having copies of your slides. They can concentrate more on your presentation and less on taking detailed notes when you supply the presentation handouts.

To print handouts, select File | Print. In the Print dialog box, move to Print What and select Handouts (two, three, or six slides per page). Make sure to check Black and White before printing. The option labeled Frame slides adds a thin border around each slide.

Handouts print in portrait format. The arrangement of slides depends on the number of slides per page you chose. Two slides per page print one above the other, half size. Three slides per page print three slides along the left side of the page, with the right side blank. Six slides per page print three slides each along the left and right sides of the page. The size of the slides in three-per-page and six-per-page is the same.

Because handouts are just printed slides, you can't change to a handout view. You can, however, format parts of your handout pages using the Handout Master (select View | Master | Handout Master). On the Handout Master, shown in Figure 33.4, you can specify a header and footer and add the date and page numbers. What you enter on the Handout Master then prints on every handout page.

33

MAKING THE PRESENTATION

FIGURE 33.4.

Change the handout format from the Handout Master.

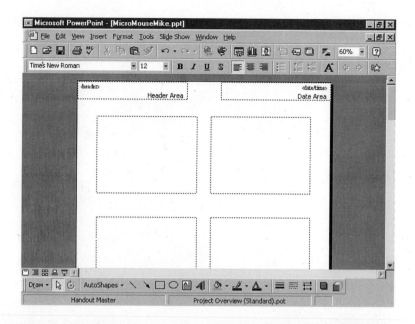

NOTE: YOU CAN'T CHANGE HANDOUT MASTER SLIDE AREAS

You can't change the slide's boxed areas on the Handout Master. The boxed areas just show the outlines of the different-sized slide areas.

Making a Presentation from a PC

Finally (imagine here either a dramatic hush or a blood-stirring drum roll, depending on your mood), this section explains how to give your presentation, showing your work to someone other than yourself, your spouse, or your roommate—someone like your boss, or her boss, or the Board of Directors, or your Marketing 101 class.

A presentation from a PC (also called an on-screen slide show or an electronic presentation) shows your slides, one at a time, moving from one slide to the next automatically or from a mouse click from you. In PowerPoint, you activate your electronic marvel from the menu bar by selecting View | Slide Show, or by clicking the Slide Show icon.

TIP: SELECT THE FIRST SLIDE BEFORE STARTING

Make sure you select the presentation's first slide before starting Slide Show from the icon. Whatever slide is active is the first slide to display.

Controlling Your Slide Show

If you want to control the way your slide show appears, select Slide Show | Set Up Show to display the Set Up Show dialog box, shown in Figure 33.5. Here you can control how PowerPoint presents the show by specifying a full screen or windowed view. In addition, you can choose to show all slides or only a portion of your slides, designating beginning and ending slide numbers. You also select how the slides will change (or advance) from one to the next and if the presentation will loop through the slides continuously until you press Esc.

FIGURE 33.5.

The Set Up Show dialog box gives you presentation control.

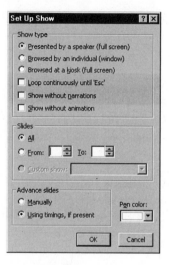

If you want complete control over your presentation, select Manually in the Advance slides section. With this setting, PowerPoint waits for your mouse click (or keystroke) before advancing to the next slide in your presentation. You can move through individual slides as quickly or as slowly as you wish. To move to the next slide, click the left mouse button or press the N key on the keyboard; press the P key to move to the previous slide.

Often, you'll need to make your presentation within certain time constraints. You'll have an overall time limit, and within that limit you'll want to devote specific amounts of time to different slides and subjects. You can set your presentation to change slides according to times you determine. To set slide timings manually, select Slide Show | Slide Transition, or right-click a slide in the Slide Sorter view and select Slide Transition.

In the Advance section of the Slide Transition dialog box, shown in Figure 33.6, select Automatically After and supply the number of seconds you wish to spend on this slide. Set the advance time for each slide. PowerPoint displays the number of seconds you've indicated for each slide below the slide in the Slide Sorter view.

FIGURE 33.6.

The Slide Transition dialog box.

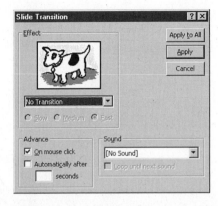

NOTE: USE SECONDS

You must enter a value in seconds. If you want your slide to display for 3 minutes, enter 180 seconds. The Slide Sorter view translates the seconds into minutes.

Rather than using this manual method of entering the timing for each slide, you can automatically set the timings as you move through the presentation. When previewing the Slide Sorter view, select Slide Show | Rehearse Timings. PowerPoint begins your presentation and displays the Rehearsal dialog box, shown in Figure 33.7.

FIGURE 33.7.

The Rehearsal dialog box lets you set presentation timings.

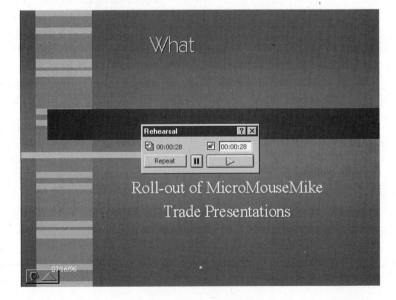

The time on the left is the cumulative time of the entire presentation so far. The time on the right is the time spent so far on the current slide. Practice what you want to say for each slide, and then click the right-arrow key to record the time and advance to the next slide. If you want to redo the timing for a slide, click the Repeat button. The time counters reset (for both the cumulative time and the current slide's time), and you can begin your timing again. Click the pause button (the one with two vertical lines) to suspend timing until you click it again.

When you've worked through your presentation, PowerPoint displays a dialog box giving the total time of the presentation and asking if you want to record the slide timings for view in Slide Sorter. When you select Yes, PowerPoint saves the slide timings and displays the number of seconds for each slide below each slide in the Slide Sorter view, as shown in Figure 33.8.

FIGURE 33.8.

The Slide Sorter view displays each slide's timing.

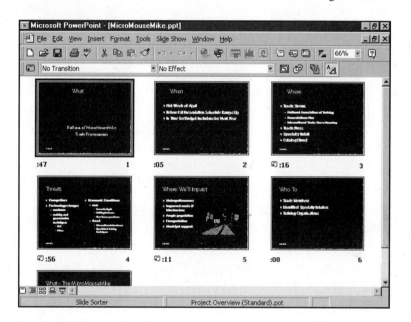

33

MAKING THE
PRESENTATION

To run your presentation using your slide timings, whether entered manually or through Rehearsal, select Use Slide Timings in the Slide Show dialog box. Your presentation runs automatically, changing slides after the times you designated.

NOTE: REHEARSE TO GET MANUAL TIMINGS

If you want to know how long each slide takes to present, but you don't want to lock yourself into the timings, rehearse your presentation to work out your speed. Don't save the timings. When actually giving your presentation, use manual advance and present each slide as you rehearse.

continues

continued

PowerPoint does have a Slide Meter feature that compares your recorded timings with your actual slide presentation speed. During your slide show, right-click and select Slide Meter. The dialog box shown in Figure 33.9 appears.

Figure 33.9.

The Slide Meter feature.

Not only does the right mouse button offer timing feedback with the Slide Meter, but you can also control the presentation's next and previous slides with the right-click pop-up menu, as well as change the mouse cursor to a pen that lets you draw and underline slide material as you present the slide show.

You can set up your presentation to run unattended, looping continuously through the slides. Rehearse and record timings, making sure you give enough time for someone to read and digest each slide, and then run your presentation using slide timings and selecting Loop continuously until 'Esc' from the Set Up Show dialog box.

TIP: USING LOOPING PRESENTATIONS

Use a looping presentation at trade shows, in information booths, or anyplace you want to show your information without giving a "live" presentation. Add well-planned animations and transitions to help keep your viewers' interest.

NOTE: STOPPING A SLIDE SHOW

To stop a slide show at any time, press the Esc key.

Branching Within Your Presentation

During an interactive slide show (one where your audience is alive and well and asking questions, instead of one where you show each slide in order, no matter what), you might want to change the order in which you show your slides. Use the Slide Navigator to move quickly from slide to slide. Right-click in the current slide, select Go, and then select Slide Navigator. The Slide Navigator, shown in Figure 33.10, lists your slides by number and title, allowing you to select a particular slide and go quickly to it. The Last slide viewed box keeps your place, noting where you were before jumping around in your presentation.

FIGURE 33.10.

The Slide Navigator.

NOTE: SLIDE SHOW KEYBOARD TECHNIQUES

You can use the P and N keys to move to the previous and next slides, respectively. However, this method takes extra time and might appear unprofessional.

When you anticipate branching to a different slide, set up the "branch" in advance by following these steps:

1. Place a drawing or clip art object in the slide from which you'll branch, as shown in Figure 33.11.

FIGURE 33.11.

A clip art object works well as a branching point.

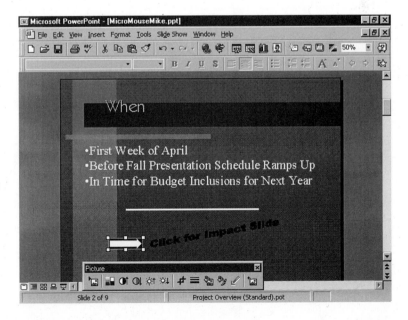

2. Select the object and then select Slide Show | Action Settings. The Action Settings dialog box, shown in Figure 33.12, determines what happens during the presentation if the presenter clicks the selected object.

FIGURE 33.12.

The Action Settings dialog box.

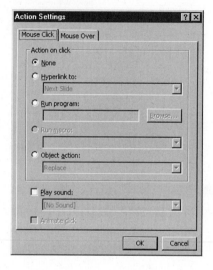

3. In the Action Settings dialog box, select one of the branching options. As you can see, PowerPoint will even send your presentation screen to the Internet to display a Web page if you insert the correct hyperlink option's URL address.

4. Click the arrow below Hyperlink To and view the options available for branching.

5. Select Slide.

6. From the Hyperlink to Slide dialog box that appears, select the slide to which you want to branch. PowerPoint displays that slide's preview so you'll know exactly what you chose.

7. Click OK twice to return to PowerPoint.

When you run your slide show, click your branch object (the cursor changes to a pointing hand when over a branching object) to jump to the designated slide.

NOTE: MULTIPLE BRANCHING OBJECTS

You may have more than one branching object in a slide.

33

MAKING THE
PRESENTATION

TIP: USE BRANCHING WITH AUDIENCE PARTICIPATION

Use this branching feature to personalize and keep high interest during your presentations. At a certain point in your presentation, have your audience vote on what they want to see next. Click the appropriate object, and your audience sees its own presentation.

Branching to Another Presentation

Within this branching concept, you might find that it makes more sense to have your branches be separate presentations. Consider branching to separate presentations when

- You want different slide templates for different branches.
- Several smaller files become easier to handle than one huge, slow file.
- Presentations you want to show already exist.
- Multiple people are creating different parts of the presentation.

Setting up a branch to another presentation is similar to, but more complicated than, branching within a presentation. To branch to another presentation, follow the next steps.

NOTE: CREATE THE OTHER PRESENTATION

These steps assume that you've already created the other presentation.

1. In the slide from which you'll branch, select Insert | Object, and then select Create from File.
2. Click Browse and select the file you want to branch to.
3. If you want changes in the branch presentation to be reflected in your current presentation, click the Link box. Otherwise, with the Link box unchecked, PowerPoint inserts the contents of the branch presentation *at that point in time* into your current presentation. Changes in the branch presentation don't appear in your current presentation.
4. Click OK to exit the Insert Object dialog box.
5. PowerPoint inserts a thumbnail of the branch presentation's first slide. Size the thumbnail as required.
6. Select the thumbnail, and then select Slide Show | Action Settings.
7. In the Action Settings dialog box, select Object Action and then Show.

When you run your slide show and click one of the thumbnails (the cursor changes to a pointing hand when it's over one of these "hot spots"), PowerPoint branches to the new presentation. Once the embedded slide show finishes, it returns control to your original presentation. To move on the next slide, click somewhere outside the thumbnail hot spot.

NOTE: MULTIPLE BRANCHING THUMBNAILS

You can have more than one branching thumbnail on a slide.

TIP: POINTERS FOR BRANCH PRESENTATION THUMBNAILS

Be creative with the branching presentations so that they display well as thumbnails. If you branch to more than one presentation from the same slide, give each presentation a different template, as shown in Figure 33.13. Make the first slide of the branch presentations a clip art or drawing object that readily communicates the subject of the presentation. Depending on how you size your thumbnails, the title of the branch presentations might not be readable, but you'll have an "icon" to represent each branch.

FIGURE 33.13.

Branch presentation thumbnails help clarify branching options.

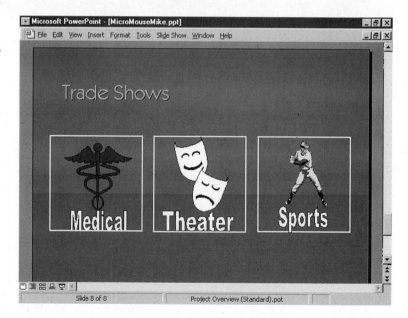

Beyond the Software: Presentation Hardware and Other Goodies

Knowing how to create your presentation using PowerPoint is well and good, but there's another big component to your presentation: the hardware you'll use to show it. At the lowest level, you can give your presentation on a desktop or laptop PC. The size of the screen or monitor and the number of people you can crowd around the display will have a considerable impact on the presentation's effectiveness. Be particularly careful with laptops with passive matrix screens. These screens can only be viewed from straight on; anyone at the edges will completely miss out on the presentation.

NOTE: NETWORK PRESENTATIONS

With Office 97, you're not limited to your own computer. You can offer presentations over a network and even over Web pages that your company publishes. Contact your network administrator for information regarding the networking and Internet options available for your presentations.

Another, more effective, hardware option for giving your presentation is the LCD panel. An LCD panel intercepts the video from a PC and displays the image on the panel. When you place the LCD panel on an overhead projector, the projector picks up the image and displays it on a wall screen. Using an LCD panel with an overhead projector allows you to show your presentation in any situation where an overhead projector is effective. Here are a couple warnings about LCD panels:

- You limit your presentation quality to the resolution of the panel.
- LCD panels can project the screen image darker than it is on the PC. A higher light output from the overhead projector can help alleviate this problem.

An LCD projector intercepts the video from a PC and projects the image, greatly magnified, onto a screen. LCD projectors give you more flexibility than the LCD panel/overhead projector arrangement, because you can place the projector farther away from the screen and get a larger projected image. As with LCD panels, the resolution of the image from an LCD projector can vary. LCD projectors cost considerably more than the LCD panel/overhead projector combination.

Using a standard mouse—or worse, a laptop's pointing device—during a presentation can be frustrating. With a mouse, you're limited by the length of the mouse cord, so you might be inappropriately tethered to the PC. I, at least, find the mouse buttons to be confusing when I give a presentation—I want the right button to advance a slide and the left button to move back a slide. Of course, I could specifically switch the mouse buttons for my presentation, but I share the presentation facilities with other groups and if I forgot to change the button configuration back, I'd be lousing *them* up.

Consider, then, one of the hand-held pointing devices specifically geared to presentation giving. These devices usually have the advance button on the right and provide cursor-moving capabilities at your fingertips. You can get cordless versions of these devices, too, so you no longer have a tether.

If you're using a big screen of some sort, think about how you will point at things on your slides. If you're close enough to the screen, you can use one of the collapsible, antenna-like pointers. Keep in mind, however, that getting that close to the screen might place you in the light source. Then, you're half-blind and your shadow might block important parts of the slide. Also, check out conditions before giving your presentation. Will your audience be able to see your pointer?

A laser pointer provides a good alternative to the antenna pointer. You can use it from where you stand so you don't block the screen and distract your audience by moving toward the screen. Laser pointers can be trickier to use than you'd think, though. You might need practice to move the pointer slowly enough so your audience can pick out what you're highlighting. Sweeping that little red dot around in circles can distract your audience or make them dizzy. Don't shine the pointer in anyone's eyes—yours included.

Interacting with Your Presentation

In addition to making your presentation interact with your audience, you can interact with your presentation in a number of ways.

Annotations

You can annotate, or write or draw on, your slides during a presentation. To turn on the annotation "pen," right-click and select Pen, or press Ctrl-P. The cursor changes to a pencil. Hold down the left mouse button and move the mouse to "write" on the presentation slide. Annotations appear on the screen only and don't change the content or appearance of the slides themselves.

TIP: ERASE SHORTCUT

To erase annotations, press E while using the annotation pen.

Meeting Minder

PowerPoint's Meeting Minder allows you to make notes about your presentation as you go along. For example, if your presentation is the agenda for a departmental meeting and you want to make minutes of the meeting and note action items as your meeting progresses, use Meeting Minder to "automate" those tasks.

You can access Meeting Minder, shown in Figure 33.14, during a presentation by right-clicking and selecting Meeting Minder. Choose the tab you want to use:

- Meeting Minutes gives you room, by slide, to take minutes.
- Similarly, Action Items provides space to cumulatively record action items determined during the meeting.

FIGURE 33.14.

Meeting Minder.

Meeting Minutes and Action Items require a little work on your part to integrate them into your presentation. Before closing your presentation, right-click and select Meeting Minder. Click the Export button to display the dialog box shown in Figure 33.15, and select the export options you'd like for Meeting Minder. Click Export Now. A Word document called "Meeting Minutes" opens, as shown in Figure 33.16. This document contains the minutes and action items you noted in Meeting Minder.

FIGURE 33.15.

Meeting Minder export options.

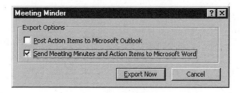

FIGURE **33.16.**

*Meeting Minder
minutes in Word.*

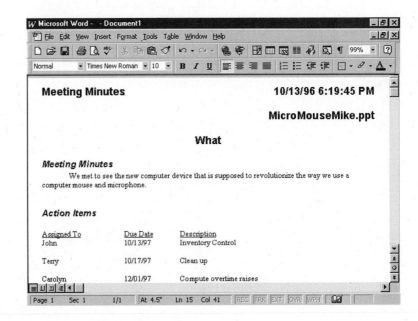

FIGURE **33.16.**

*Meeting Minder
minutes in Word.*

The Pack and Go Wizard

Quite often, in the world of electronic presentations, the computer you create your presentation on won't be the one you show it on. What if that other computer doesn't have PowerPoint? Must you lug around your PowerPoint disks or Office CD to install on the other computer, wasting your time and breaking licensing laws right and left? Must you hope and pray that your "target" computer already has PowerPoint loaded? No, all you "must" do is run the Pack and Go Wizard to package your presentation—and a PowerPoint viewer, if needed—on a disk to install on the target computer.

To run the Pack and Go Wizard, shown in Figure 33.17, select File | Pack and Go, and follow the instructions the wizard gives you. As with other Office wizards, this one is fairly self-explanatory. Pay attention, however, to the following selections in the wizard:

- Include linked files: If your presentation includes linked files, clicking this button ensures that the linked files get packed up, too.

- Embed True Type fonts: Clicking this button ensures that the fonts you use in your presentation are the same ones that show up in your presentation.

- Include PowerPoint Viewer: If the computer on which you'll show your presentation doesn't have PowerPoint, pack the viewer and you'll be able to run your presentation on that computer, too.

FIGURE 33.17.
The Pack and Go Wizard opening screen.

TIP: INCLUDE THE VIEWER

Just to be safe, it's probably a good idea to always include the viewer. You might need an extra disk to make room for it, but wouldn't you rather *know* that you'll have PowerPoint?

Once the Wizard has packed everything up, it's time to move to the target computer and unpack. Put the Pack and Go disk (or the first one, if PowerPoint produced more than one) in the disk drive and run pngsetup.exe. Specify a destination folder, and you can let the wizard do the rest.

To show your presentation (if you didn't check out your presentation right away to see if the viewer really does work), go into the directory you specified and run pptview.exe. Select the presentation, specify if you want to loop or use automatic timings, and click Show. Your presentation runs just as if it were on the machine where you created it.

CAUTION: DON'T VIEW BRANCHED SHOWS RIGHT AWAY

If you're viewing a presentation that branches to other presentations, don't try to view immediately after you've finished setting up the presentation on the target computer. You can't guarantee which of the presentations will run first.

NOTE: KEEP THE DISKS NEARBY

Keep your disk(s) handy after you've set up your Pack and Go presentation on the other machine. Despite indications to the contrary, you'll need to have the (first) disk in the disk drive when you exit the setup.

33

MAKING THE PRESENTATION

Choosing Your Output Medium

Now that you know how to do most of the mechanics of giving your presentation, it's time to examine the output medium itself: Given the choices of electronic presentations, overhead transparencies, 35mm slides, and just plain paper, which should you use when?

Electronic (On-Screen) Presentations

One of the greatest benefits of electronic presentations is flexibility. You can easily make last-minute changes—or even changes on-the-fly during the presentation. Because the file is the presentation medium, you don't have additional output worries. You have flexibility, too, in the order of your slides. Changing to different slides is no harder than bringing up the Slide Navigator and selecting where you want to go. You no longer have to click through several slides to jump over the slides you want to occasionally skip. In addition, branching allows you to jump to other parts of your presentation, or to other presentations.

As mentioned earlier, the computer on which you show an electronic presentation can be a disadvantage. If you're using a laptop to make a presentation to a group, your effectiveness is limited by the small size of the screen and the display's characteristics. A desktop computer likely has a better monitor, but you still have limitations regarding how many people can cluster around the screen.

For electronic presentations, a projection system is the way to go, if one is available. The big screen makes viewing a pleasure for all attendees, and you (the presenter) have room to move around and point things out. There is one drawback to the projection system output device: Generally, you'll darken the room for best viewing. Often, people know that they don't have to be (or look) as attentive during a darkened-room presentation; while the lights are off, your audience might be gone (mentally), too.

An additional benefit of electronic presentations is the lack of further production costs. Create the slide in your computer, and that's that. No printing, no reproduction, no ink or toner consumed.

Electronic presentations given on laptops or desktop PCs provide for the most informal presentations. Granted, a laptop-based presentation might be an excellent way to make a sales pitch to a limited number of people at a customer's site, but it's still not up to the level of other output media. Video project-based presentations are a step up on the formality scale, but they work well only for small- to mid-sized audiences.

Overhead Transparencies

Of the three output media, overhead transparencies are the second most flexible, but only in terms of changing the order of your presentation. You can swap transparencies fairly easily, but you can count out last-minute changes to the transparencies themselves. You can use markers to write on the overhead, but you're stuck with what you put on the thing originally.

Put your transparencies in some kind of sleeve or sheet protector. The sleeves provide holes for storing your overheads in binders, protect your slides from scratches, and provide extra weight to keep your slide firmly planted on the overhead projector. Make sure you use crystal-clear sleeves, though, or your slides might appear dim or discolored. Consider using the sleeves with "wings." The wings give you room to make notes about the overhead.

Many sources indicate to use a light background with dark letters for overhead transparencies. Feel free, however, to try out dark backgrounds with light text, but be certain that your overheads are readable and legible. Consider the cost of dark backgrounds, though. Colored ink or toner or film isn't cheap. Producing all those slides in color could prove to be burdensome to your budget.

Overhead transparencies still lend themselves to less-than-formal situations and smaller-sized audiences. (Would you really want to worry about putting overheads on the projector the right way out, the right way up, and completely straight, when giving an important presentation to the Board of Directors?)

35mm Slides

35mm slides probably provide the most professional presentation and are the most suitable medium for formal presentations. 35mm slides offer excellent color and image quality. You can change images more quickly using slides than overhead transparencies—and you don't have to worry about slides being crooked.

Using 35mm slides as your output medium brings up a host of issues that many of us aren't used to dealing with, however. With 35mm slides, you have to determine where and how you will get your presentation file converted into slides. You also need to decide whether you want plastic or glass mounts for your slides. Plastic mounts are cheaper than glass and are appropriate for informal presentations. Glass mounts provide sharper image focus and are less likely to pop out of focus, which can be a problem with plastic mounts. Once you have your slides, you have to arrange them and load them into cassettes, making sure you get them all in the right way. You have to worry about the possibility of all your slides falling out of their cassettes three minutes before you're due to begin.

TIP: USE NUMBERED SLIDES

Number the slides in your presentation. That way, if you have a three-minutes-before-you're-due-to-begin-type disaster, at least you'll have the numbers to guide your reloading chore.

One consideration for producing the slides themselves: Send your file to Genigraphics. Genigraphics Corporation is a service bureau that has provided PowerPoint users the necessary options to have their PowerPoint slides converted to 35mm slides, digital color overheads, posters, or large display prints. Run the Genigraphics Wizard (by selecting File | Send to

Genigraphics) and follow the instructions to get your information to Genigraphics and your output back from them.

CAUTION: YOU MIGHT NEED TO INSTALL GENIGRAPHICS

If you don't see the Genigraphics option on your File menu, you must run Office 97's Setup program once again and install the Genigraphics driver.

Summary

This chapter looked at creating and using notes and handouts to accompany your presentation. Then it concentrated on the mechanics of actually giving your presentation, including hardware considerations, adding annotations, and using the Meeting Minder. The Pack and Go Wizard allows you to move your presentation from one machine to another without all the extra baggage of including PowerPoint, too. Finally, this chapter explored some of the issues involved with different presentation output media.

Here are a few chapters where you'll find related information:

- Techniques for creating presentations are covered in Chapter 32, "Designing an Effective Presentation."
- If you want to add sounds and videos to your presentations, see Chapter 34, "Multimedia Presentations."
- Some PowerPoint customization settings are covered in Chapter 35, "Customizing PowerPoint."
- You'll learn how to run slide shows via VBA in Chapter 58, "Programming a PowerPoint Presentation."

Multimedia Presentations

IN THIS CHAPTER

I feel like Zsa Zsa Gabor's fifth husband. I know what I'm supposed to do but I don't know if I can make it interesting.

—*Al Gore*

You've seen simple animations in PowerPoint, but its multimedia capabilities go far beyond flying text, drive-in clip art, and dissolve transitions. With PowerPoint, your presentations can include sound and video, and video clips can include movies or animation.

What Is Multimedia?

Multimedia involves effects in two or more media. In today's computing world, multimedia generally means including video (or motion of some kind) and sound in a presentation, software package, or some other form of output.

Multimedia seems to have burst onto the computing scene relatively suddenly. A number of improvements in technology helped bring on this explosion of sight and sound. Some of the factors contributing to the rise of multimedia are

- Cheaper, more powerful processors
- Cheaper, improved CD-ROM technology
- Cheaper memory
- Improved sound cards
- Improved graphics cards
- Dramatically increased Internet usage, which supports multimedia

We have become used to increasingly sophisticated graphics and special effects in movies, TV, and videos. Once the technology to put motion and sound into software became affordable, multimedia took off.

PowerPoint's Help files list these minimum requirements for your computer to run multimedia presentations:

- A 486 processor running at 66MHz (a Pentium yields better video results)
- 16MB or more of memory
- 30MB of hard disk space
- A Soundblaster-compatible card
- External speakers
- A VGA 256-color graphics adapter; 16-bit or 24-bit adapters are recommended for better results with video

With several of these recommendations, more is better. The faster your processor or the more powerful (a Pentium chip as opposed to a 486 chip), the better. The more memory you have, the better. Sound cards, speakers, and graphics adapters come in different qualities. Higher-quality hardware usually results in higher-quality output. (Higher-quality hardware also results in higher prices, but such is life.)

Why Use Multimedia Presentations?

We've come to expect sophisticated audio and visual effects in our entertainment and, increasingly, in our software, including games, informative and educational software, and business applications. Multimedia is *the* thing in user-oriented output. Put somewhat bluntly, if you don't have multimedia, you're at a competitive disadvantage. Other factors being equal, someone else's product, whether it's software or a business presentation, might well be deemed better than yours if his is multimedia and yours isn't.

Perceptions (and marketing ploys) aside, we do have high expectations of what we see. If presentations don't catch and keep our interest, we become easily bored and tune out. Movement and sound—the stuff of multimedia—help catch and hold our attention.

In addition, different people learn in different ways: Some people learn by seeing (which could include reading), some learn by hearing, and others learn by doing. Although even multimedia presentations can't do much about those who learn by doing, they can address themselves to the learn-by-seeing folks by providing video clips and pictures in addition to text. Learn-by-hearing people can benefit from sounds and video sound tracks in addition to the presenter's material.

The more information you include in your presentation, the less you have to provide as the presenter. If the material you want to cover is all in the presentation, you won't have to worry about forgetting to make important points during the presentation. Similarly, if different people give the same presentation, you'll be assured of consistency among presenters if the presentation takes over most of the work.

The Trials and Tribulations of Multimedia

Multimedia can heighten audience interest in your presentation, but it can also distract. Too much motion, too much sound, too many lights, too many cameras, and too much action can produce presentations that no one wants to sit through. If they're done well, multimedia presentations can bring new interest and effectiveness to your presentations. If they're done poorly, you could lose your audience. A well-done single-media PowerPoint presentation can be far more effective than a badly done multimedia presentation.

In addition to the possibility of media overkill, multimedia brings with it hardware considerations simply not applicable to single media. You could show a single-media presentation on many existing computer systems. For a successful multimedia presentation, however, you must have a powerful-enough processor, sufficient memory, and adequate sound and graphics cards.

Multimedia-capable systems aren't as plentiful as single media-capable systems. If your presentation is part of a traveling road show and you're dependent on computer systems at your different destinations, you might find your finely tuned multimedia presentation falling flat on its face.

Multimedia presentations take up a lot of space, too. *Your* hard disk might have enough space for your wondrous creation, but will the one at your presentation site? Do you want to create and load all those backup disks? Or, if you use compression software and you don't need quite so many disks, will you remember to bring along a copy of the decompression software?

Multimedia PowerPoint Presentations

Now that we have the warnings out of the way, let's look at creating multimedia presentations in PowerPoint. Throughout this chapter, I'll assume that you've taken all the warnings to heart and that you have the appropriate multimedia hardware muscle, both for development and deployment. In addition, you should be familiar with some standard multimedia terms, such as *transition* and *video clip file*.

Basic Multimedia

You get basic multimedia capabilities with PowerPoint's slide animation and transitions. Display the Animation Effects toolbar and select Custom Animation to access these multimedia effects. Animation and transitions also add sound to your presentation. With text or object animation, the animation and sound drop-down list boxes in the Custom Animation dialog box show you the available sounds. Try to match sounds to animation effects. For example, you could team up the "Fly from right" animation effect with the sound of a car driving by. Use the Custom Animation dialog box, shown in Figure 34.1, to associate a sound with a transition. Chapter 32, "Designing an Effective Presentation," explains how to best utilize the transition effects.

FIGURE 34.1.

Adding a drive-by sound to a transition.

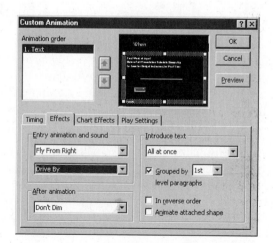

Similarly, you can add sounds to slide transitions. Select Slide Show | Slide Transition, and then select a sound from the Sound drop-down list. Checking the Loop until next sound box does just what it says—the sound repeats until some other sound replaces it.

CAUTION: DON'T OVERDO LOOPING SOUNDS

Looping sounds can get *very* irritating *very* quickly. Use them with extreme care! And don't forget to turn looping sounds off. They'll be there until another sound turns them off. If you forget to set another sound and you have breaking glass sounding throughout the rest of your presentation, you might not have an audience when the presentation finishes. Test your presentation before giving it.

NOTE: SOUNDS WITHOUT TRANSITIONS

You can add a sound to a slide transition even if you don't use a transition effect, as shown in Figure 34.2.

FIGURE 34.2.

You can have sound without a transition.

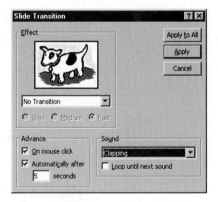

More Advanced Multimedia

You can transform your presentation into a multimedia marvel by adding audio and video clips (either live or animation) from other sources. Because these clips aren't part of the PowerPoint package, you'll need to add them as objects.

PowerPoint offers a number of ways to add video or audio clips to slides. You may do one of the following:

- Select Insert | Movies and Sounds
- Select Insert | Object | Video Clip or Insert | Object | Wave Sound

Multimedia clips are available from any number of sources. For videos, look for Video for Windows clips (those with .AVI and .MOV extensions); for sounds, look for .WAV files. The Microsoft Office 97 CD-ROM offers some samples. The Valupack folder on the CD has a wealth of goodies. In the Video folder, the Fourpalm folder contains "live" video clips. The Tcvisual folder has a number of animations. In the Audio folder, check out the Network offerings. The Effects, Elements, and Music folders contain a variety of .WAV files just begging for use as slide transitions, background music, or special effects.

If you click the Clip Gallery's Internet button, PowerPoint goes to Microsoft's Web site so that you can browse the collection of more than 2,000 graphic, sound, and video clip files. Microsoft constantly updates this site with additional files, so you'll want to check out what's there.

Controlling Your Clips

Once you've inserted your clip in a slide, you can edit the clip so that it better meets your needs. You have access to controls that can help you change both the video and sound tracks to meet your presentation's needs.

Editing Video Clips

To edit video clips, right-click the multimedia video object's icon, and then select Edit | *Movie* | Object. (What's between Edit and Object depends on the type of object you've inserted.) The Play Options dialog box, shown in Figure 34.3, appears so that you can specify the way PowerPoint 97 plays the video.

FIGURE 34.3.

This dialog box helps you determine how your video clip plays.

If you want to edit the video clip, you must click the Windows Start button to display the Start menu. Select Programs | Accessories | Media Player to start the Media Player application. When Media Player opens, load and edit your video clip object.

Because we're dealing with different kinds of media, Media Player responds differently to each kind. If you open a sound, Media Player responds with a sound editor; if you open a video, Media Player opens its video editor.

The Scale option from the Media Player menu bar (remember, we're looking at the video version) lets you select how you want to view the clip—by time, frames, or tracks. When you change the scale, the units marked on the slider change to reflect the new scale reference.

NOTE: THE ACTIVE SCALE

The slider itself doesn't indicate which scale is active, nor do the Scale menu selections. However, the caption area below the clip does.

TIP: USE THE TIME SCALE

Most people are probably more concerned with how long a clip takes than how many frames it contains. Therefore, the Time scale might be your best choice.

Selecting Edit | Options from Media Player offers you a number of ways to control or change the appearance of the video in your presentation, as shown in Figure 34.4. Select Auto Repeat to have the video player loop.

FIGURE 34.4.
*The Options
dialog box.*

If you want to control the video while it plays in your presentation, leave Control Bar On Playback checked. When the video plays in your presentation, you'll have access to simple controls—start, pause, stop, and a slider. If you choose to have the control bar, PowerPoint also displays a caption for the video. This caption defaults to the filename. You can change it if you want something a little more friendly or descriptive.

Choosing Edit | Selection lets you select exactly which part of the video you want to play. Depending on the scale you choose, the Set Selection dialog box, shown in Figure 34.5, reflects either frames or time. Click the up and down arrows next to the From, To, and Size fields to edit the video's start and stop points.

FIGURE 34.5.

The Set Selection dialog box.

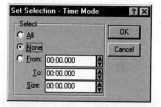

NOTE: EDITING BY FRAMES

Editing by frames could probably come in handy here. But you still need to know what frames to use as starting and stopping points.

TIP: EDIT THE VIDEO LENGTH

If the video you want is a little too long, or it's just right except for that bit at the end, edit it here to fit your needs.

Use the Start, Stop, and Pause buttons to play your clip a few times so that you can make sure it's just right before you add it to your presentation.

Editing Audio Clips

To change the volume of your system as it plays your clip, double-click the taskbar's speaker icon to open the Volume Control dialog box, shown in Figure 34.6. Adjust the sliders to control the video's volume.

While still in the Volume Control dialog box, select Options | Advanced to put the Advanced button on the Volume Control dialog box. Clicking the Advanced button opens the Advanced Controls for Volume Control dialog box, shown in Figure 34.7, where you can adjust bass and treble values.

FIGURE 34.6.

The Volume Control dialog box.

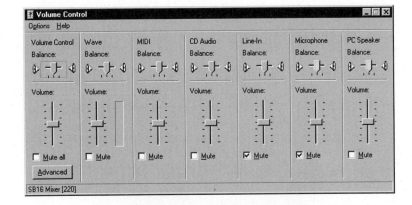

FIGURE 34.7.

Advanced controls for volume control.

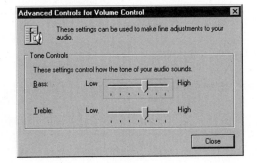

Playing Your Clips

If you insert your video or audio clips as described, you'll need to click each clip during your presentation to have them all play. Further tweaking of your clips allows them to play automatically during your presentation.

In Slide view, select a clip and right-click it. Select Action Settings from the pop-up menu. In the Action Settings dialog box, shown in Figure 34.8, select Play from the Object action dropdown list. You now won't need to click the actual clip to play it during your presentation. To play the clip, click anywhere on your presentation's screen.

For completely automatic clip playing, after you've selected the Play option in the Action Settings dialog box, display the Custom Animation dialog box, shown in Figure 34.9, by selecting Slide Show | Custom Animation. Click the Play Settings tab. To trigger the clip's play, check the Play using animation order option.

34

MULTIMEDIA PRESENTATIONS

FIGURE 34.8.

The Action Settings dialog box with play options.

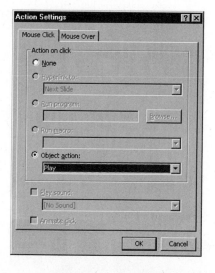

FIGURE 34.9.

Specifying the playing options.

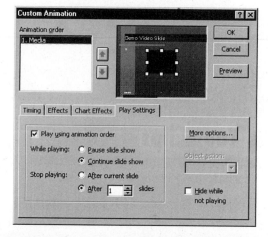

NOTE: ALLOW FOR THE EXTRA VIDEO SETUP TIME

As discussed in the section "Speed of Presentation," it takes time for PowerPoint to fire up and play media clips, particularly video clips. If you're planning the time between clips, be sure to consider this additional set-up time.

Performance and Quality Considerations

As attention-getting as multimedia is, it doesn't come without a price. Audio and video files take up a lot of disk space and require a lot of processing power. Memory, particularly the lack of it, affects performance. Multimedia presentations also rely heavily on hardware capabilities for their quality. Graphics and sound cards become important.

Monitors, on the other hand, probably become less important, at least for the presentations themselves. Although you might still have the presentation-on-a-laptop scenario, much of multimedia's impact could be lost on that tiny screen. For truly effective multimedia presentations, you'll probably need some kind of projection system. However, if you design your presentation as a stand-alone, single-person viewing station, you *will* need to be concerned about monitor size and quality.

NOTE: LAPTOPS AND PRESENTATIONS

Hooking up a laptop to an overhead projection unit does keep laptops in the multimedia game. You're still concerned with the quality of the laptop's screen, though, and then you've got the projection hardware to consider, too.

NOTE: MONITOR QUALITY

Monitor quality plays an important role in creating the presentation. If you do a lot of multimedia presentations, a large-screen, high-quality monitor will help you keep your eyesight and sanity. You'll be a lot less likely to use that monitor for the actual presentation, though, given the limited number of people you can fit around it.

Quality of Output

No matter what visuals you put in your multimedia presentation, they'll fall flat if they don't look good when played. The physical size of a video clip window affects the presentation's quality. Many video clips are no bigger than a few inches on each side. You could resize the window, of course, but there's a reason for the original dimensions. Increasing the size of a video window, particularly for a movie clip, produces a grainy image. Grainy images look blocky and blurry and don't lead to overall good impressions. Animations, depending on their level of detail, don't suffer so much from graininess, but their edges can become quite jagged. Sharp, clear pictures, therefore, will be small in relation to the overall size of the slide and screen.

Picture quality aside, you need to be concerned with the smoothness of the movie or animation. If your processor, memory, and video card constrain your video clips, they'll look jerky, pause, or skip sections. The sound might not stay in sync with the picture.

TIP: WINDOW SIZE AND BORDERS

PowerPoint helps you with window-sizing issues. Select the video object, right-click, and choose Format Picture from the pop-up menu. You can control the window as well as the video's border.

Sound reproduction can also cause problems. If you have a clip of someone giving important information verbally, you'll want your audience to hear the voice clearly. Your sound card comes into play here. Pay attention to the volume of any sound or video clips. You want your audience to hear your presentation but not be blasted away by it. Test your presentation under the conditions in which it will be played—with the same equipment, area, and background conditions if possible. Know how to get to the volume controls. You can't change the volume of a clip during a presentation, so you need to know how to control the volume through the speakers.

Speed of Presentation

It takes time for PowerPoint to set up a video clip to run. Once the clip starts, PowerPoint takes a while to fire up the object, during which time you and your audience watch the "working" cursor. When the clip is finished, it takes PowerPoint some time to close things down, too. Be sure to account for these waiting times when planning your presentation.

Hardware Considerations

In general, your presentation's quality degrades in the areas where your hardware lacks the minimum configuration discussed near the beginning of this chapter. You do have some options for improving performance, whether you're straining the capabilities of your top-end system or straining just to get your older setup to work. Here are some things to consider:

- Keep the size of your video window small. Besides the picture-quality issues, bigger windows use more system resources.
- Don't have competing media. Although a video clip with a sound track runs as a unit, an audio loop in the background could affect performance.
- Do you need both an audio and a video track? If you create your own multimedia clips rather than rely on what someone else provides, leaving off the audio can help keep quality up.

One more hardware issue is disk space. Although disk space might not affect the running of your presentation, it certainly has a bearing on creating and storing your presentation. Multimedia isn't cheap, space-wise. For example, a blank 10-slide presentation consumes 20KB of disk space. Adding a checkerboard transition to all slides has minimal impact, increasing disk space to 27KB. With a drum roll sound transition on all the slides, disk space used jumps to 46KB. Including a 5 ½-second video clip bumps the file size to 343KB.

Putting It into Practice: A Multimedia Presentation

To look at actually putting a multimedia presentation together, we will turn our attention to the MicroMouseMike, introduced in Chapter 32. The roll-out plans for the MicroMouseMike include a demonstration at the Presentations Plus trade show. Now, we'll start building that presentation.

First, some background. This presentation serves a different purpose than the one for employees, so we choose a different template. This time it's Generic. Generic is plain but contains enough color to keep the audience focused, without detracting from the video clips in the slides. A change to the Slide Master gives us an extremely legible sans serif font for all slide text. (We don't want our audience to have to work to read our slides. A trade show presents enough distractions without making it easy for our audience to tune out.) We won't worry about outlining the content. We'll assume that all that's been done and that we're putting in the multimedia parts. Figure 34.10 shows the outline for the first part of the presentation.

FIGURE 34.10.

The MicroMouseMike presentation outline.

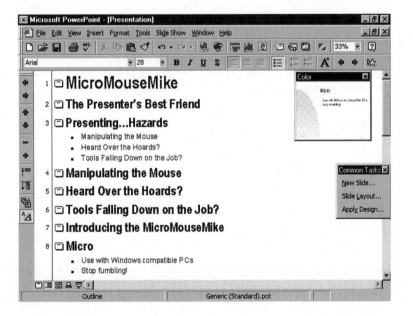

34

MULTIMEDIA
PRESENTATIONS

The MicroMouseMike presentation at the Presentations Plus trade show is designed as a fairly simple, informative presentation. The MicroMouseMike folks intend to use it to attract people to the booth and keep their attention long enough for them to learn something about the MicroMouseMike. A person will emcee the presentation, reading a script. When you use a person tied in to a separate sound system, the verbal audio requirements won't use up PC resources.

The MicroMouseMike folks have a superb presentation system, so they won't have to worry about resources otherwise. (The mighty MicroMouseMike, of course, serves as the combined mouse and microphone.)

Unless otherwise noted, the audio clips that are mentioned come from the Network folder of the Office 97 CD. All audio and video clips come from the CD's Valupack folder.

NOTE: YOU HAVE TO TRY IT TO APPRECIATE IT

This is a book, not a multimedia presentation. You can't see or hear what the next sections discuss. Use your imagination, and by all means, try out the effects yourself.

For the first slide, the presentation's introduction, we'll add a longish piece of music for the slide transition. For this, we've chosen explorer.wav from the Audio folder. In Slide Sorter view, select the first slide, right-click, select Slide Transition, and go to the Sound box in the Slide Transition dialog box. Move all the way to the bottom of the list for Other Sound, work your way through the directories to select explorer.wav, and click the Apply button. The presenter will speak over this music clip to introduce the MicroMouseMike, the "Presenter's Best Friend."

The next four slides form a group, and we add multimedia effects accordingly. Dealing with the hazards of presenting shows, broken glass forms the sound theme. Each line of text in the first of these slides flies into the sound of breaking glass (one of the "standard" sounds), and the transition from this slide to each of the next three is also broken glass. (In Slide Sorter view, select all four of the slides and add the same transition.) Because the last three slides of this group contain video clips, we won't clutter them with visual transitions, too.

The three video slides of the group contain video clips from the Fourpalm Movies folder: The first has arrowhit.avi; the second, hotcup.avi; and the third, winner.avi. Use any method discussed earlier to insert the movie objects.

The next slide, Introducing the MicroMouseMike, comes right from the employee presentation. We'll have each of the three objects fly in from the upper right, accompanied by the foghorn.wav sound from the Audio folder.

TIP: EASY ACCESS TO OTHER SOUNDS

Once you've used an "Other Sound," PowerPoint adds that file to the top of the sounds list. Scroll to the top for the foghorn sound after you've put it in the first object.

On the next slide, we'll insert separate audio objects for each line of text (see Figure 34.11). Select Slide Show | Custom Animation to time the audio clips so that they play after the presenter reads the line. We'll add doorbell.wav for the first line, glide.wav for the second, and rio.wav for the third. Line up the sound icons at the right side of the slide so that they don't distract from the main message.

FIGURE 34.11.

Three audio objects reside on the text lines.

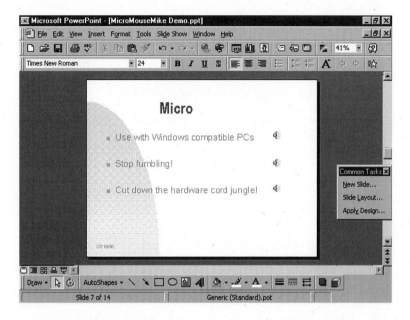

That's all we're going to cover for this presentation. As you've seen, PowerPoint offers many ways to add multimedia capabilities to presentations, and we could add much more life to our MicroMouseMike show. A few last reminders, though. Like animations and transitions, multimedia is *fun!* It's also hazardous to your presentation's health. Overused, or used poorly, multimedia can create loud (both visually and aurally), distracting, obnoxious, overbearing presentations. Don't make your multimedia presentation the modern equivalent of the neighbor's vacation slides (out of focus, poorly framed, boring). Err on the side of understatement.

Summary

Multimedia, the ability to include sound and motion in presentations, offers a lot of punch. It also requires more hardware power than a single-media presentation. Hardware weaknesses can degrade the quality of an otherwise perfectly constructed presentation.

PowerPoint's animation and transition capabilities add basic motion to presentations. You can also add sound effects to slide animations and transitions. Beyond these basic native abilities, you can add video and sound clips to your presentations as objects. Microsoft's Media Player helps you control these clips.

34

MULTIMEDIA PRESENTATIONS

Factors that influence the quality of your presentation (outside of design) include the following:

- The type of your computer's processor
- The speed of your computer's processor
- How much memory your machine has
- The quality of your graphics and sound cards

In general, the more or the higher, the better.

Problems that can show up in your presentations because of inadequate hardware include the following:

- Grainy, blurry, or blocky images
- Jagged images
- Jerky movies
- Movies that skip or pause
- Sound out of sync with the picture

In the last part of this chapter, we looked at putting multimedia objects into a presentation.

Here are a few chapters where you'll find related information:

- OfficeArt is covered in Chapter 5, "Using the OfficeArt Tools."
- To learn how to work with PowerPoint's charting tools, see Chapter 6, "Working with Microsoft Graph."
- Techniques for creating presentations are covered in Chapter 32, "Designing an Effective Presentation."
- I'll cover some techniques for running slide shows in Chapter 33, "Making the Presentation."
- Some PowerPoint customization settings are covered in Chapter 35, "Customizing PowerPoint."
- You'll learn how to control PowerPoint via VBA in Chapter 58, "Programming a PowerPoint Presentation."

Customizing PowerPoint

IN THIS CHAPTER

CHAPTER

35

*I have never wished to cater to the crowd; for what I know they do not approve, and what
they approve I do not know.*

—Epicurus

For most users, PowerPoint is just fine right out of the box. Its layout is clean and relatively
straightforward, and its default options suit most people's style. This might be why PowerPoint
doesn't come with anywhere near the number of customization options that you've seen so far
for Word, Excel, and Access. Still, it does have a few settings that you can tweak to fit the way
you work. This chapter runs through them all.

PowerPoint's View Options

As with all the Office applications, the source of PowerPoint's customization settings is the
Options dialog box, shown in Figure 35.1. You display it by selecting Tools | Options.

FIGURE 35.1.

*The View tab contains
a few settings related to
the PowerPoint
interface.*

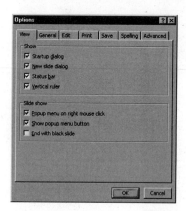

We'll begin by looking at the various controls offered in the View tab:

Startup dialog: Deactivate this check box to prevent PowerPoint from displaying at
startup its initial dialog box (the one that prompts you to either create a new presentation or open an existing presentation). In this case, PowerPoint will automatically
create a new presentation at startup and will display the New Slide dialog box.

New slide dialog: Deactivate this check box to prevent PowerPoint from displaying
the New Slide dialog box whenever you create a new presentation. In this case,
PowerPoint adds a default slide type to the presentation.

Status bar: This check box toggles the PowerPoint status bar on and off.

Vertical ruler: When this check box is activated, PowerPoint displays its vertical ruler
whenever the horizontal ruler is displayed (such as when you select a slide object). If
you'd rather see just the horizontal ruler, deactivate this check box.

NOTE: DISPLAYING THE RULER

If you don't see PowerPoint's ruler, select View | Ruler.

Popup menu on right mouse click: When this check box is activated, right-clicking the screen during a slide show displays the slide show context menu, as shown in Figure 35.2. Deactivate this check box to disable right-click access to this menu.

Show popup menu button: This check box toggles the slide show popup menu button that appears in the lower-left corner of the screen during a slide show (see Figure 35.2).

End with black slide: If you activate this check box, PowerPoint displays a black screen that has the words End of slide show, click to exit at the top. When this check box is deactivated, you're returned to PowerPoint after you finish a slide show.

FIGURE 35.2.

The popup menu button appears in the bottom-left corner of the slide show screen.

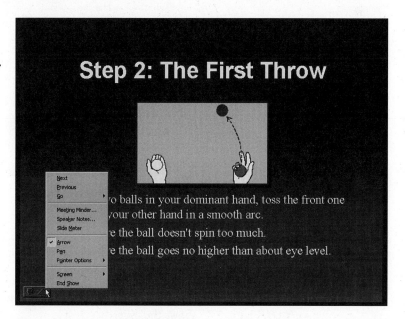

Options on the General Tab

The controls contained in the General tab, shown in Figure 35.3, set a few miscellaneous PowerPoint options:

Provide feedback with sound to screen elements: When this check box is activated, PowerPoint plays sounds associated with various program events, such as opening and closing files.

Recently used file list: Activate this check box to display at the bottom of the File menu a list of the files you've used most recently. Use the accompanying spinner to change the number of files displayed.

Macro virus protection: When this check box is activated, Excel warns you if a presentation you're about to open contains macros, and it checks those macros for viruses.

Link sounds with file size greater than x Kb: This spinner determines the threshold at which PowerPoint will no longer embed sound files in a presentation. At the default size of 100 KB, for example, sound files that are smaller than 100 KB will be embedded in the presentation, but files that are larger than that will only be linked to the presentation.

User information: Use these text boxes to enter the name and initials you want displayed in the Properties dialog box, edit tracking, comments, and so on.

FIGURE 35.3.

The General tab controls a grab bag of PowerPoint settings.

The Edit Settings

The next stop on our PowerPoint customization tour is the Edit tab, shown in Figure 35.4. These settings control various text-editing options, the Undo level, and more:

Replace straight quotes with smart quotes: When this check box is activated, PowerPoint automatically converts straight quotation marks (") into so-called "smart" (curly) quotes ("). Figure 35.5 shows the difference.

Automatic word selection: This option affects how you select text by dragging the mouse. When this check box is activated, PowerPoint will select the entire word once you've highlighted only the first part of it.

Use smart cut and paste: When this check box is turned on, PowerPoint monitors the spacing around words that you cut, paste, and delete. For example, if you paste a word beside another one, PowerPoint will insert a space between them. Similarly, if you delete the last word of a sentence, PowerPoint will ensure that no space remains before the period.

Drag-and-Drop text editing: This option affects what PowerPoint does when you drag the mouse over selected text. When this check box is activated, drag-and-drop is turned on so that dragging selected text will move the text along with the mouse pointer. (To copy the text instead, hold down the Shift key while dragging.) Deactivating this option turns off drag-and-drop, so dragging the mouse over selected text only changes the selection.

New charts take on PowerPoint font: Activating this check box tells PowerPoint to use its default font (18-point Arial) for inserted charts. If you deactivate this option, PowerPoint uses whatever fonts are defined in the chart itself.

Maximum number of undos: This spinner determines the number of Undo levels that PowerPoint will track as you work. The maximum number is 150. Note that the higher the number, the more memory and resources PowerPoint will use.

FIGURE 35.4.

The Edit tab governs a few text editing settings and a few other edit-related options.

Printing Options

If you regularly print your presentations, the options in the Print tab, shown in Figure 35.6, might prove useful. The first three options apply to all presentations:

Background printing: When this check box is activated, you're returned to PowerPoint as soon as you submit a print job, and the spooling and printing occurs behind the scenes. For faster printing, deactivate this check box. This will give the print job a higher priority, but you won't return to PowerPoint as quickly.

Print TrueType fonts as graphics: If you activate this check box, PowerPoint will send TrueType fonts to the printer as bitmaps (assuming that your printer supports this option). This might result in better-looking output at large type sizes.

Print inserted objects at printer resolution: When this check box is deactivated, PowerPoint prints embedded objects at their native resolution. If you activate this check box, PowerPoint attempts to print the objects at the printer's native resolution.

35

CUSTOMIZING
POWERPOINT

FIGURE 35.5.

The difference between "smart" quotes and straight quotes.

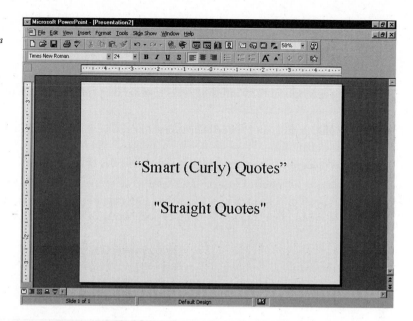

The rest of the options in the Printing tab affect only the currently open presentation:

Use the most recently used print settings: When this option is activated (the default), PowerPoint uses the same print settings that were used for the last print job. This saves you from having to define different print settings for each presentation.

Use the following default print settings: If you activate this option instead, the rest of the controls in the dialog box are activated so that you can make specific printing choices.

Print what: Use this drop-down list to choose what parts of the presentation you want to print by default.

Print hidden slides: If your presentation includes hidden slides, activate this check box to include them in the printout.

Black and white: Activate this check box to set black and white (where colors are printed as shades of gray) as the default print colors for this presentation.

Pure black and white: Activate this check box to set pure black and white (color fills are printed as white, and pictures are printed as shades of gray) as the default print colors for this presentation.

Scale to fit paper: If you activate this check box, PowerPoint scales slides that are larger or smaller than the page so that they fit the page.

Frame slides: Activate this check box to have PowerPoint display a border around each printed slide.

FIGURE 35.6.

Use the Print tab to set various PowerPoint printing options.

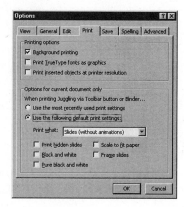

Options for Saving Your Work

This section examines the options available in the Save tab, shown in Figure 35.7:

Allow fast saves: When this check box is activated, selecting the Save command doesn't save the entire file. Instead, PowerPoint just appends any changes you've made to the end of the file. This is much quicker than saving the entire file, but it can also increase the file size considerably. To keep your PowerPoint file sizes down, deactivate this check box.

Prompt for file properties: Activate this check box to have PowerPoint display the Properties dialog box whenever you save a new presentation.

Full text search information: When this check box is turned on, PowerPoint saves search data with the presentation that lets you perform a full text search. This greatly speeds up searching but can increase the file size.

Save AutoRecover info every x minutes: With this option activated, PowerPoint periodically saves information about the presentation that lets it recover the file in the event of a system crash. Use the spinner to determine the interval PowerPoint uses to save the AutoRecover data.

Save PowerPoint files as: This drop-down list determines the default format used when you save a PowerPoint file.

35

CUSTOMIZING
POWERPOINT

FIGURE 35.7.

The Save tab provides various options related to saving your work.

Spell Check Settings

PowerPoint's spell check feature is useful for avoiding embarrassing spelling gaffes. The options in the Spelling tab, shown in Figure 35.8, let you customize how the spell checker operates:

> **Spelling:** This check box toggles PowerPoint's on-the-fly spell check on and off. The on-the-fly spell check is called AutoCorrect, and PowerPoint uses it to monitor each word you type. If the program doesn't recognize a word you type, it marks it with a wavy red underline.

> **Hide spelling errors:** This check box toggles the misspelled word indicator (the wavy red underline) on and off.

> **Suggest Always:** If you deactivate this check box, the spell checker won't suggest possible replacements for misspelled words.

> **Ignore Words in UPPERCASE:** When this check box is activated, the spell checker ignores all words typed entirely in uppercase letters. Normally, the spell checker flags words that have multiple capital letters. This feature is designed to catch strings in which the Caps Lock key IS ACTIVATED ACCIDENTALLY and words where you held down the Shift key a second too long, LIke THis. So if you often purposefully type words entirely in uppercase, activate this option.

> **Ignore Words with numbers:** When this check box is activated, the spell checker ignores all words that contain numeric values.

FIGURE 35.8.

Use the Spelling tab settings to customize the PowerPoint spell checker.

The Advanced Options

To close our look at the PowerPoint customization options, this section examines the controls found in the Advanced tab, shown in Figure 35.9:

Render 24-bit bitmaps at highest quality: When this check box is activated, Power-Point attempts to display 24-bit images at the highest possible screen resolution. If you find that your images are loading or refreshing slowly, try deactivating this check box.

Export pictures: These options control how PowerPoint exports images. Choose Best for printing to export the images for maximum print quality; choose Best for on-screen viewing to export the images for maximum display quality.

Default file location: This option determines the initial folder that appears when you first display the Open or Save As dialog boxes. To make it easy to find your Power-Point documents, save them all in a single folder and enter the full path in this text box.

FIGURE 35.9.

The Advanced tab completes our look at PowerPoint customization settings.

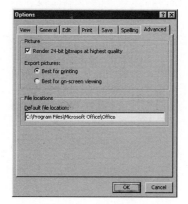

Summary

This chapter completed this book's PowerPoint coverage by running through each of the controls in the various Options dialog box tabs. Here are a few chapters where you'll find related information:

- OfficeArt is covered in Chapter 5, "Using the OfficeArt Tools."
- To learn how to work with PowerPoint's charting tools, see Chapter 6, "Working with Microsoft Graph."
- Techniques for creating presentations are covered in Chapter 32, "Designing an Effective Presentation."
- I cover some techniques for running slide shows in Chapter 33, "Making the Presentation."
- If you want to add sounds and videos to your presentations, see Chapter 34, "Multimedia Presentations."
- You'll learn how to control PowerPoint via VBA in Chapter 58, "Programming a PowerPoint Presentation."

VII
PART

Unleashing Outlook

Setting Up Outlook

IN THIS CHAPTER

CHAPTER

36

Science and technology multiply around us. To an increasing extent they dictate the languages in which we speak and think. Either we use those languages, or we remain mute.

—*J. G. Ballard*

Users of Office 95 had to rely on two separate tools to manage their electronic lives: Microsoft Exchange, the Windows 95 e-mail client, and Schedule+, the Office address book and time-management program. Although both applications were a large step up from sticky notes and postage stamps, the combination was never a satisfying one. Why? Well, let me count the ways:

- Although Windows 95's Exchange client was to be admired for its capability to combine multiple e-mail systems and faxing in a single Inbox, it was woefully lacking in features. Items such as message filtering and automatic signatures, although available for years in other clients, were nowhere to be found in Exchange. (However, the client that shipped with Exchange Server was a noticeable improvement.)

- Schedule+ had some interesting and useful features, but it suffered from a clunky interface. And its piggish use of system resources made you reluctant to leave it open all the time (usually considered a prerequisite for a scheduling tool!).

- Exchange and Schedule+ didn't know how to work with each other. For example, the programs couldn't share a common address book, or even exchange addresses via some common file format.

- Neither program was set up to properly handle the groupware services offered by Microsoft Exchange Server.

To solve these problems, Microsoft came up with a new program to replace both the Exchange client and Schedule+. It's called Outlook. Not only does it combine the functionality of Exchange and Schedule+ in a single package, but it also includes a boatload of new features that turn it into a truly useful information management tool. This chapter introduces you to Outlook and shows you how to set it up on your system. Subsequent chapters here in Part VII cover each Outlook feature.

Installing Outlook

Getting Outlook up and running on your system isn't all that hard, thanks to wizards that ease some chores and thanks to a common interface for the various information services. Here's an overview of the entire Outlook installation and configuration process:

1. Install the Outlook program and any information services you need, such as Internet Mail and Microsoft Fax.

2. Add the information services you want to use to your Windows Messaging profile.

3. Configure each information service as needed.

4. Configure Outlook as needed.

The rest of this chapter expands on each step.

Installing the Outlook Client and Information Services

You can install Outlook and the information services you need either during the Office 97 installation or from Control Panel. For the latter, you need to follow these steps:

1. From Control Panel, launch the Add/Remove Programs icon.

2. In the Add/Remove Programs Properties dialog box, make sure the Install/Uninstall tab is selected, highlight the Microsoft Office 97 item, and click the Add/Remove button. You'll be prompted to insert your Office 97 CD.

3. Insert the Office 97 CD, and then click OK. This will load the Office 97 Setup program.

4. When the Setup dialog box appears, click Add/Remove. Setup displays a list of Office 97 components.

5. In the Options list, activate the check box beside Outlook. (If you don't want to install the entire Outlook package—all 40 MB of it!—highlight Outlook, click Change Option, and then use the dialog box that appears to choose which components you want to install.)

6. Click Continue. Setup installs the Outlook files and lets you know when it's done.

7. Click OK.

Setting Up Your Default Messaging Profile

To complete the installation of Outlook, you must set up the default Windows Messaging *profile*. This profile specifies the information services you want to use, as well as the configuration of those services. Later in this chapter, I'll show you how to create new profiles that use different services and configurations.

If you're continuing the installation of Outlook, you should see the Inbox Setup Wizard dialog box, shown in Figure 36.1. If you don't see this dialog box, either double-click the desktop's Microsoft Outlook icon or select Start | Programs | Microsoft Outlook.

FIGURE 36.1.

Use this dialog box to select the services you want to use.

Make sure that the Use the following information services option is activated so that the Inbox Setup Wizard will guide you through the installation of whichever services have their check boxes activated. I won't discuss the various options for each service in detail (see Chapter 39, "Using Outlook for Faxing," for the Microsoft Fax options), but here's a rundown of what you can expect:

Microsoft Fax: You'll be asked to specify the fax/modem you want to use, whether you want incoming calls answered automatically, and your fax number.

Microsoft Exchange Server: You'll need to enter the name of your Exchange server and the name of your mailbox. You'll also be asked whether you travel with your computer. (Select Yes to enable reading and composing mail while not connected to the network.)

Microsoft Mail: The Inbox Setup Wizard will ask you to specify the location of the workgroup postoffice (enter a UNC path to the postoffice), your postoffice name (the Wizard displays a list of the users who have accounts on the postoffice), and your password.

Internet Mail: To set up this service, you need to specify whether you connect to your Internet mail server via modem or network connection, the host name or IP address of the mail server, how you want to work with Internet messages (off-line or automatic), and your Internet e-mail address, account name, and password.

The Microsoft Network Online Service: The dialog box that appears for MSN just gives you an overview of the service.

Other dialog boxes will ask you to enter a path to your personal address book file and personal folder file (your personal message store). You have two ways to proceed:

■ If you're upgrading over Exchange, make sure the displayed paths point to your existing address book file and folder file. This will ensure that all your addresses and messages are imported into Outlook.

■ If you're not upgrading over Exchange, you can just go with the default values (MAILBOX.PAB and MAILBOX.PST).

That's about it. The final Wizard dialog box shows you the services you set up. Click Finish, and Outlook will load automatically.

Adding Services After Outlook Is Installed

If you didn't include all the available information services when you configured your Outlook profile, you can easily add them later. To get started, use either of the following techniques:

■ Launch Control Panel's Mail and Fax icon to display the Windows Messaging Settings Properties dialog box, shown in Figure 36.2.

■ In Outlook, select Tools | Services. In this case, you see a dialog box named Services that includes the Services tab (see Figure 36.2).

FIGURE 36.2.

*Use the Services tab to
add new services to your
profile.*

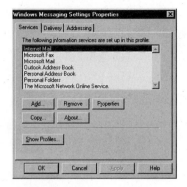

To add a service, click the Add button, highlight the service in the Add Service to Profile dialog box, shown in Figure 36.3, and click OK. Outlook then asks you to configure the service. See the next few sections to learn about the various configuration options available for each type of service.

FIGURE 36.3.

*Use this dialog box to
highlight the service you
want to add.*

Configuring Outlook's Information Services

The next few sections tell you how to configure each Outlook service (except Microsoft Fax; I'll leave that until Chapter 39). The properties you work with depend on the service, but you'll generally have to configure options such as how you connect to the service, what to do with incoming mail, and how to deliver outgoing mail.

Here are the techniques to use to display the properties sheet for a service:

- Double-click Control Panel's Mail and Fax icon to display the Windows Messaging Settings Properties dialog box, highlight the service in the Services tab, and click Properties.

- Start Outlook, select Tools | Services to display the Services dialog box, highlight the service, and click Properties.

Setting Up Microsoft Mail

The Microsoft Mail properties sheet, shown in Figure 36.4, contains eight tabs for your configuration pleasure (if that's the right word). The next few sections explain the various options.

Note that, depending on the options you work with, your changes might not go into effect until the next time you start Outlook.

FIGURE 36.4.

The Microsoft Mail properties sheet is loaded with configuration options.

Connection Properties

The options in the Connection tab determine how you connect to the workgroup postoffice.

The Enter the path to your postoffice text box should show the UNC path for your postoffice (or a local path if the postoffice is on your machine). If the path isn't correct, type the correct value, or click the Browse button and highlight the path in the Browse for Postoffice dialog box.

The other options determine how Microsoft Mail connects to the postoffice when you start Outlook. You have four choices:

Automatically sense LAN or Remote: You can use Microsoft Mail either over your local area network (LAN) or remotely by using a modem and Windows 95's Dial-Up Networking utility. If you activate this option, Outlook will attempt to determine the type of connection automatically.

Local area network (LAN): Activate this option if you're accessing your postoffice over a LAN.

Remote using a modem and Dial-Up Networking: Activate this option if you're accessing the postoffice remotely. (Note that you need to have Dial-Up Networking installed on your computer to access your postoffice remotely.

Offline: If you select this option, Outlook doesn't connect to the postoffice. This is useful if you're traveling and don't have remote access to the postoffice. You can compose messages and "send" them, and Outlook stores them until you can connect to the postoffice.

Logon Properties

The Logon tab, shown in Figure 36.5, displays the name of your postoffice mailbox and your password (or, at least, asterisks that represent your password).

FIGURE 36.5.

Use the Logon tab to configure various properties related to logging on to the postoffice.

If you want Outlook to enter your password for you automatically when you log on to the postoffice, activate the When logging on, automatically enter password check box. You might want to think twice before activating this option, because it means that anyone with access to your computer can also log on to your account.

If you want to change your password, click the Change Mailbox Password button. In the Change Mailbox Password dialog box that appears, enter your old password followed by your new one (twice).

> **TIP: ANOTHER ROUTE TO CHANGE MAILBOX PASSWORD**
>
> You can also access the Change Mailbox Password dialog box by selecting Tools | Microsoft Mail Tools | Change Mailbox Password from the Outlook window.

Delivery Properties

The Delivery tab, shown in Figure 36.6, contains various options for configuring how Microsoft Mail deals with sent and received messages:

Enable incoming mail delivery: This check box determines whether Outlook transfers messages from the postoffice to your inbox. If you don't want to receive any messages temporarily (because your disk space is running low, for example), deactivate this option.

Enable outgoing mail delivery: This check box determines whether Outlook transfers messages from your inbox to the postoffice. If you deactivate this option, Outlook stores your "sent" messages in your Outbox.

Enable delivery to: Click the Address Types button to specify which types of e-mail addresses you want Outlook to send to the postoffice. The Address Types dialog box contains check boxes for the various types of mail. If you deactivate any of these check boxes, Outlook suspends mail service for that type.

Check for new mail every *x* minute(s): This value determines how often Outlook checks the postoffice for incoming mail.

Immediate notification: If you activate this check box, Outlook notifies you immediately if mail for you arrives in the postoffice. Note that the computers involved must support the NetBIOS protocol.

Display Global Address List only: If you activate this option, Outlook displays only the addresses from the postoffice (the Global Address List). Otherwise, Outlook also displays the addresses from your Personal Address Book.

FIGURE 36.6.

The properties in the Delivery tab control the delivery and receipt of mail messages.

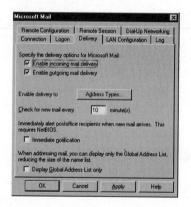

LAN Configuration Properties

When you're running Microsoft Mail over a local area network, you can use the LAN Configuration tab, shown in Figure 36.7, to set various LAN-related properties:

Use Remote Mail: Outlook normally delivers your incoming mail automatically at intervals determined by the Check for new mail every *x* minute(s) property you saw in the Delivery tab. If you activate the Use Remote Mail check box, however, Outlook doesn't download your mail automatically. Instead, you connect to the postoffice manually (by selecting Tools | Remote Mail), display the headers for the messages that are waiting for you, and download only the messages you want to read. (This procedure is explained in more detail in the next chapter.)

Use local copy: This check box determines whether Outlook uses the list of addresses stored in the postoffice. If you activate this check box, Outlook creates a copy of the postoffice address list, stores the copy on your computer, and then uses this list when you're composing messages. This is useful if your network is experiencing delays or poor performance. (To update the list, select Tools | Microsoft Mail Tools | Download Address Lists from Outlook.)

Use external delivery agent: If you activate this check box, Outlook delivers your messages by using the EXTERNAL.EXE program, which can speed up delivery times on a slow LAN. EXTERNAL.EXE is available as part of the Microsoft Mail Post Office Upgrade, which you can get from Microsoft. (This upgrade converts your Windows 95 postoffice into a full-fledged Microsoft Mail Server postoffice.)

FIGURE 36.7.

Use the LAN Configuration tab to configure Microsoft Mail on a local area network.

Log Properties

If you're having problems with Microsoft Mail, you can tell Outlook to monitor various mail events and record them in a log file. You use the Log tab, shown in Figure 36.8, to set this up:

Maintain a log of session events: Activate this check box to force Outlook to keep a log of each mail session.

Specify the location of the session log: Use this text box to specify the text file that Outlook uses to record the log.

The log includes a record of your logging in and out, messages sent and received, and any errors that occur. Here are a few lines from a typical session log:

```
12/10/96 - 6:39PM - Connection type selected: 'Automatically sense LAN or Remote'
12/10/96 - 6:39PM - You are using the connection type 'Local Area Network',
➥connected at a speed of 38400 Bytes/second.
12/10/96 - 6:39PM - Logged on to mailbox: 'Paul'.
12/10/96 - 6:39PM - Postoffice server: '\\Hermes\wgpo0000\'.
12/10/96 - 6:39PM - Checking for mail. 0 item(s) to download.
12/10/96 - 7:07PM - The Microsoft Mail Service has been disconnected from the
➥network due to a network failure.
```

```
12/10/96 - 7:08PM - You are using the connection type 'Local Area Network',
➡connected at a speed of 200000 Bytes/second.
12/10/96 - 7:08PM - The connection to the network has been restored.
12/10/96 - 7:17PM - Sent mail 'The network is up and running again'. [ID:00001231]
12/10/96 - 7:17PM - Checking for mail. 0 item(s) to download.
```

Figure 36.8.

Use the Log tab to set up a log file to monitor Microsoft Mail events.

Remote Properties

You use the properties in the Remote Configuration, Remote Session, and Dial-Up Networking tabs to set up Microsoft Mail for remote operation. Before setting any of these properties, make sure you've activated the Remote using a modem and Dial-Up Networking option in the Connection tab.

Next, select the Dial-Up Networking tab, shown in Figure 36.9. Here's a rundown of the available properties on this tab:

Use the following Dial-Up Networking connection: Use this drop-down list to choose the Dial-Up Networking connection you want to use for your remote Microsoft Mail sessions. Also note that you can use the Add Entry button to create a new Dial-Up Networking connection and the Edit Entry button to make changes to a connection.

When Dial-Up Networking fails to connect: These text boxes tell Outlook what to do if the Dial-Up Networking connection fails. Enter the number of times to retry and the interval, in seconds, between retries.

Confirm the Dial-Up Networking connection before starting a session: These options determine whether Outlook prompts you to initiate the Dial-Up Networking connection. If you select Never confirm, Outlook establishes the connection automatically without prompting you for confirmation. If you select Confirm on first session and after errors, Outlook asks you to confirm that you want to establish the connection only for the initial session and each time an error occurs. If you select Always confirm, Outlook always prompts you to confirm the connections.

36
SETTING UP
OUTLOOK

FIGURE 36.9.

Use the Dial-Up Networking tab to define how Microsoft Mail works with Dial-Up Networking.

NOTE: THE CONFIRMATION DIALOG BOX HAS USEFUL OPTIONS

When Outlook asks you to confirm the connection, the dialog box that appears gives you lots of options for the remote session. These options are check boxes that determine whether Outlook sends mail, receives mail, updates your Microsoft Mail address list, and more. So even though it might seem like a hassle to always be asked to confirm the connection, there are advantages to doing so.

Next on the agenda is the Remote Session tab, shown in Figure 36.10. These check boxes determine when Outlook starts and ends the Dial-Up Networking session:

When this service is started: If you activate this check box, the Dial-Up Networking session is initiated as soon as you start Outlook.

After retrieving mail headers: If you're using Remote Mail, activating this check box tells Outlook to end the Dial-Up Networking session as soon as Remote Mail has retrieved the waiting message headers.

After sending and receiving mail: When this check box is activated, Outlook shuts down the Dial-Up Networking session as soon as it delivers (sends and receives) mail.

When you exit: When this check box is activated, your Dial-Up Networking session is closed when you exit Outlook.

Schedule Mail Delivery: Use this button to schedule your remote Microsoft Mail sessions at regular intervals. In the Remote Scheduled Sessions dialog box that appears, click Add to display the Add Scheduled Sessions dialog box, shown in Figure 36.11. In the Use drop-down list, select your Dial-Up Networking connection. In the When drop-down list, select Every, Weekly on, or Once at. In the hours : minutes spinner, enter a time. Click OK until you're back in the Microsoft Mail properties sheet.

FIGURE 36.10.

Use the Remote Session tab to specify events that start and end your remote Microsoft Mail sessions.

FIGURE 36.11.

The Add dialog box lets you schedule remote sessions at regular intervals.

Finally, the Remote Configuration tab, shown in Figure 36.12, sets a few more options for your Microsoft Mail Dial-Up Networking session:

Use Remote Mail: Activate this check box to use Remote Mail during your Dial-Up Networking sessions.

Use local copy: If you activate this check box, Outlook creates a copy of the postoffice address list, stores the copy on your computer, and then uses this list when you're composing messages.

Use external delivery agent: If you activate this check box, Outlook delivers your messages using the EXTERNAL.EXE program, which can speed up delivery times on a slow link.

FIGURE 36.12.

The Remote Configuration tab sets a few properties that control Microsoft Mail's behavior during a connection to the remote server.

36

Setting Up Microsoft Network Mail

Compared to Microsoft Mail's properties sheet, the properties sheet for The Microsoft Network's mail service is a walk in the park, as you can see in Figure 36.13. The Transport tab contains just three options:

Download mail when e-mail starts up from MSN: When this check box is activated, if you start Outlook while you're connected to MSN, Outlook automatically downloads any waiting MSN e-mail messages.

Disconnect after Updating Headers from Remote Mail: The Microsoft Network version of Outlook's Remote Mail feature lets you connect to MSN, download the headers of any waiting messages, and transfer to your Inbox only the messages you select. If you activate this check box, Outlook disconnects you from MSN after it has obtained the message headers. This is useful for saving connect time, because you can examine the headers offline.

Disconnect after Transferring Mail from Remote Mail: If you activate this check box, Outlook disconnects you from MSN automatically after it has transferred the messages you selected in Remote Mail.

FIGURE 36.13.

*The properties sheet for
The Microsoft Network
mail service.*

The Address Book tab contains a single check box: Connect to MSN to check names. If you leave this option deactivated, Outlook accepts any MSN addresses you use as-is. If you activate this check box, however, Outlook connects to MSN to verify the addresses you select.

Setting Up Internet Mail

If you have an e-mail account with an Internet information service, you can set up Outlook to send and retrieve messages via this account. You specify most Internet Mail options—such as your e-mail address, mail server, and password—when you set up this service. However, if you need to change these values or set some of the other Internet Mail options, you'll need to display the properties sheet for Internet Mail, shown in Figure 36.14.

FIGURE 36.14.

Use the Internet Mail properties sheet to configure your Internet e-mail account for use with Outlook.

General Properties

The General properties tab covers the basic data for your account, such as your address, server, and password. Here are the fields to fill in:

Full name: This is the name that appears in the From line of the messages you send.

E-mail address: Use this field to enter your Internet e-mail address.

Internet Mail server: This is the domain name of your service provider's mail server. If your information service uses separate machines for Post Office Protocol (POP3) and Simple Mail Transport Protocol (SMTP), enter the POP3 machine in this field (and see the information on the Advanced Options button at the end of this list).

Account name: This is the name of your POP3 account on the mail server.

Password: This is the password for your POP3 account.

Message Format: If you click this button, the Message Format dialog box, shown in Figure 36.15, appears. These options determine how Outlook sends rich text messages. If you activate the Use MIME when sending messages check box, Outlook uses the MIME (Multipurpose Internet Mail Extensions) format for sending messages. If you deactivate this check box, Outlook uses Uuencode instead (this applies to both incoming and outgoing messages). You can also use the Character Set button to specify the character set to be used when you're sending messages that include extended characters (you'll usually choose either ISO 8859-1 or US ASCII).

FIGURE 36.15.

Use this dialog box to specify the format and character set to use for your Internet e-mail messages.

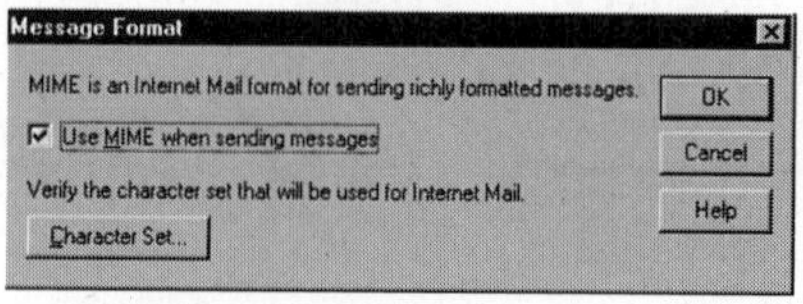

CAUTION: MIME MIGHT EMBED EXTRA CHARACTERS

If your recipients complain that your messages contain extra characters, such as equals signs (=) at the end of every line, MIME is the likely culprit. If you activate the Use MIME when sending messages option, some gateways won't correctly interpret all the characters in your message. For example, soft returns often end up with an extraneous equals sign. To fix this problem, turn off the Use MIME when sending messages option.

Advanced Options: Clicking this button displays the Advanced Options dialog box. You use the text box to specify an alternative mail server to use for outgoing mail. You need to fill this in only if your mail server doesn't process outgoing mail. For example, some Internet systems use separate computers for POP3 (incoming mail) and SMTP (outgoing mail). In this case, use the Advanced Options dialog box to enter the domain name of the SMTP machine.

Connection Properties

The Connection tab, shown in Figure 36.16, controls how Outlook connects to your Internet mail server. Here are your choices:

Connect using the network: Activate this option if you connect to the Internet via your local area network.

Connect using the modem: Activate this option if you connect to the Internet via your modem. In the Dial using the following connection drop-down list, select the Dial-Up Networking connection you want to use. (Note that you can create a new connection right from the Connection tab by clicking the Add Entry button. In addition, the Edit Entry button lets you modify an existing entry, and the Login As button lets you change the name and password for your account.)

Work off-line and use Remote Mail: When this check box is deactivated, Outlook downloads all waiting messages from your Internet mailbox. If you prefer to view your headers and then selectively download messages, activate this check box to use Outlook's Remote Mail feature.

Schedule: If you aren't using Remote Mail, click the Schedule button to set the interval at which Outlook will check for new mail. In the Schedule dialog box that appears, use the Check for new messages every x minute(s) spinner to set the interval you prefer.

Log File: This button lets you specify options that Outlook will use to keep a log of your Internet Mail sessions. In the Log File dialog box, use the Specify the level of logging you want list to choose No Logging, Basic (logs only logon and logoff times and error messages), or Troubleshooting (logs the complete transaction record between the client and server; use this option only if you're having problems, because the log file can get huge). Also, use the Specify a location for the log file text box to specify the log file to use (the default is IMAIL.LOG in your main Windows folder).

FIGURE 36.16.

Use the Connection tab to determine how Outlook connects to your Internet mail server.

A Tour of the Outlook Window

Now that you have Outlook installed and your information services are added and configured, you're ready to start working with the program. I'll begin by giving you a tour of the Outlook window.

The most important thing to remember about the Outlook layout is that everything is organized in a hierarchy of folders with the following properties:

■ The *folder banner,* shown in Figure 36.17, tells you the name of the current folder. In the default view, for example, the current folder is Inbox, which holds your delivered e-mail messages.

■ The large area below the folder banner displays the contents of the current folder (such as a series of e-mail messages for the Inbox folder).

■ You can see the contents of only one folder at a time. Outlook doesn't support multiple open folders, which keeps things simple and uncluttered.

Navigating Outlook Folders

Since Outlook is organized as a hierarchy of folders, it's important to be able to navigate this hierarchy quickly and easily. To that end, Outlook provides numerous methods for traversing the folder tree. The next few sections give you a quick run-through of the various methods available.

FIGURE 36.17.
The Outlook window is organized to make it easy to find the information you need.

Click here for a list of folders   Folder banner

Outlook Bar

Folder contents

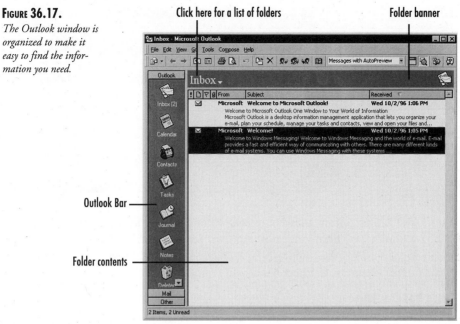

The Outlook Bar

The Outlook Bar is the vertical strip that runs down the left side of the Outlook window. Each icon in the Outlook Bar represents a folder. You can display the contents of a folder by clicking its icon.

NOTE: VIEWING MORE ICONS

If you can't see all the icons in the Outlook Bar, click the downward-pointing arrow at the bottom of the bar to scroll down.

The Outlook Bar has various "categories" of icons. The default Outlook category shows icons for the Inbox, Calendar, Contacts, Tasks, Journal, Notes, and Deleted Items folders. However, you'll notice two other buttons at the bottom of the Outlook Bar:

Mail: Click this button to view only mail-related folders in the Outlook Bar. Initially, the mail folders are Inbox, Sent Items, Outbox, and Deleted Items.

Other: Click this button to see folders for My Computer, Favorites, and any other folders in your network profile. Clicking the My Computer folder displays the drives attached to your computer, as shown in Figure 36.18.

FIGURE 36.18.

You can use Outlook as a file management tool.

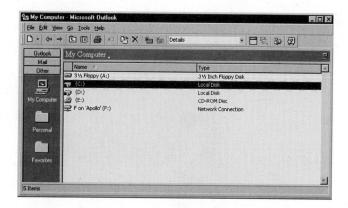

The Other folder is a significant addition to the Outlook folder hierarchy because it means that you can use Outlook as a file management tool. Any action available in Windows Explorer—copying, moving, deleting, and renaming files; formatting floppy disks; you name it—can also be performed from within the Outlook window.

Using the Folder List

The Folder list is a list of all the folders in your Personal Folders file, as well as any shared mail folders on your network. To display this list, first make sure you're in one of Outlook's folders (not, for example, in a disk folder). Then click the name of the current folder that's displayed in the folder banner, as shown in Figure 36.19. To view the contents of a folder, just click it.

FIGURE 36.19.

The Folder list shows your personal folders and shared network folders.

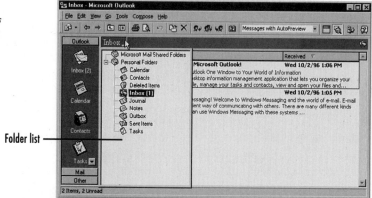

Folder list ——

NOTE: ACTIVATING THE FOLDER LIST

You can display the Folder list full-time by activating the View | Folder list command.

Browsing and Other Folder Navigation Techniques

Outlook provides a few other techniques for jumping from folder to folder. For example, you can browse folders much as you browse Web sites. You can also select specific folders via menu commands. Here are the techniques to use:

- To move back to a folder, either select Go | Back or click the Back button on the toolbar.

- To move forward to a folder, either select Go | Forward or click the Forward button on the toolbar.

- To move up one folder in the hierarchy, either select Go | Up One Level, press Backspace, or click the Up One Level button on the toolbar.

- To go to one of the standard Outlook folders, pull down the Go menu and select the folder name (for example, Inbox). Note that Outlook provides a couple of shortcut keys: press Ctrl-Shift-I for the Inbox folder and Ctrl-Shift-O for the Outbox folder.

- To go to any folder, select Go | Go to Folder (or press Ctrl-Y), use the dialog box that appears to highlight the folder you want, and click OK.

Working with Folders

Although the default folders that come with Outlook will get you off to a good start, you'll probably find that you need to modify the hierarchy to suit your needs. For example, you'll almost certainly want to create new e-mail folders so that you can properly organize your saved messages. Besides creating new folders, Outlook also lets you move and copy folders, rename folders, and delete folders. Here's a summary:

Creating a new subfolder: Select the folder in which you want to create the subfolder, and then select File | Folder | Create Subfolder (or press Ctrl-Shift-E). In the Create New Folder dialog box, enter a name and description for the folder, and then click OK.

Copying a folder: Select the folder you want to copy, and then select File | Folder | Copy *Folder* (where *Folder* is the name of the folder). In the Copy Folder dialog box, highlight the parent folder you want to use and click OK.

Moving a folder: Select the folder you want to move, and then select File | Folder | Move *Folder*. In the Move Folder dialog box, highlight the new parent folder and click OK.

Renaming a folder: Select the folder you want to rename, choose File | Folder | Rename *Folder,* enter the new name in the Rename dialog box, and click OK.

Copy a folder's design: A folder's design includes its permissions, rules, description, forms, and views. To copy these values from another folder to the current folder, select File | Folder | Copy Folder Design. In the Copy Design From dialog box, highlight the folder that has the design you want to copy, activate the check boxes for the design elements you want (for example, Permissions), and click OK.

Adding a folder to the Outlook Bar: Select the Outlook Bar category in which you want the folder to appear, choose the folder, and select File | Folder | Add to Outlook Bar. To remove an icon from the Outlook Bar, right-click it and choose Remove from Outlook Bar. When Outlook asks you to confirm, click Yes.

Deleting a folder: Select the folder you want to delete and then select File | Folder | Delete *Folder*.

TIP: USE THE FOLDER CONTENT MENU

Many of the folder-related commands are also available on the folder context menu. To see this menu, open the folder you want to work with and then right-click the folder banner.

Creating New Outlook Profiles

If you use only one or two information services and you're the only person who uses your computer for e-mail, Outlook's default messaging profile will be all you need. Having multiple profiles, however, does prove useful in plenty of situations:

■ If you do most of your e-mailing using a single service (Internet Mail, for example), you could speed up Outlook and simplify its operation by creating a profile that uses only that one service. You could then create a second profile that includes your other services, and you could load that profile only when you need it.

■ Remember that profiles store not only the services you use, but also the configurations of these services. So you could create different profiles for different configurations. For example, you could set up one profile to use Remote Mail while you're sitting at your computer. If you're going out, you could switch to a second profile that's configured to check your mail unattended.

■ If you have multiple e-mail accounts in the same service, Outlook doesn't let you add the service twice in a single profile. Instead, you need to create a new profile, add the service, and then configure it for the other account.

■ If you share your computer with other people, you can set up a profile for each person to use.

To create a new profile, follow these steps:

1. In Outlook, select Tools | Options to display the Options dialog box.

2. In the General tab, activate the Prompt for a profile to be used option (if it isn't activated already) and click OK.

3. Select File | Exit and Log Off to quit all messaging applications.

4. Restart Outlook. You'll eventually see the Choose Profile dialog box, shown in Figure 36.20.

FIGURE 36.20.

Use this dialog box to create new profiles and select the profile you want to use.

5. Later, you'll use the Profile Name drop-down list to select the profile you want to work with. For now, though, click New. The Inbox Setup Wizard appears.

6. Run through the steps I outlined earlier for setting up a profile. (Be sure to specify a different name for this profile.) When you're done, you're returned to the Choose Profile dialog box, and your new profile is selected in the Profile Name list.

TIP: HOW TO AVOID RECONFIGURING SERVICES

One of the problems with creating a new profile is that Outlook makes you reconfigure all your services again. However, you can avoid this drudgery. When you're creating your new profile, be sure to select the Manually configure information services option in the first Inbox Setup Wizard dialog box. When the Wizard prompts you to add services, just click OK. Proceed normally, but when you get back to the Choose Profile dialog box, load one of your other profiles (specifically, the profile that contains the services you want to use for this new profile). Then, when you're in Outlook later, select Tools | Services to display the Services dialog box. Highlight one of the services you want to use in your new profile, and then click Copy. In the Copy Information Service dialog box that appears, highlight the name of your new profile and click OK. Outlook copies the service and its configuration to the new profile.

7. If you want this profile to be your default (this means it will be selected automatically in the Profile Name list each time you start Outlook), click the Options >> button, and activate the Set as default profile check box in the expanded dialog box, shown in Figure 36.21.

FIGURE 36.21.

The expanded dialog box you see when you click the Options >> button.

8. If you want to run through the logon screens and options for each service at startup, activate the Show Logon screens for all information services check box.

9. Click OK. Outlook loads the profile.

Summary

This chapter introduced you to Outlook, Office 97's desktop information manager. My goal was to help you get Outlook up and running on your system. To that end, I showed you how to install the program and its information services and set up your default profile. From there, you learned how to configure Microsoft Mail, The Microsoft Network Mail, and Internet Mail. With that out of the way, I took you on a tour of the Outlook window and showed you various methods of navigating and working with Outlook's folder.

We've only just begun our Outlook journey. Here's an itinerary for the rest of the trip:

- Chapter 37, "The Ins and Outs of the Outlook Inbox," shows you the basics of using Outlook for reading, sending, and working with e-mail messages.

- Outlook is jammed with fancy e-mail features. I'll cover them all in Chapter 38, "Advanced Outlook E-Mail Topics."

- If you're interested in using Outlook to send and receive faxes, I'll show you how in Chapter 39, "Using Outlook for Faxing."

- To learn how to use the Outlook Calendar, see Chapter 40, "Places to Go: Calendar."

- Chapter 41, "People to Meet: Contacts," gives you the scoop on Outlook's impressive Contacts feature.

- You'll learn how to wield the Tasks, Journal, and Notes tools in Chapter 42, "Things to Do: Tasks, Journal, and Notes."

- I show you how to program Outlook e-mail in Chapter E3 on the CD, "Programming the Outlook Inbox."

CHAPTER 37

The Ins and Outs of the Outlook Inbox

IN THIS CHAPTER

Order and simplification are the first steps toward the mastery of a subject—the actual enemy is the unknown.

—*Thomas Mann*

It wasn't all that long ago that people were mourning the demise of letter writing. The evil twin influences of reduced leisure time and overexposure to television were usually cited as the reasons for the passing of a once-popular pastime. Now, however, letter writing is making a big comeback. That's not to say that you'll see mail carriers' mailbags groaning under the weight of epistles, postcards, and *billets-doux* as folks try to catch up on their correspondence. No, the real force behind this resurgence of the written word is *e-mail.* In corporations and colleges, at home and on the road, people who would never even consider putting pen to paper are exchanging electronic missives and messages in staggering numbers.

Office 97 users can get in on this e-mail frenzy as well. Outlook's e-mail information services let you swap messages with others on your network, or with users on remote systems such as the Internet. This chapter gets you up to speed with Outlook's e-mail capabilities by showing you around the Inbox. You'll learn how to compose messages, check for new mail, read received messages, reply to these messages, work with the Outlook Address Book, and do lots more. I'll investigate Outlook's more advanced e-mail features in the next chapter. If it's fax capabilities you're after, you'll want to read Chapter 39, "Using Outlook for Faxing."

A Tour of the Inbox

At this point, you should have Outlook installed, configured, and ready for action. You're now free to start firing off missives, notes, memos, tirades, harangues, and any other kind of digital correspondence (or *bit-spit,* as some wags like to call electronic text) that strikes your fancy. And, of course, you'll also want to read any incoming messages that others have sent your way.

Before we get that far, however, let's take a closer look at the Inbox. Assuming Outlook is up and running and that the Inbox folder is displayed, you'll see a window similar to the one shown in Figure 37.1.

You'll notice that I've activated the Mail folders in the Outlook Bar. These folders serve as storage areas for different types of messages. I'll show you how to create folders and move messages between them later in this chapter, but for now, here's a rundown of Outlook's default folders:

Inbox: This folder holds all your incoming messages. When you first start Outlook, it displays the contents of the Inbox folder by default.

Sent Items: This folder holds a copy of each message you send.

Outbox: This folder holds messages you've composed but haven't sent yet.

Deleted Items: This folder holds the items (messages and other folders) you delete.

FIGURE 37.1.

The Outlook window.

Column Headers

Mail folders

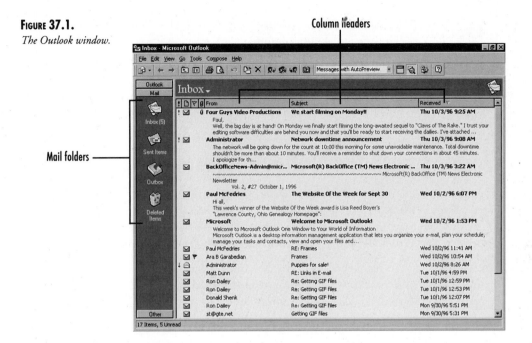

The message list shows you the messages that reside in the currently selected folder. I'll show you how to customize the columns in the next section, but for now, let's examine the default columns. The From column tells you the name or address of the person or system that sent you the message. The Subject column shows you the Subject line of the message. The Received column tells you the date and time the message was received. The left side of the message list has four other columns:

 This column tells you the priority level assigned to the message. A red exclamation point indicates a high priority, and a blue down-arrow indicates a low priority. If you don't see a symbol in this column, either the message has medium priority or no priority was assigned.

 This column tells you the message type. E-mail and editable fax messages display an envelope, noneditable fax messages display a fax icon, and system messages (such as errors and delivery notifications) use a postmark icon.

You use this column to flag messages that you want to deal with later. This is a visual indication that a message needs to be acted upon in some way, which makes it less likely that you'll delete or move the message before following up.

 A paper clip icon in this column tells you that the message contains an attachment (that is, an OLE object embedded in the message).

Working with the Outlook Address Book

As you'll see a bit later, when you compose a new message or reply to a received message, Outlook provides fields in which you can specify the recipient's address. If you have correspondents with whom you swap notes frequently, typing their e-mail addresses each time can be a pain. (This is especially true of some Internet e-mail addresses, which can be absurdly lengthy.)

Instead of typing your recipients' addresses by hand each time you compose a message, you can use Outlook's *Address Book* to store these frequently used addresses for easy recall. Here are the methods you can use to display the Address Book:

- Select Tools | Address Book.
- Press Ctrl-Shift-B.
- In the message composition window, click either the To button or the Cc button.

 - Click the Address Book button on the toolbar.

Figure 37.2 shows the Address Book window that Outlook displays. (If you're in the middle of composing a message, you'll see a slightly different version of this window.) The bulk of the window is taken up by a list of names; these are determined by the currently selected item in the Show names from the box. This box contains the various address lists you have to work with. Depending on the services you installed, you should see one or more of the following lists:

Microsoft Network: Selecting this item displays the complete list of members of The Microsoft Network. To download this list, Outlook will connect you to MSN if you're not already online.

Postoffice Address List: This is the list of users in your Microsoft Mail postoffice.

Outlook Address Book: This is a list of Contacts folders that have been set up to double as e-mail address books. Each of these folders displays the e-mail addresses that you've defined in the Contacts folder. (See Chapter 41, "People to Meet: Contacts," to learn how to set up a Contacts folder as an address book.)

Global Address List: This is a list of addresses available to all the Exchange Servers in your network.

A Microsoft Exchange Server address list: This is a list of addresses available to the Exchange Server to which your mailbox belongs. The name usually takes the form *Company Name | Domain Name | *Recipients.

Personal Address Book: You can use this list either to add new addresses or to add existing names from any of the other lists. I'll show you how this works later in this section.

FIGURE 37.2.

Use the Address Book to store your frequently used e-mail addresses.

When you select an address list, the Address Book displays the names contained in the list. If you scroll to the right, you'll see two more columns: one that tells you the type of address (such as MS for a Microsoft Mail address or SMTP for an Internet address), and another that specifies the e-mail address.

To find a specific name in the address list, use any of the following techniques:

- Move into the list and scroll through it using the scrollbars or the navigation keys (up arrow, down arrow, Page Up, and Page Down).

- In the Type Name or Select from List text box, type the first few letters of the name you want.

- Select Tools | Find (or press Ctrl-Shift-F), enter the name in the Find dialog box, and click OK.

NOTE: SPECIFIC MSN SEARCHES

You can perform more specific searches if you're working with the list of addresses from The Microsoft Network. In this case, the Find dialog box includes fields for the member ID, first name, last name, address, company name, and even sex and marital status. (However, few MSN members provide such personal details.)

The Address Book Toolbar

Before getting into the various techniques you can use to work with the Address Book, let's take a second to examine the buttons available on the Address Book toolbar. Table 37.1 spells them out.

Table 37.1. Address Book toolbar buttons.

Button	Name	Description
	New Entry	Adds a new address to the Personal Address Book.
	Find	Displays the Find dialog box.
	Properties	Displays the properties sheet for the selected address.
	Delete	Deletes the selected address.
	Add to Personal Address Book	Adds the selected address to the Personal Address Book.
	New Message	Starts a new e-mail message.
	Help	Invokes What's This? Help. After clicking this button, click a control in the Address Book window to display a Help topic related to that control.

Adding Addresses to Your Personal Address Book

Your Personal Address Book is a .PAB file that resides on your hard disk (usually in your main Windows folder under the filename MAILBOX.PAB). You use the Personal Address Book (PAB) in either of two ways: to store addresses from the other address lists, or to store new addresses.

Adding Addresses from Other Address Lists

You can use the PAB to cull addresses from one of the other address lists. For example, if you have friends on The Microsoft Network, you might want to pull their addresses out of the MSN list and store them in your PAB. This way, you don't have to load the entire MSN address list every time you want to send them a message.

To move an address from another address list into your PAB, display the appropriate list, highlight the name, and then use any of the following techniques:

- Select File | Add to Personal Address Book.

- Click the Add to Personal Address Book button on the toolbar.

- Select File | Properties (or click the toolbar's Properties button), and in the properties sheet that appears, select Personal Address Book.

- Right-click the name and select Add to Personal Address Book from the context menu.

Adding New Addresses

To store new addresses that don't exist in the other address lists, follow these steps:

1. Select File | New Entry or click the New Entry toolbar button. Outlook displays the New Entry dialog box, shown in Figure 37.3.

FIGURE 37.3.

Use this dialog box to select the type of address you want to create.

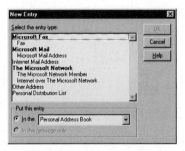

2. In the Select the entry type list, highlight the type of address you want to create and click OK. The dialog box that appears depends on the type of address you selected. For example, Figure 37.4 shows the properties sheet for an Internet Mail address.

FIGURE 37.4.

The properties sheet that Outlook displays depends on the address type you selected. This dialog box is for an Internet e-mail address.

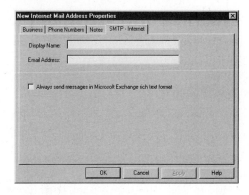

3. Fill in the address particulars. In most cases, the properties sheet also has Business, Phone Numbers, and Notes tabs you can fill out as well.

4. When you're done, click OK.

Changing the Properties of the Personal Address Book

Outlook keeps track of a few properties related to the Personal Address Book. These include the name that appears in the address list, the filename, and how names are arranged. To view these properties, select Tools | Options to display the Addressing dialog box, highlight Personal Address Book, and click Properties. Figure 37.5 shows the properties sheet that Outlook displays. Here's a summary of the available controls:

Name: This is name that appears in the list of address lists in the Address Book dialog box.

Path: This is the full pathname of the .PAB file. If you've created other .PAB files in other profiles, you can use this text box to specify a different file.

Show names by: These two options determine whether the Personal Address Book displays names by first name or last name.

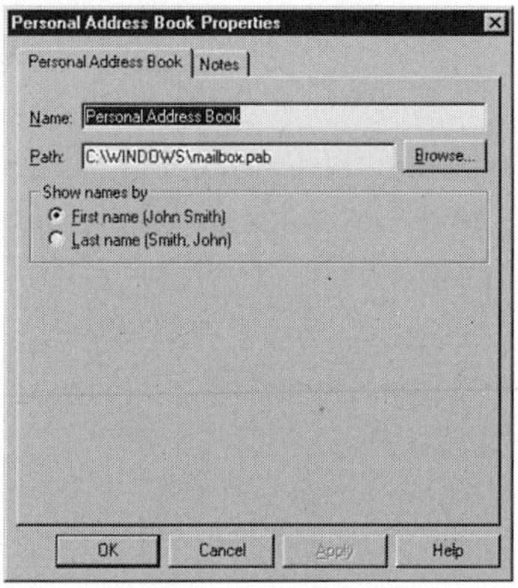

FIGURE 37.5.

Use the properties sheet to adjust some Personal Address Book options.

Outlook also provides a Notes tab you can use to add a description of the PAB or some other annotation.

TIP: SHARING A PERSONAL ADDRESS BOOK

If you use Outlook on multiple machines (say, at home and at work, or on a desktop and a notebook), don't re-create the Personal Address Book from scratch on each machine. Instead, create the PAB on one machine, and then copy the .PAB file to your other machines. If you use a different name, be sure to adjust the Path field in the PAB's properties sheet accordingly. (In case you're wondering, Outlook lets you specify a network path to a remote PAB file, but it doesn't let two installations of Outlook work with the file at the same time.)

Creating a Personal Distribution List

You'll see that the Address Book makes it a snap to include addresses in your correspondence. Even the Address Book method of choosing names can get tedious, however, if you regularly send messages to many people. For example, you might broadcast a monthly bulletin to a few dozen recipients, or you might send notes to entire departments.

To make these kinds of mass mailings easier to manage, Outlook lets you create a *personal distribution list* (PDL). This is a collection of e-mail addresses grouped under a single name. To send a message to every member of the PDL, you simply specify the PDL as the "recipient" of the message. Here are the steps to follow to create a PDL:

1. In the Address Book window, display the New Entry dialog box as described earlier.

2. At the bottom of the Select the entry type list, highlight Personal Distribution List and click OK. Outlook displays the properties sheet shown in Figure 37.6.

FIGURE 37.6.

Use this dialog box to define a new PDL.

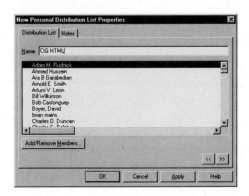

3. In the Name text box, enter the name you want to use for the PDL.

4. To include addresses (that is, *members*) in the PDL, click the Add/Remove Members button. Outlook displays the Edit Members dialog box, shown in Figure 37.7.

Figure 37.7.

Use the Edit Members dialog box to add PDL e-mail addresses.

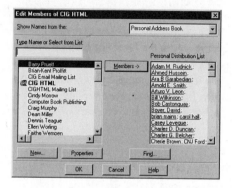

5. Use the Show Names from the box to select the address list you want to work with.

6. To add members, highlight the names and click Members->.

7. When you're done, click OK to return to the PDL properties sheet.

8. Click OK. Outlook adds the PDL to the Personal Address Book and identifies it as a PDL by placing a special icon beside the name.

Composing and Sending a New Message

Now it's time to get down to the e-mail nitty-gritty. For starters, I'll show you how to use Outlook to compose and send a message. You'll also learn how to work with the Outlook address book, how to embed objects in your messages, and how to use WordMail, the Microsoft Word replacement for the default Outlook message editor.

Composing a Message

Composing a message isn't all that different from composing a letter or memo in Word. You just need to add a few extra bits of information, such as your recipient's e-mail address and a description of your message.

To get started, either select Compose | New Mail Message or press Ctrl-N. Outlook displays a new message composition window, as shown in Figure 37.8. Here are the basic steps to follow to compose your message:

1. In the To field, enter the recipient's address. If you want to send the message to multiple recipients, separate each address with a semicolon (;).

2. In the Cc field, enter the addresses of any recipients you want to receive copies of the message. Again, separate multiple addresses with semicolons.

3. In the Subject field, enter a brief description of the message. This description will appear in the Subject column of the recipient's mail client, so make sure that it accurately describes your message.

4. Use the box below the Subject field to enter your message. Feel free to use any of the formatting options found on the Format menu or the Formatting toolbar. Remember, however, that not all systems will transfer rich text formatting.

5. To send your message, select File | Send, press Ctrl-Enter, or click the Send button on the toolbar.

FIGURE 37.8.

Use the Message window to enter the e-mail addresses of your recipients, the Subject line, and the body of the message.

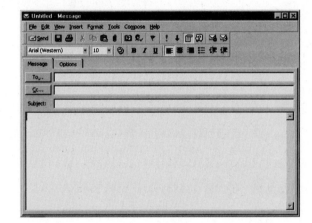

When you click Send, Outlook delivers the message to the recipient's mailbox or to the remote system (depending on the address). The exception to this rule is if you're using Outlook's Remote Mail feature (see "Retrieving Messages with Remote Mail" later in this chapter). In this case, Outlook doesn't deliver the message. Instead, it stores the message in the Outbox folder. To deliver the message, you have two choices:

- Invoke Remote Mail and initiate the mail transfer.
- Select Tools | Check for New Mail. This not only looks for new incoming messages, but also delivers all your Outbox messages.

Using the Address Book to Specify Recipients

When you're composing a message, you can use the Address Book to add recipients without having to type their addresses. First, use the techniques described earlier to display the Address Book. (Remember that when you're in the composition window, you can click the To and Cc buttons to display the Address Book.) Figure 37.9 shows the slightly different version of the Address Book that appears.

FIGURE 37.9.

This dialog box appears when you invoke the Address Book from within the message composition window.

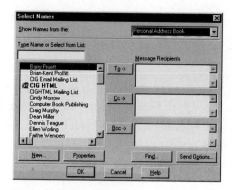

Use the Show names from the list to select the address list you want to work with. Highlight the recipient and then click one of the following buttons:

To->: Adds the recipient to the message's To field.

Cc->: Adds the name to the Cc field. ("Cc" stands for *courtesy copy*.)

Bcc->: Adds a Bcc field to the message and inserts the recipient's name in that field. ("Bcc" stands for *blind courtesy copy*. It's similar to Cc, except that addresses in this field aren't displayed to the other recipients.)

When you've added all the recipients for your message, click OK.

Inserting Objects in a Message

Outlook's OLE support means that you can insert objects into your messages. These objects are sent to the recipient using rich text format, so as long as the recipient's system supports this format (specifically, the remote gateway must be able to handle MIME or UUencode attachments, and the recipient's e-mail client must be MAPI-compliant), you can attach spreadsheets, word processing documents, graphics, files, and any other OLE object to your messages.

Depending on the type of object you want to work with, Outlook gives you three methods of inserting objects:

Inserting a file: To insert a file into the message, select Insert | File or click the toolbar's Insert File button. In the Insert File dialog box that appears, highlight the file you want to send. If you just want to include the file's text, activate the Text only option. To send the file as an attachment, activate the Attachment option. To send the file as a shortcut, activate the Shortcut option. When you click OK, Outlook embeds the file into the message as an icon.

TIP: OTHER WAYS TO E-MAIL A FILE

If you want to e-mail a file, Windows offers a couple other methods that are easier to use:

- In Explorer, right-click the file you want to send, and then select Send To | Mail Recipient.
- In any Office application, open the file you want to send and select File | Send To | Mail Recipient.

Either way, Outlook cranks out a new message and inserts the file automatically.

Inserting an Outlook item: If you want to insert an Outlook item (such as another e-mail message or contact), select Insert | Item. In the Insert Item dialog box, highlight the item you want to use; activate Text only, Attachment, or Shortcut; and click OK.

Inserting an OLE object: To insert an OLE object, select Insert | Object. In the Insert Object dialog box that appears, either select Create from new and choose the object type you want, or select Create from file and specify the filename. If you're creating a new object, Outlook invokes the appropriate application. If the application supports visual editing, the composition window assumes the characteristics (menus and toolbars) of the application. For example, Figure 37.10 shows the composition window displayed while you're creating a new Excel worksheet object.

FIGURE 37.10.

When you insert a new object for an application that supports visual editing, the message window assumes the characteristics of the application (Excel, in this case).

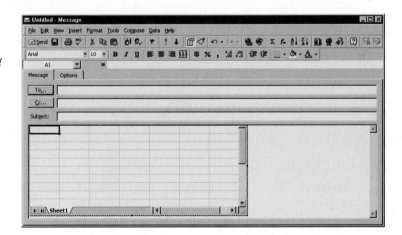

Setting Message Options

Before sending your message, you might want to specify a few extra options, such as asking for a delivery receipt or setting the importance and sensitivity levels. All of these items can be found in the Options tab of the new message, as shown in Figure 37.11. You have the following choices:

Importance: Sets the importance to Low, Normal, or High. Remember, though, that not all mail systems will honor this flag. You can also click the following toolbar buttons to set the Importance level:

 Importance: High

Importance: Low

Sensitivity: This drop-down list assigns a default sensitivity level to your messages. Select Normal (no sensitivity), Personal (nonbusiness), Private (recipients can't modify your messages when replying), or Confidential (tells the recipient that the contents of your message should be forwarded with caution).

Use voting buttons: If you activate this check box, Outlook adds "voting buttons" to the message, which let you get simple feedback from your recipients. Use the drop-down list to choose which buttons you want to use.

NOTE: VOTING BUTTONS EXPLAINED

What are voting buttons? They're a handy new feature in Outlook. If you activate the Use voting buttons check box in a message you send, the recipients will see an extra "toolbar" near the top of the message window. If you choose, say, the Approve;Reject voting buttons, this toolbar contains buttons named Approve and Reject. All the user has to do is click one of these buttons to send a response. If he clicks the Approve button, for example, you'll get a reply in which the word "Approve" has been appended to the Subject line.

Have replies sent to: Use this text box to specify an address where you want any replies sent. Click the Select Names button to choose addresses from the Address Book.

Save sent message to: Use this text box to choose a folder in which to store a copy of the message. The default folder is Sent Items, but you can choose another by clicking the Browse button.

Delivery options: Activate the Do not deliver before check box to set a date and time after which the message will be sent. Activate the Expires after check box to set a date and time after which the message will be removed from the recipient's Inbox (assuming that he hasn't yet read it by that time).

Tracking options: These check boxes tell Outlook to attach delivery and read receipts to the message. Again, not all e-mail gateways honor these receipt requests.

Categories: Click this button to display the Categories dialog box, from which you can assign one or more categories (such as Business or Personal) to the message.

FIGURE 37.11.

Use the Options tab to set various options for the message.

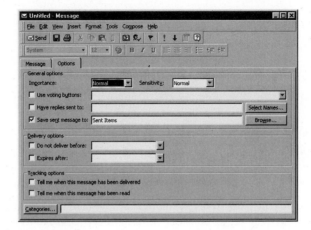

Reading Incoming Mail

Of course, you won't be spending all your time firing off notes and missives to friends and colleagues. Those people will eventually start sending messages back, and you might start getting regular correspondence from mailing lists, administrators, and other members of the e-mail community. This section shows you how to retrieve messages, read them, and then deal with them appropriately.

Retrieving Messages

As you saw in the preceding chapter, you can set up most of the mail services (with the exception of The Microsoft Network) to automatically look for messages that are waiting in your mailbox and, if any are found, to retrieve them to your Outlook Inbox folder. Also, Outlook checks for waiting messages each time you send a message to a particular service.

However, one of Outlook's little quirks (it has a few of them!) is that it doesn't have any kind of "Retrieve" command for downloading messages directly. Instead, even if you don't have any messages to send, you can get Outlook to check for incoming messages by using either of the following methods:

■ To check for messages on all your services, select Tools | Check for New Mail.

■ To check for mail on only specific services, select Tools | Check for New Mail On. In the Check for New Mail On dialog box that appears, shown in Figure 37.12, activate the check boxes for the services you want to use, and then click OK.

FIGURE 37.12.

Use this dialog box to tell Outlook to check for mail on only specific services.

Outlook connects to each service in turn, checks for waiting messages, and retrieves any it finds. (And, of course, it also sends any messages you've composed and stored in your Outbox folder.)

Retrieving Messages with Remote Mail

With each of the preceding methods, Outlook grabs any and all messages that are waiting for you and dumps them in your Inbox folder. You might not want to do this, however. For example, you might have dozens of messages waiting and you might need only one or two of them for now. Or you might have some messages that contain huge file attachments, and you might prefer to leave them on the server and then set up an unattended download overnight or while you're at lunch.

For this kind of control over your incoming messages, you have to use Outlook's Remote Mail feature. When you set up a service to use Remote Mail, Outlook doesn't retrieve your messages automatically. Instead, you must connect to the service manually. After you do, however, you can ask Remote Mail to download the headers for the waiting messages. You can then select the messages you want to retrieve and transfer only those to your inbox; the rest stay on the server.

CAUTION: MAKE SURE SENT MESSAGES ARE REALLY SENT

As I mentioned in the preceding section, Outlook always performs sending and retrieving at the same time. This means that when you're using Remote Mail, Outlook doesn't send the messages you compose. Instead, it stores them in the Outbox folder until you connect to the service via Remote Mail. The problem is that Outlook often gives you no indication that the message only went to the Outbox folder. So if you forget that you're using Remote Mail, you'll think your message is winging its way to the recipient when, all along, it hasn't gone anywhere. (I'd be embarrassed to tell you how many times I've done this!)

Starting Remote Mail

I showed you in the preceding chapter how to set up the various mail services to use Remote Mail. (Note that The Microsoft Network always uses Remote Mail.) When you've done that, you can start Remote Mail by selecting Tools | Remote Mail | Connect. Outlook displays the Remote Connection Wizard, shown in Figure 37.13. Choose which services you want to use and click Next >. The Wizard then asks whether you want to retrieve and send all messages, or retrieve only the message headers. Make your choice and click Finish.

FIGURE 37.13.

The Remote Connection Wizard will help you get Remote Mail up and running.

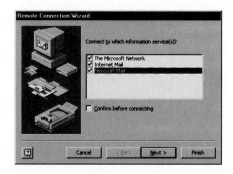

Outlook then connects to each service, retrieves either entire messages or just the headers of the waiting messages, and stores everything in the Inbox folder. If you downloaded just headers, you need to decide what to do with each message. Here are your choices:

Mark to Retrieve: If you want Outlook to retrieve a message, highlight it and select Tools | Remote Mail | Mark to Retrieve or click the Mark to Retrieve button on the Remote toolbar.

Mark to Retrieve a Copy: If you want Outlook to retrieve only a copy of the message (the original stays on the server), highlight the message and either select Tools | Remote Mail | Mark to Retrieve a Copy or click the Mark to Retrieve a Copy button on the Remote toolbar.

Mark to Delete: To delete a message, highlight it and either select Tools | Remote Mail | Mark to Delete or click the Delete toolbar button.

When that's taken care of, you can transfer the marked messages by selecting Tools | Remote Mail | Connect to start the Wizard again. Click Next >, and you'll see a list of the messages you marked, as shown in Figure 37.14. Click Finish to download the messages.

FIGURE 37.14.

This dialog box gives you a summary of the items that will be transferred.

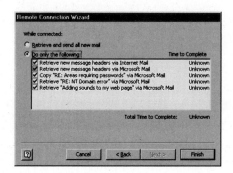

Opening a Message

At long last, you're ready to start reading your messages. In the message list, highlight the message you want to read, and then use any of the following techniques to open it:

- Select File | Open.
- Press Enter.
- Double-click the message.
- Right-click the message and select Open from the context menu.

Outlook displays that message in the window shown in Figure 37.15.

FIGURE 37.15.

Outlook uses this window to display your messages.

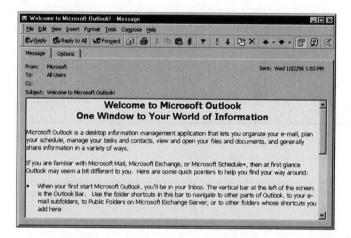

NOTE: TOGGLING MESSAGE BOLDFACE

Unread messages appear in the message list in boldface type. After you've read a message, Outlook displays it in regular type so that you know right away whether you've read it. You can toggle boldfacing on and off by selecting Edit | Mark as Read or Edit | Mark as Unread.

TIP: QUICKLY ADDING THE SENDER TO YOUR PAB

If you want to add the sender of the message to your Personal Address Book, an easy way to do so is to right-click the sender's name in the From line in the header. From the context menu that appears, select Add to Personal Address Book.

> **NOTE: A PREVIEW PANE TOOL**
>
> Microsoft has an add-in tool called the 3-Pane Extension that splits the message area in two: The top half shows the usual message list, and the bottom half shows the text of the currently highlighted message. This handy tool can be found on the Outlook "free stuff" page:
>
> `http://www.microsoft.com/OfficeFreeStuff/Outlook/`

Working with Your Messages

When you have a message open, you can do plenty of things with it (besides reading it, of course). You can print it, save it to a file, move it to another folder, delete it, and more. Most of these operations are straightforward, so I'll just summarize the basic techniques here:

Flagging the message: If you need to perform some sort of follow-up action for the message, you can set a message flag that will appear beside the message in the folder. To set the flag, select Edit | Message Flag to display the Flag Message dialog box. Use the Flag list to choose the type of flag (for example, Follow up or Reply), and use the By list to select a date by which you want to perform the action.

Reading other messages: If you have several messages you want to read, you don't have to return to the message list to navigate your messages. If you want to move on to the next message, select View | Next. The cascade menu that appears gives you a number of options. For example, to just see the next message in the list, select Item. To see the next unread message, select Unread Item. You can also view previous messages by selecting View | Previous and choosing the appropriate command from the cascade menu.

> **TIP: MESSAGE LIST SHORTCUTS**
>
> To view the next item in the message list, press Ctrl->. To view the previous item in the message list, press Ctrl-<.

Dealing with attachments: If a message has an attachment, it will appear either as an icon or as an object embedded in the message. You can use the usual OLE methods of viewing the object (assuming that you have the correct server application).

Moving a message to a different folder: In the preceding chapter, I showed you how to create new folders in Outlook. This is especially handy for e-mail messages, because you can use folders for storing related messages. To move a message to another folder, select File | Move to Folder. In the Move Item to dialog box that appears, highlight the folder you want to use, and then click OK.

Saving a message: Instead of storing the message in a folder, you might prefer to save it to a file. To do this, select File | Save As. In the Save As dialog box, select a location, enter a filename, and select a format (Text Only, Rich Text Format, Outlook Template, or Message Format).

Saving an attachment: If the message has a file attachment, select File | Save Attachments. The cascade menu that appears gives you a list of the message attachments. Select the attachment and then use the Save Attachment dialog box to select a storage location and a name for the file.

Printing a message: To print a copy of the message, select File | Print to display the Print dialog box. Enter your print options (including whether you want to print any attachments), and then click OK.

Deleting a message: If you want to get rid of the message you're reading, select File | Delete or press Ctrl-D. You can also click the toolbar's Delete button. Note that Outlook doesn't really delete the message. Instead, it just moves it to the Deleted Items folder. If you change your mind and decide to keep the message, just open the Deleted Items folder and move the message back. To permanently remove a message, open the Deleted Items folder and delete the message from there.

NOTE: CLEARING THE DELETED ITEMS FOLDER

If you find that your Deleted Items folder is overflowing with discarded messages, there are two methods you can use to "take out the trash":

- Open the Deleted Items folder and delete the items again. This time, however, the deletion is permanent, so be sure you really want these messages deleted.

- To force Outlook to clean out the Deleted Items folder every time you exit the program, select Tools | Options and display the General tab in the Options dialog box. Activate the Empty the Deleted Items folder upon exiting check box, and then click OK.

TIP: DRAG-AND-DROP TECHNIQUES

The basic drag-and-drop technique comes in handy when you're dealing with Outlook messages. For example, with drag-and-drop you can carry out these actions:

- Move messages around by dragging them from the message list and dropping them on the folder where you want them moved.

- Delete messages by dragging them from the message list and dropping them on the Deleted Items folder.

- Save messages by dragging them from the message list and dropping them on the desktop or on a folder window.

- Save file attachments by dragging them from the message and dropping them on the desktop or on a folder window.

Replying to a Message

If you receive a message from someone who needs some information from you, or if you think of a witty retort to a friend's or colleague's message, you'll want to send a reply. Instead of requiring you to create a new message from scratch, Outlook (like all e-mail programs) has a "Reply" feature that saves you the following steps:

- Outlook starts a new message automatically.

- Outlook inserts the recipient automatically.

- Outlook inserts the original Subject line but adds "RE:" to the beginning of the line to identify this message as a reply.

- Outlook adds the header and the text of the original message to the body of the new message.

Outlook gives you two Reply options:

Reply: This option sends the reply only to the person who sent the original. Any names in the Cc line are ignored. To use this option, select Compose | Reply or press Ctrl-R. You can also click the Reply button on the toolbar.

Reply to All: This option sends the reply not only to the original author, but also to anyone else mentioned in the Cc line. To use this option, select Compose | Reply to All or press Ctrl-Shift-R. You can also click the Reply to All button on the toolbar.

Figure 37.16 gives you an idea of what the composition window looks like after you select (in this case) the Reply option.

FIGURE 37.16.

Using Outlook's "Reply" command saves you lots of time when you're composing responses to messages you've received.

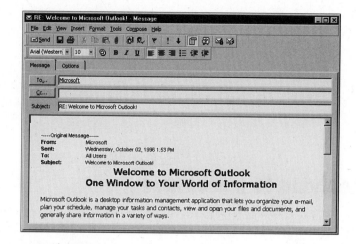

Forwarding a Message

Instead of replying to a message, you might prefer to forward it to another person. For example, you might receive a message in error, or you might think that a friend or colleague might receive some benefit from reading a message you received. Whatever the reason, you can forward a message to another address by using any of the following methods:

- Select Compose | Forward.
- Press Ctrl-F.

- Click the Forward button on the toolbar.

Outlook creates a new message, adds the original Subject line with FW: (to identify this as a forwarded message), and inserts the original text in the message body. If you like, you can add your own text as well.

Summary

This chapter took all your Outlook installation and configuration efforts from the preceding chapter and put them to good use. Specifically, you learned how to work with the Address Book, compose and send messages, read and work with incoming mail, and reply and forward messages. Check out the following chapters for related information:

- Outlook has numerous advanced features that will help you really take charge of your e-mail. I discuss topics such as sorting and filtering messages and customizing the Inbox in Chapter 38, "Advanced Outlook E-Mail Topics."

■ You can find faxing fun and foolishness in Chapter 39, "Using Outlook for Faxing."

■ You can use the Contacts folder to enter e-mail addresses and then make these addresses available as an e-mail address book. I'll show you how in Chapter 41, "People to Meet: Contacts."

■ I show you how to program Outlook e-mail in Chapter E3 on the CD, "Programming the Outlook Inbox."

Advanced Outlook E-Mail Topics

CHAPTER

38

Something deeply hidden had to be behind things.

—Albert Einstein

Back in Chapter 36, "Setting Up Outlook," I complained that the Exchange client that came with Windows 95 was woefully lacking in features. Strangely, most of the prerelease versions of Windows 95 came with a version of Exchange that was chock-full of interesting trinkets. In the end, however, Microsoft got cold feet and decided to "dumb down" the client to avoid confusing beginning-level users. Instead, they incorporated those features into the client that shipped with Exchange Server.

Outlook represents the next stage in the evolution of Microsoft's flagship e-mail client. You saw the basic functionality of this client in the preceding chapter, and now we'll turn our attention to Outlook's e-mail bells and whistles. This chapter shows you how to customize the Inbox; create automatic "signatures"; sort, filter, and group messages; and much more.

Customizing the Inbox Message Columns

The default columns in Outlook's Inbox tell you the basic information you need for any message. Much more information is available, however. For example, you might want to know the date and time the message was sent, the number of lines in the message, and the first few words of the message. All of these items and many more can be displayed as columns in the message list.

To customize Outlook's columns, select View | Field Chooser. Outlook displays the Field Chooser dialog box, shown in Figure 38.1. The drop-down list at the top of this dialog box contains various categories of message fields, so you should first select the category that contains the field you want to add. (If in doubt, you can select the All Mail fields item to see all the available fields.) Once the field is displayed, you add it to the Outlook window by dragging it from the Field Chooser and dropping it inside the column headers at the point where you want the field to appear.

FIGURE 38.1.

Use the Field Chooser dialog box to customize the columns displayed in the message list.

Here's a rundown of a few other column customization chores you can perform:

- Outlook has a "big picture" method of customizing columns. To try it, select View | Show Fields. The Show Fields dialog box that appears has two boxes: the Available fields list shows the column headings you can use, and the Show these fields in this order list shows the current column headings. Use the Add-> and <-Remove buttons to customize the field selection. You can also use the Move Up and Move Down buttons to adjust the column order.

- To remove a column, drag its header outside the column header area. (You can do this with or without the Field Chooser displayed.)

- To move a column, drag its header left or right within the column header area.

- To size a column, drag the right edge of the column's header to the left or right. If you want a column to be as wide as its widest entry, right-click the column header and choose Best Fit from the context menu.

- To change how text is aligned within a column, right-click the column's header, choose Alignment from the context menu, and then select Align Left, Align Right, or Center from the cascade menu.

Customizing Outlook's E-Mail Options

Outlook boasts a number of options for controlling e-mail, including specific options for reading and sending mail. (As you'll see in subsequent chapters, there are also options for Calendar, Journal, and many other Outlook components.) This section examines these customization options. To begin, select Tools | Options to display the Options dialog box, and then select the E-mail tab, shown in Figure 38.2. (Note that Windows 95 users will see a slightly different Options dialog box than the one shown here.)

FIGURE 38.2.

Use the Options dialog box to change a few global Outlook settings.

38

ADVANCED
OUTLOOK E-MAIL
TOPICS

The E-Mail Tab

The E-mail tab presents a mixed bag of settings that control everything from what services Outlook should check to what the program does when new mail arrives:

Check for new mail on: This box shows a list of the e-mail services you've installed. The services with activated check boxes are the ones Outlook connects to when you select Tools | Check for New Mail.

When new items arrive: These check boxes determine what Outlook does to let you know that a new message has arrived in your Inbox. These options are useful if Outlook is checking for new mail automatically. If you activate the Play a sound check box, Outlook beeps your speaker. If you activate Briefly change the mouse cursor, the cursor changes to an envelope icon for a split second (when they say briefly, they *mean* briefly). If you activate Display a notification message, you see the dialog box shown in Figure 38.3. If you click Yes, Outlook opens the first of your new messages.

FIGURE 38.3.

If you activate the Display a notification message check box, you'll see this dialog box whenever a new message arrives in your Inbox.

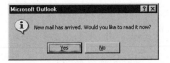

NOTE: SYSTEM TRAY ALWAYS NOTIFIES YOU OF NEW MESSAGES

No matter which options you activate in the When new items arrive group, Outlook always indicates that you have new mail by displaying an envelope icon in the taskbar's system tray.

Process delivery, read, and recall receipts on arrival: When this check box is activated, Outlook will update the "tracking status" of a message automatically. In other words, if you send a message with delivery or read receipt requests, as soon as you receive these receipts, Outlook will add the receipt information to the sent message. If you deactivate this check box, Outlook doesn't update the tracking status until you "open" the receipts.

NOTE: TRACKING THE TRACKING STATUS

To follow the tracking status of a message, display the Sent Items folder and open the message. The Tracking tab tells you which receipts have been received from which recipients.

Process requests and responses on arrival: When this check box is activated, Outlook automatically updates your Calendar when you receive a meeting request. If you sent a meeting request, Outlook automatically updates your Meeting Planner when responses are delivered. (See Chapter 40, "Places to Go: Calendar," for more information.)

Delete receipts and blank meeting responses after processing: If you activate this check box, Outlook automatically deletes delivery and read receipts as soon as you (or Outlook) process them. It also deletes any meeting request responses that have no comments.

Setting Up WordMail

Microsoft Word comes with a component called *WordMail* that replaces the standard Outlook message editor with Microsoft Word. This is a great idea, because it gives you access to some useful Word features, including on-the-fly spell checking, the grammar checker, a thesaurus, templates, AutoText, macros, and much more.

To tell Outlook that you prefer to use WordMail to compose your e-mail, display the Options dialog box, move to the E-mail tab, and activate the Use Microsoft Word as the e-mail editor check box. Figure 38.4 shows the new message composition window you'll see when you use Word as your e-mail editor.

FIGURE 38.4.

With WordMail enabled, you have most of Word's commands and features at your disposal.

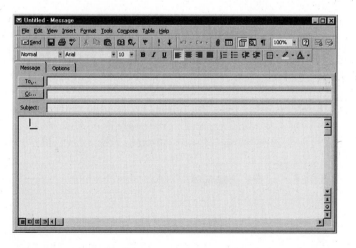

Word comes with an e-mail template called Email.dot. Each new message you create is based on the default e-mail template. You can set a different template as the default by clicking the Template button, highlighting the template in the WordMail Template dialog box, and clicking Select.

38

ADVANCED
OUTLOOK E-MAIL
TOPICS

- To add a template to the list, click the Add button, highlight the template in the Add dialog box, and click Add.
- To make changes to a template, highlight it and click Edit. Outlook starts Word and loads the template.

Outlook's Send Options

Now let's examine the various options that Outlook provides for sending e-mail. In the Options dialog box, select the Sending tab, shown in Figure 38.5. Here's a synopsis of the available options:

Font: Click this button to specify the default font to use in the message composition window.

Set importance: These options determine the default importance level of your messages. Choose High, Normal, or Low.

Set sensitivity: This drop-down list assigns a default sensitivity level to your messages. Select Normal, Personal, Private, or Confidential (I described each option in more detail in the preceding chapter).

Tell me when all messages have been delivered: If you activate this check box, you'll receive notification (a *receipt*) when the messages you sent have been delivered to the recipients' mailboxes.

Tell me when all messages have been read: If you activate this check box, you'll receive a receipt telling you when the recipients have read the messages you sent.

Save copies of messages in "Sent Items" folder: When this check box is activated, Outlook saves a copy of your message in the Sent Items folder. It's a good idea to leave this option checked, because it gives you a record of the messages you send.

In folders other than the Inbox, save replies with original message: If you activate this check box and respond to a message that's sitting in a folder other than the Inbox, Outlook saves a copy of your message in the other folder instead of in the Sent Items folder.

Save forwarded messages: Activate this check box to save a copy of each message you forward.

Here are some things to bear in mind when setting these values:

- The tracking options, sensitivity, and importance options set only the default levels. You can always change the levels for individual messages.
- Not all remote systems will honor receipt requests or forward the assigned levels of sensitivity or importance.
- Your recipients will see the assigned importance and sensitivity levels only if they're displaying the Importance and Sensitivity columns.

FIGURE 38.5.

Use the Sending tab to configure Outlook's default settings for composing and sending messages.

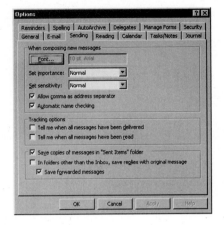

Outlook's Read Options

Outlook also has a few read-related properties. To view them, select the Reading tab, shown in Figure 38.6. Here's a review of the available controls:

When replying to a message: Use this drop-down list to determine what Outlook does with the original message when you crank out a reply. You can also click the Font button to specify the font to use for the new text you add to the response.

When forwarding a message: Again, use this drop-down list to determine what Outlook does with the original message when you forward it. You can also select a font for the text you add to the forwarded message.

After moving or deleting an open item: This list determines what Outlook does when you move or delete the message you're reading. You can choose to open the previous item (the item above the current item in the list of messages, that is), open the next item, or return to the Inbox.

Mark my comments with: If you activate this check box, the text box to the right becomes available. Any text you enter into this box is used by Outlook when you edit the original message in a reply or forward. Specifically, Outlook adds the text (enclosed in square brackets) beside the edited material. Note that this option is unavailable if you're using Word as your e-mail editor (because you can use Word's annotation feature instead).

Close original message on reply or forward: When this check box is activated, Outlook closes the original message when you reply to it or forward it.

Use US English for included message headers: If you're using a non-English version of Outlook, activate this check box to send the message header of a reply or forwarded message in English.

FIGURE 38.6.

Use the Reading tab to set various properties related to reading messages.

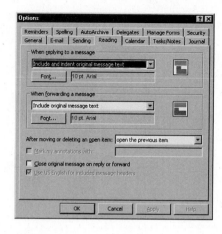

Options for Information Services

Outlook has a few options that apply to the information services you installed. To view these options, first select Tools | Services from Outlook to display the Services dialog box.

Delivery Options

The options in the Delivery tab, shown in Figure 38.7, modify a couple of settings that Outlook uses with incoming and outgoing messages:

Deliver new mail to the following location: This drop-down list determines which message store (.PST file) or mailbox is used to hold incoming messages.

Recipient addresses are processed by these information services in the following order: The list determines the order in which outgoing messages are delivered. The service at the top of the list has its messages sent first, then the next service, and so on. To change the order, highlight a service and use the Move Up and Move Down arrow buttons provided.

FIGURE 38.7.

The Delivery tab's options control what Outlook does with incoming and outgoing messages.

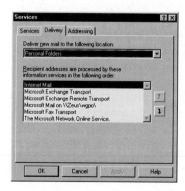

Addressing Options

The Addressing tab, shown in Figure 38.8, contains a few options that control how Outlook works with the various address lists in your Personal Address Book (which I discussed in more detail in Chapter 37, "The Ins and Outs of the Outlook Inbox"):

Show this address list first: This drop-down list determines the default address list that Outlook displays whenever you open the address book.

Keep personal addresses in: This drop-down list specifies the address book you want to use to store any addresses you create by hand.

When sending mail, check names using these address lists in the following order: Outlook can verify mail addresses before you send messages. This list determines the order Outlook uses when going through its checks. To change the order, highlight a list and use the Move Up and Move Down arrow buttons provided. To reduce the number of address lists you have to deal with, highlight a list and click Remove. If you later decide you need that list again, click Add to display the Add Address List dialog box, and then highlight the list and click the Add button.

FIGURE 38.8.

Use the Addressing tab to control how Outlook works with your address lists.

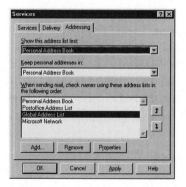

38

ADVANCED OUTLOOK E-MAIL TOPICS

Changing the Folder View

You'll often need to work with multiple, related messages. For example, you might want to see all the messages from a particular correspondent, or you might want to work with all messages that have the same Subject line (even if there's a "RE:" tacked on to the beginning). Outlook is particularly strong in this area because, as you'll see in the next few sections, it provides you with a seemingly endless number of methods for manipulating a message list.

We'll begin this section by looking at *views*. A view is just another way of looking at a message list. For example, the Unread Messages view tells Outlook to display only those messages that you haven't opened.

Outlook's default view is Messages with AutoPreview. As you've seen, this view displays each unread message by showing the header information (From, Subject, Received) followed by the first three lines of the message body. This is an excellent feature, but there are nine other pre-defined views that you might want to try out:

Messages: Displays each message on a single line showing only the header information.

By Message Flag: Splits the folder into two panes: The top pane shows the messages you've flagged (and the type of flag you've set), and the bottom pane shows the un-flagged messages. You also get an extra Message Flag column that tells you the type of flag. This is an example of a message *group*. See "Grouping the Messages" later in this chapter for more information on grouping.

Last Seven Days: Displays only those messages that you've received in the last week. This is an example of a message *filter*. See "Filtering the Messages" later in this chapter for more information on filters.

Flagged for Next Seven Days: This view filters the messages to show only those that have been flagged *and* whose flags are due within the next week. (A new Due By column tells you the due date of each flag.)

By Conversation Topic: This view groups the messages according to the "conversation" defined for each message. This applies only to Exchange Server and Microsoft Mail messages. For regular messages, the conversation is the same as the subject. For messages posted to public folders, you can define a topic that is separate from the subject line. See the section "Posting Messages to Public Folders" later in this chapter.

By Sender: This view groups the messages by the name of the person who sent each message.

Unread Messages: This view filters the messages to show only those that haven't yet been read (or marked as read).

Sent To: This view groups the messages by the name of the person to whom each message was sent.

Message Timeline: This unique view, shown in Figure 38.9, displays a timeline that lists the messages you received underneath the time you received them. The View menu has three commands—Day, Week, and Month—that you can use to customize the timeline. Alternatively, use the following toolbar buttons:

    Day (shows messages by day)

    Week (shows messages by week)

    Month (shows messages by month)

Figure 38.9.

The timeline view shows you when you received each message.

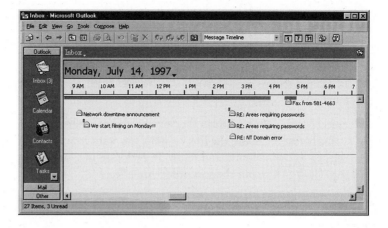

To change the view, Outlook gives you two methods:

■ Select View | Current View, and then choose the view you want from the cascade menu that appears.

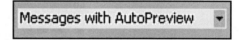

■ Use the Current View drop-down list on the toolbar.

TIP: AUTOPREVIEW IN OTHER VIEWS

You can access the AutoPreview feature in any of the views, not just Messages by Auto-Preview. Either activate the View | AutoPreview command, or click the AutoPreview button on the toolbar.

NOTE: CUSTOM VIEWS

Outlook also lets you define your own views. I'll tell you how to do this after I show you how to sort, filter, and group messages (see the section "Defining a Custom View" later in this chapter).

Sorting the Messages

By default, Outlook sorts the Inbox messages in descending order according to the values in the Received column. Similarly, messages in the Sent Items folder are sorted by the values in the Sent column. But you're free to sort the messages based on any displayed column. Here are the techniques you can use:

■ Select View | Sort to display the Sort dialog box, shown in Figure 38.10. Use the Sort items by list to choose the first column you want to use for the sort, use Then by to select a second column, and so on. In each case, activate either Ascending or Descending. Click OK to put the sort order into effect.

FIGURE 38.10.

Use this dialog box to sort your messages.

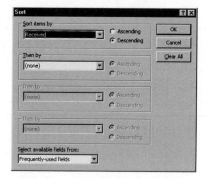

■ Click the header for the column you want to use for the sort. An arrow appears beside the column name to tell you the direction of the sort (an up arrow for ascending and a down arrow for descending).

■ Right-click the header of the column you want to use, and then select either Sort Ascending or Sort Descending from the context menu.

NOTE: SORTS ARE UNIQUE TO FOLDERS

The sort order you choose is unique to the current folder. This is convenient because it lets you set up different sort orders for different folders.

Grouping the Messages

You saw in the preceding section that Outlook comes with a few views that group related messages. For example, the By Sender view groups the messages by the name of the person who sent the message. As you can see in Figure 38.11, selecting this view transforms the message list into a display that's reminiscent of the outline views in Word or Excel. That is, each "group" has a plus sign (+) button beside it. Clicking this plus sign reveals the members of the group.

FIGURE 38.11.

The message list grouped by sender.

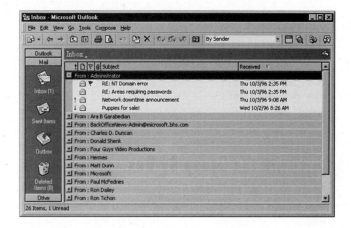

The big advantage of working with grouped messages is that Outlook treats them as a unit. This means that you can open, move, or delete all the messages in the group with a single operation.

Defining a New Grouping

Although some of the views group messages, they might not be the exact groupings you want to work with. No matter—Outlook is happy to let you define your own groupings. Just follow these steps:

1. Select View | Group By to display the Group By dialog box, shown in Figure 38.12.

FIGURE 38.12.

Use the Group By dialog box to define a new grouping for the messages.

2. Use the Select available fields from list to choose the category from which you want to select your grouping fields.

3. Use the Group items by list to choose the first field you want to use for the grouping. If you want to include the field as a column, activate the Show field in view check box. You can also activate either Ascending or Descending to sort the groups on this field.

4. To create subgroups, use one or more of the Then by lists to select other fields.

5. The Expand/collapse defaults list determines whether the groupings are displayed expanded (each message in each group is shown) or collapsed (only the groups are shown). You can also choose As last viewed to display the groups as you last had them.

6. Click OK to put the grouping into effect.

Working with the Group By Box

When you group your messages, Outlook adds the Group By box just below the folder banner, as shown in Figure 38.13. The button inside the Group By box tells you which field is being used for the grouping. Here's a summary of the various techniques you can use with the Group By box to adjust your groupings:

■ If you don't see the Group By box, either activate the View | Group By Box command, or click the Group By Box button on the toolbar.

■ Click the field button inside the Group By box to toggle the group sort order between ascending and descending.

■ To add an existing message list field to the grouping, drag the field's header into the Group By box.

■ To add any other field to the Group By box, select View | Field Chooser to display the Field Chooser dialog box, and then drag the field you want to use into the Group By box.

■ If you have multiple fields in the Group By box, you can change the subgroupings by dragging the field buttons left or right.

■ To remove the grouping, either drag the field button outside the group box or right-click the field button and choose Don't Group By This Field.

FIGURE 38.13.

You can use the Group By box to work with your groups.

The Group By box

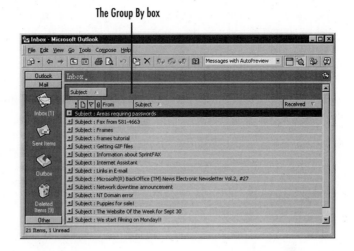

Filtering the Messages

Grouping messages often makes them easier to deal with, but you're still working with *all* the messages inside the folder. To really knock a message list down to size, you need to *filter* the messages. When we looked at views earlier, you saw that certain views displayed only selected messages. For example, choosing the Last Seven Days view reduced the message list to just those missives that were received in the last week.

As with groups, Outlook makes it easy to design your own filters. You'll soon see that filtering is one of Outlook's most powerful (and potentially complex) features. Yes, you can perform simple filters on field values, but Outlook can take you far beyond these basic filters. For example, you can filter messages based on words or phrases in the subject or body.

To get started, select View | Filter. The Filter dialog box that appears, shown in Figure 38.14, contains three tabs:

Messages: Use the controls in this tab to set message-based criteria. For example, you can enter a word or phrase in the Search for the word(s) text box and select an item from the In drop-down list (for example, subject field only). Outlook will filter messages that contain the word or phrase in the chosen item.

More Choices: This tab lets you fine-tune your filter. For example, you can set up a case-sensitive filter by activating the Match case check box. You can also filter based on priority, importance, attachments, and size.

38

ADVANCED OUTLOOK E-MAIL TOPICS

Advanced: This tab lets you set up sophisticated criteria for your filter. Use the Field list to choose a field, use the Condition list to select an operator (such as contains or is empty), and use the Value list to enter a criteria value. Click Add to List to add the criteria to the filter.

Figure 38.14.

Use the Filter dialog box to set up a custom message filter.

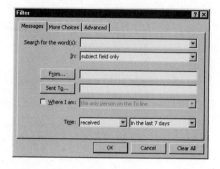

Defining a Custom View

If you go to a lot of work to set up a sort order, grouping, or filter, it seems a shame to have to repeat the process each time you want to use the same view. Happily, Outlook saves you that drudgery by letting you save custom sorts, groupings, or filters. In fact, Outlook goes one better by letting you save *combinations* of these views. In other words, you can define a view that includes a sort order, a grouping, and a filter. And, for added convenience, these views are available along with Outlook's predefined views, so they're easy to implement.

Here are the steps to follow to create a custom view:

1. If you want to apply the view to only a specific folder, select the folder.
2. Select View | Define Views to display the Define Views for *Folder* dialog box (where *Folder* is the name of the current folder).
3. Click New. Outlook displays the Create a New View dialog box, shown in Figure 38.15.

Figure 38.15.

Use this dialog box to name your view and choose the view type.

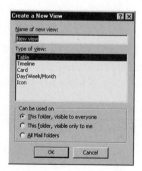

4. Use the Name of new view text box, enter a name for the view you'll be creating, and use the Type of view list to choose the view type. (For a mail folder, this will probably be Table, but feel free to try out some of the others.) Also, use the Can be used on group to select the folders to which the view will apply. Click OK to continue.

5. The View Summary dialog box, shown in Figure 38.16, contains various buttons that let you define the view specifics:

>   **Fields:** Displays the Show Fields dialog box so you can choose which fields to include in your view.
>
>   **Group By:** Displays the Group By dialog box so you can specify a grouping.
>
>   **Sort:** Displays the Sort dialog box so you can set up a sort order for the messages.
>
>   **Filter:** Displays the Filter dialog box so you can create a message filter for the view.
>
>   **Format:** Displays the Format dialog box so you can adjust the view's fonts and other formatting options.

FIGURE 38.16.

Use the buttons in the View Summary dialog box to spell out the particulars of your custom view.

38

ADVANCED
OUTLOOK E-MAIL
TOPICS

6. Click OK to return to the Define Views dialog box.

7. If you'd like to switch to the new view right away, click Apply View. Otherwise, click Close to return to Outlook.

TIP: HOW TO AVOID CREATING NEW VIEWS FROM SCRATCH

If another view exists that's similar to the custom view you want to create, there's a method you can use to save some time. Rather than creating the new view from scratch, highlight the existing view in the Define View dialog box, and then click Copy. In the Copy View dialog box that appears, enter a name for the new view and click OK. Outlook will then display the View Summary dialog box so that you can make your adjustments.

Using Rules to Process Messages Automatically

As e-mail becomes a ubiquitous feature on the business (and even home) landscape, you find that e-mail chores take up more and more of your time. And I'm not just talking about the three R's of e-mail: reading, 'riting, and responding. Basic e-mail maintenance—flagging, moving, deleting, and so on—also takes up large chunks of otherwise-productive time.

To help ease the e-mail time crunch, Outlook lets you set up "rules" that perform actions in response to specific events. Here's a list of just a few of the things you can do with rules:

- Move an incoming message to a specific folder if the message contains a particular keyword in the subject or body, or if it's from a particular person
- Automatically delete messages with a particular subject or from a particular person
- Flag messages based on specific criteria (such as keywords in the subject line or body)
- Have Outlook notify you with a custom message if an important message arrives
- Have copies of messages you send stored in a specific folder, depending on the recipient

Clearly, rules are powerful tools that shouldn't be wielded lightly or without care. Fortunately, Outlook comes with an Inbox Assistant that makes the process of setting up and defining rules almost foolproof. (Note, however, that you can use the Inbox Assistant only if you've installed the Exchange Server information service.) To get started, select Tools | Inbox Assistant. In the Inbox Assistant dialog box that appears, click Add Rule. You'll see the Edit Rule dialog box, shown in Figure 38.17.

Figure 38.17.

Use the Edit Rule dialog box to define a rule.

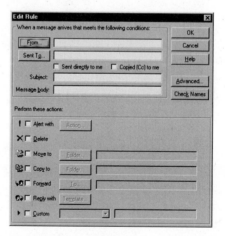

The first step is to define the criteria that will cause Outlook to invoke this rule. In other words, what conditions must an incoming message meet in order to apply the rule to that message? That's the purpose of the controls in the When a message arrives that meets the following conditions group:

From: Use this control to specify one or more e-mail addresses (or click From to choose them from the address book). In this case, Outlook will invoke the rule for any message sent from one of these addresses.

Sent To: Use this control to specify the addresses of the message recipients that will invoke the rule. You can also activate the Sent directly to me check box for messages in which your address is on the To line, and you can activate the Copied (Cc) to me check box for messages in which your address is on the Cc line.

Subject: Use this text box to enter a word or phrase that must appear in the Subject line to invoke the rule.

Message body: Use this text box to enter a word or phrase that must appear in the message body to invoke the rule.

Advanced: Clicking this button displays the Advanced dialog box, shown in Figure 38.18. These options control advanced criteria such as the size of the message, the date it was received, the Importance and Sensitivity levels, and more.

FIGURE 38.18.

Use the Advanced dialog box to set up sophisticated criteria for invoking the rule.

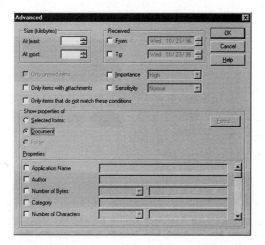

38

ADVANCED OUTLOOK E-MAIL TOPICS

Once you've determined *when* the rule will be invoked, you need to specify the *action* that Outlook will perform on the messages that satisfy these criteria. That's the job of the controls in the Perform these actions group:

Alert with: Activate this check box to have Outlook display a message when the message arrives. Clicking the Action button displays the Alert Actions dialog box, shown in Figure 38.19. You can use this dialog box to specify the message and choose a sound to play.

Delete: Activate this check box to delete the message upon arrival.

Move to: Activate this check box to move the message to a folder you specify. You can either type the folder name or click Folder to choose the folder from a dialog box.

Copy to: Activate this check box to copy the message to the specified folder.

Forward: Activate this check box to forward the message. Use the text box to specify one or more recipients, or click the To button to choose names from the address book.

Reply with: Activate this check box to generate a reply message. Click Template to choose a different e-mail template for the reply.

Custom: Activate this check box to apply a custom action to the message (such as an action supplied by a third-party vendor).

FIGURE 38.19.

Use the Alert Actions dialog box to specify a message to display and a sound to play when the message arrives.

When you're done, click OK to add the new rule to the Inbox Assistant, shown in Figure 38.20.

FIGURE 38.20.

The rules you've defined appear in the Inbox Assistant dialog box.

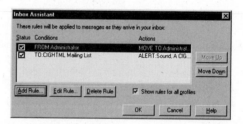

NOTE: RULE MAINTENANCE

You can use the Inbox Assistant dialog box to maintain your rules. For example, each rule you've defined has a check box beside it that toggles the rule on and off. You can change a rule by highlighting it and clicking Edit Rule. To get rid of a rule, highlight it and click Delete Rule.

NOTE: THE RULES WIZARD

Microsoft has a more advanced rules tool called the Rules Wizard. It provides more sophisticated message filtering, such as the capability to filter messages based on Internet e-mail addresses and words in the Subject line. It's the perfect "Spam killer," and you can download it from the Outlook "free stuff" page:

```
http://www.microsoft.com/OfficeFreeStuff/Outlook/
```

Creating an Automatic Signature

In e-mail circles, a *signature* is an addendum that appears as the last few lines of a message. Its purpose is to let the folks reading your e-mail know a little more about the person who sent it. Although signatures are optional, many people use them because they can add a friendly touch to your correspondence. You can put anything you like in your signature, but most people just put their name, their company name and address, other contact information (such as a fax number), and maybe a quote or two that fits in with their character.

Sounds like yet another e-mail chore, right? Not at all. Outlook has a nice feature that lets you define a signature and insert it into individual messages or into every message you send. To create a signature, follow these steps:

1. Select Tools | AutoSignature. Outlook displays the AutoSignature dialog box, shown in Figure 38.21.

FIGURE 38.21.

Use this dialog box to set up your signature.

2. Use the text box provided to enter your signature.
3. Use the Font and Paragraph buttons to format your signature text. (Remember, though, that most e-mail systems won't honor this formatting.)
4. To have Outlook add the signature to the end of every new message you compose, activate the Add this signature to the end of new messages check box.
5. If you'd also like your signature added to replies, deactivate the Don't add this signature to replies or forwarded messages check box.
6. Click OK.

If you elected not to have Outlook add the signature automatically to every new message, you can insert it by hand. When you're in the message composition window, just select Insert | AutoSignature.

Posting Messages to Public Folders

E-mail systems that operate under the aegis of Microsoft Exchange Server can have public folders that are accessible to each client on the system—assuming, that is, that these clients have installed Outlook's Microsoft Exchange Server information service. When you open the Folder List (by selecting View | Folder List), you'll see a folder named Public Folders. This is the Exchange Server container for all the public folders. In particular, this folder contains a subfolder named All Public Folders in which users can create new public folders. Figure 38.22 shows some examples.

FIGURE 38.22.

Exchange Server public folders are accessible to all clients on the network.

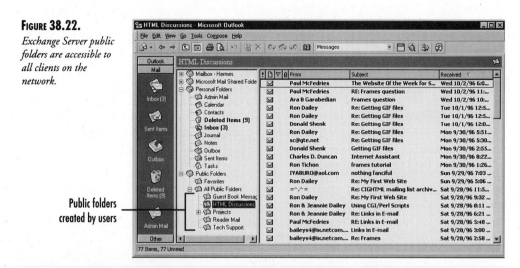

Public folders created by users

NOTE: MODIFYING PUBLIC FOLDER DATA

When working with public folders and the messages they contain, the general rule is that you can modify only items that you created yourself. For example, if you create a public folder, only you can move, rename, or delete it. Similarly, you can modify messages in someone else's public folder only if you posted those messages yourself.

However, Outlook gives the owner of each public folder a mechanism for adjusting permissions and other properties. Right-click your folder and choose Properties from the context menu. The properties sheet that appears gives you numerous options for setting up user permissions, defining the operation of the folder, and more.

Public folders are a convenient way to share e-mail among a group of users, but they can act as more than just common storage areas. Specifically, you can use a public folder to set up "conversations" between users. In this sense, a public folder becomes more like a Usenet newsgroup. Instead of sending a message to one or more e-mail recipients, you "post" the message to the folder. Others can then read the message and post replies in the same folder. A group of related posts is called a *conversation*.

Posting a message is more or less the same as composing an e-mail message. Here are the differences:

■ To post a new message to a public folder, display the folder and then select Compose | New Post in This Folder (or press Ctrl-Shift-S). In the message composition window that appears, enter a subject and the message, and then click Post.

■ To post a reply to a message in a public folder, highlight the message and then select Compose | Post Reply in This Folder. Again, enter a subject and the message, and then click Post.

Figure 38.23 shows a public folder with a few conversations going. In this example, I've switched to the By Conversation Topic view so that you can see how Outlook groups conversations. Notice, in particular, that Outlook differentiates between the Conversation field and the Subject field. This is handy, because it lets you post messages to a particular conversation, yet still write a unique Subject line.

FIGURE 38.23.

A public folder with several ongoing conversations.

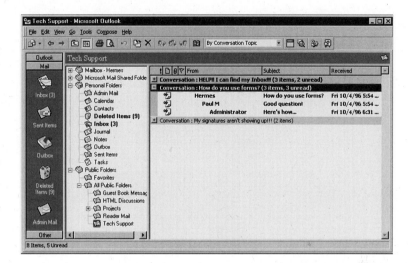

Summary

If you doubted it before, surely this chapter convinced you that Outlook is no ordinary e-mail client. The sheer wealth of gadgets and trinkets crammed into this package is impressive, to say the least. Few, if any, e-mail programs on any platform can match Outlook feature-for-feature. Here's what's in store in subsequent chapters:

■ If you'd like to learn how to use Microsoft Fax via Outlook, head for Chapter 39, "Using Outlook for Faxing."

■ You can use e-mail to plan business meetings and appointments. I'll show you how it's done in Chapter 40, "Places to Go: Calendar."

■ The Outlook Journal can record your e-mail activity. See Chapter 42, "Things to Do: Tasks, Journal, and Notes," for the nitty-gritty.

■ I show you how to program Outlook e-mail in Chapter E3 on the CD, "Programming the Outlook Inbox."

Using Outlook for Faxing

IN THIS CHAPTER

As machines become more and more efficient and perfect, so it will become clear that imperfection is the greatness of man.

—*Ernst Fischer*

Remember when, a decade or so ago, the fax (or the *facsimile,* as it was called back then) was the hottest thing around, the new kid on the telecommunications block? How amazing it seemed that we could send a letter or memo or even a picture through phone lines and have it emerge seconds later across town or even across the country. Sure, the fax that came slithering out the other end was a little fuzzier than the original, and certainly a lot slimier, but it sure beat using the post office.

Nowadays, though, faxing is just another humdrum part of the workaday world, and any business worth its salt has a fax machine on standby. Increasingly, however, dedicated fax machines are giving way to *fax/modems*—modems that have the capability to send and receive faxes in addition to their regular communications duties. Not only does this make faxing affordable for individuals and small businesses, but it also adds a new level of convenience to the whole fax experience:

- You can send faxes right from your computer without having to print the document.
- Because faxes sent via computer aren't scanned (as they are with a fax machine), the document that the recipient gets is sharper and easier to read.
- You can store incoming faxes along with the rest of your e-mail.
- You can use your printer to get a hard copy of a fax on regular paper, thus avoiding fax paper (which, besides being inherently slimy, has an annoying tendency to curl).
- You can send binary files along with your faxes (provided that both the sending and the receiving fax/modems support this feature).

If you're looking to get into the fax fast lane, look no further than Outlook's Microsoft Fax service. This chapter shows you how to install and configure Microsoft Fax, and how to use it to send and receive faxes.

Adding the Microsoft Fax Service Provider

If you chose to include Microsoft Fax in the list of information services to install with Outlook, the Inbox Setup Wizard, shown in Figure 39.1, leads you through the appropriate configuration steps.

FIGURE 39.1.

*If you installed
Microsoft Fax during
the Outlook installa-
tion, the Inbox Setup
Wizard helps you
configure the fax
service.*

If you bypassed Microsoft Fax during installation, you can easily add the Microsoft Fax service
from within Outlook. Here are the steps to follow:

1. In Outlook, select Tools | Services to display the Services dialog box.
2. Click Add. Outlook displays the Add Services to Profile dialog box.
3. Highlight Microsoft Fax and click OK. Outlook displays a dialog box that gives you a
   summary of the steps you're about to follow to configure Microsoft Fax, and it asks
   whether you want to perform the configuration now.
4. Click Yes. Outlook displays the Microsoft Fax properties sheet, shown in Figure 39.2.

FIGURE 39.2.

*You use this properties
sheet to configure
Microsoft Fax. For
now, you need enter
only your fax number
and the modem you
want to use.*

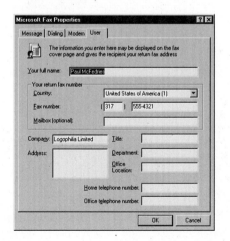

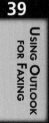

39

USING OUTLOOK
FOR FAXING

5. I'll explain the controls in this dialog box in depth in the next section. For now, you
   need to fill in only the Fax number field.
6. Select the Modem tab.

7. If you have more than one fax/modem, highlight it, select Set as Active Fax Modem, and click OK. (Again, I'll explain this tab in detail in the next section.) Outlook adds Microsoft Fax to your profile.

8. Click OK to return to Outlook, and then exit and restart Outlook.

Microsoft Fax Properties

You saw in the preceding section that Outlook requires you to specify a few properties before it will add Microsoft Fax to your profile. In this section, you'll return to the Microsoft Fax properties sheet to examine the available options in more detail. To get the properties sheet back on-screen, use either of the following techniques:

- Select Tools | Services, highlight Microsoft Fax, and click the Properties button.
- Select Tools | Microsoft Fax Tools | Options.

When Outlook displays the properties sheet, you'll see the Message tab by default, as shown in Figure 39.3. The next few sections run through each of the tabs.

FIGURE 39.3.

You use the Message tab to set options for faxes you send.

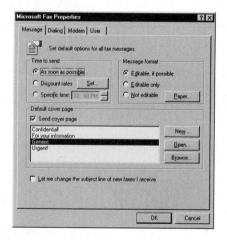

Message Properties

The Message tab contains a few properties that specify the default setup for the faxes you send. The Time to send group determines when Microsoft Fax sends your faxes. Here's a summary of what's available:

As soon as possible: Selecting this option (it's the default) means that your faxes get sent right away (or as soon as the modem is free).

Discount rates: If you choose this option, Microsoft Fax sends a fax only if the current time falls within the time when your phone rates are discounted. To specify the start and end times for your discounted phone rates, click the Set button. In the

Set Discount Rates dialog box, shown in Figure 39.4, enter the Start and End times, and click OK.

FIGURE 39.4.

Use this dialog box to specify the start and end times for your discounted phone rates.

Specific time: If you activate this option, you can use the spinner to specify a time for Microsoft Fax to send all your pending faxes.

The options in the Message format group control the format that Microsoft Fax uses to send your faxes:

Editable if possible: When this option is activated, Microsoft Fax attempts to send faxes as editable, binary documents. When connecting with the remote system, Microsoft Fax queries the machine to see whether it supports this format. (The editable document format is supported by Microsoft Fax systems and Microsoft At Work-compliant systems.) If it doesn't, Microsoft Fax sends the fax as a noneditable image. Otherwise, Microsoft Fax sends the fax as an editable, binary message, which means that

- if you send a text-only fax, the recipient can read and edit the fax just like a regular e-mail message.
- if you include a file with the fax, the file is transferred in its native format, and it appears as an attachment when the recipient views the fax.

Editable only: If you activate this option, Microsoft Fax queries the remote system to see whether it supports the editable fax format. If it doesn't, the fax transmission is canceled.

Not editable: If you activate this option, Microsoft Fax sends all your faxes in a noneditable format, as explained here:

- If the receiving system is a Group 3 fax machine, Microsoft Fax renders the fax as a bitmap image and sends it using whatever protocol the machine supports.
- If the receiving system is Microsoft Fax-compatible, the fax is sent using the Microsoft At Work rendered fax format.

For noneditable faxes, you can also click the Paper button to display the Message Format dialog box, shown in Figure 39.5. Use the options in this dialog box to specify the size, quality, and orientation of the image.

FIGURE 39.5.

Use this dialog box to specify the message format to use for noneditable faxes.

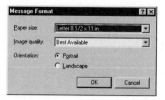

In the Default cover page group, activate the Send cover page check box to send a cover page with all your faxes. The accompanying list gives you several cover pages to choose from. I'll discuss these cover pages in more detail, and show you how to modify them and create new ones, later in this chapter (see "Working with Fax Cover Pages").

Finally, the Let me change the subject line of new faxes I receive check box determines how Microsoft Fax handles incoming noneditable faxes. The Subject line of a received noneditable fax always has the following form:

```
Fax from FaxID
```

Here, *FaxID* is either the phone number of the sending fax machine or the machine's internal fax identification string. (If Microsoft Fax can't determine either value, it displays just Fax in the Subject line.) The Let me change the subject line of new faxes I receive check box gives you the following choices:

- If this check box is deactivated, you can't change the Subject line of a noneditable fax. Moreover, opening a noneditable fax takes you directly to the Fax Viewer (see "Receiving Faxes" later in this chapter).

- If this check box is activated, you can change the Subject line of a noneditable fax. Microsoft Fax sets this up by inserting the noneditable fax as an attachment to an editable message, as shown in Figure 39.6. When you open the message, you can edit the Subject line, just as with any e-mail message.

FIGURE 39.6.

You can set up Microsoft Fax to enable editing of the Subject lines of your received faxes.

The received fax is inserted as an icon ⎯⎯⎯

The Subject line can be edited

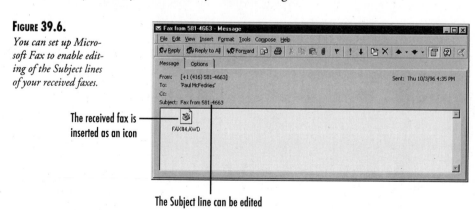

Dialing Properties

You use the Dialing tab, shown in Figure 39.7, to determine how Microsoft Fax dials fax numbers. Here are your options:

Dialing Properties: Click this button to display Windows' Dialing Properties dialog box, which lets you specify a number to dial for an outside line, set up a calling card number, and disable call waiting.

Toll Prefixes: In some locations, you must dial certain numbers that are in your area code as long distance. In other words, even though the numbers share your area code, you must dial a 1 and the area code first. If you have a fax recipient with such a number, click the Toll Prefixes button. In the dialog box that appears, highlight the appropriate prefix and click Add->. This tells Microsoft Fax to append 1 and your area code to any numbers that use this prefix.

Number of retries: This value determines the number of times Microsoft Fax attempts to send a fax if it encounters a busy signal or some other error.

Time between retries: This value determines the number of minutes Microsoft Fax waits between retries.

FIGURE 39.7.

Use the Dialing tab to specify how Microsoft Fax dials fax numbers.

39

USING OUTLOOK
FOR FAXING

Modem Properties

The Modem tab, shown in Figure 39.8, controls how Microsoft Fax works with your fax/modem. The Available fax modems list displays the installed modems on your system. If you have more than one modem, you can designate one of them as the modem used by Microsoft Fax by highlighting it and clicking the Set as Active Fax Modem button. You can also use the Add button to install another modem and the Remove button to delete a modem from the list.

FIGURE 39.8.

Use the Modem tab to tell Microsoft Fax which modem you want to use as the active fax/modem.

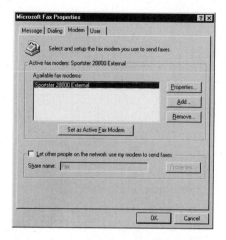

For each fax/modem, Microsoft Fax maintains several properties that determine how the program and the modem work together. To view these properties, highlight the fax/modem and then click the Properties button. Microsoft Fax displays the properties sheet shown in Figure 39.9.

FIGURE 39.9.

Use this dialog box to set various properties of the fax/modem.

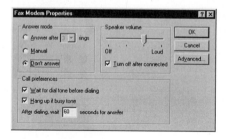

Here's a rundown of the options this dialog box provides:

Answer after *x* rings: Activate this option to tell Microsoft Fax to answer incoming calls automatically. Use the spinner to specify the ring number on which Microsoft Fax should answer the call.

Manual: If you activate this option, Microsoft Fax displays a dialog box whenever it detects an incoming call. You can use this dialog box to have Microsoft Fax either answer the call or ignore it. Use this option if you also receive voice calls on the same line.

Don't answer: If you activate this option, Microsoft Fax ignores any incoming calls. Technically, this option means that Microsoft Fax won't monitor the serial port to which the modem is attached. This is useful if you're using 16-bit communications programs that need to use the port while Outlook is running. When Microsoft Fax is monitoring a serial port for incoming calls, only 32-bit TAPI (Telephony Application Programming Interface) programs can get access to the port.

Speaker volume: This slider determines the default volume level of the modem's speaker. Also, make sure that the Turn off after connected check box is activated to avoid listening to the squeaks and squawks the two machines make while they're transferring data.

Wait for dial tone before dialing: When this check box is activated, the modem won't dial unless it can detect a dial tone, which is usually what you want. However, if your modem doesn't seem to recognize the dial tone in your current location (if you're in a different country, for example), or if you need to dial manually, deactivate this check box.

Hang up if busy tone: When this check box is activated, Microsoft Fax hangs up the connection if it detects a busy signal on the receiving end.

After dialing, wait *x* seconds for answer: This value determines how long Microsoft Fax waits for the receiving fax machine to answer the call.

If you click the Advanced button, you'll see the Advanced dialog box, shown in Figure 39.10. You shouldn't need to change any of these settings, but just in case you're having trouble faxing, here's a summary of what each control represents:

Disable high speed transmission: This check box determines whether your modem transfers data at speeds any faster than 9,600 bps. If you're having trouble with your fax transmissions, try activating this check box to restrict data transfers to 9,600 bps or less.

Disable error correction mode: This check box determines whether Microsoft Fax uses the modem's built-in error correction protocol for transmitting noneditable faxes. If your fax transmissions are unreliable, the error correction protocol might be the culprit. Try activating this check box to turn off error correction.

Enable MR compression: MR compression is used by Group 3 fax machines for faster transfers. You can activate this check box when you have a large fax to send, but bear in mind that this compression scheme makes faxes more sensitive to phone-line noise.

Use Class 2 if available: If you activate this check box, Microsoft Fax operates your modem as a Class 2 device (even though your modem might support Class 1). This can overcome some transmission problems, but it disables Microsoft Fax's binary file transfer and security features (because these aren't supported by Class 2 fax/modems).

Reject pages received with errors: If you activate this check box, Microsoft Fax rejects pages with errors that exceed the threshold specified in the Tolerance box. The lower the threshold, the fewer errors a page must have before it's accepted by Microsoft Fax.

FIGURE 39.10.

This dialog box controls various advanced modem properties.

The Modem tab also contains a Let other people on the network use my modem to send faxes check box. You can use this option to set up your modem as a fax server for your network. I'll explain how this works later in this chapter (see "Network Faxing").

User Properties

The final tab in the Microsoft Fax properties sheet is User, which you saw back in Figure 39.2. Microsoft Fax uses these properties to fill in various fields on your fax cover sheets. Also, the fields in the Your return fax number group tell the recipient which fax address to use when replying.

NOTE: THE MAILBOX FIELD

If you have a network fax server, use the Mailbox field to enter the name of your mailbox or account. That way, when your recipient replies, the incoming fax is routed to your mailbox automatically.

Sending a Fax

With Microsoft Fax installed, added to your profile, and configured to your liking, you can now start firing off faxes to everyone you know. Microsoft Fax provides three ways to send a fax:

- You can create a message using the e-mail techniques I showed you in the preceding chapter. In this case, though, the recipient's "address" is a fax phone number.
- You can use the Compose New Fax Wizard to lead you through the various faxing steps, from selecting a recipient to setting up your modem to entering your text.
- You can fax documents directly from applications.

Each of these methods requires that you specify a fax phone number as the message address, so let's first see how you add fax numbers to your Personal Address Book.

Creating Fax Addresses in Your Personal Address Book

You saw in Chapter 37, "The Ins and Outs of the Outlook Inbox," that you can use the Personal Address Book to store e-mail addresses from the other address lists (such as the list of Microsoft Network members) and for new recipients. You can also use the Personal Address Book to store fax numbers. Here are the steps to follow:

1. In Outlook, select Tools | Address Book to open the Address Book.

2. Select File | New Entry to display the New Entry dialog box.

3. In the Select the entry type list, highlight Fax and click OK. Outlook displays the New Fax Properties dialog box, shown in Figure 39.11.

4. Fill in the following fields:

    Name to show on cover page: Enter the name of the recipient. Microsoft Fax will place this entry in the To field on the fax cover sheet.

    Country code: Enter the recipient's country.

    Area code and fax number: Enter the area code and phone number of the recipient's fax machine.

    Mailbox (optional): If the recipient uses a fax server, enter his mailbox name or account number here. This information lets the server route the message appropriately.

    Dial area code, even though it's the same as mine: If the number uses the same area code as you but requires a long-distance dial, activate this check box.

FIGURE 39.11.

Use this properties sheet to fill in the particulars for the fax recipient.

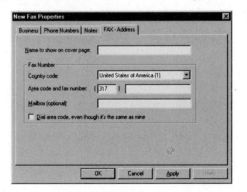

39

USING OUTLOOK FOR FAXING

5. The fax cover sheet will also include items such as the recipient's company name and business phone number, so you should also fill out the other tabs in the properties sheet.

6. When you're done, click OK.

Composing a Fax from Scratch

Microsoft Fax makes composing a new fax about as painless as any of this communications business gets. Once you've set up a fax/modem in Windows and understand the basics of putting together an e-mail message (as described in Chapter 37), you know practically everything you need to know to get the job done. The next two sections run through the two methods available for creating faxes from scratch: using the message composition window and using the Compose New Fax Wizard.

Using the Message Composition Window

You can create fax messages using the same technique I showed you in the preceding chapter for creating an e-mail message. The only differences are that your recipient's address must be a fax address, and you can set some extra options for the fax message.

To compose the fax, select Compose | New Mail Message, and in the new Message window that appears, fill in the fields as needed. When you're adding the recipient address, keep in mind that you can select names from your Personal Address Book, or you can use the Fax Addressing Wizard. To try the latter, select Tools | Fax Addressing Wizard to display the dialog box shown in Figure 39.12. Enter the recipient's name in the To text box, select the country code, enter the fax number, and click Add to List. The recipient appears in the Recipient list box. Keep adding recipients in this manner as needed, and then click Finish when you're done.

FIGURE 39.12.

Use the Fax Addressing Wizard to forge on-the-fly fax addresses.

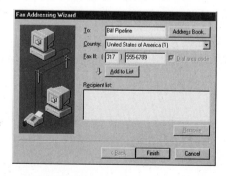

The only other difference between a fax and an e-mail message is that Microsoft Fax provides a few options you can set for each fax. To view these options, select File | Send Options to display the dialog box shown in Figure 39.13. As you can see, these options are similar to those found on the Message tab of the Microsoft Fax properties sheet, which was discussed earlier and shown in Figure 39.3. Note too that clicking the Dialing button displays properties similar to those you saw earlier in the Dialing tab, shown back in Figure 39.7.

Other than these differences, you compose the message exactly the same as you do an e-mail note. You can even insert files to go along for the ride. When you're done, make sure that your modem is ready for action, and select File | Send.

FIGURE 39.13.

Use this dialog box to specify sending options for this fax message.

NOTE: USE LARGER FONTS FOR GROUP 3 FAX MACHINES

One of the advantages of working in the message composition window is that you can adjust the font size used in your message. This won't matter if you're sending an editable fax (because the reader will view the text in his or her regular e-mail font), but it can make a big difference for noneditable faxes sent to Group 3 fax machines. These machines typically have low resolution, so they reproduce small fonts poorly. To make sure that your faxes are readable, use a 12-point or even a 14-point sans serif font (such as Arial).

Using the Compose New Fax Wizard

As an alternative to the message composition window, Microsoft Fax offers the Compose New Fax Wizard that leads you step-by-step through the entire fax-creation process. This Wizard is geared more toward novice users, but even experienced types will find it handy for quick fax notes. Here's how it works:

1. To start the Wizard, use either of the following techniques:
   - Click Windows' Start button and then select Programs | Accessories | Fax | Compose New Fax.
   - In Outlook, select Compose | New Fax.

2. The first Wizard dialog box asks you which dialing location you want to use. You can click the Dialing Properties button to either select a different location or adjust the properties of the current location. Otherwise, click Next >.

3. The next Wizard dialog box is almost identical to the Fax Addressing Wizard you worked with earlier, shown back in Figure 39.12. Either enter a fax number or use the Address Book button to choose a fax recipient from your Personal Address Book, and then click Next >.

39

USING OUTLOOK
FOR FAXING

4. The next Wizard dialog box, shown in Figure 39.14, asks whether you want a cover page. Either click No, or click Yes and highlight the cover page you want to use. You can also click the Options button to display the Send Options dialog box you learned about earlier (see Figure 39.13). Click Next > to continue.

FIGURE 39.14.

Select your cover page and send options from this Compose New Fax Wizard dialog box.

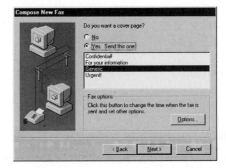

5. The Wizard now prompts you to enter the Subject line and Note for the fax, as shown in Figure 39.15. If you're using a cover page, activating the Start note on cover page check box tells Microsoft Fax to begin your note on the cover page. If you deactivate this check box, the note begins on a fresh page. Click Next >.

6. Your next chore is to specify any files you want to include with the fax transmission. Click the Add File button, highlight the file in the Open a File to Attach dialog box that appears, and click Open. Click Next > when you've added all the files you need.

7. In the last Wizard dialog box, click Finish to send your fax.

FIGURE 39.15.

Use this Wizard dialog box to enter the Subject line and Note for the fax.

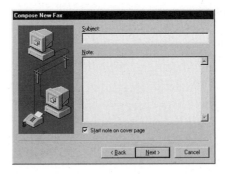

Faxing from an Application

The third method of sending a fax is to bypass Outlook altogether and send a document directly from an application. You don't need applications with special features to do this, either. That's because when you install Microsoft Fax, it adds a new printer driver to Windows 95. This printer driver, however, doesn't send a document to the printer. Instead, it renders the document as a fax and then sends it to your modem.

To try this, select File | Print in your application. When the Print dialog box appears, use the Name drop-down list to select the Microsoft Fax printer driver, as shown in Figure 39.16. When you click OK, the Compose New Fax Wizard starts so that you can specify a recipient, a cover page, and other fax options.

FIGURE 39.16.

To fax a document from an application, select File | Print and then choose the Microsoft Fax printer driver.

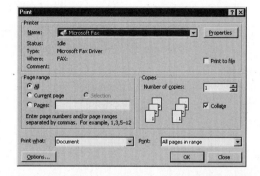

TIP: QUICK DOCUMENT FAXING

If you have a particular document you want to fax, you don't have to open its application and print to the Microsoft Fax driver. Instead, you can do this from Explorer or My Computer by right-clicking the document's filename and selecting Send To | Fax Recipient.

NOTE: WORD'S FAX TOOLS

Word comes with a few predefined fax page templates that make it easy to create attractive fax documents. To use one of these templates, select File | New from Word, and then activate the Letters & Faxes tab in the New dialog box. Note that this tab also boasts an icon for the Fax Wizard, which leads you step by step through the creation of a fax.

Working with Fax Cover Pages

I've mentioned fax cover pages a couple of times so far in this chapter, so it's time we took a closer look. In the fax world, a cover page performs the same function as an e-mail message header: It specifies who is supposed to receive the fax and who sent it. Unlike an e-mail message header, which is meant to be read and interpreted by a mail server or gateway, a fax cover sheet is meant for human consumption. In a company or department where several people share a fax machine, the cover page makes it clear which person is supposed to get the fax. And when that person does read the message, she can use the rest of the information to see who sent the fax.

Microsoft Fax comes with four prefab cover pages: Confidential!, For your information, Generic, and Urgent!. You can use these pages as circumstances dictate, you can modify them to suit your style, or you can create new pages from scratch.

> **NOTE: DON'T SEND A COVER PAGE FOR EDITABLE FAXES**
>
> You need to use a cover page only if you're sending a noneditable (bitmap) fax. If you send an editable fax, the receiving system converts it into a regular mail message (assuming, of course, that the system can deal with editable faxes), so the recipient never sees the cover page.

Starting the Fax Cover Page Editor

To edit and create fax cover pages, Microsoft Fax comes with the Fax Cover Page Editor application. To start this program, use either of the following techniques:

- Click Windows' Start button, and then select Programs | Accessories | Fax | Cover Page Editor.
- In Outlook, select Tools | Microsoft Fax Tools | Options to display the Options dialog box. In the Message tab, either select New in the Default cover page group, or highlight a cover page and click Open.

Figure 39.17 shows the window that appears. (If you don't see an open file, select File | Open and choose one of the .CPE files from your main Windows 95 folder.)

Editing a Cover Page

Keeping in mind that cover pages always get sent as bitmaps, the idea behind the Cover Page Editor is to create a template for the bitmap. So, as you might expect, the Cover Page Editor is really a graphics application that specializes in working with fax bitmaps. The templates you work with consist of three types of fields: information, text, and graphics.

Inserting Information Fields

Information fields are placeholders for data. For example, the {Sender's Company} field (information fields always appear surrounded by braces) tells Microsoft Fax to insert the name of the sender's company each time you use this cover page when you send a fax. With the Cover Page Editor, you can insert fields for recipient, sender, and message data:

- For the recipient, you can insert fields for the person's name, fax number, company, address, and much more. This information is gleaned from the properties sheet for the recipient's address (assuming that you included the address in your Personal Address Book). Select Insert | Recipient to see a complete list of the available fields.

■ For the sender, you can insert fields for the name, fax number, company, address, telephone numbers, and more. Microsoft Fax gets this data from the User tab of the Microsoft Fax properties sheet. Select Insert | Sender to see the available fields.

■ For the message, the available fields include the note text, the Subject line, the time the fax was sent, the number of pages, and the number of attachments. The Insert | Message command displays a cascade menu that lists these fields.

FIGURE 39.17.

Microsoft Fax provides the Fax Cover Page Editor so that you can edit and create cover pages to use with your faxes.

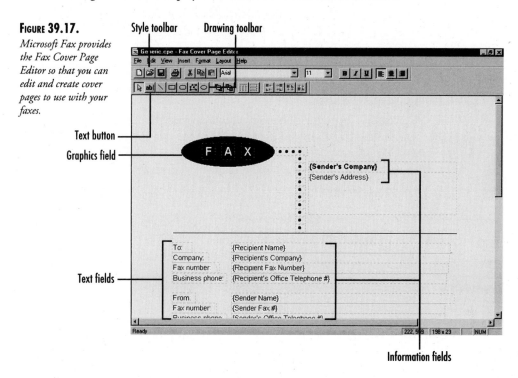

Inserting Text Fields

Text fields are text boxes that either describe the contents of each information field or provide titles, subtitles, and headings. To insert a text field, click the Text button on the Drawing toolbar, drag the mouse inside the cover page to create a box for the field, and enter your text. To change the text in an existing field, double-click it. (Note too that you can format text fields by using the buttons on the Style toolbar and by using the Format | Font and Format | Align Text commands.)

Inserting Graphics Fields

Graphics fields are bitmap objects you can use for logos or separators, or just to add some style to the cover page. The Cover Page Editor's Drawing toolbar lets you create many kinds of drawing objects, including lines, rectangles, circles, and polygons.

39

USING OUTLOOK FOR FAXING

Receiving Faxes

You saw in the previous couple of chapters how Outlook hasn't quite yet achieved its goal of becoming a universal inbox, but its support for Microsoft Mail, The Microsoft Network Mail, CompuServe, and the Internet is a pretty good start.

If you use any of these e-mail systems, tossing into the mix Outlook's support for storing received faxes in the same inbox makes Outlook an attractive messaging client. (Now, if we could just get it to field our voice mail, life would be perfect.) This section explains how Microsoft Fax handles incoming faxes and shows you how to view those faxes when they're sitting in your Inbox.

Answering Incoming Calls

How Microsoft Fax handles incoming calls from remote fax systems depends on how you set up your fax/modem. Recall that when you display the Fax Modem Properties dialog box (by clicking Properties in the Modem tab of the Microsoft Fax properties sheet), the Answer mode group boasts three options that determine how Microsoft Fax deals with incoming calls:

Answer after *x* rings: Tells Microsoft Fax to answer incoming calls automatically.

Manual: Lets you answer incoming calls manually.

Don't answer: Tells Microsoft Fax to ignore any incoming calls.

Answering Calls Automatically

Enabling the Answer after *x* rings option is the easiest way to handle incoming calls. In this mode, Microsoft Fax constantly polls the modem's serial port for calls. When it detects a call coming in, it waits for whatever number of rings you specified (which can be as few as two rings or as many as 10) and then leaps into action. Without any prodding from you, it answers the phone and immediately starts conversing with the remote fax machine. The Microsoft Fax Status window appears so that you can see the progress of the transfer, as shown in Figure 39.18.

FIGURE 39.18.

When Microsoft Fax answers an incoming fax call, this window keeps you abreast of the fax transfer.

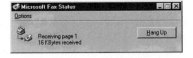

Answering Calls Manually

When you work with Microsoft Fax in manual mode, you'll see the Receive Fax Now? dialog box, shown in Figure 39.19, whenever the program detects an incoming call. To have Microsoft Fax field the call, click Yes. Otherwise, click No and answer the call yourself.

FIGURE 39.19.

In manual answer mode, Microsoft Fax displays this dialog box when it detects an incoming call.

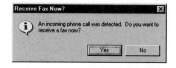

This mode is ideal if you receive both voice calls and fax calls on the same phone line. Here's the basic procedure you'll need to follow for incoming calls:

1. When the phone rings, pick up the receiver.
2. If you hear a series of tones, you know that a fax is on its way. In this case, click the Yes button in the Receive Fax Now? dialog box. If it's a voice call, click No instead.
3. After you click Yes, Microsoft Fax initializes the modem to handle the call. Wait until Microsoft Fax reports Answering call in the Microsoft Fax Status window, and then hang up the receiver. (If you hang up before this, you'll disconnect the call.)

NOTE: REDISPLAYING THE RECEIVE FAX NOW? DIALOG BOX

The Receive Fax Now? dialog box stays on-screen for seven or eight seconds. If you miss it, you can still get Microsoft Fax to take the call by clicking the Answer Now button (or by selecting Options | Answer Now) in the Microsoft Fax Status window. Again, wait until Microsoft Fax reports Answering call before hanging up the receiver.

Working in Don't Answer Mode

If you select the Don't answer option, Microsoft Fax ignores any incoming calls. If you know you have a fax coming in (if, say, you pick up the receiver and hear the tones from the remote fax machine), click the Microsoft Fax icon on the toolbar's system tray. This opens the Microsoft Fax Status window. Now either select Options | Answer Now or click the Answer Now button.

Opening Received Faxes

Depending on the size of the fax transmission and whether it's an editable fax or a bitmap, Microsoft Fax takes anywhere from a few seconds to a few minutes to process the data. Eventually, though, your fax appears in the Inbox. (For noneditable faxes, Outlook displays a fax icon in the Item Type column; editable faxes get the usual envelope icon.)

How you view the message depends on whether the fax is editable and whether Microsoft Fax is set up to allow fax Subject lines to be edited:

- If the fax is editable, it appears in the message list with the usual envelope icon in the Item Type column. To view the message, use the same techniques I outlined in the preceding chapter for e-mail messages.

39

USING OUTLOOK FOR FAXING

■ For a noneditable fax, Outlook displays a fax icon in the Item Type column. When you open the message, Outlook displays the bitmap image of the fax in the Fax Viewer, as shown in Figure 39.20.

FIGURE 39.20.

When you open a noneditable fax, Outlook uses the Fax Viewer to display the bitmap.

■ If you've enabled Subject line editing, opening the message displays an icon that represents the fax bitmap, as shown earlier in Figure 39.6. To get the fax into the Fax Viewer, double-click the icon.

Using the Fax Viewer

The Fax Viewer is basically a graphics viewer with a few extra features that let you navigate multipage faxes. Here's a quick summary of the Fax Viewer techniques you can wield to examine your faxes:

Moving the fax image: To move the fax image inside the window, first make sure that the Edit | Drag command is activated or that the Drag button is pressed. Then use the mouse to drag the image around the window.

Zooming the image: The Zoom menu contains commands that let you zoom into the image (using the Zoom In command) or out of the image (using the Zoom Out command). You can also choose specific magnifications: 25%, 50%, or 100%. To fit the image to the window, select Fit Width, Fit Height, or Fit Both. Some of these commands are also available as toolbar buttons:

                         The Zoom In button

The Zoom Out button

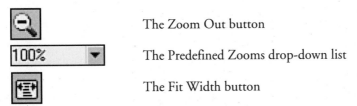 The Predefined Zooms drop-down list

 The Fit Width button

Rotating the image: For faxes that come with the wrong orientation, the Rotate menu commands let you turn the image so that you can read the fax. Select either Right or Left to rotate the image 90 degrees, or select Flip Over to rotate the image 180 degrees.

The Rotate Left button

The Rotate Right button

Inverting the image: To reverse blacks and whites in the image, select Image | Invert.

Viewing thumbnails: To get the big picture in a multipage fax, activate View | Thumbnails (or press the Show Thumbnails button). As you can see in Figure 39.21, the Fax Viewer displays small versions of each page on the left side of the screen. Click a page's thumbnail to display that page.

FIGURE 39.21.

The Fax Viewer's thumbnails view.

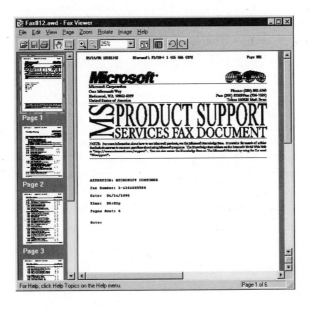

Navigating multiple pages: The Fax Viewer has a few more tricks up its sleeve for moving between pages. On the Page menu, select Next, Previous, First, and Last. You can also select the Go To command to head for a specific page number.

39

USING OUTLOOK FOR FAXING

Click this scrollbar button to move to the previous page.

Click this scrollbar button to move to the next page.

Saving the fax to a file: Instead of working with a fax from Outlook, you might prefer to save it to a separate Fax Viewer file. This makes it easy to archive the fax or include it as a file attachment in a message. To save the fax, select File | Save Copy As, select a location, enter a filename in the Save Copy As dialog box, and click Save. Note that Fax Viewer files use the .AWD extension.

Copying data to the Clipboard: The fax is a bitmap, so you might want to copy some or all of a page to the Clipboard to use in other applications. First, make sure that the Edit | Select command is activated (or that the Select button is pressed). To copy the current page as a whole, select Edit | Copy Page. If you want just part of the page, use the mouse to drag a box around the area you want, and then select Edit | Copy.

TIP: "SIGN" YOUR FAXES

One of the drawbacks of sending faxes via your computer is that you have no way to sign your documents. To get around this limitation, sign your name on a piece of paper, and then use a regular fax machine to send the signature to your computer. Display this document in the Fax Viewer, select your signature, and copy it to the Clipboard. Then open Paint and select Edit | Paste to paste your signature. Select Edit | Copy To, and save the signature to its own file. To add your signature to your faxes, select Insert | Object in the Cover Page Editor, and insert the signature's .BMP file.

Accessing Fax-on-Demand Systems

Hundreds of businesses have implemented fax-on-demand systems. These are fax servers that contain dozens or even hundreds of documents that are available for downloading. You call the system, and after perhaps negotiating a few voice menus, you enter a document number and your fax number. A few minutes later, the server calls your fax number and sends you the document. (Most systems also have catalogs you can download to get the document numbers and titles.)

In some cases, the fax server supports the Group 3 *poll-retrieve* capability. This lets a program such as Microsoft Fax connect to the server and download the document you want automatically. This feature is called *Request a Fax,* and it works like this:

1. Either select Tools | Microsoft Fax Tools | Request a Fax in Outlook or select Start | Programs | Accessories | Fax | Request a Fax. The first Request a Fax Wizard dialog box, shown in Figure 39.22, appears.

FIGURE 39.22.

The Request a Fax Wizard leads you step-by-step through a fax-on-demand session.

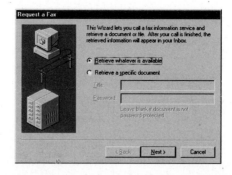

NOTE: THE SPRINTFAX MESSAGE

When you first install Microsoft Fax, a message from SprintFAX is placed in your Inbox. This message invites you to double-click an icon to get information about the SprintFAX broadcast fax service. This icon is an Object Packager package that runs the Request a Fax feature behind the scenes. This action is equivalent to selecting the Retrieve whatever is available option and calling 1-800-352-8575. If you like, you can use SprintFAX as a way to try out the Request a Fax service.

---

2. This dialog box gives you two options:

    Retrieve whatever is available: When you select this option, Microsoft Fax asks the server to send all the information it has on tap. This option is useful for fax-on-demand systems that cater to a single product.

    Retrieve a specific document: Most fax-on-demand systems have multiple documents available, so you'll need to activate this option. Use the Title text box to enter the name or number of the document you want to retrieve, and use the Password text box to enter a password if required. Click Next > when you're ready to continue.

3. Enter the name and number of the fax-on-demand system, and click Add. Alternatively, select Address Book and use your Personal Address Book to enter the number. Click Next > to move to the next dialog box.

4. The Wizard asks when you want to send the request. Select As soon as possible, When phone rates are discounted, or A specific time. (For the last choice, use the spinner to enter the time you want Microsoft Fax to make the call.) Click Next >.

5. Click Finish to send the fax request.

Network Faxing

One of the chief benefits of having networked computers is the ability to share peripherals—such as printers and CD-ROM drives—among all the machines. If you have a network and

you have multiple users who need to fax documents, Microsoft Fax lets you share a single fax/
modem on the network. The computer then becomes a *fax server* that lets any machine on the
network send faxes. (Note, however, that all received faxes stay on the fax server until the administrator can route them manually. Microsoft Fax doesn't support the routing of incoming
faxes.)

Setting Up the Fax Server

To set up a computer to operate as a fax server, follow these steps:

1. Select Tools | Microsoft Fax Tools | Options to display the Microsoft Fax properties
   sheet, and then select the Modem tab.

2. Activate the Let other people on the network use my modem to send faxes check box.

3. If you have multiple disk drives, Microsoft Fax asks which drive you want to use for
   the network fax service. Use the drop-down list provided to select the drive, and then
   click OK to return to the Microsoft Fax properties sheet. Microsoft Fax creates a new
   folder called NetFax on the drive and shares this folder with the network.

4. To change the properties of the shared network fax folder, click the Properties button
   beside the Share name box.

5. The dialog box that appears, shown in Figure 39.23, lets you change the default values
   for the Share Name and Comment (which shouldn't be necessary), as well as set up
   security for the shared folder. Note that users need full access to the shared folder in
   order to send faxes via the fax server.

FIGURE 39.23.

*Use this dialog box to
change the properties of
the shared network fax
folder.*

6. Click OK to return to the properties sheet, and then click OK again to return to
   Outlook.

Specifying the Fax Server on a Client Machine

In order for network users to send faxes via the fax server, they must specify the fax server's network path rather than a fax/modem. Here are the steps each client must follow:

1. On the client computer, start Outlook, select Tools | Microsoft Fax Tools | Options to display the Microsoft Fax properties sheet, and select the Modem tab.

2. Click the Add button. The Add a Fax Modem dialog box, shown in Figure 39.24, appears.

FIGURE 39.24.

This dialog box appears when you click the Add button.

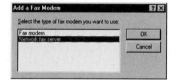

3. Highlight Network fax server, and then click OK. Microsoft Fax displays the Connect To Network Fax Server dialog box, shown in Figure 39.25.

FIGURE 39.25.

Use this dialog box to enter the network path to the fax server.

4. Enter the network path for the fax server and click OK. The network path always takes the form *ComputerName**FaxServer,* in which *ComputerName* is the network name of the fax server computer and *FaxServer* is the share name of the network fax folder. In Figure 39.25, for example, the computer name is Zeus, and the share name of the fax folder is Fax.

5. In the Modem tab, highlight the network fax server and select Set as Active Fax Modem.

6. Click OK.

Summary

This chapter ran through the features and capabilities of Microsoft Fax. I began by showing you how to add the Microsoft Fax service to your Outlook profile and then how to configure Microsoft Fax. You learned the various methods available for sending faxes, including using the message composition window, the Compose New Fax Wizard, and the Microsoft Fax printer driver. I also showed you how to edit and create cover pages to include in your faxes. From

39

USING OUTLOOK
FOR FAXING

there, you learned how to deal with incoming faxes—including Microsoft Fax's various phone-answering modes—how to open a received fax, and how to use the Fax Viewer. I closed by covering Request a Fax and network faxing.

Here's a list of chapters where you'll find related information:

- The general steps for adding and configuring services in Outlook are covered in Chapter 36, "Setting Up Outlook."

- To learn how to use Outlook for sending and retrieving e-mail, check out Chapter 37, "The Ins and Outs of the Outlook Inbox."

Places to Go: Calendar

CHAPTER 40

Punctuality is the soul of business.

—*Thomas C. Haliburton*

It seems almost redundant to describe modern life as "busy." Everyone is working harder, cramming more appointments and meetings into already packed schedules, and somehow finding the time to get their regular work done between crises. As many a management consultant has advised over the years (charging exorbitant fees to do so), the key to surviving this helter-skelter, pell-mell pace is *time management*. And although there are as many theories about time management as there are consultants, one of the keys is that you should always try to make the best use of the time available. Although that often comes down to self-discipline and prioritizing your tasks, an efficient scheduling system can sure help.

That's where Outlook's Calendar feature comes in. At first glance, Calendar just looks like an electronic version of your day planner. You move around from day to day and month to month, entering tasks and appointments at their scheduled times. But Calendar goes far beyond this simple time-keeping function. For example, you can use it to schedule meetings via e-mail and, depending on the responses, update your schedule automatically. You can put your Calendar on a public network folder so that others can see when you're available and set up appointments with you based on this information.

In other words, Calendar helps you spend less time on the process of scheduling, which gives you more time to do real work. This chapter takes you through the full spectrum of Calendar's features and functions, including setting up appointments, meetings, and events.

The Calendar Folder

When you display the Calendar folder, Outlook displays a window similar to the one shown in Figure 40.1. As you can see, Calendar is laid out more or less like a day planner or desk calendar. Here's a quick tour:

Day calendar: This half of the Calendar folder shows one day at a time, divided into half-hour intervals. The appointments and meetings you schedule will appear in this area.

Date Navigator: This area shows two months at a time (usually the current month and the next month). As its name suggests, you use the Date Navigator to change the date shown in the Day view area. Dates for which you have already scheduled appointments or meetings are shown in bold type. Note that today's date always has a red square around it.

TaskPad: You use this area to jot down quick notes to yourself. These notes aren't date-dependent, so they remain in view no matter which date is displayed in the Day calendar. See Chapter 42, "Things to Do: Tasks, Journal, and Notes," to learn how to work with tasks in Outlook.

FIGURE 40.1.

Outlook's Calendar folder.

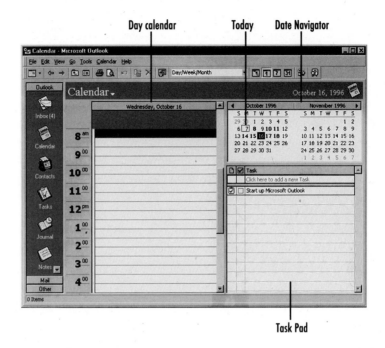

Day calendar   Today   Date Navigator

Task Pad

Using the Date Navigator

Calendar always opens with today's date displayed. However, if you want to work with a different day, the Date Navigator makes it easy. All you have to do is click a date, and Calendar will display it in the Day calendar. If the month you need isn't displayed in the Date Navigator, use either of the following techniques to pick a different month:

- Click the left-pointing arrow in the month headers to move backward one month at a time. Similarly, click the right-pointing arrow in the month headers to move forward one month at a time.

- Move the mouse pointer over one of the month headers, then press and hold down the left mouse button. A pop-up menu displays seven months—the month you clicked and the three months before and after. Drag the mouse to the month you want and release the button.

Changing the Number of Days Displayed

Calendar's default view is the Day calendar, which shows just a single day's worth of appointments and meetings. However, Calendar is quite flexible and is happy to show two days, three days, a week, or even a month at a time.

40

PLACES TO GO:
CALENDAR

The easiest way to change the view is to use Calendar's Day, Week, and Month commands:

■ For the Week calendar, select View | Week, or click the Week toolbar button (you can also press Alt-hyphen), to show the entire week (see Figure 40.2).

FIGURE 40.2.

The Week calendar.

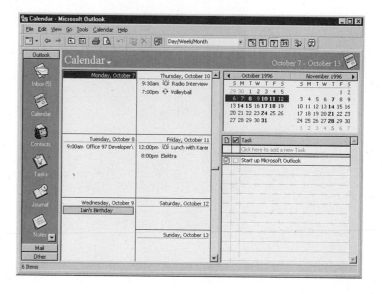

■ For the Month calendar, select View | Month, or click the Month toolbar button (you can also press Alt-=), to show the entire month (see Figure 40.3).

FIGURE 40.3.

The Month calendar.

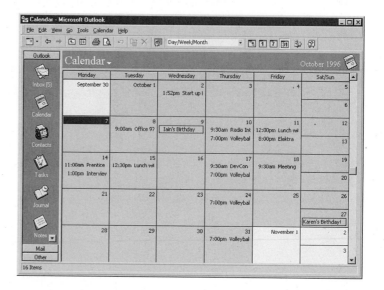

■ To return to the Day calendar, select View | Day or click the Day toolbar button.

Besides these predefined views, Outlook also lets you view however many days you want. Move the mouse pointer into the Date Navigator area and drag the pointer over the days you'd like to see. When you release the button, Outlook displays the selected days. For example, in Figure 40.4 I dragged the mouse over the 7th, 8th, and 9th.

Figure 40.4.

Outlook is happy to display whatever number of days you need.

Drag the mouse pointer over the days you want to view

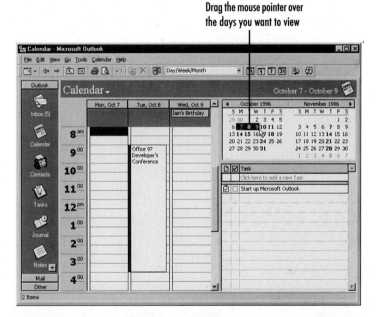

TIP: QUICKLY DISPLAY ANY NUMBER OF DAYS

You can also display x number of days by pressing Alt-x. For example, pressing Alt-3 displays the three days beginning with the currently selected day. Press Alt-0 for 10 days.

Other Navigation Techniques

To complete our look at Calendar's navigation aids, here are a few more techniques you can use:

■ To move to today's date, select Go | Go to Today or click the Go to Today button on the toolbar.

■ To move to a specific date, select Go | Go to Date, or press Ctrl-G, to display the Go To Date dialog box, shown in Figure 40.5. Enter the date you want in the Date text box, or drop down the box to display a calendar and click the date. You can also use the Show in list to select either Day Calendar, Week Calendar, or Month Calendar. Click OK to display the date.

FIGURE 40.5.

Use this dialog box to navigate to a specific date.

■ Use the keyboard shortcuts summarized in Table 40.1.

Table 40.1. Calendar's navigation keys.

Key	Action
Day Calendar	
Up arrow	Selects the previous block of time.
Down arrow	Selects the next block of time.
Tab	Selects the next appointment.
Shift-Tab	Selects the previous appointment.
Home	Selects the beginning of the work day.
End	Selects the end of the work day.
Alt-up arrow	Selects the same day in the previous week.
Alt-down arrow	Selects the same day in the next week.
Week Calendar	
Up arrow	Selects the previous day.
Down arrow	Selects the next day.
Home	Selects the first day of the week.
End	Selects the last day of the week.
Month Calendar	
Left arrow	Selects the previous day.
Right arrow	Selects the next day.
Home	Selects the first day of the week.
End	Selects the last day of the week.
Up arrow	Selects the same day of the week in the previous week.
Down arrow	Selects the same day of the week in the next week.

Items You Can Schedule in Calendar

Calendar differentiates between three kinds of items:

Appointments: An appointment is the most general Calendar item. It refers to any activity for which you set aside a block of time. Typical appointments include a lunch date, a trip to the dentist or doctor, or a social engagement. You can also create *recurring* appointments that are scheduled at regular intervals (such as weekly or monthly).

Events: An event is any activity that consumes one or more entire days. Examples include conferences, trade shows, vacations, and birthdays. In Calendar, events don't occupy blocks of time. Instead, they appear as banners above the affected days. You can also schedule recurring events.

Meetings: A meeting is a special kind of appointment to which two or more people are invited. Outlook has a Meeting Planner that lets you set up a meeting and send e-mail messages inviting people to the meeting. Outlook can then track the responses so that you know who is coming to the meeting and who isn't.

The next few sections show you how to create appointments, events, and meetings.

A Note About Public Calendar Folders

If you would like to give other people access to your schedule, Outlook lets you create public Calendar folders on Microsoft Exchange Server systems. This lets people on your network check your schedule to see when you're free or busy, which might help them schedule their own meetings and appointments.

Public Calendar folders (which you create in the Public Folders area of your Exchange Server system) are set up by default as read-only for everyone but yourself. You can change this by setting permissions on the folder. (Highlight the folder and select File | Folder | Properties. In the properties sheet that appears, use the Permissions tab to modify the access privileges for the folder.)

Note, however, that you don't need to set up a public Calendar folder to use Outlook's group scheduling features. That's because rudimentary information about your schedule is "published" on the server as you enter and adjust appointments. This information includes the times of your appointments and whether you've designated that time as "free" or "busy." This so-called *free/busy information* is used by Outlook when you're requesting or planning a meeting.

Setting Up Appointments

Outlook gives you a number of methods for creating appointments, ranging from simple text-only notes to more sophisticated examples that use features such as reminder messages.

Typing in Appointments

By far the easiest way to create an appointment is to just type it in the Day calendar in the appropriate time block. Before you start typing, however, you need to decide how much time to block out for the appointment:

- If you need only a half hour, just click inside the Day calendar at the time the appointment is scheduled to occur.
- If you need more than a half hour, drag the mouse pointer over the time blocks to select them. (You can also hold down the Shift key and use the up and down arrow keys to highlight the block.)

With your block highlighted, type in a description of the appointment. Note that pressing Enter will start a new line in the appointment description. When you're finished, you need to either click outside the time block or press Shift-Enter.

Using the Appointment Form

To attach some bells and whistles (literally!) to your appointment, you need to use Outlook's Appointment form. First, highlight the time blocks you want to devote to the appointment. (This is optional at this stage, but it will save you a couple of steps later.) Now select Calendar | New Appointment, or press Ctrl-N, to display the Appointment form, which will be similar to the one shown in Figure 40.6.

Here's a summary of the various controls on this form:

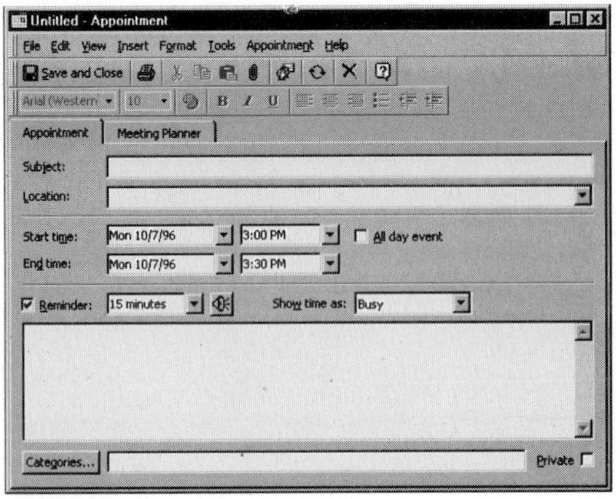

FIGURE 40.6.

Use the Appointment form to enter your new appointments.

Subject: A description of the appointment. This is the text that will appear in the Calendar.

Location: Specifies the location (such as a room number or address) for the appointment.

Start time: The date and time that the appointment starts. Entering these values is much easier if you use Outlook's AutoDate feature. For example, you can enter next Monday and Outlook will calculate the appropriate date. See the next section for more information.

End time: The date and time the appointment ends.

All day event: Activate this check box if you change your mind and want to turn the appointment into an event.

Reminder: If you'd like Outlook to remind you that your appointment is coming up, keep the Reminder check box activated. Use the drop-down list to specify how soon before the appointment the reminder should be displayed. If you'd like Outlook to play a sound, click the sound icon to select a .WAV file to be played. Figure 40.7 shows an example of a reminder message. Once you see this message, you can click Dismiss to get rid of it, Postpone to have Outlook display the reminder again in five minutes (or whatever time you choose in the Click Postpone to be reminded again in list), or Open Item to display the item in the Appointment window.

FIGURE 40.7.

An example of an Outlook Reminder message.

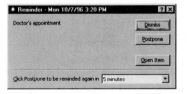

Show time as: If your schedule is set up as a public folder, you can use this drop-down list to inform others of your status during this appointment. You can select Busy, Free, Tentative (if you're not sure), or Out of Office.

Notes: You can use this large text box to enter notes about the appointment.

Categories: Use this option to classify the appointment by category (for example, Business or Personal).

Private: Activate this check box to hide the appointment from others who have access to the folder. This also prevents the appointment from being published with the rest of your free/busy information.

When you're done, click the Save and Close button to add the appointment and return to the Calendar folder.

Taking Advantage of AutoDate

One of Outlook's most interesting features is its ability to accept natural-language entries in date and time fields and to convert those entries into real dates and times. If today is October 7th, for example, entering next week in a date field will cause Outlook to enter October 14th as the date. Similarly, you can enter noon in a time field, and Outlook "knows" that you mean 12:00.

This slick feature is called *AutoDate,* and once you understand its ways, you'll find that it saves you lots of time in certain situations. I won't give you a full description of what AutoDate understands, but a few examples should give you an idea of what it can do, and you can experiment from there.

Here are some notes about entering natural-language dates:

- AutoDate will convert yesterday, today, and tomorrow into their date equivalents.

- You can shorten day names to their first three letters: sun, mon, tue, wed, thu, fri, and sat. (Notice, too, that case isn't important.) You can also shorten month names: jan, feb, mar, apr, may, jun, jul, aug, sep, oct, nov, and dec.

- To specify a date in the current week (Calendar's weeks run from Sunday through Saturday), use the keyword this (for example, this fri).

- To specify a date from last week or last month, use the keyword last (for example, last aug).

- To specify a date in the next week or month, use the keyword next (for example, next sat).

- If you want to use the first day of a week or month, use the keyword first. For example, first mon in dec will give you the first Monday in December. Similarly, use last to specify the last day of a week or month.

- To get a date that is a particular number of days, weeks, months, or years from some other date, use the keyword from (for example, 6 months from today).

- To get a date that is a particular number of days, weeks, months, or years before some other date, use the keyword before (for example, 2 days before christmas).

NOTE: AUTODATE'S BUILT-IN HOLIDAYS

Yes, AutoDate also recognizes a number of holidays that fall on the same date each year, including the following: Boxing Day, Cinco de Mayo, Christmas, Christmas Day, Christmas Eve, Halloween, Independence Day, Lincoln's Birthday, New Year's Day, New Year's Eve, St. Patrick's Day, Valentine's Day, Veterans Day, and Washington's Birthday.

- To get a date that is a particular number of days, weeks, months, or years in the past, use the keyword ago (for example, 4 weeks ago).

- AutoDate also accepts spelled-out dates, such as August 23rd and first of January. These aren't as useful, because they probably take longer to spell out than they do to enter the date in the usual format.

For time fields, keep the following points in mind:

- AutoDate will convert noon and midnight into the correct times.

- AutoDate understands military time. So if you enter 9, AutoDate converts this to 9:00 AM. However, if you enter 21, AutoDate changes it to 9:00 PM.

- Use now to specify the current time.

- You can specify time zones by using the following abbreviations: CST, EST, GMT, MST, and PST.

Creating a Recurring Appointment

If you have an appointment that occurs at a regular interval (say, weekly or monthly), Calendar lets you schedule a *recurring* appointment. For example, if you create a weekly appointment, Calendar will fill in that appointment automatically on the same day of the week at the same time for the duration you specify.

You can use two methods to schedule a recurring appointment:

- Start a new appointment by selecting Calendar | New Recurring Appointment.

- If you've already started a regular appointment, either select Appointment | Recurrence, press Ctrl-G, or click the Recurrence toolbar button.

Either way, you'll see the Appointment Recurrence dialog box, shown in Figure 40.8.

FIGURE 40.8.

Use this dialog box to set up a recurring appointment.

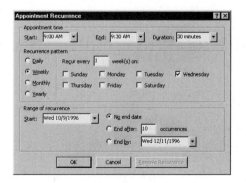

40

PLACES TO GO:
CALENDAR

Here's the nitty-gritty on the various controls in this dialog box:

Appointment time: Use the Start, End, and Duration boxes to specify the appointment time. (Note that you need to fill in only two of these three values; Outlook will figure out the third by itself.)

Recurrence pattern: Select the interval you want to use: Daily, Weekly, Monthly, or Yearly. The options to the right of these buttons will change, depending on your selection. The Weekly option, for example, asks you to enter the length of the interval in weeks, as well as the day of the week to use.

Range of recurrence: Use the Start box to tell Outlook when the recurring appointment should begin. If you want the appointment scheduled indefinitely, activate the No end date option. Otherwise, you can use End after to specify the number of appointments to schedule, or you can use End by to specify the date of the last appointment.

Click OK to return to the Appointment window to fill in the rest of the appointment details.

Scheduling an Event

As I mentioned earlier, an *event* is an activity that consumes one or more days (or, at least, the working part of those days). Some activities are obvious events: vacations, trade shows, sales meetings, and so on. But what about, say, a training session that lasts from 9:00 to 4:00. Is that an event or just a long appointment? From Outlook's point of view, there are two main differences between an appointment and an event:

- By default, an appointment is marked as "busy" time, so other people know not to schedule appointments at conflicting times. On the other hand, an event is marked as "free" time.

- Appointments are entered as time blocks in the Calendar, but events are displayed as a banner at the top of the calendar. This means that you can also schedule appointments on days that you have events.

A good example that illustrates these differences is a trade show. Suppose the show lasts an entire day and you're a sales rep who will be attending the show. You could schedule the show as a day-long appointment. However, what if you also want to visit with customers who are attending the show? In that case, it would make more sense to schedule the show as an event. This leaves the calendar open for you to schedule appointments with your customers.

Scheduling an event is very similar to setting up an appointment. To get started, select Calendar | New Event. As you can see in Figure 40.9, the Event form that appears is almost identical to the Appointment form. The only differences are that you can't specify a start and end time, and the All day event check box is activated.

Figure 40.9.

Use the Event form to schedule an event.

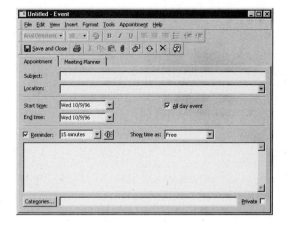

If you'd prefer to schedule a recurring event, select Calendar | New Recurring Event instead. As before, the Appointment Recurrence dialog box will appear so that you can define the interval.

Requesting a Meeting

The appointments and events that you've worked with so far haven't required you to work directly with anyone on your network or on a remote network. Yes, if you've posted a schedule to a public Exchange Server folder, others on your network can view your appointments and events (at least those that you haven't set up as private). But there might be times when you need to coordinate schedules with other people in order to arrange a meeting.

The old-fashioned method of doing this involved a phone conversation in which each person consulted his day planner to try to find a mutually free time. This isn't too bad if just two people are involved, but what if there are a dozen? Or a hundred? You could try sending out e-mail messages, but you're still looking at a coordination nightmare for a large group of people.

Outlook solves this dilemma by implementing a couple of time-saving features:

Meeting Requests: These are e-mail messages that you use to set up small meetings. They let the invitees respond to your invitation with a simple click of a button.

Meeting Planner: This more sophisticated tool is designed for coordinating larger groups. The Planner lets you see in advance the schedule of each invitee, so you can schedule a suitable time *before* inviting everyone.

The next two sections show you how to use both features.

Sending Out a New Meeting Request

If you need to set up a simple meeting that involves just a few people, a basic meeting request is all you'll need. A meeting request is an e-mail message that asks the recipients to attend a meeting on a particular day at a particular time. The recipients can then check their schedules (although Outlook does this for them automatically) and either accept or reject the request by clicking buttons attached to the message.

To start a meeting request, select Calendar | New Meeting Request or press Ctrl-Shift-Q. Outlook displays the Meeting form, shown in Figure 40.10. This form is almost identical to the appointment form you saw earlier. The only difference is that you use the To box to enter the e-mail addresses of the invitees. (Or you can click To and choose the addresses from an address book. Note that you can designate attendees who are required and attendees who are optional.) When you're done, click the Send button to mail the request.

FIGURE 40.10.

Use the Meeting form to send out a meeting request.

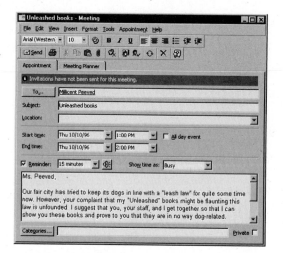

When the recipient gets the message, he'll see a window that looks something like the one shown in Figure 40.11. There are two important things to note about this message:

- The toolbar contains three buttons that define the response: Accept, Tentatively Accept, and Decline.

- When Outlook receives a meeting request, it checks your Calendar to see if the request conflicts with any existing appointments. If a conflict is present, Outlook tells you when you view the request.

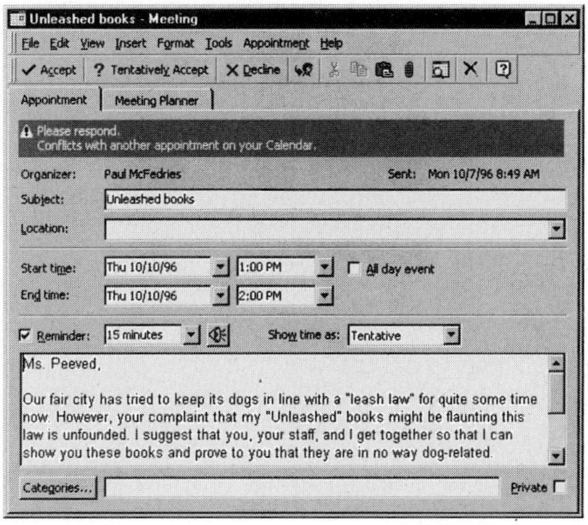

Figure 40.11.

An example of what the meeting request looks like on the recipient's end.

To respond to this request, the recipient either clicks one of the toolbar response buttons or pulls down the Appointment menu and selects one of the following options: Accept, Tentatively Accept, or Decline. Outlook then displays a dialog box similar to the one shown in Figure 40.12. It contains the following options:

Edit the response before sending: Select this option to display the Meeting Response form, which lets you enter some explanatory text in your response.

Send the response now: Select this option if you want to return the response without any explanatory text.

Don't send a response: Select this option to ignore the request (it will be deleted).

If you Accept or Tentatively Accept the meeting, Outlook adds it to your Calendar automatically.

Figure 40.12.

Use this dialog box to determine how your response is handled.

Planning a Meeting

For larger meetings, you can use Outlook's Meeting Planner to do some advance work. Specifically, you tell the Planner the names of the invitees, and Outlook queries their schedules and shows you when they're free. This lets you choose a convenient time for the meeting before sending out the request.

To plan a meeting, you have two choices:

- If you've already started a meeting request, activate the Meeting Planner tab in the Meeting form.

- If you're starting from scratch, either select Calendar | Plan a Meeting or click the Plan a Meeting button on the toolbar.

Figure 40.13 shows the Plan a Meeting window that appears when you invoke the Meeting Planner from scratch. The first thing you need to do is add all the attendees. You can either type in the person's name under your own in the All Attendees column, or you can click Invite Others to select names using an address book. As you add names, Outlook checks their schedules and fills the timeline with blocks that represent each person's existing appointments and meetings. Once you've added all the attendees, you can adjust your meeting time accordingly. There are three methods you can use:

- Enter new values in the Meeting start time and Meeting end time controls.

- In the timeline, use the mouse pointer to drag the meeting selection bars left or right. The green bar represents the meeting start time, and the red bar represents the end time.

- To have Outlook select an appropriate time automatically, use the AutoPick feature. Click << to choose an earlier time, or click AutoPick >> to choose a later time.

FIGURE 40.13.

Use this window to plan a meeting from scratch.

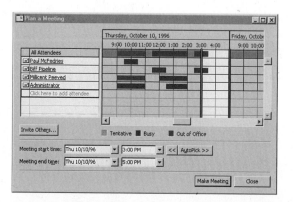

TIP: APPOINTMENTS MIGHT BE "FREE" TIME

A person's blocked time might not mean he's unavailable. For example, he might have scheduled an appointment but designated that appointment as "free" time. To find out, right-click the block. Outlook will consult the person's schedule and display a banner that tells you whether the item is "Busy" or "Free."

If you're working in the Plan a Meeting window, click Make Meeting to generate the meeting request. Fill in the fields as usual, and then click Send.

To monitor the status of the responses, double-click the meeting in your Calendar and activate the Meeting Planner tab, shown in Figure 40.14. Outlook displays a list of the attendees and their current status (Accepted, Declined, and so on). If you don't see the list of attendees, activate the Show attendee status option.

FIGURE 40.14.

Use the Meeting Planner tab to track the progress of the attendees' responses.

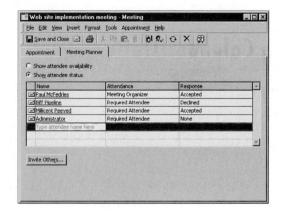

Working with Calendar's Views

As with all of Outlook's modules, you can view your schedule in several different ways. For example, you can set up the Calendar folder to show just the events you've scheduled.

The Day, Week, and Month calendars are part of Calendar's default Day/Week/Month view. To look at your appointments, events, and meetings in a new light, try one of Calendar's five other predefined views:

Active Appointments: Displays a tabular list of all the items you've scheduled, sorted by date.

Events: Displays a tabular list of scheduled events, sorted by the event's start date.

Annual Events: Displays a tabular list of all the events you've scheduled with an annual recurrence.

Recurring Appointments: Displays a tabular list of all the recurring appointments you've created.

By Category: Groups the appointments by category.

Outlook gives you two methods of changing the view:

- Select View | Current View, and then choose the view you want from the cascade menu that appears.
- Use the Current View drop-down list on the toolbar.

NOTE: CUSTOM CALENDAR VIEWS

You can also create your own views of the Calendar folder. See Chapter 38, "Advanced Outlook E-Mail Topics," to learn how to create custom views. Note, too, that when you use any of the tabular views, Outlook lets you modify the columns that are displayed in the table, as well as sort, filter, and group the appointments. Again, see Chapter 38 to learn how these operations work.

Setting Calendar Options

To help you set up Calendar to suit the way you work, Outlook offers a number of options that control things such as the first day of the week and the time interval displayed in the Day calendar. To work with these options, select Tools | Options to display the dialog box shown in Figure 40.15. (If you give this command from Calendar, the Calendar tab will be selected automatically.) Here's a summary of the available controls:

Calendar work week: These controls define your work week. Use the check boxes to select which days of the week are working days. Use the First day of week list to choose the day that you want to use as the start of each week. Use the First week of year list to specify the initial week of the year.

Calendar working hours: These are the hours in the Day calendar that are deemed working hours. (Calendar displays non-working hours with a gray background.)

Appointment defaults: The Duration value determines the interval that Calendar uses in the Day view. The Reminder value determines the default number that appears when you use a reminder with your appointments.

Date Navigator: Use the Font button to define the font used in the Date Navigator. If you activate the Show week numbers check box, Outlook displays week numbers beside each week in the Date Navigator.

Use Microsoft Schedule+ 7.0 as my primary calendar: Activate this check box to use Schedule+ 7.0 instead of Outlook's Calendar.

Time Zone: Clicking this button displays the Time Zone dialog box, in which you can specify your current time zone and even specify an additional time zone for comparison purposes.

Add Holidays: Clicking this button displays the Add Holidays to Calendar dialog box. You use it to specify holidays from various countries that you want to include in your schedule.

Advanced Scheduling: Clicking this button displays the Advanced Scheduling dialog box, shown in Figure 40.16. You can use the controls in the Processing of meeting requests group to have Outlook handle incoming meeting requests automatically. The controls in the Settings for free/busy information group determine how much of your schedule is published on the server and how often information from other people's schedules is refreshed on your machine.

FIGURE 40.15.

Use the Calendar tab to set some Calendar options.

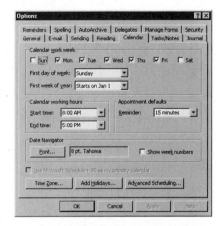

FIGURE 40.16.

The Advanced Scheduling dialog box.

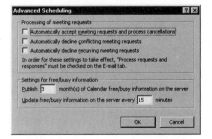

Summary

This chapter showed you how to work with Outlook's Calendar. After a brief orientation and a review of some navigation skills, you got right down to business by learning how to set up appointments (both regular and recurring), schedule events, and plan and request meetings. I finished this chapter by examining a few Calendar options and customization techniques.

Here's a list of chapters where you'll find related information:

■ Outlook's e-mail basics can be found in Chapter 37, "The Ins and Outs of the Outlook Inbox."

■ See Chapter 38, "Advanced Outlook E-Mail Topics," to learn how to display different fields; sort, group, and filter appointments; and create custom views.

■ You can create appointments and meetings with people in your Contacts list. To learn how to set up contacts in Outlook, head for Chapter 41, "People to Meet: Contacts."

■ Outlook has a separate Tasks folder that is a larger-scale version of the TaskPad. I'll show you how it works in Chapter 42, "Things to Do: Tasks, Journal, and Notes."

People to Meet: Contacts

CHAPTER 41

We cannot always assure the future of our friends; we have a better chance of assuring our future if we remember who our friends are.

—*Henry Kissinger*

When I introduced you to Outlook's e-mail capabilities in Chapter 37, "The Ins and Outs of the Outlook Inbox," I also introduced you to the Address Book. You saw that this was a convenient storage area for the e-mail addresses and fax numbers you use most often. The Address Book even gives you a few extra fields for contact information: addresses, phone numbers, and so on.

However, the Address Book looks positively pathetic when placed alongside Outlook's *real* contact management module. Called, appropriately enough, *Contacts,* this folder gives you amazing flexibility for dealing with your ever-growing network of colleagues, clients, friends, and family. So, yes, you can use Contacts to store mundane information such as phone numbers and addresses, but with over 100 predefined fields available, you can preserve the minutiae of other people's lives: their birthdays and anniversaries, the names of their spouses and children, their nicknames, and even their Web page addresses.

This chapter takes you inside the Contacts folder and shows you how to add and edit contacts; import contact data from other programs; phone, e-mail, and fax contacts; and customize your Contacts view.

Checking Out the Contacts Folder

When you first display the Contacts folder, you won't see much of anything: just your name in a box. (Outlook always adds a single contact for yourself during installation.) You'll learn how to populate the Contacts folder with new entries in the next section. Once you're done, your Contacts folder will look like the one shown in Figure 41.1.

FIGURE 41.1.

How the Contacts folder looks once you've added a few contacts.

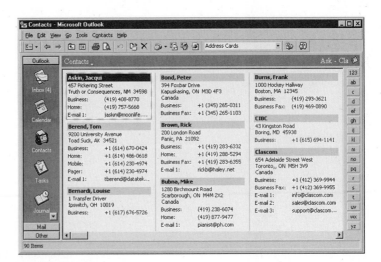

As you can see, Outlook presents each contact as an *address card* that shows some of the information you've entered: name, address, phone numbers, and e-mail address. (See the section "Customizing the Contacts Folder" to learn how to customize the fields that Outlook displays in these cards and how to change the view used in this folder.)

Here are a few techniques you can use to navigate the Contacts cards:

- Press Tab to move forward one card at a time. To move backward through the cards, press Shift-Tab.

- Press the right arrow key to move right one column at a time. Press the left arrow key to move left one column at a time.

- Press Page Up to move to the next screen. Press Page Down to move to the previous screen.

- To move to a specific letter, either press the letter's key on the keyboard or click the letter buttons on the right side of the Contacts folder.

Adding a New Contact

That next-to-empty Contacts folder is a bit depressing, so let's get right down to adding some new cards. This section shows you various methods of setting up new contacts. You'll also learn how to import contact data from other programs, including Schedule+.

Creating a New Contact from Scratch

To start a new contact, either select Contacts | New Contact or press Ctrl-N. Outlook displays the Contact window, shown in Figure 41.2.

FIGURE 41.2.

Use this window to enter data for your new contact.

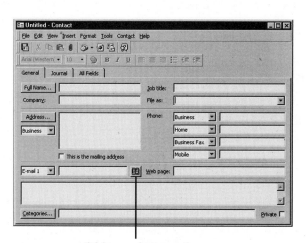

Click here to select an e-mail
address from an address book

Most of the fields you see are straightforward; you just fill in the appropriate data. However, here are a few notes about certain fields in the General tab:

> **Full Name:** Use the text box to enter the name of the contact. To enter more detailed information, click the Full Name button to display the Check Full Name dialog box, shown in Figure 41.3. This dialog box lets you enter not only separate first, middle, and last names, but also the appropriate title (Mr., Ms., and so on) and suffix (Jr., II, and so on).

Figure 41.3.

Use this dialog box to enter detailed name information.

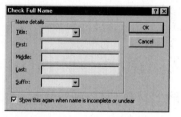

> **File as:** Outlook uses this field to determine where the contact appears alphabetically. In most cases, Outlook uses the person's last name. For example, if you enter `Biff Pipeline` in the Full Name box, Outlook will add `Pipeline, Biff` to the File as field. If Biff Pipeline is actually a company name, you can either edit the File as field directly, or you can drop down the list to select an alternative entry (for example, `Biff Pipeline`).

> **Address:** You use this field to enter the contact's street address, city, state or province, ZIP or postal code, and country. Use the drop-down list to specify whether this is a business, home, or other address. If this is the contact's mailing address, activate the This is the mailing address check box. As with the name, you can also use a dialog box to enter specific address information. In this case, click the Address button.

> **Phone:** Outlook can record no less than 18 phone numbers for each contact. The default Contact window just shows fields for the four most common numbers: Business, Home, Business Fax, and Mobile. To enter different numbers, use the drop-down lists provided to select the type of number you want to add. (If you want to add phone numbers *in addition to* the ones displayed, I'll show you how to do this later in this section.)

> **E-mail:** Use this field to enter the contact's e-mail address. Note that Outlook can hold up to three e-mail addresses for each contact (E-mail 1, E-mail 2, and E-mail 3). If this contact's e-mail address is already defined in an address book, press Ctrl-Shift-B, or click the button beside the field (see Figure 41.2). The Select Name dialog box that appears is identical to the Address Book dialog box you saw in Chapter 37. Highlight the address you want and click OK.

Web page: Use this field to enter the URL of the contact's Web page address (for example, `http://www.domain.com/user/home.html`).

Notes: Use the large text box near the bottom of the window to enter notes about this contact.

Categories: Use this field to assign each contact to a predefined category list (such as Key Customer, Suppliers, or Personal). Click the Categories button to see a list of the available categories.

The Journal tab lets you set various Journal-related options for this contact. I discuss the Journal in detail in Chapter 42, "Things to Do: Tasks, Journal, and Notes."

As I mentioned earlier, Outlook boasts over 100 fields for each contact. If a particular field you need to fill in isn't displayed in the General tab, you'll find it in the All Fields tab, shown in Figure 41.4. Use the Select from drop-down list to choose a category of fields to work with. (If you're not sure, select All Contact fields to see every available field.) Find the field you want and then enter your data in the Value column.

FIGURE 41.4.

Use the All Fields tab to fill in fields not found in the General tab.

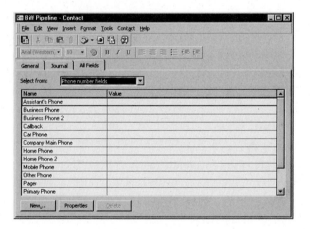

When your labors for this contact are complete, you have three ways to proceed:

- To return to the Contacts folder, select File | Close. When you're asked if you want to save your changes, click Yes.

- To continue adding contacts, select File | Save and New. In this case, Outlook adds the current contact and displays a fresh Contact window.

- If you want to add another contact from the same company, select File | Save and New in Company. Outlook again displays a new Contact window, but it copies the business-related data from the previous contact, including the company name, business address, and the business phone and fax numbers.

Importing Contact Data

If you have your contact data in some other application, chances are you'll be able to import that data into Outlook and save yourself the hassle of retyping all that information. Outlook comes with an Import and Export Wizard that makes it easy.

To get started, select File | Import and Export to display the Import and Export dialog box, shown in Figure 41.5. As you can see, this Wizard is useful for many more things than just importing contact data. You can also import message stores (.PST files) and Microsoft Mail files, as well as export Outlook data in various formats. Our concern here is to import contact information, so make sure that the Import from Schedule+ or another program or file is highlighted, and click Next >.

FIGURE 41.5.

You can use the Import and Export Wizard to grab contact data and other information.

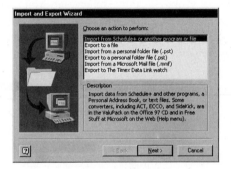

The next Wizard dialog box, shown in Figure 41.6, asks you to choose the format of the data you want to import. The Wizard can bring in data in a number of different formats:

> **Personal information managers:** You can import data from Lotus Organizer and Schedule+. Converters for other PIMs—such as ACT!, ECCO, and Sidekick—are available from Microsoft.
>
> **Database:** If the information is stored in a database, Outlook can import Access, Excel, FoxPro, and dBASE tables.
>
> **Personal Address Book:** If you've populated your Personal Address Book with a number of e-mail addresses (and other info), you can import this data into the Contacts folder.
>
> **Text files:** If that still isn't good enough, you can use your existing program to export the data into a text file (with either comma-separated or tab-separated fields), and the Wizard will import the text.

Highlight the appropriate file type, and click Next >.

41

FIGURE 41.6.

*Use this Wizard dialog
box to choose the type of
file you want to import.*

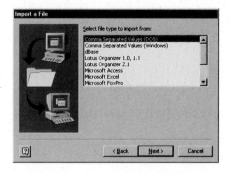

The next Wizard dialog box you see depends on the file type you choose. More than likely, however, the Wizard will ask you to specify the file you want to import, as shown in Figure 41.7. Use the File to import text box to enter the full pathname of the file (or click Browse to use the Browse dialog box to choose the file). The buttons in the Options group tell Outlook how you want to handle duplicate items (if they exist). Click Next > when you're ready to proceed.

FIGURE 41.7.

*You'll probably need to
specify which file to
import.*

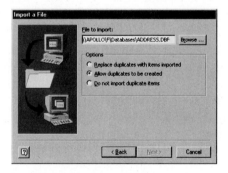

Now the Wizard asks you to choose a destination for the imported data (see Figure 41.8). Highlight a folder (this will likely be your Contacts folder, unless you've created other folders to hold contact data) and click Next >. The Wizard opens the selected file and displays the dialog box shown in Figure 41.9.

FIGURE 41.8.

*Use this dialog box to
choose a destination
folder.*

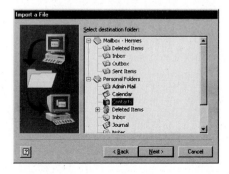

FIGURE 41.9.

The Wizard displays this dialog box when it's ready to import the data.

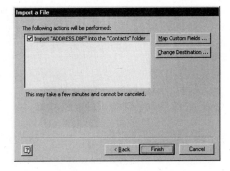

To ensure that the data is imported into the correct fields in your Contacts folder, click the Map Custom Fields button to display the dialog box shown in Figure 41.10. The From group on the left shows a single record from the data you'll be importing. (Use the Next > and < Previous buttons to see other records.) The To group on the right shows the mapping data for the Contacts folder: The Field column shows the Contacts fields, and the Mapped from column shows the related fields from the import file. To map a field, drag it from the import file and drop it on the appropriate field in the Contacts folder. When you're done, click OK to return to the Wizard.

FIGURE 41.10.

Use the Map Custom Fields dialog box to make sure the imported data gets entered into the correct Contacts fields.

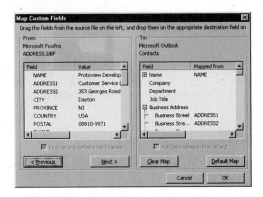

To import the data, click Finish. The Translation Monitor window will show you the progress of your import.

Editing Contact Data

Once you've added some contacts, you'll often have to edit them to either add new information or change existing information. Outlook gives you two methods of editing a contact:

■ If the field you want to edit is visible in the contact's address card, click the field. This activates "in-cell editing," which lets you make changes to the field directly.

■ To make changes to other fields, you have to open the contact. You can either double-click the contact name, or highlight the contact and do one of the following: select File | Open, press Ctrl-O, or press Enter.

NOTE: ACTIVATING IN-CELL EDITING

If clicking a field doesn't activate in-cell editing, you need to turn on this feature. To do so, select View | Format View, activate the Allow in-cell editing check box in the dialog box that appears, and click OK.

Turning the Contacts Folder into an E-Mail Address Book

At first blush, there seems to be a natural connection between Outlook's e-mail client and its Contacts folder. After all, you can enter one or more e-mail addresses for each client. And you'll see later in this chapter that it's easy to send an e-mail message to a client from within the Contacts folder (see "Working with Your Contacts").

However, if you're working in a mail folder and you compose a new message, there's no way to choose a contact as your recipient. You'd think that you ought to be able to display the Address Book (or something) and choose the contact to whom you want to send the message.

This seems like a major integration gaffe on the part of Outlook, but it turns out that you *can* use the Contacts folder as an address book. You just have to ask Outlook to do it for you. Here's how:

1. In the Contacts folder, select File | Folder | Properties for "Contacts". Outlook displays the Contacts Properties dialog box.
2. Activate the Outlook Address Book tab, shown in Figure 41.11.
3. Activate the Show this folder as an e-mail Address Book check box, and use the Name of the address book text box to specify the name that will appear in the list of address books.
4. Click OK.

To use the Contacts address book when composing a message, click To or Cc to display the Select Names dialog box, shown in Figure 41.12. Open the Show names from the drop-down list and look for Outlook Address Book. Beneath that, you'll see Contacts. When you select this item, Outlook displays the e-mail addresses from your Contacts folder. (If you have the Microsoft Fax service installed, you'll also see all the defined fax numbers.)

FIGURE 41.11.

Use the Outlook Address Book tab to turn the Contacts folder into an address book.

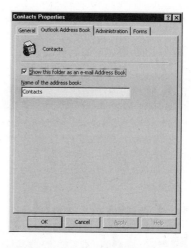

FIGURE 41.12.

The Contacts e-mail (and, in this case, fax) data can now be used as an address book.

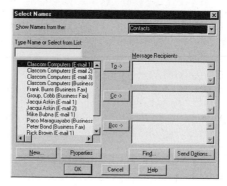

Phoning a Contact

Outlook supports TAPI (the Telephony Application Programming Interface), which means among other things that you can have Outlook dial your phone automatically via an attached modem. This feature is called AutoDialer. To use it, you need to arrange your phone cables appropriately:

- Run one phone cable from your phone to the "Phone" jack on your modem.
- Run a second phone cable from your modem's "Line" jack to the phone jack on your wall.

With that out of the way, highlight the contact you want to phone, and then do either of the following:

■ Select Tools | Dial.

■ Click the AutoDialer button on the toolbar.

Either way, you'll see a list of commands that includes the phone number (or numbers) for the contact. Select the number you want to dial. Outlook displays the New Call dialog box, shown in Figure 41.13. Before starting your call, you can use the following options in this dialog box:

Open Contact: Click this button to open the Contact window for the current contact.

Dialing Properties: Click this button to select or change Windows' dialing properties.

Dialing Options: You use this button to set up speed dial numbers. See the next section for details.

Create new Journal Entry when starting new call: Activate this check box to create an entry in Outlook's Journal for this call. See Chapter 42 to learn how to use the Journal.

FIGURE 41.13.

Use this dialog box to set dialing properties and initiate the call.

When you're ready to dial, click Start Call. Through your modem's speaker, you'll hear the phone dialing. When you see the dialog box shown in Figure 41.14, pick up your receiver and click Talk. Outlook returns you to the New Call dialog box. If you'd like to view the contact's data while talking, click Open Contact. When the call is complete, click End Call. You can either make another call at this point, or click Close to return to the Contact folder.

FIGURE 41.14.

When you see this dialog box, pick up the receiver and click Talk.

TIP: REDIALING RECENT CALLS

Outlook keeps track of the last seven calls you dialed. To redial one of these numbers, select Tools | Dial | Redial, or click the AutoDialer button and then click Redial. Select the number to redial from the cascade menu that appears.

NOTE: ON-THE-FLY DIALING

Besides phoning specific contacts, you can also use Outlook to dial numbers on-the-fly. Select Tools | Dial | New Call (or press Ctrl-Shift-D) to display the New Call dialog box. Enter the number in the Dial number text box, and then click Start Call.

Quick Connections with Speed Dial

If you have several contacts that you dial regularly, you can save a few steps by setting up their phone numbers in Outlook's Speed Dial feature. This places the numbers on the Dial menu so that they're only a few clicks away.

To create a Speed Dial number, display the New Call dialog box. (It doesn't matter how you do this. Unfortunately, Outlook gives you no direct method of defining a specific number as a Speed Dial number. It would be nice if we had, say, an "Add to Speed Dial" command, but there isn't one.) Now click the Dialing Options button to display the Dialing Options dialog box, shown in Figure 41.15. Enter a name in the Name text box, enter the phone number in the Phone number text box, and then click Add. You can add up to 20 entries.

FIGURE 41.15.

Use the Dialing Options dialog box to define your Speed Dial numbers.

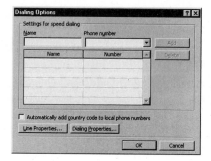

To place a call using Speed Dial, select Tools | Dial | Speed Dial, or click the AutoDialer button and choose Speed Dial. In the cascade menu that appears, choose the number you want to call.

Working with Your Contacts

You didn't go to all the trouble of entering or importing contact data just to look up someone's birthday or spouse name. No, with all that information at your fingertips, you'll want to do things that are a bit more substantial. Like what? Well, Outlook gives you lots of choices. You've already seen that you can have your modem phone a contact. However, you can also send an e-mail message to a contact, you can request a meeting, you can set up a new task, and you can surf to that person's Web page. The following list gives you a quick run-through of the methods you use to accomplish all of these tasks from within the Contacts folder. Note that in each case you should highlight the contact you want to work with beforehand.

Sending an E-Mail to a Contact: If you've defined at least one e-mail address for a client, you can send that person a message by selecting Contacts | New Message to Contact, or by clicking the New Message to Contact toolbar button. (If a contact has more than one address, Outlook displays a dialog box that tells you all the addresses will be inserted on the To line.) Outlook starts a new message and fills in the To line with the contact's e-mail address.

Requesting a Meeting with a Contact: To set up a new meeting with the contact, select Contacts | New Meeting with Contact, or click the New Meeting with Contact toolbar button (you can also press Ctrl-Shift-G). Outlook loads a new meeting request message and addresses it to the contact.

Exploring a Contact's Web Page: If the contact has a Web page and you've entered the URL in the Web page field, you can load the page into Internet Explorer right from the Contacts folder. Just select Contacts | Explore Web Page, or click the Explore Web Page toolbar button (you can also press Ctrl-Shift-X). Internet Explorer loads and displays the Web page.

Sending a Letter to a Contact: Instead of all these high-tech tasks, you might want to send an old-fashioned letter to the contact. If you select Contacts | New Letter to Contact, Outlook starts Word and loads the Letter Wizard, which takes you on a four-step journey to create the letter.

Customizing the Contacts Folder

Like all of Outlook's folders, the Contacts folder can be customized to suit the way you work. Specifically, you can specify different fields to display in the address cards, you can work with alternative views, and you can sort and filter the contacts. The rest of this chapter shows you how to perform these customization chores.

Changing the Fields Shown in the Contacts Window

The default fields shown in each address card tell you the basic information that you've defined for each contact. (Blank fields aren't shown in the address cards.) However, you've seen that Outlook lets you enter data in dozens of different fields. If the default address card layout isn't showing a field you want to see (such as the contact's Web page address), you can easily make some adjustments.

To customize Outlook's address cards, follow these steps:

1. Select View | Show Fields to display the Show Fields dialog box, shown in Figure 41.16.

FIGURE 41.16.

Use the Show Fields dialog box to customize the fields displayed in the address cards.

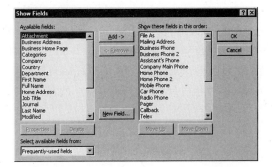

2. Use the Select available fields from drop-down list to select the category of fields you want to work with.

3. In the Available fields list, highlight a field you want to see, and click Add->.

4. To remove a field, highlight it in the Show these fields in this order list, and click <-Remove.

5. You can change the position of an address card field by highlighting it in the Show these fields in this order list, and clicking either Move Up or Move Down.

6. Repeat steps 2 through 5 to customize other fields.

7. When you're done, click OK.

Changing the Contacts View

Like the other Outlook folders, the Contacts folder has several predefined views that you can use to see the contact information in different ways. The default view is Address Cards, but there are five other views you can check out:

Detailed Address Cards: This view is similar to Address Cards, but it shows more fields for each contact, including home data, Web page, and notes. Also, multiline entries are displayed in full.

Phone List: This view displays the contacts in a tabular format with the fields as columns. The contacts are sorted by full name.

By Category: This view groups the contacts according to the values in the Categories field. Contacts within each category are sorted by the File As field.

By Company: This view groups the contacts by the Company field. Within each company, contacts are sorted by the File As field.

By Location: This view groups the contacts by country. Again, contacts within each country are sorted by the File As field.

To change the view, use either of the following methods:

■ Select View | Current View, and then choose the view you want from the cascade menu that appears.

■ Use the Current View drop-down list on the toolbar.

Sorting the Contacts

By default, Outlook sorts the contacts in ascending order according to the values in the File As field. But you're free to sort the messages based on any field. Here are the techniques you can use:

■ Select View | Sort to display the Sort dialog box, shown in Figure 41.17. Use the Sort items by list to choose the first column you want to use for the sort, use Then by to select a second column, and so on. In each case, activate either Ascending or Descending. Click OK to put the sort order into effect.

FIGURE 41.17.

Use this dialog box to sort your contacts.

■ If you're using one of the tabular views (such as Phone List), click the header for the column you want to use for the sort. An arrow appears beside the column name to tell you the direction of the sort (an up arrow for ascending and a down arrow for descending). You can also right-click the header of the column you want to use and then select either Sort Ascending or Sort Descending from the context menu.

Grouping the Contacts

You saw earlier how Outlook comes with a few views that group related messages. For example, the By Company view groups messages by the values in the Company field. As you can see in Figure 41.18, selecting this view transforms the contacts list into a tabular format where the entries for each company appear together. As with all of Outlook's groupings, you click a plus sign to expand a group and a minus sign to collapse a group.

FIGURE 41.18.

The Contacts grouped by company.

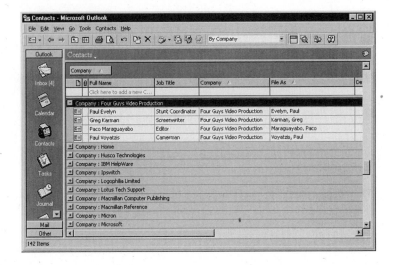

Grouping contacts is basically the same as grouping e-mail messages, so you should check out Chapter 38, "Advanced Outlook E-Mail Topics," for the details of creating groups and working with the Group By box. Bear in mind, however, that you can't group contacts when they're displayed as address cards. You have to select one of the tabular views before the grouping commands become available.

Filtering the Messages

Instead of working with the entire list of contacts, you might prefer to reduce the number of cards by filtering the list. Again, this is similar to filtering e-mail messages as described in Chapter 38, with the following differences:

- The Filter dialog box has a Contacts tab that lets you filter contacts according to specified words or phrases in any Contacts field.
- You can also filter contacts according to e-mail addresses.

Defining a Custom View

You also saw in Chapter 38 that you can save a custom sort order, grouping, or filter into a new view. Again, see that chapter for the details on this process. Note that when you're setting up your view, you'll either want to select Table (for a tabular view) or Card (for a card view).

Summary

In this chapter, you turned your attention to Outlook's Contacts folder. After a quick tour and some navigation techniques, you learned various methods of adding new contacts, including creating them from scratch and importing existing data. I also showed you how to turn the Contacts folder into an e-mail address book, how to phone a contact, how to e-mail and schedule meetings, and how to customize the Contacts folder.

Here's a list of chapters where you'll find related information:

- If you'll be sending e-mail messages from within the Contacts folder, see Chapter 37, "The Ins and Outs of the Outlook Inbox," to learn the basics of composing messages.

- I went through all the gory details of grouping, filtering, and defining custom views in Chapter 38, "Advanced Outlook E-Mail Topics."

- You saw in this chapter that you can request a meeting with a contact from within the Contacts folder. I showed you how to put together meeting requests in Chapter 40, "Places to Go: Calendar."

- If you want to set up new tasks for a contact, see Chapter 42, "Things to Do: Tasks, Journal, and Notes," to learn how to define a task.

- You can use the Journal to keep a record of your contact calls, messages, and meeting requests. I'll show you how the Journal works in Chapter 42.

Things to Do: Tasks, Journal, and Notes

CHAPTER

42

"The horror of that moment," the King went on, "I shall never, never forget!"
"You will, though," the Queen said, "if you don't make a memorandum of it."

—*Lewis Carroll*

The biggest advantage that Outlooks brings to the table is its seamless integration of e-mail, scheduling, and contact information. For the first time, Office users get these three core components of a personal information management system in a single package.

Outlook would certainly be worth the price of admission if it included just these three modules. Happily, though, there's still a lot more to discover in the Outlook package. This chapter looks at the three remaining Outlook folders: Tasks, Journal, and Notes.

Tasks: Outlook's To-Do List

It has become a time-honored tradition for the responsibly forgetful among us to write down reminders of things to do and upcoming activities. The idea behind the Tasks folder is to give you an electronic equivalent of these "to-do" lists.

If you've used Schedule+, you'll feel right at home in the Tasks folder because it's an update of the Schedule+ To-Do module. As you'll see, however, Outlook's tasks are much more sophisticated than the relatively simple To-Do list items from Schedule+. The next few sections show you how to create tasks and work with the Tasks folder.

Creating a New Task

As you can see in Figure 42.1, the Tasks folder is a simple table with four columns:

Icon: The first column shows an icon that tells you whether the item is a regular task (something you need to do), a task request (something you've asked someone else to do), or a requested task (something that someone else has asked you to do).

Complete: A column of check boxes. When a task is complete, you activate the check box to "cross off" the task.

Subject: A description of the task.

Due Date: The date by which the task must be completed.

Entering a Task into the Tasks Folder

The easiest way to create a new task is to simply enter the Subject and Due Date directly in the Tasks folder. The top line of the Tasks folder is used for entering new items. Just click below the Subject header and type in a description of the task. Then move to the Due Date column and either type in the date, use a natural-language date description (see Chapter 40, "Places to Go: Calendar"), or click the drop-down arrow to select the date from a calendar. When you press Enter, Outlook adds the item to the list of tasks.

FIGURE 42.1.

The Tasks folder: a digital to-do list.

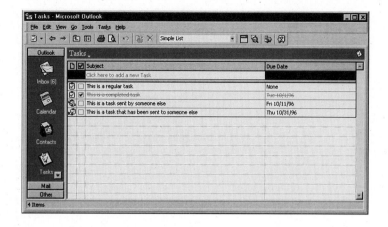

Using the Task Form

If you'd like Outlook to remind you when a task is due, or if you want to set other task options such as the priority and current status, you'll need to use the Task form, shown in Figure 42.2. You can display this form either by selecting Tasks | New Task or by pressing Ctrl-N. Here are the fields to fill in:

Subject: A description of the task. This is the text that will appear in the Tasks folder.

Due date: If you want to assign a due date to the task, activate the Due option and enter a date. You can also assign a starting date for the task by filling in the Start box. In both cases, you can use the AutoDate feature (see Chapter 40) to enter a natural-language date description.

Status: Use this drop-down list to specify the task's current status: Not Started, In Progress, Completed, Waiting on someone else, or Deferred.

Priority: Use this drop-down list to give the task either a Low, Normal, or High priority.

% Complete: Use this spinner to specify a percentage that reflects how much of the task is complete.

Reminder: If you'd like Outlook to remind you that your task is due, activate the Reminder check box. Use the two drop-down lists to specify the date and time you want the reminder displayed. If you'd like Outlook to play a sound, click the sound icon to select a .WAV file to be played.

Notes: You can use this large text box to enter notes about the task.

Categories: Use this button to classify the task by category (for example, Gifts or Phone Calls).

Private: Activate this check box to hide the task from others who have access to the folder.

When you're done, click the Save and Close button to add the task to the list.

FIGURE 42.2.

Use this form to fill in the details about the task.

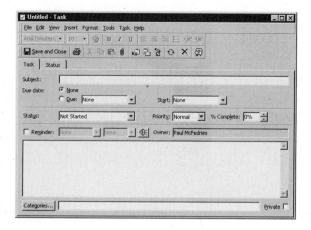

Working with Task Requests

If you're a practitioner of the fine art of delegating, you'll enjoy Outlook's Task Request feature. This feature lets you send an e-mail message to another person, requesting that he complete a specified task (which he can accept or decline). The task still appears on your task list so that you can keep tabs on its progress. For ongoing tasks, the other person can send you status reports that let you know how much of the task is complete, and Outlook will update the task accordingly.

Sending a Task Request

To create and send a task request, Outlook gives you two choices:

- To create a new task request, either select Tasks | New Task Request or press Ctrl-Shift-U.

- If you've already started a regular task, you can convert it to a task request by selecting Task | Assign Task or by clicking the Assign Task button on the toolbar.

Figure 42.3 shows the Task form that appears. This is similar to the form you saw earlier, with the following differences:

To: Use this text box to enter the name of the recipient. You can also click the To button and choose the name from an address book.

Keep an updated copy of this Task on my Task List: When this check box is activated, Outlook adds the task to your Tasks folder. If the recipient sends back any status reports, Outlook updates the task automatically.

Send me a status report when this Task is complete: When this check box is activated, Outlook will monitor the task and, when it's complete, will send a "Task Completed" status report automatically.

FIGURE 42.3.

Use the Task form to create a new task request.

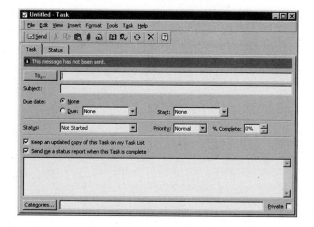

Once you've finished defining the task, click Send. When the recipient opens the task request message, he'll see a toolbar with Accept and Decline buttons. He needs to click one of these buttons (or select either Task | Accept or Task | Decline) to respond. (Outlook will ask him if he wants to edit the response before sending it.)

Sending a Status Report

If someone else has sent you a task request, and you accepted the request, Outlook adds the task to your Tasks folder automatically. To keep the requester apprised of your progress, you can send him status reports.

To begin, open the task (by double-clicking it in the Tasks folder). Make your adjustments in the Task form that appears (you'll usually change either the Status field or the % Complete field), and then do one of the following:

- Select Task | Send Status Report or click the Send Status Report toolbar button. Edit the message that appears, if necessary, and then click Send.

- Select Task | Mark Complete, or click the Mark Complete toolbar button. If the requester asked that a status report be sent upon completion of the task, his Tasks list will be updated automatically.

Working with Views in the Tasks Folder

The Tasks folder comes with no less than 10 predefined views. The Simple List view is the default, but feel free to check out the others to get a new look at your tasks:

Detailed List: This view adds new columns for the Status, % Complete, and Categories.

Active Tasks: This view shows only tasks that aren't yet complete. New columns are added for Status, Due Date, % Complete, and Categories.

Next Seven Days: This view filters the tasks to show only those with a Due Date coming up within the next week.

Overdue Tasks: This view shows only incomplete tasks that are past their due dates.

By Category: This view groups the tasks by category.

Assignment: This view filters the tasks to show only those that have been assigned by someone else.

By Person Responsible: This view groups the tasks by the "owner" of the task (that is, the person who originated the task or task request).

Completed Tasks: This view filters the tasks to show only those tasks that have been marked as complete. A field showing the Date Completed is also displayed.

Task Timeline: This view presents a timeline that shows you when the tasks are due.

To change the view, use either of the following methods:

■ Select View | Current View, and then choose the view you want from the cascade menu that appears.

■ Use the Current View drop-down list on the toolbar.

NOTE: CUSTOM TASKS FOLDER VIEWS

You can also create your own views of the Tasks folder. See Chapter 38, "Advanced Outlook E-Mail Topics," to learn how to create custom views. Note, too, that Outlook lets you modify the columns that are displayed in the Tasks folder, as well as sort, filter, and group the tasks. Again, see Chapter 38 for the details on each technique.

Options for the Tasks Folder

Outlook has a number of default values that control the look of the Tasks folder and which options are set in the various Task forms. To change these options to suit your style, select Tools | Options and head for the Tasks/Notes tab in the Options dialog box, shown in Figure 42.4. (If you invoke this command from the Tasks folder, Outlook selects the Tasks/Notes tab automatically.) Here are some explanations of the available controls:

Reminder time: This option specifies what time that Outlook will display the reminder on the day a task is due.

Set reminders on tasks with due dates: When this check box is activated, Outlook will include a reminder with any task that includes a due date.

Keep updated copies of assigned tasks on my Task list: When this check box is activated, Outlook always adds accepted task requests to your Tasks folder.

Send status reports when assigned tasks are completed: When this check box is activated, Outlook always sends a status report to the task requester when you complete the task he assigned to you.

Task color options: These controls set the color of overdue and completed tasks.

Task working hours: You can use the Status tab in the Task form to enter the number of hours you worked on a task. Outlook uses the Hours per day value to convert the hours worked value into days. For example, if Hours per day is 8 and you work 16 hours on a task, Outlook converts this to 2 days. Similarly, you use the Hours per week control to convert hours into weeks.

FIGURE 42.4.

Use the Tasks/Notes tab to set some options for the Tasks folder.

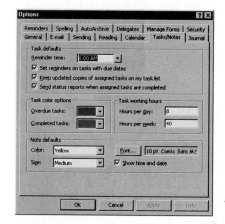

Journal: Your Outlook Diary

One of the consequences of leading a busy life is that you often can't remember what you did from one day to the next. All your phone calls, messages, tasks, activities, appointments, and meetings cease being independent actions and instead blend into an amorphous mass of busyness. If you're having trouble remembering when you worked on a particular file or made a particular phone call, you'll love Outlook's unique Journal feature.

The Journal is a diary-like module that tracks your activities on a timeline. You can set up Journal to record when you make phone calls, send e-mail messages, respond to task and meeting requests, and even when you open files in other Office applications.

Figure 42.5 shows a Journal folder set up to track various activities. As you can see, each type of activity is assigned its own group, and items are inserted into the appropriate groups as you work. You can use the following techniques to work with these items:

- To open the Journal entry, either double-click the item or right-click the item and choose Open Journal Entry from the context menu.

- If you'd prefer to open the item that the Journal entry refers to (such as an e-mail message), right-click the entry and then choose Open Item Referred To.

FIGURE 42.5.

*Use the Journal to track
your activities.*

The next few sections show you various methods of creating Journal entries.

Creating Journal Entries from Scratch

Journal is most convenient when you set it up to record your activities automatically. I'll show you how to do this later, but let's begin by learning how to create new Journal entries from scratch. Why would you need to do this? Well, the biggest reason is that Journal's automatic entries cover only certain activities. For example, Journal will create entries for meeting requests, but not for appointments and events. Also, you can use Journal to record non-Outlook activities such as conversations, ideas, and letters sent and received.

In the Journal folder, either select Journal | New Journal Entry or press Ctrl-N. Outlook displays the Journal Entry form, shown in Figure 42.6. Here are the fields you have to fill in:

Subject: Enter a description of the entry. This is the text that will appear in Journal's timeline.

Entry type: Use this drop-down list to select one of the 20 different entry types that Outlook supports.

Contact: If the entry deals with one of your contacts, use this text box to enter his name. Alternatively, click the Address Book button to the right of this text box to select a name from an address book.

Company: If the entry deals with a specific company, use this field to enter the company name.

Start time: Use these drop-down lists to specify a start time for the entry. This will determine where on the timeline the entry appears. Also, you can either select a specific duration or click Start Timer to begin timing the event. (Note that the timer *begins* at whatever value is specified in the Duration field.)

Notes: You can use this large text box to enter notes about the Journal entry.

Categories: Use this button to classify the entry by category (for example, Ideas or Phone Calls).

Private: Activate this check box to hide the entry from others who have access to the folder.

When you're done, click the Save and Close button to add the entry to the Journal.

FIGURE 42.6.

Use the Journal Entry form to set up a Journal entry from scratch.

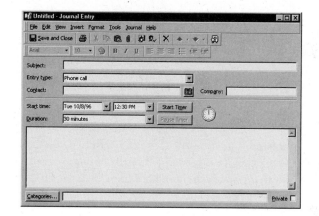

Journal and the Contacts List

You saw in the last section that you can specify one of your contacts when defining a new Journal entry. To make this a bit easier, Outlook also lets you define a new entry directly from the Contacts folder. You can also set up a contact so that all activities with this contact are recorded automatically.

To try this, move to the Contacts folder and open the contact you want to work with. In the Contact form, select the Journal tab, shown in Figure 42.7.

The table that takes up the bulk of the Journal tab displays a list of the Journal entries that exist for this contact. (You can filter this list by selecting a Journal entry type from the Show drop-down box.)

If you just want to create a new Journal entry for this contact, click New Journal Entry to display the Journal Entry form. On the other hand, you might prefer that Outlook create Journal entries automatically for this contact. To set this up, activate the Automatically record journal entries for this contact check box.

FIGURE 42.7.

Use the Journal tab to set up Journal tracking for this contact.

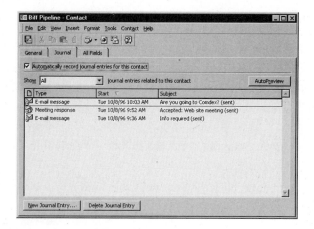

Journal and Phone Calls

Some of the items that Journal can track aren't all that useful. For example, recording e-mail entries can give you a feel for how much work you did on a given day. However, you can easily sort stored messages by date, or even display them in the Message Timeline view, so keeping Journal entries is somewhat redundant.

On the other hand, some Journal entries are indispensable because you would otherwise have no record of the activity they track. Phone calls are a good example. Although you can use Outlook to initiate phone calls (as explained in Chapter 40), potentially important details such as the date, time, and duration of the call aren't recorded.

To solve this, it's easy to create Journal entries for phone calls. One way to do this would be to create a new Journal entry just prior to making your call. However, Outlook offers an easier alternative. When you start your call and you see the New Call dialog box, shown in Figure 42.8, activate the Create new Journal Entry when starting call check box. When you click Start Call, Outlook displays the Journal Entry form, sets the Duration to 0 minutes, and starts the timer. When you complete your call, click the Save and Close button.

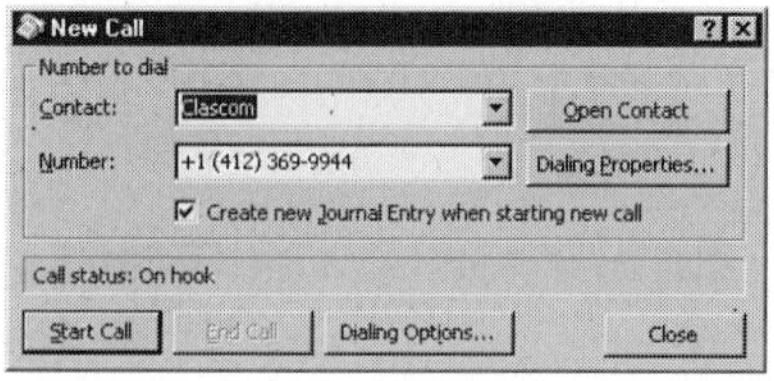

FIGURE 42.8.

You can create a Journal entry for the phone calls you initiate within Outlook.

Setting Up Journal to Create Entries Automatically

Journal is an interesting tool with some interesting potential uses. However, you might not feel like creating Journal entries for every task you perform. Similarly, you might find that you forget to record some entries.

To take some of the drudgery out of creating Journal entries, Outlook lets you set up automatic entries for certain types of activities. To see how this works, select Tools | Options. In the Options dialog box that appears, activate the Journal tab, shown in Figure 42.9. Here's a description of the controls in this tab:

> **Automatically record these items:** Place check marks beside the entry types you want Journal to record automatically.
>
> **For these contacts:** If you want to apply the selected activities to only certain contacts, activate the appropriate check boxes in this list.
>
> **Also record file from:** These check boxes determine which Office applications Journal will track. Journal will record the opening and closing times of any document related to these applications.
>
> **Double-clicking a journal entry:** These options determine what Outlook does when you double-click a Journal entry.
>
> **AutoArchive Journal Entries:** Click this button to decide what to do with old entries.

FIGURE 42.9.

Use the Journal tab to set up automatic entries.

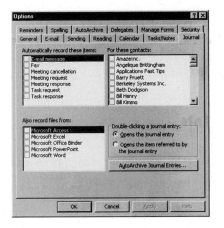

Working with Journal Views

The Journal folder comes with half a dozen predefined views. The By Type view is the default, but feel free to check out the others to get a new look at your tasks:

> **By Contact:** Groups the entries according to the contacts.
>
> **By Category:** Groups the entries by category.

Entry List: A table that shows columns for Entry Type, Subject, Start, Duration, Contact, and Categories.

Last Seven Days: A tabular view that filters the entries to show only those with a Start date within the last week.

Phone Calls: Filters the entries to show only phone calls.

To change the view, use either of the following methods:

- Select View | Current View and then choose the view you want from the cascade menu that appears.

- Use the Current View drop-down list on the toolbar.

NOTE: CUSTOM JOURNAL FOLDER VIEWS

As usual, you're free to set up custom views. I explain how in Chapter 38. Also, you can customize tabular views with new sort orders, groups, and filters. Again, Chapter 38 is the place to find out the details.

Notes: Electronic Sticky Notes

The final stop on our Outlook tour is the Notes folder. Notes are little text boxes that you can use for jotting down phone numbers, ideas, reminders, quotations, interesting words and phrases, or anything else that you need to record quickly. They're the digital equivalent of the Post-it Notes that many of us have plastered all over our monitors and walls. Best of all, Notes are independent of the Outlook window, so you can position them on your screen wherever they'll be noticed.

Creating a Note

Creating a new note is a breeze. First, open the Notes folder and select Note | New Note (or press Ctrl-N). In the yellow window that appears (see Figure 42.10), type in your text. The note will then remain on-screen, independent of the Outlook window (unless you close Outlook, of course). If you'd prefer not to see the note, click the Close button (the X in the upper-right corner).

FIGURE 42.10.

An example of an Outlook note.

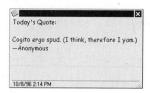

Today's Quote:

Cogito ergo spud. (I think, therefore I yam.)
—Anonymous

10/8/96 2:14 PM

Another way to create a note is to highlight some text in another application, drag the text, and then drop it inside the Notes folder.

Once your note is created, you can work with it using the following techniques:

- To change the note color, right-click the note, choose Color from the context menu, and then choose the color you want from the cascade menu.

- If you want to assign a category, right-click the note, choose Categories, and then use the Categories dialog box to assign one or more categories.

Using Notes Views

You've seen how other Outlook folders offer different views of their items, and the Notes folder is no exception. Select View | Current View, or drop down the Current View toolbar list, and then choose one of the following views:

Notes List: Displays the notes in a tabular format that shows the first few lines of note text.

Last Seven Days: A tabular view that filters the notes to show only those that were created in the last week.

By Category: Groups the notes by category.

By Color: Groups the notes by color.

Setting Notes Options

The Tasks/Notes tab in the Options dialog box (shown in Figure 42.4) sports a few Note-related controls:

Note defaults: Use the Color list to choose the default note color, and use the Size list to choose the default note size.

Font: Click this button to set the default font for the notes.

Show time and date: When this check box is activated, Outlook displays at the bottom of each note the date and time that the note was created.

Summary

This chapter closed our look at Outlook by examining the remaining three folders: Tasks, Journal, and Notes. For the Tasks folder, I showed you how to create new tasks, work with task requests, and send status reports for in-progress tasks. For the Journal, I showed you how to create entries from scratch, make the Journal and Contacts list work together, create Journal entries while making phone calls, and set up Outlook to generate Journal entries automatically. For Notes, you learned how to create notes and adjust their properties. In each folder, you also saw the various options that are available, as well as how to work with different views.

Here's a list of chapters where you'll find related information:

- See Chapter 38, "Advanced Outlook E-Mail Topics," to learn how to display different fields; sort, group, and filter folder items; and create custom views.
- I described how to use AutoDate—Outlook's natural-language date feature—in Chapter 40, "Places to Go: Calendar."

VIII
PART

Unleashing the Office Internet Tools

Understanding Web Documents

CHAPTER

43

It's given new meaning to me of the scientific term black hole.

—*Don Logan, on Web site spending*

The last couple of years have seen a huge increase in the popularity of the World Wide Web. Not only are people surfing like there's no tomorrow, but everyone from individuals to Fortune 500 corporations is rushing to set up shop in cyberspace. For individuals, a Web site is a great way to let other surfers know you're out there. (On my Web site, for example, I have data about my books, updates to the printed material, extra chapters, mailing list archives, and more.) For corporations, the Web is useful for customer contact: tech support, marketing information, product announcements, contests, and even online commerce.

However, Web technology hasn't only spurred massive growth in the Internet's public highways and byways. IT managers all over the world have come to the realization that they can leverage existing technologies such as TCP/IP, Web servers, and Web browsers to create private, internal internets—or *intranets,* as they're usually called. In fact, it's likely that the majority of corporations are sinking more money into developing intranet sites than Internet sites. Why? Well, there are many reasons:

- Once you "get" the idea of an intranet, you can usually think of dozens of ways that it can benefit your business. Corporate reporting, financial data, announcements, archives of frequently-used files (such as proprietary graphics files), scheduling, document collaboration—the list is endless.

- Intranets can work with existing content. For example, years ago I worked at a large corporation that maintained a database that had thousands of internal employee phone numbers. This database was printed each month, and a copy was distributed to everyone in the company. Needless to say, the printed version was out of date the moment the ink was dry. If we'd had an intranet, we could have created an online phone book that was updated dynamically from the database. As you'll soon see, one of the major goals of Office 97 is to allow existing documents (such as Word and Excel files) to be posted seamlessly (that is, without conversion to HTML) on intranets.

- An intranet usually doesn't have the same bandwidth limitations that exist with an Internet connection. This means that there are fewer restrictions on the number of files you can post and on the size of those files. It's also possible to provide richer content (such as multimedia files).

- An intranet, since it is by definition not connected to the public Internet, is inherently more secure (although precautions must still be taken if the network has an Internet gateway).

Given the success of both intranets and the Internet, the big question nowadays is how to deliver Web-based content quickly and cheaply, yet still maintain a high level of quality. That's where Office 97 comes in. Microsoft has crammed an amazing number of Web publishing tools into their flagship suite, so there's bound to be at least one that suits your needs. The purpose of the chapters here in Part VIII is to introduce you to each of these tools and to show you how to wield them to publish Web pages, either internally or on the Internet. First, though, this chapter presents an introduction to Web documents, including ActiveX controls and HTML tags. These basics will serve you well in the chapters to come.

First, a Few Words from the Web

Like all of the Internet's services, the Web has its own vernacular and acronyms. To make sure that we're reading from the same Web page, so to speak, here's a glossary of some common Web jargon:

applet   A Java program.

bandwidth   A measure of how much data can be stuffed through a transmission medium such as a phone line or network cable. There's only so much bandwidth to go around at any given time, so you'll see lots of Net paranoia about "wasting bandwidth." Bandwidth is measured in *bits per second.*

bit   The fundamental unit of computer information (it's a blend of the words "binary" and "digit"). Computers do all their dirty work by manipulating a series of high and low electrical currents. A high current is represented by the digit 1, and a low current is represented by the digit 0. These 1s and 0s—the bits—are used to represent absolutely everything that goes on inside your machine.

bits per second (bps)   A measure of *bandwidth.* Because it takes eight bits to describe a single character, a transmission medium with a bandwidth of, say, 8 bps would send data at the pathetically slow rate of one character per second. Bandwidth is more normally measured in kilobits per second (Kbps, or thousands of bits per second). So, for example, a 28.8 Kbps modem can handle 28,800 bits per second. In the high end, bandwidth is measured in megabits per second (Mbps, or millions of bits per second).

form   A Web document used for gathering information from the reader. Most forms have at least one text field where you can enter text data (such as your name or the keywords for a search). More sophisticated forms also include check boxes, option buttons, and command buttons.

frames   Rectangular browser areas that contain separate sections of text, graphics, and HTML.

GIF   Graphics Interchange Format. The most commonly used graphics format on the Web.

hit   A single access of a Web page. A hit is recorded for a particular Web page each time a browser displays the page.

home page   The first hypertext document displayed when you follow a link to a Web server.

hosting provider   A company that provides you with storage space (usually at a fee) for your Web pages. The company runs a *Web server* that enables surfers to view your pages.

hot list   A collection of links to cool or interesting sites that you check out regularly.

HTML (Hypertext Markup Language)   The encoding scheme used to format a Web document. The various HTML "tags" define hypertext links, reference graphics files, and designate nontext items such as buttons and check boxes.

HTTP (Hypertext Transfer Protocol)   The protocol used by the Web to transfer hypertext documents and other Net resources.

hyperlink   Another name for a hypertext link.

image map   A "clickable" *inline image* that takes you to a different page, depending on which part of the image you click.

inline image   An image displayed within a Web page.

Java   A programming language designed to create software that runs inside a Web page.

JPEG   A common Web graphics format developed by the Joint Photographic Experts Group. See also *GIF*.

link   A word or phrase that, when selected, sends the reader to a different page or to a different location on the same page.

surf   To leap from one Web page to another by furiously clicking any link in sight; to travel through cyberspace.

URL (Uniform Resource Locator)   An Internet addressing scheme that spells out the exact location of a Net resource. Most URLs take the following form:

```
protocol://host.domain/directory/file.name
```

`protocol`	The TCP/IP protocol to use for retrieving the resource (such as HTTP or FTP).
`host.domain`	The domain name of the host computer where the resource resides.
`directory`	The host directory that contains the resource.
`file.name`	The filename of the resource.

VRML   Virtual Reality Modeling Language. Used to create Web sites that are 3-D "worlds" that you "enter" using a VRML-enhanced browser. You can then use the mouse to "move" around this world in any direction.

Web server   A program that responds to requests from Web browsers to retrieve resources. This term is also used to describe the computer that runs the server program.

An HTML Primer

If you've seen some World Wide Web pages in your Internet travels, you might think you need some high-end word processor or page layout application to achieve all those fancy effects. Well, although you *can* use a sophisticated software package, the truth is that any basic text editor (such as the Notepad accessory that comes with Windows) is all you need to create attractive Web pages.

The secret is that, underneath all the bells and whistles, Web pages are relatively simple affairs. You just type in your text and then you insert markers—called *tags*—that dictate how you want things to look. For example, if you'd like a word on your page to appear in bold text, you surround that word with the appropriate tags for boldness.

In general, tags use the following format:

```
<TAG>The text to be affected</TAG>
```

The TAG part is a code (usually one or two letters) that specifies the type of effect you want. For example, the tag for bolding is <B>. So if you wanted the phrase ACME Coyote Supplies to appear in bold, you'd type the following into your document:

```
<B>ACME Coyote Supplies</B>
```

The first <B> tells the browser to display all text that follows in a bold font. This continues until the </B> is reached. The slash (/) defines this as an *end tag,* which tells the browser to turn off the effect. As you'll see, there are tags for lots of other effects, including italics, paragraphs, headings, page titles, lists, and lots more. HTML is just the sum total of all these tags.

These days you don't need to know HTML tags to create Web pages. For example, in Chapter 45, "Creating Web Documents in Word," you'll learn how to use Word's menus and toolbars to put pages together. However, you need to bear in mind that all the techniques you'll learn in that chapter are, in the end, creating HTML tags (albeit behind the scenes). So knowing a bit about how HTML tags work will help you understand what's going on in Chapter 45 and in the rest of Part VIII. And, if you're having trouble getting Word or some other Office program to get your pages just right, you can always examine the HTML code and make some adjustments by hand.

43

UNDERSTANDING
WEB DOCUMENTS

NOTE: HTML REFERENCE

This section presents only the briefest of introductions to HTML. Most of the tags I'll be talking about have a number of attributes that you can use to refine each tag's behavior. Fortunately, Internet Explorer 3 comes with the ActiveX Control Pad, which has an HTML reference that you can use to get the full story on each tag. To view this reference, start the ActiveX Control Pad (see Chapter E2 on the CD, "Web Page Programming: ActiveX and VBScript") and then select Help | HTML Reference.

The Basic Structure of Web Pages

Web pages range from dull to dynamic, inane to indispensable, but they all have the same underlying structure. This consistent structure—which, as you'll see, is nothing more than a small collection of HTML tags—is the reason why almost all browser programs running on almost all types of computers can successfully display almost all Web pages.

HTML files always start with the <HTML> tag. This tag doesn't do much except tell any Web browser that tries to read the file that it's dealing with a file that contains HTML codes. Similarly, the last line in your document will always be the </HTML> tag, which you can think of as the HTML equivalent for "The End."

The next items in the HTML tag catalog serve to divide the document into two sections: the *head* and the *body*.

The head section is like an introduction to the page. Web browsers use the head to glean various types of information about the page. Although a number of items can appear in the head section, the most common is the title of the page, which I'll talk about shortly. To define the head, you add a <HEAD> tag and a </HEAD> tag immediately below the <HTML> tag.

The body section is where you enter the text and other tags that will actually appear on the Web page. To define the body, you place a <BODY> tag and a </BODY> tag after the head section (that is, below the </HEAD> tag).

These tags define the basic structure of every Web page:

```
<HTML>

<HEAD>
Header tags go here.
</HEAD>

<BODY>
The Web page text and tags go here.
</BODY>

</HTML>
```

Adding a Title

The next item you need to add is the title of the Web page. The page's title is just about what you might think it is: the overall name of the page (not to be confused with the name of the file you're creating). If someone views the page in a graphical browser (such as Netscape or Internet Explorer), the title appears in the title bar of the browser's window.

To define a title, you surround the text with the <TITLE> and </TITLE> tags. For example, if you wanted the title of your page to be *My Home Sweet Home Page*, you'd enter it as follows:

```
<TITLE>My Home Sweet Home Page</TITLE>
```

Note that you always place the title inside the head section, so your basic HTML document will now look like this:

```
<HTML>
<HEAD>
<TITLE>My Home Sweet Home Page</TITLE>
</HEAD>
<BODY>
</BODY>
</HTML>
```

Text and Paragraphs

With your page title firmly in place, you can now think about the text you want to appear in the body of the page. For the most part, you can simply type the text between the `<BODY>` and `</BODY>` tags.

Things get a little tricky when you want to start a new paragraph. In most text editors and word processors, starting a new paragraph is a simple matter of pressing the Enter key to move to a new line. You can try doing that in your Web page, but the browsers that read your page will ignore this "white space." Instead, you have to use the `<P>` tag to tell the browser that you want to move to a new paragraph:

```
<HTML>
<HEAD>
<TITLE>My Home Sweet Home Page</TITLE>
</HEAD>
<BODY>
This text appears in the body of the Web page.
<P>
This text appears in a new paragraph.
</BODY>
</HTML>
```

Adding Formatting and Headings

HTML has lots of tags that will spruce up your page text. You saw earlier how a word or phrase surrounded by the `<B>` and `</B>` tags will appear in **bold** in a browser. You can also display text in *italics* by bracketing it with the `<I>` and `</I>` tags, and you can make your words appear in `monospace` by surrounding them with the `<TT>` and `</TT>` tags.

NOTE: MORE FONT FUN

Internet Explorer also supports the `<FONT>` tag:

`<FONT SIZE=n FACE=name COLOR=color>`

Here, `SIZE` specifies the text size, `FACE` specifies a font name, and `COLOR` specifies the text color. See the HTML reference for details on these attributes.

Like chapters in a book, many Web pages divide their contents into several sections. To help separate these sections and make life easier for the reader, you can use *headings*. Ideally, these headings act as mini-titles that convey some idea of what each section is all about. To make these titles stand out, HTML has a series of heading tags that display text in a larger, bold font. There are six heading tags in all, ranging from <H1>, which uses the largest font, down to <H6>, which uses the smallest font.

 To illustrate these text formatting and heading tags, Figure 43.1 shows how Internet Explorer displays the following text (see Formats.htm on the CD):

```
<HTML>
<HEAD>
<TITLE>My Home Sweet Home Page</TITLE>
</HEAD>
<BODY>
This text appears in the body of the Web page.
<P>
This text appears in a new paragraph.
<P>
You can create various text formatting effects,
including <B>bold text</B>, <I>italic text</I>,
and <TT>monospaced text</TT>.

<H1>An H1 Heading</H1>
<H2>An H2 Heading</H2>
<H3>An H3 Heading</H3>
<H4>An H4 Heading</H4>
<H5>An H5 Heading</H5>
<H6>An H6 Heading</H6>

</BODY>
</HTML>
```

Figure 43.1.

Examples of text formatting and heading tags.

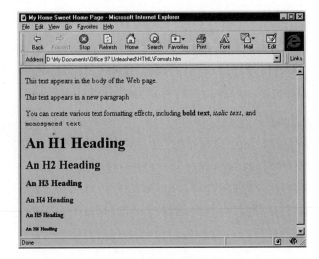

Setting Up Lists

HTML offers three different list styles: numbered lists, bulleted lists, and definition lists. This section takes you through the basics of each list type.

If you want to include a numbered list of items—a Top Ten list, bowling league standings, or any kind of ranking—don't bother adding the numbers yourself. Instead, you can use HTML *ordered lists* to make the Web browser generate the numbers for you.

Ordered lists use two types of tags:

■ The entire list is surrounded by the <OL> and </OL> tags.

■ Each item in the list is preceded by the <LI> (list item) tag.

The general setup looks like this:

```
<OL>
<LI>First item.
<LI>Second item.
<LI>Third item.
<LI>You get the idea.
</OL>
```

Of course, numbered lists aren't the only kinds of lists. If you just want to list a few points, a *bulleted list* might be more your style. They're called "bulleted" lists because a Web browser displays a small dot or square (depending on the browser) called a *bullet* to the left of each item.

The HTML tags for a bulleted list are pretty close to the ones you saw for a numbered list. As before, you precede each list item with the <LI> tag, but you enclose the entire list in the <UL> and </UL> tags. Why <UL>? Well, what the rest of the world calls a bulleted list, the HTML powers-that-be call an *unordered list.* Here's how they work:

```
<UL>
<LI>First bullet point.
<LI>Second bullet point.
<LI>Third bullet point.
<LI>And so on
</UL>
```

The final type of list is called a *definition list.* It was originally used for dictionary-like lists in which each entry had two parts: a term and a definition. However, definition lists are useful for more than just definitions.

To define the two different parts of each entry in these lists, you need two different tags. The term is preceded by the <DT> tag, and the definition is preceded by the <DD> tag:

```
<DT>Term<DD>Definition
```

You then surround all your entries with the <DL> and </DL> tags to complete your definition list. Here's how the whole thing looks:

```
<DL>
<DT>A Term<DD>Its Definition
```

```
<DT>Another Term<DD>Another Definition
<DT>Yet Another Term<DD>Yet Another Definition
<DT>Etc.<DD>Abbreviation of a Latin phrase that means "and so forth."
</DL>
```

Figure 43.2 shows how the various types of lists appear in Internet Explorer (see Lists.htm on the CD).

Figure 43.2.

How HTML lists appear in a browser.

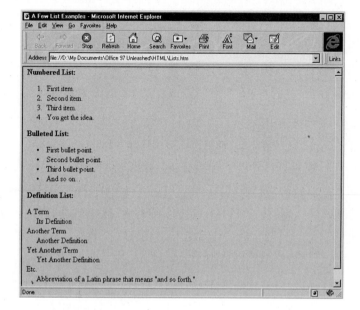

Working with Hyperlinks

As I mentioned earlier, the "H" in HTML stands for hypertext, which is dynamic text that defines a *link* to another document. The user clicks the hypertext, and the browser takes him to the linked document.

The HTML tags that set up links are <A> and </A>. The <A> tag is a little different from the other tags you've seen. Specifically, you don't use it by itself; instead, you add the address of the document to which you want to link. Here's how it works:

```
<A HREF="address">
```

Here, HREF stands for hypertext reference. Just replace *address* with the actual address of the Web page you want to use for the link (and, yes, you have to enclose the address in quotation marks). Here's an example:

```
<A HREF="http://www.mcp.com/sams/">
```

You're not done yet, though. Next you have to give the reader some descriptive link text to click on. All you do is insert the text between the <A> and </A> tags, like so:

```
<A HREF="address">Link text goes here</A>
```

Here's an example:

```
Why not head to the <A HREF="http://www.mcp.com/sams">Sams home page</A>?
```

 Figure 43.3 shows how this looks in a Web browser. Notice how the browser highlights and underlines the link text. When you point the mouse cursor at the link, the address you specified appears in the status bar (see Link.htm on the CD).

FIGURE 43.3.

How Internet Explorer displays the hypertext link.

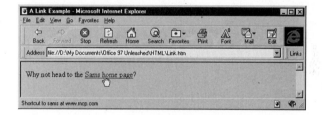

43

UNDERSTANDING WEB DOCUMENTS

NOTE: URL DEFINED

Internet addresses are called *uniform resource locators* (URLs). See the definition earlier in this chapter.

Inserting Images

If you're looking to make your Web site really stand out from the crowd, you need to go graphical with a few well-chosen images. How do you insert images if HTML files are text-only? As you'll see a bit later, all you'll really be doing (for each image you want to use) is adding a tag to the document that says, in effect, "Insert image here." This tag specifies the name of the graphics file, so the browser opens the file and displays the image.

Some computer wag once said that the nice thing about standards is that there are so many of them! Graphics files are no exception. It seems that every geek who ever gawked at a graphic has invented his own format for storing them on disk. There are images in GIF, JPEG, BMP, PCX, TIFF, DIB, EPS, and TGA formats, and those are just the ones I can think of off the top of my head. How's a budding Web page architect supposed to make sense of all this?

The good news is that the vast majority of browsers can handle only two formats: GIF and JPEG. (And some older browsers can't even handle JPEG.) Internet Explorer, however, can also work with Windows' native BMP and DIB formats.

As I mentioned earlier, there's an HTML code that tells a browser to display an image: the <IMG> tag. Here's how it works:

```
<IMG SRC="filename">
```

Here, SRC is short for "source," and *filename* is the name and path of the graphics file you want to display. For example, suppose you have an image named logo.gif and it's located in the Graphics folder. To add it to your page, you'd use the following line:

```
<IMG SRC="/Graphics/logo.gif">
```

NOTE: HANDLING NONGRAPHICAL BROWSERS

Some browsers can't handle images, and some surfers speed up their downloads by turning graphics off in their browser. In these situations, you should include a text description of the image by including the ALT attribute in the <IMG> tag:

```
<IMG SRC="filename" ALT="Alternative text">
```

Setting Up Tables

An HTML table is a rectangular grid of rows and columns in a Web page. You can enter all kinds of information into a table, including text, numbers, links, and even images. Your tables will always begin with the following basic container:

```
<TABLE>
</TABLE>
```

All the other table tags fit between these two tags. There are two things you need to know about the <TABLE> tag:

- If you want your table to show a border, use the <TABLE BORDER> tag.
- If you don't want a border, just use <TABLE>.

Once that's done, most of your remaining table chores will involve the following four-step process:

1. Add a row.
2. Divide the row into the number of columns you want.
3. Insert data into each cell.
4. Repeat steps 1 through 3 until done.

To add a row, you toss a `<TR>` (table row) tag and a `</TR>` tag (its corresponding end tag) between `<TABLE>` and `</TABLE>`:

```
<TABLE BORDER>
<TR>
</TR>
</TABLE>
```

Now you divide that row into columns by placing the `<TD>` (table data) and `</TD>` tags between `<TR>` and `</TR>`. Each `<TD>`/`</TD>` combination represents one column (or, more specifically, an individual cell in the row). Therefore, if you want a three-column table, you'd do this:

```
<TABLE BORDER>
<TR>
<TD></TD>
<TD></TD>
<TD></TD>
</TR>
</TABLE>
```

Now you enter the row's cell data by typing text between each `<TD>` tag and its `</TD>` end tag:

```
<TABLE BORDER>
<TR>
<TD>Row 1, Column1</TD>
<TD>Row 1, Column2</TD>
<TD>Row 1, Column3</TD>
</TR>
</TABLE>
```

Remember that you can put any of the following within the `<TD>` and `</TD>` tags:

- Text
- HTML text-formatting tags (such as `<B>` and `<I>`)
- Links
- Lists
- Images

 Once you've got your first row firmly in place, you simply repeat the procedure for the other rows in the table. For our sample table, here's the HTML that includes the data for all the rows (see Table.htm on the CD):

```
<TABLE BORDER>
<TR>
<TD>Row 1, Column1</TD>
<TD>Row 1, Column2</TD>
<TD>Row 1, Column3</TD>
</TR>
```

```
<TR>
<TD>Row 2, Column1</TD>
<TD>Row 2, Column2</TD>
<TD>Row 2, Column3</TD>
</TR>

<TR>
<TD>Row 3, Column1</TD>
<TD>Row 3, Column2</TD>
<TD>Row 3, Column3</TD>
</TR>
</TABLE>
```

Figure 43.4 shows the result in Internet Explorer.

FIGURE 43.4.

An HTML table in Internet Explorer.

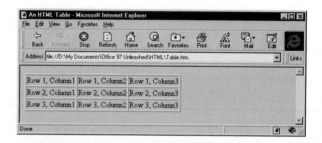

NOTE: TABLE HEADINGS

If you want to include headings at the top of each column, use `<TH>` (table heading) tags in the first row. Most browsers display text within a `<TH>/</TH>` combination in bold type. (Note, too, that you can just as easily use `<TH>` tags in the first column to create headers for each row.)

ActiveX: Making Web Pages Sing and Dance

Many people, originally stunned and amazed at the sheer wealth and diversity of information on the Web, eventually find themselves asking "Is that all there is?" The problem is that after you've read all those marketing blurbs, lists of "hot links," and let-me-tell-you-about-myself home pages, you begin to yearn for something more substantial. As you'll see in Chapter 46, "Web Forms and Databases," forms are a step in the right direction because they at least let you interact with a page.

However, 1996 was the year that pages moved away from the simple type-it-and-send-it world of forms and started performing the Web equivalent of singing and dancing. In other words, Web pages are no longer restricted to static displays of text and graphics, but instead have dynamic, kinetic, and truly *interactive* environments. Instead of being mere documents to read and look at, pages have become *programs* that you can manipulate and play with.

One of the engines that's propelling this transformation is called *ActiveX* (the technology formerly known as OLE controls). Web weavers can embed ActiveX controls right in their Web pages. These controls are miniprograms that can provide dynamic content that runs on the Web page. This content can be anything from games to stock market updates to OLE servers that let you view documents in their native format. For example, the Web page shown in Figure 43.5 shows a Web page running an ActiveX version of Minesweeper.

FIGURE 43.5.

Internet Explorer 3.0 showing a Web page with embedded ActiveX game.

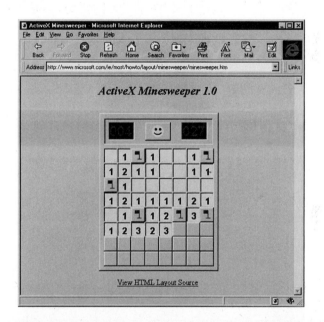

43

UNDERSTANDING WEB DOCUMENTS

NOTE: THERE'S JAVA, TOO

The other engine behind the trend toward interactive Web pages is the Java programming language. Developers can write Java programs and include them as part of a Web page. Java-enabled browsers then download these programs and run them in the page. Microsoft supports Java in Internet Explorer through the ActiveX technology. (Java applets will run inside a component called the ActiveX Java Virtual Machine.)

Here are a few advantages that ActiveX controls have over traditional software:

- The controls are sent to your browser and are started behind the scenes. You don't have to worry about installation, setup, or loading, because your browser takes care of all the dirty work for you.

- The controls are designed to be cross-platform. Whether you're running Windows, a Mac, or a UNIX platform, the controls should (eventually) run without complaint.

- Because you're always sent the latest and greatest version of the control when you access a site, you don't need to worry about upgrades and new releases.

Currently, only Internet Explorer 3.0 supports embedded ActiveX controls. However, Microsoft has signed up a whole slew of other browser companies to license the ActiveX technology. Not only that, but a company called NCompass has developed plug-in software that lets the Netscape Navigator browser support ActiveX controls (see `http://www.ncompasslabs.com/`). Combine this with the thousands of controls that already exist—and the fact that developers can create ActiveX controls without learning any new programming techniques and can create them using many different programming systems, from Visual C++ to Visual Basic (version 5.0)—and you can see that ActiveX will be ubiquitous on the Web before too long.

NOTE: MORE ACTIVEX INFORMATION

To learn about including ActiveX controls in your Web pages, see Chapter E2.

On a larger scale, Internet Explorer 3.0 is also the first application that supports Microsoft's new *Active Document* format. An Active Document is an OLE container that can hold any kind of ActiveX control. For example, Internet Explorer 3.0 is really just an empty container that can support various file types. If you load a Web page, Internet Explorer 3.0 loads its HTML parsing engine and displays the page appropriately. But it could just as easily operate as a spreadsheet engine or a word processing engine. In this case, Internet Explorer 3.0 would load the appropriate menus and toolbars for working with spreadsheet files or word processing documents. For example, Figure 43.6 shows Internet Explorer 3.0 displaying an Excel 97 worksheet. Notice that the Explorer interface changes to display Excel's menus and toolbars. (In order for this to work properly, you need to load Office 97 documents into Explorer. If you try to load documents that use the older formats, Explorer will just invoke the original application.)

Internet Explorer 3.0 is the first stage in Microsoft's long-term plan to create a seamless connection between the browser, applications, the operating system, and the Internet (or an intranet). As Figure 43.6 shows, you can now use Internet Explorer as a one-size-fits-all client for working with Office applications. Eventually, though, the browser will *become* the operating system, and the Windows desktop will be transformed into an *active desktop* that lets you view and work with local documents, network documents, Web pages, and remote documents. Remote sites will then be a simple extension of your desktop, and the browser's "surfing" metaphor will be used to navigate both locally and remotely.

FIGURE 43.6.

Internet Explorer 3.0 displaying an Excel worksheet.

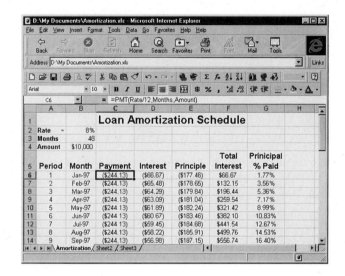

Visual Basic Scripting

ActiveX controls are a powerful way to create dynamic Web pages, but they still take a fairly high level of programming sophistication to create. For people with less programming time or inclination, Microsoft has created Visual Basic Scripting (VBScript) and provided support for this language in Internet Explorer 3.0.

VBScript is a subset of the Visual Basic programming language (in fact, it's a subset of Visual Basic for Applications). As such, it provides a simple way for developers of all skill levels to incorporate code into their Web pages. So, for example, you could run a program each time someone accesses a page, each time someone clicks a button, and so on. Developers can also use VBScript to process forms data and to access the properties and methods associated with ActiveX controls that are embedded in a Web page. And because Internet Explorer 3.0 is an ActiveX control itself, VBScript programs can control the browser's properties and methods.

I'll give you a VBScript tutorial in Chapter E2.

Summary

This chapter gave you a brief introduction to Web documents. You began with an HTML primer that covered all the basic tags, as well as text formatting, headings, lists, links, images, and tables. I then told you about ActiveX controls and the exciting plans Microsoft has in store for merging the browser and Windows. I closed with a look at VBScript.

Here's a list of chapters where you'll find related information:

- Turn to Chapter 44, "The Office 97 Internet Tools," to learn about the Web page publishing techniques and applications that ship with Office 97.
- Word's Web page building techniques are covered in Chapter 45, "Creating Web Documents in Word."
- To learn how to construct and work with forms, as well as how to use forms to query ODBC databases, see Chapter 46, "Web Forms and Databases."
- Internet Explorer includes a utility for embedding ActiveX controls in Web pages. It's called the ActiveX Control Pad, and it's covered in Chapter E2 on the CD, "Web Page Programming: ActiveX and VBScript."
- As I mentioned earlier, Chapter E2 is also the place to go for information on VBScript.
- I show you how to get connected to the Internet in Chapter E7 on the CD, "Setting Up an Internet Connection in Windows 95."

The Office 97 Internet Tools

CHAPTER

44

> *We're not forming an Internet division. To us, you know, it's like having an electricity*
> *division or a software division. The Internet is pervasive in everything that we're doing.*
>
> —*Bill Gates*

Back in Chapter 2, "What's New in Office 97," I told you that the Office 97 upgrade was first and foremost an *Internet* upgrade. That is, Microsoft spared no expense in bringing a huge number of tools and enhancements to the Office products in an effort to make the entire Office suite Net-friendly. Are these features enough to claim success? Well, you'll have to decide that for yourself as you work through the rest of the chapters here in Part VIII. It must be said, however, that pieces are still missing (at least at the time of this writing). For example, the Internet is still waiting for a standard object request broker (ORB) so that objects (such as ActiveX components) can communicate over networks. Microsoft's Distributed Component Object Model (DCOM) is designed to handle this and will likely be implemented in a future Windows release.

Along similar lines, Microsoft has yet to create a platform-independent specification for ActiveX. In other words, ActiveX controls work fine under Windows, but they don't work on other systems, such as Macintosh and UNIX. This creates quite a roadblock in ActiveX's path to becoming the Internet's object standard, because much of the Internet remains UNIX-based.

These points aside, however, there's no doubt that Office 97 is a quantum leap ahead of its predecessors in terms of creating Web content.

This chapter gets you started by examining a few of the Office 97 Web tools. You'll learn about browsing via the Office applications, inserting hyperlinks into your documents, Excel's Web Queries, saving documents in HTML format, the Web Publishing Wizard, and much more.

Browsing with Internet Explorer

There's certainly no shortage of Web browsers available, but most Office 97 users will probably opt for Internet Explorer. Why? Well, let's count the reasons:

- It comes free as part of the Office 97 suite.
- It's full to bursting with features that no other browser (with the possible exception of Netscape Navigator) can match.
- It supports many interesting new HTML innovations such as alternative fonts, floating frames, background sounds, and video. It also supports .BMP images.
- It supports ActiveX controls.
- It's an active document container, so you can use it to view and work with documents and files.

This section shows you how to use Internet Explorer, including how to navigate links, deal with files, and organize your Favorites folder.

A Tour of the Internet Explorer Screen

When you crank up Internet Explorer 3.0 (remember to establish a connection to your service provider first), you'll see the window shown in Figure 44.1.

FIGURE 44.1.

The Internet Explorer screen.

Title bar   Address bar   Standard toolbar   Links toolbar

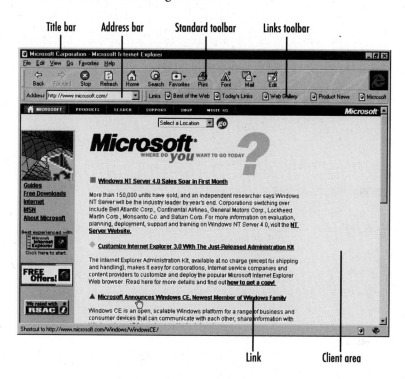

Link   Client area

Here's a summary of the main features of this screen:

Title bar: The top line of the screen shows you the title of the current Web page.

Standard toolbar: These buttons give you point-and-click access to some of Internet Explorer's main features. If you prefer to hide the toolbar (because, for example, you want more screen real estate), deactivate View | Toolbar.

Address toolbar: This area shows you the URL of the current page.

Links toolbar: This toolbar provides buttons that take you to some popular links. (If you don't see the full toolbar, use the mouse to drag the toolbar to the left.)

Client area: This is the area below the Address toolbar that takes up the bulk of the Internet Explorer screen. It's where the body of each Web page is displayed. You can use the vertical scrollbars to see more of the current document.

Link: Links to other documents (or to other places in the same document) are displayed underlined and in a different color. You select a link by clicking it. When you point to a link, Internet Explorer does two things: It changes the mouse pointer to a hand with a pointing finger, and in the Status bar it displays Shortcut to and the name of the document to which the link will take you.

Status bar: This bar lets you know Internet Explorer's current status, displays a description of the links you point to, and tells you the progress of the current Internet Explorer operation (such as downloading a file).

Navigating with Internet Explorer

Now that you're familiar with the lay of the Internet Explorer land, you can start using it to navigate sites. The next few sections take you through the various ways you can use Internet Explorer to wend your way through the Web.

Following the Links

As I said, Internet Explorer displays hypertext links in an underlined font that's a different color from the rest of the text. To follow one of these links, you have three choices:

- Click it with the mouse. (Image maps work the same way: Position the mouse pointer over the portion of the map you want to see, and then click.)
- Right-click the link and choose Open.
- Right-click the link and choose Open In New Window. This command spawns a new Internet Explorer window and opens the link URL in that window.

NOTE: OPENING A NEW WINDOW

You can open another Internet Explorer window at any time by selecting File | New Window or by pressing Ctrl-N.

Here are a few notes about working with links in Internet Explorer:

- To find out the name of the document that will open when you click a link, place the mouse pointer over the link, and the name will appear in the Status bar.
- If you want to see the full address of the link's URL, right-click the link and select Properties from the context menu.
- To copy the link's URL (for example, to reference the URL in an e-mail message), right-click the link and select Copy Shortcut from the context menu. This copies the URL to the Clipboard.
- If you select a link and then change your mind (or if a link is busy loading large graphics or animation files and you don't want to wait), you can stop the download by selecting View | Stop, by pressing Esc, or by clicking the Stop button on the toolbar.

- If you select a link and some of the objects don't load properly, you can reload the page by selecting View | Refresh, by pressing F5, or by clicking the toolbar's Refresh button.

- To e-mail a link shortcut to someone, click the link to open the page, and then select File | Send To | Mail Recipient. A new e-mail message appears that displays the URL in the Subject line and the page as an attachment. Specify a recipient and then send the message (see Chapter 37, "The Ins and Outs of the Outlook Inbox," for details).

Entering a URL

If you want to strike out for a particular Web site, you can specify a URL by using any of the following methods:

- Click inside the Address bar, delete the current URL, type the one you want, and press Enter.

- Select File | Open, or press Ctrl-O. In the Open dialog box that appears, shown in Figure 44.2, type your URL in the Open text box and click OK.

FIGURE 44.2.

Use this dialog box to enter the URL you want to see.

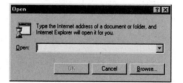

- From the Windows taskbar, select Start | Run, enter the URL in the Run dialog box, and click OK.

- If you want to open an HTML file or Office document that resides on your hard disk or your LAN, select File | Open, click the Browse button, highlight the file in the Open dialog box, and click Open.

Retracing Your Steps

After you've started leaping through the Web's cyberspace, you'll often want to head back to a previous site, or even to your start page. (MSN's Web site is the default start page, but later I'll show you how to designate any URL as your start page.) Here's a rundown of the various techniques you can use to move to and fro in Internet Explorer:

- To go back to the previous document, click the Back button on the toolbar, select Go | Back, or press Alt-left arrow.

- After you've gone back to a previous document, you can move ahead to the next document by clicking the Forward button on the toolbar, by selecting Go | Forward, or by pressing Alt-right arrow.

- To return to the start page, either click the Home toolbar button or select Go | Start Page.

44

THE OFFICE 97
INTERNET TOOLS

■ To return to a specific document you've visited, pull down the Go menu and select the document's title from the list at the bottom of the menu. If you need to see the document's URL or a larger list, select Go | Open History Folder. In the History folder that appears, double-click the document you want to open.

Creating a Shortcut to a URL

Another way to navigate Web sites via Internet Explorer is to create shortcuts that point to the appropriate URLs. You can use two methods to do this:

■ Use Internet Explorer to view the URL, and then select File | Create Shortcut. When Windows tells you that a shortcut will be placed on your desktop, click OK.

■ Copy the URL from the Address toolbar to the Clipboard, create a new Windows shortcut, and then paste the URL into the Command line text box.

■ To create a shortcut from a link, drag the link from the Web page and drop it on the desktop. Alternatively, you can right-click the link and choose Copy Shortcut from the context menu, and then right-click inside a folder and choose Paste Shortcut.

After your shortcut is in place, you can launch the Web site by double-clicking the shortcut's icon.

Using the Search Page

The navigation approaches you've tried so far have encompassed the two extremes of Web surfing: clicking links randomly to see what happens, and entering URLs to display specific sites. However, what if you're looking for information on a particular topic, but you don't know any appropriate URLs and you don't want to waste time clicking aimlessly around the Web? In this case, you'll want to put the Web to work for you. In other words, you'll want to use one of the Web's search engines to try to track down sites that contain the data you're looking for.

Conveniently, Internet Explorer contains a link that gives you easy access to a half dozen of the Web's best search engines (you can search the Microsoft and MSN Web sites as well). To view these links, select Go | Search the Web, or click the toolbar's Search the Internet button. You'll see the page shown in Figure 44.3. To try a search, enter your search text in one of the text boxes provided, and then click the Search button beside the text box. If you're not sure which search engine to try, select the choosing a search service link to see descriptions of each engine.

Dealing with Files

As you click your way around the Web, you'll find that some links don't take you to other pages but instead are tied directly to a file. In this case, you'll see the dialog box shown in Figure 44.4. If you want to view the file (for example, if you want to open a text file in Notepad), activate the Open it option. If you prefer to download the file to disk, activate Save it to disk, choose a location for the file in the Save As dialog box, and click Save.

FIGURE 44.3.

Internet Explorer displays this page when you click Search the Internet.

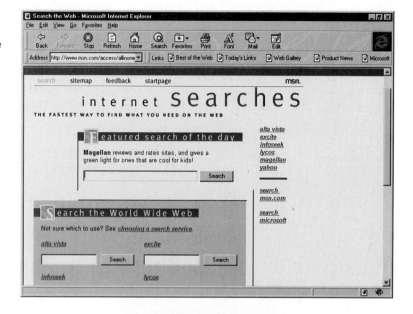

FIGURE 44.4.

You'll see this dialog box if a link is tied to a file.

44

The Favorites Folder: Sites to Remember

The sad truth is that much of what you'll see on the Web will be utterly forgettable and not worth a second look. However, there are a few gems out there waiting to be uncovered—sites you'll want to visit regularly. Instead of memorizing the appropriate URLs, jotting them down on sticky notes, or plastering your desktop with shortcuts, you can use Internet Explorer's handy Favorites feature to keep track of your choice sites.

The Favorites feature is really just a folder (you'll find it in your main Windows folder) that you use to store Internet shortcuts. The advantage of using the Favorites folder as opposed to any other folder is that you can add, view, and link to the Favorites folder shortcuts directly from Internet Explorer.

Adding a Shortcut to the Favorites Folder

When you find a site you want to declare as a favorite, select Favorites | Add To Favorites, or click the Favorites toolbar button and then choose Add To Favorites. In the Add To Favorites dialog box that appears, shown in Figure 44.5, the title of the Web page appears in the Name text box. Feel free to edit the name. If you've set up subfolders inside Favorites, click Create in>> to display a list of the subfolders. Highlight the folder you want to use to store the shortcut. When you're done, click OK.

FIGURE 44.5.

Use this dialog box to add a shortcut to the Favorites folder.

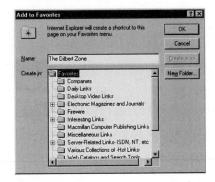

Viewing the Favorites Folder

If you want to work with the Favorites folder directly, use any of the following methods to display the folder:

- In Internet Explorer, select Favorites | Organize Favorites.
- In Explorer, highlight the Favorites subfolder either in your main Windows folder (Windows 95) or in your profile folder (Windows NT).
- Click the Favorites button and then choose Organize Favorites.

Figure 44.6 shows the Organize Favorites dialog box. From here, you can rename shortcuts, edit the contents of shortcuts (by right-clicking the shortcut and choosing Properties), delete shortcuts, and create new subfolders to organize your shortcuts.

FIGURE 44.6.

The Favorites folder stores your Internet shortcuts.

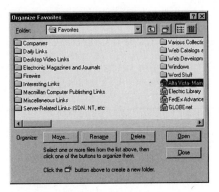

Opening an Internet Shortcut from the Favorites Folder

The purpose of the Favorites folder, of course, is to give you quick access to the sites you visit regularly. To link to one of the shortcuts in your Favorites folder, you have two choices:

- In Internet Explorer, the Favorites menu contains the complete list of your Favorites folder shortcuts. To link to a shortcut, pull down this menu and select the shortcut you want. You can also click the Favorites toolbar button and then choose the shortcut.

- Open the Favorites folder and double-click a shortcut.

Inserting Hyperlinks in Office Documents

One of the most interesting innovations in Office 97 is the capability to create hyperlinks in any kind of Office document: Word documents, Excel worksheets, Access databases, PowerPoint presentations, and even Outlook e-mail messages. This section shows you the various techniques available for inserting hyperlinks in Office documents.

Hyperlinks and Word

Word 97 now accepts hyperlinks within the body of a document. This lets you create "active" documents that allow the reader to click special text sections and "surf" to another document, which may be on the World Wide Web, your corporate intranet, or your hard drive.

For example, consider the Word document shown in Figure 44.7. As you can see, the phrase "amortization schedule" is displayed underlined and in a different color (blue). This formatting indicates that this phrase is a hyperlink. Clicking this link displays the Excel worksheet shown in Figure 44.8.

TIP: VIEWING THE LINK ADDRESS

To see where a hyperlink will take you, move the mouse pointer over the link text. After a second or two, a banner appears that tells you the name of the hyperlink document.

Word gives you no less than three methods for constructing a hyperlink:

- Use Word's AutoCorrect feature to create links automatically.
- Enter the appropriate information by hand.
- Paste information from another document.

The next few sections discuss each method.

FIGURE 44.7.

A Word document containing a hyperlink.

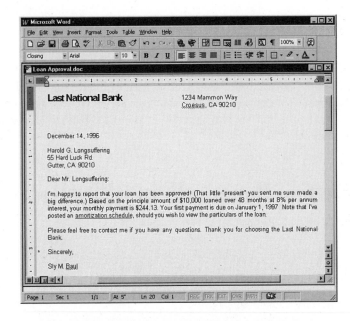

FIGURE 44.8.

Clicking the hyperlink displays this Excel worksheet.

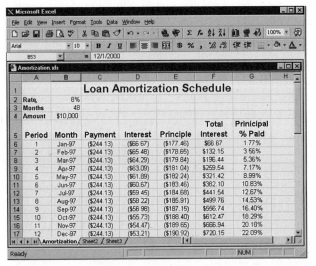

TIP: USE DRAG-AND-DROP TO CREATE LINKS

Word actually gives you a fourth method for creating a hyperlink: drag-and-drop. Just right-click and drag a file from Explorer or My Computer and drop it inside a Word document. In the context menu that appears, choose Create Hyperlink Here.

Creating a Hyperlink Using AutoCorrect

The easiest way to create a hyperlink in Word is just to type the address into your document. As long as the address is a network path or an Internet URL, Word will convert the text into a hyperlink, no questions asked.

If this doesn't work for you, you'll need to turn on this feature by following these steps:

1. Select Tools | AutoCorrect to display the AutoCorrect dialog box, shown in Figure 44.9.

FIGURE 44.9.

Use this dialog box to ensure that Word converts network paths and URLs to hyperlinks.

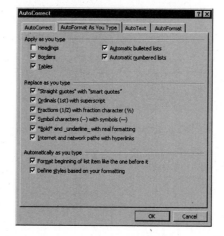

2. Activate the AutoFormat As You Type tab.
3. Activate the Internet and network paths with hyperlinks check box.
4. Click OK.

Creating a Hyperlink from Scratch

For more control over your hyperlinks, you need to use Word's Insert Hyperlink feature, which lets you specify not only link documents, but also named locations within documents (such as a named range within an Excel worksheet).

To get started, either highlight the text that you want to use for the hyperlink, or select the position in the document where you want the link to appear. Note that if you don't select any text beforehand, the link text will just be the hyperlink address.

Now you initiate the hyperlink definition either by selecting Insert | Hyperlink or by clicking the Insert Hyperlink button on Word's Standard toolbar (you can also press Ctrl-K). Word displays the Insert Hyperlink dialog box, shown in Figure 44.10, so that you can define the particulars of the hyperlink.

FIGURE 44.10.

Use the Insert Hyper-link dialog box to create your hyperlinks from scratch.

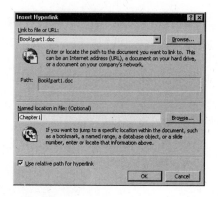

You begin by filling in the Link to file or URL text box. This is the name of the file or Web document that the user will jump to when he clicks the link. You can enter any of the following:

- A path to another Word document
- A path to a document from a different application on your hard drive
- A path to a multimedia file (such as a sound or video file)
- A network (UNC) path to a document on your company's intranet
- A URL on the World Wide Web

If you're not sure of the correct path, click the Browse button and select the file from the Link to File dialog box that appears.

The next control in the Insert Hyperlink dialog box is Named location in file. You use this optional text box to specify what part of the file you want the link to display. Note that, in Word, this feature works only for bookmarks, so you enter a bookmark name from the Word document to which you're linking. You can click Browse and choose the location from the Bookmark dialog box that appears, shown in Figure 44.11.

FIGURE 44.11.

Word hyperlinks can point to bookmarks within other Word documents.

Finally, if you activate the Use relative path for hyperlink check box, you don't need to enter a full path to the file. Instead, you need only enter a path that is relative to the Word document that contains the hyperlink. For example, suppose the Word document resides in the C:\My Documents\ folder and that you want to set up a link to a spreadsheet named Budget.xls in the C:\My Documents\Spreadsheets\ folder. With the Use relative path for hyperlink check box activated, you can enter the path for this spreadsheet as follows:

```
Spreadsheets\Budget.xls
```

This way, as long as the two documents remain in the same location relative to each other, you can move them without breaking the link.

When you're finished with the Insert Hyperlink dialog box, click OK to insert the hyperlink.

NOTE: WORKING WITH LINKS

If you right-click a hyperlink and then choose Hyperlink from the context menu, the cascade menu that appears contains the following commands:

> Open: Opens the linked document.
>
> Open in New Window: Creates a new window and then opens the linked document.
>
> Copy Hyperlink: Copies the hyperlink to the Clipboard.
>
> Add to Favorites: Displays the Add To Favorites dialog box so that you can include the link in your Favorites folder.
>
> Edit Hyperlink: Displays the Edit Hyperlink dialog box, which is identical to the Add Hyperlink dialog box.
>
> Select Hyperlink: Highlights the hyperlink text.

NOTE: INSERTED FILES PRESERVE LINKS

If you insert a file into a Word document (or into any Office document), and that file contains hyperlinks, Word will preserve the links.

Pasting a Hyperlink in Word

The final method for creating a hyperlink is to paste an object from the Clipboard. That is, you copy an object to the Clipboard—it could be a section of text, an Excel range, some records from a table, or whatever—select the spot in the document where you want the link to appear, and then select Edit | Paste Hyperlink. When you click this hyperlink, not only does Word load the application and document from which you copied the information, but it also moves to the spot in the document where the information resides.

Hyperlinks and Excel

Working with hyperlinks in Excel is more or less the same as with Word. The only major difference is that you can't type a URL or network path into a cell and have Excel convert it into a link automatically. This section examines three methods that you can use to insert hyperlinks into a worksheet.

Using the Insert Hyperlink Dialog Box

You can use the Insert Hyperlink dialog box (shown in Figure 44.11) to create hyperlinks in a cell. First, enter a word or phrase that you want to use as the link text. (If you don't do this, Excel will use the address of the hyperlink.) If you'd prefer to associate the hyperlink with an object (such as an image), click the object to select it.

Now select Insert | Hyperlink (or click the Insert Hyperlink button on Excel's Standard toolbar) to display the Insert Hyperlink dialog box, and enter the address or path of the linked document. If the document you're linking to is an Excel workbook, you can use the Named location in file text box to enter a range name.

Pasting a Hyperlink in Excel

As with Word, you can copy data to the Clipboard and then use Edit | Paste as Hyperlink to insert the data as a hyperlink.

Using the HYPERLINK Function

Excel 97 also has a new function—called HYPERLINK—that you can use to insert a hyperlink into a cell. Here's the general format for this function:

HYPERLINK(*address, Link text*)

address	The URL, local path, or network path of the document to which you want to link.
Link text	The text that will appear in the cell. If you omit this argument, Excel displays *address* instead.

For example, the following formula sets up a link to the Budget.xls workbook in the \\Server\Public folder and displays Budget Workbook in the cell:

=HYPERLINK("\\Server\Public\Budget.xls", "Budget Workbook")

Hyperlinks and Access

Unlike with Word and Excel, you can't just insert hyperlinks into Access at random. Instead, to work with hyperlinks in Access tables, you have to create a special field. Specifically, you have to create a field that uses the new Hyperlink data type (see Chapter 25, "Working with Tables"). If you're experimenting with the Northwind sample database that ships with Access, check out the Suppliers table, shown in Figure 44.12, for an example of a Hyperlink field.

FIGURE 44.12.

To add hyperlinks to an Access table, you need to create a field that uses the Hyperlink *data type.*

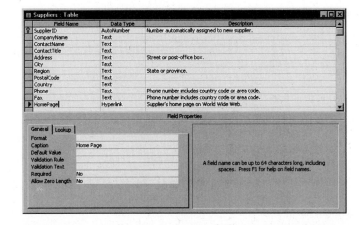

TIP: INSERTING LINKS IN DATASHEET VIEW

Rather than use Design view to add a Hyperlink column, you can do so quickly from Datasheet view by selecting Insert | Hyperlink Column.

Once the Hyperlink field is in place, you have two options for inserting a hyperlink into a cell:

- Select the cell and then type the URL, path, or network path for the document to which you want to link.

- Select Insert | Hyperlink to use the Insert Hyperlink dialog box to specify the link. If the document you're linking to is an Access database, you can use the Named location in file text box to enter the name of a table from that database.

Once the link is in place, simply click the cell to jump to the specified document. Figure 44.13 shows the Suppliers table with a few hyperlinks added.

FIGURE 44.13.

The Suppliers table with some sample hyperlinks.

Supplier ID	Company Name	Country	Home Page
1	Exotic Liquids	UK	http://www.exotic.com/
2	New Orleans Cajun Delights	USA	http://www.cajun.com/
3	Grandma Kelly's Homestead	USA	http://www.granny.net/homestead.html
4	Tokyo Traders	Japan	http://www.host.net/~tokyo/index.htm
5	Cooperativa de Quesos 'Las Cabras'	Spain	
6	Mayumi's	Japan	
7	Pavlova, Ltd.	Australia	http://www.pavlova.au/homepage.html
8	Specialty Biscuits, Ltd.	UK	
9	PB Knäckebröd AB	Sweden	http://www.knackered.com/bread.html
10	Refrescos Americanas LTDA	Brazil	
11	Heli Süßwaren GmbH & Co. KG	Germany	http://www.heli.de/
12	Plusspar Lebensmittelgroßmärkte AG	Germany	http://deutsche.net/~plusspar/
13	Nord-Ost-Fisch Handelsgesellschaft mbH	Germany	
14	Formaggi Fortini s.r.l.	Italy	
15	Norske Meierier	Norway	
16	Bigfoot Breweries	USA	#http://www.bigfoot.com/stomp.html#
17	Svensk Sjöföda AB	Sweden	
18	Aux joyeux ecclésiastiques	France	
19	New England Seafood Cannery	USA	
20	Leka Trading	Singapore	

Record: 14 ◄ 16 ► ►I ►* of 30

When working with Access hyperlinks, bear in mind that some of the normal Access editing methods don't apply. For example, you might normally edit a cell by first clicking it to get the insertion point cursor and then making changes. With a Hyperlink field, however, you can't get the cursor by clicking (because that just activates the link). Instead, you need to either use the keyboard (highlight the cell and press F2) or right-click the cell and choose Hyperlink | Select Hyperlink from the context menu.

Also, you need to be careful when you're editing a hyperlink. As you can see in Figure 44.13 (record 16), Access displays pound signs (#) around the link. Access ignores anything you enter *after* the last pound sign. So if you're adding to the address, make sure you do it within the pound signs. Note, however, that anything *before* the first pound sign is used as link text. So instead of displaying, say, a URL, you can enter a description or name.

In general, then, Access hyperlinks take the following form:

```
Link Text#link address#
```

For example, suppose you enter the following into a cell:

```
Click here to load the memo#C:\My Documents\memo.doc#
```

Access will display only Click here to load the memo in the cell.

TIP: VIEWING THE LINK ADDRESS

For a cell that's displaying link text, you can see the address to which the link points by moving the mouse pointer over the hyperlink. Access displays the address in the status bar.

Hyperlinks and PowerPoint

You can also add hyperlinks to your PowerPoint presentations. You can use two methods:

The Insert | Hyperlink command: Select some text or an image and then select this command (or click the Insert Hyperlink button on the toolbar). PowerPoint will display the usual Insert Hyperlink dialog box. Note that if the document you're linking to is a PowerPoint presentation, you can use the Named location in file text box to enter a slide name.

Pasting an object as a hyperlink: As with the other Office products, you can copy data to the Clipboard and then select Edit | Paste as Hyperlink to insert the data as a hyperlink.

Office 97 and FTP

One of Microsoft's long-term goals is to blur the distinction between resources residing on your hard drive and resources located on the Internet. For example, you know that you can map a shared network resource so that it appears to be just another drive attached to your computer. In the same way, Microsoft wants you to be able to access Internet sites so that they too appear to be another local resource.

Office 97 provides the first step toward this goal by implementing support for accessing FTP sites from within the Open and Save As dialog boxes. Specifically, you can download files from FTP sites and upload files to FTP sites all within the comfort of any Office application.

When you display the Open or Save As dialog box and drop down the Look in list (or the Save in list, as it's called in the Save As dialog box), you'll see that it contains an item called Internet Locations (FTP). Selecting this item displays a list of the FTP sites that you've defined, as shown in Figure 44.14. (I'll show you how to define FTP sites shortly.) Double-clicking one of these sites logs you into the FTP server (assuming that you have the appropriate privileges to do so) and displays the files and directories available, as shown in Figure 44.15. From here, you have two choices:

- If you're opening a file, highlight it and click Open to display it inside the Office application. (I'm assuming, of course, that the application can handle the file type you select.)

- If you're saving a file, select the location, change the name, if necessary, and click Save. This will store the file on the FTP server.

In other words, the FTP site has become a direct extension of your local computer!

Figure 44.14.

Office 97's Open and Save As dialog boxes let you work with FTP sites.

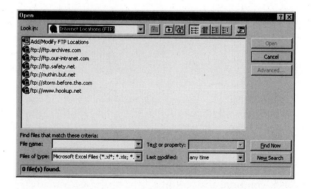

Figure 44.15.

Opening an FTP location displays the files and directories available.

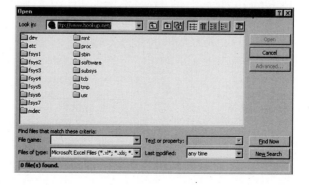

TIP: DIRECT DIRECTORY ACCESS

If you open directories while in the FTP site, the Look in list "remembers" them and displays them in a tree below the site name. Therefore, you can head directly for a particular directory by selecting it from the Look in list.

Here are the steps to follow to define an FTP location:

1. In any Office 97 application, display either the Open dialog box or the Save As dialog box.

2. Use the Look in list to select Internet Locations (FTP).

3. Double-click Add/Modify FTP Locations. You'll see the Add/Modify FTP Locations dialog box, shown in Figure 44.16.

FIGURE 44.16.

Use this dialog box to define FTP sites.

4. In the Name of FTP site text box, enter the host name of the FTP server (for example, `ftp.domain.com`).

5. Use the Log on as group to enter your login information:

   ■ If you have an account on the server, activate the User option, enter your user name in the text box provided, and enter your password in the Password text box.

   ■ If you don't have an account, but the server accepts anonymous logins, activate the Anonymous option and enter your e-mail address in the Password text box.

6. Click Add. The site is added to the FTP sites list.

7. Repeat steps 4 through 6 to define other FTP sites.

8. When you're done, click OK.

Displaying Web Pages in Excel

Excel 97 now supports the HTML format. Therefore, if a Web page contains data that you need, the easiest way to get at it is to open the page right in Excel. This section shows you how to open Web pages, explains Excel's HTML limitations, and outlines the HTML extensions that Excel supports.

Opening a Web Page in Excel

As usual, select File | Open to display the Open dialog box. After this, you have two choices:

■ If the page resides on your hard drive or local area network, use the Files of type dropdown list to choose HTML Document, highlight the file, and click Open.

■ If the page resides on the Internet or your corporate intranet, use the File name text box to enter the Web page's URL (for example, `http://www.our-intranet.com/data.html`), and then click Open.

Keep in mind, however, that Excel won't necessarily display the Web page in the same way that a browser would. Although Excel's HTML support includes most formatting tags, there are quite a few tags that it won't display. Here's a quick rundown of how Excel treats various categories of HTML tags:

■ Most character formatting tags are supported, including the tags for bold, italic, underlined, and monospaced text, as well as the `<FONT>` tag's various attributes (`COLOR`, `SIZE`, and `FONT`).

■ Heading tags are converted into the equivalent Heading styles.

■ Links are preserved intact.

■ Definition lists are displayed as two-column lists, while bulleted and numbered lists are displayed in a single column.

■ `<P>` tags convert to blank rows.

■ Most table tags and attributes are supported.

Note, however, that Excel does *not* support the tags for images and forms.

Excel's HTML Extensions

One of the most interesting innovations in Excel 97 is its support for extra features not found in the standard HTML specifications. These features serve to extend HTML to give a Web page some of Excel's native functionality. Note, however, that these extensions are available only if you view the page in Excel; Web browsers will ignore these attributes (yet still display the page normally).

These extensions affect the `<TABLE>` tag, and there are three in all: `FORMULA`, `AUTOFILTER`, and `CROSSTAB`.

The FORMULA Attribute

The FORMULA attribute is an extension of both the `<TH>` and `<TD>` tags. Recall from the last chapter that you use `<TH>` and `<TD>` to define a single cell in a table. The FORMULA attribute, as its name suggests, defines an Excel formula expression. When you use Excel to view a page that uses FORMULA, Excel enters the formula into a cell and proceeds to calculate the result. Thus, with little effort and no programming whatsoever, you can create dynamic, formula-driven Web pages.

Here's the syntax to use with the FORMULA attribute:

```
FORMULA="=expression"
```

Here, *expression* is a legal Excel expression, as shown in the following example:

```
<TABLE>
<TR>
<TH>Sales
<TH>Expenses
<TH>Profit

<TR>
<TD>100
<TD>85
<TD FORMULA="=A2-B2">Sales-Expenses
</TABLE>
```

Figure 44.17 shows how Excel displays these tags. Notice how the formula defined by the FORMULA attribute has been entered into cell C2. In contrast, Figure 44.18 shows the same page displayed in Internet Explorer. As you can see, the browser ignores the FORMULA attribute completely and just displays the text after the `<TD>` tag.

FIGURE 44.17.

Use the FORMULA *attribute to display work with Web page calculations while viewing the page in Excel.*

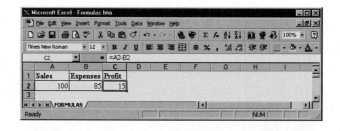

FIGURE 44.18.

Browsers ignore the FORMULA *attribute.*

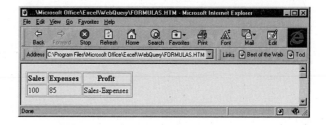

> ### NOTE: THE EXCEL WEB CONNECTIVITY KIT
>
> The examples I'm using to demonstrate Excel's extended HTML attributes are part of the Excel Web Connectivity Kit, which comes with the Office 97 Resource Kit. It is also available on the Web at this address:
>
> `http://www.microsoft.com/OfficeFreeStuff/Excel/`
>
> Note, however, that I've modified the examples slightly to suit the purposes of this chapter.

The AUTOFILTER Attribute

As explained in Chapter 19, "Working with Lists and Databases," Excel's AutoFilter features add drop-down arrows to the top of each column in a table. These arrows display lists that contain all the unique values in the column. If you select a value from one of these lists, Excel shows only those records that match the selected value.

You can add AutoFilter functionality to your Web pages by including the AUTOFILTER attribute in the <TABLE>, <TR>, <TH>, or <TD> tags. Here's the AUTOFILTER syntax:

```
AUTOFILTER="value"
```

Here, *value* is the unique value upon which you want to filter the table. Note that Excel also accepts (ALL), (BLANKS), and (NONBLANKS) for *value*. Here are some points to bear in mind:

- ■ If you use AUTOFILTER in the <TABLE> tag, the same *value* is applied to all columns. In this context, it only makes sense to use a nonspecific *value* such as (ALL) or (NONBLANKS).

- ■ If you use AUTOFILTER in the <TR> tag, the same *value* is applied to all the cells in the row.

- ■ If you use AUTOFILTER in the <TD> or <TH> tag, the *value* is used to filter only that column.

Here's an example:

```
<TABLE>
<TR>
<TD>Store #
<TD AUTOFILTER="(NONBLANKS)">Date
<TD>Channel
<TD AUTOFILTER="Brass">Division
</TABLE>
```

Figure 44.19 shows the results on some sample data. Notice how the table is filtered to include only those records where the Date column isn't blank and the Division column contains "Brass."

FIGURE 44.19.

The AUTOFILTER
attribute in action.

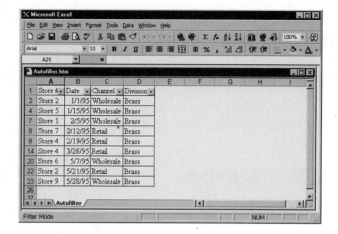

The CROSSTAB Attribute

As you learned in Chapter 20, "Creating and Customizing Pivot Tables," Excel's pivot tables are a great way to knock a large amount of data down to size. If that data happens to reside inside a Web page table, you can still apply a pivot table analysis to the numbers. The secret is Excel's CROSSTAB attribute. You use this in the <TABLE> tag. It instructs Excel to display the table's data in a pivot table. If you want Excel to display grand totals in the pivot table, add the following to the <TABLE> tag (in addition to CROSSTAB):

CROSSTABGRAND=*VALUE*

Here, *VALUE* can be NONE (no grand totals), ROW (grand totals in the rows only), COL (grand totals for the columns only), or ROWCOLUMN (grand totals for both rows and columns).

To refine the pivot table, Excel has six extensions to the <TH> and <TD> tags that define things such as the row field, column field, data field, and so on. Note that you must use these extensions in the first row of data. Here's a summary:

ROWFIELD: Use this attribute in the <TD> or <TH> tag of the column you want to use as the row field.

COLFIELD: Use this attribute in the <TD> or <TH> tag of the column you want to use as the column field.

DATAFIELD: Use this attribute in the <TD> or <TH> tag of the column you want to use as the data field.

AGGREGATOR: This attribute is used in conjunction with the DATAFIELD attribute. It defines the function Excel uses in the data field. It uses the form AGGREGATOR="*FUNCTION*", where *FUNCTION* can be SUM, AVERAGE, MAX, MIN, PRODUCT, COUNTNUMS, STDEV, STDDEVP, VAR, or VARP.

PAGEFIELD: Use this attribute in the <TD> or <TH> tag of the column you want to use as the page field.

SUBTOTAL: This attribute is used in conjunction with the ROWFIELD, COLFIELD, and PAGEFIELD attributes. It tells Excel to produce subtotals for the specified fields. You can use the same functions that I listed for the AGGREGATOR attribute.

Figure 44.20 shows the pivot table that is displayed when Excel reads the following (partial) HTML file:

```
<TABLE BORDER CROSSTAB CROSSTABGRAND=ROWCOLUMN>
<TR>
<TH ROWFIELD>Store #
<TH>Date
<TH PAGEFIELD>Channel
<TH COLFIELD>Division
<TH>Product
<TH DATAFIELD AGGREGATOR="SUM">Units
<TH>Price
```

FIGURE 44.20.

Use CROSSTAB and its associated attributes to display Web page table data in an Excel pivot table.

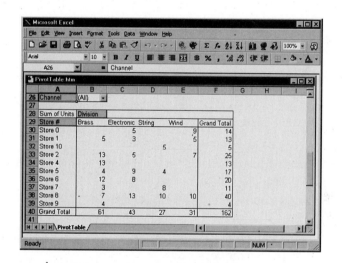

Converting Office Documents to HTML

Microsoft certainly wasn't shy about adding Web page creation tools to Office 97. You can use Word (as I'll explain in Chapter 45, "Creating Web Documents in Word"), the ActiveX Control Pad (see Chapter E2 on the CD, "Web Page Programming: ActiveX and VBScript"), and FrontPage. You can even just hand-code the HTML using Word (as long as you save the document as text-only) or even Notepad.

All these weapons are welcome additions to any Webmaster's arsenal, but what if you have existing documents, worksheets, and presentations that you want to mount on the Web? Yes, the latest version of Internet Explorer can work in conjunction with Office 97 to display these files, but not all your readers might have that capability. To make sure *anyone* who surfs to your site can access your data, you need to convert your files into the Web's *lingua franca:*

HTML. Fortunately, the Office 97 applications make this easy by including features that convert documents from their native format to HTML. This section explains the techniques that you'll use in each application.

Converting Word Documents to HTML

Word 97 does an excellent job of converting existing documents into HTML format. Character formatting (that is, those formats that are compatible with HTML) is carried out flawlessly; bullets, numbers, and tables remain intact; graphics are preserved; and, of course, hyperlinks make the journey without a hitch.

About the only thing you need to watch out for are your headings. As long as you've used Word's default heading styles (Heading 1, Heading 2, and so on), these will be transferred correctly to HTML heading tags.

Of course, there will still be a few Word knickknacks that don't survive the trip: text boxes, unusual symbols, columns, and table formulas, to name a few.

The best part is that the conversion is about as painless as these things get. Here are the steps to follow:

1. Make sure you've saved your document in Word format.
2. Select File | Save as HTML. Word displays the Save As HTML dialog box.
3. Use the Save in box to select a location for the new file.
4. Use the File name box to change the name of the file if necessary. If you don't, Word just changes the document's extension to .HTML.
5. Click Save. Depending on the original format of the file, Word might display a dialog box that warns you that you might lose formatting.
6. Click Yes to continue. You might see another dialog box, warning you that all macros associated with the document will be lost.
7. Click Yes. Word converts the document and then displays the new HTML file.

Converting Excel Ranges to HTML Tables

Excel's row-and-column format mirrors the layout of an HTML table, so it's natural that you should be able to convert a range into the appropriate HTML table tags.

Before getting started, make sure the Internet Assistant Wizard add-in is loaded. You'll know it's loaded if you see a Save as HTML command on the File menu. If you don't see this command, select Tools | Add-ins, activate the check box beside Internet Assistant Wizard in the Add-Ins dialog box, and click OK.

With the Wizard waiting in the wings, you're ready to begin the process of converting the active worksheet to an HTML file. Your first task is to decide what you want to convert:

■ If you want to convert the entire sheet, select any cell in the sheet.

- If you want to convert only a specific range, select the range.
- If you want to convert multiple ranges, select one of the ranges. You'll be able to use the Internet Assistant Wizard to select the other ranges.
- If you want to convert a chart, select the chart.

Now get the ball rolling by selecting File | Save as HTML. Excel starts the Internet Assistant Wizard and displays the dialog box shown in Figure 44.21. If you'd like to add another range or chart to the List of ranges or charts to export, click Add and use the dialog box that appears to specify the objects to convert. When you're ready to proceed, click Next >.

FIGURE 44.21.

Excel's Internet Assistant Wizard leads you through the worksheet-to-HTML conversion process.

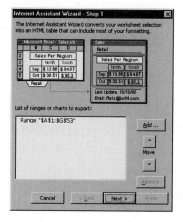

The next Wizard dialog box is shown in Figure 44.22. This dialog box gives you two choices: Convert the Excel data into a new HTML file, or insert the data into an existing file. Make your selection and click Next >.

FIGURE 44.22.

You can either create a new HTML file or insert the range into an existing file.

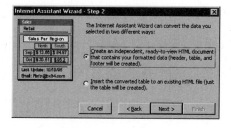

44

THE OFFICE 97
INTERNET TOOLS

At this point, you hit a fork in the Wizard's road:

- If you chose to create a new file, you'll see the dialog box shown in Figure 44.23. The top-to-bottom layout of this dialog box mirrors the layout of the new HTML file that the Wizard will create. In other words, the Title becomes the <TITLE> tag, the Header appears at the top of the page body, and so on. Fill in the fields as appropriate.

FIGURE 44.23.

Use this Wizard dialog box to fill in the particulars of your new HTML file.

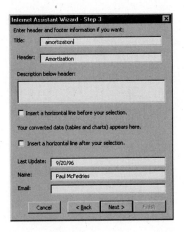

■ If you chose to insert the table into an existing HTML file, you'll see the dialog box shown in Figure 44.24. You need to use Notepad or some other text editor to insert the tag `<!--##Table##-->` into the HTML file. The Wizard uses this tag as a marker for where the table should appear. Once you've done that, either activate the Open your file directly option and enter the file's path in the text box, or activate the Open your file from your FrontPage Web option and enter the file's URL.

Either way, when you're done, click Next >.

FIGURE 44.24.

This Wizard dialog box appears if you're inserting the table into an existing file.

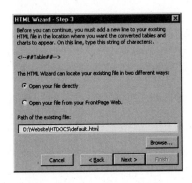

The final Wizard dialog box is shown in Figure 44.25. You have two choices:

Save the result as a HTML file: If you activate this option, enter the file's path and name in the File Path text box.

Add the result to your FrontPage Web: If you activate this option, enter the file's URL in the URL Path text box.

With that out of the way, click Finish. Excel converts the selected objects to HTML.

FIGURE 44.25.

Use the final Wizard dialog box to specify a location for the HTML file.

Converting an Access Table or Query to HTML

What if you want to convert a table or query to HTML? Or what if you want to post multiple tables or queries, or even an Access report? For all of these tasks, Access offers the Publish To The Web Wizard. This powerful Wizard lets you select multiple database objects for conversion, choose a default HTML "template" that specifies tags you want to appear in all the converted documents, create a home page for the objects, and more. You can even build dynamic forms that you can use to query the database. This section shows you how to use this Wizard. Note, however, that I'll restrict my discussion to publishing static pages. To learn how to create dynamic forms for querying, see Chapter 46, "Web Forms and Databases."

To get the show on the road, open the database you want to work with and select File | Save As HTML. Access fires up the Publish To The Web Wizard and displays the first of its dialog boxes, shown in Figure 44.26. This initial dialog box mostly just gives you an introduction to what the Wizard can do. However, if you've used the Wizard before and have saved one or more "publication profiles," the check box will be available. If you want to reuse one of your profiles, activate the check box and then highlight the profile you want to use. Click Next >.

FIGURE 44.26.

The Publish To The Web Wizard will lead you through the steps necessary for converting databases tables, queries, and reports to HTML.

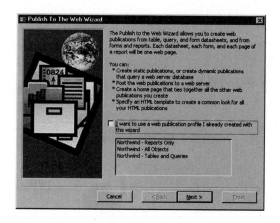

The next Wizard dialog box, shown in Figure 44.27, gives you an opportunity to choose which database objects you want to convert to HTML. Activate the check boxes for the objects that you'll be publishing to the Web, or click Select All to activate all the objects in the current tab in one fell swoop. When you're done, click Next >.

FIGURE 44.27.

Use this dialog box to choose which objects to convert.

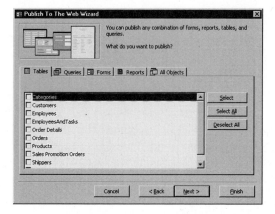

Rather than just converting each object to a plain HTML file, the Publish To The Web Wizard lets you select a "template" that it will use as the basis for all the converted database objects. This is handy, for example, if all your Web pages use a consistent layout: a company logo, copyright information, a background color or image, an image map for navigating, and so on.

You use the next Wizard dialog box, shown in Figure 44.28, to select the HTML file to use as a template. Either enter the appropriate path by hand or click Browse to select it from a dialog box. Note, too, that you're not stuck with using just a single template for all the objects. For example, you might prefer to use one template for your tables and another for your reports. To accomplish this, activate the I also want to select a different template for some of the selected objects check box. When you click Next >, the Wizard displays an extra dialog box that lets you select a template for every object that you're converting.

FIGURE 44.28.

Use this Wizard dialog box to choose a template upon which your converted files will be based.

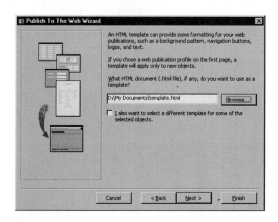

The next item on the Wizard's to-do list is to ask you whether you want to create static or dynamic pages, as shown in Figure 44.29. As I mentioned earlier, I'm covering only static pages in this chapter, so make sure the Static (HTML) publications option is activated, and click Next >. (Again, head for Chapter 46 to learn how to create .HTX files.)

FIGURE 44.29.

This dialog box lets you convert the database objects as static or dynamic files.

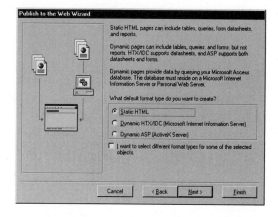

The Publish To The Web Wizard is almost ready to begin the conversion process. Your next chore is to decide how you want the documents published, as shown in Figure 44.30. If you want the files copied to a local or network folder, enter the appropriate path in the text box provided. You can also choose to run WebPost (the Web Publishing Wizard) to upload the converted objects to a remote Web server. If these options aren't available, you need to install WebPost. (See the next section to learn how this Wizard operates.) Click Next > to continue.

FIGURE 44.30.

Tell the Wizard where and how you want the documents published.

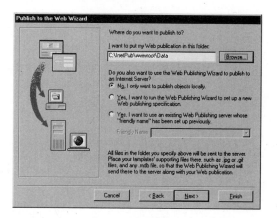

The Wizard can create a separate HTML file that serves as a "home page" for the conversion, as shown in Figure 44.31. This page contains links to all converted database objects. If you want the Wizard to create this page for you, activate the Yes, I want to create a home page check box, and then enter a name for the page in the text box provided. Click Next >.

FIGURE 44.31.
The Wizard is only too happy to create a home page that ties all the converted objects together.

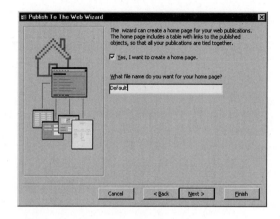

For your final task, you can save the settings you just specified in a "Web publication profile," as shown in Figure 44.32. That way, when you want to update the converted data down the road, you need only select the appropriate profile in the initial Publish To The Web Wizard dialog box. To save the profile, activate the Yes, I want to save wizard answers to a Web publication profile check box, enter a name for the profile in the text box, and click Finish.

FIGURE 44.32.
The final Wizard dialog box lets you save your settings in a Web publication profile.

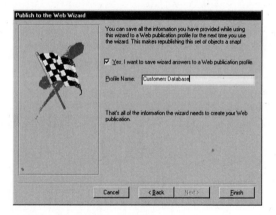

Access converts the selected objects to HTML. When that's done, if you elected to use WebPost, the Web Publishing Wizard will load.

Summary

In this chapter, you surfed through a selection of the Internet tools provided in the Office 97 package. You began with a look at Internet Explorer, including how to use it to navigate Web sites, download files, and save URLs in your Favorites folder. From there, I showed you a number of methods for inserting hyperlinks in Word, Excel, Access, and PowerPoint. Subsequent topics included working with FTP sites within Office, displaying Web pages within Excel (and

Excel's handy HTML extensions), converting Office documents to HTML, and publishing pages to your Web server.

That's a real handful, but we're not done yet. Here's a list of chapters where you'll find even more Office Web page publishing techniques:

- Chapter 45, "Creating Web Documents in Word," shows you how to use Word to create HTML pages from scratch.
- You can use Office tools to create dynamic forms that get information from the user and query databases. Chapter 46, "Web Forms and Databases," shows you how it's done.
- If you'd like to add ActiveX functionality to your pages, the easiest way is to use the ActiveX Control Pad. I provide full instructions in Chapter E2 on the CD, "Web Page Programming: ActiveX and VBScript."
- I show you how to get connected to the Internet in Chapter E7 on the CD, "Setting Up an Internet Connection in Windows 95."

Creating Web Documents in Word

CHAPTER

45

Man is a tool-using animal... Without tools he is nothing, with tools he is all.

—*Thomas Carlyle*

Microsoft Word is Office 97's all-purpose Web page wonder. Although other Office 97 programs—such as Excel and Access—are useful for creating certain types of Web documents (and, of course, for publishing existing documents—such as worksheets and tables—on the Web), you can use Word to cobble together *any* kind of Web document. Whether you just want to publish a simple text-only page or construct a feature-rich page with multimedia bells and whistles, Word is up to the task. This chapter shows you how to wield all of Word's Web-related tools.

Using the Web Page Wizard

If you need to create a professional-looking Web page, but you don't have the time or the inclination to fiddle with Word's HTML bells and whistles, the Web Page Wizard might be just what you need. This is a simple wizard that lets you choose from various Web page layouts and styles and then constructs a basic page for you. All you need to do is customize the page text and links to suit your needs.

To start the Wizard, select File | New to display the New dialog box. Activate the Web Pages tab, click the Web Page Wizard icon, and then click OK. Word creates a new document and loads the Wizard.

The first of the Wizard dialog boxes is shown in Figure 45.1. This dialog box presents a list of the various predefined Web page layouts that come with Word. As you click each layout, the document changes to reflect the new layout. When you see a layout you like, click Next to continue.

FIGURE 45.1.

Use the first Web Page Wizard dialog box to choose one of Word's predefined Web page layouts.

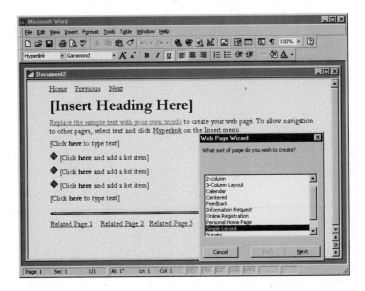

The next Wizard dialog box, shown in Figure 45.2, asks you to select a visual style for your page. The built-in styles alter the page background colors and images, fonts, bullets, horizontal lines, and more. Again, the page changes as you click each choice. Once you've made your selection, click Finish.

FIGURE 45.2.

The next Wizard dialog box presents a selection of Web page visual styles.

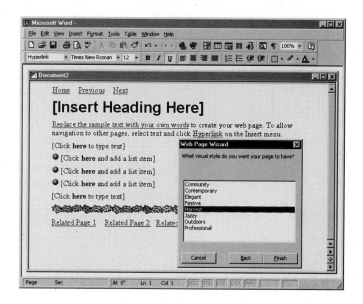

With the skeleton of your page in place, you now modify the page as follows:

- The document contains a number of placeholders: text surrounded by square brackets (for example, [Click **here** to type text]). Click the placeholders and type in your replacement text.
- For other text, you just type as you would in any normal Word document.
- The document also inserts a few hyperlinks. To edit these links, right-click a link and choose Hyperlink from the context menu.

Besides these techniques, you can also format the document using the methods I'll outline in the next section.

NOTE: MORE WEB PAGE WIZARD ACCESSORIES

Microsoft is constantly creating new accessories for the Web Page Wizard. You can download them from the Word "free stuff" site:

`http://www.microsoft.com/OfficeFreeStuff/Word/`

45

CREATING WEB
DOCUMENTS IN
WORD

Crafting Web Pages by Hand

The pages created by the Wizard are an easy way to get a head start on your Web page chores. However, you'll probably find that you have to make extensive modifications to the Wizard's creations to end up with the page you prefer. Alternatively, you may elect to bypass the Wizard altogether and create your pages from scratch. Either way, you'll have to know how to wield the myriad Web page layout and formatting tools that ship with Word. The next few sections take you through each of these tools.

Before you begin, you need to start a fresh Web document. (You could also convert an existing document into HTML format; I showed you how to do this in Chapter 44, "The Office 97 Internet Tools.") Select File | New to display the New dialog box. Activate the Web Pages tab, click the Blank Web Page icon, and click OK. Word creates a new document and adjusts its menu commands and toolbars as follows:

- New commands are added for HTML-only features. For example, the Insert menu sports a new Scrolling Text command so that you can add a "marquee" to your Web page.
- Commands and features that aren't supported by HTML are removed. So, for example, the Format | Columns command is removed because HTML doesn't support columns.

Web Page Properties: `Title` and `Base`

Each Web document has two properties that you need to think about:

`Title`: This is the text that most browsers will display in their title bar when they load your page. By default, Word sets the page title to the name you give the document when you save it (minus the .HTML extension). For example, if you name the file MyPage.html, the page title becomes MyPage.

`Base`: This is a URL or path that lets you set up relative links on your page. For example, suppose your `Base` property is set to `http://www.somehost.com/~biff/`. If you then set up a link to another.html, the browser will link to the following file:

`http://www.somehost.com/~biff/another.html`

In other words, using the `Base` property lets you enter shorter paths for your links.

To adjust the `Title` and `Base` properties, you need to select File | Properties. In the Document Properties dialog box that appears, shown in Figure 45.3, use the Title text box to enter a new title for the page, use the Base text box to enter a URL or path, and click OK.

Viewing the HTML Tags

If you were weaned on the minutiae of HTML tags and attributes, it might be hard for you to get used to Word's WYSIWYG Web display. If you'd like to get fine-tuned control over your page, or if you've just got a hankering to view the underlying HTML tags associated with your page, it's easy enough to see them. Save the document and then select View | HTML Source.

Word switches the page to the HTML source code, as shown in Figure 45.4. Feel free to edit the tags as necessary. When you're done, click the Exit HTML Source toolbar button to return to the regular view.

FIGURE 45.3.
Use this dialog box to specify the document's Title *and* Base *properties.*

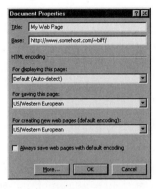

FIGURE 45.4.
You can view the HTML source for your Web pages.

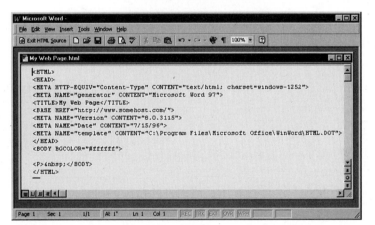

Formatting Characters

Thanks to the word processing ground upon which it sits, Word has no shortage of options for formatting characters. For basic formatting chores, you use the same tools that you would use when formatting text in your regular Word documents. In other words, you can make text bold, italic, or underlined, you can change the text color, and you can select different fonts.

NOTE: FONT SUPPORT

Not all browsers support different fonts. Internet Explorer does, but you need Netscape Navigator 3.0 or later to view different fonts. Even then, the person viewing your page needs to have the specified font installed on his or her system in order to see the font within the browser.

There are also two Web-specific text formatting tools added to the Formatting toolbar:

 Click this button to increase the font size.

 Click this button to decrease the font size.

Also, you can select one of the character styles from the Style list (see the next section for details). The Style list has entries for monospaced text (the Typewriter style), preformatted text (the Preformatted style), and more.

Setting Default Text Colors

Every Web page document uses a default color for body text and two default colors for hyperlinks: one for links that haven't been clicked on and one for links that have been clicked on. In HTML, these attributes are part of the <BODY> tag.

To set these default colors in Word, select Format | Text Colors. Word displays the Document Text Colors dialog box, shown in Figure 45.5. Use the drop-down list to set the colors you prefer, and then click OK.

FIGURE 45.5.

Use this dialog box to specify the default text colors used in your Web page.

Creating a Scrolling Text Marquee

If you're looking to grab people's attention, Word has just the thing: scrolling text. This is an area on your page where a text message scrolls (in its default behavior) from the right to left. It's something like a marquee used in theaters and other venues (which is why the HTML tag associated with this feature is called <MARQUEE>).

CAUTION: NO UNIVERSAL SUPPORT FOR SCROLLING TEXT

As of this writing, only Internet Explorer supports scrolling text. You should check your page in other browsers (especially the latest version of Netscape Navigator) before committing to this type of effect.

To set up scrolling text, select Insert | Scrolling Text. Word displays the Scrolling Text dialog box, shown in Figure 45.6. Here's a rundown of the various options:

Behavior: Determines how the text moves in the box. Select Scroll to make the text wrap. Select Slide to have the text move from one end of the box to the other. Select Alternate to have the text move back and forth within the box.

Direction: This drop-down controls whether the text moves right-to-left or left-to-right.

Background Color: Sets the background color of the scroll box.

Loop: Determines the number of times the text scrolls.

Speed: Use this slider to control the speed of the scrolling text.

Type the Scrolling Text Here: Use this text box to enter the text you want to display.

Preview: This box shows what the selected options will produce.

When you're done, click OK to add the marquee.

FIGURE 45.6.

Use this dialog box to set up scrolling text on your page.

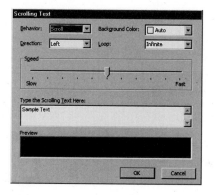

Working with Styles

Much of HTML involves applying a particular style to a section of text or an entire paragraph. For example, a heading is a style that consists of bold text in a particular font size with an extra blank line before it. So it makes sense, then, that Word uses a large collection of defined styles to insert HTML tags.

Word gives you two ways to see a list of the available styles:

- Open the Formatting toolbar's Style drop-down list.
- Select Format | Style to display the Style dialog box, shown in Figure 45.7.

In the Style dialog box, styles with a paragraph symbol (¶) next to them are paragraph styles: They apply to the entire current paragraph. Styles with an **a** beside them are text styles: They apply to the currently selected text.

For example, if you wanted to format a paragraph as a top-level heading (the <H1> tag), you'd place the cursor inside the paragraph and then apply the Heading 1 style.

FIGURE 45.7.
Much of Word's
HTML is produced
using styles.

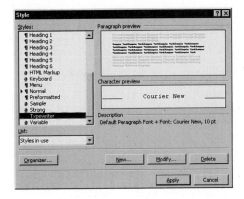

Working with Bulleted Lists

Creating a bulleted HTML list is the same as creating a bulleted list in a regular Word document. To begin, use either of the following techniques:

■ Select Format | Bullets and Numbering. In the Bulleted tab, shown in Figure 45.8, choose the bullet style you want and click OK. (As you can see, the available styles are different than the ones you get with a regular Word document. Click More to see a few extra styles.)

FIGURE 45.8.
Use this dialog box to
choose the bullet style
you want to work with.

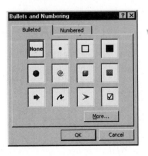

■ Click the Bullets button on the Formatting toolbar.

Word inserts the bulleted list container (the `<UL>` and `</UL>` tags) and adds the first item. Type in the item text and then press Enter to generate the next bullet automatically. Press Enter twice to end the list.

Working with Numbered Lists

As with bulleted lists, inserting a numbered list in your HTML document is no different than doing so in a regular Word document. To start the list, use either of the following techniques:

■ Select Format | Bullets and Numbering. In the Numbered tab, click the style you want, and then click OK.

■ Click the Numbers button on the Formatting toolbar.

Word inserts the numbered list container (the <OL> and </OL> tags) and adds the first item. Type in the item text and then press Enter to generate the second item automatically. Press Enter twice to end the list.

Working with Definition Lists

Definition lists operate a bit differently. Since there is no equivalent in regular Word documents, you have to use styles to build the list. Here's how it's done:

■ To insert the definition list container (the <DL> and </DL> tags), apply the Definition List style.

■ To format an item as a term (the <DT> tag), apply the Definition Term style.

■ To format an item as a definition (the <DD> tag), apply the Definition style.

Adding Images to Your Page

If you feel like enhancing your page with a nice graphic or two, Word gives you no shortage of methods to try. If you select Insert | Picture, the cascade menu that appears contains the following:

Clip Art: Choose this command to select clip art, images, sounds, or videos from the Office 97 Clip Gallery.

From File: Choose this command to select an image from the Insert Picture dialog box. You can also display this dialog box by clicking the Insert Picture button on the toolbar.

Browse Web Art Page: Choose this command to display a Web page that contains various images you can use.

From Scanner: Choose this command to capture an image from a scanner attached to your computer. You can use the Microsoft Photo Editor to spruce up the image before importing it into the document.

Chart: Choose this command to use Microsoft Graph to add a chart to your page.

Formatting an Image

Once you have your image in place, Word boasts a few formatting options that you can use to make sure the images appear exactly as you'd like. For example, you can specify a text equivalent for browsers that don't support graphics, and you can determine whether text wraps around the image.

The Picture toolbar lets you control some of these options. Here's a summary of the buttons available on this toolbar:

Button	*Name*	*What It Does*
	No Wrapping	Prevents text from wrapping around the image.
	Left Wrapping	Causes text to wrap around the left side of the image.
	Right Wrapping	Causes text to wrap around the right side of the image.
	Format Picture	Displays the Picture dialog box, shown in Figure 45.9.
	Reset Picture	Returns the image to its default settings.

FIGURE 45.9.

The Picture dialog box controls various aspects of how the image is displayed on the Web page.

Besides clicking the Format Picture button on the Picture toolbar, you can also display the Picture dialog box by clicking the image and selecting Format | Picture, or by right-clicking the image and choosing Format Picture from the context menu. The Position tab controls two formatting options:

Text wrapping: These options control how text wraps around the image. Select None, Left, or Right.

Distance from text: These options control the Vertical and Horizontal distance between the image and the surrounding text.

The Settings tab has a few more options to play with:

Link: This group shows the name of the image file. To use an absolute path that includes the drive and folder, activate the Use absolute path check box.

Picture placeholder: Use this text box to enter a text description of the image. This description will be displayed in nongraphical browsers. (This is equivalent to using the ALT attribute in the HTML <IMG> tag.)

When you're done, click OK to put the settings into effect.

Constructing Tables

Microsoft Word has been table-aware for a few years now, and the latest versions make it easy to set up and format tables in your documents. The good news for Webmasters is that Word's Web files leverage all this table know-how, so you can create HTML tables just as easily as you can create regular Word tables. Not only that, but Word also lets you adjust things such as the table borders, cell width and spacing, and more.

Inserting a Simple Table

If all you need to do is create a simple table for displaying row-and-column data, you can use Word's standard table-creation tools. First, position the cursor where you want the table to appear. Now either select Table | Insert Table, or click the Insert Table toolbar button. In the table grid that appears, drag the mouse pointer through the number of rows and columns you want. Release the mouse button to insert the table.

Drawing More Complex Tables

Most Web page tables are used for more complex tasks, such as organizing the entire page so that text and graphics line up nicely. To accomplish this, more complex tables are needed where rows and columns have varying widths, where cells span multiple rows or columns, and so on.

For these more complicated scenarios, Word has a tool that lets you draw the table to the specifications you prefer. Here's how it works:

1. Click the Tables and Borders button on the Standard toolbar to display the Tables and Borders toolbar.

2. Click the Draw Table button on the Tables and Borders toolbar. (Note that you can combine steps 1 and 2 into a single operation by selecting Table | Draw Table.)

3. Move the mouse pointer (it should now look like a pencil) to the upper-left corner where you want the table to appear, and then drag the mouse to create a box that defines the perimeter of the table.

4. Move the mouse pointer inside the table and then drag across to create a row, or drag down to create a column.

5. You can split a cell by moving the mouse pointer inside the cell and then dragging up (to split the cell vertically) or across (to split the cell horizontally). You can also click the Split Cells button and use the Split Cells dialog box to enter the number of rows and columns you want inside the cell.

6. To merge two or more cells, click the Draw Table button to deactivate it, then drag to select the cells you want to merge. Now click the Merge Cells button.

7. To make sure that two or more rows have the same height, select the rows and then click the Distribute Rows Evenly button.

8. To make sure that two or more columns have the same width, select the columns and then click the Distribute Columns Evenly button.

9. To remove a line from the table, click the Erase button and then drag along the line you want to erase. (The line turns red while you drag.)

10. Repeat steps 4 through 9 to complete the table.

Once your table is in place, Word offers a number of other tools that let you format the individual cells and the table as a whole:

■ For the table, select Table | Table Properties. In the Table Properties dialog box, shown in Figure 45.10, you can specify whether text wraps around the table by clicking an option in the Text wrapping group. Use the Surrounding text group to determine the distance between the table and the body text. Use the Background drop-down list to choose the color of the table background. Use the Space between columns spinner to set the column spacing.

FIGURE 45.10.

Use this dialog box to set some properties that apply to the table as a whole.

■ For a cell, click inside the cell and then select Table | Cell Properties. The Cell Properties dialog box lets you choose the cell's Vertical alignment, Background color, Width, and Height. You can also use the following toolbar buttons to set the vertical alignment:

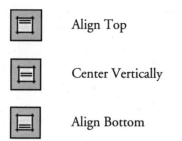 Align Top

Center Vertically

Align Bottom

- To activate the table's borders and specify the border width, select Table | Borders.
- To sort the table, select Table | Sort, and then use the Sort dialog box to specify the sort parameters. For quick sorts, use the following toolbar buttons:

 Sort Ascending

Sort Descending

- To toggle the display of gridlines on and off, either select Table | Gridlines or click the Hide/Show Gridlines button.

A Few Odds and Ends

To round out our look at Word's Web page creation techniques, this section presents a few HTML odds and ends, including horizontal rules, character codes, background colors, and more:

- To add a horizontal rule (the `<HR>` tag), select Insert | Horizontal Line and choose the line style you want from the Horizontal Line dialog box. You can also click the Horizontal Line button on the Formatting toolbar.

- To insert a character code, select Insert | Symbol. In the Symbol dialog box that appears, select (normal text) from the Font list, highlight the character you want, and click Insert.

- If you'd like to insert the current date, select Insert | Date and Time. In the Date and Time dialog box that appears, choose the format you want to use from the Available Formats list, and activate the Update Automatically (Insert as Field) check box. Activating this option tells Word to update the date each time you open the file. Click OK to insert the date.

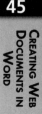

45

CREATING WEB
DOCUMENTS IN
WORD

- To paint the background with a color or image, either select Format | Background or click the Background button on the toolbar. In the palette that appears, either click a color or click Fill Effects to select an image.

Previewing Your Web Page

Word does a good job of showing you what your page will look like, but it's not entirely WYSIWYG. To a get a true representation of the page, you need to display it in a Web browser. To do this, you can either load your favorite browser and display the file, or you can use either of the following techniques to load the document automatically in your system's default browser:

- Select File | Web Page Preview.

- Click the Web Page Preview button on the Standard toolbar.

Summary

This chapter showed you how to use Microsoft Word to wield the full power and splendor of a high-end word processor to create Web pages. First I showed you various methods of inserting hyperlinks in your documents. From there, you learned how to use the Web Page Wizard to create attractive Web pages with just a few mouse clicks. For heavy-duty Web chores, you also learned how to add Web page baubles and bangles by hand, including formatting characters, styles, lists, multimedia files, and tables. I closed by showing you how to convert existing Word documents into HTML format.

Here's a list of chapters where you'll find related information:

- Many of Word's page creation techniques are the same as those used for regular documents. To find out more about these features, see Part III, "Unleashing Word."
- To learn more about HTML, see Chapter 43, "Understanding Web Documents."
- I show you how to get connected to the Internet in Chapter E7 on the CD, "Setting Up an Internet Connection in Windows 95."

Web Forms
and Databases

IN THIS CHAPTER

CHAPTER

46

> *There is a great satisfaction in building good tools for other people to use.*
>
> —*Freeman Dyson*

The Web pages we've talked about so far have been more or less static—just a collection of text and images that provide no user interaction. Still, it *is* possible to provide a very basic level of interaction by including hyperlinks in your pages (see Chapter 44, "The Office 97 Internet Tools"). Excel's HTML extensions (also covered in Chapter 44) are a step up because they let you filter HTML table data as well as work with large amounts of data in pivot table form. Beyond this, however, there lies a whole genre of interactive Web pages called *forms*. This chapter introduces you to HTML forms and shows you various Office methods of constructing them. I'll also show you how to use forms to query Web-based databases.

Understanding Forms

To understand forms, think of the humble dialog box. Most modern applications display a dialog box whenever they need to extract information from you. For example, selecting a program's Print command will most likely result in some kind of Print dialog box showing up. The purpose of this dialog box will be to pester you for information such as the number of copies you want, which pages you want to print, and so on.

A form is simply the Web page equivalent of a dialog box. It's a page that's populated with dialog box–like controls—such as text boxes, drop-down lists, and command buttons—that are used to obtain information from the reader. For example, Figure 46.1 shows a form from my Web site. This is a "guest book" that people "sign" when they visit my Web abode. (At this point it's worth mentioning that although most new browsers can handle forms, some older browsers might choke on them.)

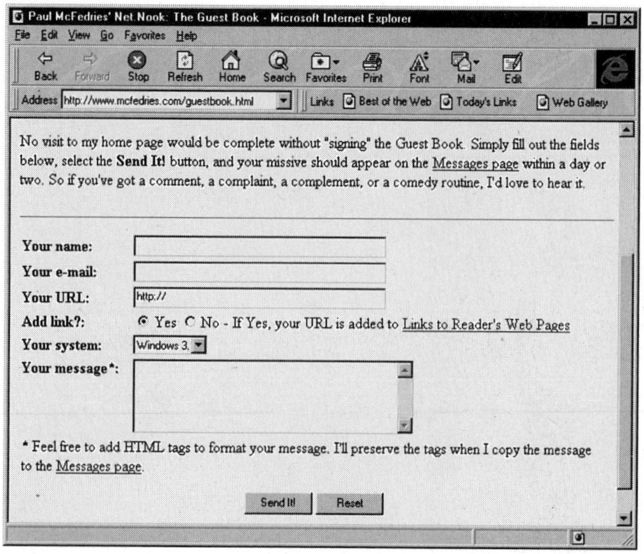

FIGURE 46.1.

A form used as a guest book.

As you can imagine, guest books are only the beginning of what you can do with forms. If you publish a newsletter or magazine, you can use forms to gather information from subscribers. If your Web site includes pages with restricted access, you can use a form to get a person's user name and password for verification. If you have information in a database, you can use a form to construct a query.

It's one thing to build a form, but it's quite another to actually make it do something useful. In other words, having a form on your Web site doesn't do you much good unless you have some way to process whatever data the user enters into the form. There are a number of ways to go about this, but the most common is to create a "script" that runs on the Web server. This script reads the form data, performs some sort of operation on the data (such as adding it to a database), and then returns some kind of "results" page (which might only be a simple "Thanks!" message). These scripts must conform to the Common Gateway Interface (CGI) standard, which defines how the browser sends the form data to the server.

CGI is a complex topic that is beyond the scope of this book. If you'd like to learn more about it, I recommend the book *HTML & CGI Unleashed* (Sams Publishing, 1995). However, if you'll be using the form to work with an Access database on Microsoft's Internet Information Server (IIS), you can use Internet Database Connector (IDC) files to query the database using the parameters entered into the form. I'll explain how this works later in this chapter. For now, though, let's see how you create forms.

Creating a Form from Scratch

In Chapter 43, "Understanding Web Documents," I introduced you to HTML tags and showed how you can use them to build attractive Web pages. There is also a whole host of tags for defining the individual controls that make up a form; I'll run through them in this section. Instead of coding your forms by hand, however, you might prefer the ease of Word's menu commands and toolbar buttons. To that end, for each form tag, I'll also provide you with the equivalent technique for creating the control in Word.

If you'll be using Word, you need to do two things to get started:

1. Open an existing HTML document or start a new one (see Chapter 45, "Creating Web Documents in Word").

2. Display the Control Toolbox by entering Word's Form Design mode. You do this by either selecting View | Form Design Mode or clicking the Form Design Mode toolbar button. (Note that Word's Form Design mode is available only for HTML documents.)

Defining the Form

In HTML, you define a form by entering the `<FORM>` and `</FORM>` tags within the body of the page. The `<FORM>` tag always includes a couple of extra attributes that tell the Web server how to process the form. Here's the general format:

```
<FORM ACTION="URL" METHOD=METHOD>
</FORM>
```

Here, the `ACTION` attribute tells the browser where to send the form's data. This will almost always be the script that you've set up to process the data. The `URL` part is the program's address.

The `METHOD` attribute tells the browser how to send the form's data to the URL specified by `ACTION`. You have two choices for `METHOD`:

> `GET`: The browser appends a question mark (?) and the data to the end of the `ACTION` attribute's URL and then requests this URL/data combination from the server.

> `POST`: The browser sends the data to the server in a separate message.

When deciding which method to use, bear in mind that each control on your form sends two things to the server: the name of the control and the data the user entered into the control. This means that a form could end up sending quite a bit of data to the server (especially if the form contains many controls or text boxes that could potentially hold long strings). However, some systems restrict the size of a URL sent to a Web server. This means that the `GET` method's URL/data combination might end up truncated. The `POST` method doesn't suffer from this problem, so you should always use it when large amounts of form data are involved. If you're not sure, use `POST`.

Let's look at an example. If you don't have a script for processing the form, you can still test the form by using one of the NCSA's public scripts. There's one for the `POST` method and one for the `GET` method. Here's how to use the `POST` method version:

```
<FORM ACTION="http://hoohoo.ncsa.uiuc.edu/htbin-post/post-query" METHOD=POST>
```

For the `GET` method, use the following:

```
<FORM ACTION="http://hoohoo.ncsa.uiuc.edu/htbin/query" METHOD=GET>
```

You can try this after you build a working form.

If you're working in Word, the `<FORM>` and `</FORM>` tags are represented by the `Top of Form` and `Bottom of Form` styles, respectively. To add these styles to your page, insert a "submit" button (as explained in the next section). Here are the general steps you'll follow each time you want to add a control:

1. Move the insertion point to where you want the control to appear.
2. Click the appropriate icon in the Control Toolbox. (You can also choose Insert | Forms and then select the control you want from the cascade menu that appears.) Word adds the control to the page.
3. Drag the control's selection bars to size the control as needed.
4. Either click the Properties button or double-click the control to display its properties sheet and then fill in the control's properties, as required. (I'll explain the various properties as we examine each control.)

Once the Top of Form and Bottom of Form styles are in place, you specify the action and method parameters by modifying the properties of the submit button, as explained in the next section.

The Submit Button

Most dialog boxes, as you probably know by now, have an OK button. Selecting this button says, in effect, "All right, I've made my choices. Now go put everything into effect." Forms also have command buttons that come in two flavors: "submit" and "reset."

A submit button is the form equivalent of an OK dialog box button. When the reader clicks the submit button, the form data is shipped out to the program specified by the <FORM> tag's ACTION attribute. Here's the simplest format for the submit button:

```
<INPUT TYPE=SUBMIT>
```

As you'll see, most form elements use some variation on the <INPUT> tag. In this case, the TYPE=SUBMIT attribute tells the browser to display a command button labeled Submit (or, on some browsers, Submit Query or Send). Note that each form can have just one submit button.

If the standard Submit label is too prosaic for your needs, you can make up your own label, as follows:

```
<INPUT TYPE=SUBMIT VALUE="Label">
```

Here, Label is the label that will appear on the button.

To insert a submit button using Word, click the Submit icon in the Control Toolbox. In the properties sheet for a submit button, shown in Figure 46.2, you can set the following properties:

    Action: The URL of the script that processes the form.

    Caption: The text that appears on the button.

    Encoding: Leave this property as is.

    HTMLName: You don't need to fill in this property.

    Method: The method used to submit the form (Get or Post).

FIGURE 46.2.

The Properties dialog box.

Using a Submit Image

A variation on the submit button theme is the *submit image*. This is similar to a submit button, but the user clicks a picture instead. Here's the general tag syntax:

```
<INPUT TYPE=IMAGE SRC="Path">
```

Here, `Path` is the path and filename of the image file.

To insert this control in Word, click the Image Submit button in the Control Toolbox. Word displays the Insert Picture dialog box. Highlight the image file you want to use and click Insert. The available properties are more or less the same as those mentioned earlier for a submit button. The only difference is that the `Caption` property is replaced by the `Source` property, which specifies the path and name of the image.

Starting Over: The Reset Button

If you plan on creating fairly large forms, you can do your readers a big favor by including a reset button somewhere on the form. A reset button clears all the data from the form's fields and re-enters any default values that you specified in the fields. (I'll explain how to set up default values for each type of field as we go along.) Here's the tag to use to include a reset button:

```
<INPUT TYPE=RESET>
```

You can create a custom label by tossing the VALUE attribute into the <INPUT> tag, as in the following example:

```
<INPUT TYPE=RESET VALUE="Start From Scratch">
```

In Word, click the Reset button in the Control Toolbox. If you'd like to change the button label, display the properties sheet and enter the text you want to use in the `Caption` property.

Using Text Boxes for Single-Line Text

For simple text entries, such as a person's name or address, use text boxes. Here's the basic format for a text box tag:

```
<INPUT TYPE=TEXT NAME="FieldName">
```

In this case, *FieldName* is a name you assign to the field that's unique among the other fields in the form. For example, to create a text box named FirstName, you'd enter the following:

```
<INPUT TYPE=TEXT NAME="FirstName">
```

 Here's some HTML code that utilizes a few text boxes to gather some information from the user (see TextBox.htm on the CD):

```
<HTML>
<HEAD>
<TITLE>Text Box Example</TITLE>
</HEAD>
<BODY>
<H3>Please tell me about yourself:</H3>
<FORM ACTION="http://hoohoo.ncsa.uiuc.edu/htbin-post/post-query" METHOD=POST>
First Name: <INPUT TYPE=TEXT NAME="FirstName">
<P>
Last Name: <INPUT TYPE=TEXT NAME="LastName">
<P>
Nickname: <INPUT TYPE=TEXT NAME="NickName">
<P>
Stage Name: <INPUT TYPE=TEXT NAME="StageName">
<P>
<INPUT TYPE=SUBMIT VALUE="Just Do It!">
<INPUT TYPE=RESET VALUE="Just Reset It!">
</FORM>
</BODY>
</HTML>
```

Figure 46.3 shows how this code looks in Internet Explorer, and Figure 46.4 shows the page that's returned by the NCSA server if you click the Just Do It! button. Notice how the page shows the names of the fields followed by the value the user entered.

FIGURE 46.3.

A form with a few text boxes.

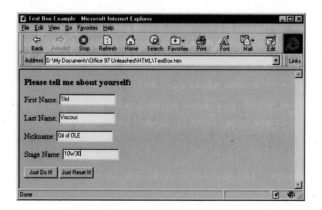

FIGURE **46.4.**

An example of the page that's returned when you send the form data to the NCSA public server.

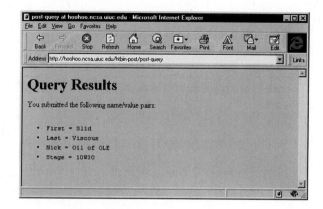

Text boxes also come with the following bells and whistles:

Setting the default value: If you'd like some text to appear in the field by default, include the VALUE attribute in the <INPUT> tag. For example, suppose you want to know the URL of the reader's home page. To include http:// in the field, you'd use the following tag:

```
<INPUT TYPE=TEXT NAME="URL" VALUE="http://">
```

Setting the size of the box: To determine the length of the text box, use the SIZE attribute. (Note that this attribute affects only the size of the box, not the length of the entry; for the latter, use the MAXLENGTH attribute.) For example, the following tag displays a text box that is 40 characters long:

```
<INPUT TYPE=TEXT NAME="Address" SIZE=40>
```

Limiting the length of the text: In a standard text box, the reader can type away until his fingers are numb. If you'd prefer to restrict the length of the entry, use the MAXLENGTH attribute. For example, the following text box is used to enter a person's age; it restricts the length of the entry to three characters:

```
<INPUT TYPE=TEXT NAME="Age" MAXLENGTH=3>
```

In Microsoft Word, you insert a text box by clicking the Text Box button in the Control Toolbox. The properties sheet for a text box control contains three properties:

HTMLName: The name of the text box.

MaxLength: The maximum number of characters the user can enter into the field.

Value: The initial value of the field.

NOTE: PASSWORD TEXT BOXES

A slight variation on the text-box theme is the password box:

`<INPUT TYPE=PASSWORD NAME="`*FieldName*`">`

This is a text box that displays only asterisks as the user types. To insert a
password box in Word, click the Password button in the Control Toolbox.

Using Text Areas for Multiline Text

If you want to give your readers extra room to type their text, or if you need multiline entries
(such as an address), you're better off using a *text area* than a text box. A text area is also a
rectangle that accepts text input, but text areas can display two or more lines at once. Here's
how they work:

```
<TEXTAREA NAME="FieldName" VALUE="Text" ROWS=TotalRows COLS=TotalCols WRAP>
</TEXTAREA>
```

Here, *FieldName* is a unique name for the field, *Text* is the initial text that appears in the field,
TotalRows specifies the total number of lines displayed, and *TotalCols* specifies the total number of columns displayed. The WRAP attribute tells the browser to wrap the text onto the next
line whenever the user's typing hits the right edge of the text area. (The WRAP attribute is supported by most browsers, but not all of them.) Note, too, that the <TEXTAREA> tag requires the
</TEXTAREA> end tag. (If you want to include default values in the text area, just enter them—
on separate lines, if necessary—between <TEXTAREA> and </TEXTAREA>.)

The following HTML tags show a text area in action (see TextArea.htm on the CD),
and Figure 46.5 shows how it looks in a browser.

```
<HTML>
<HEAD>
<TITLE>Text Area Example</TITLE>
</HEAD>
<BODY>
<H3>Today's Burning Question</H3>
<HR>
<FORM ACTION="http://hoohoo.ncsa.uiuc.edu/htbin-post/post-query" METHOD=POST>
First Name: <INPUT TYPE=TEXT NAME="FirstName">
<P>
Last Name: <INPUT TYPE=TEXT NAME="LastName">
<P>
Today's <I>Burning Question</I>: <B>Why is Jerry Lewis so popular in France?</B>
<P>
Please enter your answer in the text area below:
<BR>
<TEXTAREA NAME="Answer" ROWS=10 COLS=60 WRAP>
</TEXTAREA>
<P>
```

```
<INPUT TYPE=SUBMIT VALUE="I Know!">
<INPUT TYPE=RESET>
</FORM>
</BODY>
</HTML>
```

FIGURE 46.5.

An example of a text area.

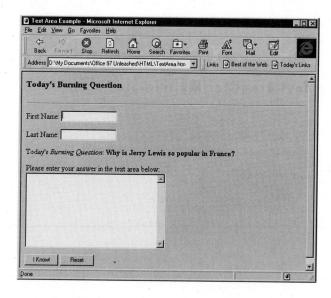

 To get a text area in Word, click the Text Area button in the Control Toolbox. In the control's properties sheet, use the `Columns` property to set the width, the `Rows` property to set the height, and the `WordWrap` property to enable or disable wrapping.

Toggling an Option On and Off with Check Boxes

If you want to elicit yes/no or true/false information from your readers, check boxes are a lot easier than having the user type in the required data. Here's the general format for an HTML check box:

```
<INPUT TYPE=CHECKBOX NAME="FieldName">
```

As usual, `FieldName` is a unique name for the field. You can also add the attribute `CHECKED` to the `<INPUT>` tag, which tells the browser to display the check box "pre-checked." Here's an example (see CheckBox.htm on the CD):

```
<INPUT TYPE=CHECKBOX NAME="Species" CHECKED>Human
```

 Notice in this example that I placed some text beside the `<INPUT>` tag. This text is used as a label that tells the reader what the check box represents. Here's a longer example that uses a few check boxes. Figure 46.6 shows how it looks.

```
<HTML>
<HEAD>
<TITLE>Check Box Example</TITLE>
</HEAD>
<BODY>
<H3>Welcome to Hooked On Phobics!</H3>
<HR>
<FORM ACTION="http://hoohoo.ncsa.uiuc.edu/htbin-post/post-query" METHOD=POST>
What's <I>your</I> phobia? (Please check all that apply):
<P>
<INPUT TYPE=CHECKBOX NAME="Ants">Myrmecophobia (Fear of ants)<BR>
<INPUT TYPE=CHECKBOX NAME="Bald">Peladophobia (Fear of becoming bald)<BR>
<INPUT TYPE=CHECKBOX NAME="Beards">Pogonophobia (Fear of beards)<BR>
<INPUT TYPE=CHECKBOX NAME="Bed">Clinophobia (Fear of going to bed)<BR>
<INPUT TYPE=CHECKBOX NAME="Chins">Geniophobia (Fear of chins)<BR>
<INPUT TYPE=CHECKBOX NAME="Flowers">Anthophobia (Fear of flowers)<BR>
<INPUT TYPE=CHECKBOX NAME="Flying">Aviatophobia (Fear of flying)<BR>
<INPUT TYPE=CHECKBOX NAME="Purple">Porphyrophobia (Fear of the color purple)<BR>
<INPUT TYPE=CHECKBOX NAME="Teeth">Odontophobia (Fear of teeth)<BR>
<INPUT TYPE=CHECKBOX NAME="Thinking">Phronemophobia (Fear of thinking)<BR>
<INPUT TYPE=CHECKBOX NAME="Vegetables">Lachanophobia (Fear of vegetables)<BR>
<INPUT TYPE=CHECKBOX NAME="Fear">Phobophobia (Fear of fear)<BR>
<INPUT TYPE=CHECKBOX NAME="Everything">Pantophobia (Fear of everything)<BR>
<P>
<INPUT TYPE=SUBMIT VALUE="Submit">
<INPUT TYPE=RESET>
</FORM>
</BODY>
</HTML>
```

FIGURE 46.6.

*Some check box
examples.*

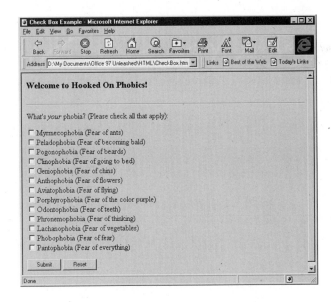

Word users can get a check box by heading for the Control Toolbox and clicking the Check Box button. In the control's properties sheet, make sure you fill in the HTMLName property, and set the Checked property to True or False.

Multiple Choice: Option Buttons

Instead of yes/no choices, you might want your readers to have a choice of three or four options. In this case, option buttons are your best bet. With option buttons, the user gets two or more choices, but he can choose only one. Here's the general format:

```
<INPUT TYPE=RADIO NAME="FieldName" VALUE="Value">
```

FieldName is the usual field name, but in this case you supply the same name to *all* the option buttons. That way, the browser knows which buttons are grouped. *Value* is a unique text string that specifies the value of the option when it's selected. In addition, you can also add CHECKED to one of the buttons to have the browser activate the option by default.

The following HTML document puts a few option buttons through their paces (see RadioBtn.htm on the CD), as shown in Figure 46.7.

```
<HTML>
<HEAD>
<TITLE>Radio Button Example</TITLE>
</HEAD>
<BODY>
<H3>Survey</H3>
<HR>
<FORM ACTION="http://hoohoo.ncsa.uiuc.edu/htbin-post/post-query" METHOD=POST>
Which of the following best describes your current salary level:
<UL>
<INPUT TYPE=RADIO NAME="Salary" VALUE="Salary1" CHECKED>Below the poverty line<BR>
<INPUT TYPE=RADIO NAME="Salary" VALUE="Salary2">Living wage<BR>
<INPUT TYPE=RADIO NAME="Salary" VALUE="Salary3">Comfy<BR>
<INPUT TYPE=RADIO NAME="Salary" VALUE="Salary4">DINK (Double Income, No Kids)<BR>
<INPUT TYPE=RADIO NAME="Salary" VALUE="Salary5">Rockefellerish<BR>
</UL>
Which of the following best describes your political leanings:
<UL>
<INPUT TYPE=RADIO NAME="Politics" VALUE="Politics1" CHECKED>So far left,
➥I'm right<BR>
<INPUT TYPE=RADIO NAME="Politics" VALUE="Politics2">Yellow Dog Democrat<BR>
<INPUT TYPE=RADIO NAME="Politics" VALUE="Politics3">Right down the middle<BR>
<INPUT TYPE=RADIO NAME="Politics" VALUE="Politics4">Country Club Republican<BR>
<INPUT TYPE=RADIO NAME="Politics" VALUE="Politics5">So far right, I'm left<BR>
</UL>
<P>
<INPUT TYPE=SUBMIT VALUE="Submit">
<INPUT TYPE=RESET>
</FORM>
</BODY>
</HTML>
```

FIGURE 46.7.

A form that uses radio buttons for multiple-choice input.

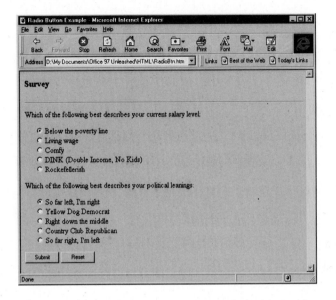

To insert a series of option buttons via Word, use the Option Button icon in the Control Toolbox. For each button that you want grouped, use the properties sheet to assign each button the same HTMLName.

Selecting from Lists

Option buttons are a great way to give your readers multiple choices, but they get unwieldy if you have more than about five or six options. For longer sets of options, you're better off using lists. Setting up a list requires a bit more work than the other form tags. Here's the general format:

```
<SELECT NAME="FieldName" SIZE=Items>
<OPTION>First item text</OPTION>
<OPTION>Second item text</OPTION>
<OPTION>And so on...</OPTION>
</SELECT>
```

For the SIZE attribute, *Items* is the number of items you want the browser to display. If you omit SIZE, the list becomes a drop-down list. If SIZE is 2 or more, the list becomes a rectangle with scrollbars for navigating the choices. Also, you can insert the MULTIPLE attribute into the <SELECT> tag. This tells the browser to allow the user to select multiple items from the list.

Between the <SELECT> and </SELECT> tags are the <OPTION>/</OPTION> tags; these define the list items. If you add the SELECTED attribute to one of the items, the browser selects that item by default.

To get some examples on the table, the following document defines no less than three selection lists (see Lists2.htm on the CD). Figure 46.8 shows what the Internet Explorer browser does with them.

```
<HTML>
<HEAD>
<TITLE>Selection List Example</TITLE>
</HEAD>
<BODY>
<H3>Putting On Hairs: Reader Survey</H3>
<HR>
<FORM ACTION="http://hoohoo.ncsa.uiuc.edu/htbin-post/post-query" METHOD=POST>
Select your hair color:<BR>
<SELECT NAME="Color">
<OPTION>Black</OPTION>
<OPTION>Blonde</OPTION>
<OPTION SELECTED>Brunette</OPTION>
<OPTION>Red</OPTION>
<OPTION>Something neon</OPTION>
<OPTION>None</OPTION>
</SELECT>
<P>
Select your hair style:<BR>
<SELECT NAME="Style" SIZE=7>
<OPTION>Bouffant</OPTION>
<OPTION>Mohawk</OPTION>
<OPTION>Page Boy</OPTION>
<OPTION>Permed</OPTION>
<OPTION>Shag</OPTION>
<OPTION SELECTED>Straight</OPTION>
<OPTION>Style? What style?</OPTION>
</SELECT>
<P>
Hair products used in the last year:<BR>
<SELECT NAME="Products" SIZE=5 MULTIPLE>
<OPTION>Gel</OPTION>
<OPTION>Grecian Formula</OPTION>
<OPTION>Mousse</OPTION>
<OPTION>Peroxide</OPTION>
<OPTION>Shoe black</OPTION>
</SELECT>
<P>
<INPUT TYPE=SUBMIT VALUE="Hair Mail It!">
<INPUT TYPE=RESET>
</FORM>
</BODY>
</HTML>
```

Word uses separate Control Toolbox buttons for list boxes and drop-down boxes:

 List Box

 Drop-down Box

FIGURE 46.8.

*A form with a few
selection list examples.*

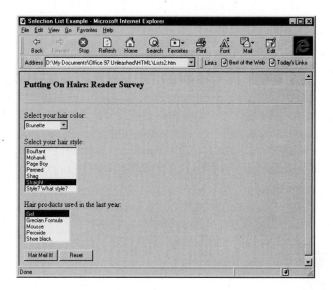

In either case, you specify the list items by opening the control's properties sheet and entering the items in the `DisplayValues` property (separate each item with a semicolon). You can also set `MultiSelect` to `True` or `False`, and you can specify the number of items shown by using the `Size` property.

Hidden Controls

If you put together a lot of forms, you might find that some of them use similar layouts and controls. For forms that are only slightly different from each other, it might not make sense to write separate scripts to handle the data. It would be nice if you could use a single script and have it branch depending on which form was being used.

An easy way to accomplish this is to include a "hidden" control in each form:

```
<INPUT TYPE=HIDDEN NAME="FieldName" VALUE="Value">
```

As the `HIDDEN` type implies, these controls aren't visible to the user. However, their `NAME` and `VALUE` attributes are sent to the script along with the rest of the form data. Consider the following example:

```
<INPUT TYPE=HIDDEN NAME="FormName" VALUE="Form A">
```

A script could test the `FormName` variable. If its value was `Form A`, it could process one set of instructions. If it was `Form B`, it could process a different set of instructions.

In Word, you can add a hidden control by clicking the Hidden button in the Control Toolbox.

Access and the Internet Database Connector

As you've seen, creating a form isn't all that hard. Unfortunately, forms become considerably trickier when it comes to processing their data. As I've said, this usually requires writing some kind of CGI script. However, if you want to use your form to query an ODBC database on the Web server, there's a way to do so without programming.

The secret is the Internet Database Connector (IDC) that's built into Microsoft's Internet Information Server (IIS). This software lets you query a data source on the server and return an HTML page that displays the results of the query. The components you need to accomplish this are simple text files that you can construct without too much effort. However, there's a way to avoid even that bit of drudgery: Access 97 has a couple of features that will create these components automatically.

Understanding the Internet Database Connector

The Open Database Connectivity (ODBC) standard lets applications query databases without having to know the specifics of how queries are constructed in the native format of the database. You just write a standard query and pass it to the ODBC driver for the data source you're using. The driver takes care of the dirty work of converting the query into something the remote database system understands.

The Internet Database Connector in IIS performs a similar function for Web-based queries. You send a query to the IIS server, it passes the data to the IDC, and the IDC uses an ODBC driver to query the data source. The resulting dynaset is passed back to the IDC, converted into a Web page, and sent to the user's browser.

To accomplish all this, you need to create two files: an IDC file that spells out the particulars of the query, and an HTX file that IIS uses as a template for the returned data. (HTX stands for "HTML extension." See "The Structure of an HTX File" later in this chapter.)

The Structure of an IDC File

An IDC file is a text file that uses the .IDC extension. It specifies various parameters for the query. There are a number of parameters, but only three are required (see the IIS documentation for explanations of the other parameters):

> Datasource: This is the name of the ODBC data source. Note that you have to use a system DSN (data source name) in order for this to work. (NT Server has an ODBC Administrator utility that you can use to create system DSNs.)

`Template`: This is the name of the HTX file that IDC uses as a template for the returned data (see the next section).

`SQLStatement`: This is the SQL command that you want the ODBC driver to execute.

Here's a typical IDC file:

```
Datasource:Northwind
Template:results.htx
SQLStatement:SELECT Customers.CompanyName, Customers.ContactName
+FROM Customers
+WHERE Customers.Country='Canada'
```

This is a query on a table named Customers in the Northwind data source. The SQL SELECT statement is designed to find only those customers for whom the Country field equals "Canada." (Note that it's okay to use multiple lines for the SQL statement; just be sure to use a plus sign (+) at the beginning of each extra line.) The dynaset produced by this query is returned in an HTML file based on the results.htx template.

The Structure of an HTX File

An HTX file is also a text file, but in this case the .HTX extension is used. HTX means "HTML extension." Why "extension"? Because HTX files are really just HTML files, except that they contain "placeholders" that specify where the data in the query dynaset is to be inserted. These placeholders are special tags that IIS understands. For the IDC file just shown, here's an HTX file that you might construct:

```
<HTML>
<HEAD>
<TITLE>Customers Located in Canada</TITLE>
</HEAD>
<BODY>
<TABLE>
<TR>
<TH>Company Name<TH>Contact Name

<%BeginDetail%>
<TR>
<TD><%CompanyName%>
<TD><%ContactName%>
<%EndDetail%>

</TABLE>
</BODY>
</HTML>
```

As you can see, this looks like a typical HTML file that defines a table with headings for each field used in the query. The difference, though, lies in the `<%BeginDetail%>` and `<%EndDetail%>` tags. These special tags tell IIS to run through each record in the dynaset. Placeholders are specified for each field in the dynaset: `<%CompanyName%>` and `<%ContactName%>`. As IIS runs through the records, it substitutes the actual field values. In the end, you're left with a pure HTML file that the browser displays.

Setting Up the Query Form

Once you have your IDC and HTX files constructed, you need to build a form that will execute the query. This is a simple matter of specifying the IDC file in the <FORM> tag's ACTION attribute, like so (the question mark signifies that this action is a query):

```
<FORM ACTION="http://www.server.com/queries/canada_cust.idc?" METHOD=POST>
```

In this case, when the user submits the form, IIS will execute the canada_cust.idc file. In other words, it will run the query that is specified in this file and then return the results.

CAUTION: FOLDERS NEED EXECUTE PERMISSION

When you place your IDC file on the server, make sure that the folder you use is set up for "execute" permission in IIS.

NOTE: IDC HYPERLINKS

Technically, you don't have to set up a form to run an IDC query. You could just create a hyperlink that points to the IDC file, like so:

```
<A HREF="http://www.server.com/queries/canada_cust.idc?">Canadian Customers</A>
```

Rather than hard-coding the SQL statement in the IDC file, you might prefer to use a parameter query. For example, instead of specifying that the query return customers for whom the Country field is "Canada," you might want to give the user the ability to specify which country value he wants to work with. To do this, you use a parameter in your SQL statement:

```
SQLStatement:SELECT Customers.CompanyName, Customers.ContactName
+FROM Customers
+WHERE Customers.Country=%ctry%
```

Now add a text box control (or whatever) to your form, and give it the same name as the SQL statement's parameter:

```
<INPUT TYPE=TEXT NAME="ctry">
```

When the user submits the form, IIS replaces %ctry% in the SELECT with whatever the user entered into the text box.

NOTE: THE JOBFORM SAMPLE APPLICATION

Microsoft has set up a sample online application that uses the IDC for querying a database of jobs. This application contains many examples of IDC files, HTX files, and forms, so it's a great way to learn how all this works. (You can even download the files and run the application on your server.) This application is called the Job Forum, and you can find it at the following address:

`http://www.microsoft.com/MSAccess/Internet/JobForum/default.htm`

Creating IDC and HTX Files in Access

Creating the requisite IDC and HTX files isn't difficult, but it's always nice to know that there are faster ways of doing something. Happily, Access 97 provides a couple of quick methods for creating IDC and HTX files automatically.

For starters, use Access to create the query that you want to run (see Chapter 26, "Querying Data," for details). Now select File | Save to HTML to load the Publish To The Web Wizard, described in Chapter 44. When the Wizard asks if you want to create static or dynamic publications, activate the Dynamic (HTX) publications option. The next Wizard dialog box prompts you for the name of the data source (among other things).

Summary

This chapter showed you how to construct and work with Web-based forms. After a brief introduction to forms, I showed you all the form tags, including the basic `<FORM>`/`</FORM>` container, submit and reset buttons, text boxes, option buttons, list boxes, and more. I also showed you how to use Word's Control Toolbox to insert each type of control into an HTML document. You then learned about the Internet Database Connector in IIS and how to construct the IDC and HTX files that you need for this service. Finally, I showed you how to use Access to make it easier to create these IDC and HTX files.

Here's a list of chapters where you'll find related information:

- To learn about the other HTML tags, see Chapter 43, "Understanding Web Documents."

- To learn more about using Word to create a Web page, see Chapter 45, "Creating Web Documents in Word."

- You can use VBScript to perform validation checks on your form before sending it to the server. I'll show you how to use VBScript in Chapter E2 on the CD, "Web Page Programming: ActiveX and VBScript."

- I show you how to get connected to the Internet in Chapter E7 on the CD, "Setting Up an Internet Connection in Windows 95."

Building and Managing an Office Web Site

CHAPTER 47

Make visible what, without you, might perhaps never have been seen.

—Robert Bresson

The chapters here in Part VIII have so far assumed that you're working either on the Internet or within the confines of an existing corporate network or intranet. What do you do if no such structure exists? What if you want to set up a Web site for a particular department or project? In particular, what do you do if you want to feature not only HTML-based pages on your Web but also Office documents in their native format?

In these and related situations, one solution is to roll up your sleeves and construct an Office Web site of your own. What's that? You thought you needed a degree in electrical engineering to run a Web site? Not at all, thanks to two powerful and easy-to-use tools: Personal Web Server and Microsoft FrontPage. This chapter shows you how to work with both of these programs to create and maintain an Office Web site.

An Overview of Personal Web Server

It has always seemed that the lot in life for Microsoft's mainstream Windows products (3.x through 95) was to be left holding the client end of the client/server stick. That's not surprising, because Windows has always been designed as a stand-alone operating system. However, one of the benefits of a (mostly) 32-bit architecture and built-in multithreading is that Windows can at least aspire to higher ground. For example, the Dial-Up Server component (available in the Microsoft Plus! kit for Windows 95) lets a Windows 95 machine act as a Dial-Up Networking host. In the first half of this chapter, you'll learn about a way to send Windows 95 even further into server territory. Specifically, I show you how to implement Personal Web Server to turn your Windows 95 client into a competent World Wide Web server.

Getting Personal Web Server

Personal Web Server is available from various sources:

- With the Office 97 Small Business Edition ValuPack
- In the Internet Explorer Starter Kit
- As a component in the Microsoft FrontPage package
- With the Windows 95 OSR2 update
- At Microsoft's Web site as an Internet Explorer 3.0 (and higher) component:

  `http://www.microsoft.com/ie/download/`

It's important to note, however, that Microsoft has released a version 1.0a for Personal Web Server that fixes a few problems in the 1.0 release. Before running Personal Web Server, be sure to download this latest version. (There's also a patch available for 1.0 users.)

NOTE: INSTALL TCP/IP NETWORKING

Personal Web Server runs both the HTTP and the FTP protocols. Before you can use Personal Web Server, you must install and configure TCP/IP on your computer. See Chapter E1 on the CD, "Office on a Network," and Chapter E7, "Setting Up an Internet Connection in Windows 95," for details. Note, as well, that Personal Web Server's administration tool is browser-based, so you need a Web browser installed on your system.

Viewing the Personal Web Server Defaults

After you install Personal Web Server and restart your computer, you see a new Personal Web Server icon in the system tray, which tells you that the server's HTTP service has started. Before you start serving pages, though, you need to understand some of the defaults that are set for Personal Web Server. Display the Personal Web Server properties sheet by using either of the following methods:

- Double-click the Personal Web Server icon in the system tray.
- Select Start | Settings | Control Panel, and then launch the Personal Web Server icon from the Control Panel window.

Either way, you see the Personal Web Server Properties dialog box, shown in Figure 47.1.

FIGURE 47.1.

Use this properties sheet to configure Personal Web Server.

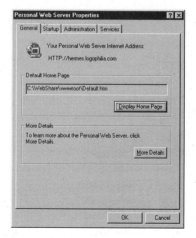

The General tab shows you the root address of your Web server. This address always takes the following form:

```
http://name.domain
```

The interpretation of this address depends on several factors. If you're on a TCP/IP network, for example, *name* is your computer's network name, and *domain* is the domain name of your TCP/IP network. In my example, the computer name is hermes and the domain name is logophilia.com, so the address of my server is http://hermes.logophilia.com. (If you'll be using Personal Web Server exclusively on an intranet, the root address uses the format http://*name*.)

NOTE: CHANGING THE COMPUTER NAME

If you don't like the name used by Personal Web Server, you can change it by right-clicking Network Neighborhood and selecting Properties. In the Network properties sheet that appears, click Identification and then use the Computer Name text box to change the name. Note, however, that changing this name might mess up either the DNS or the WINS resolution for your computer. (This doesn't apply if you're using DHCP on an intranet.)

NOTE: MY REAL WEB SERVER ADDRESS

The http://hermes.logophilia.com address is a temporary server setup for the purposes of this chapter. My full-time Web server has the following URL:

http://www.mcfedries.com/

The Default Home Page group shows you the path and filename of the HTML file that will serve as the initial page that users see when they access your root address. There are two things to note here:

- The path name of the default home page is mapped to the server's root directory. The default path of C:\WebShare\wwwroot\ corresponds to the root (/) of your Web site. In my example, the server's root directory is http://hermes.logophilia.com/, which is the same thing as C:\WebShare\wwwroot\.

- All Web servers define a default document for every directory. If a user does not specify an HTML document in the URL, the server displays the default document. For Personal Web Server, the default document is named default.htm, so the following URLs display the same document:

  http://hermes.logophilia.com/
  http://hermes.logophilia.com/default.htm

Note that you can click the Display Home Page and More Details buttons to load some pages into your browser. However, I hold off discussing the display of pages until later in this chapter. (See "Testing the Web Server" later in this chapter.)

Personal Web Server Startup

This section takes a look at the various startup options that are available with Personal Web Server. These options are divided into two categories: the Web server itself and the services it supports.

The Web Server Startup Options

As I mentioned earlier, the Web server is launched automatically each time you start Windows 95. The controls in the Startup tab of the Personal Web Server Properties sheet, shown in Figure 47.2, determine several Personal Web Server startup options:

Web Server State: This group tells you whether the Web server is currently running. Click Stop to shut down the Web server; to restart the server, click Start.

Run the Web server automatically at startup: When this check box is activated, the Web server is launched each time you start Windows 95.

Show the Web server icon on the taskbar: This check box toggles the Personal Web Server icon in the system tray on and off.

FIGURE 47.2.

Personal Web Server's startup options are found in the Startup tab.

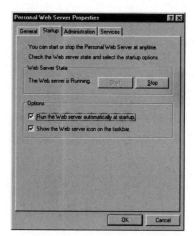

Service Startup Options

Personal Web Server supports both World Wide Web and File Transfer Protocol operations, and these are supported respectively by the HTTP and FTP protocols. Personal Web Server has a separate service to handle each protocol, and these services must be running for users to be able to access Web pages and FTP files.

The Services tab, shown in Figure 47.3, allows you to start and stop each service. To do so, highlight the service and then click either Start or Stop.

FIGURE 47.3.

You can start and stop both the FTP server and the Web (HTTP) server from the Services tab.

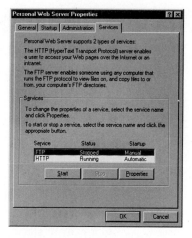

By default, the HTTP service launches automatically at startup, but the FTP service does not. To change these defaults, highlight a service, click Properties to display the service's properties sheet (Figure 47.4 shows the dialog box that appears for the HTTP service), and activate either Automatic or Manual.

FIGURE 47.4.

Use this dialog box to determine whether the HTTP service launches automatically at startup. The properties sheet for the FTP service is similar.

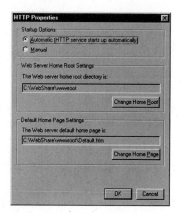

Testing the Web Server

With both the Web server and the HTTP service started, you should now check to make sure that the server works properly before moving on to more serious administration issues. The next two sections show you how to test the server on both an intranet and an Internet connection.

Testing an Intranet Connection

If you'll be using Personal Web Server on an intranet, you need to do two things before trying the Web server:

- Establish a connection to the network.
- Enable WINS resolution on the server computer. WINS (Windows Internet Name Service) maps NetBIOS computer names to IP addresses. Enabling WINS allows other computers on the intranet to find your server. (See Chapter E7 for more information.)

To test the connection, start a Web browser and enter a URL of the following form:

`http://name/`

Here, *name* is the NetBIOS name of the computer running the Web server (for example, `http://hermes/`). You should see the default Personal Web Server home page, shown in Figure 47.5.

FIGURE 47.5.

The default Personal Web Server home page.

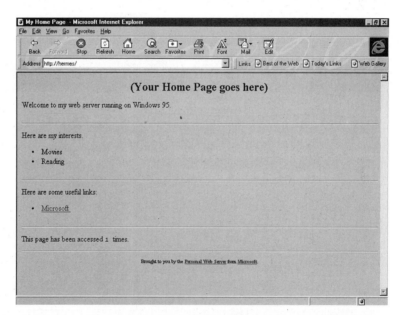

TIP: THE HOME PAGE DOES NOT APPEAR

If you don't see the home page, try entering a URL of the following format:

`http://IPaddress/`

Here, *IPaddress* is the IP address of the computer running the Web server (for example, `http://205.123.45.6/`).

continues

> continued
>
> If that still doesn't work, try the `localhost` address:
>
> `http://localhost/`

As you can see in Figure 47.5, the default.htm supplied with Personal Web Server isn't much to look at, so you need to make changes before inviting guests over to your Web home.

Testing an Internet Connection

Although I assume in this chapter that your goal is to set up an intranet-based Web site, you might want to include an Internet connection as well. If you want to use Personal Web Server to hand out Web pages to Internet-based surfers, note that you must have a static IP address. That way, the Domain Name System (DNS) can always find your computer (which isn't possible if you use DHCP or some other on-the-fly IP address assignment). If you don't have a static IP address assigned to your computer, an alternative is to set up a proxy server that uses "IP masquerading" to make it look as though your computer has a static IP address.

NOTE: THE WINGATE PROXY SERVER

A software program called Wingate lets you establish an Internet connection on one Windows 95 machine and then have other networked Windows 95 machines access the Internet through that same connection. In other words, it lets you set up a Windows 95 client as an Internet gateway. See the following Web page for more information:

`http://www.deerfield.com/wingate/`

Now establish a connection to your ISP (if necessary), load your Web browser, and enter the root address of your server. What is your root address? It's `http://` followed by the DNS name assigned to your computer. This name takes one of the following forms:

- If you're on a TCP/IP network, the name is *name.domain*, where *name* is your computer's network name and *domain* is the domain name of your TCP/IP network. In the Personal Web Server example I'm using in this chapter, the computer's name is `hermes` and the domain is `logophilia.com`, so here's my root address:

  `http://hermes.logophilia.com/`

- If you connect to an ISP, the name is usually *user.domain*, where *user* is your user name and *domain* is the domain name of your ISP (or a domain suffix supplied by the ISP). For example, given a user name of `biff` and an ISP domain of `provider.com`, here's the root address:

  `http://biff.provider.com/`

TROUBLESHOOTING: THE ROOT ADDRESS DOESN'T WORK

If the default Personal Web Server home page doesn't appear, there could be a DNS problem. As before, try connecting again using only your IP address. .

NOTE: MORE TROUBLESHOOTING IDEAS

If you still can't connect to your home page, there might be a problem with either your TCP/IP settings or your Internet connection. Head for Chapter E7 to verify that you installed and configured everything correctly, and check out the troubleshooting notes in that appendix.

Administering the Web Server

Assuming that Personal Web Server is serving up Web pages without a complaint, it's now time to get your site ready for external access. This task involves a number of administrative details, such as setting up security, establishing time-outs, mapping directories, and setting up Web site monitoring. The next few sections take you through all the Web server's administrative details.

Starting the Internet Services Administrator

Personal Web Server's Internet Services Administrator is a series of Web pages, forms, and scripts that allow you to perform all the required chores within the friendly confines of your favorite browser. To start the Administrator, use any of the following techniques:

- In the Personal Web Server properties sheet, activate the Administration tab and then click Administration.
- Right-click the Personal Web Server icon in the system tray and select Administer from the context menu.
- In your browser, enter the following URL (where *server* is the address of your Web server):

  ```
  http://server/htmla/htmla/htm
  ```

Figure 47.6 shows the Administrator page that appears.

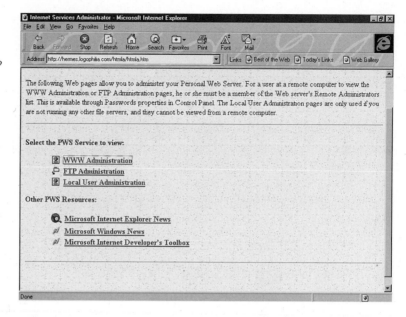

The Service Options

In the Main Administrator page, click the WWW Administration link to display the page shown in Figure 47.7. As you can see, this page has three "tabs" that represent the three aspects of Web server administration: Service, Directories, and Logging. I discuss the Service tab in this section and cover the other two tabs in the following sections. When you're done, click the OK button at the bottom of the page to put the new settings into effect.

The Service tab contains several controls related to the HTTP service. Here's a summary:

Connection timeout: This is the time, in seconds, that the Web server will allow remote users to make a successful connection. If a connection can't be made within this time frame, the Web server sends a Connection timed out error message.

Maximum Connections: This value determines the maximum number of simultaneous connections the Web server will allow.

Allow anonymous: Leave this check box activated to enable anonymous logons. In other words, people who do not have an account on your network can still access your pages. If you want to restrict your pages to those with the correct user names and passwords, clear this check box.

Basic: If you have Web pages that require client authentication (user name and password), activating this check box tells the Web server to accept user names and passwords in unencrypted form. This is a dangerous practice, but few browsers support the Windows NT Challenge/Response, discussed next.

FIGURE **47.7.**

The Service "tab" for the WWW Administration page.

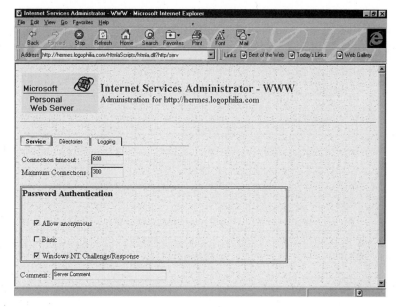

Windows NT Challenge/Response: This is a more robust form of client authentication that accepts only encrypted user names and passwords. As of this writing, the only browser that supports this method is Internet Explorer (version 2.0 and later).

NOTE: CHALLENGE/RESPONSE REQUIRES USER-LEVEL SECURITY

You can use Windows NT Challenge/Response password authentication only if the Web server computer is configured for user-level security with validation provided by a Windows NT domain. See Chapter E1 for details on setting up user-level security.

Configuring Web Folders

Personal Web Server handles folders in two different ways:

■ If a folder is a subfolder of the root (C:\WebShare\wwwroot), browsers can access the folder directly. For example, if you add a home subfolder (C:\WebShare\wwwroot\home), users can access this folder by adding home/ to the root address:

```
http://server/home/
```

■ For all other folders, you must set up an *alias* that maps the folder path to a virtual server folder. For example, the HTML files for the Administrator are located in the C:\Program Files\WebSvr\Htmla folder, and Personal Web Server maps this folder path to the /Htmla alias. This means you access this folder in a Web browser like so:

```
http://server/htmla/
```

For your Office web, you'll want to set up aliases for folders that contain the documents you want to include in the Web. Here are some ideas:

By User: Set up a Users folder and create subfolders for each user who has access to the Web. You can then set up an alias for each user. For example, suppose the user Biff stores his documents in the C:\WebShare\wwwroot\users\biff folder. If you map this folder to the /biff alias, this user's "home" directory is `http://server/biff/`.

By Department: Set up folders for each department or group that will access the Web. As with users, your best bet is to map these department folders to top-level Web paths (such as `http://server/Marketing/`).

By Project: If you have users collaborating on particular projects, set up folders for each project. In this case, you might consider creating an overall Projects folder and then adding subfolders for each project. You then map, say, C:\WebShare\wwwroot\Projects\Budget97\ to /Projects/Budget97.

By Application: If you're setting up a library of Office documents for others to use, you might want to set up folders and aliases for each Office application (Word, Excel, and so on). You can then create subfolders for various document categories (templates, faxes, invoices, and so on).

Web aliases are controlled by the Directories tab on the WWW Administrator page. As you can see in Figure 47.8, the Administrator displays a table showing the current aliases and their "real" folder paths.

To add a new folder alias, follow these steps:

1. Click the Add link. The Administrator displays the form shown in Figure 47.9.

2. Use the Directory text box to enter the path of the folder you want to work with (or click Browse to use another form to choose the folder).

3. If you want this folder to be the home directory for your Web site, activate the Home Directory option button. Otherwise, activate the Virtual Directory option and use the Directory Alias text box to enter an alias for the folder.

4. Use the Access options to determine the type of access allowed in this folder: Read and/or Execute (you need only Execute access if you'll be placing scripts within the folder).

5. Click OK to add the alias and return to the Directories tab.

Figure 47.8.

The Directories tab allows you to map aliases for the folders on your computer.

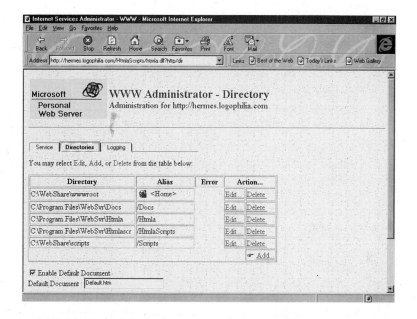

Figure 47.9.

Use this form to add new folder aliases to your web.

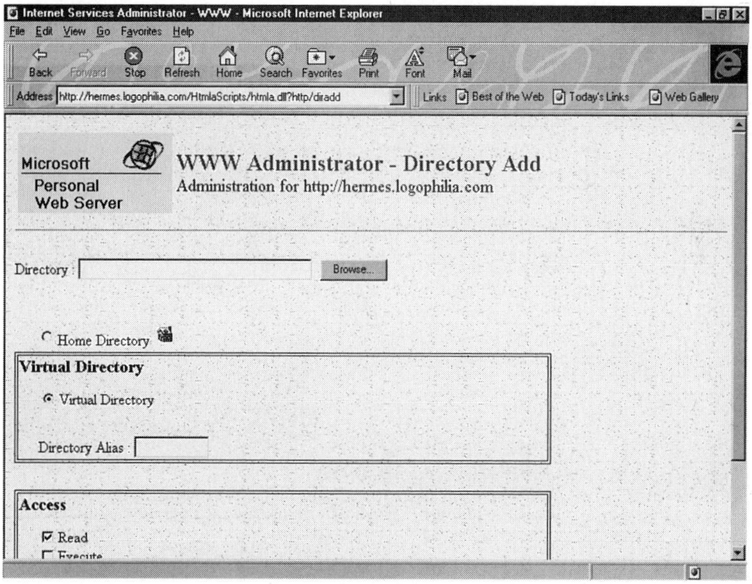

47

BUILDING AND
MANAGING AN
OFFICE WEB SITE

NOTE: WORKING WITH EXISTING ALIASES

To make changes to an existing alias, click the appropriate Edit link. The page that appears is similar to the one shown in Figure 47.9.

If you no longer need an alias, click its Delete link.

The Directories tab also includes a few other controls:

Enable Default Document: When this check box is activated, users who don't specify a document when entering a URL will be shown the default document (assuming that one exists in the folder).

Default Document: Use this text box to specify the name of the default document used in each folder. The most common names for default documents are default.htm, default.html, index.htm, and index.html.

Directory Browsing Allowed: When this check box is activated and no default document exists in a folder (or if you deactivate the Enable Default Document check box), the user sees a list of all the files in the folder.

Another Way to Set Up Web Folders

Instead of cranking up the WWW Administrator to set up Web folders, you can do it directly from Windows Explorer. Here are the steps to follow:

1. Right-click the folder you want to share and select Sharing.

2. In the dialog box that appears, activate the Shared As option and enter the alias name for the folder in the Share Name text box, as shown in Figure 47.10.

FIGURE 47.10.

You can set up Web folders directly from the folder's properties sheet.

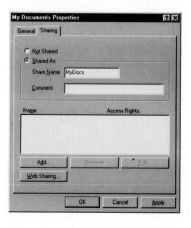

3. Click Web Sharing. Windows 95 displays the Web Sharing Folder Properties dialog box, shown in Figure 47.11.

4. Activate the Share folder for HTTP check box.

5. Activate either or both of the Read Only and Execute Scripts check boxes.

6. Click OK to return to the folder's properties sheet.

7. Click Add to display the Add Users dialog box.

8. Highlight The world and then click Read Only.

FIGURE 47.11.

Use this dialog box to specify that this folder is to be shared for the HTTP service.

9. Click OK to return to the folder's properties sheet.

10. Click OK to put the share into effect.

The Logging Options

After your Web server is chugging along and serving pages to all and sundry, you might start to wonder which pages are popular with surfers and which ones are languishing. You might also want to know if users are getting errors when they try to access your site.

You can glean all of this information and more by working with Personal Web Server's logs. A log is a text file that records all the activity on your Web site, including the IP address and computer name (if applicable) of the surfer, the file that was served, the date and time the file was shipped to the browser, and the server return code (see the next Note box). For each server request, the log file writes a sequence of comma-separated values, which means it is easy to import the file into a database or spreadsheet program for analysis.

To customize the Web server's logging, activate the Logging tab to display the form shown in Figure 47.12. Here's a review of the controls on this form:

Enable logging: The Web server maintains a log of server activity when this check box is activated.

Automatically open new log: When this check box is activated, the Web server starts a fresh log at the interval specified in the option buttons below it: Daily, Weekly, Monthly, or When the file size reaches *x* MB. If you deactivate this check box, the server uses a single log file to record all activity.

Log file directory: Use this text box to specify the folder in which the Web server will create the log files. Note that the name of each log file depends on the interval you choose for logging. If you choose monthly logging, for example, the log file for August 1997 is In0897.log.

FIGURE 47.12.

Use the Logging tab to enable monitoring of Web server activity.

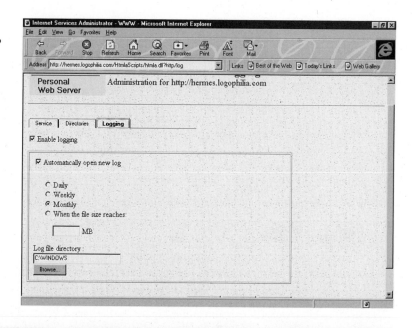

NOTE: SERVER RETURN CODES

A server return code of 200 means the document was sent successfully to the browser. For unsuccessful operations, here's a summary of some of the return codes you'll find in the log:

Return Code	What It Means
204	File contains no content
301	File moved permanently
302	File moved temporarily
400	Bad request
401	Unauthorized access
403	Access forbidden
404	File not found
500	Internal server error
501	Service not implemented
502	Bad gateway
503	Service unavailable

Web Server Security

Depending on the type of Web site you're running and the information stored in your Web pages, you might want to invest a little or a lot of time and effort in securing your site against unauthorized access. There are two basic approaches to Personal Web Server security:

- You can use the same type of access control security that is used by the computer on which Personal Web Server is running.

- You can configure Personal Web Server to use local security, which is a list of users and groups of users given specific access rights within the Web server.

Access Control Security

The easiest (and most robust) form of Web server security is the access control that's built into Windows 95 networking. As you'll learn in Chapter E1, you can configure your Windows 95 machine to use either share-level or user-level security. Specifically, if the "File and printer sharing for Microsoft Networks" service is installed, you can use either share-level security (passwords assigned to specific folders) or user-level security (users and groups assigned to shared folders with pass-through validation provided by a Windows NT server). Similar security levels are available on NetWare networks if the "File and printer sharing for NetWare Networks" service is installed. See Chapter E1 for more information on setting up access control security.

NOTE: RESHARE FOLDERS AFTER CHANGING ACCESS TYPE

As noted in Chapter E1, Windows 95 removes all folder shares after you change the access security type. This means that you'll need to reshare your aliased Web folders.

Local User Security

Local user security is a list of users (or groups of users) that are allowed access to your Web site. You use local security if your server is not on a network or if you want to keep server security separate from your computer's overall security. Personal Web Server uses local security only under either of the following conditions:

- If neither the "File and printer sharing for Microsoft Networks" service nor the "File and printer sharing for NetWare Networks" service is installed.

- If one of those services is installed, but you deactivate file and printer sharing. (To do this, right-click Network Neighborhood, select Properties, and click File and Print Sharing. In the dialog box that appears, deactivate both the "I want to be able to give others access to my files" check box and the "I want to be able to allow others to print to my printer(s)" check box.)

After local security is enabled, start the Internet Services Administrator and click the Local User Administration link. This action loads the Local User Administrator page, shown in Figure 47.13. The next couple of sections show you how to put this Administrator to work with local users and groups.

FIGURE 47.13.

Use the Local User Administrator to create lists of local users and groups for your Web site.

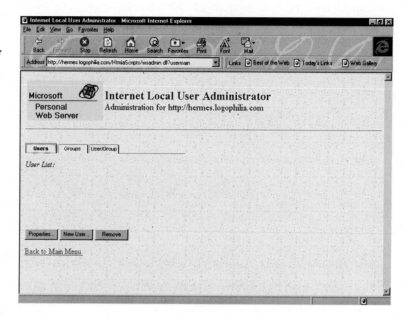

Adding a Local User

The local user list is empty initially, so you need to add users. Here are the steps to follow:

1. To get started, click the New User button. The Administrator displays the form shown in Figure 47.14.

2. Enter a unique name in the User Name field.

3. Enter the user's password in the User Password field. Note that Personal Web Server does not allow null passwords.

4. Enter the password again in the Confirm Password field.

5. Click Add to create the user and return to the Users tab.

To make changes to an existing user, highlight the user's name in the User List and then click Properties. You can delete the highlighted name from the user list by clicking Remove.

FIGURE 47.14.

Use this form to add a user to the list of local users.

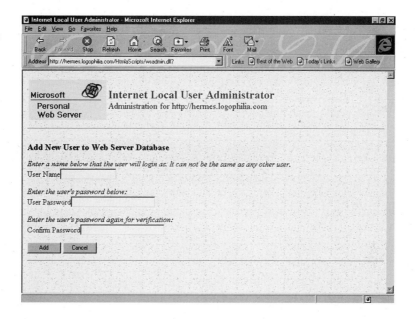

Creating a Group

Instead of working with individual users, you might prefer to work with multiple users at once by adding them to a local group. You can then specify access permissions that will apply to every member of the group.

To create a new local group, follow these steps:

1. Click the Groups tab in the Local User Administrator page.
2. Click New Group to display the form shown in Figure 47.15.

FIGURE 47.15.

Use this form to create a new local group.

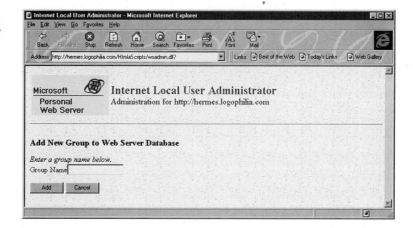

3. Enter a name for the new group in the Group Name text box.

4. Click Add to create the group and return to the Groups tab.

Now you need to populate the group with users. Here are the steps to follow:

1. Activate the User/Group tab in the Local User Administrator page. Figure 47.16 shows the form that appears.

FIGURE 47.16.

Use this form to assign users to groups.

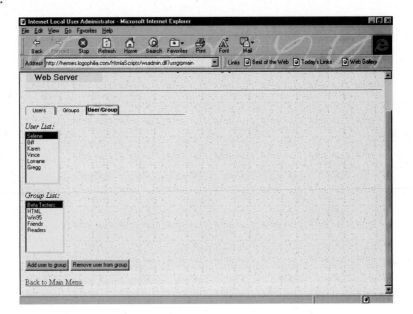

2. In the User List box, highlight the name of a user you want to add to the group.

3. In the Group List box, highlight the name of the group.

4. Click Add user to group.

5. Repeat steps 2 through 4 to add other users to the group.

Implementing Local Security

With your local users and groups set up the way you want, you now need to assign permissions for your Web folders. Here's how the job is done:

1. Right-click the folder you want to work with and select Sharing.

2. Click Add to display the Add Users dialog box.

3. Highlight the users or groups you want to give access to the folder, and then click Read Only.

4. Click OK to return to the folder's properties sheet.

5. Click OK to put the permissions into effect.

Administering the FTP Server

When the FTP service is started, remote users can download files from, and upload files to, your server. The root address of your FTP server takes the following form (where *server* is the network name or DNS name of the computer running Personal Web Server):

```
ftp://server/
```

Note that this root directory is an alias for C:\WebShare\ftproot.

Recall that Personal Web Server doesn't start the FTP service automatically. To get the service running, display the Personal Web Server properties sheet and activate the Services tab. Highlight the FTP service and then click Start.

With the service started, you can set some administrative options. To do so, launch the Internet Services Administrator and click the FTP Administration link. Figure 47.17 shows the form that appears.

FIGURE 47.17.

The FTP administration form.

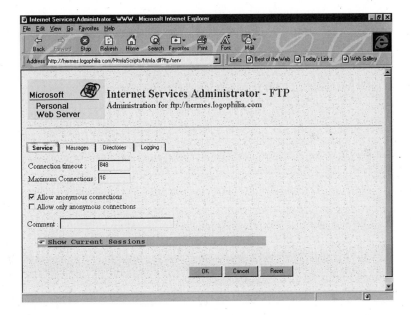

Many of the available administration options are identical to the ones you saw earlier for the Web server, so I'll just summarize the unique points about each tab:

Service: Activate the Allow anonymous connections check box to allow users to establish anonymous FTP sessions. (These are sessions in which the user logs on with the user name anonymous and the e-mail address as the password.) If you want only anonymous users, activate the Allow only anonymous connections check box. Note, too, that you can view a list of the current FTP connections by clicking the Show Current Sessions link. Figure 47.18 shows the page that appears.

Figure 47.18.

Personal Web Server can show you your current FTP connections.

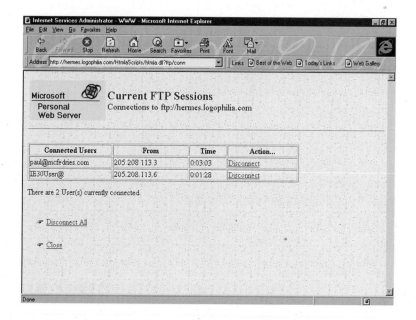

Messages: The controls in this tab specify messages that are sent to the user. The Welcome message appears when the user logs on, and the Exit message appears when the user ends the session. If the service reaches its connection limit (defined in the Service tab), Personal Web Server displays the message shown in the Maximum connections message text box.

Directories: As with the Web server, you can use the Directories tab to set up aliases for folders on your computer. You can also choose to display the FTP directory listings in either UNIX or MS-DOS format.

Logging: This tab is identical to the Logging tab for the Web server. Note, however, that the default value for starting a new log is Daily.

NOTE: FTP AND OFFICE

Don't forget that you can access your FTP server via the Open and Save As dialog boxes in the Office applications. Just set up a new FTP site and use the name of your server as the FTP address. Refer to Chapter 44, "The Office 97 Internet Tools," to learn how to add an FTP site to these dialog boxes.

One caveat, though: Because of the nature of the Office FTP service, the Open and Save As dialog boxes only show subfolders of your FTP root folder. Other folders that you've mapped as aliases won't appear. To work with aliases, you need to use a Web browser.

Remote Administration of Personal Web Server

Although you'll probably perform most of your Web and FTP server administration duties from the computer on which Personal Web Server was installed, at times you might need to make changes from another computer. You can configure Personal Web Server to allow administration either from another computer on your network or via the Internet. Here are the steps to follow:

1. If you've set up Personal Web Server to use local security, make sure that you add a user name (say, Administrator) and password to use for remote administration.

2. Select Start | Settings | Control Panel, and then launch the Passwords icon.

3. Display the Remote Administration tab, shown in Figure 47.19.

FIGURE 47.19.

Use the Remote Administration tab to activate remote administration and specify one or more administrators.

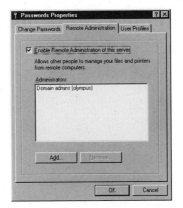

4. Make sure that the Enable Remote Administration of this server check box is activated.

5. Click Add to display the Choose Administrators dialog box.

6. Highlight your administration user (or another appropriate user name) and click Add.

7. Click OK to return to the Remote Administration tab.

8. Click OK to put the new settings into effect.

To access the Internet Services Administrator page remotely, enter the following address into a Web browser (where, as usual, *server* is the network name or DNS name of the server):

```
http://server/htmla/htmla.htm
```

NOTE: YOU CAN'T MODIFY LOCAL USER LIST REMOTELY

If you're using local security, note that you can't modify the local user list when administering the server remotely.

> **NOTE: MORE POWERFUL SOLUTIONS**
>
> Personal Web Server is fine for small Web sites that don't get much traffic. If you're planning a large site, however, you might want to consider a more powerful solution. Here are a few Windows 95 Web servers to check out:
>
> > WebSite: `http://website.ora.com/`
> >
> > Alibaba: `http://alibaba.austria.eu.net/DOCS/index.htm`
> >
> > ZBServer Pro: `http://www.zbserver.com/`
> >
> > For the latest servers, visit the TUCOWS Winsock archive: `http://tucows.mcp.com/`.

Using FrontPage to Manage Your Office Web

Many Office webs are small affairs containing just a handful of folders and no more than a few dozen documents. These mini-webs should pose no great organizational or administrative challenges. The funny thing about Web sites, however, is that they tend to grow quite quickly. Although your Web site may start off modestly enough, the ease with which you can tack on new aliases and insert new documents just about guarantees that a larger, more complex site awaits you down the road.

Naturally, the larger and more complex your Web site becomes, the greater the challenges that face the site administrator. Not only do you have to update the site's folders and files, but elements *inside* the files also require periodic maintenance. For example, many of your Web documents will contain hyperlinks to other files on your Web and possibly to remote Internet sites. If a linked document gets moved or deleted, or if an Internet address is changed or shut down, you must update your links accordingly. That's not a problem for a few files, but a large Office web may have hundreds or even thousands of hyperlinks, so manual maintenance becomes, at best, a full-time job.

If your Office web has grown to an unmanageable size, or if you suspect that it might grow unwieldy in the future, you need a tool that will help you build and maintain your site. The rest of this chapter examines just such a tool: Microsoft FrontPage.

What Is FrontPage?

FrontPage is a Web management and authoring application that's designed to handle all aspects of Web site administration. FrontPage is essentially two tools in one package:

FrontPage Editor: This is a WYSIWYG page creation tool that lets you create and edit Web pages without dealing with the intricacies of HTML.

FrontPage Explorer: You use this tool to create a FrontPage Web, which is a collection of Web documents. The FrontPage Explorer gives you a tree-like view of all the documents in your web, and, for each document, it tracks the images it uses and the hyperlinks it contains. You can use the Explorer to import and export files, maintain hyperlinks, test your web, and much more.

Because my focus in this chapter is maintaining an Office web, I don't cover the FrontPage Editor and instead concentrate solely on the FrontPage Explorer.

Notes on Installing FrontPage

The FrontPage installation procedure is relatively straightforward, so I don't give a blow-by-blow account of the entire process. Instead, here are a couple of notes to bear in mind before beginning the install:

- For best results, you should install Personal Web Server before installing FrontPage. (The FrontPage Setup program reminds you of this.)

- If you plan on implementing user-level access control, you should perform the switch from share-level control before installing FrontPage. Otherwise, you must uninstall FrontPage and then reinstall after changing the security level.

A Tour of FrontPage Explorer

The first time you start FrontPage, it examines your system to extract its host name and TCP/IP address. When that's done, you see the Getting Started with Microsoft FrontPage dialog box, shown in Figure 47.20.

FIGURE 47.20.

You see this dialog box each time you launch FrontPage.

I discuss each of the options in this dialog box later, but for now, create a quick FrontPage web so you can get a feel for the FrontPage Explorer window:

1. Make sure the From a Wizard or Template option is activated, and then click OK. The New FrontPage Web dialog box appears.

2. Highlight Learning Web and then click OK. You see the Learning FrontPage Template.

3. Use the Web Server or File Location box to enter the path of the folder in which you want to create the web. Alternatively, enter the name or address of your Web server.

4. Use the Name of New FrontPage Web text box to name the web.

5. Click OK. FrontPage creates the new web and displays it in the FrontPage window, as shown in Figure 47.21.

FIGURE 47.21.

Once you create the test web, it appears in the FrontPage Explorer window.

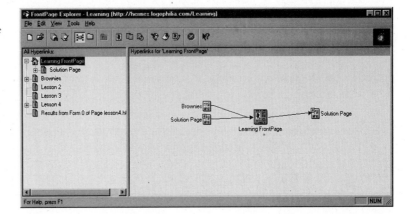

In FrontPage parlance, a *web* is a collection of related documents, including the hyperlinks, images, and other objects that reside within those documents. FrontPage Explorer's job, basically, is to give you a visual display of the various components of a particular web.

As you can see in Figure 47.21, the FrontPage Explorer window is divided into two panes, the contents of which depend on which FrontPage Explorer view you're using: *hyperlink view* or *folder view*.

Hyperlink View

Hyperlink view shows you the connections (that is, links) that exist between the web documents. The left pane gives you a hierarchical outline of the web:

- The top level of the hierarchy represents the documents in the root folder of the web.

- The web home page is shown with a house icon (see Learning FrontPage in the sample web).

- The hierarchy is set up as one or more parent/child relationships, where a document that includes a hyperlink is the parent and a document to which a hyperlink points is the child. In the sample web, the Learning FrontPage document (the parent) has a link that points to the Solution Page document (the child).

- As with Windows Explorer, click the plus sign (+) beside a document to open its branch and display the child document. Click the minus sign (–) to close the branch.
- The names shown are the titles of the HTML files. For regular Office documents, FrontPage shows the filenames.

The right pane shows the hyperlink relationships that exist within whatever document is highlighted in the left pane, as follows:

- The document icon in the middle of the pane represents the highlighted document.
- Arrows that point away from the document represent hyperlinks within the document. The arrows point to icons that represent the linked pages.
- Arrows that point to the document represent hyperlinks from other pages that refer to the document.

Folder View

A FrontPage web is really just a folder that resides within the server root, and the name of the web is the same as the name of this folder. To get a better sense of this, you can switch FrontPage Explorer to folder view by using either of the following methods:

- Select View | Folder View.

- Click the Folder View toolbar button.

As you can see in Figure 47.22, folder view looks much like Windows Explorer. The left pane shows the name of the web's folder at the top and all its subfolders beneath it. The right pane shows the name of each file in the folder along with various bits of information such as the title, size, and last modification date.

FIGURE 47.22.

The FrontPage Explorer in folder view.

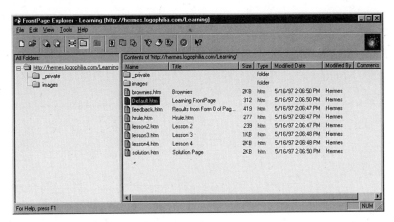

To switch back to hyperlink view, use one of these techniques:

■ Select View | Hyperlink View.

 ■ Click the Hyperlink View toolbar button.

Hyperlink View Options

To further refine the hyperlink view, FrontPage Explorer offers three extra settings:

 Hyperlinks to Images: When this setting is active, FrontPage Explorer also shows hyperlinks that point to image files. To turn on this setting, select View | Hyperlinks to Images or click the Hyperlinks to Images toolbar button.

 Repeated Hyperlinks: If a page has multiple links to the same page, FrontPage Explorer usually only shows a single link. To see all the links to that page, select View | Repeated Hyperlinks or click the Repeated Hyperlinks toolbar button.

 Hyperlinks Inside Page: When this setting is active, FrontPage Explorer also shows hyperlinks that point to an anchor within the current document. To turn on this setting, select View | Hyperlinks Inside Page or click the Hyperlinks Inside Page toolbar button.

Figure 47.23 shows an example. Here I activated the Hyperlinks to Images setting, opened the Brownies page, and highlighted Hrule.htm. Notice how the hrule.gif image appears as a link from Hrule.htm.

FIGURE 47.23.

FrontPage Explorer with the Hyperlinks to Images setting activated.

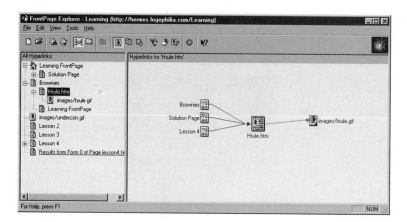

Creating a FrontPage Web

Now that you're familiar with the FrontPage Explorer layout, it's time to put it to good use by creating a FrontPage web. Before getting down to the specifics, however, you have some decisions to make in advance concerning where you want to create your web and how you want to proceed.

When thinking about where you want to create your web, you have two choices:

Create the web directly on the server: With this option, you create and work with your files directly on the Web server. Use this option if you have full-time access to the Web server. Note, however, that you'll be working with "live" server data, so any changes you make will be visible immediately to other people accessing your web on the server.

Create the web locally: With this option, you set up the web on your local hard drive. When your data is fit for public consumption, you then "publish" the web to your Web server. Take this path if you need to work offline or if you don't want incremental changes reflected in the server files.

As far as how you create your web, you again have two ways to go:

Create the web by hand: In this case, you start with an empty web and then add files to it, either by creating the files from scratch or by adding files to the Web folder (you can copy the files or use the FrontPage Explorer's Import feature).

Use a template or wizard: FrontPage comes with a number of templates and wizards that will help you get your web off the ground quickly.

The next few sections expand on all of these techniques.

47

BUILDING AND
MANAGING AN
OFFICE WEB SITE

NOTE: WHAT ABOUT THE ROOT?

Earlier in this chapter, you saw that the Web server has a root folder. How do you use FrontPage Explorer to work with files in the root folder? The secret is that FrontPage maintains a default web called the root web, which corresponds to the root folder on the server. To work with files in the root, you must first open the root web. See "Opening an Existing Web" later in this chapter.

Creating a Web by Hand

If the files you need for your web already exist, or if you'll be creating your own files from scratch, your best bet is to weave your web yourself. To get started, use any of the following techniques:

- Select File | New | FrontPage Web.
- Press Ctrl-N.

- Click the New button on the FrontPage Explorer toolbar.

You then see the New FrontPage Web dialog box, shown in Figure 47.24.

FIGURE 47.24.

Use this dialog box to choose the type of FrontPage web you want to create.

I'll discuss many of the templates and wizards available in this dialog box a bit later (see "Creating a Web with a Template or Wizard"). For now, though, you have three ways to proceed:

Normal Web: If you select this Web template, FrontPage creates a new web that has only a single, blank page that will serve as the home page for your web. (The name of this file will be whatever is defined as the default page on the server, such as default.htm.) Select this option if you don't have a home page defined for your web.

Empty Web: If you choose this Web template, FrontPage creates a new web but doesn't populate it with any files. Select this option if you already have a home page that you want to add to the web later.

Learning FrontPage: Choose this template to create a sample FrontPage web to experiment with and learn the basics of FrontPage.

When you've made your choice, click OK. The name of the dialog box that appears depends on the template you chose. For example, Figure 47.25 shows the Learning FrontPage Template dialog box. Here's a summary of the controls:

Web Server or File Location: Here's where you decide whether you want to create your web on the server or locally. To place the web on the server, enter the name or address of the Web server. To create a local web, enter the path for the folder in which you want your web created.

Connect Using SSL: If you specified a server in the preceding text box, activating this check box tells FrontPage that you want to connect to the server using the Secure Sockets Layer protocol. (This protocol ensures secure communications between FrontPage and the Web server.)

Name of New FrontPage Web: Use this text box to specify a name for your new web. Note that FrontPage creates a new folder with this name, and all web files are stored in that folder. The folder location depends on where you create your Web:

■ If you're creating your web on the server, FrontPage adds a subfolder to the server's root folder. For example, a new web named `MyWeb` has the following URL:

```
http://server/MyWeb/
```

■ If you're creating your web locally, FrontPage adds a subfolder to the folder you specified. For example, if you specified C:\Webs and your new web is named MyWeb, FrontPage creates the following folder:

```
C:\Webs\MyWeb
```

FIGURE 47.25.

Use this dialog box to enter your server name and a name for your new web.

NOTE: FRONTPAGE WEB NAMES

Here are some notes to bear in mind when choosing a name for your new web:

■ FrontPage doesn't allow you to enter spaces in the web name.

■ Restrictions on other characters and the length of the web name depend on the type of Web server you're using. If you're running Personal Web Server on a Windows 95 machine, for example, your web name must follow the usual Windows 95 naming conventions (except, as I've said, spaces are forbidden).

■ If you're using a UNIX server, note that directory names are case-sensitive. MyWeb is different from myweb.

Once you've entered your information, click OK. FrontPage then creates the new web and returns you to the FrontPage Explorer window. From here, skip down to the section "Adding Files to the Web" to see how you go about populating your web.

Creating a Web with a Template or Wizard

If you don't have any existing web pages and the idea of creating everything from scratch sounds like too much work, you can either use one of the predefined templates or else enlist the services of the FrontPage Web wizards to get you started. These templates and wizards create a set of web pages on a particular theme, which you can then customize as needed. In addition to the Normal and Empty templates discussed in the last section, FrontPage also comes with the templates and wizards discussed in the next few sections.

Corporate Presence Wizard

Use this wizard to design a Web site for a corporation. You can place basic company data on the home page and then include other pages for product and service information, feedback, searching, and more. Here's a summary of the information the wizard asks for during the creation of this type of web:

- The pages you want to include in the web. In addition to the home page, you can also add the following pages: What's New, Products/Services, Table of Contents, Feedback Form, Search Form. Subsequent wizard dialog boxes let you further customize each of these choices.

- The topics you want to place on the web's home page, such as an introduction, mission statement, company profile, and contact information.

- The common information that you want to appear at the top of each page (such as your company logo and links to the main pages) and at bottom of each page (such as a contact e-mail address and copyright information).

- The overall style of the pages (Plain, Conservative, Flashy, or Cool).

- The colors you want to use for text and links, as well as the background image to use.

- Whether you want an "under construction" icon to appear on all unfinished pages.

- Your company's name, address, phone and fax numbers, and e-mail addresses.

- Whether you want the To Do List displayed after the web is created. (I'll discuss the To Do List later in this chapter. See the section titled "The FrontPage Explorer Tools.")

Once the web is created, you need to customize the pages with specific information for your company. Figure 47.26 shows a web created using this wizard and Figure 47.27 shows how the home page appears in Internet Explorer.

FIGURE 47.26.

A Corporate Presence web.

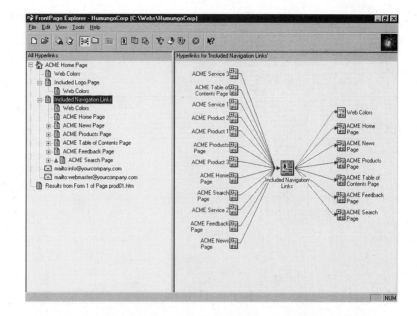

FIGURE 47.27.

The home page for the Corporate Presence web.

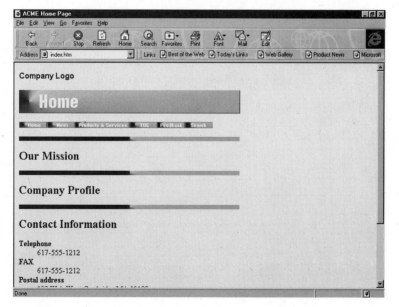

Customer Support Web

The Customer Support web is designed for companies that require customer support. It creates What's New and FAQ (Frequently Asked Questions) pages, forms for submitting suggestions and bug reports, a file download page, a discussion page, and a search form. Figure 47.28 shows part of the web and Figure 47.29 shows the home page.

FIGURE 47.28.

The Customer Support web.

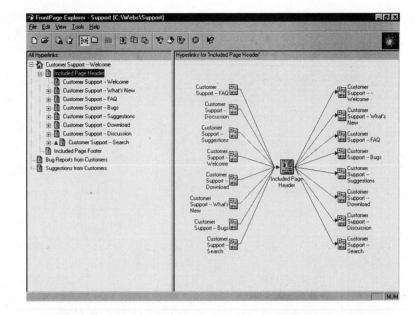

FIGURE 47.29.

The home page for the Customer Support web.

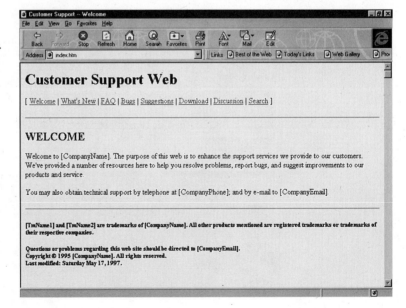

Discussion Web Wizard

If you've ever participated in a Usenet newsgroup, you know that the content of these groups is a collection of messages on a particular topic. A person sends a message to the group, another person responds to that message, someone else responds to the response, and so on. A particular series of messages and their responses is called a *thread.*

If you want to add the same message/response give-and-take to your Web site, use the Discussion Web Wizard to set it up. This wizard creates a web that has a form for submitting articles, a table of contents that shows the submitted articles, a search feature, and more. Here's a rundown of some of the data requested by this wizard:

■ The main features of the web, including a table of contents, a search form, a confirmation page, and whether you want threaded replies (which give users the ability to respond to specific articles).

■ The name of the discussion (this appears at the top of each page) and the name of the folder that is used to store the articles.

■ The fields you want to include on the submission form.

■ Whether you want the discussion available to everyone or just to registered users.

■ Some table of contents options (how you want the contents sorted and whether this page should be the home page).

■ The colors you want to use for text and links.

■ Whether you want to use frames to display the articles.

Figure 47.30 shows a web created using this wizard. Figure 47.31 shows the Submission Form.

FIGURE 47.30.

A web created with the Discussion Web Wizard.

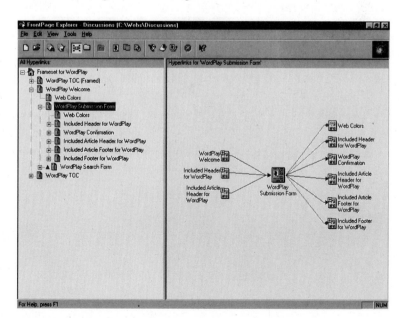

FIGURE 47.31.

The Submission Form created by the Discussion Web Wizard.

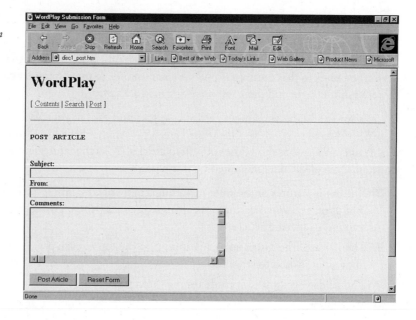

Personal Web

The Personal Web template creates a basic home page for an individual. This page includes sections on employee information, current projects, a list of hot links, personal interests, biographical and contact data, and a comments form. Figure 47.32 shows the web, and Figure 47.33 shows how the page looks in Internet Explorer.

FIGURE 47.32.

The Personal web.

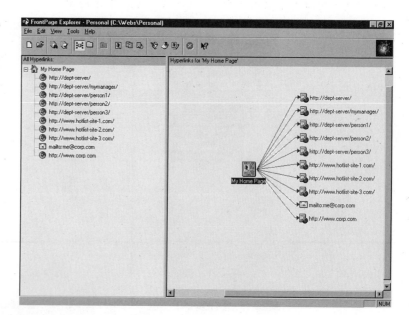

FIGURE 47.33.

How the Personal Web page looks in the browser.

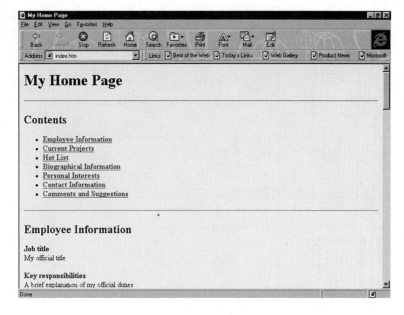

Project Web

The Project Web template is useful for creating webs related to specific projects or tasks. The home page includes a section where you can enter the latest project news, and it also includes links to the following pages: a description of the project members, the project schedule and status, the project archives, a search form, and a discussion area. Figure 47.34 shows the web and Figure 47.35 shows the unmodified home page.

FIGURE 47.34.

The Project web.

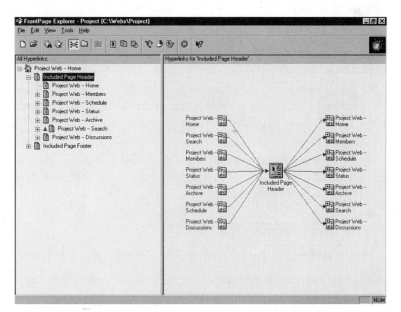

FIGURE 47.35.

The Project web home page.

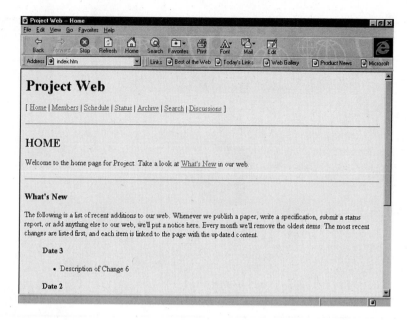

Adding Files to the Web

When you create a web by hand, you need to fill out the web by adding files. Even if you use one of the templates or wizards, you may still need to toss in some other files to get the web set up the way you want. Either way, FrontPage Explorer gives you three ways to add a file to a web: create a new file, add a file to the web's folder, and import a file or folder into the web.

Creating a New File

If you don't have any existing files that you want to include in your web, you need to build files from scratch:

- For HTML files, you can use Notepad, Word, or any other HTML editor.

- If you want to take advantage of the FrontPage server extensions, use the FrontPage Editor to create your pages. You can open the FrontPage Editor either by selecting Tools | Show FrontPage Editor or by clicking the Show FrontPage Editor toolbar button.

- To create a new graphics file, open the Image Composer application (assuming you installed it) either by selecting Tools | Show Image Editor or by clicking the Show Image Editor toolbar button.

- If you want to include a new Office document in your web, use the appropriate Office application to create the file.

Whatever method you use to create the file, you have two choices for adding it to your web:

- If your web is stored locally, save the file to the web's folder on your hard disk.

■ If your web is stored on the server, save the file to the appropriate network folder (or use FTP for remote connections).

Return to FrontPage Explorer and select View | Refresh (or press F5) to update the web and display the file.

Adding Files to the Web Folder

In the last section, you saw that adding a new file to a web was a simple matter of saving the file to the web's folder. It should come as no surprise that the secret to adding any existing file to your web is to copy or move the file into the web's folder. You have a couple of ways to proceed:

■ Use the standard Windows Explorer techniques to copy or move the file into the web folder.

■ Open the web in FrontPage Explorer and then drag the file from Windows Explorer and drop it inside the FrontPage Explorer window.

TIP: ADDING FILES TO WEB SUBFOLDERS

To add a file to a web subfolder, switch FrontPage Explorer Editor to folder view, open the subfolder you want to use, and drop the file on the Contents pane.

NOTE: YOU CAN ADD FOLDERS, AS WELL

The techniques in this section apply equally well to folders, which means you can add entire folders to your web.

Importing a File or Folder

Although adding files and folders to your web folder is a straightforward way to bulk up your web, FrontPage also offers an Import feature that makes it easy to add large numbers of files or folders. The next two sections discuss the Import command and the Import Web Wizard.

Using the Import Command

Here are the steps to follow to import files or folders using the Import command:

1. Open the web to which you want to import the files or folders.

2. Select File | Import to display the Import File to FrontPage Web dialog box.

3. To choose a file to import, click Add File, highlight the file in the Add File to Import List dialog box, and click Open. FrontPage adds the file to the import list in the Import File to FrontPage Web dialog box.

4. To choose a folder to import, click Add Folder, highlight the folder in the Browse for Folder dialog box, and click OK. FrontPage adds the folder's files to the import list in the Import File to FrontPage Web dialog box.

5. To change the relative URL used for a file displayed in the import list, highlight the file, click Edit URL, adjust the URL in the dialog box that appears, and click OK.

TIP: YOU CAN SPECIFY A NEW WEB SUBFOLDER

When you edit a URL, you can specify a new subfolder in which to store the file and FrontPage creates the folder for you automatically. For example, suppose you're importing a file named August.htm and you want to store it in a new subfolder named Schedule. To have FrontPage create this folder, select the file and edit its URL to Schedule\August.htm.

---

6. Click OK to import the files.

Using the Import Web Wizard

FrontPage also comes with an Import Web Wizard that takes you step-by-step through the process of importing a folder. Here's how it works:

1. Open the web to which you want to import the files or folders.

2. Select File | New | FrontPage Web to display the New FrontPage Web dialog box.

3. Highlight Import Web Wizard, activate the Add to the current web check box, and click OK. FrontPage launches the Import Web Wizard, shown in Figure 47.36.

Figure 47.36.

Use the first Import Web Wizard dialog box to choose the source folder you want to import.

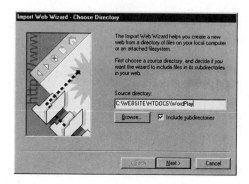

4. Use the Source directory text box to enter the path of the folder you want to import. Alternatively, click Browse, highlight the folder in the Browse for Folder dialog box, and click OK.

5. If you want FrontPage to import any subfolders, as well, make sure the Include subdirectories check box is activated.

6. Click Next.

7. The next Import Web Wizard dialog box, shown in Figure 47.37, displays a list of the files that will be imported. If it lists files you don't want to include in your web, highlight them and click Exclude.

FIGURE 47.37.

Use this Import Web Wizard to exclude any files you don't want in your web.

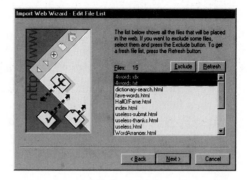

8. Click Next to display the final Import Web Wizard dialog box.
9. Click Finish to import the files.

Publishing a Web

If you elected earlier to store your web locally, you eventually need to copy the web files to the server. In FrontPage lingo, this is known as *publishing* the web, and this section shows you how it works.

To begin, open the web you want to publish, and then select File | Publish FrontPage Web to display the Publish FrontPage Web dialog box, shown in Figure 47.38.

FIGURE 47.38.

This dialog box appears when you select the Publish FrontPage Web command.

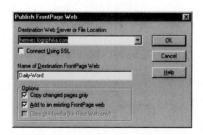

Here's a summary of the controls:

> **Destination Web Server or File Location:** Use this box to enter the name or address of the Web server.
>
> **Connect Using SSL:** Activate this check box if you want to connect to the server using the Secure Sockets Layer protocol.
>
> **Name of Destination FrontPage Web:** Use this text box to specify a name for the server web. FrontPage uses this name to create a subfolder off the server's root folder.

Copy changed pages only: This check box determines what FrontPage does if you publish a file and a file with the same name already exists on the server Web. When the check box is activated, FrontPage only publishes the file if it has changed since it was last copied to the server.

Add to an existing FrontPage web: When this check box is activated, FrontPage copies the files to an existing web on the server. In this case, use the Name of Destination FrontPage Web text box to enter the name of the existing web. If you're publishing to a new web on the server, deactivate this check box.

Copy child webs (for Root Web only): If you're working with the root web (the top level web on the server), activate this check box if you want to publish all of the root's child webs, as well. (See "Opening an Existing Web" to learn how to work with the root web.)

When you've made your selections, click OK to publish the web on the server.

Working with FrontPage Webs

Now that you've got a web or two in the books, look at some FrontPage Explorer techniques for working with your webs. The next few sections show you how to open existing webs, open web files for editing, delete web files, and delete entire webs.

Opening an Existing Web

To open a web you've created in the past, follow these steps:

1. To get started, FrontPage Explorer gives you all kinds of methods:
   - When you launch FrontPage Explorer, activate the Open Existing FrontPage Web option and click OK.
   - Select File | Open FrontPage Web.

   - Click the Open FrontPage Web toolbar button.

2. In the Open FrontPage Web dialog box that appears, use the Web Server or File Location box to specify the location of the web. Either enter the name or address of the Web server or the path for the folder that contains the web. (As usual, you can activate Connect Using SSL to set up a secure server connection.)

3. Click List Webs. FrontPage displays a list of all the webs in the specified location, as shown in Figure 47.39.

4. Highlight the web you want to open and then click OK.

Figure 47.39.

Click List Webs to see a list of all the webs in the specified location.

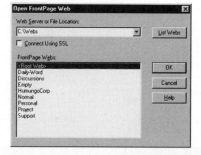

NOTE: THE ROOT WEB

As I mentioned earlier, the root web is the top-level web and it corresponds to the server's root folder. All the other webs you create are contained within this root web. To work with the root web, highlight <Root Web> in the Open FrontPage Web dialog box and click OK.

Note, as well, that once you've opened the server's root web, you can modify the server access permissions directly from FrontPage Explorer. To do this, select Tools | Permissions and use the Permissions dialog box to adjust the access privileges for users and groups.

TIP: CANCELING THE PROCEDURE

Large webs can take a long time to open. If you want to bail out of a lengthy open procedure, or if you realize you're opening the wrong web, you can stop the process by clicking the Stop button on the FrontPage Explorer toolbar.

Opening Web Files for Editing

Once you have a web open, you might find you need to make changes to a particular file. For example, FrontPage might show that a file has a broken hyperlink that you want to fix. There are two ways to open a file from the FrontPage Explorer window:

■ To open a file in its native application, either highlight the file and select Edit | Open or right-click the file and select Open from the shortcut menu. FrontPage opens HTML files in the FrontPage Editor and Office documents in their default Office application.

■ To open a file using some other application, either highlight the file and select Edit | Open With or right-click the file and select Open With from the shortcut menu. Use the Open With Editor dialog box, shown in Figure 47.40, to choose the application and then click OK.

FIGURE 47.40.

Use the Open With Editor dialog box to select the application you want to use to edit the file.

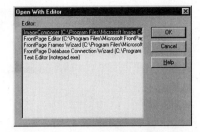

TIP: CHANGING EDITOR ASSOCIATIONS

You can change the applications that appear in the Open With Editor dialog box. Select Tools | Options to display the Options dialog box, and then activate the Configure Editors tab. Highlight the file type you want to change, click Modify, and use the Modify Editor Association dialog box to select a different application.

Deleting Web Files

If a particular file in your web has worn out its welcome, use any of the following techniques to remove the file from the web:

- Select the file and then select Edit | Delete.
- Select the file and then press Delete.
- Right-click the file and then select Delete from the shortcut menu.

Deleting a Web

Rather than deleting individual files from a web, you might prefer to delete the entire web if you no longer need it. To do this, select File | Delete FrontPage Web. FrontPage then warns you that deleting the web is permanent and asks you to confirm the deletion, as shown in Figure 47.41. Click Yes to delete the web. FrontPage Explorer then displays the Getting Started with Microsoft FrontPage dialog box so you can open an existing web or start a new one.

FIGURE 47.41.

FrontPage asks you to confirm a web deletion.

The FrontPage Explorer Tools

If what you've seen so far was all that FrontPage Explorer did, it would still be worth the money. The bird's-eye view of a web's files, objects, and links, the easy access to the files' native applications for editing, and the simplicity with which you can publish a web all make FrontPage a great addition to any Office webmaster's tool kit.

However, FrontPage Explorer has quite a few more tricks up its electronic sleeve. For example, you can use it to verify all the hyperlinks in your web files, and you can use it to replace text and check spelling across all the web files. The rest of this chapter covers these and other handy FrontPage Explorer techniques.

The To Do List

As the proprietor of a medium-sized Web site (around 3,000 files), I can tell you that a webmaster's work is never done. There are new pages to create, existing documents to convert to HTML, user feedback messages to process, scripts to write, server errors to track, and a lot of little tweaks to perform in an effort to avoid the "cobweb" label. (A cobweb site is one that hasn't been updated for a long time.)

Those of us who are organizationally challenged keep track of all these endless tasks by scribbling messages on sticky notes, flagging items in Outlook, and keeping the rest filed in our heads (where they often get lost in the clutter). Happily, FrontPage offers an alternative to this haphazard and inefficient approach: the To Do List. The feature is about what you expect: a simple list of tasks to be performed at some future date. Moreover, FrontPage maintains a To Do List for each of your webs, so you don't have to worry about getting your tasks confused.

To view the To Do List, use either of the following techniques:

- Select Tools | Show To Do List.

- Click the Show To Do List toolbar button.

Figure 47.42 shows a typical To Do List. As you can see, each task is given a name, the user name of the person assigned the task, the task priority, the page to which the task is linked, and a description of the task.

Figure 47.42.

*A FrontPage
To Do List.*

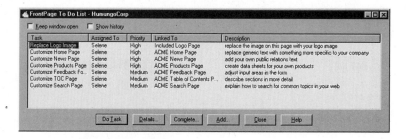

Here's a quick summary of the various methods you can use to work with the To Do List:

Creating a new, unlinked task: To add an unlinked task to the list (that is, a task that isn't linked to a particular file), click Add to display the Add To Do Task dialog box, shown in Figure 47.43. Enter a name for the task, assign it to a user, select a priority, and enter a description.

FIGURE 47.43.

Use the Add To Do Task dialog box to create a new task.

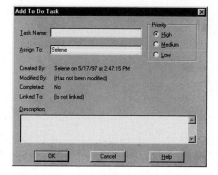

Creating a new, linked task: To add a task that's linked to a particular file, click the file in FrontPage Explorer, select Edit | Add To Do Task, and fill in the Add To Do Task dialog box.

Editing a task: To make changes to a task, highlight it in the To Do List, click Details, and use the Task Details dialog box to make your changes.

Performing a task: If a task is linked to a file, you can open that file for editing by highlighting the task and clicking Do Task. If you want to keep the To Do List on-screen while you perform each task, activate the Keep window open check box.

Marking a task as complete: When a task is done, you can mark it as complete by highlighting it in the To Do List and clicking Complete. In the Complete Task dialog box that appears, shown in Figure 47.44, either activate Mark this task as completed or activate Delete this task and then click OK. Tasks that are marked as completed become part of the To Do List's history file. You can display the history by activating the Show history check box in the To Do List window.

FIGURE 47.44.

Use this dialog box to mark a task as completed.

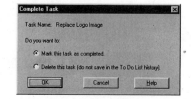

Verifying Hyperlinks

Hyperlinks are the lifeblood of any Web page. However, you don't have to spend all that much time surfing the World Wide Web before stumbling upon an inescapable fact: Broken hyperlinks are a way of Web life. Whether it's a server down for the count, a defunct account, a deleted, moved, or renamed page, or simply the wrong URL, links fail and users get frustrated.

To help reduce the hair pulling and teeth gnashing caused by broken links on your web, FrontPage has a handy feature that checks and verifies all the hyperlinks contained in a web. If changes are necessary, you can edit the links directly without loading the whole page (although you can load the whole page if you want).

Follow these steps to verify the links in the current web:

1. Select Tools | Verify Hyperlinks. This displays the Verify Hyperlinks dialog box, which contains a list of all the hyperlinks in the web.

2. Click Verify. FrontPage runs through each of the links, checks to see if they're valid, and displays the results in the Status column (OK or Broken), as shown in Figure 47.45.

FIGURE 47.45.

FrontPage uses the Status column to tell you whether a link is broken.

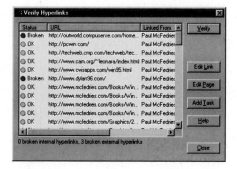

3. FrontPage gives you three options for dealing with any link:

    Edit Link: Click this button to display the Edit Link dialog box, shown in Figure 47.46. Enter the new URL, choose which pages to update (if the link is used on multiple pages), and click OK.

    Edit Page: Click this button to load the page into FrontPage Editor for adjustments.

    Add Task: Click this button to add a "Fix broken link" task to the To Do List.

4. When you're done, click Close.

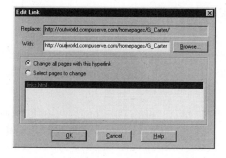

Finding Across Files

If your web contains only a few pages, it's usually easy enough to find the information you need. In a large Web site, however, locating a bit of text becomes more problematic. To help, FrontPage offers a handy Find feature that lets you search for a word or phrase across every file in your web.

To use this feature, first open the web you want to work with. Your first decision is which files in the web you want to search. FrontPage Explorer searches every file in the web by default. However, you can perform the search across only part of the web by selecting the files in advance.

You can get started by using any of the following techniques:

- Select Tools | Find.
- Press Ctrl-F.

- Click the Cross File Find toolbar button.

FrontPage displays the Find in FrontPage Web dialog box, shown in Figure 47.47. Fill in the following fields:

FIGURE 47.47.

Use the Find in FrontPage Web dialog box to specify your search text.

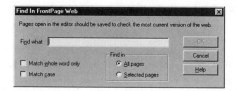

Find what: Use this text box to enter the word or phrase you want to find.

Match whole word only: When this check box is deactivated, FrontPage looks for text that *contains* the search text. If you only want to find instances that match the search text exactly, activate this check box.

Match case: Activate this check box to make your search case-sensitive.

Find in: Activate All pages to perform the search across every file in the web. Otherwise, activate Selected pages to perform the search across only the files you selected.

When you're ready to go, click OK. FrontPage scours the web for the search text and then displays the results in a Find dialog box similar to the one shown in Figure 47.48. From here, highlight a page and then click Edit Page. FrontPage loads the page into the FrontPage Editor and displays a standard Find dialog box with which you can search the file.

FIGURE 47.48.

This dialog box shows you which pages in the web contain the search text.

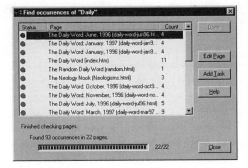

Finding and Replacing Across Files

Any Web site worth its salt has common design or content elements on most, if not all, pages. It could be a list of links to your main pages, a logo, a copyright message, or contact information. These common elements establish the overall look and feel of your pages and ensure that users always know where to find certain bits of information.

The big problem with these common tags or text is that if you want to change any of the data, you have to plow through every page on your site to do it. That's no big deal if you have just a few pages to take care of, but it's a chore of nightmarish dimensions if you have hundreds.

Fortunately, you can turn that nightmare into a pleasant dream by using FrontPage Explorer's Replace Across Files feature. This gem of a command scours an entire web for a particular piece of text and replaces it with whatever text you specify. This is perfect for updating e-mail addresses, changing GIF filenames, updating link URLs, and so on.

To use this feature, open the web you want to work with and optionally select the files you want to work with. Now select Tools | Replace, or press Ctrl-H, to display the Replace in FrontPage Web dialog box, shown in Figure 47.49. This dialog box uses the same fields as the Find dialog box, except that you also use the Replace with text box to enter the replacement text.

When you click OK, FrontPage runs through the pages, looking for the search text. When it's done, it displays a Find dialog box similar to the one shown earlier in Figure 47.48. Again, highlight the page you want to work with and then click Edit Page. This loads the FrontPage Editor and displays a standard Replace dialog box that you can use to perform the replacements.

Figure 47.49.

*Use the Replace in
FrontPage Web dialog
box to replace text
across your web files.*

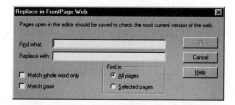

NOTE: ALSO CONSIDER INCLUDE FILES

An *include file* is a text file that contains text and HTML tags. By adding a special code to your Web pages, you can tell the server to insert the contents of the include file in strategic locations. For example, you can set up a "footer" text file that includes a standard copyright message and contact information and then add an include file code at the bottom of each of your pages. If any of this information changes, you need only change the single include file and each page shows the new data automatically. To insert such a code, select Insert | WebBot in the FrontPage Editor and then select the Include WebBot.

Checking Spelling Across Files

The Internet as a whole displays a remarkable tolerance for spelling mistakes. I suppose that's because many Netizens don't use English as their first language, so words are often spelled creatively. That doesn't mean, however, that you should tolerate misspelled words on your own site. A thorough proofread of all your pages is a must. To be safe, however, FrontPage also offers a useful feature that checks spelling across your entire web.

As with Find and Replace, first select the pages you want to check, if necessary. Then use any of the following techniques to get the spell check started:

- Select Tools | Spelling.
- Press F7.

- Click the Cross File Spelling toolbar button.

FrontPage displays the Spelling dialog box, shown in Figure 47.50. Choose whether you want to check all the pages in the web or just those you've selected, and then click Start.

Figure 47.50.

*FrontPage displays this
dialog box when you
run the Spelling
command.*

FrontPage examines each page and starts compiling a list of the words that aren't in its dictionary. When it's done, it displays the Check Spelling dialog box, shown in Figure 47.51. For each page you want to fix, highlight the page and then click Edit Page. This loads the page into the FrontPage Editor and launches a standard spell check.

Figure 47.51.

Once the spell check is complete, FrontPage displays the results.

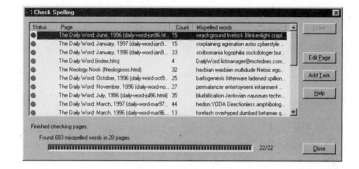

Summary

This chapter discussed a couple of tools that help you set up and maintain an Office Web site. The first half of the chapter showed you how to set up a Web server on a Windows 95 machine. After examining the Personal Web Server defaults and startup options, I showed you how to test your server. From there, you learned how to administer the Web server, set up Web server security, and administer the FTP server. I also showed you how to enable remote administration of the server.

The second half of this chapter covered FrontPage Explorer, the powerful Web creation and maintenance program. I took you on a tour of the FrontPage Explorer window and then showed you how to create a web both by hand and by using a template or wizard. From there, you learned some techniques for working with webs, including opening a web, editing files, and deleting a web. I closed with a look at a few FrontPage Explorer tools, including the To Do List, Verify Hyperlinks, Find, Replace, and Spelling.

Here's a list of chapters where you'll find related information:

- I covered the basic techniques for finding, replacing, and checking spelling in Chapter 3, "Day-to-Day Office Basics."

- For an introduction to Web pages and HTML, see Chapter 43, "Understanding Web Documents."

- To learn how to use Internet Explorer, Office FTP, and more, see Chapter 44, "The Office 97 Internet Tools."

- I show you how to set up and use your computer on a network in Chapter E1 on the CD, "Office on a Network."

- To learn about TCP/IP and Internet connections, see Chapter E7, "Setting Up an Internet Connection in Windows 95."

IX
PART

Unleashing Office Integration

Office Integration and OLE

IN THIS CHAPTER

CHAPTER

48

A man with a talent does what is expected of him, makes his way, constructs, is an engineer, a composer, a builder of bridges. It's the natural order of things that he construct objects outside himself and his family.

—May Sarton

It used to be that applications operated in splendid isolation. For example, if you needed to write a memo, you'd fire up your word processor program and start hunting and pecking. If you then realized you needed a spreadsheet to complement the text, you'd shut down the word processor, crank up your spreadsheet program, and start crunching numbers. The only tools you had at hand to connect these two documents were a paper clip and a "See attached" message.

Now, thanks to Windows wonders such as multitasking, the Clipboard, and OLE, applications have gone from isolation to collaboration. Not only can you have your word processor and spreadsheet applications running at the same time, but you can easily share data between them, to the point where you can actually place, for example, an entire spreadsheet inside a word processing document.

This willingness to share data between applications is one of Windows' best features, and it's the subject of this chapter. I'll show you the full gamut of data sharing tools, from simple cut-and-paste Clipboard techniques to sophisticated linking and embedding operations involving OLE. For Office-specific integration techniques, see Chapter 49, "Packaging Office Documents with Binder," and Chapter 50, "Working with the Office Integration Tools."

NOTE: "WINDOWS" REFERENCES

Most of the material in this chapter applies equally well to both Windows 95 and Windows NT 4.0. Therefore, whenever I mention "Windows," understand that I mean both Windows 95 and Windows NT 4.0.

Cut-and-Paste Clipboard Techniques

At its most basic level, the Clipboard is a "don't-reinvent-the-wheel" device. In other words, if you've created something that works—whether it's a bit of polished prose, an attractive graphic, or a complex spreadsheet formula—and you'd like to reuse it, don't waste time re-creating the data from scratch. Instead, you can send the existing data to the Clipboard and then insert a copy of it in a different document or even in a different application altogether.

The Clipboard is the best thing to happen to document editing since the invention of Wite-Out. If you need to restructure a letter or a spreadsheet model, the best way to do so is to move the text or cells from their current position to some other part of the document. The Clipboard makes this easy, because you can cut the data out of the document, store it on the Clipboard, and then paste it into a different location.

The next couple of sections review the specifics of cutting and copying data via the Clipboard.

Working with Data and Files

Before you can send anything to the Clipboard, you have to select the data you want to work with. How you do this depends on the data. To select a graphic, for example, you click on it.

Since you'll often use the Clipboard for copying and moving text, Office has a few generic techniques for selecting chunks of text:

- Drag the mouse over the text you want to select.
- Click at the beginning of the text, hold down the Shift key, and then click at the end of the text.
- To select a word, double-click it.
- In Word, you can use the following techniques:

  You can select an entire paragraph by triple-clicking it.

  You can select an entire line by clicking in the left margin beside the line.

  You can select the entire document by holding down Ctrl and clicking anywhere in the left margin.

- In Word (and many other Windows applications), choose Edit | Select All to select the entire document.
- Place the insertion point cursor at the beginning of the text, hold down the Shift key, and use the application's navigation keys (the arrow keys, Page Up, Page Down, and so on) to select the text.

As soon as the data is selected, you then cut or copy it (as appropriate) to the Clipboard, head for the destination (which could be a different part of the same document, a different document, or a document in another application), and paste the data from the Clipboard. Table 48.1 lists the Edit menu commands, shortcut keys, and toolbar buttons that are usually associated with these Clipboard operations.

48

OFFICE
INTEGRATION
AND OLE

Table 48.1. Commands and shortcuts for managing the Clipboard.

Command	Keyboard Shortcut	Toolbar Button	Description
Edit | Cut	Ctrl-X	✂	Removes the selected data from the document and stores it on the Clipboard.
Edit | Copy	Ctrl-C	📋	Makes a copy of the selected data and stores it on the Clipboard.
Edit | Paste	Ctrl-V	📋	Inserts the Clipboard's contents at the current position of the insertion point cursor.

TIP: DON'T FORGET THE CONTEXT MENU

Many applications also display the Cut, Copy, and Paste commands on the context menu if you right-click the selected data.

CAUTION: PASTE YOUR CUT DATA AS SOON AS POSSIBLE

Remember that each time you cut or copy a selection, the application deletes the current contents of the Clipboard. To avoid losing data after a cut, you should perform the paste operation as soon as you can.

Pasting Data in a Different Format

Clipboard data usually has a default format that's used when you select the Paste command. For example, if you send a piece of a Paint image to the Clipboard and then paste it into Word, the image is inserted using the bitmap format. However, there are often multiple formats for a given data type. Images, for example, can be bitmaps, pictures (metafiles), or DIBs.

If you'd like to use a different format when you paste data, most applications have a Paste Special command on their Edit menu. Selecting this command displays a dialog box similar to the one shown in Figure 48.1. Here, the As box lists the various formats that are available. You simply highlight the one you want and click OK. (However, you need to be careful that you don't embed the data. In many cases, the first item shown in the As list is an *object* format. If you select this item, Windows pastes the data as an embedded object. I'll discuss this in more detail when I talk about Object Linking and Embedding later in this chapter.)

FIGURE 48.1.

The Paste Special command gives you access to the other formats available with the data you're pasting from the Clipboard.

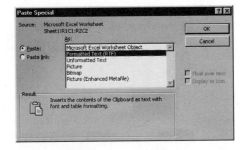

Sending Screen Shots to the Clipboard

A number of programs on the market will capture a snapshot of your screen and save it to a graphics file. (I used a program called Collage Capture to take all the screen shots in this book.) These screen captures are useful in manuals and training documentation, or just as a starting point for an image you want to create.

If you don't have a screen capture program, you can still take screen shots. Windows gives you two techniques:

- Press your keyboard's Print Screen key. This captures an image of the entire screen and sends it to the Clipboard.
- Press Alt-Print Screen. This captures only an image of the current application window and sends it to the Clipboard.

Once you've captured the screen or window, you can open a program (such as Word, PowerPoint, or Photo Editor) and paste the screen shot.

Using the Clipboard Viewer

Windows ships with a Clipboard Viewer utility that you can use to display and work with the current contents of the Clipboard. Assuming that Clipboard Viewer is installed, you can launch it by selecting Start | Programs | Accessories | Clipboard Viewer. The Clipboard Viewer window that appears displays the last piece of data you cut or copied to the Clipboard. In Figure 48.2, for example, I copied an address from the Word window, and it now appears in the Clipboard Viewer.

To see the formats that the current data supports, pull down the Display menu. You can select one of the commands to display the data in a different format. (You might see lots of dimmed commands on this menu. The data supports these formats; they just can't be displayed in the Clipboard Viewer window.)

FIGURE 48.2.

*The Clipboard Viewer
shows you the last hunk
of data that you cut or
copied.*

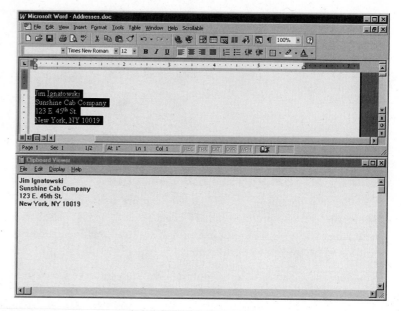

Saving the Clipboard's Contents

What do you do if you cut some data to the Clipboard and then realize you have to work with other data in the meantime? You could paste the current Clipboard contents into a different document, but that might not be convenient. Instead, you can use the Clipboard Viewer to store the current Clipboard contents in a separate Clipboard (CLP) file. You can then open this file later when you need it. Here's how it's done:

1. Select the data you want to save, and cut or copy it to the Clipboard if you haven't done so already.

2. Open the Clipboard Viewer.

3. Select File | Save As to display the Save As dialog box.

4. Select a location and enter a name for the file. Use a short name (eight characters or less), and don't add an extension.

5. Click OK.

To use the saved data down the road, fist make sure you've pasted any existing Clipboard data. Then open the Clipboard Viewer, select File | Open, and choose the file you need in the Open dialog box that appears. When the Clipboard Viewer asks if you want to clear the contents of the Clipboard, click Yes.

Deleting the Clipboard's Contents

As I mentioned earlier, the Clipboard is a memory buffer. So, of course, anything that's sitting on the Clipboard uses up some of your system's memory. If you've cut or copied a large graphic image or file, the Clipboard will be correspondingly large. If your system doesn't have much physical RAM to begin with, a massive Clipboard can slow down your system. To solve this problem, you can reduce the size of the Clipboard by using either of the following methods:

- Copy a smaller piece of data to the Clipboard (such as a single character).
- In the Clipboard Viewer, select Edit | Delete or press Delete. When the Clipboard Viewer asks if you want to clear the contents of the Clipboard, click Yes.

Understanding OLE

The Clipboard-based methods we've looked at are certainly simple ways to work, but they suffer from three major drawbacks. First, if the data gets changed in the original application, the document containing the copy will become out-of-date. This has two consequences:

- If you know that the data needs to be updated, you have to repeat the whole copy-and-paste procedure to get the latest version of the data.
- If you don't know that the data needs to be updated (for example, if someone else changes the original data without telling you), you'll be stuck with an old version of the info.

Second, what if you want to make changes to the copied data? You might be able to edit the data directly (if it's just text, for example), but more often than not you'll need to crank up the original application, change the data there, and then copy the data via the Clipboard again. However, problems can arise if you're not sure which application to use, or if you're not sure which file contains the original data.

Third, copying data between documents is often wasteful since you end up with multiple copies of the same data. You could cut the data from the original application and then paste it, but then there would be no easy way to edit the data using the original application.

It would be nice if you didn't have to worry about the updating of your shared data. It would be nice if there were a system that would accomplish three goals:

- If the data changes in the original application, update the copied data automatically.
- If you want to edit the copied data, make it easy to find both the original application and the original data file.
- Let you store nonnative data inside a document without having to maintain separate documents for the original data.

Happily, OLE—Object Linking and Embedding—meets all three goals and adds a few extra conveniences to the mix for good measure. OLE is one of Microsoft's most important technologies. It can be described without hyperbole as the foundation of all Microsoft's future development efforts in operating systems, applications, and the Internet. Understanding how OLE operates, then, is crucial to understanding not only Windows (which makes extensive use of OLE internally) but also Windows applications, which must support OLE in order to qualify for the Windows 95 or Windows NT logo.

OLE wasn't always such a big deal. Microsoft originally hoped that Dynamic Data Exchange (DDE) would carry the data-sharing torch into the future. DDE works by establishing a communications "channel" between two applications along which data can be transferred. Unfortunately, DDE failed miserably. It was slow, flaky, and inflexible, and it was a programmer's solution to what is, really, an end-user's problem.

OLE leaped into the breach by making it easy for users to share data between applications, keep shared data updated automatically, and mix multiple data types in a single document without wasting disk space. The problem, however, was that OLE was implemented only sporadically. Because Microsoft relied on individual applications to execute OLE functionality, users could never be sure of what they were getting and whether or not two applications could work together. That all changed with the release of Windows 95 and Windows NT 4.0, however, because now OLE is built right into the operating system. For example, you're working with OLE when you create a shortcut to a program or document. Not only that, but all Windows applications that deal with documents are guaranteed to be OLE-compliant, so you always know what you're getting.

First, Some Fundamentals

You'll spend the rest of this section exploring some important OLE underpinnings. Before diving into these theoretical waters, however, you should know about three crucial OLE concepts: *objects, servers,* and *containers:*

Object: In the OLE world, an object is not only data—a slice of text, a graphic, a sound, a chunk of a spreadsheet, or whatever—but also one or more functions for creating, accessing, and using that data.

Server application: The application that you use to create and edit an object. Also known as the *source application.*

Container application: The application that you use to store a linked or embedded object created with a server application. Also known as the *client application.*

With these simple fundamentals in hand, you can now take a closer look at OLE architecture. However, OLE is a large, complicated standard, and it's hideously complex to program. Lucky for you, though, unleashing OLE in Windows 95 in no way requires you to delve too deeply into this complexity. Instead, I'll restrict your look at OLE's plumbing to just the following five topics:

- Compound documents
- The Component Object Model
- OLE drag-and-drop

- OLE automation
- ActiveX controls (formerly OLE controls)

Compound Documents

A *compound document* is a document that contains, along with its native data, one or more objects that were created using other applications. The key point is that the compound document's native data and its objects can have entirely different data formats. For example, a word processing document can include a spreadsheet range object or a sound clip object. The container application doesn't need to know a thing about these alien data formats, either. All it has to know is the name of the server application that created the data and how to display the data. All this information (and more) is included free of charge as part of the object, so it's readily available to the container application.

As the name Object Linking and Embedding implies, you create a compound document by either linking objects to the document or embedding objects in the document. The next three sections explain linking and embedding in more depth, and then I'll examine four more issues related to linking and embedding: visual editing, OLE-related Clipboard formats, nested objects, and object conversion.

Understanding Linking

Linking is one of the OLE methods you can use to insert an object into a file from a container application and thus create a compound document. In this case, the object includes only the following information:

- The Registry key needed to invoke the object's server application (see "OLE and the Registry" later in this chapter for details).
- A metafile that contains GDI instructions on how to display the object. These instructions simply generate the primitives (lines, circles, arcs, and so on) that create an image of the object. These primitives are the heart of the GDI, and they form the basis of any image you see on-screen. So the container application doesn't have to know a thing about the object itself; it just follows the metafile's instructions blindly, and a perfect replica of the object's image appears.
- A pointer to the server application file (the *source document*) that contains the original data.

Linking brings many advantages to the table, but three are most relevant to our purposes. First, the link lets the container application check the source document for changes. If it finds that the data has been modified, OLE can use the link to update the object automatically. For example, suppose you insert a linked spreadsheet object into a word processor document. If you revise some of the numbers in the spreadsheet sometime down the road, the object inside the

48

OFFICE
INTEGRATION
AND OLE

document is automatically updated to reflect the new numbers. However, this updating is automatic only under certain conditions:

- If the container application is running and has the compound document open, the update is automatic.

- If the compound document isn't open when the data is changed, the object gets updated automatically the next time you open the compound document.

- Most OLE applications let you disable automatic updating either for individual documents or for the application as a whole. In this case, you need to perform the updates manually. (I'll show you how this is done later in this chapter.)

Second, since the object "knows" where to find both the server application and the source document, you can edit the object from within the container application. In most cases, double-clicking the object invokes the server and loads the appropriate source file. You can then edit the original data and exit the server application, and your object is, once again, updated automatically.

Third, since the source data exists in a separate file, you can easily reuse the data in other compound documents, and you can edit the data directly from within the server application.

Understanding Embedding

One of the problems associated with linking is that if you distribute the compound document, you also have to distribute the source document. Similarly, if you move the source document to a different location on your system, the link breaks. (However, you can edit the link to reflect the new location.)

NOTE: LINK TRACKING

Microsoft promises that future versions of Windows will support *link tracking*. This means that the operating system will monitor links and update them automatically if you move a source file to a new location.

Embedding solves these problems by inserting an object not only with the server's Registry information and the metafile for displaying the object, but also with the object's *data*. This way, everything you need to display and work with the object exists within the object itself. There's no need for a separate source file, so you can distribute the compound document knowing that the recipient will receive the data intact.

In fact, embedding lets you *create* server objects from within the container application. If you're working with Word for Windows, for example, you can insert a new spreadsheet object right from Word. OLE will start Excel so that you can create the new object, but when you exit Excel, the object will exist only within the Word compound document. There will be no separate Excel file.

Note that many applications can operate only as OLE servers. This means that they aren't standalone applications and therefore have no way to create files on their own. They exist only to create OLE objects for compound documents. Microsoft Office ships with several examples of these applications, including WordArt and Microsoft Graph.

Should You Link or Embed?

Perhaps the most confusing aspect of OLE is determining whether you should link your objects or embed them. As you've seen, the only major difference between linking and embedding is that a linked object stores only a pointer to its data, while an embedded object stores its own data internally.

With this in mind, you should link your objects if any of the following situations apply:

■ You want to keep your compound documents small. The information stored in a linked object—the pointers to the server and source document, and the metafile—consume only about 1.5 KB, so very little overhead is associated with linking. (If you're using WordPad as the container, you can check this out for yourself. Click the object and select Edit | Object Properties, or right-click the object and select Object Properties from the context menu. The properties sheet that appears shows you the size of the object, as shown in Figure 48.3.)

48

OFFICE INTEGRATION AND OLE

FIGURE 48.3.
The WordPad properties sheet for a linked object. Notice that the linked object takes up only 1.5 KB.

■ You're sure the source document won't be moved or deleted. To maintain the link, OLE requires that the source file remain in the same place. If the document gets moved or deleted, the link is broken. (Although, as I've said, most OLE applications let you reestablish the link by modifying the path to the source document.)

■ You need to keep the source file as a separate document in case you want to make changes to it later, or in case you need it for other compound documents. You're free to link an object to as many container files as you like. If you think you'll be using the source data in different places, you should link it to maintain a separate file.

■ You won't be sending the compound document via e-mail or floppy disk. Again, OLE expects the linked source data to appear in a specific place. If you send the compound document to someone else, he might not have the proper source file to maintain the link.

Similarly, you should embed your objects if any of the following situations apply:

■ You don't care how big your compound documents get. Embedding works best in situations in which you have lots of hard disk space and lots of memory. For example, Figure 48.4 shows the WordPad properties sheet for an embedded object. This is the same Excel worksheet that was linked in Figure 48.4, but you can see that the embedded object is much larger.

FIGURE 48.4.

The WordPad properties sheet for an embedded object. Because embedded objects store their own data, they're much larger than linked objects.

■ You don't need to keep the source file as a separate document. If you need to use the source data only once, embedding it means you can get rid of the source file (or never have to create one in the first place) and reduce the clutter on your hard disk.

■ You'll be sending the compound documents and you want to make sure the object arrives intact. If you send a file containing an embedded object, the other person will see the data complete and unaltered. If he wants to edit the object, however, he'll need to have the server application installed.

NOTE: OLE NEEDS MEMORY

Whether you link or embed, OLE will still put a strain on your system's memory resources. Although Microsoft has made some strides in improving the efficiency of the OLE standard, the memory cost is still high. You'll need a minimum of 12 MB of physical RAM to achieve anything approaching reasonable performance out of OLE.

Linking and Embedding via the Clipboard

As you'll learn later in this chapter (see "Working with OLE"), you can paste data from the Clipboard to a container document as either a linked or embedded object. The secret to this is that when you cut or copy an OLE object to the Clipboard, the server application also throws in a few extra formats that the container application can use to link or embed the object. Table 48.2 lists a few of these OLE-related formats.

Table 48.2. OLE-related Clipboard formats.

Format	Description
Embed Source	A copy of the server object to be used for embedding.
Filename	The name of a file that was sent to the Clipboard.
Link Source	The link to the server.
Link Source Descriptor	A description of the link.
Native	The format that the source application uses to store the data internally.
Object Descriptor	Describes the object, including its class ID and size.

Visual Editing

In the original incarnation of OLE, double-clicking an object opened a new window for the server application and loaded the source document (if the object was linked) or loaded the object's data (if the object was embedded). This process is called *open editing*.

When OLE 2.0 debuted a couple of years ago, it introduced the idea of *visual editing* (also known as *in-place editing*). When you double-click an embedded object, instead of your seeing the server application in a separate window, certain features of the container application's window are temporarily hidden in favor of the server application's features. (Linked objects still use open editing.) Here's a summary of the changes that occur in the container application:

- The document window's title bar changes to tell you what kind of object you're now working with. (Not all applications do this.)
- The menu bar (with the exception of the File and Window menus) is replaced by the server application's menu bar.
- The toolbars are replaced by the server application's toolbars.

Essentially, the container application "becomes" the server application while still maintaining the object's context in the compound document. Let's look at an example. First, Figure 48.5 shows the normal Microsoft Excel window.

FIGURE 48.5.

The Microsoft Excel window before you insert an object.

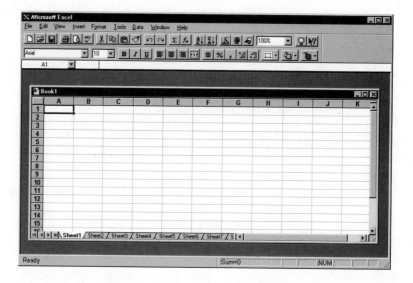

If you now insert a Microsoft Word document into Excel, OLE changes the menu bar and toolbars from Excel's to Word's, as you can see in Figure 48.6. However, the rest of the Excel interface—including the row and column headers, the underlying worksheet cells, and the sheet tabs—remain visible to give context to the embedded object. (To exit visual editing, click outside the object.)

FIGURE 48.6.

During visual editing, the Excel window assumes many features of the Word window.

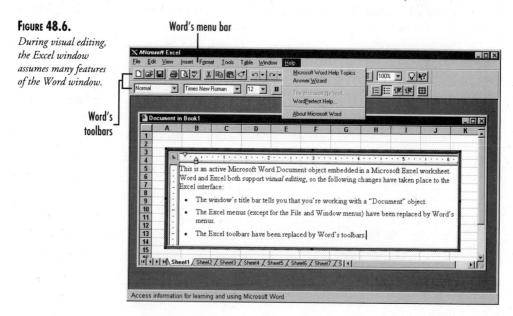

Nested Objects

Once you've opened the server application to create or edit an object, most of the server's features become available. (During visual editing, you can't access server features that relate to files and windows; that's why the container application's File and Window menus don't change.) In particular, if the server application can also double as a container application, you have access to the server features that let you insert linked or embedded objects. In other words, you can double-click an object to activate the server application, and you can then insert a linked or embedded object inside the existing object. This is called *nesting objects*. OLE has no limit on the number of nesting levels you can use.

For example, Figure 48.7 shows a WordArt object nested inside the Word Document object that's embedded in an Excel worksheet.

FIGURE 48.7.

OLE lets you nest objects within objects.

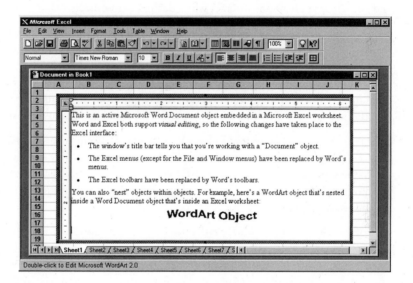

Object Conversion

I mentioned earlier that if you send a compound document to another person, he won't be able to edit the linked or embedded objects unless he has the appropriate server application. However, that's not true in all cases. OLE has a feature called *object conversion* that lets OLE servers convert objects into formats they can work with.

For example, suppose you embed an Excel worksheet into a Word document. If you then send the resulting compound document to a colleague, she'll be able to read the document as long as she has Word. If she wants to edit the embedded worksheet, however, she might not need Excel. All she needs is a spreadsheet program that's capable of converting Excel worksheet objects into the program's native object format.

OFFICE INTEGRATION AND OLE

Note as well that object conversion can also be used by the server application to convert its own objects, as follows:

- To convert an existing object to a related format. In Excel, for example, you can convert a Worksheet object to a Chart object, and vice versa.

- To upgrade older objects to a new format. If a server enhances its objects with extra functionality, for example, it can use object conversion to upgrade existing objects so that they too have access to the same functions.

The Component Object Model

The Component Object Model (COM) is the heart and soul of OLE. It defines not only the standards that server applications use to create objects, but also the mechanisms by which server and container applications interact when dealing with objects.

These features are implemented as *interfaces,* which are collections of related functions. A server application makes an OLE component (that is, an object) available by implementing an interface for the component. When a container application needs to work with a server's OLE components, it just uses the appropriate interface. The container application doesn't have to know anything about the underlying structure of the component. It just works with the interface functions and the linking or embedding (or whatever) happens in a consistent manner.

This is analogous to the way Windows itself operates. To make an operating system component available to the user, Windows implements an interface. For example, to give you access to the file system, Windows offers the Explorer (or My Computer) interface. You don't have to know anything about how Explorer was programmed or what internal data structures it uses; you just have to manipulate the interface.

One of the chief features of COM is that the interfaces it supports are extensible. In other words, when a vendor upgrades its components, it doesn't change the existing behavior of the interface; it just adds new functionality. (This is done either by extending an existing interface or by creating new interfaces; container applications can query the server to find out what's new.) This way, container applications know they can work with a server reliably and that an interface function used today will work exactly the same 10 years from now. The *OLE Programmer's Reference* says that, metaphorically, an object's interface acts like a "contract" that guarantees its behavior for prospective container applications.

(This explains why Microsoft has dropped version numbering from OLE. A new version number for a software product implies that the underlying functionality of the product has changed. However, thanks to its extensibility, that will never happen with OLE because existing functions will always work the same. So, in a sense, you'll never get a "new" version of OLE, just a better implementation of the existing version.)

The starting point for COM is the *class factory.* This is an object in the server application that creates instances of OLE components. When you tell your container application that you want to insert a particular object, the container notifies the appropriate server's class factory that an instance of the object is required. The class factory then creates the object and informs the container application of the appropriate interface to use in order to access the new object.

After the class factory has done its work, the server and container communicate (with COM as the intermediary) through various interfaces. These interfaces control a number of OLE features, including compound documents, visual editing, how data is transferred between server and container, how an object is stored in the container, how the server notifies the container of changes, and many more.

OLE Drag-and-Drop

You can use the Clipboard to do the OLE thing, but in keeping with Windows' drag-and-drop nature, the latest OLE applications also let you use drag-and-drop to insert linked or embedded objects. This lets you perform OLE chores without having to resort to the Cut, Copy, and Paste commands and without using the Clipboard. Windows supports three kinds of OLE drag-and-drop:

> **Inter-window:** You drag a selected object from the server application's window and drop it on the container application's window.

> **Inter-object:** You drag a selected object and drop it on another object to produce a nested object. Or you can "un-nest" an object by dragging it out of an object.

> **Icons:** You drag a selected object and drop it on a desktop icon, such as a printer or a disk drive.

OLE Automation

The beauty of OLE is not only how easy it is to insert objects in a container application (especially via drag-and-drop), but the access you have to the object's original tools. With a simple double-click, you can edit the object with the full power of the server's menus and commands.

But, until recently, the one thing that was missing was the ability to control the server via macros. If you program in, say, VBA (Visual Basic for Applications), it would be nice to be able to create new objects using VBA procedures. This is especially true if you're developing corporate applications for end-users. Editing or creating an object, whether you use visual editing or open editing, has meant that you must at least be familiar with the server application. And although *you* might be willing to spend time and effort learning a new program, the users of your VBA applications might not be.

This has all changed with the advent of OLE automation. Applications that support OLE automation "expose" their objects to VBA (and any other applications and development tools that support the OLE automation standard). So just as VBA can recognize and manipulate, say, an Excel worksheet range (a Range object), it can also recognize and manipulate objects from other OLE automation applications. VISIO, for example, exposes a number of objects to VBA, including its documents, pages, shapes, and windows. Access 7.0 exposes dozens of objects, including its forms and reports. Also, the Binder application that ships with Office supports OLE automation and exposes its sections as objects.

Each of these objects has its own collection of properties and actions (or *methods,* as they're called among OLE automationists) that can be read or altered. For example, you can use OLE automation to create a new PowerPoint presentation object and then use the Add method of the Slides object to add a slide object to the presentation.

Although only a few applications now support OLE automation, it's widely believed that this will be *the* standard for application interoperability in the not-too-distant future. Certainly, any other applications that use VBA will be OLE-automated (and Microsoft has stated publicly that VBA will soon be a part of all its major applications), and many other applications will expose their objects (the way VISIO, Access, and PowerPoint do).

ActiveX Controls

As an Office 97 user, you've probably gasped at the disk real estate that the applications gobble up. Consider just the executable files: MSACCESS.EXE, 2.85 MB; EXCEL.EXE, 5.33 MB; POWERPNT.EXE, 3.33 MB; WINWORD.EXE, 5.07 MB. These behemoth files are indicative of the biggest disease facing software today: code bloat. Each new iteration of an application (and I don't mean to pick on Office; *every* application suffers from this) crams in more bells, more whistles, and more gee-aren't-our-programmers-clever features. If you can use these new baubles, the toll on your hard disk free space is probably worth it. More likely, however, you might use one or two of the new features, and the rest you couldn't care less about. In the end, most software programs follow the old 80-20 rule: you spend 80 percent of your time using 20 percent of the features.

In response to user complaints, the software industry is finally doing something about this problem. Someday soon you'll be able to install only the features you'll actually use and consign the rest to the obscurity they deserve. The engine behind this change is *component-based software.* These are small software modules that perform specific tasks. For example, a spell-checking component would do nothing but check an application's spelling. By combining such modules, you can create a customized version of a software package that's tailored to your needs.

The current standard for these software components is the ActiveX control (formerly known as the OLE control). These are prebuilt OLE objects that developers can plug into existing applications. These objects expose various properties and actions, so the developer can manipulate how the program appears and works with the user. This functionality will eventually come to the end-user as well, allowing you to mix and match components to create a package that contains only the features you need.

The first place you'll see ActiveX controls in action is on the Internet. In version 3 of Microsoft's Internet Explorer World Wide Web browser, when developers insert ActiveX controls into Web pages, Internet Explorer downloads them to the user's computer and executes them. This technique is used mostly to spice up Web pages with dynamic content, such as an animation or an order form that includes running totals.

OLE and the Registry

Windows makes extensive use of the Registry to store all kinds of information about your system. So it will come as no surprise that the Registry plays a big part in OLE as well.

Programmatic Identifier Keys

Most OLE-related Registry data can be found in the HKEY_CLASSES_ROOT key (an alias of HKEY_LOCAL_MACHINE\SOFTWARE\Classes). HKEY_CLASSES_ROOT consists of a long list of extensions, followed by an equally long list of file types, which are known, officially, as *programmatic identifiers*. For example, Figure 48.8 shows the key for the programmatic ID for an Excel worksheet.

FIGURE 48.8.

The programmatic ID keys contain lots of useful OLE info.

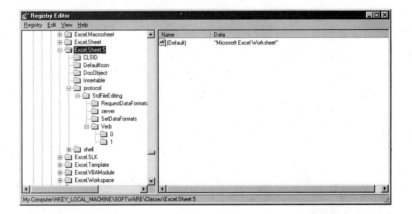

48

OFFICE INTEGRATION AND OLE

The key's default value is the name of the file type that the programmatic ID represents (Microsoft Excel Worksheet in Figure 48.8). Here's a rundown of the OLE-related subkeys that you'll find in the programmatic ID key:

CLSID: This is the object's *class ID,* a 16-byte (32 hexadecimal digit) value that's also known as the object's Globally Unique Identifier (GUID). As the latter name implies, CLSIDs are values that uniquely identify an object. The value of the CLSID key points to a subkey of the HKEY_CLASSES_ROOT\CLSID key (discussed in a moment).

NOTE: HOW CLSID VALUES ARE GENERATED

CLSIDs are either assigned by Microsoft or generated by a program that comes in the Microsoft Software Development Kit. How can a vendor be sure that its object's CLSID is unique? Well, if you get the value from Microsoft, Microsoft can check its database to ensure uniqueness. All Microsoft-generated CLSID values use the following format (where *xxxxxxxx* is a unique sequence of eight hexadecimal digits):

`{xxxxxxxx-0000-0000-C000-000000000046}`

If you use the program, consider how each value is generated. The first eight digits are random, the next four digits are generated by the current date and time, and the last 20 digits are generated based on the hardware details of the developer's computer. That combination is about as unique as it gets!

Insertable: This key is a flag that tells COM that this type of object can be inserted into a container document. When you select Insert | Object, COM gathers all the objects that have the Insertable key and displays them in the Object dialog box.

DefaultIcon: If you elect to insert an object as an icon, OLE uses the data in this key to determine which icon to display.

StdExecute\server: This subkey gives the container application the pathname of the server application to be used to execute the object.

StdFileEditing\server: This subkey gives the container application the pathname of the server application to be used to edit the object.

Verb: This subkey lists the actions you can take with a linked or embedded object. Most objects have two verbs: Edit (which activates visual editing) and Open (which activates open editing). Others—such as AVIFile (video files) and SoundRec (audio files)—also have a Play verb that plays the object.

CLSID Keys

As I said, the CLSID subkey contains a setting that points to a subkey of HKEY_CLASSES_ROOT\CLSID. For example, the Excel worksheet object's CLSID subkey points to the following key, as shown in Figure 48.9:

`HKEY_CLASSES_ROOT\CLSID\{00020810-0000-0000-C000-000000000046}`

FIGURE 48.9.

Each OLE object has a subkey in the `HKEY_CLASSES_ROOT\ CLSID` *key.*

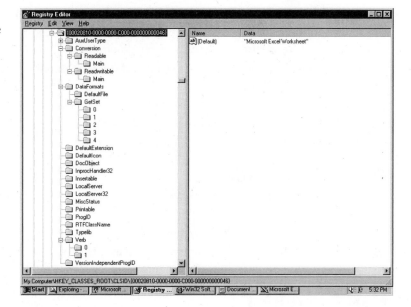

The default value of this key is the name of the object. The subkeys contain lots of OLE-related data. Here's a summary of a few of these keys:

AuxUserType: Alternative (shorter) names for the object type.

Conversion: Information used during object conversion. Items in the `Readable` subkey are formats that the server application can convert into the object's format; items in the `Readwritable` subkey are file formats that the server can convert the object into.

DataFormats: The data formats supported by the server application. Most of the formats are listed as integer values that correspond to default formats defined by Windows.

DefaultExtension: The default extension for this type of object. If you leave off the extension when you enter a filename in the Insert Object dialog box (described later), OLE tacks on the extension specified in this subkey.

DefaultIcon: If you elect to insert an object as an icon, OLE uses the data in this key to determine which icon to display. (This is the same as `DefaultIcon` in the programmatic ID subkey, discussed earlier.)

InProcHandler and InProcHandler32: In-process handlers (DLL files) used to help the server and container applications communicate. `InProcHandler` is for 16-bit server applications; `InProcHandler32` is for 32-bit applications.

InProcServer and InProcServer32: In-process servers (DLL files) that a container application can call instead of a full-blown server application.

Insertable: This key is a flag that tells COM that this type of object can be inserted into a container document. When you select Insert | Object, COM gathers all the objects that have the `Insertable` key and displays them in the Object dialog box. (This is the same as `Insertable` in the programmatic ID subkey, discussed earlier.)

LocalServer and LocalServer32: The full pathname of the server application. 32-bit applications need only the `LocalServer32` subkey, but the `LocalServer` subkey is also added for backwards compatibility with 16-bit container applications.

ProgID: A pointer to the object's programmatic ID.

Verb: This subkey lists the actions you can take with a linked or embedded object. (This is the same as `Verb` in the programmatic ID subkey, discussed earlier.)

Working with OLE

After all that OLE theory, you're due for some hands-on techniques. To that end, I'll spend the rest of this chapter showing you how to put OLE to work creating compound documents. I'll run through several methods of both linking and embedding objects, I'll talk about editing those objects, and I'll show you how to maintain links.

Linking an Object

If you have data you'd like to share between applications, and you feel that linking is the best way to go, Windows gives you two methods: linking via the Clipboard, and inserting a linked file. The next two sections discuss each method. Then I'll show you how to work with and maintain your links.

Linking via the Clipboard

You saw earlier in this chapter how to use the Clipboard's cut, copy, and paste methodology to transfer static data between applications. However, the Clipboard is no slouch when it comes to OLE data transfers. If the original application is an OLE server, a cut or copy operation passes not only the selected data to the Clipboard, but also formats such as Object Descriptor, Link Source, and Link Source Descriptor (see Table 48.2). A container application can use these formats to determine whether the object on the Clipboard can be linked, and to perform the actual linking.

Once you've placed the data on the Clipboard, switch to the container application and position the cursor where you want the data to be pasted. Now select Edit | Paste Special to display the Paste Special dialog box, shown in Figure 48.10.

FIGURE 48.10.

*Use the Paste Special
dialog box to paste
Clipboard data as a
linked object.*

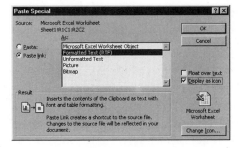

The As box lists the various formats available for the data, but you can ignore most of them. To establish a link between the container and the server, activate the Paste Link option. Usually, most of the formats will disappear, and you'll be left with only the object format. If you'd like the data to appear as an icon in the container document, activate the Display As Icon check box. When you're ready, click OK to paste the linked object into the container, as shown in Figure 48.11.

FIGURE 48.11.

*A linked object
displayed as an icon.*

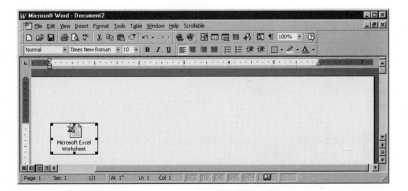

NOTE: LINKING VIA DRAG-AND-DROP

The Office applications let you embed objects by dragging them from a server and dropping them on a container. For example, if you highlight a worksheet range in Excel, you can drag the range to Word and drop it inside a document. Note that this moves the data to the container. If you want to copy the data, hold down Ctrl while you drag the mouse.

Inserting a File as a Linked Object

Instead of pasting part of a document as a linked object, you might prefer to insert an entire file as a linked object. For example, if you insert a linked Excel worksheet into a Word document, the container object will reflect *any* changes made to the original worksheet, including data added or removed, global formatting adjustments, and so on.

Also, there are situations in which you have no choice but to insert a file. For example, you can't insert part of a bitmap as a linked object; instead, you have to insert the entire file.

Here are the basic steps to follow to insert a file as a linked object:

1. In the container application, position the cursor where you want the file inserted.
2. Select Insert | Object.
3. Select the Create from File tab, as shown in Figure 48.12.

FIGURE 48.12.

The Object dialog box from Word 97. You use the Create from File tab to insert a file object in the container.

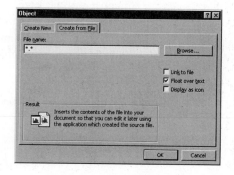

4. Enter the filename of the file you want to link. You can also click the Browse button to choose the file from a dialog box.
5. Activate the Link to File check box.
6. In Word, if you want the object to "float," activate the Float over text check box. If you deactivate this check box, text flows around the object.
7. If you want the linked file to appear as an icon, activate the Display as Icon check box.
8. Click OK to insert the linked file object.

Managing Links

All container applications that support object linking also give you some kind of method to manage document links. This involves updating a link so that the container displays the most recent changes, changing a link's source, determining how links are updated in the container, and breaking links you no longer need to maintain.

In most container applications, you manage links by selecting Edit | Links. You'll see a Links dialog box similar to the one shown in Figure 48.13 (this is the Links dialog box from Word). Here's a rundown of the basic link management chores you can perform:

Changing the link update method: By default, links are updated automatically. In other words, if both the source and the container are open, whenever the source data changes, the data in the container also changes. If you would prefer to update the container document by hand, highlight the link and activate the Manual option.

Updating the link: If you've set a link to Manual, or if the server document isn't open, you can make sure a link contains the latest and greatest information by highlighting it and clicking the Update Now button.

Changing the link source: If you move the source document, you'll need to modify the link so that it points to the new location. You can do this by highlighting the appropriate link and clicking the Change Source button.

Breaking a link: If you no longer want to maintain a link between the source and the container, you can break the link. This will leave the data intact, but changes made to the original data will no longer be reflected in the container. To break a link, highlight it and click the Break Link button.

FIGURE 48.13.

Container applications that support object linking have a Links dialog box that you can use to maintain the links.

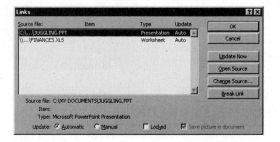

Embedding an Object

If you prefer to embed an object instead of linking it, Windows gives you three or four methods to choose from (depending on the server application): the Clipboard, drag-and-drop, inserting a new embedded object, and inserting an embedded file.

Embedding via the Clipboard

Assuming that the original application is an OLE server, a cut or copied object in the Clipboard includes not only link-related formats, but also a few formats that let a container application embed the data (such as the Embed Source format). Again, the container application can use these formats to perform the embedding.

To embed data that's been placed on the Clipboard, switch to the container application, position the cursor where you want the data to be pasted, and select Edit | Paste Special. In the Paste Special dialog box that appears, select the object format from the As list (this format should be highlighted by default) and make sure that the Paste option is activated. Also, if you'd like the data to appear as an icon in the container document, activate the Display As Icon check box. When you're ready, click OK to paste the embedded object into the container.

Inserting a New Embedded Object

If the object you want to embed doesn't exist, and you don't need to create a separate file, OLE lets you insert the new object directly into the container application. Here's how it works:

1. In the container application, move the cursor to where you want the new object to appear.

2. Select Insert | Object to display the Object dialog box, shown in Figure 48.14.

FIGURE 48.14.

Use this dialog box to select the type of embedded object you want to create.

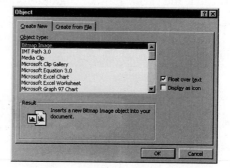

3. The Object type list displays all the available objects on your system. (Recall that Windows generates this list by looking for all the Registry entries in HKEY_CLASSES_ROOT that have an Insertable subkey.) Highlight the type of object you want to create.

4. Click OK. Windows starts the server application for the object type you selected. The server will either appear in-place or in a separate window.

5. Create the object you want to embed.

6. Exit the server application. If you were working with the server using visual editing, click outside the object. Otherwise, select File | Exit & Return to *document*, where *document* is the name of the active document in the container application.

Inserting an Embedded File

You can insert an entire existing file (as opposed to an object within a file) as an embedded object. This is useful if you want to make changes to the file from within the container without disturbing the original. Follow these steps:

1. In the container document, position the cursor where you want to embed the object.

2. Select Insert | Object to display the Object dialog box.

3. Select the Create from File tab.

4. Enter the filename of the file you want to embed. You can also click the Browse button to choose the file from a dialog box.

5. If you want the linked file to appear as an icon, activate the Display as icon check box.

6. Click OK to insert the linked file object.

Editing a Linked or Embedded Object

If you need to make some changes to a linked or embedded object, you can use the container application to launch the server application and load the object automatically. (Remember, too, that for a linked object you can always run the server application and work with the object directly.) How you do this depends on the application, but here are a few methods that work for most OLE containers:

- Double-click the object.

- Select the object, pull down the Edit menu, and then select either Linked *ObjectType* Object (for a linked object) or *ObjectType* Object (for an embedded object). In both cases, *ObjectType* is the type of object you selected (for example, Bitmap Image or Worksheet). From the cascade menu that appears, select Edit. If the server application supports visual editing, this will launch the object in-place.

- Select the object, pull down the Edit menu, and then select either the Linked *ObjectType* Object command (for a linked object) or the *ObjectType* Object command (for an embedded object). In the cascade menu that appears, select Open. For servers that support the Open verb, this will launch the object in a separate window.

- Right-click the object, select either Linked *ObjectType* Object or *ObjectType* Object, and select either Edit or Open.

48

OFFICE
INTEGRATION
AND OLE

NOTE: EDIT ISN'T ALWAYS THE DEFAULT VERB

Sometimes, when you double-click an object (such as a sound file or a video file), Windows will play the object instead of editing it. In this case, you can edit the object only by using the appropriate Edit command.

Summary

This chapter showed you how to share Office data in Windows. We began with the Clipboard, and I showed you how to cut, copy, and paste data between Windows applications. I also gave you a quick tour of the Clipboard Viewer. We then turned our attention to OLE. I gave you an extensive look at OLE theory—including compound documents, objects, linking, embedding, and the Component Object Model—and then I showed you how to put OLE to good use in your Office applications.

Here's a list of chapters where you'll find related information:

- You'll learn how to use the Binder as an OLE container in Chapter 49, "Packaging Office Documents with Binder."

- You'll find Office-specific integration techniques in Chapter 50, "Working with the Office Integration Tools."

- For information on mailing and routing Office files, see Chapter 51, "Mailing and Routing Documents."

- I show you how to share your work in networked environments in Chapter 52, "Sharing Your Work."

- To learn how to use VBA to integrate Office documents, see Chapter E6 on the CD, "Integrating Office Applications with VBA."

CHAPTER 49

Packaging Office Documents with Binder

Union may be strength, but it is mere blind brute strength unless wisely directed.

—*Samuel Butler*

In the discussion of the Microsoft Office Shortcut Bar in Chapter 7, "More Office Tools," you saw how Microsoft has moved away from looking at applications as separate programs through the implementation of the New and Open dialog boxes, which are used in all Office applications.

With the Office Binder application, Microsoft has gone a step further. Taking a cue from the business office environment, Office Binder collects documents in an electronic three-ring binder. This application combines your documents into one file by using extensions to OLE technology. Combining the different application documents into one file lets you open, save, print, or mail them as one unit.

A binder about a business meeting might include an invitation, an address list, an agenda, some presentation slides, the meeting minutes, and a wrap-up memo. The binder captures information at and about every stage of the meeting, from scheduling to following up on action items. If you're working with a coworker to schedule the meeting, having all the information in one location makes collaboration easier. The sample templates that come with Office Binder include one called Proposal and Marketing Plan, which is organized as just described. Figure 49.1 shows a sample Proposal and Marketing Plan binder. More information about the templates provided with Office Binder can be found in the "Office Binder Templates" section of this chapter.

FIGURE 49.1.

A sample Proposal and Marketing Plan binder.

Each document in a binder is called a *section*. Sections can be rearranged, renamed, added, deleted, hidden, and printed. The information in each section is stored inside the binder file. No auxiliary files are used. For this reason, the binder files can get rather large. When binder files contain lots of graphics, they can become prohibitively large. For example, they might take up more space than is available on a floppy disk.

> **NOTE: BINDER FILE EXTENSIONS**
>
> When using Windows Explorer to view the file system, you need to know what the file extensions stand for. Here are the three extensions that Office Binder uses:
>
> | Extension | File Type |
> | --- | --- |
> | .OBD | Binder document |
> | .OBT | Binder template |
> | .OBZ | Binder Wizard (a binder template that includes macros) |

Office Binder Advantages

Office Binder has many advantages over simply grouping files in a Windows folder.

Consistent Section Order

You can arrange the sections of a binder in any order you like. This order is saved with the binder file. When you group documents in a folder, the operating system controls and limits the ways you can order or sort the documents. For example, if you want to sort documents that begin with numbers, you need to add leading zeros (for example, 001, 050, 400) so that they sort correctly. There is no way to do a reverse sort so that higher numbers appear first.

Consecutive Page Numbers

Using binders lets you print sections with consecutive page numbers. This includes all of the different types of applications. An Excel spreadsheet that follows a Word document will start its page number wherever the Word document ends.

Easier E-Mail Transfer

When using electronic mail to transmit information, it's usually much easier to send one file than many files. In any case, using only one file (the binder) makes it impossible to forget to send one of the needed documents.

More Efficiency

Opening one file (the binder) is more efficient than opening several files; therefore, moving between documents is faster.

Using Briefcase

You can use the Briefcase file synchronization program, part of Windows 95, to allow several people to work on the same binder at once. Each person using the binder copies it to the local Briefcase from a network file server. Then, each user can work on his or her own sections. When the original file is updated using Briefcase, only the changed sections are updated.

If the same section has been changed in both the original file and the personal file, you'll be asked how to handle the situation.

Global Spell Checking

With the new Spell It feature, each section is automatically checked for spelling as it is created. Therefore, there is no spell-check feature for the entire binder.

Office Binder Limitations

There are also some limitations to binders. This section discusses a few of them.

Disabled Features

Some application features are disabled inside the Office Binder program. For example, to reduce possible confusion, the individual application status bars are disabled. Only the Office Binder status bar is visible when a section is being edited.

You also can't create or edit macros inside the sections. In order to do this, you need to save the section to a separate file, add the macro or edit an existing one, and then reattach the section to the binder.

TIP: SAVING SECTIONS

Select Section | Save As to save a section as a separate document. Then select Section | Add From File to reattach it.

Large Physical Files

Office Binder files have a tendency to grow quite large. This causes the physical file to sprawl all over your hard disk as the file becomes fragmented. If you notice that a binder takes a long time to load, follow these steps to eliminate the fragmentation:

1. Open the binder.
2. Select File | Save Binder As to save the binder with a new name.
3. Delete the old binder file.
4. Rename the new binder with the old binder name.

Security

Office Binder circumvents any security you might have set up for your documents. When you add a password-protected document to a binder, the binder asks you to type in the password. Binder never asks for the password again—the document is no longer secure.

> **NOTE: PROTECTION IS DISABLED**
>
> The Protect and Unprotect menu options are still active inside the binder. They just don't protect anything.

You can gain a small measure of security by setting the read-only attribute of the binder file using the Windows Explorer. To do this, right-click the file, select Properties, and then check the read-only check box on the General tab. However, doing this still allows someone to re-name the file and save another in its place.

A stronger security measure is to store the binder on a read-only network drive. Talk with your network administrator about this possibility.

The Office Binder Menus

Office Binder is an OLE container application. This means that when you edit a document, the menu bar changes to reflect the application that is responsible for that particular document. In addition to its four standard menus (File, Go, Section, and Help), each application (Word, Excel, and PowerPoint) adds some of its own menu commands.

> **NOTE: SOME INTERFACE ELEMENTS ARE SUPPRESSED IN BINDER**
>
> Each application is subservient to Office Binder. This means, among other things, that the status area is suppressed. For example, Word normally shows the current page and section number in the status area. When you look at a Word document in Office Binder, this information isn't displayed.

A binder combines the documents of other Office applications. Therefore, when Office Binder is started with a blank binder, its menus consist of options that relate to opening a new or existing binder, changing binder properties, adding sections, and accessing some help selections. After the first section is added, more options become available.

The File Menu

The File menu has options to manipulate the binder as a whole:

- New Binder: Lets you select the type of binder you want to create. The standard types are Blank, Proposal and Marketing Plan, and Report.

- Open Binder: Lets you select an existing binder to open. The binder can be on your computer, on a computer in your company's network, or on the Internet (if you have access).

- Save Binder: Saves the current binder.

- Save Binder As: Lets you specify a filename for your binder. You can save your binder on your computer or on your corporate network. If you have access to the Internet, you can save files to an FTP site, providing that you have access rights to the site and the site allows users to save files. To do so, choose Internet Locations (FTP) from the Save in list box in the Save Binder As dialog box.

- Binder Page Setup: You use this option to add a header and a footer to sections in your binder, to control page numbering, and to control which sections of the binder can be printed. You can turn headers or footers off for specific sections. You can number all sections' pages consecutively or number each section's pages separately. Finally, you can set up the Print Binder command to print all sections or only the sections selected in the binder's left pane.

- Binder Print Preview: Shows you how your binder's sections will look when you print them. Figure 49.2 shows an example of a Word document in print preview. Notice the Binder Print Preview floating toolbar, which you can use to move among the binder's documents and to exit print preview mode.

FIGURE 49.2.

A Word document in print preview via its binder.

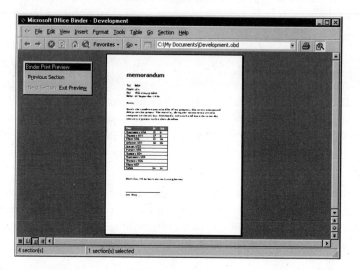

- Print Binder: Displays a dialog box that lets you select a printer as well as determine the number of copies and collating sequence. In addition, you can request to print only the current section or all sections. This dialog box also controls whether the page numbering is consecutive or restarts for each section.

■ Send To: You use this submenu to send or route a binder to others via e-mail and to place a binder in a Microsoft Exchange public folder.

> Mail Recipient: Sends the binder to someone via e-mail.

> Routing Recipient: Routes the binder to others for review. You can choose to send the binder to recipients in turn. In other words, when one reviewer finishes, the binder automatically goes to the next reviewer so that each reviewer can see the previous revisions. You can also choose to send the binder to all reviewers at once. When everyone has reviewed the binder, it comes back to you.

> Exchange Folder: Posts the binder to a Microsoft Exchange or Outlook folder to make the binder available to others.

■ Binder Properties: Displays the Microsoft Office Binder Properties dialog box, shown in Figure 49.3.

There are five tabs from which to choose:

> General: Displays the binder name, location, creation date, last modified data, and the size in bytes.

> Summary: Includes input fields for the binder's title, subject, author information, manager information, company information, category names, keywords, and comments.

> Statistics: Displays the binder creation date, last modified date, last access date, last printed date, who last saved it, and other information such as the number of pages, paragraphs, and lines.

Contents: Displays the section names that are in your binder.

Custom: Includes input fields for adding custom properties to the binder. You can access a drop-down list of 27 properties by clicking the down arrow next to the Name field. You can add as many other properties to the list as you like.

The Summary and Custom tabs both let you set property values. Depending on your point of view, the most important use for the properties might be for documentation. For example, corporate auditors need to know who the last person to modify a document was and when the document was last changed.

Most users, however, will probably use the properties to help them find documents in the future. If you consistently fill in the property information, you can use the new search facilities in the New and Open dialog boxes to find documents quickly.

Figure 49.3.

The Microsoft Office Binder Properties dialog box for a binder called Development.

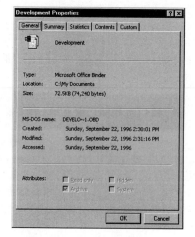

- Binder Options: You use this option to control whether binders print as a single job or as individual jobs corresponding to the binder's objects, and where binders are stored by default. You can also use this option to choose whether to show Office Binder's status bar, the left pane, and the left pane buttons in the current binder.

- Close: Closes Office Binder. If any sections have been changed, you're given a chance to save them.

The Go Menu

The Go menu is Office Binder's link to the Internet and your corporate intranet. Use its commands to view Internet or intranet information in Office Binder.

> **NOTE: USING BINDER WITH THE INTERNET**
>
> To use Office Binder with the Internet or a corporate intranet, you must have Internet Explorer installed, or you must have Word installed with Web page authoring tools. Additionally, to use Office Binder with the Internet, you must have a connection to the Internet, either via a dedicated line or by using a modem.

You can also use the Go menu to work with binders stored on your computer. The Go menu has the following commands:

- Open: Opens a selected hypertext link or lets you type a link to a document or folder to open. If your computer is connected to the Internet or a corporate intranet, you can open resources such as World Wide Web pages there too.

- Back: Opens the previous file in the history list, a list of the 10 files you most recently jumped to using hyperlinks or that you opened using the Web toolbar.

- Forward: Opens the next file in the history list.

- Start Page: Opens the start page you selected.

- Search the Web: Opens the search page you selected. A search page gives you a fast way to find information on the Internet or your company's intranet, even when you don't know where the information is located.

- Set Start Page: Sets the currently open page as your start page.

- Set Search Page: Sets the currently open page as your search page.

- Show Web Toolbar: Displays the Web toolbar in Office Binder.

The Section Menu

The Section menu lets you manipulate each section as an individual element. Here are its options:

- Add: Adds an Excel chart or worksheet, a PowerPoint presentation, or a Word document to the open binder.

  This option doesn't let you choose a template on which to base your new document. If you need to use a specific template, create the document using the New dialog box (as described in Chapter 3) and then use the Add From File menu option.

  You can also add sections by dragging and dropping documents from the file system. If you drop an unknown document type, Word will try to convert it automatically to a Word document.

- Add From File: Adds an existing document to the binder. It's important to realize that making changes to the new section *does not* change the original document. This is because the section is stored in the binder file along with the other sections.

49

PACKAGING OFFICE
DOCUMENTS WITH
BINDER

- Delete: Deletes the selected section(s). A confirmation message is displayed so as to avoid accidental deleting.

- Duplicate: Duplicates the selection. A dialog box will ask you where in the section list the new section should be inserted.

- Rename: Lets you rename the selected section. You can also rename a section by double-clicking the section name under the icon.

- Rearrange: Lets you rearrange the order of the sections. You can also rearrange sections by right-clicking a section icon and then dragging it to a new location. A small arrow appears to the right of the section list, indicating where the section will be inserted when you stop dragging.

- Next Section: Opens the next section in the binder.

- Previous Section: Opens the previous section in the binder.

- Hide: Hides the active section. A hidden section is not displayed in the section list.

- Unhide Section: Displays a dialog box listing the hidden sections. You can select one section to unhide. This section will become the active section.

- Page Setup: Lets you modify the page size, margins, and other page settings. The dialog box that is displayed changes according to the application that is being used to edit the active section.

- Print Preview: Shows you how the current section will look when you print it.

- Print: Prints the current sections. The options in the Print dialog box change according to the application that is being used to edit the active section.

- Save As File: Lets you save the active section to a separate file. Changes to the new file *will not* be reflected in the binder.

- View Outside: Moves the editing window out of Office Binder's window. This way, you can see two sections at once. Also, this makes the application's status area visible and all the application menu options available.

- Section Properties: Displays the Section Properties dialog box. This dialog box is exactly like the Binder Properties dialog box, except that the information is pulled from the section instead of the binder as a whole.

- Select All: Selects all the sections.

The Help Menu

The Help menu options change to reflect which application is being used to edit the active section. Here are the two basic options:

- Contents and Index: Displays the Office Binder Help dialog box, which has three tabs: Contents, Index, and Find.

■ About Office Binder: Displays the Office Binder version number and product ID. There are also buttons for getting system information and information about tech support.

Unbinding Binders

If you right-click a binder (.OBD) file in a folder or on your desktop, you'll see the Unbind option on the context menu. This option splits a binder into its individual parts using the section names as the filenames. Making changes to the individual files doesn't change the original binder. The individual files are stored in the same folder as the binder.

Common Problems with Office Binder

The Office Binder program has its share of problems that might arise. This section discusses a few of the more common ones.

The Binder Is Too Large to Print

If you encounter this problem, simply print the binder in sections, a few at a time. The page numbers will still be consecutive if you have the headers or footers set up correctly.

The Page Numbers Don't Print

The usual reason for this problem is that one of the binder sections doesn't have page numbering enabled.

Incorrect Page Numbers

When you print with consecutive page numbers, the initial page number for each section is determined by Office Binder. If you explicitly reset the page numbering inside the section, the page numbers will be incorrect.

To fix this problem, remove the explicit page number setting from the appropriate section. Select File | Binder Print Preview to determine which section is causing the problem.

The Binder Is Too Large to E-Mail

Sending a binder through your e-mail system might be impractical because of its size. If you need to do this often, consider writing a macro to unbind the individual sections, e-mail them, and then recombine them. You might also consider placing the file in an Outlook shared folder.

External OLE Links Are Not Supported

Although it's possible to embed an OLE object in a binder section, you can't link a document to a binder section. Linking between two sections in the same binder *is* possible.

Problems with Opening Binders or Sections

If you've run into a problem opening a binder or a section, try unbinding the binder and then double-clicking each separate file to determine which section has the problem. When the section with the problem is found, delete that section from the binder. Alternatively, you can create a new binder and add each section to it.

Office Binder Templates

An Office Binder template is the foundation you use to build your own binders. Near the beginning of this chapter, you read about the Proposal and Marketing Plan template. Microsoft has also supplied a template for Report binders. If you use a template to start your binder, remember that you aren't limited to the sections already provided. You can add or delete sections as needed. Table 49.1 shows what sections each template provides.

Table 49.1. The Office Binder templates.

Template Name	Sections	Application
Proposal and Marketing	Cover Letter	Word
	Quote	Excel
	Slide Show	PowerPoint
	Referrals	Word
	Details	Word
	Follow-up	Word
Report	Cover Letter	Word
	Executive Summary	Word
	Slide Show	PowerPoint
	Analysis	Word
	Data	Excel

You can select any of these templates from the Binders tab of the New Office Document dialog box, shown in Figure 49.4. (Click the first button on the Office shortcut bar to see this dialog box.)

Creating an Office Binder Template

Using templates can save you time, because designing a report or deciding which sections need to be in a presentation can take a significant amount of effort. In order to reduce the effort needed in the future, save your work in template form.

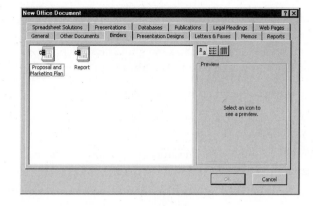

FIGURE 49.4.

The New Office Document dialog box showing the Office Binder templates.

You can create your own Office Binder template by following these steps:

1. Create a binder with the sections that you want to save for the future.
2. Select File | Save Binder As.
3. Change the Save As Type field to Binder Templates.
4. Double-click the Binders folder.
5. Enter a filename for your binder. Remember that you can use long filenames.
6. Click Save.

If you would like to create a preview for your template, be sure to check the Save Preview Picture option on the Summary tab of the Section Properties dialog box in the first section of the binder.

TIP: HARD DISK SPACE SAVER

To save hard disk space, only the first section should have the Save Preview Picture option checked.

Summary

The Office Binder application will probably prove to be of great use to you. Its advantages are numerous, especially if you take the time to create templates beforehand.

Anytime you have a recurring document, take a moment to decide whether creating a template now will save time later.

49

PACKAGING OFFICE DOCUMENTS WITH BINDER

Microsoft will undoubtedly improve Office Binder, so you can look forward to additional functionality as well as more types of documents available to include as sections. For example, wouldn't it be nice to have pictures and sound files independent of Word or PowerPoint? Third-party vendors also will be able to add features to Office Binder.

Here are a few chapters that contain related information:

■ Basic integration and OLE concepts can be found in Chapter 48, "Office Integration and OLE."

■ You'll find more data on Office integration in Chapter 50, "Working with the Office Integration Tools."

■ For more detailed information on mailing and routing Office files, see Chapter 51, "Mailing and Routing Documents."

■ To learn how to use VBA to integrate Office documents, see Chapter E6 on the CD, "Integrating Office Applications with VBA."

Working with the Office Integration Tools

CHAPTER 50

We are continually faced with a series of great opportunities disguised as insoluble problems.

—John W. Gardner

In the Office 97 package, the links between the major programs are even tighter and more integrated than before. Microsoft's goal with this new Office suite (and, indeed, with all of Windows 95) is to turn the user's attention away from working with applications and more toward working with documents. This is a laudable goal, because for too long now users have been shaping their documents to fit the application they were using rather than the other way around. We need to start thinking of applications as mere tools that help us achieve a particular result.

To that end, the Office applications boast three features that can help you focus on your documents:

- The applications themselves share a common user interface. For example, the menu structures and toolbar buttons in all the Office programs are nearly identical. Also, many of the Office programs share common modules, such as the spell checker.

- Support for OLE 2 in all the Office applications makes it easier to create and maintain compound documents.

- The addition of the Binder application (which I discussed in the preceding chapter) makes it easy to combine related documents from multiple applications into a single file for distribution.

Although most of your Office data-sharing will follow the basic OLE steps we looked at in Chapter 48, "Office Integration and OLE," a few shortcuts and techniques are specific to the Office applications. This chapter fills you in on the details.

Word's Integration Tools

As the Office application in charge of memos, letters, summaries, and reports, Word is often required to integrate data from external sources, whether it's data for a mail merge, an Excel range that illustrates a calculation, or a graphic inserted from the Clip Gallery or some other source. Most of these tasks can be accomplished using the basic cut-and-paste and OLE techniques outlined in Chapter 48. However, Word has a few other integration tools up its sleeve, and this section will tell you about them.

Using Mail Merge

It seems that I receive a boilerplate letter just about every day. I know you've seen them too—written as though a person and not a company was sending it to you. Its tone is personal, with just a hint of friendliness. Don't you wonder how it's done?

The company sending the mail starts with a database that contains your name and address.

Usually, they'll also have stored some other data about you: your buying habits, credit history, and so on.

The process in this example is similar—except for the friendliness, that is. What you're going to create is a dunning letter to be sent out from a fictional legal office. It will remind its recipients of their agreement and their fiscal performance to date, and then request that they bring their account up to date.

The process itself is simple. You first create a database and then create a document. Into the document you place field names derived from the database. Finally, you have Word merge the two into a collection of individualized letters that it can print out to hard copy.

Starting with the Letter

The first step to creating this boilerplate letter is to open Word—if it isn't already—and enter the following text in a new document, as shown in Figure 50.1:

```
Dear [],
How are things in []? Well, we hope.
Just to bring you up to date, we'd like to remind you that it's been quite a while
since we [] your lawsuit for you. As you may remember, you agreed to pay us [] % of
your winnings, as well as []% of the expenses involved.
So far, you have paid us [] from a total amount owed of []. We would appreciate it
if you would bring your account up to date as soon as possible.
Sincerely,
[]
Attorney at Law
```

FIGURE 50.1.

The boilerplate letter before fields are added.

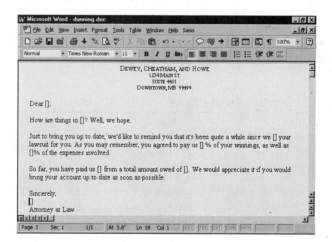

> **NOTE: USING SQUARE BRACKETS**
>
> You'll notice that square brackets ([ ])are used as placeholders in the text. I've found over the years that it's easier to simply write a letter—even a boilerplate one—by letting the words and thoughts flow, rather than stopping every few words to go through the process of adding a field. To do that, however, you need to have a way of keeping track of where the data will eventually go—hence, the brackets.

Save the letter as DUNNING. With that done, you can move on to the next part of the process.

Creating the Database

The next thing you want to do is to open Microsoft Access to create the database. To do so, follow these steps:

1. Open Access. In the Microsoft Access dialog box, in the Create a New Database Using frame, select Blank database and then click OK. Access displays its File New Database dialog box.

2. In the filename text box, give your new database the name attorney.mdb and then click Create. Access creates a new, empty database.

3. In the Database container, click New. Access displays its New Table dialog box.

4. Select Design View and click OK. Access displays a new, blank table in Design view. Create its fields according to Table 50.1.

5. Save the table as Client Info. Although it isn't necessary to incorporate a primary key in this case, you may use the Name field if you want.

Table 50.1. The database scheme for the DUNNING.DOC letter.

Field Name	Type	Length	Description
Name	Text	50	Client's name
Address	Text	50	Client's address
City	Text	50	Client's city
State	Text	50	Client's state
Zip	Text	50	Client's ZIP code
Result	Text	50	Case result
Contingency percentage	Number (Long)	4	Contingency percentage owed by client
Expense percentage	Number (Long)	4	Expense percentage owed by client

Field Name	Type	Length	Description
Amount paid	Currency	8	Amount paid on account
Account amount	Currency	8	Total amount billable to client
Attorney	Text	50	Attorney assigned to the case

Entering Data into Your Database

Next, you'll populate your database with data. Do the following:

1. Start Access and call up the Attorney database.
2. From the database container, click the Tables tab if it isn't already active.
3. Double-click the Client Info table name or click the Open button. Access displays the table in Datasheet view.
4. Enter data into the Client Info table, one row at a time, according to Table 50.2.
5. Save the file after you've entered all the client information.

NOTE: USING A FORM FOR DATA ENTRY

If you don't like entering data row-by-row, you can use a form instead. Click Access's AutoForm button, and Access will automatically create one for you. See Chapter 27, "Creating and Using Simple Forms," for more information.

Automatically Sending the Data to Word

After you enter data in Access, sending it to Word is as simple as clicking the Office Links button, as shown in Figure 50.2. When you click this button, Access creates an automatic DDE link with Word and then creates a file or table and sends over the data in the form of a Word table.

FIGURE 50.2.

The Office Links button automatically connects parts of Microsoft Office.

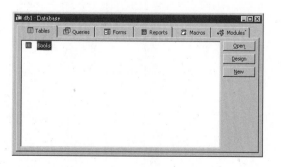

Table 50.2. Names and addresses for the dunning letter.

Name	Address	City	State	Zip	Result	Contingency Percentage	Expense Percentage	Amount Paid	Account Amount	Attorney
Joe Blow	123 Fifth St	Hadleyville	OR	88032	Lost	33	100	$63,000.00	$120,000.00	Will Cheatham
Irving Feeblebottom	12450 Maple Ave	Hill Valley	OR	88232	Won	33	25	$1,200.00	$3,000,000.00	Will Cheatham
Bill Barnes	233 Chopman Blvd	Pullman	WA	98002	Won	40	100	$300.00	$6,000.00	Andy Howe
George Johnson	543 Thurman Ave	Seattle	WA	98022	Lost	33	28	$1,200.00	$40,000.00	Andy Howe

That procedure is fine, but you are going to send data from Access to Word in a more structured way. Read the next section.

Merging Data with Word

After you complete a letter and a database is in place, it's time to make the two work together.

As you probably know, an Access database is comprised of one or more tables. Each table, in turn, is comprised of records (rows) made up of fields (columns). To get Word and Access working together, you have to establish a link between them. You can establish this link from Access (as you did a moment ago when you used Office Links to connect Access and Word), or you can set up the link from Word. To establish the link from Word, click the Mail Merge Helper button on the Mail Merge toolbar, and then click the Get Data button in the Data Source section. Select Open Data Source and choose the Attorney database and the appropriate table.

Then, in your Word document, you need to insert placeholders that will accept the contents of the database's fields, one record per each Word document.

> ### NOTE: YOU DON'T NEED TO USE ALL THE FIELDS
>
> It isn't necessary to use all the fields in your database in your merged letter. To prove that's so, you aren't going to use all the fields in the attorney database in your letter.

Start by inserting the placeholders. To do so, follow these steps:

1. Open Word and call up the boilerplate letter, DUNNING.DOC.
2. Select Tools | Mail Merge. Word displays the Mail Merge Helper dialog box, shown in Figure 50.3.

FIGURE 50.3.
The Mail Merge Helper dialog box, ready to do your bidding.

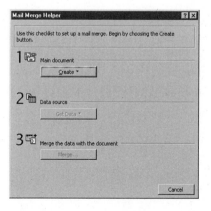

3. In the Main document, click Create. Word displays a list of the types of documents you can create using Mail Merge; select Form Letters. When Word prompts you to indicate which file you want to use as the main document, click the Active Window button. Word displays the file, ready for you to edit.

4. Just above the document, you'll see the Word Mail Merge toolbar. Move your cursor to the first [ ] placeholder, delete it, and click the Insert Merge Field button on the Mail Merge toolbar, as shown in Figure 50.4. Word displays in a list all the fields from your Attorney database.

FIGURE 50.4.

You can choose any field from the database to insert into your document.

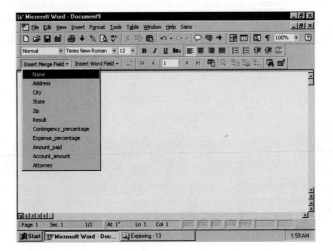

5. Choose the Name field. Word closes the list of fields and inserts a linked field placeholder in your document.

6. In the same way, insert the following fields into the appropriate places in your letter:

> City
>
> Result
>
> Contingency_percentage
>
> Expense_percentage
>
> Amount_paid
>
> Account_amount

When you're done, the letter should look like the one shown in Figure 50.5.

FIGURE 50.5.

The DUNNING.DOC letter with field placeholders in place.

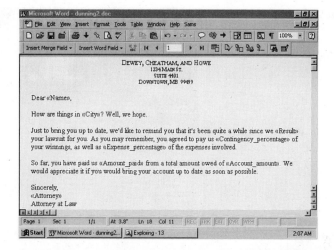

Access databases also can contain queries, the results of which look and behave very much like tables. For DDE and OLE purposes, you can use the results of an Access query in the same way you would an Access table. See Chapter 26, "Querying Data."

Finishing Up Your Mail Merge

What comes next is something I've always been fascinated with. Click the View Merged Data button on the Mail Merge toolbar. (It's the one with the ABC on it.) Word exchanges its display of the field placeholder names with the data actually stored in each field.

After the data from the database is in your letter, you can print it—or any of its pages—just as you would any other Word document, as shown in Figure 50.6.

Remember that each record in the Attorney database provides data for a single document. To accommodate this, Word automatically creates another identical document for each record. It strings them along, page after page, in one now-longer document. If you want, you can page through this longer document by clicking the database navigation keys on the Mail Merge toolbar.

50

THE OFFICE
INTEGRATION
TOOLS

FIGURE 50.6.

*The DUNNING.DOC
letter, all ready to put
people on edge.*

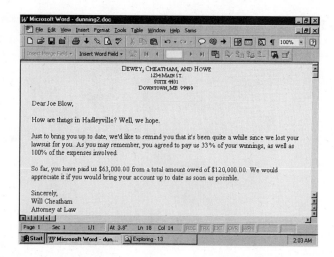

Inserting Excel Data into Word

The scenario for the following example is this: You've been assigned to create a report forecasting the billable hours and revenue generated for the year by each of the three partner attorneys. Because it's a report, you want to write it in Word. But because you know that to complete the assignment you'll need to crunch numbers, you'll want to use a spreadsheet application. This is not a problem.

As you know from other chapters in this book, Excel is the spreadsheet application that comes as part of the Microsoft Office software package. It is one of the most comprehensive, complete, and easy-to-use applications of its type. When you use Excel with Word, you are marrying the two families of software that made microcomputers viable.

I don't mean to torture the metaphor, but the "bond" that holds this marriage together is OLE. When you place an Excel spreadsheet object in your Word document, it's almost like you're placing a little piece of Excel there—and that's what is actually going on.

Excel, being the server application in this case, is exposing to Word its spreadsheet object. Word then behaves as a client application and incorporates that object into one of its documents. The result is symbiosis.

Next, you are going to create a spreadsheet in Excel and link it into Word. Then while the spreadsheet is in Word, you'll edit the spreadsheet—just as if it were still part of Excel (which it actually is!).

NOTE: WHY WE'RE LINKING

You might remember from Chapter 48 that you can link or embed an object into your document. There are two reasons you're going to link your spreadsheet. First, when you embed an object, it—and all its size—becomes part of the container document. It can grow to enormous proportions in no time. Second, forecast numbers often need to be changed. If you link the spreadsheet, someone else can change the numbers using Excel, and the changes will be immediately reflected in your document the next time you open it.

Unlike Word, Excel really lends itself to keeping track of numbers. Your project will use it to do that; in this case, the billable hours and revenue generated by the legal firm of Dewey, Cheatham, and Howe (with apologies to The Three Stooges).

NOTE: THE WORKBOOK'S ON THE CD

 This Excel spreadsheet can be found on the CD-ROM that accompanies this book. If you'd like, you can open that file and follow along rather than reenter everything on the spreadsheet.

The spreadsheet contains three parts. The first is a section devoted to the hourly rate for each of the three partners. The second is a total of each of their billable hours by calendar quarter. The third is a simple multiplication of the first two sections, yielding the revenue generated by each partner. Figure 50.7 shows a sample of the spreadsheet in its final form.

FIGURE 50.7.

The sample spreadsheet.

	A	B	C	D	E	F
1	**Attorney Fiscal Performance**					
2						
3	**Hourly Rate**					
4	Andrew Howe	$250.00				
5	Candace Dewey	$300.00				
6	William Cheatham	$325.00				
7						
8	**Billable hours**	**Subtotal**	**1st Quarter**	**2nd Quarter**	**3rd Quarter**	**4th Quarter**
9	Andrew Howe	2,500	625	645	600	630
10	Candace Dewey	2,615	640	650	655	670
11	William Cheatham	2,860	750	720	700	690
12	**Total**	7,975				
13						
14	**Revenue Earned**	**Subtotal**	**1st Quarter**	**2nd Quarter**	**3rd Quarter**	**4th Quarter**
15	Andrew Howe	$ 625,000.00	$ 156,250.00	$ 161,250.00	$ 150,000.00	$ 157,500.00
16	Candace Dewey	$ 784,500.00	$ 192,000.00	$ 195,000.00	$ 196,500.00	$ 201,000.00
17	William Cheatham	$ 929,500.00	$ 243,750.00	$ 234,000.00	$ 227,500.00	$ 224,250.00
18	**Total**	$2,339,000.00				
19						
20						

50

THE OFFICE INTEGRATION TOOLS

To get on your way, follow these steps:

1. Load and run Excel, opening it to a blank spreadsheet.

2. Move to cell A1 (the upper leftmost cell). In it, type `Attorney Fiscal Performance`. If you want, you can format the text in that cell in bold by clicking the Bold button on the formatting toolbar.

3. Move to cell A3 and type `Hourly Rate`. Again, you might want to format this in bold so that it stands out.

4. Continuing down to A4, enter data into rows 4, 5, and 6 according to Table 50.3. Entries in bold type represent column or subsection headings.

Table 50.3. Hourly rates.

	A	B
3	**Hourly Rate**	
4	Andrew Howe	$250.00
5	Candace Dewey	$300.00
6	William Cheatham	$325.00

5. Save the spreadsheet as Attorney.xls.

6. Move to cell A8 and enter data according to Table 50.4, leaving the attorney data for column B blank for now.

Table 50.4. Billable hours.

	A	B	C	D	E	F
8	**Billable Hours**	**Subtotal**	**1st Quarter**	**2nd Quarter**	**3rd Quarter**	**4th Quarter**
9	Andrew Howe		625	645	600	630
10	Candace Dewey		640	650	655	670
11	William Cheatham		750	720	700	690

7. Move to cell A14 and enter data according to Table 50.5, leaving the attorney revenue data blank for now.

Table 50.5. Revenue earned.

	A	B	C	D	E	F
14	**Revenue Earned**	**Subtotal**	**1st Quarter**	**2nd Quarter**	**3rd Quarter**	**4th Quarter**
15	Andrew Howe					
16	Candace Dewey					
17	William Cheatham					

8. Save the spreadsheet.

When you're done, your spreadsheet should look like the one shown in Figure 50.8.

FIGURE 50.8.

Your spreadsheet before you do the math.

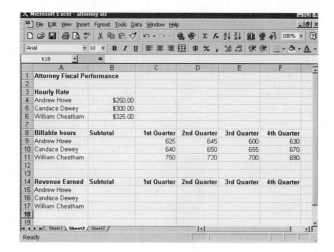

Calculating the Sums

After you have a basic spreadsheet, it's time to do the math. You enter the formulas that will compute the revenue earned for each attorney, and that will add up the columns of billable hours and revenue earned.

To do this, follow these steps:

1. Create a formula that will sum the billable hours for each attorney. With your spreadsheet active, move to cell B9. In it, type the following formula:

   `=SUM(C9..F9)`

   Press Enter. Excel sums the four cells to the right of cell B9 and displays the resulting value. That takes care of attorney Andrew Howe.

2. Do the same thing for the other two attorneys. With cell B9 highlighted, press Ctrl-C. Excel copies the contents of that cell to the Clipboard.

3. Move to cell B10 and highlight it. Drag the cursor so that it and cell B11 are highlighted. You can tell which cells are selected by the dashed line Excel draws around them.

4. Press Ctrl-V. Excel copies into the two highlighted cells the formula from cell B9 that you copied to the Clipboard. As soon as the information is pasted into the cells, Excel sums the four cells to the right and displays the resulting values. With that, the data for the other two attorneys' data is taken care of.

5. Now you need to do the same thing regarding their revenue earned. Move to cell B15. With it highlighted, drag your cursor down two more cells to B17.

6. When all three cells are selected (you'll see the same dashed line around them), press Ctrl-V. Excel copies into those cells the same formula from the Clipboard, performs the same sum function on the four cells to their right, and displays zeros (see Figure 50.9)! Don't worry—zeros are fine for now, because you haven't done the multiplication to figure out how much revenue for the firm each attorney has generated.

FIGURE 50.9.

The spreadsheet with the additions done.

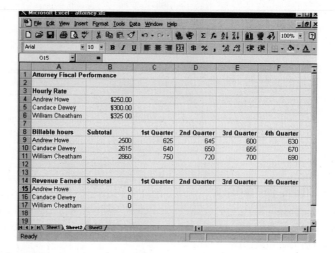

Calculating the Multiplication

It might seem a bit backward to do the multiplication after you do the addition, but it's not. Actually, in this type of spreadsheet situation, there's really no first and second. All the math must be done before you arrive at the information you need.

First, you need to create a formula to multiply each attorney's first quarter revenue earned. Do the following:

1. Move to cell C15. In it, type the following formula:

   =C9*$B$4

   Excel multiplies the contents of cell C9 with the contents of cell B4 and displays the result in the highlighted cell C15.

NOTE: EXCEL'S RELATIVE REFERENCING

You might be wondering about the dollar signs ($)used in the multiplication formula. Excel, in its internal figuring, "thinks" in relative terms. For example, the relationship between cell C15 (where you want to see the result) and the cell containing Andrew Howe's hourly rate is to Excel "one cell over, and five cells up from the one that's highlighted now."

That relative thinking works fine for arriving at the figure for his first quarter revenue earned. It breaks down, however, when you try to figure the second and subsequent quarter figures. For that reason, dollar signs are used to tell Excel to use the contents of cell B4 absolutely—in other words, to use exactly that cell's contents in the multiplication. You'll find more information on this in Chapter 16, "Manipulating Formulas and Functions."

2. Move to cell C16 and type the following formula:

   =C10*$B$5

   Excel multiplies the contents of cell C10 with the contents of cell B5 and displays the result in the highlighted cell C16.

3. Move to cell C17 and type the following formula:

   =C11*$B$6

   Excel multiplies the contents of cell C11 with the contents of cell B6 and displays the result in the highlighted cell C17.

Next, you need to copy these formulas to arrive at the figures for each of the other three quarters. To do so, follow these steps:

1. Move up to cell C15. With it highlighted, drag down two cells to cell C17 so that all three cells are selected.

2. Press Ctrl-C. Excel places the contents of the selected cells onto the Clipboard.

3. Move to cell D15. Drag and select all the cells from it to cell F17, and then press Ctrl-V. Excel copies the formulas from the Clipboard, performs the multiplication, and displays the resulting values, as shown in Figure 50.10.

FIGURE 50.10.

Your spreadsheet with the multiplication completed.

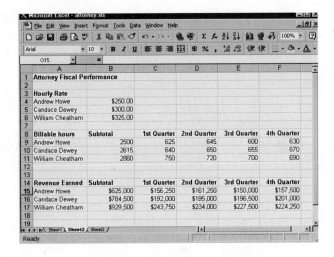

Next, you'll run two quick totals just to satisfy your curiosity. One is for the total hours worked by the attorneys, and another is for the total revenue generated:

1. Move to cell A12 and type Total.

2. With the cell still highlighted, press Ctrl-B to make bold the cell's text font.

3. Click the Align Right button on the Formatting toolbar to realign the cell's text font.

4. Move to cell B12. Click the Autosum button on the formula toolbar. Excel assumes that you want to sum the three cells above B12, so you can simply press Enter to accept that. Excel does the addition and displays the result in cell B12.

5. Select both cells A12 and B12 and then press Ctrl-C. Excel copies to the Clipboard the formulas from both cells.

6. Move to cell A18 and press Ctrl-V. Excel copies the formulas from the Clipboard, performs the addition, and displays the result in cell B18, as shown in Figure 50.11.

With that, you are finished with the spreadsheet part of this example. Next, you move on to the report.

Creating a Report

Now that your background data is ready, it's time to create a report that you can use to explain it.

Start with one of Word's built-in report templates. To begin creating a report, follow these steps:

1. In Word, select File | New and click the Reports tab. The New dialog box, shown in Figure 50.12, appears.

2. Dewey, Cheatham, and Howe is a contemporary legal firm, so double-click Contemporary Report to select it. Word displays the report template, ready for you to modify, as shown in Figure 50.13.

	A	B	C	D	E	F
3	Hourly Rate					
4	Andrew Howe	$250.00				
5	Candace Dewey	$300.00				
6	William Cheatham	$325.00				
8	Billable hours	Subtotal	1st Quarter	2nd Quarter	3rd Quarter	4th Quarter
9	Andrew Howe	2500	625	645	600	630
10	Candace Dewey	2615	640	650	655	670
11	William Cheatham	2860	750	720	700	690
12	Total	7,975				
14	Revenue Earned	Subtotal	1st Quarter	2nd Quarter	3rd Quarter	4th Quarter
15	Andrew Howe	$625,000	$156,250	$161,250	$150,000	$157,500
16	Candace Dewey	$784,500	$192,000	$195,000	$196,500	$201,000
17	William Cheatham	$929,500	$243,750	$234,000	$227,500	$224,250
18	Total	$2,339,000				

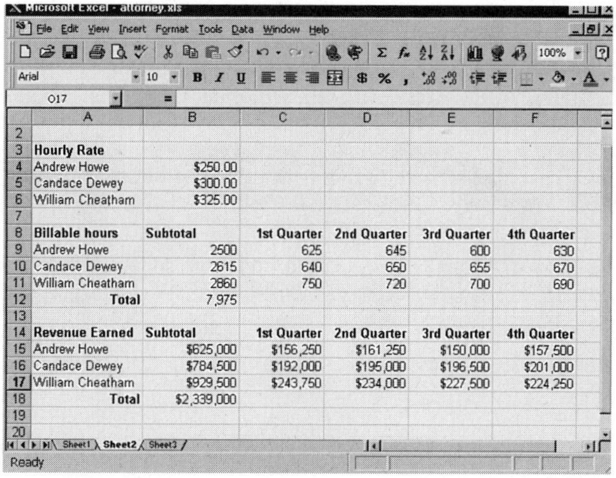

FIGURE 50.11.
The finished spreadsheet.

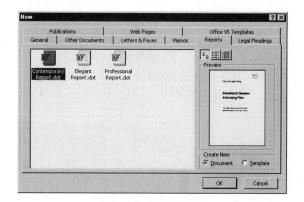

FIGURE 50.12.
Click a report template to get started.

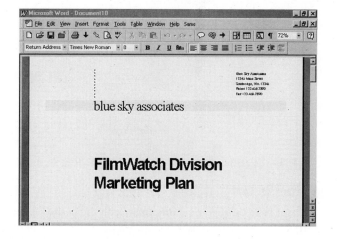

FIGURE 50.13.
The contemporary report document template before modification.

3. Just to be safe, save the file as Fiscal Report.doc.

Modifying the Report

The template Word calls up is a good start. Now you need to modify the report so that it reflects the name and address of the example legal firm. To do so, perform the following steps:

> **NOTE: THE TEMPLATE IS ON THE CD**
>
> This document template can be found on the CD that accompanies this book.

1. Move to the name and address frame at the top right of the form, and change it to the following:

   Dewey, Cheatham, and Howe

   1234 Main St.

   Suite 4401

   Downtown, MB 99499

2. Move to the blue sky associates logo and change it to Dewey, Cheatham, and Howe.

3. Move to the FilmWatch Division report title and change it to Firm Fiscal Report, as shown in Figure 50.14.

FIGURE 50.14.

The contemporary report document template after you make modifications.

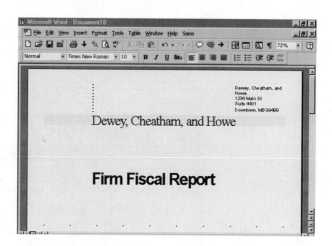

4. Delete all the remaining text found on succeeding pages in the document.

Writing the Report

With the front page finished, it's time to actually write the report. My personal philosophy is that reports are tools to convey specific information—not tomes to be digested. In other words, with business reports, less is more. This example follows that philosophy.

> **NOTE: YOU DON'T NEED TO WRITE A REPORT**
>
> In this example, you don't actually write text for the report. You probably already know how to type, so there's no point to entering the text, especially when the task at hand is to embed an Excel spreadsheet. You can, however, work along with this example, using the document template you've just modified.

Assume that—without your actually having to do so—you are writing a report forecasting the firm's fiscal performance. You continue to write, until you get to the point in the report where you want to insert the spreadsheet that you created. To insert the spreadsheet, do the following:

1. Select Insert | Object. Word displays the Object dialog box, shown in Figure 50.15.

FIGURE 50.15.

The Object dialog box, ready to call up your spreadsheet.

2. Click the Create from File tab. Enable the Link to file check box. This creates an OLE link between the spreadsheet and your Word document.

3. In the File name text box, type `Attorney.xls`. If necessary, you can click the Browse button to find the spreadsheet file on your hard disk.

4. Click OK, and the magic begins.

An Automagical Occurrence

When creating an OLE link, what happens in the background is—to me, at least—fascinating. The following is a simplified version of what occurs:

1. Word starts Excel, passing to it the name of the Attorney.xls spreadsheet file.

2. Excel looks for and finds the Attorney.xls spreadsheet file, loads it into memory, and then exposes it (makes it available as an object) to Word.

3. Word takes over the spreadsheet object, figures out how much room on your document it will take, creates a frame of that size, inserts the spreadsheet into that frame, and displays it for you, as shown in Figure 50.16. Voilà!

50

THE OFFICE INTEGRATION TOOLS

FIGURE 50.16.

Your spreadsheet inserted into a Word document.

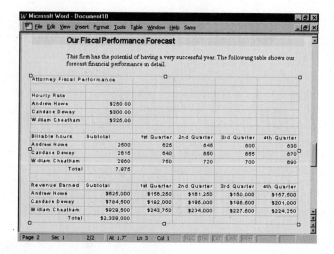

Editing a Spreadsheet from Within Word

You know, it never fails: Under time pressure, you create the report just short of the deadline, and someone comes to you with a last-minute change. This must happen frequently at Microsoft, because they've included in the Word and OLE business a quick and easy way to deal with the situation—you can edit the spreadsheet right while it's in your Word document.

Suppose you need to make a change to the spreadsheet. The firm has discovered that it can get another $10 per hour out of Candace Dewey's clients. Also, ol' Willy Cheatham has been losing too many cases lately. His hourly rate has got to come down by $20. To make these changes, follow these steps:

1. Move to the spreadsheet in your document and double-click it. Word unhides Excel (which has actually been running, hidden, all along) and displays in it your spreadsheet.

2. Move to cell B5 and increase Dewey's rate by $10 so that it now is $310. Excel recalculates all the numbers, dependent on the value in cell B5.

3. Move to cell B6 and decrease Cheatham's rate by $20 so that it now is $305. Excel recalculates all the numbers, dependent on the value in cell B6.

4. Save the spreadsheet.

After you make your changes, press Alt-Tab until Word is in the foreground of your desktop. Notice that because the spreadsheet and Word document are linked, OLE has already made the changes in your report for you, as shown in Figure 50.17.

Looking over the spreadsheet object in your report, there's one other thing that would really improve its appearance. I refer, of course, to those rather obtrusive gridlines Excel inserts by default.

FIGURE 50.17.

Your spreadsheet, with its numbers reflecting the latest information.

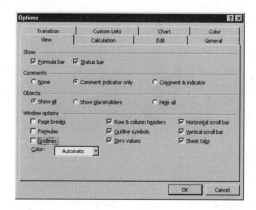

Our Fiscal Performance Forecast					

This firm has the potential of having a very successful year. The following table shows our forecast financial performance in detail.

Attorney Fiscal Performance

Hourly Rate					
Andrew Howe	$250.00				
Candace Dewey	$310.00				
William Cheatham	$305.00				

Billable hours	Subtotal	1st Quarter	2nd Quarter	3rd Quarter	4th Quarter
Andrew Howe	2500	625	645	600	630
Candace Dewey	2615	640	650	655	670
William Cheatham	2860	750	720	700	690
Total	7,975				

Revenue Earned	Subtotal	1st Quarter	2nd Quarter	3rd Quarter	4th Quarter
Andrew Howe	$625,000	$156,250	$161,250	$150,000	$157,500
Candace Dewey	$810,650	$198,400	$201,500	$203,050	$207,700
William Cheatham	$872,300	$228,750	$219,600	$213,500	$210,450
Total	$2,307,950				

Modifying the Format of an Object

Taking out the spreadsheet gridlines in your Word document is as easy as if you were doing it in Excel. The reason is—of course—that because it's a linked OLE document, you're actually doing it in Excel. To modify the format, perform the following steps:

1. Double-click the spreadsheet object in your report. Word calls up Excel and displays the linked spreadsheet.

2. Select Tools | Options. Excel displays the Options dialog box, shown in Figure 50.18.

FIGURE 50.18.

Excel's Options dialog box.

3. Select the View tab. Disable the Gridlines check box. Excel removes the gridlines from your spreadsheet—both in Excel and in your report, as shown in Figure 50.19.

4. Save the spreadsheet in Excel.

FIGURE 50.19.

Your cleanly formatted report.

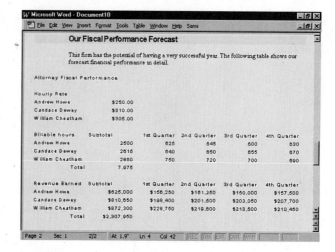

Adding a Chart to the Report

When you get right down to it, the purpose of a report is to quickly and efficiently transmit information to your reader. As for being quick and efficient in transferring numerical concepts, words simply don't cut it as well as pictures do. For that reason, take an extra moment to embellish your report with a pie chart created from the Excel spreadsheet. Do the following:

1. Call up the spreadsheet in Excel. (Remember that you can do this by double-clicking the spreadsheet object in Word, or by opening it directly from within Excel.)

2. Use the Excel Chart Wizard to create a pie chart from the subtotaled billable hours for the three attorneys: cells A9 through B11.

3. After you create the chart, select it and press Ctrl-C to copy it to the Clipboard.

4. Open your report in Word and then move to where you want your report to appear. When there, press Ctrl-V. Word copies the pie chart into your spreadsheet, as shown in Figure 50.20.

5. Save the report.

FIGURE 50.20.

Your report now contains a chart.

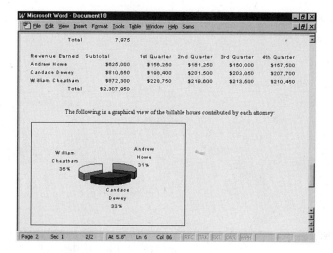

Integrating Data Within Excel

Excel doesn't exist in a vacuum. You often have to import data to Excel from other applications (such as a database file or a text file from a mainframe). And, just as often, you have to export Excel data to other programs (such as a word processor or a presentation graphics package). Although these tasks usually are straightforward, you still can run into some problems. Therefore, Excel provides some features that can help you avoid these problems. This section looks at the various ways you can exchange data between Excel and other applications.

Working with Word

As the word processor in the Office group, Microsoft Word is a popular choice as a client application because worksheets, ranges, and charts are often used to back up statements in a proposal or memo. However, exchanging data between Word and Excel isn't always straightforward, because, depending on how you paste the information, it's often hard to predict the result. To help out, the next couple of sections tell you exactly what to expect when sharing data between Word and Excel.

Exporting an Excel Range to Word

When you copy a range in Excel and then from Word select Edit | Paste Special, the Paste Special dialog box gives you five data types to use for the paste. To help you decide which option is best for you, Table 50.6 summarizes each data type.

Table 50.6. Data types available for pasting an Excel range.

Data Type	Description
Microsoft Excel Worksheet Object	Embeds the range as a Worksheet object.
Formatted Text (RTF)	Pastes the range as a Word table and preserves existing formatting.
Unformatted Text	Pastes the range as plain text with tabs separating each column and line feeds separating each row.
Picture	Inserts the range as a picture. Use this data type instead of Bitmap to preserve memory and keep screen redraws fast.
Bitmap	Inserts the range as a bitmap image. The only advantage over the Picture data type is that the bitmap image shows you exactly what the Excel range looks like.

NOTE: PASTING A CHART

If you copy an Excel chart to the Clipboard, Word's Paste Special dialog box offers you three data types: Microsoft Excel Chart Object, Picture, and Bitmap.

Importing Text from Word

Copying Word text to the Clipboard and then pasting it into Excel is straightforward. The Paste Special dialog box gives you a choice of four data types, as described in Table 50.7.

Table 50.7. Data types available for pasting Word text.

Data Type	Description
Microsoft Word Document Object	Embeds the text as a document object.
	Inserts the text as a picture.
Picture	Pastes the text as unformatted text.
Text	Places text separated by tabs into separate columns. Places paragraphs into separate rows.

TIP: PASTING SHORTCUT

When Word text is on the Clipboard, selecting Excel's Edit | Paste command is the same as selecting Edit | Paste Special and choosing the Text data type.

NOTE: PASTING A WORD TABLE TO A RANGE

If you copy a Word table to the Clipboard and you would prefer to insert the content of each table cell into its own worksheet cell, use the Text data type when pasting.

Creating a New Excel Worksheet in Word

In Chapter 48, I showed you how to embed a new object in a client document by using the client application's Insert | Object command. If you want to embed a new Excel worksheet object in a Word document, you can use Word's Insert | Object command and choose Microsoft Excel Worksheet as the object type. If you have a mouse handy, however, Word gives you an even easier way to embed a new worksheet object:

1. In Word, position the cursor at the spot where you want the worksheet object to appear.

2. Move the mouse pointer over the Insert Microsoft Excel Worksheet button on Word's Standard toolbar, and then press and hold down the left mouse button. A grid appears below the toolbar.

3. Each grid cell represents a cell in the range. To define the size of the range you want, drag the mouse pointer into the grid and highlight the appropriate number of rows and columns you want, as shown in Figure 50.21.

4. Release the mouse button. Word embeds the range and activates in-place inserting.

5. Enter your data, formulas, and formatting using the Excel menus, toolbars, and formula bar.

6. When you're done, click outside the object.

The Relationship Between Linking and Word Bookmarks

When you link an object in a worksheet, Excel sets up a remote reference formula to keep track of the link. For a Word object, this formula takes the following general form:

```
=Word.Document.6¦DocumentName!'!BookmarkName'
```

Here, *DocumentName* is the full pathname of the Word document containing the original text, and *BookmarkName* is the name of a special bookmark that Excel creates in the Word document.

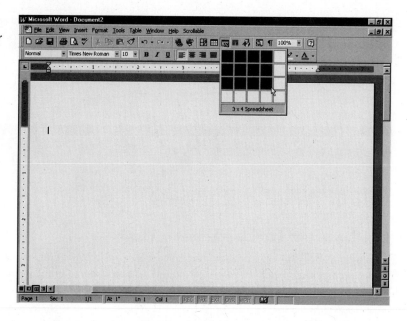

FIGURE 50.21.

Drag the mouse pointer into the grid to define the number of rows and columns in your embedded range.

For example, if this is the first time you've linked text from a particular document, Excel creates a bookmark named OLE_LINK1. (To see this for yourself, display the Word document, select Edit | Bookmark, highlight the OLE_LINK1 bookmark in the Bookmark dialog box, and click the Go To button. Word takes you right to the linked text.)

If you already have bookmarks set up in a Word document, you can create your own remote reference formulas from scratch:

1. In Excel, select a range with enough rows to hold all the paragraphs in your bookmarked text. (If the text contains tabs, you'll need to select enough columns as well.)

2. In the formula bar, enter the remote reference formula. Make sure that you enter the full pathname for the document (the drive, folder, and filename), as well as the bookmark name.

3. Press Ctrl-Shift-Enter. Excel pastes the text into the selected range.

Working with PowerPoint

Exchanging data between Excel and PowerPoint uses methods similar to those for Word. Here are a few things to bear in mind:

■ When you're pasting a range, PowerPoint's Paste Special dialog box gives you the same data type choices as Word.

■ PowerPoint tends to insert worksheets and charts as rather small objects. To see the range properly, you need to increase the size of the object.

■ If you want to insert a new worksheet object into a slide, you can use PowerPoint's Insert Microsoft Excel Worksheet button on its Standard toolbar. This button works just like the one on Word's Standard toolbar.

Using Excel to Work with Access

If your database needs to extend only to simple, flat-file tables, Excel's built-in database capabilities probably will do the job. For larger table and relational features, however, you'll want to use a more sophisticated application, such as Access. The next couple of sections show you how to share data between Excel and Access.

Exporting Excel Data to Access

To transfer Excel data into Access, you can use either the Clipboard or Access's Import Spreadsheet Wizard feature.

To use the Clipboard method, you need to set up an Access table with the same number of fields as there are columns in the range you want to copy. When that's done, follow these steps to paste the data into the table:

1. In Excel, copy the data to the Clipboard.
2. In Access, open the table (datasheet view), move to the new record at the bottom of the table, and select the first field.
3. Select Edit | Paste Append. Access pastes the data into the table and displays a dialog box that lets you know how many records are about to be added.
4. Click Yes to return to the table.

CAUTION: ACCESS IGNORES EXTRA COLUMNS

If the Excel range you're copying has more columns than there are fields in the Access table, Access ignores the extra columns.

To use the Import Spreadsheet Wizard method, follow these steps:

1. In Excel, close the workbook you'll be importing if it's currently open.
2. In Access, select File | Get External Data | Import. Access displays the Import dialog box.
3. Highlight Microsoft Excel (*.xls) in the Files of type list.
4. Highlight the workbook you want to import, and then click Import. Access starts the Import Spreadsheet Wizard, as shown in Figure 50.22.

50

THE OFFICE
INTEGRATION
TOOLS

FIGURE 50.22.

Use the first Import Spreadsheet Wizard dialog box to tell Access the name of the worksheet or range you want to import.

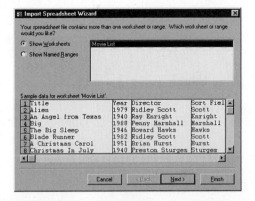

TIP: A FASTER WAY TO THE WIZARD

You can bypass steps 1 through 4 if you've loaded Excel's AccessLinks add-in file. With this add-in loaded, select a cell inside the table you want to export, and then select Data | Convert to Access to start the Import Spreadsheet Wizard.

5. Either activate the Show Worksheets option and highlight the worksheet you want to import, or activate the Show Named Ranges option and highlight the named range you want to import. When you're done, click Next > to display the next Import Spreadsheet Wizard dialog box.

6. If the first row of the worksheet or range contains the field names you want to use, activate the First Row Contains Column Headings check box, and then click Next >.

7. In the next Wizard dialog box, activate In a New Table if you want to import the data to a new table. Otherwise, activate In an Existing Table and choose the table from the list provided. When you're done, click Next > to display the Import Spreadsheet Wizard dialog box, shown in Figure 50.23.

FIGURE 50.23.

Use this Import Spreadsheet Wizard dialog box to specify information about each field you're importing.

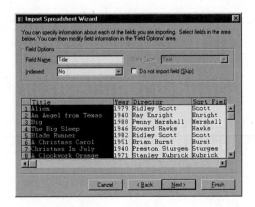

8. For each field (column), enter a field name and specify whether the field should be indexed. If you want the Wizard to bypass a field, activate the Do not import field (Skip) check box. To select a different field, click on the field's header. When you're done, click Next > to move to the next dialog box.

9. The next Wizard dialog box lets you specify a primary key for the new table. You have three choices (click Next > when you've made your choice):

> **Let Access add Primary Key:** Choose this option to tell Access to create a new field (called ID) to use as the primary key.

> **Choose my own Primary Key:** Choose this option to select a primary key from one of the existing fields (which you select from the associated drop-down list).

> **No Primary Key:** Choose this option if you don't want to specify a primary key for the new table.

10. In the final Import Spreadsheet Wizard dialog box, enter a name for the new table in the Import to Table text box. If you'd like the Wizard to analyze the structure of the table (to look for data redundancies and other relational issues), activate the I would like a wizard to analyze... check box. When you're ready, click Finish. Access creates the new table and displays a dialog box.

11. Click OK to return to the database.

Importing Data from Access

Transferring table records from Access to Excel can also be done in one of two ways: with the Clipboard or with the Analyze It With MS Excel feature. Here's a rundown of the Clipboard method:

1. In Access, open the table (datasheet view) and select the records you want to import.

2. Select Edit | Copy to place the records on the Clipboard.

3. In Excel, select the destination for the records.

4. Select Edit | Paste. Excel pastes the field names in the current row and the records in separate rows below.

The Analyze It With MS Excel feature can convert an Access database object into an Excel worksheet and open the new sheet in Excel all in one step. To try this out, open the datasheet, form, or report that you want to convert, and then do one of the following:

■ Select Tools | OfficeLinks | Analyze It With MS Excel.

■ Click the OfficeLinks button in the toolbar and then select Analyze It With MS Excel.

Access converts the table into an Excel worksheet, activates Excel, and then loads the new worksheet.

Importing Text Files into Excel

When you import text data, Excel usually breaks up the file according to the position of the carriage-return and line-feed characters. This means that each line in the text file gets inserted into a cell. In most cases, this is not the behavior you want. For example, if you've downloaded some stock data, you need the date, volume, and pricing values in separate columns.

Instead of making you divide each line by hand, Excel includes a TextWizard tool that can parse text files in the usual step-by-step fashion of the wizards. How you use the TextWizard depends on the text's format. There are two possibilities:

- Delimited text: Each field is separated by characters such as commas, spaces, or tabs.

- Fixed-width text: The fields are aligned in columns.

If you're not sure which type of file you're dealing with, just start the TextWizard as described in either of the following two procedures. In most cases, the TextWizard can determine the data type for you.

To import a text file (or to convert worksheet text into columns), follow these steps:

1. To open the text file, select File | Open, and then select the file from the Open dialog box. (To help out, select the Text Files option from the list labeled Files of type.) Excel displays the Text Import Wizard - Step 1 of 3 dialog box, shown in Figure 50.24.

FIGURE 50.24.

Use the Text Import Wizard - Step 1 of 3 dialog box to select the type of text file you're importing.

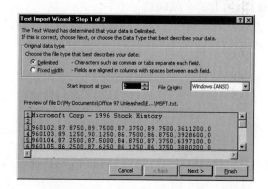

Or, if you want to convert worksheet text, select the text and then choose Data | Text to Columns. Excel displays the Convert Text to Columns Wizard - Step 1 of 3 dialog box.

2. In the Original data type group, activate either Delimited or Fixed width.

3. If you're importing a text file, enter a number in the spinner labeled Start import at row, and then select the file's native environment from the File Origin drop-down list.

4. Click the Next > button to move to the wizard's Step 2 of 3 dialog box, shown in Figure 50.25.

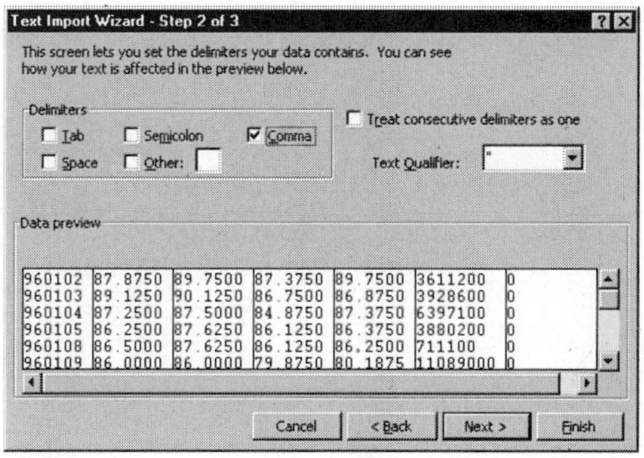

FIGURE 50.25.

The Text Import Wizard - Step 2 of 3 dialog box for delimited data.

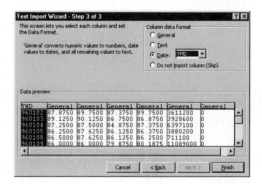

5. If you're using a delimited file, select the appropriate delimiting character from the Delimiters check boxes. If the data includes text in quotation marks, select the appropriate quotation mark character from the Text Qualifier list.

   If you're using a fixed-width file, you can set up the column breaks by using the following techniques:

   > To create a column break, click inside the Data preview area at the spot where you want the break to occur.
   >
   > To move a column break, drag it to the new location.
   >
   > To delete a column break, double-click it.

6. Click the Next > button to move to the wizard's Step 3 of 3 dialog box, shown in Figure 50.26.

FIGURE 50.26.

Use the Step 3 of 3 dialog box to select and format the columns.

7. Select each column and then choose one of the options from the Column data format group. (You select a column by clicking the column header.) If you don't want a column imported, activate the Do not import column (Skip) option.

8. Click Finish. Excel imports the text file, as shown in Figure 50.27.

50

THE OFFICE INTEGRATION TOOLS

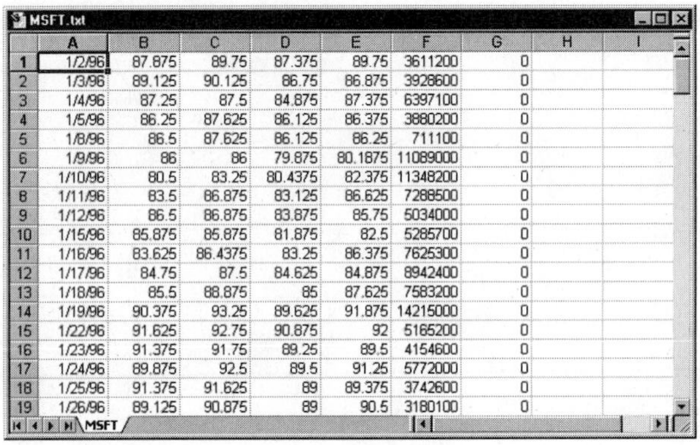

	A	B	C	D	E	F	G	H	I
1	1/2/96	87.875	89.75	87.375	89.75	3611200	0		
2	1/3/96	89.125	90.125	86.75	86.875	3928600	0		
3	1/4/96	87.25	87.5	84.875	87.375	6397100	0		
4	1/5/96	86.25	87.625	86.125	86.375	3880200	0		
5	1/8/96	86.5	87.625	86.125	86.25	711100	0		
6	1/9/96	86	86	79.875	80.1875	11089000	0		
7	1/10/96	80.5	83.25	80.4375	82.375	11348200	0		
8	1/11/96	83.5	86.875	83.125	86.625	7288500	0		
9	1/12/96	86.5	86.875	83.875	85.75	5034000	0		
10	1/15/96	85.875	85.875	81.875	82.5	5285700	0		
11	1/16/96	83.625	86.4375	83.25	86.375	7625300	0		
12	1/17/96	84.75	87.5	84.625	84.875	8942400	0		
13	1/18/96	85.5	88.875	85	87.625	7583200	0		
14	1/19/96	90.375	93.25	89.625	91.875	14215000	0		
15	1/22/96	91.625	92.75	90.875	92	5165200	0		
16	1/23/96	91.375	91.75	89.25	89.5	4154600	0		
17	1/24/96	89.875	92.5	89.5	91.25	5772000	0		
18	1/25/96	91.375	91.625	89	89.375	3742600	0		
19	1/26/96	89.125	90.875	89	90.5	3180100	0		

FIGURE 50.27.
The text file imported into Excel.

PowerPoint Integration Techniques

Through OLE (object linking and embedding) you can insert all or part of another Office application's file (an object) in a PowerPoint presentation. OLE also lets you edit or update the information in that object. The main differences between linking and embedding involve

- Which application stores the object's information
- How information in the object gets updated

With linking, the parent application—the one in which the object was created—stores the object's information. The host application—the one in which the object is placed—only receives a copy of the object that refers to the original. The parent application updates the data in the object; the linked copy in the host application reflects any changes made in the original application. In PowerPoint, as with other Office applications, you use the Paste Special command to link objects.

Embedding, on the other hand, stores the object and its data in the host application file itself; the object becomes part of the host file. You update information in the object by double-clicking on the object; the object's application opens so that you can edit its data. When you close the object, the change is reflected in the host application. With embedding, the original file remains unaffected by changes to the object. You use the Paste command to embed objects.

Building Presentations from Word Documents

Using OLE, you can use Word documents to build PowerPoint presentations. In general, you can look at three ways to create PowerPoint presentations from Word documents:

- Straight text
- Outlines
- Tables

Linking and Embedding Word Text

Blocks of Word text, when placed in a PowerPoint slide, look like blocks of Word text, as shown in Figure 50.28. No fancy transformations happen when you link or embed. Normal font sizes in documents don't make for easy reading in a presentation, nor do paragraphs provide the concise, bullet-point style that's effective for presentation reading. In short, straight Word text often doesn't make sense for linking or embedding in a PowerPoint presentation.

FIGURE 50.28.

Embedded Word text.

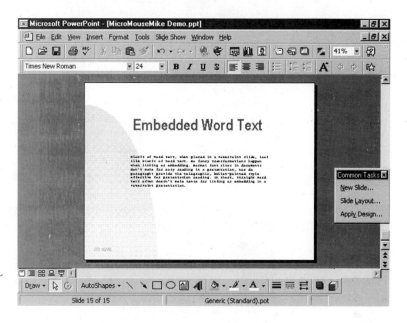

However, there are a few instances in which linking or embedding Word text in a presentation makes sense. A document with a particular format could make an effective addition to a presentation. For example, a meeting agenda produced through Word's Agenda Wizard might be reproduced in a presentation given during the meeting (see Figures 50.29 and 50.30). Or, you might want to display printed quotes in a presentation, where the text format of the object creates more of an impact.

To embed Word text in a PowerPoint slide, copy the text you want to embed in the slide. In PowerPoint, paste the text into the desired slide. You can use any Office method of pasting the text: Right-click in your document and select Paste from the pop-up menu, select Edit | Paste, or press Ctrl-V.

50

THE OFFICE
INTEGRATION
TOOLS

FIGURE 50.29.

*A Word agenda
document.*

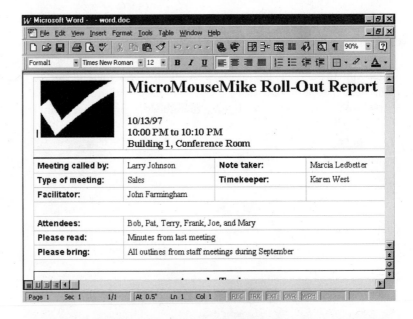

FIGURE 50.30.

*Word's agenda text in a
PowerPoint slide.*

To paste the text into the slide in a different format, select Edit | Paste Special from PowerPoint. In the Paste Special dialog box that appears, shown in Figure 50.31, leave the Paste button active, and select the format you'd like to use for the pasted text:

■ The Picture option pastes the text into the slide as a drawing-type object.

■ Formatted Text preserves any formatting (bold, italic, or fonts) and pastes the text at default presentation text size.

■ Unformatted Text pastes the text into the slide at the presentation's default text size and formatting style.

FIGURE 50.31.

Paste Special formats.

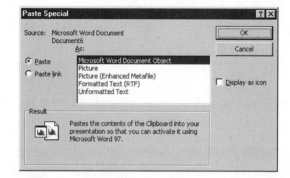

To link Word text in a PowerPoint slide, copy the text you want to link in the slide. In PowerPoint, select Edit | Paste Special and choose Paste Link.

> **NOTE: WORD DOCUMENTS AS OBJECTS**
>
> You can link or embed entire Word files in a PowerPoint slide. To do so, select Insert | Object. Click the Create from File button. Click Browse to select the file. Click OK to embed the file. Select Link, and then click OK to link the file.

Embedding Word Outlines

Word outlines, when specially embedded in a PowerPoint presentation, become presentation outlines: Heading 1 text lines become slide titles, and Heading 2 and lower lines form the bulleted lines. Office provides two ways to embed Word outlines in PowerPoint presentations—one from the Word side and the other from the PowerPoint side.

> **NOTE: IT'S THE HEADINGS THAT COUNT**
>
> This embedding uses the heading styles to create slides. You don't necessarily have to work from Outline view in Word.

In Word, select File | Send To | Microsoft PowerPoint. Word saves the file in a special format called *rich text format* (the file has an .RTF extension), which PowerPoint can read as a slide. Word starts PowerPoint (if you don't already have it loaded), and PowerPoint then opens the

.RTF file. You don't have to choose which file will be opened, because Word automatically tells PowerPoint which file to open. A new presentation opens with the Word document's Heading 1 style for the titles, Heading 2 style for the highest text levels, and so on.

CAUTION: POWERPOINT IGNORES OTHER STYLES

If the Word document contains styles other than Heading 1 through Heading 6, PowerPoint ignores that text.

To build a presentation from a Word outline while in PowerPoint, select Insert | Slides from Outline. Navigate through the directory structure to find your Word file, and then select Insert. The Word file outline becomes slides in the active presentation.

NOTE: EMBEDDED OUTLINES CAN'T BE EDITED AS WORD DOCUMENTS

Once you've embedded a Word outline into a PowerPoint presentation, you can't double-click the object to edit it. The outline has become multiple slides, so you have no one object to click. Also, there is no need to be able to edit the outline through Word; PowerPoint has all the capabilities necessary for manipulating the outline.

Embedding Word Tables

You can embed Word tables from the PowerPoint side. You insert a Word table object in a PowerPoint slide by choosing Slide Layout and choosing a slide layout for a table, as shown in Figure 50.32, or by selecting Insert | Microsoft Word Table. The Insert Word Table dialog box lets you specify the number of columns and rows in the table. Click OK, and a Word table of the specified dimensions appears. As with other embedded objects, editing takes place within Word; the table object itself exists in the PowerPoint slide.

FIGURE 50.32.

A table slide layout.

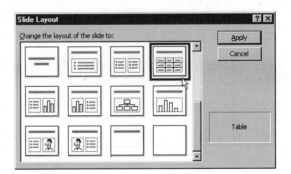

Adding Excel Charts

You can also link and embed Excel charts in PowerPoint slides. To link an Excel chart in a PowerPoint slide, open the Excel worksheet, select and copy the chart, move to the PowerPoint slide, select File | Paste Special, and choose Paste Link. When you double-click the linked chart, its parent worksheet opens, and you can edit the Excel file. Any changes to the Excel file that update the chart are reflected in the chart in the PowerPoint slide.

To embed an existing Excel chart in a PowerPoint slide, open the Excel worksheet, select and copy the chart, move to the PowerPoint slide, and click the presentation's chart area. PowerPoint prompts you to double-click. If you double-click, PowerPoint opens a new datasheet view. Instead of editing the datasheet, you can paste an Excel worksheet into the chart by selecting Edit | Import File and selecting the Excel worksheet or chart. If you double-click the embedded chart, the Excel chart will open within the PowerPoint slide, as shown in Figure 50.33. Edit the chart or worksheet to make changes to the chart in the slide. Changes to the embedded chart do not affect the original Excel file from which you copied the chart.

FIGURE 50.33.

An embedded chart.

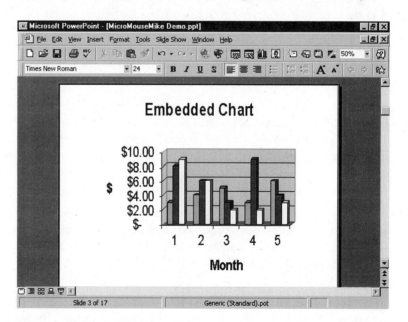

You can also embed a new Excel chart in a PowerPoint slide. Select Insert | Object, and then select Microsoft Excel Chart. PowerPoint embeds a new default chart into the slide. Double-click the chart to open it and change the data to meet your needs.

50

THE OFFICE
INTEGRATION
TOOLS

NOTE: INSERT CHARTS ONE AT A TIME

If you select several charts from a worksheet and try to link or embed them in a slide, PowerPoint gets confused and doesn't recognize the type of object you're dealing with. If you continue, PowerPoint pastes the charts in the slide as a picture. To put several linked or embedded charts on a single slide, link or embed them one at a time.

Using Access to Work with Other Office Applications

One question that always comes up when you're looking at integrating data and/or applications is which way the integration should go. In other words, should you bring Excel data into Access or bring the Access data into Excel? With Office 97, there is little difficulty in working with the data either way. However, you can usually figure out the best way to go by thinking about how you work (or how the person for whom you're designing your application works). If you normally do a lot of data entry or sophisticated queries, you probably should remain in Access. If you mainly crunch numbers or do trend analysis, you should stay in Excel. The application you're most comfortable working with should be your interface.

Another consideration is whether you want to actually move the data or just create a link to it. In general, if the data will be updated often in both applications, you'll want to create a link. That way, you'll avoid doing a lot of imports, exports, and reconciliations. On the other hand, if you're just trying to put out some information for a report or you're moving the data to a particular platform from which it will be worked on in the future, moving the data through some form of export and import is probably your best option.

In the next sections you'll learn how to move data between Access 97 and the other Office 97 applications using somewhat more powerful methods than cutting and pasting. After you learn these methods, you'll know how to integrate the Office 97 tools more tightly in order to build custom solutions to your problems.

Using Access to Work with Word

Access and Word tend to be used together in a business setting because of the need to track things such as mailing addresses (which Word doesn't do well) and creating memos and reports (which Word does do well). Because of this, several different methods are available for sharing data between the two applications.

Using the Mail Merge Wizard

The first way to share data between the two applications is to use the Microsoft Word Mail Merge Wizard (if you're using Microsoft Word 6 or later) to create a mail merge document.

Once this link has been established, you can open your document in Microsoft Word at any time to print a new batch of form letters, labels, and so on using the current data in Microsoft Access.

To set up this link, first highlight the data source you want to export: Either click the name of a table in the Table tab, or click the name of a query in the Query tab. Then either select Tools | OfficeLinks | Merge It With MS Word, or click the Merge It With MS Word toolbar button. Figure 50.34 shows the Mail Merge Wizard dialog box that appears. You have two choices:

> **Link your data to an existing Microsoft Word document:** Select this option to link the data to an existing mail merge document. In this case, the Wizard displays the Select Microsoft Word Document dialog box so that you can choose the document.
>
> **Create a new document and then link the data to it:** Select this option to create a fresh mail merge file in Word. In this case, the Wizard starts Microsoft Word so that you can create the new document.

FIGURE 50.34.

Use the Mail Merge Wizard to link Access data to a Word mail merge document.

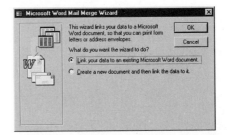

NOTE: MAIL MERGE INSTRUCTIONS

To learn how to create mail merge documents in Word, see the section "Using Mail Merge" earlier in this chapter.

Creating a Mail Merge Data Source File

Another way to export Microsoft Access data, which can be used by any version of Microsoft Word, is to create a mail merge data source file. This file can then be used with Word's mail merge feature. Although this method is a little more complex, it provides more flexibility because the resulting file can be sent to remote or networked users. It also lets you archive information on who was sent what, if this is an essential part of your business.

To export to a Microsoft Word mail merge data source file from Access, you need to do the following:

1. Open the Database window in Access for the database you want to work with and then click the name of the table or query you want to export.

2. Select File | Save As/Export. Access displays the Save As dialog box, shown in Figure 50.35.

FIGURE 50.35.

*The Save As dialog box
for a table.*

3. Activate the To an External File or Database option and click OK. Access displays the Save Table *TableName* In dialog box (where *TableName* is the name of the table you selected in step 1).

4. In the Save as type list, select Word for Windows Merge.

5. Use the Save in and File name controls to enter a location and name for the new file.

6. Click Export.

When you click the Export button, Microsoft Access creates the data source containing the field names and all the data from your table.

When you create a Word mail merge file, Access uses the field names from the table or query. Because Word for Windows has different formatting rules than Access, field names longer than 20 characters are truncated, and characters other than letters, numbers, and underscores are converted to underscores.

In a Word mail merge file, the first record in the file—the header row—contains the field names. All the other records are data rows. The field names in the header row must match the field names in the main document. If they don't match, edit the field names either in the export file (you can open this in Word for Windows) or in the main document so that they do match.

Creating a Rich Text Format File

Using a rich text format file to share data between Access and Word is very similar to the method just described, but it's designed to handle the output of a datasheet, form, or report in which you want to carry the data as well as the formatting. A rich text format (.RTF) file preserves formatting such as fonts, colors, and styles. .RTF files can be opened with Microsoft Word (version 6 or later) as well as other Windows word processing and desktop publishing programs.

As an example, I'll export the Products By Category report from the Northwind sample database, shown in Figure 50.36. To create an .RTF file from Access, follow the steps given in the preceding section. When you get to the Save Table...In dialog box, select Rich Text Format in the Save as type drop-down list. Figure 50.37 shows the .RTF file loaded into Word 6.

FIGURE 50.36.

The Products By Category report.

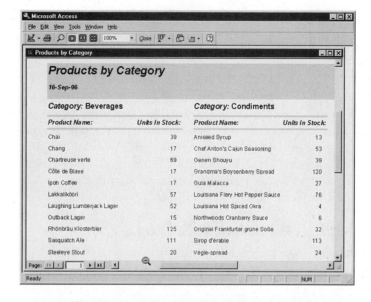

FIGURE 50.37.

The report exported to an .RTF file and loaded into Word.

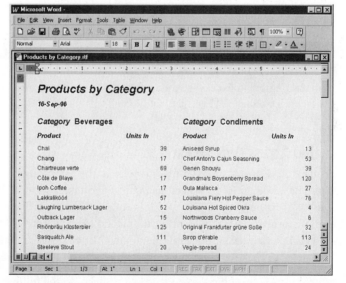

NOTE: USING A MACRO

You can also use the OutputTo action in a macro to save an object in another application's file format (such as RTF). When you use this action, you specify the type of database object you want to output, the name of the object, the output format, and the name of the output file. To learn more about using macros in Access, read Chapter 30, "Creating Access Macros."

50

THE OFFICE
INTEGRATION
TOOLS

Creating an .RTF File and Autoloading Word

By going through the process somewhat differently, you can create an .RTF file as well as load Word automatically in order to start working on the file. This is particularly useful if you're building an application in which you want to use Word's text-editing capabilities without having the user load Word by hand.

To try this out, click the name of the table, query, form, or report you want to save and load into Microsoft Word. To save a section of a datasheet, open the datasheet and select a portion of it. Now select Tools | OfficeLinks | Publish It With MS Word. (For tables and queries, you can also click the Publish It With MS Word button on the toolbar.) The output is saved as an .RTF file in the default database folder (or the last folder you selected in a save or export operation). Then Word starts automatically and opens the file.

Using Access to Work with Excel

Chapter 19, "Working with Lists and Databases," and Chapter 21, "Using Microsoft Query," explained how to work with data in Excel. However, Excel's database capabilities are limited to "flat file" operations only. If you need the relational power of Access, you'll need to know how to move data back and forth between the two programs. The following sections explain how you can work with Excel .XLS files.

> **NOTE: THE IMPORT SPREADSHEET WIZARD**
>
> I discussed importing Excel worksheets using the Import Spreadsheet Wizard earlier in this chapter. See the section "Exporting Excel Data to Access."

Exporting Access Data to Excel

Exporting Access data to an .XLS file is similar to the technique used for exporting forms, reports, and datasheets to RTF. As you might imagine, tables and queries are converted to a basic Excel list. For forms and reports, saving output to Microsoft Excel version 5.0 or later preserves most formatting (such as fonts and colors). Also, report group levels are saved as Microsoft Excel outline levels. For example, Figure 50.38 shows an Access report with grouping levels. Figure 50.39 shows the same report exported to an Excel worksheet with outline levels.

To export to an Access object to an Excel worksheet, do the following:

1. In the Database window, click the object you want to export.
2. Select File | Save As/Export. Access displays the Save As dialog box.
3. Activate the To an External File or Database option and click OK.
4. In the Save as type list, select either Microsoft Excel 5-7 or Microsoft Excel 97.
5. Use the Save in and File name controls to enter a location and a name for the new file.
6. Click Export.

FIGURE 50.38.

A grouped report in Access.

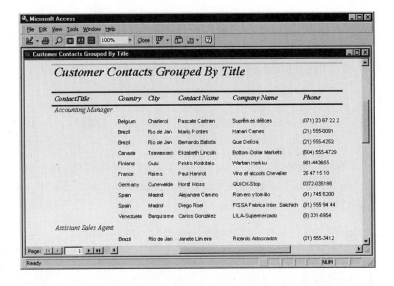

FIGURE 50.39.

The exported report showing outline levels in Excel.

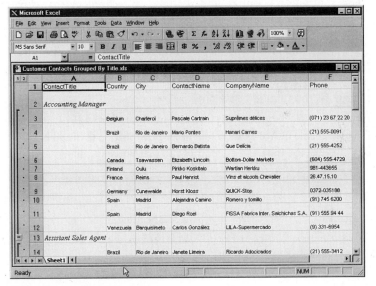

Creating an .XLS File and Autoloading Excel

Just like Word, Excel can be automatically loaded with the information exported to it. To try this, click the name of the table, query, form, or report you want to save and load into Microsoft Excel. To save a section of a datasheet, open the datasheet and select a portion of it. Now select Tools | OfficeLinks | Analyze It With MS Excel. (For tables and queries, you can also click the Analyze It With MS Excel button on the toolbar.) The output is saved as an .XLS file in the default database folder (or the last folder you selected in a save or export operation). Then Excel starts automatically and opens the file.

The end result looks the same as if the file had been exported and then loaded. This method saves a couple of steps and also makes it easier to integrate Excel into an overall solution.

Using Excel's AccessLinks Add-In

As part of the overall philosophy of more tightly integrating the various Office 97 elements, Excel comes with an add-in program called AccessLinks (ACCLINK.XLA). It is designed to make working directly with Access forms and reports easier. To use AccessLinks, you must have both Access 97 and Excel 97 installed. If this add-in isn't loaded, here's how to do it:

1. Switch to Excel and select Tools | Add-ins. Excel displays the Add-Ins dialog box.
2. In the Add-Ins available list, activate the AccessLinks Add-In check box.
3. Click OK.

When Excel loads AccessLinks, you'll see three new commands on the Data menu: Access Form, Access Report, and Convert To Access. (In addition to looking at AccessLinks, we'll also look at other ways to link information between Excel and Access in this chapter.)

These solutions rely on the underlying OLE technology that is part of the Office 97 (and Windows 95) architecture. OLE (which stands for object linking and embedding) has been around for a while. In the previous version of OLE (2.x), Access could work with other OLE applications, but now the latest version allows Access to be an OLE server. What this means is that Access 97 can more closely control what happens with data coming in and going out.

Using Access Forms in Excel

In Chapter 19, I showed you how to enter data into a list using Excel's standard form. The forms available in Access are much more powerful, so it would be nice if you could use them to enter your Excel data. The good news is that you can, thanks to the AccessLinks add-in.

The first step is to create a new Access form from Excel that is built around the linkage of the spreadsheet. To do this, follow these steps:

1. In Excel, select a cell in your worksheet list.
2. Select Data | Access Form. Excel displays the Create Microsoft Access Form dialog box, shown in Figure 50.40.

FIGURE 50.40.

The Data | Access Form command displays this dialog box.

3. Activate either the New database option or the Existing database option. For the latter, type the name and path of the database file in the text box provided (or use the Browse button).

4. Click OK.

5. Access is loaded with a defined link to the spreadsheet.

6. The Access Form Wizard is then loaded using the linked table with data from the spreadsheet. The Wizard guides you through building a data entry form for the Excel list (see Chapter 27, "Creating and Using Simple Forms," for details). You can enter additional data into the list by clicking the Forms button, which is placed on the worksheet by the Access Form Wizard.

Be aware that a significant amount of time can pass between steps 3 and 4, and again between steps 4 and 5. So, if it seems that nothing is happening, wait a couple of minutes and see what happens before killing the process.

Once you have a form created, you might want to use it again. To do so, simply click one of the cells and then click the Forms button on your worksheet. If Excel can't find the form, the Locate Microsoft Access Form dialog box lets you browse your folders for the .MDB file that is linked with your worksheet.

Using Access Reports in Excel

Using Access reports is very similar to using Access forms. Here's the procedure:

1. Select a cell in your worksheet list.

2. Select Data | Access Reports. A dialog box similar to the one shown in Figure 50.40 will prompt you for the database in which to put the link and report.

3. Activate either the New database or the Existing database option. For the latter, type the name and path of the database file in the text box provided (or use the Browse button).

4. Click OK.

5. Access is loaded with a defined link to the spreadsheet.

6. The Access Report Wizard is then loaded using the linked table with data from the worksheet. It then guides you through building a report for the Excel data (see Chapter 28, "Designing and Customizing Reports," for the specifics).

Once you have a report created, you might want to use it again. To do so, simply click one of the cells and then click the Report button that was placed on your worksheet.

50

THE OFFICE
INTEGRATION
TOOLS

Creating an Access Table from Excel Data

In the future, if you'll be working primarily with a set of data from Access, your best bet is to create an Access table from your Excel worksheet. Here's the procedure:

1. Select a cell in your worksheet list.
2. Select Data | Convert To Access. Excel displays the Convert to Microsoft Access dialog box.
3. Activate either the New database or the Existing database option. For the latter, type the name and path of the database file in the text box provided (or use the Browse button).
4. Click OK.
5. The Import Spreadsheet Wizard is then loaded (along with Access). This wizard guides you through the steps for permanently converting your Excel data to an Access table in a database.

Linking Access Tables to Excel Data

You might already have linked tables between different Access databases or between an Access database and an external database such as DB2, Oracle, or Paradox. You can use this same process to link your table to an Excel worksheet.

To do so, begin by opening the database in which you want to create the link. Then select File | Get External Data | Link Tables. Access displays the Link dialog box, in which you choose Microsoft Excel from the Files of type list, highlight the workbook that contains the data you want to link to, and then click Link. From here, the Link Spreadsheet Wizard is loaded. This wizard is identical to the Import Spreadsheet Wizard you saw earlier.

When you're done, you'll notice that the Tables tab for your database has a new icon for the table you linked to. In this case, though, the table has a small Excel icon next to it. This indicates that it's a linked table (in other words, it's linked to an Excel spreadsheet).

Word, Excel, Access, and OLE Objects

When it comes to using Word and Excel with Access, there are two main ways to share data:

- Through the exporting and importing procedures covered earlier
- Through object linking and embedding using an OLE Object field

This section discusses the second method.

The first step to linking or embedding is to open the table that will be storing the data and insert a field that has the OLE Object data type. From there, display the datasheet, click a record in the OLE Object field, and select Insert | Object. Access displays the Insert Object dialog box, shown in Figure 50.41.

FIGURE 50.41.

Use this dialog box to embed or link an OLE object.

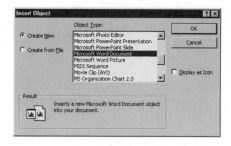

At this stage, you have two options:

■ To embed a new OLE object, make sure that the Create New option is activated, use the Object Type list to select an object type, and click OK. Access loads the appropriate application so that you can create the object. When you're done, select File | Close and Return to *Table*: Table (where *Table* is the name of the current Access table).

■ For an existing OLE object, activate the Create from File option. Access adjusts the dialog box to display a File text box in which you enter the path to the file. If you want to insert the file as a linked object, activate the Link check box; otherwise, Access will insert the file as an embedded object.

In both cases, you can also activate the Display as Icon check box to insert the object as an icon. Note, however, that you'll see the icon only if you display the table in a form. Figure 50.42 shows a sample form that displays several OLE objects (two for Word and two for Excel) that illustrate the difference between inserting as an icon and inserting in the usual way.

FIGURE 50.42.

A form showing several examples of OLE Object data.

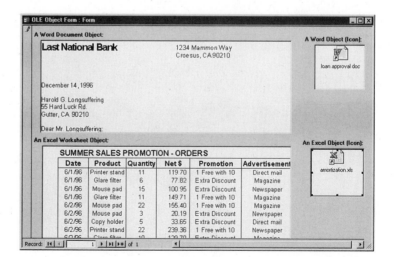

Summary

This chapter closed our look at Office integration by examining the various data sharing tools that come with each of the major Office applications.

Here's a list of chapters where you'll find related information:

- Basic integration and OLE concepts can be found in Chapter 48, "Office Integration and OLE."

- You'll learn how to use the Binder as an OLE container in Chapter 49, "Packaging Office Documents with Binder."

- You'll find Office-specific integration techniques in Chapter 50, "Working with the Office Integration Tools."

- For information on mailing and routing Office files, see Chapter 51, "Mailing and Routing Documents."

- I show you how to share your work in networked environments in Chapter 52, "Sharing Your Work."

- To learn how to use VBA to integrate Office documents, see Chapter E6 on the CD, "Integrating Office Applications with VBA."

X PART

Unleashing the Networked Office

Mailing and Routing Documents

CHAPTER 51

> *You could read Kant by yourself, if you wanted; but you must share a joke with some one else.*
>
> —*Robert Louis Stevenson*

Sometimes you need to distribute your documents to coworkers, clients, and customers. When this need arises, you'll want to accomplish your task in the most efficient way possible. This chapter looks at the various ways you can distribute your documents electronically through both e-mail and faxing.

First, we'll take a look at WordMail. After you install WordMail as your preferred e-mail editor, sending e-mail messages is a snap. Next, we'll explore the reasons why you might want to route a document and what it takes to do so. Suppose that you've just finished the budget proposal for next year and you want to let the other members of your project team review it. By routing your proposal, you can have others review an electronic version of your document, make revisions, and add comments, and then you'll automatically get it back when they're finished.

Using Word as an E-Mail Editor

With WordMail, you can use special toolbar buttons and commands to send, read, forward, and reply to e-mail messages using Microsoft Word. You can also use Word's reviewing options (such as notes, annotations, revisions, highlighter, and so on), which make it easier for you to read comments from individuals when sending and receiving e-mail messages.

Installing WordMail

To use Word as an e-mail editor, you must have Microsoft Exchange installed as your Windows Messaging client. Exchange is loaded when you install Windows 95. In Office 95, it also served as the user interface to manage Microsoft Mail, Internet Mail, Windows faxing, and connections to The Microsoft Network. However, Office 97 includes a desktop information manager called Outlook that handles these functions. Outlook is essentially a dressed-up version of Exchange with a much more intuitive user interface, as well as the contact management and scheduling features of Schedule+. For more information on Outlook, see Chapter 36, "Setting Up Outlook."

In addition to having Exchange loaded, you must have selected the WordMail option in Exchange when you installed Word. If you didn't check this option when you installed Word, follow these steps to do so:

1. Run the Microsoft Office Setup program or the Word Setup program.
2. If you've previously installed Microsoft Office, click the Add/Remove button.
3. Activate the Microsoft Word check box, and then click the Change Option button.
4. In the Options dialog box, activate the WordMail in Exchange check box.
5. Click OK.

NOTE: SWITCHING MAIL EDITORS

As soon as you've installed WordMail, you can switch between the Outlook mail editor and the WordMail editor. Simply run Outlook and select Tools | Options to display the Options dialog box, shown in Figure 51.1. Click the E-mail tab. Activate or deactivate the Use Microsoft Word as the e-mail editor check box.

FIGURE 51.1.

You can easily switch between WordMail and the Outlook e-mail editor using the Options dialog box.

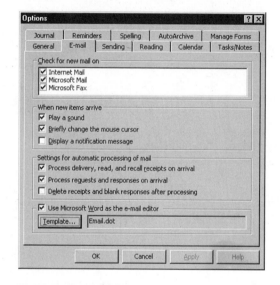

Sending a WordMail Message

Once you have WordMail installed as your preferred e-mail editor, you can send an e-mail message using WordMail just as you would using the Outlook editor. However, you might experience a decrease in system performance if you have 16MB of memory or less. To send a WordMail message, simply select File | Send To and choose Mail Recipient from any Microsoft Office application. Alternatively, you can select Compose | New Mail Message from Outlook. Figure 51.2 shows the WordMail compose window.

This window has all the features and functionality of the Outlook editor, coupled with the familiarity of Word toolbars and commands. As you'll see later in this chapter, you can even attach a template to the WordMail editor so that your favorite styles and formatting features are handy.

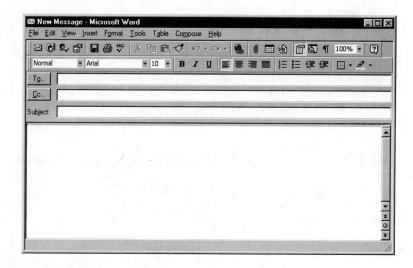

The WordMail Properties Dialog Box

The WordMail Properties dialog box, shown in Figure 51.3, sets properties for e-mail messages. In this example, a file named Proposal is being sent by e-mail. By setting various options in this dialog box, you can control how your messages are sent, receive return receipts when messages are delivered and read, and even notify recipients of messages that are highly sensitive or confidential. Select File | Properties from the WordMail compose window to display the Properties dialog box and set the various options for your WordMail messages.

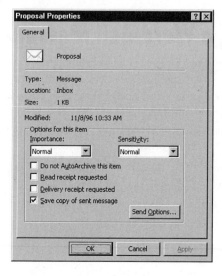

These are the options in the Properties dialog box:

- Type: Displays the type of message.
- Location: Displays the name of the folder in which the message is stored.
- Size: Displays the size of the message.
- Modified: Displays the date and time that the message was most recently modified.
- Importance: High indicates a high level of importance for a message. The message will display a red exclamation point (!) in the Importance column of the recipient's inbox. Normal indicates a normal level of importance. Low indicates a low level of importance. The message will display a down arrow in the Importance column of the recipient's inbox.
- Sensitivity: Select a level of sensitivity from this list box to let the recipient know whether the message is normal, personal, private, or confidential. The security level and type of message will appear in the Sensitivity column of the recipient's inbox.
- Do not AutoArchive this item: Activate this check box if you don't want the message moved to the archive folder.
- Read receipt requested: Activate this check box if you want to be notified when the recipient opens the message you sent.
- Delivery receipt requested: Activate this check box if you want to be notified when the message you sent has been delivered.
- Save copy of sent message: Activate this check box if you want to save a copy of each message you send.
- Apply: Click this button to apply the selected options to the message without closing the Properties dialog box.

Changing How WordMail Messages Look

WordMail comes with some generic templates for writing e-mail messages. If you often find yourself reformatting your e-mail messages for greater impact, you might want to change the default template that WordMail uses. You can do this by using one of the following methods:

- Set the template to use one of the various templates that ship with Word.
- Create a new template and set it as the default. For more information on how to create a Word template, see Chapter 10, "Document Patterns and Presentations."
- Edit one of the existing templates.

WordMail Templates

The following steps show you how to change the templates used with WordMail:

1. In Outlook, select Tools | Options and click the E-mail tab to display the Options dialog box, shown in Figure 51.1.
2. Click the Template button and locate the template you want to use.
3. Click Select to return to the Options dialog box.

Creating an Automatic Signature

Not only can you customize the templates in WordMail, but you can also create an automatic "signature" that can be appended to your electronic message. This signature can include formatted text, graphic images such as a company logo, and even a scanned image of your handwritten signature. WordMail makes adding an automatic signature a snap, as you'll see in the following procedure:

1. Open the WordMail compose window.
2. Enter and format the text as you want it to appear on your e-mail messages. If you want to include an image in your signature, import that graphic using Insert | Picture.
3. Select the text, including any graphics.
4. Select Tools | Auto Signature. Word displays the AutoSignature dialog box, shown in Figure 51.4.

FIGURE 51.4.

Use the AutoSignature dialog box to create an automatic signature for your e-mail messages.

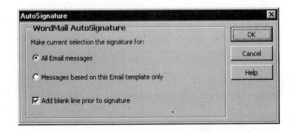

5. Select whether you want to include an automatic signature on all e-mail messages or just e-mail messages based on your e-mail template, and whether you want to add a blank line before the signature.
6. Click OK. You now have an automatic signature that will be appended to your e-mail messages.

Routing Documents

You can use Office applications (that is, Excel, Word, PowerPoint, and Access) with Microsoft Exchange (or other compatible mail packages) to send an online copy of a document. The recipients can then comment on, revise, or add to the document, and it will be routed back to you via e-mail. You might want to route a document if you have a long review period or a short list of reviewers. Other advantages you receive by routing a document include the following:

- You automatically receive a routing status message as each recipient forwards your document.

- You ensure that each recipient is reminded to forward the document to the next recipient.

NOTE: ROUTING REQUIREMENTS

Document routing might not work across e-mail gateways. To use document routing, you need a mail system that is compatible with the Messaging Application Programming Interface (MAPI) or Vendor-Independent Messaging (VIM). Exchange is a MAPI-compatible mail system, and Lotus cc:Mail is an example of a VIM-compatible mail system.

Preparing Documents for Review

Before you route your Word document, you might want to prepare it for review. This makes it easier to track the changes that recipients make in a document. Revision marks show where text or graphics have been added, deleted, or moved. You can also protect the document from permanent changes.

Preparing a document for review is easy:

1. Open the document you want to prepare for review.
2. Select Tools | Protect Document.
3. If you want to let reviewers change a document, and you want to track their changes with revision marks, click the Tracked Changes button. If you don't want reviewers to change the contents of the document but you want to let them add comments, click the Comments button. If you've created a form, click the Forms button and then click Sections to clear the check boxes of the sections you don't want to protect. If you want others to only add revisions and annotations without changing the contents, enter a password.

NOTE: PROTECTED FORMS CAN STILL BE FILLED IN

If you protect your form with a password, users who don't know the password will still be able to enter information in the form fields.

> **CAUTION: UNPROTECTED DOCUMENTS CAN BE MODIFIED**
>
> If you don't protect your document with a password, anyone can unprotect the document and make undocumented revisions without your knowledge by selecting Tools | Unprotect Document.

4. Click OK to protect your document.

The Routing Slip

When you route a document, you specify a series of recipients on a routing slip. Exchange sends the document to the first person on the routing slip. When that person is done with the document, he or she sends it, and the routing slip automatically addresses the document to the next person on the routing slip. The document eventually finds its way back to you after each person has reviewed it. Although you can also route other Office documents, the following procedure shows you how to route a Word document:

1. Open the file you want to route.

2. Select File | Send To and click Routing Recipient.

3. You might be asked which Exchange profile you want to use. If so, choose the profile and then click OK. The Routing Slip dialog box, shown in Figure 51.5, appears.

FIGURE 51.5.

Use the Routing Slip dialog box to select recipients and route a document.

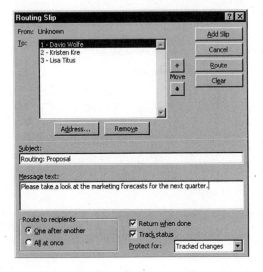

4. Click the Address button to display the Address Book.

5. Highlight a recipient and then click To->. When you're done selecting recipients, click OK to return to the Routing Slip dialog box.

TIP: CHANGE THE RECIPIENT ORDER

If you want to change the order in which recipients will receive your document, highlight a recipient's name in the To box and use one of the Move arrows to move the name up or down in the list.

6. Adjust the Subject text, if necessary, and enter an explanatory message in the Message text area.

7. If you want the document returned to you after the last recipient has worked with it, enable the Return when done check box. If you would like to receive a message each time a recipient routes the document to the next person, enable the Track status check box.

8. When you're ready, click the Route button. If you want to attach a routing slip and route the document at a later time, click the Add Slip button.

NOTE: ROUTING TO GROUPS

If you have group aliases set up in your Personal Address Book, you can select a group alias as the recipient. However, all members of the group alias are considered one recipient, so they will all receive the document at the same time. To route the document to members of a group alias one after another, send it to the individual members, not to the alias.

Sending a Document

Once a routing slip is attached, follow these steps to route a document:

1. Select File | Send To and click Next Routing Recipient to display the Send dialog box, shown in Figure 51.6.

FIGURE 51.6.

The Send dialog box, used to send a routed document.

2. If you want to route the document, select the option Route document to. If you want to send the document to someone without routing it, select the option Send copy of document without using the routing slip.

3. Click OK.

Opening a Routed Document

If you've just received a routed document, it will appear as an attachment to an e-mail message. To open a routed document, follow your e-mail program's instructions. If you're using Exchange, double-click the document icon to open the document attached to a mail message.

Editing a Routing Slip

If you've added a routing slip or received a routed document, the File | Add Routing Slip command changes to File | Edit Routing Slip. There might be occasions when you need to edit the routing slip. For example, one of the recipients on the list might be on vacation next week. Rather than have the document sit in that person's mailbox until he gets back, you can move him to the end of the list or delete his name from the list. The following procedure shows you how to edit a routing slip:

1. Select File | Send To and click Other Routing Recipient to display the Routing Slip dialog box (shown in Figure 51.5).

2. If you want to delete a name from the list of recipients, highlight the name in the To box and click the Remove button. To change the routing order, highlight a name in the To box and use the Move arrows to move the name up or down in the list. To delete the routing slip, click the Clear button.

3. Click Route if you want to send the document, or click Add Slip to save your changes and send the document at a later time.

Sending Form Letters from Word to Fax Numbers and E-Mail Addresses

There might be occasions when you need to distribute a document to a large list of fax numbers or e-mail addresses. (This is sometimes referred to as *broadcasting*.) For example, you might want to transmit a time-critical press release to a number of local media sources, send a proposal out for bid to a list of suppliers, or send price-sensitive product information to your customers. One way to accomplish this is to send the same document to all the people on your fax or e-mail address list. An even better way is to harness the power of Word's Mail Merge feature and personalize each document with information specific to the recipient.

Before you can broadcast a document, you need to successfully create a main document and link it to a data source. For more information on how to set up a mail merge document, see

Mailing and Routing Documents

CHAPTER 51

1181

51

MAILING AND
ROUTING
DOCUMENTS

Chapter 13, "Word as a Publisher." To illustrate the process of broadcasting a document, I created a merge document called Price List (see Figure 51.7) as the main document with the Personal Address Book as the data source.

FIGURE 51.7.
*A Word main doc-
ument ready to be
merged with a data
source.*

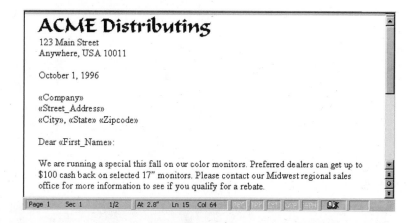

TIP: USE MERGE FOR MULTIPLE ENCLOSURES

You can use Word's merge feature to send several different documents to the same recipient as enclosures. For example, your main document might be a cover sheet that includes merge fields specific to the recipient. You might also want to send a second promotional page and a third page listing retail outlets. By inserting one or more INCLUDETEXT fields in the main document, Word inserts the contents of the documents specified by the INCLUDETEXT fields.

Here are the steps for merging a document to a list of fax numbers or e-mail addresses:

1. With the main document in the active window, select Tools | Mail Merge to display the Mail Merge Helper dialog box, shown in Figure 51.8.

2. To avoid processing records that don't contain a fax number or e-mail address, click the Query Options button. Word displays the Query Options dialog box, shown in Figure 51.9.

3. Select the Filter Records tab. In the Field box, select the data field that contains the fax number or e-mail address. In the example using the Personal Address Book as the data source, the Primary_Fax field contains the fax number. In the Comparison box, select "is not blank" to filter out records that don't have a fax number or e-mail address.

4. Click OK to return to the Mail Merge Helper dialog box.

FIGURE 51.8.

*The Mail Merge
Helper dialog box.*

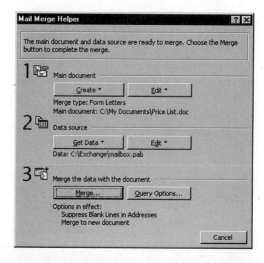

FIGURE 51.9.

*Use the Query Options
dialog box to filter data
records that don't con-
tain a fax number or
e-mail address.*

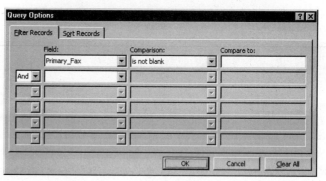

5. In the Mail Merge Helper dialog box, click Merge to display the Merge dialog box,
   shown in Figure 51.10.

FIGURE 51.10.

*The Merge dialog box,
used to select an
electronic message
system.*

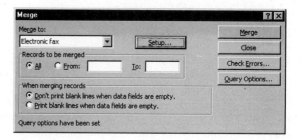

6. In the Merge to box, select Electronic fax (or Electronic mail if you want to broadcast
   e-mail messages). If you're using another mail system, select the electronic message
   system you want to use.

Mailing and Routing Documents

CHAPTER 51

1183

51

MAILING AND
ROUTING
DOCUMENTS

7. Click Setup to display the Merge To Setup dialog box, shown in Figure 51.11. In the box labeled Data field with Mail/Fax address, select the data field that contains the fax number or e-mail address. Again, the Primary_Fax field is selected for this example. Click OK to return to the Merge dialog box.

FIGURE 51.11.

The Merge To Setup dialog box.

CAUTION: PREVENT LOST FORMATTING

To preserve the formatting of a merged document transmitted by fax or e-mail, activate the check box labeled Send document as an attachment. Otherwise, Word inserts the document text in the mail message and doesn't retain the document formatting.

8. In the Merge dialog box, click Merge.

TIP: BYPASS THE COVER SHEET TO SAVE MONEY

If the merge document will contain the recipient's name and company name, you can save money on long distance faxes by not including a cover sheet. Simply start Exchange and select Tools | Microsoft Fax Tools | Options to display the Microsoft Fax Properties dialog box. Select the Message tab and deactivate the Send Cover Page check box.

Summary

This chapter showed you various techniques for distributing your documents electronically. You learned how to install and use WordMail, as well as how to route a document and send faxes from your desktop. Here are some related chapters to investigate:

- Word's Mail Merge feature is covered in Chapter 13, "Word as a Publisher."
- To learn about Outlook's e-mail capabilities, see Chapter 37, "The Ins and Outs of the Outlook Inbox," and Chapter 38, "Advanced Outlook E-Mail Topics."
- To learn more about faxing, see Chapter 39, "Using Outlook for Faxing."
- If you need some networking know-how, head to Chapter E1 on the CD, "Office on a Network."

Sharing Your Work

IN THIS CHAPTER

CHAPTER 52

All who joy would win
Must share it,—Happiness was born a twin.

—Lord Byron

Sharing your work no longer means just simply putting a file out where others can get to it. This chapter explores the ways in which Microsoft Office extends the capabilities of your network. It also covers the use of document properties, implements methods to find files quickly, and demonstrates how to share your work through mail.

Sharing Your Files

The most common method of sharing work is to use shared network directories. This might be your own directory that you provide as a shared resource, or a centrally shared directory on a server. The concept of sharing files has been around since the inception of networks. The hurdle users face with this method occurs when the number of shared directories and files increases. Finding the file you want can be challenging. It was even more difficult on operating systems where you were limited to an eight-character name and a three-character extension. By now, you know that you aren't bound by these limits under Windows 95.

Filenames and Properties

With the use of long filenames and document properties, you can assign descriptive information to Microsoft Office documents. It might be beneficial to your office to implement a standard way of naming files and to encourage the use of file properties. To access file properties in Word, Excel, PowerPoint, and Access, select File | Properties. Figure 52.1 shows the properties for a Word document. Word is used as the basis for the following examples.

FIGURE 52.1.

Document properties.

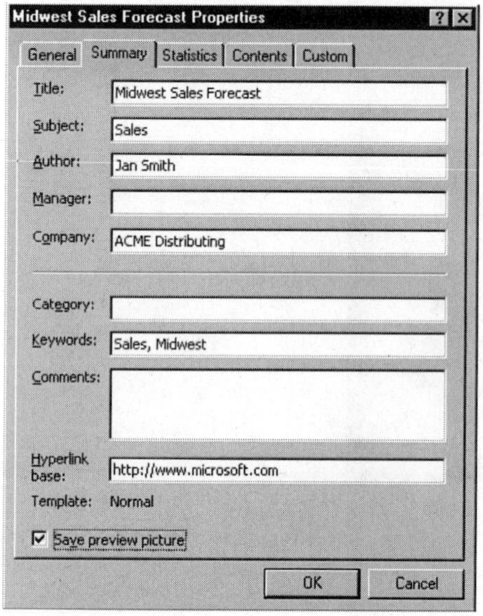

These are the default properties that Microsoft Office provides. Some of the fields are automatically filled in, such as the title and author. The title is based on the first line of text in your document. This might not always be what you want, but at least Office has made an attempt. If you don't like the title Office has selected for you, replace it with a more descriptive one. The author field is based on the information you provided when you initially set up Office. If you want to change the default name, select Tools | Options. In the Options dialog box that appears, make your changes in the User Information tab.

Figure 52.1 has other information filled in, such as subject and keywords. The more information you provide, the easier it will be to track down lost files. As mentioned earlier, you might want to make a company-wide decision as to how to best utilize these fields. The usefulness of properties will become more apparent when we discuss file searches and file indexes later in this chapter.

New to the Properties dialog box in Office 97 applications is the Hyperlink base address box. A hyperlink is used to jump to a location in the same file or another file. It's represented by colorful underlined text or a graphic. You click a hyperlink to jump to a location in a file, another file, or even a URL location on the World Wide Web. You should enter the base address for all relative hyperlinks with the current document.

If you don't find a property that suits your needs, you can use custom properties. Figure 52.2 shows the addition of a custom property called "Client." If you drop down the Name list box, you will find that Microsoft Office has predefined some custom properties for you. If none of these properties suits your needs, you can supply your own. You can also select the type of value to be associated with the name from the Type list box: Text, Date, Number, or Yes/No. For example, you could create a custom property that tracks whether the document has been approved for release. In this case, you could create a custom property named "Approved" and make it a Yes/No value. This would let you perform a search for all documents that hadn't been approved.

With this knowledge of document properties, you should be able to set up a standard way for users to save their work. For example, a law office might want to use a custom property named Client to help track files. A columnist might use the built-in property Category as a place to enter the type of article he or she is writing (for example, Movie Review, Variety, Editorial, and so on). It's up to you how to best implement properties.

TIP: AUTOMATIC PROPERTIES PROMPT

If you want to be prompted automatically for the properties the first time a document is saved, select Tools | Options. In the Options dialog box that appears, choose the Save tab and enable Prompt for Document Properties.

52

SHARING YOUR WORK

FIGURE 52.2.

Adding a custom property.

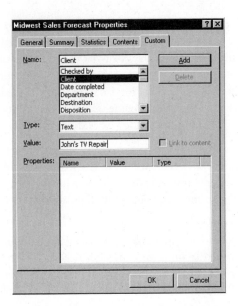

Using the Find Fast Utility

You might not know this, but the Microsoft Office Find Fast utility is probably running on your computer right now. The Find Fast utility is installed during the Office setup process and runs automatically in the background, indexing all your Office documents. Because you have put a lot of work into giving your documents descriptive names and useful properties, the indexes that Find Fast creates let you search quickly for documents based on any number of parameters.

If Find Fast is installed, it will be located in your Startup folder. To access Find Fast, look in Control Panel. If you can't find it, you might want to install it. To do this, run Microsoft Office Setup and select Add/Remove. To add the Find Fast utility, highlight Office Tools and click the Change Option button. Figure 52.3 shows the Find Fast utility in the list of optional Office tools. Select Find Fast and continue with the setup.

NOTE: LOCATING THE STARTUP FOLDER

Files placed in the Startup folder run automatically every time Windows 95 boots. To find the Startup folder, use Windows Explorer to open the folder in which Windows is installed, and then open the \Start Menu\Programs\StartUp subfolder.

FIGURE 52.3.

Installing the Find Fast utility.

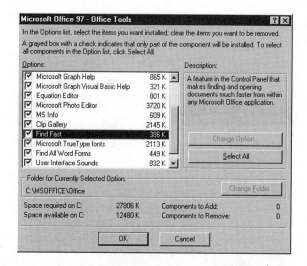

NOTE: DON'T CONFUSE FIND FILE WITH FIND

The index's file searching capabilities aren't related to the Find function accessed from the Windows 95 Start button. The indexes are used when you open a file from within Microsoft Office.

Find Fast creates hidden .ff* files in the root directories that you specify for indexing. The default is to place the index file at the root directory of each hard drive. If you run the Find Fast utility from Control Panel, you will see the directories being indexed. Figure 52.4 shows drives C: and D: being indexed.

FIGURE 52.4.

The Find Fast utility shows which directories are being indexed.

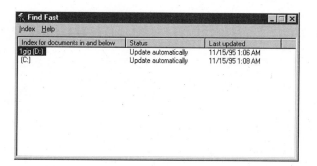

The index will cover files in and below each specified path. You can create indexes anywhere you like. However, keep in mind that searches will be more thorough if users can point to one main directory and search it and all underlying directories. On the other hand, it might be inefficient to have Find Fast search every directory when it performs updates. If you plan to save all your Microsoft Office documents in a directory called My Documents, you can instruct Fast Find to index in and below that directory only. Within the My Documents directory, you can create subdirectories to further organize your work. Be assured that Find Fast will index those as well.

NOTE: YOU CAN'T CREATE CHILD INDEXES WITHIN PARENT INDEXES

After you create a Find Fast index, you can't create any indexes in subdirectories. Find Fast will warn you that the index you're trying to create is in the scope of one of its parent directories. There is no need to create indexes below a parent index. If you want to create multiple indexes, you need to delete any indexes in parent directories.

Network drives can be indexed the same way as your local drive. The following are the ways in which you can maintain an index on a network drive:

- If the computer that is sharing its directory has Office installed, the computer can maintain the index just as it is maintained on a user's local drive. This would be the case in a peer-to-peer network in which a user has shared one of his local directories and has made it available to others.

- A user with Microsoft Office can be designated to create the index and keep it updated. To create an index, use the Find Fast utility in Control Panel and select Index | Create Index. Figure 52.5 shows an index being added to the \\SERVER1\ PUBLIC directory. This user should be running the Find Fast utility at all times (this is done automatically if Find Fast is in the Startup folder, as mentioned earlier) in order to keep the index current. Only one computer needs to maintain the index. Don't let several users update the same index. You might want to make this an administrative activity by granting write access to the administrator only.

FIGURE 52.5.

Creating a Find Fast index on a network directory.

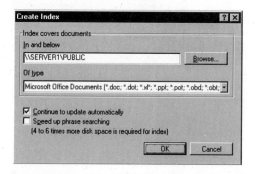

- If the directory is being accessed from Windows NT Server, you can obtain the Find Fast NT service from the Microsoft Office Resource Kit. Because it runs as a service, Find Fast will run in the background without requiring a user to log onto the server.

This is the most efficient way to maintain the indexing, because the processing is off-loaded to the server, thus reducing network traffic and removing the burden from a user's workstation. Remember that all users must have at least read permissions at the directory level where the index files are located. Keep in mind that the indexes are created in and below the specified path.

> ### CAUTION: AVOID RUNNING BOTH VERSIONS
>
> Don't install Find Fast NT and the Find Fast single-user version that ships with Microsoft Office on the same computer. Delete the single-user version from the Startup group to prevent it from running.

Finding Files

At this point you've done a great job of setting up your network, you've convinced people to use document properties, and you've set up Find Fast indexing for quick and comprehensive searches—and users are creating documents left and right. It's time to put Office's file search capabilities to the test.

Using Word as an example again, select File | Open. The Open dialog box, shown in Figure 52.6, appears. The basic search criteria available in this first screen include File name and Text or property. You can select a specific directory in which to search or select a root directory to search in and below. One thing to be aware of is the Commands and Settings button in the upper-right corner (the button has a drop-down menu with a check mark over it). From the drop-down menu, select Search Subfolders.

FIGURE 52.6.

The Open dialog box.

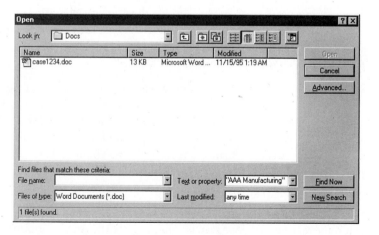

By default, subfolders are not searched. The speed of the searches performed here is due to the Find Fast indexes you created earlier. The Text or property field lets you search for text that is in the body of the document or in one of the properties you defined in your document. It was mentioned earlier that a law firm might use a custom property, Client, to label their documents. In this field, they would enter the client name, and the results of the search would return documents related to a specific client. If your search text contains spaces, place quotation marks around the phrase, as in "AAA Manufacturing".

Because you haven't defined where you want the words "AAA Manufacturing" to appear, you might find files that contain the words "AAA Manufacturing" in the body of the text. You can narrow down the search by clicking the Advanced button. Figure 52.7 shows how you have narrowed the search criteria to look for "AAA Manufacturing" in the Client property only.

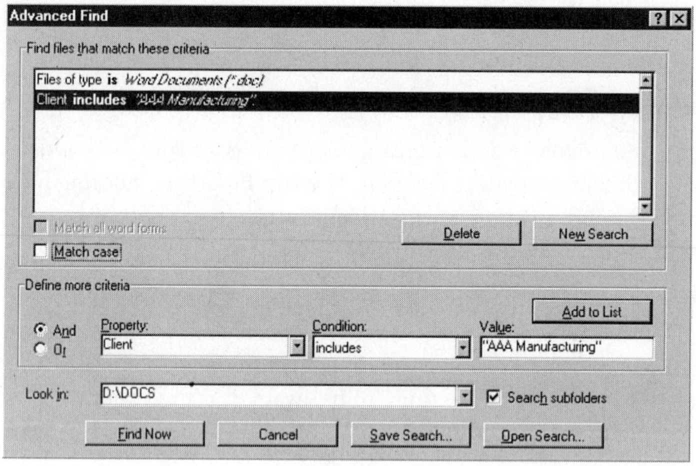

Figure 52.7.

The Advanced Find Dialog box lets you build very specific search criteria.

You can create precise searches by defining the property, condition, and value. Every time you define the criteria, you click Add to List. If you enable the And option when adding a subsequent criterion, the files found will logically satisfy both criteria. Use the Or option to create a search that matches either criterion.

For example, you might want to find documents with the Client property matching "AAA Manufacturing" and that were written by Jan Smith. In this case, you would set the Property to `Client` and the Value to `"AAA Manufacturing"` and click Add to List. Then, for the subsequent criteria, you would set the condition to And, type `Author` for the Property, and enter `"Jan Smith"` as the value. Again, click Add to List. You have now created a logical search that will search for specific documents that match the conditions you have created.

When you click Find Now, the search will commence and return you to the original File Open dialog box. The files found that match the criteria will be presented in the list view. If you want to further modify your search, you can click the Advanced button again to change your last search.

If at any time you feel you have created an advanced search that will be useful in the future, be sure to save the search for later retrieval. Click the Save Search button at the bottom of the

Advanced Find dialog box. Give the search a name and click OK. You can retrieve the search at any time by clicking Open Search.

Shared Workbooks in Excel

When files are shared over a network, you eventually will encounter a dialog box warning you that another user already has the file open. The options presented to you include opening the file in read-only mode, creating a copy of the file, or waiting for the user to finish with the document. None of these options are appealing when you're trying to get work done. Excel 97 provides an alternative to hunting down the person who has the document open: shared workbooks. A shared workbook can be opened and edited by multiple users simultaneously.

You can insert data, insert and delete ranges, and sort data in a shared workbook. Be aware that formatting cells and entering formulas aren't allowed; therefore, you should format your ranges and edit your formulas before designating a workbook as a shared list. These operations are disabled because they would interfere with other users using the workbook.

After you place the workbook on a shared network resource, you can designate the workbook as a shared list by following these steps:

1. From Excel, select Tools | Share Workbook. The Share Workbook dialog box appears, as shown in Figure 52.8.

FIGURE 52.8.

The Share Workbook dialog box in Excel 97 lets you use multiuser editing.

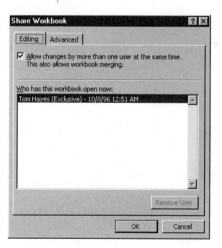

2. In the Editing tab, activate the check box that allows editing by more than one person at a time.

3. Click OK. At this point, Excel will require you to save the workbook.

4. When Excel returns you to the workbook, you will notice that [Shared] is appended to the workbook's title bar.

> **CAUTION: WATCH FOR READ-ONLY FILES**
>
> If you receive the error message Can't access read-only document *filename*.xls when attempting to open the Shared Lists dialog box, it might be because you have opened a workbook as read-only. Either you don't have read/write permission for the network directory, or you explicitly opened the file as read-only. In the File Open dialog box, be sure you haven't selected Open Read Only on the Commands and Settings menu.

Working with a Shared List

Now that your workbook is set up as a shared workbook, try opening the workbook on multiple users' machines. To see which users are accessing the file, select Tools | Shared Workbook and then choose the Editing tab. Figure 52.9 shows a sample list of users who currently have the workbook open.

FIGURE 52.9.

Select the Editing tab to view which users are currently accessing the shared workbook.

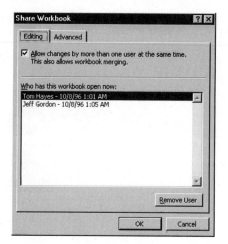

If you want to update the workbook with each user's changes, select File | Save. If the update includes changes made by others, Excel will inform you.

If two users have edited the same cell, the Resolve Conflicts dialog box, shown in Figure 52.10, will appear. Figure 52.10 shows that you and another user have made a change to cell H11. In this example, you have entered a value of 18000, and the other user has entered a value of 22000. Click the Accept All Mine button to keep your work, or click Accept All Others to allow the changes made by the other user. If you want to track these conflicts, select Tools | Share Workbook. In the Advanced tab, activate the Keep change history for radio button and specify a number of days. You can customize how the changes are tracked by selecting Tools | Track Changes | Highlight Changes.

FIGURE 52.10.

The Resolve Conflicts dialog box appears when multiple users have changed the same cell range.

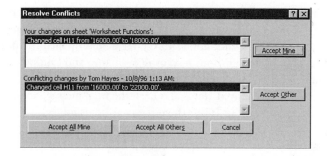

Using Mail to Share Documents

Mail provides a great vehicle to distribute documents throughout your workgroup. The two methods that are discussed here are selecting File | Send To to mail a document, and routing a document.

Using the Send To Menu Option to Mail Documents

There is no need to exit the Office application that you're currently using in order to send mail. Every Office application lets you mail the document you currently have open. With your document open, select File | Send To. If the Choose Profile dialog box appears, select the profile you use to send mail. Figure 52.11 shows the mail message that is created in Microsoft Exchange. Notice that the document has been automatically inserted into the body of the text. You aren't limited to sending only the document—you can add comments and attachments within the body of the message.

FIGURE 52.11.

The mail message created using File | Send To places your document in the body of the text.

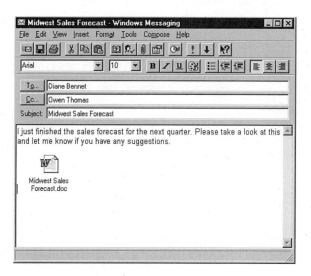

When the intended recipient receives the mail message, he simply double-clicks the document's icon to open the file. The recipient can store the document in one of two ways: by using Save As from within the Office application after he has opened the document, or by moving the mail message to a folder. Both Microsoft Exchange and Outlook let you create custom folders in addition to the standard Inbox, Outbox, Sent Items, and Deleted Items. You can create your own folder, such as Saved Items. To keep the mail message for a period of time, simply drag mail messages from your Inbox to your Saved Items folder. This is a great way to temporarily archive documents you're interested in. I say temporarily because you don't want to eat away at the resources your mail server (or workgroup postoffice) provides. For more information on Outlook, see Part VII, "Unleashing Outlook."

Routing Documents

When you use Send to mail a document, each recipient receives his or her own copy of the original. Routing a document lets you distribute a single copy of the original. You can control the recipients and the order in which the document is sent. See Chapter 51, "Mailing and Routing Documents," for further routing techniques.

Summary

This chapter showed you how to add properties to your Microsoft Office documents. These properties help users locate documents on shared directories. This chapter also examined how file-searching performance can be improved by implementing the Find Fast utility. You should have a better understanding of how the Find Fast utility works, as well as how to create and manage the Find Fast indexes. This chapter also covered the shared lists capabilities in Excel that let multiple users work on the same workbook.

Here's a list of related chapters:

- To learn more about Outlook's e-mail features, see Chapter 37, "The Ins and Outs of the Outlook Inbox," and Chapter 38, "Advanced Outlook E-Mail Topics."

- If you need some networking knowledge, head to Chapter E1 on the CD, "Office on a Network."

- Be sure to examine Chapter 51, "Mailing and Routing Documents," for other ways to share your documents using mail.

XI
PART

Unleashing Office Application Development with VBA

Getting Started with VBA

CHAPTER

53

He has accomplished half who has made a beginning; dare to be wise; begin!

—Horace

When Excel 5 was released in 1994, developers and power users were thrilled to see that it included the first iteration of Microsoft's new macro language: Visual Basic for Applications (VBA). Most folks discarded the creaky old Excel 4 macro language without a second thought and waited eagerly for Microsoft to fulfill its promise to make VBA the common macro language for all its applications.

Other Office products were slowly brought into the VBA fold, but it's only with the release of Office 97 that Microsoft has finally achieved its goal. Now all of the Big Four—Word, Excel, Access, and PowerPoint—have a VBA development environment at their core. Not only that, but Microsoft is now licensing VBA as a separate product—called VBA 5.0—that other companies can incorporate into their own applications. As I wrote this, a number of developers had leaped willingly onto the VBA 5.0 bandwagon, including such heavyweights as Adobe, Autodesk, Micrografx, and Visio. And as if that weren't enough, Microsoft has also created a version of VBA—called VBScript—to use a scripting tool for Web pages.

There is little doubt, then, that VBA plays a huge role in Microsoft's future plans. Anyone interested in truly unleashing the power of the Office applications and of Web pages will need to learn the VBA language. The good news is that VBA combines both power and ease-of-use. So even if you've never programmed before, you won't find it hard to create useful procedures that let your Office applications perform like they never have before.

This chapter introduces you to this powerful tool. I'll begin by showing you how to use VBA to record simple macros that help automate routine tasks. To get the most out of VBA, however, you need to do some programming. To that end, this chapter gets you started by showing you how to use VBA variables and operators and how to write simple command macros and user-defined functions. It also shows you the basic syntax of VBA statements, operators, and objects.

What Is a Macro?

A *macro* is a small program that contains a list of instructions that you want a program to perform. Like DOS batch files, macros combine several operations into a single procedure that you can invoke quickly. (Many people also refer to macros as *scripts*.) This list of instructions is composed mostly of *macro statements* that are closely related to program commands. Some of these statements perform specific macro-related tasks, but most just correspond to menu commands and dialog box options. For example, VBA's `ActiveWindow.Close` function works just like File | Close.

How Does VBA Fit In?

VBA is a programming environment designed specifically for application macros. As I said, VBA is now the standard language in the Office suite. The advantage of this is obvious: A standard language means that, no matter which program you use, you have to learn only one set of state-ments and techniques. And it also means that applications will get along better than they ever have, because VBA "knows" the functions and commands used by every program.

The power of VBA is clear, but perhaps its biggest advantage is that it's easier to use than most programming languages (including the old macro languages used in Word, Excel, and Access). If you don't want to do any programming, VBA lets you record macros and attach them to buttons either on the worksheet or on a toolbar. You can also create dialog boxes by simply drawing the appropriate controls onto a document or onto a separate "user form." Other vi-sual tools let you customize menus and toolbars as well, so you have everything you need to create simple applications without writing a line of code.

Of course, if you want to get the most out of VBA, you'll need to augment your interface with programming code. Unlike WordBasic or the Excel 4.0 macro language, VBA is a full-blown programming environment that includes most high-level programming constructs as well as every access to every feature in the application. Add the powerful debugging tool and the abil-ity to create a Help system, and you have everything you need to create professional-level Of-fice applications.

The Two Types of Macros

VBA macros come in two flavors: *command macros* and *user-defined functions*. Here's a sum-mary of the differences:

- Command macros (which also are known as Sub procedures for reasons that will become clear later in this chapter) are the most common type of macro. They usually contain statements that are the equivalent of menu options and other program commands. The distinguishing feature of command macros is that, like regular program commands, they have an effect on their surroundings. (In Excel, for example, this would mean the current worksheet, the workspace, and so on.) Whether it's formatting some text, printing a document, or creating custom menus, command macros *change* things. I show you how to create command macros in the section "Writing Your Own Command Macro."

- User-defined functions (also called Function procedures) work just like a program's built-in functions. Their distinguishing characteristic is that they accept arguments, manipulate those arguments, and then return a result. A properly designed function macro has no effect on the current environment. I show you how to create these functions in the section "Creating User-Defined Functions with VBA."

Recording a VBA Macro

By far the easiest way to create a command macro is to use the Macro Recorder. With this method, you just run through the task you want to automate (including selecting text, run-ning menu commands, and choosing dialog box options), and the Recorder translates every-thing into the appropriate VBA statements. These are copied to a separate area called a *module* where you can then replay the entire procedure any time you like. The following steps show you how to record a command macro in Word, Excel, or PowerPoint.

NOTE: ACCESS IS UNIQUE

Access implements VBA differently than do Word, Excel, and PowerPoint. Therefore, most of the instructions in this chapter only apply to the latter three applications. I'll show you how to work with Access VBA macros in Chapter E5 on the CD, "VBA Database Programming in Access."

1. Either select Tools | Macro | Record New Macro or click the Record Macro button on the Visual Basic toolbar. You'll see the Record Macro dialog box. Figure 53.1 shows the Excel version.

Figure 53.1.

Use the Record Macro dialog box to name and describe your macro.

2. The application proposes a name for the macro (such as Macro1), but you can use the Macro name text box to change the name to anything you like. (You must follow a few naming conventions, though: The name can have no more than 255 characters, the first character must be a letter or an underscore (_), and no spaces or periods are allowed.)

3. Word and Excel let you assign shortcuts to the macro:

    ■ In Word, click Toolbars to add a button for the macro to a toolbar, or click Keyboard to assign a shortcut key to the macro.

    ■ In Excel, enter a letter in the Shortcut key: Ctrl+ text box.

4. Use the Store macro in drop-down list box to specify where the macro will reside.

5. Enter a description of the macro in the Description text box.

6. Click OK. The application returns you to the document, displays Recording or REC in the status bar, and displays the Stop Recording Macro toolbar.

7. Perform the tasks you want to include in the macro.

8. When you finish the tasks, select Tools | Macro | Stop Recording, or click the Stop Macro button.

Viewing the Resulting Module

When you record a macro, the application creates a "VBA project." This is a container that includes both the document you used for the macro and a special object called a *module* that contains the macro code.

To see your macro, select Tools | Macro | Macros (or press Alt-F8) to display the Macro dialog box. In the Macro Name list, highlight the macro you just recorded, and then click the Edit button. The application opens the Visual Basic Editor window, opens the module, and displays the macro. As you can see in Figure 53.2, the application (Excel, in this case) translates your actions into VBA code and combines everything into a single macro.

FIGURE 53.2.

A sample recorded macro.

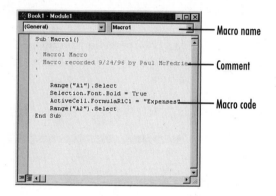

A typical macro has the following features:

Comments: The first few lines begin with a quotation mark ('), which tells Excel that these lines are *comments* that aren't processed when you run the macro. In each recorded macro, the comments display the name of the macro and the description you entered in the Record New Macro dialog box.

Sub/End Sub: These keywords mark the beginning (Sub) and end (End Sub) of a macro. The Sub keyword is the reason why command macros also are called Sub procedures.

Macro name: After the Sub keyword, Excel enters the name of the macro followed by a left and right parenthesis (the parentheses are used for *arguments,* as you'll see later).

Macro code: The main body of the macro (in other words, the lines between the Sub and End Sub lines) consists of a series of statements. These are Excel's interpretations of the actions you performed during the recording. In the example, four actions were performed:

1. Cell A1 was selected.
2. The cell was formatted as boldface.
3. The string Expenses was typed into the cell.
4. The Enter key was pressed (which moved the selection down to cell A2).

Editing a Recorded Macro

As you're learning VBA, you'll often end up with recorded macros that don't turn out quite right the first time. Whether the macro runs a command it shouldn't or is missing a command altogether, you'll often have to patch things up after the fact.

A VBA module is more like a word-processing document than a worksheet, so you make changes the same way you would in a word processor or text editor. If your macro contains statements that you want to remove, just delete the offending lines from the module.

Touring the Visual Basic Editor

The Visual Basic Editor represents an entirely new way of looking at the VBA universe. The idea was to create a separate, integrated VBA development environment modeled after the layout of Microsoft's Visual Basic programming environment. To that end, the Visual Basic Editor is divided into three areas, as shown in Figure 53.3: the Project Explorer, the Properties window, and the work area.

FIGURE 53.3.

The Visual Basic Editor is a complete programming environment.

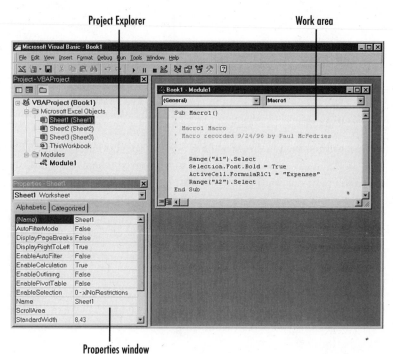

Project Explorer

Work area

Properties window

The Project Explorer

The Project Explorer area shows a hierarchical view of the contents of the current VBA project. (If you don't see the Project Explorer, either select View | Project Explorer, press Ctrl-R, or click the Project Explorer button on the toolbar.)

These contents include the open application objects (worksheets, documents, slides, and so on) and any modules that have been created either by recording a macro or by creating one from scratch (explained in a moment). The Project Explorer toolbar contains three icons that let you work with the objects in the tree:

 Click the View Code button to open a module window that contains the VBA code associated with the selected object.

 Click the View Object button to switch back to the original application and display the selected object.

 Click the Toggle Folders button to alternate the Project Explorer display between a hierarchical view of the objects and a simple list of all the objects.

The Properties Window

The Properties window shows the various properties available for whatever object is highlighted in the Project Explorer. (If you don't see the Properties window, either select View | Properties Window, press F4, or click the Properties Window button on the toolbar.)

The Properties window is divided into two areas. The left side of the window shows you the names of all the properties associated with the object, and the right side shows you the current value of the property. To change the value of a property, click in the appropriate box on the right side of the window and then either type in the new value or select it from a drop-down list (the method you use depends on the property).

Bear in mind that these are "design-time" properties you're setting. In other words, these are the property values that will be in effect before you run a macro. As you'll see in Chapter 54, "Understanding Objects," you can also change an object's properties within a program (that is, at *runtime*).

The Work Area

The rest of the Visual Basic Editor window is taken up by the work area. This is where the modules you work with are displayed. Other VBA objects—such as the custom dialog boxes and user forms that you create yourself—also appear in this area.

To get a module to appear in the work area, highlight it in the Project Explorer and then use any of the following techniques:

- Click the View Code button on the Project Explorer toolbar.
- Select View | Code.
- Press F7.
- Double-click the module.

Writing Your Own Command Macro

Although the Macro Recorder makes it easy to create your own homegrown macros, there are plenty of macro features that you can't access with mouse or keyboard actions or by selecting menu options. In Excel, for example, VBA has a couple dozen information macro functions that return data about cells, worksheets, workspaces, and more. Also, the VBA control functions let you add true programming constructs such as looping, branching, and decision-making.

To access these macro elements, you need to write your own VBA routines from scratch. This is easier than it sounds, because all you really need to do is enter a series of statements in a module. The next two sections take you through the various steps.

NOTE: A PARADOX

Although the next two sections tell you how to create VBA macros, I realize there's an inherent paradox here: How can you write your own macros when you haven't learned anything about them yet? Making you familiar with VBA's statements and functions is the job of the last half of this chapter and the other six chapters here in Part XI. The next two sections will get you started, and you can use this knowledge as a base on which to build your VBA skills in subsequent chapters.

Creating a New Module

If you want to enter your macro in an existing module, just display the window as described in the section "Viewing the Resulting Module." If you want to start a new module, first use either of the following techniques to display the Visual Basic Editor (if you're not there already):

- Select Tools | Macro | Visual Basic Editor.
- Click the Visual Basic Editor toolbar button.

TIP: TOGGLING BETWEEN VBA AND THE APPLICATION

You can also get to the Visual Basic Editor by pressing Alt-F11. In fact, this key combination is a toggle that switches you between the Visual Basic Editor and the original application.

Once you have the Visual Basic Editor displayed, select Insert | Module to open a new module window.

TIP: YOU CAN IMPORT VISUAL BASIC FILES

If you've used Visual Basic before, you can leverage your existing code by importing modules into your project. Select File | Import, use the Import File dialog box to highlight the appropriate .BAS file, and click Open.

Writing a Command Macro

With a module window open and active, follow these steps to write your own command macro:

1. Place the insertion point where you want to start the macro.

2. If you want to begin your macro with a few comments that describe what the macro does, type a single quotation mark (') at the beginning of each comment line.

3. To start the macro, type Sub, followed by a space and the name of the macro. When you press Enter at the end of this line, Excel automatically adds a pair of parentheses at the end of the macro name. It also tacks on an End Sub line to mark the end of the procedure.

4. Between the Sub and End Sub lines, type the VBA statements you want to include in the macro. For clarity, indent each line by pressing the Tab key at the beginning of the line.

When you press Enter to start a new line, VBA analyzes the line you just entered and performs three chores:

- It formats the colors of each word in the line: VBA keywords are blue, comments are green, and all other text is black.

- VBA keywords are converted to their proper case. For example, if you type end sub, VBA converts this to End Sub when you press Enter.

- It checks for syntax errors. VBA signifies a syntax error either by displaying a dialog box to let you know what the problem is, or by not converting a word to its proper case or color.

53

GETTING STARTED
WITH **VBA**

> **TIP: ALWAYS ENTER KEYWORDS IN LOWERCASE**
>
> By always entering VBA keywords in lowercase letters, you'll be able to catch typing errors by looking for keywords that VBA doesn't recognize (that is, the ones that remain in lowercase).

Running a VBA Macro

The Office applications offer several methods of running your VBA macros. Here's a quick rundown:

- Select Tools | Macro | Macros (or press Alt-F8) to display the Macro dialog box. Use the Macro Name list to highlight the macro you want to run, and then click the Run button.

- In a module, place the insertion point anywhere inside the macro, and then either select Run | Run Sub/User Form, press the F5 key, or click the Run Sub/User Form button on the Visual Basic Editor toolbar.

- If you assigned a shortcut key to the macro, press the key combination.

- If you added a new command to the Tools menu for the macro, select the command.

Creating User-Defined Functions with VBA

The Office applications come with a large number of built-in functions. Excel, for example, has hundreds of functions—one of the largest function libraries of any spreadsheet package. However, even with this vast collection, you'll still find that plenty of applications aren't covered. For example, you might need to calculate the area of a circle of a given radius, or the gravitational force between two objects. You could, of course, easily calculate these things on a worksheet, but if you need them frequently, it makes sense to define your own functions that you can use anytime. The next four sections show you how it's done.

Understanding User-Defined Functions

As I mentioned earlier, the defining characteristic of user-defined functions is that they return a result. They can perform any number of calculations on numbers, text, logical values, or whatever, but they're not allowed to affect their surroundings. In a worksheet, for example, they can't move the active cell, format a range, or change the workspace settings. In fact, anything you can access using the application menus is off-limits in a user-defined function.

So what *can* you put in a user-defined function? All of the application's built-in functions are fair game, and you can use any VBA function that isn't the equivalent of a menu command or desktop action.

All user-defined functions have the same basic structure, as shown in Figure 53.4. This is a function named `HypotenuseLength` that calculates the length of a right triangle's hypotenuse given the other two sides.

FIGURE 53.4.

A user-defined function that calculates the length of a right triangle's hypotenuse.

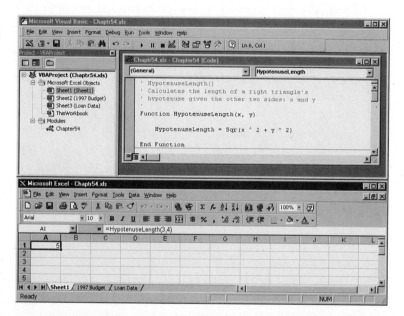

NOTE: THE CODE IS ON THE CD

You'll find the code for the `HypotenuseLength` function, as well as all the other procedures in this chapter, on this book's CD. In the CHAPTR53.XLS file, look in the module named Chapter53.

Here's a summary of the various parts of a user-defined function:

The `Function` statement: This keyword identifies the procedure as a user-defined function. The `Function` keyword is the reason that user-defined functions also are called `Function` procedures.

The function name: This is a unique name for the function. Names must begin with an alphabetic character, they can't include a space or a period, and they can't be any longer than 255 characters.

The function arguments: Just as many application functions accept arguments, so do user-defined functions. Arguments are typically one or more values that the function uses as the raw materials for its calculations. You always enter arguments between parentheses after the function name, and you separate multiple arguments with commas.

The VBA statements: This is the code that actually performs the calculations. Each expression is a combination of values, operators, variables, and VBA or application functions that produce a result.

The return value: User-defined functions usually return a value. To do this, include a statement in which you set the name of the function equal to an expression. For example, in the HypotenuseLength function, the following statement defines the return value:

```
HypotenuseLength = Sqr(x ^ 2 + y ^ 2)
```

The End Function keywords: These keywords indicate the end of the function procedure.

All your user-defined functions will have this basic structure, so you need to keep three things in mind when designing these kinds of macros:

- What arguments will the macro take?
- What formulas will you use within the macro?
- What value or values will be returned?

Writing User-Defined Functions

User-defined functions can't contain menu commands, mouse actions, or keyboard actions. This means, of course, there is no way to record user-defined functions. You have to create them by hand. This process is very similar to creating a command macro from scratch. Here are the general steps to follow when you write a user-defined function:

1. Open the module you want to use for the function.

2. Place the insertion point where you want to start the macro.

3. If you like, enter one or more comments that describe what the macro does. Be sure to type a single quotation mark (') at the beginning of each comment line.

4. Start the macro by typing Function followed by a space and then the name of the macro. If your function uses arguments, enclose them in parentheses after the function name (be sure to separate each argument with a comma). When you press Enter, VBA adds the End Function statement.

5. Enter the VBA statements that you want to include in the function. As with Sub procedures, you should indent each line for clarity by pressing the Tab key at the beginning of the line.

Employing User-Defined Functions

You'll probably find that user-defined functions are most useful in Excel. In this case, you can employ these functions only within worksheet formulas or in other VBA statements. You have two choices:

- In the cell, enter the function the same way you would any of Excel's built-in functions. In other words, enter the name of the function and then the necessary arguments enclosed in parentheses. In Figure 53.4, the window at the bottom shows the HypotenuseLength function in action. Cell A1 contains the following formula:

```
=HypotenuseLength(3,4)
```

- Select Insert | Function, highlight All in the Function category list, and select the macro from the Function name list. Click OK and enter the arguments. When you're done, click OK.

An Introduction to VBA Programming

Although it's possible to create useful VBA applications without programming, most macro developers occasionally have to write at least a little bit of code. And it goes without saying that if you hope to build anything even remotely complex or powerful, a knowledge of VBA programming is a must. The rest of this chapter gets you started with some programming fundamentals. If you combine these with the objects I discuss in Chapter 54, and the control structures I talk about in Chapter 55, "Controlling VBA Code and Interacting with the User," you'll have a solid base from which to explore further programming topics.

VBA Procedures

The basic unit of VBA programming is the *procedure,* which is a block of code in a module that you reference as a unit. Earlier in this chapter you learned about the two types of procedures: command macros (also known as Sub procedures) and user-defined functions (or Function procedures).

The Structure of a Procedure

To recap what you learned earlier, a Sub procedure is allowed to modify its environment, but it can't return a value. Here is the basic structure of a Sub procedure:

```
Sub ProcedureName (argument1, argument2, ...)
    [VBA statements]
End Sub
```

For example, Listing 53.1 shows a Sub procedure that enters some values for a loan in various ranges and then adds a formula to calculate the loan payment.

Listing 53.1. A sample Sub procedure.

```
Sub EnterLoanData()
    Range("IntRate").Value = .08
    Range("Term").Value = 10
    Range("Principal").Value = 10000
    Range("Payment").Formula = "=PMT(IntRate/12, Term*12, Principal)"
End Sub
```

A Function procedure, on the other hand, can't modify its environment, but it does return a value. Here is its structure:

```
Function ProcedureName (argument1, argument2, ...)
    [VBA statements]
    ProcedureName = returnValue
End Function
```

For example, Listing 53.2 is a Function procedure that sums two ranges, stores the results in variables named totalSales and totalExpenses (see the section "Working with Variables"), and then uses these values and the fixedCosts argument to calculate the net margin.

Listing 53.2. A sample Function procedure.

```
Function CalcNetMargin(fixedCosts)
    totalSales = Application.Sum(Range("Sales"))
    totalExpenses = Application.Sum(Range("Expenses"))
    CalcNetMargin = (totalSales-totalExpenses-fixedCosts)/totalSales
End Function
```

Calling a Procedure

Once you've written a procedure, you can use it either in a worksheet formula or in another procedure. This is known as *calling* the procedure.

Calling a Procedure Name in the Same Project

If a procedure exists in a module that is contained in the current VBA project, you call it by entering the procedure name and then including any necessary arguments. For example, as you learned earlier, you can call the HypotenuseLength procedure from a worksheet cell by entering a formula such as this:

```
=HypotenuseLength(3,4)
```

If you like, you can also call a procedure from another procedure. For example, the following VBA statement sets a variable named TotalPerimeter equal to the total perimeter of a right triangle that has two sides of length X and Y:

```
TotalPerimeter = X + Y + HypotenuseLength(X,Y)
```

If the procedure exists in a different module, but it has the same name as a procedure in the current module, you need to preface the call with the name of the module that contains the procedure:

```
ModuleName.ProcedureName
```

For example, the following statement calls the CalcNetMargin function from another module:

```
Module.CalcNetMargin(100000)
```

Calling a Procedure in Another Project

If you have a VBA statement that needs to call a procedure in another project, you first need to set up a *reference* to the project. Doing so gives you access to all the project's procedures. The following steps show you what to do:

1. Display the Visual Basic Editor for the project you want to work with.
2. Select Tools | References. The References dialog box appears, as shown in Figure 53.5.

FIGURE 53.5.

Use the References dialog box to set up a reference to another project.

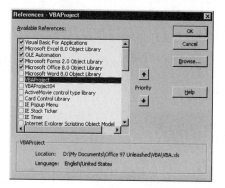

3. If the project is from the same application and is open, it will appear in the Available References list. Highlight the project and activate its check box. If the project isn't open, click the Browse button, choose the project you want from the Add Reference dialog box that appears, and then click Open to return to the References dialog box.
4. Click OK to return to the Visual Basic Editor. You'll see the project added to the Project Explorer.

> ## CAUTION: PROJECT NAMES MUST BE UNIQUE
>
> If the project you select in the References dialog box has the same name as the project in the current document, VBA will display an error message, because no two open projects can have the same name. To avoid this, make sure you give each of your VBA projects a unique name. To rename a project, use either of the following methods:
>
> - Click the project name in the Project Explorer and then use the Name property in the Properties window to change the name.
>
> - Highlight one of the project's objects in the Project Explorer and then select Tools | *ProjectName* Properties, where *ProjectName* is the name of the project. In the Project Properties dialog box that appears, enter the new name in the Project Name text box and then click OK.

Once you have the reference established, you call the procedure the same way you call the procedures in the current project. If the two projects have procedures with the same names, you need to add the project's name, surrounded by square brackets ([ ]), to the call:

```
[ProjectName].ProcedureName
```

For example, the following statement calls the HypotenuseLength function in the project named VBAProject:

```
[VBAProject].HypotenuseLength(3,4)
```

Visual Basic Editor Techniques for Easier Coding

If in the past you've used either Visual Basic for Applications or Visual Basic, you'll be pleased to know that the new Visual Basic Editor boasts a number of handy features that make it easier than ever to create and work with procedures. The next few sections discuss four of these features: IntelliSense, comment blocks, Find, and bookmarks.

Taking Advantage of IntelliSense

VBA 5.0's new IntelliSense feature is like a mini version of the VBA Help system. It offers you assistance with VBA syntax either on-the-fly or on-demand. You should find this an incredibly useful tool because, as you'll see as you work through this book, VBA contains dozens of statements and functions, and VBA-enabled programs offer hundreds of objects to work with. Few people can commit all this to memory, and it's a pain to be constantly looking up the correct syntax. IntelliSense helps by giving you hints and alternatives as you type. To see what I mean, let's look at the five types of IntelliSense help available.

List Properties/Methods

In Chapter 54, you'll learn how to work with the objects that each VBA-enabled application makes available. In particular, you'll learn about *properties* and *methods*, which, put simply, define the characteristics of each object. (In broad terms, properties describe an object's appearance, and methods describe what you can do with an object.)

As you'll see, however, each object can have dozens of properties and methods. To help you code your procedures correctly, IntelliSense can display a list of the available properties and methods as you type your VBA statements. To try this, activate a module in the Visual Basic Editor and type application followed by a period (.). As shown in Figure 53.6, VBA will display a pop-up menu. The items on this menu are the properties and methods that are available for the Application object. Use the following methods to work with this menu:

- Keep typing to display different items in the list. In Excel, for example, if you type cap, VBA highlights Caption in the list.
- Double-click an item to insert it into your code.
- Highlight an item (by clicking it or by using the up and down arrow keys) and then press Tab to insert the item and continue working on the same statement.
- Highlight an item and then press Enter to insert the item and start a new line.
- Press Esc to remove the menu without inserting an item.

FIGURE 53.6.

IntelliSense displays the available properties and methods as you type.

Note that if you press Esc to remove the pop-up menu, VBA won't display it again for the same object. If you would like to display the menu again, use any of the following techniques:

- Select Edit | List Properties/Methods.
- Press Ctrl-J.
- Right-click the module and choose List Properties/Methods.
- Click the List Properties/Methods button on the Edit toolbar.

NOTE: DISPLAYING THE EDIT TOOLBAR

VBA doesn't display the Edit toolbar by default. To display it, either select View | Toolbars | Edit or right-click any toolbar and choose Edit from the shortcut menu.

53

GETTING STARTED WITH VBA

List Constants

IntelliSense has a List Constants feature that's similar to List Properties/Methods. In this case, you get a pop-up menu that displays a list of the available constants for a property or method. (A *constant* is a fixed value that corresponds to a specific state or result. See the later section "Working with Variables" to learn more about them.) For example, type the following in a module:

```
Application.ActiveWindow.WindowState=
```

Figure 53.7 shows the pop-up menu that appears in Excel. This is a list of constants that correspond to the various settings for a window's WindowState property. For example, you would use the xlMaximized constant to maximize a window. You work with this list using the same techniques that I outlined for List Properties/Methods.

If you need to display this list manually, use any of the following methods:

- Select Edit | List Constants.
- Press Ctrl-Shift-J.
- Right-click the module and choose List Constants.

- Click the List Constants button on the Edit toolbar.

FIGURE 53.7.

The List Constants feature in action.

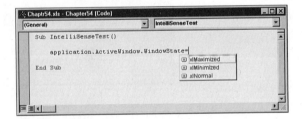

Parameter Info

You learned earlier that a user-defined function typically takes one or more arguments (or parameters) to use in its internal calculations. Many of the functions and statements built into VBA also use parameters, and some have as many as a dozen separate arguments! The syntax of such statements is obviously very complex, so it's easy to make mistakes. To help you when you're entering a user-defined function or one of VBA's built-in functions or statements, IntelliSense provides the Parameter Info feature. As its name implies, this feature displays information on the parameters you can utilize in a function. To see an example, enter the following text in any Excel module:

```
activecell.formula=pmt(
```

As soon as you type the left parenthesis, a banner pops up that tells you the available arguments for (in this case) VBA's `Pmt` function, as shown in Figure 53.8. Here are the features of this banner:

- The current argument is displayed in bold. When you enter an argument and then type a comma, VBA displays the next argument in bold.
- Arguments that are optional are surrounded by square brackets ([ ]).
- The various `As` statements (for example, `As Double`) tell you the *data type* of each argument. I'll explain data types in the next chapter.
- To remove the banner, press Esc.

FIGURE 53.8.

The Parameter Info feature shows you the defined arguments for the current function or statement.

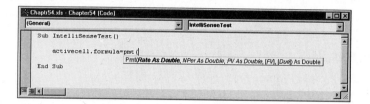

As usual, IntelliSense also lets you display this information by hand. Here are the techniques to use:

- Select Edit | Parameter Info.
- Press Ctrl-Shift-I.
- Right-click the module and choose Parameter Info.
- Click the Parameter Info button on the Edit toolbar.

Quick Info

IntelliSense also has a Quick Info feature that's similar to Parameter Info. In this case, though, Quick Info provides not only a list of function parameters, but also the syntax of *any* VBA statement, as well as the value of a constant. See Figure 53.9.

FIGURE 53.9.

Quick Info can help you with constant values as well as statement syntax and function parameters.

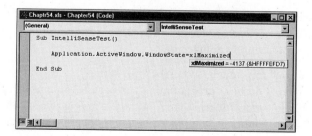

53

GETTING STARTED WITH VBA

Here are the methods you can use to display the Quick Info banner:

- Select Edit | Quick Info.
- Press Ctrl-I.
- Right-click the module and choose Quick Info.

- Click the Quick Info button on the Edit toolbar.

Complete Word

The last of the IntelliSense features is Complete Word. You use this feature to get VBA to complete a keyword that you've started typing, thus saving some wear and tear on your typing fingers. To use Complete Word, just type in the first few letters of a keyword and do one of the following:

- Select Edit | Complete Word.
- Press Ctrl-Spacebar.
- Right-click the module and choose Complete Word.

- Click the Complete Word button on the Edit toolbar.

If the letters you typed are enough to define a unique keyword, IntelliSense fills in the rest of the word. For example, if you type `appl` and run Complete Word, IntelliSense changes your typing to `Application`. However, if there are multiple keywords that begin with the letters you typed, IntelliSense displays a pop-up menu that you can use to select the word you want.

Working with Comment Blocks

Although comments aren't executed when you run a procedure, they still have an important role to play in VBA programming. In particular, you can use comments to document a procedure:

- You can provide an overall explanation of what the procedure does.
- You can detail any assumptions you've made about how the procedure runs, as well as any background information necessary to operate the procedure.
- You can explain the arguments the procedure uses, if any.
- You can create a "running commentary" throughout the procedure that explains what the procedure is doing and why.

Why go to all this trouble? Well, the VBA language uses a fairly straightforward syntax, but it still suffers (as do most programming languages) from an inherent crypticness. So although *you* might know exactly what your program is trying to accomplish, other people will have a harder time deciphering your code. A copiously commented procedure removes some of this burden and makes it easier for other people to work with your procedures. Not only that, but you'll find that comments are an invaluable tool for getting up to speed when you haven't looked at a procedure for six months.

However, there is yet another way that comments are useful: to prevent VBA from executing troublesome statements. If you're pulling your hair out trying to figure out why a particular statement won't run properly, it's often best to just skip the statement altogether and come back to it later. Or you might want to try an alternative statement. Either way, tacking an apostrophe onto the beginning of the statement is all you need to do in order to "comment out" the pesky line and move on to more productive matters.

Suppose, however, that instead of a single line of troublesome code you have 10 lines, or even 20 or 30. Again, you can bypass these lines by commenting them out, but it's pain to have to insert apostrophes at the beginning of every line. To relieve you of this hassle, VBA 5.0 has a new Comment Block feature that can toggle commenting on and off for any number of statements. To use this feature, highlight the statements you want to work with and then do one of the following:

■ To comment out the statements, click the Comment Block button on the Edit toolbar.

■ To uncomment the statements, click the Uncomment Block button on the Edit toolbar.

Finding Code

Once you gain experience with VBA, you'll find that your modules and procedures will become larger and more complex. If you ever find yourself lamenting a long-lost piece of code adrift in some huge megamodule, the folks who designed VBA can sympathize (probably because it has happened to *them* a time or two). In fact, they were even kind enough to build a special Find feature into VBA to help you search for missing code. Find can look for a word or phrase in a procedure, module, or even an entire project. There's even a Replace feature that you can use to replace one or more instances of a word or phrase with another word or phrase.

Using the Find Feature

If you need to find some code in a module that has only a relatively small number of statements, it's usually easiest just to scroll through the module using the mouse or keyboard. But if you're dealing with a few dozen or even a few hundred statements, or with a module that contains dozens of procedures and functions, don't waste your time rummaging through the statements by hand. The Visual Basic Editor's Find feature lets you search for a key word or phrase.

When you're ready to begin, you can select Edit | Find, press Ctrl-F, or click the Find button on the toolbar. The Find dialog box appears, as shown in Figure 53.10.

FIGURE 53.10.

Use the Find dialog box to hunt for code in a procedure, module, or project.

Here's a summary of the various controls in this dialog box:

Find What: Use this text box to enter the word or phrase you want to find.

Search: The options in this group define the *search scope,* which tells VBA where to conduct its search. The options are Current Procedure, Current Module, Current Project, and Selected Text.

Direction: If you suspect that the code you want is below the current insertion point, select Down. If you think the code is above the current insertion point, select Up. If you're not sure, select All to run through the entire search scope.

Find Whole Word Only: When this check box is deactivated, VBA looks for text that contains the search text. For example, if your search text is *work,* VBA would match *worksheet* and *ThisWorkbook.* If you want to find only words that match the search text exactly, activate this check box.

Match Case: Activate this check box to make your searches case-sensitive.

Use Pattern Matching: Activate this check box if you want to use VBA's pattern-matching feature, which supports the following characters:

Character	What It Matches
?	Any single character.
*	Zero or more characters.
#	Any single digit.
[character-list]	Any single character in *character-list*, which can be either a series of characters (for example, [aeiou]) or a range (for example, [a-m]).
[!character-list]	Any single character not in *character-list*.

Replace: Clicking this button displays the Replace dialog box (see the next section).

Find Next: Click this button to find the next instance of your search text. (In this case, "next" depends on whether you're searching up or down.)

When you start the search, VBA highlights the first instance of your search text if it finds a match. If this is the instance you want, click Cancel. Otherwise, you can continue searching by clicking the Find Next button. If VBA can't find the search text, it lets you know when it has reached the bottom of the search scope (if you're searching down) or the top of the search scope (if you're searching up). Click Yes to search the rest of the scope. If VBA still can't find the search text, it displays a message to let you know.

TIP: SEARCHING IDEAS

Searching for code is a straightforward affair, but VBA gives you lots of options. To make things easier, here are a couple of things to keep in mind when using the Find feature:

- For best results, don't try to match an entire statement. A word or two is usually all you really need.

- If you're not sure how to spell a word, just use a piece of it. Access will still find `Application` if you search for just app (although it will also find keywords such as `AppActivate` and `DDEAppReturnCode`).

Using the Replace Feature

One of the VBA features you'll probably come to rely on the most is *find and replace*. This means that VBA seeks out a particular bit of code and then replaces it with something else. This might not seem like a big deal for a statement or two, but if you need to change a couple of dozen instances of a variable name, it can be a real time-saver.

Happily, replacing data is very similar to finding it. To get started, you can either click the Replace button in the Find dialog box or select Edit | Replace (you can also press Ctrl-H). You'll see the Replace dialog box, shown in Figure 53.11. Enter the data you want to search for in the Find What text box and then enter the data you want to replace it with in the Replace With text box. The other options are similar to those in the Find dialog box. When you're ready to go, click one of the following buttons:

Find Next: Click this button to find the next match without performing a replacement.

Replace: Click this button to replace the currently highlighted data and then move on to the next match.

Replace All: Click this button to replace every instance of the search text with the replacement text. If you click this button, VBA will display a dialog box telling you how many replacements were made (assuming that the search text was found). Click OK to dismiss the dialog box.

53

GETTING STARTED WITH VBA

FIGURE 53.11.

Use the Replace dialog box to search for and replace code.

Working with Variables

Your VBA procedures often will need to store temporary values for use in later statements and calculations. For example, you might want to store values for total sales and total expenses to use later in a gross margin calculation. In VBA, as in most programming languages, you store temporary values in *variables*. This section explains this important topic and shows you how to use variables in your VBA procedures.

Declaring Variables

Declaring a variable tells VBA the name of the variable you're going to use. You declare variables by including Dim statements (Dim is short for *dimension*) at the beginning of each Sub or Function procedure. A Dim statement has the following syntax:

```
Dim variableName
```

`variableName` is the name of the variable. The name must begin with an alphabetic character, it can't be longer than 255 characters, it can't be a VBA keyword, and it can't contain a space or any of the following characters:

```
. ! # $ % & @
```

For example, the following statement declares a variable named totalSales:

```
Dim totalSales
```

NOTE: VARIABLE CASE CONSIDERATIONS

To avoid confusing variables with the names of objects, properties, or methods, many programmers begin their variable names with a lowercase letter. This is the style used in this book.

Also note that VBA preserves the case of your variable names throughout a procedure. For example, if you declare a variable named totalSales and you later enter this variable name as, say, totalsales, VBA will convert the name to totalSales automatically as part of its syntax checking. This means two things:

- If you want to change the case used in a variable, change the *first* instance of the variable (usually the Dim statement).

- Once you've declared a variable, you should enter all subsequent references to the variable entirely in lowercase. Not only is this easier to type, but you'll immediately know if you've misspelled the variable name if you see that VBA doesn't change the case of the variable name once you enter the line.

Most programmers set up a declaration section at the beginning of each procedure and use it to hold all their Dim statements. Then, once the variables have been declared, you can use them throughout the procedure.

Listing 53.3 shows a `Function` procedure that declares two variables—`totalSales` and `totalExpenses`—and then uses Excel's `Sum` function to store a range sum in each variable. Finally, the `GrossMargin` calculation uses each variable to return the function result.

Listing 53.3. A function that uses variables to store the intermediate values of a calculation.

```
Function GrossMargin()
    ' Declarations
    Dim totalSales
    Dim totalExpenses
    ' Code
    totalSales = Application.Sum(Range("Sales"))
    totalExpenses = Application.Sum(Range("Expenses"))
    GrossMargin = (totalSales - totalExpenses) / totalSales
End Function
```

In the `GrossMargin` function, notice that you store a value in a variable with a simple assignment statement of the following form:

```
variableName = value
```

NOTE: DECLARING GLOBAL VARIABLES

If you want to use a variable in all the procedures in a module, place the declaration at the top of the module before your first procedure. This is called a *global* declaration.

53

GETTING STARTED
WITH VBA

Variable Data Types

The *data type* of a variable determines the kind of data the variable can hold. Table 53.1 lists all the VBA data types.

Table 53.1. The VBA data types.

Data Type	Storage Size	Type-Declaration Character	Description
Boolean	2 bytes		Takes one of two logical values: `True` or `False`.
Byte	1 byte		Used for small, positive integer values (from 0 to 255).

continues

Table 53.1. continued

Data Type	Storage Size	Type-Declaration Character	Description
Currency	8 bytes	@	Used for monetary or fixed-decimal calculations where accuracy is important. The value range is from −922,337,203,685,477.5808 to 922,337,203,685,477.5807.
Date	8 bytes		Used for holding date data. The range is from January 1, 0100 to December 31, 9999. When setting a value to a Date variable, enclose the date in pound signs (for example, newDate = #1/15/97#).
Double	8 bytes	#	Double-precision floating point. Negative numbers range from −1.79769313486232E308 to −4.94065645841247E−324. Positive numbers range from 4.94065645841247E−324 to 1.79769313486232E308.
Integer	2 bytes	%	Used for integer values in the range −32,768 to 32,767.
Long	4 bytes	&	Large integer values. The range is from −2,147,483,648 to 2,147,483,647.
Object	4 bytes		Refers to objects only.
Single	4 bytes	!	Single-precision floating point. Negative numbers range from −3.402823E38 to −1.401298E−45. Positive numbers range from 1.401298E−45 to 3.402823E38.
String	1 byte per	$	Holds string values. The character strings can be up to 64K.

Data Type	Storage Size	Type-Declaration Character	Description
Variant (number)	16 bytes		Can take any kind of data.
Variant (string)	22 bytes plus 1 byte per character		Can take any kind of data.

You specify a data type by including the As keyword in a Dim statement. Here is the general syntax:

```
Dim variableName As DataType
```

    variableName   The name of the variable.

    DataType   One of the data types from Table 53.1.

For example, the following statement declares a variable named textString to be of type String:

```
Dim textString As String
```

Using Array Variables

An array is a group of variables of the same data type. Why would you need to use an array? Well, suppose you wanted to store 20 employee names in variables to use in a procedure. One way to do this would be to create 20 variables named, say, employee1, employee2, and so on. However, it's much more efficient to create a single employee array variable that can hold up to 20 names. Here's how you would do so:

```
Dim employee(19) As String
```

As you can see, this declaration is very similar to one you would use for a regular variable. The difference is the 19 enclosed in parentheses. The parentheses tell VBA that you're declaring an array, and the number tells VBA how many elements you'll need in the array. Why 19 instead of 20? Well, each element in the array is assigned a *subscript,* where the first element's subscript is 0, the second is 1, and so on, up to, in this case, 19. So the total number of elements in this array is 20.

You use the subscripts to refer to any element simply by enclosing its index number in the parentheses, like so:

```
employee(0) = "Ponsonby"
```

By default, the subscripts of VBA arrays start at 0 (this is called the *lower bound* of the array) and run up to the number you specify in the Dim statement (this is called the *upper bound* of the array). If you would prefer your array index numbers to start at 1, include the following statement at the top of the module (that is, before declaring your first array and before your first procedure):

```
Option Base 1
```

Another way to specify a specific lower bound is to add the To keyword to your array declaration. Here's the syntax:

```
Dim arrayName(LowerBound To UpperBound) As DataType
```

arrayName	The name of the array variable.
LowerBound	A long integer specifying the lower bound of the array.
UpperBound	A long integer specifying the upper bound of the array.
DataType	One of the data types from Table 53.1.

For example, here's a declaration that creates an array variable with subscripts running from 50 to 100:

```
Dim myArray(50 To 100) As Currency
```

Dynamic Arrays

What do you do if you're not sure how many subscripts you'll need in an array? You could guess at the correct number, but that will almost always leave you with one of the following problems:

- If you guess too low and try to access a subscript higher than the array's upper bound, VBA will generate an error message.
- If you guess too high, VBA will still allocate memory to the unused portions of the array, so you'll waste precious system resources.

To avoid both of these problems, you can declare a *dynamic* array by leaving the parentheses blank in the Dim statement:

```
Dim myArray() As Double
```

Then, when you know the number of elements you need, you can use a ReDim statement to allocate the correct number of subscripts (notice that you don't specify a data type in the ReDim statement):

```
ReDim myArray(52)
```

The following is a partial listing of a procedure named PerformCalculations. This procedure declares calcValues as a dynamic array and totalValues as an integer. Later in the procedure, totalValues is set to the result of a function procedure named GetTotalValues. The ReDim statement then uses totalValues to allocate the appropriate number of subscripts to the calcValues array.

```
Sub PerformCalculations()
    Dim calcValues() As Double, totalValues as Integer
    .
    .
    .
    totalValues = GetTotalValues()
    ReDim calcValues(totalValues)
    .
    .
    .
End Sub
```

NOTE: PRESERVING ARRAY VALUES

The ReDim statement reinitializes the array so that any values stored in the array are lost. If you want to preserve an array's existing values, use ReDim with the Preserve option:

```
ReDim Preserve myArray(52)
```

NOTE: DETERMINING ARRAY BOUNDS

If your program needs to know the lower bound and the upper bound of an array, VBA provides a couple of functions that can do the job:

LBound(*arrayName*)	Returns the lower bound of the array given by *arrayName*.
UBound(*arrayName*)	Returns the upper bound of the array given by *arrayName*.

Multidimensional Arrays

If you enter a single number between the parentheses in an array's Dim statement, VBA creates a *one-dimensional* array. But you also can create arrays with two or more dimensions (60 is the maximum). For example, suppose you wanted to store both a first name and a last name in your employees array. To store two sets of data with each element, you would declare a two-dimensional array, like so:

```
Dim employees(19,1) As String
```

The subscripts for the second number work like the subscripts you've seen already. In other words, they begin at 0 and run up to the number you specify. So this Dim statement sets up a "table" (or a *matrix,* as it's usually called) with 20 "rows" (one for each employee) and two "columns" (one for the first name and one for the last name). Here are two statements that initialize the data for the first employee:

```
employees(0,0) = "Biff"
employees(0,1) = "Ponsonby"
```

Working with Constants

Constants are values that don't change. They can be numbers, strings, or other values, but, unlike variables, they keep their value throughout your code. VBA recognizes two types of constants: built-in and user-defined.

Using Built-In Constants

Many properties and methods have their own predefined constants. For Word objects, these constants begin with the letters wd. For Excel objects, they begin with the letters xl. For VBA objects, they begin with vb.

For example, Excel's Window object recognizes three built-in constants for its WindowState property: xlNormal (to set a window to its normal state), xlMaximized (to maximize a window), and xlMinimized (to minimize a window). To maximize the active window, for example, you would use the following statement:

```
ActiveWindow.WindowState = xlMaximized
```

Creating User-Defined Constants

To create your own constants, use the Const statement:

```
Const CONSTANTNAME = expression
```

CONSTANTNAME	The name of the constant. Most programmers use all-uppercase names for constants.
expression	The value (or a formula that returns a value) that you want to use for the constant.

For example, the following statement creates a constant named DISCOUNT and assigns it the value 0.4:

```
Const DISCOUNT = 0.4
```

VBA Operators

Just as you use operators such as addition (+) and multiplication (*) to build formulas in Excel worksheets and Word tables, so too do you use operators to combine functions, variables, and values in a VBA statement. VBA operators fall into four general categories: arithmetic, comparison, logical, and miscellaneous.

Arithmetic Operators

VBA's arithmetic operators are similar to those you've been using in your worksheets. Table 53.2 lists each of the arithmetic operators you can use in your VBA statements.

Table 53.2. The VBA arithmetic operators.

Operator	Name	Example	Result
+	Addition	10+5	15
-	Subtraction	10-5	5
-	Negation	-10	-10
*	Multiplication	10*5	50
/	Division	10/5	2
%	Percentage	10%	0.1
^	Exponentiation	10^5	100000
Mod	Modulus	10 Mod 5	0

The Mod operator works like Excel's MOD() worksheet function. In other words, it divides one number by another and returns the remainder. Here's the general form to use:

```
result = dividend Mod divisor
```

dividend	The number being divided.
divisor	The number being divided into dividend.
result	The remainder of the division.

For example, 16 Mod 5 returns 1 because 5 goes into 16 three times with a remainder of 1.

Comparison Operators

You use the comparison operators in a statement that compares two or more numbers, text strings, cell contents, or function results. If the statement is true, the result of the formula is given the logical value True (which is equivalent to any nonzero value). If the statement is false, the formula returns the logical value False (which is equivalent to 0). Table 53.3 summarizes VBA's comparison operators and shows you how they can be used with both numeric and string values.

Table 53.3. The VBA comparison operators.

Operator	Name	Example	Result
=	Equal to	10=5	False
>	Greater than	10>5	True
<	Less than	10<5	False
>=	Greater than or equal to	"a">="b"	False
<=	Less than or equal to	"a"<="b"	True
<>	Not equal to	"a"<>"b"	True

53

GETTING STARTED WITH VBA

Logical Operators

You use the logical operators to combine or modify True/False expressions. Table 53.4 summarizes VBA's logical operators.

Table 53.4. The VBA logical operators.

Operator	General Form	What It Returns
And	*Expr1* And *Expr2*	True if both *Expr1* and *Expr2* are True; False otherwise.
Eqv	*Expr1* Eqv *Expr2*	True if both *Expr1* and *Expr2* are True or if both *Expr1* and *Expr2* are False; False otherwise.
Imp	*Expr1* Imp *Expr2*	False if *Expr1* is True and *Expr2* is False; True otherwise.
Or	*Expr1* Or *Expr2*	True if at least one of *Expr1* and *Expr2* is True; False otherwise.
Xor	*Expr1* Xor *Expr2*	False if both *Expr1* and *Expr2* are True or if both *Expr1* and *Expr2* are False; True otherwise.
Not	Not *Expr*	True if *Expr* is False; False if *Expr* is True.

Summary

This chapter introduced you to VBA, Office 97's powerful macro language and development environment. I showed you how to record, write, and run a macro, how to create procedures and user-defined functions, and how to work with variables and operators. You'll find related information in the following chapters:

■ Objects are one of the most important concepts in VBA. To learn how they work, see Chapter 54, "Understanding Objects."

■ VBA, like any programming language worth its salt, contains a number of statements that control program flow and allow user interaction. I discuss these statements in Chapter 55, "Controlling VBA Code and Interacting with the User."

■ You can run procedures from custom menus and toolbars. I show you how in Chapter 59, "Creating a Custom User Interface."

■ To help ensure that your code is problem-free, I'll show you various techniques for trapping errors and debugging procedures in Chapter E4 on the CD, "Debugging VBA Procedures."

■ You'll find a complete list of VBA's built-in statements in Appendix D, "VBA Statements." For a list of VBA's functions, head for Appendix E, "VBA Functions."

Understanding Objects

IN THIS CHAPTER

CHAPTER 54

> *We live in a world of things, and our only connection with them is that we know how to manipulate or to consume them.*

> —*Erich Fromm*

Many of your VBA procedures will perform calculations using simple combinations of numbers, operators, and the host application's built-in functions. You'll probably find, however, that most of your code manipulates the application environment in some way, whether it's formatting document text, entering data in a worksheet range, or setting application options. Each of these items—the document, the range, the application—is called an *object* in VBA. Objects are perhaps the most crucial concept in VBA programming, and I explain them in detail in this chapter.

NOTE: FOR MORE INFORMATION

For more information, consult Chapter 4, "Working with Objects," of my book *Visual Basic for Applications Unleashed* (Sams Publishing, 1997), which contains more comprehensive information on objects.

What Is an Object?

The dictionary definition of an object is "anything perceptible by one or more of the senses, especially something that can be seen and felt." Now, of course, you can't feel anything in an Office application, but you can see all kinds of things. To VBA, an object is anything in an application that you can see *and* manipulate in some way. For example, an Excel range is something you can see, and you can manipulate it by entering data, changing colors, setting fonts, and so on. A range, therefore, is an object.

What *isn't* an object? The Office programs are so customizable that most things you can see qualify as objects, but not everything does. For example, the Maximize and Minimize buttons in document windows aren't objects. Yes, you can operate them, but you can't change them. Instead, the window itself is the object, and you manipulate it so that it is maximized or minimized.

You can manipulate objects in VBA in any of the following three ways:

- You can make changes to the object's *properties*.
- You can make the object perform a task by activating a *method* associated with the object.
- You can define a procedure that runs whenever a particular *event* happens to the object.

To help you understand properties, methods, events, and objects, I'll put things in real-world terms. Specifically, look at your computer as though it were an object. For starters, you can think of your computer in one of two ways: as a single object or as a *collection* of objects (such as the monitor, the keyboard, the system unit, and so on).

If you want to describe your computer as a whole, you mention the name of the manufacturer, the price, the color, and so on. Each of these items is a *property* of the computer. You can also use your computer to perform tasks, such as writing letters, crunching numbers, and playing games. These are the *methods* associated with your computer. There are also a number of things that happen to the computer that cause it to respond in predefined ways. For example, when you click the On button, the computer runs through its Power On Self-Test, initializes its components, and so on. The actions to which the computer responds automatically are its *events*.

The sum total of all these properties, methods, and events gives you an overall description of your computer. In a more general sense, you can think of a generic "computer" object, which also (in an abstract way) has the same properties, uses the same methods, and responds to the same events. This more abstract form is called a *class*. A specific computer object is called an *instance* of the computer class.

Your computer is also a collection of objects, each with its own properties, methods, and events. The CD-ROM drive, for example, has various properties, including its speed and data rate. Its methods are actions such as ejecting a disc and adjusting the sound level. A CD-ROM event might be inserting a disc that contains an AUTORUN.INF file that causes the disc's program to run automatically.

In the end, you have a complete description of the computer: what it looks like (its properties), how you interact with it (its methods), and to what actions it responds (its events).

The Object Hierarchy

As you've seen, your computer's objects are arranged in a hierarchy with the most general object (the computer as a whole) at the top. Lower levels progress through more specific objects (such as the system unit, the motherboard, and the processor).

Each Office application's objects are also arranged in a hierarchy. The most general object—the Application object—refers to the program itself. In Excel, for example, the Application object contains no fewer than 15 objects, some of which are outlined in Table 54.1. Notice that, in most cases, each object is part of a *collection* of similar objects.

54

UNDERSTANDING
OBJECTS

Table 54.1. Some Excel objects in the `Application` object.

Object	Collection	Description
AddIn	AddIns	An Excel add-in file. The `AddIns` collection refers to all the add-ins available to Excel (in other words, all the add-ins listed in the Add-Ins dialog box).
Dialog	Dialogs	A built-in Excel dialog box. The `Dialogs` object is a collection of all the Excel built-in dialog boxes.
Name	Names	A defined range name. The `Names` object is the collection of all the defined names in all open workbooks.
Window	Windows	An open window. The `Windows` object is the collection of all the open windows.
Workbook	Workbooks	An open workbook. The `Workbooks` object is the collection of all the open workbooks.
WorksheetFunction	None	A container for Excel's built-in worksheet functions.

Most of the objects in Table 54.1 have objects beneath them in the hierarchy. A Workbook object, for example, contains Worksheet objects and possibly `Chart` objects. Similarly, a Worksheet object contains many objects of its own, such as Range objects and possibly an Outline object.

To specify an object in the hierarchy, you usually start with the uppermost object and add the lower objects, separated by periods. For example, here's one way you can specify the range B2:B5 on the worksheet named `"Sheet1"` in the workbook named `"Book1"`:

```
Application.Workbooks("Book1").Worksheets("Sheet1").Range("B2:B5")
```

As you'll see, there are ways to shorten such long-winded "hierarchical paths."

Working with Object Properties

Every object has a defining set of characteristics. These characteristics are called the object's *properties*, and they control the appearance and position of the object. For example, each Window object has a `WindowState` property you can use to display a window as maximized, minimized, or normal. Similarly, a Word Document object has a `Name` property to hold the filename, a `Saved` property that tells you whether the document has changed since the last save, a `Type` property to hold the document type (regular or template), and many more.

When you refer to a property, you use the following syntax:

`Object.Property`

For example, the following expression refers to the `ActiveWindow` property of the `Application` object:

`Application.ActiveWindow`

One of the most confusing aspects of objects and properties is that some properties do double duty as objects. Figure 54.1 uses an Excel example to illustrate this. The `Application` object has an `ActiveWindow` property that tells you the name of the active window. However, `ActiveWindow` is also a Window object. Similarly, the Window object has an `ActiveCell` property that specifies the active cell, but `ActiveCell` is also a Range object. Finally, a Range object has a `Font` property, but a font is also an object with its own properties (`Italic`, `Name`, `Size`, and so on).

FIGURE 54.1.

Some properties can also be objects.

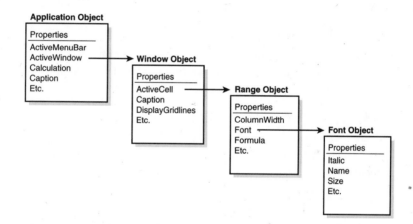

In other words, lower-level objects in the object hierarchy are really just properties of their parent objects. This idea will often help you reduce the length of a hierarchical path (and thus reduce the abuse your typing fingers must bear). For example, consider the following object path:

`Application.ActiveWindow.ActiveCell.Font.Italic`

Here, an object such as `ActiveCell` implicitly refers to the `ActiveWindow` and `Application` objects, so you can knock the path down to size as follows:

`ActiveCell.Font.Italic`

Setting the Value of a Property

To set a property to a certain value, you use the following syntax:

`Object.Property=value`

Here, `Object` is a hierarchical path that specifies the object you want to work with, `Property` is the name of the property you want to change, and `value` is an expression that returns the value to which you want to set the property. This value can be any of VBA's recognized data types, including the following:

- A numeric value. For example, the following statement sets the size of the font in the active cell to 14:

  ```
  ActiveCell.Font.Size = 14
  ```

- A string value. The following example sets the font name in the active cell to Times New Roman:

  ```
  ActiveCell.Font.Name = "Times New Roman"
  ```

- A logical value (in other words, `True` or `False`). The following statement turns on the `Italic` property in the active cell:

  ```
  ActiveCell.Font.Italic = True
  ```

Returning the Value of a Property

Sometimes you need to know the current setting of a property before changing the property or performing some other action. You can find out the current value of a property by using the following syntax:

```
variable=Object.Property
```

Here, `Object` and `Property` are defined as they were before, and `variable` is a variable or another property. For example, the following statement stores the contents of the active cell in a variable named `cellContents`:

```
cellContents = ActiveCell.Value
```

Working with Object Methods

An object's properties describe what the object is, whereas its *methods* describe what the object *does.* For example, in Word you can spell-check a `Document` object using the `CheckSpelling` method. Similarly, you can sort a `Table` object using the `Sort` method.

How you refer to a method depends on whether the method uses any arguments. If it doesn't, the syntax is similar to that of properties:

```
Object.Method
```

For example, the following statement saves the active document:

```
ActiveDocument.Save
```

If the method requires arguments, you use the following syntax:

```
Object.Method (argument1, argument2, ...)
```

NOTE: WHEN TO USE METHOD PARENTHESES

Technically, the parentheses around the argument list are necessary only if you'll be storing the result of the method in a variable or object property.

For example, Word's Document object has a Close method that you can use to close a document programmatically. Here's the syntax:

```
Object.Close(SaveChanges, OriginalFormat, RouteDocument)
```

Object	A Document object.
SaveChanges	A constant that specifies whether the file is saved before closing.
OriginalFormat	A constant that specifies whether the file is saved in its original format.
RouteDocument	A True or False value that specifies whether the document is routed to the next recipient.

NOTE: FORMATTING REQUIRED ARGUMENTS

For many VBA methods, not all the arguments are required. For the Close method, for example, only the **SaveChanges** argument is required. Throughout this book, I differentiate between required and optional arguments by displaying the required arguments in bold type.

For example, the following statement prompts the user to save changes, saves the changes (if applicable) in the original file format, and routes the document to the next recipient:

```
ActiveDocument.Close wdPromptToSaveChanges, wdOriginalFormat, True
```

To make your methods clearer to read, you can use VBA's predefined *named arguments*. For example, the syntax of the Close method has three named arguments: SaveChanges, OriginalFormat, and RouteDocument. Here's how you use them in the preceding example:

```
ActiveDocument.Close SaveChanges:=wdPromptToSaveChanges, _
    OriginalFormat:=wdOriginalFormat, _
    RouteDocument:=True
```

Notice how the named arguments are assigned values with the := operator.

54

UNDERSTANDING OBJECTS

> **NOTE: THE CODE CONTINUATION CHARACTER**
>
> Note the use of the underscore (_) in the preceding example. This is VBA's *code continuation character*, and it's useful for breaking long statements into multiple lines for easier reading. One caveat, though: Make sure that you add a space before the underscore, or VBA will generate an error.

> **TIP: USE NAMED ARGUMENTS IN ANY ORDER**
>
> Another advantage to using named arguments is that you can enter the arguments in any order you want, and you can ignore any arguments you don't need (except necessary arguments, of course).

Handling Object Events

In simplest terms, an *event* is something that happens to an object. For example, opening an Excel workbook is an event for that workbook. Don't confuse a method with an event, however. Yes, Excel has an Open method that you can use to open a workbook, but this method only *initiates* the procedure; the actual process of the file being opened is the event. Note, too, that events can happen either programmatically (by including the appropriate method in your code) or by user intervention (by selecting, say, File | Open).

In VBA, the event itself isn't as important as how your procedures *respond* to the event. In other words, you can write special procedures called *event handlers* that run every time a particular event occurs. In a workbook, for example, you can specify event handlers not just for opening the file, but also for other events such as activating the workbook window, saving the file, inserting a new worksheet, closing the file, and so on.

For example, Figure 54.2 shows a module window for a workbook. (Specifically, it's the module window for the project's ThisWorkbook object.) Notice that the module window has two drop-down lists just below the title bar:

Object list: This list tells you what kind of object you're working with. If you select (General) in this list, you can use the module window to enter standard VBA procedures and functions. If you select an object from this list, however, you can enter event handlers for the object.

Procedure list: This list tells you which procedure is active in the module. If you select (General) in the Object list, the Procedure list contains all the standard VBA procedures and functions in the module. If you select an object in the Object list, however, the Procedure list changes to show all the events recognized by the object.

FIGURE 54.2.

An example of an event procedure. Here, this procedure runs each time the workbook is opened.

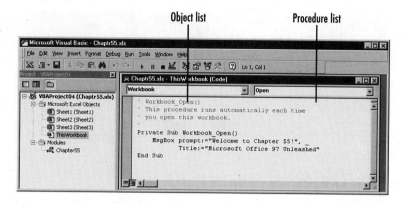

In Figure 54.2, I selected Workbook in the Object list, so the Procedure list contains all the events recognized by the Workbook object. For the Open event, I inserted a MsgBox statement into the Workbook_Open event handler. This statement displays a message each time the workbook is opened. (I show you how to use MsgBox in Chapter 55, "Controlling VBA Code and Interacting with the User.")

Working with Object Collections

A *collection* is a set of similar objects. For example, Excel's Workbooks collection is the set of all the open Workbook objects. Similarly, the Worksheets collection is the set of all Worksheet objects in a workbook. Collections are objects, too, so they have their own properties and methods, and you can use the properties and methods to manipulate one or more objects in the collection.

The members of a collection are called the *elements* of the collection. You can refer to individual elements using either the object's name or using an *index*. For example, the following statement closes a workbook named Budget.xls:

```
Workbooks("Budget.xls").Close
```

On the other hand, the following statement uses an index to make a copy of the first picture object in the active worksheet:

```
ActiveSheet.Pictures(1).Copy
```

If you don't specify an element, VBA assumes you want to work with the entire collection.

54

UNDERSTANDING OBJECTS

> **NOTE: USE COLLECTIONS TO REFER TO OBJECTS**
>
> It's important here to reiterate that you can't refer to many application objects by themselves. Instead, you must refer to the object as an element in a collection. For example, when referring to the Budget.xls workbook, you can't just use Budget.xls. You have to use `Workbooks("Budget.xls")` so that VBA knows you're talking about a currently open workbook.

The Object Browser

The Object Browser is a handy tool that shows you the objects available for your procedures as well as the properties, methods, and events for each object. (Technically, it shows you the various *classes* of objects available.) You can also use it to move quickly between procedures and to paste code templates into a module.

To display the Object Browser, activate the Visual Basic Editor and then either select View | Object Browser or click the Object Browser button on the Visual Basic toolbar. (You can also press F2.) You see the Object Browser dialog box, shown in Figure 54.3.

FIGURE 54.3.

VBA's Object Browser.

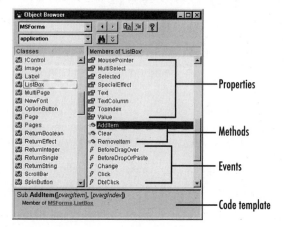

Object Browser Features

Here's a rundown of the Object Browser's features:

Libraries and projects: This drop-down list contains all the libraries and projects referenced by any module in the current document. A *library* is a file that contains information about the objects in an application. You usually see several libraries in this list: for example, the library for the current application, which lists the application objects you can use in your code; the VBA library, which lists the functions and language constructs specific to VBA; and the MSForms library, which contains objects related to building user forms. (See Chapter 59, "Creating a Custom User Interface.")

Search text: You can use this text box to enter a search string.

Classes: When you select a library, the Classes list shows the available object classes in the library. If you select a VBA project instead, the Classes list shows objects in the project.

Members: When you highlight a class in the Classes list, the Members list shows the methods, properties, and events available for that class. (Each member type has a different icon; refer to Figure 54.3.) When you highlight a module, Members shows the procedures contained in the module. To move to one of these procedures, double-click it.

Code template: The bottom of the Object Browser window displays code templates that you can paste into your modules. These templates list the method, property, event, or function name followed by the appropriate named arguments, if there are any. You can paste this template into a procedure and then edit the template. (Note, too, that the code template area also includes hyperlinks to related topics. Click one of these links to display the topic.)

Working with the Object Browser

The point of the Object Browser is to give you an easy way to see the available objects in a given library, as well as view the various properties, methods, and events associated with each object. However, the Object Browser is more than just an information resource because you can also use it to learn more about VBA as well as take some of the drudgery out of coding. Here's a quick list of a few techniques you can use with the Object Browser:

Control the Members list: The Members list has two views: grouped (all the properties, methods, and events together) and alphabetical. To toggle between these views, right-click the Object Browser and choose the Group Members command.

Search the objects: As I mentioned earlier, you can enter search text to look for specific items. Once you enter your text, use the following Object Browser buttons:

Click this button to begin the search. VBA expands the Object Browser dialog box to show the search results, as shown in Figure 54.4. Click an item to display it in the Members list.

Click this button to hide the list of found search items.

Click this button to display the list of found search items.

FIGURE 54.4.

When you search, the Object Browser displays an extra panel that shows the matching items.

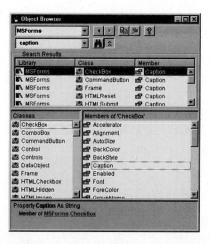

TIP: WHOLE-WORD SEARCHES

If you prefer that VBA match only whole words in your searches, right-click the Object Browser and activate the Find Whole Words Only command.

Browse the objects: You can use the following buttons to move back and forth through the members you've highlighted in the current Object Browser session:

 Click this button to move backward through the members you've seen.

 Click this button to move forward through the members you've seen.

 Copy an item: For members with long names, you can use the Object Browser's Copy feature to copy the member name to the Clipboard for easy pasting into your procedures. To use this feature, highlight the member and then either right-click the Object Browser and click Copy or click the Copy button.

 Get help for an item: If you want to know more about the highlighted member or class, you can invoke the Help system topic for that item. To do this, either right-click the Object Browser and click Help or click the Help button.

Referencing Additional Object Libraries

The default list of libraries that you see in the Object Browser is by no means a complete list. Depending on the applications and controls installed on your system, dozens of object libraries might be available. You saw in Chapter 53, "Getting Started with VBA," that you need to set up a reference to another VBA project in order to use procedures from that project. It's the same with object libraries: To use their objects, you must first set up a reference to the appropriate library file. (Yes, the library then appears in the Object Browser's list of libraries and projects.) Here are the steps to follow:

1. Either select Tools | References or right-click the Object Browser and choose References from the context menu. VBA displays the References dialog box.

2. In the Available References list, activate the check box for each object library you want to use.

3. Click OK to return to the Visual Basic Editor.

Assigning an Object to a Variable

As you learned in Chapter 53, you can declare a variable as an Object data type by using the following form of the Dim statement:

```
Dim variableName As Object
```

Once you set up your object variable, you can assign an object to it using the Set statement. Set has the following syntax:

```
Set variableName = ObjectName
```

    variableName   The name of the variable.

    ObjectName   The object you want to assign to the variable.

For example, the following statements declare a variable named budgetSheet to be an Object and then assign it to the 1997 Budget worksheet in the Budget.xls workbook:

```
Dim budgetSheet As Object
Set budgetSheet = Workbooks("Budget.xls").Worksheets("1997 Budget")
```

TIP: DECLARE SPECIFIC OBJECT TYPES

For faster performance, use specific object types instead of the generic Object type in your Dim statements. For example, the following statement declares the budgetSheet variable to be type Worksheet:

```
Dim budgetSheet As Worksheet
```

Working with Multiple Properties or Methods

Because most objects have many different properties and methods, you often need to perform multiple actions on a single object. This is accomplished easily with multiple statements that set the appropriate properties or run the necessary methods. However, this can be a pain if you have a long object name.

For example, take a look at the FormatRange procedure shown in Listing 54.1. This procedure formats a range in the Sheet1 worksheet with six statements. The Range object name—Worksheets("Sheet1").Range("B2:B5")—is quite long and is repeated in all six statements.

Listing 54.1. A procedure that formats a range.

```
Sub FormatRange()
    Worksheets("Sheet1").Range("B2:B5").Style = "Currency"
    Worksheets("Sheet1").Range("B2:B5").WrapText = True
    Worksheets("Sheet1").Range("B2:B5").Font.Size = 16
    Worksheets("Sheet1").Range("B2:B5").Font.Bold = True
    Worksheets("Sheet1").Range("B2:B5").Font.Color = RGB(255, 0, 0) ' Red
    Worksheets("Sheet1").Range("B2:B5").Font.Name = "Times New Roman"
End Sub
```

NOTE: THIS CHAPTER'S CODE LISTINGS

You'll find the code for Listing 54.1, as well as all the other procedures in this chapter, on this book's CD-ROM. Look for the file named Chaptr54.xls. If you don't have Excel, use the text file named Chaptr54.bas.

NOTE: THE RGB FUNCTION

When you want to specify colors in VBA, use the RGB function:

RGB(*red, green, blue*)

red	An integer value between 0 and 255 that represents the red component of the color.
green	An integer value between 0 and 255 that represents the green component of the color.
blue	An integer value between 0 and 255 that represents the blue component of the color.

To shorten this procedure, VBA provides the With statement. Here's the syntax:

```
With object
    [statements]
End With
```

object	The name of the object.
statements	The statements you want to execute on *object*.

The idea is that you strip out the common object and place it on the `With` line. Then all the statements between `With` and `End With` need only reference a specific method or property of that object. In the `FormatRange` procedure, the common object in all six statements is `Worksheets("Sheet1").Range("B2:B5")`. Listing 54.2 shows the `FormatRange2` procedure, which uses the `With` statement to strip out this common object and make the previous macro more efficient.

Listing 54.2. A more efficient version of `FormatRange()`.

```
Sub FormatRange2()
    With Worksheets("Sheet1").Range("B2:B5")
        .Style = "Currency"
        .WrapText = True
        .Font.Size = 16
        .Font.Bold = True
        .Font.Color = RGB(255, 0, 0) 'Red
        .Font.Name = "Times New Roman"
    End With
End Sub
```

The Application Object

You'll see plenty of objects when you turn your attention to specific Office objects in Chapters 56 through 58 and Chapter E5 on the CD. For now, though, take a look at an object that is common to all programs: the `Application` object. The `Application` object refers to the application as a whole; therefore, it acts as a container for all the program's objects. However, the `Application` object does have a few useful properties and methods of its own, and many of these members are applicable to all the Office applications.

Properties of the Application Object

The `Application` object has dozens of properties that affect a number of aspects of the program's environment. For starters, any control in the application's Options dialog box (select Tools | Options) has an equivalent `Application` object property. For example, the `StatusBar` property takes a `True` or `False` value that toggles the status bar on or off.

Here's a rundown of a few other `Application` object properties you'll use most often in your VBA code:

`Application.ActivePrinter` returns or sets the name of the application's current printer driver.

`Application.ActiveWindow` returns a `Window` object that represents the window that currently has the focus.

`Application.Caption` returns or sets the name that appears in the title bar of the main application window. In Excel, for example, to change the title bar caption from "Microsoft Excel" to "ACME Coyote Supplies," you'd use the following statement:

```
Application.Caption = "ACME Coyote Supplies"
```

`Application.Dialogs` returns the collection of all the application's built-in dialog boxes. See Chapter 55 to learn how to display these dialog boxes from your VBA procedures.

`Application.DisplayAlerts` determines whether the application displays alert dialog boxes. For example, if your code deletes an Excel worksheet, Excel usually displays an alert box asking you to confirm the deletion. To suppress this alert box and force Excel to accept the default action (which is, in this case, deleting the sheet), set the `DisplayAlerts` property to `False`.

NOTE: ALERTS ARE RESTORED AUTOMATICALLY

The application restores the `DisplayAlerts` property to its default state (`True`) when your procedure finishes. If you prefer to turn the alerts back on before then, set the `DisplayAlerts` property to `True`.

`Application.Height` returns or sets the height, in points, of the application window.

`Application.Left` returns or sets the distance, in points, of the left edge of the application window from the left edge of the screen.

`Application.Path` returns the path of the `Application` object. In other words, it tells you the drive and folder where the application's executable file resides (such as C:\Program Files\Microsoft Office\Office). Note that the returned path does not include a trailing backslash (\).

`Application.ScreenUpdating` returns or sets the application's screen updating. When `ScreenUpdating` is set to `True` (the default), the user sees the results of all your code actions: cut-and-paste operations, drawing objects added or deleted, formatting, and so on. Applications look more professional (and are noticeably faster) if the user just sees the end result of all these actions. To do this, turn off screen updating (by setting the `ScreenUpdating` property to `False`), perform the actions, and turn screen updating back on.

`Application.Top` returns or sets the distance, in points, of the top of the application window from the top of the screen.

`Application.UsableHeight` returns or sets the maximum height, in points, that a window can occupy within the application's window. In other words, this is the height of the application window less the vertical space taken up by the title bar, menu bar, toolbars, status bar, and so on.

`Application.UsableWidth` returns or sets the maximum width, in points, that a window can occupy within the application's window. This is the width of the application window less the horizontal space taken up by items such as the vertical scroll bar.

`Application.Version` returns the version number of the application.

`Application.Visible` is a `Boolean` value that either hides the application (`False`) or displays the application (`True`).

`Application.Width` returns or sets the width, in points, of the application window.

`Application.Windows` is the collection of all the application's open Window objects.

`Application.WindowState` returns or sets the state of the main application window. This property is controlled via three built-in constants that vary between applications:

Window State	Excel	Word	PowerPoint
Maximized	xlMaximized	wdWindowStateMaximize	ppWindowMaximized
Minimized	xlMinimized	wdWindowStateMinimize	ppWindowMinimized
Normal	xlNormal	wdWindowStateNormal	ppWindowNormal

Methods of the Application Object

The `Application` object features a few dozen methods that perform actions on the program's environment. Here's a summary of the most common methods:

`Application.CheckSpelling`: When used with the Word or Excel `Application` object, the `CheckSpelling` method checks the spelling of a single word using the following syntax (note that Word's method has a few extra arguments):

`Application.CheckSpelling(`***word***`,`*customDictionary*`,`*ignoreUppercase*`)`

word	The word you want to check.
customDictionary	The filename of a custom dictionary that the application can search if ***word*** wasn't found in the main dictionary.
ignoreUppercase	Set to `True` to tell the application to ignore words in all uppercase.

For example, the code shown in Listing 54.3 gets a word from the user, checks the spelling, and tells the user whether the word is spelled correctly. (You can also use this property with a `Document`, `Worksheet`, or `Range` object, as described in Chapter 56, "Programming Word," and Chapter 57, "Excel VBA Techniques." Also, see Chapter 55 to learn more about the `InputBox` function.)

Listing 54.3. A procedure that checks the spelling of an entered word.

```
Sub SpellCheckTest()
    Dim word2Check As String, result As Boolean
    word2Check = InputBox("Enter a word:")
```

continues

Listing 54.3. continued

```
    result = Application.CheckSpelling(word2Check)
    If result = True Then
        MsgBox "'" & word2Check & "' is spelled correctly!"
    Else
        MsgBox "Oops! '" & word2Check & "' is spelled incorrectly."
    End If
End Sub
```

`Application.EnableCancelKey` controls what the application does when the user presses Esc (or Ctrl+Break), which, under normal circumstances, interrupts the running procedure. If you don't want the user to interrupt a critical section of code, you can disable the Esc key (and Ctrl+Break) by setting the `EnableCancelKey` property to `xlDisabled`. (Note that I'm using the Excel constants here; see the Object Browser for the appropriate constants in other applications.) To restore interrupts to their default state, set the `EnableCancelKey` property to `xlInterrupt`. You can also set `EnableCancelKey` to `xlErrorHandler` to run an error-handler routine established by the `On Error Go To` statement. For details on the `On Error Go To` statement, see Chapter E4 on the CD, "Debugging VBA Procedures."

CAUTION: LEAVE ESC ENABLED DURING TESTING

Wield the `EnableCancelKey` property with care. If you disable the Esc key and your code ends up in an infinite loop, there's no way to shut down the procedure short of shutting down Excel itself. Therefore, while you're testing and building your application, you should always make sure the `EnableCancelKey` property is set to `True`.

`Application.Help` displays the application's Help system.

`Application.Quit` quits the application. If there are any open documents with unsaved changes, the application asks whether you want to save the changes. To prevent this, either save the documents before running the `Quit` method or set the `DisplayAlerts` property to `False`. (In the latter case, note that the application does *not* save changes to the workbooks. Also, Word's version of `Quit` accepts an argument that specifies whether to save changes.)

`Application.Repeat` repeats the user's last action. This is equivalent to selecting Edit | Repeat.

The Window Object

Another object that's common to almost all applications is the Window object, which represents an open window in an application. Note that this isn't the same as an open document. Rather, the Window object is just a container for a document, so the associated properties and methods have no effect on the document data. You can use VBA to change the window state (maximized or minimized), size and move windows, navigate open windows, and much more. In the next section, I show you how to specify a Window object in your code; you'll also look at some Window object properties and methods.

Specifying a Window Object

If you need to perform some action on a window or change a window's properties, you need to tell the application which window you want to use. VBA gives you two ways to do this:

Use the Windows object: The Windows object is the collection of all the open windows in the application. To specify a window, either use its index number (as given by the numbers beside the windows on the application's Windows menu) or enclose the window caption (in other words, the text that appears in the window's title bar) in quotation marks. For example, if the Budget.xls window is listed first in the Window menu, the following two statements are equivalent:

```
Windows(1)
Windows("Budget.xls")
```

Use the ActiveWindow object: The ActiveWindow object represents the window that currently has the focus.

Opening a New Window

If you need to create a new window, use the Window object's NewWindow method:

Window.NewWindow

Window   The Window object from which you want to create the new window.

Note that this argument is optional in some applications. In Word, for example, if you omit *Window*, the active window is used.

Window Object Properties

Here's a rundown of some common properties associated with Window objects:

Window.Caption returns or sets the text that appears in the title bar of the specified *Window*.

Window.Height returns or sets the height, in points, of the specified *Window*.

Window.Left returns or sets the distance, in points, of the left edge of the specified *Window* from the left edge of the application window.

Window.Top returns or sets the distance, in points, of the top of the specified *Window* from the top of the application window.

Window.UsableHeight returns or sets the maximum height, in points, that data can occupy within the specified *Window*.

54

UNDERSTANDING OBJECTS

Window.UsableWidth returns or sets the maximum width, in points, that data can occupy within the specified *Window*.

Window.Visible is a Boolean value that either hides the specified *Window* (False) or displays the *Window* (True).

Window.Width returns or sets the width, in points, of the specified *Window*.

Window.WindowNumber returns the window number of the specified *Window*. For example, a window named Chaptr54.xls:2 has window number 2.

Window.WindowState returns or sets the state of the specified *Window*. See the Application.WindowState property, discussed earlier, for a list of the constants that control this property.

Window Object Methods

Window objects have a few methods that you can use to control your windows programmatically. Here are a few methods that you'll use most often:

Window.Activate activates the specified open *Window*. For example, the following statement activates the Finances.xls window:

```
Windows("Finances.xls").Activate
```

Window.Close closes the specified *Window*.

Window.LargeScroll scrolls through the specified *Window* by screens, using the following syntax:

Window.LargeScroll(*Down, Up, ToRight, ToLeft*)

Window	The Window object you want to scroll.
Down	The number of screens to scroll down.
Up	The number of screens to scroll up.
ToRight	The number of screens to scroll to the right.
ToLeft	The number of screens to scroll to the left.

Window.SmallScroll scrolls through the specified *Window* by lines, using the following syntax:

Window.SmallScroll(*Down, Up, ToRight, ToLeft*)

The arguments are the same as those in the LargeScroll method.

Summary

This chapter discussed the all-important topic of objects and how to work with them in your VBA procedures. After reading some introductory information on objects and the object hierarchy, you learned about the three member types of any object class: properties, methods, and events. I also showed you how to use the Object Browser, how to assign objects to variables, and how to work with multiple properties or methods. I closed this chapter with a look at the properties and methods of the `Application` and `Window` objects. Here's a list of chapters where you'll find related information:

- The `With...End With` statement is an example of a VBA control structure. I discuss a few more of these control structures in Chapter 55, "Controlling VBA Code and Interacting with the User."

- I cover Word's object hierarchy in Chapter 56, "Programming Word."

- Excel's objects are the topic of Chapter 57, "Excel VBA Techniques."

- For PowerPoint objects, check out Chapter 58, "Programming a PowerPoint Presentation."

- If you want to use VBScript to program Web pages, I take you through the Scripting Object Model in Chapter E2 on the CD, "Web Page Programming: ActiveX and VBScript."

- The object hierarchy associated with Outlook's e-mail feature is the subject of Chapter E3 on the CD, "Programming the Outlook Inbox."

- I discuss Access objects in Chapter E5 on the CD, "VBA Database Programming in Access."

- Tables, queries, and other database-related items have their own object hierarchy called Data Access Objects. You'll learn how to work with this model in Chapter E5.

Controlling VBA Code and Interacting with the User

CHAPTER 55

IN THIS CHAPTER

O, it is excellent
To have a giant's strength, but it is tyrannous
To use it like a giant.

—*William Shakespeare*

One of the advantages of writing your own VBA procedures instead of simply recording them is that you end up with much more control over what your code does and how it performs its tasks. In particular, you can create procedures that make decisions based on certain conditions and that can perform *loops*—the repeated running of several statements. This chapter shows you how to work with these so-called *control structures*.

Another advantage of rolling your own code is that you can establish some level of interaction with whoever uses the program. For example, you can display messages and prompt the user for information. The second half of this chapter shows you various VBA methods of interacting with the user.

Code That Makes Decisions

A smart procedure performs tests on its environment and then decides what to do next based on the results of each test. For example, suppose you've written a Function procedure that uses one of its arguments as a divisor in a formula. You should test the argument before using it in the formula to make sure that it isn't 0 (to avoid producing a Division by zero error). If it is zero, you could then display a message that alerts the user to the illegal argument.

Using If...Then to Make True/False Decisions

Simple true/false decisions are handled by the If...Then statement. You can use either the single-line syntax:

```
If condition Then statement
```

or the *block* syntax:

```
If condition Then
    [statements]
End If
```

condition	You can use either a logical expression that returns True or False, or you can use any expression that returns a numeric value. In the latter case, a return value of zero is functionally equivalent to False, and any nonzero value is equivalent to True.
statement(s)	The VBA statement or statements to run if condition returns True. If condition returns False, VBA skips over the statements.

Whether you use the single-line or block syntax depends on the statements you want to run if the *condition* returns a True result. If you have only one statement, you can use either syntax. If you have multiple statements, you must use the block syntax.

Listing 55.1 shows a revised version of the GrossMargin procedure from Chapter 53, "Getting Started with VBA." This version—called GrossMargin2—uses If...Then to check the totalSales variable. The procedure calculates the gross margin only if totalSales is not zero.

Listing 55.1. An If...Then example.

```
Function GrossMargin2()
    Dim totalSales
    Dim totalExpenses
    totalSales = Application.Sum(Range("Sales"))
    totalExpenses = Application.Sum(Range("Expenses"))

    If totalSales <> 0 Then
        GrossMargin2 = (totalSales - totalExpenses) / totalSales
    End If
End Function
```

NOTE: THIS CHAPTER'S CODE LISTINGS

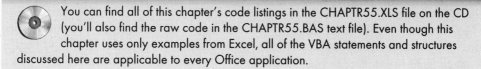

You can find all of this chapter's code listings in the CHAPTR55.XLS file on the CD (you'll also find the raw code in the CHAPTR55.BAS text file). Even though this chapter uses only examples from Excel, all of the VBA statements and structures discussed here are applicable to every Office application.

Using If...Then...Else to Handle a False Result

Using the If...Then statement to make decisions adds a powerful new weapon to your VBA arsenal. However, this technique suffers from an important drawback: A False result only bypasses one or more statements; it doesn't execute any of its own. This is fine in many cases, but there will be times when you need to run one group of statements if the condition returns True and a different group if the result is False. To handle this, you need to use an If...Then...Else statement:

```
If condition Then
    [TrueStatements]
Else
    [FalseStatements]
End If
```

condition	The test that returns True or False.
TrueStatements	The statements to run if *condition* returns True.
FalseStatements	The statements to run if *condition* returns False.

If the *condition* returns True, VBA runs the group of statements between If...Then and Else. If it returns False, VBA runs the group of statements between the Else and the End If.

Let's look at an example. Suppose you want to calculate the future value of a series of regular deposits (using VBA's FV function), but you want to differentiate between monthly deposits and quarterly deposits. Listing 55.2 shows a Function procedure called FutureValue that does the job.

Listing 55.2. A procedure that uses If...Then...Else.

```
Function FutureValue(Rate, Nper, Pmt, Frequency)
    If Frequency = "Monthly" Then
        FutureValue = FV(Rate / 12, Nper * 12, Pmt / 12)
    Else
        FutureValue = FV(Rate / 4, Nper * 4, Pmt / 4)
    End If
End Function
```

The first three arguments—Rate, Nper, and Pmt—are, respectively, the annual interest rate, the number of years in the term of the investment, and the total deposit available annually. The fourth argument, Frequency, is either "Monthly" or "Quarterly". The idea is to adjust the first three arguments based on the Frequency. For example, if Frequency is "Monthly", you need to divide the interest rate by 12, multiply the term by 12, and divide the annual deposit by 12. The If...Then...Else statement runs a test on the Frequency argument:

```
If Frequency = "Monthly" Then
```

If this is True, the function adjusts Rate, Nper, and Pmt accordingly and returns the future value. Otherwise, a quarterly calculation is assumed, and different adjustments are made to the arguments.

Using Select Case to Make Multiple Decisions

The problem with If...Then...Else is that normally you can make only a single decision. This statement calculates a single logical result and performs one of two actions. But there are plenty of situations that require multiple decisions before you can decide which action to take.

One solution is to use the And and Or operators to evaluate a series of logical tests. For example, the FutureValue procedure probably should test the Frequency argument to make sure it's either "Monthly" or "Quarterly" and not something else. The following If...Then statement uses the Or operator to accomplish this:

```
If Frequency = "Monthly" Or Frequency = "Quarterly" Then
```

If Frequency doesn't equal either of these values, the entire condition returns False, and the procedure can return a message to the user.

This approach works, but you're really only performing multiple logical tests; in the end, you're still making a single decision. A better approach is to use VBA's Select Case statement:

```
Select Case TestExpression
   Case FirstExpressionList
        [FirstStatements]
    Case SecondExpressionList
       [SecondStatements]...
    Case Else
        [ElseStatements]
End Select
```

TestExpression	This expression is evaluated at the beginning of the structure. It must return a value (logical, numeric, string, and so on).
ExpressionList	A list of one or more expressions in which each expression is separated by a comma. VBA examines each element in the list to see whether one matches the *TestExpression*. These expressions can take any one of the following forms:

Expression
Expression To Expression
Is LogicalOperator Expression

The To keyword defines a range of values (for example, 1 To 10). The Is keyword defines an open-ended range of values (for example, Is >= 100).

Statements	These are the statements VBA runs if any part of the associated *ExpressionList* matches the *TestExpression*. VBA runs the optional *ElseStatements* if no *ExpressionList* matches the *TestExpression*.

NOTE: HANDLING MULTIPLE MATCHES

If more than one *ExpressionList* contains an element that matches the *TestExpression*, VBA runs only the statements associated with the *ExpressionList* that appears first in the Select Case structure.

For example, suppose you want to write a procedure that converts a raw score into a letter grade according to the following table:

Raw Score	Letter Grade
80 and over	A
Between 70 and 79	B
Between 60 and 69	C
Between 50 and 59	D
Less than 50	F

Listing 55.3 shows the `LetterGrade` procedure, which uses a `Select Case` statement to make the conversion.

Listing 55.3. A procedure that makes multiple decisions using a `Select Case` statement.

```
Function LetterGrade(rawScore)
    Select Case rawScore
        Case Is < 0
            LetterGrade = "ERROR! Score less than 0!"
        Case Is < 50
            LetterGrade = "F"
        Case Is < 60
            LetterGrade = "D"
        Case Is < 70
            LetterGrade = "C"
        Case Is < 80
            LetterGrade = "B"
        Case Is <= 100
            LetterGrade = "A"
        Case Else
            LetterGrade = "ERROR! Score greater than 100!"
    End Select
End Function
```

Functions That Make Decisions

Much of what is discussed in this chapter involves ways to make your procedures cleaner and more efficient. These are laudable goals for a whole host of reasons, but the following are the main ones:

- Your code will execute faster.
- You'll have less code to type.
- Your code will be easier to read and maintain.

This section looks at three powerful VBA functions that can increase the efficiency of your procedures: `IIf`, `Choose`, and `Switch`.

The IIf Function

You've seen how the decision-making prowess of the If...Then...Else structure lets you create "intelligent" procedures that can respond appropriately to different situations. However, sometimes If...Then...Else just isn't efficient. For example, suppose you want to test the computer on which your code is running to see if it has a flawed Pentium chip. (Some older Pentium processors contain a bug in their floating-point unit that causes incorrect calculations in some rare circumstances.) Here's a code fragment that includes an If...Then...Else structure that performs this test:

```
Dim flawedPentium As Boolean
If (4195835 - (4195835/3145727) * 3145727) <> 0 Then
    flawedPentium = True
Else
    flawedPentium = False
End If
```

As it stands, there is nothing wrong with this code. However, it seems like a lot of work to go through just to assign a value to a variable. For these types of situations, VBA 5.0 has a new IIf function that's more efficient. IIf, which stands for "Inline If," performs a simple If test on a single line:

IIf (***condition***, ***TrueResult***, ***FalseResult***)

condition	A logical expression that returns True or False.
TrueResult	The value returned by the function if ***condition*** is True.
FalseResult	The value returned by the function if ***condition*** is False.

Listing 55.4 shows a function procedure that checks for a faulty Pentium machine by using IIf to replace the If...Then...Else statement just shown.

Listing 55.4. A function that uses IIf to test for a faulty Pentium chip.

```
Function FlawedPentium() As Boolean
    FlawedPentium = IIf((4195835 - (4195835/3145727) * 3145727), True, False)
End Function
```

If the calculation returns a nonzero value, the chip is flawed; therefore, IIf returns True. Otherwise, the chip is okay, so IIf returns False.

The Choose Function

In the preceding section, I showed you how the IIf function is an efficient replacement for If...Then...Else when all you need to do is assign a value to a variable based on the results of the test. Suppose now you have a similar situation with the Select Case structure. In other words, you want to test a number of possible values and assign the result to a variable.

55

CONTROLLING VBA CODE

VBA has a `Weekday` function that returns the current day of the week as a number. What if you want to convert that number into the name of the day (convert 1 into Sunday, for example)? Here's a procedure fragment that will do so:

```
Dim weekdayName As String
Select Case Weekday(Now)
    Case 1
        weekdayName = "Sunday"
    Case 2
        weekdayName = "Monday"
    Case 3
        weekdayName = "Tuesday"
    Case 4
        weekdayName = "Wednesday"
    Case 5
        weekdayName = "Thursday"
    Case 6
        weekdayName = "Friday"
    Case 7
        weekdayName = "Saturday"
End Select
```

Again, this seems like *way* too much effort for a simple variable assignment. And, in fact, it *is* too much work now that VBA 5.0's new `Choose` function is available. `Choose` encapsulates the essence of the preceding `Select Case` structure—the test value and the various possible results—into a single statement. Here's the syntax:

```
Choose(index, value1, value2,...)
```

index	A numeric expression that determines which of the values in the list is returned. If *index* is 1, *value1* is returned. If *index* is 2, *value2* is returned (and so on).
value1, value2...	A list of values from which `Choose` selects the return value. The values can be any valid VBA expression.

Listing 55.5 shows a function called `WeekdayName` that returns the day name by using `Choose` to replace the `Select Case` structure just shown.

Listing 55.5. A function that uses the Choose function to select from a list of values.

```
Function WeekdayName(weekdayNum As Integer) As String
    WeekdayName = Choose(weekdayNum, "Sunday", "Monday", _
        "Tuesday", "Wednesday", "Thursday", "Friday", "Saturday")
End Function
```

The Switch Function

`Choose` is a welcome addition to the VBA function library, but its use it limited because of two constraints:

- You can use `Choose` only when the ***index*** argument is a number or a numeric expression.
- `Choose` can't handle logical expressions.

To illustrate why the last point is important, consider the `Select Case` structure used earlier in this chapter to convert a test score into a letter grade:

```
Select Case rawScore
    Case Is < 0
        LetterGrade = "ERROR! Score less than 0!"
    Case Is < 50
        LetterGrade = "F"
    Case Is < 60
        LetterGrade = "D"
    Case Is < 70
        LetterGrade = "C"
    Case Is < 80
        LetterGrade = "B"
    Case Is <= 100
        LetterGrade = "A"
    Case Else
        LetterGrade = "ERROR! Score greater than 100!"
End Select
```

At first blush, this structure seems to satisfy the same inefficiency criteria I mentioned earlier for `If...Then...Else` and `Select Case`. In other words, each `Case` runs only a single statement, and that statement serves only to assign a value to a variable. The difference, though, is that the `Case` statements use logical expressions, so you can't use `Choose` to make this code more efficient.

However, you *can* use VBA 5.0's new `Switch` function to do the job:

```
Switch(expr1, value1, expr2, value2,...)
```

expr1, expr2...	These are logical expressions that determine which of the values in the list is returned. If ***expr1*** is `True`, ***value1*** is returned. If ***expr2*** is `True`, ***value2*** is returned (and so on).
value1, value2...	A list of values from which `Switch` selects the return value. These values can be any valid VBA expression.

`Switch` trudges through the logical expressions from left to right. When it comes across the first `True` expression, it returns the value that appears immediately after the expression. Listing 55.6 puts `Switch` to work to create a more efficient version of the `LetterGrade` function.

Listing 55.6. A procedure that uses the Switch function to convert a test score into a letter grade.

```
Function LetterGrade2(rawScore As Integer) As String
    LetterGrade2 = Switch( _
        rawScore < 0, "ERROR! Score less than 0!", _
        rawScore < 50, "F", _
        rawScore < 60, "D", _
        rawScore < 70, "C", _
        rawScore < 80, "B", _
        rawScore <= 100, "A", _
        rawScore > 100, "ERROR! Score greater than 100!")
End Function
```

Code That Loops

You've seen in this chapter and in previous chapters that it makes sense to divide your VBA chores and place them in separate procedures or functions. That way, you need to write the code only once and then call it any time you need it. This is known in the trade as *modular programming,* and it saves time and effort by helping you avoid reinventing too many wheels.

There are also wheels to avoid reinventing *within* your procedures and functions. For example, consider the following code fragment:

```
MsgBox "The time is now " & Time
Application.Wait Now + TimeValue("00:00:05")
MsgBox "The time is now " & Time
Application.Wait Now + TimeValue("00:00:05")
MsgBox "The time is now " & Time
Application.Wait Now + TimeValue("00:00:05")
```

> **NOTE: THE WAIT METHOD**
>
> This code fragment uses the Excel `Application` object's `Wait` method to produce a delay. The argument `Now + TimeValue("00:00:05")` pauses the procedure for about five seconds before continuing.

This code does nothing more than display the time, delay for five seconds, and repeat this two more times. Besides being decidedly useless, this code just reeks of inefficiency. It's clear that a far better approach would be to take just the first two statements and somehow get VBA to repeat them as many times as necessary.

The good news is that not only is it possible to do this, but VBA also gives you a number of different methods of performing this so-called *loop.* You'll investigate each of these methods in the next few sections.

Using Do...Loop Structures

What do you do when you need to loop but you don't know in advance how many times to repeat the loop? This could happen if, for example, you want to loop only until a certain condition is met, such as encountering a blank cell. The solution is to use a Do...Loop.

The Do...Loop has four different syntaxes:

```Do While condition```
```[statements]```
```Loop```
	Checks *condition* before entering the loop. Executes the *statements* only while *condition* is True.

```Do```
```[statements]```
```Loop While condition```
	Checks *condition* after running through the loop once. Executes the *statements* only while *condition* is True. Use this form when you want the loop to be processed at least once.

```Do Until condition```
```[statements]```
```Loop```
	Checks *condition* before entering the loop. Executes the *statements* only while *condition* is False.

```Do```
```[statements]```
```Loop Until condition```
	Checks *condition* after running through the loop once. Executes the *statements* only while *condition* is False. Again, use this form when you want the loop to be processed at least once.

Listing 55.7 shows a procedure called BigNumbers that runs down a worksheet column and changes the font color to magenta whenever a cell contains a number greater than or equal to 1,000.

Listing 55.7. A procedure that uses a Do...Loop to process cells until it encounters a blank cell.

```
Sub BigNumbers()
    Dim rowNum As Integer, colNum As Integer, currCell As Range
    rowNum = ActiveCell.Row                              'Initialize row #
    colNum = ActiveCell.Column                           'Initialize column #
    Set currCell = ActiveSheet.Cells(rowNum, colNum)     'Get first cell
    Do While currCell.Value <> ""                        'Do while not empty
        If IsNumeric(currCell.Value) Then                'If it's a number,
            If currCell.Value >= 1000 Then               'and it's a big one,
                currCell.Font.Color = RGB(255, 0, 255)   'color font magenta
            End If
        End If
        rowNum = rowNum + 1                              'Increment row #
        Set currCell = ActiveSheet.Cells(rowNum, colNum) 'Get next cell
    Loop
End Sub
```

55

CONTROLLING
VBA CODE

The idea is to loop until the procedure encounters a blank cell. This is controlled by the following Do While statement:

```
Do While currCell.Value <> ""
```

currCell is an object variable that is Set using the Cells method (which I described in the preceding chapter). Next, the first If...Then uses the IsNumeric function to check if the cell contains a number, and the second If...Then checks if the number is greater than or equal to 1,000. If both conditions are True, the font color is set to magenta—RGB(255,0,255).

Using For...Next Loops

The most common type of loop is the For...Next loop. You use it when you know exactly how many times you want to repeat a group of statements. The structure of a For...Next loop looks like this:

```
For counter = start To end [Step increment]
    [statements]
Next [counter]
```

counter	A numeric variable used as a *loop counter*—a number that counts how many times the procedure has gone through the loop.
start	The initial value of counter. This is usually 1, but you can enter any value.
end	The final value of counter.
increment	This optional value defines an increment for the loop counter. If you leave this out, the default value is 1. Use a negative value to decrement counter.
statements	The statements to execute each time through the loop.

The basic idea is simple. When VBA encounters the For...Next statement, it follows this five-step process:

1. Set counter equal to start.
2. Test counter. If it's greater than end, exit the loop (that is, process the first statement after the Next statement). Otherwise, continue. If increment is negative, VBA checks to see whether counter is less than end.
3. Execute each statement between the For and Next statements.
4. Add increment to counter. Add 1 to counter if increment is not specified.
5. Repeat steps 2 through 4 until done.

Listing 55.8 shows a simple Sub procedure—LoopTest—that uses a For...Next statement. Each time through the loop, the procedure uses the StatusBar property to display the value of Counter (the loop counter) in the status bar. (See the section "Using VBA to Get and Display Information" to learn more about the `StatusBar` property.) When you run this procedure, `Counter` gets incremented by 1 each time through the loop, and the new value gets displayed in the status line.

Listing 55.8. A simple For...Next loop.

```
Sub LoopTest()
    Dim counter
    For counter = 1 To 10
    'Display the message
        Application.StatusBar = "Counter value: " & counter
    ' Wait for 1 second
        Application.Wait Now + TimeValue("00:00:01")
    Next counter
    Application.StatusBar = False
End Sub
```

The following are some notes on `For...Next` loops:

- If you use a positive number for *increment* (or if you omit *increment*), *end* must be greater than or equal to *start*. If you use a negative number for *increment, end* must be less than or equal to *start*.

- If *start* equals *end,* the loop will execute once.

- As with `If...Then...Else` structures, indent the statements inside a `For...Next` loop to increase readability.

- To keep to a minimum the number of variables defined in a procedure, always try to use the same name for all your `For...Next` loop counters. The letters *i* through *n* traditionally are used for counters in programming. For greater clarity, you might want to use names such as `counter`.

- For the fastest loops, don't use the counter name after the `Next` statement. If you'd like to keep the counter name for clarity (which I recommend), precede the name with an apostrophe (') to comment out the name, like this:

```
For counter = 1 To 10
    [statements]
Next 'counter
```

- If you need to break out of a `For...Next` loop before the defined number of repetitions is complete, use the `Exit For` statement, described in the section "Using `Exit For` or `Exit Do` to Exit a Loop."

Using For Each...Next Loops

A useful variation of the `For...Next` loop is the `For Each...Next` loop, which operates on a collection of objects. You don't need a loop counter, because VBA just loops through the individual

55

CONTROLLING
VBA CODE

elements in the collection and performs on each element whatever operations are inside the loop. Here's the structure of the basic For Each...Next loop:

```
For Each element In group
    [statements]
Next [element]
```

element	A variable used to hold the name of each element in the collection.
group	The name of the collection.
statements	The statements to be executed for each element in the collection.

As an example, let's create a command procedure that converts a range of text into proper case (that is, the first letter of each word is capitalized). This function can come in handy if you import mainframe text into your worksheets, because mainframe reports usually appear entirely in uppercase. This process involves three steps:

1. Loop through the selected range with For Each...Next.

2. Convert each cell's text to proper case. Use Excel's PROPER() function to handle this:

   PROPER(*text*)

   text is the text to convert to proper case.

3. Enter the converted text into the selected cell. You do so by setting the Range object's Value property.

Listing 55.9 shows the resulting procedure, ConvertToProper. Note that this procedure uses the Selection object to represent the currently selected range.

Listing 55.9. A Sub procedure that uses For Each...Next to loop through a selection and convert each cell to proper case.

```
Sub ConvertToProper()
    Dim cellObject As Object
    For Each cellObject In Selection
        cellObject.Value = Application.Proper(cellObject)
    Next
End Sub
```

Using Exit For or Exit Do to Exit a Loop

Most loops run their natural course and then the procedure moves on. There might be times, however, when you want to exit a loop prematurely. For example, you might come across a certain type of value, or an error might occur, or the user might enter an unexpected value. To exit a For...Next loop or a For Each...Next loop, use the Exit For statement. To exit a Do...Loop, use the Exit Do statement.

Listing 55.10 shows a revised version of the `BigNumbers` procedure, which exits the `Do...Loop` if it comes across a cell that isn't a number.

Listing 55.10. In this version of the `BigNumbers` procedure, the `Do...Loop` is terminated with the `Exit Do` statement if the current cell isn't a number.

```
Sub BigNumbers2()
    Dim rowNum As Integer, colNum As Integer, currCell As Range
    rowNum = ActiveCell.Row                         'Initialize row #
    colNum = ActiveCell.Column                      'Initialize column #
    Set currCell = ActiveSheet.Cells(rowNum, colNum)  'Get first cell
    Do While currCell.Value <> ""                   'Do while not empty
        If IsNumeric(currCell.Value) Then           'If it's a number,
            If currCell.Value >= 1000 Then          'and it's a big one,
                currCell.Font.Color = RGB(255, 0, 255)  'color font magenta
            End If
        Else                                        'If it's not,
            Exit Do                                 'exit the loop
        End If
        rowNum = rowNum + 1                         'Increment row #
        Set currCell = ActiveSheet.Cells(rowNum, colNum) 'Get next cell
    Loop
End Sub
```

NOTE: EXITING PROCEDURES

If you want to exit a procedure before reaching `End Sub` or `End Function`, use `Exit Sub` or `Exit Function`.

Using VBA to Get and Display Information

A well-designed application not only makes intelligent decisions and streamlines code with loops but also keeps the user involved. It should display messages at appropriate times and ask the user for input. When interacting with the application, the user feels that he or she is a part of the process and has some control over what the program does—which means that the user won't lose interest in the program and will be less likely to make careless mistakes. The rest of this chapter takes you through various methods of giving and receiving user feedback.

Displaying Information to the User

Displaying information is one of the best (and easiest) ways to keep your users involved. If an operation will take a long time, keep the user informed of the operation's time and progress. If a user makes an error (for example, enters the wrong argument in a user-defined function), he should be gently admonished so that he will be less likely to repeat the error.

VBA gives you three main ways to display information: the `Beep` statement, the `StatusBar` property, and the `MsgBox` function.

Beeping the Speaker

VBA's most rudimentary form of communication is the simple, attention-getting beep. It's Excel's way of saying "Ahem!" or "Excuse me!" and it's handled, appropriately enough, by the Beep statement.

For example, Listing 55.11 shows the RecalcAll procedure that recalculates all the open workbooks and then sounds three beeps to mark the end of the process.

Listing 55.11. A procedure that recalculates all open workbooks and then sounds three beeps.

```
Sub RecalcAll()
    Dim i As Integer
    Application.Calculate
    For i = 1 To 3
        Beep
        ' Pause for 2 seconds between beeps
        Application.Wait Now + TimeValue("00:00:02")
    Next i
End Sub
```

Displaying a Message in the Status Bar

In Word and Excel, you can use the Application object's StatusBar property to display text messages in the status bar at the bottom of the screen. This gives you an easy way to keep the user informed about what a procedure is doing or how much is left to process.

Listing 55.12, an example of the StatusBar property, shows a revised version of the ConvertToProper procedure. The goal is to display a status bar message of the form Converting cell *x* of *y*, in which *x* is the number of cells converted so far and *y* is the total number of cells to be converted.

Listing 55.12. A procedure that uses the StatusBar property to inform the user of the progress of the operation.

```
Sub ConvertToProper2()
    Dim cellVar As Object
    Dim cellsConverted As Integer, totalCells As Integer
    ' Initialize some variables
    cellsConverted = 0
    totalCells = Selection.Count
    For Each cellVar In Selection
        cellVar.Formula = Application.Proper(cellVar)
        cellsConverted = cellsConverted + 1
        Application.StatusBar = "Converting cell " & _
                                cellsConverted & " of " & _
                                totalCells
    Next
    Application.StatusBar = False
End Sub
```

The `cellsConverted` variable tracks the number of cells converted, and the `totalsCells` variable stores the total number of cells in the selection (given by `Selection.Count`).

The `For Each...Next` loop does three things:

- It converts one cell at a time to proper case.
- It increments the `cellsConverted` variable.
- It sets the `StatusBar` property to display the progress of the operation. (Note the use of the concatenation operator (`&`) to combine text and variable values.)

When the loop is done, the procedure sets the `StatusBar` property to `False` to clear the status bar.

Displaying a Message Using `MsgBox`

The problem with using the `StatusBar` property to display messages is that it's often a bit too subtle. Unless the user knows to look in the status bar, he or she might miss your messages altogether. When the user really needs to see a message, you can use the `MsgBox` function:

`MsgBox(`**`prompt`**`,buttons,title,helpFile,context)`

`prompt`	The message you want to display in the dialog box.
`buttons`	A number or constant that specifies, among other things, the command buttons that appear in the dialog. (See the next section.) The default value is `0`.
`title`	The text that appears in the dialog box title bar. If you omit the title, VBA uses "Microsoft Excel."
`helpFile`	The text that specifies the Help file that contains the custom help topic. If you enter `helpFile`, you also have to include `context`. If you include `helpFile`, a Help button appears in the dialog box.
`context`	A number that identifies the help topic in `helpFile`.

For example, the following statement displays the message dialog box shown in Figure 55.1:

`MsgBox "You must enter a number between 1 and 100!",,"Warning"`

FIGURE 55.1.

A simple message dialog box produced by the `MsgBox` *function.*

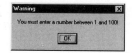

NOTE: PARENTHESES REMINDER

The MsgBox function, like all VBA functions, needs parentheses around its arguments only when you use the function's return value. See the section later in this chapter called "Getting Return Values from the Message Dialog Box."

TIP: BREAK PROMPT TEXT INTO MULTIPLE LINES

For long prompts, VBA wraps the text inside the dialog box. If you would like to create your own line breaks, use VBA's Chr function and the carriage-return character (ASCII 13) between each line:

```
MsgBox "First line" & Chr(13) & "Second line"
```

Setting the Style of the Message

The default message dialog box displays only an OK button. You can include other buttons and icons in the dialog box by using different values for the *buttons* parameter. Table 55.1 lists the available options.

Table 55.1. The MsgBox *buttons* parameter options.

Constant	Value	Description
		Buttons
vbOKOnly	0	Displays only an OK button (the default).
vbOKCancel	1	Displays the OK and Cancel buttons.
vbAbortRetryIgnore	2	Displays the Abort, Retry, and Ignore buttons.
vbYesNoCancel	3	Displays the Yes, No, and Cancel buttons.
vbYesNo	4	Displays the Yes and No buttons.
vbRetryCancel	5	Displays the Retry and Cancel buttons.
		Icons
vbCritical	16	Displays the Critical Message icon.
vbQuestion	32	Displays the Warning Query icon.
vbExclamation	48	Displays the Warning Message icon.
vbInformation	64	Displays the Information Message icon.
vbDefaultButton1	0	The first button is the default.
vbDefaultButton2	256	The second button is the default.
vbDefaultButton3	512	The third button is the default.

Constant	Value	Description
		Icons
`vbApplicationModal`	0	The user must respond to the message box before continuing work in the current application.
`vbSystemModal`	4096	All applications are suspended until the user responds to the message box.

You derive the *buttons* argument in one of two ways:

- By adding up the values for each option
- By using the VBA constants separated by plus signs (+)

For example, Listing 55.13 shows a procedure named `ButtonTest`, and Figure 55.2 shows the resulting dialog box. Here, three variables—*msgPrompt, msgButtons,* and *msgTitle*—store the values for the `MsgBox` function's **prompt,** *buttons,* and *title* arguments. In particular, the following statement derives the *buttons* argument:

```
msgButtons = vbYesNoCancel + vbQuestion + vbDefaultButton2
```

You also could derive the *buttons* argument by adding up the values that these constants represent (3, 32, and 256, respectively), but the procedure becomes less readable that way.

Listing 55.13. A procedure that creates a message dialog box.

```
Sub ButtonTest()
    Dim msgPrompt As String, msgTitle As String
    Dim msgButtons As Integer, msgResult As Integer
    msgPrompt = "Are you sure you want to copy" & Chr(13) & _
                "the selected files to drive A?"
    msgButtons = vbYesNoCancel + vbQuestion + vbDefaultButton2
    msgTitle = "Copy Files"
    msgResult = MsgBox(msgPrompt, msgButtons, msgTitle)
End Sub
```

FIGURE 55.2.

The dialog box that is displayed when you run the code in Listing 55.13.

Getting Return Values from the Message Dialog Box

A message dialog box that displays only an OK button is straightforward. The user either clicks OK or presses Enter to remove the dialog from the screen. The multibutton styles are a little different, however; the user has a choice of buttons to select, and your procedure should have a way to find out what the user chose.

55

CONTROLLING
VBA CODE

You do this by storing the MsgBox function's return value in a variable. Table 55.2 lists the seven possibilities.

Table 55.2. The MsgBox function's return values.

Constant	Value	Button Selected
vbOK	1	OK
vbCancel	2	Cancel
vbAbort	3	Abort
vbRetry	4	Retry
vbIgnore	5	Ignore
vbYes	6	Yes
vbNo	7	No

To process the return value, you can use an If...Then...Else or Select Case structure to test for the appropriate values. For example, the ButtonTest procedure shown earlier used a variable called *msgResult* to store the return value of the MsgBox function. Listing 55.14 shows a revised version of ButtonTest that uses a Select Case statement to test for the three possible return values. (Note that the vbYes case runs a procedure named CopyFiles. The ButtonTest procedure assumes that the CopyFiles procedure already exists elsewhere in the module.)

Listing 55.14. This example uses Select Case to test the return values of the MsgBox function.

```
Sub ButtonTest2()
    Dim msgPrompt As String, msgTitle As String
    Dim msgButtons As Integer, msgResult As Integer
    msgPrompt = "Are you sure you want to copy" & Chr(13) & _
                "the selected files to drive A?"
msgButtons = vbYesNoCancel + vbQuestion + vbDefaultButton2
    msgTitle = "Copy Files"
    msgResult = MsgBox(msgPrompt, msgButtons, msgTitle)
    Select Case msgResult
        Case vbYes
            CopyFiles
        Case vbNo
            Exit Sub
        Case vbCancel
            Application.Quit
    End Select
End Sub
```

Getting Input from the User

As you've seen, the MsgBox function lets your procedures interact with the user and get some feedback. Unfortunately, this method limits you to simple command-button responses. For more varied user input, you need to use more sophisticated techniques.

Prompting the User for Input

The `InputBox` function displays a dialog box with a message that prompts the user to enter data, and it provides a text box for the data itself. The syntax for this method appears as the following:

`InputBox(`**`prompt`**`,title,default,xpos,ypos,helpFile,context)`

`prompt`	The message you want to display in the dialog box.
`title`	The text that appears in the dialog box title bar. The default value is the null string (nothing).
`default`	The default value displayed in the text box. If you omit `default`, the text box is displayed empty.
`xpos`	The horizontal position of the dialog box from the left edge of the screen. The value is measured in points (there are 72 points in an inch). If you omit `xpos`, the dialog box is centered horizontally.
`ypos`	The vertical position, in points, from the top of the screen. If you omit `ypos`, the dialog is centered vertically in the current window.
`helpFile`	The text specifying the Help file that contains the custom help topic. If you enter `helpFile`, you also have to include `context`. If you include `helpFile`, a Help button appears in the dialog box.
`context`	A number that identifies the help topic in `helpFile`.

For example, Listing 55.15 shows a procedure called `GetInterestRate` that uses the `InputBox` method to prompt the user for an interest rate value. Figure 55.3 shows the dialog box that appears.

Listing 55.15. A procedure that prompts the user for an interest rate value.

```
Function GetInterestRate()
    Dim done As Boolean
    ' Initialize the loop variable
    done = False
    While Not done
        ' Get the interest rate
        GetInterestRate = Application.InputBox( _
                    prompt:="Enter an interest rate between 0 and 1:", _
                    title:="Enter Interest Rate", _
                    type:=1)
        ' First, check to see if the user cancelled
        If GetInterestRate = "" Then
            Exit Function
        Else
            ' Make sure the entered rate is betwen 0 and 1
```

continues

55

CONTROLLING
VBA CODE

Listing 55.15. continued

```
            If GetInterestRate >= 0 And GetInterestRate <= 1 Then
                done = True
            End If
        End If
    Wend
End Function
```

FIGURE 55.3.

*A dialog box generated
by the* InputBox
function.

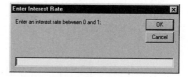

The InputBox method returns one of the following values:

- The value entered into the text box if the user clicked OK
- An empty string if the user clicked Cancel

In Listing 55.15, the result of the InputBox method is stored in the GetInterestRate function. The procedure first checks to see if InputBox returned the empty string (""). If so, the Exit Function statement bails out of the procedure. Otherwise, an If...Then statement checks to make sure the number is between 0 and 1. If it is, the done variable is set to True so that the While...Wend loop will exit; if the number isn't between 0 and 1, the procedure loops and the dialog box is redisplayed.

NOTE

Excel has its own version of InputBox that's an Application object method. It has the same syntax as the VBA InputBox function, except that it tacks on an extra argument—*type*:

Application.InputBox(**prompt**,title,default,xpos,ypos,helpFile,context,type)

   type   A number that specifies the data type of the return value, as follows:

type	Data Type
0	Formula
1	Number
2	Text (the default)
4	Boolean (True or False)
8	Reference (a Range object)
16	Error value
32	An array of values

Accessing an Application's Built-In Dialog Boxes

Many VBA methods are known as *dialog box equivalents* because they let you select the same options that are available in an application's built-in dialog boxes. Using dialog box equivalents works fine if your procedure knows which options to select, but there are times when you might want the user to specify some of the dialog box options.

For example, if your procedure will print a document (using the `PrintOut` method), you might need to know how many copies the user wants or how many pages to print. You could use the `InputBox` method to get this data, but it's usually easier to just display the Print dialog box.

The built-in dialog boxes are Dialog objects, and `Dialogs` is the collection of all the built-in dialog boxes. To reference a particular dialog box, use one of the predefined application constants. Table 55.3 lists a few of the more common ones from Word and Excel.

Table 55.3. Some of Excel's built-in dialog box constants.

Word Constant	Excel Constant	Dialog Box
wdDialogFormatFont	xlDialogFont	Font
wdDialogFileNew	xlDialogNew	New
wdDialogFileOpen	xlDialogOpen	Open
wdDialogFilePageSetup	xlDialogPageSetup	Page Setup
wdDialogEditPasteSpecial	xlDialogPasteSpecial	Paste Special
wdDialogFilePrint	xlDialogPrint	Print
wdDialogFilePrintSetup	xlDialogPrinterSetup	Printer Setup
wdDialogFileSaveAs	xlDialogSaveAs	Save As
wdDialogInsertObject	xlDialogObject	Object
wdDialogFormatStyle	xlDialogStyle	Style
wdDialog	xlDialogSort	Sort

NOTE: DIALOG BOX CONSTANTS

To see a complete list of constants for Word and Excel's built-in dialog boxes, first open the Object Browser. In the list of libraries, select the application, and then highlight <globals> in the Classes list. In the Member list, look for the *xx*Dialog constants, where *xx* varies between applications: wdDialog for Word, xlDialog for Excel.

55

CONTROLLING
VBA CODE

To display any of these dialog boxes, use the Dialog object's Show method. For example, the following statement displays Excel's Print dialog box:

```
Application.Dialogs(xlDialogPrint).Show
```

If the user clicks Cancel to exit the dialog box, the Show method returns False. This means that you can use Show inside an If statement to determine what the user did:

```
If Not Application.Dialogs(xlDialogPrint).Show Then
    MsgBox "File was not printed"
End If
```

Summary

This chapter showed you how to take command of your VBA code by using control structures and user interaction. To make logical (true/false) decisions, use If...Then or If...Then...Else. To make multiple decisions, use Select Case. I also included material on three decision-making functions: IIf, Choose, and Switch. To loop through a section of code, use Do...Loop, For...Next, or For Each...Next loops. If you need to exit a loop, use either the Exit For or Exit Do statement. User interaction is handled by the Beep function, the MsgBox function, the InputBox method, and the built-in dialog boxes.

To get some related information, tune in to the following chapters:

- This chapter used quite a few Excel objects as examples. To get the full scoop on these and other Excel objects, see Chapter 57, "Excel VBA Techniques."

- To get maximum control over your code's user interaction, you'll need to build your own custom dialog boxes. To find out how, see Chapter 59, "Creating a Custom User Interface."

- A big part of procedure control involves anticipating potential user errors. You'll learn more about this topic in Chapter E4 on the CD, "Debugging VBA Procedures."

Programming Word

IN THIS CHAPTER

Writing is a dreadful Labour, yet not so dreadful as Idleness.

—*Thomas Carlyle*

With the advent of Office 97, Word for Windows programmers finally get to ditch the hoary WordBasic macro language in favor of the relative comforts and power of VBA. Now developers building Word-based applications and power users writing Word macros can take advantage of a modern language that exposes a vast array of objects—from documents to paragraphs to sentences. Not only that, but the simplistic macro development window that was the bane of all Word programmers has given way to the Visual Basic Editor and its large collection of useful tools. Similarly, the clunky Dialog Box Editor has now been relegated to the dustbin of Word programming history and replaced by the user forms of VBA 5.0. (See Chapter 59, "Creating a Custom User Interface.")

All of this is great news for people who program Word and who have grown tired of the all-too-glaring limitations of WordBasic. This chapter will serve as your introduction to the Word-specific capabilities of VBA. In case you've used WordBasic in the past, I begin with a look at the transition to VBA so you can get up to speed quickly. The rest of this chapter examines some specific Word objects and their properties, methods, and events.

The Transition from WordBasic to VBA

The first thing you need to know about the transition from the WordBasic way of doing things to the VBA way is that you don't have to bother with it if you really don't want to. In other words, if you prefer to keep programming Word via WordBasic, you can go right ahead because VBA has a built-in mechanism that lets you continue using WordBasic commands and syntax in your macros. This mechanism is a new object called WordBasic that includes methods that correspond to all the WordBasic statements and functions.

For example, consider the following snippet of WordBasic code:

```
StartOfDocument
Insert "Introduction"
Style "Heading 1"
InsertPara
```

These statements move the insertion point to the top of the document, insert the word "Introduction" and format it with the Heading 1 style, and insert a new paragraph. Here's how the equivalent statements look in VBA:

```
With WordBasic
    .StartOfDocument
    .Insert "Introduction"
    .Style "Heading 1"
    .InsertPara
End With
```

As you can see, all you have to do is append WordBasic. to a WordBasic statement to transform it into a method of the WordBasic object.

In fact, this is precisely how Word handles existing WordBasic macros. If you open a template that contains WordBasic procedures and functions, you see a few messages in Word's status bar telling you that the program is "converting" these macros. All this means is that Word is tacking on `WordBasic.` to each statement.

Of course, if you truly want to unleash Word for Windows programming, you need to leave WordBasic behind and start using native VBA statements and functions. The biggest advantage of doing this (and the biggest hurdle WordBasic programmers face) is that you gain access to all of Word's objects. WordBasic really is just a list of a few hundred commands that all exist on the same "level" without any kind of hierarchy. In VBA, on the other hand, statements must take into account the hierarchical nature of the Word object model, from the `Application` object at the top, down through lower-level objects such as Document and Paragraph.

This means you need to let go of the traditional way of programming in WordBasic, which involves moving the insertion point to a specific spot and then, say, inserting text or a paragraph or selecting a section of text and then applying formatting to that selection. With Word's object model, you can usually refer to objects without moving the insertion point or selecting anything. For example, here's a VBA code fragment that performs the same tasks as the WordBasic fragment shown previously:

```
With ActiveDocument.Paragraphs(1).Range
    .InsertBefore "Introduction"
    .Style = "Heading 1"
    .InsertParagraphAfter
End With
```

With these ideas in mind, you can now turn to the real meat of this chapter: the Word for Windows object model. The sheer size of the hierarchy (Word has nearly 200 separate objects) prevents me from covering every object, property, and method. However, you'll spend the majority of your Word programming time dealing with a few key objects, and it's to these objects that I turn my attention in the rest of this chapter.

Word's Application Object

In Chapter 54, "Understanding Objects," you learned about some `Application` object properties and methods that are common to all VBA-enabled applications. However, Word also has quite a few unique properties and methods; I discuss some of them in this section.

Properties of the Application Object

Here's a rundown of a few `Application` object properties that might prove useful in your VBA applications:

> `ActivePrinter` returns or sets the name of the active printer. (Note that to set the active printer, you must specify the name of an existing Windows printer.) The following statement sets the active printer:
>
> ```
> ActivePrinter = "HP LaserJet 5P/5MP PostScript local on LPT1:"
> ```

`Application.CapsLock` returns `True` if the Caps Lock key is activated.

`Application.NumLock` returns `True` if the Num Lock key is activated.

`Application.StartupPath` returns or sets the path of Word's startup folder.

`Application.UserInitials` returns or sets the initials of the user. Word uses these initials when constructing comment marks.

Methods of the Application Object

The Word `Application` object comes with quite a few methods. Here are a few of the more useful ones:

`Application.ChangeFileOpenDirectory` specifies the folder that appears by default in the Open dialog box the next time the user selects File | Open. Here's the syntax:

`Application.ChangeFileOpenDirectory(`***Path***`)`

Path	The path of the folder that appears in the Open dialog box.

In the following example, the `Dir` function is first used to test whether a folder exists. If it does, the `ChangeFileOpenDirectory` method sets the folder as the File | Open default:

```
If Dir("C:\My Documents\") <> "" Then
    Application.ChangeFileOpenDirectory "C:\My Documents\"
End If
```

`Application.OnTime` runs a procedure at a specified time, using the following syntax:

`Application.OnTime(`***When, Name,*** `Tolerance)`

When	The time (and date, if necessary) you want the procedure to run. Enter a date/time serial number.
Name	The name (entered as text) of the procedure to run when the time given by ***When*** arrives.
`Tolerance`	If Word isn't ready to run the procedure at ***When***, it keeps trying for the number of seconds specified by `Tolerance`. If you omit `Tolerance`, VBA waits until Word is ready.

The easiest way to enter a time serial number for ***When*** is to use the `TimeValue` function:

`TimeValue(`***Time***`)`

Time	A string representing the time you want to use (such as `"5:00PM"` or `"17:00"`).

For example, the following formula runs a procedure called `MakeBackup` at 5:00 p.m.:

```
Application.OnTime _
    When:=TimeValue("5:00PM"), _
    Name:="MakeBackup"
```

TIP: RUNNING A PROCEDURE AFTER A SPECIFIED INTERVAL

If you want the OnTime method to run after a specified time interval (for example, an hour from now), use Now + TimeValue(*Time*) for *When* (where *Time* is the interval you want to use). For example, the following statement schedules a procedure to run in 30 minutes:

```
Application.OnTime _
    When:=Now + TimeValue("00:30"), _
    Name:="MakeBackup"
```

Application.Move moves the Word application window according to the following syntax:

Application.Move(*Left, Top*)

> *Left*   The horizontal screen position, in points, of the left edge of the application window.
>
> *Top*   The vertical screen position, in points, of the top edge of the application window.

Note that this method causes an error if the window is maximized or minimized. Listing 56.1 shows a procedure that checks to see whether the application window is maximized or minimized. If it's not maximized or minimized, the procedure moves the window into the top-left corner of the screen.

Listing 56.1. A procedure that moves the Word window into the top-left corner of the screen.

```
Sub TopLeftCorner()
    With Application
        If .WindowState <> wdWindowStateMaximize _
            And .WindowState <> wdWindowStateMinimize _
            Then .Move 0, 0
    End With
End Sub
```

Application.Resize changes the size of the Word application window. Here's the syntax:

Application.Resize(*Width, Height*)

> *Width*   The new width of the application window, in points.
>
> *Height*   The new height of the application window, in points.

As with the Move method, this method raises an error if the application window is maximized or minimized.

Application.Quit quits Word. If there are any open documents with unsaved changes, Word asks whether you want to save the changes. To prevent this, either save the documents before running the Quit method (I'll tell you how to save documents in the next section) or set the DisplayAlerts property to False. (In the latter case, note that Word does *not* save changes to the documents.)

Working with Document Objects

In Microsoft Word, the Document object appears directly below the Application object in the object hierarchy. You can use VBA to create new documents, open or delete existing documents, save and close open documents, and more. The next section takes you through various techniques for specifying documents in your VBA code; then you'll look at some Document object properties, methods, and events.

Specifying a Document Object

If you need to do something with a document, or if you need to work with an object contained in a specific document (such as a section of text), you need to tell Word which document you want to use. VBA gives you three ways to do this:

Use the Documents object: The Documents object is the collection of all open document files. To specify a particular document, either use its index number (where 1 represents the first document opened) or enclose the document name in quotation marks. For example, if Memo.doc was the first document opened, the following two statements are equivalent:

```
Documents("Memo.doc")
Documents(1)
```

Use the ActiveDocument object: The ActiveDocument object represents the document that currently has the focus.

Use the ThisDocument object: The ThisDocument object represents the document where the VBA code is executing. If your code deals only with objects residing in the same document as the code itself, you can use the ActiveDocument object. However, if your code deals with other documents, use ThisDocument whenever you need to make sure that the code affects only the document containing the procedure.

Opening a Document

To open a document file, use the Open method of the Documents collection. The Open method has ten arguments you can use to fine-tune your document openings, but only one of these is mandatory. Here's the simplified syntax showing the one required argument (for the rest of the arguments, look up the Open method in the VBA Help system):

```
Documents.Open(FileName)
```

FileName   The full name of the document file, including the drive and folder that contain the file.

For example, to open a document named Letter.doc in the current drive and folder, you use the following statement:

```
Documents.Open "Letter.doc"
```

Creating a New Document

If you need to create a new document, use the `Documents` collection's `Add` method:

```
Documents.Add(Template, NewTemplate)
```

Template	This optional argument specifies the template file to use as the basis for the new document. Enter a string that spells out the path and name of the .DOT file. If you omit this argument, Word creates the new document based on the Normal template.
NewTemplate	If you set this argument to `True`, Word creates a new template file.

Document Object Properties

Most Document object properties return collections of other objects. For example, the `Words` property is a collection of all the words in a document, and the `Bookmarks` property is a collection of all the bookmarks in the document. Here's a list of a few other common properties associated with Document objects:

Document.`GrammarChecked` returns `True` if the entire document has been grammar-checked; returns `False` otherwise.

Document.`Name` returns the filename of the document.

Document.`Path` returns the path of the document file.

> **NOTE: NEW, UNSAVED DOCUMENTS**
>
> A new, unsaved document's `Path` property returns an empty string (`""`).

Document.`Saved` determines whether changes have been made to a document since it was last saved.

Document.`SpellingChecked` returns `True` if the entire document has been spell-checked; returns `False` otherwise.

Document Object Methods

Document objects have dozens of methods that let you do everything from saving a document to closing a document. Here are the methods you'll use most often:

Document.`Activate` activates the specified open *Document*. For example, the following statement activates the Tirade.doc document:

```
Documents("Tirade.doc").Activate
```

`Document`.CheckGrammar checks the grammar in the specified `Document`.

`Document`.CheckSpelling checks the spelling in the specified `Document`. This method contains a number of optional arguments that let you set various spell-check options. (See "Checking Spelling and Grammar with VBA" later in this chapter.)

`Document`.Close closes the specified `Document`. This method uses the following syntax:

Document.Close(*SaveChanges, OriginalFormat, RouteDocument*)

Document	The Document object you want to close.
SaveChanges	If the document has been modified, this argument determines whether Word saves those changes:

wdSaveChanges	Saves changes before closing.
wdDoNotSaveChanges	Doesn't save changes.
wdPromptToSaveChanges	Asks the user whether he wants to save changes.

OriginalFormat	Specifies the format to use when saving the document:

wdOriginalFormat	Saves the document using its original format.
wdWordDocument	Saves the document in Word format.
wdPromptUser	Asks the user whether he wants to save the document in its original format.

RouteDocument	If set to `True`, this argument tells Word to route the document to the next recipient.

`Document`.Goto returns a Range object (see "The Range Object" later in this chapter) that represents the start of a specified position in the `Document`. Here's the syntax:

Document.GoTo(*What, Which, Count, Name*)

Document	The Document object with which you want to work.
What	The type of item to go to. Word uses 17 different constants for this argument. Here's a list of the most common ones you'll use:

        wdGoToBookmark

        wdGoToComment

        wdGoToEndnote

        wdGoToField

        wdGoToFootnote

        wdGoToGraphic

```
wdGoToLine

wdGoToObject

wdGoToPage

wdGoToSection

wdGoToTable
```

Which   A constant that determines how Word goes to the new range:

wdGoToAbsolute	Uses the absolute position of the item.
wdGoToFirst	Goes to the first instance of the item.
wdGoToLast	Goes to the last instance of the item.
wdGoToNext	Goes to the next instance of the item.
wdGoToPrevious	Goes to the previous instance of the item.
wdGoToRelative	Use the relative position of the item.

Count   A positive value that represents the number of the item. For example, the line number of *What* is wdGoToLine.

Name   The name of the item, if *What* is wdGoToBookmark, wdGoToComment, wdGoToField, or wdGoToObject.

For example, the following statement goes to the second line in the active document:

```
ActiveDocument.Goto _
    What:=wdGoToLine, _
    Which:=wdGoToAbsolute, _
    Count:=2
```

On the other hand, the following statement goes to the second line from the current position in the active document:

```
ActiveDocument.Goto _
    What:=wdGoToLine, _
    Which:=wdGoToRelative, _
    Count:=2
```

Document.PrintOut prints the specified *Document* using the following syntax:

Document.PrintOut(*Range, From, To, Copies, Pages, ActivePrinter, PrintToFile*)

Document   The Document object you want to print.

Range   Specifies the range of text to print, as follows:

wdPrintAllDocument	Prints the entire document.
wdPrintCurrentPage	Prints only the current page.
wdPrintFromTo	Prints a range of pages from a starting page number (see the *From* argument) to an ending page (see the *To* argument).

	wdPrintRangeOfPages	Prints a range of pages (see the *Pages* argument).
	wdPrintPrintSelection	Prints only the currently selected text.
From		If *Range* is wdPrintFromTo, this argument specifies the page number from which to start printing.
To		If *Range* is wdPrintFromTo, this argument specifies the page number of the last page to print.
Copies		The number of copies to print. The default value is 1.
Pages		If *Range* is wdPrintRangeOfPages, this argument specifies the page range (for example, 4-8,10).
ActivePrinter		Specifies the printer to use.
PrintToFile		If True, Word prints the document to a file and prompts the user for a filename.

Document.PrintPreview displays the specified *Document* in the Print Preview window.

Document.Save saves the specified *Document*. If the document is new, use the SaveAs method instead.

Document.SaveAs saves the specified *Document* to a different file. Here's the simplified syntax for the SaveAs method (to see all 11 arguments in their full syntax, look up the SaveAs method in the VBA Help system):

Document.SaveAs(**FileName**)

Document	The Document object you want to save to a different file.
FileName	The full name of the new document file, including the drive and folder where you want the file to reside.

Listing 56.2 shows a procedure named MakeBackup that uses the SaveAs method, as well as a few other methods and properties of the Document object.

Listing 56.2. A procedure that creates a backup copy of the active document on a floppy disk.

```
Sub MakeBackup()
    Dim backupFile As String
    Dim currFile As String
    With ActiveDocument
        '
        ' Don't bother if the document is unchanged or new
        '
        If .Saved Or .Path = "" Then Exit Sub
        '
        ' Mark current position in document
        '
        .Bookmarks.Add Name:="LastPosition"
        '
        ' Turn off screen updating
        '
```

```
        Application.ScreenUpdating = False
        '
        ' Save the file
        '
        .Save
        '
        ' Store the current file path, construct the path for the
        ' backup file, and then save it to Drive A
        '
        currFile = .FullName
        backupFile = "A:\" + .Name
        .SaveAs FileName:=backupFile
    End With
    '
    ' Close the backup copy (which is now active)
    ActiveDocument.Close
    '
    ' Reopen the current file
    '
    Documents.Open FileName:=currFile
    '
    ' Return to pre-backup position
    '
    ActiveDocument.GoTo What:=wdGoToBookmark, Name:="LastPosition"
End Sub
```

After declaring a couple of variables, this procedure checks to see whether the backup operation is necessary. In other words, if the document has no unsaved changes (the Saved property returns True) or if it's a new, unsaved document (the Path property returns ""), bail out of the procedure.

Otherwise, a new Bookmark object is created to save the current position in the document, screen updating is turned off, and the file is saved.

You're now ready to perform the backup. First, the currFile variable is used to store the full path name of the document, and the path name of the backup file is built with the following statement:

```
backupFile = "A:\" + .Name
```

This is used to save the file to drive A. Note that this statement is easily customized to save the file to a different hard disk or even a network drive. (For the latter, use a UNC network path name in place of A:\.)

The actual backup takes place via the SaveAs method, which saves the document to the path given by backupFile. From there, the procedure closes the backup file, reopens the original file, and uses the GoTo method to return to the original position within the document.

NOTE: SCHEDULING REGULAR BACKUPS

Rather than run MakeBackup by hand, you might consider using the OnTime method to schedule backups at specific times or at regular intervals.

NOTE: TRAPPING ERRORS

The MakeBackup procedure should probably check to see whether there is a disk in drive A for running the SaveAs method. I show you how to account for this type of error in Chapter E4 on the CD, "Debugging VBA Procedures."

Document Object Events

Document objects respond to three different events: Close, Open, and New. Here's a quick run-down on each event:

NOTE: ENTERING EVENT HANDLER CODE

Remember that you don't create event handlers in a regular VBA module. Instead, you follow these steps:

1. In the Visual Basic Editor's Project Explorer, highlight the Document object you want to work with. For the document containing the VBA code, highlight ThisDocument.

2. SelectView | Code, press F7, or click the View Code button in the Project Explorer.

3. In the code window that appears, use the Object drop-down list (the one on the left) to select the Document object.

4. Use the Procedure drop-down list (the one on the right) to select the event you want to work with. VBA adds the event handler's procedure stub to the code window.

5. Enter your event-handler code within the procedure stub.

Close fires when the user selects File | Close or when your code runs the Document object's Close method. Note that the statements you define inside the event handler run before the workbook is closed and before the user is asked to save changes. Here's the procedure stub of the event handler:

```
Private Sub Document_Close()
    <Event handler code goes here>
End Sub
```

New applies only to templates, and it fires when the user creates a new document based on the template or when your code runs the Document object's Add method and specifies this template. Here's the procedure stub used by the event handler:

```
Private Sub Document_New()
    <Event handler code goes here>
End Sub
```

Open fires when the user selects File | Open or when your code runs the Document object's Open method. Here's the procedure stub of the event handler:

```
Private Sub Document_Open()
    <Event handler code goes here>
End Sub
```

Objects That Represent Text in Word

Although you can add lines, graphics, and other objects to a document, text is what Word is all about. It won't come as any surprise to you that Word has a truckload of objects that give you numerous ways to work with text. The next few sections take you through a few of these objects.

The Range Object

If you've used VBA with Excel, you probably know that Excel has no separate object to represent a cell. Instead, a cell is considered just an instance of the generic Range class.

Along similar lines, Word has no separate objects for its most fundamental text units: the character and the word. Like Excel, Word considers these items to be instances of a generic class, which is also called the Range object. A Range object is defined as a contiguous section of text in a document, so it can be anything from a single character to an entire document.

There are two basic methods for returning a Range object: the Document object's Range method and the Range property.

The Range Method

The Document object has a Range method that lets you specify starting and ending points for a range. Here's the syntax:

Document.Range(*Start,End*)

Document	The Document object.
Start	The starting character position. Note that the first character in a document is at position 0.
End	The ending character position.

For example, the following statements use the myRange object variable to store the first 100 characters in the active document:

```
Dim myRange As Range
myRange = ActiveDocument.Range(0, 99)
```

The Range Property

Many Word objects have a Range property that returns a Range object, including the Paragraph and Selection objects (discussed later). This is important because these objects lack certain properties and methods that are handy for manipulating text. For example, the Paragraph object doesn't have a Font property. The Range object does, however, so you format a paragraph's font programmatically by referring to its Range property:

```
ActiveDocument.Paragraphs(1).Range.Font.Italic = True
```

This statement formats the first paragraph in the active document with italic text. (I discuss the Paragraphs collection in a moment.)

Range Object Properties

The Range object's properties include many of the standard text formatting commands. Here's a brief review of just a few of these properties:

Range.Bold returns True if the specified *Range* is formatted entirely as bold; returns False if no part of the range is bold; returns wdUndefined if only part of the range is formatted as bold. You can also set this property using True (for bolding), False (to remove bolding), or wdToggle (to toggle the current setting between True and False).

Range.Case returns or sets the case of the specified *Range*. This property uses various Word constants, including wdLowerCase, wdTitleSentence, wdTitleWord, wdToggleCase, and wdUpperCase.

Range.Characters returns a Characters collection that represents all the characters in the *Range*. (See the section titled "The Characters Object.")

Range.End is the position of the last character in the *Range*.

Range.Font returns or sets a Font object that specifies the character formatting used in the *Range*.

Range.Italic returns True if the specified *Range* is formatted entirely as italic; returns False if no part of the range is italic; returns wdUndefined if only part of the range is formatted as italic. You can also set this property using True (for italics), False (to remove italics), or wdToggle (to toggle the current setting between True and False).

Range.Paragraphs returns a Paragraphs collection that represents all the Paragraph objects in the *Range*. (See the section titled "The Paragraph Object.")

Range.Sentences returns a Sentences collection that represents all the Sentence objects in the *Range*. (See the section titled "The Sentences Object.")

Range.Start is the position of the first character in the *Range*.

Range.Text returns or sets the text in the *Range*.

Range.Words returns a Words collection that represents all the words in the *Range*. (See the section titled "The Words Object.")

Range Object Methods

Because it's the fundamental text object, it's not surprising that the Range object boasts a large number of methods that you can use to manipulate text. Here are a few of the ones you'll use most often:

Range.CheckGrammar checks the grammar in the specified *Range*.

Range.CheckSpelling checks the spelling in the specified *Range*. This method contains a number of optional arguments that let you set various spell-check options. (See "Checking Spelling and Grammar with VBA" later in this chapter.)

Range.Collapse: If the *Range* is currently selected, use this method to remove the selection and position the cursor according to the following syntax:

Range.Collapse(*Direction*)

Range	The Range object.
Direction	Specifies where you want the cursor to end up. Use wdCollapseStart to position the cursor at the beginning of the **Range** (this is the default). Use wdCollapseEnd to position the cursor at the end of the **Range**.

NOTE: THE SELECTION OBJECT

The Selection object represents the currently selected text. To select text programmatically, use the Range object's Select method (discussed at the end of this section).

Range.Copy copies the *Range* to the Clipboard.

Range.Cut cuts the *Range* from the document and places it on the Clipboard.

Range.Delete: If used without arguments, this method deletes the entire *Range*. However, you can fine-tune your deletions by using the following syntax:

Range.Delete(*Unit*,*Count*)

Range	The Range object containing the text you want to delete.
Unit	A constant that specifies whether you're deleting characters (use wdCharacter) or entire words (use wdWord). If you omit this argument, VBA assumes you're deleting characters.
Count	The number of units to delete. Use a positive number to delete forward; use a negative number to delete backward.

Range.InsertAfter inserts text after the specified *Range*:

Range.InsertAfter(**Text**)

Range	The Range object after which you want to insert the text.
Text	The text to insert.

Range.InsertBefore inserts text before the specified *Range*:

Range.InsertBefore(**Text**)

Range	The Range object before which you want to insert the text.
Text	The text to insert.

Range.Paste pastes the contents of the Clipboard at the current *Range* position. To avoid overwriting the currently selected *Range*, use the Collapse method before pasting.

Range.Select selects the specified *Range*.

The Characters Object

The `Characters` object is a collection that represents all the characters in whatever object is specified. For example, `ActiveDocument.Paragraphs(1).Characters` is the collection of all the characters in the Range object given by `ActiveDocument.Paragraphs(1)` (the first paragraph in the active document). Other objects that have the `Characters` property are Document and `Selection`.

Because `Characters` is a collection, you refer to individual characters by including an index number (`Characters(50)`, for example). The following statement formats the first character in the active document to point size 20:

```
ActiveDocument.Words(1).Font.Size = 20
```

To count the number of characters in the specified object, use the `Count` property:

```
totalChars = Documents("Chapter1.doc").Characters.Count
```

This example sets the variable `totalChars` equal to the number of characters in the Chapter1.doc file.

Listing 56.3 shows another example that uses the `Characters` object. In this case, the function procedure named `CountCharacters` takes on an `Object` argument named `countObject` and a `String` argument named `letter`. The procedure determines the number of instances of `letter` that occur within `countObject`.

Listing 56.3. A function that counts the number of instances of a specified character in an object.

```
Function CountCharacters(countObject As Object, letter As String) As Long
    Dim i As Long, char As Range
    i = 0
    For Each char In countObject.Characters
        If char = letter Then i = i + 1
    Next char
    CountCharacters = i
End Function
Sub TestCountCharacters()
    MsgBox CountCharacters(ActiveDocument, "e")
End Sub
```

The Words Object

The `Words` object is a collection that represents all the words in whatever object is specified. For example, `ActiveDocument.Words` is the collection of all the words in the active document. Other objects that have the `Words` property are `Paragraph`, `Range`, and `Selection`.

You refer to individual words by using an index number with the `Words` collection. As I mentioned earlier, however, this doesn't return a "Word" object; there is no such thing in Microsoft Word's VBA universe. Instead, individual words are classified as `Range` objects. (See "The Range Object" earlier in this chapter.)

The following statement formats the first word in the active document as bold:

```
ActiveDocument.Words(1).Font.Bold = True
```

To count the number of words in the specified object, use the Count property:

```
totalWords = Documents("Article.doc").Words.Count
```

The Sentences Object

The next rung on Word's text object ladder is the Sentences object. This is a collection of all the sentences in whatever object you specify, whether it's a Document, Range, or Selection.

As with Words, you refer to specific members of the Sentences collection using an index number, and the resulting object is a Range. For example, the following statement stores the active document's first sentence in the firstSentence variable:

```
firstSentence = ActiveDocument.Sentences(1)
```

Again, you can use the Count property to return the total number of sentences in an object. In the following procedure fragment, the Count property determines the last sentence in a document:

```
With Documents("Remarks.doc")
    totalSentences = .Sentences.Count
    lastSentence = .Sentences(.totalSentences)
End With
```

The Paragraph Object

From characters, words, and sentences, you make the next logical text leap: paragraphs. A Paragraph object is a member of the Paragraphs collection, which represents all the paragraphs in the specified Document, Range, or Selection. As with the other text objects, you use an index number with the Paragraphs object to specify an individual paragraph.

Paragraph Properties

Word's various paragraph formatting options are well-represented in the large set of properties available for the Paragraph object. Here are a few useful ones:

Paragraph.KeepTogether returns or sets whether the specified *Paragraph* object remains together on the same page when Word repaginates the document.

Paragraph.KeepWithNext returns or sets whether the specified *Paragraph* remains on the same page with the following paragraph when Word repaginates the document.

Paragraph.LeftIndent returns or sets the left indent (in points) of the specified *Paragraph*.

Paragraph.LineSpacing returns or sets the line-spacing setting (in points) for the specified *Paragraph*.

Paragraph.RightIndent returns or sets the right indent (in points) for the specified *Paragraph*.

Paragraph.SpaceAfter returns or sets the spacing (in points) after the specified *Paragraph*.

Paragraph.SpaceBefore returns or sets the spacing (in points) before the specified *Paragraph*.

Paragraph.Style returns or sets the style of the specified *Paragraph*. Word has a huge number of constants that represent its predefined styles. For example, to set the Heading 1 style, you use the wdStyleHeading1 constant. To see the other constants, search for wdBuiltInStyle in the Object Browser.

The following procedure fragment applies several properties to the active paragraph (recall that the InchesToPoints function converts values expressed in inches to the equivalent value expressed in points):

```
With Selection.Range
    .LeftIndent=InchesToPoints(1)
    .LineSpacing=12
    .SpaceAfter=6
    .Style=wdStyleNormal
End With
```

Paragraph Methods

To finish our look at the Paragraph object, here are a few methods you can wield in your code:

Paragraph.Indent indents the specified *Paragraph* to the next tab stop.

Paragraph.Next moves forward in the document from the specified *Paragraph* to return a *Paragraph* object:

Paragraph.Next(*Count*)

Paragraph	The Paragraph object from which you want to move.
Count	The number of paragraphs to move forward.

Paragraph.Outdent outdents the *Paragraph* to the previous tab stop.

Paragraph.Previous moves backward in the document from the specified *Paragraph* to return a Paragraph object:

Paragraph.Previous(*Count*)

Paragraph	The Paragraph object from which you want to move.
Count	The number of paragraphs to move backward.

Paragraph.Space1 sets the specified *Paragraph* to single-spaced.

Paragraph.Space15 sets the specified *Paragraph* to 1.5-line spacing.

Paragraph.Space2 sets the specified *Paragraph* to double-spaced.

Checking Spelling and Grammar with VBA

Because words are at the heart of Word, it makes sense that there are a number of properties and methods for checking spelling and grammar via your VBA procedures. The rest of this chapter looks at the various features Word VBA makes available for spelling and grammar checks.

Spell-Checking a Document or Range

To check the spelling in a Document object or a Range object, VBA offers the `CheckSpelling` method, which initiates the spell-check procedure:

`Object``.CheckSpelling(`*`CustomDictionary, IgnoreUppercase, AlwaysSuggest,`*
➥*`CustomDictionaryX`*`)`

Object	The Document or Range object you want to check.
CustomDictionary	The filename of a custom dictionary that the application can search if a word isn't found in the main dictionary.
IgnoreUppercase	Set this argument to True to tell Word to ignore words entirely in uppercase.
AlwaysSuggest	Set this argument to True to tell Word to always suggest alternative spellings for misspelled words.
CustomDictionaryX	The name or names of one or more extra custom dictionaries. Here, *X* can be any value between 2 and 10.

Spell-Checking a Word

If you want to spell-check only a specific word or phrase, use the following alternative syntax for the `CheckSpelling` method:

`Application``.CheckSpelling(`**`Word`**`,` *`CustomDictionary, IgnoreUppercase, MainDictionary,`*
➥*`CustomDictionaryX`*`)`

`Word`	The word or phrase you want to check.
CustomDictionary	The filename of a custom dictionary that the application can search if **`Word`** isn't found in the main dictionary.
IgnoreUppercase	Set this argument to True to tell Word to ignore words entirely in uppercase.
MainDictionary	The name of the main dictionary Word should use to check **`Word`**.
CustomDictionaryX	The name or names of one or more extra custom dictionaries. Here, *X* can be any value between 2 and 10.

Checking Grammar

To start a grammar check on a Document or Range object, use the `CheckGrammar` method:

`Object.CheckGrammar`

> `Object`   The Document or Range object you want to check.

If you prefer to check the grammar of a string, use the alternative syntax:

`Application.CheckGrammar(String)`

> `String`   The text you want to check.

Summary

This chapter took you on a tour of the new VBA implementation in Word 97. After I discussed the transition from WordBasic to VBA, you learned about Word's `Application` object, including a few useful properties and methods. From there, I went through a number of Word-specific objects, including the Document, Range, `Characters`, `Words`, `Sentences`, and Paragraph objects. I closed with a look at spell- and grammar-checking from VBA.

Here's a list of chapters where you'll find related information:

- For a general discussion of VBA objects, see Chapter 54, "Understanding Objects."
- To learn how to integrate Word with other Office applications, see Chapter E6 on the CD, "Integrating Office Applications with VBA."

Excel VBA Techniques

IN THIS CHAPTER

> *Now here, you see, it takes all the running you can do, to keep in the same place. If you want to get somewhere else, you must run at least twice as fast as that!*
>
> *—Lewis Carroll*

If you're using VBA in Excel, most of your procedures will eventually do *something* to the Excel environment. They might open a workbook, rename a worksheet, select a cell or range, enter a formula, or even set some of Excel's options. Therefore, knowing how VBA interacts with Excel is crucial if you ever hope to write useful routines. This chapter looks closely at that interaction as I show you how to work with all the most common Excel objects, including the Workbook, Worksheet, and Range objects.

Excel's Macro Options

Before you get to the object fun and games, take a quick look at the various options that Excel provides for recording macros. At this point in your VBA career, you might be wondering why you would even bother with recorded macros. After all, the first four chapters here in Part XI served to expand your VBA horizons so that you could glimpse the larger world of application programming. Isn't the macro recorder just for novices?

You'd be surprised. The developer's never-ending quest for efficiency applies not just to his programs but also to his programming. For example, if you need to put together a few lines of code that manipulate some Excel objects, but you're not sure of the correct syntax, it might take you a few minutes to look up the objects either in this chapter or in the Excel help system. However, there's a good chance you can run through those same actions in the macro recorder in just a few seconds. You can then paste the resulting code into your procedure and edit accordingly. With the macro recorder's existence now fully justified, examine the available options.

Assigning a Shortcut Key

To assign a shortcut key to an existing macro (or change a macro's current shortcut key) from Excel, select Tools | Macro | Macros (or press Alt-F8). In the Macro Name dialog box, highlight the macro and click Options to display the Macro Options dialog box, shown in Figure 57.1. Use the Shortcut key Ctrl+ text box to enter the letter you want to use with Ctrl for the key combination. For example, if you enter e, you can run the macro by pressing Ctrl-E. Note that Excel shortcut keys are case-sensitive. In other words, if you enter E in the Ctrl+ text box, you must press Ctrl-Shift-E to run the macro.

FIGURE 57.1.

Use the Macro Options dialog box to assign a shortcut key to a macro.

CAUTION: AVOID SHORTCUT KEY CONFLICTS

Make sure you don't specify a shortcut key that conflicts with Excel's built-in shortcuts (such as Ctrl-B for Bold or Ctrl-C for Copy). If you use a key that clashes with an Excel shortcut, Excel overrides its own shortcut and runs your macro instead (provided, that is, that the workbook containing the macro is open).

There are only seven letters not assigned to Excel commands which you can use with your macros: e, j, k, l, m, q, t, and y. You can get extra shortcut keys by using uppercase letters. For example, Excel differentiates between Ctrl-b and Ctrl-B (or, more explicitly, Ctrl-Shift-b). Note, however, that Excel uses four built-in Ctrl-Shift shortcuts: A, F, O, P.

You can also use the OnKey method to trigger a macro when the user presses a specific key combination. See the section "Running a Procedure When the User Presses a Key" for details.

While you're in the Macro Options dialog box, you can also use the Description text box to add some descriptive text about the macro. (This text appears in the Description area of the Macro dialog box when you highlight the macro.)

Recording with Relative References

By default, Excel uses absolute references during recording. For example, if you select cell A4, the macro recorder translates this action into the following VBA statement:

```
Range("A4").Select
```

On the other hand, you might prefer that all your cell references be relative to a specific cell. That way, you can apply the code to a different range just by selecting a different cell before running the macro.

To do this, you need to tell Excel to use relative references during recording. First, select the cell that you want to use as the starting point. Then begin your recording in the usual manner (in other words, select Tools | Macros | Record New Macro, fill in the Record Macro dialog box, and click OK). When the Stop Recording toolbar appears, click the Relative Reference button and then perform the macro actions normally.

For macros that use relative references, VBA translates cell-related actions as an "offset" from cell A1. For example, suppose you began the macro with cell A1 selected and then you clicked cell A4 during the recording. VBA translates this action into the following VBA statement:

```
ActiveCell.Offset(3,0).Range("A1").Select
```

VBA uses the Offset method to refer to a range that's a specified number of rows and columns from the current cell. I tell you more about this method later in this chapter (see "Working with Range Objects").

New VBA Features in Excel 97

Excel (along with Project) was in the first wave of Microsoft applications to become VBA-enabled. Subsequent Excel versions have tweaked the VBA object model and added new statements and functions to reflect both the new features in Excel and the continuing evolution of the VBA language. Excel 97 is no exception; I'll highlight some of the major changes in this section.

Excel 97's VBA object model has a few significant changes from the Excel 95 model. These changes include not only revisions both major and minor to existing objects, but also some completely new objects. Here's a rundown of the changes to the most important objects:

CommandBars: This is a new object in Excel 97 (it's common to every Office application). It's a collection that contains all the menu bars, toolbars, and shortcut menus defined in Excel. It replaces the old MenuBars and Toolbars objects (although, for backward compatibility, the properties and methods associated with these objects still work in Excel 97).

UserForms: This is a new object in the VBA hierarchy. It represents the user forms (dialog boxes) that you create using the Visual Basic Editor (see Chapter 59, "Creating a Custom User Interface"). It replaces the DialogSheets object used in previous versions of Excel.

Hyperlinks: In keeping with the Web-based focus of Office 97, the object models of Excel 97 and all the Office applications include the Hyperlinks object, which represents (in Excel's case) all the hyperlinks used in a worksheet or range.

Shapes: This new collection represents all the drawing objects you can create in Excel: lines, ovals, rectangles, and so on. It replaces the individual drawing objects used in previous versions.

Comment: This object represents Excel 97's new Comments feature, which replaces the old cell notes feature.

FormatCondition: You use this new object to control the conditional range formatting feature, which is new to Excel 97.

Range: This object includes a number of new properties and methods, including the AddComment method (for adding a comment to a cell), the Comment property (for accessing an existing comment), the FormatConditions property (to read or set the conditional formatting in a range), and the Merge method (for merging cells).

RecentFiles: You can use this new object to access Excel's list of recently used files.

Validation: This new object supports the new range validation feature in Excel 97.

WorksheetFunction: You use this new object to access Excel's worksheet functions. (In previous versions, these functions were contained directly in the Application object.) See "Accessing Worksheet Functions" later in this chapter.

Excel's Application Object

In Chapter 54, "Understanding Objects," I described a few Application object properties and methods that are common to all VBA applications. As you can imagine, though, each application has its own unique set of properties and methods for the Application object. Excel is no exception, and you saw quite a few in the preceding section. This section shows you a few more.

Accessing Worksheet Functions

VBA has dozens of functions of its own, but its collection is downright meager compared to the hundreds of worksheet functions available with Excel. If you need to access one of these worksheet functions, VBA makes them available via a property of the Application object called WorksheetFunctions. Each function works exactly as it does on a worksheet; the only difference is that you must append Application. to the name of the function.

> **NOTE: YOUR OLD VBA PROCEDURES WILL STILL WORK**
>
> I mentioned earlier that WorksheetFunctions is a new element in the VBA 5.0 object model. Previous versions accessed Excel's worksheet functions via the Application object directly. However, there's no immediate need to go back and rewrite your old procedures because VBA 5.0 still supports the old model. There's no telling how long this support will remain in VBA, however, so you should probably put this change on your "to do" list. (This is a perfect example of how the Visual Basic Editor's Replace feature comes in handy. See Chapter 53, "Getting Started with VBA," for details.)

For example, to run the SUM() worksheet function on the range named Sales and store the result in a variable named totalSales, you use the following statement:

```
totalSales = Application.WorksheetFunctions.Sum(Range("Sales"))
```

> **CAUTION: USE VBA'S FUNCTIONS TO AVOID ERRORS**
>
> The WorksheetFunctions object includes only those worksheet functions that don't duplicate an existing VBA function. For example, VBA has a UCase$ function that's equivalent to Excel's UPPER() worksheet function (both convert a string into uppercase). In this case, you must use VBA's UCase$ function in your code. If you try to use Application.WorksheetFunctions.Upper, you receive the error message Object doesn't support this property or method.

> **NOTE: A LIST OF VBA FUNCTIONS**
>
> For a complete list of VBA functions, see Appendix E, "VBA Functions."

Other Properties of the Application Object

In addition to the properties you saw earlier that control many of Excel's workspace options, the Application object has dozens of other properties that affect a number of aspects of the Excel environment. Here's a rundown of some Application object properties you'll use most often in your VBA code:

Application.CutCopyMode returns or sets Excel's Cut or Copy mode status. If your code copies a Range object and then pastes it (as described later in this chapter), Excel stays in Copy mode after the paste. This means that it displays a moving border around the range and displays Select destination and press ENTER or choose Paste in the status bar. If you prefer not to confuse the user with these Copy mode indicators, you can take Excel out of Copy mode (or Cut mode, if you cut the range) by running the following statement:

Application.CutCopyMode = False

Application.MemoryFree returns the amount of system memory that is still available to Excel.

Application.MemoryTotal returns the total amount of system memory (used and free) that is available to Excel.

Application.MemoryUsed returns the amount of system memory that is being used by Excel.

Application.MouseAvailable returns True if a mouse is present on the system.

Application.OperatingSystem returns the name and version number of the current operating system. This is a useful way of determining whether your procedure should run a feature specific to Windows 95 or to the Macintosh version of Excel.

Methods of Excel's Application Object

The Application object features a few dozen methods that perform actions on the Excel environment. Here's a summary of the most common methods:

Calculate calculates all the open workbooks. Note that you don't need to specify the Application object. You can just enter Calculate by itself.

Application.DoubleClick is equivalent to double-clicking the current cell. If in-cell editing is activated, running this method opens the cell for editing; otherwise, running this method opens the cell's comment (if it has one) for editing.

`Application.Quit` quits Excel. If any open workbooks have unsaved changes, Excel asks whether you want to save the changes. To prevent this, either save the workbooks before running the `Quit` method (I tell you how to save workbooks in the section "Manipulating Workbook Objects") or set the `DisplayAlerts` property to `False`. (In the latter case, note that Excel does *not* save changes to the workbooks.)

`Application.SaveWorkspace` saves the current workspace. Here's the syntax:

`Application.SaveWorkspace(`***Filename***`)`

> ***Filename***   The name of the workspace file.

`Application.Volatile`: When inserted inside a user-defined function, the `Volatile` method tells Excel to recalculate the function every time the worksheet is recalculated. If you don't include the `Volatile` method, Excel only recalculates the function whenever its input cells change. (Here, the input cells are those cells passed directly to the function as arguments. This doesn't apply to any other cells used indirectly in the calculation.) Use the following statement (inside a user-defined function) to change a function's behavior from volatile to nonvolatile:

`Application.Volatile False`

`Application.Wait` pauses a running macro until a specified time is reached. Here's the syntax:

`Application.Wait(`***Time***`)`

> ***Time***   The time when you want to macro to resume running.

For example, if you want your procedure to delay for five seconds, you use the following statement:

`Application.Wait Now + TimeValue("00:00:05")`

Some Event-Like Methods

The `Application` object comes with several methods that are "event-like." In other words, they respond to outside influences such as the press of a key. This section looks at two of these methods: `OnKey` and `OnTime`.

Running a Procedure When the User Presses a Key

As discussed earlier in this chapter (see the section "Excel's Macro Options"), Excel lets you assign a Ctrl-*key* shortcut to a procedure. However, this method has two major drawbacks:

- Excel uses some Ctrl-*key* combinations internally, so your choices are limited.

- It doesn't help if you want your procedures to respond to "meaningful" keys such as Delete and Esc.

57

EXCEL VBA
TECHNIQUES

To remedy these problems, use the `Application` object's `OnKey` method to run a procedure when the user presses a specific key or key combination:

```
Application.OnKey(Key, Procedure)
```

Key   The key or key combination that runs the procedure. For letters, numbers, or punctuation marks, enclose the character in quotes (for example, `"a"`). For other keys, see Table 57.1.

Procedure   The name (entered as text) of the procedure to run when the user presses a key. If you enter the null string (`""`) for *Procedure*, a key is disabled. If you omit *Procedure*, Excel resets the key to its normal state.

Table 57.1. Key strings to use with the OnKey method.

Key	What to Use
Backspace	`"{BACKSPACE}"` or `"{BS}"`
Break	`"{BREAK}"`
Caps Lock	`"{CAPSLOCK}"`
Delete	`"{DELETE}"` or `"{DEL}"`
Down arrow	`"{DOWN}"`
End	`"{END}"`
Enter (keypad)	`"{ENTER}"`
Enter	`"~"` (tilde)
Esc	`"{ESCAPE}"` or `"{ESC}"`
Help	`"{HELP}"`
Home	`"{HOME}"`
Insert	`"{INSERT}"`
Left arrow	`"{LEFT}"`
Num Lock	`"{NUMLOCK}"`
Page Down	`"{PGDN}"`
Page Up	`"{PGUP}"`
Right arrow	`"{RIGHT}"`
Scroll Lock	`"{SCROLLLOCK}"`
Tab	`"{TAB}"`
Up arrow	`"{UP}"`
F1 through F12	`"{F1}"` through `"{F12}"`

You can also combine these keys with the Shift, Ctrl, and Alt keys. You just precede these codes with one or more of the codes listed in Table 57.2.

Table 57.2. Symbols that represent Alt, Ctrl, and Shift in OnKey.

Key	What to Use
Alt	% (percent)
Ctrl	^ (caret)
Shift	+ (plus)

For example, pressing Delete usually wipes out only a cell's contents. If you want a quick way of deleting everything in a cell (contents, formats, comments, and so on), you could set up (for example) Ctrl-Delete to do the job. Listing 57.1 shows three procedures that accomplish this:

SetKey: This procedure sets up the Ctrl-Delete key combination to run the DeleteAll procedure. Notice how the *Procedure* argument includes the name of the workbook; therefore, this key combination operates in any workbook.

DeleteAll: This procedure runs the Clear method on the current selection.

ResetKey: This procedure resets Ctrl-Delete to its default behavior.

Listing 57.1. Procedures that set and reset a key combination using the OnKey method.

```
Sub SetKey()
    Application.OnKey _
        Key:="^{Del}", _
        Procedure:="Chaptr57.xls!DeleteAll"
End Sub
Sub DeleteAll()
    Selection.Clear
End Sub
Sub ResetKey()
    Application.OnKey _
        Key:="^{Del}"
End Sub
```

NOTE: THIS CHAPTER'S CODE LISTINGS

You can find all the listings in this chapter in the workbook Chaptr57.xls, which is on the CD-ROM that comes with this book. If you don't have Excel and you want to view these listings anyway (although I can't imagine why!), you can also find them in the file Chaptr57.bas.

Running a Procedure at a Specific Time

If you need to run a procedure at a specific time, use the OnTime method:

```
Application.OnTime(EarliestTime, Procedure, LatestTime, Schedule)
```

EarliestTime	The time (and date, if necessary) you want the procedure to run. Enter a date/time serial number.
Procedure	The name (entered as text) of the procedure to run when the *EarliestTime* arrives.
LatestTime	If Excel isn't ready to run the procedure at *EarliestTime* (in other words, if it's not in Ready, Cut, Copy, or Find mode), it keeps trying until *LatestTime* arrives. If you omit *LatestTime*, VBA waits until Excel is ready. Enter a date/time serial number.
Schedule	A logical value that determines whether the procedure runs at *EarliestTime*. If *Schedule* is True or omitted, the procedure runs. Use False to cancel a previous OnTime setting.

The easiest way to enter the time serial numbers for *EarliestTime* and *LatestTime* is to use the TimeValue function:

```
TimeValue(Time)
```

Time	A string representing the time you want to use (such as "5:00PM" or "17:00").

For example, the following formula runs a procedure called Backup at 5:00 p.m.:

```
Application.OnTime _
    EarliestTime:=TimeValue("5:00PM"), _
    Procedure:="Backup"
```

TIP: RUNNING A PROCEDURE AFTER A SPECIFIED INTERVAL

If you want the OnTime method to run after a specified time interval (for example, an hour from now), use Now + TimeValue(*Time*) for *EarliestTime* (where *Time* is the interval you want to use). For example, the following statement schedules a procedure to run in 30 minutes:

```
Application.OnTime _
    EarliestTime:=Now + TimeValue("00:30"), _
    Procedure:="Backup"
```

Manipulating Workbook Objects

Workbook objects appear directly below the Application object in Excel's object hierarchy. You can use VBA to create new workbooks, open or delete existing workbooks, save and close open workbooks, and much more. The next section takes you through various techniques for specifying workbooks in your VBA code; then you'll look at some Workbook object properties, methods, and events.

Specifying a Workbook Object

If you need to perform some action on a workbook, or if you need to work with an object contained in a specific workbook (such as a worksheet), you need to tell Excel which workbook you want to use. VBA gives you no fewer than three ways to do this:

Use the Workbooks object: The Workbooks object is the collection of all the open workbook files. To specify a workbook, either use its index number (where 1 represents the first workbook opened) or enclose the workbook name in quotation marks. For example, if the Budget.xls workbook were the first workbook opened, the following two statements are equivalent:

```
Workbooks(1)
Workbooks("Budget.xls")
```

Use the ActiveWorkbook object: The ActiveWorkbook object represents the workbook that currently has the focus.

Use the ThisWorkbook object: The ThisWorkbook object represents the workbook where the VBA code is executing. If your code only deals with objects residing in the same workbook as the code itself, you can use the ActiveWorkbook object. However, if your code deals with other workbooks, use ThisWorkbook whenever you need to make sure that the code affects only the workbook containing the procedure.

Opening a Workbook

To open a workbook file, use the Open method of the Workbooks collection. The Open method has a dozen arguments you can use to fine-tune your workbook openings, but only one of these arguments is mandatory. Here's the simplified syntax showing the one required argument (for the rest of the arguments, look up the Open method in the VBA help system):

```
Workbooks.Open(FileName)
```

FileName	The full name of the workbook file, including the drive and folder that contain the file.

For example, to open a workbook named Data.xls in the current drive and folder, you use the following statement:

```
Workbooks.Open "Data.xls"
```

> **NOTE: WORKING WITH DRIVES AND FOLDERS**
>
> You can use VBA to change the default drive and folder. To change the drive, use the ChDrive function. For example, the statement ChDrive "D" changes the current drive to D.
>
> To change the current folder (directory), use the ChDir function. For example, the statement ChDir "\My Documents\Worksheets" changes the default folder to \My Documents\ Worksheets on the current drive. If you need to know the name of the current directory, use the CurDir function.

Creating a New Workbook

If you need to create a new workbook, use the Workbooks collection's Add method:

```
Workbooks.Add(Template)
```

Template is an optional argument that determines how the workbook is created. If *Template* is a string specifying an Excel file, VBA uses the file as a template for the new workbook. You can also specify one of the following constants:

xlWBATWorksheet	Creates a workbook with a single worksheet.
xlWBATChart	Creates a workbook with a single chart sheet.
xlWBATExcel4MacroSheet	Creates a workbook with a single Excel 4 macro sheet.
xlWBATExcel4IntlMacroSheet	Creates a workbook with a single Excel 4 international macro sheet.

Here's a sample statement that uses the Add method to open a new workbook based on Excel's Invoice.xlt template file:

```
Workbooks.Add "C:\Program Files\Microsoft Office" & _
    "\Templates\Spreadsheet Solutions\Invoice.xlt"
```

Workbook Object Properties

Here's a rundown of some common properties associated with Workbook objects:

Workbook.FullName returns the full path name of the *Workbook*. The full path name includes the workbook's path (the drive and folder in which the file resides) and the filename.

Workbook.Name returns the filename of the *Workbook*.

Workbook.Path returns the path of the *Workbook* file.

NOTE: THE PATH FOR A NEW WORKBOOK

A new, unsaved workbook's Path property returns an empty string (" ").

Workbook.ProtectStructure returns True if the structure of the *Workbook* is protected; returns False otherwise. (To learn how to use code to protect a workbook, see the next section, which discusses the Workbook object's Protect method.)

Workbook.ProtectWindows returns True if the window size and position of the *Workbook* are protected; returns False otherwise. (See the description of the Protect method to learn how to protect windows programmatically.)

Workbook.Saved determines whether changes have been made to the *Workbook* since it was last saved. If changes have been made, Saved returns False.

TIP: CLOSING WITHOUT SAVING CHANGES

The Saved property is read/write. Therefore, besides reading the current value of Saved, you can also set Saved to either True or False. For example, to allow the user to close a workbook (by selecting File | Close) without saving changes and without Excel asking if she wants to save changes, set the workbook's Saved property to True. (See also the Workbook object's Close method, discussed in the next section.)

Workbook Object Methods

Workbook objects have dozens of methods that let you do everything from saving a workbook to closing a workbook. Here are a few methods that you'll use most often:

Workbook.Activate activates the specified open *Workbook*. For example, the following statement activates the Finances.xls workbook:

```
Workbooks("Finances.xls").Activate
```

Workbook.Close closes the specified *Workbook*. This method uses the following syntax:

Workbook.Close(*SaveChanges, FileName, RouteWorkbook*)

Workbook	The Workbook object you want to close.
SaveChanges	If the workbook has been modified, this argument determines whether Excel saves those changes:

True	Saves changes before closing.
False	Doesn't save changes.
Omitted	Asks the user whether she wants to save changes.

`FileName`	Save the workbook under this filename.
`RouteWorkbook`	Routes the workbook according to the following values:

`True`	Sends the workbook to the next recipient.
`False`	Doesn't send the workbook.
Omitted	Asks the user whether she wants to send the workbook.

`Workbook.PrintOut` prints the specified `Workbook` using the following syntax:

`Workbook.PrintOut(From, To, Copies, Preview, ActivePrinter, PrintToFile,`
➥`Collate)`

`Workbook`	The Workbook object you want to print.
`From`	The page number from which to start printing.
`To`	The page number of the last page to print.
`Copies`	The number of copies to print. The default value is 1.
`Preview`	If `True`, Excel displays the Print Preview window before printing. The default value is `False`.
`ActivePrinter`	Specifies the printer to use.
`PrintToFile`	If `True`, Excel prints the workbook to a file and prompts the user for a filename.
`Collate`	If `True`, and `Copies` is greater than 1, Excel collates the copies.

`Workbook.PrintPreview` displays the specified `Workbook` in the Print Preview window.

`Workbook.Protect` protects the specified `Workbook`. The `Protect` method uses the syntax shown here:

`Workbook.Protect(Password, Structure, Windows)`

`Workbook`	The Workbook object you want to protect.
`Password`	A text string that specifies the (case-sensitive) password to use with the protection.
`Structure`	If `True`, Excel protects the workbook's structure.
`Windows`	If `True`, Excel protects the workbook's windows.

`Workbook.Save` saves the specified `Workbook`. If the workbook is new, use the `SaveAs` method instead.

`Workbook.SaveAs` saves the specified `Workbook` to a different file. Here's the simplified syntax for the `SaveAs` method (to see all nine arguments in the full syntax, look up the `SaveAs` method in the VBA Help system):

Workbook.SaveAs(*FileName*)

Workbook	The Workbook object you want to save to a different file.
FileName	The full name of the new workbook file, including the drive and folder where you want the file to reside.

`Workbook.Unprotect` unprotects the specified *Workbook*. Here's the syntax:

Workbook.Unprotect(*Password*)

Workbook	The Workbook object you want to unprotect.
Password	The protection password.

Workbook Object Events

Workbook objects respond to a number of events, including opening, closing, activating, de-activating, printing, and saving. Here's a quick look at a few of these events:

`Activate` fires when the workbook gains the focus within Excel:

- ■ When the user selects the workbook from the Window menu
- ■ When your code runs the workbook's `Activate` method
- ■ When the user opens the workbook or when your code runs the workbook's `Open` method

Note that this event doesn't fire if the workbook has the focus in Excel and the user switches to Excel from a different application. Here's the event-handler procedure stub that appears when you select the `Activate` event in a workbook's code module:

```
Private Sub Workbook_Activate()
    <Event handler code goes here>
End Sub
```

NOTE: ENTERING EVENT HANDLER CODE

It's worth repeating that you don't create these event handlers in a regular VBA module. Instead, you follow these steps:

1. In the Visual Basic Editor's Project Explorer, highlight the object you want to work with. For the workbook containing the VBA code, highlight ThisWorkbook.

2. Select View | Code, press F7, or click the View Code button in the Project Explorer.

3. In the code window that appears, use the Object drop-down list (the one on the left) to select the Workbook object.

4. Use the Procedures drop-down list (the one on the right) to select the event you want to work with. VBA adds the event handler's procedure stub to the code window.

5. Enter your event-handler code within the procedure stub.

BeforeClose fires when the user selects File | Close or when your code runs the workbook's Close method. Note that the statements you define inside the event handler run before the workbook is closed and before the user is asked to save changes. Here's the procedure stub of the event handler:

```
Private Sub Workbook_BeforeClose(Cancel As Boolean)
    <Event handler code goes here>
End Sub
```

Cancel is a Boolean value that determines whether the workbook is closed. If you set Cancel to True during this procedure, Excel won't close the workbook.

BeforePrint fires when the user selects File | Print or when your code runs the workbook's PrintOut method. The statements you define inside the event handler run before the workbook is printed and before the Print dialog box appears. Here's the event handler's procedure stub:

```
Private Sub Workbook_BeforePrint(Cancel As Boolean)
    <Event handler code goes here>
End Sub
```

Cancel is a Boolean value that determines whether the workbook is printed. If you set Cancel to True during this procedure, Excel won't print the workbook.

BeforeSave fires when the user selects either File | Save or File | Save As or when your code runs the workbook's Save or SaveAs methods. The statements you define inside the event handler run before the workbook is saved. Here's the procedure stub:

```
Private Sub Workbook_BeforeSave(ByVal SaveAsUI As Boolean Cancel As Boolean)
    <Event handler code goes here>
End Sub
```

SaveAsUI	A Boolean value that determines whether Excel displays the Save As dialog box during a Save As operation.
Cancel	A Boolean value that determines whether the workbook is saved. If you set Cancel to True during this procedure, Excel won't save the workbook.

Deactivate fires when the workbook loses the focus within Excel (for example, if the user creates a new workbook or activates another open workbook). This event doesn't fire if the user switches to a different application. Note as well that Excel first switches to the other workbook and *then* runs the event handler. Here's the event-handler procedure stub:

```
Private Sub Workbook_Deactivate()
    <Event handler code goes here>
End Sub
```

NewSheet fires when the user creates a new sheet in the workbook (for example, by selecting Insert | Worksheet) or when your code runs the Add method of the Worksheets object. (See "Dealing with Worksheet Objects" later in this chapter.) This event also fires when the user or your code creates a chart in a new sheet. Note that the statements you define inside the event handler run *after* the new sheet is inserted.

Here's the procedure stub used by the event handler:

```
Private Sub Workbook_NewSheet(ByVal Sh As Object)
    <Event handler code goes here>
End Sub
```

Sh is an `Object` value that represents the new sheet. *Sh* can be either a Workbook object or a Chart object.

`Open` fires when the user selects File | Open or when your code runs the workbook's `Open` method. Here's the procedure stub of the event handler:

```
Private Sub Workbook_Open()
    <Event handler code goes here>
End Sub
```

Dealing with Worksheet Objects

Worksheet objects contain a number of properties, methods, and events you can exploit in your code. These include options for activating and hiding worksheets, adding new worksheets to a workbook, and moving, copying, and deleting worksheets. The next few sections discuss these and other worksheet operations.

Specifying a Worksheet Object

If you need to deal with a worksheet in some way, or if your code needs to specify an object contained in a specific worksheet (such as a range of cells), you need to tell Excel which worksheet you want to use. To do this, use the `Worksheets` object. `Worksheets` is the collection of all the worksheets in a particular workbook. To specify a worksheet, either use its index number (where 1 represents the first worksheet tab, 2 the second worksheet tab, and so on) or enclose the worksheet name in quotation marks. For example, if `Sheet1` is the first worksheet, the following two statements are equivalent:

```
Workbooks(1)
Worksheets("Sheet1")
```

If you need to work with multiple worksheets (say, to set up a 3-D range), use VBA's `Array` function with the `Workbooks` collection. For example, the following statement specifies the `Sheet1` and `Sheet2` worksheets:

```
Wordsheets(Array("Sheet1","Sheet2"))
```

Creating a New Worksheet

The `Worksheets` collection has an `Add` method you can use to insert new sheets into the workbook. Here's the syntax for this method:

```
Worksheets.Add(Before, After, Count, Type)
```

> *Before*   The sheet before which the new sheet is added. If you omit both *Before* and *After,* the new worksheet is added before the active sheet.

After	The sheet after which the new sheet is added. Note that you can't specify both the *Before* and *After* arguments.
Count	The number of new worksheets to add. VBA adds one worksheet if you omit *Count*.
Type	The type of worksheet. You have three choices: xlWorksheet (the default), xlExcel4MacroSheet, or xlExcel4IntlMacroSheet.

In the following statement, a new worksheet is added to the active workbook before the Sales sheet:

```
Worksheets.Add Before:=Worksheets("Sales")
```

Properties of the Worksheet Object

Take a tour through some of the most useful properties associated with Worksheet objects:

Worksheet.Name returns or sets the name of the specified *Worksheet*. For example, the following statement renames the Sheet1 worksheet to 1994 Budget:

```
Worksheets("Sheet1").Name = "1994 Budget"
```

Worksheet.Outline returns an Outline object that represents the outline for the specified *Worksheet*.

NOTE: WORKING WITH THE OUTLINE OBJECT

Once you have the Outline object, use the ShowLevels method to select an outline level. For example, the following statement displays the second outline level for the Net Worth worksheet:

```
Worksheets("Net Worth").Outline.ShowLevels 2
```

Here are some other outline-related properties and methods you can use:

Range.AutoOutline automatically creates an outline for the specified *Range* object.

Window.DisplayOutline: Set this property to True to display the outline for the specified *Window* object.

Range.ClearOutline clears the outline for the specified *Range* object.

Worksheet.ProtectContents returns True if the specified *Worksheet* is protected. To set this property (and the next few protection-related properties), run the Worksheet object's Protect method.

Worksheet.ProtectDrawingObjects returns True if the drawing objects on the specified *Worksheet* are protected.

`Worksheet.ProtectionMode` returns `True` if user-interface-only protection is activated for the specified `Worksheet`.

`Worksheet.ProtectScenarios` returns `True` if the scenarios in the specified `Worksheet` are protected.

`Worksheet.StandardHeight` returns the standard height of all the rows in the specified `Worksheet`.

`Worksheet.StandardWidth` returns the standard width of all the columns in the specified `Worksheet`.

`Worksheet.UsedRange` returns a Range object that represents the used range in the specified `Worksheet`.

`Worksheet.Visible` controls whether the user can see the specified `Worksheet`. Setting this property to `False` is equivalent to selecting Format | Sheet | Hide. For example, to hide a worksheet named Expenses, you use the following statement:

```
Worksheets("Expenses").Visible = False
```

To unhide the sheet, set its `Visible` property to `True`.

Methods of the Worksheet Object

Here is a list of some common Worksheet object methods:

`Worksheet.Activate` makes the specified `Worksheet` active (so that it becomes the `ActiveSheet` property of the workbook). For example, the following statement activates the Sales worksheet in the Finance.xls workbook:

```
Workbooks("Finance.xls").Worksheets("Sales").Activate
```

`Worksheet.Calculate` calculates the specified `Worksheet`. For example, the following statement recalculates the Budget 1997 worksheet:

```
Worksheets("Budget 1997").Calculate
```

`Worksheet.CheckSpelling` displays the Spelling dialog box to check the spelling on the specified `Worksheet`. Here is the syntax of this version of the `CheckSpelling` method:

`Worksheet``.CheckSpelling(`*`CustomDictionary`*`, `*`IgnoreUppercase`*`, `*`AlwaysSuggest`*`)`

Worksheet	The worksheet you want to check.
CustomDictionary	The filename of a custom dictionary that Excel can search if a word can't be found in the main dictionary.
IgnoreUppercase	Set to `True` to tell Excel to ignore words entirely in uppercase.
AlwaysSuggest	Set to `True` to tell Excel to display a list of suggestions for each misspelled word.

`Worksheet.Copy` copies the specified `Worksheet` using the following syntax:

`Worksheet``.Copy(`*`Before`*`, `*`After`*`)`

Worksheet	The worksheet you want to copy.
Before	The sheet before which the sheet will be copied. If you omit both *Before* and *After*, VBA creates a new workbook for the copied sheet.
After	The sheet after which the new sheet is added. You can't specify both the *Before* and *After* arguments.

In the following statement, the Budget 1997 worksheet is copied to a new workbook:

```
Worksheets("Budget 1997").Copy
```

Worksheet.Delete deletes the specified *Worksheet*. For example, the following statement deletes the active worksheet:

```
ActiveSheet.Delete
```

Worksheets.FillAcrossSheets enters data or formatting in a range that applies to the specified *Worksheets*. This method uses the following syntax:

Worksheets.FillAcrossSheets(**Range**, *Type*)

Worksheets	The Worksheets object you want to work with.
Range	The Range object in which you want to fill the data or formatting. Note that the specified range must be within one of the sheets specified in **Worksheets**.
Type	An optional argument that specifies what you want to fill:

xlFillWithAll	Fills the sheets with both the contents and the formatting contained in **Range**. This is the default value.
xlFillWithContents	Fills the sheets with just the contents of **Range**.
xlFillWithFormats	Fills the sheets with just the formatting of **Range**.

For example, the following statement fills the contents of range A1:D5 of worksheet Sheet1 across worksheets named Sheet1, Sheet2, and Sheet3:

```
Worksheets(Array("Sheet1", "Sheet2", "Sheet3")).FillAcrossSheets _
    Range:=Worksheets("Sheet1").Range("A1:D5"), _
    Type:=xlFillWithContents
```

Worksheet.Move moves the specified *Worksheet* using the following syntax:

Worksheet.Move(*Before, After*)

Worksheet	The worksheet you want to move.
Before	The sheet before which the sheet will be moved. If you omit both *Before* and *After*, VBA creates a new workbook for the moved sheet.

After	The sheet after which the new sheet is added. You can't specify both the *Before* and *After* arguments.

In the following statement, the Budget 1997 worksheet is moved before the Budget 1996 worksheet:

```
Worksheets("Budget 1997").Move Before:=Worksheets("1996 Budget")
```

Worksheet.Protect sets up protection for the specified *Worksheet*. Here's the syntax to use:

```
Worksheet.Protect(Password, DrawingObjects, Contents, Scenarios,
➥UserInterfaceOnly)
```

Worksheet	The worksheet you want to protect.
Password	A text string that specifies the (case-sensitive) password to use with the protection.
DrawingObjects	Set to True to protect the worksheet's drawing objects.
Contents	Set to True to protect the worksheet's cell contents.
Scenarios	Set to True to protect the worksheet's scenarios.
UserInterfaceOnly	Set to True to protect the worksheet's user interface but not its macros.

For example, the following statement protects the Payroll worksheet's contents and scenarios and sets up a password for the protection:

```
Worksheets("Payroll").Protect _
    Password:="cheapskate", _
    Contents:=True, _
    Scenarios:=True
```

Worksheet.Select selects the specified *Worksheet*.

Worksheet.SetBackgroundPicture adds a bitmap image to the background of the specified *Worksheet*. Here is the syntax:

```
Worksheet.SetBackgroundPicture(FileName)
```

Worksheet	The worksheet you want to use.
FileName	The filename of the bitmap image you want to use.

For example, the following statement sets the background image of Sheet1 to C:\Windows\Clouds.bmp:

```
Worksheets("Sheet1").SetBackgroundPicture "C:\Windows\Clouds.bmp"
```

Worksheet.Unprotect unprotects the specified *Worksheet*. Here's the syntax:

```
Worksheet.Unprotect(Password)
```

Worksheet	The Worksheet object you want to unprotect.
Password	The protection password.

57

EXCEL VBA
TECHNIQUES

Worksheet Object Events

Worksheet objects respond to several events, including activating and deactivating the worksheet, calculating the worksheet, and making a change to the worksheet. Here's a rundown of a few of these events:

Activate fires when the worksheet gains the focus within Excel (such as when the user clicks the worksheet's tab or when your code runs the worksheet's Activate method). Note that this event doesn't fire in the following situations:

- When the user switches from one workbook to another
- When the user switches to Excel from a different application

Here's the syntax of this procedure:

```
Private Sub Worksheet_Activate()
    <Event handler code goes here>
End Sub
```

Calculate fires when the specified worksheet recalculates, which in turn depends on whether any user-defined function was set up as a volatile function. (See the discussion of the Application object's Volatile method earlier in this chapter.) If no function is volatile, the Calculate event fires as follows:

- When the user reenters a cell containing a formula—that is, when the user highlights the cell, presses F2 to activate in-cell editing, and presses Enter.
- When the value of any input cell changes. An input cell is a cell that is referenced in a formula or used as an argument in a function.
- When your code runs the worksheet's Calculate method.

If a user-defined function has been set up as volatile, the Calculate event fires not only in the preceding situations, but also when the following occurs:

- When the user presses F9 or, in the Calculation tab of the Options dialog box, clicks the Calc Now button or the Calc Sheet button.
- When the value of a cell that is used indirectly in a calculation changes.

Here's the procedure stub of the event handler:

```
Private Sub Worksheet_Calculate()
    <Event handler code goes here>
End Sub
```

For example, Listing 57.2 shows the event handler defined for the 1997 Budget worksheet in Chaptr57.xls. The procedure watches a value named GrossMargin (cell B16 in the 1997 Budget worksheet). If, after a recalculation, this value dips below 20 percent, the procedure displays a warning message.

Listing 57.2. A Calculate event handler that monitors the GrossMargin cell.

```
Sub CheckMargin()
    With Range("GrossMargin")
        If .Value < 0.2 Then
            .Select
            MsgBox "Gross Margin is below 20%!"
        End If
    End With
End Sub
```

Change fires when the user changes the value of any cell in the worksheet or when your code changes the Value property of a cell. (See "Working with Range Objects" later in this chapter.) Here's the event-handler procedure stub:

```
Private Sub Worksheet_Change(ByVal Target As Excel.Range)
    <Event handler code goes here>
End Sub
```

Target is a Range object that represents the cell in which the new value was entered.

Listing 57.3 shows a sample event handler for the 1997 Budget worksheet. In this case, the code checks whether the user entered a numeric value in Column B. If not, a message is displayed and the Target cell is selected again.

Listing 57.3. A Change event handler that ensures the user enters only numeric values in Column B.

```
Private Sub Worksheet_Change(ByVal Target As Excel.Range)
    With Target
        '
        ' Make sure we're in Column B
        '
        If .Column = 2 Then
            '
            ' The value must be a number
            '
            If Not IsNumeric(.Value) Then
                MsgBox "Please enter a number in cell " & _
                    .Address & "!"
                .Select
            End If
        End If
    End With
End Sub
```

Deactivate fires when the worksheet loses the focus within Excel (for example, if the user clicks the tab of another worksheet or if your code runs the Activate method for another worksheet). Note that Excel first switches to the other worksheet and *then* runs the event handler. Here's the event-handler procedure stub:

```
Private Sub Worksheet_Deactivate()
    <Event handler code goes here>
End Sub
```

Working with Range Objects

Mastering cell and range references is perhaps the most fundamental skill to learn when working with spreadsheets. After all, most worksheet tasks involve cells, ranges, and range names. However, this skill takes on added importance when you're dealing with VBA procedures. When you're editing a worksheet directly, you can easily select cells and ranges with the mouse or the keyboard, or you can paste range names into formulas. In a procedure, however, you always have to describe—or even calculate—the range you want to select.

What you describe is the most common of all VBA objects: the Range object. A Range object can be a single cell, a row or column, a selection of cells, or a 3-D range. The following sections look at various techniques that return a Range object, as well as a number of Range object properties and methods.

Returning a Range Object

Much of your VBA code will concern itself with Range objects of one kind or another. Therefore, you need to be well-versed in the various techniques that are available for returning Range objects, whether they are single cells, rectangular ranges, or entire rows and columns. This section takes you through each of these techniques.

Using the Range Method

The `Range` method is the most straightforward way to identify a cell or range. It has two syntaxes. The first requires only a single argument:

```
Worksheet.Range(Name)
```

> *Worksheet* The Worksheet object to which the `Range` method applies. If you omit *Worksheet*, VBA assumes that the method applies to the `ActiveSheet` object.
>
> ***Name*** A range reference or name entered as text.

For example, the following statements enter a date in cell B2 and then create a data series in the range B2:E10 of the active worksheet (I'll discuss the `Formula` and `DataSeries` methods in more detail later):

```
Range("B2").Value = #01/01/95#
Range("B2:B13").DataSeries Type:=xlDate, Date:=xlMonth
```

The `Range` method also works with named ranges. For example, the following statement clears the contents of a range named `Criteria` in the Data worksheet:

```
Worksheets("Data").Range("Criteria").ClearContents
```

The second syntax for the `Range` method requires two arguments:

```
Worksheet.Range(Cell1, Cell2)
```

Worksheet	The Worksheet object to which the Range method applies. If you omit *Worksheet*, VBA assumes that the method applies to the ActiveSheet object.
Cell1, Cell2	The cells that define the upper-left corner (***Cell1***) and lower-right corner (***Cell2***) of the range. Each can be a cell address as text, a Range object consisting of a single cell, or an entire column or row.

The advantage of this syntax is that it separates the range corners into individual arguments. This lets you modify each corner under procedural control. For example, you can set up variables named upperLeft and lowerRight and then return Range objects of different sizes:

```
Range(upperLeft,lowerRight)
```

Using the Cells Method

The Cells method returns a single cell as a Range object. Here's the syntax:

```
Object.Cells(RowIndex, ColumnIndex)
```

Object	A Worksheet or Range object. If you omit *Object*, the method applies to the ActiveSheet object.
RowIndex	The row number of the cell. If *Workbook* is a worksheet, a ***RowIndex*** of 1 refers to row 1 on the sheet. If *Object* is a range, ***RowIndex*** 1 refers to the first row of the range.
ColumnIndex	The column of the cell. You can enter a letter as text or a number. If *Object* is a worksheet, a ***ColumnIndex*** of "A" or 1 refers to column A on the sheet. If *Object* is a range, a ***ColumnIndex*** of "A" or 1 refers to the first column of the range.

For example, the following procedure fragment loops five times and enters the values Field1 through Field5 in cells A1 through E1:

```
For colNumber = 1 To 5
    Cells(1, colNumber).Value = "Field" & colNumber
Next colNumber
```

TIP: A SHORTER CELL REFERENCE

You can also refer to a cell by enclosing an A1-style reference in square brackets ([ ]). For example, the following statement checks the spelling of the text in cell C4 of the active worksheet:

```
ActiveSheet.[C4].CheckSpelling
```

> **NOTE: THE CELLS COLLECTION**
>
> The `Cells` method has a second syntax that doesn't require arguments: `Object.Cells`. When `Object` is a worksheet, this method returns a collection of all the cells in the sheet.

Returning a Row

If you need to work with entire rows or columns, VBA has several methods and properties you can use. In each case, the object returned is a `Range`.

The most common way to refer to a row in VBA is to use the `Rows` method. This method uses the following syntax:

`Object.Rows(Index)`

> *Object*   The Worksheet or Range object to which the method applies. If you omit *Object*, VBA uses the `ActiveSheet` object.
>
> *Index*   The row number. If *Object* is a worksheet, an *Index* of 1 refers to row 1 on the sheet. If *Object* is a range, an *Index* of 1 refers to the first row of the range. If you omit *Index*, the method returns a collection of all the rows in *Object*.

For example, Listing 57.4 shows a procedure named `InsertRangeRow`. This procedure inserts a new row before the last row of whatever range is passed as an argument (`rangeObject`). This is a useful subroutine in programs that need to maintain ranges (such as an Excel list).

Listing 57.4. A procedure that uses the Rows method to insert a row before the last row of a range.

```
Sub InsertRangeRow(rangeObject As Range)
    Dim totalRows As Integer, lastRow As Integer
    With rangeObject
        totalRows = .Rows.Count          ' Total rows in the range
        lastRow = .Rows(totalRows).Row   ' Last row number
        .Rows(lastRow).Insert            ' Insert before last row
    End With
End Sub
Sub InsertTest()
    InsertRangeRow ThisWorkbook.Worksheets("Sheet1").Range("Test")
End Sub
```

After declaring the variables, the first statement uses the `Rows` method without the *Index* argument to return a collection of all the rows in `rangeObject` and uses the `Count` property to get the total number of `rangeObject` rows:

```
totalRows = rangeObject.Rows.Count
```

The second statement uses the totalRows variable as an argument in the Rows method to return the last row of rangeObject, and then the Row property returns the row number:

```
lastRow = rangeObject.Rows(totalRows).Row
```

Finally, the last statement uses the Insert method to insert a row before lastRow. (Insert has three different syntaxes. See the help system for details.)

To use InsertRangeRow, you need to pass a Range object to the procedure. For example, the InsertRange procedure shown at the end of Listing 57.4 inserts a row into a range named Test.

NOTE: ANOTHER WAY TO RETURN A ROW

You can also use the EntireRow property to return a row. The syntax *Range*.EntireRow returns the entire row or rows that contain the *Range* object. This is most often used to mimic the Shift-Spacebar shortcut key that selects the entire row that includes the active cell. To do this, you use the following statement:

```
ActiveCell.EntireRow.Select
```

Returning a Column

To return a column, use the Columns method. The syntax for this method is almost identical to that of the Rows method:

```
Object.Columns(Index)
```

Object	The Worksheet or Range object to which the method applies. If you omit *Object*, VBA uses the ActiveSheet object.
Index	The column number. If *Object* is a worksheet, an *Index* of "A" or 1 refers to column A on the sheet. If *Object* is a range, *Index* "A" or 1 refers to the first column of the range. If you omit *Index*, the method returns a collection of all the columns in *Object*.

For example, the following statement sets the width of column B on the active worksheet to 20:

```
Columns("B").ColumnWidth = 20
```

NOTE: ANOTHER WAY TO RETURN A COLUMN

The syntax *Range*.EntireColumn returns the entire column or columns that contain the specified *Range* object.

Using the `Offset` Method

When defining your Range objects, you often won't know the specific range address to use. For example, you might need to refer to the cell that's two rows down and one column to the right of the active cell. You can find out the address of the active cell and then calculate the address of the other cell, but VBA gives you an easier (and more flexible) way: the `Offset` method. `Offset` returns a Range object that is offset from a specified range by a certain number of rows and columns. Here is its syntax:

Range`.Offset(`*RowOffset, ColumnOffset*`)`

Range	The original Range object.
RowOffset	The number of rows to offset *Range*. You can use a positive number (to move down), a negative number (to move up), or `0` (to use the same rows). If you omit *RowOffset*, VBA uses `0`.
ColumnOffset	The number of columns to offset *Range*. Again, you can use a positive number (to move right), a negative number (to move left), or `0` (to use the same columns). If you omit *ColumnOffset*, VBA uses `0`.

For example, the following statement formats the range B2:D6 as bold:

```
Range("A1:C5").Offset(1,1).Font.Bold = True
```

Listing 57.5 shows a procedure called `ConcatenateStrings` that concatenates two text strings. This is handy, for instance, if you want to combine a list with separate first and last name fields.

Listing 57.5. A procedure that uses the `Offset` method to concatenate two text strings.

```
Sub ConcatenateStrings()
    Dim string1$, string2$
    ' Store the contents of the cell 2 to the left of the active cell
    string1$ = ActiveCell.Offset(0, -2)
    ' Store the contents of the cell 1 to the left of the active cell
    string2$ = ActiveCell.Offset(0, -1)
    ' Enter combined strings (separated by a space) into active cell
    ActiveCell.Value = string1$ & " " & string2$
End Sub
```

The procedure begins by declaring `string1$` and `string2$`. (The `$` type declaration characters automatically declare these variables as string types; see Chapter 53 for details.) The next statement stores in `string1$` the contents of the cell two columns to the left of the active cell by using the `Offset` method as follows:

```
String1$ = ActiveCell.Offset(0, -2)
```

Similarly, the next statement stores in `string2$` the contents of the cell one column to the left of the active cell. Finally, the last statement combines `string1$` and `string2$` (with a space in between) and stores the new string in the active cell.

Selecting a Cell or Range

If you've used the Excel 4.0 macro language, you know that most of its range operations require you to first select the range and then do something to it. For example, changing the font to Times New Roman in the range B1 to B10 of the active sheet requires two commands:

```
=SELECT(!$B$1:$B$10)
=FORMAT.FONT("Times New Roman")
```

VBA, however, lets you access objects directly without selecting them first. This means that your VBA procedures rarely have to select a range. You can perform the preceding example with a single (and faster) VBA statement:

```
Range("B1:B10").Font.Name = "Times New Roman"
```

Sometimes, however, you do need to select a range. For example, you might need to display a selected range to the user. To select a range, use the `Select` method:

Range.Select

> *Range*   The Range object you want to select.

For example, the following statement selects the range A1:E10 in the Sales worksheet:

```
Worksheets("Sales").Range("A1:E10").Select
```

TIP: RETURNING THE SELECTED RANGE

To return a Range object that represents the currently selected range, use the `Selection` property. For example, the following statement applies the Times New Roman font to the currently selected range:

```
Selection.Font.Name = "Times New Roman"
```

Defining a Range Name

In VBA, range names are `Name` objects. To define them, you use the `Add` method for the `Names` collection (which is usually the collection of defined names in a workbook). Here is an abbreviated syntax for the `Names` collection's `Add` method (this method has 11 arguments; see the VBA Reference in the help system):

```
Names.Add(Text, RefersTo)
```

> *Text*   The text you want to use as the range name.
>
> *RefersTo*   The item to which you want the name to refer. You can enter a constant, a formula as text (such as `"=Sales-Expenses"`), or a worksheet reference (such as `"Sales!A1:C6"`).

For example, the following statement adds the range name `SalesRange` to the `Names` collection of the active workbook:

```
ActiveWorkbook.Names.Add _
    Text:="SalesRange", _
    RefersTo:="=Sales!$A$1$C$6"
```

More Range Object Properties

Some of the examples you've seen in the last few sections have used various Range object properties. Here's a review of a few more properties you're likely to use often in your VBA code:

Range.`Address` returns the address, as text, of the specified *Range*.

Range.`Column` returns the number of the first column in the specified *Range*.

Range.`Count` returns the number of cells in the specified *Range*.

Range.`CurrentArray` returns a Range object that represents the entire array in which the specified *Range* resides.

CAUTION: TEST FOR AN ARRAY

If the specified range isn't part of an array, the `CurrentArray` property generates a `No cell found` error message. To prevent this error, use the `HasArray` property to test whether the range is part of an array. If the range is part of an array, `HasArray` returns `True`.

Range.`CurrentRegion` returns a Range object that represents the entire region in which the specified *Range* resides. A range's "region" is the area surrounding the range that is bounded by at least one empty row above and below and at least one empty column to the left and right.

Range.`Formula` returns or sets a formula for the specified *Range*.

Range.`FormulaArray` returns or sets an array formula for the specified *Range*.

Range.`NumberFormat` returns or sets the numeric format in the specified *Range*. Enter the format you want to use as a string, as shown in the following statement:

```
Worksheets("Analysis").Range("Sales").NumberFormat = _
    "$#,##0.00_);[Red]($#,##0.00)"
```

Range.`Row` returns the number of the first row in the specified *Range*.

Range.`Value` returns or sets the value in the specified *Range*.

More Range Object Methods

Here's a look at a few more methods that should come in handy in your VBA procedures:

Range.`Cut` cuts the specified *Range* to the Clipboard or to a new destination. The `Cut` method uses the following syntax:

Range.`Cut(Destination)`

| ***Range*** | The Range object to cut. |
| *Destination* | The cell or range where you want the cut range to be pasted. |

For example, the following statement cuts the range A1:B3 and moves it to the range B4:C6:

```
Range("A1:B3").Cut Destination:=Range("B4")
```

Range.Copy copies the specified *Range* to the Clipboard or to a new destination. Copying a range is similar to cutting a range. Here's the syntax for the Copy method:

Range.Copy(*Destination*)

| ***Range*** | The range to copy. |
| *Destination* | The cell or range where you want the copied range to be pasted. |

Range.Clear removes everything from the specified *Range* (contents, formats, and comments).

Range.ClearComments removes the cell comments for the specified *Range*.

Range.ClearContents removes the contents of the specified *Range*.

Range.ClearFormats removes the formatting for the specified *Range*.

Range.DataSeries creates a data series in the specified *Range*. The DataSeries method uses the following syntax:

Range.DataSeries(*Rowcol, Type, Date, Step, Stop, Trend*)

Range	The range to use for the data series.
Rowcol	Use xlRows to enter the data in rows or xlColumns to enter the data in columns. If you omit *Rowcol,* Excel uses the size and shape of **Range.**
Type	The type of series. Enter xlLinear (the default), xlGrowth, xlChronological, or xlAutoFill.
Date	The type of date series, if you used xlChronological for the *Type* argument. Your choices are xlDay (the default), xlWeekday, xlMonth, or xlYear.
Step	The step value for the series (the default value is 1).
Stop	The stop value for the series. If you omit *Stop,* Excel fills the range.
Trend	Use True to create a linear or growth trend series. Use False (the default) to create a standard series.

Range.FillDown uses the contents and formatting from the top row of the specified *Range* to fill down into the rest of the range.

Range.FillLeft uses the contents and formatting from the rightmost column of the specified *Range* to fill left into the rest of the range.

Range.FillRight uses the contents and formatting from the leftmost column of the specified *Range* to fill right into the rest of the range.

Range.FillUp uses the contents and formatting from the bottom row of the specified *Range* to fill up into the rest of the range.

Range.Insert inserts cells into the specified *Range* using the following syntax:

***Range*.Insert(*Shift*)**

Range	The range into which you want to insert the cells.
Shift	The direction you want to shift the existing cells. Use either xlShiftToRight or xlShiftDown. If you omit this argument, Excel determines the direction based on the shape of ***Range***.

Range.Resize resizes the specified *Range*. Here's the syntax for this method:

***Range*.Resize(*RowSize*, *ColSize*)**

Range	The range to resize.
RowSize	The number of rows in the new range.
ColSize	The number of columns in the new range.

For example, suppose you use the InsertRangeRow procedure from Listing 57.4 to insert a row into a named range. In most cases, you want to redefine the range name so that it includes the extra row you added. Listing 57.6 shows a procedure that calls InsertRangeRow and then uses the Resize method to adjust the named range.

Listing 57.6. A procedure that uses Resize to adjust a named range.

```
Sub InsertAndRedefineName()
    With ThisWorkbook.Worksheets("Sheet1")
        InsertRangeRow .Range("Test")
        With .Range("Test")
            Names.Add _
                Name:="Test", _
                RefersTo:=.Resize(.Rows.Count + 1)
        End With
        .Range("Test").Select
    End With
End Sub
```

In the Names.Add method, the new range is given by the expression .Resize(.Rows.Count + 1). Here, the Resize method returns a range that has one more row than the Test range.

Summary

This chapter showed you how to use VBA to manipulate Excel. You examined various properties and methods for common objects, including the `Application`, Workbook, Worksheet, and Range objects. Here are some chapters to check out for related information:

- You can find general Excel techniques in Part IV, "Unleashing Excel."
- For a general discussion of VBA objects, see Chapter 54, "Understanding Objects."
- You'll learn how to integrate Excel with other Office applications in Chapter E6 on the CD, "Integrating Office Applications with VBA."

57

EXCEL VBA
TECHNIQUES

Programming a PowerPoint Presentation

IN THIS CHAPTER

[When juggling] there are great possibilities for creativity, with hundreds of original patterns and variations.

—*Charles Lewis (Carlo)*

Previous versions of Office didn't make incorporating PowerPoint presentations into your VBA applications easy, because there was no way to program PowerPoint directly. Instead, you had to work with a different VBA-enabled application (such as Excel), use OLE automation to expose PowerPoint's objects, and manipulate those objects via the automation interface. It worked, but it was a slow and unintuitive way to program.

That's all changed with Office 97. Although you can still manipulate PowerPoint via OLE automation (see Chapter E6 on the CD, "Integrating Office Applications with VBA"), PowerPoint 97 is now fully programmable thanks to its built-in VBA engine. It comes with all the VBA tools I've discussed so far—the macro recorder, the Visual Basic Editor, support for Microsoft Forms, and so on—so all your newfound VBA knowledge can be put to good use programming presentations.

This chapter shows you how to leverage that knowledge in the PowerPoint environment by examining a few PowerPoint objects and their associated properties, methods, and events.

PowerPoint's Application Object

Chapter 54, "Understanding Objects," ran through some `Application` object properties and methods that are common to all VBA-enabled applications. You've also seen in the last two chapters how Word and Excel have a few unique `Application` object members. PowerPoint's `Application` object has just a few unique properties and no unique methods. Here's a list of some of PowerPoint's unique properties:

> `ActivePresentation` returns a Presentation object that represents the presentation file which currently has the focus within PowerPoint. See "PowerPoint's Presentation Object" later in this chapter to learn about the properties and methods of the Presentation object.

> `ActivePrinter` returns or sets the name of the active printer. (Note that to set the active printer, you must specify the name of an existing Windows printer.) The following statement sets the active printer:

> `ActivePrinter = "HP LaserJet 5P/5MP PostScript local on LPT1:"`

> `Presentations` returns the `Presentations` object, which is the collection of all open presentations.

> `SlideShowWindows` returns the `SlideShowWindows` object, which is the collection of all open slide show windows.

PowerPoint's Presentation Object

In PowerPoint, the Presentation object represents a presentation file (.PPT) that is open in the PowerPoint application window. You can use VBA to create new presentations, open or delete existing presentations, save and close presentations, and more. The next section takes you through various techniques for specifying presentations in your VBA code; then you'll look at some Presentation object properties and methods.

Specifying a Presentation Object

If you need to do something with a presentation, or if you need to work with an object contained in a specific presentation (such as a slide), you need to tell PowerPoint which presentation you want to use. VBA gives you three ways to do this:

> **Use the `Presentations` object:** The `Presentations` object is the collection of all open presentation files. To specify a particular presentation, either use its index number (where 1 represents the first presentation opened) or enclose the presentation filename in quotation marks. For example, if Proposal.ppt was the first presentation opened, the following two statements are equivalent:

```
Presentations("Proposal.ppt")
Presentations(1)
```

> **Use the `ActivePresentation` object:** The `ActivePresentation` object represents the presentation that currently has the focus.

> **Use the `Presentation` property:** Open slide show windows have a `Presentation` property that returns the name of the underlying presentation. For example, the following statement uses the `currPres` variable to store the name of the presentation in the first slide show window:

```
currPres = SlideShowWindows(1).Presentation
```

Opening a Presentation

To open a presentation file, use the `Open` method of the `Presentations` collection. The `Open` method has several arguments you can use to fine-tune your presentation openings, but only one of these arguments is mandatory. Here's the simplified syntax showing the one required argument (for the rest of the arguments, look up the `Open` method in the VBA help system):

```
Presentations.Open(FileName)
```

Here, *FileName* is the full name of the presentation file, including the drive and folder that contain the file. For example, to open a presentation named Proposal.ppt in the C:\My Documents\ folder, you use the following statement:

```
Presentations.Open "C:\My Documents\Proposal.ppt"
```

Creating a New Presentation

If you need to create a new presentation, use the Presentations collection's Add method:

```
Presentations.Add(WithWindow)
```

WithWindow is a Boolean value that determines whether the presentation is created in a visible window. Use True for a visible window (this is the default); use False to hide the window.

Presentation Object Properties

Here's a list of a few common properties associated with Presentation objects:

Presentation.FullName returns the full path name of the specified Presentation. The full path name includes the presentation's path (the drive and folder in which the file resides) and the filename.

Presentation.HandoutMaster returns a Master object that represents the handout master for the specified Presentation.

Presentation.HasTitleMaster returns True if the specified Presentation has a title master.

Presentation.Name returns the filename of the Presentation.

Presentation.NotesMaster returns a Master object that represents the notes master for the specified Presentation.

Presentation.Path returns the path of the Presentation file.

> **NOTE: THE PATH OF A NEW PRESENTATION**
>
> A new, unsaved presentation's Path property returns an empty string ("").

Presentation.Saved determines whether changes have been made to the specified Presentation since it was last saved.

Presentation.SlideMaster returns a Master object that represents the slide master for the specified Presentation.

Presentation.Slides returns a Slides object that represents the collection of Slide objects contained in the specified Presentation.

Presentation.SlideShowSettings returns a SlideShowSettings object that represents the slide show setup options for the specified Presentation.

Presentation.TemplateName returns the name of the design template underlying the specified Presentation.

Presentation.TitleMaster returns a Master object that represents the title master for the specified Presentation.

Presentation Object Methods

A Presentation object has methods that let you save the presentation, close it, print it, and more. Here are the methods you'll use most often:

Presentation.AddTitleMaster adds a title master to the specified *Presentation*. Note that VBA generates an error if the presentation already has a title master, so your code should use the HasTitleMaster property to check for an existing title master before running this method, as shown in the following procedure fragment:

```
With ActivePresentation
    If Not .HasTitleMaster Then .AddTitleMaster
End With
```

Presentation.ApplyTemplate applies a design template to the specified *Presentation*. This method uses the following syntax:

Presentation.ApplyTemplate(***FileName***)

Presentation	The Presentation object to which you want to apply the template.
FileName	The full name of the template (.POT) file.

For example, the following statement applies the Dads Tie template to the active presentation:

```
ActivePresentation.ApplyTemplate _
    "C:\Microsoft Office\Templates\Presentation Designs\Dads Tie.pot"
```

Presentation.Close closes the specified *Presentation*. If the file has unsaved changes, PowerPoint asks the user whether he wants to save those changes.

Presentation.NewWindow opens a new window for the specified *Presentation*.

Presentation.PrintOut prints the specified *Presentation* using the following syntax:

Presentation.PrintOut(*From, To, Copies, PrintToFile, Collate*)

Presentation	The Presentation object you want to print.
From	The page number from which to start printing.
To	The page number of the last page to print.
Copies	The number of copies to print. The default value is 1.
PrintToFile	The name of a file to which you want the presentation printed.
Collate	If this argument is True and *Copies* is greater than 1, VBA collates the copies.

Presentation.Save saves the specified Presentation. If the presentation is new, use the SaveAs method instead.

Presentation.SaveAs saves the specified *Presentation* to a different file. Here's the syntax for the SaveAs method:

Presentation.SaveAs(*FileName*, *FileFormat*, *EmbedTrueTypeFonts*)

Presentation	The Presentation object you want to save to a different file.
FileName	The full name of the new presentation file, including the drive and folder where you want the file to reside.
FileFormat	The PowerPoint format to use for the new file. Use one of the following constants:

ppSaveAsAddIn	Add-in (.PPA)
ppSaveAsPowerPoint3	PowerPoint 3.0 (.PPT)
ppSaveAsPowerPoint4	PowerPoint 4.0 (.PPT)
ppSaveAsPowerPoint7	PowerPoint 95 (.PPT)
ppSaveAsPresentation	PowerPoint Show (.PPS)
ppSaveAsRTF	Rich Text Format (.RTF)
ppSaveAsTemplate	Template (.POT)

EmbedTrueTypeFonts	If True, PowerPoint embeds the presentation's TrueType fonts in the new file.

The Juggling Application

Throughout this chapter, I put the PowerPoint objects, methods, and properties that I talk about to good use in an application that builds an entire presentation from scratch. This presentation will consist of a series of slides that provide instructions on how to juggle.

The code for the application consists of five procedures:

Main: This procedure ties the entire application together by calling each of the other procedures in the module.

CreateJugglingPresentation: This procedure creates a new Presentation object and saves it.

CreateJugglingSlides: This procedure adds the slides to the presentation and then formats them.

SetUpFirstPage: This procedure adds and formats text for the presentation title page.

SetUpJugglingPages: This procedure adds and formats a title, picture, and instruction text for each of the four pages that explain how to juggle.

RunJugglingSlideShow: This procedure asks the user whether he or she wants to run the slide show and then runs it if Yes is chosen.

To get started, Listing 58.1 shows the Main procedure.

Listing 58.1. This procedure ties everything together by calling each of the code listings individually.

```
' Global variable
Dim pres As Presentation
Sub Main()
    '
    ' Create the presentation file
    '
    CreateJugglingPresentation
    '
    ' Add the slides
    '
    AddJugglingSlides
    '
    ' Set up the title page
    '
    SetUpStartPage
    '
    ' Set up the Juggling pages
    '
    SetUpJugglingPages
    '
    ' Save it and then run it
    '
    pres.Save
    RunJugglingSlideShow
End Sub
```

First, the pres variable is declared as a Presentation object. Notice that this variable is defined at the module level so that it can be used in all the procedures in the module. Then Main begins by calling the CreateJugglingPresentation procedure, shown in Listing 58.2. From there, the other procedures (discussed later in this chapter) are called and the presentation is saved.

Listing 58.2. This procedure creates a new presentation and then saves it.

```
Sub CreateJugglingPresentation()
    Dim p As Presentation
    '
    ' If the old one is still open, close it without saving
    '
    For Each p In Presentations
        If p.Name = "Juggling" Then
            p.Saved = True
            p.Close
        End If
    Next p
    '
    ' Create a new Presentation object and store it in pres
    '
    Set pres = Presentations.Add
    pres.SaveAs FileName:="Juggling.ppt"
End Sub
```

A `For Each...Next` loop runs through each open presentation and checks the `Name` property. If it equals Juggling.ppt, you know the file is already open. If it's open (say, from running the application previously), the procedure closes it without saving it. The `pres` variable is `Set` and then the presentation is saved using the `SaveAs` method.

NOTE: THE JUGGLING APPLICATION CODE

You can find the presentation and code used in this chapter's sample application on the CD-ROM that accompanies this book. Look for the Chaptr58.ppt file (or Chaptr58.bas if you don't have PowerPoint but still want to examine the code).

Working with PowerPoint Slide Objects

PowerPoint presentations consist of a series of slides. In PowerPoint VBA, a slide is a Slide object that contains a number of properties and methods that you can wield in your code. These include options for setting the slide's layout, specifying the transition effect, and copying and deleting slides. The next few sections discuss these and other slide techniques.

Specifying a Slide

To work with a slide, you need to specify a Slide object. For a single slide, the easiest way to do this is to use the `Slides` object. `Slides` is the collection of all the slides in a particular presentation. To specify a slide, either use the slide's index number (where 1 represents the first slide in the presentation, 2 the second slide, and so on), or enclose the slide name in quotation marks. For example, if Slide1 is the first slide, the following two statements are equivalent:

```
ActivePresentation.Slides("Slide1")
ActivePresentation.Slides(1)
```

Alternatively, you can specify a slide by using its *slide ID* number. PowerPoint assigns a unique ID to each slide you create. As you'll see later when you look at slide properties, this value is stored in the `SlideID` property of each Slide object. To refer to a slide by its ID number, use the `FindBySlideID` method of the `Slides` object:

Presentation`.Slides.FindBySlideID(`*SlideID*`)`

> *Presentation*   The Presentation object that contains the slide.
>
> *SlideID*   The slide's ID number.

I show you an example of this method in the next section when I discuss how to create a new slide. If you need to work with multiple slides (say, to apply a particular layout to all the slides), use the `Range` method of the `Slides` object:

Presentation`.Slides.Range(`*Index*`)`

Presentation	The Presentation object that contains the slides.
Index	An array that specifies the slides.

For the *Index* argument, use VBA's `Array` function with multiple instances of any of the following: slide index numbers, slide names, or slide ID numbers. For example, the following statement specifies the slides named `Slide1` and `Slide2`:

```
ActivePresentation.Slides.Range(Array("Slide1","Slide2"))
```

TIP: WORKING WITH ALL SLIDES

To work with every slide in the presentation, use the `Range` method without an argument, as in this example:

```
ActivePresentation.Slides.Range
```

You can also use the Presentation object's `SlideMaster` property to work with the slide master. This will change the default settings for every slide in the presentation.

Creating a New Slide

Once you create a presentation, you need to populate it with slides. To insert a new Slide object into a presentation, use the `Add` method of the `Slides` collection:

Presentation`.Slides.Add(`*Index, Layout*`)`

Presentation	The Presentation object in which you want to add the slide.
Index	The index number of the new slide within the `Slides` object. Use 1 to make this the first slide; use `Slides.Count + 1` to make this the last slide.
Layout	A constant that specifies the layout of the new slide. PowerPoint defines over two dozen constants, including `ppLayoutText` (for a text-only slide), `ppLayoutChart` (for a chart slide), and `ppLayoutBlank` (for a blank slide). Look up the `Add` method in the VBA help system to see the full list of constants.

The following statements add an organization chart slide to the end of the active presentation:

```
With ActivePresentation.Slides
    .Add Index:=.Count + 1, Layout:=ppLayoutOrgchart
End With
```

Here's another example of the Add method that saves the new slide's ID number:

```
With ActivePresentation.Slides
    newSlideID = .Add(1, ppLayoutText).SlideID
End With
```

Inserting Slides from a File

Instead of creating slides from scratch, you might prefer to pilfer one or more slides from an existing presentation. The InsertFromFile method lets you do this. It uses the following syntax:

***Presentation*.Slides.InsertFromFile(*FileName*, *Index*, *SlideStart*, *SlideEnd*)**

Presentation	The Presentation object in which you want to add the slides.
FileName	The name of the file (including the drive and folder) that contains the slides you want to insert.
Index	The index number of an existing slide in ***Presentation***. The slides from ***FileName*** are inserted after this slide.
SlideStart	The index number of the first slide in ***FileName*** that you want to insert.
SlideEnd	The index number of the last slide in ***FileName*** that you want to insert.

For example, the following procedure fragment inserts the first five slides from Budget.ppt at the end of the active presentation:

```
With ActivePresentation.Slides
    .InsertFromFile _
        FileName:="C:\Presentations\Budget.ppt", _
        Index:=.Count, _
        SlideStart:=1, _
        SlideEnd:=5
End With
```

Slide Properties

To let you change the look and feel of your slides, PowerPoint VBA offers a number of Slide object properties. These properties control the slide's layout, background, color scheme, name, and more. This section describes a few of the more useful Slide object properties:

NOTE: A RANGE OF SLIDES ACTS AS A SINGLE SLIDE

If you specify multiple slides using the Range method described earlier, PowerPoint returns a SlideRange object that references the slides. This object has the same properties and methods as a Slide object, so you can work with multiple slides the same way that you work with a single slide.

Slide.Background returns or sets the background of the specified *Slide*. Note that this property actually returns a ShapeRange object. (See "Dealing with Shape Objects" later in this chapter.)

You usually use this property with the slide master to set the background for all the slides in the presentation. For example, the following statements store the slide master background in a variable and then use the Shape object's Fill property to change the background patter for all the slides in the active presentation:

```
Set slideBack = ActivePresentation.SlideMaster.Background
slideBack.Fill.PresetGradient _
    Style:=msoGradientHorizontal, _
    Variant:=1, _
    PresetGradientType:=msoGradientFire
```

If you just want to change the background for a single slide, you must first set the slide's FollowMasterBackground property to False:

```
With ActivePresentation.Slides(1)
    .FollowMasterBackground = False
    .Background.Fill.PresetGradient _
        Style:=msoGradientHorizontal, _
        Variant:=1, _
        PresetGradientType:=msoGradientFire
End With
```

Slide.DisplayMasterShapes returns or sets whether the specified *Slide* displays the Shape objects defined on the slide master. If True, objects on the slide master (such as text, graphics, and OLE objects) also appear on the slide.

Slide.FollowMasterBackground: As mentioned earlier, this property returns or sets whether the specified *Slide* uses the same Background property as the slide master. Set this property to False to set a unique background for an individual slide.

Slide.Layout returns or sets the layout for the specified *Slide*. Again, see the VBA help system for the full list of layout constants.

Slide.Master returns the slide master for the specified *Slide*. The following two statements are equivalent:

```
ActivePresentation.SlideMaster
ActivePresentation.Slides(1).Master
```

Slide.Name returns or sets the name of the specified *Slide*.

Slide.NotesPage returns a SlideRange object that represents the notes page for the specified *Slide*.

Slide.Shapes returns a Shapes collection that represents all the Shape objects on the specified *Slide*.

Slide.SlideID returns the ID number of the specified *Slide*.

Slide.SlideIndex returns the index number of the specified *Slide* within the Slides collection.

Slide.SlideShowTransition returns a SlideShowTransition object that represents the transition special effects used for the specified *Slide* during a slide show.

58

PROGRAMMING A POWERPOINT PRESENTATION

The Juggling Application: Creating the Slides

Listing 58.3 shows the AddJugglingSlides procedure, which adds four slides to the juggling presentation (represented, remember, by the pres variable) and then uses the SlideMaster object to set the default background for the slides.

Listing 58.3. A procedure that adds the slides to the juggling presentation and formats them.

```
Sub AddJugglingSlides()
    Dim i As Integer
    With pres
        With .Slides
            '
            ' Add the opening slide
            '
            .Add(Index:=1, Layout:=ppLayoutTitle).Name = "Opener"
            '
            ' Now add the slides for each step
            '
            For i = 1 To 4
                .Add(Index:=i + 1, Layout:=ppLayoutTitle).Name = "Juggling" & i
            Next i
        End With
        '
        ' Set the background for all the slides
        '
        .SlideMaster.Background.Fill.PresetGradient _
            Style:=msoGradientHorizontal, _
            Variant:=1, _
            PresetGradientType:=msoGradientNightfall
    End With
End Sub
```

Slide Methods

PowerPoint VBA defines a half dozen Slide object methods that let you copy slides, delete slides, export slides, and more. Here's the complete list:

Slide.Copy copies the specified *Slide* to the Clipboard. If you then want to paste the slide into another presentation, use the Paste method of the Slides object:

Presentation.Slides.Paste(*Index*)

| *Presentation* | The Presentation object into which you want to paste the slide. |
| *Index* | The index number of the slide before which the slide will be pasted. |

For example, the following statements copy the first slide from the 1996 Budget presentation and paste it before the first slide in the 1997 Budget presentation:

```
Presentations("1996 Budget").Slides(1).Copy
Presentations("1997 Budget").Slides.Paste 1
```

`Slide`.`Cut` cuts the specified `Slide` from the presentation and places it on the Clipboard. Again, use the `Slides`.`Paste` method to paste the slide into another presentation.

`Slide`.`Delete` deletes the specified `Slide`.

`Slide`.`Duplicate`: Use this method to make a copy of the specified `Slide` in the same presentation. The new slide is added to the presentation immediately after the specified `Slide`. Note, too, that this method returns a SlideRange object that refers to the new slide.

`Slide`.`Export` exports the specified `Slide` to a file in a graphics format of your choice. Here's the syntax:

`Slide`.`Export(FileName, FilterName, ScaleWidth, ScaleHeight)`

Slide	The Slide object you want to export.
FileName	The name of the exported file, possibly including the drive and folder. (If you omit the drive and folder, the slide is exported to the current folder.) Note that you don't need to add a file extension. PowerPoint adds whatever extension is appropriate according to the **FilterName** you use.
FilterName	The graphics format to use for the exported file. Use the registered extension for the graphics format (such as .JPG for a JPEG file).
ScaleWidth	A number that determines the factor by which the slide is scaled horizontally during the export. For example, a value of 2 doubles the width of the slide in the exported file.
ScaleHeight	A number that determines the factor by which the slide is scaled vertically during the export.

The following statement exports the first slide in the active presentation to a file named Summary.jpg in the C:\Graphics folder:

```
ActivePresentation.Slides(1).Export _
    FileName:="C:\Graphics\Summary", _
    FilterName:="JPG"
```

`Slide`.`Select` selects the specified `Slide`. Note that the presentation window must be displayed in a view that supports this method. For example, this method fails in Slide view, but it works in Outline or Slide Sorter view. Here's some code that uses the ViewType property to change the view of the active window to Slide Sorter and then selects a slide:

```
ActiveWindow.ViewType = ppViewSlideSorter
ActivePresentation.Slides(3).Select
```

58

PROGRAMMING
A POWERPOINT
PRESENTATION

Dealing with Shape Objects

PowerPoint slides are really just a collection of objects: titles, text boxes, pictures, OLE objects, labels, lines, curves, and so on. In PowerPoint VBA, each of these items is a Shape object. Therefore, to get full slide control in your VBA procedures, you must know how to add, edit, format, and otherwise manipulate these objects. That's the goal of this section.

Specifying a Shape

You must specify a Shape object before you can work with it. The techniques you use for this are similar to those I outlined earlier for Slide objects.

For a single shape, use the Shapes object, which is the collection of all Shape objects on a particular slide. To specify a shape, either use the shape's index number (where 1 represents the first shape added to the slide, 2 is the second shape, and so on), or enclose the shape name in quotation marks. For example, if Rectangle 1 is the first shape, the following two statements are equivalent:

```
ActivePresentation.Shapes("Rectangle 1")
ActivePresentation.Shapes(1)
```

If you need to work with multiple shapes, use the Range method of the Shapes object:

Slide.Shapes.Range(*Index*)

Slide	The Slide object that contains the shapes.
Index	An array that specifies the shapes.

As with multiple slides, use VBA's Array function for the *Index* argument:

```
Presentations(1).Slides(1).Shapes.Range(Array("Oval 1","TextBox 2"))
```

> **TIP: WORKING WITH ALL SHAPES**
>
> To work with every shape in the slide, use the Range method without an argument:
> ```
> Presentations(1).Slides(1).Shapes.Range
> ```

Adding Shapes to a Slide

The Slides object has 14 different methods you can use to insert shapes into a slide. Many of these methods use similar arguments, so before I list the methods, take a quick tour of the common arguments:

BeginX	For connectors and lines, the distance (in points) from the shape's starting point to the left edge of the slide window.
BeginY	For connectors and lines, the distance (in points) from the shape's starting point to the top edge of the slide window.

EndX	For connectors and lines, the distance (in points) from the shape's ending point to the left edge of the slide window.
EndY	For connectors and lines, the distance (in points) from the shape's ending point to the top edge of the slide window.
FileName	The path and name of the file used to create the shape (such as a picture or an OLE object).
Height	The height of the shape (in points).
Left	The distance (in points) of the left edge of the shape from the left edge of the slide window.
Orientation	The orientation of text within a label or text box. For horizontal text, use the constant msoTextOrientationHorizontal; for vertical text, use the constant msoTextOrientationVerticalFarEast.
SafeArrayOfPoints	For curves and polylines, this is an array of coordinate pairs that specify the vertices and control points for the object.
Top	The distance (in points) of the top edge of the shape from the top edge of the slide window.
Width	The width of the shape (in points).

Here's a list of the Shapes object methods and arguments that you can use to create shapes:

Slide.Shapes.AddCallout adds a callout to the specified *Slide* using the following syntax:

Slide.Shapes.AddCallout(***Type***, ***Left***, ***Top***, ***Width***, ***Height***)

Type	A constant that specifies the type of callout to add:	
	msoCalloutOne	A single-segment callout that can only be oriented horizontally or vertically.
	msoCalloutTwo	A single-segment callout that can be oriented in any direction.
	msoCalloutThree	A double-segment callout.
	msoCalloutFour	A triple-segment callout.

Slide.Shapes.AddComment adds a comment to the specified *Slide* using the following syntax:

Slide.Shapes.AddComment(***Left***, ***Top***, ***Width***, ***Height***)

`Slide`.Shapes.AddConnector adds a connector to the specified `Slide` using the following syntax:

`Slide`.Shapes.AddConnector(***Type, BeginX, BeginY, EndX, EndY***)

Type	A constant that specifies the connector type:

msoConnectorCurve	A curved connector.
msoConnectorElbow	A connector with an elbow.
msoConnectorStraight	A straight connector.

NOTE: CONNECTING A CONNECTOR

The AddConnector method returns a Shape object that represents the new connector. You use this object's ConnectorFormat property to set up the beginning and ending points of the connector. In other words, you use the ConnectorFormat.BeginConnect and ConnectorFormat.EndConnect methods to specify the shapes attached to the connector.

`Slide`.Shapes.AddCurve adds a curved line to the specified `Slide` using the following syntax:

`Slide.Shapes.AddCurve(***SafeArrayOfPoints***)`

`Slide`.Shapes.AddLabel adds a label to the specified `Slide` using the following syntax

`Slide.Shapes.AddLabel(***Orientation, Left, Top, Width, Height***)`

NOTE: LABEL TEXT

I'll show you how to add text to a label and text box in the section "Some Shape Properties."

`Slide`.Shapes.AddLine adds a straight line to the specified `Slide` using the following syntax:

`Slide.Shapes.AddLine(***BeginX, BeginY, EndX, EndY***)`

`Slide`.Shapes.AddMediaObject adds a multimedia file to the specified `Slide` using the following syntax:

`Slide.Shapes.AddMediaObject(***FileName***, Left, Top, Width, Height)`

`Slide`.Shapes.AddOLEObject adds an OLE object to the specified `Slide` using the following syntax:

`Slide.Shapes.AddOLEObject(Left, Top, Width, Height, ClassName, FileName,`
`➥DisplayAsIcon, IconFileName, IconIndex, IconLabel, Link)`

Here's a summary of the extra arguments used in this method:

`ClassName`	The class name or programmatic ID for the OLE object.
`FileName`	The file to use to create the OLE object.
`DisplayAsIcon`	Set to `True` to display the object as an icon. The default value is `False`.
`IconFileName`	If `DisplayAsIcon` is `True`, this is the file that contains the icon.
`IconIndex`	If `DisplayAsIcon` is `True`, this is the index of the icon within `IconFileName`.
`IconLabel`	If `DisplayAsIcon` is `True`, this is the label that appears beneath the icon.
`Link`	If you specify a `FileName`, set this argument to `True` to set up a link to the original file. The default value is `False`.

`Slide.Shapes.AddPicture` adds a graphic to the specified `Slide` using the following syntax:

```
Slide.Shapes.AddPicture(FileName, LinkToFile, SaveWithDocument, Left, Top,
➥Width, Height)
```

Here's a summary of the extra arguments used in this method:

`LinkToFile`	Set this argument to `True` to set up a link to the original file. If this argument is `False`, an independent copy of the picture is stored in the slide.
`SaveWithDocument`	Set this argument to `True` to save the picture with the presentation. Note that this argument must be `True` if **`LinkToFile`** is `False`.

`Slide.Shapes.AddPolyline` adds an open polyline or a closed polygon to the specified `Slide` using the following syntax:

```
Slide.Shapes.AddPolyline(SafeArrayOfPoints)
```

`Slide.Shapes.AddShape` adds an `AutoShape` to the specified `Slide` using the following syntax:

```
Slide.Shapes.AddShape(Type, Left, Top, Width, Height)
```

Here, the **`Type`** argument is a constant that specifies the `AutoShape` you want to add. PowerPoint VBA defines dozens of these constants. To see the full list, look up the `AutoShapeType` property in the VBA help system.

`Slide.Shapes.AddTextbox` adds a text box to the specified `Slide` using the following syntax:

```
Slide.Shapes.AddTextbox(Left, Top, Width, Height)
```

Slide.Shapes.AddTextEffect adds a WordArt text effect to the specified *Slide* using the following syntax:

```
Slide.Shapes.AddTextEffect(PresetTextEffect, Text, FontName, FontSize,
➥FontBold, FontItalic, Left, Top)
```

Here's a summary of the extra arguments used in this method:

PresetTextEffect	A constant that specifies one of WordArt's preset text effects. Look up this method in the VBA help system to see the few dozen constants that are available.
Text	The WordArt text.
FontName	The font applied to *Text*.
FontSize	The font size applied to *Text*.
FontBold	Set to True to apply bold to *Text*.
FontItalic	Set to True to apply italics to *Text*.

Slide.Shapes.AddTitle adds a title to the specified *Slide*. This method takes no arguments. However, be aware that the AddTitle method raises an error if the slide already has a title. To check in advance, use the HasTitle property, as shown in the following example:

```
With ActivePresentation.Slides(1).Shapes
    If Not .HasTitle Then
        .AddTitle.TextFrame.TextRange.Text = "New Title"
    End If
End With
```

Some Shape Properties

PowerPoint VBA comes equipped with over three dozen Shape object properties that control characteristics such as the dimensions and position of a shape, whether a shape displays a shadow, and the shape name. Take a quick look at a few of these properties:

Shape.AnimationSettings returns an AnimationSettings object that represents the animation effects applied to the specified *Shape*. AnimationSettings contains various properties that apply special effects to the shape. The following is a sampler. (See the VBA help system for the complete list as well as the numerous constants that work with these properties.)

■ AdvanceMode: A constant that determines how the animation advances. The two choices are automatically (in other words, after a preset amount of time; use ppAdvanceOnTime) or when the user clicks the slide (use ppAdvanceOnClick). For the latter, you can specify the amount of time by using the AdvanceTime property.

■ AfterEffect: A constant that determines how the shape appears after the animation is complete.

■ Animate: A Boolean value that turns the shape's animation on (True) or off (False).

■ **AnimateTextInReverse**: When this `Boolean` value is `True`, PowerPoint builds the text animation in reverse order. For example, if the shape is a series of bullet points and this property is `True`, the animation displays the bullet points from last to first.

■ **EntryEffect**: A constant that determines the special effect applied initially to the shape's animation. For example, you can make the shape fade in by using the `ppEffectFade` constant.

■ **TextLevelEffect**: A constant that determines the paragraph level that gets animated.

■ **TextUnitEffect**: A constant that determines how PowerPoint animates text: by paragraph, by word, or by letter.

Shape.`AutoShapeType`: For an AutoShape object, this property returns or sets the shape type for the specified *Shape*.

Shape.`Fill` returns a FillFormat object that represents the fill formatting for the specified *Shape*. The FillFormat object defines numerous methods you can wield to apply a fill to a shape:

■ `OneColorGradient` sets the fill to a one-color gradient.

■ `Patterned` sets the fill to a pattern.

■ `PresetGradient` sets the fill to one of PowerPoint's preset gradients.

■ `PresetTextured` sets the fill to one of PowerPoint's preset textures.

■ `Solid` sets the fill to a solid color. After running this method, use the `Fill.ForeColor` property to set the fill color.

58

PROGRAMMING
A POWERPOINT
PRESENTATION

NOTE: WORKING WITH COLORS

PowerPoint's color properties (such as `ForeColor`) return a ColorFormat object. This object represents either the color of a one-color object or the background or foreground color of an object with a pattern or gradient. To set a color, use the ColorFormat object's `RGB` property and VBA's `RGB` function to set a red-green-blue value, as in this example:

```
Shapes(1).Fill.Solid.ForeColor.RGB = RGB(255,0,0)
```

■ `TwoColorGradient` sets the fill to a two-color gradient.

■ `UserPicture` sets the fill to a graphics file that you specify.

■ `UserTexture` sets the fill to a specified graphics image that gets tiled to cover the entire shape.

Shape.`HasTextFrame`: A `Boolean` value that tells you if the specified *Shape* has a text frame (`True`) or not (`False`). See the `TextFrame` property, discussed later.

Shape.`Height` returns or sets the height, in points, for the specified *Shape*.

Shape.Left returns or sets the distance, in points, between the left edge of the bounding box of the specified *Shape* and the left edge of the presentation window.

Shape.Name returns or sets the name for the specified *Shape*.

Shape.Shadow returns a ShadowFormat object that represents the shadow for the specified *Shape*. The ShadowFormat object contains various properties that control the look of the shadow. For example, Shadow.ForeColor controls the shadow color and Shadow.Visible is a Boolean value that turns the shadow on (True) or off (False).

Shape.TextEffectFormat: For a WordArt object, this property returns a TextEffectFormat object that represents the text effects of the specified *Shape*.

Shape.TextFrame returns a TextFrame object for the specified *Shape*. A text frame is an area within a shape that can hold text. The frame's text, as a whole, is represented by the TextRange object, and the actual text is given by the Text property of the TextRange object. This rather convoluted state of affairs means that you need to use the following property to a refer to a shape's text:

Shape.TextFrame.TextRange.Text

For example, the following statements add to the active presentation a new slide that contains only a title, and then they set the title text to 1997 Budget Proposal:

```
With ActivePresentation.Slides
    With .Add(1, ppLayoutTitleOnly).Shapes(1)
        .TextFrame.TextRange.Text = "1997 Budget Proposal"
    End With
End With
```

Also note that the TextFrame object has a number of other properties that control the text margins, orientation, word wrap, and more.

Shape.Top returns or sets the distance, in points, between the top edge of the bounding box of the specified *Shape* and the top edge of the presentation window.

Shape.Type returns or (in some cases) sets the shape type for the specified *Shape*.

Shape.Visible: A Boolean value that makes the specified *Shape* either visible (True) or invisible (False).

Shape.Width returns or sets the width, in points, for the specified *Shape*.

The Juggling Application: Creating the Title Page

To put some of these properties through their paces, Listing 58.4 shows the juggling application's SetUpStartPage procedure.

Listing 58.4. A procedure that sets up the text and animation settings for the first page of the juggling presentation.

```
Sub SetUpStartPage()
    Dim shapeTitle As Shape
    Dim shapeSubTitle As Shape
    With pres.Slides("Opener")
```

```
        Set shapeTitle = .Shapes(1)     ' The title
        Set shapeSubTitle = .Shapes(2)  ' The subtitle
        '
        ' Add the title text
        '
        With shapeTitle.TextFrame.TextRange
            .Text = "Juggling"
            With .Font
                .Name = "Arial"
                .Size = 44
                .Bold = True
                .Color.RGB = RGB(255, 255, 255)
            End With
        End With
        '
        ' Set the title animation
        '
        With shapeTitle.AnimationSettings
            .Animate = True
            .AdvanceMode = ppAdvanceOnTime
            .AdvanceTime = 0
            .TextUnitEffect = ppAnimateByCharacter
            .EntryEffect = ppEffectFlyFromLeft
        End With
        '
        ' Add the subtitle text
        '
        With shapeSubTitle.TextFrame.TextRange
            .Text = "A Step-By-Step Course"
            With .Font
                .Name = "Arial"
                .Size = 36
                .Bold = True
                .Color.RGB = RGB(255, 255, 255)
            End With
        End With
        '
        ' Set the subtitle animation
        '
        With shapeSubTitle.AnimationSettings
            .Animate = True
            .AdvanceMode = ppAdvanceOnTime
            .AdvanceTime = 0
            .TextUnitEffect = ppAnimateByWord
            .EntryEffect = ppEffectFlyFromBottom
        End With
    End With
End Sub
```

The first slide is named Opener, and this is the object used through most of the procedure. The shapeTitle variable is Set to the slide's title—Shapes(1)—and the shapeSubTitle variable is Set to the subtitle text box—Slides(2).

From there, the title's TextFrame property is used to add and format the title text. Then its AnimationSettings property is used to animate the text. A similar sequence of code adds text, formatting, and animation to the subtitle.

Some Shape Methods

The Shape object comes with a number of methods that let you perform actions such as copying, deleting, and flipping slides. Here's a list of some of the more useful methods:

`Shape.Apply` applies to the specified `Shape` the formatting that was captured from another shape using the `PickUp` method (described later).

`Shape.Copy` copies the specified `Shape` to the Clipboard. If you then want to paste the shape into another slide, use the `Paste` method of the `Shapes` object:

`Slide``.Shapes.Paste`

> **`Slide`** The Slide object into which you want to paste the shape.

`Shape.Cut` cuts the specified `Shape` from the slide and places it on the Clipboard. Use the `Shapes.Paste` method to paste the shape into another slide.

`Shape.Delete` deletes the specified `Shape`.

`Shape.Duplicate` makes a copy of the specified `Shape` in the same slide. The new shape is added to the `Shapes` object immediately after the specified `Shape`. Note, too, that this method returns a Shape object that refers to the new shape.

`Shape.Flip` flips the specified `Shape` around its horizontal or vertical axis. Here's the syntax:

`Shape``.Flip(`*`FlipCmd`*`)`

> **`Shape`** The Shape object you want to flip.
>
> **`FlipCmd`** A constant that determines how the shape is flipped. Use either `msoFlipHorizontal` or `msoFlipVertical`.

`Shape.IncrementLeft` moves the specified `Shape` horizontally using the following syntax:

`Shape``.IncrementLeft(`*`Increment`*`)`

> **`Shape`** The Shape object you want to move.
>
> **`Increment`** The distance, in points, that you want the shape moved. Use a positive number to move the shape to the right; use a negative number to move the shape to the left.

`Shape.IncrementRotation` rotates the specified `Shape` around its z-axis using the following syntax:

`Shape``.IncrementRotation(`*`Increment`*`)`

> **`Shape`** The Shape object you want to move.
>
> **`Increment`** The number of degrees you want the shape rotated. Use a positive number to rotate the shape clockwise; use a negative number to rotate the shape counterclockwise.

Shape.IncrementTop moves the specified *Shape* vertically using the following syntax:

Shape.IncrementTop(**Increment**)

> **Shape** The Shape object you want to move.
>
> **Increment** The distance, in points, that you want the shape moved. Use a positive number to move the shape down; use a negative number to move the shape up.

Shape.PickUp copies the formatting of the specified *Shape*. Use the Apply method (discussed earlier) to apply the copied formatting to a different object.

Shape.Select selects the specified *Shape* using the following syntax:

Shape.Select(*Replace*)

> **Shape** The Shape object you want to select.
>
> *Replace* A Boolean value that either adds the shape to the current selection (False) or replaces the current selection (True). True is the default.

The Juggling Application: Creating the Instructions

To continue the juggling application, the SetUpJugglingPages procedure, shown in Listing 58.5, is run. This procedure serves to set up the title, picture, and instruction text for each of the four instruction slides.

Listing 58.5. A procedure that sets up the titles, pictures, and text instructions for each of the juggling slides.

```
Sub SetUpJugglingPages()
    Dim thisPres As Presentation
    Dim slideTitle As Shape
    Dim slidePicture As Shape
    Dim slideText As Shape
    Dim i As Integer
    For i = 1 To 4
        With pres.Slides("Juggling" & i)
            '
            ' Get pictures from Chaptr58.ppt
            '
            Set thisPres = Presentations("Chaptr58.ppt")
            thisPres.Slides(1).Shapes(i + 1).Copy
            .Shapes.Paste
            '
            ' Adjust the layout and then set the Shape variables
            '
            .Layout = ppLayoutObjectOverText
            Set slideTitle = .Shapes(1)
            Set slideText = .Shapes(2)
            Set slidePicture = .Shapes(3)
            '
```

continues

Listing 58.5. continued

```
        ' Add the title text
        '
        With slideTitle.TextFrame.TextRange
            Select Case i
                Case 1
                    .Text = "Step 1: The Home Position"
                Case 2
                    .Text = "Step 2: The First Throw"
                Case 3
                    .Text = "Step 3: The Second Throw"
                Case 4
                    .Text = "Step 4: The Third Throw"
            End Select
            With .Font
                .Name = "Arial"
                .Size = 44
                .Bold = True
                .Color.RGB = RGB(255, 255, 255)
            End With
        End With
        '
        ' Set the picture animation and shadow
        '
        With slidePicture
            With .AnimationSettings
                .Animate = True
                .AdvanceMode = ppAdvanceOnTime
                .AdvanceTime = 0
                .EntryEffect = ppEffectFade
            End With
            With .Shadow
                .ForeColor.RGB = RGB(0, 0, 0)
                .OffsetX = 10
                .OffsetY = 10
                .Visible = True
            End With
        End With
        '
        ' Add the instruction text
        '
        With slideText.TextFrame.TextRange
            Select Case i
            Case 1
            .Text = "Place two balls in your dominant hand, " & _
                "one in front of the other." & Chr(13) & _
                "Hold the third ball in your other hand." & Chr(13) & _
                "Let your arms dangle naturally and bring your " & _
                "forearms parallel to the ground (as though you " & _
                "were holding a tray.)" & Chr(13) & _
                "Relax your shoulders, arms, and hands."
            Case 2
            .Text = "Of the two balls in your dominant hand, " & _
                "toss the front one towards your other hand " & _
                "in a smooth arc." & Chr(13) & _
                "Make sure the ball doesn't spin too much." & Chr(13) & _
                "Make sure the ball goes no higher than about eye level."
```

```
            Case 3
            .Text = "Once the first ball reaches the top of its arc, " & _
                "toss the ball in your other hand." & Chr(13) & _
                "Throw the ball towards your dominant hand, making " & _
                "sure that it flies UNDER the first ball." & Chr(13) & _
                "Again, try not to spin the ball and make sure it goes " & _
                "no higher than eye level."
            Case 4
            .Text = "Now for the tricky part (!). Soon after you release " & _
                "the second ball, the first ball will approach your " & _
                "hand. Go ahead and catch the first ball." & Chr(13) & _
                "When the second ball reaches its apex, throw the " & _
                "third ball (the remaining ball in your dominant hand) " & _
                "under it." & Chr(13) & _
                "At this point, it just becomes a game of catch-and-" & _
                "throw-under, catch-and-throw-under. Have fun!"
            End Select
            With .Font
                .Name = "Times New Roman"
                .Size = 24
                .Bold = False
                .Color.RGB = RGB(255, 255, 255)
            End With
        End With
    End With
    Next i
End Sub
```

A `For...Next` loop runs through each of the four instructional slides. (Recall that earlier the `CreateJugglingSlides` procedure gave these slides the names `Juggle1` through `Juggle4`.) Here's a summary of the various chores that are run within this loop:

1. The first task is to load the pictures that illustrate each step. You can find these pictures on the slide in Chaptr58.ppt. To get them into the juggling presentation, the code uses the `Copy` method to copy each one from Chaptr58.ppt to the Clipboard, and then it uses the `Paste` method to add the picture to the juggling slide. When that's done, the slide's `Layout` property is set to `ppLayoutObjectOverText`, and the three variables that represent the three shapes on each slide are `Set`.

2. Next, the title text is added. Here, a `Select Case` structure is used to add a different title to each slide, and then the text is formatted.

3. The picture is animated, and a shadow is added.

4. The last chunk of code uses another `Select Case` to add the appropriate instructions for each slide, and then the instruction text is formatted.

Operating a Slide Show

With your presentation created and saved, slides added and set up, and shapes inserted and formatted, your file is just about ready to roll. All that remains is to add a few slide show settings and transition effects. This section shows you how to do that as well as how to run your slide show when it's complete.

Slide Show Transitions

Each Slide object has a `SlideShowTransition` property that determines how the slide advances during a slide show. This property is actually a `SlideShowTransitions` object, and you set up the transition effect by modifying this object's properties. Here's a list of the key properties:

> *Slide*`.SlideShowTransition.AdvanceOnClick`: For the specified *Slide*, this property returns or sets whether the slide advances when it's clicked. Set this property to `True` to advance the slide by clicking it.

> *Slide*`.SlideShowTransition.AdvanceOnTime`: For the specified *Slide*, this property returns or sets whether the slide advances after a period of time has elapsed (as set by the `AdvanceTime` property). Set this property to `True` to advance the slide after a period of time.

> *Slide*`.SlideShowTransition.AdvanceTime`: This property returns or sets the amount of time, in seconds, after which the specified *Slide* advances, assuming that the `AdvanceOnTime` property is set to `True`.

NOTE: ENABLING ADVANCE ON TIME

To allow a slide to advance based on time, you also need to set the `SlideShowSettings` object's `AdvanceMode` property to `ppSlideShowUseSlideTimings`. This object is a property of the Presentation object, and I'll discuss it in detail in the section "Slide Show Settings."

> *Slide*`.SlideShowTransition.EntryEffect`: A constant that determines the special effect used in the transition for the specified *Slide*. Look up this property in the VBA help system to see the dozens of available constants.

> *Slide*`.SlideShowTransition.Hidden`: This property returns or sets whether the specified *Slide* is hidden during the slide show. Use `True` to hide the slide or `False` to make the slide visible.

> *Slide*`.SlideShowTransition.Speed`: This property returns or sets the speed of the transition for the specified *Slide*. Use one of the following constants:

- `ppTransitionSpeedFast`
- `ppTransitionSpeedMedium`
- `ppTransitionSpeedSlow`
- `ppTransitionSpeedMixed`

Slide Show Settings

The Presentation object has a `SlideShowSettings` property that controls various global settings for the slide show. This property is actually a `SlideShowSettings` object and the settings are the properties of this object. Here's a rundown of the settings you'll use most often:

Presentation.SlideShowSettings.AdvanceMode returns or sets how the slides advance for the specified *Presentation*. Use ppSlideShowManualAdvance to advance slides manually (by clicking) or ppSlideShowUseSlideTimings to advance slides based on the AdvanceTime property for each slide. You can also use the ppSlideShowRehearseNewTimings constant to run the slide show in Rehearsal mode (which lets you set the timings by advancing the slides manually).

Presentation.SlideShowSettings.EndingSlide returns or sets the index number of the last slide that is displayed in the slide show for the specified *Presentation*.

Presentation.SlideShowSettings.LoopUntilStopped returns or sets whether the slide show for the specified *Presentation* plays continuously. Set this property to True to play the slide show in a continuous loop until the user presses Esc; set this property to False to play the slide show just once.

Presentation.SlideShowSettings.PointerColor returns or sets the color of the mouse pointer during the slide show for the specified *Presentation*. For example, the following statements set the color of the slide show pointer to red:

```
With ActivePresentation.SlideShowSettings
    .PointerColor.RGB = RGB(255, 0, 0)
End With
```

Presentation.SlideShowSettings.ShowType returns or sets the slide show type for the specified *Presentation*. Use ppShowTypeSpeaker (for the standard, full-screen slide show), ppShowTypeWindow (to run the slide show in a window), or ppShowTypeKiosk (to run the slide show in kiosk mode: full screen with a continuous loop).

Presentation.SlideShowSettings.ShowWithAnimation returns or sets whether the slide show for the specified *Presentation* uses the animation settings applied to each slide's shapes. Set this property to True to enable animation; use False to disable animation.

Presentation.SlideShowSettings.ShowWithNarration returns or sets whether the slide show for the specified *Presentation* uses narration. Set this property to True to enable narration; use False to disable narration.

Presentation.SlideShowSettings.StartingSlide returns or sets the index number of the first slide that is displayed in the slide show for the specified *Presentation*.

Running the Slide Show

At long last you're ready to display the presentation's slide show for all to see. To do so, simply invoke the Run method of the SlideShowSettings object:

Presentation.SlideShowSettings.Run

For example, Listing 58.6 shows the last of the juggling application's procedures. In this case, the procedure presents a dialog box that asks the user if he or she wants to run the slide show. If Yes is clicked, some transition effects are applied to the instruction slides and then the Run method is invoked.

Listing 58.6. This procedure asks the user if he or she wants to run the presentation's slide show.

```
Sub RunJugglingSlideShow
    If MsgBox("Start the slide show?", vbYesNo, "Juggling") = vbYes Then
        With pres
            .Slides("Juggling1").SlideShowTransition.EntryEffect =
            ➥ppEffectBlindsHorizontal
            .Slides("Juggling2").SlideShowTransition.EntryEffect =
            ➥pEffectCheckerboardAcross
            .Slides("Juggling3").SlideShowTransition.EntryEffect =
            ➥ppEffectBoxIn
            .Slides("Juggling4").SlideShowTransition.EntryEffect =
            ➥ppEffectStripsLeftDown
            .SlideShowSettings.Run
        End With
    End If
End Sub
```

Summary

This chapter showed you the ins and outs of PowerPoint VBA. You began with a look at a few properties of PowerPoint's Application object. From there, I went through a number of PowerPoint-specific objects, including the Presentation, Slide, and Shape objects. I closed by showing you how to work with slide shows in your VBA code. Throughout this chapter, I illustrated the concepts with a sample application that creates a PowerPoint presentation from scratch.

Here's a list of chapters where you'll find related information:

■ For a few PowerPoint pointers, head for Part VI, "Unleashing PowerPoint."

■ For a general discussion of VBA objects, including how to work with For Each...Next loops, see Chapter 54, "Understanding Objects."

■ I showed you how to work with For...Next and Select Case in Chapter 55, "Controlling VBA Code and Interacting with the User."

■ To learn how to integrate PowerPoint with other Office applications, see Chapter E6 on the CD, "Integrating Office Applications with VBA."

Creating a Custom User Interface

IN THIS CHAPTER

CHAPTER 59

The system designer suffers because the better his system does its job, the less its users know of its existence.

—*Gerald M. Weinberg*

VBA procedures are only as useful as they are convenient. There isn't much point in creating a procedure that saves you (or your users) a few keystrokes if you (or they) have to expend a lot of time and energy hunting down a routine. Shortcut keys are true time-savers, but some applications (such as Excel) have only a limited supply to dole out (and our brains can memorize only so many Ctrl-*key* combinations).

Instead, you need to give some thought to the type of user interface you want to create for your VBA application. The interface includes not only the design of the documents but also three other factors that let the user interact with the model: dialog boxes, menus, and toolbars. Although you certainly can give the user access to the application's built-in dialogs, menus, and toolbars, you'll find that you often need to create your own interface elements from scratch. This chapter shows you how to use VBA 5.0's new Microsoft Forms feature to create custom dialog boxes and input forms. You'll also learn how to set up custom menus and toolbars.

Understanding Custom Forms and Dialog Boxes

The InputBox function you learn about in Chapter 55, "Controlling VBA Code and Interacting with the User," works fine if you need just a single item of information, but what if you need four or five? What if you want the user to choose from a list of items? In some cases, you can use the application's built-in dialog boxes (which I also discussed in Chapter 55), but these might not have the exact controls you need, or they might have controls to which you don't want the user to have access.

The solution is to build your own dialog boxes. You can add as many controls as you need (including list boxes, option buttons, and check boxes), and your procedures will have complete access to all the results. Best of all, the Visual Basic Editor (VBE) makes constructing even the most sophisticated dialog boxes as easy as dragging the mouse pointer. The next few sections show you how to create dialog boxes and integrate them into your applications.

Forms and Dialog Boxes in VBA 5.0

In VBA 5.0, dialog boxes are called *forms* (or *user forms*). This more general term is in keeping with the more general nature of these objects in the latest incarnation of VBA. Yes, you can use a form as a dialog box to ask the user for confirmation or to set a few options. You can also use forms as data entry screens or query-building mechanisms. In this sense, a VBA form is a close cousin to the form objects that have been available in Access from Day One. In recognition of this, I forego the term "dialog box" and instead use the term "form" throughout the rest of this chapter. (The exception to this is when I discuss built-in application dialog boxes.)

NOTE: EXCEL 95'S DIALOG SHEETS

If you've created form objects and worked with Dialog objects in Excel's previous versions of VBA, don't worry—your procedures and objects will still work as they always have. However, VBA 5.0's forms are completely different, so the following discussion will be new to you. You'll find, however, that VBA 5.0 forms are easier to create and much more powerful than the relatively primitive dialog boxes available previously.

Adding a Form to Your Project

Forms are separate objects that you add to your VBA projects. To do this, open the Visual Basic Editor and either select Insert | UserForm or drop down the Insert toolbar button and select UserForm. As you can see in Figure 59.1, VBA performs the following tasks in response to this command:

- It adds a Forms branch to the project tree in the Project Explorer.
- It creates a new UserForm object and adds it to the Forms branch.
- It displays the form in the work area.
- It displays the Toolbox.

FIGURE 59.1.

Selecting Insert | UserForm adds a new form to the project.

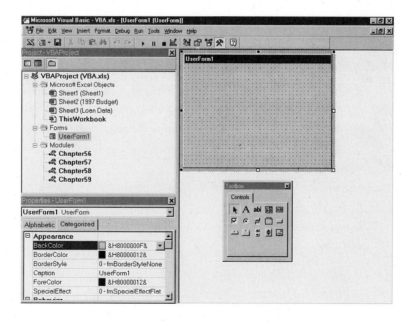

Changing the Form's Design-Time Properties

One of Microsoft's design goals in VBA 5.0 was to create a common user interface between the Visual Basic Editor and Visual Basic 5.0, the stand-alone programming environment. To that end, forms (and all the control objects you can add to a form) have an extensive list of properties that you can manipulate by entering or selecting values in the Properties window. (Recall that you display the Properties window by selecting View | Properties Window or by pressing F4.)

For a form, there are more than 30 properties arranged into seven categories (in the Properties window, activate the Categories tab to see the properties arranged by category), as described in the next few sections.

NOTE: CONTROLLING FORM PROPERTIES PROGRAMMATICALLY

Besides modifying form properties at design time, you can also modify many of the properties at runtime by including the appropriate statements in your VBA procedures. I talk about this in greater detail later in this chapter. (See the section "Using a Form in a Procedure.")

The Appearance Category

The properties in the Appearance category control the look of the form:

BackColor sets the color of the form's background. For all color properties, you can either enter the hexadecimal equivalent of the color you want (surround by & signs) or click the drop-down arrow to display a color menu. In this menu, you can choose either a predefined color from the System tab or a built-in color from the Palette tab.

BorderColor sets the color of the form's border. Note that for this property to have any effect, you have to assign a border to the form using the BorderStyle property.

BorderStyle: Choose fmBorderStyleSingle to apply a border around the form. Use fmBorderStyleNone for no border.

Caption specifies the text that's displayed in the form's title bar.

ForeColor sets the default color of text used in the form's controls.

SpecialEffect controls how the form appears in relation to the form window (for example, raised or sunken).

The Behavior Category

The properties in the Behavior category control two aspects of how the user interacts with the form:

Cycle determines what happens when the user presses Tab while the focus is on the last control in the form. If this property is set to fmCycleAllForms and the form has multiple pages, focus is set to the first control on the next page. If this property is set to fmCycleCurrentForm, focus is set to the first control on the current page.

Enabled: Set this property to True to enable the form or False to disable it.

The Font Category

The Font property determines the default font used throughout the form. When you activate this property, click the three-dot (...) button to display the Font dialog box from which you can select the font, style, size, and effects.

The Misc Category

As its name implies, the Misc category contains a collection of properties that don't fit anywhere else:

Name: You use this property to refer to the form in your VBA code.

TIP: USE DESCRIPTIVE NAMES

Although you might be tempted to stick with the default form name supplied by VBA (such as UserForm1), your code will be easier to read if you give the form a more descriptive name. Indeed, this advice applies not only to forms but to *all* controls.

DrawBuffer is the number of pixels that VBA sets aside in memory for rendering the frame. You can enter an integer value between 16,000 and 1,048,576.

HelpContextID specifies the topic number in a help file that refers to the help topic for the form.

MouseIcon assigns a picture that will appear as the mouse pointer whenever the pointer is inside the form. Note that you must also set the MousePointer property to fmMousePointerCustom.

MousePointer determines the appearance of the mouse pointer when the pointer is inside the form.

Tag defines a hidden string that is assigned to the form. You can use this string to specify extra information about the form that isn't available with the other properties (such as a version number, the creation date or developer name, or a description of the form's purpose).

WhatsThisButton: When this property is set to True, VBA displays a "What's This?" help button (it has a question mark) in the upper-right corner, which signifies that What's This? help is available for the form.

WhatsThisHelp: When this property is set to True, VBA displays a pop-up help window when the user clicks a control after clicking the "What's This?" help button. The displayed text is defined in a custom help file.

Zoom specifies a percentage by which the form is enlarged (for values between 100 and 400) or reduced (for values between 10 and 100).

The Picture Category

In the Picture category, use the Picture property to set a background image for the form. (Again, click the three-dot button to select a picture file from a dialog box.) The other properties determine how the picture is displayed:

PictureAlignment specifies where on the form the picture is displayed.

PictureSizeMode specifies how the picture is displayed relative to the form. Use fmPictureSizeModeClip to crop any part of the picture that's larger than the form; use fmPictureSizeModeStretch to stretch the picture so that it fits the entire form; use fmPictureSizeModeZoom to enlarge the picture until it hits the vertical or horizontal edge of the form.

PictureTiling: For small images, set this property to True to fill the background with multiple copies of the image.

The Position Category

The properties in the Position category specify the dimensions of the form (Height and Width) and the position of the form within the application window. For the latter, you can either use the StartUpPosition property to center the form relative to the application window (CenterOwner) or to the screen (CenterScreen), or you can choose Manual and specify the Left and Top properties. (The latter two properties set the form's position in points from the application window's left and top edges.)

The Scrolling Category

The properties in the Scrolling category determine whether the form displays scroll bars and, if it does, what format the scroll bars have:

KeepScrollBarsVisible determines which of the form's scroll bars remain visible even if they aren't needed.

ScrollBars determines which scroll bars are displayed on the form.

ScrollHeight specifies the total height of the form's scrollable region. For example, if the form's Height property is set to 200 and you set the ScrollHeight property to 400, you double the total vertical area available in the form.

ScrollLeft: If ScrollWidth is greater than the width of the form, use the ScrollLeft property to set the initial position of the horizontal scroll bar's scroll box. For example, if the ScrollWidth is 200, setting ScrollLeft to 100 starts the horizontal scroll bar at the halfway position.

ScrollTop: If ScrollHeight is greater than the height of the form, use the ScrollTop property to set the initial position of the vertical scroll bar's scroll box.

ScrollWidth specifies the total width of the form's scrollable region.

VerticalScrollBarSide determines whether the vertical scroll bar appears on the right or left side of the window.

Working with Controls

Now that your form is set up with the design-time properties you need, you can get down to the brass tacks of form design. In other words, you can start adding controls to the form, adjusting those controls to get the layout you want, and setting the design-time properties of each control. I discuss the unique characteristics of each type of control later in this chapter. (See the section "Types of Form Controls.") For now, though, I run through a few techniques that you can apply to any control.

Inserting Controls on a Form

The new form object is an empty shell that doesn't become a useful member of society until you populate it with controls. As with the form-building tools in Word and Access, the idea is that you use this shell to "draw" the controls you need. Later, you can either link the controls directly to other objects (such as Excel worksheet cells) or create procedures to handle the selections.

The Toolbox contains buttons for all the controls you can add to a form. Here are the basic steps to follow to add any control to the form:

1. Click the button you want to use.

2. Move the mouse pointer into the form and position it where you want the top-left corner of the control to appear.

3. Drag the mouse pointer. VBA displays a gray border indicating the outline of the control.

4. When the control is the size and shape you want, release the mouse button. VBA creates the control and gives it a default name (such as CheckBox*n*, where *n* signifies that this is the *n*th check box you've created on this form).

> **TIP: ADDING MULTIPLE COPIES OF A CONTROL**
>
> If you want to add multiple instances of the same type of control, double-click the appropriate Toolbox button. The button remains pressed, and you can draw as many instances of the control as you need. When you're done, click an empty part of the Toolbox to reset the control.

Common Control Properties

Later in this chapter, I'll run through each of the default controls and explain their unique features. However, a few properties are common to many of the controls. Many of these properties perform the same functions as those I outlined for a form earlier in this chapter. These properties include the following: `BackColor`, `ForeColor`, `SpecialEffect`, `Enabled`, `Font`, `HelpContextID`, `MouseIcon`, `MousePointer`, `Tag`, `Picture`, `PicturePosition`, `Height`, `Width`, `Left`, and `Top`. (Note that the latter two are relative to the left and top edges of the form.)

Here's a list of a few other properties that are common to some or all of the default controls:

> `Accelerator` determines the control's accelerator key. (In other words, the user will be able to select this control by holding down Alt and pressing the specified key.) The letter you enter into this property will appear underlined in the control's caption.

> **TIP: ACCELERATORS FOR CONTROLS WITHOUT CAPTIONS**
>
> Some controls (such as list boxes and text boxes) don't have a `Caption` property. However, you can still assign an accelerator key to these controls by using a `Label` control. I'll show you how this is done when I discuss labels in the section "Types of Form Controls."

> `AutoSize`: If this property is set to `True`, the control resizes automatically to fit its text (as given by the `Caption` property).

> `BackStyle` determines whether the control's background is opaque (use `fmBackStyleOpaque`) or transparent (use `fmBackStyleTransparent`).

> `ControlSource`: In the VBE, this property specifies which cell is used to hold the control's data. You can enter either a cell reference or a range name.

> **CAUTION: AVOID CONTROL SOURCE FOR SAFER CODE**
>
> The value of a cell linked to a control changes whenever the value of the control changes, even when the user clicks Cancel to exit the form. It's usually better (and safer) to assign the value of a control to a variable and then, if appropriate, place the value in the cell under program control.

Caption sets the control's text.

ControlTipText sets the "control tip" that pops up when the user lets the mouse pointer linger over the control for a second or two.

Locked: Set this property to True to prevent the user from editing the current value of the control.

TabIndex determines where the control appears in the tab order (in other words, the order in which VBA navigates through the controls when the user presses the Tab key). See the next section.

TabStop determines whether the user can navigate to the control by pressing Tab. If this property is set to False, the user won't be able to select the control using the Tab key.

Visible determines whether the user can see the control (True) or not (False).

Setting the Tab Order

As you know, you can navigate a form by pressing the Tab key. The order in which the controls are selected is called the *tab order*. VBA sets the tab order according to the order you create the controls on the form. You'll often find that this order isn't what you want to end up with, so the VBE lets you control the tab order yourself. The following procedure shows you how it's done:

1. Select View | Tab Order. (You can also right-click an empty part of the form and select Tab Order from the shortcut menu.) The VBE displays the Tab Order dialog box, shown in Figure 59.2.

FIGURE 59.2.

Use the Tab Order dialog box to set the order in which the user navigates the form when pressing the Tab key.

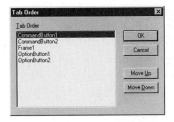

2. In the Tab Order list, highlight the control you want to work with.

3. Click Move Up to move the item up in the tab order, or click Move Down to move the control down.

4. Repeat steps 2 and 3 for other controls you want to move.

5. Click OK.

Adding Controls to the Toolbox

At first, the Toolbox just displays the default set of controls. However, Office 97 ships with a number of extra controls—including a collection of ActiveX controls—that you can add to the Toolbox. Also, you can use any other controls installed on your system (such as those installed with Visual Basic, for example) in your Toolbox.

To add another control to the Toolbox, click the Toolbox to activate it, and select Tools | Additional Controls. In the Additional Controls dialog box, shown in Figure 59.3, use the Available Controls list to activate the check boxes beside each control you want to add, and then click OK. The controls appear as icons in the Toolbox and you can use them exactly as you do the default controls.

FIGURE 59.3.

*The Additional
Controls dialog box
displays a complete list
of the available controls
on your system.*

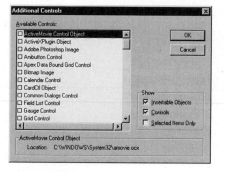

Handling Form Events

An *event-driven* language is one in which code can respond to specific events, such as a user's clicking a command button or selecting an item from a list. The procedure can then take appropriate action, whether it's validating the user's input or asking for confirmation of the requested action. Previous versions of VBA had only rudimentary event handlers and therefore could hardly be described as event-driven. VBA 5.0, however, is fully event-driven thanks to its support of many different kinds of events. For example, a form responds to more than 20 separate events, including activating and deactivating the form, displaying the form, clicking the form, and resizing the form.

For each event associated with an object, VBA has set up stub procedures called *event handlers*. These procedures are really just Sub and End Sub statements. You process the event by filling in your own VBA code between these statements. Here are the steps to follow:

1. Click the object for which you want to define an event handler.
2. Either select View | Edit Code or double-click the object. (You can also right-click the object and select Edit Code from the shortcut menu.) VBA displays the code module for the object, as shown in Figure 59.4.

FIGURE 59.4.

For each event, VBA defines a stub procedure. You define the procedure by entering code into this stub.

3. Use the procedure drop-down list (the one on the right) to select the event you want to work with.

4. Enter the rest of the procedure code between the Sub and End Sub statements.

Types of Form Controls

The default Toolbox offers 14 different controls for your custom forms. The next few sections introduce you to each type of control and show you the various options and properties associated with each object.

Command Buttons

Most forms include command buttons to let the user accept the form data (an OK button), cancel the form (a Cancel button), or execute some other command at a click of the mouse.

To create a command button, use the CommandButton tool in the Toolbox. A command button is a CommandButton object that includes many of the common control properties mentioned earlier as well as the following design-time properties (among others):

Cancel: If this property is set to True, the button is selected when the user presses Esc.

Caption returns or sets the text that appears on the button face.

Default: If this property is set to True, the button is selected when the user presses Enter. Also, the button is displayed with a thin black border.

Labels

You use labels to add text to the form. To create labels, use the Label button in the Toolbox to draw the Label object, and then edit the Caption property. Although labels are mostly used to display text, you can also use them to name controls that don't have their own captions—such as text boxes, list boxes, scroll bars, and spinners.

It's even possible to define an accelerator key for the label and have that key select another control. For example, suppose you want to use a label to describe a text box, but you also want to define an accelerator key that the user can press to select the text box. The trick is that you must first create a label and set its Accelerator property. You then create the text box immediately after. Because the text box follows the label in the tab order, the label's accelerator key will select the text box.

TIP: ACCELERATORS FOR EXISTING CONTROLS

To assign a label and accelerator key to an existing control, add the label and then adjust the tab order so that the label comes immediately before the control in the tab order.

Text Boxes

Text boxes are versatile controls that let the user enter text, numbers, cell references, and formulas. To create a text box, use the TextBox button in the Toolbox. Here are a few useful properties of the TextBox object:

EnterFieldBehavior determines what happens when the user tabs into the text box. If you select 0 (fmEnterFieldBehaviorSelectAll), the text within the field is selected. If you select 1 (fmEnterFieldBehaviorRecallSelect), only the text that the user selected the last time he was in the field will be selected.

EnterKeyBehavior: When set to True, this property lets the user start a new line within the text box by pressing Enter. (Note that this is applicable only if you set MultiLine to True.) When this property is False, pressing Enter moves the user to the next field.

MaxLength determines the maximum number of characters that the user can enter.

MultiLine: Set this property to True to let the user enter multiple lines of text.

PasswordChar: If this property is set to True, the text box displays the user's entry as asterisks.

Text returns or sets the text inside the text box.

WordWrap: When this property is True, the text box wraps to a new line when the user's typing reaches the right edge of the text box.

Frames

You use frames to create groups of two or more controls. There are three situations in which frames come in handy:

To organize a set of controls into a logical grouping: Let's say your form contains controls for setting program options and obtaining user information. You could help the user make sense of the form by creating two frames: one to hold all the controls for the program options and one to hold the controls for the user information.

To move a set of controls as a unit: When you draw controls inside a frame, these controls are considered part of the Frame object. Therefore, when you move the frame, the controls move right along with it. This can make it easier to rearrange multiple controls on a form.

To organize option buttons: If you enter multiple option buttons inside a frame (see the next section), VBA treats them as a group and therefore allows the user to activate only one of the options.

To create a frame, click the Frame button in the Toolbox and then drag a box inside the form. Note that you use the Frame object's `Caption` property to change the caption that appears at the top of the box.

Option Buttons

Option buttons are controls that usually appear in groups of two or more; the user can select only one of the options. To create an option button, use the `OptionButton` tool. You can determine whether an option button starts off activated or deactivated by setting the `Value` property. If it's `True`, the option is activated; if it's `False`, the option is deactivated.

In order for option buttons to work effectively, you need to group them so that the user can select only one of the options at a time. VBA gives you three ways to do this:

- Create a frame and then draw the option buttons inside the frame.
- Use the same `GroupName` property for the options you want to group.
- If you don't draw the option buttons inside a frame or use the `GroupName` property, VBA treats all the option buttons in a form as one group.

TIP: INSERTING UNFRAMED OPTION BUTTONS

If you already have one or more "unframed" option buttons on your form, you can still insert them into a frame. Just select the buttons, cut them to the Clipboard, select the frame, and paste. VBA will add the buttons to the frame.

Check Boxes

Check boxes let you include options that the user can toggle on or off. To create a check box, use the `CheckBox` button in the Toolbox.

As with option buttons, you can control whether a check box is initially activated (checked). Set its `Value` property to `True` to activate the check box or to `False` to deactivate it.

Toggle Buttons

A toggle button is a cross between a check box and a command button. Click it once, and the button stays pressed; click it again, and the button returns to its normal state. You create toggle buttons by using the ToggleButton tool in the Toolbox.

You control whether a toggle button is initially activated (pressed) by setting its `Value` property to `True` to press the button or to `False` to "unpress" the button.

List Boxes

VBA offers two different list objects you can use to present the user with a list of choices: a ListBox and a ComboBox.

The ListBox Object

The ListBox object is a simple list of items from which the user selects an item or items. Use the ListBox button to create a list box. Here are some ListBox object properties to note:

ColumnCount: The number of columns in the list box.

ColumnHeads: If this property is True, the list columns are displayed with headings.

MultiSelect: If this property is True, the user may select multiple items in the list.

RowSource determines the items that appear in the list. In Excel, enter a range or a range name.

Text sets or returns the selected item.

The ComboBox Object

The ComboBox object is a control that combines a text box with a list box. The user clicks the drop-down arrow to display the list box and then selects an item from the list or enters an item in the text box. Use the ComboBox button to create this control.

Because ComboBox is actually two separate controls, the available properties are an amalgam of those discussed earlier for a text box and a list box. You can also work with the following properties that are unique to a ComboBox object:

ListRows determines the number of items that appear when the user drops the list down.

MatchRequired: If this property is True, the user can only enter values from the list. If it's False, the user can enter new values.

Style determines the type of ComboBox. Use 0 (fmStyleDropDownCombo) for list that includes a text box; use 2 (fmStyleDropDownList) for a list only.

List Box Techniques

How do you specify the contents of a list if the RowSource property isn't applicable (that is, if you're not working in Excel or if the data you want in the list isn't part of an Excel range)? In this case, you must build the list at runtime. You can use the AddItem method, described later in this section, or you can set the List property. For the latter, you must specify an array of values. For example, the following statements use a form's Initialize event to populate a list box with the days of the week:

```
Private Sub UserForm_Initialize()
    ListBox1.List() = Array("Monday", "Tuesday", "Wednesday", "Thursday",
    ➥"Friday", "Saturday", "Sunday")
End Sub
```

List boxes also have a few useful methods for controlling from your VBA code the items that appear in a list box:

AddItem adds an item to the specified list box. Here's the syntax:

object.AddItem(**text**,*index*)

object	The name of the ListBox object to which you want to add the item.
text	The item's text.
index	The new item's position in the list. If you omit this argument, VBA adds the item to the end of the list.

Clear removes all the items from the specified list box.

RemoveItem removes an item from the specified list box using the following syntax:

object.RemoveItem(**index**)

object	The ListBox object from which you want to remove the item.
index	The index number of the item you want to remove.

Scroll Bars

Scroll bars are usually used to navigate windows, but by themselves you can use them to enter values between a predefined maximum and minimum. Use the ScrollBar button to create either a vertical or horizontal scroll bar. Here's a rundown of the ScrollBar object properties you'll use most often in your VBA code:

LargeChange returns or sets the amount that the scroll bar value changes when the user clicks between the scroll box and one of the scroll arrows.

Max returns or sets the maximum value of the scroll bar.

Min returns or sets the minimum value of the scroll bar.

SmallChange returns or sets the amount that the scroll bar value changes when the user clicks one of the scroll arrows.

Value returns or sets the current value of the scroll bar.

Spin Buttons

A spin button is similar to a scroll bar in that the user can click the button's arrows to increment or decrement a value. To create a spin button, use the SpinButton tool in the Toolbox. The properties for a SpinButton object are the same as those for a ScrollBar (except that there is no LargeChange property).

Most spin buttons have a text box control beside them to give the user the choice of entering the number directly or selecting the number by using the spin button arrows. You have to use VBA code to make sure that the values in the text box and the spinner stay in synch. (In other words, if you increment the spinner, the value shown in the text box increments as well and vice versa.)

To do this, you have to add event-handler code for both controls. For example, suppose you have a text box named `TextBox1` and a spin button named `SpinButton1`. Listing 59.1 shows the basic event-handler code that will keep the values of these two controls synchronized.

Listing 59.1. Event-handler code that keeps a text box and a spin button in synch.

```
Private Sub TextBox1_Change()
    SpinButton1.Value = TextBox1.Value
End Sub
Private Sub SpinButton1_Change()
    TextBox1.Value = SpinButton1.Value
End Sub
```

TabStrip and MultiPage Controls

I mentioned earlier that you can use frames to group related controls visually and help the user make sense of the form. However, there are two situations in which frames fall down on the job.

The first situation is when you need the form to show multiple sets of the same (or similar) data. For example, suppose you have a form that shows values for sales and expense categories. You might want the form to be capable of showing separate data for various company divisions. One solution is to create separate frames for each division and populate each frame with the same controls, but this is clearly inefficient. A second solution is to use a list or a set of option buttons. This will work, but it might not be obvious to the user how he is supposed to display different sets of data, and these extra controls just serve to clutter the frame. A better solution is to create a tabbed form in which each tab represents a different set of data.

The second situation is when you have a lot of controls. In this case, even the judicious use of frames won't be enough to keep your form from becoming difficult to navigate and understand. In situations where you have a large number of controls, you're better off creating a tabbed form that spreads the controls over several tabs.

In both of these situations, the tabbed form solution acts much like the tabbed dialog boxes you work with in Windows, Office, and other modern programs. To create tabs in your forms, VBA offers two controls: `TabStrip` and `MultiPage`.

The TabStrip Control

The `TabStrip` is an ideal way to give the user an intuitive method of displaying multiple sets of data. The basic idea behind the `TabStrip` control is that as the user navigates from tab to tab, the visible controls remain the same, and only the data displayed inside each control changes. The advantage here is that you need to create only a single set of controls on the form, and you use code to adjust the contents of these controls.

You create a TabStrip by clicking the TabStrip button in the Toolbox and then dragging the mouse until the strip is the size and shape you want. Here are a few points to keep in mind:

- The best way to set up a TabStrip is to add it as the first control on the form and then add the other controls inside the TabStrip.

- If you already have controls defined on the form, draw the TabStrip over the controls and then select Format | Order | Send to Back to send the TabStrip to the bottom of the z-order.

- You can also display a series of buttons instead of tabs. To use this format, select the TabStrip and change the Style property to fmTabStyleButtons (or 1).

Figure 59.5 shows a form that contains a TabStrip control and an Excel worksheet that shows budget data for three different divisions. The goal here is to use the TabStrip to display budget data for each division as the user selects the tabs.

FIGURE 59.5.

Using the form's TabStrip *to display budget data from the three divisions in the Excel worksheet.*

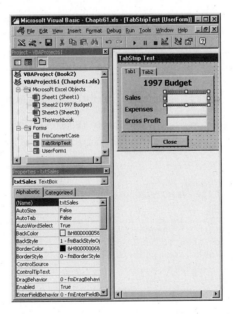

The first order of business is to use code to change the tab captions, add a third tab, and enter the initial data. Listing 59.2 shows an Initialize event procedure that does just that.

Listing 59.2. An `Initialize` event procedure that sets up a `TabStrip`.

```
Private Sub UserForm_Initialize()
    '
    ' Rename the existing tabs
    '
    With TabStrip1
        .Tabs(0).Caption = "Division I"
        .Tabs(1).Caption = "Division II"
        '
        ' Add a new tab
        '
        .Tabs.Add "Division III"
    End With
    '
    ' Enter the initial data for Division I
    '
    With Worksheets("1997 Budget")
        txtSales = .[B2]
        txtExpenses = .[B12]
        txtGrossProfit = .[B13]
    End With
End Sub
```

The code first uses the `Tabs` collection to change the captions of the two existing tabs. The `Tabs` collection represents all the tabs in a `TabStrip`, and you refer to individual tabs using an index number (where the first tab is 0, the second is 1, and so on). Then the `Tabs` collection's `Add` method is used to add a third tab titled Division III to the `TabStrip`. Finally, the three text boxes within the `TabStrip` (named `txtSales`, `txtExpenses`, and `txtGrossProfit`) are set to their respective values for Division I in the 1997 Budget worksheet.

Now you must set up a handler for when the user clicks a tab. This fires a `Change` event for the `TabStrip`, so you use this event handler to adjust the values of the text boxes, as shown in Listing 59.3.

Listing 59.3. A `Change` event procedure that modifies the controls within a `TabStrip` whenever the user selects a different tab.

```
Private Sub TabStrip1_Change()
    With Worksheets("1997 Budget")
        Select Case TabStrip1.Value
            Case 0
                '
                ' Enter the data for Division I
                '
                txtSales = .[B2]
                txtExpenses = .[B12]
                txtGrossProfit = .[B13]
            Case 1
                '
                ' Enter the data for Division II
                '
                txtSales = .[C2]
                txtExpenses = .[C12]
```

```
                txtGrossProfit = .[C13]
                Case 2
                '
                ' Enter the data for Division III
                '
                txtSales = .[D2]
                txtExpenses = .[D12]
                txtGrossProfit = .[D13]
        End Select
    End With
End Sub
```

Here, a Select Case checks the Value property of the TabStrip (where the first tab has the value 0, the second tab has the value 1, and so on). Figure 59.6 shows the form in action. (See "Displaying the Form" later in this chapter to learn how to run a form.)

FIGURE 59.6.

Clicking each tab displays the data for the appropriate division.

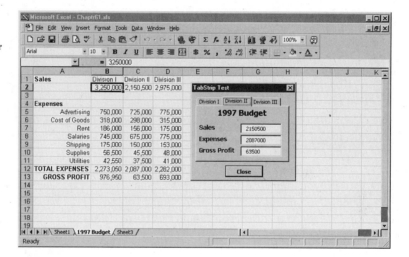

The MultiPage Control

The MultiPage control is similar to a TabStrip in that it displays a series of tabs along the top of the form. The major difference, however, is that each tab represents a separate form (called a *page*). Therefore, you use a MultiPage control whenever you want to display a different set of controls each time the user clicks a tab.

You add a MultiPage control to your form by clicking the MultiPage button in the Toolbox and then dragging the mouse until the control is the size and shape you want.

It's important to remember that each page in the control is a separate object (a Page object). Each time you select a page, the values that appear in the Properties window apply only to the selected page. For example, the Caption property determines the text that appears in the page's tab. Also, you set up a page by selecting it and then drawing controls inside the page. (If you have controls on the form already, you can put them inside a page by cutting them to the Clipboard, selecting the page, and pasting the controls.)

Working with a `MultiPage` control in code is similar to working with a `TabStrip`:

- The `Pages` collection represents all the pages inside a `MultiPage` control. You refer to individual pages using their index number.
- Use the `Pages.Add` method to add more pages to the control.
- When the user selects a different tab, the `MultiPage` control's `Change` event fires.

Using a Form in a Procedure

After you create your form, the next step is to incorporate your handiwork into some VBA code. This involves three separate techniques:

- Displaying the form
- Handling events while the form is displayed
- Processing the form results

Displaying the Form

Each UserForm object has a `Show` method that you use to display the form to the user. For example, to display a form named `UserForm1`, you use the following statement:

`UserForm1.Show`

Alternatively, you might want to load the form into memory but keep it hidden from the user. For example, you might need to perform some behind-the-scenes manipulation of the form before showing it to the user. You can do this by executing the `Load` statement:

Load *Form*

> *Form*   The name of the form you want to load.

This statement brings the form object into memory and fires the form's `Initialize` event. From there, you can display the form to the user at any time by running the form's `Show` method as discussed above.

TIP: DISPLAYING A FORM BY HAND

Before getting to the code stage, you might want to try your form to make sure it looks okay. To do this, activate the form and then either select Tools | Run Sub/UserForm, press F5, or click the Run Sub/UserForm button on the toolbar.

Handling Events While the Form Is Displayed

Once the user has the form in front of him, your code should watch for and react to events. Although you'll rarely have to account for every possible event, you should keep an eye on a few common ones.

For starters, here are a few form events that are often handy to trap:

Click fires when the user clicks an empty part of the form.

DblClick fires when the user double-clicks an empty part of the form.

Initialize fires when the form loads (that is, after you run the Show method). Use this event to set up the controls' and the form's properties at runtime.

KeyDown fires when the user presses and holds down a key or key combination. The event handler is passed two values:

  ■ A KeyCode variable that contains the ANSI code of the key. (See Appendix F, "The Windows ANSI Character Set.")

  ■ A Shift variable that tells you which of the following keys was also pressed:

> *Key:* Shift *value*
>
> Shift: fmShiftMask or 1
>
> Ctrl: fmCtrlMask or 2
>
> Alt: fmAltMask or 4

To check for a combination, use the sum of the values. For example, use 3 to see if both Shift and Ctrl were pressed.

KeyPress fires when the user presses and releases a key. The event handler is passed a variable named KeyANSI that represents the ANSI value of the key that was pressed.

KeyUp is similar to KeyDown, except that it fires when the user releases the key or key combination that he had previously held down.

MouseDown fires when the user presses and holds down a mouse button. The event handler is passed four variables:

  ■ Button specifies the button that was pressed (fmButtonLeft or 1 for the left button, fmButtonRight or 2 for the right button, or fmButtonMiddle or 4 for the middle button).

  ■ Shift specifies whether any combination of Shift, Ctrl, and Alt was also pressed. (See the description of the KeyDown event.)

  ■ X specifies the horizontal position, in points, of the mouse pointer from the left edge of the form.

  ■ Y specifies the vertical position, in points, of the mouse pointer from the top edge of the form.

MouseMove is similar to MouseDown, except that it fires when the user moves the mouse pointer within the form window.

MouseUp is similar to MouseDown, except that it fires when the user releases the mouse button.

Resize fires when the user resizes the form. You might want to use this event to adjust the relative sizes of your controls to account for the new form size.

Control objects support most of the events in this list for a form and quite a few others. Here's a quick look at a few that you should find useful:

AfterUpdate fires after the user has changed the control's data. Note, however, that this event occurs after the BeforeUpdate event and before the Exit event.

BeforeUpdate fires before the data in a control is updated with the user's changes. The event procedure passes a Cancel variable which, if you set it to True, voids the update and returns the user to the control. This event is particularly useful if the control is bound to, say, a worksheet cell and you want to validate the entry before allowing changes to the cell.

Change fires when the Value property of a control changes. See Table 59.1 for a list of controls with the Value property.

Enter fires just before the control gets the focus.

Exit fires just before the control loses the focus. The event procedure passes a Cancel variable which, if you set it to True, leaves the focus on the control.

Unloading the Form

Once the user fills out the form, you'll probably want her to click a command button to put whatever values she entered into effect. Alternatively, she could click some sort of Cancel button to dismiss the form without affecting anything.

However, just clicking a command button doesn't get rid of the form—even if you set up a command button with the Default or Cancel property set to True. Instead, you have to add the following statement to the event handler for the command button:

```
Unload Me
```

The Unload command tells VBA to dismiss the form. Note that the Me keyword refers to the form in which the event handler resides. For example, the following event handler processes a click on a command button named cmdCancel:

```
Private Sub cmdCancel_Click()
    Dim result as Integer
    result = MsgBox("Are you sure you want to Cancel?", vbYesNo + vbQuestion)
    If result = vbYes Then Unload Me
End Sub
```

You should note, however, that simply unloading a form doesn't remove the form object from memory. To ensure proper cleanup (technically, to ensure that the form object class fires its internal `Terminate` event), Set the form object to `Nothing`. For example, the following two lines `Show` the `frmConvertCase` form and then `Set` it to `Nothing` to ensure termination:

```
frmConvertCase.Show
Set frmConvertCase = Nothing
```

Processing the Form Results

When the user clicks OK or Cancel (or any other control that includes the `Unload Me` statement in its `Click` event handler), you usually need to examine the form results and process them in some way.

Obviously, how you proceed depends on whether the user has clicked OK or Cancel because this almost always determines whether the other form selections should be accepted or ignored:

- If OK is clicked, the `Click` event handler for that button can process the results. In other words, it can read the `Value` property for each control (for example, by storing them in variables for later use in the program or by entering the values into the VBE cells).

- If Cancel is clicked, the code can move on without processing the results. (As shown earlier, you can include code to ask the user if he's sure he wants to cancel.)

Table 59.1 lists all the controls that have a `Value` property and describes what kind of data gets returned.

Table 59.1. `Value` properties for some form controls.

Object	What It Returns
CheckBox	`True` if the check box is activated; `False` if it's deactivated; `Null` otherwise.
ComboBox	The position of the selected item in the list (where 1 is the first item).
ListBox	The position of the selected item in the list (where 1 is the first item).
MultiPage	An integer that represents the active page (where 0 is the first page).
OptionButton	`True` if the option is activated; `False` if it's deactivated; `Null` otherwise.
ScrollBar	A number between the scroll bar's minimum and maximum values.
SpinButton	A number between the spinner's minimum and maximum values.
TabStrip	An integer that represents the active tab (where 0 is the first tab).
TextBox	The value entered in the box.
ToggleButton	`True` if the button is pressed; `False` otherwise.

For example, Figure 59.7 shows the Convert Case form created in the Visual Basic Editor. The idea behind this form is to convert the selected cells to proper case, uppercase, or lowercase, depending on the option chosen.

FIGURE 59.7.

A custom form that lets the user change the case of the selected worksheet cells.

To load this form, I created a macro named `ConvertCase` that contains the two statements shown earlier:

```
frmConvertCase.Show
Set frmConvertCase = Nothing
```

Here, `frmConvertCase` is the name of the form shown in Figure 59.7. The three option buttons are named `optProper`, `optUpper`, and `optLower`; the OK button is named `cmdOK`. Listing 59.4 shows the event handler that runs when the user clicks OK.

Listing 59.4. A procedure that processes the Convert Case custom form.

```
Private Sub cmdOK_Click()
    Dim c As Range
    For Each c In Selection
        If optProper.Value = True Then
            c.Value = StrConv(c, vbProperCase)
        ElseIf optUpper.Value = True Then
            c.Value = StrConv(c, vbUpperCase)
        ElseIf optLower.Value = True Then
            c.Value = StrConv(c, vbLowerCase)
        End If
    Next 'c
    Unload Me
End Sub
```

The procedure runs through the selected cells, checking to see which option button was chosen, and then converts the text by using VBA's `StrConv` function:

`StrConv(`**`String, Conversion`**`)`

`String`	The string you want to convert.
`Conversion`	A constant that specifies the case you want:

`vbProperCase`	Proper Case
`vbUpperCase`	UPPERCASE
`vbLowerCase`	lowercase

Menus, Toolbars, and VBA 5.0

In Chapter 8, "Customizing the Office Menus and Toolbars," I showed you how to modify the Office menus and toolbars, including how to assign macros to menu items and toolbar buttons. However, sometimes it might be inconvenient, impractical, or downright impossible to make design-time modifications to a user's menus or toolbars. What do you do in these situations if you want to give the user pull-down menu or toolbar access to your application's procedures? Easy: Get your application to build its own menus, cascade menus, commands, and toolbars at runtime. For example, the document that contains your VBA application has an Open event that you can use to construct the necessary menu structure each time the user runs the application, as well as a Close event to remove the custom items when the application shuts down.

TIP: ATTACH TOOLBARS TO EXCEL WORKBOOKS

If you're building an Excel application, there *is* a way to distribute custom toolbars with your project:

1. Activate the workbook to which you want to attach the custom toolbar.
2. Select Tools | Customize and choose the Toolbars tab in the Customize dialog box.
3. Highlight your custom toolbar and then click Attach. Excel displays the Attach Toolbars dialog box.
4. Highlight the custom toolbar and then click Copy.
5. Click OK.

NOTE: WHICH APPLICATION?

In this chapter, I use the word "application" in two contexts: your VBA application and the underlying application in which your VBA code runs (such as Word or Excel). To avoid confusion, I refer to the underlying application as the *container application*.

The secret of controlling menus and toolbars programmatically is a new object in VBA 5.0: CommandBars. This Microsoft Office 97 object is a collection that represents all the command bars in the current application, where a "command bar" can be any of the following: a menu bar, a shortcut menu, or a toolbar. This single object replaces the multiple objects used in older versions of Excel (such as MenuBars and Toolbars), although code that uses these older objects still works in VBA 5.0.

You can use the properties and methods of the CommandBars collection to make modifications to the container application's menus and toolbars within procedures. This includes not only simulating the basic design-time techniques of adding menus, commands, and toolbars but also some techniques that are only available at runtime, such as renaming, disabling, and enabling menus and commands. The rest of this chapter takes you on a brief tour of some of these techniques.

NOTE: REFERENCE THE OFFICE OBJECT LIBRARY

Because CommandBars is a Microsoft Office 97 object, you won't be able to use it unless you've established a reference to the Office object library. This is usually set up automatically when you install Office 97. However, if you don't see the CommandBars object in the Object Browser, select Tools | References from the Visual Basic Editor and use the References dialog box to activate the reference for the Microsoft Office 8.0 Object Library.

Understanding Command Bars

To work with command bars effectively, you'll likely need to change the way you think about menu bars, shortcut menus, and toolbars. In other words, instead of thinking of these as distinct objects, you need to start thinking of them as variations on the same theme. What theme? Well, for lack of anything better, how about the palette-of-controls-that-you-click-to-perform-an-action theme? Think about it. Whether it's a menu bar, a shortcut menu, or a toolbar, you interact with the object in the same way: You click a control (a menu bar item, a menu command, a toolbar button, and so on) and something happens (a menu pulls down, a command is executed, a cascade menu appears, a pop-up box appears, and so on).

This, in a nutshell, is why Microsoft decided to gather menu bars, shortcut menus, and toolbars under the umbrella of the CommandBars object. Each of these items is now a CommandBar object, and the only difference between them is that each has a different Type property.

In a similar vein, the objects that can appear on a command bar—menu commands, toolbar buttons, pop-up boxes, drop-down menus, and so on—are called *controls*, and they're all variations of the new CommandBarControl object.

Specifying a Command Bar

As with any collection object, you use the CommandBars object to specify individual members of the collection (which are CommandBar objects, in this case). You can specify either an index number or the name of the command bar. For example, both of the following statements refer to the menu bar that appears when the focus is on an Excel worksheet:

```
CommandBars(1)
CommandBars("Worksheet Menu Bar")
```

Unlike most collections, the index numbers used in the CommandBars object aren't all that useful. For example, Excel's Worksheets collection contains all the worksheets in a workbook, and the index numbers correspond to the order the sheets appear in the workbook. In the CommandBars collection, however, the index numbers for the built-in menus and toolbars have been assigned by the container application's design team, so they have no intrinsic meaning. This means that you usually have to refer to individual CommandBar objects by their names:

Custom CommandBar objects: Any menu or toolbars that you create at runtime can also be named within the code. Therefore, your procedures always know the names of these objects.

Built-in toolbars: The names of the container application's built-in toolbars are easy enough to figure out. The name of the toolbar is just the text that appears in the toolbar's title bar (when the toolbar is floating, that is).

Built-in menu bars and shortcut menus: The container application supplies a name for each built-in menu bar and shortcut menu, but there's no easy method for determining the names of these objects.

To help you solve the latter problem, Listing 59.5 presents an Excel procedure that runs through the entire CommandBars collection and displays the name, type, and index number for each command bar.

Listing 59.5. A procedure that runs through Excel's CommandBars collection and writes the name, type, and index number of each command bar.

```
Sub ListExcelCommandBars()
    Dim i As Integer
    Dim cb As CommandBar
    Dim cbType As String
    i = 0
    For Each cb In CommandBars
        Select Case cb.Type
            Case msoBarTypeNormal      '0
                cbType = "Toolbar"
            Case msoBarTypeMenuBar      '1
                cbType = "Menu Bar"
            Case msoBarTypePopup      '2
                cbType = "Shortcut Menu"
        End Select
        With Worksheets("Sheet1").[a2]
            .Offset(i, 0) = cb.Name
            .Offset(i, 1) = cbType
            .Offset(i, 2) = cb.Index
        End With
        i = i + 1
    Next
    Set cb = Nothing
End Sub
```

NOTE: LISTING WORD'S COMMAND BARS

If you want to list the command bars in Word, substitute the `With...End With` statement in Listing 59.5 with the following (see either Chaptr59.doc or Chaptr59.bas on the CD):

```
With ActiveDocument.Paragraphs(2).Range
    With .ParagraphFormat.TabStops
        .Add Position:=InchesToPoints(2)
        .Add Position:=InchesToPoints(3.5)
    End With
    .InsertAfter cb.Name & vbTab
    .InsertAfter cbType & vbTab
    .InsertAfter cb.Index
    .InsertParagraphAfter
End With
```

Properties of the CommandBars Object

Before you get to the properties and methods of individual command bars, examine a few properties of the `CommandBars` object. These properties control the look and feel of all the command bars, including the animation style used with menus, whether buttons display tooltips, and more:

`CommandBars.ActiveMenuBar` returns a CommandBar object that represents the active menu bar in the container application.

`CommandBars.Count` returns the number of command bars in the `CommandBars` collection.

`CommandBars.DisplayKeysInTooltips` returns or sets whether the container application includes a control's shortcut key inside the tooltip that is displayed when the user hovers the mouse pointer over the control. Use `True` to include the shortcut key.

`CommandBars.DisplayTooltips` returns or sets whether the container application displays a tooltip when the user hovers the mouse pointer over a command bar control. Use `True` to display tooltips.

`CommandBars.LargeButtons` returns or sets whether the container application displays large toolbar buttons. Use `True` to display the large buttons.

`CommandBars.MenuAnimationStyle` returns or sets the animation style the container application uses for pulled-down menus. Use one of the following constants:

`msoMenuAnimationUnfold`	Unfold
`msoMenuAnimationSlide`	Slide
`msoMenuAnimationNone`	None
`msoMenuAnimationRandom`	Switches randomly between Unfold, Slide, and None

Working with Command Bars

Now that you're familiar with the `CommandBars` object, you can put it to good use creating your own custom command bars and modifying the container application's built-in command bars. This section shows you how to perform these actions.

Creating a New Command Bar

Whether you want to create a new toolbar, shortcut menu, or menu bar, the procedure is exactly the same. In other words, you invoke the `Add` method of the `CommandBars` object and use it to specify the type of command bar you want. Here's the syntax:

```
CommandBars.Add(Name, Position, MenuBar, Temporary)
```

Name	The name you want to use for the new command bar. Although this argument is optional, it's always a good idea to include it so that you can be sure of the command bar's name. Otherwise, the container application assigns a generic name such as `Custom1`.
Position	Determines where the command bar appears within the container application's window:

`msoBarTop`	Command bar is docked at the top of the window.
`msoBarBottom`	Command bar is docked at the bottom of the window.
`msoBarLeft`	Command bar is docked on the left side of the window.
`msoBarRight`	Command bar is docked on the right side of the window.
`msoBarFloating`	Command bar is undocked.
`msoBarPopup`	Command bar is a shortcut menu.
`msoBarMenuBar`	(Macintosh only) Command bar replaces the system menu bar.

MenuBar	A `Boolean` value that determines whether the new command bar replaces the active menu bar. Use `True` to replace the menu bar; use `False` to leave the active menu bar in place (this is the default).

    Temporary   A `Boolean` value that determines when the command bar is deleted. Use `True` to have the command bar deleted when the container application is closed; use `False` to keep the command bar (this is the default).

For example, Listing 59.6 shows a procedure that uses the `Add` method to create a new temporary toolbar named My Toolbar. Before doing so, the procedure runs through the `CommandBars` collection to make sure there is no existing command bar with the same name. (The container application generates an error if you attempt to create a new command bar with the name of an existing command bar.)

Listing 59.6. A procedure that creates a new toolbar after first checking to see if a command bar with the same name already exists.

```
Sub AddToolbar()
    Dim cb As CommandBar
    Dim cbExists As Boolean
    cbExists = False
    For Each cb In CommandBars
        If cb.Name = "My Toolbar" Then
            cbExists = True
            Exit For
        End If
    Next cb
    If cbExists Then
        MsgBox "A command bar named ""My Toolbar"" already exists!"
    Else
        Set cb = CommandBars.Add( _
            Name:="My Toolbar", _
            Position:=msoBarFloating, _
            Temporary:=True)
    End If
    Set cb = Nothing
End Sub
```

Command Bar Properties

Whether you're dealing with one of the container application's built-in command bars or a custom command bar that you've created via code, you can exploit a number of CommandBar object properties in your VBA procedures. Here's a look a few useful ones:

    CommandBar`.BuiltIn` returns `True` if the specified *CommandBar* is native to the container application; returns `False` for custom command bars.

    CommandBar`.Controls` returns a `CommandBarControls` object that represents the collection of all the controls contained in the specified *CommandBar*.

    CommandBar`.Enabled`: When this property is `True`, the user can work with the specified *CommandBar*. The command bar is disabled when this property is set to `False`.

    CommandBar`.Height` returns or sets the height, in pixels, for the specified *CommandBar*.

This property only has an effect on a non-empty command bar. Also, note that setting this property results in an error in two situations:

- If the command bar is docked (in other words, the command bar's `Position` property isn't set to `msoBarFloating`; see the `Position` property, discussed later).

- If the command bar is protected against resizing (in other words, the command bar's `Protection` property is set to `msoNoResize`; see the `Protection` property, discussed later).

Here's a procedure fragment that checks a command bar's `Position` and `Protection` properties before changing the height:

```
With CommandBars("My Toolbar")
    If .Position = msoBarFloating And _
        Not .Protection = msoBarNoResize Then
        .Height = 100
    End If
End With
```

CommandBar.`Index` returns the index number in the `CommandBars` collection for the specified *CommandBar*.

CommandBar.`Left`: If the command bar is floating, this property returns or sets the distance, in pixels, of the left edge of the specified *CommandBar* from the left edge of the screen (not the container application window). If the command bar is docked, this property returns the distance from the left edge of the docking area.

CommandBar.`Name` returns or sets the name of the specified *CommandBar*.

CommandBar.`Position` returns or sets the position of the specified *CommandBar*. This property uses the same constants that I outlined earlier for the `Position` argument in the `CommandBars` object's `Add` method.

CommandBar.`Protection` returns or sets the protection options for the specified *CommandBar*. You use these options to prevent (or allow) user customization of the object. When setting this property, use any one of the following constants (or you can apply multiple levels of protection by using the sum of two or more constants):

Protection	Value	Resulting Protection
msoBarNoProtection	0	None
msoBarNoCustomize	1	Prevents the user from adding, modifying, or deleting controls.
msoBarNoResize	2	Prevents the user from resizing the command bar.
msoBarNoMove	4	Prevents the user from moving the command bar.
msoBarNoChangeVisible	8	Prevents the user from hiding or unhiding the command bar.

continues

Protection	*Value*	*Resulting Protection*
msoBarNoChangeDock	16	Prevents the user from docking or undocking the command bar.
msoBarNoVerticalDock	32	Prevents the user from docking the command bar on the left or right side of the window.
msoBarNoHorizontalDock	64	Prevents the user from docking the command bar on the top or bottom of the window.

CommandBar.RowIndex returns or sets the row number in the docking area for the specified *CommandBar*. You use this property to determine where in the docking area your command bar will appear. You can use any positive integer or the constant msoBarRowFirst (to place the command bar at the beginning of the docking area) or msoBarRowLast (to place the command bar at the end of the docking area).

CommandBar.Top: If the command bar is floating, this property returns or sets the distance, in pixels, of the top edge of the specified *CommandBar* from the top edge of the screen (*not* the container application window). If the command bar is docked, this property returns the distance from the top edge of the docking area.

CommandBar.Type returns the object type for the specified *CommandBar*, as follows:

msoBarTypeNormal	Toolbar
msoBarTypeMenuBar	Menu bar
msoBarTypePopup	Shortcut menu

CommandBar.Visible returns or sets whether the specified *CommandBar* is visible. Use True to display the command bar; use False to hide the command bar. Note that VBA sets this property to False by default when you create a custom command bar.

CommandBar.Width returns or sets the width, in pixels, for the specified CommandBar. This property only has an effect on a non-empty command bar and, as with Height, this property results in an error if the command bar is docked or if the command bar is protected against resizing.

Deleting a Custom Command Bar

Unless you specify otherwise, the command bars you create become a permanent part of the container application. This might be a desirable situation in certain circumstances. For example, if your VBA application contains utilities that are applicable to any document in the container application, it makes sense to give the user full-time access to the procedures.

On the other hand, your procedures might be applicable only while the VBA application is running. In this case, there are a number of reasons why you should delete the command bars when your application shuts down:

- You avoid confusing the user with extra command bars.
- You prevent damage to the user's other files that might be caused by running one of your procedures on a document that wasn't designed for your application.
- You save memory and resources.

I mentioned earlier that you can create your command bars with the Add method's Temporary argument set to True. This tells the container application to delete the command bar upon exiting. For immediate deleting, however, use the CommandBar object's Delete method:

CommandBar.Delete

CommandBar is the custom CommandBar object that you want to delete. Note that you can't delete built-in command bars.

Resetting a Built-In Command Bar

If you make changes to one of the container application's built-in command bars, you can restore the command bar to its default state by using the Reset method:

CommandBar.Reset

CommandBar is the built-in CommandBar object you want to reset. For example, Listing 59.7 shows the CleanUpCommandBars procedure that loops through the CommandBars collection and performs one of two tasks. If the command bar is built-in, it's restored to its default state; if the command bar is a custom object, it's deleted.

Listing 59.7. A procedure that runs through the CommandBars collection and resets the built-in command bars and deletes the custom command bars.

```
Sub CleanUpCommandBars()
    Dim cb As CommandBar
    For Each cb In CommandBars
        If cb.BuiltIn Then
            cb.Reset
        Else
            cb.Delete
        End If
    Next cb
    Set cb = Nothing
End Sub
```

Working with Command Bar Controls

At this point, your custom command bars aren't particularly useful because they can't do much of anything. In other words, they don't contain any controls that the user can click or otherwise execute. This section solves that problem by giving you the lowdown on VBA's command bar controls and by showing you how to add and modify custom command bar controls.

The Microsoft Office 97 object model divides command bar controls into three categories:

> CommandBarButton is an object that the user clicks to execute a command or run a procedure. Menu commands and toolbar buttons are examples of CommandBarButton objects.

> CommandBarPopup is an object that the user clicks to display a menu of items. Examples of CommandBarPopup objects are menu bar commands and menu commands that display cascade menus.

> CommandBarComboBox takes one of three forms: a text box into which the user enters text (for example, the Name text box in the Modify Selection menu; see Figure 8.5 in Chapter 8); a drop-down list from which the user selects an item; or a combo box that combines a text box and a drop-down list (for example, the Font and Font Size controls on the Formatting toolbar in Word and Excel).

Specifying a Control

As you learned earlier, each CommandBar object has a `Controls` property that returns the collection of all the controls on the command bar. You use this collection to specify individual controls using their index number, where `Controls(1)` is the first control on the command bar, `Controls(2)` is the second control, and so on. In each case, a CommandBarControl object is returned.

Another way to specify a control is to use the CommandBar object's `FindControl` method:

CommandBar.FindControl(*Type, Id, Tag, Visible, Recursive*)

CommandBar	The CommandBar object in which you want to search.
Type	A constant that specifies the type of CommandBarControl object you want to find. For custom controls, use one of the following constants that correspond to the control types discussed previously: `msoControlButton`, `msoControlPopup`, `msoControlEdit`, `msoControlDropdown`, or `msoControlComboBox`. For built-in controls, Office also defines quite a number of other constants. To see these constants, look up the `Type` property of the CommandBarControl object in the Office VBA help system.

Id	This is a unique identifier that the container application supplies for each control. This identifier is returned by the CommandBarControl object's Id property.
Tag	Specifies the Tag property of the control you want to find.
Visible	Use True to search only for controls that are visible; use False to search for hidden controls as well (this is the default).
Recursive	Use True to search not only the command bar, but also all of its cascade menus and pop-up menus; use False to search only the command bar (this is the default).

If FindControl is successful, it returns a CommandBarControl object for the first control that matches your search criteria. If the search fails, FindControl returns the value Nothing.

Adding a Control to a Command Bar

When customizing command bars, you can take a number of different routes:

- You can modify a built-in command bar by adding built-in controls.
- You can modify a built-in command bar by adding custom controls that execute your VBA procedures.
- You can modify a custom command bar by adding built-in controls.
- You can modify a custom command bar by adding custom controls.

Whichever route you take, you insert a control into a command bar by using the Controls object's Add method:

CommandBar.Controls.Add(*Type, Id, Parameter, Before, Temporary*)

| *CommandBar* | The CommandBar object into which you want to insert the control. |
| *Type* | A constant that determines the type of custom control to add: |

msoControlButton	CommandBarButton
msoControlPopup	CommandBarPopup
msoControlEdit	CommandBarComboBox
msoControlDropdown	CommandBarComboBox
msoControlComboBox	CommandBarComboBox

| *Id* | An integer that specifies the built-in control you want to add. |

Parameter	You use this argument to send a parameter to a built-in control. (The container application uses this parameter to modify how it runs the command associated with the control.) For custom controls, you can use this argument to send information to the procedure associated with the control.
Before	The index number of the control before which the new control will be added. If you omit this argument, VBA adds the control to the end of the command bar.
Temporary	A Boolean value that determines when the control is deleted. Use True to have the control deleted when the container application is closed; use False to keep the control (this is the default).

For example, the following statement adds a CommandBarButton object to the end of the toolbar named My Toolbar:

```
CommandBars("My Toolbar").Controls.Add Type:=msoControlButton
```

The Command Bar Info Utility

One of the problems you face when working with command bars and controls is that you're often flying blind. For example, you saw earlier that there's no easy way to tell the name of a menu bar or shortcut menu. Similarly, you can't add a built-in control to a command bar unless you know its Id property, but VBA gives you no easy way to determine this property.

To help you out, I put together a small utility that solves this dilemma. In Chaptr59.xls on this book's CD-ROM, you see a form named CommandBarInfo. If you run this form, you see the dialog box shown in Figure 59.8. The idea is that you use the Name list to select the name of a command bar and then use the Caption list to choose a control. The labels beneath this list tell you the control's Id, Type, and Index properties.

FIGURE 59.8.

Use the Command Bar Info utility to find out the Id *property of a built-in control.*

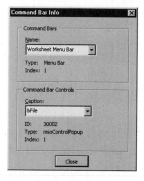

Control Properties

To make your custom controls do something useful, you have to set a few properties. For example, you'll want to specify the procedure to run when the user clicks the control, and you'll probably want to define a tooltip for a your toolbar-based controls. Here's a quick rundown of these and other control properties:

`Control.BeginGroup` returns `True` if the specified `Control` is at the beginning of a group of controls on a command bar. If `True`, the underlying application displays a separator bar before the `Control`.

`Control.BuiltIn` returns `True` if the specified `Control` is native to the container application; returns `False` for custom controls.

`Control.Caption` returns or sets the caption for specified `Control`. If the control is a menu bar command or a menu command, the `Caption` property determines the command text, so you should include an ampersand before the letter you want to use as an accelerator key:

```
Set newMenu = CommandBars(1).Controls.Add(Type:=msoControlPopup)
newMenu.Caption = "&My Menu"
```

NOTE: BUTTON CAPTION IS DEFAULT TOOLTIP

If the control is a toolbar button, the `Caption` property sets the default text used as the control's tooltip. Note, however, that each control also has a `ToolTipText` property that you can use to manipulate the tooltip text.

`Control.Controls`: If the specified `Control` is a CommandBarPopup object, this property returns the collection of all the controls on the pop-up. For example, you can use this property to return all the menu items in a pull-down menu.

`Control.DropDownLines`: If the specified `Control` is a `CommandBarComboBox` object, this property returns or sets the number of items that appear when the user drops down the list.

`Control.DropDownWidth`: If the specified `Control` is a CommandBarComboBox object, this property returns or sets the width of the control, in pixels.

`Control.Enabled`: When this property is `True`, the user can work with the specified `Control`. The control is disabled when this property is set to `False`.

59

CREATING A CUSTOM USER INTERFACE

Control.FaceId: If the specified *Control* is a CommandBarButton object, this property returns or sets the ID number of the icon on the button's face. Note that this number is the same as the control's Id property in most cases.

Control.Id: As you've seen, this property returns a unique ID for the specified built-in *Control*. Note that all custom controls return 1 for the Id property.

Control.Index returns the index number in the Controls collection for the specified *Control*.

Control.List(**Index**): If the specified *Control* is a CommandBarComboBox object, this property returns or sets the value of the list item given by **Index** (where 0 is the first item).

Control.ListCount: If the specified *Control* is a CommandBarComboBox object, this property returns the number of items in the list.

Control.ListIndex: If the specified *Control* is a CommandBarComboBox object, this property returns or sets the selected item in the list.

Control.OnAction returns or sets the name of the VBA procedure that executes when the user clicks the specified Control. Listing 59.8 shows a procedure that adds a new command to the Tools menu.

Listing 59.8. A procedure that modifies the Tools menu by adding a command to execute the RunCommandBarInfo procedure.

```
Sub AddToolsMenuCommand()
    Dim cb As CommandBar
    Dim menuTools As CommandBarControl
    Dim ctrl As CommandBarControl
    Dim ctrlExists As Boolean
    ctrlExists = False
    '
    ' Get the Tools menu (ID=30007)
    '
    Set menuTools = Application.CommandBars.FindControl(Id:=30007)
    '
    ' Make sure the command doesn't exist
    '
    For Each ctrl In menuTools.Controls
        If ctrl.Caption = "Command &Bar Info" Then
            ctrlExists = True
            Exit For
        End If
    Next ctrl
    '
    ' If the command doesn't exist, add it
    '
    If Not ctrlExists Then
        Set ctrl = menuTools.Controls.Add(Type:=msoControlButton)
        With ctrl
            .Caption = "Command &Bar Info"
            .OnAction = "RunCommandBarInfo"
        End With
```

```
    End If
    Set cb = Nothing
End Sub
' This procedure runs the CommandBarInfo utility.
'
Sub RunCommandBarInfo()
    CommandBarInfo.Show
End Sub
```

The procedure first checks to see if the command already exists. It does this by using the FindControl method to find the Tools menu (which the Command Bar Info utility tells us has ID 30007) and then using a For Each...Next loop to check the Caption of each item on the menu. If the command doesn't exist, the Add method tacks it onto the end of the menu, the Caption property is set to Command &Bar Info, and the OnAction property is set to RunCommandBarInfo. The latter procedure appears at the end of the listing and it just runs the Show method to display the CommandBarInfo form.

Control.ShortcutText: If the specified *Control* is a CommandBarButton object that appears on a menu, this property returns or sets the shortcut key text that appears to the right of the control.

Control.State: If the specified *Control* is a CommandBarButton object, this property returns or sets the appearance of the button:

msoButtonUp	Unpressed
msoButtonDown	Pressed
msoButtonMixed	Mixed

Control.Style: If the specified *Control* is a CommandBarButton object, this property returns or sets how the container application displays the button:

msoButtonAutomatic	Using the container application's default display
msoButtonIcon	With an icon only
msoButtonCaption	With a caption only
msoButtonIconandCaption	With both an icon and a caption

Control.Text: If the specified *Control* is a CommandBarComboBox object, this property returns or sets the text that appears in the text box part of the control.

Control.ToolTipText returns or sets the tooltip text for specified *Control*.

Control.Type returns the object type for the specified *Control*. To see a complete list of control types, open the code window for the CommandBarInfo form and examine the ControlType function.

Control.Visible returns or sets whether the specified *Control* is visible. Use True to display the control; use False to hide the control.

59

CREATING A
CUSTOM USER
INTERFACE

Control Methods

To complete your examination of controls, this section looks at a few methods associated with controls. With these methods, you can copy and move a control, execute the action that underlies a control, set the focus on a control, delete a control, and more. Here's the rundown:

`Control.AddItem`: If the specified `Control` is a CommandBarComboBox object, this method adds an item to the control's list using the following syntax:

`Control.AddItem(`**`Text, `**`Index)`

Control	The control to which you want to add the list item.
Text	A string that specifies the item to be added to the list.
Index	The position of the new item in the list. If you omit this argument, VBA adds the item to the end of the list.

`Control.Clear`: If the specified `Control` is a CommandBarComboBox object, this method clears the contents of the list. Note that you can't apply this method to a built-in control.

`Control.Copy` makes a copy of the specified `Control` using the following syntax:

`Control.Copy(`*`Bar, Before`*`)`

Control	The control you want to copy.
Bar	The CommandBar object to which you want to copy the control. If you omit this argument, VBA makes a copy of this control on the command bar that contains **Control**.
Before	The index number of the control before which the copied control will be inserted. If you omit this argument, VBA adds the control to the end of the command bar.

`Control.CopyFace`: If the specified `Control` is a CommandBarButton object, this method copies the icon on the button's face to the Clipboard. You can then use the `PasteFace` method (which appears later in this list) to apply the copied face to another button.

`Control.Delete` deletes the specified `Control` using the following syntax:

`Control.Delete(`*`Temporary`*`)`

Control	The control you want to delete.
Temporary	A `Boolean` value that determines the permanence of the deletion. If you use `True`, VBA deletes the control but then restores the control the next time the container application is started. If you use `False`, VBA deletes the control permanently (this is the default).

Control.Execute runs the built-in command or VBA procedure associated with the specified *Control*.

Control.Move moves the specified *Control* using the following syntax:

Control.Move(*Bar*, *Before*)

Control	The control you want to move.
Bar	The CommandBar object to which you want to move the control. If you omit this argument, VBA moves the control to the end of the command bar that contains **Control**.
Before	The index number of the control before which the moved control will be inserted. If you omit this argument, VBA adds the control to the end of the command bar.

Control.PasteFace: If the specified *Control* is a CommandBarButton object, this method pastes the current contents of the Clipboard onto the button's face. You usually use this method after having first copied another button's face to the Clipboard using the CopyFace method (which appears earlier in this list).

Control.RemoveItem: If the specified *Control* is a CommandBarComboBox object, this method removes an item from the list using the following syntax:

Control.RemoveItem(***Index***)

Control	The control from which you want to remove the item.
Index	The number of the item that you want to remove.

Control.Reset restores the specified *Control* to its default state.

Control.SetFocus sets the focus on the specified Control.

Summary

This chapter showed you how to use VBA to create a custom user interface. I began by discussing VBA 5.0's new Microsoft Forms feature. After a brief introduction to user forms, I showed you how to add a form to your project and how to set a number of form design-time properties. From there, I turned your attention to controls, and you learned numerous techniques for working with the various Toolbox objects. After a brief discussion of form event handlers, I took you on a tour of the various control types that are available in the Toolbox. You then learned how to handle forms inside your VBA procedures.

The rest of the chapter rounded out your VBA user interface education by showing you how to wield Office 97's CommandBars object model to create custom command bars and controls and to modify the container application's built-in command bars and controls.

Here's a list of chapters where you'll find related information:

- I go through some basic user interface features—such as the `MsgBox` and `InputBox` functions—in Chapter 55, "Controlling VBA Code and Interacting with the User." This chapter also shows you how to access the built-in dialog boxes available in VBA applications.

- Handling form results often means using loops and control structures (such as `If...Then...Else` and `Select Case`). I explain these VBA statements in Chapter 55.

IN THIS PART

Appendixes

What's in the Office 97 ValuPack

IN THIS APPENDIX

APPENDIX A

In addition to the major applications I've discussed throughout this book, Office 97 also comes with a ValuPack that's loaded with dozens of extra goodies. This appendix outlines most of these extras. To see the complete list, head for the \ValuPack folder on your Office CD-ROM.

Wizards and Template Files

Office Small Business Edition offers dozens of additional wizards and templates to augment those in the basic Office package. There are .DOT and .WIZ files for Word, .XLT files for Excel, .POT files for PowerPoint, and .OFT files and forms for Outlook. You'll find all of these files in the \ValuPack\Template folder in your Small Business Edition disc.

In addition to the Office templates, the Small Business Edition CD-ROM also includes the following wizards and templates:

Avery Wizard: This is a Word add-in that makes it easier to work with Avery labels. See \ValuPack\AveryWiz.

Microsoft Office Upgrade Wizard: If you're upgrading from a previous version of Office, this wizard, shown in Figure A.1, eases the upgrade path by removing older Office files or components that are no longer needed. You'll find this wizard in the \ValuPack\OffClean folder.

FIGURE A.1.

Use the Microsoft Office Upgrade Wizard to clean out your old Office files.

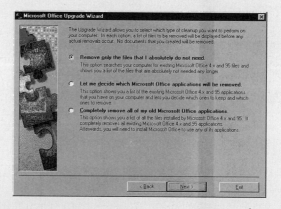

Microsoft Office Binder templates: The \ValuPack\Binders\A4 folder contains a couple of binder templates—Meeting Organizer and Proposal and Marketing Plan—that can save time when creating these kinds of binders.

Microsoft Web Publishing Wizard: This wizard makes it easy to publish Web pages to an Internet service provider or Web hosting provider. See \ValuPack\WebPost.

Timex Data Link Watch Wizard: The Timex Data Link Watch can receive information from Outlook. To make it easier to export appointments, tasks, anniversaries, and reminders, use the Timex Data Link Watch Wizard, found in \ValuPack\Timex.

Multimedia Files and Utilities

If you want to add a bit of pizzazz to your Office documents or Web pages, the ValuPack has a large number of images, sounds, utilities, and other multimedia marvels. Here's a summary:

ActiveMovie: This is Microsoft's next-generation digital video technology. It supports not only the current video standards, including AVI and QuickTime, but also MPEG and the new ActiveMovie Streaming Format. To install the ActiveMovie control, see \ValuPack\AMovie.

ActiveMovie publishing: The ValuPack also includes the Publish to ActiveMovie Stream Format tool, which publishes PowerPoint presentations to ASF format. Users with the ActiveMovie control installed can view your presentation streamed over the Internet or an intranet. ("Streamed" means that the movie is displayed in real time without first downloading the entire file.) See \ValuPack\Asf.

Animated cursors: This is a collection of animated cursors. You'll find the installation program in \ValuPack\Cursors.

Animated GIF files: The ValuPack boasts a number of animated GIF images, which are essentially multiple GIF files amalgamated into a single file and played in sequence to create an animation. They're in the \ValuPack\AnimGIFs folder.

Netscape ActiveX Plug-In: This plug-in module enables the Netscape Web browser to work with ActiveX controls. The installation program is in the \ValuPack\ AXPlugIn folder.

Office 97 sounds: This is a collection of sound files that get associated with various Office application events. The installation program is in \ValuPack\Sounds.

PowerPoint Animation Player: This plug-in enables your Web browser to view animations created with PowerPoint. The installation program is in the \ValuPack\ PPTAnim folder.

PowerPoint Custom Soundtrack: This is a PowerPoint add-in that enables you to set up custom soundtracks to play with your presentations. Look for the setup program in the \ValuPack\MusicTrk folder.

PowerPoint RealAudio: This add-in gives PowerPoint the capability to play Real-Audio files. (RealAudio is a streaming audio format common on the World Wide Web.) The installation program is in the \ValuPack\RealAud folder, and there's a small collection of RealAudio files in the \ValuPack\RealAud\RaSounds folder.

Textures: For a list of JPEG images suitable for Web page or document backgrounds, see \ValuPack\Textures.

TrueType fonts: You'll find a large number of TrueType font files in the \ValuPack\ MSFonts folder.

Viewers and Converters

The ValuPack comes with the following Office viewers and converters:

Outlook converters: These converters enable you to import ACT!, ECCO, and SideKick files, as well as import and export Journal entries, Notes items, and Inbox messages. The installation program is in the \ValuPack\Convert\Outlook folder.

PowerPoint Viewer: This viewer enables you to view PowerPoint slide shows even if you don't have PowerPoint installed. The installation program is in the \ValuPack\ PPT4View folder.

Word 97 converter: This tool enables you to convert Word 97 documents to Word 95 format (or Word 6.x format for NT and the Mac). The installation program is in the \ValuPack\Wrd97Cnv folder.

Word Viewer: This viewer enables you to view Word documents even if you don't have Word installed. The installation program is in the \ValuPack\WordView folder.

Microsoft Camcorder

Microsoft Camcorder is a screen-capture utility with a twist: it enables you to capture screen shots in real time and play them back as a movie. This is perfect for demonstrating computer-based techniques for training and customer support. Camcorder creates AVI video files by default, but you can also create stand-alone movies (EXE files) that anyone can play.

More ValuPack Extras

To complete your look at the extra knickknacks that come with the Small Business Edition ValuPack, here's a list of a few more files and tools available on the CD:

Additional VBA help files: The \ValuPack\MoreHelp folder contains help files that provide information on the object models and some VBA programming considerations for Outlook, Binder, Microsoft Graph, and Microsoft Map.

Building Applications with Microsoft Access 97: This online book, shown in Figure A.2, tells developers how to create database solutions using Access. To view this book, open the following Web page:

```
\ValuPack\Access\BldApps\default.htm
```

FIGURE A.2.

Building Applications with Microsoft Access 97 is an online book that shows you how to develop database applications using Access.

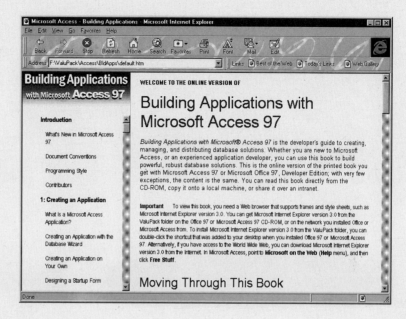

Data Access Pack: This is a setup program that enables you to install ODBC drivers for external data access. You'll find the installation program in the \ValuPack\DataAcc folder.

Internet controls help file: The \ValuPack\Access\WebHelp folder contains a help file that tells you how to use VBA to program the Web Browser and Internet Explorer ActiveX controls.

cc:Mail information service: The ValuPack includes an information service that enables you to use Outlook to retrieve and send cc:Mail messages. You'll find the installation program in the \ValuPack\CCMail folder.

Office 97 Small Business Edition

IN THIS APPENDIX

APPENDIX B

As you've seen in this book, Microsoft Office is a sprawling, complex package with more than enough muscle to handle most business tasks and problems. However, every business has its own unique needs and concerns, so getting the most out of previous versions of Office often meant doing two things:

- Creating custom solutions in the form of templates, worksheet models, add-ins, macros, and Access or VBA applications.
- Augmenting the Office applications with other programs (such as a page layout application).

Microsoft recognized this fact, so it decided to help out by putting together new Office packages designed to appeal to specific market segments. This appendix discusses one of these packages, Office 97 Small Business Edition, which Microsoft hopes will meet the needs of small business owners and the self-employed. (I discuss Office 97 Developer Edition in Appendix C.)

About the Small Business Edition

The Small Business Edition is a two-CD set that starts with the Office 97 Standard Edition components: Word, Excel, PowerPoint, and Outlook. It also includes many of the other common Office tools: Internet Explorer, Binder, the Office Shortcut bar, WordArt, the Clip Gallery, Graph, Equation Editor, Photo Editor, Query, Organization Chart, and Visual Basic for Applications.

The Small Business Edition also includes three extra applications—Publisher, Small Business Financial Manager, and Automap Streets Plus—and an online book called *Doing Business on the Internet*. I'll discuss these extra features in the next few sections.

Microsoft Publisher

Microsoft Word contains a number of tools that help you set up interesting pages. Using features such as frames, columns, graphics, and tables, you can impose a particular layout on a page and so create basic flyers, letterheads, and résumés. As powerful as Word is, it just wasn't designed to handle true page layout tasks with anything resembling efficiency. If you regularly put together newsletters, brochures, business cards, and the like, you're better off switching to a dedicated page layout application.

The problem, though, is that small businesses and the self-employed are often subject to the constraints imposed by a small budget. High-end page layout programs with their equally high-end price tags might be out of reach for all but the most well-heeled. Microsoft's solution to this dilemma was to bundle its Publisher page layout application with the Small Business Edition. Publisher is a powerful program that provides you with a huge array of tools for creating sophisticated single-page and multi-page documents. Best of all, Publisher comes with a large cast of page wizards that are only too happy to lead you step-by-step through the creation of everything from basic business cards to full-blown Web sites.

When you launch Publisher, the program displays the dialog box shown in Figure B.1. From here, you have four ways to proceed:

- To start a new publication and have a page wizard lead you through it, make sure the PageWizard tab is showing, highlight the type of publication you want, and click OK.

- To start with a fresh page, activate the Blank Page tab, shown in Figure B.2, highlight the type of page you want, and click OK.

- If you have an existing document you want to amend, activate the Existing Publication tab, highlight the file, and click OK.

- To work with the default blank publication, click Cancel.

FIGURE B.1.

You see this dialog box each time you start Publisher.

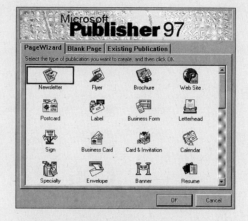

FIGURE B.2.

Use the Blank Page tab to start a new publication using a specific page layout.

Figure B.3 shows the Publisher screen with a publication in progress. In addition to the page that appears in the middle of the window, you also see the following screen elements:

Toolbox: Use these tools to add frames for text, pictures, tables, or WordArt images or to insert shapes.

Standard toolbar: Use these tools for standard program operations as well as some basic image manipulation.

Formatting toolbar: Use these tools to format the current selection.

Page controls: Use these controls to navigate multipage publications and to zoom into and out of a page.

Help window: This window gives you quick access to Help system topics related to your current task. Use the Hide Help button in the lower-right corner to close this window. (Click Show Help to display it again.)

FIGURE B.3.
The Publisher screen.

Standard toolbar

Formatting toolbar

Toolbox

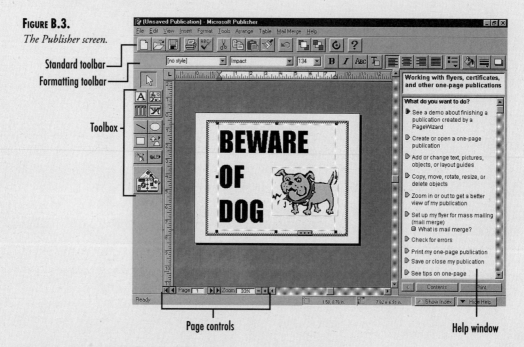

Page controls   Help window

Small Business Financial Manager

Most small businesses and self-employed professionals use some accounting package to record and monitor their financial activity and to balance their books. The Office Small Business Edition includes a set of Excel add-ins—called the Small Business Financial Manager—that give you extra tools for importing data from various accounting programs. This feature lets you use Excel's data analysis tools to examine your data and extract the information you need. If Excel's built-in tools don't do the job, the Small Business Financial Manager comes with a few of its own what-if analysis tools, as well as a wizard that helps you create dynamic financial reports.

When you install the Small Business Financial Manager, Excel sprouts a new Accounting menu that contains the following commands:

Import Wizard: This command launches a wizard that takes you through the steps of importing accounting data into a worksheet. Figure B.4 shows the Import your Accounting Data dialog box that appears. When you import the data, Excel stores it in an Access database for later use within the Small Business Financial Manager.

FIGURE B.4.

Use the Import Wizard to load your accounting data into Excel.

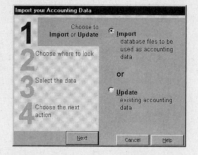

Report Wizard: This command runs the Report Wizard, which helps you prepare a number of financial reports, including a trial balance, an income statement, cash flow, and a balance sheet. Figure B.5 shows the first of the wizard's dialog boxes.

FIGURE B.5.

The Report Wizard makes it easy to create sophisticated financial reports.

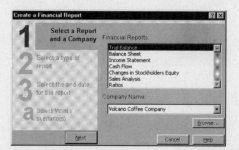

What-If Wizard: This command launches the What-If Wizard, which helps you set up a new worksheet that contains various controls for creating what-if scenarios. Figure B.6 shows an example of the worksheet that the wizard creates.

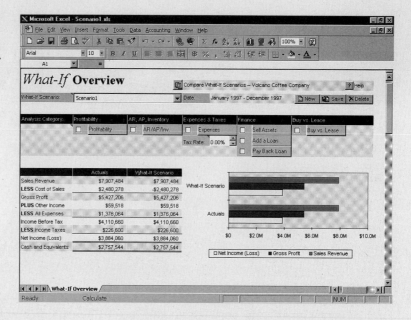

Insert Balance: Use this command to insert an account balance into a worksheet. Figure B.7 shows the dialog box from which you select the account balance you want to work with.

Recalculate Reports: Run this command to update your reports with the latest accounting data.

Remap Data: Use this command to change the way the Small Business Financial Manager aggregates your account balance information. Choosing this command displays the Map Your Accounts dialog box, shown in Figure B.8. You use this dialog box to move one or more account codes into the category you use for your account balances.

FIGURE B.8.

*Use the Map Your
Accounts dialog box to
move account codes
from one category to
another.*

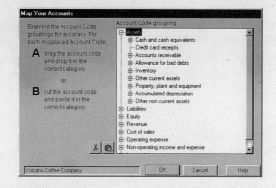

Automap Streets Plus

If your business requires you to travel regularly, you know the value of a good map for getting around in a strange city. Now imagine converting your favorite paper maps into electronic form so that you can easily view and search them. Toss in a database that contains tens of thousands of U.S. city locations—including restaurants and hotels—and the capability to map a route from one location to another, and you have the Automap Streets Plus application that comes with Office Small Business Edition.

Figure B.9 shows the main Automap Streets Plus window. Here's a summary of what each option does:

Find an Address: This command lets you search the Automap Streets Plus database for a particular address. If the program finds a match, it displays a map of the city and points out the address, as shown in Figure B.10.

Highlight a Route: Use this command to use the Automap Streets Plus highlighter to mark a route between two locations. Automap Streets Plus tells you the distance between the two points.

Find a Place: This command lets you search for a city, state, airport, museum, park, or just about any other named place you can imagine.

Find Yellow Pages Listings: This command is available only if you upgrade to the Deluxe version of Automap Streets Plus.

Import Pushpins from File: This command imports address information from a text or .CSV file and then adds "pushpins" to your maps that point out where you can find each address. For example, you could export your Outlook Contacts folder to a .CSV file and then import the data into Automap Streets Plus.

View the Map: This command displays the current Automap Streets Plus map.

WebLinks: This command launches your Web browser so you can access Web sites devoted to hundreds of cities.

Introduction: This command displays a series of help topics that give you an overview of Automap Streets Plus.

Automap Trip Planner Demo: This command gives you a demonstration of Automap Trip Planner. This tool lets you plan the best route from Point A to Point B, gives you a list of sights to see along the way, establishes an itinerary, estimates fuel costs, and more. It also offers a number of predefined routes.

Subscription: This command gives you information and instructions on setting up an Automap Streets Plus subscription, which means the latest maps are sent to you annually so you always have the most up-to-date information.

Figure B.9.

The main Automap Streets Plus window.

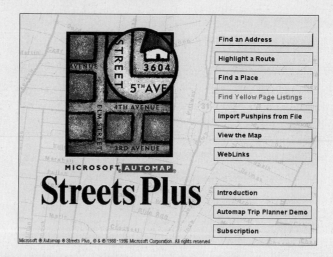

Figure B.10.

When you search for an address, Automap Streets Plus points it out on a map of the city.

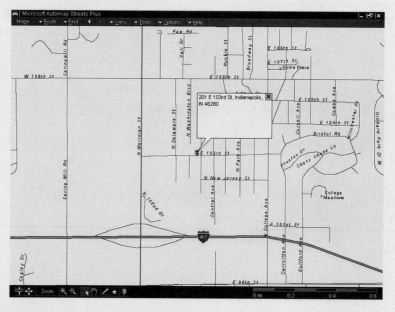

Doing Business on the Internet

Doing Business on the Internet is an electronic book that tells you how to get your business on the Internet, how to set up your Web site, and how to attract customers to your site. To view this book properly, you should copy the contents of the \ValuPack\Internet folder on the Small Business Edition disc to your Web server. Launch your Web browser and load the following page (where *server* is the name or address of your Web server):

```
http://server/Internet/default.htm
```

Figure B.11 shows the page that appears. Use the image map links on the left to display other pages in the book.

FIGURE B.11.

The home page of
Doing Business on the
Internet.

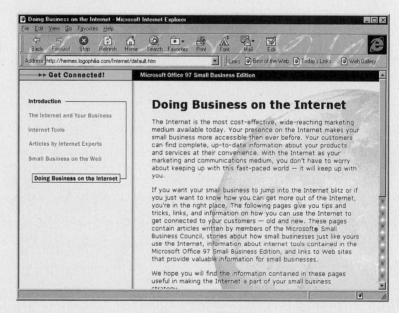

Office 97 Developer Edition

APPENDIX C

If you made your way through the chapters in Part XI, "Unleashing Office Application Development with VBA," you know that Office has become a powerful development environment for creating custom business applications. Thanks to features such as cross-application support for VBA, the powerful editing and debugging tools in the Visual Basic Editor, the common forms builder, and a massive Office object model, building dynamic, powerful solutions has never been easier.

The result is a fast-growing Office application development community with an appetite for more information and tools. To help satisfy that appetite (at least for now; developers *always* need more information), Microsoft has released a developer-oriented variation on the Office theme. It's called Microsoft Office 97 Developer Edition, and it's a two-CD set that comes with Office 97 Professional on one disc and a set of developer tools on the other. You also get two printed manuals—*Microsoft Office 97 Visual Basic Programmer's Guide* and *Building Applications with Microsoft Access 97*—that provide information, tips, and techniques for creating Office applications.

This appendix briefly describes the programming tools that are unique to the Developer Edition. After installation, you can access most of these tools by selecting Start | Programs | Microsoft ODE Tools.

Access Runtime Engine

The Access runtime engine lets you distribute Access applications and run them on machines that don't have Access installed. This runtime engine is royalty-free, and it provides full Access database support, which means that your application will run exactly as it does in the full Access environment. However, a number of restrictions are placed on the runtime environment:

- None of the database object design views are available.
- The Database, Macro, and Module windows are hidden.
- The Access Help system isn't included. You must provide your own custom help files.
- The Access toolbars aren't available. Again, you must create custom toolbars with your application.
- The View, Format, and Tools menus are hidden, as are any commands from the Edit, Insert, and Records menus that let the user change your application's objects.
- Visual Basic error handling is disabled. This means that your application shuts down if a runtime error occurs. Therefore, you need to set up error handlers within your code (as described in Chapter E4 on the CD, "Debugging VBA Procedures").
- The use of the Shift key to disable AutoExec macros at startup is disabled. The key combinations listed in Table C.1 are also disabled.

Table C.1. Key combinations that are disabled in the Access runtime environment.

Key Combination	Description
Alt-F1	Displays the Database window.
Alt-F2	Runs the File | Save As command.
Ctrl-Break	Stops macro execution.
Ctrl-Enter	Opens the design view window for the selected object.
Ctrl-F11	Switches between the built-in and custom menu bars.
Ctrl-G	Displays the Debug window.
Ctrl-N	Runs the File | New command.
Shift-F12	Saves a database object.

The easiest way to use the Access runtime engine is to include it as a component using the Setup Wizard.

Setup Wizard

The Setup Wizard is an Access application that leads you through the steps necessary to create a custom setup program that installs your Office application. This setup program not only installs the appropriate files, but it also creates shortcuts and updates the appropriate Registry settings.

When you launch the Setup Wizard, Access loads and you see the Setup Wizard dialog box, shown in Figure C.1. (The Setup Wizard application also checks your system to see whether you have a source code control program installed. If you don't, you see a dialog box at startup that warns you that the source code controls are unavailable.)

FIGURE C.1.

*The initial Setup
Wizard dialog box.*

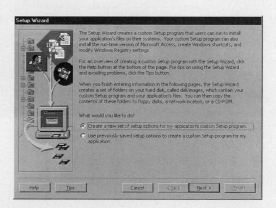

Take a quick Setup Wizard test drive so that you can see the features of this application. Because you're just starting out, make sure the Create a new set... option is activated, and then click Next. As you can see in Figure C.2, the next step is to tell the wizard which files to include in your application. You can also set a number of options, including the installation path, whether existing files should be overwritten, and more.

Figure C.2.

Use this Setup Wizard dialog box to choose the files that are part of your application.

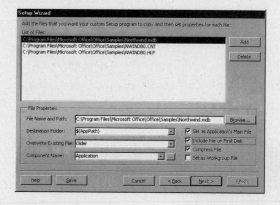

You use the next wizard dialog box, shown in Figure C.3, to specify shortcuts that you want the setup program to create. Note, too, that for Access database applications you can also install a runtime version of Access (more on this later).

Figure C.3.

Use this wizard dialog box to specify shortcuts for your application.

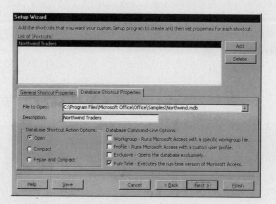

Next you specify the Registry keys and values that the setup program should create (see Figure C.4). You can use these keys to store application settings, default values, and other items that you want stored between uses of your application.

FIGURE C.4.

This wizard dialog box lets you define Registry entries for your application.

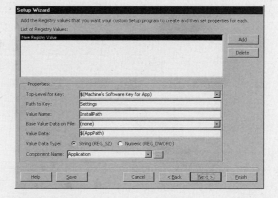

From here, you select the components to install with your application, and then you use the dialog box shown in Figure C.5 to name and describe the components, as well as decide which installation type each component should be included in (Typical, Compact, or Custom).

FIGURE C.5.

You use this dialog box to set up the application's components.

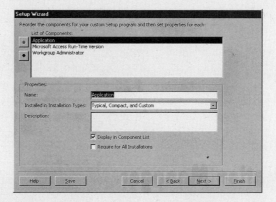

As you can see in Figure C.6, the Setup Wizard also asks you a few questions about your application, including its name, version number, default install folder, and more.

FIGURE C.6.

The Setup Wizard queries you for information about your application.

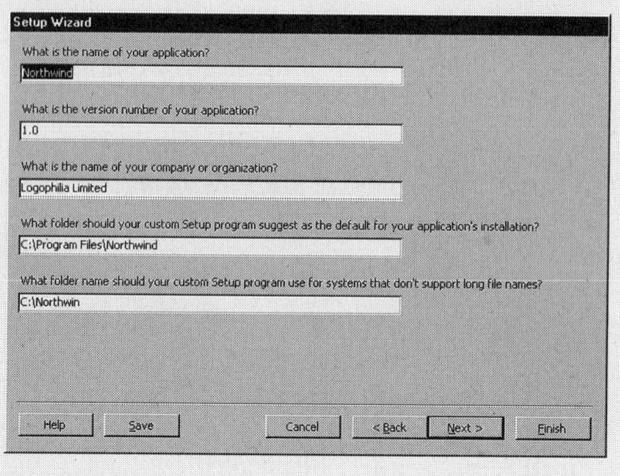

After another dialog box in which you can specify an executable file to run after the setup program is complete, you get to the last Setup Wizard dialog, shown in Figure C.7. Here, the wizard wants to know where it should create the disk images that you'll use to distribute your application. You also get the opportunity to save the setup template for use with other applications.

FIGURE C.7.

The last of the Setup Wizard's dialog boxes asks you where you want the disk images created.

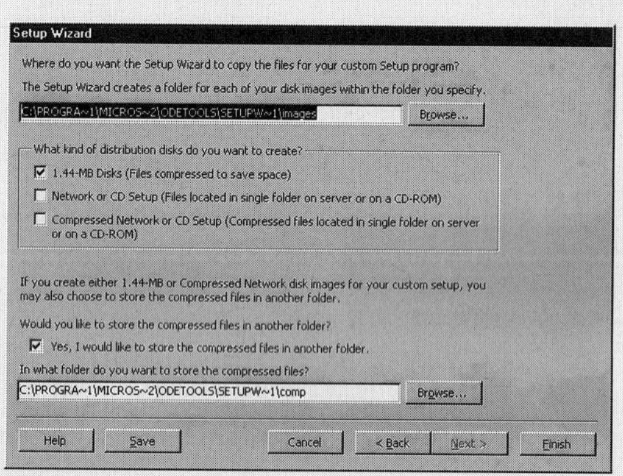

Replication Manager

In Chapter 24, "An Access Database Primer," I showed you how to work with the Access replication feature, which lets you create *replicas*—"special copies" of a database. You can then distribute these replicas to users in different locations so they can work on their copy of the database independent of other users. Replicas allow for data synchronization so that all the replicas can be combined into a single entity, incorporating all the changes that have been introduced in the individual users' copies.

If you find that you use replication frequently, you'll want to take a look at the Replication Manager application that comes with the Office Developer Edition. Replication Manager lets you set up and maintain replicated databases via an easy-to-use graphical interface. You get an intuitive visual display of your replica sets, commands for administering replicas, point-and-click synchronization (via a tool called the Synchronizer), and even an easy method for synchronizing replicas over the Internet.

When you launch Replication Manager for the first time, the Configure Microsoft Replication Manager Wizard appears, as shown in Figure C.8. Here's a summary of the configuration information this wizard sets up:

- Whether you want support for indirect synchronization
- Whether you want to replicate databases across the Internet
- The name and location of the Synchronizer log file
- The Synchronizer's name and whether you want it to start automatically when you start Windows

FIGURE C.8.

The first time you run Replication Manager, this wizard leads you through the configuration process.

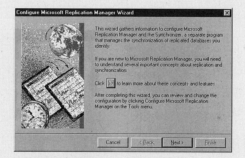

Once you complete the configuration chores, a window appears so that you can convert a database to a design master or create a replica set. (Click Close to get to the Replication Manager window.)

If you haven't done so already, your first task is to convert an existing database to a design master. Select Tools | Convert Database to Design Master. Replication Manager prompts you to select the database and then runs the Convert Database to Design Master Wizard, shown in Figure C.9. Here's a summary of the choices this wizard lets you enter:

- Whether you want to create a backup copy of the database
- A description of the replica set
- The database objects you want available in the replica set
- Whether you want your replicas created as read/write or read-only

FIGURE C.9.

The Convert Database to Design Master Wizard takes you through the conversion process.

Once that's done, you can then create a new replica by selecting File | New Replica. Replication Manager launches the New Replica Wizard, which takes you step-by-step through the replication procedure:

1. Specify the source and destination for the new replica (see Figure C.10).
2. Set up the replica to be read/write or read-only.
3. Decide whether you want to use Synchronizer to manage the replica.

FIGURE C.10.

Use the New Replica Wizard dialog box to create a replica.

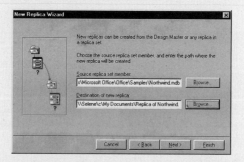

Once the replica set is established, it appears as an icon in the Replication Manager window, along with any unmanaged replications, as shown in Figure C.11. From here, you can use the menu commands to synchronize the replicas, open other replica sets, edit the databases, and more.

FIGURE C.11.

Replicas and replica sets appear as icons in the Replication Manager window.

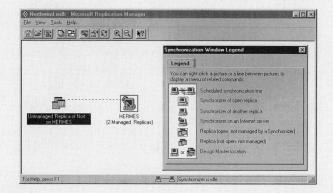

ActiveX Controls

The Office Developer Edition comes with a dozen additional ActiveX controls that you can insert into your forms. The available objects include the following:

CommonDialog: This control gives you access to the following Windows common dialog boxes: Open, Save As, Color, Font, Print, and the Windows Help engine. For example, if your CommonDialog control is named `CommonDialog1`, the method `CommonDialog1.ShowOpen` displays the Open dialog box.

ImageList: You use this control to set up a central image repository for your application. The images are stored as `ImageList` objects within this control, and you can then assign these objects to the `Picture` property of other form objects.

Internet Transfer: This control implements the HTTP and FTP Internet protocols. This means that you can use your form to retrieve HTML pages and download and upload files on FTP sites.

ListView: This control lets you display objects using one of four different views: Large Icons, Small Icons, List, or Report. These views are similar to the views you can select when working within Explorer or any folder window.

ProgressBar: This control displays a progress indicator during lengthy operations.

RichTextBox: This control is essentially a text editor that also lets the user add formatting to the text. You can use this control to open and save both ASCII and RTF text files.

Slider: This control lets you add a slider to your form.

StatusBar: This control implements a status bar that you can place at the bottom of your form. You can divide the status bar object into multiple panels and then use constants to specify the data you want to display in each panel (Caps Lock status, Num Lock status, the current date and time, and so on).

TabStrip: This control replaces the default TabStrip control that comes with VBA 5.0.

Toolbar: Use this control to add a toolbar to your form. You specify the buttons by creating a Buttons collection for the toolbar object. You can then either assign text to the buttons or else use images from an ImageList object.

TreeView: This control lets you display a hierarchical object list, which is perfect for showing folder trees or any objects that have a hierarchical relationship.

UpDown: This control replaces the default SpinButton control that comes with VBA 5.0.

Winsock: This control gives you access to TCP (Transfer Control Protocol) and UDP (User Datagram Protocol) services from your VBA application.

Help Workshop

Many VBA objects let you reference custom help topics. This is a welcome addition to any Office application, but it has traditionally been a difficult one to implement because help files have always been tricky to work with. To help out, the Office Developer Edition comes with the Help Workshop, an application that provides a front end for building custom Windows help files.

Here are the basic steps you use to create a help file for your Office application (consult the help system for more information on each step):

1. In Word, open a new file.
2. For each topic, enter a topic ID (a number sign (#) followed by a topic name), followed by the topic text, followed by a hard page break.
3. Add links, index entries, and other topic specifications.
4. When you're done, save the file in RTF format.
5. Run the Help Workshop by selecting Start | Programs | Microsoft ODE Tools | Microsoft Help Workshop.
6. Create a new help project by selecting File | New, highlighting Help Project, clicking OK, and entering a name for the .HPJ file in the dialog box that appears.
7. In the Help Workshop window, click Files, click Add, highlight the RTF topics file you created earlier, and click Open.
8. Create a new Contents file by selecting File | New, highlighting Help Contents, clicking OK, and filling in the window that appears.
9. In the Help file project window, shown in Figure C.12, click Save and Compile to create your Help file.

FIGURE C.12.
The Help Workshop lets you create help files without messy API calls.

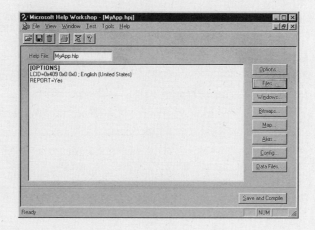

Win32 API Viewer

The Win32 API is a collection of more than 1,500 Sub and Function procedures that provide access to many Windows services. These procedures reside in a series of *dynamic link libraries* (DLLs) that form the core of the Windows 95 and Windows NT operating systems. (Most of the Win32 API can be found in just three files: GDI32.dll, Kernel32.dll, and User32.dll.) Windows programs use these routines for such basic services as creating windows; opening, reading, and writing files; editing Registry entries; and much more. In fact, your VBA procedures make extensive use of the Win32 API, although the underlying mechanism is hidden from you. When you display a user form, create a menu, use Shell to start a program, and so on, VBA translates these actions into calls to the Win32 API behind the scenes.

Because the Win32 API exists in files that are external to the VBA environment, you must specify a function and its DLL before you can use the function in your code. This is not unlike automation, in which you must set up a reference to an external object library before you can use the library's objects. With API functions, however, you create a "reference" by setting up a *declaration* for the function. This declaration must provide the following information:

- The name of the Function or Sub procedure
- The DLL in which the procedure resides
- The arguments (and their data types) used by the procedure
- The data type of the value that is returned by the procedure (Function procedure only)

To accomplish this, VBA provides the Declare statement. You must place this statement at the module level, and you use one of the following syntaxes, depending on whether you want to work with a Sub or Function procedure:

```
Declare Sub Name Lib "LibName" Alias "AliasName" (ArgList)

Declare Function Name Lib "LibName" Alias "AliasName" (ArgList) As Type
```

C

**OFFICE 97
DEVELOPER
EDITION**

Name	The name of the Sub or Function procedure you want to use. (Note that these names are case-sensitive.)
LibName	The name of the DLL file in which the procedure can be found (for example, kernel32).
AliasName	An alternative name for the procedure.
ArgList	A list of arguments (along with their respective data types) that are passed to the procedure.
Type	The data type of the value returned by a Function procedure.

For example, the following statement declares a function named Beep from the kernel32 DLL:

```
Declare Function Beep Lib "kernel32" Alias "Beep" (ByVal dwFreq As Long, ByVal
➥dwDuration As Long) As Long
```

As you can see, these Declare statements can be quite complex (and Beep is one of the simpler functions!). Fortunately, the Office Developer Edition comes with the Win32 API Viewer application, which gives you a complete list of the appropriate Declare statements (as well as the constants and custom data types used in the API).

When you first run the API Viewer (by selecting Start | Programs | Microsoft ODE Tools | Win32 API Viewer), the window that appears is empty. To load it with the API data, select File | Load Database File, highlight the Win32api.mdb file (which should be in the /ODETools/ Win32 API Viewer subfolder of your main Office folder), and then click Open.

To use the API Viewer, follow these steps:

1. Use the API Type list to select the type of data you want (Constants, Declares, or Types).

2. Use the Available Items list to highlight the API item you want to work with.

3. Click Add to add the item to the Selected Items list, as shown in Figure C.13.

FIGURE C.13.

The API Viewer gives you copy-and-paste access to the full Win32 API.

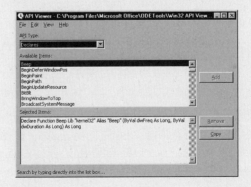

4. Repeat steps 2 and 3 to add other items to the list.

5. Click Copy to send the selected items to the Clipboard.

6. Return to your application and paste the data.

Source Code Control Integration

With the Developer Edition, you can integrate your Access applications with a source code control system—such as Visual SourceSafe—that allows development teams to work together.

The basic idea behind source code control is that all the master copies of the database objects are kept in a central project. Each developer can then "check out" an object (such as a form), which means that they work on a local copy of the object. Others can't access the object until the developer checks it back in to the project. (The exception here is the module object. Multiple developers can work on a module, and you can then merge the changes into the master copy of the module.)

Other source code control features include the capability to view the history of changes made to an object, create version objects, revert objects to previous versions, and visually compare the different versions of an object.

VBA Statements

APPENDIX D

Throughout Part XI, "Unleashing Office Application Development with VBA," I introduced you to various VBA statements. These statements appeared on an "as-needed" basis whenever I wanted to explain a particular VBA topic (such as the control structures we looked at in Chapter 55, "Controlling VBA Code and Interacting with the User"). Although I covered many VBA statements in this book, a bit of VBA's 89-statement repertoire was overlooked. However, most of the missing statements are either obscure or rarely used (such as the repugnant GoTo statement). (Note that, in this context, a *statement* is any VBA keyword or construct that isn't a function, object, property, or method.)

In an effort to put some finishing touches on our VBA coverage, this appendix presents a brief, but complete, look at every VBA statement. You can get full explanations and examples from the Statements section of the VBA Help file.

Table D.1. VBA statements.

Statement	Description
AppActivate *title, wait*	Activates the running application with the title or task ID given by *title*.
Beep	Beeps the speaker.
Call *name, argumentlist*	Calls the *name* procedure. (Because you can call a procedure just by using its name, the Call statement is rarely used in VBA programming.)
ChDir *path*	Changes the current directory (folder) to *path*.
ChDrive *drive*	Changes the current drive to *drive*.
Close *filenumberlist*	Closes one or more I/O files opened with the Open statement.
Const *CONSTNAME*	Declares a constant variable named *CONSTNAME*.
Date = *date*	Changes the system date to *date*.
Declare *name*	Declares a procedure from a dynamic link library (DLL).
DefBool *letterrange*	A module-level statement that sets the default data type to Boolean for all variables that begin with the letters in *letterrange* (for example, DefBool A-F).
DefByte *letterrange*	Sets the default data type to Byte for all variables that begin with the letters in *letterrange*.
DefCur *letterrange*	Sets the default data type to Currency for all variables that begin with the letters in *letterrange*.
DefDate *letterrange*	Sets the default data type to Date for all variables that begin with the letters in *letterrange*.

Statement	Description
DefDbl *letterrange*	Sets the default data type to Double for all variables that begin with the letters in *letterrange*.
DefInt *letterrange*	Sets the default data type to Integer for all variables that begin with the letters in *letterrange*.
DefLng *letterrange*	Sets the default data type to Long for all variables that begin with the letters in *letterrange*.
DefObj *letterrange*	Sets the default data type to Object for all variables that begin with the letters in *letterrange*.
DefSng *letterrange*	Sets the default data type to Single for all variables that begin with the letters in *letterrange*.
DefStr *letterrange*	Sets the default data type to String for all variables that begin with the letters in *letterrange*.
DefVar *letterrange*	Sets the default data type to Variant for all variables that begin with the letters in *letterrange*.
Dim *varname*	Declares a variable named *varname*.
Do...Loop	Loops through one or more statements while a logical condition is True.
DoEvents	Yields execution to the operating system so that it can process pending events from other applications (such as keystrokes and mouse clicks).
End *keyword*	Ends a procedure, function, or control structure.
Erase *arraylist*	Frees the memory allocated to a dynamic array or reinitializes a fixed-size array.
Err = *errornumber*	Sets Err (the current error status) to *errornumber*.
Error *errornumber*	Simulates an error by setting Err to *errornumber*.
Exit *keyword*	Exits a procedure, function, or control structure.
FileCopy *source, destination*	Copies the *source* file to *destination*.
For Each...Next	Loops through each member of a collection.
For...Next	Loops through one or more statements until a counter hits a specified value.
Function	Declares a user-defined function procedure.

continues

Table D.1. continued

Statement	Description
Get #*filenumber, varname*	Reads an I/O file opened by the Open statement into a variable.
GoSub...Return	Branches to and returns from a subroutine within a procedure. (However, creating separate procedures makes your code more readable.)
GoTo *line*	Sends the code to the line label given by *line*.
If...Then...Else	Runs one of two sections of code based on the result of a logical test.
Input #*filenumber, varlist*	Reads data from an I/O file into variables.
Kill *pathname*	Deletes the file *pathname* from a disk.
Let *varname = expression*	Sets the variable *varname* equal to *expression*. Let is optional and is almost never used.
Line Input #*filenumber, var*	Reads a line from an I/O file and stores it in *var*.
Load	Loads a user form into memory without displaying it.
Lock #*filenumber, recordrange*	Controls access to an I/O file.
LSet *stringvar = string*	Left-aligns a string within a String variable.
LSet *var1 = var2*	Copies a variable of one user-defined type into another variable of a different user-defined type.
Mid	Replaces characters in a String variable with characters from a different string.
MidB	Replaces byte data in a String variable with characters from a different string.
MkDir *path*	Creates the directory (folder) named *path*.
Name *oldpathname* As *newpathname*	Renames a file or directory (folder).
On Error	Sets up an error-handling routine.
On...GoSub, On...GoTo	Branches to a line based on the result of an expression.
Open *pathname,* etc.	Opens an input/output (I/O) file.
Option Base 0¦1	Determines (at the module level) the default lower bound for arrays.
Option Compare Text¦Binary	Determines (at the module level) the default mode for string comparisons.

Statement	Description
Option Explicit	Forces you to declare all variables used in a module. Enter this statement at the module level.
Option Private	Indicates that the module is private and can't be accessed by other procedures outside the module. Enter this statement at the module level.
Print #*filenumber*	Writes data to an I/O file.
Private *varname*	Declares the *varname* variable to be a private variable that can be used only in the module in which it's declared. Enter this statement at the module level.
Property Get	Declares a property procedure.
Property Let	Assigns a value to a property in a property procedure.
Property Set	Sets a reference to an object in a property procedure.
Public *varname*	Makes the *varname* variable available to all procedures in a module.
Put #*filenumber, varname*	Writes data from the variable *varname* to an I/O file.
Randomize *number*	Initializes the random-number generator. Omit *number* to get a different random number each time.
ReDim *varname*	Reallocates memory in a dynamic array.
Rem *comment*	Tells VBA that the following text is a comment. The apostrophe (') is more widely used.
Reset	Closes all I/O files that were opened with Open.
Resume	After an error, resumes program execution at the line that caused the error.
Return	See GoSub...Return.
RmDir *path*	Deletes a directory (folder).
RSet *stringvar = string*	Right-aligns a string within a String variable.
SaveSetting *appname*, etc.	Retrieves a setting from the Windows Registry.
Seek #*filenumber, position*	Sets the current position in an I/O file.

continues

Table D.1. continued

Statement	Description
Select Case	Executes one of several groups of statements based on the value of an expression.
SendKeys *string, wait*	Sends the keystrokes given by *string* to the active application.
Set *objectvar = object*	Assigns an *object* to an Object variable named *objectvar*.
SetAttr *pathname, attr*	Assigns the attributes given by *attr* (for example, vbReadOnly) to the file given by *pathname*.
Static *varname*	Declares *varname* to be a variable that will retain its value as long as the code is running.
Stop	Places VBA in Pause mode.
Sub	Declares a procedure.
Time = *time*	Sets the system time to *time*.
Type *varname*	Declares a user-defined data type. (Used at the module level only.)
Unload	Removes a user form from memory.
Unlock *#filenumber, recordrange*	Removes access controls on an I/O file.
While...Wend	Loops through a block of code while a condition is True.
Width *#filenumber, width*	Assigns an output line width to an I/O file.
With...End With	Executes a block of statements on a specified object.
Write *#filenumber*	Writes data to an I/O file.

VBA Functions

Although I discussed quite a few VBA functions in Part XI, "Unleashing Office Application Development with VBA," I was by no means exhaustive in my coverage. VBA boasts over 160 built-in functions that cover data conversion, dates and times, math, strings, and much more. This appendix presents a categorical list of each VBA function and the arguments it uses. You can get full explanations and examples for all the functions in the Functions section of the VBA Help file.

Table E.1. Conversion functions.

Function	*What It Returns*
CBool(*expression*)	An *expression* converted to a Boolean value.
CByte(*expression*)	An *expression* converted to a Byte value.
CCur(*expression*)	An *expression* converted to a Currency value.
CDate(*expression*)	An *expression* converted to a Date value.
CDbl(*expression*)	An *expression* converted to a Double value.
CInt(*expression*)	An *expression* converted to an Integer value.
CLng(*expression*)	An *expression* converted to a Long value.
CSng(*expression*)	An *expression* converted to a Single value.
CStr(*expression*)	An *expression* converted to a String value.
CVar(*expression*)	An *expression* converted to a Variant value.
CVDate(*expression*)	An *expression* converted to a Date value. (Provided for backward compatibility. Use CDate instead.)
CVErr(*errornumber*)	A Variant of subtype Error that contains *errornumber*.

Table E.2. Date and time functions.

Function	*What It Returns*
Date	The current system date as a Variant.
Date$()	The current system date as a String.
DateAdd(*interval, number, date*)	A Date value derived by adding *number* time intervals to *date*.
DateDiff(*interval, date1, date2,...*)	The number of time intervals between *date1* and *date2*.
DatePart(*interval, date,...*)	The *interval* (month, quarter, and so on) given by *date*.

Function	*What It Returns*
DateSerial(*year, month, day*)	A Date value for the specified *year*, *month*, and *day*.
DateValue(*date*)	A Date value for the *date* string.
Day(*date*)	The day of the month given by *date*.
Hour(*time*)	The hour component of *time*.
Minute(*time*)	The minute component of *time*.
Month(*date*)	The month component of *date*.
Now	The current system date and time.
Second(*time*)	The second component of *time*.
Time	The current system time as a Variant.
Time$	The current system time as a String.
Timer	The number of seconds since midnight.
TimeSerial(*hour, minute, second*)	A Date value for the specified *hour*, *minute*, and *second*.
TimeValue(*time*)	A Date value for the *time* string.
Weekday(*date*)	The day of the week, as a number, given by *date*.
Year(*date*)	The year component of *date*.

Table E.3. Error functions.

Function	*What It Returns*
Erl	A value that specifies the line number where the most recent error occurred.
Err	A value that specifies the runtime error number of the most recent error.
Error(*errornumber*)	The error message, as a Variant, that corresponds to the *errornumber*.
Error$(*errornumber*)	The error message, as a String, that corresponds to the *errornumber*.

Table E.4. File and directory functions.

Function	What It Returns
CurDir(*drive*)	The current directory as a Variant.
CurDir$(*drive*)	The current directory as a String.
Dir(***pathname***, *attributes*)	The name, as a Variant, of the file or directory (folder) specified by ***pathname*** and satisfying the optional *attributes* (for example, vbHidden). Returns Null if the file or directory doesn't exist.
Dir$(***pathname***, *attributes*)	The name, as a String, of the file or directory (folder) specified by ***pathname*** and satisfying the optional *attributes* (for example, vbHidden). Returns Null if the file or directory doesn't exist.
EOF(***filenumber***)	True if the end of file specified by ***filenumber*** has been reached; False otherwise.
FileAttr(***filenumber***, ***returnType***)	The file mode (if ***returnType*** is 1) or the file handle (if ***returnType*** is 2) of the file given by ***filenumber***.
FileDateTime(***pathname***)	The Date that the file given by ***pathname*** was created or last modified.
FileLen(***pathname***)	The length, in bytes, of the file given by ***pathname***.
FreeFile(*rangenumber*)	The next file number available to the Open statement.
GetAttr(***pathname***)	An integer representing the attributes of the file given by ***pathname***.
Loc(***filenumber***)	The current read/write position in an open I/O file.
LOF(***filenumber***)	The size, in bytes, of an open I/O file.
Seek(***filenumber***)	The current read/write position, as a Variant, in an open I/O file.
Shell(***pathname***, *windowstyle*)	The task ID of the executed program given by ***pathname***.

Table E.5. Financial functions.

Function	What It Returns
DDB(*cost, salvage, life, period*, factor)	Returns the depreciation of an asset over a specified period using the double-declining balance method.
FV(*rate, nper, pmt*, pv, type)	Returns the future value of an investment or loan.
IPmt(*rate, per, nper, pv*, fv, type)	Returns the interest payment for a specified period of a loan.
IRR(*values*, guess)	Returns the internal rate of return for a series of cash flows.
MIRR(*values, finance_rate, reinvest_rate*)	Returns the modified internal rate of return for a series of periodic cash flows.
NPer(*rate, pmt, pv*, fv, type)	Returns the number of periods for an investment or loan.
NPV(*rate, value1*, value2...)	Returns the net present value of an investment based on a series of cash flows and a discount rate.
Pmt(*rate, nper, pv*, fv, type)	Returns the periodic payment for a loan or investment.
PPmt(*rate, per, nper, pv*, fv, type)	Returns the principal payment for a specified period of a loan.
PV(*rate, nper, pmt*, fv, type)	Returns the present value of an investment.
Rate(*nper, pmt, pv*, fv, type, guess)	Returns the periodic interest rate for a loan or investment.
SLN(*cost, salvage, life*)	Returns the straight-line depreciation of an asset over one period.
SYD(*cost, salvage, life, period*)	Returns sum-of-years digits depreciation of an asset over a specified period.

E

VBA FUNCTIONS

Table E.6. Math functions.

Function	What It Returns
Abs(*number*)	The absolute value of *number*.
Atn(*number*)	The arctangent of *number*.
Cos(*number*)	The cosine of *number*.
Exp(*number*)	*e* (the base of the natural logarithm) raised to the power of *number*.
Fix(*number*)	The integer portion of *number*. If *number* is negative, Fix returns the first negative integer greater than or equal to *number*.
Hex(*number*)	The hexadecimal value, as a Variant, of *number*.
Hex$(*number*)	The hexadecimal value, as a String, of *number*.
Int(*number*)	The integer portion of *number*. If *number* is negative, Int returns the first negative integer less than or equal to *number*.
Log(*number*)	The natural logarithm of *number*.
Oct(*number*)	The octal value, as a Variant, of *number*.
Oct$(*number*)	The octal value, as a String, of *number*.
Rnd(*number*)	A random number.
Sgn(*number*)	The sign of *number*.
Sin(*number*)	The sine of *number*.
Sqr(*number*)	The square root of *number*.
Tan(*number*)	The tangent of *number*.

Table E.7. Miscellaneous functions.

Function	What It Returns
Array(*arglist*)	A Variant array containing the values in *arglist*.
Choose(*index*, *choice1*, etc.)	Returns a value from a list of choices.
CreateObject(*class*)	An Automation object of type *class*.
Environ(*envstring¦number*)	A String value that represents the operating system environment variable given by *envstring* or *number*.
Format(*expression*, *format*)	The *expression*, as a Variant, according to the string *format*.
Format$(*expression*, *format*)	The *expression*, as a String, according to the string *format*.

Function	What It Returns
GetAllSettings(**appname, section**)	Retrieves from the Registry all the settings in the specified **section**.
GetObject(*pathname, class*)	The Automation object given by *pathname* and *class*.
GetSetting(**appname**, etc.)	Retrieves a setting from the Registry.
IIf(**expr, truepart, falsepart**)	Returns **truepart** if **expr** is True; returns **falsepart** otherwise.
Input(**number, #filenumber**)	**number** characters, as a Variant, from the I/O file given by **filenumber**.
Input$(**number, #filenumber**)	**number** characters, as a String, from the I/O file given by **filenumber**.
InputB(**number, #filenumber**)	**number** bytes, as a Variant, from the I/O file given by **filenumber**.
InputB$(**number, #filenumber**)	**number** bytes, as a String, from the I/O file given by **filenumber**.
InputBox(**prompt**, etc.)	Prompts the user for information.
IsArray(**varname**)	True if **varname** is an array.
IsDate(**expression**)	True if **expression** can be converted into a date.
IsEmpty(**expression**)	True if **expression** is empty.
IsError(**expression**)	True if **expression** is an error.
IsMissing(**argname**)	True if the argument specified by **argname** was not passed to the procedure.
IsNull(**expression**)	True if **expression** is the null string ("").
IsNumeric(**expression**)	True if **expression** is a number.
IsObject(**expression**)	True if **expression** is an object.
LBound(**arrayname, dimension**)	The lowest possible subscript for the array given by **arrayname**.
MsgBox(**prompt**, etc.)	The button a user selects from the MsgBox dialog box.
Partition(**number, start, stop,...**)	Returns a String that indicates where **number** occurs within a series of ranges.
QBColor(**color**)	Returns the RGB color code that corresponds to **color** (a number between 1 and 15).

continues

Table E.7. continued

Function	What It Returns
RGB(*red*, *green*, *blue*)	The color that corresponds to the *red*, *green*, and *blue* components.
Switch(*expr1*, *value1*, etc.)	Evaluates the expressions (*expr1* and so on) and returns the associated value (*value1* and so on) for the first expression that evaluates to True.
Tab(*n*)	Positions output for the Print # statement or the Print method.
TypeName(*varname*)	A string that indicates the data type of the *varname* variable.
UBound(*arrayname*, *dimension*)	The highest possible subscript for the array given by *arrayname*.
VarType(*varname*)	A constant that indicates the data type of the *varname* variable.

Table E.8. String functions.

Function	What It Returns
Asc(*string*)	The ANSI character code of the first letter in *string*.
AscB(*string*)	The byte corresponding to the first letter in *string*.
AscW(*string*)	The Unicode character code of the first letter in *string*.
Chr(*charcode*)	The character, as a Variant, that corresponds to the ANSI code given by *charcode*.
Chr$(*charcode*)	The character, as a String, that corresponds to the ANSI code given by *charcode*.
ChrB(*charcode*)	The byte that corresponds to the ANSI code given by *charcode*.
ChrW(*charcode*)	The Unicode character that corresponds to the ANSI code given by *charcode*.
InStr(*start*, *string1*, *string2*)	The character position of the first occurrence of *string2* in *string1*, starting at *start*.
InStrB(*start*, *string1*, *string2*)	The byte position of the first occurrence of *string2* in *string1*, starting at *start*.

Function	What It Returns
LCase(***string***)	***string*** converted to lowercase as a Variant.
LCase$(***string***)	***string*** converted to lowercase as a String.
Left(***string, length***)	The leftmost ***length*** characters from ***string*** as a Variant.
Left$(***string, length***)	The leftmost ***length*** characters from ***string*** as a String.
LeftB(***string***)	The leftmost ***length*** bytes from ***string*** as a Variant.
LeftB$(***string***)	The leftmost ***length*** bytes from ***string*** as a String.
Len(***string***)	The number of characters in ***string***.
LenB(***string***)	The number of bytes in ***string***.
LTrim(***string***)	A string, as a Variant, without the leading spaces in ***string***.
LTrim$(***string***)	A string, as a String, without the leading spaces in ***string***.
Mid(***string, start,*** *length*)	*length* characters, as a Variant, from ***string*** beginning at ***start***.
Mid$(***string, start,*** *length*)	*length* characters, as a String, from ***string*** beginning at ***start***.
MidB(***string, start,*** *length*)	*length* bytes, as a Variant, from ***string*** beginning at ***start***.
MidB$(***string, start,*** *length*)	*length* bytes, as a String, from ***string*** beginning at ***start***.
Right(***string, length***)	The rightmost ***length*** characters from ***string*** as a Variant.
Right$(***string, length***)	The rightmost ***length*** characters from ***string*** as a String.
RightB(***string, length***)	The rightmost ***length*** bytes from ***string*** as a Variant.
RightB$(***string, length***)	The rightmost ***length*** bytes from ***string*** as a String.
RTrim(***string***)	A string, as a Variant, without the trailing spaces in ***string***.

E

VBA FUNCTIONS

continues

Table E.8. continued

Function	*What It Returns*
RTrim$(*string*)	A string, as a String, without the trailing spaces in *string*.
Space(*number*)	A string, as a Variant, with *number* spaces.
Space$(*number*)	A string, as a String, with *number* spaces.
Str(*number*)	The string representation, as a Variant, of *number*.
Str$(*number*)	The string representation, as a String, of *number*.
StrComp(*string2, string2, compare*)	A value indicating the result of comparing *string1* and *string2*.
String(*number, character*)	*character,* as a Variant, repeated *number* times.
String$(*number, character*)	*character,* as a String, repeated *number* times.
Trim(*string*)	A string, as a Variant, without the leading and trailing spaces in *string*.
Trim$(*string*)	A string, as a String, without the leading and trailing spaces in *string*.
UCase(*string*)	*string* converted to uppercase as a Variant.
UCase$(*string*) ·	*string* converted to uppercase as a String.
Val(*string*)	The number contained in *string*.

The Windows ANSI Character Set

This appendix presents the Windows ANSI character set. Table F.1 lists the ANSI numbers from 32 to 255. The first 32 numbers—0 to 31—are reserved for control characters such as ANSI 13, the carriage return. There are three columns for each number:

Column	Description
Text	The ANSI characters that correspond to normal text fonts such as Arial (Excel's default font), Courier New, and Times New Roman.
Symbol	The ANSI characters for the Symbol font.
Wingdings	The ANSI characters for the Wingdings font.

To enter these characters into your worksheets, you can use any of the following four methods:

■ For the ANSI numbers 32 through 127, you can either type the character directly using the keyboard, or hold down the Alt key and type the ANSI number using the keyboard's numeric keypad.

■ For the ANSI numbers 128 through 255, hold down the Alt key and use the keyboard's numeric keypad to enter the ANSI number, including the leading 0 shown in the table. For example, to enter the registered trademark symbol (ANSI 174), you would press Alt-0174.

■ Use the CHAR(*number*) worksheet function, where *number* is the ANSI number for the character you want to display.

■ In a Visual Basic procedure, use the Chr(*charcode*) function, where *charcode* is the ANSI number for the character.

Table F.1. The Windows ANSI character set.

ANSI	Text	Symbol	Wingdings
32			
33	!	!	✎
34	"	∀	✂
35	#	#	✀
36	$	∃	✆
37	%	%	♤
38	&	&	▭
39	'	∋	⚲
40	(	(	☎
41	)	)	☏

ANSI	Text	Symbol	Wingdings
42	*	*	
43	+	+	
44	,	,	
45	-	−	
46	.	.	
47	/	/	
48	0	0	
49	1	1	
50	2	2	
51	3	3	
52	4	4	
53	5	5	
54	6	6	
55	7	7	
56	8	8	
57	9	9	
58	:	:	
59	;	;	
60	<	<	
61	=	=	
62	>	>	
63	?	?	
64	@	≅	
65	A	A	
66	B	B	
67	C	X	
68	D	Δ	
69	E	E	
70	F	Φ	
71	G	Γ	
72	H	H	
73	I	I	
74	J	ϑ	
75	K	K	
76	L	Λ	
77	M	M	
78	N	N	
79	O	O	
80	P	Π	
81	Q	Θ	

continues

Table F.1. continued

ANSI	Text	Symbol	Wingdings
82	R	Ρ	✿
83	S	Σ	⬤
84	T	Τ	❄
85	U	Υ	✝
86	V	ς	✠
87	W	Ω	✤
88	X	Ξ	✢
89	Y	Ψ	✿
90	Z	Z	☾
91	[	[	☯
92	\	∴	ॐ
93	]	]	✻
94	^	⊥	♈
95	_	_	♉
96	`	‾	♊
97	a	α	♋
98	b	β	♌
99	c	χ	♍
100	d	δ	♎
101	e	ε	♏
102	f	φ	♐
103	g	γ	♑
104	h	η	♒
105	i	ι	♓
106	j	φ	er
107	k	κ	&
108	l	λ	●
109	m	μ	○
110	n	ν	■
111	o	o	□
112	p	π	□
113	q	θ	□
114	r	ρ	□
115	s	σ	◆
116	t	τ	◆
117	u	υ	◆
118	v	ϖ	❖
119	w	ω	◆
120	x	ξ	⊠
121	y	ψ	◲
122	z	ζ	⌘

ANSI	Text	Symbol	Wingdings
123	{	{	✪
124	|	|	●
125	}	}	"
126	~	~	"
127			▯
0128			⓪
0129			①
0130	,		②
0131	ƒ		③
0132	„		④
0133	…		⑤
0134	†		⑥
0135	‡		⑦
0136	^		⑧
0137	‰		⑨
0138	Š		⑩
0139	‹		❶
0140	Œ		❷
0141			❸
0142			❹
0143			❺
0144			❻
0145	'		❼
0146	'		❽
0147	"		❾
0148	"		❿
0149	•		❿
0150	–		ℭℨ
0151	—		ℨ℩
0152	˜		ℨ℩
0153	™		ℭℨ
0154	š		❧
0155	›		❦
0156	œ		❧
0157			❧
0158			·
0159	Ÿ		•
0160			
0161	¡	ϒ	○
0162	¢	′	◉
0163	£	≤	●
0164	¤	⁄	◉

continues

Table F.1. continued

ANSI	Text	Symbol	Wingdings
0165	¥	∞	◎
0166	¦	*f*	○
0167	§	♣	■
0168	¨	♦	□
0169	©	♥	◣
0170	ª	♠	✦
0171	«	↔	★
0172	¬	←	✳
0173	–	↑	✹
0174	®	→	✸
0175	¯	↓	✵
0176	°	°	✛
0177	±	±	✚
0178	²	″	◆
0179	³	≥	⌑
0180	´	×	◈
0181	µ	∝	✪
0182	¶	∂	☆
0183	·	•	◔
0184	¸	÷	◕
0185	¹	≠	◕
0186	º	≡	◕
0187	»	≈	◕
0188	¼	…	◕
0189	½	⏐	◕
0190	¾	—	◕
0191	¿	↵	◕
0192	À	ℵ	◕
0193	Á	ℑ	◕
0194	Â	ℜ	◕
0195	Ã	℘	☘
0196	Ä	⊗	☙
0197	Å	⊕	☘
0198	Æ	∅	☙
0199	Ç	∩	☘
0200	È	∪	☙
0201	É	⊃	☙
0202	Ê	⊇	☙
0203	Ë	⊄	✤
0204	Ì	⊂	◼
0205	Í	⊆	✾
0206	Î	∈	✿

ANSI	Text	Symbol	Wingdings
0207	Ï	∉	
0208	Ð	∠	
0209	Ñ	∇	
0210	Ò	®	
0211	Ó	©	
0212	Ô	™	
0213	Õ	∏	
0214	Ö	√	
0215	×	·	
0216	Ø	¬	
0217	Ù	∧	
0218	Ú	∨	
0219	Û	⇔	
0220	Ü	⇐	
0221	Ý	⇑	
0222	Þ	⇒	
0223	ß	⇓	
0224	à	◊	
0225	á	⟨	
0226	â	®	
0227	ã	©	
0228	ä	™	
0229	å	Σ	
0230	æ	(	
0231	ç			
0232	è			
0233	é	⌈	
0234	ê			
0235	ë	⌊	
0236	ì	(	
0237	í	⟨	
0238	î			
0239	ï			
0240	ð			
0241	ñ	⟩	
0242	ò	∫	
0243	ó	⌠	
0244	ô			
0245	õ	⌡	
0246	ö	)	
0247	÷			
0248	ø	)	

continues

Table F.1. continued

ANSI	Text	Symbol	Wingdings
0249	ù	⌉	▫
0250	ú	⎮	▫
0251	û	⌋	✘
0252	ü	⌉	✔
0253	ý	⎭	⊠
0254	þ	⌋	☑
0255	ÿ		▦

I

INDEX

Symbols

B

X-Z

MACMILLAN COMPUTER PUBLISHING USA

A VIACOM COMPANY

Technical Support:

If you need assistance with the information in this book or with a CD/Disk accompanying the book, please access the Knowledge Base on our Web site at **http://www.superlibrary.com/general/support**. Our most Frequently Asked Questions are answered there. If you do not find the answer to your questions on our Web site, you may contact Macmillan Technical Support **(317) 581-3833** or e-mail us at **support@mcp.com**.

What's on the CD-ROM

The companion CD-ROM contains an assortment of third-party tools and product demos. The disc creates a new program group for this book and utilizes the Windows 95 Explorer. Using the icons in the program group and Windows Explorer, you can view information concerning products and companies and install programs with just a few clicks of the mouse.

To create the program group for this book, follow these steps:

Windows 95 and NT 4.0 Installation Instructions

1. Insert the disc into your CD-ROM drive.

2. If Windows 95 or Windows NT 4.0 is installed on your computer and the AutoPlay feature is enabled, a Program Group for this book is automatically created whenever you insert the disc into your CD-ROM drive. Follow the directions provided in the installation program.

   If AutoPlay is not enabled, using Windows Explorer, choose Setup.exe from the root level of the CD-ROM to create the Program Group for this book.

3. Double-click the Browse the CD-ROM icon in the newly created Program Group to access the installation programs of the software or reference material included on this CD-ROM.

4. To review the latest information about this CD-ROM, double-click the About this CD-ROM icon.

Technical Support

If you need assistance with the information in this book or with the CD-ROM that accompanies this book, please access the Knowledge Base on our Web site at

http://www.superlibrary.com/general/support

Our most Frequently Asked Questions are answered there. If you do not find the answer to your questions on our Web site, you may contact Macmillan Technical Support at (317) 581-3833 or e-mail us at support@mcp.com.

NOTE

If you have trouble reading from our CD-ROM, try to clean the data side of the CD-ROM with a clean, soft cloth. One cause of this problem is dirt disrupting the access of the data on the disc. If the problem still exists, whenever possible, insert this CD-ROM into another computer to determine if the problem is with the disc or your CD-ROM drive.

Another common cause of this problem might be that you have outdated CD-ROM drivers. In order to update your drivers, first verify the manufacturer of your CD-ROM drive from your system's documentation. If you're using Windows 95 or Windows NT 4.0, you may also check your CD-ROM manufacturer by going to \Settings\Control Panel\System and selecting Device Manager. Double-click the CD-ROM option, and you will see information on the manufacturer of your drive.

You may download the latest drivers from your manufacturer's Web site or from

http://www.windows95.com